# Great Britain
## &
# Ireland
## 2012

# Contents

## FURTHER INFORMATION

## TOWNS from A to Z

## MAPS

# How to use this guide

## TOURIST INFORMATION

Distances from the main towns, tourist
offices, local tourist attractions,
means of transport,
golf courses
and leisure activities...

## HOTELS

From 🏨🏨🏨 to 🏠, 🏠:
categories of comfort.
In red 🏨🏨🏨 ... 🏠, 🏠:
the most pleasant.

## RESTAURANTS
## AND PUBS

From XXXXX to X, 🍺:
categories of comfort.
In red XXXXX ... X, 🍺:
the most pleasant.

## STARS

| | |
|---|---|
| ❀❀❀ | Worth a special journey. |
| ❀❀ | Worth a detour. |
| ❀ | A very good restaurant. |

## GOOD FOOD
## AND ACCOMMODATION
## AT MODERATE PRICES

| | |
|---|---|
| 😋 | Bib Gourmand |
| 🏩 | Bib Hotel |

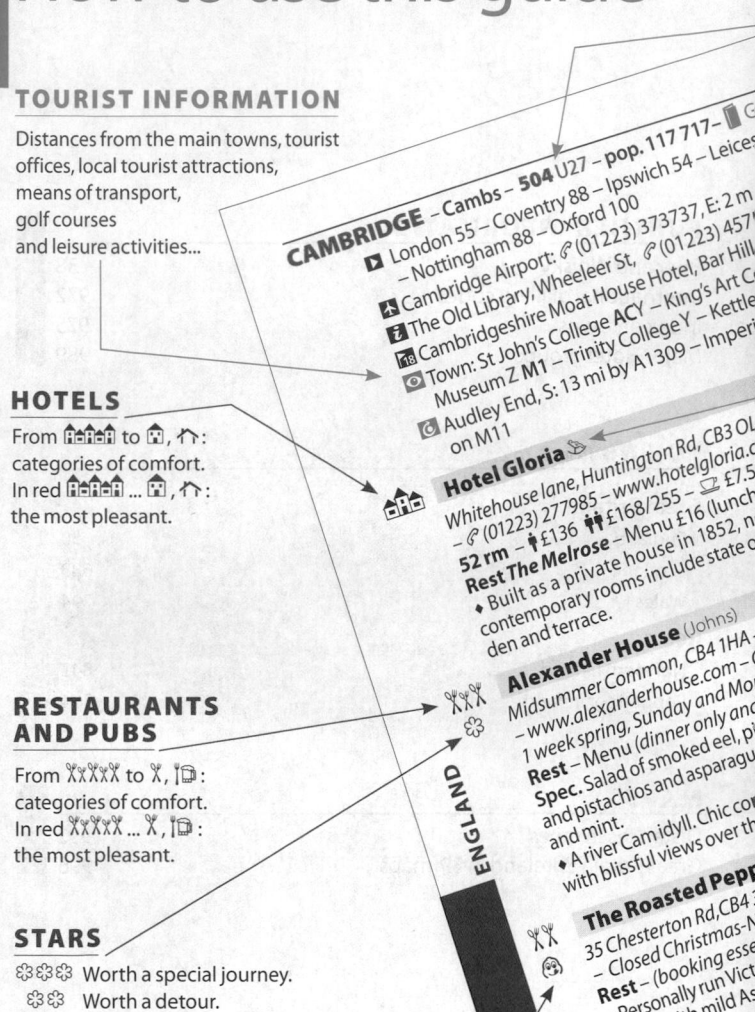

**CAMBRIDGE – Cambs – 504** U27 **– pop. 117 717–**

▶ London 55 – Coventry 88 – Ipswich 54 – Leices
– Nottingham 88 – Oxford 100

✈ Cambridge Airport: 𝒞 (01223) 373737, E: 2 m

🏛 The Old Library, Wheeleer St, 𝒞 (01223) 457

ⓘ Cambridgeshire Moat House Hotel, Bar Hill

🔞 Town: St John's College AC Y – King's Art C
Museum Z **M1** – Trinity College Y – Kettle

👁 Audley End, S: 13 mi by A1309 – Imperi
on M11

**Hotel Gloria** 🏨
Whitehouse lane, Huntington Rd, CB3 0L
– 𝒞 (01223) 277985 – www.hotelgloria.c
**52 rm** – †£136 ††£168/255 – 🛏 £7.5
**Rest The Melrose** – Menu £16 (lunch
♦ Built as a private house in 1852, n
contemporary rooms include state o
den and terrace.

**Alexander House** (Johns)
Midsummer Common, CB4 1HA
– www.alexanderhouse.com – C
1 week spring, Sunday and Mo
**Rest** – Menu (dinner only and
**Spec.** Salad of smoked eel, p
and pistachios and asparagu
and mint.
♦ A river Cam idyll. Chic co
with blissful views over th

**The Roasted Pepp**
35 Chesterton Rd, CB4 3
– Closed Christmas-N
**Rest** – (booking esse
♦ Personally run Vict
dishes with mild As

at Histon North: 3 m on

**Blue House**
44 High St, CB3
– Closed 2 wee
**22 rm** – †£3
♦ Red-brick t
overlooks r
preserves.

**CANTERBUR**
▶ Lor

Feli

4

**OTHER MICHELIN PUBLICATIONS**

References for the Michelin map
and Green Guide which cover the area.

**12**A2

vich 61

nbridge.gov.uk

9988 X

Backs YZ – Fitzwilliam

– Queen's College **ACZ**

um, Duxford, S: 9 mi

**LOCATING THE TOWN**

Locate the town on the regional map
at the end of the guide
(map number and coordinates).

**QUIET HOTELS**

🐾 Quiet hotel.
🐾 Very quiet hotel.

🍴 🌳 & 👤 **P** *VISA* 🍴 **①**    Z**d**

: 1,5 m by A1307

**LOCATING
THE ESTABLISHMENT**

Located on the town plan
(coordinates and letters
giving the location).

20/35.50

ern and stylish public areas. The

kies. Sleek restaurant overlooks gar-

🍴 🍴 *VISA* **AE** **①**    Y**a**

9 245

s Christmas, 2 weeks August,

**DESCRIPTION OF THE
ESTABLISHMENT**

Atmosphere, style,
character and specialities.

–Saturday) £30/50 🍴

d apple purée. Braised turbot with peanuts

of apricot, Strawberry sorbet, fraises des bois

ning room with smart first floor bar and terrace

*VISA* 🍴 **AE** **①**    Y**c**

**PRICES**

3) 351872 – www.roastedpepper.co.uk

Sunday

only) Menu £25

**FACILITIES
AND SERVICES**

use with smartly clad tables. Classic French and Italian

s, served at reasonable prices.

🍴 **P** 🍴

ambridge

ut rest

23) 262164 – www.bluehousefarm.com

–New Year

house on a working farm...with beautiful blue windows; house

y garden room for breakfast, including home-made bread and

ooms.

**604** R29 – **pop. 47 123 (inc. Frimley)** – 📗 Great Britain    **9**D2

ghton 76 – Dover 15 – Maidstone 28 – Margate 17

🍴 🍴 🍴 🍴 & 👤 **P** *VISA* 🍴 **①**

15 2BG, East: 0.75 m off Portsmouth Rd (A325)

www.felixhall.com

🍴 £6.50

ner only) £19/28    staircase leads to the bedrooms; some

re bright and modern. 19C res-

5

# The MICHELIN guide's commitments

## Experienced in quality

Whether it is in Japan, the USA, China or Europe our inspectors use the same criteria to judge the quality of the hotels and restaurants and use the same methods of visiting. The guide can only boast this worldwide reputation thanks to its commitment to the readers and we would like to stress these here :

## The MICHELIN guide's commitments:

**Anonymous inspections:** our inspectors make regular and anonymous visits to hotels and restaurants to gauge the quality of products and services offered to an ordinary customer. They settle their own bill and may then introduce themselves and ask for more information about the establishment. Our readers' comments are also a valuable source of information, which we can then follow up with another visit of our own.

**Independence:** To remain totally objective for our readers, the selection is made with complete independence. Entry into the guide is free. All decisions are discussed with the Editor and our highest awards are considered at a European level.

**Selection and choice:** The guide offers a selection of the best hotels and restaurants in every category of comfort and price. This is only possible because all the inspectors rigorously apply the same methods.

**Annual updates:** All the practical information, the classifications and awards are revised and updated every single year to give the most reliable information possible.

**Consistency:** The criteria for the classifications are the same in every country covered by the MICHELIN guide.

The sole intention of Michelin is to make your travels both safe and enjoyable.

# Dear Reader,

## Dear Reader,

Having kept up-to-date with the latest developments in the hotel and restaurant scenes, we are pleased to present this new, improved and updated edition of the Michelin Guide.

Since the very beginning, our ambition has remained the same each year: to accompany you on all of your journeys and to help you choose the best establishments to both stay and eat in, across all categories of comfort and price; whether that's a friendly guesthouse or luxury hotel, a lively gastropub or fine dining restaurant.

To this end, the Michelin Guide is a tried-and-tested travel planner, its primary objective being to provide first-hand experience for you, our readers. All of the establishments selected have been rigorously tested by our team of professional inspectors, who are constantly seeking out new places and continually assessing those already listed.

Every year the guide recognises the best places to eat, by awarding them one ✿, two ✿✿ or three ✿✿✿ stars. These lie at the heart of the selection and highlight the establishments producing the best quality cuisine – in all styles – taking into account the quality of ingredients, creativity, mastery of techniques and flavours, value for money and consistency.

Other symbols to look out for are the Bib Gourmand ⊛ and the Bib Hotel , which point out establishments that represent particularly good value; here you'll be guaranteed excellence but at moderate prices.

We are committed to remaining at the forefront of the culinary world and to meeting the demands of our readers. As such, we are very interested to hear your opinions on the establishments listed in our guide. Please don't hesitate to contact us, as your contributions are invaluable in directing our work and improving the quality of our information.

We continually strive to help you on your journeys.

Thank you for your loyalty and happy travelling with the 2012 edition of the Michelin Guide.

Consult the MICHELIN guide at www.ViaMichelin.com
and write to us at:
themichelinguide-gbirl@uk.michelin.com

# Classification & awards

## CATEGORIES OF COMFORT

The Michelin guide selection lists the best hotels and restaurants in each category of comfort and price. The establishments we choose are classified according to their levels of comfort and, within each category, are listed in order of preference.

| | | |
|---|---|---|
| 🏨🏨🏨 | XXXXX | Luxury in the traditional style |
| 🏨🏨 | XXXX | Top class comfort |
| 🏠🏠 | XXX | Very comfortable |
| 🏠 | XX | Comfortable |
| 🏠 | X | Quite comfortable |
| | 🍴 | Pubs serving good food |
| ⌂ | | Other recommended accommodation (Guesthouses, farmhouses and private homes) |
| without rest. | | This hotel has no restaurant |
| with rm | | This restaurant also offers accommodation |

## THE AWARDS

To help you make the best choice, some exceptional establishments have been given an award in this year's Guide. They are marked ✿, ☺, 🏨 . For those awarded a Bib Hotel, the mention **"rm"** appears in the description of the establishment.

### THE BEST CUISINE

Michelin stars are awarded to establishments serving cuisine, of whatever style, which is of the highest quality. The cuisine is judged on the quality of ingredients, the skill in their preparation, the combination of flavours, the levels of creativity, the value for money and the consistency of culinary standards.

For every restaurant awarded a star we include 3 specialities that are typical of their cooking style. These specific dishes may not always be available.

| | |
|---|---|
| ✿✿✿ | **Exceptional cuisine, worth a special journey** |
| | One always eats extremely well here, sometimes superbly. |
| ✿✿ | **Excellent cooking, worth a detour** |
| ✿ | **Very good cooking in its category** |

Occasionally "Rising Stars " will feature. These are establishments that we feel have the potential for a higher award. Once they can produce their high standard of cooking on a consistent basis they could me our future stars.

### GOOD FOOD AND ACCOMMODATION AT MODERATE PRICES

| | |
|---|---|
| ☺ | **Bib Gourmand** |
| | Establishment offering good quality cuisine for under £28 or €40 in the Republic of Ireland (price of a 3 course meal not including drinks). |

    **Bib Hotel**
    Establishment offering good levels of comfort and service, with most rooms priced at under £90 or under €115 in the Republic of Ireland (price of a room for 2 people, including breakfast).

## PLEASANT HOTELS AND RESTAURANTS

Symbols shown in red indicate particularly pleasant or restful establishments: the character of the building, its décor, the setting, the welcome and services offered may all contribute to this special appeal.

⋔, 🏠 to 🏨🏨🏨    **Pleasant hotels & guesthouses**

🍴, 💥 to 💥💥💥💥💥    **Pleasant restaurants & pubs**

## OTHER SPECIAL FEATURES

As well as the categories and awards given to the establishment, Michelin inspectors also make special note of other criteria which can be important when choosing an establishment.

### LOCATION

If you are looking for a particularly restful establishment, or one with a special view, look out for the following symbols:

    🐾    **Quiet hotel**
    🐾    **Very quiet hotel**
    ≼    **Interesting view**
    ≼    **Exceptional view**

### WINE LIST

If you are looking for an establishment with an excellent wine list, look out for the following symbol:

    🍇    **Particularly interesting wine list**
    This symbol might cover the list presented by a sommelier in a luxury restaurant or that of a simple pub or restaurant where the owner has a passion for wine. The two lists will offer something exceptional but very different, so beware of comparing them by each other's standards.

### SMOKING
In Great Britain and the Republic of Ireland the law prohibits smoking in all pubs, restaurants and hotel public areas.

# Facilities
# & services

| | |
|---|---|
| **30 rm** | Number of rooms |
| | Lift (elevator) |
| AC | Air conditioning (in all or part of the establishment) |
| | Fast Internet access in bedrooms |
| | Wi-fi Internet access in bedrooms |
| | Establishment at least partly accessible to those of restricted mobility |
| | Special facilities for children |
| | Meals served in garden or on terrace |
| | An extensive facility for relaxation and well-being |
| | Sauna – Exercise room |
| | Swimming pool: outdoor or indoor |
| | Garden – Park |
| | Tennis court – Golf course and number of holes |
| | Fishing available to hotel guests. A charge may be made |
| | Equipped conference room |
| | Private dining rooms |
| | Hotel garage (additional charge in most cases) |
| **P** | Car park for customers only |
| | No dogs allowed (in all or part of the establishment) |
| | Nearest Underground station (in London) |
| *May - October* | Dates when open, as indicated by the hotelier |

# Prices

Prices quoted in this guide were supplied in summer 2011 and apply to low and high seasons. They are subject to alteration if goods and service costs are revised. By supplying the information, hotels and restaurants have undertaken to maintain these rates for our readers.

In some towns, when commercial, cultural or sporting events are taking place the hotel rates are likely to be considerably higher.

Prices are given in £ sterling, except for the Republic of Ireland where euros are quoted.

All accommodation prices include both service and V.A.T. All restaurant prices include V.A.T. Service is also included when an **s** appears after the prices.

Where no **s** is shown, prices may be subject to the addition of a variable service charge which is usually between 10 % - 15 %.

(V.A.T. does not apply in the Channel Islands).

Out of season, certain establishments offer special rates. Ask when booking.

## RESERVATION AND DEPOSITS

Some hotels will require a deposit which confirms the commitment of both the customer and the hotelier. Ask the hotelier to provide you with all the terms and conditions applicable to your reservation in their written confirmation.

## CREDIT CARDS

Credit cards accepted by the establishment:

AE ① ⓜⓒ *VISA*  American Express – Diners Club – MasterCard – Visa

## ROOMS

| | | |
|---|---|---|
| rm 🛉 | 50/90 | Lowest price 50 and highest price 90 for a comfortable single room |
| rm 🛉🛉 | 70/120 | Lowest price 70 and highest price 120 for a double or twin room for 2 people |
| rm ⌁ | 55/85 | Full cooked breakfast (whether taken or not) is included in the price of the room |
| ⌁ | 6 | Price of breakfast |

## SHORT BREAKS

Many hotels offer a special rate for a stay of two or more nights which comprises dinner, room and breakfast usually for a minimum of two people. Please enquire at hotel for rates.

## RESTAURANT

**Set meals:** lowest price £13, highest price £28, usually for a 3 course meal. The lowest priced set menu is often only available at lunchtimes.

**A la carte meals:** the prices represent the range of charges from a simple to an elaborate 3 course meal.

| | |
|---|---|
| **s** | Service included |
| 🎭 | Restaurants offering lower priced pre and/or post theatre menus |

↑: Dinner in this category of establishment is sometimes communal and meals are not always available every evening. It will generally be a limited menu, served at a set time, to residents only. Lunch is rarely offered. Many will not be licensed to sell alcohol.

# Information on localities

## GENERAL INFORMATION

| | |
|---|---|
| ✉ **York** | Postal address |
| **501** M27, ⑩ | Michelin map and co-ordinates or fold |
| ▮ Great Britain | See the Michelin Green Guide Great Britain |
| **pop. 1057** | Population |
| | Source: 2001 Census (Key Statistics for Urban Areas) |
| | Crown copyright 2004 |
| BX **a** | Letters giving the location of a place on a town plan |
| 🏌18 | Golf course and number of holes (handicap sometimes required, telephone reservation strongly advised) |
| ☀ ≼ | Panoramic view, viewpoint |
| ✈ | Airport |
| ⛴ | Shipping line (passengers & cars) |
| ⛴ | Passenger transport only |
| 𝑖 | Tourist Information Centre |

## STANDARD TIME

In winter, standard time throughout the British Isles is Greenwich Mean Time (GMT). In summer, British clocks are advanced by one hour to give British Summer Time (BST). The actual dates are announced annually but always occur over weekends in March and October.

## TOURIST INFORMATION

### STAR-RATING

| | |
|---|---|
| ★★★ | Highly recommended |
| ★★ | Recommended |
| ★ | Interesting |
| AC | Admission charge |

### LOCATION

| | |
|---|---|
| 👁 | Sights in town |
| ⟳ | On the outskirts |
| N, S, E, W | The sight lies North, South, East or West of the town |
| A 22 | Take road A 22, indicated by the same symbol on the Guide map |
| 2mi. | Distance in miles (In the Republic of Ireland kilometres are quoted). |

# Plan key

@ ● a  Hotels – restaurants

## SIGHTS

| | |
|---|---|
| ■ ⌐ | Place of interest |
| ⛪ ✝ | Interesting place of worship Catholic-Protestant |

## ROADS

|  |  |
|---|---|
| M 1 | Motorway |
| ❹ ❹ | Numbered junctions: complete, limited |
|  | Dual carriageway with motorway characteristics |
| ▬▬ | Main traffic artery |
| A 2 | Primary route (GB) and National route (IRL) |
| ◄ ⌐=====⌐ | One-way street – Unsuitable for traffic or street subject to restrictions |
| ⇒ ▭ ···→ | Pedestrian street – Tramway |
| Piccadilly P P&R | Shopping street – Car park – Park and Ride |
| ╪ ╪╪ ╪╪ | Gateway – Street passing under arch – Tunnel |
| 15.5 | Low headroom (16'6" max.) on major through routes |
| ▭ 🚂 | Station and railway |
| o++++o o-■-■-o | Funicular – Cable-car |
| ⚠ B | Lever bridge – Car ferry |

## VARIOUS SIGNS

|  |  |
|---|---|
| 🛈 | Tourist Information Centre |
| ⛪ ☪ ✡ | Church/Place of worship - Mosque – Synagogue |
| ⊤ ∴ | Communications tower or mast – Ruins |
| ▭ ⊡ | Garden, park, wood – Cemetery |
| ○ 🏇 🏌 | Stadium - Racecourse - Golf course |
| ▶ ⛸ | Golf course (with restrictions for visitors) – Skating rink |
| ≋ ▣ | Outdoor or indoor swimming pool |
| ◄ 🌿 | View – Panorama |
| ■ ○ ⊞ 🌂 | Monument – Fountain – Hospital – Covered market |
| ⚓ ♆ | Pleasure boat harbour – Lighthouse |
| ✈ ⊖ ● 🚌 | Airport – Underground station – Coach station |
| 🚢 | Ferry services: passengers and cars |
| ✉ | Main post office |
| ▭ | Public buildings located by letter: |
| C H J | County Council Offices – Town Hall – Law Courts |
| M T U | Museum – Theatre – University, College |
| POL. | Police (in large towns police headquarters) |

## LONDON

| | |
|---|---|
| **BRENT** WEMBLEY | Borough – Area |
| | Borough boundary |
| ▬▬▬ | Congestion Zone – Charge applies Monday-Friday 07.00-18.00 |
| ⊖ | Nearest Underground station to the hotel or restaurant |

# Starred establishments 2012

The colour corresponds to the establishment
with the most stars in this location.

London — This location has at least one 3 star restaurant ✹✹✹

Dublin — This location has at least one 2 star restaurant ✹✹

Edinburgh — This location has at least one 1 star restaurant ✹

Lochinver

Sleat

Fort William

Dalry

Ballantrae

Portpatrick

NORTHERN
IRELAND

Malahide

Dublin

REPUBLIC
OF IRELAND

Ardmore

GUERNSEY

JERSEY

La Pulente • St Helier

ISLES OF SCILLY

Rock

Portscatho

SHETLAND ISLANDS

ORKNEY ISLANDS

Nairn

SCOTLAND

Auchterarder

Peat Inn

Elie

Balloch

Edinburgh

Leith

Pooley Bridge

Windermere

Ramsgill-in-Nidderdale

Oldstead

Cartmel

Bolton Abbey

Ilkley

Langho

South Dalton

Birkenhead

ENGLAND

Sheffield

Llandrillo

Chester

Baslow

Nottingham

Montgomery

Morston

Clipsham

Hunstanton

Birmingham

Hambleton

Ludlow

Royal Leamington Spa

Titley

Winchcombe

Cambridge

VALES

Eldersfield

Upper Slaughter

Cheltenham

Murcott

Woburn

Llanddewi Skirrid

Welwyn Garden City

Whitebrook

Great Milton

Malmesbury

Sprigg's Alley

Marlow

Bristol

London

Colerne

Chew Magna

Castle Combe

Shinfield

Ascot

Seasalter

Little Bedwyn

Bray

Ripley

Faversham

Knowstone

Bagshot

Biddenden

Winchester

Cranbrook

Chagford

Petersfield

Emsworth

Cuckfield

Bodiam

Dorchester

Beaulieu

Horsham

Torquay

Ventnor

# Starred establishments

## ✾✾✾

### → England

| | |
|---|---|
| **Bray** | Fat Duck |
| **Bray** | Waterside Inn |
| **London / City of Westminster** | Alain Ducasse at The Dorchester |
| **London / Kensington and Chelsea** | Gordon Ramsay |

## ✾✾

### → England

| | |
|---|---|
| **Cambridge** | Midsummer House |
| **Chagford** | Gidleigh Park |
| **Cheltenham** | Le Champignon Sauvage |
| **London / City of Westminster** | L'Atelier de Joël Robuchon |
| **London / City of Westminster** | Le Gavroche |
| **London / City of Westminster** | Hibiscus |
| **London / City of Westminster** | Hélène Darroze at The Connaught |
| **London / City of Westminster** | Marcus Wareing at The Berkeley |
| **London / City of Westminster** | Square |
| **London / Kensington and Chelsea** | Ledbury |
| **Malmesbury** | Whatley Manor |
| **Marlow** | Hand and Flowers  **N** |
| **Nottingham** | Restaurant Sat Bains  **N** |
| **Oxford / Great Milton** | Le Manoir aux Quat' Saisons |
| **Rock** | Restaurant Nathan Outlaw |

### → Scotland

| | |
|---|---|
| **Auchterarder** | Andrew Fairlie at Gleneagles |

### → Republic of Ireland

| | |
|---|---|
| **Dublin** | Patrick Guilbaud |

---

→ **N** *New*

# → England

| | |
|---|---|
| **Ascot** | Coworth Park |
| **Bagshot** | Michael Wignall at The Latymer (at Pennyhill Park Hotel) |
| **Baslow** | Fischer's at Baslow Hall |
| **Bath / Colerne** | The Park (at Lucknam Park Hotel) |
| **Beaulieu** | The Terrace (at Montagu Arms Hotel) |
| **Beverley / South Dalton** | Pipe and Glass Inn |
| **Biddenden** | West House |
| **Birkenhead** | Fraiche |
| **Birmingham** | Purnell's |
| **Birmingham** | Simpsons |
| **Birmingham** | Turners |
| **Blackburn / Langho** | Northcote |
| **Blakeney / Morston** | Morston Hall |
| **Bodiam** | Curlew |
| **Bolton Abbey** | Burlington (at Devonshire Arms Country House Hotel) |
| **Bourton-on-the-Water / Upper Slaughter** | Lords of the Manor |
| **Bray** | Royal Oak |
| **Bristol** | Casamia |
| **Castle Combe** | Manor House H. and Golf Club |
| **Chester** | Simon Radley at The Chester Grosvenor |
| **Chew Magna** | Pony and Trap |
| **Chinnor / Sprigg's Alley** | Sir Charles Napier |
| **Clipsham** | The Olive Branch and Beech House |
| **Cranbrook** | Apicius |
| **Cuckfield** | Ockenden Manor |
| **Dorchester** | Sienna |
| **Eldersfield** | Butchers Arms |
| **Emsworth** | 36 on the Quay |
| **Faversham** | Read's |
| **Grange-over-Sands / Cartmel** | L'Enclume |
| **Horsham** | The Pass (at South Lodge Hotel) |
| **Hunstanton** | The Neptune |
| **Ilkley** | Box Tree |
| **Jersey / La Pulente** | Atlantic |
| **Jersey / St Helier** | Bohemia (at Club Hotel and Spa) |
| **Jersey / St Helier** | Tassili (at Grand Hotel) |
| **Kington / Titley** | The Stagg Inn |
| **London / Bromley** | Chapter One |
| **London / Camden** | Hakkasan Hanway Place |
| **London / Camden** | Pied à Terre |
| **London / City of London** | Club Gascon |
| **London / City of London** | Rhodes Twenty Four |
| **London / City of Westminster** | Amaya |
| **London / City of Westminster** | Apsleys |

| | | |
|---|---|---|
| **London / City of Westminster** | Arbutus | |
| **London / City of Westminster** | L'Autre Pied | |
| **London / City of Westminster** | Benares | |
| **London / City of Westminster** | Dinner by Heston Blumenthal | **N** |
| **London / City of Westminster** | Galvin at Windows | |
| **London / City of Westminster** | Gauthier - Soho | |
| **London / City of Westminster** | Greenhouse | |
| **London / City of Westminster** | Hakkasan Mayfair | **N** |
| **London / City of Westminster** | Kai | |
| **London / City of Westminster** | Locanda Locatelli | |
| **London / City of Westminster** | Maze | |
| **London / City of Westminster** | Murano | |
| **London / City of Westminster** | Nobu (at The Metropolitan Hotel) | |
| **London / City of Westminster** | Nobu Berkeley St | |
| **London / City of Westminster** | Pollen Street Social | **N** |
| **London / City of Westminster** | Pétrus | |
| **London / City of Westminster** | Quilon | |
| **London / City of Westminster** | Rhodes W1 (Restaurant) | |
| **London / City of Westminster** | Semplice | |
| **London / City of Westminster** | Seven Park Place | |
| **London / City of Westminster** | Sketch (The Lecture Room and Library) | |
| **London / City of Westminster** | Tamarind | |
| **London / City of Westminster** | Texture | |
| **London / City of Westminster** | Umu | |
| **London / City of Westminster** | Wild Honey | |
| **London / City of Westminster** | Yauatcha | |
| **London / City of Westminster** | Zafferano | |
| **London / Hammersmith and Fulham** | Harwood Arms | |
| **London / Hammersmith and Fulham** | River Café | |
| **London / Hounslow** | La Trompette | |
| **London / Islington (Borough of)** | North Road | **N** |
| **London / Islington (Borough of)** | St John (Clerkenwell) | |
| **London / Kensington and Chelsea** | Kitchen W8 | |
| **London / Kensington and Chelsea** | Rasoi | |
| **London / Richmond-upon-Thames** | The Glasshouse | |
| **London / Richmond-upon-Thames** | Petersham Nurseries Café | |
| **London / Tower Hamlets** | Galvin La Chapelle | |
| **London / Tower Hamlets** | Viajante | |
| **London / Wandsworth (Borough of)** | Chez Bruce | |
| **Ludlow** | Mr Underhill's at Dinham Weir | |
| **Marlborough / Little Bedwyn** | Harrow at Little Bedwyn | |
| **Marlow** | Adam Simmonds at Danesfield House | |
| **Murcott** | Nut Tree | |
| **Oakham / Hambleton** | Hambleton Hall | |
| **Oldstead** | Black Swan | **N** |
| **Pateley Bridge / Ramsgill-in-Nidderdale** | Yorke Arms | |
| **Petersfield** | JSW | |
| **Portscatho** | Driftwood | **N** |

| | |
|---|---|
| **Reading / Shinfield** | L'Ortolan |
| **Ripley (Surrey)** | Drake's |
| **Royal Leamington Spa** | Mallory Court |
| **Sheffield** | Old Vicarage |
| **South Molton / Knowstone** | The Masons Arms |
| **Torquay** | Room in the Elephant |
| **Ullswater / Pooley Bridge** | Sharrow Bay Country House |
| **Welwyn Garden City** | Auberge du Lac |
| **Whitstable / Seasalter** | The Sportsman |
| **Wight (Isle of) / Ventnor** | Hambrough |
| **Winchcombe** | 5 North St |
| **Winchester** | The Black Rat |
| **Windermere** | Holbeck Ghyll |
| **Woburn** | Paris House |

## → Scotland

| | | |
|---|---|---|
| **Ballantrae** | Glenapp Castle | **N** |
| **Balloch** | Martin Wishart at Loch Lomond (at Cameron House Hotel) | **N** |
| **Dalry** | Braidwoods | |
| **Edinburgh** | Castle Terrace | **N** |
| **Edinburgh** | Number One (at Balmoral Hotel) | |
| **Edinburgh** | 21212 | |
| **Edinburgh / Leith** | Kitchin | |
| **Edinburgh / Leith** | Martin Wishart | |
| **Elie** | Sangster's | |
| **Fort William** | Inverlochy Castle | |
| **Lochinver** | Albannach | |
| **Nairn** | Boath House | |
| **Peat Inn** | Peat Inn | |
| **Portpatrick** | Knockinaam Lodge | |
| **Skye (Isle of) / Sleat** | Kinloch Lodgee | |

## → Wales

| | | |
|---|---|---|
| **Abergavenny / Llanddewi Skirrid** | Walnut Tree | |
| **Llandrillo** | Tyddyn Llan | |
| **Monmouth / Whitebrook** | Crown at Whitebrook | |
| **Montgomery** | The Checkers | **N** |

## → Republic of Ireland

| | |
|---|---|
| **Ardmore** | House (at Cliff House Hotel) |
| **Dublin** | Chapter One |
| **Dublin** | L'Ecrivain |
| **Dublin** | Thornton's (at The Fitzwilliam Hotel) |
| **Malahide** | Bon Appétitt |

# Bib Gourmand 2012

• Places with at least one Bib Gourmand establishment.

Kilberry

NORTHERN
IRELAND
Ballyclare
Holywood
Belfast

Warrenpoint

Roundstone

REPUBLIC
OF IRELAND
Dublin
Stepaside

Lisdoonvarna

Clonegall

Adare

Dingle

Lismore

Duncannon

Durrus

Kinsale

GUERNSEY
St Saviour

JERSEY

Padstow

St. Ives

Freathy

Penzance

SCOTLAND

Glasgow
Edinburgh
Sorn
Peebles

SHETLAND
ISLANDS

ORKNEY
ISLANDS

Durham
Hurworth-on-Tees
Masham
Thornton
Ferrensby
Sutton-on-the-Forest
Wiswell
Leeds
Beverley
Bury
Oldham
Sheffield
Alderley Edge

ENGLAND
Stathern
Burnham Market
Itteringham
Wymondham
Stamford
Ingham
Bruntingthorpe
Stanton
East Haddon
Stoke Holy Cross
Bury St. Edmunds
Woolhope
Tewkesbury
Little
Wilbraham
Aldeburgh
Stow-on-the-Wold
Brecon
Oxford
Kelvedon
Tetbury
Seer Green
Cardiff
Bristol
Toot Baldon
London
Backwell
Bray
Wells
East
Chisenbury
Longstock
Preston
Candover
Ramsgate
Bruton
Romsey
Droxford
West Hoathly
Rockbeare
Wimborne
St. Giles
Hove
Henfield
Brighton
Hastings and St Leonards

VALES

# Bib Gourmand

## Good food at moderate prices

→ England

| | |
|---|---|
| Aldeburgh | Lighthouse |
| Alderley Edge | The Wizard |
| Backwell | New Inn |
| Beaconsfield / Seer Green | Jolly Cricketers |
| Beverley | Whites |
| Blackpool / Thornton | Twelve |
| Bray | Hinds Head |
| Brighton | Chilli Pickle |
| Brighton / Hove | Ginger Pig |
| Brighton / Hove | Meadow |
| Bristol | Flinty Red **N** |
| Bristol | Greens' Dining Room |
| Bruntingthorpe | The Joiners **N** |
| Bruton | At The Chapel |
| Burnham Market | Hoste Arms |
| Bury | Waggon |
| Bury St Edmunds | Pea Porridge |
| Cambridge / Little Wilbraham | Hole in the Wall |
| Clitheroe / Wiswell | Freemasons |
| Darlington / Hurworth-on-Tees | Bay Horse |
| Droxford | Bakers Arms |
| Durham | Bistro 21 |
| East Chisenbury | Red Lion Freehouse |
| East Haddon | Red Lion **N** |
| Exeter / Rockbeare | Jack in the Green Inn |
| Guernsey / St Saviour (Guernsey) | Pavilion |
| Hastings and St. Leonards | St Clements |
| Henfield | Ginger Fox |
| Ingham | Ingham Swan **N** |
| Itteringham | Walpole Arms |
| Kelvedon | George and Dragon |
| Knaresborough / Ferrensby | General Tarleton Inn |
| Leeds | Piazza by Anthony |
| London / Brent | Sushi-Say **N** |
| London / Camden | Bradley's |
| London / Camden | Giaconda Dining Room |
| London / Camden | Great Queen Street |
| London / Camden | Market |
| London / Camden | Salt Yard |
| London / City of London | Goldfish City |
| London / City of London | 28°-50° |
| London / City of Westminster | Al Duca |
| London / City of Westminster | Bar Trattoria Semplice |
| London / City of Westminster | Barrafina **N** |
| London / City of Westminster | Benja Bangkok Table |
| London / City of Westminster | Bocca di Lupo |
| London / City of Westminster | da Polpo **N** |
| London / City of Westminster | Dehesa |
| London / City of Westminster | Hereford Road |
| London / City of Westminster | Iberica |
| London / City of Westminster | Kateh **N** |
| London / City of Westminster | Koya **N** |
| London / City of Westminster | Opera Tavern **N** |
| London / City of Westminster | Polpo |
| London / City of Westminster | Terroirs |
| London / City of Westminster | Trishna **N** |
| London / Hammersmith and Fulham | Azou **N** |
| London / Hounslow | Charlotte's Bistro |
| London / Islington (Borough of) | Comptoir Gascon |
| London / Islington (Borough of) | Drapers Arms |

→ **N** *New*

| | |
|---|---|
| **London / Islington (Borough of)** | 500 |
| **London / Islington (Borough of)** | Medcalf |
| **London / Islington (Borough of)** | Morito |
| **London / Islington (Borough of)** | Trullo |
| **London / Lambeth** | Canton Arms |
| **London / Lewisham** | Chapters |
| **London / Merton** | Fox and Grapes **N** |
| **London / Richmond-upon-Thames** | Brown Dog |
| **London / Richmond-upon-Thames** | Mango and Silk |
| **London / Richmond-upon-Thames** | Simply Thai |
| **London / Southwark (Borough of)** | Anchor and Hope |
| **London / Southwark (Borough of)** | José **N** |
| **London / Southwark (Borough of)** | Zucca |
| **London / Tower Hamlets** | Brawn **N** |
| **London / Tower Hamlets** | Cafe Spice Namaste |
| **London / Tower Hamlets** | Galvin Café a Vin |
| **London / Tower Hamlets** | St John Bread and Wine **N** |
| **London / Wandsworth (Borough of)** | Triphal **N** |
| **Masham** | Vennell's |
| **Melton Mowbray / Stathern** | Red Lion Inn |
| **Millbrook / Freathy** | View |
| **Norwich / Stoke Holy Cross** | Wildebeest Arms |
| **Oldham** | White Hart Inn |
| **Oxford** | Anchor **N** |
| **Oxford** | Magdalen Arms |
| **Oxford / Toot Baldon** | Mole Inn |
| **Padstow** | Rick Stein's Café |
| **Penzance** | Untitled by Robert Wright **N** |
| **Preston Candover** | Purefoy Arms |
| **Ramsgate** | Age and Sons |
| **Romsey** | Three Tuns **N** |
| **St Ives** | Black Rock |
| **Sheffield** | Artisan |
| **Stamford** | Jim's Yard |
| **Stanton** | Leaping Hare |
| **Stockbridge / Longstock** | Peat Spade Inn |

| | |
|---|---|
| **Stow-on-the-Wold** | Old Butchers |
| **Sutton-on-the-Forest** | Rose and Crown |
| **Tetbury** | Gumstool Inn |
| **Tewkesbury** | Owens **N** |
| **Wells** | Old Spot |
| **West Hoathly** | Cat Inn |
| **Wimborne St Giles** | Bull Inn |
| **Woolhope** | Butchers Arms |
| **Wymondham** | Berkeley Arms **N** |

## → Scotland

| | |
|---|---|
| **Edinburgh** | Dogs |
| **Glasgow** | Stravaigin **N** |
| **Kintyre (Peninsula) / Kilberry** | Kilberry Inn |
| **Peebles** | Osso |
| **Sorn** | Sorn Inn n |

## → Wales

| | |
|---|---|
| **Brecon** | Felin Fach Griffin **N** |
| **Cardiff** | chai st **N** |
| **Cardiff** | Mint and Mustard **N** |

## → Northern Ireland

| | |
|---|---|
| **Ballyclare** | Oregano |
| **Belfast** | Cayenne |
| **Holywood** | Fontana **N** |
| **Warrenpoint** | Restaurant 23 |

## → Republic of Ireland

| | |
|---|---|
| **Adare** | White Sage |
| **Clonegall** | Sha Roe Bistro |
| **Dingle** | Chart House |
| **Dublin** | Pichet |
| **Dublin** | Pig's Ear |
| **Duncannon** | Aldridge Lodge |
| **Durrus** | Good Things Café |
| **Kinsale** | Fishy Fishy Cafe |
| **Lisdoonvarna** | Wild Honey Inn |
| **Lismore** | O'Brien Chop House |
| **Roundstone** | O'Dowd's |
| **Stepaside** | Box Tree **N** |

# Bib Hotel

## Good accommodation at moderate prices

---

## → England

| | |
|---|---|
| **Aldeburgh / Friston** | Old School |
| **Barnard Castle** | Homelands |
| **Bodmin** | Bokiddick Farm |
| **Bourton-on-the-Water** | Coombe House |
| **Bovey Tracey** | Brookfield House |
| **Bungay / Earsham** | Earsham Park Farm |
| **Bury St Edmunds / Beyton** | Manorhouse |
| **Cheddleton** | Choir Cottage |
| **Deddington** | Old Post House |
| **Devizes / Potterne** | Blounts Court Farm |
| **Doddington** | Old Vicarage |
| **Earl Stonham** | Bays Farm |
| **Eastbourne** | Brayscroft |
| **Harrogate / Kettlesing** | Knabbs Ash |
| **Hartland** | Golden Park |
| **Henfield / Wineham** | Frylands |
| **Hexham** | West Close House |
| **Holbeach** | Pipwell Manor |
| **Kenilworth** | Victoria Lodge |
| **Kirkwhelpington** | Shieldhall |
| **Leyburn** | Clyde House |
| **Longtown** | Bessiestown Farm |
| **Morpeth / Longhorsley** | Thistleyhaugh Farm |
| **Oxhill** | Oxbourne House |
| **Penrith** | Brooklands |
| **Pickering** | Bramwood |
| **Ripon** | Sharow Cross House |
| **Ross-on-Wye / Kerne Bridge** | Lumleys |

| | |
|---|---|
| **Salisbury / Little Langford** | |
| | Little Langford Farmhouse |
| **Scarborough** | Alexander |
| **Southend-on-Sea** | Beaches |
| **Stow-on-the-Wold** | Number Nine |
| **Stow-on-the-Wold /** | |
| **Lower Swell** | Rectory Farmhouse **N** |
| **Torquay** | Colindale |
| **Tynemouth** | Martineau |
| **Wallingford** | North Moreton House |
| **Wareham** | Gold Court House |
| **Warwick** | Charter House **N** |
| **Wells / Easton** | |
| **(Somerset)** | Beaconsfield Farm |
| **Whitby / Briggswath** | Lawns |
| **York** | Alexander House |

## → Scotland

| | |
|---|---|
| **Anstruther** | Spindrift |
| **Auchencairn** | Balcary Mews |
| **Ayr** | Coila |
| **Ayr** | No.26 The Crescent |
| **Ballater** | Moorside House |
| **Blairgowrie** | Gilmore House |
| **Carnoustie** | The Old Manor |
| **Crieff** | Merlindale |
| **Dunkeld** | Letter Farm |
| **Forres / Dyke** | Old Kirk |
| **Glendevon** | Tormaukin |

---

| | |
|---|---|
| **Jedburgh** | Willow Court |
| **Kingussie** | Hermitage |
| **Montrose** | 36 The Mall |
| **Nairn** | Bracadale House |
| **Peebles** | Rowanbrae |
| **Perth** | Taythorpe |
| **Pitlochry** | Dunmurray Lodge |
| **Skye (Isle of) / Broadford** | Tigh an Dochais |
| **Skye (Isle of) / Dunvegan** | Roskhill House |
| **Stevenston** | Ardeer Farm Steading |
| **Stonehaven** | Beachgate House **N** |
| **Strathpeffer** | Craigvar |
| **Thornhill** | Gillbank House |
| **Ullapool** | Point Cottage |
| **Wick** | The Clachan |

## ➜ Wales

| | |
|---|---|
| **Aberaeron** | Llys Aero |
| **Betws Garmon** | Betws Inn |
| **Colwyn Bay** | Rathlin Country House |
| **Dolgellau** | Tyddyn Mawr |
| **Llandudno** | Abbey Lodge |
| **Llandudno** | Lympley Lodge |
| **Llanuwchllyn** | Eifionydd |

| | |
|---|---|
| **Ruthin** | Firgrove |
| **Whitton** | Pilleth Oaks **N** |

## ➜ Northern Ireland

| | |
|---|---|
| **Bangor** | Cairn Bay Lodge |
| **Belfast** | Ravenhill House |
| **Crumlin** | Caldhame Lodge |

## ➜ Republic of Ireland

| | |
|---|---|
| **Ballyvaughan** | Drumcreehy House |
| **Bansha** | Rathellen House |
| **Carlow** | Barrowville Town House **N** |
| **Castlegregory** | Shores Country House |
| **Donegal** | Ardeevin |
| **Dundalk** | Rosemount |
| **Kinsale / Barrells Cross** | Rivermount House |
| **Oughterard** | Railway Lodge |
| **Oughterard** | Waterfall Lodge |
| **Portlaoise** | Ivyleigh House **N** |
| **Toormore** | Fortview House |
| **Tramore** | Glenorney |
| **Wexford** | McMenamin's Townhouse **N** |

# Particularly pleasant hotels & guesthouses

## → England

| | |
|---|---|
| Dogmersfield | Four Seasons |
| London / City of Westminster | Berkeley |
| London / City of Westminster | Claridge's |
| London / City of Westminster | Connaught |
| London / City of Westminster | Dorchester |
| London / City of Westminster | Four Seasons |
| London / City of Westminster | Mandarin Oriental Hyde Park |
| London / City of Westminster | Ritz |
| London / City of Westminster | Savoy |
| New Milton | Chewton Glen |
| Oxford / Great Milton | Le Manoir aux Quat' Saisons |
| Taplow | Cliveden |

## → England

| | |
|---|---|
| Ascot | Coworth Park |
| Aylesbury | Hartwell House |
| Bath / Colerne | Lucknam Park |
| Bourton-on-the-Water / Lower Slaughter | Lower Slaughter Manor |
| Chagford | Gidleigh Park |
| Cheltenham | Ellenborough Park |
| Jersey / St Saviour (Jersey) | Longueville Manor |
| London / City of Westminster | Goring |
| London / City of Westminster | One Aldwych |
| London / City of Westminster | Soho |
| Lyndhurst | Lime Wood |
| Malmesbury | Whatley Manor |
| Newbury | Vineyard at Stockcross |
| North Bovey | Bovey Castle |
| Ston Easton | Ston Easton Park |

## → Scotland

| | |
|---|---|
| Ballantrae | Glenapp Castle |
| Eriska (Isle of) | Isle of Eriska |
| Fort William | Inverlochy Castle |

## → Republic of Ireland

| | |
|---|---|
| Ballyfin | Ballyfin |
| Dublin | Merrion |
| Kenmare | Park |
| Killarney | Killarney Park |

## → England

| | |
|---|---|
| Abberley | Elms |
| Amberley | Amberley Castle |
| Bath | Bath Priory |
| Beaulieu | Montagu Arms |
| Bolton Abbey | Devonshire Arms Country House |
| Bourton-on-the-Water / Upper Slaughter | Lords of the Manor |
| Broadway | Buckland Manor |
| Castle Combe | Manor House H. and Golf Club |
| Dedham | Maison Talbooth |
| Evershot | Summer Lodge |
| Gillingham | Stock Hill Country House |
| Guernsey / St Peter Port | Old Government House H. and Spa |
| Jersey / La Pulente | Atlantic |
| London / Camden | Charlotte Street |
| London / Camden | Covent Garden |

| | |
|---|---|
| **London / City of Westminster** | Dukes |
| **London / City of Westminster** | Halkin |
| **London / City of Westminster** | Stafford |
| **London / Kensington and Chelsea** | Blakes |
| **London / Kensington and Chelsea** | The Capital |
| **London / Kensington and Chelsea** | Draycott |
| **London / Kensington and Chelsea** | The Milestone |
| **London / Kensington and Chelsea** | The Pelham |
| **Newcastle upon Tyne** | Jesmond Dene House |
| **Oakham / Hambleton** | Hambleton Hall |
| **Reading** | Forbury |
| **Royal Leamington Spa** | Mallory Court |
| **Scilly (Isles of)** | St Martin's on the Isle |
| **Tetbury** | Calcot Manor |
| **Ullswater / Pooley Bridge** | Sharrow Bay Country House |
| **Winchester / Sparsholt** | Lainston House |

| | |
|---|---|
| **Windermere / Bowness-on-Windermere** | Gilpin H. and Lake House |
| **Yarm** | Judges Country House |
| **York** | Middlethorpe Halll |

## → Scotland

| | |
|---|---|
| **Blairgowrie** | Kinloch House |
| **Edinburgh** | Prestonfield |
| **Gullane** | Greywalls |
| **Torridon** | The Torridon |

## → Wales

| | |
|---|---|
| **Llandudno** | Bodysgallen Hall |
| **Llangammarch Wells and Spa** | Lake Country House |

## → Republic of Ireland

| | |
|---|---|
| **Ardmore** | Cliff House |
| **Ballyvaughan** | Gregans Castle |
| **Dublin** | Dylan |
| **Gorey (Wexford)** | Marlfield House |
| **Mallow** | Longueville House |

## → England

| | |
|---|---|
| **Ambleside** | The Samling |
| **Bath** | Queensberry |
| **Bigbury-on-Sea** | Burgh Island |
| **Blakeney / Morston** | Morston Hall |
| **Brampton** | Farlam Hall |
| **Burnham Market** | Hoste Arms |
| **Chester** | Green Bough |
| **Cirencester / Barnsley** | Barnsley House |
| **Cuckfield** | Ockenden Manor |
| **Frome** | Babington House |
| **Helmsley** | Feversham Arms |
| **Horley** | Langshott Manor |
| **Lewdown** | Lewtrenchard Manor |
| **London / Kensington and Chelsea** | Egerton House |
| **London / Kensington and Chelsea** | Knightsbridge |
| **London / Kensington and Chelsea** | The Levin |
| **London / Kensington and Chelsea** | Number Sixteen |
| **Newquay / Mawgan Porth** | Scarlet |
| **North Walsham** | Beechwood |

| | |
|---|---|
| **Orford** | Crown and Castle |
| **Portscatho** | Driftwood |
| **Rushlake Green** | Stone House |
| **St Mawes** | Hotel Tresanton |
| **Scilly (Isles of)** | Hell Bay |
| **Southampton / Netley Marsh** | Hotel TerraVina |
| **Stratford-upon-Avon** | Arden |
| **Tavistock / Milton Abbot** | Hotel Endsleigh |
| **Torquay / Maidencombe** | Orestone Manor |
| **Wareham** | Priory |
| **Windermere** | Holbeck Ghyll |

## → Scotland

| | |
|---|---|
| **Abriachan** | Loch Ness Lodge |
| **Achiltibuie** | Summer Isles |
| **Arran (Isle of)** | Kilmichael Country House |
| **Lochearnhead / Balquhidder** | Monachyle Mhor |
| **Nairn** | Boath House |
| **Port Appin** | Airds |
| **Portpatrick** | Knockinaam Lodge |
| **Skye (Isle of) / Sleat** | Kinloch Lodge |

## → Wales

| | |
|---|---|
| **Llandudno** | Osborne House |
| **Machynlleth** | Ynyshir Hall |
| **Narberth** | Grove |
| **Swansea / Llanrhidian** | Fairyhill |

## → Republic of Ireland

| | |
|---|---|
| **Ballingarry** | Mustard Seed at Echo Lodge |
| **Kinsale** | Perryville House |

## → England

| | |
|---|---|
| **Ashwater** | Blagdon Manor |
| **Bourton-on-the-Water** | Dial House |
| **Burnham Market** | Vine House |
| **Chillington** | whitehouse |
| **Dartmouth / Kingswear** | Nonsuch House |
| **Helmsley / Harome** | Cross House Lodge |
| **Keswick / Portinscale** | Swinside Lodge |
| **Ludlow** | De Grey's Town House |
| **Lynton / Martinhoe** | Old Rectory |
| **Porlock** | Oaks |
| **Salisbury /** | |
| **Teffont Magna** | Howard's House |

## → Wales

| | |
|---|---|
| **Betws-y-Coed** | Tan-y-Foel Country House |
| **Dolgellau** | Ffynnon |

## → Republic of Ireland

| | |
|---|---|
| **Bagenalstown** | Kilgraney Country House |
| **Castlelyons** | Ballyvolane House |
| **Dingle** | Emlagh Country House |
| **Lahinch** | Moy House |

## → Scotland

| | |
|---|---|
| **Kelso / Ednam** | Edenwater House |
| **Kirkbean** | Cavens |
| **Mull (Isle of) / Tiroran** | Tiroran House |
| **Tain / Cadboll** | Glenmorangie House |

## → England

| | |
|---|---|
| **Arnside** | Number 43 |
| **Ash** | Great Weddington |
| **Austwick** | Austwick Hall |
| **Beverley** | Burton Mount |
| **Blackpool** | Number One St Lukes |
| **Bridport /** | |
| **Burton Bradstock** | Norburton Hall |
| **Brighton** | Kemp Townhouse |
| **Broad Oak** | Fairacres |
| **Cheltenham** | Thirty Two |
| **Chipping Campden /** | |
| **Broad Campden** | Malt House |
| **Clun** | Birches Mill |
| **Crackington Haven** | Manor Farm |
| **Cranbrook** | Cloth Hall Oast |
| **East Hoathly** | Old Whyly |
| **Hawkshead / Far Sawrey** | West Vale |
| **Haworth** | Ashmount Country House |
| **Ivychurch** | Olde Moat House |
| **Kendal** | Beech House |
| **Kilham** | Kilham Hall |
| **Lavenham** | Lavenham Priory |
| **Ledbury / Kynaston** | Hall End |
| **Lizard** | Landewednack House |
| **Marazion / Perranuthnoe** | Ednovean Farm |
| **Marazion / St Hilary** | Ennys |
| **Moreton-in-Marsh** | Old School |
| **North Bovey** | Gate House |
| **North Lopham** | Church Farm House |
| **Padstow** | Treann |

| | |
|---|---|
| **Padstow** | Treverbyn House |
| **Padstow** | Woodlands Country House |
| **Pershore / Eckington** | Eckington Manor |
| **Pickering** | 17 Burgate |
| **Pickering /** | |
| **Levisham** | Moorlands Country House |
| **Pillerton Priors** | Fulready Manor |
| **Ripon** | Sharow Cross House |
| **St Austell / Tregrehan** | Anchorage House |
| **Shrewsbury** | Pinewood House |
| **Stow-on-the-Wold /** | |
| **Lower Swell** | Rectory Farmhouse |
| **Stratford-upon-Avon** | Cherry Trees |
| **Tavistock / Chillaton** | Tor Cottage |
| **Teignmouth** | Thomas Luny House |
| **Thursford Green** | Holly Lodge |
| **Warkworth** | Roxbro House |
| **Wold Newton** | Wold Cottage |

## → Scotland

| | |
|---|---|
| **Ballantrae** | Cosses Country House |
| **Bute (Isle of) / Ascog** | Balmory Hall |
| **Connel** | Ards House |
| **Drumbeg** | Blar na Leisg at Drumbeg House |
| **Edinburgh** | One Royal Circus |
| **Fort William** | Grange |
| **Fortrose** | Water's Edge |
| **Grantown-on-Spey** | Dulaig |
| **Islay (Isle of) / Ballygrant** | Kilmeny |
| **Linlithgow** | Arden House |
| **Lochinver** | Ruddyglow Park Country House |

| | |
|---|---|
| **Mainland (Orkney Islands) /** | |
| **Harray** | Holland House |
| **Mull (Isle of) / Gruline** | Gruline Home Farm |
| **Skirling** | Skirling House |
| **Skye (Isle of) / Bernisdale** | Spoons |
| **Strathpeffer** | Craigvar |
| **Tain / Nigg** | Wemyss House |

## → Wales

| | |
|---|---|
| **Aberaeron** | 3 Pen Cei |
| **Anglesey (Isle of) / Beaumaris** | Cleifiog |
| **Anglesey (Isle of) /** | |
| **Menai Bridge** | Neuadd Lwyd |
| **Betws-y-Coed /** | |
| **Penmachno** | Penmachno Hall |
| **Dolfor** | Old Vicarage |
| **Dolgellau** | Tyddyn Mawr |
| **Pwllheli / Boduan** | Old Rectory |
| **St Clears** | Coedllys Country House |

## → Northern Ireland

| | |
|---|---|
| **Ballintoy** | Whitepark House |
| **Dungannon** | Grange Lodgel |

## → Republic of Ireland

| | |
|---|---|
| **Castlegregory** | Shores Country House |
| **Cong** | Ballywarren House |
| **Fethard** | Mobarnane House |
| **Kenmare** | Sallyport House |
| **Toormore** | Fortview House |

# Particularly pleasant restaurants & pubs

## XXXXX

→ England

| | |
|---|---|
| **London / City of Westminster** | The Ritz Restaurant |

## XXXX

→ England

| | |
|---|---|
| **Bath / Colerne** | The Park (at Lucknam Park Hotel) |
| **Bolton Abbey** | Burlington (at Devonshire Arms Country House Hotel) |
| **Bray** | Waterside Inn |
| **London / City of Westminster** | Hélène Darroze at The Connaught |
| **London / City of Westminster** | Marcus Wareing at The Berkeley |

→ Republic of Ireland

| | |
|---|---|
| **Dublin** | Patrick Guilbaud |

## XXX

→ England

| | |
|---|---|
| **Baslow** | Fischer's at Baslow Hall |
| **Birmingham** | Simpsons |
| **Blackburn / Langho** | Northcote |
| **Cambridge** | Midsummer House |
| **Dedham** | Le Talbooth |
| **Faversham** | Read's |
| **Ilkley** | Box Tree |
| **Lavenham** | Great House |
| **London / City of London** | Coq d'Argent |
| **London / City of Westminster** | Cecconi's |
| **London / City of Westminster** | Pétrus |
| **London / City of Westminster** | Quo Vadis |
| **London / City of Westminster** | The Wolseley |
| **London / Hackney** | Boundary |
| **London / Kensington and Chelsea** | Bibendum |
| **London / Kensington and Chelsea** | The Capital Restaurant (at The Capital Hotel) |
| **London / Tower Hamlets** | Galvin La Chapelle |

| Pateley Bridge / Ramsgill-in-Nidderdale | Yorke Arms |
| **Petersfield** | JSW |
| **Reading / Shinfield** | L'Ortolan |
| **Skipton / Hetton** | Angel Inn and Barn Lodgings |
| **Ston Easton** | Sorrel (at Ston Easton Park Hotel) |
| **Welwyn Garden City** | Auberge du Lac |
| **Winteringham** | Winteringham Fields |
| **Woburn** | Paris House |

→ Scotland

| **Edinburgh** | 21212 |
| **Peat Inn** | Peat Inn |
| **St Andrews** | Seafood |

→ Wales

| **Llandrillo** | Tyddyn Llan |

→ England

| **Alkham** | Marquis |
| **Arlingham** | Old Passage Inn |
| **Bath / Colerne** | Brasserie (at Lucknam Park Hotel) |
| **Bildeston** | Bildeston Crown |
| **Brockenhurst** | The Pig |
| **Burnham Market** | Hoste Arms |
| **Bury St Edmunds** | Maison Bleue |
| **Cheltenham** | Daffodil |
| **Grange-over-Sands / Cartmel** | L'Enclume |
| **Grantham / Great Gonerby** | Harry's Place |
| **Grantham / Hough-on-the-Hill** | Brownlow Arms |
| **Kibworth Beauchamp** | Firenze |
| **Kirkby Lonsdale** | Hipping Hall |
| **London / Camden** | Mon Plaisir |
| **London / City of Westminster** | Le Café Anglais |
| **London / City of Westminster** | Clos Maggiore |
| **London / City of Westminster** | J. Sheekey |
| **London / City of Westminster** | Rules |
| **London / City of Westminster** | Wild Honey |
| **London / Hammersmith and Fulham** | River Café |
| **Ludlow** | Mr Underhill's at Dinham Weir |
| **Malmesbury** | Le Mazot (at Whatley Manor Hotel) |
| **Newquay / Watergate Bay** | Fifteen Cornwall |
| **Padstow** | Paul Ainsworth at No.6 |
| **Padstow** | The Seafood |
| **St Mawes** | Restaurant Tresanton (at Hotel Tresanton) |
| **Sark** | La Sablonnerie |
| **Stanton** | Leaping Hare |
| **Yeovil / Barwick** | Little Barwick House |

→ Scotland

| **Kingussie** | Cross at Kingussie |
| **Lochinver** | Albannach |
| **Skye (Isle of) / Dunvegan** | Three Chimneys and The House Over-By |

## ➔ England

| | |
|---|---|
| **Alton / Lower Froyle** | The Anchor Inn |
| **Ambleside** | Drunken Duck Inn |
| **Barnard Castle / Romaldkirk** | Rose and Crown |
| **Bath / Combe Hay** | Wheatsheaf |
| **Baughurst** | Wellington Arms |
| **Beverley / South Dalton** | Pipe and Glass Inn |
| **Bolnhurst** | Plough at Bolnhurst |
| **Bray** | Hinds Head |
| **Burford / Swinbrook** | Swan Inn |
| **Cambridge / Little Wilbraham** | Hole in the Wall |
| **Chichester / Chilgrove** | Fish House |
| **Chichester / East Lavant** | The Royal Oak Inn |
| **Cirencester / Barnsley** | Village Pub |
| **Cirencester / Sapperton** | Bell |
| **Clipsham** | The Olive Branch and Beech House |
| **Clitheroe / Wiswell** | Freemasons |
| **East Garston** | Queen's Arms |
| **Helmsley / Harome** | Star Inn |
| **Kendal / Crosthwaite** | Punch Bowl Inn |
| **Keyston** | Pheasant |
| **Lydford** | Dartmoor Inn |
| **Marlow** | Hand and Flowers |
| **Mistley** | Mistley Thorn |
| **Old Warden** | Hare and Hounds |
| **Oldstead** | Black Swan |
| **Oxford / Fyfield** | White Hart |
| **Skipton / Hetton** | Angel Inn |
| **South Molton / Knowstone** | The Masons Arms |
| **Stockbridge / Longstock** | Peat Spade Inn |
| **Stoke-by-Nayland** | Crown |
| **Stow-on-the-Wold / Nether Westcote** | Feathered Nest |
| **Sutton-on-the-Forest** | Rose and Crown |
| **Tarr Steps** | Tarr Farm Inn |
| **Windermere / Troutbeck** | Queen's Head |
| **Woolhope** | Butchers Arms |

## ➔ Wales

| | |
|---|---|
| **Aberaeron** | Harbourmaster |
| **Brecon** | Felin Fach Griffin |
| **Skenfrith** | Bell at Skenfrith |

## ➔ Republic of Ireland

| | |
|---|---|
| **Kinsale** | Toddies at The Bulman |

# Further information

# Beer...

It's no exaggeration to say that beer and its consumption has pretty much defined popular conception of the British character for hundreds of years. From humble ale-house, via ubiquitous urban tavern, to agreeable coaching inn – all manner of drinking establishments have lined the British highway and byway since medieval times. As an example of the popularity of the properties of ale, by the fourteenth century there were over 350 taverns in London alone, while exactly 400 years ago you could have wandered round the capital's Square Mile and found over a thousand alehouses.

The quality of the beverage proffered to thirsty customers has varied as much as the fixtures and fittings but, generally speaking, the production of beer has followed a time-honoured recipe of four ingredients: barley, hops, yeast and water. The perfect pint begins with barley - the classic beer-making grain - and a clean, plentiful water supply coming together in a maltings, creating sugar for fermentation. The result looks like thin porridge; this boiling sludge is then filtered to a brown, hazy liquid called sweet wort.

Malt imparts sweetness to a beer and so, to give it balance, the addition of hops provides a bitter element to the mix. The hops need to be boiled to release their bitterness; it's at this point the true process of brewing is enacted. Eventually, the 'hopped wort' is cooled and filtered, in preparation for the key operation: fermentation. To ferment the beer, the brewers' little miracle-worker – yeast – is added to the fermentation vessels. Yeast is a living micro-organism, and its great claim to fame (apart from filling jars of Marmite!) is being able to convert the sugars into alcohol, carbon dioxide gas and a host of subtle flavours. With real ale, a secondary fermentation takes place when the finished product is safely ensconced in its barrel or cask, a process known as conditioning which happens before it leaves the brewery, and later, as it lies in the pub cellar. The final link in the chain is the publican, who (hopefully) oversees that decent pint gushing enticingly from the hand pump!

# ... and Whisky

Translated from the Gaelic term 'water of life', whisky depends for its very existence on the classic qualities of H2O. The local water supply dictates the nature of your glass of whisky; above and beyond that, the characteristics of the drink itself can range from spicy and aromatic to stylish and fruity, from light and fragrant to seaweedy and peaty. The classic Scotch whisky - only produced in the ideal natural environment of Scotland - makes full use of plentiful water supplies: barley is steeped in water for two to three days to turn it into malt, and then dried in a kiln traditionally fuelled by peat, before being ground in a mill.

The milled malt is called grist, and when hot water is added, the mixture is fed into a mash tun. This is where the sugars from malting dissolve, and the resulting solution – wort – oozes through the floor of the tun, to be passed into large wooden or stainless steel vessels. Add yeast, and fermentation occurs, with the sugars turning to alcohol. By now, this looks something like beer, but when it's distilled – a two-pronged process in which condensing vapours are captured - any resemblance to ale is long gone! By the time the different parts of the distillation are gathered together and redistilled, the resultant liquid – the new-make whisky – is ready to spend the next three years (by law) in oak casks maturing: the wood enhances the final aroma and flavour. Whisky makers enjoy a certain pact with the heavens: as the liquid matures, some of it evaporates into the ether, and this is known as the 'Angels' Share'…

Irish whiskey (note the extra 'e') differs slightly from the Scottish version, and not just in the spelling. It's traditionally made from cereals, and peat is hardly ever used in the malting process, so there's a lack of the smoky, earthy characteristics found over the Irish Sea. It's also encouraged to sit around for a much longer time: the maturation period is seven years, more than twice that of Scotch.

# YOU ALREADY KNOW THE MICHELIN GUIDE, NOW FIND OUT ABOUT THE MICHELIN GROUP

# The Michelin Adventure

It all started with rubber balls! This was the product made by a small company based in Clermont-Ferrand that André and Edouard Michelin inherited, back in 1880. The brothers quickly saw the potential for a new means of transport and their first success was the invention of detachable pneumatic tyres for bicycles. However, the automobile was to provide the greatest scope for their creative talents. Throughout the 20th century, Michelin never ceased developing and creating ever more reliable and high-performance tyres, not only for vehicles ranging from trucks to F1 but also for underground transit systems and aeroplanes.

From early on, Michelin provided its customers with tools and services to facilitate mobility and make travelling a more pleasurable and more frequent experience. As early as 1900, the Michelin Guide supplied motorists with a host of useful information related to vehicle maintenance, accommodation and restaurants, and was to become a benchmark for good food. At the same time, the Travel Information Bureau offered travellers personalised tips and itineraries.

The publication of the first collection of roadmaps, in 1910, was an instant hit! In 1926, the first regional guide to France was published, devoted to the principal sites of Brittany, and before long each region of France had its own Green Guide. The collection was later extended to more far-flung destinations, including New York in 1968 and Taiwan in 2011.

In the 21st century, with the growth of digital technology, the challenge for Michelin maps and guides is to continue to develop alongside the company's tyre activities. Now, as before, Michelin is committed to improving the mobility of travellers.

## MICHELIN TODAY

### WORLD NUMBER ONE TYRE MANUFACTURER
• 70 production sites in 18 countries
• 111,000 employees from all cultures and on every continent
• 6,000 people employed in research and development

# Moving
## for a world

Moving forward means developing tyres with better road grip and shorter braking distances, whatever the state of the road.

## CORRECT TYRE PRESSURE

**RIGHT PRESSURE**

- Safety
- Longevity
- Optimum fuel consumption

-0,5 bar

- Durability reduced by 20% (- 8,000 km)

-1 bar

- Risk of blowouts
- Increased fuel consumption
- Longer braking distances on wet surfaces

# forward together
## where mobility is safer

It also involves helping motorists take care of their safety and their tyres. To do so, Michelin organises "Fill Up With Air" campaigns all over the world to remind us that correct tyre pressure is vital.

## WEAR

### DETECTING TYRE WEAR

The legal minimum depth of tyre tread is 1.6mm.

Tyre manufacturers equip their tyres with tread wear indicators, which are small blocks of rubber moulded into the base of the main grooves at a depth of 1.6mm.

Tyres are the only point of contact between vehicle and road.

**The photo below shows the actual contact zone.**

NEW TYRE

WORN TYRE
(1,6 mm tread)

*If the tread depth is less than 1.6mm, tyres are considered to be worn and dangerous on wet surfaces.*

# Moving forward
## means sustainable mobility

By 2050, Michelin aims to cut the quantity of raw materials used in its tyre manufacturing process by half and to have developed renewable energy in its facilities. The design of MICHELIN tyres has already saved billions of litres of fuel and, by extension, billions of tonnes of $CO_2$.

Similarly, Michelin prints its maps and guides on paper produced from sustainably managed forests and is diversifying its publishing media by offering digital solutions to make travelling easier, more fuel efficient and more enjoyable!

The group's whole-hearted commitment to eco-design on a daily basis is demonstrated by ISO 14001 certification.

Like you, Michelin is committed to preserving our planet.

# Chat with Bibendum

Go to
www.michelin.com/corporate/fr
Find out more about Michelin's
history and the latest news.

## QUIZ

Michelin develops tyres for all types of vehicles. See if you can match the right tyre with the right vehicle…

Solution: A-6 / B-4 / C-2 / D-1 / E-3 / F-7 / G-5

# Great Britain

England

Channel Islands • Isle of Man

**ABBERLEY** – Worcestershire – **503** M27 – **pop. 654** – ⊠ Worcester    **18** B2
▶ London 137 mi – Birmingham 27 mi – Worcester 13 mi

🏨 **Elms** ⊗    ◁ 🚗 🕭 🎧 🖳 🕙 📻 🎰 Là ✗ ⇕ 🖐 **P** **VISA** **◯◯** **AE**
West : 2 mi on A 443 ⊠ WR6 6AT – ℰ (01299) 896 666
– www.theelmshotel.co.uk
**23 rm** (dinner included) ⊑ – ☗£ 200/315 ☗☗£ 330/510
**Rest** *Brooke Room* – see restaurant listing
**Rest** *Pear Terrace* – Carte £ 22/25
♦ Impressive Queen Anne house built in 1710. Inside, modern colours and fabrics blend seamlessly with traditional furnishings. Bedrooms are split between the house and old stables, and most boast pleasant country views. Choice of modern fine dining, or snacks and more traditional dishes in informal Pear Terrace – that latter set within an impressive spa. Child friendly.

✗✗ **Brooke Room** – at Elms Hotel    ◁ 🚗 🕭 **P** **VISA** **◯◯** **AE**
West : 2 mi on A 443 ⊠ WR6 6AT – ℰ (01299) 896 666
– www.theelmshotel.co.uk
**Rest** – Menu £ 21/49 – Carte £ 17/49
♦ Fine dining room set in an impressive Queen Anne house designed by Sir Gilbert White in 1710. Straightforward menu offers dishes of a modern persuasion. Homemade goat's cheese is a feature.

---

**ABBOTSBURY** – Dorset – **503** M32 – **pop. 422**    **3** B3

▶ London 146 mi – Bournemouth 44 mi – Exeter 50 mi – Weymouth 10 mi
◎ Town★★ - Chesil Beach★★ - Swannery★ **AC** – Sub-Tropical Gardens★ **AC**
🄲 St Catherine's Chapel★, 0.5 mi uphill (30 mn rtn on foot). Maiden Castle★★ (◁★)
NE : 7.5 m

🏠 **Abbey House** without rest ⊗    🚗 🕙 🖐 **P**
Church St ⊠ DT3 4JJ – ℰ (01305) 871 330 – www.theabbeyhouse.co.uk
– March-November
**5 rm** ⊑ – ☗£ 110 ☗☗£ 110
♦ Historic stone house; part-15C abbey infirmary. Garden holds a unique Benedictine water mill. Breakfast room with low beamed ceiling and fireplace. Cosy bedrooms.

---

**ABINGDON** – Oxfordshire – **503** Q28 – **pop. 36 010** ▮ Great Britain    **10** B2
▶ London 64 mi – Oxford 6 mi – Reading 25 mi
▤ from Abingdon Bridge to Oxford (Salter Bros. Ltd) 2 daily (summer only)
🄳 Abbey Close ℰ (01235) 52 27 11, www.abingdon.gov.uk
🄳 Drayton Park Drayton Steventon Rd, ℰ (01235) 55 06 07
◎ Town★ – County Hall★

**at Marcham** West : 3 mi on A 415

🏠 **Rafters** without rest    🖐 🖐 **P** **VISA** **◯◯** **◯**
Abingdon Rd, on A 415 ⊠ OX13 6NU – ℰ (01865) 391 298
– www.bnb-rafters.co.uk
**4 rm** ⊑ – ☗£ 52/85 ☗☗£ 120
♦ Modern, well-equipped bedrooms; the superior room, with luxury bathroom and balcony, is best. Friendly owner offers substantial, locally sourced breakfast. Massage chair for relaxation.

---

**ABINGER COMMON** – Surrey – **504** S30    **7** D2
▶ London 32 mi – Croydon 26 mi – Barnet 62 mi – Ealing 44 mi

🍴 **Abinger Hatch**    🚗 🕙 ⇄ **P** **VISA** **◯◯** **AE**
Abinger Ln ⊠ RH5 6HZ – ℰ (01306) 730 737 – www.theabingerhatch.com
**Rest** – Menu £ 15 (weekdays) – Carte £ 22/31
♦ Set in prime walking country, this attractive 18C inn has been lovingly restored and now oozes country gentility. The bar is the best spot to enjoy the flavoursome country cooking, from lamb pie to gooseberry fool. Hampers available.

ENGLAND

## ABINGER HAMMER – Surrey – **504** S30         **7** C2

▶ London 35 mi – Brighton 40 mi – Dover 91 mi – Portsmouth 50 mi

XX **Drakes on the Pond**     AC P VISA ⓪

*Dorking Rd, on A 25* ✉ *RH5 6SA –* ✆ *(01306) 731 174*
*– www.drakesonthepond.com – Closed 2 weeks August, Christmas-New Year,*
*Sunday and Monday*
**Rest** – Menu £ 26 (lunch) – Carte £ 42/53
◆ Long-standing neighbourhood restaurant – formerly a cowshed – run by husband and wife: he cooks, she leads front of house. Long, narrow room with bright walls. Simply presented, classic dishes.

## ALDEBURGH – Suffolk – **504** Y27 – pop. 2 654      **15** D3

▶ London 97 mi – Ipswich 24 mi – Norwich 41 mi

🖪 152 High St ✆ (01728) 45 36 37, www.aldeburgh-uk.com

🖪 ThorpenessHotel and Golf Course Thorpeness, ✆ (01728) 45 21 76

🏨 **Wentworth**     ≪ 🚗 🏠 ⅄ rm, ⁞¶ P VISA ⓪ AE ⓪

*Wentworth Rd.* ✉ *IP15 5BD –* ✆ *(01728) 452 312*
*– www.wentworth-aldeburgh.com*
**35 rm** ⬙ – ♦£ 92/132 ♦♦£ 150/170
**Rest** – Menu £ 15/24 – Carte lunch £ 21/30
◆ Carefully furnished, traditional seaside hotel; coast view bedrooms are equipped with binoculars and all have a copy of 'Orlando the Marmalade Cat'; a story set in the area. Formal dining room offers mix of brasserie and classic dishes.

🏨 **Brudenell**     ≪ 🏠 🖥 ⁞¶ VISA ⓪ AE ⓪

*The Parade* ✉ *IP15 5BU –* ✆ *(01728) 452 071 – www.brudenellhotel.co.uk*
**44 rm** ⬙ – ♦£ 80/159 ♦♦£ 147/314    **Rest** – Carte £ 23/34
◆ Contemporary hotel situated right on the beach, with a relaxed ambience and superb sea views. Bedrooms feature modern bathrooms and up-to-date facilities. Informal, split-level bar/restaurant offers an accessible menu of modern classics to suit every taste.

X **Lighthouse**     🏠 AC VISA ⓪ AE
☺

*77 High St* ✉ *IP15 5AU –* ✆ *(01728) 453 377 – www.lighthouserestaurant.co.uk*
*– Closed lunch 1 January and lunch 26 December*
**Rest** – *(booking essential)* Carte £ 20/31
◆ Busy, unpretentious bistro boasts a wealth of Suffolk produce from local meats to Aldeburgh cod and potted shrimps. Rustic, flavourful dishes with strong Mediterranean influences. Good choice of wines, amiable service and a warm, relaxing ambience.

**at Friston** Northwest : 4 mi by A 1094 on B 1121 – ✉ Aldeburgh

⌂ **Old School** without rest     🚗 ⅏ P
🏠

✉ *IP17 1NP –* ✆ *(01728) 688 173 – www.fristonoldschool.co.uk*
**3 rm** ⬙ – ♦£ 60/72 ♦♦£ 80
◆ Red-brick former school house with pleasant gardens. Good-sized bedrooms boast attractive furnishings, modern bathrooms and nice views. Communal breakfasts include a 'Full Suffolk', locally smoked kippers and milk from the nearby dairy. Run by lovely owners.

## ALDERLEY EDGE – Cheshire East – **502** N24 – pop. 5 280    **20** B3

▶ London 187 mi – Chester 34 mi – Manchester 14 mi – Stoke-on-Trent 25 mi

🖪 Wilmslow Mobberley Great Warford, ✆ (01565) 87 21 48

🏨 **Alderley Edge**     🚗 🖥 ⅏ ⁞¶ 🎿 P VISA ⓪ ⓪

*Macclesfield Rd* ✉ *SK9 7BJ –* ✆ *(01625) 583 033 – www.alderleyedgehotel.com*
*– Closed 25-26 December*
**49 rm** – ♦£ 90/130 ♦♦£ 145/180, ⬙ £ 18 – 1 suite
**Rest** *Alderley* – see restaurant listing
◆ Well-run, early Victorian country house in affluent village. Smart landscaped gardens; compact, fairly formal interior. Modern, leather-furnished guest areas. More classically styled bedrooms.

**ENGLAND** (vertical text in left margin)

XXX **Alderley** – at Alderley Edge Hotel    🖼 ᴷᴷ **P** 🛏 𝚟𝚒𝚜𝚊 ⓪⊙ AE ⓪
✉ SK9 7BJ – 𝒞 (01625) 583 033 – www.alderleyedgehotel.com
– *Closed 25-26 December and Sunday dinner*
**Rest** – Menu £ 24/35 – Carte approx. £ 46⅛
◆ Formal restaurant with full-length windows and long-standing reputation. Modern British menus display some interesting combinations and unusual twists. Good value lunch and daily evening menus.

🍴 **The Wizard**    🖼 ⌂ **P** 𝚟𝚒𝚜𝚊 ⓪⊙
⊛ *Macclesfield Rd, Southeast : 1.25 mi on B 5087* ✉ SK10 4UB – 𝒞 (01625) 584 000
– www.ainscoughs.co.uk – *Closed 25 December*
**Rest** – Carte £ 25/38
◆ Characterful, dog-friendly, 200 year old pub with flag floors, wood beams and open fires. Seasonal menu of traditional dishes, including pub favourites and the occasional Mediterranean influence. Small tapas-style plates provide nibbles for drinkers.

---

**ALDERNEY** – Alderney – **503** Q33 – pop. 2 400 – see Channel Islands

---

**ALDFIELD** – North Yorkshire – **502** P21 – see Ripon

---

**ALFRISTON** – East Sussex – **504** U31 – pop. 1 721 – ✉ Polegate    **8** A3
▶ London 66 mi – Eastbourne 9 mi – Lewes 10 mi – Newhaven 8 mi

XX **Moonrakers** with rm    ⌂ ⁽ᵗ⁾ 𝚟𝚒𝚜𝚊 ⓪⊙
*High St* ✉ BN2 5TD – 𝒞 (01323) 871 199 – www.moonrakersrestaurant.co.uk
– *Closed January, Sunday dinner, Monday and Tuesday*
**1 rm** ☲ – ♥♥£ 155/215    **Rest** – *(booking essential)* Menu £ 19/35
◆ Charming 16C cottage with heavy beams, inglenook fireplace and lovely terrace. Interesting dishes display classic flavour combinations with modern twists. Ingredients are handled with care. A stylish, beamed bedroom with sitting room occupies the first floor.

XX **Wingrove House** with rm    🖼 ⌂ ⁽ᵗ⁾ **P** 𝚟𝚒𝚜𝚊 ⓪⊙ AE
*High St* ✉ BN26 5TD – 𝒞 (01323) 870 276 – www.wingrovehousealfriston.com
– *Closed 25 December*
**5 rm** ☲ – ♥£ 95 ♥♥£ 155
**Rest** – *(closed Sunday dinner in winter)* Carte £ 21/30
◆ Imposing colonial-style house; personally run, with relaxed, informal feel. Spacious, contemporary brasserie, wood-floored lounge and pleasant terrace. Modern menu of brasserie dishes served by a bright team. Understated, stylish bedrooms; some with balconies.

🍴 **George Inn** with rm    🖼 ⌂ ᴷᴷ rm, ⁽ᵗ⁾ 𝚟𝚒𝚜𝚊 ⓪⊙
*High St* ✉ BN26 5SY – 𝒞 (01323) 870 319 – www.thegeorge-alfriston.com
– *Closed 25-26 December*
**6 rm** ☲ – ♥£ 75/90 ♥♥£ 125/145    **Rest** – Carte £ 24/32
◆ Characterful 14C stone and timber pub in a delightful village on the Southdown Way. Menu offers sharing boards and restaurant-style dishes, with pub classics appearing as specials. Comfy, simply furnished bedrooms; Bob Hall, with its 13C murals, is the best.

---

**ALKHAM** – Kent – **504** X30 – pop. 607    **9** D2
▶ London 72 mi – Bexley 61 mi

XX **Marquis** with rm    🖼 🛇 rm, 🛇 rm, ⁽ᵗ⁾ **P** 𝚟𝚒𝚜𝚊 ⓪⊙ AE
*Alkham Valley Rd* ✉ CT15 7DF – 𝒞 (01304) 873 410
– www.themarquisatalkham.co.uk – *Closed Monday lunch*
**10 rm** ☲ – ♥£ 145/185 ♥♥£ 145/235    **Rest** – Menu £ 23/43
◆ Fashionable former pub with smart bar, stylish dining room and relaxed atmosphere. Accomplished cooking features classical combinations with original touches; portions are generous and presentation is modern. A six course tasting menu is available. Chic, sexy bedrooms boast luxurious bathrooms.

## ALNWICK – Northumberland – **501** O17 – **pop. 7 767** ▯ Great Britain **24** B2

▶ London 320 mi – Edinburgh 86 mi – Newcastle upon Tyne 34 mi

ℹ️ 2 The Shambles ℰ(01665) 510 6 65, www.visitalnwick.org.uk

🏌 Swansfield Park, ℰ(01665) 60 26 32

◉ Town ★ - Castle★★ **AC**

◉ Dunstanburgh Castle★ **AC**, NE : 8 mi by B 1340 and Dunstan rd (last 2.5 mi on foot)

⌂ **Greycroft** without rest    🚗 ⚡ ᵗⁱⁱ **P** 𝚟𝚒𝚜𝚊 ⓸

Croft Pl, via Prudhoe St ⊠ NE66 1XU – ℰ (01665) 602 127 – www.greycroft.co.uk
– Closed Christmas
**6 rm** ⌕ – **♦**£ 60 **♦♦**£ 110

♦ Quiet 19C house, 5min walk from Alnwick castle. Bedrooms individually decorated to a high standard, including a delightful family room. Breakfast in airy conservatory overlooking walled garden. Hospitable owners.

⌂ **Aln House** without rest    🚗 ⚡ ᵗⁱⁱ **P** 𝚟𝚒𝚜𝚊 ⓸

South Rd, Southeast : 0.75 mi by B 6346 on Newcastle rd ⊠ NE66 2NZ
– ℰ (01665) 602 265 – www.alnhouse.co.uk – Closed 24-26 December
**6 rm** ⌕ – **♦**£ 55/80 **♦♦**£ 80/95

♦ Semi-detached Edwardian house with mature front and rear gardens, close to the castle and town centre. Homely lounge enhanced by personal touches. Individually appointed, immaculately kept bedrooms with smart bold feature walls.

✗✗ **Blackmore's** with rm    🏠 ᵗⁱⁱ 🛁 **P** 𝚟𝚒𝚜𝚊 ⓸

24 Bondgate Without ⊠ NE66 1PN – ℰ (01665) 602 395
– www.blackmoresofalnwick.com – Closed 25 December
**14 rm** ⌕ – **♦**£ 50/100 **♦♦**£ 115/135   **Rest** – Carte £ 18/24 **s**

♦ 18C stone building with modern, open-plan interior and central bar. Bistro serves menu of mainly pub classics; first floor restaurant, with interesting display of clocks, offers more ambitious fare. Well-kept, contemporary bedrooms in chocolate tones.

### at North Charlton North : 6.75 mi by A 1 – ⊠ Alnwick

⌂ **North Charlton Farm** without rest ✏    ← 🚗 🦘 ⚡ **P**

⊠ NE67 5HP – ℰ (01665) 579 443 – www.northcharltonfarm.co.uk – Closed
Christmas
**3 rm** ⌕ – **♦**£ 80 **♦♦**£ 80

♦ Attractive house on working farm with agricultural museum. Offers traditional accommodation. Each bedroom is individually decorated and has countryside views.

### at Chathill North : 8.75 mi by A 1 off B 6347

🏨 **Doxford Hall H. and Spa** ✏    🚗 🦘 📺 ⁿ 🏊 & rm, ⚡ 🛁 **P**

⊠ NE67 5DN – ℰ (01665) 589 700       𝚟𝚒𝚜𝚊 ⓸ 🅰🅴 ⓞ
– www.doxfordhall.com
**30 rm** ⌕ – **♦**£ 150 **♦♦**£ 175 – 1 suite
**Rest** *George Runciman* – Menu £ 25 (lunch) – Carte dinner £ 37/50

♦ 18C house with recent extensions, well-appointed spa and immaculately kept formal gardens. Spacious bedrooms, styled to complement original house; all have mod cons including flat screens, while impressive feature beds add a sense of luxury. Interesting modern cuisine served in formal dining room.

---

## ALSTONEFIELD – Staffordshire – **504** O24 – **pop. 274**     **19** C1

▶ London 157 mi – Birmingham 66 mi – Liverpool 77 mi – Leeds 88 mi

🍴 **George**    🚗 🏠 **P** 𝚟𝚒𝚜𝚊 ⓸

⊠ DE6 2FX – ℰ (01335) 310 205 – www.thegeorgeatalstonefield.com – Closed
25 December
**Rest** Carte £ 20/39

♦ Simply furnished, family-run pub with roaring fire and relaxed, cosy atmosphere. Daily changing menus offer well-priced, down-to-earth dishes; good 'on toast' section at lunch.

## ALTON – Hampshire – **504** R30 – pop. 16 051       **6** B2

▶ London 53 mi – Reading 24 mi – Southampton 29 mi – Winchester 18 mi

🛈 7 Cross and Pillory Lane ✆ (01420) 8 84 48, www.visit-hampshire.co.uk

🏌 Old Odiham Rd, ✆ (01420) 8 20 42

### at Lower Froyle Northeast : 4.5 mi by A 31

🍴 **The Anchor Inn** with rm      🚗 ☂ 📶 **P** 💳 **VISA 🔅 AE ①**
✉ GU34 4NA – ✆ (01420) 23 261 – www.anchorinnatlowerfroyle.co.uk – Closed 25 December

**5 rm** ⬜ – †£ 90/130 ††£ 120/150    **Rest** – Carte £ 27/35

◆ Part-whitewashed, part-tile hung 14C building in pretty countryside, boasting low beams, open fires and bric-a-brac aplenty. Good-sized menus offer classic pub dishes with a refined edge; cooking is hearty and flavoursome. Bedrooms are fittingly characterful.

## ALTRINCHAM – Greater Manchester – **502** N23 – pop. 40 695     **20** B3

▶ London 191 mi – Chester 30 mi – Liverpool 30 mi – Manchester 8 mi

🛈 20 Stamford New Rd ✆ (0161) 912 59 31, www.altrincham.org.uk

🏌 Altrincham Municipal Timperley Stockport Rd, ✆ (0161) 928 07 61

🏌 Dunham Forest Oldfield Lane, ✆ (0161) 928 26 05

🏌 Ringway Hale Barns Hale Mount, ✆ (0161) 980 26 30

🍴 **Victoria**                   💳 **VISA 🔅 AE**
29 Stamford St ✉ WA14 1EX – ✆ (0161) 613 18 55 – Closed 1 January, 26 December and Sunday dinner

**Rest** – Carte £ 24/33

◆ Traditional looking pub in a quiet part of town, with flowers on the windowsills, a few pavement tables and an appealing, single-roomed interior with a wooden bar at its centre. Menu offers light bites and classics with a modern twist.

### at Little Bollington Southwest : 3.25 mi on A 56 – ✉ Altrincham

🏠 **Ash Farm** without rest ☜      🚗 📶 **P** 💳 **VISA 🔅**
Park Ln ✉ WA14 4TJ – ✆ (0161) 929 92 90 – www.ashfarm.co.uk
– Closed 22 December-2 January

**3 rm** ⬜ – †£ 49/61 ††£ 77/86

◆ 18C former farmhouse with large garden, modern pine-furnished breakfast room and comfy, boho lounge. Traditional, antique-furnished bedrooms have a pleasant country house style. Friendly owners.

## ALVESTON – Warwickshire – **504** O/P27 – see Stratford-upon-Avon

## AMBERLEY – West Sussex – **504** S31 – pop. 525 – ✉ Arundel    **7** C2

▌ Great Britain

▶ London 56 mi – Brighton 24 mi – Portsmouth 31 mi

🄲 Bignor Roman Villa (mosaics★) **AC**, NW : 3.5 mi by B 2139 via Bury

🏰 **Amberley Castle** ☜     🚗 🕭 ✕ 📶 ♨ **P** 💳 **VISA 🔅 AE**
Southwest : 0.5 mi on B 2139 ✉ BN18 9LT – ✆ (01798) 831 992
– www.amberleycastle.co.uk

**13 rm** ⬜ – †£ 230/285 ††£ 465/520 – 6 suites

**Rest Queen's Room** – see restaurant listing

◆ Stunning 12C castle displaying original stonework, battlements and evidence of a moat. Charming grounds with lovely gardens, lakes and a croquet lawn, matched inside by a characterful array of rooms packed with armour and heraldic antiques. Sumptuous bedrooms boast spa baths and a palpable sense of history.

🍴🍴🍴 **Queen's Room** – at Amberley Castle Hotel     🚗 🕭 **P** 💳 **VISA 🔅 AE**
Southwest : 0.5 mi on B 2139 ✉ BN18 9LT – ✆ (01798) 831 992
– www.amberleycastle.co.uk

**Rest** – (booking essential) Menu £ 33/63

◆ Elegant dining room with a barrel-vaulted ceiling, lancet windows and an open fire, set within a stunning 12C castle. Ambitious modern menu; dishes are complex and arrive artfully presented.

▶ London 278 mi – Carlisle 47 mi – Kendal 14 mi

**ℹ** Market Cross *𝒞* (015394) 3 25 82, www.amblesideonline.co.uk

**◉** Lake Windermere★★ – Dove Cottage, Grasmere★ **AC** AY **A** – Brockhole National
Park Centre★ **AC**, SE : 3 mi by A 591 AZ. Wrynose Pass★★, W : 7.5 mi by A 593 AY
– Hard Knott Pass★★, W : 10 mi by A 593 AY

Plan on next page

---

**🏨** **The Samling** ⊛ ⇐ 🚗 🕭 **P** **VISA** **⦿** **AE** **⦿**
*Ambleside Rd, South : 1.5 mi on A 591 ⊠ LA23 1LR – 𝒞 (015394) 31 922*
*– www.thesamlinghotel.co.uk*
**9 rm** ⌂ – ✝£ 175/265 ✝✝£ 190/280 – 2 suites
**Rest** *– (booking essential for non-residents)* Menu £ 35/60
♦ Located on the hillside, with a lovely lake outlook and fantastic views from the
hot tub. Highly individual bedrooms range from classical and characterful to bold
and eye-catching; all boast excellent facilities. Intimate dining room, with attentive, structured service.

**🏠** **Lakes Lodge** without rest 🕉 **P** **VISA** **⦿** **AE**
*Lake Rd ⊠ LA22 0DB – 𝒞 (015394) 33 240 – www.lakeslodge.co.uk*
*– Closed 19-27 December* AZ**s**
**16 rm** ⌂ – ✝£ 60/130 ✝✝£ 75/150
♦ Three-storey townhouse on the roadside. Modern, stylish bedrooms with bright
fabrics and compact bathrooms; great views from number 10. Newer basement
rooms boast wall-sized Lakeland images.

**🏠** **Riverside** without rest ⊛ ⇐ 🚗 🕉 🎙 **P** **VISA** **⦿**
*Under Loughrigg ⊠ LA22 9LJ – 𝒞 (015394) 32 395*
*– www.riverside-at-ambleside.co.uk – Closed 12 December-31 January*
**6 rm** ⌂ – ✝£ 65/98 ✝✝£ 85/116 BY**s**
♦ Homely, mid-Victorian slate house with steep lawned garden and fire-lit
lounge; set in a peaceful riverside road. Bedroom 2 with its four-poster and double-aspect views is best. Lovely owners.

**🏠** **Red Bank** without rest 🚗 🕉 🎙 **P**
*Wansfell Rd ⊠ LA22 0EG – 𝒞 (015394) 34 637 – www.red-bank.co.uk*
**3 rm** ⌂ – ✝£ 60/70 ✝✝£ 80/100 AZ**r**
♦ Well-maintained guest house close to centre of town. Small seating area with
wood burning stove; breakfast room overlooks the garden. 3 colour-themed bedrooms with compact, modern bathrooms.

**✕✕** **Log House** with rm 🎃 🕉 rm, 🎙 **VISA** **⦿** **AE**
*Lake Rd ⊠ LA22 0DN – 𝒞 (015394) 31 077 – www.loghouse.co.uk*
*– Closed 3 January-1 February, 25-26 December and Monday* BY**v**
**3 rm** ⌂ – ✝£ 60/93 ✝✝£ 60/93 **Rest** *– (dinner only)* Carte £ 25/39
♦ Attractive cream-painted log cabin, imported from Norway over 100 years ago
as a studio for artist Alfred Heaton Cooper. Modern, Mediterranean-influenced
menus; sit in the raised rear area. Simple bedrooms – Room 1 is most characterful; Room 3 has the best view.

**🍴** **Drunken Duck Inn** with rm ⇐ 🚗 🕭 🎃 🕉 rm, 🎙 **P** **VISA** **⦿**
*Barngates, Southwest : 3 mi by A 593 and B 5286 on Tarn Hows rd*
*⊠ LA22 0NG – 𝒞 (01539) 436 347 – www.drunkenduckinn.co.uk*
*– Closed 25 December*
**17 rm** ⌂ – ✝£ 117/150 ✝✝£ 230/295
**Rest** *– (booking essential)* Carte £ 22/46
♦ Attractive pub in beautiful Lakeland countryside with fire-lit bar and two formal, linen-laid dining rooms. Simple lunches and elaborate dinners with prices
to match; generous cooking and attentive service. Ales brewed on-site. Boutique, country house bedrooms – some with patios, all with squashy beds and
country views.

**ENGLAND**

**AMERSHAM (Old Town)** – Buckinghamshire – **504** S29
– pop. 21 470

▶ London 29 mi – Aylesbury 16 mi – Oxford 33 mi

▣ Little Chalfont Lodge Lane, ✆ (01494) 76 48 77

**11 D2**

XX **Artichoke** 🅐🅒 ⇔ 🆅🆂🅰 ⬤ 🅰🅔
*9 Market Sq ⊠ HP7 0DF – ℰ (01494) 726 611 – www.artichokerestaurant.co.uk*
*– Closed 2 weeks late August, 1 week Christmas, Sunday and Monday*
**Rest** – *(booking essential at dinner)* Menu £ 25/44 – Carte lunch £ 33/46
♦ 16C red-brick house in a picturesque town, with an artichoke etched on its
window. A narrow beamed room with cream-painted walls and polished tables
leads through to a more modern extension. Ambitious modern dishes arrive
nicely presented.

X **Gilbey's** 🏠 🅐🅒 ⇔ 🆅🆂🅰 ⬤
⊠ HP7 0DF – ℰ (01494) 727 242 – www.gilbeygroup.com
**Rest** – *(booking essential)* Menu £ 24 (weekdays) – Carte £ 30/43
♦ Part of a former 17C school, this busy neighbourhood restaurant is cosy and
informal with modern artwork on walls. Eclectic range of British cooking with
global influences.

---

**AMPLEFORTH** – North Yorkshire – **502** Q21 – see Helmsley

---

**ANSTEY** – Hertfordshire – **504** Q25 **12** B2
🄳 London 38 mi – Croydon 71 mi – Barnet 35 mi – Ealing 47 mi

⛰ **Anstey Grove Barn** without rest 🦢 🚗 🕭 🕅 🐱 🅿 🆅🆂🅰 ⬤ 🅰🅔 ⓪
*East : 0.5 mi on Meesden rd ⊠ SG9 0BJ – ℰ (01763) 848 828*
*– www.ansteygrovebarn.co.uk*
**6 rm** ⌸ – †£ 65 ††£ 80
♦ Converted barn on what was once a working pig farm. Simply furnished,
homely bedrooms named after breeds of pig; the best is Old Yorkshire with its
four-poster and roll-top bath.

ENGLAND

---

**APPLEBY-IN-WESTMORLAND** – Cumbria – **502** M20 – pop. 2 862 **21** B2
🄳 London 285 mi – Carlisle 33 mi – Kendal 24 mi – Middlesbrough 58 mi
🄵 Boroughgate ℰ (017683) 5 11 77, www.visitcumbria.com
🄵🄸 Appleby Brackenber Moor, ℰ (017683) 5 14 32

🏠🏠🏠 **Appleby Manor Country House** 🦢 ≤ 🚗 🏠 🕅 🆚 🅿
*Roman Rd, East : 1 mi by B 6542 and Station Rd* 🆅🆂🅰 ⬤ 🅰🅔 ⓪
⊠ CA16 6JB – ℰ (017683) 51 571 – www.applebymanor.co.uk – Closed
*Christmas*
**31 rm** ⌸ – †£ 95/100 ††£ 150/250 **Rest** – Carte £ 27/36 s
♦ Family-run, Victorian gentleman's residence with mature gardens and more recent extensions. Spacious, traditionally styled guest areas; small leisure suite. Bedrooms in original house are the most characterful. Two-roomed, formal restaurant
offers classical menus.

🏠🄷 **Tufton Arms** 🦢 🕅 🆚 🅿 🆅🆂🅰 ⬤ 🅰🅔 ⓪
*Market Sq ⊠ CA16 6XA – ℰ (017683) 51 593 – www.tuftonarmshotel.co.uk*
*– Closed 24-27 December*
**20 rm** ⌸ – †£ 77/95 ††£ 130/210
**Rest** – Menu £ 30 (dinner) – Carte £ 18/33
♦ 16C former coaching inn in traditional market town boasts contemporary interior; chic, comfortable bedrooms in bold colours. Fishing, shooting and stalking
can be arranged. Easy-going menu served in modern dining room.

---

**APPLEDORE** – Devon – **503** H30 – pop. 2 187 **2** C1
🄳 London 228 mi – Barnstaple 12 mi – Exeter 46 mi – Plymouth 61 mi
👁 Town ★

⛰ **West Farm** without rest 🚗 🕅
*Irsha St, West : 0.25 mi ⊠ EX39 1RY – ℰ (01237) 425 269 – Closed*
*Christmas-New Year*
**3 rm** ⌸ – †£ 67 ††£ 100
♦ 17C house, boasting particularly pleasant garden at the back, in a charming little coastal village. Delightfully appointed sitting room. Bedrooms feel comfortable
and homely.

## APPLETREEWICK – North Yorkshire – 502 O21

22 B2

▶ London 236 mi – Harrogate 25 mi – Skipton 11 mi

⌂ **Knowles Lodge** without rest ⅏ ⟨ ⟩ 🅿 VISA ◍◍
South : 1 mi on Bolton Abbey rd ⊠ BD23 6DQ – ✆ (01756) 720 228
– www.knowleslodge.com
**4 rm** ⌷ – †£ 60 ††£ 100
♦ Unusual Canadian ranch-house style guesthouse, clad in timber and sited in
quiet dales location. Large sitting room with fine outlook. Cosy bedrooms have
garden views.

## ARKHOLME – Lancashire

20 A1

▶ London 254 mi – Birmingham 140 mi – Liverpool 71 mi – Leeds 99 mi

▯ **Redwell Inn** ⟨ ⟩ 🅿 VISA ◍◍
Southwest : 1 mi on B 6254 ⊠ LA6 1BQ – ✆ (015242) 21 240
– www.redwellinnarkholme.co.uk
**Rest** – (booking advisable) Menu £ 16 (lunch) – Carte £ 16/39
♦ Attractive 16C stone inn with rustic bar and more formal dining room. Son
cooks while mum and dad look after front of house. Menus offer something for
everyone, from nibbles such as a homemade Scotch egg with HP sauce to a classic fish pie.

## ARLINGHAM – Gloucestershire – 503 M28 – pop. 377 – ⊠ Gloucester

4 C1

▶ London 120 mi – Birmingham 69 mi – Bristol 34 mi – Gloucester 16 mi

✕✕ **Old Passage Inn** with rm ⅏ ⟨ ⟩ AC 🅿 VISA ◍◍ AE
Passage Rd, West : 0.75 mi ⊠ GL2 7JR – ✆ (01452) 740 547
– www.theoldpassageinn.com – Closed 25-26 December and Monday
**3 rm** – †£ 60/110 ††£ 80/140, ⌷ £ 8
**Rest** – Seafood – Menu £ 20 (weekdays) – Carte £ 34/55
♦ Sweet, green painted former inn by the River Severn – its terrace is a great place
to watch the famous Severn Bore. Bright yellow décor, red tiled floors and eye-
catching local art for sale. Good-sized seafood menus offer simply prepared dishes
of top notch produce. Well-equipped modern bedrooms boast pleasant views.

## ARMSCOTE – Warwickshire – 504 P27

19 C3

▶ London 91 mi – Birmingham 36 mi – Oxford 38 mi

⌂ **Willow Corner** without rest ⟨ ⟩ 🅿
⊠ CV37 8DE – ✆ (01608) 682 391 – www.willowcorner.co.uk – Restricted
opening in winter
**3 rm** ⌷ – †£ 50/65 ††£ 70/85
♦ Cream-washed cottage in a small village, with low-beamed guest areas and
homely décor. Original features include mullioned windows and a stable door.
Cottagey bedrooms boast good facilities and thoughtful touches.

## ARNSIDE – Cumbria – 502 L21 – pop. 2 301

21 A3

▶ London 257 mi – Liverpool 74 mi – Manchester 69 mi – Bradford 97 mi

⌂ **Number 43** ⟨ ⟩ VISA ◍◍
43 The Promenade ⊠ LA5 0AA – ✆ (01524) 762 761 – www.no43.org.uk
**6 rm** ⌷ – †£ 100 ††£ 185  **Rest** – Menu £ 23
♦ Stylishly converted Victorian townhouse boasting superb estuary and fell
views. Contemporary bedrooms with smart bathrooms, quality furnishings and
good facilities. Comfy, open-plan lounge and dining room. Home-cooked meals
by arrangement; lighter sharing platters every evening. Have breakfast on glass-
enclosed terrace.

## ARUNDEL – West Sussex – 504 S31 – pop. 3 297 ▮ Great Britain

7 C2

▶ London 58 mi – Brighton 21 mi – Southampton 41 mi – Worthing 9 mi
▯ 61 High St ✆ (01903) 88 22 68, www.arundel.org.uk
◉ Castle ★★ AC

XX **Town House** with rm    🕪 VISA ☎ ⓪
*65 High St ⊠ BN18 9AJ – ☏ (01903) 883 847 – www.thetownhouse.co.uk*
*– Closed 2 weeks February, 2 weeks October, 25-26 December, 1 January, Sunday and Monday*
**4 rm** ⌑ – ♦£ 75 ♦♦£ 130   **Rest** – Menu £ 20/30
◆ Early 17C house displaying original sugar glass windows and impressive Renaissance ceiling with gilded walnut panelling. Smartly laid, intimate dining room. Confidently executed, tried-and-tested dishes with a classical base. Modern, well-equipped bedrooms.

**at Burpham** Northeast : 3 mi by A 27 – ⊠ Arundel

🏠 **Burpham Country House** 🐾    ≼ 🚗 🎇 ⁽ᵖ⁾ P VISA ☎
*The Street ⊠ BN18 9RJ – ☏ (01903) 882 160 – www.burphamcountryhouse.com*
*– Closed January and 25-26 December*
**9 rm** ⌑ – ♦£ 80/95 ♦♦£ 120/140
**Rest** – *(closed Sunday and Monday) (dinner only)* Carte £ 25/31
◆ Reputedly a hunting lodge for the Duke of Norfolk, this tranquil hotel constitutes the ideal 'stress remedy break'. Calm, pastel-coloured bedrooms overlook exquisite gardens. Seasonal menu of classic dishes served in dining room and conservatory.

🍺 **George and Dragon**    P VISA ☎
*Main St ⊠ BN18 9RR – ☏ (01903) 883 131 – www.gdinn.co.uk*
**Rest** – Carte £ 25/46
◆ It's all in the name: a good old-fashioned English pub with a rustic bar, linen-clad dining room and relaxed feel. Cooking features British classics, old pub favourites and daily specials.

**ASCOT** – Windsor and Maidenhead – **504** R29 – pop. 15 761    **11** D3
▶ London 36 mi – Reading 15 mi
🏌 Mill Ride Ascot, ☏ (01344) 88 67 77

🏨🏨 **Coworth Park** 🐾    ≼ 🚗 🐕 🖥 🌐 🐎 ♨ ✕ 🛎 ₺ rm, ⚙ 🅰️🅲 ⁽ᵖ⁾ 🧖 P
⁂    *London Rd, East : 2.75 mi on A 329 ⊠ SL5 7SE*    VISA ☎ AE ⓪
*– ☏ (01344) 876 600 – www.coworthpark.com*
**57 rm** – ♦£ 195/500 ♦♦£ 195/500, ⌑ £ 25 – 13 suites
**Rest Barn** – see restaurant listing
**Rest John Campbell at Coworth Park** – Menu £ 30 (weekday lunch)/60 🐾
**Spec.** Duck with cherries and water chestnuts. Halibut with oyster, chorizo and seaweed. Hay chocolate mousse with rose and blood orange sorbets.
◆ 17C property set in 246 acres and boasting its own championship polo pitches. Comfortable, stylish guest areas; superb spa. Beautiful bedrooms feature bespoke furniture, marble bathrooms and a high level of facilities. Fine dining restaurant serves inventive cooking with plenty of original touches.

XX **Ascot Oriental**    🍴 🅰️🅲 ⇔ P VISA ☎ AE
*East : 2.25 mi on A 329 ⊠ SL5 0PU – ☏ (01344) 621 877*
*– www.ascotoriental.com – Closed 25-26 December*
**Rest** – Chinese – Menu £ 29 – Carte £ 32/47
◆ Professionally run restaurant with calming décor. Extensive menu combines old customer favourites with newer, more original dishes; excellent Cantonese choices. Clean, flavoursome cooking.

XX **Barn** – at Coworth Park Hotel    ≼ 🍴 🅰️🅲 P VISA ☎ AE
*London Rd, East : 2.75 mi on A 329 ⊠ SL5 7SE – ☏ (01344) 876 600*
*– www.coworthpark.com*
**Rest** – Carte £ 30/35
◆ An informal alternative to the fine dining restaurant, this buzzy, rustic room's floor-to-ceiling windows let in plenty of light and offer views over the fields. Menu offers classics like steak and fish and chips.

**ENGLAND**

XX **Ascot Grill**       🛱 AC VISA ⓪ AE
*6 Hermitage Par, High St* ✉ *SL5 7HE* – ℰ *(01344) 622 285* – *www.ascotgrill.co.uk*
*– Closed 25-26 December, 1 January and Sunday*
**Rest** – Menu £ 16 (lunch) – Carte £ 21/52
♦ Set at the end of a 1950s shopping parade. Slick interior with leather, silk and velvet furnishings; floor-to-ceiling windows open onto a pleasant pavement terrace. Wide-ranging modern grill menu offers seafood, steak and vegetarian dishes.

---

**ASENBY** – North Yorkshire – see Thirsk

---

**ASH** – Kent – **504** X30      **9** D2
▶ London 70 mi – Canterbury 9 mi – Dover 15 mi

⌂ **Great Weddington**      🚗 ※ ⁽ᵗ⁾ P̄ VISA ⓪ AE
*Northeast : 0.5 mi by A 257 on Weddington rd* ✉ *CT3 2AR* – ℰ *(01304) 813 407*
*– www.greatweddington.co.uk – Closed Christmas-New Year*
**4 rm** ⌣ – ♦£ 75/95 ♦♦£ 100/125    **Rest** – Menu £ 40
♦ Charming Regency country house, ideally located for Canterbury and Dover. Well appointed drawing room and terrace. Thoughtfully furnished, carefully co-ordinated rooms. Communal dining room; owner an avid cook.

---

**ASHBOURNE** – Derbyshire – **502** O24 – **pop. 5 020** ▌ Great Britain    **16** A2
▶ London 146 mi – Birmingham 47 mi – Manchester 48 mi – Nottingham 33 mi
▮ 13 Market Pl ℰ (01335) 34 36 66, www.visitpeakdistrict.com
◉ Dovedale★★ (Ilam Rock★) NW : 6 mi by A 515

🏨 **Callow Hall** ⌖      ⪕ 🚗 🐕 ⌖ 🛱 ⁽ᵗ⁾ P̄ VISA ⓪ AE
*Mappleton Rd, West : 0.75 mi by Union St (off Market Pl)* ✉ *DE6 2AA*
*– ℰ (01335) 300 900 – www.callowhall.co.uk*
**15 rm** ⌣ – ♦£ 140 ♦♦£ 190 – 1 suite    **Rest** – Menu £ 25/45 – Carte £ 37/43
♦ Victorian country house in 44 acres of gardens, fields and woodland. Individually styled bedrooms boast original features, well-appointed bathrooms, and quality fabrics and furnishings. Daily changing menus feature local produce and tasty home-smoked salmon.

XX **dining room**      VISA ⓪
*33 St Johns St* ✉ *DE6 1GP* – ℰ *(01335) 300 666*
*– www.thediningroomashbourne.co.uk – Closed Sunday-Wednesday*
**Rest** – *(dinner only) (booking essential)* Menu £ 40/48
♦ Modern, stylish décor blends agreeably with period features including a cast iron range and 17C salt safe. Well-sourced, seasonal ingredients inform intricate modern dishes on 8 or 16 course tasting menus.

---

**ASHBURTON** – Devon – **503** I32 – **pop. 3 309**      **2** C2
▶ London 220 mi – Exeter 20 mi – Plymouth 25 mi
◉ Dartmoor National Park★★

X **Agaric** with rm      🛱 VISA ⓪
*30 and 36 North St* ✉ *TQ13 7QD* – ℰ *(01364) 654 478*
*– www.agaricrestaurant.co.uk – Closed first 2 weeks August, 2 weeks Christmas, Sunday-Tuesday and Saturday lunch*
**4 rm** ⌣ – ♦£ 50/65 ♦♦£ 130    **Rest** – *(booking essential)* Carte £ 32/39
♦ 200 year-old house, selling home-made jams, fudge and olives. Relaxed neighbourhood restaurant using a blend of cooking styles. Very stylish, individually themed bedrooms.

---

**ASHFORD** – Kent – **504** W30 – **pop. 58 936**      **9** C2
▶ London 56 mi – Canterbury 14 mi – Dover 24 mi – Hastings 30 mi
**Access** Channel Tunnel : Eurostar information and reservations ℰ (08705) 186186
▮ 18 The Churchyard ℰ (01233) 62 91 65, www.visitheartofkent.com

**Eastwell Manor** ⚜ ← 🚗 🐕 ⛳ 🏊 ⊕ 🏇 🛴 ✕ 📷 🎮 📶 ♨ 🅿️ 🇻🇮🇸🇦 ⊕⊕ AE
*Eastwell Park, Boughton Lees, North : 3 mi by A 28 on A 251*
✉ TN25 4HR – 𝒞 (01233) 213 000 – www.eastwellmanor.co.uk
**20 rm** ⊑ – ♦£ 190 ♦♦£ 295 – 22 suites – ♦♦♦£ 445
**Rest** *Manor* – Menu £ 20/27 – Carte approx. £ 50
**Rest** *Pavilion* – 𝒞 (01233) 213 100 – Carte £ 21/31
• Impressive manor house with Tudor origins, surrounded by manicured gardens and extensive parkland. Rebuilt in 1926 following a fire but some superb plaster ceilings and stone fireplaces remain. Characterful guest areas and luxurious bedrooms. Sizeable spa and golf course. Choice of wood-panelled restaurant complete with pianist or more casual brasserie and terrace.

**ASHFORD-IN-THE-WATER** – Derbyshire – **502** O24 – **see Bakewell**

**ASHPRINGTON** – Devon – **503** J32 – **see Totnes**

**ASHWATER** – Devon – **503** H31                                                    **2** C2
▶ London 218 mi – Bude 16 mi – Virginstow 3 mi

**Blagdon Manor** ⚜ ← 🚗 🐕 🏇 🅿️ 🇻🇮🇸🇦 ⊕⊕
*Northwest : 2 mi by Holsworthy rd on Blagdon rd* ✉ EX21 5DF – 𝒞 (01409)
*211 224 – www.blagdon.com – Closed January, Monday and Tuesday*
**7 rm** ⊑ – ♦£ 85 ♦♦£ 195    **Rest** – *(booking essential)* Menu £ 20/38
• Proudly run former farmhouse in peaceful, rural location. Modern country house bedrooms, spotlessly kept, named after surrounding villages. Library, lounges and flag-floored bar. Classically-based cooking with a modern touch, served in dining room with conservatory extension.

**ASKRIGG** – North Yorkshire – **502** N21 – **pop. 1 002** – ✉ **Leyburn**    **22** A1
▶ London 251 mi – Kendal 32 mi – Leeds 70 mi – Newcastle upon Tyne 70 mi

**Yorebridge House** 🚗 🐕 🏇 ✕ ♨ 🅿️ 🇻🇮🇸🇦 ⊕⊕ ⊕
*Bainbridge, West : 1 mi* ✉ DL8 3EE – 𝒞 (01969) 652 060
*– www.yorebridgehouse.com*
**11 rm** ⊑ – ♦£ 225 ♦♦£ 250
**Rest** – *(booking essential for non residents)* Menu £ 45 (dinner) – Carte £ 23/45
• Lovingly restored former school with warm, hospitable owners. Modern, stylish and comfortable interior. Individually designed bedrooms, some with hot tubs. Locally sourced produce in relaxing dining room.

**ASTON CANTLOW** – Warwickshire – **503** O27 – **pop. 1 843**    **19** C3
▮ Great Britain
▶ London 106 mi – Birmingham 20 mi – Stratford-upon-Avon 5 mi
◪ Mary Arden's House★ **AC**, SE : 2 mi by Wilmcote Lane and Aston Cantlow Rd

**King's Head** 🚗 🏇 🇻🇮🇸🇦 ⊕⊕
*21 Bearley Rd* ✉ B95 6HY – 𝒞 (01789) 488 242 – www.thekh.co.uk – Closed 25
*December and Sunday dinner*
**Rest** – Carte £ 22/31
• Characterful black and white timbered, part 15C inn, set in a picturesque village. Seasonal menus feature traditional pub dishes, with local meats and fish to the fore. Regular duck suppers.

**ASTON ROWANT** – Oxfordshire – **504** R28 – **pop. 2 512**    **11** C2
▶ London 45 mi – Coventry 69 mi

**Lambert Arms** 🚗 🛴 ♿ ⅙ rm, 🆎 ♨ 🅿️ 🇻🇮🇸🇦 ⊕⊕ AE ⊕
*London Rd, on A 40* ✉ OX49 5SB – 𝒞 (01844) 351 496
*– www.bespokehotels.com*
**42 rm** – ♦£ 79/119 ♦♦£ 109/129, ⊑ £ 7    **Rest** – Carte £ 20/37
• Traditional, half-timbered roadside inn with large mews extension to rear. Bedrooms are split between the two; newer mews rooms are spacious, modern and ideal for business travellers. Rustic bar and restaurant serve accessible, pub-style dishes. Cheery staff.

ENGLAND

## ASTON TIRROLD – Oxfordshire
**10** B3
▶ London 58 mi – Reading 16 mi – Streatley 4 mi

🏠 **Sweet Olive at The Chequers Inn**    ☎ P̄ VISA ⊕ AE
Baker St ✉ OX11 9DD – *𝒞 (01235) 851 272 – www.sweet-olive.com*
*– Closed 3 weeks February, 2 weeks July, Sunday dinner and Wednesday*
**Rest** – *(booking essential)* Carte £ 25/35
◆ Red-brick Victorian pub at heart of the village; cosy, welcoming and popular with the locals. Gallic owners offer French-influenced menu and interesting selection of fine wines.

---

## ATCHAM – Shropshire – **503** L25 – see Shrewsbury

---

## ATTLEBOROUGH – Norfolk – **504** X26 – pop. 6 530
**15** C2
▶ London 101 mi – Norwich 19 mi – Ipswich 42 mi – Peterborough 87 mi

✕ **Mulberry Tree** with rm    ☎ 🎶 P̄ VISA ⊕ AE
Station Rd ✉ NR17 2AS – *𝒞 (01953) 452 124 – www.the-mulberry-tree.co.uk*
*– Closed 24 December-2 January and Sunday*
**5 rm** ☐ – ♦£ 75 ♦♦£ 100    **Rest** – Carte £ 27/34
◆ Contemporary bar/restaurant set in imposing brick-built property with pleasant terrace and bowling green. Bar menu popular at lunch. À la carte offers attractively presented, globally influenced, modern dishes. Stylish, very comfortable bedrooms.

---

## AUGHTON – Lancashire – **502** L23 – pop. 8 342
**20** A2
▶ London 217 mi – Liverpool 13 mi – Manchester 40 mi – Bradford 68 mi

✕✕ **Swan Inn** with rm    ☎ 🛎 AC 🎶 ➴ P̄ VISA ⊕ AE
2 Springfield Rd ✉ L39 6ST – *𝒞 (01695) 421 450 – www.mpwtheswan.co.uk*
**12 rm** ☐ – ♦£ 50/70 ♦♦£ 60/140
**Rest** – Menu £ 16/20 (weekday dinner) – Carte approx. £ 25
◆ Sizeable, smartly refurbished restaurant with linen-laid tables; its walls decorated with cartoons from Marco Pierre White's private collection. Accessible menu of modern British cooking with some locally influenced dishes. Stylish, contemporary bedrooms.

---

## AUSTWICK – North Yorkshire – **502** M21 – pop. 467
**22** A2
– ✉ Lancaster (lancs.)
▶ London 259 mi – Kendal 28 mi – Lancaster 20 mi – Leeds 46 mi

🏠 **Traddock** ⌖    ☞ 🎶 P̄ VISA ⊕
✉ LA2 8BY – *𝒞 (015242) 51 224 – www.thetraddock.co.uk*
**12 rm** ☐ – ♦£ 85/105 ♦♦£ 145/185
**Rest** – *(booking essential for non-residents)* Carte £ 22/35
◆ Georgian country house – formerly a private residence – named after an old horse trading paddock. Modern interior with bright, airy lounges. Bedrooms boast feature beds, rural views and roll-top baths. Formal dining room serves modern versions of old classics.

🏠 **Austwick Hall**    ☞ 🎶 🎶 P̄ VISA ⊕
Southeast : 0.5 mi on Townend Ln ✉ LA2 8BS – *𝒞 (015242) 51 794*
*– www.austwickhall.co.uk*
**5 rm** ☐ – ♦£ 170 ♦♦£ 185    **Rest** – Menu £ 29
◆ Characterful house in a delightful village on the edge of the dales and surrounded by tiered gardens and woodland. Spacious, antique-furnished bedrooms; one with a roll-top bath affording views down the garden. Nothing is too much trouble for the friendly owners. Tea on arrival. Dinner includes a local cheese selection.

🏠 **Wood View** without rest    ☞ P̄ VISA ⊕
The Green ✉ LA2 8BB – *𝒞 (015242) 51 190 – www.woodviewbandb.com*
*– Restricted opening in winter*
**5 rm** ☐ – ♦£ 48/55 ♦♦£ 84
◆ In a charming spot on the village green, the cottage dates back to 17C with many of the original features still in place including exposed rafters in several bedrooms.

ENGLAND

## AXMINSTER – Devon – **503** L31 – **pop. 4 952**                    2 D2
▶ London 156 mi – Exeter 27 mi – Lyme Regis 5 mi – Taunton 22 mi
◉ Lyme Regis★ - The Cobb★, SE : 5.5 mi by A 35 and A 3070

### ✗ **River Cottage Canteen**                                    🆅🅸🆂🅰 ⓐⓑ
*Trinity Sq ⊠ EX13 5AN – ℰ (01297) 631 715 – www.rivercottage.net – Closed*
*dinner Sunday and Monday*
**Rest** – Carte £ 19/44
◆ Busy restaurant, deli and coffee shop owned by Hugh Fearnley-Whittingstall.
Simple, industrial-style room with mismatched furniture. Blackboards change
twice-daily, offering gutsy, flavoursome country cooking and showcasing local
produce.

## AYLESBURY – Buckinghamshire – **504** R28 – **pop. 69 021**          11 C2
▌ Great Britain
▶ London 46 mi – Birmingham 72 mi – Northampton 37 mi – Oxford 22 mi
🄸 Kings Head Passage off Market Square ℰ (01296) 33 05 59,
www.visitbuckinghamshire.org
🆂 Weston Turville New Rd, ℰ (01296) 42 40 84
🆂 Aylesbury Golf Centre Bierton Hulcott Lane, ℰ (01296) 39 36 44
◉ Waddesdon Manor★★, NW : 5.5 mi by A 41 – Chiltern Hills★

### 🏨 **Hartwell House** ⚘        ≤ 🚗 🐎 🐎 🖼 🌐 🐟 🏋 ⅋ 📷 ⅋ 📡 🔱 🅿
*Oxford Rd, Southwest : 2 mi on A 418 ⊠ HP17 8NR*                   🆅🅸🆂🅰 ⓐⓑ 🅰🅴
*– ℰ (01296) 747 444 – www.hartwell-house.com*
**36 rm** ⊑ – ♥£ 160/200 ♥♥£ 260 – 10 suites
**Rest** *Soane* – Menu £ 23/33 – Carte dinner £ 43/53 s
◆ Where Louis XVIII, exiled King of France, was once resident. Impressive palatial
house in 90 acres of parkland, boasting luxurious lounges, ornate furnishings and
magnificent, antique-filled bedrooms. Restaurant offers good value lunches and
traditional country house cooking.

## AYLESFORD – Kent – **504** V30                                    8 B1
▶ London 37 mi – Maidstone 3 mi – Rochester 8 mi

### ✗✗✗ **Hengist**                                   🅰🅲 ⇌ 🆅🅸🆂🅰 ⓐⓑ 🅰🅴 ①
*7-9 High St ⊠ ME20 7AX – ℰ (01622) 719 273 – www.hengistrestaurant.co.uk*
*– Closed Monday*
**Rest** – Menu £ 15 (lunch) – Carte £ 32/38
◆ Converted 16C town house, elegantly appointed throughout, with bonus of exposed rafters and smart private dining room upstairs. Accomplished modern
cooking with seasonal base.

## AYLSHAM – Norfolk – **504** X25 – **pop. 5 504**                   15 D1
▶ London 128 mi – Norwich 13 mi – Ipswich 57 mi – Stevenage 105 mi

### ⌂ **Old Pump House** without rest                   🚗 ⅋ 📡 🅿 🆅🅸🆂🅰 ⓐⓑ
*2 Holman Rd ⊠ NR11 6BY – ℰ (01263) 733 789 – www.theoldpumphouse.com*
*– Closed Christmas*
**5 rm** ⊑ – ♥£ 80/98 ♥♥£ 98/120
◆ Well-run Georgian house with the original village water pump still standing outside. Tastefully furnished throughout: bedrooms boast fine reproduction oak furniture – one boasts a four-poster. The owners have a passion for antiques and art.

## AYNHO – Northamptonshire – **504** Q28 – **pop. 632**             16 B3
▶ London 73 mi – Birmingham 66 mi – Leicester 62 mi – Coventry 48 mi

### 🏨 **Cartwright**                               ⌂ ⅋ 📡 🔱 🅿 🆅🅸🆂🅰 ⓐⓑ 🅰🅴
*1-5 Croughton Rd ⊠ OX17 3BE – ℰ (01869) 811 885*
*– www.oxfordshire-hotels.co.uk*
**21 rm** ⊑ – ♥£ 80/120 ♥♥£ 140/150   **Rest** – Menu £ 17/21 – Carte £ 21/34
◆ Modernised 16C inn, ideally placed for Silverstone and Bicester Village. Spacious bedrooms come with complimentary wi-fi and are split between main
house and rear conversion. Dining is an informal affair, with a seasonal menu of
robust dishes.

ENGLAND

**AYSGARTH** – North Yorkshire – **502** O21                                    **22** A1
▶ London 249 mi – Ripon 28 mi – York 56 mi

🏠   **George and Dragon Inn** with rm                    ☆ **P** *VISA* ⓩ ⓪
⌧ *DL8 3AD* – ☏ *(01969) 663 358* – www.georgeanddragonaysgarth.co.uk
– *Closed 2 weeks January*
**7 rm** ☞ – †£ 40/55  ††£ 80/90    **Rest** – Menu £ 13 (lunch) – Carte £ 20/30
♦ Laid-back coaching inn set in the National Park, close to the breathtaking River
Ure waterfalls. Unfussy pub classics include plenty of local meats, game and
proper old-fashioned puddings. Comfy, individually styled bedrooms; some with
whirlpool baths.

---

**BABBACOMBE** – Torbay – **503** J32 – see Torquay

---

**BACKWELL** – North Somerset – **503** L29 – pop. 5 455                        **3** B2
▶ London 127 mi – Bristol 9 mi – Cardiff 48 mi – Swansea 83 mi

🏠   **New Inn**                                        ☆ **P** *VISA* ⓩ **AE** ⓪
😊   86 West Town Rd ⌧ *BS48 3BE* – ☏ *(01275) 462 199*
– www.newinn-backwell.co.uk – *Closed 2 weeks January, 25-26*
*December, Sunday dinner and Monday*
**Rest** – Menu £ 16/24 – Carte £ 27/40
♦ Pretty 18C stone pub with warm farmhouse feel, welcoming open-fired bar
and more formal dining area with 'tea room' atmosphere. Cooking is in a stylishly
modern vein, featuring appealing menus of precisely prepared, elegant dishes
and interesting side plates.

---

**BAGSHOT** – Surrey – **504** R29 – pop. 5 247                                 **7** C1
▶ London 37 mi – Reading 17 mi – Southampton 49 mi
🏳 Windlesham Grove End, ☏ (01276) 45 22 20

🏨🏨   **Pennyhill Park** ✍        ≼ 🗋 🕭 ⌫ 🗵 ⊕ 🏊 ✂ 🖻 ﺣ ⍐ ☕ 🅿 *VISA* ⓩ **AE**
London Rd, Southwest : 1 mi on A 30 ⌧ *GU19 5EU* – ☏ *(01276) 471 774*
– www.exclusivehotels.co.uk
**112 rm** – †£ 195/295  ††£ 295, ☞ £ 21 – 11 suites
**Rest** *Michael Wignall at The Latymer* ✿
**Rest** *Brasserie* – see restaurant listing
♦ Impressive 19C manor house set in 123 acres. Classical guest areas display
modern touches; spacious bedrooms boast period furnishings and great views.
Have afternoon tea in the comfy lounge before heading for one of the best spas
in Europe.

✂✂✂✂   **Michael Wignall at The Latymer** – at Pennyhill Park Hotel          🖵
✿    London Rd, Southwest : 1 mi on A30 ⌧ *GU19 5EU*          ☆ **AC** **P** *VISA* ⓩ **AE**
– ☏ *(01276) 486 156* – www.exclusivehotels.co.uk
– *Closed 1-16 January, Sunday, Monday, lunch Tuesday and Saturday*
**Rest** – *(booking essential)* Menu £ 34/60
**Spec.** Poached chicken, smoked eel and horseradish emulsion. Saddle of rabbit
and glazed veal belly with butternut squash purée. Poached pear, liquorice ice
cream and crisp pear cannelloni.
♦ Elegant hotel dining room with oak-clad walls, glass-enclosed chef's table,
quality place settings and formal service. Cooking is careful, precise and uses
only top quality ingredients. The menu is concise and offers ambitious, original
dishes that are full of flavour.

✂   **Brasserie** – at Pennyhill Park Hotel            ≼ 🗋 🕭 **P** *VISA* ⓩ **AE**
London Rd, Southwest : 1 mi on A 30 ⌧ *GU19 5EU* – ☏ *(01276) 471 774*
– www.exclusivehotels.co.uk – *Closed Saturday lunch*
**Rest** – *(buffet lunch)* Carte £ 34/48
♦ Spacious hotel dining room set in an impressive 19C manor house that lies
within 123 acres of grounds. Stylish, modern décor with doors opening out onto
the garden. Appealing brasserie menu.

ENGLAND

**BAKEWELL** – Derbyshire – **502** O24 – **pop. 3 676** ▯ Great Britain **16** A1

▶ London 160 mi – Derby 26 mi – Manchester 37 mi – Nottingham 33 mi

ℹ Bridge St ℘ (01629) 81 65 58, www.peakdistrict.gov.uk

◙ Chatsworth ★★★ (Park and Garden ★★★) **AC**, NE : 2.5 mi by A 619 – Haddon Hall ★★ **AC**, SE : 2 mi by A 6

## at Ashford-in-the-Water Northwest : 1.75 mi by A 6 and A 6020 – ⊠ Bakewell

**Riverside House**    🐾 ℀ **P** VISA ⚌ AE
*Fennel St ⊠ DE45 1QF – ℘ (01629) 814 275 – www.riversidehousehotel.co.uk*
**14 rm** ⊑ – †£ 155 ††£ 195
**Rest** *Riverside Room* – Menu £ 15/45
 ♦ Homely former shooting lodge with gardens running down to the river. Cosy open-fired bar and elegant drawing room. Well-furnished bedrooms with good extras – some have views, some in the wing open onto a terrace. Classical dining takes place over several rooms.

**River Cottage** without rest    🐾 ℀ ᵗ **P** VISA ⚌
*Buxton Rd ⊠ DE45 1QP – ℘ (01629) 813 327 – www.rivercottageashford.co.uk*
**4 rm** ⊑ – †£ 80/95 ††£ 100/135
 ♦ Traditional stone cottage by the River Wye, with delightful gardens and terrace. Bedrooms blend modern furnishings and antique furniture. Complimentary wines and afternoon tea.

## BALSALL COMMON – West Midlands – see Coventry

## BAMBURGH – Northumberland – **501** O17 – **pop. 582** ▯ Great Britain **24** B1

▶ London 337 mi – Edinburgh 77 mi – Newcastle upon Tyne 51 mi

◙ Castle ★ **AC**

**Lord Crewe Arms**    🕭 **AC** rest, ℀ ᵗ **P** VISA ⚌
*Front St ⊠ NE69 7BL – ℘ (01668) 214 243 – www.lordcrewe.co.uk*
*– February-October*
**17 rm** ⊑ – †£ 65/105 ††£ 85/150
**Rest** – *(bar lunch)* Carte £ 16/35
 ♦ Privately owned, 17C former coaching inn, in the shadow of the Norman castle. Spacious, comfy lounge and contemporary bedrooms. Characterful, beamed bar is more rustic in style and offers a traditional menu.

## at Waren Mill West : 2.75 mi on B 1342 – ⊠ Belford

**Waren House** ⌘    ≤ 🐾 ᵗ 🏋 **P** VISA ⚌ AE
*⊠ NE70 7EE – ℘ (01668) 214 581 – www.warenhousehotel.co.uk*
**12 rm** (dinner included) ⊑ – †£ 110/150 ††£ 190/235 – 3 suites
**Rest** – *(dinner only)* Menu £ 35
 ♦ Personally run, antique-furnished country house set in beautiful, tranquil gardens. Bedrooms, named after the owners' family members, mix classic and modern styles: some have four-posters and coastal views. Formal dining room boasts ornate ceiling; menus showcase local ingredients.

## BAMPTON – Devon – **503** J31 – **pop. 1 617** **2** D1

▶ London 189 mi – Exeter 18 mi – Minehead 21 mi – Taunton 15 mi

**Bark House**    🐾 **P** VISA ⚌
*Oakfordbridge, West : 3 mi by B 3227 on A 396 ⊠ EX16 9HZ – ℘ (01398) 351 236*
*– www.thebarkhouse.co.uk – Closed 1 week January and 1 week November*
**6 rm** ⊑ – †£ 54/64 ††£ 70/100
**Rest** – *(closed Monday) (dinner only and Sunday lunch) (booking essential for non-residents)* Menu £ 22
 ♦ Simple, homely hotel; formerly used as a wood store for the local tannery. Bedrooms boast contemporary fabrics and modern bathrooms. One leads to a small garden; another has a balcony. Honest home cooking, coupled with good bin ends from the owner's wine business.

**Quarrymans Rest** with rm                    rm, P VISA AE
*Briton St* ✉ *EX16 9LN –* ✆ *(01398) 331 480 – www.thequarrymansrest.co.uk*
*– Closed 25 December and Sunday dinner*
**3 rm** ⊑ – †£ 55/65 ††£ 65/85   **Rest** – Carte £ 23/31 **s**
♦ 17C inn with relaxed, open-fired bar/lounge and more formal, intimate restaurant. Locally sourced produce to the fore on seasonal menu of tried-and-tested classics, with the occasional Asian influence. Clean, fresh, uncluttered bedrooms.

---

**BANBURY** – Oxfordshire – **503** P27 – **pop. 43 867** 🏴 Great Britain          **10** B1
▶ London 76 mi – Birmingham 40 mi – Coventry 25 mi – Oxford 23 mi
🛈 Spiceball Park Rd ✆ (01295) 25 98 55, www.visitnorthoxfordshire.com
🏌 Cherwell Edge Chacombe, ✆ (01295) 71 15 91
◉ Upton House★ **AC**, NW : 7 mi by A 422

**at Sibford Gower** West : 8 mi by B 4035 – ✉ Banbury

**Wykham Arms**                                    P VISA 
*Temple Mill Rd.* ✉ *OX15 5RX –* ✆ *(01295) 788 808 – www.wykhamarms.co.uk*
*– Closed Monday except bank holidays*
**Rest** – Carte £ 23/31
♦ Thatched stone pub set down country lanes in a small village. Featuring local produce, menus range from bar snacks and lights bites to the full 3 courses. Good range of wines by the glass.

---

**BARNARD CASTLE** – Durham – **502** O20 – **pop. 6 714** 🏴 Great Britain     **24** A3
▶ London 258 mi – Carlisle 63 mi – Leeds 68 mi – Middlesbrough 31 mi
🛈 Flatts Rd ✆ (01833) 69 09 09, www.teesdalediscovery.com
🏌 Harmire Rd, ✆ (01833) 63 83 55
◉ Bowes Museum★ **AC**
◉ Raby Castle★ **AC**, NE : 6.5 mi by A 688

**Homelands**                                        VISA AE
*85 Galgate* ✉ *DL12 8ES –* ✆ *(01833) 638 757*
*– www.homelandsguesthouse.co.uk – Closed 25 September-2 October and 15 December-15 January*
**5 rm** ⊑ – †£ 43/67 ††£ 78   **Rest** – Menu £ 20
♦ Victorian terraced house on the main road through the town, just a short drive from Raby Castle. Immaculately maintained interior with cosy lounge. Individually furnished bedrooms are compact but well-priced; four are in the house, the fifth, at the end of a long, mature rear garden. Home-cooked dinners by arrangement.

**at Greta Bridge** Southeast : 4.5 mi off A 66 – ✉ Barnard Castle

**Morritt**                                    rm, P VISA 
✉ *DL12 9SE –* ✆ *(01833) 627 232 – www.themorritt.co.uk*
**27 rm** ⊑ – †£ 110/120 ††£ 179/200
**Rest *Morritt*** – see restaurant listing
**Rest *Bistro/Bar*** – Carte approx. £ 23
♦ Personally run, 19C former coaching inn displaying a pleasant mix of old and new. Individually designed bedrooms blend contemporary décor with antique furnishings, and boast four-posters or other interesting bedsteads. Oak panelled restaurant serves modern menu; all-day snacks offered in the bistro and bar.

**Morritt** – at Morritt Hotel                          P VISA 
✉ *DL12 9SE –* ✆ *(01833) 627 232 – www.themorritt.co.uk*
**Rest** – Carte £ 30/35
♦ Smart oak-panelled dining room with dark wood beams and a lovely parquet floor, set within a charming coaching inn. Modern menu relies on local ingredients and dishes arrive well-presented.

ENGLAND

**at Hutton Magna** Southeast : 7.25 mi by A 66

🏠 **Oak Tree Inn**  　　　　　　　　　　**P** 𝘃𝘪𝘴𝘢 ⦿ 𝔸𝔼
  ✉ DL11 7HH – ☎ (01833) 627 371 – Closed 24-27 December, 31 December,
  1 January and Monday
  **Rest** – (dinner only) (booking essential) Carte £ 27/34
  ♦ Small but charming whitewashed pub consisting of a single room. Run by a
  husband and wife team; he cooks, while she serves. Cooking is hearty and flavoursome with a rustic French feel.

**at Romaldkirk** Northwest : 6 mi by A 67 on B 6277 – ✉ Barnard Castle

🏠 **Rose and Crown** with rm  　　　　　　🚗 **P** 𝘃𝘪𝘴𝘢 ⦿
  ✉ DL12 9EB – ☎ (01833) 650 213 – www.rose-and-crown.co.uk – Closed 24-26
  December
  **12 rm** ⌂ – †£ 95/125 ††£ 135/185
  **Rest** – Carte £ 22/33 **s**
  **Rest The Restaurant** – (dinner only and Sunday lunch) Menu £ 19/35 **s**ॐ
  ♦ Quintessential 18C English inn with atmospheric bar and horse brasses; set by a
  Saxon church and surrounded by three village greens. Both bar and rear brasserie
  serve classical fare; more formal restaurant offers seasonally changing four course
  dinner menu. Bedrooms boast designer décor, flat screen TVs and Bose radios.

**BARNSLEY** – Gloucestershire – **503** O28 – see Cirencester

**BARRASFORD** – Northumberland　　　　　　　　　　　24 A2
▶ London 309 mi – Newcastle upon Tyne 29 mi – Sunderland 42 mi
  – Middlesbrough 66 mi

🏠 **Barrasford Arms** with rm  　　　🚗 🏠 🍴 rm, ¶¹ **P** 𝘃𝘪𝘴𝘢 ⦿ ⓪
  ✉ NE48 4AA – ☎ (01434) 681 237 – www.barrasfordarms.co.uk – Closed
  January, 25-26 December, Monday February-March, Sunday dinner, Monday
  lunch and bank holidays
  **7 rm** ⌂ – †£ 50/65 ††£ 85
  **Rest** – Menu £ 16 (weekday lunch) – Carte £ 22/30
  ♦ Close to Kielder Water and Hadrian's Wall, this personally run 19C stone inn
  has a traditional, homely atmosphere. Pub classics served at lunch; more substantial dishes at dinner. Modern, comfortable bedrooms.

**BARTON-ON-SEA** – Hampshire – **503** P31　　　　　　6 A3
▶ London 108 mi – Bournemouth 11 mi – Southampton 24 mi – Winchester 35 mi

✗✗ **Pebble Beach** with rm  　　　　　　⬅ 🏠 𝔸ℂ **P** 𝘃𝘪𝘴𝘢 ⦿ 𝔸𝔼
  Marine Dr ✉ BH25 7DZ – ☎ (01425) 627 777 – www.pebblebeach-uk.com
  **4 rm** – †£ 70 ††£ 100, ⌂ £ 6.50　**Rest** – Seafood – Carte £ 17/41
  ♦ Large, split-level restaurant with open-plan kitchen, fish tank and white baby
  grand piano. Metal-furnished terrace boasts impressive Solent and Isle of Wight
  views. Extensive, seasonally changing menus centred around local seafood.
  Good-sized, homely bedrooms.

**BARWICK** – Somerset – **503** M31 – see Yeovil

**BASHALL EAVES** – Lancashire – **502** M23 – see Clitheroe

**BASLOW** – Derbyshire – **502** P24 – pop. 1 184 – ✉ Bakewell　　16 A1
▌ Great Britain
▶ London 161 mi – Derby 27 mi – Manchester 35 mi – Sheffield 13 mi
◉ Chatsworth★★★ (Park and Garden★★★) **AC**

### 🏠 Cavendish ⟪ 🍴 ⟫ ♨ 🍸 🛜 🐕 🅿 VISA ⓸ AE

*Church Ln, on A 619* ✉ *DE45 1SP* – ℰ *(01246) 582 311*
*– www.cavendish-hotel.net*
**23 rm** – ♟£ 140/154 ♟♟£ 177/230, ⌷ £ 18.90 – 1 suite
**Rest** *The Gallery* – see restaurant listing
**Rest** *Garden Room* – Carte £ 26/31
♦ Elegant hotel on the Chatsworth Estate, boasting lovely parkland views. Bedrooms have a cosy, country house feel and a slightly contemporary edge. Some of the furniture and paintings come from Chatsworth House. Formal restaurant serves traditional menus; Garden Room offers all-day dining and afternoon teas.

### ✕✕✕ Fischer's at Baslow Hall with rm 🍴 🍸 🅿 VISA ⓸
### ✿

*Calver Rd, on A 623* ✉ *DE45 1RR* – ℰ *(01246) 583 259*
*– www.fischers-baslowhall.co.uk* – Closed 25-26 and 31 December
**10 rm** ⌷ – ♟£ 105/145 ♟♟£ 155/225 – 1 suite
**Rest** – *(closed Sunday dinner to non-residents and Monday lunch) (booking essential)* Menu £ 34/72
**Spec.** Deep-fried crab in kadaif pastry, caramelised pork belly and Pedro Ximenez vinegar. Goosnargh duck à l'orange. English strawberries three ways with a camomile tea panna cotta.
♦ Edwardian manor house with impressive formal grounds and walled vegetable garden. Classically based and accomplished cooking, with the occasional modern twist, uses much local produce. Comfortable bedrooms in main house; garden rooms larger.

### ✕✕✕ The Gallery – at Cavendish Hotel ⟪ 🍴 🅿 VISA ⓸ AE

*Church Ln, on A 619* ✉ *DE45 1SP* – ℰ *(01246) 582 311*
*– www.cavendish-hotel.net*
**Rest** – Menu £ 41
♦ Fine dining restaurant in an elegant hotel on the Chatsworth Estate, which boasts views out across the parkland. Dishes have a traditional base but presentation and techniques are more modern.

### ✕ Rowley's 🍴 🅿 VISA ⓸

*Church St* ✉ *DE45 1RY* – ℰ *(01246) 583 880* – *www.rowleysrestaurant.co.uk*
*– Closed Sunday dinner*
**Rest** – *(booking advisable)* Menu £ 26 (lunch) – Carte £ 26/35
♦ Contemporary restaurant and bar set over two floors; downstairs with view of open plan kitchen. Modern menu, with produce sourced from in and around Peak District.

---

## BASSENTHWAITE – Cumbria – **501** K19 – pop. 433     **21** A2
▶ London 300 mi – Carlisle 24 mi – Keswick 7 mi

### 🏠 Pheasant 🍴 🐾 📺 rest, 🍸 🕻 🅿 VISA ⓸

*Southwest : 3.25 mi by B 5291 on Wythop Mill Rd* ✉ *CA13 9YE* – ℰ *(017687) 76 234* – *www.the-pheasant.co.uk* – Closed 24-25 December
**15 rm** ⌷ – ♟£ 90/125 ♟♟£ 150/220
**Rest** *Bistro at The Pheasant* – Carte £ 22/33
**Rest** *Dining Room* – *(dinner only and Sunday lunch)* Menu £ 35
♦ 16C whitewashed coaching inn with hugely characterful bars, comfy lounge and traditional styled bedrooms – some with lovely country views. Home-cooked dishes in laid-back, oak-furnished Bistro. Daily changing menu and garden outlook in more formal Dining Room.

### 🏠 Overwater Hall ✍ ⟪ 🍴 🐾 🍸 🅿 VISA ⓸

*Northeast : 2.5 mi by Uldale rd on Overwater rd* ✉ *CA7 1HH*
*– ℰ (017687) 76 566* – *www.overwaterhall.co.uk* – Closed 2-16 January
**11 rm** (dinner included) ⌷ – ♟£ 110/170 ♟♟£ 220/300
**Rest** – *(closed Monday lunch)* Menu £ 48 (dinner) – Carte lunch £ 24/31
♦ Castellated Georgian manor house built in 1811, set in 18 acres of mature gardens. Three good-sized lounges, one with a bar. Large, boldly patterned bedrooms with rich fabrics and good quality bathrooms. Formal dining room offers a traditional country house menu.

# BATH

See city maps on following pages                                        4 C2

ENGLAND

**Bath and North East Somerset** – pop. 80 488 – **503** M29 – **504** M29 – 🗍 Great Britain
▶ London 119 – Bristol 13 – Southampton 63 – Taunton 49

## 🛈 Tourist Information

Abbey Chambers, Abbey Church Yard ℰ(0906) 711 20 00, www.visitbath.co.uk

## Golf Courses

🔟 Tracy Park Wick Bath Rd, ℰ(0117) 9 37 18 00
🔟 Lansdown, ℰ(01225) 42 21 38
🔟 Entry Hill, ℰ(01225) 83 42 48

## ◎ SIGHTS

**In the town :** City★★★ · Royal Crescent★★★ AV · The Circus★★★ AV · Museum of Cos-
tume★★★ **AC** AV**M7** · Roman Baths★★ **AC** BX**D** · Holburne Museum★★ Y**M5** ·
Pump Room★ BX**B** · Assembly Rooms★ AV · Bath Abbey★ BX · Pulteney Bridge★ BV
· Lansdown Crescent★★ Y · Camden Crescent★ Y

**On the outskirts :** American Museum at Claverton★★ **AC** E : 3 mi by A 36 Y

**In the surrounding area :** Corsham Court★★ AC, NE : 8.5 mi by A 4 · Dyrham Park★
**AC**, N : 6.5 mi by A 4 and A 46

---

🏨🏨🏨 **Royal Crescent**        ⇐ 🚗 🔲 🕪 🕭 ℐ˅ 💆 🛎 🗚 ℗˚ 💆 🅿 💳 ⓦ 🆎 ⓞ
16 Royal Cres ⊠ BA1 2LS – ℰ (01225) 823 333 – www.royalcrescent.co.uk
**35 rm** 🖵 – ♛♛£ 199/595 – 10 suites                                    AV**a**
**Rest** *Dower House* – see restaurant listing
♦ Professionally run townhouse in sweeping Georgian crescent, boasting smart
fire-lit entrance, period drawing room/library and stylish spa. Elegant Georgian
bedrooms display antiques.

🏨🏨🏨 **Bath Spa**        🚗 🏠 🔲 🕪 🕭 💆 🛎  க rm, 🗚 rest, 🕉 ℗˚ 💆 🅿 💳 ⓦ 🆎
Sydney Rd ⊠ BA2 6JF – ℰ (0844) 879 91 06 – www.macdonaldhotels.co.uk
**118 rm** – ♛£ 153/215 ♛♛£ 153/320, 🖵 £ 18 – 11 suites                Y**z**
**Rest** *Vellore* – (dinner only) (booking essential) Carte £ 40/50
**Rest** *Alfresco* – (lunch only and dinner Friday-Saturday) Carte £ 26/33
♦ Impressive 19C mansion in mature gardens, with newer wing. Period lounges
and contemporary bedrooms; full butler service in Imperial Suites. Superb spa. Impressive, formal Georgian dining room with Corinthian columns. Informal Alfresco
offers classic grill menu.

69

*(M4, M5)* **A 46** STROUD

CHIPPENHAM **A 4**

UPPER WESTON

M⁶

Lansdown Lane

Swainswick Lane

CHARLCOMBE

Bailbrook Lane

TOLL BRIDGE

WESTON

High St

Lansdown Road

St. Saviours Rd

Gloucester Rd

Road

Avon

BATHAMPTON

**A 4** BRISTOL

Kelston Rd

Newbridge Hill

Combe Park

LANSDOWN CRESCENT

CAMDEN CRESCENT

London Rd

A 36 Warminster

Road

**A 36** WARMINSTER

Y

Newbridge Rd

Dover

Up. Bristol

Road

ROYAL VICTORIA PARK Rd

M⁶

🗖18

Y

Newton Road

Bristol Rd A 36

A 4

North

Bathwick

Hill

Road

The Avenue

TWERTON

The Hollow

Widcombe Hill

A 3062

U

Whiteway

Englishcombe

Lane

A 367

Greenway La

🗖9

PRIOR PARK

Rd

RUSH HILL Frome

Wellsway

Claverton Down

N

BATH

B3110

Bradford Road

A 3062

COMBE DOWN

0       1 km
0       1 mile

**A 367** EXETER

---

 **Bath Priory**  🍴 🏡 ⌨ 🦞 🕥 🏊 ♨ ♿ ♨ **P** **VISA** 🅐🅔 ⓘ

*Weston Rd ⊠ BA1 2XT – ℰ (01225) 331 922 – www.thebathpriory.co.uk*
**27 rm** ⌨ – ♛♛ £ 430/645                                                    Yc
**Rest** – Menu £ 35/75 ♨

♦ Impressive Georgian house with mature gardens, classical guest areas, sumptuous sitting room and smart spa. Luxurious bedrooms blend the traditional and the modern. Designer bathrooms. Two dining rooms; the smaller more romantic, the larger more modern. Ambitious cooking uses some unexpected combinations.

---

 **Homewood Park**  🍴 🕊 ⌨ 🦞 🕥 🏊 ⓦ **P** **VISA** 🅐🅔 ⓘ

*Abbey Ln, Hinton Charterhouse, Southeast : 6.5 mi on A 36 ⊠ BA2 7TB*
*– ℰ (01225) 723 731 – www.homewoodpark.co.uk*
**19 rm** ⌨ – ♛ £ 215 ♛♛ £ 255 – 2 suites
**Rest** – Menu £ 22/55 **s**

♦ Remotely set country house with fashionable interior. Charming guest areas – many boasting open fires – and contemporary bedrooms with bold colour schemes. Superb spa and treatment facilities. Dining split between 3 rooms. Modern dishes are stylishly presented.

---

**Queensberry**  🍴 ⑁ ⅌ **P** **VISA** 🅐🅔

*Russel St ⊠ BA1 2QF – ℰ (01225) 447 928 – www.thequeensberry.co.uk*
**29 rm** – ♛ £ 135/195 ♛♛ £ 135/480, ⌨ £ 15                          AVx
**Rest** *Olive Tree* – see restaurant listing

♦ Long-standing Georgian townhouse in the city centre, run by a friendly well-versed team. Guest areas include a snug lounge, well-appointed sitting rooms and a bar, all with a contemporary feel. Funky, individually designed bedrooms have nice designer touches, plasma TVs, digital radios and a host of extras.

# BATH

ENGLAND

| | |
|---|---|
| ...mbury | BX 2 |
| ...rgyle St | BV 3 |
| ...ennett St | AV 4 |
| ...ridge St | BVX 6 |
| ...oad Quay | BX 7 |
| ...harles St | AX 10 |
| ...harlotte St | AV 12 |
| ...heap St | BX 13 |
| ...hurchill Bridge | BX 14 |
| ...rcus Pl | AV 16 |
| ...ay St | AV |
| ...rand Parade | BX 17 |
| ...reat Stanhope St | AV 18 |
| Green St | BV 21 |
| Guinea Lane | BV 23 |
| Henry St | BX 24 |
| Lower Borough Walls | BX 26 |
| Milsom St | ABV |
| Monmouth Pl | AVX 28 |
| Monmouth St | AX 30 |
| New Bond St | BX 31 |
| New Orchard St | BX 32 |
| Nile St | AX 34 |
| Northgate St | BVX 35 |
| Old Bond St | BX 36 |
| Orange Grove | BX 38 |
| Pierrepont St | BX 39 |
| Quiet St | BV 40 |
| Russel St | AV 42 |
| Southgate Shopping Centre | BX |
| Southgate St | BX 43 |
| Terrace Walk | BX 46 |
| Union St | BX 47 |
| Upper Borough Walls | BX 48 |
| Westgate Buildings | AX 49 |
| Westgate St | ABX 50 |
| Wood St | AV 52 |
| York St | BX 53 |

## Dukes

*Great Pulteney St ⊠ BA2 4DN – ℰ (01225) 787 960*
*– www.dukesbath.co.uk*                                    BV**n**

**13 rm** ⌑ – †£ 99/123 ††£ 139/179 – 4 suites
**Rest *Cavendish*** – Menu £ 10 (lunch) – Carte £ 24/45

♦ Welcoming Palladian-style townhouse with period furnishings and plenty of charm. Bedrooms, named after famous Dukes, feature bold prints, heavy fabrics and antiques; some have four-posters. Dining room opens onto a patio area and offers a modern, formal menu.

A good night's sleep without spending a fortune? Look for Bib Hotel 🏠.

ENGLAND

### Oldfields without rest
102 Wells Rd ⊠ BA2 3AL – ✆ (01225) 317 984 – www.oldfields.co.uk – Closed 24-25 December
**16 rm** – ♦£ 55/70 ♦♦£ 65/170                                                    Zu
♦ Spaciously elegant Victorian house with comfy, well-furnished drawing room, breakfast room boasting 'Bath rooftops' view and bedrooms that exude a high standard of comfort.

### Apsley House without rest
141 Newbridge Hill ⊠ BA1 3PT – ✆ (01225) 336 966 – www.apsley-house.co.uk – Closed 24-25 December                                                    Yx
**12 rm** – ♦£ 125/150 ♦♦£ 175/200
♦ Built for the Duke of Wellington and staffed with the unobtrusive calm of an English private house. Spacious individual rooms; two open onto a peaceful, mature rear garden.

### Cheriton House without rest
9 Upper Oldfield Pk ⊠ BA2 3JX – ✆ (01225) 429 862 – www.cheritonhouse.co.uk
**12 rm** – ♦£ 60/95 ♦♦£ 85/165                                                    Zu
♦ Immaculately kept house with 19C origins, run by very charming hosts. Comfortable, sizeable rooms and lounge, with some fine tiled fireplaces. Breakfast in the conservatory.

### Dorian House without rest
1 Upper Oldfield Pk ⊠ BA2 3JX – ✆ (01225) 426 336 – www.dorianhouse.co.uk – Closed 24-25 December                                                    Zu
**13 rm** – ♦£ 69/99 ♦♦£ 99/165
♦ Charming 19C house featuring original stained glass. Music-related memorabilia in reception. Well-appointed bedrooms display good attention to detail; some are Victorian in style, others more modern. Delightful conservatory breakfast room.

### Villa Magdala without rest
Henrietta Rd ⊠ BA2 6LX – ✆ (01225) 466 329 – www.villamagdala.co.uk – Closed 1 week Christmas                                                    BVr
**18 rm** – ♦£ 110/130 ♦♦£ 130/150
♦ Named after Napier's 1868 victory. Well-equipped rooms, floral furnishings; carefully preserved ornate balustrade and showpiece bedroom with four-poster and chaise longue.

### One Three Nine without rest
139 Wells Rd ⊠ BA2 3AL – ✆ (01225) 314 769 – www.139bath.co.uk – Closed 24-25 December                                                    Zr
**10 rm** – ♦£ 65/170 ♦♦£ 75/180
♦ Unassuming Victorian building conceals the chic, bold décor of a stylish boutique hotel. Individually styled bedrooms may include four-posters or spa baths. Excellent terrace breakfast.

### Lavender House without rest
17 Bloomfield Pk, (off Bloomfield Rd) ⊠ BA2 2BY – ✆ (01225) 314 500 – www.lavenderhouse-bath.com                                                    Zs
**4 rm** – ♦£ 65 ♦♦£ 90/120
♦ Edwardian house hidden way from the town centre, in a residential area. Snug sitting room and pleasant breakfast room boasting a characterful 17C sideboard. Comfortable bedrooms have delightful designer wallpapers and nice extra touches.

### Athole House without rest
33 Upper Oldfield Pk ⊠ BA2 3JX – ✆ (01225) 320 000 – www.atholehouse.co.uk
**4 rm** – ♦£ 70/100 ♦♦£ 100/130                                                    Zi
♦ Spacious, bay windowed Victorian guesthouse with large garden, away from city centre. Bright breakfast room; conservatory lounge. Light, airy, contemporary bedrooms.

XXXX **Dower House** – at Royal Crescent Hotel     🍴 🛜 AC ⇔ VISA ☺ AE ⓸
*16 Royal Cres* ✉ *BA1 2LS* – ☎ *(01225) 823 333* – *www.royalcrescent.co.uk*
**Rest** – Menu £ 28/56🍽     AV**a**
♦ Plush, contemporary dining room with swish bar, spacious lounge and lovely garden. Creative, seasonal cooking is underpinned by a French base. Attentive, understated service.

XX **Olive Tree** – at Queensberry Hotel     AC ⇔ VISA ☺ AE
*Russel St* ✉ *BA1 2QF* – ☎ *(01225) 447 928* – *www.thequeensberry.co.uk*
*– Closed Monday lunch*     AV**x**
**Rest** – Menu £ 23 (lunch) – Carte £ 44/59
♦ Stylish restaurant set within an established boutique townhouse hotel. Split into two rooms, with elegantly laid tables and contemporary artwork hung on the walls. Modern menus display Mediterranean influences. Pleasant team.

X **Bistro La Barrique**     🛜 AC VISA ☺
*31 Barton St* ✉ *BA1 1HG* – ☎ *(01225) 463 861* – *www.bistrolabarrique.co.uk*
*– Closed 25-26 December, 1 January, second week January and Sunday*
*October-April*     AX**a**
**Rest** – French – Carte £ 21/27
♦ Unpretentious bistro-style restaurant, with sheltered courtyard for terrace dining. Small, good value menu of 'petits plats'; classic French dishes with some Mediterranean twists.

X **Casanis**     🛜 VISA ☺
*4 Saville Row* ✉ *BA1 2QP* – ☎ *(01225) 780 055* – *www.casanis.co.uk*
*– Closed 25-26 December, 1 week January, 1 week August, Sunday and*
*Monday*     AV**n**
**Rest** – French – *(booking essential)* Menu £ 19 (lunch) – Carte £ 27/38
♦ Sweet French bistro set in an elegant Georgian building near the Assembly Rooms. Exposed wooden floors, clothed tables and a tiny rear courtyard. Skilful cooking of classic French dishes.

🍴 **Marlborough Tavern**     🛜 VISA ☺
*35 Marlborough Buildings* ✉ *BA1 2LY* – ☎ *(01225) 423 731*
*– www.marlborough-tavern.com – Closed 25 December*     AV**z**
**Rest** – *(booking advisable)* Menu £ 15 (lunch) – Carte £ 26/34
♦ Spacious, modern pub next to the park and Royal Crescent, boasting funky flock wallpaper, scrubbed wooden floors and local artwork. Unfussy, hearty, classical dishes use very local produce.

🍴 **White Hart**     🛜 VISA ☺
*Widcombe Hill* ✉ *BA2 6AA* – ☎ *(01225) 338 053* – *www.whitehartbath.co.uk*
*– Closed 25-26 December, Sunday dinner and bank holidays*     Z**o**
**Rest** – *(booking essential at dinner)* Carte £ 13/29
♦ Appealing pub on south east edge of the city centre, with a local following and a neighbourhood feel. Generous portions of hearty cooking; smaller tapas plates also popular.

**at Box** Northeast : 4.75 mi on A 4 - Y – ✉ Bath

🍴 **The Northey**     🍴 🛜 P VISA ☺ AE
*Bath Rd* ✉ *SN13 8AE* – ☎ *(01225) 742 333* – *www.ohhcompany.co.uk*
*– Closed 25-26 December*
**Rest** – Carte £ 22/30
♦ Traditional-looking, family-run stone coaching inn with open-plan interior, large dining room and vast bar. Appealing monthly menus feature unfussy, seasonal British dishes; fish is a strength.

ENGLAND

**at Colerne** Northeast : 6.5 mi by A 4 - Y - Batheaston rd and Bannerdown Rd
– ⊠ Chippenham

🏠🏠🏠 **Lucknam Park** 🦆   ⟨≲ 🚗 🔊 🎏 🕸 ⛩ 🏄 🗶 ♞ 🎿 **P** **VISA** **◯◯** **AE** **①**
*North : 0.5 mi on Marshfield rd* ⊠ *SN14 8AZ –* ✆ *(01225) 742 777*
*– www.lucknampark.co.uk*
**36 rm** – 🛉£ 315  🛉🛉£ 495, ⚏ £ 22 – 5 suites
**Rest** *The Park* 🌼 **Rest** *Brasserie* – see restaurant listing
♦ Grand Palladian mansion with tree-lined drive, rich décor, luxurious furnishings
and sumptuous fabrics. Top class facilities include impressive spa complex and renowned equestrian centre. Extremely comfortable bedrooms.

𝕏𝕏𝕏𝕏 **The Park** – at Lucknam Park Hotel   ⟨≲ 🚗 🔊 **P** **VISA** **◯◯** **AE** **①**
🌼
*North : 0.5 mi on Marshfield rd* ⊠ *SN14 8AZ –* ✆ *(01225) 742 777*
*– www.lucknampark.co.uk – Closed Sunday dinner*
**Rest** – *(dinner only and Sunday lunch) (booking essential)* Menu £ 70
**Spec.** Poached langoustines, potato mousse, asparagus and caviar. Loin of lamb
with crushed peas, morels and garlic. Cannelloni of lemon, summer berries
and crème fraîche sorbet.
♦ Located within an impressive mansion, an opulent dining room with skilled,
amiable service and a knowledgeable kitchen team. Classical menus display
modern European influences, with dishes expertly crafted from locally sourced
farm produce.

𝕏𝕏 **Brasserie** – at Lucknam Park Hotel   🕸 **P** **VISA** **◯◯** **AE** **①**
*North : 0.5 mi on Marshfield rd* ⊠ *SN14 8AZ –* ✆ *(01225) 742 777*
*– www.lucknampark.co.uk – Closed 25-26 December and 1 January*
**Rest** – Menu £ 21 (lunch) – Carte £ 33/53
♦ Linen-laid brasserie in state-of-the-art spa complex, boasting spacious bar-
lounge and airy dining room with full-length windows. Precise, modern cooking
in well-judged combinations; healthy options available. BBQs on the terrace in
summer. Clued-up service.

**at Monkton Combe** Southeast : 4.5 mi by A 36 - Y – ⊠ Bath

🍴🏠 **Wheelwrights Arms** with rm   🕸 🗶 rm, 🎙 **P** **VISA** **◯◯**
*Church Ln* ⊠ *BA2 7HB –* ✆ *(01225) 722 287 – www.wheelwrightsarms.co.uk*
**7 rm** ⚏ – 🛉£ 85/95  🛉🛉£ 150   **Rest** – Carte £ 22/30 **s**
♦ Charming 18C former carpenter's workshop in a sleepy little village, displaying
exposed stone walls, parquet floors and open fires. Wide-ranging, traditional menus; mainly fish specials. Individually designed bedrooms are modern with rustic
overtones.

**at Combe Hay** Southwest : 5 mi by A 367 – ⊠ Bath

🍴🏠 **Wheatsheaf** with rm   🚗 🕸 **P** **VISA** **◯◯**
⊠ *BA2 7EG –* ✆ *(01225) 833 504 – www.wheatsheafcombehay.com – Closed 1
week January, 24-25 December, Sunday dinner and Monday except bank
holidays*
**3 rm** ⚏ – 🛉£ 120  🛉🛉£ 150   **Rest** – Carte £ 23/37
♦ A modern take on the classical country pub; remotely set in a pretty village,
with chic styling, open fires, comfy sofas and a relaxed atmosphere. Contemporary presentation of flavourful, seasonal dishes. Spacious, modern bedrooms
boast a quality feel.

---

**BATTLE** – East Sussex – **504** V31 – **pop. 5 190** 📗 Great Britain                **8 B3**
▶ London 55 mi – Brighton 34 mi – Folkestone 43 mi – Maidstone 30 mi
🔳 Battle and Bexhill TIC, Battle Abbey, High St ✆ (01424) 77 37 21,
www.battle-sussex.co.uk
◉ Town ★ – Abbey and Site of the Battle of Hastings ★ **AC**

## ❌❌ Nobles     🛜 VISA ⦿ AE ⦿

*17 High St ⊠ TN33 OAE – ℰ (01424) 774 422 – www.noblesrestaurant.co.uk*
*– Closed Sunday dinner and bank holidays*
**Rest** – Menu £ 15 (weekday lunch) – Carte £ 24/39
♦ Simple, tasteful eatery with terrace, in heart of historical high street. Regularly changing menus offer unfussy classical dishes of local, seasonal produce, with the occasional twist.

---

## BAUGHURST – Hampshire     6 B1

▶ London 61 mi – Camberley 28 mi – Farnborough 27 mi

### 🍽 Wellington Arms     🚗 🛜 P VISA ⦿

*Baughurst Rd, Southwest : 0.5 mi ⊠ RG26 5LP – ℰ (0118) 982 01 10*
*– www.thewellingtonarms.com – Closed Sunday dinner*
**Rest** – *(booking essential)* Menu £ 19 (weekday lunch) – Carte £ 18/34
♦ Smart, cream pub boasting its own pigs, chickens, bees, herb beds and vegetable gardens. Produce is strictly local and home-grown/reared/made. Blackboard menus feature 6 dishes per course, which are replaced as produce runs out. Cooking is generous and satisfying.

---

## BEACONSFIELD – Buckinghamshire – 504 S29 – pop. 12 292     11 D3

▶ London 26 mi – Aylesbury 19 mi – Oxford 32 mi

🏌 Beaconsfield Seer Green, ℰ (01494) 67 65 45

**ENGLAND**

### 🏨 Crazy Bear     🔟 AK 🛜 📶 ♨ P VISA ⦿ AE

*73 Wycombe End ⊠ HP9 1LX – ℰ (01494) 673 086*
*– www.crazybeargroup.co.uk*
**10 rm** – ♦£ 345 ♦♦£ 430, ⊔ £ 19.50
**Rest** *Thai* **Rest** *English* – see restaurant listing
♦ Unique hotel with sumptuous, over-the-top style and plush, idiosyncratic furnishings. Moody, masculine bedrooms blend original features with rich fabrics and leather; copper baths fill from the ceiling. Flamboyant bars and Thai or English restaurant – with caviar and expensive wines, the sky's the limit.

### ❌❌ English – at Crazy Bear Hotel     🛜 AK P VISA ⦿ AE

*73 Wycombe End ⊠ HP9 1LX – ℰ (01494) 673 086*
*– www.crazybeargroup.co.uk*
**Rest** – *(booking advisable)* Menu £ 19 (lunch) – Carte £ 31/59
♦ Lavishly styled restaurant in a truly theatrical hotel. Flamboyant, sumptuous furnishings and a unique, quirky style. Extensive menus rely on specialist suppliers and their own farm produce.

### ❌❌ Thai – at Crazy Bear Hotel     ⇔ P VISA ⦿ AE

*73 Wycombe End ⊠ HP9 1LX – ℰ (01494) 673 086 – www.crazybeargroup.co.uk*
**Rest** – Thai – *(dinner only) (booking essential)* Carte £ 29/36
♦ Chicly decorated hotel restaurant boasting chandeliers, flock wallpapers, snakeskin handrails and studded leather chairs. Thai dishes dominate although influences are drawn from all over Asia.

---

## at Seer Green Northeast : 2.5 mi by A 355 – ⊠ Buckinghamshire

### 🍽 Jolly Cricketers     🛜 P VISA ⦿ AE

😊 *24 Chalfont Rd ⊠ HP9 2YG – ℰ (01494) 676 308 – Closed 2 weeks January,*
*Sunday dinner and Monday*
**Rest** – *(booking advisable)* Carte £ 23/39
♦ Charming Victorian pub filled with a host of cricketing memorabilia; even the menu is divided into 'Openers, Main Play and Lower Order'. Warming open fire and friendly staff. Appealing cooking pleasingly balances a selection of classics with more modern choices.

BEACONSFIELD

## at **Wooburn Common** Southwest : 3.5 mi by A 40 – ⊠ Beaconsfield

🏠 **Chequers Inn** ⌖     🚗 🚳 ⚸ 📶 **P** **VISA** **⬤⬤** **AE** **①**
*Kiln Ln, Southwest : 1 mi on Bourne End rd ⊠ HP10 0JQ – ℰ (01628) 529 575*
*– www.chequers-inn.com – Closed 25 December and 1 January*
**17 rm** – ♦£ 100 ♦♦£ 108, ⌕ £ 9.95    **Rest** – Menu £ 18/26 – Carte £ 28/39
♦ Attractive 17C red-brick former inn: family-owned and run since 1975. Cosy beamed bar and spacious, leather-furnished lounge. Good-sized bedrooms boast flat screen TVs and wi-fi. Choice of bar snacks, or more ambitious dishes in the clothed rear restaurant.

---

**BEAMHURST** – Staffordshire – see Uttoxeter

---

**BEAMINSTER** – Dorset – **503** L31 – pop. 2 791      **3** B3
▶ London 154 mi – Exeter 45 mi – Taunton 30 mi – Weymouth 29 mi
🏌 Chedington Court South Perrott, ℰ (01935) 89 14 13

🏨 **BridgeHouse**     🚗 🚳 ⚸ **P** **VISA** **⬤⬤** **AE**
*3 Prout Bridge ⊠ DT8 3AY – ℰ (01308) 862 200 – www.bridge-house.co.uk*
**14 rm** ⌕ – ♦£ 86/150 ♦♦£ 180/215
**Rest** – Menu £ 25 (lunch) – Carte dinner £ 30/44
♦ Hugely characterful 13C former priest's house, with newer extensions. Traditionally furnished, flag-floored lounges boast inglenook fireplaces. Mix of classical and modern bedrooms. Linen-laid restaurant with conservatory and terrace offers brasserie-style menu.

✕ **Wild Garlic**     **VISA** **⬤⬤**
*4 The Square ⊠ DT8 3AS – ℰ (01308) 861 446 – www.thewildgarlic.co.uk*
*– Closed 25-26 December, 1 January and Sunday-Tuesday*
**Rest** – (booking essential) Menu £ 22 (lunch) **s** – Carte £ 31/41 **s**
♦ Pretty, rustic restaurant in charming town; ask for a window table overlooking the square. Run by 2009 Masterchef winner, who is a keen forager. Appealing menu supplemented by blackboard specials.

---

**BEARSTED** – Kent – **504** V30 – see Maidstone

---

**BEAULIEU** – Hampshire – **503** P31 – pop. 726 – ⊠ Brockenhurst    **6** B2
📗 Great Britain
▶ London 102 mi – Bournemouth 24 mi – Southampton 13 mi – Winchester 23 mi
◉ Town★★ - National Motor Museum★★ **AC**
◉ Buckler's Hard★ (Maritime Museum★ **AC**) SE : 2 m

🏨 **Montagu Arms**     🚗 ⚸ 📶 🏊 **P** **VISA** **⬤⬤** **AE**
*Palace Ln ⊠ SO42 7ZL – ℰ (01590) 612 324 – www.montaguarmshotel.co.uk*
**18 rm** ⌕ – ♦£ 140/160 ♦♦£ 198 – 4 suites
**Rest** *The Terrace*✿ **Rest** *Monty's Inn* – see restaurant listing
♦ Well-run 18C inn which boasts a characterful parquet-floored reception and wood-panelled lounge. Lovely rear gardens are overlooked by a wicker-furnished conservatory and paved terrace. Traditional country house style bedrooms successfully marry antique furniture with modern facilities. Good level of service.

✕✕✕ **The Terrace** – at Montagu Arms Hotel     🚗 🚳 **P** **VISA** **⬤⬤** **AE**
✿ *Palace Ln ⊠ SO42 7ZL – ℰ (01590) 612 324 – www.montaguarmshotel.co.uk*
*– Closed Tuesday lunch and Monday*
**Rest** – Menu £ 25 (lunch) – Carte dinner £ 63/69
**Spec.** Cannelloni of braised rabbit with glazed spring vegetables and black pudding. Honey roast duck with smoked pecans, tamarind and date purée. Passion fruit and white chocolate cheesecake.
♦ Traditional country house dining room with wood-panelled lounge. Good-sized, linen-laid tables; polite, efficient service. Lovely garden outlook from terrace. Precisely prepared, top quality produce used in refined, classically based dishes with modern touches.

✗ **Monty's Inn** at Montagu Arms Hotel    🚘 **P** 𝗩𝗜𝗦𝗔 ⓒⓔ 𝗔𝗘
*Palace Ln* ✉ *SO42 7ZL* – ☎ *(01590) 612 324* – *www.montaguarmshotel.co.uk*
**Rest** – Carte £ 25/38
♦ Set within a large red-brick inn in a pleasant town, an informal hotel restaurant serving home-cooked classics. Meats are free range and from nearby farms; eggs are from their own chickens.

**BEELEY** – Derbyshire – pop. 165      **16** B1
▶ London 160 mi – Derby 26 mi – Matlock 5 mi

🍴 **Devonshire Arms** with rm    🏡 📶 **P** 𝗩𝗜𝗦𝗔 ⓒⓔ 𝗔𝗘
*Devonshire Sq* ✉ *DE4 2NR* – ☎ *(01629) 733 259* – *www.devonshirebeeley.co.uk*
**8 rm** 🛏 – ❖£ 114/134 ❖❖£ 197/217   **Rest** – Carte £ 19/35🏵
♦ Stone inn close to Chatsworth House and owned by the Estate. Rustic bar; modern extension with lovely views. Unusual starters followed by classics and daily 'market' dishes. Tasty afternoon teas. Beamed bedrooms in main house; larger, brighter rooms next door.

**BELCHFORD** – Lincolnshire – **502** T24 – ✉ Horncastle    **17** C1
▶ London 169 mi – Horncastle 5 mi – Lincoln 28 mi

🍴 **Blue Bell Inn**    🏡 **P** 𝗩𝗜𝗦𝗔 ⓒⓔ
*1 Main Rd* ✉ *LN9 6LQ* – ☎ *(01507) 533 602* – Closed 2 weeks mid-January
**Rest** – Carte £ 20/27
♦ A traditionally styled whitewashed pub, popular with walkers on the Viking Way. Numerous blackboard menus list sandwiches, pub favourites and more ambitious choices.

**BELFORD** – Northumberland – **501** O17 – **pop. 1 177**    **24** A1
▶ London 335 mi – Edinburgh 71 mi – Newcastle upon Tyne 49 mi
🏌 Belford South Rd, ☎ (01668) 21 33 23

⌂ **Market Cross** without rest    🚘 📶 𝗩𝗜𝗦𝗔 ⓒⓔ
*1 Church St* ✉ *NE70 7LS* – ☎ *(01668) 213 013* – *www.marketcross.net*
**4 rm** 🛏 – ❖£ 50/80 ❖❖£ 80/110
♦ 200 year-old stone house in rural town centre. Warmly decorated lounge, homely touches in tasteful bedrooms. Wide, locally inspired breakfast choice in cosy pine surroundings.

**BELPER** – Derbyshire – **502** P24 – **pop. 21 938**    **16** B2
▶ London 141 mi – Birmingham 59 mi – Leicester 40 mi – Manchester 55 mi

**at Shottle** Northwest : 4 mi by A 517 – ✉ Belper

🏠 **Dannah Farm Country House** without rest 🌿    🚘 🐾 🏊 📶 **P**
*Bowmans Lane, North : 0.25 mi by Alport rd* ✉ *DE56 2DR*   𝗩𝗜𝗦𝗔 ⓒⓔ
– ☎ *(01773) 550 273* – *www.dannah.co.uk* – Closed 24-26 December
**4 rm** 🛏 – ❖£ 79/110 ❖❖£ 165/210 – 4 suites
♦ Family-run converted farmhouse - part of a working farm. Spacious, contemporary bedrooms are diverse in style; the two level Studio suite includes hot tub and spiral staircase.

**BENENDEN** – Kent – **504** V30    **8** B2
▶ London 55 mi – Croydon 49 mi – Barnet 81 mi – Ealing 85 mi

⌂ **Ramsden Farm** without rest 🌿    ≤ 🚘 🏊 📶 **P**
*Dingleden Ln, Southeast : 1 mi by B 2086* ✉ *TN17 4JT* – ☎ *(01580) 240 203*
– *www.ramsdenfarmcottage.co.uk*
**3 rm** 🛏 – ❖£ 70/120 ❖❖£ 85/120
♦ Attractive clapperboard house with modern styling, a refreshingly relaxed air and fine countryside views. Spacious, up-to-date bedrooms; luxurious, modern bathrooms with underfloor heating.

**BEPTON** – West Sussex – see Midhurst

ENGLAND

## BERKHAMSTED – Hertfordshire – **504** S28 – pop. 18 800     **12** A2
▌ Great Britain

▶ London 34 mi – Aylesbury 14 mi – St Albans 11 mi

◉ Whipsnade Wild Animal Park★ **AC**, N : 9.5 mi on A 4251, B 4506 and B 4540

※※   **The Gatsby**        VISA ◉◉ AE

*97 High St ⌧ HP4 2DG – ℰ (01442) 870 403 – www.thegatsby.net*
*– Closed 25-26 December*

**Rest** – Menu £ 21 (lunch) – Carte £ 32/44

♦ Charming cinema built in 1938 and sympathetically converted to incorporate a trendy art deco bar and glamorous restaurant. Dine among elegant columns and ornate plasterwork. Menus offer detailed, classically based dishes with modern twists.

---

## BERWICK-UPON-TWEED – Northumberland – **501** O16     **24** A1
– pop. 13 031 ▌ Great Britain

▶ London 349 mi – Edinburgh 57 mi – Newcastle upon Tyne 63 mi

🛈 106 Marygate ℰ (01289) 33 07 33, www.visitnorthumberland.com

🏌 Goswick, ℰ (01289) 38 72 56

🏌 Magdalene Fields, ℰ (01289) 30 61 30

◎ Town★★ - Walls★

◉ Foulden★, NW : 5 mi – Paxton House (Chippendale furniture★) **AC**, W : 5 mi by A 6105, A 1 and B 6461. St Abb's Head★★ (≤★), NW : 12 mi by A 1, A 1107 and B 6438 - SW : Tweed Valley★★ – Eyemouth Museum★ **AC**, N : 7.5 mi by A 1 and A 1107 – Holy Island★ (Priory ruins★ **AC**, Lindisfarne Castle★ **AC**), SE : 9 mi by A 1167 and A 1 – Manderston★ (stables★), W : 13 mi by A 6105 - Ladykirk (Kirk o'Steil★), SW : 8.5 mi by A 698 and B 6470

※   **1 Sallyport** with rm        (🅟) VISA ◉◉ AE ①

*1 Sallyport, off Bridge St ⌧ TD15 1EZ – ℰ (01289) 308 827*
*– www.sallyport.co.uk*

**6 rm** ⌑ – ♦£ 85 ♦♦£ 150    **Rest** – Carte £ 19/31 s

♦ Pair of listed 17C houses on a cobbled alley, in the older part of town. All-day café-cum-bistro with cake and pastry counter. Bright, modern restaurant with vivid fabrics and polished tables. Daily changing menus have a classical base. Funky, boutique bedrooms feature interesting modern artwork and extras.

---

## BEVERLEY – East Riding of Yorkshire – **502** S22 – pop. 29 110     **23** D2
– ⌧ Kingston-Upon-Hull ▌ Great Britain

▶ London 188 mi – Kingston-upon-Hull 8 mi – Leeds 52 mi – York 29 mi

🛈 34 Butcher Row ℰ (01482) 86 74 30, www.yorkshire.com

🏌 The Westwood, ℰ (01482) 86 87 57

◎ Town★ - Minster★★ – St Mary's Church★

⌂   **Burton Mount** without rest        ⬚ ✤ 🅟 VISA ◉◉

*Malton Rd, Cherry Burton , Northwest : 2.75 mi by A 164, B 1248 on Leconfield rd*
*⌧ HU17 7RA – ℰ (01964) 550 541 – www.burtonmount.co.uk*

**5 rm** ⌑ – ♦£ 64 ♦♦£ 91

♦ Homely, red-brick house overlooking large, mature gardens. Dining room boasts French windows opening onto the terrace. Comfy bedrooms display heavy fabrics and dark wood furniture. Good breakfasts; dinners of well sourced local produce cooked on the Aga.

※※   **Whites** with rm        VISA ◉◉
☺

*12a North Bar Without ⌧ HU17 7AB – ℰ (01482) 866 121*
*– www.whitesrestaurant.co.uk – Closed 1 week Christmas, 1 week August, Sunday and Monday*

**4 rm** ⌑ – ♦£ 100 ♦♦£ 125

**Rest** – (booking advisable) Menu £ 18/28 – Carte dinner £ 33/37

♦ Small, friendly restaurant beside the old city walls, its plain décor contrasting nicely with black wood tables and eye-catching glass art. Good value weekday set menu uses lesser-known cuts; à la carte offers more complex dishes. Smart, modern bedrooms, some with bespoke furniture; rooftop terrace breakfast.

ENGLAND

**at Tickton** Northeast : 3.5 mi by A 1035 – ⊠ Kingston-Upon-Hull

🛏️ **Tickton Grange** 🚗 🕭 🖄 🕃 ۩ ⚓ 🅿 VISA ⓪ AE ⓪
⊠ HU17 9SH – 𝒞 (01964) 543 666 – www.beverleyticktongrange.co.uk
**21 rm** 🛌 – 🛉£ 95 🛉🛉£ 140
**Rest** *Champagne* – Menu £ 25/35
◆ Warm, welcoming, family-run hotel. Bedrooms blend Georgian and contemporary architecture, and display antique and period-inspired furniture. Richly swagged fabrics and open fires in an inviting lounge. Dine in Georgian style; large bay windows look onto the lawn.

**at South Dalton** Northwest : 5 mi by A 164 and B 1248 – ⊠ Beverley

📙 **Pipe and Glass Inn** (James Mackenzie) with rm 🚗 🕎 🖄 rm, 🅿
🕄 West End ⊠ HU17 7PN – 𝒞 (01430) 810 246 VISA ⓪
– www.pipeandglass.co.uk – Closed 2 weeks January,
25 December, Sunday dinner and Monday except bank holidays
**2 rm** – 🛉£ 140 🛉🛉£ 160 **Rest** – Carte £ 34/45
**Spec.** Wild rabbit, langoustine and Jerusalem artichoke crumble, pickled girolle salad. Rump of lamb with a 'Hotch Potch' of spring vegetables, pearl barley and crispy mutton belly. Lemon verbena posset, East Yorkshire sugar cakes
◆ Warm, bustling and inviting pub, personally run by experienced owners. Generous portions of carefully executed, flavourful cooking with judicious use of local, seasonal and traceable produce. Luxury, designer bedrooms boast all mod cons and have their own patios overlooking estate woodland. Breakfast served in bedrooms.

**BEYTON** – Suffolk – **504** W27 – **see Bury St Edmunds**

**BIBURY** – Gloucestershire – **503** O28 – **pop. 570** – ⊠ Cirencester 4 D1
🛑 Great Britain
▶ London 86 mi – Gloucester 26 mi – Oxford 30 mi
◉ Village ★

🛏️ **Swan** 🚗 🕎 🖃 🗎 🕋 ⚓ 🅿 VISA ⓪ AE ⓪
⊠ GL7 5NW – 𝒞 (01285) 740 695 – www.cotswold-inns-hotels.co.uk/swan
**18 rm** 🛌 – 🛉£ 140/200 🛉🛉£ 160/280 – 4 suites
**Rest** *Café Swan* – see restaurant listing
**Rest** *Gallery* – (dinner only) Menu £ 33 – Carte £ 28/35
◆ Ivy-clad former coaching inn with private garden and trout stream, set in a delightful village. Cosy lounges and clubby, leather-furnished bar. Mix of cottagey character and contemporary touches in bedrooms; the best are in the annexes, opt for a duplex suite. Choice of formal restaurant or relaxed brasserie.

🍴 **Café Swan** – at Swan Hotel 🚗 🅿 VISA ⓪ AE ⓪
⊠ GL7 5NW – 𝒞 (01285) 740 695 – www.cotswold-inns-hotels.co.uk/swan
**Rest** – Carte £ 28/35
◆ Set in a delightful Cotswold village, a relaxed, modern brasserie within a 17C coaching inn. Lovely flagstone courtyard complete with water fountain. Menu of light bites and brasserie dishes.

🏠 **Cotteswold House** without rest 🚗 🖄 🕋 🅿 VISA ⓪
Arlington, on B 4425 ⊠ GL7 5ND – 𝒞 (01285) 740 609
– www.cotteswoldhouse.net
**3 rm** 🛌 – 🛉£ 55 🛉🛉£ 75
◆ Set in a pleasant garden outside the picturesque village. Homely, spotless and modestly priced bedrooms, comprehensively remodelled behind a Victorian façade. Friendly, welcoming owner.

**BIDDENDEN** – Kent – **504** V30 – **pop. 2 205** 🛑 Great Britain 9 C2
▶ London 52 mi – Ashford 13 mi – Maidstone 16 mi
◉ Bodiam Castle ★★, S : 10 mi by A 262, A 229 and B 2244 – Sissinghurst Garden ★,
W : 3 mi by A 262 – Battle Abbey ★, S : 20 mi by A 262, A 229, A 21 and A 2100

ENGLAND

⋔ **Barclay Farmhouse** without rest       🍴 ⚙ ⁛ **P** 𝘝𝘐𝘚𝘈 ⓒⓞ
*Woolpack Corner, South : 0.5 mi by A 262 on Benenden rd* ✉ *TN27 8BQ*
*– 𝒞 (01580) 292 626 – www.barclayfarmhouse.co.uk*
**3 rm** ⚏ – ♦£ 65 ♦♦£ 90
♦ Set in an acre of pleasant garden: well-priced, very comfortable accommodation with fine French oak flooring and furniture. Inventive breakfasts in the barn conversion.

✗ **West House** (Graham Garrett)           **P** 𝘝𝘐𝘚𝘈 ⓒⓞ
𝕊 *28 High St* ✉ *TN27 8AH – 𝒞 (01580) 291 341*
*– www.thewesthouserestaurant.co.uk – Closed Christmas-New Year, 2*
*weeks summer, Saturday lunch, Sunday dinner and Monday*
**Rest** – Menu £ 25/38
**Spec.** Grilled calves tongue, salt-baked beetroot and smoked anchovy dressing. Slow-cooked pork belly, sherry soaked prunes, cauliflower and chorizo. White chocolate and honeycomb parfait with dark chocolate sorbet.
♦ Pretty part-16C former weavers' cottages in picturesque village. Charming beamed interior with inglenook and modern artwork. Concise seasonal menu; confident and technically skilled cooking allows the ingredients to shine.

🕍 **The Three Chimneys**       🍴 🍽 **P** 𝘝𝘐𝘚𝘈 ⓒⓞ ⓞ
*Hareplain Rd, West : 1.5 mi by A 262* ✉ *TN27 8LW – 𝒞 (01580) 291 472*
*– www.thethreechimneys.co.uk – Closed 25 and dinner 31 December*
**Rest** – *(booking essential)* Carte £ 25/36
♦ Delightful pub with charming terrace and garden, dating back to 1420 and boasting a roaring fire, dimly lit low-beamed rooms and an old world feel. Largely British dishes and nursery puddings.

---

**BIGBURY** – Devon – **503** I33                           **2** C3
▶ London 195 mi – Exeter 41 mi – Plymouth 22 mi
🅖 Kingsbridge★, E : 13 mi by B 3392 and A 379

✗ **Oyster Shack**           🍽 **P** 𝘝𝘐𝘚𝘈 ⓒⓞ 𝗔𝗘
*Milburn Orchard Farm, Stakes Hill, East : 1 mi on Easton rd* ✉ *TQ7 4BE*
*– 𝒞 (01548) 810 876 – www.oystershack.co.uk – Closed 3 January-2 February*
**Rest** – Seafood – *(booking essential)* Carte £ 30/35
♦ Eccentric venue; half a lovely covered terrace, decorated with fishing nets. Seafood, particularly local oyster dishes; classic and modern dishes using the freshest produce.

---

**BIGBURY-ON-SEA** – Devon – **503** I33 – pop. 600 – ✉ Kingsbridge     **2** C3
▶ London 196 mi – Exeter 42 mi – Plymouth 23 mi

🏨 **Burgh Island** ॐ      ≤ 🍴 🕭 🍽 🏠 ※ 🖪 ⚙ ⁛ **P** 𝘝𝘐𝘚𝘈 ⓒⓞ
*South : 0.5 mi by sea tractor* ✉ *TQ7 4BG – 𝒞 (01548) 810 514*
*– www.burghisland.com*
**15 rm** (dinner included) ⚏ – ♦£ 300/460 ♦♦£ 620 – 10 suites
**Rest** – *(dinner only and Sunday lunch) (booking essential for non-residents)*
Menu £ 60
♦ Unique Grade II listed 1930s country house in private island setting: stylishly romantic art deco interior. Charmingly individual rooms with views: some have fantastic style. Ballroom dining: dress in black tie. Owners pride themselves on accomplished cooking.

🏠 **Henley** ॐ        ≤ 🍴 ⁛ **P** 𝘝𝘐𝘚𝘈 ⓒⓞ 𝗔𝗘
*Folly Hill* ✉ *TQ7 4AR – 𝒞 (01548) 810 240 – www.thehenleyhotel.co.uk*
*– April-October*
**5 rm** ⚏ – ♦£ 80 ♦♦£ 144
**Rest** – *(dinner only) (booking essential for non-residents)* Menu £ 36
♦ Charming hotel with superb views over Burgh Island and Bolt Tail. Homely lounge, wicker-furnished conservatory and comfy bedrooms that cross New England and English Country styles; Room 2 boasts double-aspect views. Concise, unfussy dinners use local ingredients.

ENGLAND

▶ London 85 mi – Bury St Edmunds 18 mi – Ipswich 15 mi

XX    **Bildeston Crown** with rm                                    🛋 ᴕ ⁿ⁾ 🅿 *VISA* 🐼 🅰🅴
       *104 High St ⊠ IP7 7EB – ℰ (01449) 740 510 – www.thebildestoncrown.co.uk*
       *– Closed dinner 25-26 December and 1 January*
       **12 rm** 🖵 – †£ 70/150 ††£ 150/250
       **Rest** – Menu £ 24 (lunch) – Carte £ 33/45
       ♦ Old beamed inn with lovely courtyard. Stylish, modern interior with 2 bars, a
       smart lounge and formal restaurant; warm colours and open fires feature. Choose
       from classics, an ambitious à la carte or tasting menu. Elaborate, artistic cooking.
       Luxurious bedrooms boast bold colours, designer furniture and chic bathrooms.

---

**BIRKENHEAD** – Merseyside – **502** K23 – **pop. 83 729**                        **20** A3
▶ London 222 mi – Liverpool 2 mi
**Access** Mersey Tunnels (toll)
🚢 to Liverpool and Wallasey (Mersey Ferries) frequent services daily
🏌 Arrowe Park Woodchurch, ℰ (0151) 677 15 27
🏌 Prenton Golf Links Rd, ℰ (0151) 609 34 26

Plan : see Liverpool p. 3

XXX   **Fraiche** (Marc Wilkinson)                                              🛋 *VISA* 🐼
 ৩    *11 Rose Mount, Oxton, Southwest : 2.25 mi by A 552 and B 5151 ⊠ CH43 5SG*
       *– ℰ (0151) 652 29 14 – www.restaurantfraiche.com – Closed 25 December, 1-7*
       *July, Monday and Tuesday*
       **Rest** – *(dinner only and lunch Friday-Saturday) (booking essential)*
       Menu £ 27/65
       **Spec.** Arctic char, yuzu jelly and watermelon. Anjou pigeon, textures of artichoke
       and pickled mushrooms. Rhubarb and celery sorbet, vanilla mousse and wild
       strawberries.
       ♦ Stylish, sophisticated restaurant displaying interesting glass friezes. Choice of 3
       set menus. Creative, modern dishes use excellent quality ingredients from around
       the globe. Unusual combinations; impressive presentation. Knowledgeable, per-
       sonable service.

ENGLAND

# BIRMINGHAM

See city maps on following pages

**ENGLAND**

West Midlands – pop. **942 766** – **503** O26 – **504** O26 – ▯ Great Britain

▶ London 122  – Bristol 91  – Liverpool 103  – Manchester 86

**🛈 Tourist Information**

150 New St ✆(0121) 202 50 00, www.visitbirmingham.com

**Airport**

✈ Birmingham International Airport : ✆ (0844) 576 6000, E : 6 ½ m. by A 45 DU

**Golf Courses**

🏌 Edgbaston Church Rd, ✆(0121) 454 17 36
🏌 Hilltop Handsworth Park Lane, ✆(0121) 554 44 63
🏌 Hatchford Brook Sheldon Coventry Rd, ✆(0121) 743 98 21

**◎ SIGHTS**

**In the town :** City★  •  Museum and Art Gallery★★ LY**M2**  •  Barber Institute of Fine Arts★★ EX**U**

**On the outskirts :** Aston Hall★★ FVM

**In the surrounding area :** Black Country Museum★, Dudley, NW : 10 mi by A 456 and A 4123 AU • Bournville★, SW : 4 mi on A 38 and A 441

82

# INDEX OF STREET NAMES IN BIRMINGHAM

ENGLAND

# BIRMINGHAM AND
# WOLVERHAMPTON

ENGLAND

**BIRMINGHAM**
See following pages

A 41 WOLVERHAMPTON

M 5

BRISTOL. M 5

A 457

V

SMETHWICK

A 456 (M 5), KIDDERMINSTER

X

ENGLAND

A 4123 WOLVERHAMPTON

1 km
1/2 mile

B 4124

Oxhill Rd
Church Lane
Rookery
Wellington Road
A 4040
Birchfield Road
PERRY BARR
Aldridge Road
Aston Lane
Brookvale

Island
Holyhead
HANDSWORTH
Hamstead Road
Witton
ASTON
M
Aston Expressway
Lichf

Booth St.
Rabone Lane
Boulton Rd
Soho Rd
Villa Rd
Lozells Rd
High St
Victoria
Aston Rd.

Rolfe St.
High
Cape
Heath St
Green Rd
Winson Rd
Lodge Rd
Hockley Circus
10
New John St West
A 4540
54
13

SMETHWICK
Cape Hill
Dudley Rd
Spring Hill
Icknield Port Rd
A 4540
9
A 41
12
20
22
50
15
A 47
40

A 4030
Rotton Rd
A 4040
Icknield Port Rd
A 4540
7
Icknield
A 457
U
36
MILLENNIUM POINT

Beakwood
Sandon Rd
City Rd
Portland Rd
ROTTON PARK RESERVOIR
Ladywood
Middleway
Broad St.
Bristol St.
24
High St
15

Hagley Rd
A 456
Westfield Rd
Norfolk Rd
Rd
6
Middleway
5
Broad St
42
A 38
3
A 4540
19

Lordswood
A 4040
55
Harborne
High St.
Metchley Lane
Harborne Lane
Church Rd
14
Canal
Priory Rd
Bristol Road
A 441
2
Haden Way
Highgate
1
15
14

Court Oak Rd
HARBORNE
Harborne Park Rd
EDGBASTON
18
Bristol
Edgbaston Rd
Pershore Rd
Rea
Salisbury Rd
Moseley Rd
A 435
MOSELEY
Wake Rd

U
Alcester Rd
KING'S HEATH

Oak Tree La.
Bristol Road
Linden Rd
Fordhouse Lane
Pershore
Vicarage Rd
High St.
Alcester
Addison Rd

## BIRMINGHAM

BIRMINGHAM

200 m
0
200 yards

**ENGLAND**

### Hyatt Regency   ← 🖥 ⊕ ⓓ ⓕ ⓛ ⓖ rm, 🔠 ⚒ 🎧 ⚙ 🏊 🚗 VISA ⓒⓞ AE ⓞ
2 Bridge St ⊠ B1 2JZ – ℰ (0121) 643 12 34
– www.birmingham.regency.hyatt.com                                           KZa
**315 rm** – ♦£ 95/219 ♦♦£ 95/219, � £ 18 – 4 suites
**Rest** *Aria* – Menu £ 15 (weekday lunch)/20 – Carte £ 25/41
♦ Striking mirrored exterior. Glass enclosed lifts offer panoramic views. Size-able rooms with floor to ceiling windows. Covered link with International Convention Centre. Contemporary style restaurant in central atrium; modish cooking.

### Malmaison   ⊕ ⓕ ⓛ ⓖ ⓒ 🔠 ⚙ 🏊 VISA ⓒⓞ AE ⓞ
Mailbox, 1 Wharfside St ⊠ B1 1RD – ℰ (0121) 246 50 00
– www.malmaison.com                                                          LZe
**184 rm** – ♦£ 150/180 ♦♦£ 150/295, ⊆ £ 15 – 1 suite
**Rest** *Brasserie* – see restaurant listing
♦ One of the few new-build Malmaisons, set next to designer clothes and home-ware shops on the site of the old Royal Mail sorting office. Contemporary, dark-hued bedrooms; the suite has a mini-cinema. Small spa offers good range of treatments.

### Hotel Du Vin   ⓕ ⓛ ⓖ ⓒ 🔠 ⚙ 🏊 VISA ⓒⓞ AE ⓞ
25 Church St ⊠ B3 2NR – ℰ (0121) 200 06 00 – www.hotelduvin.com
**66 rm** – ♦£ 99/170 ♦♦£ 99/170, ⊆ £ 14.50                               LYe
**Rest** *Bistro* – see restaurant listing
♦ Characterful former eye hospital in a relaxed, boutique style. Richly hued bed-rooms named after wine companies and estates; one suite boasts an 8 foot bed, 2 roll-top baths and a gym. Small cellar bar/pub and comfy Bubble Bar for champagne.

### Mint   ⓕ ⓛ ⓖ ⓒ rm, 🔠 ⚙ 🎧 ⚙ 🚗 VISA ⓒⓞ AE ⓞ
1 Brunswick Sq, Brindley Pl ⊠ B1 2HW – ℰ (0121) 643 10 03
– www.minthotel.com                                                          KZb
**238 rm** – ♦£ 225 ♦♦£ 225, ⊆ £ 14
**Rest** *City Café* – ℰ (0121) 633 63 00 – Menu £ 15/20 – Carte £ 24/33
♦ In heart of vibrant Brindley Place; the spacious atrium with bright rugs and blond wood sets the tone for equally stylish bedrooms. Corporate friendly with many meeting rooms. Eat in restaurant, terrace or bar.

### Simpsons (Andreas Antona) with rm   🚗 🏠 🔠 rest, 🅿 VISA ⓒⓞ AE
🕸 20 Highfield Rd, Edgbaston ⊠ B15 3DU – ℰ (0121) 454 34 34
– www.simpsonsrestaurant.co.uk – Closed 25-26 December and bank holidays
**4 rm** – ♦£ 160 ♦♦£ 225                                                    EXe
**Rest** – Contemporary – (closed Sunday dinner) Menu £ 35/38
– Carte £ 47/54 🍷
**Spec.** Seared scallops, lime beurre noisette and borage. Fillet of Aberdeenshire beef, braised short rib. Macaé chocolate and praline mousse.
♦ Smart Georgian mansion with stylish lounges, pleasant garden terrace and summer house. Tables are well-spaced; service is formal and efficient. Classical menu displays Mediterranean influences, contemporary twists and excellent pro-duce. Spacious bedrooms boast French country styling.

### Purnell's (Glynn Purnell)   🔠 ⚙ VISA ⓒⓞ AE
🕸 55 Cornwall St ⊠ B3 2DH – ℰ (0121) 212 97 99 – www.purnellsrestaurant.com
– Closed 1-14 August, 1 week Easter, 1 week Christmas, Saturday lunch,
Sunday and Monday                                                            LYb
**Rest** – Modern – Menu £ 26/46
**Spec.** Poached egg yolk with smoked haddock, cornflakes, milk foam and curry oil. Daube of beef, English lettuce and leeks, fondue of leeks and crème fraîche. Warm dark chocolate mousse and torte, mango sorbet.
♦ Passionately run, stylish restaurant in sizeable red-brick property with large lounge. Refined and modern cooking displays plenty of original and individual touches. The tasting menus are particularly innovative in style.

XXX **Opus**                                    AC ⇄ VISA ⓪ AE ⓪
*54 Cornwall St* ⊠ *B3 2DE* – ℰ *(0121) 200 2323* – *www.opusrestaurant.co.uk*
*– Closed 24 December-early January, Saturday lunch, Sunday and bank holidays*
**Rest** – Modern – Menu £ 25 – Carte £ 30/42                        LY**z**
♦ Set in the heart of the financial district; its name means 'hard work'. Floor-to-
ceiling windows, cocktail bar and chef's table. Daily changing modern menus of
precisely prepared, wholesome dishes.

XXX **Asha's**                                       ⇄ VISA ⓪ AE
*12-22 Newhall St* ⊠ *B3 3LX* – ℰ *(0121) 200 27 67* – *www.ashasuk.co.uk* – *Closed
lunch Saturday and Sunday*                                          LY**m**
**Rest** – Indian – Menu £ 13/25 – Carte £ 26/48
♦ Smart restaurant with delightful décor and vivid artwork. Owned by renowned
artiste/gourmet Asha Bhosle. Authentic North West Indian cuisine cooked by
chefs originally from that region.

XXX **Edmunds**                                  🏠 AC VISA ⓪ AE
*6 Central Sq, Brindley Pl* ⊠ *B1 2JB* – ℰ *(0121) 633 49 44*
*– www.edmundsrestaurant.co.uk* – *Closed 1 week January, 1 week April, 2 weeks
summer, Saturday lunch, Sunday and Monday*                          KZ**x**
**Rest** – Modern European – Menu £ 20/43
♦ Formal restaurant in heart of city. Smart interior with neutral décor and modern lighting. Immaculately laid tables boast fine china and glassware. Smart, attentive staff.

XX **Carters of Moseley**                         AC VISA ⓪ AE ⓪
*2c St Mary's Row, Wake Green Rd* ⊠ *B13 9EZ* – ℰ *(0121) 449 8885*
*– www.cartersofmoseley.co.uk* – *Closed 26-31 December, 31 July-16 August,
Sunday dinner and Monday*                                           FX**a**
**Rest** – *(booking advisable)* Menu £ 18 (lunch and early dinner)
– Carte £ 32/47 **s**
♦ Smart suburban conversion with dark banquette seating, black ash tables,
large wine wall and neighbourhood bistro feel. Modern British cooking relies
largely on Cornish ingredients; afternoon tea – on Saturdays – is done very well.

XX **Turners** (Richard Turner)                        AC VISA ⓪
🥨
*69 High St, Harborne* ⊠ *B17 9NS* – ℰ *(0121) 426 44 40*
*– www.turnersofharborne.com* – *Closed Sunday and Monday*          EX**a**
**Rest** – Modern – *(booking essential)* Menu £ 30/60
**Spec.** Confit leg and rillette of rabbit, crayfish and vanilla. Roast veal, sweetbreads,
cheek and white asparagus. Strawberry Arctic roll.
♦ Neat neighbourhood restaurant in suburban parade, with wood panels, etched
mirrors and velvet chairs. Menus offer refined, flavoursome dishes of accomplished, classical cooking with modern touches; only tasting menus are offered Saturday night. Formal, structured service.

XX **Loves**                                          ⇄ VISA ⓪
*The Glasshouse, Canal Sq* ⊠ *B16 8FL* – ℰ *(0121) 454 51 51*
*– www.loves-restaurant.co.uk* – *Closed 2 weeks January, 2 weeks Easter, 2 weeks
August, Sunday and Monday*                                          JZ**a**
**Rest** – Inventive – Menu £ 25/43
♦ Situated on the ground floor of an apartment block on the canal basin, with
spacious, contemporary interior and smartly laid tables. Cooking uses modern
techniques and presentation.

XX **Lasan**                                           VISA ⓪ AE
*3-4 Dakota Buildings, James St, St Pauls Sq* ⊠ *B3 1SD* – ℰ *(0121) 212 36 64*
*– www.lasangroup.com* – *Closed 25 December and Saturday lunch*
**Rest** – Indian – Carte £ 40/56                                   KY**a**
♦ Jewellery quarter restaurant of sophistication and style; good quality ingredients allow the clarity of the spices to shine through in this well-run Indian establishment.

**ENGLAND**

XX **Bank**  ☞ AC ☐ ⇔ VISA ●● AE
4 Brindley Pl ⊠ B1 2JB – ℰ (0121) 633 44 66 – www.bankrestaurants.com
– Closed 26 December and 1 January  KZ**u**
**Rest** – Modern – Menu £ 15 (lunch and early dinner) – Carte £ 27/39
◆ Well-run, contemporary bar-restaurant. Striking glass squares hang from the dining room ceiling, its full-length windows overlooking the canal and terrace. Eclectic seasonal menu with weekly specials and influences from Asia and the Med.

XX **Bistro** – at Hotel Du Vin  VISA ●● AE
25 Church St ⊠ B3 2NR – ℰ (0121) 200 06 00 – www.hotelduvin.com
**Rest** – French – Carte £ 21/34⌘  LY**e**
◆ Classically styled hotel restaurant in striking 19C former eye hospital. Walls are filled with wine-related memorabilia and there's a hidden courtyard. French bistro menu; extensive wine list.

XX **Brasserie** – at Malmaison Hotel  AC VISA ●● AE ①
Mailbox, 1 Wharfside St ⊠ B1 1RD – ℰ (0121) 246 50 00 – www.malmaison.com
**Rest** – British – Menu £ 18 (lunch) – Carte £ 29/41  LZ**e**
◆ Bustling hotel brasserie that's particularly popular with lunchtime shoppers and local workers. Simple, rustic British menu. Private dining and wine tasting rooms ideal for corporate clients.

**ENGLAND**

> Undecided between two equivalent establishments in the same town?
> Within each category, establishments are classified in our order of
> preference: the best first.

---

# BISHOP'S STORTFORD – Hertfordshire – **504** U28 – pop. 35 325   **12** B2
▌ Great Britain
▶ London 34 mi – Cambridge 27 mi – Chelmsford 19 mi – Colchester 33 mi
✈ Stansted Airport : ℰ (0844) 3351803, NE : 3.5 m
🛈 2 Market Square ℰ (01279) 65 58 31, www.bishopsstortford.org
🖼 Audley End ★★ **AC**, N : 11 mi by B 1383

X **Lemon Tree**  AC ⇔ P VISA ●● AE ①
14-16 Water Ln ⊠ CM23 2LB – ℰ (01279) 757 788 – www.lemontree.co.uk
– Closed 25-27 December, 1 January, Sunday dinner and bank holidays
**Rest** – Menu £ 20 (weekday dinner) – Carte £ 27/46
◆ Friendly little restaurant in a 200 year old house, hidden in the town centre. Characterful interior with comfy bar-lounge and several beamed dining areas. Seasonal menus offer a good choice of unfussy, classical dishes; good value lunch.

---

# BISHOPSTONE – Swindon – **503** P29 – see Swindon

---

# BLACKBURN – Blackburn with Darwen – **502** M22 – pop. 105 085   **20** B2
▶ London 228 mi – Leeds 47 mi – Liverpool 39 mi – Manchester 24 mi
🛈 50-54 Church St ℰ (01254) 68 80 40, www.visitblackburn.co.uk
🏌 Pleasington, ℰ (01254) 20 21 77
🏌 Wilpshire 72 Whalley Rd, ℰ (01254) 24 82 60
🏌 Great Harwood Harwood Bar, Whalley Rd, ℰ (01254) 88 43 91

🍴 **Clog & Billycock**  ☞ P VISA ●● AE
Billinge End Rd, Pleasington, West : 2 mi by A 677 ⊠ BB2 6QB
– ℰ (01254) 201 163 – www.theclogandbillycock.com – Closed 25 December
**Rest** – Carte £ 20/33
◆ Spacious, modern, open-plan pub. Extensive menus offer plenty of choice and display a strong Lancastrian slant; cooking is rustic and generous. Most produce is sourced from within 20 miles.

**at Langho** North : 4.5 mi on A 666 – ⊠ Whalley

XXX  **Northcote** (Nigel Haworth) with rm  🚗 🕹 ⁇ 🅿 VISA ⚫ AE
❀  *Northcote Rd, North : 0.5 mi on A 59 at junction with A 666 ⊠ BB6 8BE*
*– 𝒞 (01254) 240 555 – www.northcote.com – Closed 25 December*
**14 rm** 🖵 – †£ 185/225 ††£ 220/270
**Rest** – Menu £ 25 (weekday lunch) – Carte £ 42/66 ❀
**Spec.** Roast halibut with Lancashire cheese fondue and bacon tempura. New season's lamb wlth asparagus, tomato and a mint relish. Roast pineapple and Eccles
cake ice cream
♦ Smartly refurbished restaurant in red-brick Victorian house. Traceability and
food miles are all-important to this team, with regional ingredients and local suppliers the stars of the show; some produce travelling only a few metres from their
own organic gardens. Elegant, contemporary bedrooms boast designer touches.

**at Mellor** Northwest : 3.25 mi by A 677 – ⊠ Blackburn

🏠  **Stanley House**  🚗 🕹 🕹 rm, 🔟 ⁇ ⁇ 🍴 🅿 VISA ⚫ AE
*Southwest : 0.75 mi by A 677 and Further Lane ⊠ BB2 7NP – 𝒞 (01254) 769 200*
*– www.stanleyhouse.co.uk*
**12 rm** 🖵 – †£ 155/180 ††£ 185/285
**Rest** *Grill on the Hill* – *(closed Sunday dinner and Monday ) (dinner only and*
*Sunday lunch)* Carte £ 25/44
♦ Attractive 17C manor house boasting superb countryside views and stylish, individually designed bedrooms; some featuring original beams or mullioned windows. Old farmhouse building houses the function rooms, a casual bar-lounge
and terrace. Grill restaurant affords great views over the grounds to the coast.

🏠  **Millstone**  🕹 ⁇ ⁇ 🅿 VISA ⚫ AE ⓪
*Church Ln ⊠ BB2 7JR – 𝒞 (01254) 813 333 – www.millstonehotel.com*
**22 rm** 🖵 – †£ 99 ††£ 125 – 1 suite  **Rest** – Carte £ 25/34
♦ Attractive sandstone former coaching inn set in a quiet village. Pub-style bar
with log fire and comfy sofas. Cosy, well-kept bedrooms have matching floral patterns and good modern facilities. Traditional wood-panelled dining room offers
accessible menu.

**ENGLAND**

**BLACKPOOL** – Blackpool – **502** K22 – pop. 142 283 🗒 Great Britain  **20** A2
📍 London 246 mi – Leeds 88 mi – Liverpool 56 mi – Manchester 51 mi
✈ Blackpool Airport : 𝒞 (0844) 4827171, S : 3 mi by A 584
🛈 1 Clifton St 𝒞 (01253) 47 82 22, www.visitblackpool.com
⛳ Blackpool Park North Park Drive, 𝒞 (01253) 39 79 16
⛳ Poulton-le-Fylde Breck Rd, Myrtle Farm, 𝒞 (01253) 89 24 44
👁 Tower ★ **AC** AY **A**

Plan on next page

🏠  **Number One South Beach**  🎐 🕹 rm, ⁇ ⁇ 🅿 VISA ⚫
*4 Harrowside West ⊠ FY4 1NW – 𝒞 (01253) 343 900*
*– www.numberonehotels.com*  BZ**v**
**13 rm** 🖵 – †£ 81/145 ††£ 125/155 – 1 suite
**Rest** – *(dinner only and Sunday lunch)* Carte £ 21/27
♦ Modernised hotel set back off promenade. Contemporary interior with stylish,
boldly coloured bedrooms; two with four-posters. Superb bathrooms boast whirlpool baths and TVs. Interesting menus are largely made up of free range, organic
and fair trade produce.

  **Number One St Lukes** *without rest*  🚗 ⁇ ⁇ 🅿 VISA ⚫
*1 St Lukes Rd ⊠ FY4 2EL – 𝒞 (01253) 343 901 – www.numberoneblackpool.com*
**3 rm** 🖵 – †£ 70/120 ††£ 100/130  AZ**a**
♦ Engagingly run, enticingly stylish guesthouse. The good value nature of the establishment is further enhanced by an elegant breakfast room and luxuriously appointed bedrooms.

# BLACKPOOL

ENGLAND

FLEETWOOD

ST. ANNES

**at Thornton** Northeast : 5.5 mi by A 584 - BY - on B 5412 – ✉ **Blackpool**

XX    **Twelve**        *VISA* ◉◉ AE

😊 *Marsh Mill, Fleetwood Rd North, North : 0.5 mi on A 585 ✉ FY5 4JZ – ℰ (01253) 821 212 – www.twelve-restaurant.co.uk – Closed first 2 weeks January and Monday*
**Rest** – *(dinner only and Sunday lunch)* Menu £ 28 – Carte £ 30/48
♦ Spacious restaurant where brick walls, exposed pipework and grey beams contribute to a slightly industrial feel. Passionately run by dynamic owner and friendly team. Good value menus offer interesting, well-executed modern dishes with the odd innovative touch.

---

**BLAKENEY** – Norfolk – **504** X25 – pop. 1 628 – ✉ Holt      **15** C1

▶ London 127 mi – King's Lynn 37 mi – Norwich 28 mi

🏨🏨🏨    **Blakeney**      ⪦ 🖙 🖥 🖧 ✎ 🖳 ⁝ ﹪ 🗜 **P** *VISA* ◉◉ AE ⓪

*The Quay ✉ NR25 7NE – ℰ (01263) 740 797 – www.blakeneyhotel.co.uk*
**63 rm** (dinner included) ⌑ – ♦£ 134/219 ♦♦£ 292/318
**Rest** – *(closed to non-residents 24-28 December dinner and 31 December-1 January)* Menu £ 28 – Carte lunch £ 20/25
♦ Traditional, privately owned hotel in a great quayside location, affording views over the estuary and salt marshes. Various comfortable lounges and bar with subtle modern touches. Individually designed bedrooms, some with balconies or sea views. Formal dining room offers good outlook and a wide-ranging menu.

ENGLAND

⬆    **Blakeney House** without rest      🖙 ﹪ **P** *VISA* ◉◉

*High St ✉ NR25 7NX – ℰ (01263) 740 561 – www.blakeneyhouse.com – Closed Christmas and 1 week early January*
**8 rm** ⌑ – ♦£ 80/95 ♦♦£ 120/150
♦ Substantial Victorian house tucked away in a tranquil spot on the High Street. Spacious, individually decorated, up-to-date bedrooms. Pleasant breakfast room with garden views.

XX    **Moorings**      AC *VISA* ◉◉

*High St ✉ NR25 7NA – ℰ (01263) 740 054 – www.blakeney-moorings.co.uk – Closed 3 weeks January, Tuesday-Thursday November-March, Sunday except bank holidays and Monday dinner*
**Rest** – *(light lunch) (booking essential)* Carte £ 26/36
♦ Bright village bistro near the quayside, offering popular light lunches. Classical dinner menu boasts unfussy, seasonal dishes, including game and local seafood. Tasty puddings.

🍺    **White Horse** with rm      🖙 ﹪ **P** *VISA* ◉◉ AE

*4 High St ✉ NR25 7AL – ℰ (01263) 740 574 – www.blakeneywhitehorse.co.uk – Closed 25 December*
**9 rm** ⌑ – ♦£ 50/80 ♦♦£ 70/140    **Rest** – *(booking advisable)* Carte £ 20/34
♦ Brick and flint former coaching inn set by the harbour. Traditional, hearty pub favourites on lunch menu. Evening à la carte features seasonal dishes and some interesting combinations. Modern bedrooms come in various shapes and sizes.

**at Cley next the Sea** East : 1.5 mi on A 149 – ✉ Holt

🏠    **Cley Windmill** ⑤      ⪦ 🖙 ﹪ **P** *VISA* ◉◉

*The Quay ✉ NR25 7RP – ℰ (01263) 740 209 – www.cleywindmill.co.uk*
**8 rm** ⌑ – ♦£ 189 ♦♦£ 189
**Rest** – *(dinner only) (booking essential to non residents)* Menu £ 33
♦ Restored 18C redbrick windmill in salt marshes with a viewing gallery: a birdwatcher's paradise. Neatly kept rooms, full of character, in the mill, stable and boatshed. Flagstoned dining room; communal table.

**at Wiveton** South : 1 mi by A149 on Wiveton Rd

🏠 **Wiveton Bell** with rm      🛜 🍽 📶 **P** 📷 **VISA** 💳 **AE**
*Blakeney Rd ⊠ NR25 7TL – 𝒞 (01263) 740 101 – www.wivetonbell.com – Closed 25 December*
**4 rm** 🍵 – ♦£ 90/140 ♦♦£ 90/140    **Rest** – *(booking essential)* Carte £ 21/29
• Characterful pub with colourful garden; surrounded by salt marshes and nature reserves. Comfy, modern bar and airy conservatory. Menus offer traditional British dishes with some international influences. Charming bedrooms come with a tuck-box for breakfast in bed.

**at Morston** West : 1.5 mi on A 149 – ⊠ Holt

🏨 **Morston Hall** (Galton Blackiston) 🌾      🚃 📶 **P** 📷 **VISA** 💳 **AE**
🌸 *The Street ⊠ NR25 7AA – 𝒞 (01263) 741 041 – www.morstonhall.com*
*– Closed 1-27 January and 24-26 December*
**13 rm** *(dinner included)* 🍵 – ♦£ 200/230 ♦♦£ 350/380
**Rest** – *(dinner only and Sunday lunch) (booking essential) (set menu only)*
Menu £ 60
**Spec.** Ox tongue and broad bean purée with petit pois and shallot jus. Canon of lamb with sweetbreads and wild garlic jus. Black cherry sorbet with morello consommé, nougatine and pistachios.
• Attractive country house with manicured gardens and antique-filled guest areas. Annexed bedrooms are largest, most luxurious and display subtle contemporary touches. Formal 4 course daily menu offers well-balanced, local, seasonal dishes. Cooking is classical, sophisticated and exhibits a delicate, modern touch.

---

**BLANDFORD FORUM** – Dorset – **503** N31 – pop. 9 854      **4 C3**
▶ London 124 mi – Bournemouth 17 mi – Dorchester 17 mi – Salisbury 24 mi
ℹ️ 1 Greyhound Yard 𝒞 (01258) 45 47 70, www.visit-dorset.org.uk
🏌️ Ashley Wood Wimborne Rd, 𝒞 (01258) 45 22 53
◉ Town ★
🔵 Kingston Lacy ★★ **AC**, SE : 5.5 mi by B 3082 – Royal Signals Museum ★, NE : 2 mi by B 3082. Milton Abbas ★, SW : 8 mi by A 354 – Sturminster Newton ★, NW : 8 mi by A 357

🏠 **Portman Lodge** without rest      🍽 📶 **P**
*Whitecliff Mill St ⊠ DT11 7BP – 𝒞 (01258) 453 727 – www.portmanlodge.co.uk*
*– Closed 2 weeks spring and Christmas*
**3 rm** 🍵 – ♦£ 60 ♦♦£ 70
• Red-brick guesthouse boasting many original Victorian features. Guest areas display artefacts from the owners' travels. Plush breakfast room or terrace dining in summer. Classical bedrooms.

**at Farnham** Northeast : 7.5 mi by A 354 – ⊠ Blandford Forum

🏠 **Farnham Farm House** without rest 🌾      ⬅ 🚃 🕙 🎿 🍽 🐾 **P**
*North : 1 mi by Shaftesbury rd ⊠ DT11 8DG – 𝒞 (01725)*     **VISA** 💳 **AE**
*516 254 – www.farnhamfarmhouse.co.uk – Closed 25-26 December*
**3 rm** 🍵 – ♦£ 70 ♦♦£ 90
• Attractive farmhouse in peaceful location. Homely, individually furnished bedrooms with country views. Swimming pool and therapy centre on site. Breakfast features local produce; picnics available.

🏠 **Museum Inn** with rm      🛜 **P** 📷 **VISA** 💳
*⊠ DT11 8DE – 𝒞 (01725) 516 261 – www.museuminn.co.uk*
**8 rm** 🍵 – ♦£ 110 ♦♦£ 165    **Rest** – *(bookings not accepted)* Carte £ 30/34
• Part-thatched 17C country pub, in a picture postcard village. Menu offers British classics with a Mediterranean edge; cooking is seasonal, unfussy and local. Bedrooms range from small and cottagey, to spacious with a four-poster.

---

**BLEDINGTON** – Gloucestershire – **503** P28 – see Stow-on-the-Wold

## BLETSOE – Bedford – **504** S27

▶ London 65 mi – Croydon 102 mi – Barnet 54 mi – Ealing 63 mi

↑ **Bourne End Farm** without rest  ≤ 🚗 🔲 🐾 📶 **P**
*North : 1.5 mi by A 6 on Bourne End rd ⊠ MK44 1QS –* ℰ *(01234) 783 184*
*– www.bourneendfarm.co.uk*
**3 rm** ⬚ – ✝£ 60/80 ✝✝£ 85/90
♦ Spotless house in over 400 acres of arable farmland; comfortable, simply furnished bedrooms with showers; cosy lounge and charming hosts. Communal farm breakfast in dining room.

## BLOCKLEY – Gloucestershire – **503** O27 – pop. 1 668
**– ⊠ Moreton-In-Marsh**

4 D1

▶ London 91 mi – Birmingham 39 mi – Oxford 34 mi

🏠 **Lower Brook House**  🚗 🐾 📶 **P** VISA ⓒ AE
*Lower St ⊠ GL56 9DS –* ℰ *(01386) 700 286 – www.lowerbrookhouse.com*
*– Closed 16-27 December*
**6 rm** ⬚ – ✝£ 80/190 ✝✝£ 80/190
**Rest** – *(closed Sunday) (dinner only)* Carte £ 25/33
♦ Personally run, adjoining 17C Cotswold stone cottages with large inglenooks, exposed beams and flagged floors. Hugely characterful and stylish from every aspect. Individually appointed bedrooms take on a more contemporary style. Imaginative evening menus of local Cotswold produce.

## BODIAM – East Sussex – **504** V30  Great Britain

8 B2

▶ London 58 mi – Cranbrook 7 mi – Hastings 13 mi
◎ Castle★★
◎ Battle Abbey★, S : 10 mi by B 2244, B 2089, A 21 and minor rd – Rye★★, SW : 13 mi by A 268

✗✗ **Curlew**  🚗 **P** VISA ⓒ
🌼 *Junction Rd, Northwest : 1.5 mi at junction with B 2244 ⊠ TN32 5UY*
*–* ℰ *(01580) 861 394 – www.thecurlewrestaurant.co.uk – Closed 2 weeks January and Monday*
**Rest** – British – Menu £ 21 (lunch) – Carte £ 29/35 ⅋
**Spec.** Double-baked cheese soufflé. Jacob's ladder, beef dripping potatoes and coleslaw. Douglas fir pine parfait, chocolate sorbet.
♦ Stylish restaurant with laid-back lounge, cow motif wallpaper and bespoke leather banquettes. Concise British menu offers accomplished, classically based dishes, interpreted in modern ways. Preparation is careful, execution is precise and presentation is appealing.

## BODMIN – Cornwall – **503** F32 – pop. 12 778

1 B2

▶ London 270 mi – Newquay 18 mi – Plymouth 32 mi – Truro 23 mi
🅩 Mount Folly ℰ (01208) 7 66 16, www.bodminlive.com
◎ St Petroc Church★
◎ Bodmin Moor★★ – Lanhydrock★★, S : 3 mi by B 3269 – Blisland★ (Church★), N : 5.5 mi by A 30 and minor roads – Pencarrow★, NW : 4 mi by A 389 and minor roads – Cardinham (Church★), NE : 4 mi by A 30 and minor rd – St Mabyn (Church★), N : 5.5 mi by A 389, B 3266 and minor rd. St Tudy★, N : 7 mi by A 389, B 3266 and minor rd

🏠 **Trehellas House**  🚗 🔲 🐾 **P** VISA ⓒ AE
*Washaway, Northwest : 3 mi on A 389 ⊠ PL30 3AD –* ℰ *(01208) 72 700*
*– www.trehellashouse.co.uk*
**12 rm** ⬚ – ✝£ 47/76 ✝✝£ 75/180
**Rest** – *(closed Monday lunch)* Menu £ 15 (lunch) – Carte £ 26/38 **s**
♦ Relaxed, personally run country house with keen owners. Bedrooms divided between main house and converted stable. Cosy and cottagey feel without being chintzy. Traditional cooking; venison a speciality.

## Bokiddick Farm without rest ⌖ ⬚ ⬚ ⬚ ⬚ P VISA ⬚

*Lanivet, South : 5 mi by A 30 following signs for Lanhydrock and Bokiddick*
✉ *PL30 5HP –* ✆ *(01208) 831 481 – www.bokiddickfarm.co.uk – Closed Christmas*
**5 rm** ⬚ – †£ 45/50 ††£ 70/80
♦ Traditional farmhouse on a working dairy farm, where you are guaranteed a very warm welcome. Homely, spotlessly kept bedrooms with fridges – 3 in the main house; 2 larger rooms in the old barn. Hearty breakfasts taken overlooking the garden. Cream tea on arrival.

---

# BOLNHURST – Bedford                                    12 A1
▶ London 64 mi – Bedford 8 mi – St Neots 7 mi

## Plough at Bolnhurst ⬚ ⬚ P VISA ⬚ ⬚

*Kimbolton Rd, South : 0.5 mi on B 660* ✉ *MK44 2EX –* ✆ *(01234) 376 274 – www.bolnhurst.com – Closed 2 weeks January, Sunday dinner and Monday*
**Rest** – Menu £ 19/25 – Carte £ 27/37⬚
♦ Smart, cosy whitewashed pub with rustic bar, modern restaurant, lovely garden and bustling atmosphere. Menus change with the seasons but always feature a 28-day aged Aberdeenshire steak selection, strong Mediterranean influences and good old fashioned puddings.

---

**ENGLAND**

# BOLTON ABBEY – North Yorkshire – 502 O22 – pop. 117    22 B2
– ✉ **Skipton** ▌ Great Britain
▶ London 216 mi – Harrogate 18 mi – Leeds 23 mi – Skipton 6 mi
◉ Bolton Priory★ AC

## Devonshire Arms Country House ⌖ ⬚ ⬚ ⬚ ⬚ ⬚ ⬚ ⬚ ⬚ ⬚

✉ *BD23 6AJ –* ✆ *(01756) 710 441* ⬚ ⬚ ⬚ P VISA ⬚ AE ⬚
– *www.devonshirehotels.co.uk*
**38 rm** (dinner included) ⬚ – †£ 206/249 ††£ 249/332 – 2 suites
**Rest** *Burlington*⬚ **Rest** *Brasserie* – see restaurant listing
♦ Fine period coaching inn, with antique-furnished guest areas and vast art collection. Compact bedrooms in extension, recently refurbished in bright, contemporary country house style. Refurbishment to continue in main house. Good spa and leisure. Smooth service.

## Burlington – at Devonshire Arms Country House Hotel ⬚ ⬚ P

✉ *BD23 6AJ –* ✆ *(01756) 710 441* VISA ⬚ AE ⬚
– *www.devonshirehotels.co.uk – Closed Monday*
**Rest** – *(dinner only and Sunday lunch) (booking essential)* Menu £ 65⬚
**Spec.** Scallops with celeriac and smoked eel. Lamb with broccoli purée, goat's cheese and tomato. Caramelised apple with blackcurrant sorbet and Calvados cream.
♦ Elegant, antique-filled dining room with polished tables and oil paintings. Structured, formal service. Ambitious, creative cooking captures modern trends; elaborate dishes are artistically presented, displaying the chef's obvious passion.

## Brasserie – at Devonshire Arms Country House Hotel ⬚ ⬚ ⬚ AC P

✉ *BD23 6AJ –* ✆ *(01756) 710 710* VISA ⬚ AE ⬚
– *www.devonshirehotels.co.uk*
**Rest** – Carte £ 23/31
♦ A contrast to the restaurant in atmosphere and design. This is a modern, vividly decorated brasserie; the kitchen produces carefully prepared, satisfying brasserie favourites.

---

# BOLTON-BY-BOWLAND – Lancashire – 502 M/N22 ▌ Great Britain    20 B2
▶ London 246 mi – Blackburn 17 mi – Skipton 15 mi
◉ Skipton - Castle★, E : 12 mi by A 59 – Bolton Priory★, E : 17 mi by A 59

**Middle Flass Lodge** 🌾     🚗 🗱 🏺 **P** **VISA** **⊛**
*Settle Rd, North : 2.5 mi by Clitheroe rd on Settle rd ⊠ BB7 4NY*
*– 𝒞 (01200) 447 259 – www.middleflasslodge.co.uk*
**7 rm** 🛏 – **†**£ 45/52 **††**£ 68/75   **Rest** – Menu £ 30
♦ Friendly, welcoming owners in a delightfully located barn conversion. Plenty of
beams add to rustic effect. Pleasantly decorated, comfy rooms with countryside
outlook. Blackboard's eclectic menu boasts local, seasonal backbone.

---

**BONCHURCH** – Isle of Wight – **504** P32 – see Wight (Isle of)

---

**BORDON** – Hampshire      **504** R 30
▶ London 54 mi – Croydon 57 mi – Barnet 67 mi – Ealing 49 mi

 **Groomes** 🌾     ≤ 🚗 ქ 🏺 **P** **VISA** **⊛** **AE**
*Frith End, North : 2.75 mi by A 325 on Frith End Sand Pit rd ⊠ GU35 0QR*
*– 𝒞 (01420) 489 858 – www.groomes.co.uk*
**7 rm** 🛏 – **†**£ 90 **††**£ 150   **Rest** – Carte £ 28/39
♦ Former farmhouse set in 185 acres, with lawned gardens and wood-furnished
terrace. Good-sized bedrooms boast modern facilities; some have free-standing
roll-top baths. Two tables of six for communal dining; set menus of home-cooked
dishes make use of local produce.

---

**BOREHAM** – Essex – **504** V27 – see Chelmsford

---

**BOROUGHBRIDGE** – North Yorkshire – **502** P21 – pop. 3 311    **22** B2
▶ London 215 mi – Leeds 19 mi – Middlesbrough 36 mi – York 16 mi
🛈 2 Fishergate 𝒞 (01423) 323 3 73, www.boroughbridge.org.uk

✗✗ **thediningroom**     🏠 **VISA** **⊛**
*20 St James's Sq ⊠ YO51 9AR – 𝒞 (01423) 326 426*
*– www.thediningroomonline.co.uk – Closed 26 December, 1 January, Sunday
dinner and Monday*
**Rest** – *(dinner only and Sunday lunch) (booking essential)* Menu £ 30
♦ Characterful, bow-fronted cottage with courtyard terrace. Modern lounge-bar
and intimate beamed restaurant. Set price menu offers hearty, boldly flavoured,
Mediterranean-influenced dishes.

**at Roecliffe** West : 1 mi

 **Crown Inn** with rm     🗱 🏺 **P** **VISA** **⊛**
*⊠ YO51 9LY – 𝒞 (01423) 322 300 – www.crowninnroecliffe.com – Closed
Sunday dinner*
**4 rm** 🛏 – **†**£ 82/97 **††**£ 114/120   **Rest** – Carte £ 25/30
♦ Smart 16C inn with stylish country interior, set by a delightful village green.
Good-sized menus offer a nice balance of meat and fish, and a dedicated 'meat
free' selection. Well-chosen wine list. Smart bedrooms with antique-style furnish-
ings and feature beds.

---

**BOSCASTLE** – Cornwall – **503** F31      **1** B2
▶ London 260 mi – Bude 14 mi – Exeter 59 mi – Plymouth 43 mi
◉ Village ★
◉ Poundstock Church ★ – Tintagel Old Post Office ★

🏠 **Boscastle House** without rest     ≤ 🚗 🗱 🏺 **P** **VISA** **⊛** **AE**
*Tintagel Rd, South : 0.75 mi on B 3263 ⊠ PL35 0AS – 𝒞 (01840) 250 654*
*– www.boscastlehouse.com – Closed 2 weeks Christmas*
**6 rm** 🛏 – **†**£ 90 **††**£ 120
♦ Modern styling in a detached Victorian house. Bedrooms are light and spacious, with roll-top baths and walk-in showers. Hearty breakfasts, cream teas and
a calm, relaxing air.

ENGLAND

↑ **Trerosewill Farm** without rest ⚓     ⪡ 🚲 🍷 ❧ ⁽ᵗ⁾ 📶 **P** 🅥🅘🅢🅐 ⬤⬤
*Paradise, South : 1 mi off B 3263* ✉ *PL35 0BL –* ☏ *(01840) 250 545*
*– www.trerosewill.co.uk – April-September*
**9 rm** �375 – ♦£ 58/82 ♦♦£ 92/108
♦ Modern guesthouse on 50 acre working farm, affording fine views of the coast and close to good clifftop walks. Conservatory breakfast room. Bedrooms in matching patterns, some with jacuzzis.

↑ **Old Rectory** without rest ⚓     🚲 **P** 🅥🅘🅢🅐 ⬤⬤
*St Juliot, Northeast : 2.5 mi by B 3263* ✉ *PL35 0BT –* ☏ *(01840) 250 225*
*– www.stjuliot.com – Restricted opening in winter*
**4 rm** �375 – ♦£ 35/70 ♦♦£ 80/98
♦ Lovely house with beautiful Victorian walled garden, originally built for the rector of St Juliot's church. Characterful bedrooms; one with a courtyard, another with a four-poster. Breakfasts use garden produce. Thomas Hardy once stayed.

---

**BOSHAM** – West Sussex – **504** R31 – see Chichester

---

**BOSTON SPA** – West Yorkshire – **502** P22 – pop. 5 952      **22** B2
▶ London 127 mi – Harrogate 12 mi – Leeds 12 mi – York 16 mi

↑ **Four Gables** without rest ⚓     🚲 ⁽ᵗ⁾ **P**
*Oaks Ln, West : 0.25 mi by A 659* ✉ *LS23 6DS –* ☏ *(01937) 845 592*
*– www.fourgables.co.uk – Closed Christmas-New Year*
**4 rm** �375 – ♦£ 60 ♦♦£ 83/93
♦ Down a quiet private road, a Grade II listed Arts and Crafts house with period fireplaces, stripped oak and terracotta tile floors. Traditional, individually decorated rooms. Manicured garden.

Guesthouses ↑ don't provide the same level of service as hotels. They are often characterised by a warm welcome and a décor which reflects the owner's personality. Those shown in red ↑ are particularly pleasant.

---

**BOUGHTON MONCHELSEA** – Kent – pop. 2 863      **8** B2
▶ London 46 mi – Southend-on-Sea 60 mi – Basildon 48 mi – Maidstone 4 mi

✗✗ **Mulberry Tree**     🚲 🏠 **P** 🅥🅘🅢🅐 ⬤⬤
*Hermitage Lane, South : 1.5 mi by Park Lane and East Hall Hill* ✉ *ME17 4DA –* ☏ *(01622) 749 082 – www.themulberrytreekent.co.uk – Closed first 2 weeks January, Sunday dinner and Monday*
**Rest** – Menu £ 18 (weekdays) – Carte £ 28/35
♦ Remotely located restaurant with stylish bold design, smart bar, large terrace and screened kitchen footage. Modern British menus provide a good choice of confidently prepared, accomplished dishes crafted from well-sourced ingredients.

---

**BOURN** – Cambridgeshire – **504** T27 – pop. 1 764      **14** A3
▶ London 58 mi – Croydon 87 mi – Barnet 44 mi – Ealing 57 mi

🍴 **Willow Tree**     🚲 🏠 **P** 🅥🅘🅢🅐 ⬤⬤ ⓞ
*29 High St* ✉ *CB23 2SQ –* ☏ *(01954) 719 775 – www.thewillowtreebourn.com*
**Rest** – Carte £ 18/38
♦ Quirky pub with life-sized cow model in the garden and gilt mirrors, chandeliers and Louis XV style furniture inside. Menus range from old pub classics to much more ambitious modern dishes.

▶ London 114 mi – Bristol 76 mi – Southampton 34 mi

✈ Bournemouth (Hurn) Airport : ✆ (01202) 364000, N : 5 mi by Hurn - DV

🛈 Westover Rd ✆ (0845) 0 51 17 00, www.bournemouth.co.uk

🏊 Queens Park Queens Park West Drive, ✆ (01202) 30 26 11

🏊 Meyrick Park Central Drive, ✆ (01202) 78 60 00

◉ Compton Acres★★ (English Garden ✦★★★) **AC** AX – Russell-Cotes Art Gallery and Museum★★ **AC** DZ **M1** - Shelley Rooms **AC** EX **M2**

ⓒ Poole★, W : 4 mi by A 338 – Brownsea Island★ (Baden-Powell Stone ✦★★) **AC**, by boat from Sandbanks BX or Poole Quay – Christchurch★ (Priory Church★) E : 4.5 mi on A 35. Corfe Castle★, SW : 18 mi by A 35 and A 351 – Lulworth Cove★ (Blue Pool★) W : 8 mi of Corfe Castle by B 3070 – Swanage★, E : 5 mi from Corfe Castle by A 351

Plans on following pages

### 🏨 Bournemouth Highcliff Marriott    ⟨ ⟩ ⟨symbols⟩

*St Michael's Rd, West Cliff* ✉ BH2 5DU    ⟨symbols⟩
– ✆ (01202) 557 702 – www.bournemouthhighcliffmarriott.co.uk          CZ**z**
**157 rm** ⌀ – ♦£ 150 ♦♦£ 170 – 3 suites
**Rest** *Highcliff Grill* – see restaurant listing
◆ Set on the clifftop, this grand old seaside hotel has a funicular linking it directly to the beach. Smart guest areas and airy modern bedrooms; some with lovely sea views. Leisure club boasts a tennis court and indoor and outdoor pools.

### 🏨 Miramar    ⟨symbols⟩ rm, ⟨symbols⟩

*19 Grove Rd, East Overcliff* ✉ BH1 3AL – ✆ (01202) 556 581
– www.miramar-bournemouth.com          DZ**u**
**43 rm** (dinner included) ⌀ – ♦£ 52/111 ♦♦£ 104/212    **Rest** – Menu £ 19/31
◆ Along the handsome lines of a grand Edwardian villa, with award winning gardens. Large, well-cared for bedrooms – a few with curved balconies – have bright, modern décor. Pleasant sun terrace faces the sea. Dining room offers a good outlook and a traditional menu.

### 🏨 Green House    ⟨symbols⟩

*4 Grove Rd* ✉ BH1 3AX – ✆ (01202) 498 900 – www.thegreenhousehotel.com
**32 rm** ⌀ – ♦£ 99/180 ♦♦£ 155/240          DZ**n**
**Rest** *Green Room* – see restaurant listing
◆ Bright, eco-friendly hotel, set in a small Victorian property and run by an enthusiastic team. Contemporary interior features reclaimed and eco-furnishings, including chairs made from old video game consoles and vegetable ink wallpapers.

### 🏠 Urban Beach    ⟨symbols⟩

*23 Argyll Rd* ✉ BH5 1EB – ✆ (01202) 301 509 – www.urbanbeach.co.uk
**12 rm** ⌀ – ♦£ 72 ♦♦£ 174/180    **Rest** – Carte £ 28/37          DX**a**
◆ Laid-back hotel with large decked terrace, set close to the beach and town. Unremarkable exterior hides spacious designer bedrooms and stylish, luxury bathrooms. Small reception is located in the trendy bar/bistro. Large menu of modern classics and steaks.

### ✗✗✗ Highcliff Grill – at Bournemouth Highcliff Marriott Hotel    ⟨symbols⟩

*St Michael's Rd, West Cliff* ✉ BH2 5DU – ✆ (01202)
557 702 – www.bournemouthhighcliffmarriott.co.uk          CZ**z**
**Rest** – (dinner only and Sunday lunch) Carte £ 27/49 **s**
◆ Stylish grill restaurant set within a landmark hotel on the clifftop and offering superb sea views. Modern steak and seafood orientated menu; dishes arrive well-presented and in a modern vein.

### ✗✗ Edge    ⟨symbols⟩

*2 Studland Rd, (4th Floor)* ✉ BH4 8JA – ✆ (01202) 757 007
– www.edgerestaurant.co.uk          CX**s**
**Rest** – Carte £ 30/44
◆ Stylish, trendy restaurant on top floor of apartment block, with floor to ceiling windows and excellent views. Seafood-based menu; modern dishes styled on classic combinations.

ENGLAND

ST MALO, CHERBOURG, JERSEY, GUERNSEY

SWANAGE

# BOURNEMOUTH
# AND POOLE

ENGLAND

**ENGLAND**

Wimborne Road
BEAR CROSS
KINSON
Poole Lane
East Howe Lane
Coombe Av
Leybourne Av.
Kinson Rd
Redhill Av
Redhill Drive
REDHILL PARK
Northbourne
Whitelegg Way
Redhill
A 3060
Broadway Lane
Castle Lane West
Castle Lane
CASTLE POINT
Woodbury
Cooper Dean
West
Blackwater Junction
Hurn Road
Moors
Stour
Ringwood Spur Rd
18
9
A 35 LYNDHURST
ALLISDOWN
Columbia Road
Kinson Road
MOORDOWN
Yeoman
Wimborne Rd
East Way
Queen's
Park Avenue
CHARMINSTER
West Way
allisdown
allisdown Rbt
University Road
Boundary Road
Boundary
Talbot
Talbot Av.
East Avenue
Wimborne Rd
WINTON
Alma Rd
Charminster
Springbourne
Wessex Way
QUEEN'S PARK
18
KING'S PARK
Central Drive
16
Alder Road
Glentenmss Rd
Wessex
Holdenhurst Rd
Ashley Rd
King's Park Drive
Christchurch Rd
SOVEREIGN SHOPPING CENTRE
57
WEST SOUTHBOURNE
MEYRICK PARK
31
56
66
70
48
46
58
**BOURNEMOUTH**
Christchurch
Parkwood Rd
BOSCOMBE
10
8
61
62
Lindsay Rd
Albemarle Road
The Avenue
73
BRANKSOME PARK
WESTBOURNE
12
West Cliff Rd
S
X
POOLE BAY

---

A 347
A 338
Cavendish Road
30
BOURNEMOUTH Way Rd
Southcote Rd
MEYRICK PARK
18
RICHMOND HILL
Wimborne Road
Dean Park Road
ST PAULS
52
Knyveton Road
Derby Rd
A 35
Y
9
Wessex
Way
A 338
Wessex
Way
30
Oxford Rd
Holdenhurst Rd
BOURNEMOUTH WEST
A 338
64
UPPER CENTRAL GARDENS
Bourne Av.
H
55
47
Old Christchurch Road
34
28
56
35
Christchurch Rd
Poole Hill
43
13
63
23
36
Gervis Road
35
West Hill
Tregonwell Rd
LOWER CENTRAL GARDENS
24
27
53
75
68
Bath Rd
49
East Grove
36
Overcliff Drive
Durley Chine Rd
17
45
20
20
T
M
Undercliff
Z
West Cliff Rd
51
INTERNATIONAL CENTRE
WATERFRONT COMPLEX
West Undercliff Promenade
T
N
0    400 m
0    400 yards

**ENGLAND**

XX **Green Room** – at Green House Hotel    🀫 AK P VISA ⚅ AE
*4 Grove Rd* ⊠ *BH1 3AX* – ☏ *(01202) 498 900* – *www.thegreenhousehotel.com*
**Rest** – *(light lunch Monday-Saturday)* Carte approx. £ 32    DZ**n**
♦ Large restaurant set within an eco-friendly hotel. Modern menus display innovative touches; the tasting option is popular. All ingredients come from within a
50 miles radius and wines are biodynamic. Snack-style menu in the bar at lunch.

X **West Beach**    ⇐ 🀫 VISA ⚅ AE
*Pier Approach* ⊠ *BH2 5AA* – ☏ *(01202) 587 785* – *www.west-beach.co.uk*
– *Closed 25 December*    DZ**c**
**Rest** – Seafood – *(booking essential)* Carte £ 23/57
♦ Popular seafood restaurant on the beach, with folding glass doors and a
decked terrace. Always bustling. Fish and shellfish caught locally; some in front
of the restaurant itself.

## BOURTON ON THE HILL – Gloucestershire – see Moreton-in-Marsh

## BOURTON-ON-THE-WATER – Gloucestershire – **503** O28    **4 D1**
– pop. 3 093 ▌ Great Britain
▶ London 91 mi – Birmingham 47 mi – Gloucester 24 mi – Oxford 36 mi
◉ Town ★
◪ Northleach (Church of SS. Peter and Paul★, Wool Merchants' Brasses★), SW : 5 mi
by A 429

🛏 **Dial House**    🚗 🀫 P VISA ⚅ AE
*The Chestnuts, High St* ⊠ *GL54 2AN* – ☏ *(01451) 822 244*
– *www.dialhousehotel.com*
**15 rm** ⊔ – ♦£ 145 ♦♦£ 245
**Rest** – *(booking essential for non-residents)* Menu £ 15/20 – Carte £ 31/43
♦ House of Cotswold stone – the oldest in the village – with lovely lawned gardens and drawing room. Bedrooms mix of the contemporary and the floral; those
in original house are the most characterful. Refined cooking makes good use of
local ingredients.

🛏 **Coombe House** without rest    🚗 ℅ (📶) P VISA ⚅
*Rissington Rd* ⊠ *GL54 2DT* – ☏ *(01451) 821 966* – *www.coombehouse.net*
– *Restricted opening in winter*
**5 rm** ⊔ – ♦£ 50/60 ♦♦£ 70/90
♦ Spacious 1920s detached house, not far from the delightful village centre. Traditional lounge and first floor terrace; breakfast room boasts full-length leaded
windows overlooking the pleasant garden. Simple but immaculately kept bedrooms offer good comforts.

### at Lower Slaughter Northwest : 1.75 mi by A 429 – ⊠ Cheltenham

🛏 **Lower Slaughter Manor** ⌖    🚗 🀫 ℀ P VISA ⚅ AE
⊠ *GL54 2HP* – ☏ *(01451) 820 456* – *www.lowerslaughter.co.uk*
**19 rm** ⊔ – ♦£ 250/765 ♦♦£ 250/1020
**Rest Sixteen58** – Menu £ 39/65 – Carte £ 29/49
♦ Beautiful listed part-17C manor in warm Cotswold stone with lovely garden.
Open fires and period detail throughout; furnishings and fabrics are rich yet con-
temporary. Smart, boldly coloured bedrooms; those in the coach house are larger
and more modern. Elegant dining room with French-influenced menu.

🛏 **Washbourne Court**    🚗 🀫 (📶) 🀫 P VISA ⚅ AE
⊠ *GL54 2HS* – ☏ *(01451) 822 143* – *www.washbournecourt.co.uk*
**26 rm** ⊔ – ♦£ 135/225 ♦♦£ 135/235 – 4 suites
**Rest** – *(bar lunch Monday-Saturday)* Menu £ 45
♦ Stone-built former manor house with pleasant cottage annexes. Stylish interior
boasts marble floored reception, contemporary bedrooms, comfy lounges and
low-beamed bar with terrace. Local produce a feature in the dark wood-furnished
dining room.

**at Upper Slaughter** Northwest : 2.5 mi by A 429 – ⊠ Bourton-On-The-Water

**Lords of the Manor** ♨     🗭 🗲 🍴 ⚗ P̄ VISA ⓪ Æ ⓘ

⊠ GL54 2JD – ℰ (01451) 820 243 – www.lordsofthemanor.com
**24 rm** ⌷ – ♦£ 195 ♦♦£ 195/380 – 2 suites
**Rest** – (dinner only and Sunday lunch) (booking essential for non-residents)
Menu £ 65
**Spec.** Crab lasagne with coriander, fennel and crab bisque. Rib and cheek of beef, snails, ceps and red wine sauce. Raspberry soufflé, Eton mess and raspberry ripple ice cream.
♦ Charming and attractive 17C former rectory set in pretty Cotswold village, with neat and mature gardens. Comfortable sitting rooms and subtly contemporary bedrooms. Formal dining room where the classically based cooking is given a modern twist.

---

## BOVEY TRACEY – Devon – 503 I32 – pop. 4 514 – ⊠ Newton Abbot    2 C2

▶ London 214 mi – Exeter 14 mi – Plymouth 32 mi
🛈 Stover Bovey Rd, Newton Abbot, ℰ (01626) 35 24 60
◉ St Peter, St Paul and St Thomas of Canterbury Church★
ⓒ Dartmoor National Park★★

**Brookfield House** without rest ♨     🗭 ⚘ ⁿ P̄ VISA ⓪

Challabrook Ln, Southwest : 0.75 mi by Brimley rd ⊠ TQ13 9DF – ℰ (01626) 836 181 – www.brookfield-house.com – February-November
**3 rm** ⌷ – ♦£ 51/55 ♦♦£ 72/80
♦ Early Edwardian house on a private road in a peaceful part of town. Set behind electric gates, in two acres of attractive gardens, it has a simple, classically styled interior and large, immaculately appointed bedrooms; popular 'Iris' catches the sun all day.

---

## BOWLAND BRIDGE – Cumbria – ⊠ Cumbria    21 A2_3

▶ London 269 mi – Liverpool 86 mi – Preston 48 mi – Blackpool 60 mi

**Hare & Hounds** with rm     🗭 🍴 ⁿ P̄ VISA ⓪

⊠ LA11 6NN – ℰ (015395) 68 333 – www.hareandhoundsbowlandbridge.co.uk
**3 rm** ⌷ – ♦£ 80 ♦♦£ 100
**Rest** – Carte £ 22/27
♦ Charming 17C Lakeland pub in a delightful village. Large front terrace leads through into a rustic, open-fired inner hung with old village photos and hop bines. Menus offer typical, hearty favourites and most produce is locally sourced. Bedrooms are well-equipped and elegant; some boast roll-top baths.

---

## BOWNESS-ON-WINDERMERE – Cumbria – 502 L20 – see Windermere

## BOX – Bath & North East Somerset – 503 N29 – see Bath

## BRADFIELD – Essex – see Mistley

## BRADFORD-ON-AVON – Wiltshire – 503 N29 – pop. 9 072    4 C2

▶ London 118 mi – Bristol 24 mi – Salisbury 35 mi – Swindon 33 mi
🛈 50 St Margarets St ℰ (01225) 86 57 97, www.bradfordonavon.co.uk
◉ Town★★ - Saxon Church of St Lawrence★★ - Tithe Barn★ – Bridge★
ⓒ Great Chalfield Manor★ (All Saints★) **AC**, NE : 3 mi by B 3109 – Westwood Manor★ **AC**, S : 1.5 mi by B 3109 – Top Rank Tory (≼★). Bath★★★, NW : 7.5 mi by A 363 and A 4 – Corsham Court★★ **AC**, NE : 6.5 mi by B 3109 and A 4

ENGLAND

**Woolley Grange**   🚲 🕭 🖭 🍴 ⊛ 🏊 ♨ 🅿 VISA ⓒⓞ AE
*Woolley Green, Northeast : 0.75 mi by B 3107 on Woolley St* ✉ *BA15 1TX*
*– 𝒞 (01225) 864 705 – www.woolleygrangehotel.co.uk*
**19 rm** ⊆ – ♦£ 120/227 ♦♦£ 315/395 – 7 suites   **Rest** – Menu £ 20/43
♦ Modern art, period furniture: innumerable charming details spread through the rooms of a beautiful Jacobean manor. This is a hotel very much geared to families. Classic British cooking in restaurant, conservatory or terrace.

**Bradford Old Windmill**   ≼ 🚲 ⅏ ⽷ 🅿 VISA ⓒⓞ
*4 Masons Lane, on A 363* ✉ *BA15 1QN* – 𝒞 *(01225) 866 842*
*– www.bradfordoldwindmill.co.uk – March-October*
**3 rm** ⊆ – ♦£ 70/105 ♦♦£ 80/125   **Rest** – Menu £ 25 **s**
♦ 1807 windmill in redressed local stone; Gothic windows and restored bridge. Rooms and circular lounge, stacked with books and curios, share a homely, unaffected quirkiness. Flavourful vegetarian menus.

**at Holt** East : 2 mi on B 3107 – ✉ Bradford-On-Avon

**Tollgate Inn** with rm   🚲 🕭 ⅏ 🅿 VISA ⓒⓞ
*Ham Grn* ✉ *BA14 6PX* – 𝒞 *(01225) 782 326 – www.tollgateholt.co.uk – Closed Sunday dinner and Monday*
**4 rm** ⊆ – ♦£ 60/110 ♦♦£ 110
**Rest** – *(booking essential)* Menu £ 20 (weekday lunch) – Carte £ 23/35
♦ 16C pub featuring a cosy, fire-lit bar, two traditional dining rooms and a delightful terrace and garden. Daily changing menu focuses on local produce, with light bites at lunch and more robust dishes at dinner. Comfortable, thoughtfully appointed bedrooms.

**BRADWELL** – **504** O24 – pop. 1 728 – ✉ **Derbyshire**                **16** A1
▶ London 170 mi – Birmingham 99 mi – Liverpool 66 mi – Leeds 48 mi

**Samuel Fox** with rm   🕭 ⅏ ⽷ 🅿 VISA ⓒⓞ
*Stretfield Rd* ✉ *S33 9JT* – 𝒞 *(01433) 621 562 – www.samuelfox.co.uk*
**4 rm** ⊆ – ♦£ 75 ♦♦£ 115   **Rest** – Menu £ 15 (lunch) – Carte £ 19/29
♦ Smart, stone-built inn with the fresh, light feel of a French bistro. Set price lunch menu and evening à la carte offer simple, flavourful dishes, with game in the winter and fish specials in the summer. Efficient, cheery service. Comfortable modern bedrooms.

**BRAITHWAITE** – Cumbria – **502** K20 – see Keswick

**BRAMFIELD** – Suffolk – **504** Y27 – pop. 1 778 – ✉ Ipswich                **15** D2
▶ London 215 mi – Ipswich 27 mi – Norwich 28 mi

**Queen's Head**   🕭 🅿 VISA ⓒⓞ AE
*The Street* ✉ *IP19 9HT* – 𝒞 *(01986) 784 214 – www.queensheadbramfield.co.uk – Closed 25 December*
**Rest** – Carte £ 21/30
♦ Characterful, personally run, cream-washed pub set in the heart of a small village. Local, seasonal produce informs the classical daily menu; organic ingredients are used where possible.

**BRAMPFORD SPEKE** – Devon                **2** D2
▶ London 184 mi – Cardiff 110 mi – Plymouth 50 mi – Torbay 29 mi

**Lazy Toad Inn**   🚲 🕭 🅿 VISA ⓒⓞ
✉ *EX5 5DP* – 𝒞 *(01392) 841 591 – www.thelazytoad@btinternet.com – Closed 3 weeks January, Sunday dinner, Monday and bank holidays*
**Rest** – Carte £ 24/29
♦ Sweet little pub with cobbled courtyard, which uses vegetables from its own polytunnel and lambs raised in its smallholding. Homemade pork scratchings in the bar; cooking displays some Asian influences – even the pak choi is homegrown.

ENGLAND

**BRAMPTON** – Cumbria – **501** L19 – **pop. 3 965** ▯ Great Britain          **21** B1

▶ London 317 mi – Carlisle 9 mi – Newcastle upon Tyne 49 mi
🛈 Market Pl 𝒞 (016977) 34 33, www.visitcumbria.com
🏌 Talkin Tarn, 𝒞 (016977) 22 55
ⓒ Hadrian's Wall★★, NW : by A 6077

🏨    **Farlam Hall** ⌓                              ⪍ 🗘 🐾 **P** 𝗩𝗜𝗦𝗔 **⦿** **AE**
*Southeast : 2.75 mi on A 689* ✉ *CA8 2NG –* 𝒞 *(016977) 46 234*
*– www.farlamhall.co.uk – Closed 4-18 January and 25-30 December*
**12 rm** (dinner included) ⌁ – ♦£ 160/190 ♦♦£ 360
**Rest** – *(dinner only) (booking essential for non-residents)* Menu £ 45🍴
 ♦ Long-standing, family-owned Victorian country house. Comfortable guest areas
overlook ornamental gardens and lake. Traditionally decorated bedrooms boast
Bose radios and flat screen TVs. Fine, formal dining in sumptuous restaurant. Attentive, pristine service.

**BRANCASTER STAITHE** – Norfolk                     **15** C1

▶ London 131 mi – King's Lynn 25 mi – Boston 57 mi – East Dereham 27 mi

🍴    **White Horse** with rm                        ⪍ 🗘 🐾 **P** 𝗩𝗜𝗦𝗔 **⦿**
✉ *PE31 8BY –* 𝒞 *(01485) 210 262 – www.whitehorsebrancaster.co.uk*
**15 rm** ⌁ – ♦£ 77/97 ♦♦£ 96/134   **Rest** – *(booking essential)* Carte £ 22/28
 ♦ Elevated position affords beautiful coastal views from rear conservatory and
terrace, while landscaped front terrace boasts parasols, heaters and lights. Varied
menu with local seafood. Up-to-date, comfortable bedrooms.

🍴    **Jolly Sailors**                              🗘 🐾 **P** 𝗩𝗜𝗦𝗔 **⦿**
✉ *PE31 8BJ –* 𝒞 *(01485) 210 314 – www.jollysailorsbrancaster.co.uk*
**Rest** – Carte £ 17/23 **s**
 ♦ Characterful, rustic pub with welcoming open fire. Simple menu ranges from
light bites such as a ploughman's, to freshly made pizzas and pub classics; all fol-
lowed by tasty nursery puddings.

**BRAY** – Windsor and Maidenhead – **504** R29 – **pop. 8 121**     **11** C3
– ✉ **Maidenhead**

▶ London 34 mi – Reading 13 mi

Plan : see Maidenhead

🍴🍴🍴🍴  **Waterside Inn** (Alain Roux) with rm        ⪍ 🔤 🐾 **P** 𝗩𝗜𝗦𝗔 **⦿** **AE** **①**
🏵🏵🏵 *Ferry Rd* ✉ *SL6 2AT –* 𝒞 *(01628) 620 691 – www.waterside-inn.co.uk – Closed 26
*December-2 February*                                    X**s**
**9 rm** ⌁ – ♦£ 210/450 ♦♦£ 210/450 – 2 suites
**Rest** – French – *(closed Tuesday except dinner June-August and Monday)*
*(booking essential)* Menu £ 58/148 – Carte £ 112/161🍴
**Spec.** Tronçonnettes de homard poêlées minute au Porto blanc. Filets de laper-
eau grillés, sauce à l' armagnac et aux marrons glacés. Péché Gourmand selon
"Alain" et "Michel".
 ♦ Few restaurants can match this glorious setting on the Thames, with the terrace an enchanting spot for an aperitif. Enjoy classic French cuisine, prepared
with great care, in elegant surroundings. Service is charming and expertly organised. Luxurious bedrooms are spacious and chic.

🍴🍴🍴  **Fat Duck** (Heston Blumenthal)                  𝗩𝗜𝗦𝗔 **⦿** **AE** **①**
🏵🏵🏵 *High St* ✉ *SL6 2AQ –* 𝒞 *(01628) 580 333 – www.fatduck.co.uk – Closed 2 weeks
*Christmas-New Year, Sunday dinner and Monday*                 X**e**
**Rest** – *(booking essential 2 months in advance) (set menu only)* Menu £ 160🍴
**Spec.** Mock turtle soup. 'Sound of the Sea'. Black Forest gâteau with kirsch ice
cream.
 ♦ Low-beamed, converted pub where history and science combine in an exciting,
innovative alchemy of contrasting flavours and textures. It's very stimulating and
involving; the attentive team are on hand to guide you through the experience.

ENGLAND

## Caldesi in Campagna ⌂ VISA ⓒ AE

*Old Mill Ln* ⊠ *SL6 2BG* – ☏ *(01628) 788 500 – www.caldesi.com – Closed Sunday dinner and Monday* **Xx**
**Rest** – Italian – Menu £ 20 (lunch) – Carte £ 21/37
♦ Welcoming former pub with smart interior, conservatory and decked garden with wood fired oven. Flavoursome Italian cooking displays Ligurian, Tuscan and Sicilian influences.

## Hinds Head ⇔ P VISA ⓒ AE ①

*High St* ⊠ *SL6 2AB* – ☏ *(01628) 626 151 – www.hindsheadhotel.co.uk – Closed 25-26 December and Sunday dinner* **Xe**
**Rest** – *(booking essential)* Menu £ 28 – Carte £ 32/48
♦ Set at the heart of a pretty village. Dark panelling and log fires provide a char-acterful, almost medieval feel. Food is down-to-earth, with classic, comforting dishes and traditional desserts. Dishes are fiercely British and big on flavour; rich, simple and satisfying.

## Royal Oak ⌂ P VISA ⓒ AE

*Paley Street, Southwest : 3.5 mi by A 308, A 330 on B 3024* ⊠ *SL6 3JN* – ☏ *(01628) 620 541 – www.theroyaloakpaleystreet.com – Closed Sunday dinner*
**Rest** – Menu £ 23 (weekday lunch) – Carte £ 41/61 ⌘
**Spec.** Lasagne of rabbit with wild mushrooms and chervil. Roast turbot with sam-phire, cockles and mussels. Yorkshire rhubarb trifle.
♦ A warm and welcoming beamed dining pub, with service that gets the tone just right. The menu champions British produce and is very appealing. This is skilled, confident cooking which sensibly avoids over-elaboration; game is han-dled deftly.

## Crown ⌂ P VISA ⓒ AE ①

*High St* ⊠ *SL6 2AH* – ☏ *(01628) 621 936 – www.thecrownatbray.co.uk*
**Rest** – Carte £ 21/35 **Xa**
♦ Charmingly restored 16C building, formerly 2 cottages and a bike shop. Dark oak columns and low beams in the bar; lighter cottage style dining room. Cook-ing is robust, flavoursome and British.

**at Bray Marina** Southeast : 2 mi by B 3208, A 308 - X - **on Monkey Island Lane** – ⊠ **Bray-On-Thames**

## Riverside Brasserie ⌂ P VISA ⓒ AE ①

*(follow road through the marina)* ⊠ *SL6 2EB* – ☏ *(01628) 780 553* – *www.riversidebrasserie.co.uk – April-September*
**Rest** – *(booking essential)* Carte £ 37/52
♦ Marina boathouse, idyllically set on the banks of the Thames. Very simply ap-pointed interior and decked terrace. Inventive cooking in informal, busy and buzzy surroundings.

---

**BRAYE** – **503** Q33 – **see Channel Islands (Alderney)**

---

**BRAY MARINA** – **Buckinghamshire** – **see Bray**

---

**BREARTON** – **North Yorkshire** – **pop. 141** **22** B2
▶ London 216 mi – Leeds 23 mi – Sheffield 67 mi – Manchester 77 mi

## Malt Shovel ⌂ P VISA ⓒ

*Main St* ⊠ *HG3 3BX* – ☏ *(01423) 862 929 – www.themaltshovelbrearton.co.uk* – *Closed 25 December, 1 January, Monday, Tuesday and dinner Sunday*
**Rest** – Carte £ 20/40
♦ Quirky, shabby-chic pub run by the Bleikers, who also own the famous smoke-house. Classical dishes with continental flavours; lots of smoked seasonal pro-duce. Tapas-style small plates at lunch.

ENGLAND (side tab)

## BREEDON ON THE HILL – Leicestershire – pop. 958    16 B2
– ✉ Castle Donington

▶ London 121 mi – Birmingham 35 mi – Sheffield 57 mi – Manchester 95 mi

### Three Horseshoes Inn    ⌷ P VISA ◉◉
*44-46 Main St ✉ DE73 8AN – ☏ (01332) 695 129 – www.thehorseshoes.com*
*– Closed 25-26 December, 1 January and Sunday dinner*
**Rest** – Carte £ 20/39

◆ Large, highly characterful, whitewashed pub with numerous interlinking rooms, cosy fires and pleasant terrace. Blackboard menus display robust, classical dishes of flavoursome, seasonal produce.

---

## BRENTWOOD – Essex – 504 V29 – pop. 47 593    13 C2

▶ London 22 mi – Chelmsford 11 mi – Southend-on-Sea 21 mi
ℹ 44 High St ☏ (01277) 20 03 00, www.visitessex.com
⛳ Bentley G. & C.C. Ongar Rd, ☏ (01277) 37 31 79
⛳ Warley Park Little Warley Magpie Lane, ☏ (01277) 22 48 91

### Marygreen Manor    ⌷ ⌖ rm, ⛶ ⌖ 🛜 ⌖ P VISA ◉◉ AE ①
*London Rd, Southwest : 1.25 mi on A 1023 ✉ CM14 4NR – ☏ (01277) 225 252*
*– www.marygreenmanor.co.uk*
**44 rm** – †£ 160 ††£ 160, ⌷ £ 15
**Rest** *Tudors* – Menu £ 18/42

◆ Mock-Tudor house with 15C origins; once owned by a servant of Catherine of Aragon. Charming open-fired rooms, ornate plaster ceilings and carved wood panelling. Bedrooms split between the house and courtyard; the former, more characterful. Rustic, formal restaurant offers elaborate, classically based dishes.

---

## BRIDGNORTH – Shropshire – 502 M26 – pop. 11 891 ▮ Great Britain    18 B2

▶ London 146 mi – Birmingham 26 mi – Shrewsbury 20 mi – Worcester 29 mi
ℹ Listley St ☏ (01746) 76 32 57, www.visitbridgnorth.co.uk
⛳ Stanley Lane, ☏ (01746) 76 33 15
◉ Ironbridge Gorge Museum★★ **AC** (The Iron Bridge★★ - Coalport China Museum★★ - Blists Hill Open Air Museum★★ - Museum of the Gorge and Visitor Centre★) NW : 8 mi by B 4373

### at Worfield Northeast : 4 mi by A 454 – ✉ Bridgnorth

### Old Vicarage ⌖    ⌷ ⌷ ⌖ rm, 🛜 P VISA ◉◉
*✉ WV15 5JZ – ☏ (01746) 716 497 – www.oldvicarageworfield.com*
**14 rm** ⌷ – †£ 73/85 ††£ 120/175
**Rest** – *(closed Sunday dinner) (booking essential)* Menu £ 22/39 – Carte £ 35/43
◆ Antiques, rare prints and rustic pottery: a personally run Edwardian parsonage in a rural setting with thoughtfully appointed bedrooms, some in the coach house. Delightful orangery dining room overlooking garden; modern British cooking.

---

## BRIDPORT – Dorset – 503 L31 – pop. 12 977    3 B3

▶ London 150 mi – Exeter 38 mi – Taunton 33 mi – Weymouth 19 mi
ℹ 47 South St ☏ (01308) 42 49 01, www.visit-dorset.org.uk
⛳ Bridport and West Dorset West Bay East Cliff, ☏ (01308) 42 25 97
◉ Mapperton Gardens★, N : 4 mi by A 3066 and minor rd. Lyme Regis★ - The Cobb★, W : 11 mi by A 35 and A 3052

### Roundham House without rest    ⌷ 🛜 P VISA ◉◉
*Roundham Gdns, West Bay Rd, South : 1 mi by B 3157 ✉ DT6 4BD*
*– ☏ (01308) 422 753 – www.roundhamhouse.co.uk – May-October*
**8 rm** ⌷ – †£ 58/93 ††£ 125
◆ Sizeable Edwardian house displaying rich colours and period furnishings. Comfy lounge; modern bedrooms with bold feature walls and good comforts. Elevated position offers pleasant country views.

### ✗ Riverside     ≼ 🕭 VISA ⓦ

*West Bay, South : 1.75 mi by B 3157* ⊠ *DT6 4EZ –* ✆ *(01308) 422 011*
*– www.thefishrestaurant-westbay.co.uk – Closed 2 December-10 February,*
*Sunday dinner and Monday except bank holidays*
**Rest** – Seafood – *(booking essential)* Menu £ 26 (weekday lunch)
– Carte £ 30/60

♦ Long-standing seafood restaurant with harbour views; accessed via a bridge. Good value daily menu offers extremely fresh, straightforward dishes crafted from local produce. Plenty of choice.

### 🏠 Bull with rm     🕭 ℅ P VISA ⓦ AE

*34 East St* ⊠ *DT6 3LF –* ✆ *(01308) 422 878 – www.thebullhotel.co.uk*
**19 rm** ⌷ – ✝£ 85/175 ✝✝£ 195/195    **Rest** – Carte £ 25/40

♦ Boutique, Regency style inn displaying an eclectic mix of period features and chic, contemporary décor. Local meats and Lyme Bay fish are showcased in classic brasserie dishes. Uniquely styled, modern bedrooms boast bold feature walls and stylish bathrooms.

**at Burton Bradstock** Southeast : 2 mi by B 3157

### 🏠 Norburton Hall without rest ⟿     ≼ 🚃 ℅ (ⁿ) P VISA ⓦ

*Shipton Ln* ⊠ *DT6 4NQ –* ✆ *(01308) 897 007 – www.norburtonhall.com*
**3 rm** ⌷ – ✝£ 110/190 ✝✝£ 110/220

♦ Spacious Edwardian Arts and Crafts house with coastal views and 6 acres of mature grounds. Woodwork, ornate carvings and period furniture abound; classical bedrooms, modern shower rooms.

---

**BRIGGSWATH** – North Yorkshire – **502** S20 – see Whitby

---

**BRIGHOUSE** – West Yorkshire – **502** O22 – pop. 32 360      **22** B2
▶ London 213 mi – Bradford 12 mi – Burnley 28 mi – Leeds 15 mi
⛳ Crow Nest Park Hove Edge Coach Rd, ✆ (01484) 40 11 21

### ✗✗ Brook's     ⟷ VISA ⓦ

*6 Bradford Rd* ⊠ *HD6 1RW –* ✆ *(01484) 715 284 – www.brooks-restaurant.co.uk*
*– Closed 10 days January, 10 days summer and Sunday*
**Rest** – *(dinner only)* Menu £ 20 (weekdays) – Carte £ 20/31

♦ Long-standing, very personally run restaurant, where eclectic art fills the walls. Pleasant wine bar and upstairs lounge. Robust, tasty, interesting dishes; kangaroo and zebra sometimes feature.

---

**BRIGHTON AND HOVE** – Brighton and Hove – **504** T31      **8** A3
**– pop. 127 035** ▌ Great Britain
▶ London 53 mi – Portsmouth 48 mi – Southampton 61 mi
✈ Shoreham Airport : ✆ (01273) 467373, W : 8 mi by A 27 AV
🛈 Royal Pavilion Shops ✆ (01273) 29 25 95, www.visitbrighton.com
⛳ East Brighton Roedean Rd, ✆ (01273) 60 48 38
⛳ The Dyke Devil's Dyke Rd, Devil's Dyke, ✆ (01273) 85 72 96
⛳ Hollingbury Park Ditchling Rd, ✆ (01273) 55 20 10
⛳ Waterhall Waterhall Rd, ✆ (01273) 50 86 58
👁 Town★★ - Royal Pavilion★★★ **AC** CZ – Seafront★★ – The Lanes★ BCZ –
  St Bartholomew's★ **AC** CX **B**
🔄 Devil's Dyke (≼★) NW : 5 mi by Dyke Rd (B 2121) BY

Plans on following pages

ENGLAND

### Hotel du Vin
🏠 AC 👤 SÁ ⁽ᵗ⁾ VISA ⓒⓞ AE ⓞ

2-6 Ship St ✉ BN1 1AD – ℰ (01273) 718 588 – www.hotelduvin.com
**49 rm** – ♦£ 110/190 ♦♦£ 140/250, � £ 15                    CZa
**Rest** *Bistro* – see restaurant listing
♦ Set on the promenade and made up of various different buildings; the oldest being a 17C former arts club. Cavernous bar-lounge with gothic style and mezzanine lounge with terrace. Comfy, contemporary bedrooms; some in their next door pub.

### Drakes
🏠 ⩽ AC 🚭 ⁽ᵗ⁾ VISA ⓒⓞ AE

43-44 Marine Par ✉ BN2 1PE – ℰ (01273) 696 934 – www.drakesofbrighton.com
**20 rm** – ♦£ 115/145 ♦♦£ 225/275, ⊻ £ 12.50                    CZu
**Rest** *Restaurant* – see restaurant listing
♦ Pair of 18C townhouses on the promenade. Stylish, modern interior with cocktail bar. Chic bedrooms boast bamboo flooring, wooden feature walls, good mod cons and wet rooms; city or sea views.

### Myhotel Brighton without rest
🏠 🛗 🚭 ⁽ᵗ⁾ SÁ ⓒⓞ AE

17 Jubilee St ✉ BN1 1GE – ℰ (01273) 900 300 – www.myhotels.com
**80 rm** – ♦£ 160 ♦♦£ 160, ⊻ £ 9.50                    CYz
♦ Contemporary glass cube, set in the heart of town. Whacky, designer interior with relaxed vibe and stylish bar. Quirky, minimalist bedrooms boast the latest technological extras.

### Kemp Townhouse without rest
⁽ᵗ⁾ VISA ⓒⓞ AE

21 Atlingworth St ✉ BN2 1PL – ℰ (01273) 681 400
– www.kemptownhousebrighton.com                    CZn
**9 rm** ⊻ – ♦£ 75/95 ♦♦£ 95/215
♦ Stylish, very personally run 19C townhouse. Bedrooms have an uncluttered, classic style and compact wet rooms; those facing the front are larger and more comfortable. 2 four-posters.

### Paskins without rest
⁽ᵗ⁾ VISA ⓒⓞ AE

18-19 Charlotte St ✉ BN2 1AG – ℰ (01273) 601 203 – www.paskins.co.uk
**19 rm** ⊻ – ♦£ 55/75 ♦♦£ 95/105                    CVe
♦ Quirky, personally run guesthouse. Small, modern bedrooms are simply furnished and well-kept. Showers only – to save water – and eco-toiletries. Organic breakfast features homemade sausages.

### brightonwave without rest
🚭 ⁽ᵗ⁾ VISA ⓒⓞ AE

10 Madeira Pl ✉ BN2 1TN – ℰ (01273) 676 794 – www.brightonwave.com
– Closed 25-26 December                    CZs
**8 rm** ⊻ – ♦£ 65/120 ♦♦£ 100/175
♦ Personally run Victorian townhouse featuring ever-changing artwork. Contemporary bedrooms: the front facing and garden rooms are the largest and most comfortable. One modern four-poster.

### Restaurant – at Drakes Hotel
XX AC ⇄ VISA ⓒⓞ AE

43-44 Marine Par ✉ BN2 1PE – ℰ (01273) 696 934
– www.therestaurantatdrakes.co.uk                    CZu
**Rest** – (booking advisable) Menu £ 40
♦ Set in hotel basement, this cool, contemporary eatery conveys a soft, moody atmosphere. The menus present a good balanced choice of modern British dishes with Gallic twists.

### Gingerman
XX AC VISA ⓒⓞ AE ⓞ

21A Norfolk Sq ✉ BN1 2PD – ℰ (01273) 326 688
– www.gingermanrestaurants.com – Closed 25 December, 2 weeks in winter and
Monday                    BZi
**Rest** – (booking essential) Menu £ 18/32
♦ Tucked away off the promenade; French and Mediterranean flavours to the fore in a confident, affordable, modern repertoire: genuine neighbourhood feel.

ENGLAND

# BRIGHTON AND HOVE

ENGLAND

CENTRE

BRIGHTON

HOVE

ST. ANN'S WELL GARDENS

ROYAL
PAVILION

THE LANES

CHURCHILL SQ.
SHOPPING CENTRE

THE BRIGHTON
CENTRE

King's

A 259

A 2073

A 259

A 259

B 2066

113

ENGLAND

❌ **Terre à Terre**  ⚏ 🅰🅲 VISA ⓒⓞ AE ⓞ
*71 East St ✉ BN1 1HQ – ☏ (01273) 729 051 – www.terreaterre.co.uk*
*– Closed 25-26 December and Monday in winter*  CZe
**Rest** – Vegetarian – *(booking essential)* Menu £ 30 (lunch) – Carte £ 24/32
◆ Relaxed, friendly restaurant decorated in warm burgundy colours. Appealing menu of tasty, original vegetarian dishes which include items from Japan, China and South America. Generous portions.

❌ **Sam's of Sevendials**  ⚏ ⇔ VISA ⓒⓞ
*1 Buckingham Pl ✉ BN1 3TD – ☏ (01273) 885 555*
*– www.samsofsevendials.co.uk – Closed 25 December and Sunday dinner*
**Rest** – Menu £ 14 (weekday lunch) – Carte £ 21/32  BXa
◆ Former bank on street corner: the vault now acts as function room. Light, airy feel with high ceiling. Modern menus with local ingredients admirably to fore. Good value lunch.

❌ **Due South**  ≤ ⚏ 🅰🅲 ⇔ VISA ⓒⓞ AE
*139 King's Rd Arches ✉ BN1 2FN – ☏ (01273) 821 218 – www.duesouth.co.uk*
*– Closed 25-26 December*  BZx
**Rest** – Menu £ 20 (lunch) – Carte £ 22/39
◆ Set beside the beach, with pleasant arch interior: the best tables upstairs facing a half-moon window and overlooking sea. Modern, seafood-based menus rely on local and organic produce.

❌ **Sam's of Brighton**  VISA ⓒⓞ AE
*1 Paston Pl ✉ BN2 1HA – ☏ (01273) 676 222 – www.samsofbrighton.co.uk*
*– Closed 25 December*  CVa
**Rest** – Menu £ 14 (lunch and early dinner) – Carte £ 22/33
◆ Simple neighbourhood eatery boasting three enormous candelabras. Simple menu of classical, seasonal dishes. Early brunch on offer at the weekend and a concise à la carte at noon.

❌ **Chilli Pickle**  ⚏ 🅰🅲 VISA ⓒⓞ AE
🈂 *17 Jubilee St ✉ BN1 1GE – ☏ (01273) 900 383 – www.thechillipickle.com*
*– Closed 25 December*  CYz
**Rest** – Indian – Carte £ 17/37
◆ Simple, relaxed restaurant with passionate chef, buzzy vibe and friendly, welcoming service. Oft-changing menu of tasty, thoughtfully prepared, authentic Indian dishes, with delicate spicing and good quality ingredients. Great selection of beers and teas.

❌ **Riddle and Finns**  ⚏ VISA ⓒⓞ AE
*12b Meeting House Ln ✉ BN1 1HB – ☏ (01273) 323 008*
*– www.riddleandfinns.co.uk*  CZi
**Rest** – Seafood – Carte £ 35/70
◆ Informal and simply decorated, with white tiles, bar stools and high, marble-topped tables for communal dining. Well-executed, classical seafood dishes; polite, attentive service.

❌ **Blenio Bistro**  ⚏ VISA ⓒⓞ AE
*87-93 Dyke Rd ✉ BN1 3JE – ☏ (01273) 220 220 – www.bleniobistro.com*
*– Closed 2 weeks late June-early July, Monday and Tuesday*  BXc
**Rest** – Carte £ 29/34
◆ Friendly, passionately run neighbourhood bistro. Simply furnished, with exposed brick, food-related art and pleasant terrace. Regularly changing menu ranges from snacks to the full 3 courses.

❌ **Bistro** – at Hotel du Vin  VISA ⓒⓞ AE ⓞ
*2-6 Ship St ✉ BN1 1AD – ☏ (01273) 718 588 – www.hotelduvin.com*
**Rest** – *(booking essential)* Carte £ 25/37 ⟁  CZa
◆ Relaxed brasserie located within a part-17C, part-gothic hotel on the promenade; in summer, make for the hidden courtyard. Extensive wine list accompanies a menu of British brasserie classics.

### The Ginger Dog   *VISA* **CO** **AE** **①**
*12 College Pl* ⊠ *BN2 1HN – ℰ (01273) 620 990*
*– www.gingermanrestaurants.com – Closed 25 December*   **CVs**
**Rest** – Carte £ 18/30
♦ Warm and welcoming shabby-chic pub; part of the growing local 'Ginger' empire. Fresh produce is to the fore on the menu, which is mostly in a British vein but with the odd nod to Italy.

## at Hove

### XX Meadow   *VISA* **CO**
*64 Western Rd* ⊠ *BN3 2JQ – ℰ (01273) 721 182*
*– www.themeadowrestaurant.co.uk – Closed 24-31 December, Sunday dinner and Monday*   **AYo**
**Rest** – Carte £ 22/34
♦ Airy, split-level dining room with small shop. Its name symbolises the chef's vision to support local producers – the 'grass roots' of the restaurant. Beasts are bought in whole; some items are from his parents' garden or foraged for. Unfussy, British cooking.

### X Graze   *AK* ⇄ *VISA* **CO** **AE**
*42 Western Rd* ⊠ *BN3 1JD – ℰ (01273) 823 707 – www.graze-restaurant.co.uk*
*– Closed 1 January*   **AYz**
**Rest** – Menu £ 32
♦ Lively neighbourhood eatery with quirky, informal feel. Cooking is elaborate and adventurous: good value midweek menu; 7 course tapas-style tasting menu must be ordered in advance for lunch.

### Ginger Pig   *VISA* **CO** **AE** **①**
*3 Hove St* ⊠ *BN3 2TR – ℰ (01273) 736 123 – www.gingermanrestaurants.com*
*– Closed 25 December*   **AVc**
**Rest** – Carte £ 24/34
♦ Smart building by the seafront – formerly a hotel – boasting a mortar ship relief and beautifully restored revolving door. Menus offer precise, flavoursome British dishes and vegetarians are well-catered for. Great value set menus. Service copes well under pressure.

ENGLAND

# BRISTOL

City of Bristol – pop. 420 556 – **503** M29 – **504** M29 – ▯ Great Britain

▶ London 121 – Birmingham 91

**ℹ Tourist Information**

Harbourside ✆(0333) 321 01 01, www.visitbristol.co.uk

**Airport**

✈ Bristol Airport : ✆ (0871) 334 4444, SW : 7 m. by A 38 AX

**Bridge**

Severn Bridge (toll)

**Golf Courses**

▤ Short Lodge GC Carsons Rd, ✆(0117) 956 55 01

▤ Clifton Beggar Clifton Bush Lane, Failand, ✆(01275) 39 34 74

## ◉ SIGHTS

**In the town**

City★★ • St Mary Redcliffe★★ DZ • At-Bristol★★ CZ • Brandon Hill★★ AX • Georgian House★★ AX**K** • Bristol Museum★★ CZ**M3** • Brunel's ss Great Britain and Maritime Heritage Centre★ **AC** AX**S2** • The Old City★ CYZ : Theatre Royal★★ CZ**T** • Merchant Seamen's Almshouses★ CZ**Q** • St Stephen's Church★ CY**S1** • St John the Baptist★ CY • College Green★ CYZ• City Museum and Art Gallery★ AX**M1**

**On the outskirts**

Clifton★★ AX •Clifton Suspension Bridge★★ (toll) • RC Cathedral of St Peter and St Paul★★ **F1** • Bristol Zoological Gardens★★ **AC**

**In the surrounding area**

Bath★★★, SE : 13 mi by A 4 BX

# INDEX OF STREET NAMES IN BRISTOL

ENGLAND

# BRISTOL

LONDON M 4 A 4174 (A 432) > A 432 CHIPPING - SODBURY

M 4 NEWPORT

A 38 GLOUCESTER, (M 5)

A 4018 GLOUCESTER (M 5)

A 4162 (M 5)

WINTERBOURNE

MANGOTSFIELD
Heath
A 4107
Bromley
B 4058
Beacon Lane

B 4421

Oldendale Rd
B 4465
FISHPONDS 79
76
A 432
BROOMHILL

STOKE GIFFORD
Mead Rd
North Rd
B 4057
Hatchet Road
Lane
B 4057
Gipsypatch Lane

HAMBROOK
Stoke Lane
Hambrook Lane
New Road
Filton
A 4174

Coldharbour Lane Stoke Lane

Bristol Rd
Park Rd
Frenchay Rd
B 4058
M 32 (Park way)
Park Rd

LOCKLEAZE
STAPLETON
Station Rd
Avenue
Filton
Road

FILTON
North
Gloucester Rd
BRITISH AEROSPACE
A 38

BRISTOL FILTON AIRPORT

Muller
B 4052
ASHLEY
Rd

HORFIELD
Filton Rd
W. Avenue
B 4469

Monks Park Av
B 4056
Monks Road
Pen Park Rd

SOUTHMEAD
Greystoke Avenue
Southmead
Wellington Hill
Kenmare
HENLEAZE
EASTFIELD
BISHOPSTON
Coldharbour Rd

BRENTRY
Knole Lane
Charlton Road
Passage

WESTBURY ON TRYM
Eastfield Rd
Westbury Rd
B 4054

THE MALL
Cribbs Causeway
Station Road
Crow Lane
HENBURY
Botany Bay Lane
Henbury
B 4055 M
Station Road
Falcondale Road
Camond
Lane
STOKE BISHOP
Stoke

M 5

1 km
1/2 mile
0
0

118

ENGLAND

Soundwell

Thickv

Causeway

Lodge Rd

42

SPEEDWELL

CLAY HILL

EASTVILLE

B 4485

Charlton Rd

Two Mile Hill Rd

Bell Hill Rd

3

29

73

KINGSWOOD

B 4046

Regent St.

Kingsway

Bryant's Hill

High Street

CONHAM

49

A 4174

BATH

A 4

BATH

Avon

TROOPERS HILL

Broomhill

Road

BRISLINGTON

RETAIL PARK

Newbridge Road

Wick Road

Allison Road

Sandy Park Road

21

Bath Road

Callington Road

B 3119

A 37 WELLS

B

St George's Park

B 4469

A 420

Church Road

Road

Fishponds

Gloucester

M 32

Shopping Centre

Easton Way

Stapleton Road

41

St Philip's Causeway

A 4320

22

Feeder Road

Old Bath Road

Wells

Wells Rd.

Airport Rd

P

Airport Rd

A 4174 (A 38)

B 4052

B 4051

Ashley Rd

Gloucester

20

72

COTHAM

Victoria Park

KNOWLE

St John's L.

B 3122

KNOWLE WEST

57

 A

Whiteladies Rd.

8

B 4467

M¹

U

Queen's Rd

BRANDON HILL

Anchor Rd

K

S²

56

7

26

Coronation Road

East St

West St

44

67

Hartcliffe Way

A 4174

Bedminster

BEDMINSTER

ZOOLOGICAL GARDENS

F¹

28

B 3129

CLIFTON VILLAGE

25

62

63

Hotwell Rd

A4

ASHTON GATE

Winterstoke Road

Bedminster Down Rd

A 370

A 3029

A 38 TAUNTON

AIRPORT

Clifton Down

Portway

CLIFTON SUSPENSION BRIDGE (TOLL)

Avon

B 3129

ASHTON PARK

Long Ashton Rd.

A 369

A 370

A 3128 CLEVEDON

**ENGLAND**

### 🏠 Hotel du Vin   🖪 AC ⟨ 📶 🛁 🅿 🚗 VISA 🐷 AE

*The Sugar House* ✉ BS1 2NU – ℰ (0117) 925 55 77 – www.hotelduvin.com
**40 rm** – 🛏£ 125/195, 🛏🛏£ 125/195, 🍽 £ 14.50                                      CY**e**
**Rest** *Bistro* – see restaurant listing
◆ Characterful 18C former sugar refinery on the inner ring road. Classical Hotel du Vin styling, with a wine-theme running throughout. Dark-hued bedrooms and duplex suites boast Egyptian linen; one has twin roll-top baths. Cosy lounge bar.

### 🏠 Brigstow Bristol   ⟨ 🖪 👌 rm, AC ⟨⟩ 🛁 VISA 🐷 AE ⓞ

*5-7 Welsh Back* ✉ BS1 4SP – ℰ (0117) 929 10 30 – www.mercure.com
**115 rm** – 🛏£ 69/150 🛏🛏£ 69/150, 🍽 £ 17 – 1 suite                                 CY**n**
**Rest** *Ellipse* – Menu £ 18 **s** – Carte £ 22/37 **s**
◆ Smart city centre hotel in charming riverside location. Stylish public areas typified by lounges and mezzanine. Modern, brightly coloured bedrooms are full of curves: both bedrooms and bathrooms feature plasma TVs. Modern brasserie and bar overlook river.

### XX Casamia (Jonray and Peter Sanchez-Iglesias)   VISA 🐷

*38 High St, Westbury-on-Trym, Northwest : 2 mi by A 4018* ✉ BS9 3DZ
– ℰ (0117) 959 28 84 – www.casamiarestaurant.co.uk – Closed Sunday and Monday                                                                                              AV**e**
**Rest** – Italian influences – (dinner only and Saturday lunch) (booking advisable set menu only) Menu £ 25/68
**Spec.** Beetroot, barley, iced yoghurt and pickled fennel. Salmon, Italian garnish and cauliflower. Pine nut panna cotta.
◆ Proudly and professionally run former trattoria; simply decorated, with linen-covered tables and leather-furnished bar for aperitifs. Skilful, innovative, flavoursome cooking from ambitious brothers. Reinterpreted dishes display Italian influences.

### XX Bordeaux Quay (The Restaurant)   🖆 VISA 🐷 AE

*VShed, Canons Way (1st Floor)* ✉ BS1 5UH – ℰ (0117) 943 12 00
– www.bordeaux-quay.co.uk                                                                          CZ**e**
**Rest** – (dinner only) Carte £ 27/42
◆ Huge harbourside emporium that's 100% organic. Ground floor houses deli, bakery, cookery school and relaxed bar. Linen-laid restaurant above offers seasonal, Mediterranean-influenced menu.

### XX Bell's Diner   VISA 🐷 AE

*1-3 York Rd, Montpelier* ✉ BS6 5QB – ℰ (0117) 924 03 57 – www.bellsdiner.co.uk
– Closed 24-30 December, lunch Monday and Saturday, Sunday and bank holidays                                                                                                AX**s**
**Rest** – (booking essential at dinner) Menu £ 38
◆ Shabby-chic neighbourhood restaurant, characterfully decorated with old bottles and flour sacks. Modern, French-inspired menus include a serious tasting selection – accompanied by wine flights.

### XX Bistro – at Hotel du Vin   🖆 🅿 VISA 🐷 AE

*The Sugar House* ✉ BS1 2NU – ℰ (0117) 925 55 77 – www.hotelduvin.com
**Rest** – (booking essential) Carte £ 22/38🕸                                             CY**e**
◆ Traditional hotel bistro with Queen Anne style chairs, polished wood tables and a pleasant courtyard terrace, set within an 18C former sugar refinery. Menus offer tried-and-tested bistro classics.

### X Riverstation   🍴 🖆 VISA 🐷 ⓞ

*The Grove, Harbourside* ✉ BS1 4RB – ℰ (0117) 914 44 34
– www.riverstation.co.uk – Closed 24-26 December and Sunday dinner
**Rest** – Menu £ 16/20 – Carte £ 25/34                                                    CZ**c**
◆ Great riverside location: watch canal boats pass by from the terrace. Bar offers all day dining with breakfast, brunch and meze plates. Upstairs café offers more substantial modern European fare.

X **Rockfish Grill**                                   AC VISA ◯◯ AE
128 Whiteladies Rd ⊠ BS8 2RS – ℰ (0117) 973 73 84 – www.rockfishgrill.co.uk
– Closed 25-29 December, 1 January, Monday and Sunday dinner          AXc
**Rest** – Seafood – (booking essential) Carte £ 24/39
♦ Well-run and busy, with polite, friendly service. Daily changing menus focus on fresh, simply prepared fish and seafood, cooked in the charcoal josper oven. Owners' fishmongers is adjacent.

X **Culinaria**                                              VISA ◯◯
1 Chandos Rd, Redland ⊠ BS6 6PG – ℰ (0117) 973 79 99
– www.culinariabristol.co.uk – Closed 2 weeks summer, 1 week spring, 1 week autumn, 1 week Christmas and Sunday-Wednesday          AXx
**Rest** – Menu £ 20 (lunch) – Carte £ 28/35
♦ Combined deli and eatery; the personally run diner is informal with lots of light and space. Sound cooking behind a collection of Mediterranean, English and French dishes.

X **Flinty Red**                                       AC VISA ◯◯ AE
34 Cotham Hill ⊠ BS6 6LA – ℰ (0117) 923 87 55 – www.flintyred.co.uk
– Closed 1 January, last week August, 25-28 December, Monday lunch and Sunday          AXn
**Rest** – Mediterranean – Carte £ 20/30
♦ Combined effort of two couples; one pair are independent wine merchants, the other, chefs. Simple, rustic interior and friendly, knowledgeable team. Concise daily menu of Mediterranean small plates. Unfussy cooking relies on quality local produce and features well-used, lesser-known cuts. Tempting wine list.

X **Greens' Dining Room**                                  VISA ◯◯ ◯
25 Zetland Rd ⊠ BS6 7AH – ℰ (0117) 924 64 37 – www.greensdiningroom.com
– Closed 1 week Christmas, Sunday and Monday          AXe
**Rest** – (booking essential) Carte £ 19/31
♦ Family-run neighbourhood eatery set in residential area, with an intimate, homely interior and a convivial atmosphere. Good value, daily changing menu: unfussy, Italian-influenced dishes rely on natural flavours and carefully sourced produce. Chatty service.

🍺 **Albion Public House and Dining Rooms**          ⛱ ⇔ VISA ◯◯ AE
Boyces Ave, Clifton Village ⊠ BS8 4AA – ℰ (0117) 973 35 22
– www.thealbionclifton.co.uk – Closed 25 December and Monday lunch
**Rest** – (booking essential) Menu £ 31 (dinner) – Carte £ 31/40          AXv
♦ Trendy Grade II listed pub at the heart of the village. Unfussy, highly seasonal menu changes twice a day; everything is homemade. BBQs held on the pleasant terrace every Sunday evening.

🍺 **Kensington Arms**                                  ⛱ VISA ◯◯ AE
35-37 Stanley Rd ⊠ BS6 6NP – ℰ (0117) 944 64 44
– www.thekensingtonarms.co.uk – Closed 25-26 December and Sunday dinner
**Rest** – Carte £ 29/37          AXi
♦ Welcoming neighbourhood pub with traditional bar, impressive high-ceilinged dining room and charming Victorian style. Menus change every two months and have a strong British and seasonal base.

🍺 **Robin Hood's Retreat**                              ⛱ VISA ◯◯ AE
197 Gloucester Rd ⊠ BS7 8BG – ℰ (0117) 924 86 39
– www.robinhoodsretreat.co.uk – Closed 25 December          AXa
**Rest** – (booking advisable at dinner) Menu £ 14 (lunch) – Carte £ 25/33
♦ Red-brick, Victorian pub in busy part of city, with characterful bar and relaxed atmosphere. Daily changing menus offer hearty, flavourful interpretations of British classics.

**BROAD CAMPDEN** – Gloucestershire – see Chipping Campden

## BROAD OAK – East Sussex – 504 V31

8 B3

▶ London 62 mi – Hastings 8 mi – Rye 7 mi

⌂ **Fairacres** without rest     ⨳ ⚘ ⁕ **P**
*Udimore Rd, on B 2089 ⊠ TN31 6DG – ℰ (01424) 883 236*
*– www.fairacresrye.co.uk – Closed Christmas-New Year*
**3 rm** ⌿ – †£ 56/70 ††£ 88/110
  ◆ Listed 17C cottage in picture-postcard pink. Big breakfasts under low beams.
Individual rooms: one overlooks superb magnolia tree in garden. All have many
thoughtful extras.

## BROADSTAIRS – Kent – 504 Y29 – pop. 22 712

9 D1

▶ London 77 mi – Canterbury 18 mi – Ramsgate 2 mi

⌂ **Belvidere Place** without rest     ⚘ ⁕ **VISA** ◉◉
*Belvidere Rd. ⊠ CT10 1PF – ℰ (01843) 579 850 – www.belvidereplace.co.uk*
**5 rm** ⌿ – †£ 120 ††£ 180
  ◆ Centrally located Georgian house with charming owner, green credentials and
eclectic, individual style. Bohemian, shabby-chic lounge boasts a retro football table. Spacious bedrooms mix modern facilities with older antique furnishings.

⌂ **Burrow House** without rest     ⚘ ⁕ **P** **VISA** ◉◉ **AE**
*Granville Rd ⊠ CT10 1QD – ℰ (01843) 601 817 – www.burrowhouse.com*
**4 rm** ⌿ – †£ 80/95 ††£ 95/175
  ◆ Tastefully restored and subtly modernised Victorian house close to seafront.
Bedrooms blend contemporary décor and fine antique furniture. Gourmet dinners
by arrangement. Substantial breakfasts.

## BROADWAY – Worcestershire – 503 O27 – pop. 2 496 ▐ Great Britain

19 C3

▶ London 93 mi – Birmingham 36 mi – Cheltenham 15 mi – Oxford 38 mi
ℹ 1 Cotswold Court ℰ (01386) 85 29 37, www.broadway-cotswolds.co.uk
◉ Town★
🄖 Country Park (Broadway Tower ❋★★★), SE : 2 mi by A 44 – Snowshill
Manor★ (Terrace Garden★) AC, S : 2.5 m

🏠 **Buckland Manor** ⌾     ≼ ⨳ ❨ ⚘ ✆ **P** **VISA** ◉◉ **AE**
*⊠ WR12 7LY – ℰ (01386) 852 626 – www.bucklandmanor.com*
**14 rm** ⌿ – †£ 195/290 ††£ 495/515
**Rest** – *(booking essential for non-residents)* Menu £ 23 (lunch)
– Carte £ 37/55 ⌀
  ◆ Secluded part 13C country house with beautiful gardens. Individually furnished
bedrooms boast high degree of luxury. Fine service throughout as old-world se-
renity prevails. Restaurant boasts elegant crystal, fine china and smooth service.

🏠 **Lygon Arms**     ⨳ ⬜ ⓐ ⌾ ℔ ❨ **AC** rest, ⁕ ⅏ **P** ◉◉ **AE** ⓪
*High St ⊠ WR12 7DU – ℰ (01386) 852 255*
*– www.barcelo-hotels.co.uk/lygonarms*
**72 rm** ⌿ – †£ 104/265 ††£ 144/305 – 6 suites
**Rest** *Goblets* – see restaurant listing
**Rest** *Great Hall* – *(closed Saturday lunch)* Carte £ 35/57 **s**
  ◆ Superbly enticing, quintessentially English coaching inn with many 16C archi-
tectural details in its panelled, beamed interiors, and in rooms that Charles I and
Cromwell once stayed in. Refined dining amongst baronial splendours, including
a minstrels' gallery.

🏠 **Broadway**     ⨳ ⌂ ⁕ **P** **VISA** ◉◉ **AE** ⓪
*The Green ⊠ WR12 7AA – ℰ (01386) 852 401 – www.cotswold-inns-hotels.co.uk*
**19 rm** ⌿ – †£ 115/155 ††£ 155/215
**Rest** *Courtyard* – Menu £ 13/28 – Carte £ 22/31
  ◆ Characterful 16C inn set on the green in the heart of the village; originally an
abbot's retreat. Classically styled guest areas. Crisp, light colour schemes in more
modern bedrooms. Timbered, horse racing themed bar. Modern British cooking
and good value lunches.

ENGLAND

⌂ **Olive Branch** without rest     🖥 ⁽ᵗ⁾ P VISA ⓒⓞ AE
*78 High St ✉ WR12 7AJ – ☏ (01386) 853 440*
*– www.theolivebranch-broadway.com*
**8 rm** ⌸ – ♦£ 55/85 ♦♦£ 88/110
◆ Welcoming guesthouse run by experienced husband and wife team; formerly a
1950s staging post. Pleasantly cluttered bedrooms with thoughtful extras – one
has a small veranda. Rustic, characterful dining room with homemade cakes at
breakfast.

⌂ **Windrush House** without rest     🚗 🖥 ⁽ᵗ⁾ P VISA ⓒⓞ AE
*Station Rd ✉ WR12 7DE – ☏ (01386) 853 577 – www.windrushhouse.com*
*– Closed January and Christmas*
**5 rm** ⌸ – ♦£ 75 ♦♦£ 90
◆ Fresh, modern guesthouse with landscaped garden, set in a picturesque village. Comfortable lounge. Light, airy bedrooms come with homemade biscuits;
some boast wrought iron beds.

✕✕ **Russell's** with rm     🏠 AC ⁽ᵗ⁾ P VISA ⓒⓞ AE
*20 High St ✉ WR12 7DT – ☏ (01386) 853 555 – www.russellsofbroadway.co.uk*
*– Closed Sunday dinner*
**7 rm** ⌸ – ♦£ 80/98 ♦♦£ 245/300    **Rest** – Menu £ 16 (lunch) – Carte £ 26/36
◆ Behind the splendid Cotswold stone façade lies a stylish modern restaurant
with terrace front and rear. Seasonally influenced, regularly changing menus.
Smart, comfy bedrooms.

✕✕ **Goblets** – at Lygon Arms Hotel     P VISA ⓒⓞ AE ⓞ
*High St ✉ WR12 7DU – ☏ (01386) 854 418*
*– www.barcleo-hotels.co.uk/lygonarms.co.uk – Closed Monday*
**Rest** – *(booking essential)* Carte £ 22/28 **s**
◆ Characterfully firelit in rustic dark oak. Modern dining room at front more at-
mospheric than one to rear. Menus of light, tasty, seasonal dishes offered.

**ENGLAND**

---

**BROCKENHURST** – Hampshire – **503** P31 – pop. 2 865 🔳 Great Britain    **6 A2**
▶ London 99 mi – Bournemouth 17 mi – Southampton 14 mi – Winchester 27 mi
🔢 Brockenhurst Manor Sway Rd, ☏ (01590) 62 33 32
◪ New Forest★★ (Rhinefield Ornamental Drive★★, Bolderwood Ornamental
Drive★★)

🏨 **Rhinefield House** 🦢     🚗 🕊 ⌕ 🏠 Ⅰ₆ ✕ & 🖥 ⁽ᵗ⁾ ♨ P VISA ⓒⓞ AE
*Rhinefield Rd, Northwest : 3 mi ✉ SO42 7QB – ☏ (01590) 625 600*
*– www.rhinefieldhousehotel.co.uk*
**50 rm** ⌸ – ♦£ 99/255 ♦♦£ 109/265 – 1 suite
**Rest** *Armada* – *(dinner only and Sunday lunch)* Menu £ 36 – Carte £ 48/58
**Rest** *The Brasserie* – Carte £ 25/48
◆ Impressive country house with ornamental pond, parterres and yew maze, in
40 acres of tranquil forest parkland. Period features include ornate wood carvings. Contemporary bedrooms boast the latest mod cons; rooms in the original house are more characterful. Fine dining in Armada. Relaxed Brasserie with
terrace.

🏨 **New Park Manor** 🦢     ← 🚗 🕊 ⌕ 🖪 ⊕ 🏠 Ⅰ₆ ⁽ᵗ⁾ ♨ P VISA ⓒⓞ AE ⓞ
*Lyndhurst Rd, North : 1.5 mi on A 337 ✉ SO42 7QH – ☏ (01590) 623 467*
*– www.newparkmanorhotel.co.uk*
**24 rm** (dinner included) ⌸ – ♦£ 120/220 ♦♦£ 190/255
**Rest** *The Stag* – Menu £ 20/43 **s**
◆ Extended, elegantly proportioned former hunting lodge built by Charles II on
his return from France. Classic bedrooms in the main house; those in the Forest
Wing are more contemporary. Candlelit fine dining.

### 🏠 Cloud                                    🔒 🛇 ♨ P VISA ⓒⓞ

*Meerut Rd* ✉ *SO42 7TD* – ☎ *(01590) 622 165 – www.cloudhotel.co.uk*
*– Closed 27 December-13 January*
**18 rm** ⌸ – **†**£ 81/170 **††**£ 162/176
**Rest** *Encore* – Menu £ 18/30
◆ Well-kept hotel made up of four cottages, set on the edge of a pretty New Forest town; photos attest to the owner's past as a tiller girl. Neat, tidy bedrooms. Busy, linen-laid restaurant with conservatory extension and theatrical theme; traditional menus.

### 🏠 Cottage Lodge *without rest*              🚗 ⬢ ⑩ P VISA ⓒⓞ ⓘ

*Sway Rd* ✉ *SO42 7SH* – ☎ *(01590) 622 296 – www.cottagelodge.co.uk – Closed Christmas*
**15 rm** ⌸ – **†**£ 80/100 **††**£ 140/160
◆ 350 year old former forester's cottage in the heart of the village: proudly run by welcoming owner. Low oak-beamed ceiling, cosy snug bar and large, neatly appointed rooms.

### ✗✗ The Pig *with rm* ⬢                  ≤ 🚗 ⑩ 🔒 🛇 ⑩ P VISA ⓒⓞ ⒶⒺ ⓘ

*Beaulieu Rd, East : 1 mi on B 3055* ✉ *SO42 7QL* – ☎ *(01590) 622 354*
*– www.thepighotel.co.uk*
**26 rm** – **†**£ 125/175 **††**£ 175/225, ⌸ £ 15   **Rest** – Menu £ 20/30
◆ Georgian house in 14 acres of mature gardens, in charming New Forest setting. Relaxed dining, where the kitchen makes good use of local produce. Keen, attentive service. Stylish, modern lounges; attractive terraces. Spacious, contemporary bedrooms offer a good level of facilities.

### ✗✗ Thatched Cottage *with rm*              🔒 ⑩ P VISA ⓒⓞ ⒶⒺ

*16 Brookley Rd* ✉ *SO42 7RR* – ☎ *(01590) 623 090 – www.thatchedcottage.co.uk*
**6 rm** – **†**£ 30/90 **††**£ 140, ⌸ £ 10
**Rest** – *(closed Sunday dinner, Monday and Tuesday) (booking essential)*
Menu £ 29 – Carte £ 21/29
◆ Long-standing restaurant set in traditional, very individually styled 17C farmhouse, with wood-furnished terrace and open kitchen. Classic dishes on locally sourced menu. Cottage-style bedrooms.

---

**BROCKTON** – Shropshire – see Much Wenlock

---

**BROMESWELL** – Suffolk – see Woodbridge

---

**BROMFIELD** – Shropshire – **503** L26 – see Ludlow

---

**BROUGHTON GIFFORD** – Wiltshire                            **4** C2
▶ London 109 mi – Bristol 31 mi – Cardiff 64 mi – Southampton 81 mi

### 🍴 Fox                                       🚗 🔒 P VISA ⓒⓞ

*The Street* ✉ *SN12 8PN* – ☎ *(01225) 782 949*
*– www.thefox-broughtongifford.co.uk – Closed 25 December, 1 January, Sunday dinner and Monday*
**Rest** – *(booking essential at weekends)* Menu £ 18 (lunch) – Carte £ 24/39
◆ Raising the profile of this pub, both locally and farther afield, has been a labour of love for its young owner. Cooking is simple, unfussy and fresh, using what's in the garden: salad leaves, fruits, chickens and pigs.

---

**BRUNDALL** – Norfolk – **504** Y26 – pop. 5 832                **15** D2
▶ London 118 mi – Great Yarmouth 15 mi – Norwich 8 mi

### ✗✗ Lavender House                          ⬥ P VISA ⓒⓞ

*39 The Street* ✉ *NR13 5AA* – ☎ *(01603) 712 215 – www.lavenderhouse.co.uk*
*– Closed 26 December-8 January, Sunday dinner, Monday and Tuesday*
**Rest** – *(dinner only and Sunday lunch) (booking advisable)* Menu £ 40
◆ Characterful low-ceilinged thatched cottage with comfy lounge and bar, cosy dining rooms and impressive 8-seater table in kitchen. Original monthly menus display interesting modern twists.

ENGLAND

## BRUNTINGTHORPE – Leicestershire 🏛 Great Britain          16 B3

▶ London 96 mi – Leicester 10 mi – Market Harborough 15 mi
🎭 Leicester - Museum and Art Gallery★, Guildhall★ and St Mary de Castro Church★, N : 11 mi by minor rd and A 5199

### 🏠 The Joiners                                    P̄ VISA ⓒⓞ
Church Walk ⊠ LE17 5QH – 𝒞 (0116) 247 82 58 – www.thejoinersarms.co.uk
– Closed Sunday dinner and Monday
**Rest** – (booking essential) Menu £ 14 (lunch) – Carte £ 26/30
♦ Neat and tidy whitewashed pub with characterful interior. Good value menus offer a mix of refined pub classics and brasserie-style dishes, cooked and presented in a straightforward manner.

## BRUSHFORD – Somerset – 503 J30 – see Dulverton

## BRUTON – Somerset – 503 M30 – pop. 2 982          4 C2

▶ London 118 mi – Bristol 27 mi – Bournemouth 44 mi – Salisbury 35 mi
🎭 Stourhead★★★ AC, W : 8 mi by B 3081

### ✕ At The Chapel                                      VISA ⓒⓞ AE
High St ⊠ BA10 0AE – 𝒞 (01749) 814 070 – www.atthechapel.co.uk
– Closed Sunday dinner
**Rest** – Carte £ 21/32
♦ Stylish, informal restaurant in former 18C chapel, with bakery to one side and wine shop to the other. Well-priced, daily menus offer rustic, Mediterranean-influenced dishes; wood-fired breads, pizzas and cakes a speciality. Friendly team.

## BRYHER – 503 A/B34 – see Scilly (Isles of)

## BUCKDEN – Cambridgeshire – 504 T27 – pop. 2 385 – ⊠ Huntingdon    14 A2

▶ London 65 mi – Bedford 15 mi – Cambridge 20 mi – Northampton 31 mi

### 🏨 George                         🎙 🕻 🕭 P̄ ⓒⓞ AE
High St ⊠ PE19 5XA – 𝒞 (01480) 812 300 – www.thegeorgebuckden.com
**12 rm** 🛏 – †£ 100/120 ††£ 150
**Rest** Brasserie – see restaurant listing
♦ Delightfully restored former 19C coaching inn with stylish, contemporary look, typified by leather tub chairs and sofas. Smart bedrooms are all named after famous Georges.

### ✕ Brasserie – at George Hotel                    🕭 P̄ VISA ⓒⓞ AE
High St ⊠ PE19 5XA – 𝒞 (01480) 812 300 – www.thegeorgebuckden.com
**Rest** – Menu £ 18 (lunch) – Carte dinner £ 27/42
♦ Spacious, modern brasserie serving a range of dishes, from traditional English game to coq au vin and even tempura of squid. French windows lead to a courtyard, creating an airy feel.

## BUCKHORN WESTON – Dorset          4 C3

▶ London 117 mi – Poole 36 mi – Bath 33 mi – Weymouth 37 mi

### 🏠 Stapleton Arms with rm            🗐 🕭 ✵ P̄ VISA ⓒⓞ AE
Church Hill ⊠ SP8 5HS – 𝒞 (01963) 370 396 – www.thestapletonarms.com
– Closed 25-26 December
**4 rm** 🛏 – †£ 72/96 ††£ 90/120   **Rest** – Carte £ 21/28
♦ Stylish, shabby-chic pub with elegant dining room; muddy boots, dogs and children are all welcome. Wide-ranging menu offers traditional choices with some Mediterranean touches. Spacious, contemporary bedrooms – some boast underfloor heating.

## BUCKINGHAM – Buckinghamshire – 503 Q27 – pop. 12 512          11 C1
🏛 Great Britain
▶ London 64 mi – Birmingham 61 mi – Northampton 20 mi – Oxford 25 mi
🏌 Silverstone Stowe Silverstone Rd, 𝒞 (01280) 85 00 05
🏌 Tingewick Rd, 𝒞 (01280) 81 55 66
🎭 Stowe Gardens★★, NW : 3 mi by minor rd. Claydon House★ AC, S : 8 mi by A 413

🏠🏠 **Villiers**  🔇 🛗 rm, 🆎 rest, 🍴 📶 🛅 🅿 💳 🍷 🆎

*3 Castle St* ✉ *MK18 1BS* – 𝒞 *(01280) 822 444* – www.oxfordshire-hotels.co.uk
**49 rm** ⬜ – ♦£ 130/160 ♦♦£ 170/180 – 3 suites
**Rest** *Villiers* – *(closed dinner 25 December)* Menu £ 17/21
– Carte dinner £ 29/34

◆ Professionally run hotel on central street. Spacious, bedrooms vary in style: some boasting original beams and eaves; all equally comfy with large, well-kept bathrooms. Modern restaurant offers appealing British menu. Locals often pop in to the lounges for coffee.

---

**BUCKLAND MARSH** – Oxfordshire – pop. 2 243  **10** A2

▶ London 76 mi – Faringdon 4 mi – Oxford 15 mi

⛽ **Trout at Tadpole Bridge** with rm  🔋 📶 🅿 💳 🍷

✉ *SN7 8RF* – 𝒞 *(01367) 870 382* – www.troutinn.co.uk – *Closed 25-26 December and Sunday dinner November-March*
**6 rm** ⬜ – ♦£ 70/80 ♦♦£ 120/150  **Rest** – Carte £ 22/34

◆ Smart pub with attractive garden leading down to the Thames. Concise menu consists of classic Gallic dishes with contemporary touches; seafood and game often feature as specials. Comfy bedrooms exceed expectations. Private moorings available.

---

**BUCKLAND NEWTON** – Dorset – **503** M31 – pop. 618  **4** C3

▶ London 214 mi

⛽ **Gaggle of Geese**  🔋 📶 🅿 💳 🍷

✉ *DT2 7BS* – 𝒞 *(01300) 345 249* – www.thegaggle.co.uk – *Closed 25 December*
**Rest** – Carte £ 19/27

◆ Shabby-chic pub with skittle alley and relaxed, boho feel. Vegetable garden, orchard and paddocks supply the kitchen; hearty pub dishes but refined presentation. Hosts regular village events.

---

**BUDE** – Cornwall – **503** G31 – pop. 3 681  **1** B2

▶ London 252 mi – Exeter 51 mi – Plymouth 50 mi – Truro 53 mi

ℹ The Crescent 𝒞 (01288) 35 42 40, www.visitbude.info

⛳ Burn View, 𝒞 (01288) 35 20 06

👁 The Breakwater★★ – Compass Point (≤★)

🏞 Poughill★ (church★★), N : 2.5 mi - E : Tamar River★★ – Kilkhampton (Church★), NE : 5.5 mi by A 39 – Stratton (Church★), E : 1.5 mi – Launcells (Church★), E : 3 mi by A 3072 – Marhamchurch (St Morwenne's Church★), SE : 2.5 mi by A 39 – Poundstock★ (≤★★, church★, guildhouse★), S : 4.5 mi by A 39. Morwenstow (cliffs★★, church★), N : 8.5 mi by A 39 and minor roads - Jacobstow (Church★), S : 7 mi by A 39

🏠🏠 **Falcon**  ≤ 🔋 🔇 🍴 📶 🛅 🅿 💳 🍷

*Breakwater Rd* ✉ *EX23 8SD* – 𝒞 *(01288) 352 005* – www.falconhotel.com
– *Closed 25 December*
**29 rm** ⬜ – ♦£ 65/83 ♦♦£ 130/140 – 1 suite
**Rest** – *(bar lunch Monday-Saturday)* Carte £ 21/30 **s**

◆ An imposing, personally run hotel with the proudly traditional character of a bygone age. Contemporary and classic blend in bedrooms. Separate private garden. Formal dining.

✕✕ **Sea Fever**  💳 🍷

*Summerleaze Cres.* ✉ *EX23 8HJ* – 𝒞 *(01288) 352 893* – www.sea-fever.co.uk
– *Closed 2 weeks January-February, 1 week November, Sunday and Monday*
**Rest** – Menu £ 24 – Carte £ 26/33

◆ Modern hotel restaurant with striking black, white and grey flowered wallpaper and purple, brushed velvet banquettes. Choice of classics on the à la carte, more ambitious dishes on the tasting menu or a mix of the two on the set selection.

ENGLAND

**BUDLEIGH SALTERTON** – Devon – **503** K32 – **pop. 4 801**    **2** D2

▶ London 182 mi – Exeter 16 mi – Plymouth 55 mi

🛈 Fore St ℰ (01395) 44 52 75, www.visitbudleigh.com

🏌 East Devon Links Rd, Budleigh Salterton, ℰ (01395) 44 33 70

◉ East Budleigh (Church★), N : 2.5 mi by A 376 – Bicton★ (Gardens★) **AC**,
N : 3 mi by A 376

---

⌂   **Long Range**        🚗 & rm, 🕾 📶 **P** *VISA* ⬤⬤

    *5 Vales Rd, by Raleigh Rd* ✉ *EX9 6HS* – ℰ *(01395) 443 321*
    *– www.thelongrangehotel.co.uk – Restricted opening in winter*
    **9 rm** ⌓ – †£ 60/80 ††£ 100/112   **Rest** – Carte £ 19/30
    ♦ Homely and unassuming guesthouse, personally run in quiet residential street.
    Sun lounge with bright aspect, overlooking broad lawn and neat borders. Simple,
    unfussy rooms. Tasty, locally sourced dishes in a comfy dining room.

---

**BUNBURY** – **502** M24 – **pop. 1 308** – ✉ **Tarporley**    **20** A3

▶ London 183 mi – Birmingham 68 mi – Liverpool 39 mi – Sheffield 87 mi

---

🍺   **Yew Tree Inn**        🏠 **P** *VISA* ⬤⬤

    *Long Ln, Spurstow* ✉ *CW6 9RD* – ℰ *(01829) 260 274*
    *– www.theyewtreebunbury.com*
    **Rest** – Carte £ 23/28
    ♦ Attractive part red brick, part black and white timbered pub with central bar
    and smaller rustic rooms surrounding it. Extensive menus offer local and home-
    made produce. Regular themed events.

---

**BUNGAY** – Suffolk – **504** Y26 – **pop. 4 895** ▮ Great Britain    **15** D2

▶ London 108 mi – Beccles 6 mi – Ipswich 38 mi

◉ Norwich★★ - Cathedral★★, Castle Museum★, Market Place★, NW : 15 mi by B
1332 and A 146

---

🍺   **Castle Inn** with rm        🏠 📶 **P** *VISA* ⬤⬤

    *35 Earsham St* ✉ *NR35 1AF* – ℰ *(01986) 892 283 – www.thecastleinn.net*
    *– Closed 25 December*
    **4 rm** ⌓ – †£ 70 ††£ 100
    **Rest** – *(closed Sunday dinner)* Menu £ 19 (lunch) – Carte £ 20/30
    ♦ Sky-blue pub with open-plan dining area and intimate rear bar. Fresh, simple
    and seasonal country based cooking; the Innkeeper's platter of local produce is a
    perennial favourite. Tasty homemade cakes and cookies on display. Homely, com-
    fortable bedrooms.

**at Earsham** Southwest : 3 mi by A 144 and A 143 – ✉ **Bungay**

---

⌂   **Earsham Park Farm** without rest ⬥    ≤ 🚗 🐾 📶 **P** *VISA* ⬤⬤

    *Old Railway Rd, on A 143* ✉ *NR35 2AQ* – ℰ *(01986) 892 180*
    *– www.earsham-parkfarm.co.uk*
    **4 rm** ⌓ – †£ 51/61 ††£ 82/102
    ♦ Appealing red-brick farmhouse on a working farm. Country-style interior dis-
    plays sculptures and stencilling by the charming owner. Individually furnished
    bedrooms boast attractive furnishings. Extensive breakfasts include their own
    homemade bacon and sausages.

---

**BURCOMBE** – Wiltshire – **see Salisbury**

---

**BURFORD** – Oxfordshire – **503** P28 – **pop. 1 171**    **10** A2

▶ London 76 mi – Birmingham 55 mi – Gloucester 32 mi – Oxford 20 mi

🛈 Sheep St ℰ (01993) 82 35 58, www.burfordcotswolds.co.uk

🏌 Burford Golf Club, ℰ (01993) 82 25 83

---

🏨   **Bay Tree**        🚗 🏠 📶 ♨ **P** *VISA* ⬤⬤ **AE** ⓪

    *Sheep St* ✉ *OX18 4LW* – ℰ *(01993) 822 791*
    *– www.cotswold-inns-hotels.co.uk/bay-tree*
    **18 rm** ⌓ – †£ 120/130 ††£ 170/210 – 3 suites
    **Rest** – Menu £ 16/32 – Carte £ 24/31
    ♦ Characterful, creeper-clad 16C house with coaching inn style, antique furnish-
    ings and original features. Two front lounges with vast stone fireplaces. Comfort-
    able bedrooms. Light, airy restaurant overlooking beautiful landscaped garden.

### Burford House

*99 High St ⊠ OX18 4QA – ℰ (01993) 823 151 – www.burfordhouse.co.uk*
**8 rm** ⌂ – †£ 128/193 ††£ 165/205
**Rest** – (closed Sunday) (lunch only and dinner Thursday-Saturday)
Menu £ 17/36 – Carte approx. £ 20
♦ Characterful 17C B&W timbered townhouse. Lounge and garden room have a subtle, contemporary edge, while comfy, individually decorated bedrooms are more traditional in style. Good breakfasts, homely lunches and gourmet dinners in informal restaurant.

### Cotland House without rest

*Fulbrook Hill, Fulbrook, Northeast : 0.5 mi on A 361 ⊠ OX18 4BH*
*– ℰ (01993) 822 382 – www.cotlandhouse.com*
**4 rm** ⌂ – †£ 70 ††£ 75/95
♦ Bright, modern house in Cotswold stone; its cool, light décor tinged with Gallic style. Neatly kept by friendly owner, with candles, magazines, fresh flowers and top-name toiletries.

### Lamb Inn with rm

*Sheep St ⊠ OX18 4LR – ℰ (01993) 823 155 – www.cotswold-inns-hotels.co.uk*
**17 rm** ⌂ – †£ 155 ††£ 270   **Rest** – Menu £ 25/39 – Carte £ 25/38
♦ 15C weavers' cottage set in a charming town. Bar offers light bites and afternoon tea; the restaurant, a daily market and set menu. Ambitious cooking is robust and classically based. Bedrooms are cosy; Rosie has its own garden.

### Highway Inn with rm

*117 High St ⊠ OX18 4RG – ℰ (01993) 823 661 – www.thehighwayinn.co.uk*
*– Closed first 2 weeks January and 25-26 December*
**9 rm** ⌂ – †£ 79/99 ††£ 89/140   **Rest** – Carte £ 24/34
♦ Characterful, personally run beamed inn dating from 1480. Simple, honest cooking of pub classics, with an emphasis on local produce; tasty nursery puddings. Classic, cosy bedrooms.

### Carpenter's Arms

*Fulbrook Hill, Northeast : 0.5 mi on A 361 ⊠ OX18 4BH – ℰ (01993) 823 275*
*– www.thecarpentersarmsfulbrook.com*
**Rest** – Menu £ 17 (lunch) – Carte £ 21/27
♦ Its unassuming outer appearance gives little clue as the warm, inviting style within. Expect robust and competitively prices dishes, from grilled chops to cod with chickpea stew. Personally run.

**at Swinbrook** East : 2.75 mi by A 40 – ⊠ Burford

### Swan Inn with rm

*⊠ OX18 4DY – ℰ (01993) 823 339 – www.theswannswinbrook.co.uk*
*– Closed 25-26 December*
**6 rm** ⌂ – †£ 80/120 ††£ 120   **Rest** – Carte £ 20/35
♦ Wisteria-clad, honey-coloured pub on the riverbank boasting a lovely garden filled with fruit trees. Charming interior displays an open oak frame and exposed stone walls hung with old photos. Daily menu features the latest local produce and a modern take on older recipes. Well-appointed bedrooms have a luxurious feel.

---

## BURLTON – Shropshire – ⊠ Shrewsbury                                18 B1
▶ London 235 mi – Shrewsbury 10 mi – Wrexham 20 mi

### Burlton Inn with rm

*⊠ SY4 5TB – ℰ (01939) 270 284 – www.burltoninn.com – Closed 25 December*
**6 rm** ⌂ – †£ 85 ††£ 105   **Rest** – (closed Sunday dinner) Carte £ 21/30
♦ Characterful 18C whitewashed inn with pleasant terrace and pretty fountain. Keenly priced menus feature unfussy classical cooking, with lighter snacks at lunch and more adventurous dishes in the evening. Neat, wood-furnished bedrooms boast large bathrooms.

## BURNHAM MARKET – Norfolk – **504** W25 – pop. 898 📗 Great Britain    **15** C1

▶ London 128 mi – Cambridge 71 mi – Norwich 36 mi

🏙 Lambourne Dropmore Rd, 𝒞 (01628) 66 67 55

🅖 Holkham Hall★★ **AC**, E : 3 mi by B 1155

🏨 **Hoste Arms**    🖃 🗓 **P** 𝕍𝕀𝕊𝔸 ⊕❸

*The Green* ✉ *PE31 8HD* – 𝒞 *(01328) 738 777* – *www.hostearms.co.uk*
**34 rm** ☲ – 🛉£ 192/210 🛉🛉£ 261/281 – 1 suite
**Rest** *Hoste Arms*☺ – see restaurant listing
◆ Extended 17C inn, in the heart of a pretty village. Stylish, comfortable bedrooms boast a high level of facilities and include the eye-catching Zulu wing with its South African themed décor. Smart beauty and wellness spa features treatment rooms and a relaxing outdoor seating area.

🏠 **Vine House** without rest    🗚 🛇 **P** 𝕍𝕀𝕊𝔸 ⊕❸

*The Green* ✉ *PE31 8HD* – 𝒞 *(01328) 738 777*
– *www.vinehouseboutiquehotel.co.uk*
**6 rm** ☲ – 🛉£ 149/232 🛉🛉£ 213/298 – 1 suite
◆ Stylish, comfortable and elegant rooms with great bathrooms at this extended Georgian house. Evening butler service for drinks. Reception and meals at Hoste Arms opposite.

🏠 **Railway Inn** without rest    **P** 𝕍𝕀𝕊𝔸 ⊕❸

*Creake Rd* ✉ *PE31 8HD* – 𝒞 *(01328) 738 777* – *www.hostearms.co.uk*
**8 rm** ☲ – 🛉£ 80/141 🛉🛉£ 97/152
◆ Former station house with derelict platform and carriage to rear. Stylish, contemporary bedrooms boast bold feature walls, modern furniture, retro fittings and good facilities.

🍴🍴 **Hoste Arms**    🎴 🗚 ⇆ **P** 𝕍𝕀𝕊𝔸 ⊕❸
◉
*The Green* ✉ *PE31 8HD* – 𝒞 *(01328) 738 777* – *www.hostearms.co.uk*
**Rest** – *(booking advisable)* Carte £ 25/30🏮
◆ Extensive restaurant offering a choice of dining areas, including a rustic bar, informal conservatory and Moroccan garden. Classically based menus feature global influences, with an emphasis on local produce. Friendly, polite service.

---

## BURNHAM-ON-CROUCH – Essex – **504** W29    **13** D2

▶ London 53 mi – Croydon 58 mi – Barnet 61 mi – Ealing 74 mi

🍴🍴 **Contented Sole**    𝕍𝕀𝕊𝔸 ⊕❸

*80 High St* ✉ *CM0 8AA* – 𝒞 *(01621) 786 900* – *www.contentedsole.co.uk*
– *Closed 26 December-18 January, Sunday dinner and Tuesday*
**Rest** – Menu £ 22 (weekdays) – Carte £ 33/43
◆ 18C house that's been a draw for diners since the '60s. Traditional interior with old beams and oak panelling. Unfussy cooking uses flavourful seasonal ingredients in familiar combinations.

---

## BURNSALL – North Yorkshire – **502** O21 – pop. 108 – ✉ Skipton    **22** A2

▶ London 223 mi – Bradford 26 mi – Leeds 29 mi

🏠 **Devonshire Fell**    ≤ 🖃 📶 🗓 **P** 𝕍𝕀𝕊𝔸 ⊕❸ 𝔸𝔼 ⓪

✉ *BD23 6BT* – 𝒞 *(01756) 729 000* – *www.devonshirefell.co.uk*
**10 rm** ☲ – 🛉£ 103/144 🛉🛉£ 144/196 – 2 suites
**Rest** – *(light lunch Monday-Saturday)* Carte £ 26/42
◆ Stone-built hotel – once a club for 19C mill owners – decorated with bold colours and striking, contemporary artwork. Spacious bedrooms boast dale views. Formal, linen-clad conservatory and more funky, modern brasserie; wide-ranging, modern menu.

🍸 **Red Lion** with rm    ≤ 🖃 🍴 📶 🗓 **P** 𝕍𝕀𝕊𝔸 ⊕❸

✉ *BD23 6BU* – 𝒞 *(01756) 720 204* – *www.redlion.co.uk*
**21 rm** ☲ – 🛉£ 70/90 🛉🛉£ 113/158 – 4 suites    **Rest** – Carte £ 20/37
◆ Appealing stone inn on the riverbank with cosy bar, laid-back lounge and formally dressed dining room. Extensive menus offer local meat/fish/game, pub favourites and daily specials. Classic bedrooms have modern overtones; the annexe rooms are more contemporary.

---

## BURPHAM – West Sussex – **504** S30 – see Arundel

## BURRINGTON – Devon – 503 I31 – pop. 533  2 C1
▶ London 260 mi – Barnstaple 14 mi – Exeter 28 mi – Taunton 50 mi

🏨 **Northcote Manor** 🌿  ≼ 🚗 🕭 ✗ 👍 rm, 🏄 🅿 VISA ☻ AE
*Northwest : 2 mi on A 377* ✉ *EX37 9LZ* – ☎ *(01769) 560 501*
*– www.northcotemanor.co.uk*
**14 rm** 🖵 – 🛏£ 110/170 🛏🛏£ 160/215 – 1 suite
**Rest** – *(booking essential)* Menu £ 42 (dinner) – Carte £ 20/34
♦ Creeper-clad hall in the Torr Valley, dating from 1716. Fine fabrics and antiques
in elegant, individually styled rooms; attention to well-judged detail lends air of
idyllic calm. Country house restaurant features eye-catching murals.

## BURTON BRADSTOCK – Dorset – 503 L31 – see Bridport

## BURTON-UPON-TRENT – Staffordshire – 502 O25 – pop. 43 784  19 C1
▶ London 128 mi – Birmingham 29 mi – Leicester 27 mi – Nottingham 27 mi
🛈 Market Place ☎ (01283) 50 80 00, www.eaststaffsbc.gov.uk
🏌 Branston G. & C.C. Burton Rd, ☎ (01283) 52 83 20
🏌 Craythorne Stretton Craythorne Rd, ☎ (01283) 56 43 29

**at Stretton** Northwest : 3.25 mi by A 5121 (A 38 Derby) – ✉ Burton-Upon-Trent

🏨 **Dovecliff Hall** 🌿  ≼ 🚗 🕭 🐾 🅰🅸 rest, ¶° 🏄 🅿 VISA ☻ AE
*Dovecliff Rd* ✉ *DE13 0DJ* – ☎ *(01283) 531 818 – www.dovecliffhallhotel.co.uk*
**15 rm** 🖵 – 🛏£ 99 🛏🛏£ 120
**Rest** – *(closed Sunday dinner)* Menu £ 19/22 – Carte £ 30/43
♦ Imposing, listed 1790s house with lovely gardens and spacious rooms, nestling
in an elevated position above the Trent. Airy bedrooms, most boasting garden
vistas. Formal dining rooms in restaurant and delightful orangery.

## BURY – Greater Manchester – 502 N23 – pop. 60 718  20 B2
▶ London 211 mi – Leeds 45 mi – Liverpool 35 mi – Manchester 9 mi
🛈 Market St ☎ (0161) 253 51 11, www.visitbury.com
🏌 Greenmount, ☎ (01204) 88 37 12

✗ **Waggon**  ⇔ 🅿 VISA ☻ AE
😊 *131 Bury and Rochdale Old Rd, Birtle, East : 2 mi on B 6222* ✉ *BL9 6UE*
*– ☎ (01706) 622 955 – www.thewaggonatbirtle.co.uk – Closed 26 December-2*
*January, 2 weeks summer, Monday and Tuesday*
**Rest** – *(dinner only and lunch Thursday, Friday and Sunday)* Menu £ 17 (lunch
and weekday dinner) – Carte £ 24/36
♦ Unprepossessing façade hides a pleasantly decorated eatery with good value,
no-nonsense cooking featuring a decidedly strong Lancashire base and the famous Bury Black Pudding.

## BURY ST EDMUNDS – Suffolk – 504 W27 – pop. 36 218  15 C2
▌ Great Britain
▶ London 79 mi – Cambridge 27 mi – Ipswich 26 mi – Norwich 41 mi
🛈 6 Angel Hill ☎ (01284) 76 46 67, www.visit-burystedmunds.co.uk
🏌 The Suffolk Golf and Spa Hotel Fornham St Genevieve, ☎ (01284) 70 67 77
◎ Town★ - Abbey and Cathedral★
◎ Ickworth House★ **AC**, SW : 3 mi by A 143

🏨 **Angel**  🎏 👍 ¶° 🏄 🅿 VISA ☻ AE
*3 Angel Hill* ✉ *IP33 1LT* – ☎ *(01284) 714 000 – www.theangel.co.uk*
**73 rm** 🖵 – 🛏£ 115/130 🛏🛏£ 130/220 – 1 suite
**Rest** *Eaterie* – see restaurant listing
♦ 15C coaching inn with attractive creeper-clad Georgian façade, set opposite Abbey Gardens. Relaxed, contemporary interior with open-fired lounge. No two bedrooms are the same; some are modern in style, others are classic four-poster suites.

ENGLAND

**Ounce House** without rest
*Northgate St* ✉ *IP33 1HP* – ✆ *(01284) 761 779* – *www.ouncehouse.co.uk*
**5 rm** ⬚ – ♦£ 85/95 ♦♦£ 130/135
◆ Two 1870s houses knocked together; well furnished with Victorian elegance. Spacious, individually styled bedrooms; well-chosen antiques contribute to a characterful interior.

**Maison Bleue**
*30-31 Churchgate St* ✉ *IP33 1RG* – ✆ *(01284) 760 623* – *www.maisonbleue.co.uk*
*– Closed 3 weeks January, 2 weeks summer, Sunday and Monday*
**Rest** – Seafood – Menu £ 20/32 – Carte £ 29/43
◆ 17C glass-fronted house with blue canopies, set in the heart of town. Chic, pastel grey colour scheme with modern landscapes. Well-presented cooking displays classic French roots, with fish the main element of the monthly changing menu. Formal, efficient service.

**Pea Porridge**
*28-29 Cannon St* ✉ *IP33 1JR* – ✆ *(01284) 700 200* – *www.peaporridge.co.uk*
*– Closed last week December, first week January, 2 weeks summer, Sunday and Monday*
**Rest** – *(booking advisable)* Menu £ 16 (weekday dinner) – Carte £ 26/30
◆ Charming restaurant in cosy 19C brick cottage – a former bakery – well run by husband and wife team. Tasty, seasonal, country-style cooking with a strong Mediterranean bias. Great value lunch menus. Biodynamic and organic old world wines. Efficient service.

**Eaterie** – at Angel Hotel
*3 Angel Hill* ✉ *IP33 1LT* – ✆ *(01284) 714 000* – *www.theangel.co.uk*
**Rest** – Menu £ 18 (lunch) – Carte £ 27/45
◆ Informal bistro in an attractive 15C coaching inn, where Dickens once stayed. Bright room boasts a long bar and modern artwork. Accessible menu offers modern European brasserie-style dishes.

**at Ixworth** Northeast : 7 mi by A 143 – ✉ Bury St Edmunds

**Theobalds**
*68 High St* ✉ *IP31 2HJ* – ✆ *(01359) 231 707* – *www.theobaldsrestaurant.co.uk*
*– Closed 1 week early summer, Monday and dinner Sunday*
**Rest** – *(dinner only and lunch Sunday and Friday)* Menu £ 29 – Carte £ 31/36
◆ Beamed part 16C cottage with a cosy firelit lounge. Friendly service and well-judged seasonal menus combine heartwarming favourites and contemporary dishes.

**at Beyton** East : 6 mi by A 14 – ✉ Bury St Edmunds

**Manorhouse** without rest
*The Green* ✉ *IP30 9AF* – ✆ *(01359) 270 960* – *www.beyton.com*
**4 rm** ⬚ – ♦£ 50/60 ♦♦£ 73/80
◆ Attractive, part-15C Suffolk longhouse with large rear garden, overlooking the village green. Cosy beamed lounge-cum-breakfast room with huge fireplace, sofas and individual dining tables. Spacious, understated bedrooms have a rustic feel; 2 are in the old barn.

**at Whepstead** South : 4.5 mi by A 143 on B 1066

**The White Horse**
*Rede Rd* ✉ *IP29 4SS* – ✆ *(01284) 735 760* – *www.whitehorsewhepstead.co.uk*
*– Closed 1 week in January, 25-26 December and Sunday dinner*
**Rest** – Carte £ 12/20
◆ Cheerfully run 17C village pub; choose between a characterful beamed room and the brighter Gallery with local artists' work. The kitchen's strength lies in the more conventional dishes.

ENGLAND

**at Horringer** Southwest : 3 mi on A 143 – ⊠ Bury St Edmunds

🏠🏠🏠  **Ickworth** ♨  ← 🚗 🕭 🖾 ⚡ 🕸 🛁 ☂ ☂ 🛋 💠 **P** VISA ☻ AE ⓪
⊠ IP29 5QE – ℰ (01284) 735 350 – www.lckworthhotel.co.uk
**26 rm** ☲ – ♦£ 110/310 ♦♦£ 120/345 – 12 suites
**Rest** Fredericks – (dinner only) Menu £ 43 **s**
**Rest** Conservatory – Carte £ 25/36
◆ Family-orientated hotel set in the east wing of a grand 200 year old mansion:
formerly home to the Marquise of Bristol and now owned by the National Trust.
Set in 1,800 acres it boasts three airy drawing rooms and comfy bedrooms with
views. Smart Fredericks overlooks gardens. Casual dining in impressive former
orangery.

---

**BUSHEY** – Hertfordshire – **504** S29 – pop. 17 001                          **12** A2
▶ London 18 mi – Luton 21 mi – Watford 3 mi
🔟 Bushey Hall Bushey Hall Drive, ℰ (01923) 22 22 53
🔟 Bushey G. & C.C. High St, ℰ (020) 8950 22 83

Plan : see Greater London (North-West) 1

✗✗  **Alpine**  🕭 AC **P** VISA ☻ AE
135 High Rd ⊠ WD23 1JA – ℰ (020) 8950 2024
– www.thealpinerestaurant.co.uk – Closed 26-27 December, dinner 25 December
and Monday                                                                      BT**c**
**Rest** – Italian – Menu £ 17/24 – Carte £ 30/35
◆ Long-standing family restaurant with low lighting, bold wallpaper and contemporary fabrics. Honest Italian menu displays influences from Sicily and Emi-
lia-Romagna, ranging from family classics to more modern interpretations; homemade pasta.

---

**BUTTERMERE** – Cumbria – **502** K20 – pop. 139 – ⊠ Cockermouth        **21** A2
▶ London 306 mi – Carlisle 35 mi – Kendal 43 mi

🏠  **Wood House** ♨  ← 🚗 🔊 🕸 **P**
Northwest : 0.5 mi on B 5289 ⊠ CA13 9XA – ℰ (017687) 70 208
– www.wdhse.co.uk – April-October
**3 rm** ☲ – ♦£ 70 ♦♦£ 110    **Rest** – Menu £ 29 **s**
◆ 16C house in a wonderfully serene lakeside setting with stunning views. Well-
appointed lounge; antique furnished bedrooms. Meals cooked on the Aga using
fresh seasonal, local ingredients and served family-style around an antique table.

---

**BUXHALL** – Suffolk – see Stowmarket

---

**BUXTON** – Derbyshire – **502** O24 – pop. 20 836                             **16** A1
▶ London 172 mi – Derby 38 mi – Manchester 25 mi – Stoke-on-Trent 24 mi
🛈 The Cultural Quarter ℰ (01298) 2 51 06, www.visitbuxton.co.uk
🔟 Buxton and High Peak Townend, ℰ (01298) 2 62 63

🏠  **Buxton's Victorian** without rest  🕸 📶 **P** VISA ☻
3A Broad Walk ⊠ SK17 6JE – ℰ (01298) 78 759 – www.buxtonvictorian.co.uk
– Closed Christmas-New Year
**7 rm** ☲ – ♦£ 54/70 ♦♦£ 94/100
◆ Charming Victorian house built in 1860 for the Duke of Devonshire. Cosy
lounge and breakfast room with views over boating lake and bandstand. Bedrooms boast period furniture.

🏠  **Grendon** without rest  🚗 🕸 📶 **P** VISA ☻
Bishops Ln. , Southeast : 0.75 mi by A 53 ⊠ SK17 6UN – ℰ (01298) 78 831
– www.grendonguesthouse.co.uk – Closed January
**5 rm** ☲ – ♦£ 50/70 ♦♦£ 80/95
◆ Cosy Edwardian house on edge of town, built for a wealthy mill owner in the
1900s, with period features and pleasant gardens. Comfortable, traditionally furnished bedrooms.

## CALLINGTON – Cornwall – **503** H32 – pop. 4 048　　　　　**2** C2

▶ London 237 mi – Exeter 53 mi – Plymouth 15 mi – Truro 46 mi

ℵℵ　**Langmans**　　　　　　　　　　　　　　　　　_VISA_ ⚙ _AE_
*3 Church St* ✉ *PL17 7RE* – ✆ *(01579) 384 933* – *www.langmansrestaurant.co.uk*
*– Closed Sunday-Wednesday*
**Rest** – *(dinner only) (booking essential) (set menu only)* Menu £ 38
♦ Quaint double-fronted shop conversion; run by husband and wife team. Pre-dinner drinks in lounge followed by 6 course tasting menu in rear dining room. Refined, precise cooking.

## CALLOW HILL – Worcestershire　　　　　　　　　　　　　**19** C3

▶ London 120 mi – Birmingham 26 mi – Coventry 35 mi – Wolverhampton 27 mi

🍺　**Royal Forester** with rm　　　　　　🛜 📶 **P** _VISA_ ⚙ _AE_ ⓘ
✉ *DY14 9XW* – ✆ *(01299) 266 286* – *www.royalforesterinn.co.uk*
**7 rm** ⛶ – ✝£ 55　✝✝£ 79
**Rest** – Menu £ 15 (weekdays) – Carte dinner £ 24/38
♦ Pub dating from 1411; rustic dining room, relaxed atmosphere and bright, contemporary bar with grand piano. Simple, flavourful cooking and informative, bi-monthly menu. Fresh, modern, food-themed bedrooms; Aubergine, Pear and Cherry are the largest.

## CALNE – Wiltshire – **503** O29 – pop. 13 789　　　　　　**4** C2

▶ London 91 mi – Bristol 33 mi – Southampton 63 mi – Swindon 17 mi
🄲 Bowood House★ **AC**, (Library ⩽★) SW : 2 mi by A 4 – Avebury★★ (The Stones★, Church★) E : 6 mi by A 4

🏨　**Bowood** 🐾　　　🚲 🐶 🛋 📺 🐾 🛗 ⭐ 🍽 🐶 📶 🄰 _VISA_ ⚙ _AE_
*Derry Hill, West : 3 mi by A 4 on Derry Hill rd* ✉ *SN11 9PQ* – ✆ *(01249) 822 228*
*– www.bowood-hotel.co.uk*
**43 rm** ⛶ – ✝£ 155/205　✝✝£ 175/285
**Rest** *Shelburne* – *(dinner only and Sunday lunch)* Carte £ 28/50
**Rest** *Clubhouse Brasserie* – Menu £ 25 (dinner) – Carte lunch £ 19/40
♦ Smart, professionally run, purpose-built hotel in grounds of Lord and Lady Lansdowne's Estate. Contemporary country house styling. Spacious bedrooms; some with balconies. Modern British cooking in formal Shelburne, with attractive terrace. Brasserie menu in golf clubhouse.

## CAMBER – E. Sussex – **504** W31 – see Rye

## CAMBRIDGE – Cambridgeshire – **504** U27 – pop. 117 010　　**14** B3
▮ Great Britain

▶ London 55 mi – Coventry 88 mi – Ipswich 54 mi – Kingston-upon-Hull 137 mi
✈ Cambridge City Airport : ✆ (01223) 373765, E : 2 mi on A 1303 X
🄸 Paes Hill ✆ (0871) 2 26 80 06, www.visitcambridge.org
🄸🄸 Cambridge Menzies Hotel Bar Hill, ✆ (01954) 78 00 98
◉ Town★★★ – St John's College★★★ **AC** Y – King's College★★ (King's College Chapel★★★) Z The Backs★★ YZ – Fitzwilliam Museum★★ Z **M1** – Trinity College★★ Y – Clare College★ Z **B** – Kettle's Yard★ Y **M2**
– Queen's College★ **AC** Z
🄲 Audley End★★, S : 13 mi on Trumpington Rd, A 1309, A 1301 and B 1383
– Imperial War Museum★, Duxford, S : 9 mi on M 11

Plan on next page

🏨　**Hotel du Vin**　　　　　　　　　　🛗 ⭐ 🄰 📶 ⭐ ⚙ _AE_
*15-19 Trumpington St* ✉ *CB2 1QA* – ✆ *(01223) 227 330* – *www.hotelduvin.com*
**41 rm** – ✝£ 150/220　✝✝£ 150/380, ⛶ £ 15　　　　　　　　**Z**e
**Rest** *Bistro* – see restaurant listing
♦ Row of ex-university owned 18C houses; now a smart, stylish hotel. Contemporary bedrooms feature wine theme; 'Brown Brothers' comes with its own cinema. Relaxing, clubby bar.

# CAMBRIDGE

## COLLEGES

ENGLAND

**Hotel Felix** ⌖  　　　　🛏 📶 📺 🧖 🅿 𝑉𝐼𝑆𝐴 ⦿ 𝔸𝔼

*Whitehouse Ln, Huntingdon Rd, Northwest : 1.5 mi by A 1307* ✉ *CB3 0LX*
*– ℰ (01223) 277 977 – www.hotelfelix.co.uk*
**52 rm** – 🕴£ 160 🕴🕴£ 295, ⬜ £ 8
**Rest *Graffiti*** – see restaurant listing
♦ Set in 3 acres of gardens, a substantial Victorian mansion that was once a private house. Stylish, contemporary lounge and bar hung with modern art. Large, comfortable, boutique bedrooms with good mod cons; only four are in the main house.

**Varsity**  　　🔟 🐾 🍴 🔗 & rm, 🅰🅲 ℀ 📶 𝑉𝐼𝑆𝐴 ⦿ 𝔸𝔼 ⓪

*Thompson's Ln* ✉ *CB5 8AQ – ℰ (01223) 306 030 – www.thevarsityhotel.co.uk*
**46 rm** ⬜ – 🕴£ 160/180 🕴🕴£ 160/180 – 2 suites　　　　　　　Y**x**
**Rest *River Bar*** – Carte £ 21/38 **s**
♦ Boutique hotel on banks of the River Cam. Smart spa, stylish roof terrace and tranquil lounge with complimentary drinks. Bedrooms with designer bathrooms; some boast coffee machines, fresh orchids and balconies. Informal restaurant.

🏵🏵🏵  **Midsummer House** (Daniel Clifford)　　　🍴 ⇔ 𝑉𝐼𝑆𝐴 ⦿ 𝔸𝔼
❀❀
*Midsummer Common* ✉ *CB4 1HA – ℰ (01223) 369 299*
*– www.midsummerhouse.co.uk – Closed 2 weeks December, Sunday, Monday*
*and lunch Tuesday*　　　　　　　　　　　　　　　　　　　　　　　Y**a**
**Rest** – Menu £ 40/75🌼
**Spec.** Seared scallop, celeriac, truffle, Granny Smith and caramel. Rack of lamb, courgette and basil purée, essence of lovage. Mango and Douglas fir cream, white chocolate cookies.
♦ Charming and idyllic location beside the River Cam; conservatory dining with fresh, bright feel. Visually impressive dishes reveal cooking that is confidently crafted; flavours are clear and pronounced. Tasting menu only Fri/Sat. Service is formal and well-timed.

🍴🍴🍴  **Alimentum**　　　　　　　　　　　🅰🅲 𝑉𝐼𝑆𝐴 ⦿ 𝔸𝔼

*152-154 Hills Rd* ✉ *CB2 8PB – ℰ (01223) 413 000*
*– www.restaurantalimentum.co.uk – Closed 23-30 December, Sunday May-Oct*
*and bank holidays*　　　　　　　　　　　　　　　　　　　　　　　X**a**
**Rest** – Menu £ 20 (lunch and early dinner)/40🌼
♦ Sleek, stylish restaurant with striking red and black décor and spacious cocktail bar. Modern menu has French base; dishes are clean and unfussy with some innovative touches.

🍴🍴  **Restaurant 22**　　　　　　　　　　🅰🅲 ⇔ 𝑉𝐼𝑆𝐴 ⦿ 𝔸𝔼

*22 Chesterton Rd* ✉ *CB4 3AX – ℰ (01223) 351 880 – www.restaurant22.co.uk*
*– Closed 24 December-2 January, Sunday and Monday*　　　　　　　Y**c**
**Rest** – (booking essential) Menu £ 30
♦ Converted Victorian house with distinctive dining room decorated in rich colours. Monthly changing classical menu; tasty, good value French-influenced dishes. Formal service.

🍴🍴  **Bistro** – at Hotel du Vin　　　　　　　　🍴 🅰🅲 ⦿ 𝔸𝔼

*15-19 Trumpington St* ✉ *CB2 1QA – ℰ (01223) 227 330 – www.hotelduvin.com*
**Rest** – Menu £ 20 (lunch) – Carte £ 25/46🌼　　　　　　　　　　Z**e**
♦ Spacious brasserie with black banquettes and walls filled with wine memorabilia. Classic dishes presented in a modern style, with French undertones. Relaxed, buzzy ambience.

🍴🍴  **Graffiti** – at Hotel Felix　　　　　　🍴 🍴 🅿 𝑉𝐼𝑆𝐴 ⦿ 𝔸𝔼

*Whitehouse Ln, Huntingdon Rd, Northwest : 1.5 mi by A 1307* ✉ *CB3 0LX*
*– ℰ (01223) 277 977 – www.hotelfelix.co.uk*
**Rest** – Menu £ 18 (lunch) – Carte £ 25/39
♦ Dark wood furnished restaurant hung with contemporary art. Cosy fire for colder months and south facing terrace the perfect spot in summer. Interesting modern menu with Mediterranean twists.

ENGLAND

✗ **Cotto**                                      🛦 VISA ⓿ AE
*183 East Rd ✉ CB1 1BG – ℰ (01223) 302 010 – www.cottocambridge.co.uk*
*– Closed August, 25 December-10 January, Sunday, Monday, dinner*
*Tuesday-Wednesday and Saturday lunch*                    **Za**
**Rest** – *(booking essential)* Menu £ 40 (dinner) **s** – Carte lunch £ 24/36 **s**
♦ By day, a café serving homemade pastries, platters and snacks. By night, a res-
taurant with large illuminated canvases and a weekly set menu of well-prepared,
classically based dishes that showcase excellent ingredients. Very personally run.

**at Histon** North : 3 mi on B 1049 - X – ✉ **Cambridge**

✗✗ **Phoenix**                                      AC P VISA ⓿
*20 The Green ✉ CB4 9JA – ℰ (01223) 233 766 – Closed 25-26 December*
**Rest** – Chinese – Menu £ 20/28 – Carte £ 44/72
♦ Popular Chinese restaurant in former pub on village green. Comfortable,
homely inner. Polite, smartly attired staff. Vast menu with plenty of Peking and
Sichuan favourites.

**at Horningsea** Northeast : 4 mi by A 1303 - X - and B 1047 on Horningsea rd
– ✉ **Cambridge**

🍺 **Crown and Punchbowl** with rm          🚗 🍴 ☾ ⁂ P VISA ⓿ AE
*High St ✉ CB25 9JG – ℰ (01223) 860 643 – www.thecrownandpunchbowl.co.uk*
*– Closed 26 December-1 January, dinner Sunday and bank holiday Monday*
**5 rm** ⬚ – ♦£ 75 ♦♦£ 95    **Rest** – Carte £ 25/33
♦ Homely dining pub with relaxed service. Dishes display European influences
and arrive in a mix of classic and more ambitious styles. Daily fish specials and a
mix and match sausage board. Simple, tidy bedrooms are handy for the airport.

**at Little Wilbraham** East : 7.25 mi by A 1303 - X – ✉ **Cambridge**

🍺 **Hole in the Wall**                          🍴 P VISA ⓿
*2 High St ✉ CB21 5JY – ℰ (01223) 812 282 – www.the-holeinthewall.com*
*– Closed 2 weeks January, 2 weeks September-October, Sunday dinner and*
*Monday except lunch on bank holidays*
**Rest** – Carte £ 23/29
♦ Characterful 15C pub with sympathetically designed extension, set well off the
beaten track. Beamed ceilings feature throughout and there's a large brick fireplace with wood burning stove. Traditionally prepared local produce; satisfying,
flavoursome dishes.

**at Madingley** West : 4.5 mi by A 1303 - X – ✉ **Cambridge**

🍺 **Three Horseshoes**                          🚗 🍴 P VISA ⓿ AE
*High St ✉ CB23 8AB – ℰ (01954) 210 221*
*– www.threehorseshoesmadingley.com*
**Rest** – *(booking advisable)* Carte £ 22/38 ❀
♦ Attractive thatched pub with bustling atmosphere. Concise bar menu and daily
changing, Italian à la carte, featuring straightforward combinations and fresh,
tasty dishes.

---

**CAMPSEA ASH** – Suffolk                               **15** D3
▶ London 101 mi – Norwich 46 mi – Southend-on-Sea 76 mi – Ipswich 16 mi

🏠 **Old Rectory** ❧                             🚗 ☾ P VISA ⓿
*Station Rd ✉ IP13 0PU – ℰ (01728) 746 524 – www.theoldrectorysuffolk.com*
*– Closed 25 December-2 Jan*
**7 rm** ⬚ – ♦£ 75 ♦♦£ 120/140
**Rest** – *(closed Saturday and Sunday)* *(dinner only)* *(set menu only)* Menu £ 30
♦ Former Georgian rectory; now a stylish hotel with attractive gardens. Contem-
porary bedrooms; Oak is the most luxurious. Striking dining room with open fire.
Dinner served on an ad hoc basis, so arrange when booking. Set 3 course menu;
accomplished home cooking.

## CANTERBURY – Kent – **504** X30 – pop. 41 784 ▮ Great Britain  **9** D2

▶ London 59 mi – Brighton 76 mi – Dover 15 mi – Maidstone 28 mi

ℹ Buttermarket ✆ (01227) 37 81 00, www.canterbury.co.uk

◉ City★★★ - Cathedral★★★ Y - St Augustine's Abbey★★ **AC** YZ **K** – King's School★ Y – Mercery Lane★ Y **12** - Christ Church Gate★ Y **D** – Museum of Canterbury★ **AC** Y **M1** – St Martin's Church★ Y **N** – West Gate Towers★ **AC** Y **R**

---

### 🏠 **Abode Canterbury**     ₤₅ 📶 ₤ 🗚 ℗ 💵 🆚 ⓒ Ⓐ Ⓓ

*30-33 High St ⊠ CT1 2RX –* ✆ *(01227) 766 266*
*– www.michaelcaines.com*                                        Y**a**
**72 rm** – ╬£ 99/155, ╬╬£ 99/155, ☕ £ 14 – 1 suite
**Rest** *Michael Caines* – see restaurant listing

♦ Centrally located former coaching inn; heavily beamed, yet with a stylish, modern, boutique feel. Contemporary bedrooms, comfortable champagne bar and atmospheric first floor lounge.

⌂ **Magnolia House** without rest　　　🍴 📺 🛜 📶 **P** VISA ⓪ AE
*36 St Dunstan's Terr.* ⊠ *CT2 8AX –* 𝒞 *(01227) 765 121*
*– www.magnoliahousecanterbury.co.uk – Closed 25-26 December*　　Y**s**
**6 rm** ⌿ – 🛏£ 55/70 🛏🛏£ 125

♦ Creamwashed Georgian house in residential area close to town. Lounge is filled with local information; breakfast room overlooks the walled garden. Neat, tidy bedrooms offer good facilities, including flat screen TVs, CD players and fridges.

✕✕ **Michael Caines** – at Abode Canterbury Hotel　　AC VISA ⓪ AE ①
*High St* ⊠ *CT1 2RX –* 𝒞 *(01227) 826 684 – www.michaelcaines.com – Closed*
*Sunday dinner*　　　Y**a**
**Rest** – Menu £ 14 (lunch) – Carte £ 37/47

♦ Enjoy a glass of Champagne in smart bar before repairing to the upmarket restaurant to enjoy modern British cooking utilising a variety of styles and classical techniques.

✕ **Goods Shed**　　　　　　　**P** VISA ⓪ AE ①
*Station Rd West, St Dunstans* ⊠ *CT2 8AN –* 𝒞 *(01227) 459 153*
*– www.thegoodsshed.net – Closed 25 December, 1 January, Sunday dinner and*
*Monday*　　　Y**x**
**Rest** – Carte £ 27/30

♦ Once derelict railway shed, now a farmers' market that's open all day. Its eating area offers superbly fresh produce with no frills and real flavours very much to the fore.

**at Lower Hardres** South : 3 mi on B 2068 - Z – ⊠ Canterbury

🍴 **Granville**　　　　　🍴 🍴 AC **P** VISA ⓪ AE
*Street End* ⊠ *CT4 7AL –* 𝒞 *(01227) 700 402 – www.thegranvillecanterbury.com*
*– Closed Sunday dinner and Monday*
**Rest** – Carte £ 21/34

♦ Sizeable, family-run pub with Scandinavian-style, open-plan interior. Constantly evolving blackboard menu offers generous portions of unfussy, traditional dishes; veg is from the allotment.

---

**CARBIS BAY** – Cornwall – **503** D33 – see St Ives

---

**CARLISLE** – Cumbria – **501** L19 – pop. 71 773 ▯ Great Britain　　**21** B1
▶ London 317 mi – Blackpool 95 mi – Edinburgh 101 mi – Glasgow 100 mi
🛫 Carlisle Airport 𝒞 (01228) 573641, NW : 5.5 mi by A 7 - BY - and B 6264
ℹ Green Market 𝒞 (01228) 62 56 00, www.discovercarlisle.co.uk
🏌 Aglionby, 𝒞 (01228) 51 30 29
🏌 Stony Holme St Aidan's Rd, 𝒞 (01228) 62 55 11
🏌 Dalston Hall Dalston, 𝒞 (01228) 71 01 65
◉ Town★ - Cathedral★ (Painted Ceiling★) AY **E** – Tithe Barn★ BY **A**
◉ Hadrian's Wall★★, N : by A 7 AY

⌂ **Number Thirty One**　　　　📺 📶 VISA ⓪ ①
*31 Howard Pl* ⊠ *CA1 1HR –* 𝒞 *(01228) 597 080 – www.number31.co.uk*
**4 rm** ⌿ – 🛏£ 65 🛏🛏£ 90　**Rest** – Menu £ 25　　　BY**a**

♦ Well-appointed, bay-windowed Victorian townhouse with sumptuous lounge and warm, immaculately-kept bedrooms. The large, comfortable Red Room on the top floor is the best. Richly decorated dining room with window onto plant-filled terrace.

**at High Crosby** Northeast : 5 mi by A 7 - BY - and B 6264 off A 689 – ⊠ Carlisle

🏠 **Crosby Lodge Country House** ⬙　　≤ 🍴 📶 **P** VISA ⓪ AE
*Crosby-on-Eden* ⊠ *CA6 4QZ –* 𝒞 *(01228) 573 618 – www.crosbylodge.co.uk*
*– Closed 25 December-10 January*
**11 rm** ⌿ – 🛏£ 90/105 🛏🛏£ 200/250
**Rest** – *(Sunday dinner residents only)* Carte £ 36/52

♦ Grade II listed, castellated house built in 1802. Warm ambience and welcoming hostess. Traditionally furnished lounge. Comfortable bedrooms with pleasant countryside outlook. Richly coloured dining room with polished brass around fireplace. Classic, homecooked food includes renowned sweet trolley.

CARLISLE

GLASGOW (M 6) **A 7** LONGTOWN, EDINBURGH

ENGLAND

## CARLTON HUSTHWAITE – North Yorkshire – 502 Q21    22 B2

▶ London 230 mi – Leeds 51 mi – Middlesbrough 32 mi – York 20 mi

### Carlton Bore    P VISA ©©

✉ YO7 2BW – ℰ (01845) 501 265 – www.carltonbore.co.uk – Closed first 2 weeks January
**Rest** – Menu £ 16 (lunch) – Carte £ 23/32
♦ Characterful 17C stone inn offering appealing menu of well-priced, generously proportioned pub favourites. Three brightly decorated rooms and a warm, welcoming atmosphere.

## CARLTON-IN-COVERDALE – North Yorkshire – 502 O21 – see Middleham

## CARLYON BAY – Cornwall – 503 F33 – see St Austell

## CARTHORPE – North Yorkshire    22 B1

▶ London 228 mi – Leeds 49 mi – Middlesbrough 40 mi – York 34 mi

### Fox and Hounds    P VISA ©©

✉ DL8 2LG – ℰ (01845) 567 433 – www.foxandhoundscarthorpe.co.uk – Closed 25 December, first week January and Monday
**Rest** – Menu £ 17 (weekdays) – Carte £ 21/32
♦ Family run, ivy-clad stone pub with a real sense of history. Menus offer a huge array of choice, with meats from the local butcher, flour milled nearby and produce from the village dairy.

## CARTMEL – Cumbria – 502 L21 – see Grange-over-Sands

## CASTLE CARY – Somerset – **503** M30 – pop. 3 056     **4** C2

▶ London 127 mi – Bristol 28 mi – Wells 13 mi

⌂ **Clanville Manor** without rest     🚗 🐶 ⅀ 🦆 🛜 P VISA ⦿⦿
*West : 2 mi by B 3152 and A 371 on B 3153* ✉ *BA7 7PJ* – 𝓒 *(01963) 350 124*
*– www.clanvillemanor.co.uk – Closed Christmas and New Year*
**4 rm** ⊑ – ♦£ 40/110 ♦♦£ 80/110
♦ 18C house, charmingly cluttered. Heirlooms and antiques abound. Breakfasts served from the Aga. Walled garden boasts heated pool. Individual bedrooms, including four-poster.

**at Lovington** *West : 4 mi by B 3152 and A 371 on B 3153* – ✉ **Castle Cary**

🏚 **The Pilgrims at Lovington** with rm     🏠 ⅙ rm, ⅌ 🐱 P VISA ⦿⦿
✉ *BA7 7PT* – 𝓒 *(01963) 240 597* – *www.thepilgrimsatlovington.co.uk – Closed first 2 weeks of October, Sunday dinner, Monday and lunch Tuesday*
**5 rm** ⊑ – ♦£ 90 ♦♦£ 120/130    **Rest** – Carte £ 24/39
♦ Pristine and personally run; its unprepossessing outward appearance masking a charming interior. Appealing menu of British/Mediterranean dishes made with quality local produce. Comfortable, contemporary bedrooms, luxurious bathrooms and substantial breakfasts.

## CASTLE COMBE – Wiltshire – **503** N29 – pop. 347 – ✉ **Chippenham**    **4** C2

▶ London 110 mi – Bristol 23 mi – Chippenham 6 mi
◉ Village ★★

🏬 **Manor House H. and Golf Club** 🐾     🚗 🐶 🦢 🏠 ✗ 🖼 🛜 🏌 P
✿ ✉ *SN14 7HR* – 𝓒 *(01249) 782 206*     VISA ⦿⦿ AE
*– www.exclusivehotels.co.uk*
**44 rm** ⊑ – ♦£ 255 ♦♦£ 255 – 4 suites
**Rest** *The Bybrook* – *(closed Monday lunch)* Menu £ 30/60
**Spec.** Seared scallops with cauliflower purée and agrodolce dressing. Slow cooked loin of veal, braised red cabbage and sweetbreads. Baked apple terrine, apple doughnut and date ice cream
♦ Fine period manor house in 365 acres of formal gardens and parkland. Interior exudes immense charm and style, with oak panelling and a host of open-fired lounges. Uniquely styled, luxurious bedrooms; many in the courtyard. Large dining room offers refined, carefully prepared dishes with a classical base. Slick service.

🏠 **Castle Inn**     🏠 ⅌ 🐱 VISA ⦿⦿ AE
✉ *SN14 7HN* – 𝓒 *(01249) 783 030* – *www.castle-inn.info – Closed 25 December*
**11 rm** ⊑ – ♦£ 80/165 ♦♦£ 195    **Rest** – *(bar lunch)* Carte £ 24/34
♦ A hostelry dating back to the 12C in the middle of a delightful and historic village. Wooden beams and much character throughout. Breakfast in conservatory. Large and varied menu served in rustic bar.

## CASTLE EDEN – Durham     **24** B3

▶ London 265 mi – Sunderland 15 mi – Newcastle upon Tyne 28 mi
– Middlesbrough 18 mi

🏚 **Castle Eden Inn**     🚗 P VISA ⦿⦿ AE
*Stockton Rd* ✉ *TS27 4SD* – 𝓒 *(01429) 835 137* – *www.castleedeninn.com*
**Rest** – Carte £ 22/31
♦ A substantial building with a modern interior. The large, stylish bar and elegant dining room share the same extensive menu, which offers everything from shepherds pie to local oysters, and uses trusted regional suppliers.

## CATEL/CASTEL – **503** P33 – see Channel Islands (Guernsey)

## CAUNTON – Nottinghamshire – **502** R24 – see Newark-on-Trent

## CERNE ABBAS – Dorset – 503 M31

**4** C3

▶ London 132 mi – Bristol - 60 mi – Cardiff 115 mi – Southampton 58 mi

🍴 **New Inn**                                          🚗 🛋 **VISA** **⨀** **AE** **①**
*14 Long St ⊠ DT2 7JF – ℰ (01300) 341 274 – www.newinncerneabbas.com*
*– Restricted opening in winter*
**Rest** – Carte £ 21/29
◆ Sizeable pub set in picture postcard village, with exposed beams, decked terrace and vast garden. Freshly prepared, traditional dishes make good use of locally sourced produce.

---

## CHADDESLEY CORBETT – Worcestershire – 503 N26 – see Kidderminster

---

## CHADWICK END – West Midlands – 503 O26

**19** C2

▶ London 106 mi – Birmingham 13 mi – Leicester 40 mi – Stratford-upon-Avon 16 mi

🍴 **Orange Tree**                                      🚗 🛋 **P** **VISA** **⨀**
*Warwick Rd, on A 4141 ⊠ B93 0BN – ℰ (01564) 785 364*
*– www.lovelypubs.co.uk – Closed 25 December and Sunday dinner*
**Rest** – *(booking essential)* Menu £ 16 (lunch and early dinner) – Carte £ 17/36
◆ Large, contemporary pub with neat gardens, spacious terrace and buzzing atmosphere. Wide-ranging menu offers several dishes in two sizes, with tasty spit roast chicken a speciality.

---

## CHAGFORD – Devon – 503 I31 – pop. 1 417

**2** C2

▶ London 218 mi – Exeter 17 mi – Plymouth 27 mi
🅖 Dartmoor National Park★★

ENGLAND

🏨 **Gidleigh Park** (Michael Caines) 🏡        ← 🚗 🎧 ➘ ✗ 🔥 rm, 📶 **P**
❀❀ *Northwest : 2 mi by Gidleigh Rd ⊠ TQ13 8HH*                    **VISA** **⨀** **AE** **①**
*– ℰ (01647) 432 367 – www.gidleigh.com*
**23 rm** 🛋 – †£ 300 ††£ 525 – 1 suite
**Rest** – *(booking essential)* Menu £ 52/110🈺
**Spec.** Salmon with Oscietra caviar, salmon jelly and Greek yoghurt vinaigrette. Salt cod, crab, chorizo, samphire and lemon purée. Caramel and cardamom parfait, milk chocolate mousse and cardamom foam.
◆ Lovingly restored and extremely comfortable Arts and Crafts house set in 100 acres. Luxurious bedrooms boast impressive bathrooms; some have a balcony. Formal restaurant, where classical French menus showcase skilfully prepared, quality local produce. Tasting menu for Michael Caines' signature dishes.

🍴🍴 **22 Mill Street** with rm                              **VISA** **⨀** **AE**
*22 Mill St ⊠ TQ13 8AW – ℰ (01647) 432 244 – www.22millst.com*
**2 rm** – †£ 90/119 ††£ 99/149, 🛋 £ 10
**Rest** – *(booking essential)* Menu £ 22/42
◆ Smart, intimate restaurant on high street of scenic village, right in the heart of Dartmoor. Fresh and unfussy, with formally laid tables. An array of modern menus offer simply cooked, seasonal classics. Comfortable, rustic-style bedrooms.

### at Sandypark Northeast : 2.25 mi on A 382 – ⊠ Chagford

🏨 **Mill End**                                        🚗 ➘ 📶 **P** **VISA** **⨀** **AE**
*on A 382 ⊠ TQ13 8JN – ℰ (01647) 432 282 – www.millendhotel.com – Closed*
*4-19 January*
**13 rm** 🛋 – †£ 75 ††£ 130/160 – 1 suite   **Rest** – *(dinner only)* Menu £ 40
◆ Well-maintained house with pleasant gardens; its comfy, antique-furnished lounge retaining a traditional charm. Classically styled bedrooms in original house; larger, more modern rooms in extension. A modern take on the classics in the bright, linen-laid restaurant.

🏠 **Parford Well** without rest 🏡                          🚗 ✗ 📶
*on Drewsteignton rd ⊠ TQ13 8JW – ℰ (01647) 433 353 – www.parfordwell.co.uk*
**3 rm** 🛋 – †£ 50/90 ††£ 90/95
◆ Tastefully maintained with superbly tended gardens. Elegant sitting room has plenty of books and French windows to garden. Two breakfast rooms. Homely, immaculate bedrooms.

**at Easton** Northeast : 1.5 mi on A 382 – ⊠ Chagford

介 **Easton Court** without rest ⊜ 🅿 💳 ⊙⊙
Easton Cross ⊠ TQ13 8JL – 𝒞 (01647) 433 469 – www.easton.co.uk
**5 rm** ⊡ – †£ 60/70 ††£ 80/85
♦ Well appointed accommodation and a high ceilinged lounge overlooking the
immaculate gardens. Home made marmalade a speciality. Friendly atmosphere.

# CHANNEL ISLANDS – 503 L/M33

## ALDERNEY – Alderney – 503 M32                                                    5 B1
🛫 Aurigny Air Services 𝒞 (01481) 822886
🄸 States Office, Island Hall, Royal Connaught Sq 𝒞 (01481) 822 8 11,
www.visitalderney.com
👁 Braye Bay★ – Mannez Garenne (≼★ from Quesnard Lighthouse) – Telegraph
Bay★ – Vallee des Trois Vaux★ – Clonque Bay★

## BRAYE – Alderney                                                                   5 B1

🄷🄷 **Braye Beach** ॐ                     ≼ 🕼 🌭 🍸 rm, ♔ 🕍 🅿 💳 ⊙⊙ 🄰🄴 ⊙
⊠ GY9 3XT – 𝒞 (01481) 824 300 – www.brayebeach.com
**27 rm** ⊡ – †£ 80/190 ††£ 100/260   **Rest** – Carte £ 18/32 **s**
♦ Smart, contemporary hotel set on edge of beach. Vaulted basement houses a
series of lounges and a 19-seat cinema. Modern European cooking with a subtle
seafood slant.

## GUERNSEY – Guernsey – 503 L32 – pop. 58 867                                        5 A2
🛫 Guernsey Airport 𝒞 (01481) 237766, Aurigny Air 𝒞 (01481) 822 886
🚢 from St Peter Port to France (St Malo) and Jersey (St Helier) (Condor Ferries Ltd) 2
weekly – from St Peter Port to France (Dielette) (Manche Iles Express) (summer
only) (60 mn) – from St Peter Port to Herm (Herm Seaway) (25 mn) – from St Peter
Port to Sark (Isle of Sark Shipping Co. Ltd) (45 mn) – from St Peter Port to Jersey
(St Helier) (HD Ferries) (1hr) – from St Peter Port to Jersey (St Helier) (Condor
Ferries Ltd) daily
🚢 from St Peter Port to France (St Malo) and Jersey (St Helier) (Condor Ferries Ltd)
– from St Peter Port to Jersey (St Helier) and Weymouth (Condor Ferries Ltd)
🄸 North Esplanade 𝒞 (01481) 72 35 52, www.visitguernsey.com
👁 Island★ - Pezeries Point★★ – Icart Point★★ – Côbo Bay★★ - St Martin's Point★★
– St Apolline's Chapel★ – Vale Castle★ – Fort Doyle★ – La Gran'mere du
Chimquiere★ – Rocquaine Bay★ – Jerbourg Point★

## CATEL/CASTEL – Guernsey                                                            5 A2

🄷🄷 **Cobo Bay** ≼ 🕼 🌭 🕍 🄰🄺 rest, 🍸 ♔ 🅿 💳 ⊙⊙ 🄰🄴
Cobo Coast Rd ⊠ GY5 7HB – 𝒞 (01481) 257 102 – www.cobobayhotel.com
– Closed January-February
**34 rm** ⊡ – †£ 49/120 ††£ 69/190
**Rest** – Menu £ 29 (dinner) – Carte lunch £ 22/31
♦ Modern hotel on sandy Cobo Bay; an ideal location for families. The rooms are
pleasant with bright décor and some have the delightful addition of seaview bal-
conies. Romantic dining with views of sunsets.

## FERMAIN BAY – Guernsey                                                             5 A2

🄷🄷🄷 **Fermain Valley** ≼ ⊜ 🄽 🌭 🕍 & 🍸 ♔ 🕍 🅿 💳 ⊙⊙ 🄰🄴
Fermain Ln ⊠ GY1 1ZZ – 𝒞 (01481) 235 666 – www.fermainvalley.com
**45 rm** ⊡ – †£ 131/183 ††£ 175/245
**Rest Valley** – see restaurant listing
♦ Stylish, comfortable hotel with beautiful gardens, hidden in a picturesque valley and affording pleasant bay views through the trees. Well-equipped bedrooms
are widely dispersed; 'Gold' rooms boast balconies. Colonial-style bar and lounge.

ENGLAND

XX **Valley** – at Fermain Valley Hotel                 ≼ 🚗 🏠 AC **P** VISA ⊙⊙ AE
*Fermain Ln* ⊠ *GY1 1ZZ* – 𝒞 *(01481) 235 666* – *www.fermainvalley.com*
**Rest** – Menu £ 25 **s** – Carte £ 25/36 **s**
♦ Informal hotel restaurant with beautiful multi-level terrace and lovely sea views. Accessible menu offers fresh fish and simple grills. A fine array of Beken yacht photos hang on the walls.

**KINGS MILLS** – Guernsey                                                    **5** A2

🛏 **Fleur du Jardin** with rm                🚗 🏠 ⅀ ⁇ **P** VISA ⊙⊙ AE ⓞ
*Grand Moulins* ⊠ *GY5 7JT* – 𝒞 *(01481) 257 996* – *www.fleurdujardin.com*
**17 rm** � – ♦£ 65/89 ♦♦£ 90/138 – 1 suite   **Rest** – Carte £ 21/27
♦ Attractive inn with stylish terrace, lovely landscaped gardens and several charming, adjoining rustic rooms. Menu ranges from homemade burgers to sea bass and tasty island seafood specials. Stylish New England themed bedrooms; there's even a heated outdoor pool.

**ST MARTIN** – Guernsey – pop. 6 267                                          **5** A2
▶ St Peter Port 2 mi

🏠 **Bella Luce** ⌂                     🚗 🏠 ⅀ ⁇ ⁇ **P** VISA ⊙⊙ AE ⓞ
*La Fosse* ⊠ *GY4 6EB* – 𝒞 *(01481) 238 764* – *www.bellalucehotel.com* – *Closed 2-16 January*
**23 rm** ⊑ – ♦£ 112/132 ♦♦£ 140/320
**Rest** *Bella Luce* – Menu £ 25 – Carte dinner £ 27/39
♦ Originally a Norman manor house; with a cosy beamed bar, cellar-like lounge and stylish, intimate interior featuring voluptuous velvets. Opulent bedrooms boast modern bathrooms. Pleasant gardens with pool. Bella Luce offers an eclectic array of modern dishes.

🏠 **La Barbarie** ⌂                          🚗 🏠 ⅀ ⁇ ⁇ **P** VISA
*Saints Bay* ⊠ *GY4 6ES* – 𝒞 *(01481) 235 217* – *www.labarbariehotel.com* – *March-October*
**26 rm** ⊑ – ♦£ 65/82 ♦♦£ 79/114 – 1 suite   **Rest** – *(bar lunch)* Carte £ 30/37
♦ Stone-built former priory with a welcoming, cottagey style. Characterful bar; well-kept pool and terrace. Bedrooms are traditional and comfortable. Seafood a speciality.

XX **Auberge**                           ≼ 🚗 🏠 **P** VISA ⊙⊙ AE ⓞ
*Jerbourg Rd* ⊠ *GY4 6BH* – 𝒞 *(01481) 238 485* – *www.theauberge.gg* – *Closed 24 December-1 February and Sunday dinner*
**Rest** – *(booking essential)* Menu £ 19 (dinner) – Carte £ 27/45
♦ Superbly located informal modern restaurant, with attractive terrace boasting tranquil sea and island views. Artistic dishes display bold flavours. Quality island-caught fish is a favourite.

**ST PETER PORT** – Guernsey                                                  **5** A2
🛈 Rohais St Pierre Park, 𝒞 (01481) 72 70 39
👁 Town★★ - St Peter's Church★ Z – Hauteville House★ **AC** Z – Castle Cornet★ (≼★) **AC** Z
🗁 Saumarez Park★ (Guernsey Folk Museum★), W : 2 mi by road to Catel Z – Little Chapel★, SW : 2.25 mi by Mount Durand road Z

Plan on next page

🏠 **Old Government House H. & Spa**        🚗 🏠 ⅀ ⊕ ⁇ ⅃♠ ⅃ 🖶 🛗 ᱼ rm,
*St Ann's Pl* ⊠ *GY1 2NU* – 𝒞 *(01481)*          AC rm, ⁇ rest, ⁇ ⅃♠ **P** VISA ⊙⊙ AE
*724 921* – *www.theoghhotel.com*                                            **Y**a
**61 rm** ⊑ – ♦£ 143/215 ♦♦£ 180/280 – 1 suite
**Rest** *Governors* – *(dinner only) (booking essential)* Menu £ 45 – Carte £ 35/48
**Rest** *Brasserie* – 𝒞 *(01481) 738 604* – Carte £ 28/46
♦ Fine 18C building; classically furnished, with many of its original features restored. Glorious ballroom, well-equipped spa and individually styled bedrooms with modern bathrooms. Intimate fine dining in Governors, where ambitious cooking has a French base. Smart yet informal Brasserie, with delightful outside terrace.

ENGLAND

143

## ✕✕ **Nautique**    ◁ VISA ⚫ Æ

*Quay Steps* ⊠ *GY1 2LE –* ℰ *(01481) 721 714 – www.lenautiquerestaurant.co.uk*
*– Closed Saturday lunch and Sunday*    Z**r**

**Rest** – Menu £ 19 (lunch) – Carte £ 31/39

◆ Quayside former warehouse with pleasant marina view and characterful, nautically themed interior; ask for a window seat. Large menu of generously sized, classic dishes, with fish a feature.

## ✕✕ **Pier 17**    ◁ 🍴 AC VISA ⚫ Æ

*Albert Pier* ⊠ *GY1 1AD –* ℰ *(01481) 720 823 – www.pier17restaurant.com*
*– Closed Sunday*    Z**x**

**Rest** – Carte £ 26/32

◆ Set at the end of a substantial stone pier in the centre of Guernsey harbour. Conservatory extension affords superb water views and the two terraces catch the last of the suns rays. Traditionally based, seasonal dishes.

**Swan Inn**                                          🛜 VISA ⓦ ⑪

*St Julian's Ave* ✉ *GY1 1WA –* ☏ *(01481) 728 969 – Closed 25 December and Sunday*                                                                    Y**x**
**Rest** – Carte £ 12/18
• Smart Victorian pub with bottle-green façade, traditional styling and good value early week menu. Choose hearty, satisfying dishes in the bar or more ambitious fare in the dining room.

## St Saviour – Guernsey                                            5 A2

▶ St Peter Port 4 mi

**Farmhouse**                      🍽 🛜 ⚒ 🅰🅲 ⚒ 🆆 ⚒ 🅿 VISA ⓦ AE

*Route des Bas Courtils* ✉ *GY7 9YF –* ☏ *(01481) 264 181 – www.thefarmhouse.gg*
**14 rm** ⚏ – ♦£ 109/145 ♦♦£ 109/265
**Rest** – Menu £ 25 – Carte dinner £ 21/42
• Former farm restyled in boutique vein. Stylish, sumptuous bedrooms with high-tech amenities; bathrooms with heated floors. Pleasant garden and pool; terrace and kitchen garden. Contemporary cooking with international edge uses island's finest produce in eclectic ways.

**Pavilion**                                    🍽 🛜 🅿 VISA ⓦ
(❀)
*Le Gron* ✉ *GY7 9RN –* ☏ *(01481) 264 165 – www.thepavilion.co.gg – Closed 2 weeks January, Christmas and Monday in winter*
**Rest** – *(lunch only and dinner Friday-Saturday)* Menu £ 23 – Carte £ 20/28 **s**
• Farmhouse-style restaurant displaying exposed stone and beams. Menus offer something for everyone, from tea and cakes to full 3 courses. Fresh, simple, intelligent cooking. Desserts a must.

## HERM – Herm – 503 M33                                           5 A2

🚢 to Guernsey (St Peter Port) (Herm Seaway) (20 mn)
◉ Le Grand Monceau ★

**White House** ⅌              ≤ 🍽 🕭 🛜 ⚒ 🆆 ⚒ 🆆 VISA ⓦ

✉ *GY1 3HR –* ☏ *(01481) 750 075 – www.herm.com – April-7 October*
**40 rm** (dinner included) ⚏ – ♦£ 79/144 ♦♦£ 158/292
**Rest** *Conservatory* – *(booking essential)* Menu £ 20/28 – Carte £ 40/50
**Rest** *Ship Inn* – *(booking advisable)* Carte £ 16/29
• Hotel with real country house feel: the beach extends to the door. Guernsey and Jethou can be viewed from the lounge. Attractive rooms. Formal Conservatory with seafood emphasis. Relaxed Ship Inn.

## JERSEY – C.I. – 503 L33 – pop. 85 150                             5 B2

🛫 States of Jersey Airport : ☏ (01534) 446 000
🚢 from St Helier to France (St Malo) (Condor Ferries Ltd) (summer only) – from St Helier to France (St Malo) (Condor Ferries Ltd) 3 weekly - from Gorey to France (Carteret) (Manche Iles Express) (summer only) (60mn) – from St Helier to Guernsey (St Peter Port) (Condor Ferries Ltd) (50 mn) – from St Helier to Guernsey (St Peter Port) (Condor Ferries Ltd) daily
🚢 from St Helier to France (St Malo) and Guernsey (St Peter Port) (Condor Ferries Ltd) – from St Helier to Sark (Condor Ferries Ltd) (50 mn) – from St Helier to Guernsey (St Peter Port) and Weymouth (Condor Ferries Ltd)
ℹ St Helier ☏ (01534) 44 88 77, www.jersey.com
◉ Island ★★ - Jersey Zoo ★★ **AC** – Jersey Museum ★ - Eric Young Orchid Foundation ★ – St Catherine's Bay ★ (≤ ★★) – Grosnez Point ★ - Devil's Hole ★ – St Matthews Church, Millbrook (glasswork ★) – La Hougue Bie ★ (Neolithic tomb ★ **AC**) - Waterworks Valley - Hamptonne Country Life Museum ★ – St Catherine's Bay ★ (≤ ★★) – Noirmont Point ★

## Gorey – Saint Martin                                             5 B2

▶ St Helier 4 mi
◉ Mont Orgueil Castle ★ (≤ ★★) **AC** – Jersey Pottery ★

145

**ENGLAND**

### Moorings
*Gorey Pier* ⌧ *JE3 6EW* – ℰ *(01534) 853 633* – *www.themooringshotel.com*
**15 rm** ⌸ – ♦£ 58/109 ♦♦£ 115/150    **Rest** – Menu £ 17/23 – Carte £ 30/46
◆ Located at the base of Gorey Castle, overlooking the waterfront, once the heart of the oyster fishing industry. Well-priced; the first floor bedrooms have terraces. Pleasant decked area at front of restaurant.

### Sumas
*Gorey Hill* ⌧ *JE3 6ET* – ℰ *(01534) 853 291* – *www.sumasrestaurant .com*
*– Closed 23 December-20 January and dinner Sunday*
**Rest** – *(booking essential)* Menu £ 20 (weekdays) – Carte £ 34/39
◆ One of the best known eateries on the island, set overlooking the harbour. Huge sliding glass doors and small heated terrace. Good value lunch and early evening menu. Local produce includes fresh island seafood; unfussy cooking displays Mediterranean influences.

### Castle Green
*La Route de la Cote* ⌧ *JE3 6DR* – ℰ *(01534) 840 218*
*– www.castlegreenjersey.co.uk – Closed 25 December, 1 January and Sunday dinner*
**Rest** – Carte £ 22/34
◆ Relaxed, friendly restaurant above Gorey Harbour, with decked terrace and southerly sea panorama. Accessible menu of modern classics, with plenty of Mediterranean dishes and fish specials.

### Bass and Lobster
*Gorey Coast Rd* ⌧ *JE3 6EU* – ℰ *(01534) 859 590* – *www.bassandlobster.com*
*– Closed Monday lunch and Sunday*
**Rest** – Menu £ 13/16 – Carte £ 27/43
◆ Bright, modern 'foodhouse' close to the beach. Seasonal island produce; fresh, tasty seafood and shellfish dominate the menu. Fantastic oysters; good value lunches. Smooth, effective service.

**GREEN ISLAND** – Saint Clement                                    **5** B2

### Green Island
*St Clement* ⌧ *JE2 6LS* – ℰ *(01534) 857 787* – *www.greenisland.je – Closed 23 December-3 January, Sunday dinner and Monday*
**Rest** – Mediterranean – *(booking essential)* Menu £ 19/24 – Carte £ 32/45
◆ Charming, personally run restaurant with terrace and seaside kiosk. Internationally influenced dishes and seafood specials showcase island produce. Flavours are bold and perfectly judged.

**GROUVILLE** – Grouville                                    **5** B2
▶ St Helier 3 mi

### Cafe Poste
*La Rue de la ville ès Renauds* ⌧ *JE3 9FY* – ℰ *(01534) 859 696*
*– www.cafeposte.co.uk – Closed 14 November-1 December, Monday and Tuesday*
**Rest** – Carte £ 22/41
◆ Popular neighbourhood restaurant – formerly a post office – with French country themed interior and cosy fire in winter. Eclectic menus include plenty of well-crafted seafood creations.

**ROZEL BAY** – Saint Martin                                    **5** B2
▶ St Helier 6 mi

### Chateau La Chaire
*Rozel Valley* ⌧ *JE3 6AJ* – ℰ *(01534) 863 354* – *www.chateau-la-chaire.co.uk*
**12 rm** ⌸ – ♦£ 85/130 ♦♦£ 95/255 – 2 suites    **Rest** – Menu £ 15/43
◆ Impressive 19C country house and gardens; drawing room features original plaster ceiling. More contemporary bedrooms blend chic styling with period furniture; Room 2 has a delightful balcony. Conservatory dining room with popular terrace; good use of island ingredients.

## St Aubin – Saint Brelade
5 B2

▶ St Helier 4 mi

🏨 **Somerville** ⬅ 🚗 ⛵ 🖥 AC rest, 🛁 📶 **P** VISA ⓪ AE

*Mont du Boulevard, South : 0.75 mi via harbour* ✉ *JE3 8AD* – ✆ *(01534) 741 226*
*– www.dolanhotels.com*
**56 rm** ⬚ – †£ 56/176 ††£ 99/219
**Rest** *Tides* – Menu £ 16/30 **s** – Carte £ 38/45 **s**
◆ Grand 19C hotel in stunning position above the town, with superb view over
St Aubin Bay. Stylish public areas and bright bedrooms. The dining room features
subtle, contemporary styling; most tables offer a view. Modern menus, with lobster specials in season.

🏨 **Panorama** without rest ⬅ 🚗 🛁 📶 VISA ⓪ AE ①

*La Rue du Crocquet* ✉ *JE3 8BZ* – ✆ *(01534) 742 429*
*– www.panoramajersey.com – Mid-April to October*
**14 rm** ⬚ – †£ 60/120 ††£ 120/160
◆ Charming, personally run and immaculately kept hotel offering stunning bay
and castle views and an extraordinary collection of teapots. Individually decorated
bedrooms and comprehensive breakfasts.

## St Brelade's Bay – Saint Brelade
5 B2

▶ St Helier 6 mi

◉ Fishermen's Chapel (frescoes★)

🏨 **L'Horizon** ⬅ 🖥 ⓦ ♨ 🏋 ❌ 🍴 🛁 🏃 🛁 📶 🐕 **P** VISA ⓪ AE ①

✉ *JE3 8EF* – ✆ *(01534) 743 101 – www.handpickedhotels.co.uk/lhorizon*
**99 rm** ⬚ – †£ 90/175 ††£ 180/290 – 7 suites
**Rest** *Grill* **Rest** *Brasserie* – see restaurant listing
◆ Long-standing hotel located right on the beachfront and boasting stunning
views out over the bay. Luxurious interior with extensive guest areas and subtle
modern styling. Choose a deluxe bedroom, as they come with balconies and sea
views.

🏨 **St Brelade's Bay** ⬅ 🚗 ⛵ ❌ 🍴 🏃 🛁 📶 🛁 **P** VISA ⓪ AE

*La Route de la Baie* ✉ *JE3 8EF* – ✆ *(01534) 746 141*
*– www.stbreladesbayhotel.com*
**80 rm** ⬚ – †£ 88/179 ††£ 206/364 – 5 suites
**Rest** *Bay* – (closed Monday and Tuesday lunch ) Menu £ 17/30 – Carte £ 27/40
◆ Traditional seafront hotel boasting charming gardens filled with tropical plants
and superb panoramic views across the bay. Original parquet floors and ornate
plaster ceilings blend nicely with a modernised lounge and contemporary bedrooms. Formal restaurant offers impressive sea view and a classical menu.

🍴🍴🍴 **Grill** – at L'Horizon Hotel ⬅ AC **P** VISA ⓪ AE ①

✉ *JE3 8EF* – ✆ *(01534) 743 101 – www.handpicked.co.uk/lhorizon – Closed*
*Sunday and Monday*
**Rest** – (dinner only) Menu £ 45
◆ Stylish restaurant with a formal atmosphere, located inside a long-standing ho-
tel which boasts lovely views across the bay. Modern British menu with a focus
on fresh, locally caught seafood.

🍴 **Oyster Box** ⬅ 🍴 AC VISA ⓪ AE ①

*La Route de la Baie* ✉ *JE3 8EF* – ✆ *(01534) 743 311 – www.oysterbox.co.uk*
*– Closed 25-26 December, 1 January and dinner Sunday-Monday October-April*
**Rest** – (booking essential) Carte £ 26/36
◆ Glass-fronted eatery with pleasant heated terrace, set on the promenade and
affording superb views over St Brelade's Bay. Stylish, airy interior hung with sail
cloths and fishermen's floats. Laid-back, friendly service. Accessible seasonal
menu features plenty of fish and shellfish; oysters are a speciality.

🍴 **Brasserie** – at L'Horizon Hotel ⬅ 🍴 AC **P** VISA ⓪ AE ①

✉ *JE3 8EF* – ✆ *(01534) 494 413 – www.handpicked.co.uk/lhorizon*
**Rest** – Menu £ 25/33
◆ Informal brasserie in a well-established beachfront hotel. A delightful terrace
provides the perfect spot when the sun is shining. Extensive, accessible menu offers something for everyone.

ENGLAND

147

## ✗ Crab Shack
⟨icons⟩

*La Route de la Baie* ✉ *JE3 8EF –* ℰ *(01534) 744 611*
*– www.crabshackjersey.co.uk – Closed 25-26 December, 1 January and Monday dinner except bank holidays*
**Rest** *– (booking advisable)* Carte £ 19/26
♦ Scaled down version of next door Oyster Box, superbly sited on the beachfront. Choose a cosy booth or bench outside; relaxed, family friendly atmosphere. Prime island produce features in accessible modern dishes, with seafood a speciality.

## ST HELIER – Saint Helier                                                        5 B2

👁 Jersey Museum★ **AC** Z - Elizabeth Castle (⟨icon⟩★) **AC** Z – Fort Regent (⟨icon⟩★ **AC**) Z
🅖 St Peter's Valley - German Underground Hospital★ **AC**, NW : 4 mi by A 1, A 11
St Peter's Valley rd and C 112

## 🏨 Grand
⟨icons⟩

*The Esplanade* ✉ *JE2 3QA –* ℰ *(01534) 722 301 – www.grandjersey.com*
**117 rm** ⌑ – ♦£ 125/225 ♦♦£ 215/225 – 6 suites                    **Yu**
**Rest** *Tassili* ✿ – see restaurant listing
**Rest** *Victoria's* – *(dinner only)* Menu £ 25 – Carte £ 25/44
♦ Welcoming Victorian hotel with large terrace, overlooking St Aubin's Bay. Stylish, modern interior with chic champagne bar, well-equipped spa and corporate cinema. Contemporary bedrooms in bold colours; some with balconies and sea views. Fine dining in sophisticated Tassili; Mediterranean menu in Victoria's.

## 🏨 Club Hotel & Spa
⟨icons⟩

*Green St* ✉ *JE2 4UH –* ℰ *(01534) 876 500 – www.theclubjersey.com – Closed 24-30 December*                                                         **Ze**
**44 rm** – ♦£ 99/215 ♦♦£ 99/215, ⌑ £ 7.50 – 2 suites
**Rest** *Bohemia* ✿ – see restaurant listing
♦ Well-run, fresh, modern hotel with pleasant poolside terrace. Bedrooms differ considerably but all are sleek and contemporary with good amenities and luxurious bathrooms.

## 🏨 Royal Yacht
⟨icons⟩

*Weighbridge* ✉ *JE2 3NF –* ℰ *(01534) 720 511 – www.theroyalyacht.com*
**109 rm** ⌑ – ♦£ 140 ♦♦£ 230 – 2 suites                             **Zb**
**Rest** *Sirocco* – *(dinner only and Sunday lunch)* Menu £ 25 – Carte £ 39/60
**Rest** *Grill* – *(closed 25 December)* Carte £ 13/29
♦ Set overlooking the harbour, with contemporary interior and splendid spa. The most spacious bedrooms look to the harbour; the quietest over the inner courtyard; suites feature hot tubs. Formal dining in first floor Sirocco, with its enviable view and Mediterranean menu. Nautical style in Grill, with steaks a speciality.

## 🏨 Eulah Country House without rest
⟨icons⟩

*Mont Cochon, Northwest : 2 mi by A 1 on B 27* ✉ *JE2 3JA –* ℰ *(01534) 626 626 – www.eulah.co.uk – Closed 20 December-4 January*
**9 rm** ⌑ – ♦£ 145/185 ♦♦♦£ 170/230
♦ Informally run Edwardian country house proves pleasantly unconventional. Stylish combined lounge and breakfast room, luxurious bedrooms and superb views of St Aubin's Bay.

## ✗✗✗ Bohemia – at Club Hotel & Spa
✿✿
⟨icons⟩

*Green St* ✉ *JE2 4UH –* ℰ *(01534) 880 588 – www.bohemiajersey.com – Closed 24-30 December, Sunday and lunch bank holiday Mondays*                  **Ze**
**Rest** – Menu £ 24/55
**Spec.** Curry salted scallops with coconut dhal, onion bhaji and apple salad. Lamb with minted peas, goat's cheese and honeycomb. Valrhona dark chocolate tart with raspberries and tarragon ice cream.
♦ This stylish restaurant has been extended to include a chef's table. Comfy bar and very attentive serving team. Top quality produce is showcased in cooking that is well-judged and clever, without being gimmicky. Good choice of wines by the glass.

**ENGLAND** *(side tab)*

## ST HELIER

0 — 300 m
0 — 300 yards

**Tassili** – at Grand Hotel   AC VISA oo AE ①

*The Esplanade* ✉ JE4 8WD – ℰ (01534) 722 301 – www.grandjersey.com
*– Closed Sunday and Monday*                                                           Y**u**

**Rest** – *(dinner only) (booking essential)* Carte £ 49/85

**Spec.** Lobster 'Caesar' salad with shellfish linguini. Quail with boudin noir, foie gras and cauliflower cheese. Banana cake with lime jelly, coconut cream and piña colada sorbet.

◆ Small, sophisticated hotel restaurant. Intimate atmosphere with aubergine colour scheme and vibrant artwork. Accomplished, innovative modern cooking uses local island produce in precisely executed, interesting and visually impressive combinations. Proud, knowledgeable service.

149

## St Saviour – Saint Saviour                                          5 B2

▶ St Helier 1 mi

### 🏠🏠🏠 Longueville Manor        🚗 🕭 🍴 ⅃ ✗ 🖂 ⟨⟩ 🅿 💳 ⬤⬤ 🆎 ⓪
*Longueville Rd, on A 3* ✉ *JE2 7WF* – ☎ *(01534) 725 501*
*– www.longuevillemanor.com*
**28 rm** 🍽 – ✝£ 195/315 ✝✝£ 220/460 – 2 suites
**Rest** – Menu £ 25/55 **s**🍴
♦ Exemplary part 13C manor for a special stay; every detail from furnishings to service is considered. Sumptuous rooms, delightful garden, poolside terrace. Panelled restaurant and terrace room overlooking garden; locally-inspired classics with modern twists.

## La Haule – Saint Peter                                          5 B2

### 🏠🏠 La Haule Manor without rest        ← 🚗 ⅃ ✗ ⟨⟩ 🅿 💳 ⬤⬤ 🆎 ⓪
*St Aubin's Bay* ✉ *JE3 8BS* – ☎ *(01534) 741 426* – *www.lahaulemanor.com*
*– March-October*
**16 rm** 🍽 – ✝£ 74/92 ✝✝✝£ 118/172
♦ Attractive, extended Georgian house with fine coastal outlook. Period style sitting room; stylish breakfast room; large basement bar. Airy, well-kept bedrooms with good view.

## La Pulente – Saint Brelade                                          5 B2

▶ St Helier 7 mi
⛳ Les Mielles G. & C.C. St Ouens Bay, ☎ (01534) 48 27 87

### 🏠🏠🏠 Atlantic 🍃        ← 🚗 🕭 ⅃ 🎏 🛏 ℔ ✗ 🖂 ✗ ⟨⟩ 🏊 🅿 💳 ⬤⬤ 🆎 ⓪
❀   *Le Mont de la Pulente, on B 35* ✉ *JE3 8HE* – ☎ *(01534) 744 101*
*– www.theatlantichotel.com – Closed 3 January-2 February*
**49 rm** 🍽 – ✝£ 150/200 ✝✝£ 250/350 – 1 suite
**Rest** *Ocean* – *(booking essential)* Menu £ 25/50
**Spec.** Roasted Jersey fish and shellfish with saffron aioli and lobster cappuccino. Selection of Jersey beef, dauphinoise purée and beef marmite. Nougatine of raspberry, vanilla cream and raspberry sorbet.
♦ Stylish hotel in stunning location with attentive team of personable staff. Public areas have relaxed, intimate feel and bedrooms are cool and fresh; some with patio, others a balcony. Elegant dining room serving delicious, well-crafted dishes, which display a real understanding of flavour. Smooth, professional service.

## SARK – Sark – 503 L33                                          5 A2

🚢 to Guernsey (St Peter Port) (Isle of Sark Shipping Co. Ltd) (summer only) (45 mn)
🚢 to Jersey (St Helier) (Condor Ferries Ltd) (50 mn)
🛈 Sark Tourism Visitor Centre ☎ (01481) 83 23 45, www.sark.info
👁 Island★★ - La Coupée★★★ – Port du Moulin★★ - Creux Harbour★
– La Seigneurie★ **AC** – Pilcher Monument★ – Hog's Back★

### ✗✗ Sablonnerie with rm 🍃        🚗 🕭 💳 ⬤⬤
*Little Sark* ✉ *GY9 0SD* – ☎ *(01481) 832 061* – *www.lasablonnerie.com*
*– mid-April-mid-October*
**20 rm** (dinner included) 🍽 – ✝£ 70/218 ✝✝£ 139/290 – 2 suites
**Rest** – *(booking essential)* Menu £ 30 – Carte £ 25/37
♦ Charming, whitewashed 16C former farmhouse with beautiful gardens. Cosy, beamed interior with a comfortable lounge for aperitifs. Regularly changing, five course menu offers a classic style of cooking using produce from their own farm. Prompt service. Neat, tidy bedrooms; Room 14, in the former stables, is the best.

## CHANNEL TUNNEL – Kent – 504 X30 – see Folkestone

## CHAPEL-EN-LE-FRITH – Derbyshire – **504** O24 – pop. 6 581    **16** A1

▣ London 175 mi – Sheffield 27 mi – Manchester 21 mi – Stoke-on-Trent 34 mi

⌂    **High Croft** without rest    ⪍ ⪕ ⁏⁏ 🄿 𝓥𝓘𝓢𝓐 ⓒⓑ 🄰🄴 ⓘ
*Manchester Rd, West : 0.75 mi on B 5470* ⊠ *SK23 9UH –* ℰ *(01298) 814 843*
*– www.highcroft-guesthouse.co.uk*
**4 rm** ⌣ – ♦£ 65 ♦♦£ 85/105
• Edwardian house with Arts and Crafts features and lovely mature garden. Comfortable bedrooms overlook surrounding hills and valleys; Atholl suite – a four-poster with tub – is best.

## CHARLTON – West Sussex – **504** R31 – see Chichester

## CHARMOUTH – Dorset – **503** L31 – pop. 1 497 – ⊠ Bridport    **3** B3

▣ London 157 mi – Dorchester 22 mi – Exeter 31 mi – Taunton 27 mi

🏠    **White House**    ⪕ ⁏⁏ 🄿 𝓥𝓘𝓢𝓐 ⓒⓑ
*2 Hillside, The Street* ⊠ *DT6 6PJ –* ℰ *(01297) 560 411*
*– www.whitehousehotel.com – Restricted opening in winter*
**6 rm** ⌣ – ♦£ 60/90 ♦♦£ 90/120    **Rest** – *(dinner only)* Menu £ 35
• Gleaming white Regency villa close to the Jurassic Coast, personally run by a friendly couple. Bedrooms feature cast iron/sleigh beds and flat screen TVs. Comfortable sitting room in period style. More modern, wood-furnished dining room; classic menus.

⌂    **Abbots House** without rest    ⪍ ⪕ ⓒ⁏⁏ 🄿 𝓥𝓘𝓢𝓐 ⓒⓑ
*The Street* ⊠ *DT6 6QF –* ℰ *(01297) 560 339 – www.abbotshouse.co.uk – Closed last 2 weeks December and January*
**3 rm** ⌣ – ♦£ 120 ♦♦£ 120
• Dating back to 1480 – originally an annexe of Forde Abbey. Cosy beamed, panelled lounge; conservatory breakfast room overlooks well-tended gardens and a working model railway. Spacious, stylish bedrooms offer homemade treats and a memento.

## CHATHILL – Northumberland – see Alnwick

## CHATTON – Northumberland – **502** O17 – pop. 438    **24** A1

▣ London 336 mi – Sunderland 63 mi – Newcastle upon Tyne 52 mi
 – South Shields 57 mi

⌂    **Chatton Park House** without rest 🝙    ⪍ ⪕ ⁏⁏ 🄿 𝓥𝓘𝓢𝓐 ⓒⓑ
*(East : 5 mi on B 6348 , Wooler Rd.)* ⊠ *NE66 5RA –* ℰ *(01688) 215 507*
*– www.chattonpark.com – Closed 23-26 and 31 December and 1 January*
**3 rm** ⌣ – ♦£ 100/110 ♦♦£ 150/170 – 1 suite
• Fine period house built in the 1750s, set in 4 acres of formal gardens and mature grounds. Smart parquet-floored hallway, huge, open-fired sitting room and airy breakfast room. Spacious bedrooms blend modern décor with original features.

## CHEDDLETON – Staffordshire – **502** N24 – pop. 2 719 – ⊠ Leek    **19** C1

▣ London 125 mi – Birmingham 48 mi – Derby 33 mi – Manchester 42 mi

⌂    **Choir Cottage** without rest    ⪍ ⪕ ⁏⁏ 🄿
🝙   *Ostlers Lane, via Hollow Lane, (opposite Red Lion on A 520)* ⊠ *ST13 7HS*
*–* ℰ *(01538) 360 561 – www.choircottage.co.uk*
**3 rm** ⌣ – ♦£ 65/69 ♦♦£ 79/90
• 17C stone cottage, once owned by the church and let to the needy, with the rent paying for new choir gowns. Smart, modern guest areas. 2 four-poster bedrooms in the old cottage; 1 more contemporary room in a newer building. All boast private outdoor seating.

## CHELMSFORD – Essex – **504** V28 – pop. 99 962    **13** C2

▣ London 33 mi – Cambridge 46 mi – Ipswich 40 mi – Southend-on-Sea 19 mi
🛈 Unit 3, Dukes Walk, Duke St ℰ (01245) 28 34 00, www.chelmsford.gov.uk

ENGLAND

151

## ✗✗ Barda 🛍 AC VISA ⦿⦿

*30-32 Broomfield Rd ⊠ CM1 1SW – ℰ (01245) 357 799*
*– www.barda-restaurant.com – Closed Sunday and Monday*
**Rest** – Menu £ 18 – Carte £ 26/35

♦ Keenly run, contemporary restaurant with a large decked terrace. Simple, flavoursome dishes on offer at lunchtimes; more interesting, international cooking with modern touches at dinner.

**at Boreham** Northeast : 3.5 mi on B 1137 (Springfield Rd)

## 🏨 Lion Inn 🛍 ᔕ rm, AC ⅍ ⦿⦆ P VISA ⦿⦿

*Main Rd ⊠ CM3 3JA – ℰ (01245) 394 900 – www.lioninnhotel.co.uk – Closed 26 December*
**15 rm** � – ♦£ 89 ♦♦£ 150 **Rest** – Carte £ 22/30

♦ Keenly run, extended former pub with eco-friendly credentials and a French feel. Soundproofed bedrooms blend contemporary fabrics with reproduction furniture. Large open-plan lounge/brasserie with buzzy atmosphere; short menu of appealing, pub-style dishes.

---

## CHELTENHAM – Gloucestershire – 503 N28 – pop. 104 968      4 C1

▮ Great Britain

▶ London 99 mi – Birmingham 48 mi – Bristol 40 mi – Gloucester 9 mi

🛈 77 Promenade ℰ (01242) 52 28 78, www.visitcheltenham.com

🏌 Cleeve Hill, ℰ (01242) 67 20 25

🏌 Cotswold Hills Ullenwood, ℰ (01242) 51 52 64

◎ Town★

◎ Sudeley Castle★ (Paintings★) AC, NE : 7 mi by B 4632 A

## 🏨🏨 Ellenborough Park ᔕ    🛏 🍸 🍷 🍽 ☕ 🏊 Ŀ₅ ᔕ ᔕ AC ⦿⦆ ᔕ P

*Southam, Northeast : 2.75 mi on B 4632 ⊠ GL52 3NH*    VISA ⦿⦿
*– ℰ (01242) 545 454 – www.ellenboroughpark.com*    AXa
**62 rm** ⊻ – ♦£ 240 ♦♦£ 850
**Rest** *Beaufort* **Rest** *Tudor Club Brasserie* – see restaurant listing

♦ Part-16C, part-timbered manor house, with stone conversions, an understated, Indian-themed spa and large grounds stretching down to the racecourse. Beautifully furnished guest areas have an elegant, classical style; Nina Campbell designed bedrooms boast superb bathrooms, the latest mod cons and plenty of extras. Excellent levels of service from a smartly attired team.

## 🏨🏨 Hotel du Vin 🛍 ᔕ AC ⦿⦆ P VISA ⦿⦿ AE

*Parabola Rd ⊠ GL50 3AQ – ℰ (01242) 588 450 – www.hotelduvin.com*
**48 rm** – ♦£ 135/190 ♦♦£ 135/190, ⊻ £ 14 – 1 suite    BYc
**Rest** *Bistro* – see restaurant listing

♦ Attractive Regency house in an affluent residential area next to the Ladies College. Shabby-chic styling with leather-furnished bar and comfy lounge. Individually designed, well-equipped, wine-themed bedrooms; some with baths in the room.

## 🏨🏨 Montpellier Chapter ⦿⦿ 🛍 ᔕ rm, AC ⦿⦆ P VISA ⦿⦿ AE

*Bayshill Rd ⊠ GL50 3AS – ℰ (01242) 527 788 – www.chapterhotels.com*
**61 rm** – ♦£ 125 ♦♦£ 440, ⊻ £ 10    BZr
**Rest** – Menu £ 15 (lunch) – Carte £ 25/36

♦ Extended Regency townhouse with retro lounges and large conservatory. Light wood furnished bedrooms come with Nespresso machines, complimentary mini bars and in-room info on an iPod touch. Dine on British dishes at marble-topped tables or on one of two terraces.

## 🏨 Hotel 🛍 AC ⅍ ⦿⦆ P VISA ⦿⦿ AE ⦿

*38 Evesham Rd ⊠ GL52 2AH – ℰ (01242) 518 898 – www.thehoteluk.co.uk*
**12 rm** – ♦£ 155/495 ♦♦£ 155/495, ⊻ £ 19    CYr
**Rest** *Parkers* – see restaurant listing

♦ Stylish, modern hotel displaying bold, contemporary colours and striking furniture. Black marble floored reception, comfortable lounge and smart bar. Bedrooms – named after dukes and dignitaries – boast chic styling, good modern facilities and smart bathrooms.

CHELTENHAM

ENGLAND

153

ENGLAND

### Beaumont House without rest
🛄 📶 P VISA 🆗 AE
56 Shurdington Rd ⊠ GL53 0JE – ℰ (01242) 223 311 – www.bhhotel.co.uk
**16 rm** 🖵 – †£ 79/85 ††£ 170/249
AXu
♦ Keenly run Georgian house with comfy drawing room and bar; breakfast room overlooks lawned garden. Refurbished bedrooms are stylish and contemporary with excellent bathrooms.

### Lypiatt House without rest
🛄 📶 P VISA 🆗 AE
Lypiatt Rd ⊠ GL50 2QW – ℰ (01242) 224 994 – www.staylypiatt.co.uk
**10 rm** 🖵 – †£ 78/95 ††£ 95/130
BZc
♦ A privately owned, serene Victorian house with friendly service. Bedrooms on the top floor with dormer roof tend to be smaller than those on the other floors. Soft, pale colours.

### Butlers without rest
🛄 📶 P VISA 🆗
Western Rd ⊠ GL50 3RN – ℰ (01242) 570 771 – www.butlers-hotel.co.uk
**9 rm** 🖵 – †£ 55/65 ††£ 95/155
BYv
♦ Personally managed hotel where bedrooms constitute a peaceful haven with stylish drapes and canopies. Rooms named after famous butlers; some overlook wooded garden to rear.

### Thirty Two without rest
📶 P VISA 🆗 AE
32 Imperial Sq ⊠ GL50 1QZ – ℰ (01242) 771 110 – www.thirtytwoltd.com
– Closed 25-26 December
BZe
**3 rm** – †£ 155 †††£ 155, 🖵 £ 10 – 1 suite
♦ Immaculate Regency house overlooking grassy city square. Stylish, beautifully appointed bedrooms with furniture designed by owner; superb bathrooms. Excellent facilities and extra touches.

### Hanover House without rest
🛄 📶 P
65 St George's Rd ⊠ GL50 3DU – ℰ (01242) 541 297 – www.hanoverhouse.org
– Closed one week Christmas and Easter
BYu
**3 rm** 🖵 – †£ 70 ††£ 100
♦ Early Victorian townhouse, perfectly located for seeing the city. Comfortable family lounge filled with books and portraits; spacious, tastefully furnished bedrooms. Organic breakfasts.

### Georgian House without rest
📶 P VISA 🆗 AE ①
77 Montpellier Terr ⊠ GL50 1XA – ℰ (01242) 515 577 – www.georgianhouse.net
– Closed 19 December-3 January
BZs
**3 rm** 🖵 – †£ 70/85 ††£ 85/115
♦ Smart, terraced Georgian house, hospitably run, in sought-after Montpellier area. Good-sized bedrooms decorated in authentic period style. Comfy, elegant communal rooms.

### Le Champignon Sauvage (David Everitt-Matthias)
AC VISA 🆗 AE ①
🏵🏵
24-28 Suffolk Rd ⊠ GL50 2AQ – ℰ (01242) 573 449
– www.lechampignonsauvage.com – Closed 3 weeks June, 10 days
Christmas, Sunday and Monday
BZa
**Rest** – Menu £ 32 (lunch and weekday dinner)/60
**Spec.** Dexter beef tartare and corned beef, wasabi cream. Winchcombe venison, salt and burdock baked golden beetroot, roasted quince. Rhubarb poached with hibiscus, mascarpone cream, gin and tonic sorbet.
♦ Firmly established restaurant with professional service from a well-versed team. Confident, accomplished cooking is underscored by a classical base but dishes have personality and are visually impressive. Some ingredients are foraged for by the chef.

### Lumière
AC VISA 🆗 AE
Clarence Par ⊠ GL50 3PA – ℰ (01242) 222 200 – www.lumiere.cc
– Closed 2 weeks January, 2 weeks summer, Tuesday lunch, Sunday and Monday
**Rest** – (booking essential) Menu £ 25/45
BCYz
♦ Elegant, comfortable and personally run restaurant, decorated in chic browns and leather. Cooking is modern, original and inventive, and makes excellent use of local suppliers.

XXX **Beaufort** – at Ellenborough Park Hotel    🛋 🕭 AK P VISA ⓤⓞ AE
*Southam, Northeast : 2.75 mi on B 4632* ✉ *GL52 3NH* – ✆ *(01242) 545 454*
*– www.ellenboroughpark.com – Closed Sunday dinner and Monday lunch*
**Rest** – Menu £ 24/50 **s**      AX**a**
♦ Formal dining room in a part-16C, part-timbered manor house, displaying original stone fireplaces, stained glass windows and dark wood panelling. Classical menu relies on local ingredients.

XX **Daffodil**    AK VISA ⓤⓞ AE ①
*18-20 Suffolk Par* ✉ *GL50 2AE* – ✆ *(01242) 700 055* – *www.thedaffodil.com*
*– Closed 1-14 January, 25 December and Sunday*      BZ**u**
**Rest** – Menu £ 16 (lunch and early dinner) – Carte £ 24/45
♦ Originally a 1920s art deco cinema, now a very pleasant restaurant with its kitchen in the former screen area and a stylish lounge in what was the old balcony. Brasserie-style dishes display worldwide influences. Service is attentive.

XX **Parkers** – at The Hotel    🍴 AK P VISA ⓤⓞ AE ①
*38 Evesham Rd* ✉ *GL52 2AH* – ✆ *(01242) 518 898* – *www.thehoteluk.co.uk*
**Rest** – Menu £ 20/40 – Carte £ 41/57      CY**r**
♦ Smart, stylish restaurant with plain walls, minimalist styling and bright pink, brushed velvet chairs. French-based menus make good use of local produce. Pleasant enclosed rear terrace.

XX **Curry Corner**    🍴 AK VISA ⓤⓞ AE
*133 Fairview Rd* ✉ *GL52 2EX* – ✆ *(01242) 528 449* – *www.thecurrycorner.com*
*– Closed 25 December, lunch Friday and Monday except bank holiday*
**Rest** – Bangladeshi – Menu £ 20 (lunch) – Carte £ 35/51      CY**a**
♦ Long-standing, family run restaurant in smart Regency townhouse. Authentic, flavoursome dishes from across India, Persia and Bangladesh. Imported spices are ground and roasted every morning.

XX **Tudor Club Brasserie** – at Ellenborough Park Hotel    🛋 🕭 AK P
*Southam, Northeast : 2.75 mi on B 4632* ✉ *GL52 3NH*    VISA ⓤⓞ AE
*– ✆ (01242) 545 454 – www.ellenboroughpark.com*      AX**a**
**Rest** – Carte £ 22/37 **s**
♦ Informal brasserie with low timbered ceiling and wood-clad walls, set within a part-16C, part-timbered manor house. Décor incorporates a sports and 'Cresta Run' theme. Classic brasserie dishes.

XX **Bistro** – at Hotel du Vin    AK P VISA ⓤⓞ AE
*Parabola Rd* ✉ *GL50 3AQ* – ✆ *(01242) 588 450* – *www.hotelduvin.com*
**Rest** – Menu £ 18 (lunch) – Carte £ 25/36 🏵      BY**c**
♦ Bistro-style restaurant in an attractive Regency hotel. Eye-catching chandelier made from wine glasses; paved terrace for warmers days. Classical French menu accompanied by a good wine list.

X **Royal Well Tavern**    AK VISA ⓤⓞ AE ①
*5 Royal Well Pl* ✉ *GL50 3DN* – ✆ *(01242) 221 212*
*– www.theroyalwelltavern.com – Closed 25 December and Sunday dinner*
**Rest** – Menu £ 13 (lunch and early dinner) – Carte £ 27/32      BY**e**
♦ Tucked away in side street close to theatre. Bustling contemporary eatery; a fusion of gentleman's club and brasserie. Rustic modern menu of carefully prepared dishes; many in two sizes.

X **Brosh**    VISA ⓤⓞ ①
*8 Suffolk Par  Montpellier* ✉ *GL50 2AB* – ✆ *(01242) 227 277*
*– www.broshrestaurant.co.uk – Closed Christmas and New Year*      BZ**o**
**Rest** – Mediterranean – *(dinner only)* Carte £ 16/37
♦ Keenly run restaurant with atmospheric interior: dimmed lights and flickering candles in the evening make for a great vibe. Eastern Mediterranean and Middle Eastern cooking features mezze.

**ENGLAND**

**at Cleeve Hill** Northeast : 4 mi on B 4632 - AX – ✉ Cheltenham

🏠 **Cleeve Hill** without rest  ≤ 🚗 🕸 🖐 **P** 𝚟𝚒𝚜𝚊 ⊚ 𝔸𝔼

✉ GL52 3PR – ✆ (01242) 672 052 – www.cleevehill-hotel.co.uk

**10 rm** ☕ – 🛏£ 50/98 🛏🛏£ 85/120

♦ Edwardian house in elevated spot; most bedrooms have views across Cleeve Common and the Malvern Hills. Breakfast room is in the conservatory; admire the landscape over coffee.

✗✗ **Malvern View** with rm  ≤ 🚗 🕸 🖐 **P** 𝚟𝚒𝚜𝚊 ⊚ 𝔸𝔼 ⓪

✉ GL52 3PR – ✆ (01242) 672 017 – www.malvernview.com
– Closed 26 December-14 January, Sunday and Monday

**6 rm** ☕ – 🛏£ 55/75 🛏🛏£ 80/130  **Rest** – Carte £ 26/36

♦ Sandstone house with views out across the Malvern countryside towards Cleeve Hill. Concise menu of classically based dishes; hearty, flavoursome cooking. Boutique-style bedrooms boast bold feature walls and modern facilities; Room 1 is the largest. Friendly service.

**at Shurdington** Southwest : 3.75 mi on A 46 - AX – ✉ Cheltenham

🏠🏠🏠 **Greenway** 🐾  🚗 🕭 ⊕ 🕸 🖐 🖐 **P** 𝚟𝚒𝚜𝚊 ⊚ 𝔸𝔼 ⓪

✉ GL51 4UG – ✆ (01242) 862 352 – www.thegreenway.co.uk

**16 rm** ☕ – 🛏£ 125/250 🛏🛏£ 125/420 – 1 suite  **Rest** – Menu £ 26/53

♦ Ivy-clad Elizabethan manor house set in large grounds and peaceful lawned gardens. Spacious, classically styled lounges and drawing rooms. Bedrooms have a typical country house feel. Smart spa facility. Garden and lily pond on view from formal restaurant.

**CHERITON FITZPAINE** – 503 J31 – ✉ Devon  **2** C2

▶ London 182 mi – Cardiff 108 mi – Plymouth 59 mi – Swansea 144 mi

🏠 **Devon Wine School** 🐾  🚗 🕸 ✗ 🖐 **P** 𝚟𝚒𝚜𝚊 ⊚

Redyeates Farm, North : 0.75 mi by Way Rd turning left down unmarked road after Redyeates cross roads. ✉ EX17 4HG – ✆ (01363) 866 742
– www.devonwineschool.co.uk – Closed 2 weeks July

**5 rm** ☕ – 🛏🛏£ 85/100  **Rest** – Menu £ 35

♦ Delightful 17C farmhouse in idyllic rural spot; offering residential wine school run by a Master of Wine. Fresh, modern bedrooms; Saint Amour has its own private terrace and roll-top bath. Set dinner menu served at large table in vaulted barn.

**CHESTER** – Cheshire West and Chester – 502 L24 – pop. 80 624  **20** A3

📗 Great Britain

▶ London 207 mi – Birkenhead 7 mi – Birmingham 91 mi – Liverpool 21 mi

🆑 Vicars Lane ✆ (01244) 40 21 11, www.visitchester.com

⛳ Upton-by-Chester Upton Lane, ✆ (01244) 38 11 83

⛳ Curzon Park, ✆ (01244) 67 77 60

👁 City★★ - The Rows★★ B – Cathedral★ B – City Walls★ B

🅲 Chester Zoo★ **AC**, N : 3 mi by A 5116

Plans on following pages

🏠🏠🏠🏠 **Chester Grosvenor**  ⊕ 🕸 🄻♨ 🔊 🖐 🄰 🕸 🖐 🖐 **P** 𝚟𝚒𝚜𝚊 ⊚ 𝔸𝔼 ⓪

Eastgate ✉ CH1 1LT – ✆ (01244) 324 024 – www.chestergrosvenor.com
– Closed 25-26 December  **B**a

**76 rm** – 🛏£ 230 🛏🛏£ 360, ☕ £ 25 – 4 suites

**Rest Simon Radley at Chester Grosvenor**❀ **Rest Brasserie** – see restaurant listing

♦ 19C hotel with grand black and white timbered façade; set close to the cathedral and historic city centre. Lavish interior displays rich décor, impressive antiques and luxurious bedrooms.

_(map of Chester area)_

## Doubletree by Hilton Chester

Warrington Rd, Northeast : 2 mi on A 56 ⊠ CH2 3PD
– ℰ (01244) 408 800 – www.doubletree-hilton.co.uk/chester  A **s**
**140 rm** – †£ 79/190 ††£ 79/230, � £ 13
**Rest** – Menu £ 20 (dinner) **s** – Carte £ 22/32 **s**
**Rest** *Marco Pierre White Steakhouse Bar & Grill* – Beef specialities –
ℰ (01244) 408 830 *(closed Sunday dinner) (dinner only and Sunday lunch)*
Carte £ 33/52

♦ Smart, stylish hotel offering sleek, spacious bedrooms with super king-sized beds, bright white décor and modern facilities. State-of-the-art conference facilities. Superb spa with well-equipped leisure club. Modern steakhouse set in 18C manor house. Informal brasserie.

## Abode Chester

Grosvenor Rd ⊠ CH1 2DJ – ℰ (01244) 347 000 – www.abodehotels.co.uk
**85 rm** – †£ 99/195 ††£ 99/550, ⊒ £ 14  B **z**
**Rest** *Michael Caines* – see restaurant listing
**Rest** *MC Café Bar & Grill* – Carte £ 19/31

♦ Imposing modern hotel opposite the castle and the racecourse; a short walk into the city. Four categories of bedroom; Enviable and Fabulous are the best. Ask for a room with a racecourse view. Ground floor MC Café Grill & Bar offers a modern brasserie menu.

CHESTER

### Green Bough

🛇 ⁽ᵗ⁾ 🖧 **P** 🅿 VISA ⓒ AE

*60 Hoole Rd, on A 56 ⊠ CH2 3NL – ℰ (01244) 326 241 – www.greenbough.co.uk – Closed 1 January, 25 and 31 December*                At

**12 rm** � – ✝£ 95/125 ✝✝£ 195/245 – 3 suites

**Rest *Olive Tree*** – see restaurant listing

♦ Red-brick Victorian house on the edge of the city. Comfortable, homely lounge with over 50 whiskies behind the bar. Bedrooms vary greatly in their décor, from traditional country house styling to bold contemporary designs – all with a high level of facilities and extra touches. Polite, friendly service.

### Dragonfly without rest

🛇 ⁽ᵗ⁾ VISA ⓒ AE

*94 Watergate St ⊠ CH1 2LF – ℰ (01244) 346 740 – www.hoteldragonfly.com*

**7 rm** – ✝£ 170 ✝✝✝£ 170, ⊒ £ 10                Br

♦ Stylish boutique townhouse. Georgian cornicing and flag/parquet floors blend with contemporary art and chic black breakfast tables. Spacious, modern bedrooms boast iPod docks and huge showers.

### Mitchell's of Chester without rest

🛇 ⁽ᵗ⁾ **P** 🅿 VISA ⓒ AE

*28 Hough Grn, Southwest : 1 mi by A 483 on A 5104 ⊠ CH4 8JQ – ℰ (01244) 679 004 – www.mitchellsofchester.com – Closed 21-29 December*                Av

**7 rm** ⊒ – ✝£ 40/80 ✝✝£ 65/90

♦ Large Victorian house, attractively restored and privately run. Homely breakfast room; lounge comes complete with parrot. Individually decorated bedrooms continue Victoriana feel.

158

**XXXX** **Simon Radley at Chester Grosvenor**  `AC` `P` `VISA` `OO` `AE` `OD`
£3  *Eastgate* ✉ *CH1 1LT* – ✆ *(01244) 324 024 – www.chestergrosvenor.com*
*– Closed January-February, 25-26 December, Sunday and Monday*  **Ba**
**Rest** – *(dinner only)* Menu £ 69 ⚜
**Spec.** Pigeon pie, cep duxelle and velouté of truffles. Noisette butter poached skate, wild garlic and langoustines. Manjari chocolate with pistachio cream, almond milk ice and rose jelly.
♦ Smart restaurant with fabric-covered walls, plush furnishings, stylish cocktail lounge and formal, detailed service. Quality ingredients come together in sophisticated dishes that boast creative, innovative touches. Attractive, modern presentation.

**XX** **Michael Caines** – at Abode Chester Hotel  `⪡` `AC` `⇔` `VISA` `OO` `AE` `OD`
*Grosvenor Rd, (Fifth Floor)* ✉ *CH1 2DJ* – ✆ *(01244) 405 820*
*– www.michaelcaines.com – Closed Sunday*  **Bz**
**Rest** – Menu £ 14 (lunch) – Carte £ 27/47
♦ Fashionable spot for city dining, located on fifth floor of hotel. Menus combine a French base with a modern edge; try the tasting menu to fully appreciate the flavourful, artistic cooking.

**XX** **Brasserie** – at Chester Grosvenor Hotel  `AC` `P` `VISA` `OO` `AE` `OD`
*Eastgate* ✉ *CH1 1LT* – ✆ *(01244) 324 024 – www.chestergrosvenor.com*
*– Closed January- February and 25-26 December*  **Ba**
**Rest** – Carte £ 33/53
♦ Attractive, classically styled Parisian brasserie with hand-painted glass skylight and pleasant buzzy ambience. Menus feature traditional British, French and Mediterranean dishes.

**XX** **Oddfellows** with rm  `(¶)` `VISA` `OO` `AE`
*20 Lower Bridge St* ✉ *CH1 1RS* – ✆ *(01244) 400 001 – www.oddfellows.biz*
**4 rm** – †£ 115/250 ††£ 115/250, � £ 13  **Bc**
**Rest** – Carte £ 24/41 **s**
♦ Quirky, uniquely styled 17C house with impressive façade. Atmospheric restaurant and stylish bar; Bedouin tents in garden. Modern British dishes come with wine recommendations. Well-equipped bedrooms have eccentric, modern style; some boast double roll-top baths.

**XX** **Olive Tree** – at Green Bough Hotel  `P` `VISA` `OO` `AE`
*60 Hoole Rd, on A 56* ✉ *CH2 3NL* – ✆ *(01244) 326 241 – www.greenbough.co.uk*
*– Closed 1 January, 25 and 31 December*  **At**
**Rest** – *(dinner only)* Menu £ 25 – Carte £ 38/45
♦ Stylish, two-roomed fine dining restaurant; it's décor inspired by Italy. Mediterranean-based menus use local, seasonal ingredients. Start with canapés in the lounge or on the rooftop garden.

**X** **Joseph Benjamin**  `VISA` `OO` `AE`
*134-140 Northgate St* ✉ *CH1 2HT* – ✆ *(01244) 344 295*
*– www.josephbenjamin.co.uk – Closed Monday*  **Bu**
**Rest** – *(lunch only and dinner Thursday -Saturday)* *(booking essential)*
Carte £ 24/33
♦ Bistro, deli and cookshop, named after its two passionate owners. Simple, light décor mirrors the style of cooking. Monthly menu of well-judged, satisfying dishes and tasty homemade pastries.

**XX** **Upstairs at the Grill**  `AC` `⇔` `VISA` `OO` `AE`
*70 Watergate St* ✉ *CH1 2LA* – ✆ *(01244) 344 883 – www.upstairsatthegrill.co.uk*
*– Closed 25 December*  **Bn**
**Rest** – Beef specialities – *(dinner only and lunch Friday-Sunday)* Carte £ 22/34
♦ Unique, buzzy restaurant adorned with cow paraphernalia. Prime quality steaks – including rib-eye, sirloin, chateaubriand and rare breeds – come with expert guidance. Clubby cocktail bar.

**ENGLAND**

XX **1539**     ⟨ 🐾 Ⓐ🄲 🄿 𝒗𝒊𝒔𝒂 ⊛ 🄰🄴

*The Racecourse* ⊠ *CH1 2LY – ℰ (01244) 304 611 – www.restaurant1539.co.uk*
*– Closed Sunday dinner*     B**e**
**Rest** – Carte £ 23/33
♦ Stylish and spacious modern brasserie set in a stand of the racecourse, with smartly furnished, decked terraces and panoramic views. Modern British cooking makes use of local produce.

---

# CHESTERFIELD – Derbyshire – 502 P24 – pop. 70 260 ▌ Great Britain   16 B1
▶ London 152 mi – Derby 24 mi – Nottingham 25 mi – Sheffield 12 mi
🔟 Grassmoor North Wingfield Rd, ℰ (01246) 85 60 44
Ⓖ Bolsover Castle★ **AC**, E : 5 mi by A 632

XX **Non Solo Vino**     Ⓐ🄲 𝒗𝒊𝒔𝒂 ⊛ 🄰🄴

*417 Chatsworth Rd, Brampton* ⊠ *S40 3AD – ℰ (01246) 276 760*
*– www.nonsolovino.co.uk – Closed 25 December, 1 January, Sunday dinner and Monday*
**Rest** – Italian – Menu £ 20 (lunch) – Carte £ 25/44 ⌘
♦ Originally a wine shop specialising in Italian wines, now also incorporates a bright, contemporary restaurant. Adventurous, modern cooking features Italian classics with a twist. Unsurprisingly, offers an interesting, well-priced wine list.

---

# CHESTER-LE-STREET – Durham – 502 P19 – pop. 36 049   24 B2
▶ London 275 mi – Durham 7 mi – Newcastle upon Tyne 8 mi
🔟 Lumley Park, ℰ (0191) 388 32 18
🔟 Roseberry Grange Grange Villa, ℰ (0191) 370 06 60

🏰 **Lumley Castle** 🦢     🚗 🕸 🛜 ♨ 🄿 𝒗𝒊𝒔𝒂 ⊛ 🄰🄴 ⓪

*East : 1 mi on B 1284* ⊠ *DH3 4NX – ℰ (0191) 389 11 11*
*– www.lumleycastle.com – Closed 24-27 December*
**73 rm** 🖵 – †£ 69/145 ††£ 115/250 – 1 suite
**Rest** *Black Knight* – *(closed Saturday lunch)* Carte £ 25/46
♦ Norman castle, without additions, underscoring its uniqueness. Rich, gothic interiors of carved wood, chandeliers, statues, tapestries, rugs. Rooms imbued with atmosphere. Restaurant offers classical dishes with an original twist.

---

# CHEW MAGNA – Bath and North East Somerset – 503 M29   4 C2
– pop. 1 187
▶ London 128 mi – Bristol 9 mi – Cardiff 52 mi – Bournemouth 89 mi

🍴 **Pony & Trap** (Josh Eggleton)     🚗 🏠 🄿 𝒗𝒊𝒔𝒂 ⊛
☸ *Knowle Hill, Newtown, South : 1.25 mi on Bishop Stuttard rd* ⊠ *BS40 8TQ*
*– ℰ (01275) 332 627 – www.theponyandtrap.co.uk – Closed Sunday dinner in winter and Monday except bank holidays*
**Rest** – *(booking essential)* Carte £ 19/36
**Spec.** Scallops with hodge podge, parsnip purée and apple salad. Pressed breast of lamb, sweetbreads and sautéed liver with aubergine salad and red wine sauce. Cardamom panna cotta, layered chocolate mousse cake and macerated strawberries.
♦ Cosy whitewashed pub in a tiny hamlet; its oversized dining room windows offering lovely country views. Twice-daily menu of extremely fresh, seasonal produce, including locally sourced, hung and smoked meats and fish. Classical cooking with clean, clear flavours.

🍴 **Bear & Swan**     🏠 🄿 𝒗𝒊𝒔𝒂 ⊛ 🄰🄴

*13 South Par* ⊠ *BS40 8SL – ℰ (01275) 331 100 – www.bearandswan.co.uk*
*– Closed Sunday dinner*
**Rest** – Carte £ 22/35
♦ Well-established village pub with delightful open-fired bar, candlelit dining room and loyal local following. Choice of fresh, homemade British pub classics or more European-influenced dishes.

ENGLAND

▶ London 69 mi – Brighton 31 mi – Portsmouth 18 mi – Southampton 30 mi

🛈 29a South St ℰ (01243) 77 58 88, www.visitchichester.org

🏌 Goodwood Kennel Hill, ℰ (01243) 75 51 33

🏌 Chichester Golf Centre Hunston Village, ℰ (01243) 53 38 33

👁 City★★ – Cathedral★★ BZ **A** – St Mary's Hospital★ BY **D** – Pallant House★ **AC** BZ **M**

🅖 Fishbourne Roman Palace★★ (mosaics★) **AC** AZ **R**. Weald and Downland Open Air Museum★★ **AC**, N : 6 mi by A 286 AY

---

### 🛏 **Ship**                    🛎 🕸 🛜 🏊 **P** *VISA* 🄌 🄰🄴

57 North St ⊠ PO19 1NH – ℰ (01243) 778 000 – www.theshiphotel.net

**36 rm** ⬚ – †£ 88/110 ††£ 110/135                    BY**s**

**Rest** – Menu £ 18 – Carte £ 23/29

♦ Grade II listed building, formerly home to one of Nelson's men. Some Georgian and Regency features remain, including a cantilevered wrought iron staircase. Stylish, contemporary bedrooms. Airy brasserie with modern menu; meat and game from nearby estate.

---

### ✗✗ **Brasserie Blanc**                    🀫 🄰🄲 🕸 *VISA* 🄌 🄰🄴

Richmond House, The Square ⊠ PO19 7SJ – ℰ (01243) 534 200 – www.brasserieblanc.com – Closed 25 December                    BZ**z**

**Rest** – French – Menu £ 14/16 – Carte £ 18/38

♦ Classically styled brasserie with lovely terrace, tucked away in a modern cobbled square. Impressive open-kitchen and display of artisan provisions for sale. Tasty, rustic French cooking.

---

### ✗✗ **Comme ça**                    🀫 🀫 🕸 ⇔ **P** *VISA* 🄌

67 Broyle Rd, on A 286 ⊠ PO19 6BD – ℰ (01243) 788 724 – www.commeca.co.uk – Closed 1 week Christmas-New Year, Sunday dinner and Monday                    AY**c**

**Rest** – French – Menu £ 25/35

♦ Stalwart of the local dining scene for many years. Classical French cooking ministered by Normand chef. Family lunches on Sundays; good value pre-theatre menu. Eat in the airy conservatory.

**ENGLAND**

---

## CHICHESTER

ENGLAND

## ✗ Field and Fork at Pallant House Gallery 🛜 VISA ◑ AE
*9 North Pallant ⊠ PO19 1TJ – ℰ (01243) 770 827 – www.fieldandfork.co.uk – Closed 25 December, Monday and dinner Sunday, Tuesday and Wednesday*
**Rest** – Menu £ 22/25 – Carte £ 20/34                                        BZc
♦ Modern restaurant in striking Queen Anne building, with delightful courtyard and adjoining art gallery. Light dishes at lunch; more formal dinner menu. Fresh, seasonal produce used with care.

### at Mid Lavant North : 2 mi on A286

## ↑ Rooks Hill without rest 🛜 ⅏ P VISA ◑ AE
*Lavant Rd ⊠ PO18 OBQ – ℰ (01243) 528 400 – www.rookshill.co.uk – Closed 26 December-8 January*
**3 rm** ⌂ – †£ 85/135 ††£ 135/175
♦ Charming Grade II listed guesthouse with mix of contemporary styling and original features. Breakfast room opens into lovely terrace/garden. Well appointed bedrooms with attractive bathrooms. Large buffet breakfast.

## 🍴 Earl of March 🛜 P VISA ◑ AE
⊠ PO18 OBQ – ℰ (01243) 533 993 – www.theearlofmarch.com – Closed Sunday dinner
**Rest** – Menu £ 23 (early dinner) **s** – Carte £ 30/39 **s**
♦ 18C inn with perfect blend of country character and contemporary styling. Terrace with amazing views of the South Downs. Good quality, seasonal produce used in classic British dishes.

### at East Lavant North : 2.5 mi off A 286 - AY – ⊠ Chichester

## 🍴 The Royal Oak Inn with rm 🛜 P VISA ◑ AE
*Pook Ln ⊠ PO18 0AX – ℰ (01243) 527 434 – www.royaloakeastlavant.co.uk*
**8 rm** ⌂ – †£ 110/185 ††£ 275/275
**Rest** – *(closed 25 December)* Menu £ 21 (lunch) – Carte £ 25/47
♦ 18C whitewashed inn with rustic, laid-back feel; arrive early for a spot by the fire. Cooking is fairly refined but steaks play an important role. There are interesting vegetarian options, a good cheese selection and plenty of wines by the glass. Spacious bedrooms are comfy and well-equipped; breakfast is a treat.

### at Charlton North : 6.25 mi by A 286 - AY – ⊠ Chichester

## 🍴 Fox Goes Free 🛜 P VISA ◑ AE
⊠ PO18 0HU – ℰ (01243) 811 461 – www.thefoxgoesfree.com
**Rest** – Carte £ 21/32
♦ Charming 17C flint pub with lovely South Downs outlook, pleasant garden and many original features. Dishes range from simple pub classics to more substantial local offerings; some to share.

### at Chilgrove North : 6.5 mi by A 286 on B 2141

## 🍴 Fish House with rm 🛜 ⅏ P VISA ◑
⊠ PO18 9HX – ℰ (01243) 519 444 – www.thefishhouse.co.uk
**15 rm** ⌂ – †£ 85/240 ††£ 150/240
**Rest** – Seafood – Menu £ 22 (lunch) – Carte £ 28/60
♦ Characterful and low beamed, with marble topped bar, oyster counter, fish tanks and stylish dining room. Classical seafood à la carte with international touches. Individually styled bedrooms boast espresso machines, iPod docks and private hot tubs in the garden.

### at Tangmere East : 2 mi by A 27 - AY – ⊠ Chichester

## ✗✗ Cassons 🛜 P VISA ◑ AE
*Arundel Rd, Northwest : 0.25 mi off A 27 (westbound) ⊠ PO18 0DU – ℰ (01243) 773 294 – www.cassonsrestaurant.co.uk – Closed 26-30 December, Tuesday lunch, Sunday dinner and Monday*
**Rest** – Menu £ 20/31 – Carte £ 39/50
♦ Rustic restaurant with linen-laid tables and exposed brick walls. Set price menus offer generous, hearty dishes with bold flavours. Cooking is classically based but employs modern techniques.

**at Sidlesham** South : 5 mi on B 2145 - AZ

⌂ **Landseer House** without rest ♨     📶 🅿 VISA ☺☺
*Cow Ln, South : 1.5 mi by B2145 and Keynor Lane* ✉ *PO20 7LN* – ✆ *(01243)*
*641 525 – www.landseerhouse.co.uk*
**6 rm** 🛏 – ♦£ 80 ♦♦£ 175
♦ Delightful guesthouse with large conservatory and unusual furniture; set in 4½
acres of gardens by a nature reserve and harbour. Two bedrooms in the courtyard. Views to the Isle of Wight.

🍴 **Crab and Lobster** with rm     📶 🅿 VISA ☺☺ AE
*Mill Ln* ✉ *PO20 7NB* – ✆ *(01243) 641 233 – www.crab-lobster.co.uk*
**4 rm** 🛏 – ♦£ 80 ♦♦£ 180
**Rest** – *(booking advisable)* Menu £ 22 (weekday lunch) – Carte £ 28/51
♦ Historic inn, superbly located on a nature reserve, with pretty gardens and a
light, relaxed feel. Seasonal menu focuses on seafood. Very comfortable bedrooms
have a modern, minimalist style; one has its own garden and an open fired stove.

**at Bosham** West : 4 mi by A 259 - AZ – ✉ **Chichester**

🏨 **Millstream**     ♨ & rm, AK rest, ℅ 📶 🅿 VISA ☺☺ AE ⓪
*Bosham Ln* ✉ *PO18 8HL* – ✆ *(01243) 573 234 – www.millstream-hotel.com*
**32 rm** 🛏 – ♦£ 85/129 ♦♦£ 149/169 – 3 suites
**Rest** – Menu £ 25/33 – Carte £ 25/43
♦ Attractive hotel with a pretty garden that backs onto a stream bobbing with
ducks. Cosy bedrooms display individually co-ordinated fabric furnishings, sand-
wash fitted furniture and large windows. Seasonal, daily changing menus.

**at Funtington** Northwest : 4.75 mi by B 2178 - AY - on B 2146 – ✉ **Chichester**

🍴🍴 **Hallidays**     🅿 VISA ☺☺
*Watery Ln* ✉ *PO18 9LF* – ✆ *(01243) 575 331 – www.hallidays.info – Closed 1*
*week spring, 2 weeks summer, Saturday lunch, Sunday dinner, Monday*
*and Tuesday*
**Rest** – Menu £ 21/26 – Carte £ 28/34
♦ A row of part-13C thatched cottages; confident and keen chef delivers a lively
medley of frequently changing menus. Modern meals sit alongside classics; local
produce plays a key role.

---

**CHIDDINGFOLD** – Surrey – **504** S30 – pop. 2 128     **7** C2
▶ London 47 mi – Guildford 10 mi – Haslemere 5 mi

🍴 **Swan Inn** with rm     🏠 AK ℅ 📶 🅿 VISA ☺☺ AE
*Petworth Rd* ✉ *GU8 4TY* – ✆ *(01428) 684 688*
*– www.theswaninnchiddingfold.com*
**10 rm** 🛏 – ♦♦£ 100/125    **Rest** – Carte £ 22/29
♦ Elegant tile-hung pub with 200 year old history and up-to-date interior. Local
Surrey set pop in for crab cakes or the 'terrine of the day' at lunch; à la carte
changes daily, depending on the latest local produce available. Bedrooms are
cool and contemporary.

---

**CHIEVELEY** – West Berkshire – **503** Q29     **10** B3
▶ London 60 mi – Newbury 5 mi – Swindon 25 mi

🍴🍴 **Crab at Chievely** with rm     🏠 ℅ 📶 🅿 VISA ☺☺ AE
*The Square, West : 2.5mi by School Rd on B 4494* ✉ *RG20 8UE* – ✆ *(01635)*
*247 550 – www.chieveley.com*
**13 rm** 🛏 – ♦£ 195 ♦♦£ 195/215
**Rest** – Seafood – Menu £ 20 (lunch) – Carte £ 35/70
♦ Thatched former inn, a characterful venue, located on a country road lined
with wheat fields. Atmospheric restaurant is filled with seafaring memorabilia
and offers a seafood-orientated menu. Highly original bedrooms are themed
around famous hotels.

---

**CHILGROVE** – West Sussex – **504** R31 – see Chichester

**CHILLATON** – Devon – **503** H32 – see Tavistock

*ENGLAND*

## CHILLINGTON – Devon – 503 I33       2 C3

▶ London 217 mi – Plymouth 26 mi – Torbay 20 mi – Torquay 22 mi

🏠 **whitehouse**      🚗 🏡 📶 **P** VISA ⚈

✉ TQ7 2JX – 🖅 (01548) 580 505 – www.whitehousedevon.com – Closed 3-31 January
**6 rm** 🍽 – ♦£ 160/180 ♦♦£ 180/250
**Rest** – (booking advisable for non residents) Carte £ 25/38
♦ Sizeable Georgian house with modern furnishings, relaxed atmosphere and beautiful gardens. Sumptuous, well appointed bedrooms, with large baths and handmade toiletries. Lovely dining room with casual, airy feel and appealing menu.

## CHINNOR – Oxfordshire – 504 R28 – pop. 5 407 ▌Great Britain      11 C2

▶ London 45 mi – Oxford 19 mi

◪ Ridgeway Path★★

### at Sprigg's Alley Southeast : 2.5 mi by Bledlow Ridge rd – ✉ Chinnor

🍴 **Sir Charles Napier**      🚗 🏡 **P** VISA ⚈ AE

❀ ✉ OX39 4BX – 🖅 (01494) 483 011 – www.sircharlesnapier.co.uk – Closed 24-26 December, Sunday dinner and Monday except bank holidays
**Rest** – (booking advisable) Menu £ 25 (weekdays) – Carte £ 35/51⅛
**Spec.** Scallops with salt cod brandade, sweet and sour lentils. Duck breast and pithivier with carrot purée, rhubarb and ginger. Vanilla yoghurt, citrus jelly and honeycomb.
♦ Attractive flint pub in a small hillside hamlet, with a hint of eccentricity in its decoration. Pleasant terrace and delightful gardens for summer; log fires and candlelight in winter. Polished and boldly flavoured French based dishes are prepared with obvious skill. Gem of a wine list.

## CHIPPENHAM – Wiltshire – 503 N29 – pop. 33 189      4 C2

▶ London 106 mi – Bristol 27 mi – Southampton 64 mi – Swindon 21 mi

🛈 Market Place 🖅 (01249) 66 59 70, www.visitwiltshire.co.uk

◪ Monkton Park (Par Three), 🖅 (01249) 65 39 28

◉ Yelde Hall★

◪ Corsham Court★★ **AC**, SW : 4 mi by A 4 – Sheldon Manor★ **AC**, W : 1.5 mi by A 420 – Biddestone★, W : 3.5 mi – Bowood House★ **AC** (Library ≼★) SE : 5 mi by A 4 and A 342. Castle Combe★★, NW : 6 mi by A 420 and B 4039

### at Stanton St Quintin North : 5 mi by A 429 – ✉ Chippenham

🏨 **Stanton Manor** ⌂      🚗 🕭 🏡 📶 🕭 **P** VISA ⚈

✉ SN14 6DQ – 🖅 (01666) 837 552 – www.stantonmanor.co.uk
**23 rm** 🍽 – ♦£ 180 ♦♦£ 180    **Rest** – Menu £ 20/28
♦ Extended 19C manor in formal gardens; popular as a wedding venue. Appealing range of bedrooms, geared to corporate market; the deluxe rooms considerably better than the standards. Elegant restaurant uses produce from the garden.

## CHIPPING CAMPDEN – Gloucestershire – 503 O27 – pop. 1 943      4 D1
▌Great Britain

▶ London 93 mi – Cheltenham 21 mi – Oxford 37 mi – Stratford-upon-Avon 12 mi

🛈 Old Police Station 🖅 (01386) 84 12 06, www.chippingcampdenonline.org

◉ Town★

◪ Hidcote Manor Garden★★ **AC**, NE : 2.5 m

🏨 **Cotswold House H. and Spa**      🚗 🏡 📺 ⚈ 🅰 ⌀ 🕭 **P** VISA ⚈ AE

The Square ✉ GL55 6AN – 🖅 (01386) 840 330 – www.cotswoldhouse.com
**25 rm** 🍽 – ♦£ 500 ♦♦£ 500 – 3 suites
**Rest** *Hicks'* – see restaurant listing
**Rest** *Juliana's* – (closed Sunday-Wednesday) (dinner only) Menu £ 50
♦ Enviably stylish Regency townhouse with graceful spiral staircase winding upwards to luxurious rooms, some very modern, boasting every mod con imaginable. Chic spa and impressive service. Formal though stylish Juliana's for accomplished cooking with an original style.

**Kings** 　　　　　　　　　　　　　　　☞ ☜ ⑪ **P** *VISA* ◉◉ **AE**

*The Square* ✉ *GL55 6AW* – ℰ *(01386) 840 256* – *www.kingscampden.co.uk*

**19 rm** ⌂ – **†**£ 97/115 **††**£ 145/175

**Rest** *Kings* – see restaurant listing

◆ Beautiful Cotswold stone townhouse with stylish, boutique interior. Bedrooms in the main house mix antiques with modern facilities and some boast sleigh beds; rooms in the cottage at the end of the garden are more contemporary.

**Seymour House** without rest 　　　　　　　☞ ☜ **P** *VISA* ◉◉

*High St* ✉ *GL55 6AG* – ℰ *(01386) 840 064* – *www.seymourhousebandb.co.uk* – *Closed Christmas-New Year*

**4 rm** ⌂ – **†**£ 90 **††**£ 120/140

◆ Welcoming Cotswold stone house with early 18C origins. Spacious hall, homely lounge and good-sized bedrooms with modern facilities – 3 are in the eaves. Lovely garden and breakfast terrace.

**Staddlestones** without rest 　　　　　　　　　☞ ⑪ **P**

*7 Aston Rd, North : 0.5 mi by B 4081 on B 4035* ✉ *GL55 6HR* – ℰ *(01386) 849 288* – *www.staddle-stones.com*

**3 rm** ⌂ – **†**£ 65 **††**£ 85

◆ Attractive sandstone war veteran's cottage. Individually decorated bedrooms with high level of facilities; large annexed suite boasts comfy lounge and country views. Afternoon tea on arrival.

**Kings** – at Kings Hotel 　　　　　　☞ ☗ ✿ **P** *VISA* ◉◉ **AE**

*The Square* ✉ *GL55 6AW* – ℰ *(01386) 840 256* – *www.kingscampden.co.uk*

**Rest** – Menu £ 30 – Carte £ 18/29

◆ Appealing restaurant in a stylish boutique townhouse. Rustic interior boasts exposed stone walls, wooden beams and a large inglenook fireplace. Modern British menus use top quality ingredients and dishes are refined and flavoursome.

**Hicks'** – at Cotswold House H. and Spa 　　　　☞ ☗ **AC P** *VISA* ◉◉ **AE**

*The Square* ✉ *GL55 6AN* – ℰ *(01386) 840 330* – *www.cotswoldhouse.com*

**Rest** – *(booking essential)* Carte £ 19/50

◆ Named after a local benefactor. Open all day serving locals and residents from a varied modern menu. Morning coffees, afternoon teas and homemade cake available. Booking essential.

**Eight Bells Inn** with rm 　　　　　　　　☗ ⑪ **P** *VISA* ◉◉

*Church St* ✉ *GL55 6JG* – ℰ *(01386) 840 371* – *www.eightbellsinn.co.uk* – *Closed 25 December*

**7 rm** ⌂ – **†**£ 60/95 **††**£ 125　**Rest** – Carte £ 23/34

◆ 14C pub close to the historic high street in an old wool merchant's town. Cooking is traditionally British – pies are the real thing, puddings are comforting and specials are just that, so arrive early. Bedrooms combine plenty of character with good mod cons.

**at Mickleton** North : 3.25 mi by B 4035 and B 4081 on B 4632 – ✉ Chipping Campden

**Three Ways House** 　　　☞ 🕅 ⅙ rm, **AC** ⑪ ⚲ **P** *VISA* ◉◉ **AE** ⓪

✉ *GL55 6SB* – ℰ *(01386) 438 429* – *www.threewayshousehotel.com*

**48 rm** ⌂ – **†**£ 85/125 **††**£ 145/240

**Rest** – *(bar lunch Monday-Saturday)* Menu £ 37

◆ Built in 1870 and renowned as the home of the Pudding Club. Two types of bedroom, split between the original house and modern block; all are very comfy and modern – opt for one of the pudding-themed rooms. Informal bar-cum-brasserie boasts antique tiled floor. Formal arcaded dining room offers weekly menu.

**Nineveh Farm** without rest 　　　　　　　☞ ☜ **P** *VISA* ◉◉

*Southwest : 0.75 mi by B 4632 on B 4081* ✉ *GL55 6PS* – ℰ *(01386) 438 923* – *www.stayinthecotswolds.co.uk*

**6 rm** ⌂ – **†**£ 65/85 **††**£ 75/95

◆ Georgian farmhouse in pleasant garden. Warm welcome; local information in residents' lounge. Comfortable rooms with view in main house or with French windows in garden house.

ENGLAND

**at Ebrington** East : 2 mi by B 4035

🍴 **Ebrington Arms** with rm                    ◫ 🛆 ⚒ ⒫ P VISA ⊙⊚
   ⊠ GL55 6NH – ℰ (01386) 593 223 – www.theebringtonarms.co.uk
**3 rm** 😑 – 🛏£ 95/105 🛏🛏£ 110/120   **Rest** – Carte – £ 21/31
   ◆ Proper village local with beamed, flag-floored bar at its hub, set in charming
chocolate box village. Robust, traditional dishes use local ingredients and up-to-
date techniques. Bedrooms have country views; Room 3, with four-poster bed
and luxury bathroom, is best.

**at Paxford** Southeast : 3 mi by B 4035 – ⊠ Chipping Campden

🍴 **Churchill Arms** with rm                    🛆 ⚒ ⒫ VISA ⊙⊚
   ⊠ GL55 6XH – ℰ (01386) 594 000 – www.thechurchillarms.com – Closed 25
December
**4 rm** 😑 – 🛏£ 60/75 🛏🛏£ 80/95   **Rest** – (bookings not accepted) Carte £ 20/36
   ◆ Traditional stone inn set in a lovely location, boasting homely, rustic interior
and great views. Cooking displays a real mix of influences, from pub classics to
more restaurant-style dishes. Cosy bedrooms with good outlooks – can be noisy
before closing time.

**at Broad Campden** South : 1.25 mi by B 4081 – ⊠ Chipping Campden

🏠 **Malt House** without rest ✎                  ◫ ⚒ ⒫ P VISA ⊙⊚
   ⊠ GL55 6UU – ℰ (01386) 840 295 – www.malt-house.co.uk – Closed
Christmas-New Year
**7 rm** 😑 – 🛏£ 95 🛏🛏£ 165
   ◆ For a rare experience of the countryside idyll, this 16C malting house is a must.
Cut flowers from the gardens on view in bedrooms decked out in fabrics to de-
light the eye.

**at Weston Subedge** Northwest : 3 mi by B 4081, B 4035 on B 4632

🍴 **Seagrave Arms** with rm                    🛆 ⚒ ⒫ P VISA ⊙⊚ AE
   Friday St ⊠ GL55 6QH – ℰ (01386) 840 192 – www.seagravearms.co.uk – Closed
first week January and Monday
**6 rm** 😑 – 🛏£ 95/115 🛏🛏£ 95/115   **Rest** – Carte £ 26/32
   ◆ Part Georgian coach house that's been attractively refurbished. Compact but
cosy, with open-fired bar, wood-furnished dining rooms and polite, formal service.
Concise menu of ambitious, complex, restaurant-style dishes. Stylish, modern
bedrooms are well-equipped.

---

**CHIPPING NORTON** – Oxfordshire – **503** P28 – pop. 5 688                    **10** A1
▶ London 77 mi – Oxford 22 mi – Stow-on-the-Wold 9 mi

🍴 **Wild Thyme**                                                VISA ⊙⊚
   10 New St ⊠ OX7 5LJ – ℰ (01608) 645 060 – www.wildthymerestaurant.co.uk
   – Closed 2 weeks January, 1 week Spring, Sunday and Monday
**Rest** – (booking advisable) Carte £ 25/39
   ◆ Friendly little restaurant off the high street with rustic scrubbed tables and tiny
courtyard garden. Wholesome regional British cooking with Mediterranean influences; tasty homemade breads.

🍴 **Masons Arms**                                          ◫ 🛆 ⒫ P VISA ⊙⊚
   Banbury Rd, Swerford, Northeast : 5 mi on A 361 ⊠ OX7 4AP – ℰ (01608)
683 212 – www.masons-arms.com – Closed Sunday dinner
**Rest** – Menu £ 15 (lunch) – Carte £ 20/30
   ◆ Stone-built inn with vast garden and pleasant countryside views. Good value
menus display an eclectic mix of straightforward dishes, ranging from the traditional to the more exotic. All produce is traceable, meats are rare breed and
breads/desserts are homemade.

---

**CHORLEY** – Lancashire – **502** M23 – pop. 33 424                    **20** A2
▶ London 222 – Blackpool 30 – Liverpool 33 – Manchester 26
🏌 Duxbury Park Duxbury Hall Rd, ℰ (01257) 26 53 80
🏌 Shaw Hill Hotel G. & C.C. Whittle-le-Woods Preston Rd, ℰ (01257) 26 92 21

XX **Red Cat**　　　　　　　　　　　　　　　　　　P VISA ☺ AE ⑩
*Blackburn Rd, Whittle-Le-Woods, Northeast : 2.5 mi  on A 674* ✉ *PR6 8LL*
*–* ☎ *(01257) 263 966 – www.theredcat.co.uk*
**Rest** – Menu £ 22 (lunch) – Carte £ 29/45
♦ Restored pub with original beams, stone walls and brick fireplaces. Unfussy,
modern dishes display good ingredients and sound cooking in well presented,
classic combinations.

---

**CHORLTON-CUM-HARDY** – Greater Manchester – **502** N23 – **see Manchester**

---

**CHRISTCHURCH** – Dorset – **503** O31 – **pop. 40 208**　　　　　**4** D3
▶ London 111 mi – Bournemouth 6 mi – Salisbury 26 mi – Southampton 24 mi
🛈 49 High St ☎ (01202) 47 17 80, www.visitchristchurch.info
🏞 Highcliffe Castle Highcliffe-on-Sea 107 Lyminqton Rd, ☎ (01425) 27 29 53
🖼 Riverside Ave, ☎ (01202) 43 64 36
👁 Town ★ - Priory ★
🗺 Hengistbury Head ★ (≤★★) SW : 4.5 mi by A 35 and B 3059

🏠 **Christchurch Harbour**　≤ 🛥 🏠 ☒ ☺ 🏠 £ᵩ 🍴 ☒ rm, AK rm, ☆ ⑩
*95 Mudeford, East : 2 mi* ✉ *BH23 3NT*　　　　　　🏔 P VISA ☺ AE ⑩
*–* ☎ *(01202) 483 434 – www.christchurch-harbour-hotel.co.uk*
**64 rm** 🛏 – ♦£ 120/190 ♦♦£ 130/290
**Rest** *Jetty* – see restaurant listing
**Rest** – Menu £ 18 (lunch) – Carte £ 28/37
♦ Busy hotel in a great spot, with pleasant drinks terrace and chic spa. Contemporary styling and plush bedrooms; choose between 'Inland' or 'Harbour'; the latter boasting either a balcony or terrace. Restaurant offers classically based cuisine.

🏠 **Captain's Club**　≤ ☺ 🏠 ☒ ☒ AK ⑩ 🏔 P VISA ☺ AE
*Wick Ferry, Wick Ln* ✉ *BH23 1HU –* ☎ *(01202) 475 111*
*– www.captainsclubhotel.com*
**17 rm** – ♦£ 169 ♦♦£ 199, 🛏 £ 16 – 12 suites
**Rest** *Tides* – see restaurant listing
♦ Eye-catching hotel displaying striking art deco and nautical influences. Floor to
ceiling windows throughout; attractive river views. Sleek, unfussy bedrooms and
suites. Stylish spa.

🏠 **Kings**　　　　　　　　　　🖻 ☒ rm, AK rest, ☆ 🕻 VISA ☺ AE
*18 Castle St* ✉ *BH23 1DT –* ☎ *(01202) 588 933*
*– www.thekings-christchurch.co.uk*
**20 rm** (dinner included) 🛏 – ♦£ 105/155 ♦♦£ 115/165
**Rest** *Jacks* – Menu £ 16 (lunch) – Carte £ 21/35
♦ Lovingly restored late 17C former coaching inn, in the heart of the town, overlooking the priory, ruins and bowling green. Pretty, boutique style and well-appointed, contemporary bedrooms. Appealing ground floor bar and brasserie.

🏠 **Druid House** without rest　　　　🛥 ☆ ⑩ P VISA ☺ AE
*26 Sopers Ln* ✉ *BH23 1JE –* ☎ *(01202) 485 615 – www.druid-house.co.uk*
**9 rm** 🛏 – ♦£ 40/80 ♦♦£ 70/110
♦ Bright, fresh inner in contrast to its exterior. Modern, slightly kitsch breakfast
room; light, airy conservatory sitting room and smart bar. Spacious bedrooms,
two with balconies.

XXX **Jetty** – at Christchurch Harbour Hotel　　　≤ 🏠 P VISA ☺ AE ⑩
*95 Mudeford, East : 2 mi* ✉ *BH23 3NT –* ☎ *(01202) 483 434*
*– www.christchurch-harbour-hotel.co.uk*
**Rest** – Menu £ 22 (lunch) – Carte £ 28/53
♦ Contemporary, eco-friendly restaurant in a fantastic waterside setting. Local,
seasonal produce includes crabs from just over the bay. Tasty specials are cooked
on the josper charcoal grill.

**ENGLAND**

XXX **Tides** – at Captain's Club Hotel  ⩿ 🕭 🔟 **P** 🆅🆂🅰 ⓾ 🅰🅴
*Wick Ferry, Wick Ln* ⊠ *BH23 1HU –* ℰ *(01202) 475 111*
*– www.captainsclubhotel.com*
**Rest** – Menu £ 19/26 – Carte £ 22/44
♦ Stylish restaurant with water feature wall, oversized windows and river views.
Modern, well judged cooking offers a wide choice, good combinations and some
unusual formats.

XX **Splinters**  ⇳ 🆅🆂🅰 ⓾ 🅰🅴
*12 Church St* ⊠ *BH23 1BW –* ℰ *(01202) 483 454 – www.splinters.uk.com*
*– Closed 1-10 January, Sunday and Monday*
**Rest** – Menu £ 17/27 – Carte £ 27/39
♦ Family-run restaurant in cobbled street with bar, lounge and several cosy, characterful rooms; one with intimate booths. Unfussy, classical cooking uses good ingredients. Interesting wine list.

---

**CHURCH ENSTONE** – Oxfordshire – ⊠ **Chipping Norton**　　**10** B1
▶ London 72 mi – Banbury 13 mi – Oxford 38 mi

🍴 **Crown Inn**  🕭 **P** 🆅🆂🅰 ⓾
*Mill Ln* ⊠ *OX7 4NN –* ℰ *(01608) 677 262 – Closed 25-26 December, 1 January*
*and Sunday dinner*
**Rest** – Carte £ 19/29
♦ 17C inn set among pretty stone houses in a picturesque village. Meat, fruit and
veg come from local farms and seafood is a speciality. Lunch offers pub favourites; tasty puddings are homemade.

---

**CHURCH STRETTON** – Shropshire – **502** L26 – pop. 3 841　　**18** B2
▌ Great Britain
▶ London 166 mi – Birmingham 46 mi – Hereford 39 mi – Shrewsbury 14 mi
🔟 Trevor Hill, ℰ (01694) 72 22 81
◎ Wenlock Edge★, E : by B 4371

XX **Studio**  🕭 🕭 🆅🆂🅰 ⓾
⊠ *SY6 6BY –* ℰ *(01694) 722 672 – www.thestudiorestaurant.net*
*– Closed 3 weeks January, 1 week spring, 1 week autumn, Christmas-New Year*
*and Sunday-Tuesday*
**Rest** – (dinner only) Menu £ 29
♦ Personally run former art studio; walls enhanced by local artwork. Pleasant
rear terrace for sunny lunches. Tried-and-tested dishes: much care taken over lo-
cal produce.

---

**CIRENCESTER** – Gloucestershire – **503** O28 – pop. 15 861　　**4** D1
▌ Great Britain
▶ London 97 mi – Bristol 37 mi – Gloucester 19 mi – Oxford 37 mi
ℹ Corinium Museum Park Street ℰ (01285) 65 41 80, www.cirencester.gov.uk
🔟 Bagendon Cheltenham Rd, ℰ (01285) 65 24 65
◉ Town★ – Church of St John the Baptist★ – Corinium Museum★ (Mosaic
pavements★) **AC**
◎ Fairford : Church of St Mary★ (stained glass windows★★) E : 7 mi by A 417

🏠 **No 12** without rest  🕭 🕸 📶 🆅🆂🅰 ⓾
*12 Park St* ⊠ *GL7 2BW –* ℰ *(01285) 640 232 – www.no12cirencester.co.uk*
**4 rm** 🖵 – ♦£ 70 ♦♦£ 95/110
♦ 16C property with Georgian façade, in the centre of a historic Roman town. Delightful rear walled garden. Excellent organic breakfast. Stylish rooms charmingly
blend old and new.

🏠 **Old Brewhouse** without rest  ♿ 🕸 📶 **P** 🆅🆂🅰 ⓾ 🅰🅴
*7 London Rd* ⊠ *GL7 2PU –* ℰ *(01285) 656 099 – www.theoldbrewhouse.com*
**10 rm** 🖵 – ♦£ 56 ♦♦£ 68
♦ 17C former brewhouse in busy central spot, with characterful cluttered interior.
Cottage-style bedrooms – most with wrought iron beds – or more modern rooms
in the extension, set around a small courtyard. Two stone-faced breakfast rooms.

X **Made by Bob**  VISA ⓒⓞ AE
*Unit 6, The Corn Hall, 26 Market Pl ⊠ GL7 2NY – 𝒞 (01285) 641 818
– www.foodmadebybob.com – Closed 25-26 December, 1 January and Sunday*
**Rest** *– (lunch only and dinner Thursday-Friday)* Carte £ 27/37
♦ Large deli crammed with produce and an informal eatery boasting an open kitchen. Everything is homemade or locally sourced, from tasty breakfasts and light lunches to more structured dinners.

**at Barnsley** Northeast : 4 mi by A 429 on B 4425 – ⊠ Cirencester

🏠 **Barnsley House** 🍃  ← 🚗 🏠 ⑩ 🏠 🏖 🏖 📶 🐾 P VISA ⓒⓞ AE ①
⊠ GL7 5EE – 𝒞 (01285) 740 000 – www.barnsleyhouse.com
**11 rm** ⌸ – †£ 247 ††£ 265/495 – 7 suites
**Rest** – Menu £ 24 (lunch) – Carte £ 29/47
♦ Impressive 17C Cotswold manor house. Contemporary interior, with hi-tech bedrooms; largest and most modern in annexed courtyard. Well-kept gardens, hydrotherapy pool, cinema. Dining room has pleasant outlook. Modern, interesting menus.

🍽 **Village Pub** with rm  🏠 🏖 P VISA ⓒⓞ AE
⊠ GL7 5EF – 𝒞 (01285) 740 421 – www.thevillagepub.co.uk
**6 rm** ⌸ – †£ 95/150 ††£ 95/150  **Rest** – Carte £ 24/31
♦ Stylish pub with open fires and cosy feel. Appealing, daily changing menu of modern British dishes, with irresistible nibbles, locally sourced meats, charcuterie from Highgrove and comforting desserts. Individually decorated bedrooms; Six has a four-poster.

**at Sapperton** West : 5 mi by A 419 – ⊠ Cirencester

🍽 **Bell**  🚗 🏠 ⇆ P VISA ⓒⓞ
⊠ GL7 6LE – 𝒞 (01285) 760 298 – www.foodatthebell.co.uk – Closed 25 December and Sunday dinner November-March
**Rest** – Carte £ 24/35 🏖
♦ Charming pub in a pretty village. Wide-ranging, daily changing menu and seafood specials take on a refined yet rustic style, relying on local and regional produce. Interesting wine list.

---

**CLANFIELD** – Oxfordshire – **503** P28 – **pop. 1 709**  **10** A2
▶ London 75 mi – Oxford 24 mi – Swindon 16 mi

🏠 **Cotswold Plough**  🚗 🐾 📶 P VISA ⓒⓞ AE
*Bourton Rd, (on A 4095) ⊠ OX18 2RB – 𝒞 (01367) 810 222
– www.cotswoldploughhotel.com – Closed 24-28 December*
**11 rm** ⌸ – †£ 89 ††£ 175
**Rest** *Restaurant* – see restaurant listing
♦ Charming hotel with delightful stone façade, located in the heart of a pretty village. Serene lounge with period fireplace. Comfortable, characterful bedrooms with a modern touch.

XX **Restaurant** – at Cotswold Plough Hotel  🚗 🏠 P VISA ⓒⓞ AE
*Bourton Rd, (on A 4095) ⊠ OX18 2RB – 𝒞 (01367) 810 222
– www.cotswoldploughhotel.com – Closed 24-28 December*
**Rest** – Menu £ 13 (lunch) – Carte £ 22/31
♦ Accomplished modern cooking; strong on fish and game. Dining over several rooms at polished tables; pre and post-prandial drinks by the fire. Friendly, informal service.

---

**CLAVERING** – Essex – **504** U28 – **pop. 1 663** – ⊠ Saffron Walden  **12** B2
▶ London 44 mi – Cambridge 25 mi – Colchester 44 mi – Luton 29 mi

🍽 **Cricketers** with rm  🚗 🏠 🐾 rm, 🏖 📶 P VISA ⓒⓞ AE
⊠ CB11 4QT – 𝒞 (01799) 550 442 – www.thecricketers.co.uk – Closed 25-26 December
**14 rm** ⌸ – †£ 68 ††£ 95/115  **Rest** – Carte £ 24/34
♦ Attractive whitewashed pub exuding old-world charm. Straightforward cooking is precise and flavoursome. Local produce is key – all veg comes from their son Jamie Oliver's garden. Simple modern bedrooms in courtyard, more traditional rooms in the pavilion.

## CLEARWELL – Gloucestershire                                    4 C1

▶ London 138 mi – Birmingham 85 mi – Bristol 31 mi – Cardiff 46 mi

### Tudor Farmhouse

*High St* ✉ *GL16 8JS –* ✆ *(01594) 833 046 – www.tudorfarmhousehotel.co.uk – Closed 24-27 December*
**20 rm** ☑ – †£ 85/95 ††£ 100/175
**Rest** – Menu £ 34 (dinner) – Carte lunch £ 18/32
♦ Converted farm buildings in the heart of the Forest of Dean. Character bedrooms in original farmhouse feature beams, uneven floors and antique furniture. More modern bedrooms in two outbuildings. Restaurant offers classic, French-influenced dishes with a twist.

---

## CLEEVE HILL – Gloucestershire – 503 N28 – see Cheltenham

---

## CLENT – Worcestershire – 504 N26 ▮ Great Britain           19 C2

▶ London 127 mi – Birmingham 12 mi – Hagley 2 mi

◪ Black Country Museum★, N : 7 mi by A 491 and A 4036 – Birmingham★ - Museum and Art Gallery★★, Aston Hall★★, NE : 10 mi by A 491 and A 456

### Bell & Cross

*Holy Cross, West : 0.5 mi off A 491 (northbound carriageway) (Bromsgrove rd)*
✉ *DY9 9QL –* ✆ *(01562) 730 319 – www.bellandcrossclent.co.uk – Closed 25 December and dinner 26, 31 December, 1 January and Sunday*
**Rest** – Menu £ 17 (weekdays) – Carte £ 21/31
♦ Charming pub down a maze of lanes, with colourful window boxes and country views. Light bites and pub classics at lunch; more ambitious dishes at dinner. Influences range from Asia to the Med.

---

## CLEY-NEXT-THE-SEA – Norfolk – 504 X25 – see Blakeney

---

## CLIFTON – Cumbria – 502 L20 – see Penrith

---

## CLIPSHAM – Rutland                                          17 C2

▶ London 101 mi – Leicester 35 mi – Coventry 72 mi – Nottingham 38 mi

### The Olive Branch & Beech House (Sean Hope) with rm

*Main St* ✉ *LE15 7SH –* ✆ *(01780) 410 355 – www.theolivebranchpub.com*
**6 rm** ☑ – †£ 98/118 ††£ 175/205
**Rest** – (booking essential) Menu £ 21/28 – Carte £ 25/41
**Spec.** Warm salad of honey and mustard chicken, olives and lemon. Whole baked sea bass, chickpea and chorizo caponata. Sticky toffee pudding, vanilla ice cream.
♦ Characterful, rustic pub with charming garden, which really captures the heart of the local community. Well-prepared, classically based dishes are flavoursome and robust, and display plenty of respect for fresh, local ingredients. Stylish bedrooms include a host of extras and the homemade breakfasts are a delight.

---

## CLITHEROE – Lancashire – 502 M22 – pop. 14 697            20 B2

▶ London 64 mi – Blackpool 35 mi – Manchester 31 mi

𝒊 Church Walk ✆ (01200) 42 55 66, www.visitlancashire.com

▦ Whalley Rd, ✆ (01200) 42 26 18

### Heathcotes Grill & Bar

*Ethos House, York St.* ✉ *BB7 2DL –* ✆ *(01200) 452 440 – www.heathcotesgrillandbar.co.uk – Closed Sunday and Monday*
**Rest** – Menu £ 14 (lunch and early dinner) – Carte approx. £ 25
♦ Stylish split-level restaurant with contemporary lighting, open kitchen and smart horseshoe bar. Good value menus offer classics with a modern touch, and local meats/fish from the wood grill.

**at Grindleton** Northeast : 3 mi by A 671

🛏 **Duke of York Inn**    🏡 **P** VISA ⦵ AE
*Brow Top ⊠ BB7 4QR – 𝒞 (01200) 441 266 – www.dukeofyorkgrindleton.com*
*– Closed 25 December, Monday except bank holidays and Tuesday following*
*bank holidays*
**Rest** – Menu £ 14 – Carte £ 24/39
◆ Ivy-clad pub in the heart of the Trough of Bowland, with views to Pendle Hill. Rustic bar and light, contemporary dining room. Good choice on seasonal menu, with plenty of regional dishes.

**at Wiswell** South : 3.75 mi by A 671

🛏 **Freemasons**    🏡 ⇆ VISA ⦵
⊛ *8 Vicarage Fold ⊠ BB7 9DF – 𝒞 (01254) 822 218*
*– www.freemasonswiswell.co.uk – Closed Monday except bank holidays*
**Rest** – Menu £ 17 (weekdays) – Carte £ 28/46
◆ Delightful pub, hidden away on a narrow lane. Flag floors, low beams and open fires downstairs; elegant, antique-furnished dining rooms upstairs. Interesting menu features modern versions of traditional pub dishes. Skilful cooking, with clear flavours. Charming service.

**at Bashall Eaves** Northwest : 3 mi by B6243

🛏 **Red Pump Inn** with rm    🏡 ℅ 🛜 **P** VISA ⦵
*Clitheroe Rd ⊠ BB7 3DA – 𝒞 (01254) 826 227 – www.theredpumpinn.co.uk*
*– Closed 2 weeks January and Monday except bank holidays*
**3 rm** ⊡ – †£ 75/95 ††£ 95/115
**Rest** – Menu £ 15 (weekdays) – Carte £ 18/28
◆ One of the oldest pubs in the Ribble Valley, with traditional restaurant, rustic bar and charming fire-lit snug. Local produce features on seasonal menus, with game a speciality. Spacious bedrooms boast good facilities and views of Pendle Hill or Longridge Fell.

---

**CLOVELLY** – Devon – **503** G31 – pop. 439 – ⊠ Bideford    **1** B1
▶ London 241 mi – Barnstaple 18 mi – Exeter 52 mi – Penzance 92 mi
◉ Village ★★
◉ SW : Tamar River ★★. Hartland : Hartland Church ★ - Hartland Quay ★ (viewpoint ★★) - Hartland Point ⩽ ★★★, W : 6.5 mi by B 3237 and B 3248 – Morwenstow (Church ★, cliffs ★★), SW : 11.5 mi by A 39

🏠 **Red Lion**    ⩽ 🏡 ℅ 🛜 **P** VISA ⦵
*The Quay ⊠ EX39 5TF – 𝒞 (01237) 431 237 – www.clovelly.co.uk*
**11 rm** (dinner included) ⊡ – †£ 112/115 ††£ 188/198
**Rest** – (dinner only) Menu £ 30
◆ Cosy little hotel/inn on the quayside; a superb location. All rooms enjoy sea and harbour views and are dressed in soft, understated colours, providing a smart resting place. Simple dining room looks out to harbour.

---

**CLUN** – Shropshire – **503** K26    **18** A2
▶ London 173 mi – Church Stretton 16 mi – Ludlow 16 mi

⌂ **Birches Mill** without rest ⊗    ℘ ℅ 🛜 **P** VISA ⦵
*Northwest : 3 mi by A 488, Bicton rd, Mainstone rd and Burlow rd ⊠ SY7 8NL*
*– 𝒞 (01588) 640 409 – www.birchesmill.co.uk – April-October*
**3 rm** ⊡ – †£ 72/82 ††£ 82/92
◆ High quality comforts in remote former corn mill: interior has characterful 17C/18C structures. Flagged lounge with lovely inglenook. Simple but tastefully decorated rooms.

---

**COCKERMOUTH** – Cumbria – **501** J20 – pop. 7 446    **21** A2
▶ London 306 mi – Carlisle 25 mi – Keswick 13 mi
🄳 Market St 𝒞 (01900) 82 26 34, www.cockermouth.org.uk
🄸 Embleton, 𝒞 (017687) 7 62 23

ENGLAND

**at Lorton** Southeast : 4.25 mi by B 5292 – ⊠ Cockermouth

🏠 **Winder Hall Country House** ᠅    ← 🛋 🕸 📶 **P** _VISA_ ⊙⊙ 𝖠𝖤
on B 5289 ⊠ CA13 9UP – 𝒞 (01900) 85 107 – www.winderhall.co.uk
**7 rm** ⌁ – ♦£ 170/185 ♦♦£ 170/185
**Rest** – (booking essential for non-residents) Menu £ 25/35 **s**
♦ Part-Jacobean manor house with mullioned windows and tranquil garden. Comfortable lounge and high quality bedrooms retain rich history of house and include two four-posters. Oak panelled dining room overlooks garden. Local produce well-used in homemade dishes. Relaxed, friendly service.

🏠 **New House Farm**    ← 🛋 📖 📶 **P** _VISA_ ⊙⊙
South : 1.25 mi on B 5289 ⊠ CA13 9UU – 𝒞 (01900) 85 404
– www.newhouse-farm.com
**5 rm** ⌁ – ♦£ 50/90 ♦♦£ 99/160    **Rest** – Menu £ 30
♦ Very well appointed, richly decorated guesthouse with hot tub in garden. Sumptuous bedrooms; one with double jacuzzi, two with four-posters. Fine furnishings and roll-top baths. Aga-cooked breakfasts and home-cooked evening meals. Tea rooms just next door.

🏠 **Old Vicarage**    🛋 📶 📶 **P** _VISA_ ⊙⊙
Church Ln, North : 0.5 mi by B 5289 on Lorton Church rd ⊠ CA13 9UN
– 𝒞 (01900) 85 656 – www.oldvicarage.co.uk – Restricted opening in winter
**8 rm** ⌁ – ♦£ 80/135 ♦♦£ 135    **Rest** – Menu £ 32
♦ Well-kept Victorian house in beautiful countryside spot. Comfortable lounge and hospitable owners. Sympathetically modernised bedrooms; four-postered Room 1 is the best. Dining room offers lovely fell views and home-cooked, local produce.

---

**COCKLEFORD** – Gloucestershire – ⊠ Cheltenham    4 C1
▶ London 95 mi – Bristol 48 mi – Cheltenham 7 mi

🍴 **The Green Dragon Inn** with rm    🛋 🍴 📶 rm, 📶 🏋 **P** _VISA_ ⊙⊙ 𝖠𝖤
⊠ GL53 9NW – 𝒞 (01242) 870 271 – www.green-dragon-inn.co.uk – Closed dinner 25-26 December and 1 January
**9 rm** ⌁ – ♦£ 70 ♦♦£ 95    **Rest** – (booking essential) Carte £ 26/32
♦ Characterful stone pub with huge open fires and carved mice hidden in the woodwork – the hallmark of designer Robert 'Mouseman' Thompson. Hearty lunches; unusual starters; generous, meaty mains. Simple, modern bedrooms; one boasts a super king-sized bed.

---

**COGGESHALL** – Essex – **504** W28 – pop. 3 919 – ⊠ Colchester    13 C2
▶ London 49 mi – Braintree 6 mi – Chelmsford 16 mi – Colchester 9 mi

🍴🍴 **Baumanns Brasserie**    _VISA_ ⊙⊙ 𝖠𝖤
4-6 Stoneham St ⊠ CO6 1TT – 𝒞 (01376) 561 453
– www.baumannsbrasserie.co.uk – Closed first 2 weeks January, Monday and Tuesday
**Rest** – Menu £ 15/24 – Carte £ 28/36
♦ Characterful 16C building, its walls packed with pictures and prints. Tasty cooking, made using local produce, brings out classic flavour combinations. Speedy service.

**at Pattiswick** Northwest : 3 mi by A 120 (Braintree Rd) – ⊠ Coggeshall

🍴 **Compasses at Pattiswick**    🛋 🍴 ♿ **P** _VISA_ ⊙⊙
Compasses Rd ⊠ CM77 8BG – 𝒞 (01376) 561 322
– www.thegreatpubcompany.co.uk
**Rest** – Carte £ 23/30
♦ Smart, rural pub with cheery service. Cooking is simple and honest, with plenty of effort put into sourcing local ingredients. Pheasant is from local shoots and venison from the woods behind.

---

**COLERNE** – Wiltshire – **503** M29 – see Bath (Bath & North East Somerset)

---

**COLN ST ALDWYNS** – Gloucestershire – **503** O28 – pop. 260    4 D1
– ⊠ Cirencester
▶ London 101 mi – Bristol 53 mi – Gloucester 20 mi – Oxford 28 mi

**New Inn at Coln** 🏠 ⑴ P VISA ⓒⓞ ⓘ

✉ GL7 5AN – 𝒞 (01285) 750 651 – www.new-inn.co.uk
**14 rm** ⌷ – ♦£ 130/150 ♦♦£ 170
**Rest** – *(bar lunch) (booking essential for non-residents)* Carte £ 24/35

♦ Charming 16C foliage-clad coaching inn, in a delightful little village. Characterful guest areas and bold modern bedrooms – some with exposed beams, stone walls or brass beds; those in the extension are quieter, with country views. Extensive list of bar meals or more formal menu in contemporary restaurant.

---

**COLSTON BASSETT** – Nottinghamshire – **502** R25 – pop. 239 **16** B2
– ✉ Nottingham

▶ London 129 mi – Leicester 23 mi – Lincoln 40 mi – Nottingham 15 mi

🏠 **The Martins Arms** 🍴 🏠 P VISA ⓒⓞ AE

*School Ln* ✉ NG12 3FD – 𝒞 (01949) 81 361 – www.themartinsarms.co.uk
– *Closed dinner 25 December and Sunday dinner*
**Rest** – Carte £ 27/33

♦ Creeper-clad pub in charming village, with cosy, fire-lit bar and period furnished dining rooms. Menu has strong masculine base, with the occasional Italian influence or global flavour.

---

**COLTISHALL** – Norfolk – **504** Y25 – pop. 2 161 – ✉ Norwich **15** D1

🔲 Great Britain

▶ London 133 mi – Norwich 8 mi

◉ Norfolk Broads★

🏠🏠 **Norfolk Mead** ⚘ ≤ 🍴 ⑴ ⑴ P VISA ⓒⓞ AE

✉ NR12 7DN – 𝒞 (01603) 737 531 – www.norfolkmead.co.uk – *Closed 25-26 December*
**13 rm** ⌷ – ♦£ 75 ♦♦£ 150
**Rest** – *(closed Saturday lunch, Sunday dinner and Monday)* Menu £ 20 (lunch) – Carte £ 25/35

♦ Restful 18C manor with an otter lake and gardens leading down to the River Bure. Bedrooms are individually colour-themed. Room 7 boasts a jacuzzi and lovely views. Candlelit restaurant looks out over the grounds.

---

**COLTON** – North Yorkshire – see Tadcaster

---

**COLWALL** – Herefordshire – see Great Malvern

---

**COLYFORD** – Devon – **503** K31 – ✉ Colyton 🔲 Great Britain **2** D2

▶ London 168 mi – Exeter 21 mi – Taunton 30 mi – Torquay 46 mi

◉ Colyton★ (Church★), N : 1 mi on B 3161 – Axmouth (≤★), S : 1 mi by A 3052 and B 3172

🏠 **Swallows Eaves** 🍴 ⑴ ⑴ P VISA ⓒⓞ

*Swan Hill Rd* ✉ EX24 6QJ – 𝒞 (01297) 553 184 – www.swallowseaves.co.uk
**8 rm** ⌷ – ♦£ 48/90 ♦♦£ 90/110
**Rest** *Reeds* – *(closed Sunday and Monday lunch)* Menu £ 28 (dinner) – Carte lunch £ 18/26

♦ Unusual grey shale-coated 1920s house, with views from some rooms over the Axe Valley: listen out for birdsong on the marshes. Fully refurbished guest areas – bedrooms and bathrooms to follow. Menus feature locally sourced meats, fish and vegetables.

---

**COMBE HAY** – Bath and North East Somerset – see Bath

---

**CONEYTHORPE** – North Yorkshire – see Knaresborough

---

**CONGLETON** – Cheshire East – **502** N24 – pop. 25 400 🔲 Great Britain **20** B3

▶ London 183 mi – Liverpool 50 mi – Manchester 25 mi – Sheffield 46 mi

🄸 High St 𝒞 (01260) 27 10 95, www.cheshirepeakdistrict.com

🄹 Biddulph Rd, 𝒞 (01260) 27 35 40

◉ Little Moreton Hall★★ **AC**, SW : 3 mi by A 34

ENGLAND

ENGLAND

XX **Pecks**  🚗 Ⓐ ♻ 🅿 VISA ⦿ AE
*Newcastle Rd, Moreton, South : 2.75 mi on A 34* ⊠ *CW12 4SB –* ℰ *(01260) 275 161 – www.pecksrest.co.uk – Closed 25-30 December, Sunday dinner and Monday*
**Rest** – Menu £ 21 (lunch) – Carte £ 24/44
♦ Airy, modish restaurant with unique style. À la carte lunch; monthly changing 5/7 course set dinner at 8pm sharp. Traditional homemade dishes use good produce and arrive in generous portions.

X **L'Endroit**  🎯 🅿 VISA ⦿ ⓪
*70-72 Lawton St* ⊠ *CW12 1RS –* ℰ *(01260) 299 548 – www.lendroit.co.uk – Closed 2 weeks February-March, 1 week June, 1 week September, Sunday, Monday and lunch Saturday*
**Rest** – French – Menu £ 12 (lunch) – Carte £ 22/29
♦ Welcoming restaurant with warm décor, upmarket bistro-style and small patio. Seasonally changing à la carte displays tasty, well-done dishes with strong French undertones. Good value lunch.

---

**CONSTABLE BURTON** – North Yorkshire – **502** O21 – see Leyburn

---

**CONSTANTINE BAY** – Cornwall – **503** E32 – see Padstow

---

**COOKHAM** – Windsor and Maidenhead – **504** R29 – pop. 5 304      **11** C3
– ⊠ **Maidenhead** ▮ Great Britain

▶ London 32 mi – High Wycombe 7 mi – Oxford 31 mi – Reading 16 mi
🚢 to Marlow, Maidenhead and Windsor (Salter Bros. Ltd) (summer only)
👁 Stanley Spencer Gallery★ **AC**

🏠 **White Oak**  🎯 🅿 VISA ⦿ AE
*Pound Ln* ⊠ *SL6 9QE –* ℰ *(01628) 523 043 – www.thewhiteoak.co.uk – Closed dinner Sunday and bank holidays*
**Rest** – Menu £ 19 (weekdays) – Carte £ 25/29
♦ Smart, contemporary pub with neutral hues and lovely terrace. Straightforward pub-style dishes feature quality meats and unfussy accompaniments, and include tasty sharing boards and assiettes.

---

**COOKHAM DEAN** – Windsor and Maidenhead ▮ Great Britain      **11** C3
▶ London 32 mi – High Wycombe 7 mi – Oxford 31 mi – Reading 16 mi
🖼 Windsor Castle★★★, Eton★★ and Windsor★, S : 5 mi by B 4447, A 4 (westbound) and A 308

🏨 **Sanctum on the Green**  🚗 🎯 ⊒ 🐀 🅿 VISA ⦿ AE ⓪
*The Old Cricket Common* ⊠ *SL6 9NZ –* ℰ *(01628) 482 638 – www.sanctumonthegreen.com*
**9 rm** ⊒ – †£ 120 ††£ 160/220
**Rest** – *(booking essential)* Menu £ 20 – Carte £ 26/41
♦ Part-timbered, part red-brick property with large terraces and heated outdoor pool, hidden away in a quiet village. Contemporary furnishings contrast with old beams. Stylish, boutique bedrooms come in bold colours. Two lounges, smart dining room and conservatory; classic dishes arrive in a modern style.

---

**CORBRIDGE** – Northumberland – **501** N19 – pop. 2 800      **24** A2
▮ Great Britain
▶ London 300 mi – Hexham 3 mi – Newcastle upon Tyne 18 mi
🖪 Hill St ℰ (01434) 63 28 15, www.thisiscorbridge.co.uk
🖼 Hadrian's Wall★★, N : 3 mi by A 68 – Corstopitum★ **AC**, NW : 0.5 m

🅓 **Duke of Wellington** with rm    ☐ 📶 **P** VISA ◕◕
*Newton, East : 3 mi by A 6350 and A 69* ✉ *NE43 7UL –* ✆ *(01661) 844 446*
*– www.thedukeofwellingtoninn.co.uk*
**7 rm** ☑ – †£ 90/100 ††£ 120/135
**Rest** – *(booking advisable)* Carte £ 22/32 **s**
♦ A single track leads to this remote inn, which is reported to be the county's oldest licensed premises, dating from the early 1600s. Rescued by a local, it's now a smart, modern pub offering good food – try the local lamb or roe deer for dinner. Stylish, luxurious bedrooms.

**at Great Whittington** North : 5.5 mi by A 68 off B 6318 – ✉ Corbridge

🅓 **Queens Head Inn**    ☐ ☐ **P** VISA ◕◕
✉ *NE19 2HP –* ✆ *(01434) 672 267 – www.the-queens-head-inn.co.uk – Closed Sunday dinner, Monday and Tuesday*
**Rest** – Carte £ 17/33
♦ Dating from 1615, with cosy bar and bric à brac filled dining room. Menu offers everything from stotties to duck spring rolls, with lamb and beef from farm next door. Friendly service.

**CORFE CASTLE** – Dorset – **503** N32 – **pop. 1 335** – ✉ Wareham    **4** C3
▶ London 129 mi – Bournemouth 18 mi – Weymouth 23 mi
◉ Castle ★ ( ≤ ★★) **AC**

🏨 **Mortons House**    ☐ ☐ & rm, ☆ **P** VISA ◕◕
*45 East St* ✉ *BH20 5EE –* ✆ *(01929) 480 988 – www.mortonshouse.co.uk*
**19 rm** ☑ – †£ 80/100 ††£ 150/160 – 2 suites
**Rest** – Menu £ 38 – Carte lunch £ 25/37
♦ Elizabethan manor built in the shape of an "E" in the Queen's honour. Wood-panelled drawing room. Range of different bedrooms, some themed: the Victoria room boasts an original Victorian bath. Traditional, formal dining room offers views out over the courtyard.

**CORNHILL-ON-TWEED** – Northumberland – **501** N17 – **pop. 317**    **24** A1
▌ Scotland
▶ London 345 mi – Edinburgh 49 mi – Newcastle upon Tyne 59 mi
◉ Ladykirk (Kirk o'Steil ★), NE : 6 mi by A 698 and B 6470

🏨 **Tillmouth Park** ⌖    ≤ ☐ ♨ **P** VISA ◕◕
*Northeast : 2.5 mi on A 698* ✉ *TD12 4UU –* ✆ *(01890) 882 255*
*– www.tillmouthpark.co.uk – Closed 2 January-29 March*
**14 rm** ☑ – †£ 79/205 ††£ 225
**Rest Library** – *(dinner only and Sunday lunch)* Carte £ 20/44
♦ Traditional 19C country house in 15 acres of grounds; set in prime shooting-/fishing country. Welcoming interior with characterful stained glass and grand staircases. Spacious bedrooms boast modern bathrooms. Wood-panelled restaurant serves à la carte dinners and a set lunch on Sunday.

🏠 **Coach House**    ☐ & rm, **P** VISA ◕◕
*Crookham, East : 4 mi on A 697* ✉ *TD12 4TD –* ✆ *(01890) 820 293*
*– www.coachhousecrookham.com – February-November*
**11 rm** ☑ – †£ 50/70 ††£ 88/110
**Rest** – *(dinner only) (booking essential for non-residents)* Menu £ 24
♦ Keenly run, small hotel set around a courtyard, converted from a collection of old farm buildings, including a 1680s dower house. Lounge with honesty bar in stable block; where the bedrooms are larger and more modern. Cosy breakfast-/dining room in original house.

**CORSE LAWN** – Worcestershire – **see** Tewkesbury (Glos.)

ENGLAND

## CORTON DENHAM – Somerset – **504** M31 – pop. 210 – ⊠ Sherborne    **4** C3
▶ London 123 mi – Bristol 36 mi – Cardiff 110 mi – Southampton 84 mi

### 🛏 **Queens Arms** with rm    ☆ VISA ◉◉ AE
⊠ DT9 4LR – *ℰ (01963) 220 317 – www.thequeensarms.com*
**5 rm** ⌂ – ♦£ 75/95 ♦♦£ 95/120    **Rest** – *(booking advisable)* Carte £ 22/28
◆ Charming 18C stone pub run by an enthusiastic owner, who takes care not to out-price the locals. Lunch focuses on one or two hearty courses, while the evening menu offers a more formal three course selection. Bedrooms are charming, well-appointed and good value.

## COTEBROOK – Cheshire West and Chester – see Tarporley

## COVENTRY – West Midlands – **503** P26 – pop. 267 755 📗 Great Britain    **19** D2
▶ London 100 mi – Birmingham 18 mi – Bristol 96 mi – Leicester 24 mi
🛈 Priory Street *ℰ (024) 7622 72 64, www.visitcoventry.co.uk*
🔒 Windmill Village Allesley Birmingham Rd, *ℰ (024) 7640 40 41*
🔒 Sphinx Sphinx Drive, *ℰ (024) 7645 13 61*
◉ City★ - Cathedral★★★ **AC** – Old Cathedral★ – Museum of British Road Transport★ **AC**

### at **Shilton** Northeast : 6.75 mi by A 4600 - on B 4065 – ⊠ Coventry

### ⋔ **Barnacle Hall** without rest    ⍃ ⌘ 🅿
*Shilton Ln. , West : 1 mi by B 4029 following signs for garden centre* ⊠ CV7 9LH
– *ℰ (024) 7661 2629 – www.barnaclehall.co.uk – Closed 24 December-2 January*
**3 rm** ⌂ – ♦£ 35/45 ♦♦£ 65/75
◆ Interesting part-16C farmhouse in rural location. Westerly facing 18C stone façade; remainder 16/17C. Beamed rooms have countryside outlook and farmhouse style furnishings.

### at **Balsall Common** West : 6.75 mi by B 4101 – ⊠ Coventry

### 🛏 **White Horse**    ☆ 🅿 VISA ◉◉ AE
*Kenilworth Rd* ⊠ CV7 7DT – *ℰ (01676) 533 207 – www.thewhitehorseatbc.co.uk*
**Rest** – Carte £ 22/30
◆ Striking black and white timbered pub with decked terrace, spacious modern interior and paved rear dining area. Easy-to-read menus display British pub classics and some Mediterranean influences.

## COVERACK – Cornwall – **503** E33    **1** A3
▶ London 300 mi – Penzance 25 mi – Truro 27 mi

### 🏠 **Bay**    ⪡ ⍃ ⅙ rm, ⋯ 🅿 VISA ◉◉
*North Corner* ⊠ TR12 6TF – *ℰ (01326) 280 464 – www.thebayhotel.co.uk*
*– Closed 1-22 December and 3 January-29 February*
**13 rm** (dinner included) ⌂ – ♦£ 88/150 ♦♦£ 210/240 – 2 suites
**Rest** – *(bar lunch)* Menu £ 30
◆ Imposing Victorian country house located in a pretty fishing village and boasting views over the bay. Homely lounge and bar. Spotless, modern bedrooms with a slight New England style. Dining room and conservatory offer classical daily menu and fish specials.

## COWLEY – Gloucestershire – **504** N28    **4** C1
▶ London 105 mi – Swindon 28 mi – Gloucester 14 mi – Cheltenham 6 mi

### 🏘 **Cowley Manor** ⌖    ⍃ ⍟ ⌇ ▥ ◉ ⍦ ⌱ ⇱ 🍴 ⫘ 🅿 VISA ◉◉ AE ⓪
⊠ GL53 9NL – *ℰ (01242) 870 900 – www.cowleymanor.com*
**22 rm** ⌂ – ♦£ 150/250 ♦♦£ 150/595 – 8 suites    **Rest** – Carte £ 25/38
◆ Impressive Regency house. 55 acres; beautiful gardens. Retro interior, bold colours, obscure fittings, excellent mod cons. Stylish bedrooms, some with balconies/lake views, most with huge bathrooms. Spa, 2 pools and sun terrace. Semi-formal restaurant with paved terrace serves classic British dishes.

## COWSHILL – Durham – **502** N19    **24** A3
▶ London 295 mi – Newcastle upon Tyne 42 mi – Stanhope 10 mi
– Wolsingham 16 mi

ENGLAND

↑ **Low Cornriggs Farm** ॐ     ≤ ⊟ ⅏ ⅏ ⅏ **P** **VISA** **⦿⦿**
*Weardale, Northwest : 0.75 mi on A 689* ⊠ *DL13 1AQ –* ℰ *(01388) 537 600*
*– www.cornriggsfarm.co.uk – Closed 24-26 December, 31 December and 1*
*January*
**3 rm** ⊟ – **♥**£ 44 **♥♥**£ 64    **Rest** – Menu £ 18 **s**
♦ Stone-built 300 year-old farmhouse boasting some superb views over Teesdale.
Conservatory dining room for summer use. Cosy, pine-furnished bedrooms.
Beamed dining room offers hearty, home-cooked, organic dishes.

---

# CRACKINGTON HAVEN – Cornwall – 503 G31 – ⊠ Bude    1 B2
▶ London 262 mi – Bude 11 mi – Plymouth 44 mi – Truro 42 mi
◉ Poundstock★ (≤★★, church★, guildhouse★), NE : 5.5 mi by A 39 – Jacobstow
(Church★), E : 3.5 m

↑ **Manor Farm** without rest ॐ     ≤ ⊟ ⅏ ⅏ **P**
*Southeast : 1.25 mi by Boscastle rd taking left turn onto Church Park Rd after*
*1 mi then taking first right onto unmarked lane* ⊠ *EX23 0JW*
*–* ℰ *(01840) 230 304 – Closed 25 December*
**3 rm** ⊟ – **♥**£ 45 **♥♥**£ 80
♦ Appears in the Domesday Book and belonged to William the Conqueror's half
brother. A lovely manor in beautifully manicured grounds. Affable owner and
comfortable rooms.

---

# CRANBROOK – Kent – 504 V30 – pop. 4 225 ▯ Great Britain    8 B2
▶ London 53 mi – Hastings 19 mi – Maidstone 15 mi
ℹ Stone St ℰ (01580) 71 25 38, www.cranbrook.org
◉ Sissinghurst Castle★ **AC**, NE : 2.5 mi by A 229 and A 262

↑ **Cloth Hall Oast** ॐ     ⊟ ⅏ ⅏ ⅏ **P**
*Coursehorn Ln, East : 1 mi by Tenterden rd* ⊠ *TN17 3NR –* ℰ *(01580) 712 220*
*– www.clothhalloast.co.uk – Closed Christmas*
**3 rm** ⊟ – **♥**£ 55/70 **♥♥**£ 125    **Rest** – Menu £ 25
♦ Superbly restored oast house that was rebuilt in 2001. Antiques, family photos
and fine artwork fill the drawing room. Bedrooms are well-equipped but retain
some original character; one boasts a splendid four-poster bed. Communal breakfasts and dinners at an antique table, set below restored rafters in the main hall.

XX **Apicius** (Tim Johnson)     **AC** **VISA** **⦿⦿**
❀ *23 Stone St* ⊠ *TN17 3HE –* ℰ *(01580) 714 666 – www.restaurant-apicius.co.uk*
*– Closed 2 weeks August, 2 weeks Christmas-New Year, Saturday lunch, Sunday*
*dinner, Monday and Tuesday*
**Rest** – Menu £ 30/36
**Spec.** Ham hock ballotine, spring pea velouté and foie gras mousse. Roast fillet of
halibut, ceps and artichokes. Poached white peach, lavender infused savarin and
vanilla ice cream.
♦ Named after Roman author of world's first cookbook. Cosy interior mixes original features with modern style. Passionate, well balanced, precise cooking uses local ingredients.

**at Sissinghurst** Northeast : 1.75 mi by B 2189 on A 262 – ⊠ Cranbrook

X **Rankins**     **VISA** **⦿⦿**
*The Street, on A 262* ⊠ *TN17 2JH –* ℰ *(01580) 713 964*
*– www.rankinsrestaurant.com – Closed Monday, Tuesday and bank holidays*
**Rest** – *(dinner only and Sunday lunch) (booking essential)* Carte £ 26/35
♦ Well-run village restaurant, immaculately kept by knowledgeable, personable
owners. Concise set menus display hearty, traditional dishes with the odd Mediterranean touch. Desserts a speciality.

---

# CRAYKE – North Yorkshire – see Easingwold

**ENGLAND**

**CRICKLADE** – Wiltshire – **503** O29 **4** D1
▶ London 89 mi – Birmingham 86 mi – Bristol 54 mi – Cardiff 87 mi

🛏 **Red Lion** with rm                                                      VISA ⓂⓄ
74 High St ✉ SN6 6DD – ℰ (01793) 750 776 – Closed Sunday Dinner
**5 rm** ⬜ – 🛉£ 75 🛉🛉£ 75   **Rest** – (booking essential) Carte £ 21/33
◆ Very charming 17C pub, just off the Thames path. 9 real ales and 30 speciality
beers in the low-beamed bar; beer pairings for every dish in the airy dining room.
Classical cooking uses extremely local produce. Comfortable bedrooms are located in the old stables.

**CROCKERTON** – Wiltshire – **see Warminster**

**CROFT-ON-TEES** – North Yorkshire – **502** P20 – **see Darlington**

**CROPSTON** – Leicestershire – **502** Q25 **16** B2
▶ London 106 mi – Birmingham 49 mi – Sheffield 67 mi – Leicester 6 mi

🏠 **Horseshoe Cottage Farm**                          🚿 ⅀ 🛰 **P** VISA ⓂⓄ
Roecliffe Rd, Hallgates, Northwest : 1 mi on Woodhouse Eaves rd ✉ LE7 7HQ
– ℰ (0116) 235 00 38 – www.horseshoecottagefarm.com
**3 rm** ⬜ – 🛉£ 63 🛉🛉£ 95   **Rest** – Menu £ 21
◆ Extended farmhouse in pleasant countryside location beside Bradgate Country
Park. Comfortable lounge; homely touches in spacious, traditional bedrooms.
Home-cooked food in communal dining room; local produce well used, including
some from the vegetable garden.

**CROSTHWAITE** – Cumbria – **502** L21 – **see Kendal**

**CRUDWELL** – Wiltshire – **503** N29 – **see Malmesbury**

**CUCKFIELD** – West Sussex – **504** T30 – **pop. 3 266** **7** D2
▶ London 40 mi – Brighton 15 mi

🏨 **Ockenden Manor** ⬍             🚿 🐾 ⅀ rest, 📞 🔧 **P** VISA ⓂⓄ ⒶⒺ Ⓞ
✿     ✉ RH17 5LD – ℰ (01444) 416 111 – www.ockenden-manor.co.uk
**25 rm** ⬜ – 🛉£ 124 🛉🛉£ 400 – 3 suites
**Rest** – (booking essential at lunch) Menu £ 28/55
**Spec.** English asparagus, boudin blanc, chicken oysters and morels. Sea bass, wild
leaf garlic gnocchi, tomato fondue and razor clam gratin. Strawberry millefeuille.
◆ Part-Elizabethan manor house dating back to the 16C, set in 9 acres of parkland and boasting pleasant South Downs views. Elegant open-fired sitting room,
cosy wood-panelled bar and antique-furnished bedrooms. Contemporary orangery dining room opens onto the gardens and offers refined seasonal cooking
with well-balanced flavours and good attention to detail.

🍴 **Cuckoo**                                              🍴 VISA ⓂⓄ ⒶⒺ
1 Broad St ✉ RH17 5LJ – ℰ (01444) 414 184 – www.cuckoorestaurant.co.uk
– Closed 1 week January, 1 week late August, Saturday lunch, Sunday dinner
and Monday
**Rest** – Menu £ 19 (lunch) – Carte £ 27/31
◆ Charming 17C cottage in heart of pretty village, with log fire, fresh flowers, personable owner and informal ambience. Tasty, modern British cooking uses fresh,
seasonal produce.

**CUDDINGTON** – Buckinghamshire – **503** M24 ▌Great Britain **11** C2
▶ London 48 mi – Aylesbury 6 mi – Oxford 17 mi
◪ Waddesdon Manor★★ **AC**, NE : 6 mi via Cuddington Hill, Cannon's Hill,
Waddesdon Hill and A 41

🛏 **Crown**                                                      **P** VISA ⓂⓄ
Aylesbury Rd ✉ HP18 0BB – ℰ (01844) 292 222
– www.thecrowncuddington.co.uk – Closed Sunday dinner
**Rest** – Carte £ 20/30
◆ Attractive thatched pub with traditional styling, welcoming atmosphere and
friendly team. Seasonal menus display hearty comfort food in the winter and lighter dishes in the summer.

**CURY** – Cornwall – **503** E33 – see Helston

**CUTNALL GREEN** – Worcestershire – **503** N27 – see Droitwich Spa

**DARGATE** – Kent – see Faversham

**DARLEY** – North Yorkshire – **502** O21                                    22 B2

▶ London 217 mi – Harrogate 8 mi – Ripon 16 mi

⌂    **Cold Cotes** without rest ⌖        ⌷ ⌲ ⌖ **P** _VISA_ ◉◉
*Cold Cotes Rd, Felliscliffe, South : 2 mi by Kettlesing rd, going straight over*
*crossroads and on Harrogate rd* ✉ HG3 2LW – ✆ *(01423) 770 937*
*– www.coldcotes.com*
**6 rm** ⌸ – ✝£ 50/60 ✝✝£ 87/99
♦ Remotely set former farmhouse in colourful, well-tended gardens; the owners
love gardening and run a small plant nursery. Smart bedrooms provide good
comforts; those in the house are small suites, those in the barn conversion are
open-plan.

**DARLEY ABBEY** – Derby – **502** P25 – see Derby

**DARLINGTON** – Darlington – **502** P20 – pop. 86 082                    22 B1

▶ London 251 mi – Leeds 61 mi – Middlesbrough 14 mi
– Newcastle upon Tyne 35 mi
✈ Teesside Airport : ✆ (08712) 242426, E : 6 mi by A 67
🛈 Horsemarket ✆ (01325) 38 86 66, www.visitdarlington.com
🏌 Blackwell Grange Briar Close, ✆ (01325) 46 44 58
🏌 Stressholme Snipe Lane, ✆ (01325) 46 10 02

**at Croft-on-Tees** South : 4.25 mi on A 167 – ✉ Darlington

🏠    **Clow Beck House** ⌖       ◁ ⌷ ⌲ ⌿ & rm, ⌖ ⌶ **P** _VISA_ ◉◉ ⌶⌷
*Monk End Farm, West : 0.75 mi by A 167 off Barton rd* ✉ DL2 2SW – ✆ *(01325)*
*721 075 – www.clowbeckhouse.co.uk – Closed 24 December-3 January*
**13 rm** ⌸ – ✝£ 85 ✝✝£ 135
**Rest** – *(dinner only) (residents only)* Carte £ 28/39 **s**
♦ Collection of converted farm buildings not far from the River Tees. Welcoming
owners and homely interior. Immaculately kept, tastefully furnished bedrooms
come with iPod docks, bathrobes and chocolates. Home-cooked dinners with a
puzzle supplied while you wait.

**at Hurworth-on-Tees** South : 5.5 mi by A 167

🏨    **Rockliffe Hall** ⌖      ⌷ ⌲ ⌿ ⌶ ◉ ⌿ ↕ 🏌 ⌶ & rm, ⌶⌷ ⌖ ⌶ ⌲ **P**
✉ DL2 2DU – ✆ *(01325) 729 999 – www.rockliffehall.com*    _VISA_ ◉◉ ⌶⌷ ◉
**60 rm** ⌸ – ✝£ 165/275 ✝✝£ 165/440
**Rest** *Kenny Atkinson at The Orangery* – see restaurant listing
**Rest** *Waterhouse Bistro* – Menu £ 28 **s** – Carte £ 27/29 **s**
**Rest** *Clubhouse* – Menu £ 28 **s** – Carte £ 20/25 **s**
♦ Impressive red-brick property in 376 acres of grounds, boasting a championship golf course, state-of-the-art leisure facilities and spa. Grand guest areas and
characterful bedrooms in original Victorian house; modern bedrooms in extensions. Bright, airy bistro offers light, modern dishes. The Clubhouse is aimed at
golfers and ranges from sandwiches to Sunday lunch.

🍴🍴🍴  **Kenny Atkinson at The Orangery** – at Rockliffe Hall Hotel    ⌷
✉ DL2 2DU – ✆ *(01325) 729 999*    ⌲ ⌶⌷ **P** _VISA_ ◉◉ ⌶⌷
*– www.rockliffehall.com – Closed Sunday*
**Rest** – *(dinner only)* Menu £ 48/70 **s**
♦ Restored Victorian orangery set within an impressive hotel, boasting a formal
bar and spacious dining room with well-spaced tables and views over the golf
course. Complex cooking displays modern techniques. Live piano music accompanies.

⌂ **Bay Horse**   ⌂ ⌂ **P** VISA ⓒ AE
45 The Green ⌂ DL2 2AA – ⌂ (01325) 720 663
– www.thebayhorsehurworth.com – Closed Sunday dinner
**Rest** – Menu £ 17 (lunch) – Carte £ 25/33
♦ Smart village pub with pleasant terrace and gardens. Wide-ranging menu offers largely hearty classics; presentation ranges from simple and rustic to more
modern and intricate.

**at Headlam** Northwest : 8 mi by A 67 – ⌂ Gainford

⌂⌂⌂ **Headlam Hall** ⌂   ⌂ ⌂ ⌂ ⌂ ⌂ ⌂ ⌂ ⌂ ⌂ ⌂ & rm, ⌂ ⌂ ⌂ **P**
⌂ DL2 3HA – ⌂ (01325) 730 238 – www.headlamhall.co.uk   VISA ⓒ AE
– Closed 24-26 December
**36 rm** ⌂ – ♦£ 95 ♦♦£ 145 – 4 suites   **Rest** – Carte £ 26/40
♦ Part-Georgian, part-Jacobean manor house in a delightful, secluded countryside setting, with charming walled gardens. Period interior furnishings and antiques. Good leisure facilities. Country house restaurant in four distinctively decorated rooms.

**at Summerhouse** Northwest : 7.5 mi on B 6279

XX **Raby Hunt** with rm   **P** VISA ⓒ AE
⌂ DL2 3UD – ⌂ (01325) 374 237 – www.rabyhuntrestaurant.co.uk – Closed 1
week spring, 1 week autumn, 25-26 December, 1 January, Sunday dinner and
Monday-Wednesday lunch
**2 rm** ⌂ – ♦£ 70/110 ♦♦£ 110
**Rest** – (booking advisable) Menu £ 18 (lunch) – Carte £ 31/44
♦ Pleasant inn located in a rural hamlet, now a family-run restaurant with elegant
dining room, small bar and walls decorated with local art. Self-taught chef creates
a weekly changing menu of complex, ambitious dishes. Comfy bedrooms have a
cosy, homely feel.

# DARTMOUTH – Devon – 503 J32 – pop. 6 008   2 C3
▣ London 236 mi – Exeter 36 mi – Plymouth 35 mi
▣ Mayor's Ave ⌂ (01803) 83 42 24, www.discoverdartmouth.com
▣ Town★★ (⌂★) - Old Town - Butterwalk★ - Dartmouth Castle (⌂★★★) **AC**
▣ Start Point (⌂★), S : 13 mi (including 1 mi on foot)

⌂⌂⌂ **Dart Marina**   ⌂ ⌂ ⌂ ⌂ ⌂ ⌂ & rm, AC rest, ⌂ ⌂ **P** VISA ⓒ
Sandquay ⌂ TQ6 9PH – ⌂ (01803) 832 580 – www.dartmarina.com
**49 rm** ⌂ – ♦£ 119/170 ♦♦£ 140/200
**Rest River Restaurant** – see restaurant listing
**Rest Wildfire** – Carte £ 31/42 **s**
♦ Modern, laid-back hotel converted from an old boat works and chandlery.
Smart, contemporary bedrooms boast lovely outlooks over either river or marina;
many also boast balconies. Small spa and leisure centre. Formal restaurant or
more casual brasserie specialising in steaks, which opens out onto a terrace.

⌂⌂ **Royal Castle**   ⌂ ⌂ **P** VISA ⓒ
11 The Quay ⌂ TQ6 9PS – ⌂ (01803) 833 033 – www.royalcastle.co.uk
**25 rm** ⌂ – ♦£ 100/110 ♦♦£ 190/210   **Rest** – Carte £ 25/34
♦ Modernised 15C coaching inn: once two buildings, now joined by a smart glass
atrium. Boldly coloured bedrooms with good comforts – some have jacuzzi baths.
Two bars: one for drinkers only, one serving all-day dishes. Restaurant offers modern takes on old classics.

XX **Seahorse**   ⌂ AC VISA ⓒ AE
5 South Embankment ⌂ TQ6 9BH – ⌂ (01803) 835 147
– www.seahorserestaurant.co.uk – Closed Monday, Sunday dinner and Tuesday lunch
**Rest** – Seafood – (booking essential) Menu £ 20 (lunch and early dinner)
– Carte £ 32/46
♦ Picturesque location overlooking estuary/harbour; some al fresco tables. Classic
bistro dishes with strong seafood slant; cooked in charcoal oven. Twice daily
menu; simplicity is key.

ENGLAND

XX **Angelique** with rm     ⟨ 𝒮 📶 VISA ⓐ AE

*2 South Embankment* ⊠ *TQ6 9BH* – 𝒞 *(01803) 839 425*
*– www.angeliquedartmouth.co.uk – Closed Sunday dinner, Tuesday lunch and Monday*
**7 rm** ⌂ – †£ 85/125 ††£ 95/125    **Rest** – Menu £ 29/56
♦ Split-level, wood-furnished restaurant with open kitchen and lovely estuary outlook; all tables share the view. Attractively presented dishes showcase local produce: choose from a set selection, concise à la carte or fish tasting menu. Large bedrooms, 5mins down the road, take on a modern, boutique style.

XX **River Restaurant** – at Dart Marina Hotel    ⟨ 🕾 AK P VISA ⓐ

*Sandquay* ⊠ *TQ6 9PH* – 𝒞 *(01803) 832 580* – *www.dartmarina.com*
**Rest** – *(dinner only and Sunday lunch)* Menu £ 17/33
♦ Stylish, linen-clad restaurant overlooking the river; popular with those mooring their boats in the marina. Menu offers modern versions of old classics and showcases local, seasonal produce.

X **Jan and Freddies Brasserie**               VISA ⓐ

*10 Fairfax Pl* ⊠ *TQ6 9AD* – 𝒞 *(01803) 832 491*
*– www.janandfreddiesbrasserie.co.uk – Closed January and Sunday except before bank holidays*
**Rest** – *(booking advisable)* Carte £ 18/35
♦ Bright, stylish brasserie in the town centre, with welcoming service and a personal touch. Menus are classically based, with dishes crafted from local, seasonal produce.

X **Annabelles Kitchen**         ⟨ VISA ⓐ AE ⓞ

*24 South Embankment* ⊠ *TQ6 9BB* – 𝒞 *(01803) 833 540*
*– www.annabelleskitchen.co.uk – Closed 2 weeks February, 1 week November, Sunday, Monday and lunch Tuesday*
**Rest** – *(booking essential)* Carte £ 26/33
♦ Occupying a prime estuary facing spot is this laid-back little eatery, run by a husband and wife team. Their philosophy is based around sourcing local and seasonal ingredients and keeping the dishes simple.

If you are looking for particularly pleasant accommodation,
book a hotel shown in red : ⚷, 🏠… 🏰🏰.

**at Kingswear** East : via lower ferry – ⊠ Dartmouth

🏠 **Nonsuch House**     ⟨ 🚗 𝒮 📶 VISA ⓐ

*Church Hill, from lower ferry take first right onto Church Hill before Steam Packet Inn* ⊠ *TQ6 0BX* – 𝒞 *(01803) 752 829* – *www.nonsuch-house.co.uk*
**4 rm** ⌂ – †£ 100/125 ††£ 125/150
**Rest** – *(closed Tuesday, Wednesday and Saturday) (dinner only) (residents only)* Menu £ 38 **s**
♦ Charming Edwardian house run by friendly, hands-on owners; and boasting lovely views over the castle, town and sea. Bright Mediterranean style décor blends nicely with original features. Spacious, well-appointed bedrooms – one has a small balcony. Local, seasonal cooking in conservatory dining room.

**at Strete** Southwest : 4 mi on A 379 – ⊠ Dartmouth

🍴 **Kings Arms**        🚗 🕾 P VISA ⓐ

*Dartmouth Rd* ⊠ *TQ6 0RW* – 𝒞 *(01803) 770 377*
*– www.kingsarms-dartmouth.co.uk – Closed Sunday dinner and Monday in winter*
**Rest** – Carte £ 20/34
♦ Dour exterior hides gem of a pub serving wide-ranging menu with focus on seafood; locally caught, simply cooked and very tasty. Delightful rear garden with fantastic coastal views.

▶ London 31 mi – Luton 15 mi – Stevenage 6 mi

🏠 **Coltsfoot Country Retreat** ॐ          ⌷ ◐ ⌷ ₺ rm, ⅍ ᵞ **P** 𝚅𝙸𝚂𝙰 ⊙⊙ 𝙰𝙴
*Coltsfoot Ln, Bulls Grn, South : 0.75 mi by Bramfield Rd* ✉ *SG3 6SB* – ☏ *(01438)*
*212 800 – www.coltsfoot.com*
**15 rm** ⌷ – ♦£ 110 ♦♦£ 135
**Rest** – *(closed Sunday) (dinner only) (booking essential)* Menu £ 33
– Carte £ 25/50
♦ Stylish hotel, once a working farm, in 40 rural acres. Lounge bar with log-burn-
ing stove. Comfortable, rustic bedrooms spread around the central courtyard:
some boast terraces; No.15 was where the prize bull was once kept. Main barn
houses restaurant. Concise modern menus employ good seasonal produce.

🍴 **Tilbury**                              ⌷ ⌷ **P** 𝚅𝙸𝚂𝙰 ⊙⊙ 𝙰𝙴
*Watton Rd* ✉ *SG3 6TB* – ☏ *(01438) 815 550 – www.thetilbury.co.uk – Closed*
*Sunday dinner*
**Rest** – Menu £ 18 (lunch) – Carte £ 25/33
♦ Local, seasonal produce leads the way at Paul Bloxham's pub. Menus change
regularly and feature a real mix of dishes, from classical steaks to adventurous
stuffed lobster and scallop sea bass.

▶ London 79 mi – Coventry 23 mi – Leicester 31 mi – Northampton 13 mi
🏌 Norton Rd, ☏ *(01327) 70 28 29*
🏌 Hellidon Lakes H. & C.C. Hellidon, ☏ *(01327) 26 25 50*
🏌 Staverton Park Staverton, ☏ *(01327) 30 20 00*

🏨 **Fawsley Hall** ॐ       ≤ ⌷ ◐ ⌷ ⑨⑩ ⋔ ₺₺ ⅍ ₺ ᵞ ⅃ **P** 𝚅𝙸𝚂𝙰 ⊙⊙ 𝙰𝙴
*Fawsley, South : 6.5 mi by A 45 off A 361* ✉ *NN11 3BA* – ☏ *(01327) 892 000*
*– www.fawsleyhall.com*
**56 rm** ⌷ – ♦£ 185 ♦♦£ 355 – 2 suites
**Rest** *Equilibrium* **Rest** *Bess's Brasserie* – see restaurant listing
♦ Set in 2,000 peaceful acres, a luxurious Tudor manor house boasting Georgian
and Victorian wings. Cavernous grand hall and exclusive leisure club/spa. Well-
appointed bedrooms vary from wing to wing: most characterful are in the
main house.

🍴🍴🍴 **Equilibrium** – at Fawsley Hall Hotel        ⌷ ◐ ₺ **P** 𝚅𝙸𝚂𝙰 ⊙⊙ 𝙰𝙴
*Fawsley, South : 6.5 mi by A 45 off A 361* ✉ *NN11 3BA* – ☏ *(01327) 892 000*
*– www.fawsleyhall.com – Closed Sunday and Monday*
**Rest** – *(dinner only) (booking essential)* Carte £ 34/46
♦ Spread over two characterful rooms, an intimate hotel restaurant set within a
grand Tudor manor house. European menu offers both traditional combinations
and dishes with more innovative touches.

🍴🍴 **Bess's Brasserie** – at Fawsley Hall Hotel       ⌷ ◐ ₺ **P** 𝚅𝙸𝚂𝙰 ⊙⊙ 𝙰𝙴
*Fawsley, South : 6.5 mi by A 45 off A 361* ✉ *NN11 3BA* – ☏ *(01327) 892 000*
*– www.fawsleyhall.com*
**Rest** – Carte £ 21/35
♦ Situated in the heart of an impressive manor house, a smart yet informal hotel
dining room boasting an impressive stone fireplace. Menu offers brasserie classics; some in a choice of dish size.

**at Staverton** Southwest : 2.75 mi by A 45 off A 425 – ✉ Daventry

🏠 **Colledges House**                    ⌷ ⅍ ᵞ **P** 𝚅𝙸𝚂𝙰 ⊙⊙
*Oakham Ln, off Glebe Ln* ✉ *NN11 6JQ* – ☏ *(01327) 702 737*
*– www.colledgeshouse.co.uk*
**4 rm** ⌷ – ♦£ 68/70 ♦♦£ 98/106   **Rest** – Menu £ 32
♦ Part 17C house in a quiet village. Full of charm with antiques, curios, portraits
and an inglenook fireplace. Homely bedrooms are in the main house and an adjacent cottage. Evening meals served at elegant oak table.

**DEAL** – Kent – **504** Y30 – pop. 29 248

▶ London 78 mi – Canterbury 19 mi – Dover 8 mi – Margate 16 mi

🄯 129 High St ✆ (01304) 36 95 76, www.deal.gov.uk

🄯 Walmer & Kingsdown Kingsdown The Leas, ✆ (01304) 37 32 56

### Dunkerley's
≼ ⚿ 📶 VISA ⊙ AE ⊙
*19 Beach St* ⊠ *CT14 7AH* – ✆ *(01304) 375 016* – *www.dunkerleys.co.uk*
**16 rm** ⌑ – ♦£ 70/80 ♦♦£ 100/150
**Rest** *Restaurant* – see restaurant listing
◆ The hotel faces the beach and the Channel. Bedrooms are comfortably furnished and the principal rooms have jacuzzis. Comfortable bar offers a lighter menu than the restaurant.

### Number One without rest
⚿ 📶 VISA ⊙
*1 Ranelagh Rd* ⊠ *CT14 7BG* – ✆ *(01304) 364 459*
– *www.numberonebandb.co.uk*
**4 rm** ⌑ – ♦£ 80 ♦♦£ 100
◆ Former boarding house close to the promenade, refurbished in a contemporary style. Understated bedrooms boast bold feature wallpaper, luxury bathrooms, fine bed linen and stimulating art.

### Restaurant – at Dunkerley's Hotel
🏠 AC VISA ⊙ AE ⊙
*19 Beach St* ⊠ *CT14 7AH* – ✆ *(01304) 375 016* – *www.dunkerleys.co.uk*
– *Closed Sunday dinner and Monday*
**Rest** – Seafood – Menu £ 16/28
◆ With views of the Channel, the restaurant is best known for preparing locally caught seafood, although non-seafood options are also available. Wide ranging wine list.

**at Worth** Northwest : 5 mi by A 258

### Solley Farm House without rest
🚗 ⚿ 📶 P VISA ⊙
*The Street* ⊠ *CT14 ODG* – ✆ *(01304) 613 701* – *www.solleyfarmhouse.co.uk*
**3 rm** ⌑ – ♦£ 85/90 ♦♦£ 120/130
◆ 300 year old house, overlooking the village pond and church. Full of character and charm, with a very welcoming owner. Organic breakfasts served on the terrace in summer.

**DEDDINGTON** – Oxfordshire – **503** Q28 – pop. 1 595

▶ London 72 mi – Birmingham 46 mi – Coventry 33 mi – Oxford 18 mi

### Old Post House without rest
🚗 ⌛ P
*New St, on A4260* ⊠ *OX15 OSP* – ✆ *(01869) 338 978* – *www.oldposthouse.co.uk*
**3 rm** ⌑ – ♦£ 60 ♦♦£ 85
◆ Charming 17C sandstone house with mullioned windows and beautiful walled garden. Comfy, open-fired lounge and spacious, classically styled bedrooms. Outdoor pool by prior arrangement. Tea and cake on arrival; tasty Aga-cooked breakfasts and homemade preserves.

**DEDHAM** – Essex – **504** W28 – pop. 1 847 – ⊠ **Colchester**
▌ Great Britain

▶ London 63 mi – Chelmsford 30 mi – Colchester 8 mi – Ipswich 12 mi

🄖 Stour Valley★ – Flatford Mill★, E : 6 mi by B 1029, A 12 and B 1070

### Maison Talbooth 🖘
≼ 🚗 ⌛ ⊙ ✗ ⚿ 📶 P VISA ⊙ AE ⊙
*Stratford Rd, West : 0.5 mi* ⊠ *C07 6HN* – ✆ *(01206) 322 367*
– *www.milsomhotels.com*
**12 rm** ⌑ – ♦£ 200 ♦♦£ 405
**Rest** *Le Talbooth* – see restaurant listing
◆ Quiet, Victorian country house with intimate atmosphere, lawned gardens and views over river valley. Some rooms are smart and contemporary, others more traditional in style.

**ENGLAND**

🏠 **Milsoms** 🍴 🥘 AC rest, 📶 🔥 P VISA 👁 AE

*Stratford Rd, West : 0.75 mi* ✉ *CO7 6HW –* 📞 *(01206) 322 795*
*– www.milsomhotels.com*
**15 rm –** 🛏£ 117 🛏🛏£ 184, ☐ £ 16
**Rest –** *(bookings not accepted)* Carte £ 21/41
◆ Modern hotel overlooking Constable's Dedham Vale with attractive garden and stylish lounge. Bright, airy and welcoming rooms feature unfussy décor and modern colours. Likeably modish, wood-floored bistro.

🍴🍴🍴 **Le Talbooth** 🍴 🥘 ✿ P VISA 👁 AE ⓞ

*Gun Hill, West : 0.5 mi* ✉ *C07 6HP –* 📞 *(01206) 323 150*
*– www.milsomhotels.com – Closed Sunday dinner October-June*
**Rest –** Menu £ 29 (lunch) – Carte £ 39/57 ❀
◆ Part Tudor house in attractive riverside setting. Exposed beams and real fires contribute to the traditional atmosphere. Menus combine the classic and the more modern. Well chosen wine list.

🍺 **Sun Inn** with rm 🍴 🥘 🍴 📶 P VISA 👁 AE

*High St* ✉ *CO7 6DF –* 📞 *(01206) 323 351 – www.thesuninndedham.com*
*– Closed 25-26 December*
**5 rm** ☐ **–** 🛏£ 65/110 🛏🛏£ 75/160
**Rest –** Menu £ 15 (weekdays) – Carte £ 25/35
◆ Sunny-coloured pub in idyllic village location. Italian-themed à la carte features simple, tasty dishes. Bar board menu offers sandwiches, terrines and tarts. Contemporary bedrooms.

## DENHAM – Buckinghamshire – **504** S29 – **pop. 2 269** ▌ Great Britain    **11** D3

▶ London 20 mi – Buckingham 42 mi – Oxford 41 mi
◉ Windsor Castle★★★, Eton★★ and Windsor★, S : 10 mi by A 412

🍺 **Swan Inn** 🍴 🥘 P VISA 👁 AE

*Village Rd* ✉ *UB9 5BH –* 📞 *(01895) 832 085 – www.swaninndenham.co.uk*
*– Closed 25-26 December*
**Rest –** *(booking essential)* Carte £ 23/28
◆ Wisteria-clad, red-brick Georgian pub with pleasant terrace and gardens. Menus change with the seasons and offer plenty of interest; sides are appealing and pudding is a must.

## DERBY – Derby – **502** P25 – **pop. 247 530** ▌ Great Britain    **16** B2

▶ London 132 mi – Birmingham 40 mi – Coventry 49 mi – Leicester 29 mi
✈ Nottingham East Midlands Airport, Castle Donington : 📞 (0871) 919 9000, SE : 12 mi by A 6 X
ℹ Market Pl 📞 (01332) 25 58 02, www.visitderby.co.uk
▪ Sinfin Wilmore Rd, 📞 (01332) 76 63 23
▪ Mickleover Uttoxeter Rd, 📞 (01332) 51 60 11
▪ Kedleston Park Quardon Kedlston, 📞 (01332) 84 00 35
▪ Breadsall Priory H. & C.C. Morley Moor Rd, 📞 (01332) 83 61 06
▪ Allestree Park Allestree Allestree Hall, 📞 (01332) 55 06 16
◉ City★ – Museum and Art Gallery★ (Collection of Derby Porcelain★) YZ **M1** – Royal Crown Derby Museum★ **AC** Z **M2**
◉ Kedleston Hall★★ **AC**, NW : 4.5 mi by Kedleston Rd X

🏠 **Cathedral Quarter** 🏠 ▐ AC 🍴 📶 🔥 VISA 👁 AE ⓞ

*16 St. Marys Gate* ✉ *DE1 3JR –* 📞 *(01332) 546 080 – www.finessecollection.com*
**38 rm** ☐ **–** 🛏£ 60/120 🛏🛏£ 80/200    Y**x**
**Rest** *Opulence* – *(closed Sunday dinner and Monday)* Menu £ 16/20 – Carte £ 27/41
◆ Boutique-style hotel retaining original features like mosaic floors and marble pillars. Bedrooms vary in size but all are furnished in a contemporary style with pastel shades. First floor Opulence boasts wood panelling and a 10-seater chef's table. Modern menus.

# DERBY

# CENTRE

ENGLAND

**at Darley Abbey** North : 2.5 mi off A 6 - X – ⊠ Derby

XX **Darleys**      AK P VISA ◎◎
*Darley Abbey Mill* ⊠ *DE22 1DZ* – 𝒞 *(01332) 364 987* – *www.darleys.com*
– *Closed 25 December-15 January, Sunday dinner and bank holidays*
**Rest** – *(booking advisable)* Menu £ 20 *(lunch)* – Carte £ 33/46
♦ Popular weir-side restaurant with river views. Attractive terrace, modern bar-
lounge and traditional dining room. Great value lunches and more ambitious
modern European dishes in the evening.

---

**DEVIZES** – Wiltshire – **503** O29 – pop. 15 272     **4** C2
▶ London 98 mi – Bristol 38 mi – Salisbury 25 mi – Southampton 50 mi
🛈 Market Pl 𝒞 (01380) 72 94 08, www.devizes.org.uk
🖼 Erlestoke, 𝒞 (01380) 83 10 69
◉ St John's Church★★ – Market Place★ – Wiltshire Heritage Museum★ **AC**
◐ Potterne (Porch House★★) S : 2.5 mi by A 360 – E : Vale of Pewsey★.
Stonehenge★★★ **AC**, SE : 16 mi by A 360 and A 344 – Avebury★★ (The Stones★,
Church★) NE : 7 mi by A 361

**at Potterne** South : 2.25 mi on A 360 – ⊠ Devizes

⛫ **Blounts Court Farm** without rest ॐ     🚗 🐾 � 🛜 📶 P VISA ◎◎
🏠 *Coxhill Ln* ⊠ *SN10 5PH* – 𝒞 *(01380) 727 180* – *www.blountscourtfarm.co.uk*
**3 rm** 🖵 – ♦£ 45/82 ♦♦£ 75/82
♦ Delightfully run farmhouse set on a 150 acre working farm. Snug inner consists
of a cosy lounge and spacious breakfast room filled with clocks and curios;
framed pastels and country photos abound. Warm, comfy, well-kept bedrooms
pay good attention to detail.

**at Rowde** Northwest : 2 mi by A 361 on A 342 – ⊠ Devizes

🍺 **George & Dragon** with rm     🚗 🍽 P VISA ◎◎
*High St* ⊠ *SN10 2PN* – 𝒞 *(01380) 723 053*
– *www.thegeorgeanddragonrowde.co.uk* – *Closed Sunday dinner*
**3 rm** – ♦£ 85/125 ♦♦£ 85/125, 🖵 £ 8
**Rest** – Seafood – *(booking essential)* Menu £ 19 – Carte £ 21/39
♦ Rustic and cosy 16C coaching inn with open fires, solid stone floors and
wooden beams. Oft-changing menu has strong emphasis on seafood, with fish
delivered daily from Cornwall. Old-world charm meets modern facilities in the individually designed bedrooms.

---

**DIDSBURY** – Greater Manchester – **502** N23 – see Manchester

---

**DITCHEAT** – Somerset     **4** C2
▶ London 124 mi – Bath 29 mi

🍺 **Manor House Inn** with rm     🚗 🍽 📶 P VISA ◎◎ AE
⊠ *BA4 6RB* – 𝒞 *(01749) 860 276* – *www.manorhouseinn.co.uk* – *Closed 25*
*December, Sunday dinner and restricted opening Christmas-New Year*
**3 rm** 🖵 – ♦£ 55/85 ♦♦£ 85    **Rest** – Carte £ 21/31
♦ Welcoming, equestrian-themed pub set on the Somerset Levels. Traditional
open fires and a restored skittle alley are coupled with honest classical cooking
and locally sourced produce. Former stables house cosy bedrooms with good
mod cons.

---

**DITCHLING** – West Sussex – **504** T31 – pop. 2 027     **7** D2
▶ London 47 mi

⛫ **Tovey Lodge** without rest ॐ     ⪻ 🚗 🖵 🛜 📶 P VISA ◎◎
*Underhill Ln, South : 1 mi by B 2112 off Ditchling Beacon rd* ⊠ *BN6 8XE*
– 𝒞 *(08456) 120 544* – *www.sussexcountryholidays.co.uk*
**5 rm** 🖵 – ♦£ 110/150 ♦♦£ 125/165
♦ Luxuriously appointed, keenly run house with mature gardens and pleasant
views. Bedrooms boast modern technology and luxurious bathrooms; Maple,
with its balcony, is the best.

ENGLAND

## DODDINGTON – Kent – **504** W30                                9 C2
▶ London 50 mi – Croydon 51 mi – Barnet 73 mi – Ealing 87 mi

⌂ **Old Vicarage** without rest ⌖                    ⌷ ⌷ ⌷ **P** _VISA_ ⌷ **AE**
*Church Hill* ⌷ ME9 0BD – ⌀ (01795) 886 136
– www.oldvicaragedoddington.co.uk – Closed 24 December-2 January
**3 rm** ⌷ – †£ 58/65 ††£ 79/89
♦ Grade II listed former vicarage for the 12C church, where wooden beams, exposed stone and period features blend with modern furnishings. Impressive hall, comfy lounge and striking antique dining table. Large bedrooms boast coffee machines and Bose sound systems.

## DOGMERSFIELD – Hampshire                                      7 C1
▶ London 44 mi – Farnham 6 mi – Fleet 2 mi

🏠🏠🏠 **Four Seasons** ⌖        ⌷ ⌷ ⌷ ⌷ ⌷ ⌷ ⌷ ⌷ ⌷ ⌷ ⌷ ⌷ ⌷ ⌷ **P**
*Dogmersfield Park, Chalky Ln* ⌷ RG27 8TD – ⌀ (01252)        _VISA_ ⌷ **AE** ⌷
853 000 – www.fourseasons.com/hampshire
**111 rm** – †£ 195/265 ††£ 195/265, ⌷ £ 25 – 22 suites
**Rest** *Seasons* – (closed dinner Sunday and Monday) (dinner only and Sunday lunch) Carte £ 45/70
♦ Part Georgian splendour in extensive woodlands; many original features in situ. Superb spa facilities: vast selection of leisure pursuits. Luxurious, highly equipped bedrooms. Restaurant has thoroughly modish, relaxing feel.

## DONCASTER – South Yorkshire – **502** Q23 – pop. 67 977       23 C3
▶ London 173 mi – Kingston-upon-Hull 46 mi – Leeds 30 mi – Nottingham 46 mi
🛬 Robin Hood Airport : ⌀ (0871) 220 2210, SE : 7m off A638
ℹ 38-40 High St ⌀ (01302) 73 43 09, www.visitdoncaster.com
🏌 Doncaster Town Moor Belle Vue Bawtry Rd, ⌀ (01302) 53 37 78
🏌 Crookhill Park Conisborough, ⌀ (01709) 86 29 79
🏌 Wheatley Amthorpe Rd, ⌀ (01302) 83 16 55
🏌 Owston Park Owston Owston Lane, Carcroft, ⌀ (01302) 33 08 21

🏠🏠🏠 **Mount Pleasant**        ⌷ ⌷ ⌷ ⌷ rm, ⌷ rest, ⌷ ⌷ ⌷ **P** _VISA_ ⌷ **AE** ⌷
*Great North Rd, Southeast : 6 mi on A 638* ⌷ DN11 0HW – ⌀ (01302) 868 696
– www.mountpleasant.co.uk
**54 rm** ⌷ – †£ 79/99 ††£ 99/169 – 2 suites
**Rest** *Garden* – Carte £ 27/41
♦ Well-run, privately owned hotel with spacious inner. Comfortable, individually styled bedrooms: one with a five-poster bed; some with jacuzzi baths or saunas. Pleasant wellness centre and treatment rooms. Large formal dining room offers extensive, classical menu.

## DONHEAD-ST-ANDREW – Wiltshire – **503** N30                   4 C3
▶ London 115 mi – Bournemouth 34 mi – Poole 32 mi – Bath 37 mi

🍴 **Forester Inn**                          ⌷ ⌷ **P** _VISA_ ⌷ **AE** ⌷
*Lower St* ⌷ SP7 9EE – ⌀ (01747) 828 038
– www.theforesterdonheadstandrews.co.uk – Closed Sunday dinner
**Rest** – Menu £ 19 (weekdays) – Carte £ 23/31
♦ Gloriously rustic 13C thatched pub. Menus display a strong seafood base, with constantly changing Brixham fish and a set 3 course selection. Charcuterie and tapas dishes on offer in the bar.

## DORCHESTER – Dorset – **503** M31 – pop. 17 861               4 C3
▶ London 135 mi – Bournemouth 27 mi – Exeter 53 mi – Southampton 53 mi
ℹ 11 Antelope Walk ⌀ (01305) 26 79 92, www.visit-dorchester.co.uk
🏌 Came Down, ⌀ (01305) 81 34 94
◉ Town★ - Dorset County Museum★ **AC**
◉ Maiden Castle★★ (⌀★) SW : 2.5 mi – Puddletown Church★, NE : 5.5 mi by A 35. Moreton Church★★, E : 7.5 mi – Bere Regis★ (St John the Baptist Church★ - Roof★★) NE : 11 mi by A 35 – Athelhampton House★ **AC**, NE : 6.5 mi by A 35 - Cerne Abbas★, N : 7 mi by A 352 – Milton Abbas★, NE : 12 mi on A 354 and by-road

ENGLAND

🏠 **Yalbury Cottage**    ≈ 🛜 📱 **P** 𝐕𝐈𝐒𝐀 ⓒⓞ
*Lower Bockhampton, East : 3.75 mi by A 35 ⊠ DT2 8PZ – 𝒞 (01305) 262 382
– www.yalburycottage.com – Closed 23-27 December*
**8 rm** ⌂ – ♦♦£ 70/85 ♦♦♦£ 100/115
**Rest** – *(closed Sunday and Monday to non-residents) (dinner only)* Menu £ 36
♦ Welcoming thatched cottage with a small garden, set in a quiet hamlet. Characterful beamed lounge with a gas-fire. Modern, comfortable bedrooms are located in the extension. Linen-clad dining room offers a set menu; most produce is sourced from within nine miles.

🏠 **Little Court** without rest    ≈ 🍵 ✗✗ 🍴 🛜 📱 𝐕𝐈𝐒𝐀 ⓒⓞ
*5 Westleaze, Charminster, North : 1 mi by A 37, turning right at Loders garage
⊠ DT2 9PZ – 𝒞 (01305) 261 576 – www.littlecourt.net*
**8 rm** ⌂ – ♦♦£ 99 ♦♦♦£ 99/109
♦ Lutyens style house boasting Edwardian wood/brickwork, leaded windows and mature gardens with a pool and tennis court. Bedrooms display original features and modern furnishings; one four-poster.

✗✗ **Sienna** (Russell Brown)    𝐀𝐂 𝐕𝐈𝐒𝐀 ⓒⓞ
✿ *36 High West St ⊠ DT1 1UP – 𝒞 (01305) 250 022 – www.siennarestaurant.co.uk
– Closed 2 weeks spring, 2 weeks autumn, Sunday and Monday*
**Rest** – *(booking essential)* Menu £ 29/43
**Spec.** Veal with white beans and pickled carrots. Fillet of brill with scallops, Jersey Royals and asparagus. Selvatica chocolate tasting plate.
♦ Small high street restaurant with frosted glass façade, intimate interior and smartly laid tables. Choice of concise à la carte or 6 course tasting menu. Precise cooking uses top quality local produce and classic flavour combinations. Polite, measured service.

**at Winterbourne Steepleton** West : 4.75 mi by B 3150 and A 35 on B 3159
– ⊠ Dorchester

🏠 **Old Rectory** without rest    ≈ ✗ 📱
*⊠ DT2 9LG – 𝒞 (01305) 889 468 – www.theoldrectorybandb.co.uk – Closed 1
week Christmas*
**4 rm** ⌂ – ♦♦£ 60 ♦♦♦£ 100
♦ Attractive house in pretty village; cross the brook and enter mature gardens. Comfy lounge and conservatory breakfast room. Immaculate bedrooms with homely, modern décor and smart bathrooms.

---

**DORRIDGE** – West Midlands – **503** O26 – ⊠ **Birmingham**    **19 C2**
▶ London 109 mi – Birmingham 11 mi – Warwick 11 mi

✗✗ **Forest** with rm    ☞ 𝐀𝐂 rest, 🍴 ♨ 📱 𝐕𝐈𝐒𝐀 ⓒⓞ 𝐀𝐄
*25 Station Approach ⊠ B93 8JA – 𝒞 (01564) 772 120 – www.forest-hotel.com
– Closed 25 December and Sunday dinner*
**12 rm** – ♦♦£ 95 ♦♦♦£ 125    **Rest** – Menu £ 16 (weekdays) – Carte £ 21/29
♦ Attractive red-brick and timber former pub with a busy ambience. Food is its backbone: modern classics served in stylish bar and restaurant. Cool, modern bedrooms.

---

**DOUGLAS** – Douglas – **502** G21 – see Man (Isle of)

---

**DOVER** – Kent – **504** Y30 – pop. 35 338 ▌ Great Britain    **9 D2**
▶ London 76 mi – Brighton 84 mi
🚢 to France (Calais) (P & O Stena Line) frequent services daily (1 h 15 mn) – to France (Calais) (SeaFrance S.A.) frequent services daily (1 h 30 mn) – to France (Boulogne) (SpeedFerries) 3-5 daily (50 mn)
🛈 Biggin 𝒞 (01304) 20 51 08, www.whitecliffscountry.org.uk
◙ Castle ★★ AC Y
◙ White Cliffs, Langdon Cliffs, NE : 1 mi on A 2 Z and A 258

# DOVER

**ENGLAND**

**at St Margaret's at Cliffe** Northeast : 4 mi by A 258 - Z – ⊠ Dover

**Wallett's Court Country House**

*West Cliffe, Northwest : 0.75 mi on Dover rd* ⊠ *CT15 6EW* — 𝒞 *(01304) 852 424* – *www.wallettscourt.com* – *Closed 24-26 December*
**17 rm** ⊇ – **†**£ 90/150 **††**£ 150/290

**Rest** *The Restaurant* – *(dinner only and Sunday lunch)* Menu £ 22/40 ⌘

◆ Heavily beamed 17C country house with characterful lounge and comfy bar. Four-poster bedrooms in main house; rustic rooms in annexes; most luxurious rooms above pleasant spa. Atmospheric restaurant with smartly laid tables offers ambitious, original, modern menu.

**DOWNTON** – Hampshire – **503** P31 – see Lymington

189

**DREWSTEIGNTON** – Devon – **503** I31 – pop. 668                              **2** C2

▶ London 190 mi – Plymouth 56 mi – Torbay 35 mi – Exeter 15 mi

XX   **Old Inn** with rm                                              (¹⁰ VISA ⚫⚪

☒ EX6 6QR – ℰ (01647) 281 276 – www.old-inn.co.uk – *Closed 2 weeks winter and Sunday-Tuesday*
**3 rm** ⌂ – †£ 70 ††£ 90/100
**Rest** – *(dinner only) (booking essential)* Menu £ 43

♦ Having run 22 Mill Street in Chagford, the owners moved to this delightful cottage in an idyllic English village. Anthea is a natural hostess and clearly loves the place; Duncan's classically based cooking is gutsy, boldly flavoured and generous, and his set menu sings seasonality.

---

**DROITWICH SPA** – Worcestershire – **503** N27 – pop. 22 585                  **19** C3

▶ London 129 mi – Birmingham 20 mi – Bristol 66 mi – Worcester 6 mi

🄳 Victoria Sq ℰ (01905) 77 43 12, www.cotswolds.info

🄸🄸 Droitwich G. & C.C. Ford Lane, ℰ (01905) 77 43 44

**at Cutnall Green** North : 3 mi on A 442 – ☒ Droitwich Spa

🄸⌂   **Chequers**                                              ⚞ 🏠 **P** VISA ⚫⚪

*Kidderminster Rd* ☒ WR9 0PJ – ℰ (01299) 851 292
– www.chequerscutnallgreen.co.uk – *Closed 25 December, dinner 26 December and 1 January*
**Rest** – Menu £ 17 (weekdays) – Carte £ 21/30

♦ Cosy roadside pub, run by the former England football team chef and his wife. Asian-influenced menus offer light bites and pub classics, with more adventurous fish and offal-based specials.

**at Hadley Heath** Southwest : 4 mi by Ombersley Way, A 4133 and Ladywood rd – ☒ Droitwich Spa

⌂   **Old Farmhouse** without rest ⌂                    ⚞ ℅ ℅ (¹⁰ **P**

☒ WR9 0AR – ℰ (01905) 620 837 – www.theoldfarmhouse.uk.com – *Closed 25 December-1 February*
**5 rm** ⌂ – †£ 40/45 ††£ 75

♦ Converted farmhouse in quiet and rural location. Spacious comfortable rooms, three in the main house and two, more private and perhaps suited to families, in the annexe.

---

**DROXFORD** – Hampshire – **504** Q31                                         **6** B2

▶ London 79 mi – Southampton 21 mi – Portsmouth 16 mi – Basingstoke 37 mi

🄸⌂   **Bakers Arms**                                              🏠 **P** VISA ⚫⚪

☺   *High St* ☒ SO32 3PA – ℰ (01489) 877 533 – www.thebakersarmsdroxford.com
– *Closed Sunday dinner and Monday*
**Rest** – Carte £ 25/31

♦ Proudly run, traditional village pub with open-plan bar, Chesterfield sofas and roaring log fire; decorative beer adverts, Victorian photographs and stag heads. Unfussy, filling dishes rely on locally sourced produce. Friendly, polite service. Local ales.

---

**DRY DODDINGTON** – Lincolnshire – **see Grantham**

---

**DULVERTON** – Somerset – **503** J30 – pop. 1 870                            **3** A2

▶ London 198 mi – Barnstaple 27 mi – Exeter 26 mi – Minehead 18 mi

👁 Village★

🄲 Exmoor National Park★★ - Tarr Steps★★, NW : 6 mi by B 3223

🄸⌂   **Woods**                                                    🏠 VISA ⚫⚪

*4 Banks Sq* ☒ TA22 9BU – ℰ (01398) 324 007 – *Closed dinner 1 January and 26 December*
**Rest** – Carte £ 16/25

♦ Delightful pub displaying charming décor and smart hand-made furniture. Regularly changing, classical Gallic menu uses both French and local, traceable produce; meat is from the owner's farm.

**at Brushford** South : 1.75 mi on B 3222 – ⊠ Dulverton

⟨ **Three Acres Country House** without rest 　　　⌂ ⌘ ⌘ **P** _VISA_ ⊚⊚
⊠ TA22 9AR – ℰ (01398) 323 730 – www.threeacrescountryhouse.co.uk
**6 rm** ⌨ – ⍾**£** 75 ⍾⍾**£** 120
♦ Remotely set guesthouse boasting nearly 3 acres of mature gardens/parkland. Comfy lounge, small bar, pine-furnished breakfast room and pleasant terrace. Large, cosy bedrooms with country views.

---

**DUNSTER** – Somerset – **503** J30 – pop. 848　　　　　　　　　　　　**3** A2
▶ London 185 mi – Minehead 3 mi – Taunton 23 mi
◉ Town★★ - Castle★★ **AC** (upper rooms ⩽★) - Water Mill★ **AC**
　- St George's Church★ - Dovecote★

⟨ **Exmoor House** without rest 　　　　　　　　　　⌘ ⌘ _VISA_ ⊚⊚
12 West St ⊠ TA24 6SN – ℰ (01643) 821 268 – www.exmoorhousedunster.co.uk
– March-25 December
**6 rm** ⌨ – ⍾**£** 50 ⍾⍾**£** 85
♦ Terraced Georgian house on the main street of a historic town; run by warm, welcoming owners. Comfy, chintzy lounge and spacious pine-furnished breakfast room. Cosy, well-kept bedrooms.

---

**DURHAM** – Durham – **501** P19 – pop. 42 100 ▯ Great Britain　　　　**24** B3
▶ London 267 mi – Leeds 77 mi – Middlesbrough 23 mi
　– Newcastle upon Tyne 20 mi
ℹ 2 Millennium Pl ℰ (0191) 384 37 20, www.thisisdurham.com
🅁 Mount Oswald South Rd, ℰ (0191) 386 75 27
◉ City★★★ - Cathedral★★★ (Nave★★★, Chapel of the Nine Altars★★★, Sanctuary Knocker★) B – Oriental Museum★★ **AC** (at Durham University by A 167) B – City and Riverside (Prebends' Bridge ⩽★★★ A , Framwellgate Bridge ⩽★★ B)
　– Monastic Buildings (Cathedral Treasury★, Central Tower⩽★) B
　– Castle★ (Norman chapel★) **AC** B
🆚 Hartlepool Historic Quay★, SE : 14 mi by A 181, A 19 and A 179

Plan on next page

ENGLAND

🏠 **Farnley Tower** 　　　　　　　⌂ ⌘ **P** _VISA_ ⊚⊚ _AE_ ⓪
The Avenue ⊠ DH1 4DX – ℰ (0191) 375 00 11 – www.farnley-tower.co.uk
**13 rm** ⌨ – ⍾**£** 65/75 ⍾⍾**£** 85/95　　　　　　　　　　　　A**c**
**Rest Gourmet Spot** – ℰ (0191) 384 66 55 (closed Sunday-Monday) (dinner only) Menu £ 25/38
♦ Spacious Victorian house in quiet residential area close to city centre. Modern, airy, well-equipped bedrooms with a good degree of comfort. Gourmet Spot, stylish and slick in black granite and leather, serves original, modern cuisine.

⟨ **Cathedral View Town House** without rest 　　　⌂ ⌘ ⌘ _VISA_ ⊚⊚
212 Lower Gilesgate ⊠ DH1 1QN – ℰ (0191) 386 95 66
– www.cathedralview.com – Closed 24 December-4 January　　　　B**n**
**6 rm** ⌨ – ⍾**£** 70/100 ⍾⍾**£** 90/125
♦ Cosy, welcoming, Georgian townhouse with terraced garden, set in the older part of the city near the centre. Attractive breakfast room with good views; extensive menu includes daily specials. Spacious, individually named rooms.

⟨ **Castle View** without rest 　　　　　　　⌘ ⌘ _VISA_ ⊚⊚ ⓪
4 Crossgate ⊠ DH1 4PS – ℰ (0191) 386 88 52 – www.castle-view.co.uk
– Closed 15 December-10 January　　　　　　　　　　　　　A**e**
**6 rm** ⌨ – ⍾**£** 55/70 ⍾⍾**£** 80/90
♦ Attractive Georgian townhouse set beside a Norman castle, off a steep cobbled hill, reputedly once the vicarage to adjacent church. Have breakfast on the terrace in summer. Individually furnished bedrooms.

## DURHAM

NEWCASTLE-UPON-TYNE (A 167)
CONSETT

A 691

SUNDERLAND

A 177 (A 167) DARLINGTON

A 691 CROOK, (A 167)

A 690 CROOK, (A 167)

## ✗✗ Finbarr's
⚐ P VISA ⓪⓪ AE

*Waddington St, Flass Vale* ⊠ *DH1 4BG –* ℰ *(0191) 370 9999*
*– www.finbarrsrestaurant.co.uk*                                          **Ax**
**Rest** *– (booking advisable)* Menu £ 17 *(lunch)* – Carte £ 22/45
♦ Hidden in a hotel outside the city and leased by the owner. Spacious modern
dining room with monochrome photos and well-spaced, smartly laid tables.
Modern, bi-monthly menus display strong French influences. Smooth, professional service.

## ✗ Bistro 21
⚐ ⇔ P VISA ⓪⓪ AE
⊕

*Aykley Heads House, Aykley Heads, Northwest : 1.5 mi by A 691 and B 6532*
⊠ *DH1 5TS –* ℰ *(0191) 384 43 54 – www.bistrotwentyone.co.uk – Closed Sunday*
*and bank holidays*
**Rest** *– (booking essential)* Menu £ 19 *(weekdays)* – Carte £ 23/44
♦ Popular restaurant in former stables of 17C villa, with French farmhouse styling
and enclosed courtyard. Fresh, uncomplicated cooking; neatly presented classics.
Good value lunch/midweek menu.

Enjoy good food without spending a fortune! Look out for the Bib Gourmand ⊕
symbol to find restaurants offering fine cuisine at special prices !

## EARL STONHAM – Suffolk – 504 X27      **15** C3

▶ London 91 mi – Ipswich 12 mi – Colchester 33 mi – Clacton-on-Sea 38 mi

⋔    **Bays Farm** without rest ✍      ✍ ⁽ᵗ⁾ **P** **VISA** ◑ **AE**

🍴    *Forward Grn, Northwest : 1 mi by A1120 on Broad Green Rd* ✉ *IP14 5HU*
     *– 𝒞 (01449) 711 286 – www.baysfarmsuffolk.co.uk*
     **4 rm** ⊑ – ♦£ 50/100 ♦♦£ 60/110
     ♦ 17C farmhouse with kitchen garden, set in 4 attractive acres. Characterful interior with comfy lounge and beamed dining room. Individually styled bedrooms; annexed 'Hayloft' is the most luxurious. Communal breakfasts of local produce and homemade bread and jam.

---

## EARSHAM – Norfolk – 504 Y26 – see Bungay

---

## EASINGWOLD – North Yorkshire – 502 Q21 – pop. 3 975 – ✉ York    **23** C2

▶ London 217 mi – Leeds 38 mi – Middlesbrough 37 mi – York 14 mi

🛈 Chapel Lane 𝒞 (01347) 82 15 30, www.visit-easingwold.com

🖊₁₈ Stillington Rd, 𝒞 (01347) 82 24 74

⋔    **Old Vicarage** without rest       ✍ ⁽ᵗ⁾ ⁽ᵗ⁾ **P**

     *Market Pl* ✉ *YO61 3AL – 𝒞 (01347) 821 015*
     *– www.oldvicarage-easingwold.co.uk – Closed 2 weeks Christmas-New Year*
     **4 rm** ⊑ – ♦£ 80/85 ♦♦£ 100/105
     ♦ Spacious, part Georgian country house with walled rose garden and adjacent croquet lawn. Immaculately kept throughout with fine period antiques in the elegant sitting room.

**at Crayke** East : 2 mi on Helmsley Rd – ✉ York

🍴    **Durham Ox** with rm       ⁽ᵗ⁾ ⁽ᵗ⁾ **P** **VISA** ◑ **AE**

     *Westway* ✉ *YO61 4TE – 𝒞 (01347) 821 506 – www.thedurhamox.com – Closed 25 December*
     **5 rm** ⊑ – ♦£ 80 ♦♦£ 100    **Rest** – *(booking essential)* Carte £ 24/35
     ♦ 300 year old, family run pub set in a sleepy hamlet. Regularly changing à la carte features hearty dishes of fresh seafood, local meats, Crayke game and tasty spit-roast chicken. Bedrooms are set in old farm cottages; some are suites, some have jacuzzis.

---

## EAST CHILTINGTON – East Sussex – see Lewes

---

## EAST CHISENBURY – Wiltshire      **4** D2

▶ London 92 mi – Bristol 51 mi – Southampton 53 mi – Reading 51 mi

🍴    **Red Lion Freehouse**       ✍ ⁽ᵗ⁾ **P** **VISA** ◑

❄   ✉ *SN9 6AQ – 𝒞 (01980) 671 124 – www.redlionfreehouse.com*
     **Rest** – *(booking advisable)* Menu £ 18 (lunch) – Carte £ 25/33
     ♦ Delightful thatched pub with exposed beams, wood burner and a pretty garden. Enthusiastic owners cook pleasingly down-to-earth dishes, precisely composed and packed with flavour. Daily changing, seasonal à la carte, great value lunch menu and Sunday roasts.

---

## EAST END – Hampshire – see Lymington

---

## EAST GARSTON – West Berkshire      **10** B3

▶ London 69 mi – Bristol 58 mi

🍴    **Queen's Arms** with rm       ✍ ⁽ᵗ⁾ ⁽ᵗ⁾ **P** **VISA** ◑ **AE**

     ✉ *RG17 7ET – 𝒞 (01488) 648 757 – www.queensarmshotel.co.uk – Closed 25 December*
     **8 rm** ⊑ – ♦£ 90/130 ♦♦£ 120/130    **Rest** – Carte £ 22/32
     ♦ A quintessentially English inn with an atmospheric, antique-furnished bar, which celebrates country pursuits. Rustic British dishes might include shepherd's pie or rib-eye steak; the lunch menu is particularly good value. Superb bedrooms and a generous breakfast.

---

## EAST GRINSTEAD – West Sussex – 504 T30 – pop. 26 222      **7** D2

▶ London 48 mi – Brighton 30 mi – Eastbourne 32 mi – Lewes 21 mi

🖊₁₈ Copthorne Borers Arm Rd, 𝒞 (01342) 71 25 08

**Gravetye Manor** ⚜  ← 🍷 ⚐ 🕭 🍸 ⚒ 🛜 **P** 🇻 ⊗ 🇦
*Vowels Ln, Southwest : 4.5 mi by B 2110 taking second turn left towards West Hoathly* ✉ *RH19 4LJ* – ✆ *(01342) 810 567 – www.gravetyemanor.co.uk*
**18 rm** 🍽 – ⭐£ 200 ⭐⭐£ 240/550
**Rest** – *(booking essential)* Menu £ 25/37 – Carte approx. £ 55 ❀
♦ Elizabethan manor house surrounded by 35 acres of gardens and 1,000 acres of forestry land. Wood-panelled guest areas display heavy fabrics. Traditionally appointed bedrooms boast large beds. Afternoon tea and all day dining in lounges. Classical dining room.

---

**EAST HADDON** – Northamptonshire                    **16** B3
▶ London 76 mi – Birmingham 47 mi – Leicester 32 mi – Coventry 34 mi

🏠  **Red Lion** with rm                    🚗 🍴 ⚒ 🛜 **P** 🇻 ⊗ 🇦
😊  *Main St* ✉ *NN6 8BU* – ✆ *(01604) 770 223 – www.redlioneasthaddon.co.uk*
**5 rm** 🍽 – ⭐£ 80 ⭐⭐£ 95/120    **Rest** – *(closed Sunday dinner )* Carte £ 20/26
♦ Thatched, honey-stone inn set in an attractive village and boasting pretty gardens and a pleasing mix of exposed wood and slate. With the chef and owner both having worked at Rhodes 24, food is taken seriously, and menus offer upgraded pub classics. Warm, welcoming bedrooms; one in the adjacent 18C cottage.

---

**EAST HENDRED** – Oxfordshire – **503** P29 – see Wantage

---

**EAST HOATHLY** – East Sussex – **504** U31 – pop. 1 206        **8** B3
▶ London 60 mi – Brighton 16 mi – Eastbourne 13 mi – Hastings 25 mi

🏠  **Old Whyly** ⚜                    🍴 ⚐ 🌳 ⚒ 🛜 **P**
*London Rd, Northwest : 0.5 mi, turning right after post box on right, taking centre gravel drive after approx. 400 metres* ✉ *BN8 6EL* – ✆ *(01825) 840 216 – www.oldwhyly.co.uk*
**3 rm** – ⭐£ 73/95 ⭐⭐£ 135    **Rest** – Menu £ 33
♦ Charming red-brick house built in 1760, set in beautiful grounds and very personally run by its delightful owner. Guest areas mix the classic and the contemporary. Bedrooms are individually designed around a theme: choose from Tulip, French or Chinese. Stylish, minimalist dining room with homemade yoghurts and jams at breakfast and daily changing 3 course dinners.

---

**EAST KENNETT** – Wiltshire – see Marlborough

---

**EAST LAVANT** – West Sussex – see Chichester

---

**EAST WITTON** – North Yorkshire – **502** O21 – ✉ Leyburn        **22** B1
▶ London 238 mi – Leeds 45 mi – Middlesbrough 30 mi – York 39 mi

🏠  **Blue Lion** with rm                    🚗 🍴 🛜 **P** 🇻 ⊗
✉ *DL8 4SN* – ✆ *(01969) 624 273 – www.thebluelion.co.uk*
**15 rm** 🍽 – ⭐£ 70 ⭐⭐£ 145    **Rest** – *(booking essential)* Carte £ 23/44 **s**
♦ Charming, characterful countryside pub. Daily-changing menu features a tasty mix of classic and modern dishes, all with seasonality and traceability at their core. Bedrooms – in the pub and outbuildings – are warm and cosy.

---

**EASTBOURNE** – East Sussex – **504** U31 – pop. 106 562 ▯ Great Britain    **8** B3
▶ London 68 mi – Brighton 25 mi – Dover 61 mi – Maidstone 49 mi
ℹ Cornfield Rd ✆ (01323) 41 54 50, www.visiteastbourne.com
⛳ Royal Eastbourne Paradise Drive, ✆ (01323) 74 40 45
⛳ Eastbourne Downs East Dean Rd, ✆ (01323) 72 08 27
⛳ Eastbourne Golfing Park Lottbridge Drove, ✆ (01323) 52 04 00
◉ Seafront ★
◉ Beachy Head ★★★, SW : 3 mi by B 2103 Z

# EASTBOURNE

**ENGLAND**

**CENTRE**

0        300 m
0        300 yards

**BUILT UP AREA**

0        1 km
0        1/2 mile

BEACHY HEAD, SEVEN SISTERS

195

**Grand**  ≤ ⌂ ⌧ ⌧ 🌐 🏊 ⛨ 🖴 🖃 🖶 rm, 🖧 📞 🖁 🅿 VISA 🌐 AE ①
*King Edward's Par.* ⊠ BN21 4EQ – ℰ (01323) 412 345
– www.grandeastbourne.com – *Closed first 2 weeks January*  Zx
**131 rm** ⌨ – †£ 169/525 ††£ 199/555 – 10 suites
**Rest** *Mirabelle* – see restaurant listing
**Rest** *Garden Restaurant* – Menu £ 22/38 – Carte £ 31/63
♦ Built in 1871 and offering all its name promises. Retains many original features, including ornate plasterwork, column-lined corridors and a Great Hall. Classical bedrooms; pay the extra for a sea view. Lavish lounges, smart cocktail bar and formal restaurant.

**Brayscroft**  ⅍ 📞 VISA 🌐
*13 South Cliff Ave* ⊠ BN20 7AH – ℰ (01323) 647 005 – www.brayscrofthotel.co.uk
**6 rm** ⌨ – †£ 36/65 ††£ 72/80  **Rest** – Menu £ 15  Zn
♦ Spacious Edwardian house located close to the seafront, gardens and pier. Traditional lounge and dining room display antiques and Italian artwork. Comfortable, classically styled bedrooms. Evening meals by daily arrangement; tailored to each guest, they feature fresh, local, free range ingredients.

**Mirabelle** – at The Grand Hotel  🅰🅲 🅿 VISA 🌐 AE ①
*King Edward's Par.* ⊠ BN21 4EQ – ℰ (01323) 435 066 – www.grandeastbourne.com
– *Closed first 2 weeks January, Sunday and Monday*  Zx
**Rest** – (booking essential) Menu £ 24/40 – Carte £ 40/65 ⅌
♦ Plush fabrics and linen-laid tables with monogrammed silverware; formal dress code and professional team. Seasonal classics or 6 course tasting menu at dinner. Rich, well-executed cooking.

**at Jevington** Northwest : 6 mi by A 259 - Z - on Jevington Rd – ⊠ Polegate

**Hungry Monk**  🅰🅲 ⇔ 🅿 VISA 🌐 AE
*The Street* ⊠ BN26 5QF – ℰ (01323) 482 178 – www.hungrymonk.co.uk – *Closed 24-26 December, Monday and bank holidays*
**Rest** – (booking essential) Menu £ 22 (lunch) – Carte approx. £ 35
♦ Charming 14C cottages with terrace, cosy lounges, traditional main room and several private rooms. Country style cooking with modern European edge. Allegedly the birthplace of banoffee pie.

**EASTGATE** – Durham – **502** N19  **24** A3
▶ London 288 mi – Bishop Auckland 20 mi – Newcastle upon Tyne 35 mi
– Stanhope 3 mi

**Horsley Hall** ⍝  ≤ ⌂ ⌧ ⅍ 🅿 VISA 🌐 AE ①
*Southeast : 1 mi by A 689* ⊠ DL13 2LJ – ℰ (01388) 517 239
– www.horsleyhall.co.uk – *Closed 22 December-2 January*
**7 rm** ⌨ – †£ 75/85 ††£ 140
**Rest** – (closed Sunday) (booking essential for non residents) Menu £ 20/30
♦ Attractive ivy-clad former hunting lodge with 14C origins, built for the Bishop of Durham. Impressive hall; superb stained glass; mix of simple, cosy bedrooms – two with Edwardian bathrooms. Baronial style dining room boasts impressive ornate ceiling.

**EASTON** – Devon – **503** I31 – see Chagford

**EASTON** – Somerset – see Wells

**EASTON ON THE HILL** – Northamptonshire  **17** C2
▶ London 94 mi – Birmingham 75 mi – Leicester 30 mi – Coventry 61 mi

**Exeter Arms** with rm  ⌂ ⌧ ⅍ 📞 🅿 VISA 🌐
*21 Stamford Rd* ⊠ PE9 3NS – ℰ (01780) 756 321 – www.theexeterarms.net
– *Closed Sunday dinner*
**6 rm** ⌨ – †£ 70/150 ††£ 90/200  **Rest** – Carte £ 23/38
♦ Sympathetically yet stylishly restored 18C inn adorned with copper pans, enamel signs and hop bines. Eat in the snug candlelit restaurant or stylish conservatory. Choose from the chef's signature dishes, tasty pizzas or 'home comforts'. Stylish, well-appointed bedrooms boast smart modern bathrooms.

**EBRINGTON** – Gloucestershire – **504** O27 – see Chipping Campden

ENGLAND

## ECCLESTON – Lancashire – 502 L23 – pop. 4 708
20 A2

▶ London 219 mi – Birmingham 103 mi – Liverpool 29 mi – Preston 11 mi

⌂ **Parr Hall Farm** without rest     🛋 ⅌ ⁽ᵗ⁾ **P** **VISA** ⓒⓞ
*Parr Ln.* ✉ *PR7 5SL* – ℰ *(01257) 451 917* – *www.parrhallfarm.com*
**10 rm** ⌕ – ┆£ 40 ┆┆£ 70
♦ Welcoming, red-brick former farmhouse. Low-beamed, pine-furnished breakfast room. Bedrooms, located in the adjacent barn conversion, boast country style fabrics and modern bathrooms.

## ECKINGTON – Derbyshire – 502 P24 – pop. 16 684
16 B1

▶ London 155 mi – Leeds 49 mi – Sheffield 10 mi – Manchester 58 mi

⍟ **Inn at Troway**     🛋 ☕ **P** **VISA** ⓒⓞ
*Snowdon Ln, Southeast : 7.5 mi by A 6135, B 6052 and B 6056* ✉ *S21 5RU*
*– ℰ (01246) 290 751 – www.relaxeatanddrink.co.uk*
**Rest** – *(booking advisable)* Menu £ 15 (lunch and early dinner) – Carte £ 19/36
♦ Early Victorian pub in picturesque location with delightful countryside views. Hearty, satisfying dishes on wide-ranging menu. Fine selection of local ales; helpful local staff.

## ECKINGTON – Worcestershire – 504 N27 – see Pershore

## EDINGTON – Wiltshire – 503 N30
4 C2

▶ London 105 mi – Bristol 43 mi – Cardiff 76 mi – Southampton 64 mi

⍟ **Paulet Arms** with rm     🛋 ☕ **AC** rest, ⅌ ⁽ᵗ⁾ **⅍ P** **VISA** ⓒⓞ **AE**
*47 Westbury Rd* ✉ *BA13 4PG* – ℰ *(01380) 830 940* – *www.pauletarms.co.uk*
*– Closed Sunday dinner and Monday*
**3 rm** – ┆£ 80/110 ┆┆£ 150/185, ⌕ £ 12.95
**Rest** – Menu £ 13 (lunch) – Carte £ 24/35
♦ Some Americans buy football clubs – in this small village, one bought a pub and then spent a fortune doing it up. Lunch is best enjoyed in the bar; dinner is quite a formal affair but the cooking is skilled and the ingredients clearly top-notch. Smart, boutique-style bedrooms.

## EGHAM – Surrey – 504 S29 – pop. 27 666
7 C1

▶ London 29 mi – Reading 21 mi

🏨 **Great Fosters**     ◔ ☒ ※ **AC** ⅌ ⁽ᵗ⁾ **⅍ P** **VISA** ⓒⓞ **AE** ⓞ
*Stroude Rd, South : 1.25 mi by B 388* ✉ *TW20 9UR* – ℰ *(01784) 433 822*
*– www.greatfosters.co.uk*
**41 rm** – ┆£ 135/215 ┆┆£ 215, ⌕ £ 19.50 – 2 suites
**Rest** *Oak Room* – see restaurant listing
♦ Elizabethan mansion built as a hunting lodge for Henry VIII. Charming inner with original features; spacious guest areas offer lovely garden views. Medieval-style bedrooms boast feature beds.

XX **Monsoon**     **AC** **VISA** ⓒⓞ **AE**
*20 High St* ✉ *TW20 9DT* – ℰ *(01784) 432 141*
*– www.monsoonrestaurantegham.co.uk*
**Rest** – Indian – Carte £ 12/22
♦ Smart, stylish restaurant that prides itself on immaculate upkeep and personable service. Contemporary artwork enlivens the walls. Freshly cooked, authentic Indian dishes.

XX **Oak Room** – at Great Fosters Hotel     ◔ 🛋 **P** **VISA** ⓒⓞ **AE** ⓞ
*Stroude Rd, South : 1.25 mi by B 388* ✉ *TW20 9UR* – ℰ *(01784) 433 822*
*– www.greatfosters.co.uk – Closed Saturday lunch*
**Rest** – Menu £ 27/56
♦ Spacious 16C oak-framed dining room with cosy bar and delightful terrace. Charming period features, immaculately laid tables and formal service. Skilful, modern cooking; complex combinations.

## ELDERSFIELD – Worcestershire

▶ London 124 mi – Birmingham 63 mi – Liverpool 145 mi – Bristol 52 mi

🍴 **Butchers Arms** (James Winter)   🚗 **P** VISA ⊕⊕
✿
*Lime Street, Southeast : 1 mi ⊠ GL19 4NX – ℰ (01452) 840 381
– www.thebutchersarms.net – Closed 2 weeks early January, 2 weeks late
August, Sunday dinner September-May, Tuesday lunch and Monday*
**Rest** – *(booking essential)* Carte £ 34/43
**Spec.** Middle White pig's cheek with crackling and Bramley apples. Fillet of beef
with foie gras and wild mushrooms. Orange marmalade pudding with Drambuie
custard.

◆ Pleasant red-brick pub with a traditional feel, run by a husband and wife team,
where everyone comes for the great atmosphere and the terrific food. Everything
from bread to ice cream is homemade; the cooking is clever and dishes full of flavour. But hurry, only 25 diners can be accommodated.

## ELLAND – West Yorkshire – **502** O22 – pop. 14 554 – ⊠ Halifax

▶ London 204 mi – Bradford 12 mi – Burnley 29 mi – Leeds 17 mi
🏌 Hullen Edge Hammerstones Leach Lane, ℰ (01422) 37 25 05

✕✕ **La Cachette**   AC VISA ⊕⊕
*31 Huddersfield Rd ⊠ HX5 9AW – ℰ (01422) 378 833
– www.lacachette-elland.com – Closed 2 weeks August, 26 December-9 January,
Sunday and bank holidays*
**Rest** – Menu £ 22 (dinner) – Carte £ 23/38 ⅋

◆ Long-standing, well-run bistro. Spacious bar and dining rooms display Gallic
décor and memorabilia. Extensive choice from daily/weekly menus and specials.
Classical, seasonal French cooking.

## ELTISLEY – Cambridgeshire – **507** T27

▶ London 70 mi – Leicester 62 mi

🍴 **Eltisley**   🚗 🛏 VISA ⊕⊕ ⊕
*2 The Green ⊠ PE19 6TG – ℰ (01480) 880 308 – www.theeltisley.co.uk
– Closed Monday in winter and Sunday dinner*
**Rest** – Carte £ 22/37

◆ Chic and stylish gastropub beside a village green. Simple, unfussy cooking relies on quality, local produce to speak for itself; everything from starters to desserts is homemade.

## ELTON – Cambridgeshire – **504** S26

▶ London 84 mi – Peterborough 11 mi – Bedford 40 mi – Kettering 24 mi

🍴 **Crown Inn** with rm   🛏 ⊕ **P** VISA ⊕⊕ AE ⓪
*8 Duck St ⊠ PE8 6RQ – ℰ (01832) 280 232 – www.thecrowninn.org
– Closed Sunday dinner and Monday lunch*
**5 rm** ⬜ – ♦£ 65 ♦♦£ 95   **Rest** – Carte £ 21/26

◆ 17C honey-stone pub in a delightful country parish, with thatched roof, cosy
inglenook and laid-back feel. Extensive menus offer British classics and some
Mediterranean influences. Smart, individually styled bedrooms – some with feature beds or roll-top baths.

## ELY – Cambridgeshire – **504** U26 – pop. 13 954 📖 Great Britain

▶ London 74 mi – Cambridge 16 mi – Norwich 60 mi
🛈 29 St Mary's St ℰ (01353) 66 20 62, www.visitely.org.uk
🏌 107 Cambridge Rd, ℰ (01353) 66 27 51
◉ Cathedral★★ **AC**
◉ Wicken Fen★, SE : 9 mi by A 10 and A 1123

✕ **Boathouse**   ← 🛏 AC ⅋ VISA ⊕⊕
*5-5a Annesdale ⊠ CB7 4BN – ℰ (01353) 664 388 – www.theboathouseely.co.uk
– Closed Christmas*
**Rest** – Menu £ 19 (weekdays) – Carte £ 22/32

◆ A riverside setting makes for a charming ambience: bag a table on the terrace
if you can. Inside there's a display of old Oxford and Cambridge oars. Worldwide
menus benefit from numerous creative touches.

ENGLAND

**at Little Thetford** South : 2.75 mi by A 10 – ⊠ Ely

↑ **Springfields** without rest      🚗 ⁄⁄ (ᵗᵖ) 🅿
*Ely Rd, North : 0.5 mi on A 10 ⊠ CB6 3HJ – ℰ (01353) 663 637 – Closed*
*10 days Christmas- New Year*
**3 rm** ☐ – ⅈ£ 55 ⅈⅈ£ 75
♦ Welcoming, curio-filled bungalow in pleasant gardens; a perfect home from
home. Immaculately kept bedrooms are decorated around colour themes and
boast tea trays laid with Wedgwood and Minton China. Take breakfast among
the Cranberry Glass collection or in the courtyard.

**at Sutton Gault** West : 8 mi by A 142 off B 1381 – ⊠ Ely

🗋 **Anchor Inn** with rm      🚗 ☆ ⁄⁄ (ᵗᵖ) 🅿 𝘝𝘐𝘚𝘈 ⬤⬤ 𝘈𝘌
⊠ CB6 2BD – ℰ (01353) 778 537 – www.anchor-inn-restaurant.co.uk
**4 rm** ☐ – ⅈ£ 89/99 ⅈⅈ£ 115/155
**Rest** – Menu £ 18 (weekday lunch) – Carte £ 25/34
♦ Riverside pub dating back to 1650 and the creation of the Hundred Foot Wash.
Tempting menu complemented by daily fish specials. For a pleasant river outlook
head for the wood-panelled rooms to the front of the bar. Neat, pine-furnished
bedrooms include two suites; one with river views.

---

**EMSWORTH** – Hampshire – **504** R31 – pop. 18 310      **6** B2
▶ London 75 mi – Brighton 37 mi – Portsmouth 10 mi – Southampton 22 mi

🍴🍴🍴 **36 on the Quay** (Ramon Farthing) with rm      ≤ 𝘝𝘐𝘚𝘈 ⬤⬤ ①
ॐ *47 South St, The Quay ⊠ PO10 7EG – ℰ (01243) 375 592*
*– www.36onthequay.co.uk – Closed 2 weeks January, 1 week May, 1 week*
*November, 24-26 December, Sunday and Monday*
**6 rm** – ⅈ£ 75/90 ⅈⅈ£ 100/110    **Rest** – *(booking essential)* Menu £ 29/55
**Spec.** Duck egg, lentils and duck liver torchon with truffle dressing. Turbot and
shrimps with parsley sauce and bacon foam. Dark chocolate cube with banana
ice cream
♦ Long-standing quayside restaurant run by experienced chef-owner. Elegant bar-
lounge and intimate linen-laid restaurant in neutral hues. Concise à la carte of
well-executed, classical dishes in flavoursome, tried-and-tested combinations. Contemporary bedrooms with good comforts; be ready to order breakfast at check-in.

🍴 **Fat Olives**      ☆ 𝘝𝘐𝘚𝘈 ⬤⬤
*30 South St ⊠ PO10 7EH – ℰ (01243) 377 914 – www.fatolives.co.uk – Closed 2*
*weeks late June, 1 week Christmas, 1 week spring, Sunday and Monday*
**Rest** – *(booking essential)* Menu £ 20 (lunch) – Carte £ 29/41
♦ Small terraced house with a welcoming ambience. Simply decorated with
wood floor and rough plaster walls. Tasty modern British menu and, yes, fat olives
are available!

---

**EPSOM** – Surrey – **504** T30 – pop. 64 493      **7** D1
▶ London 17 mi – Guildford 16 mi
🏌 Longdown Lane South Epsom Downs, ℰ (01372) 72 16 66
🏌 Horton Park G & C.C. Hook Rd, ℰ (020) 8393 84 00

🏨 **Chalk Lane**      🚗 ☆ (ᵗᵖ) ♨ 🅿 𝘝𝘐𝘚𝘈 ⬤⬤ 𝘈𝘌
*Chalk Ln., Southwest : 0.5 mi by A 24 and Woodcote Rd ⊠ KT18 7BB*
*– ℰ (01372) 721 179 – www.chalklanehotel.com*
**22 rm** ☐ – ⅈ£ 90/145 ⅈⅈ£ 135/200
**Rest** – *(closed Saturday lunch)* Menu £ 19 (lunch) – Carte £ 30/43
♦ At the foot of the Epsom Downs and near to the racecourse. Quality furnish-
ings throughout; the neatly kept bedrooms are most comfortable. Smart, modern
dining room.

XX **Le Raj**                    `AK` `VISA` `OO` `AE`
*211 Fir Tree Rd, Epsom Downs, Southeast : 2mi by B 289 and B 284 on B 291*
✉ *KT17 3LB* – ℰ *(01737) 371 371* – *www.lerajrestaurant.co.uk*
**Rest** – Bangladeshi – Carte £ 30/51
♦ Original, interesting menu makes good use of fresh ingredients and brings a modern style to traditional Bangladeshi cuisine. Smart, vibrant, contemporary interior décor.

---

## ERMINGTON – Devon – 503 I32                    2 C2
▶ London 216 mi – Plymouth 11 mi – Salcombe 15 mi

XX **Plantation House** with rm          `⊞` `⇪` `☏` `P` `VISA` `OO` `AE`
*Totnes Rd, Southwest : 0.5 mi on A 3121* ✉ *PL21 9NS* – ℰ *(01548) 831 100*
– *www.plantationhousehotel.co.uk*
**8 rm** ⊑ – †£ 69/105 ††£ 180/230
**Rest** – *(dinner only) (booking essential for non-residents)* Menu £ 38 **s**
♦ Appealing, converted Georgian rectory with smart gardens and terraced seating area. Personally run. Sound cooking of locally sourced ingredients. Individually styled bedrooms.

---

## ETTINGTON – Warwickshire – 504 P27 – pop. 953                    19 C3
▶ London 95 mi – Birmingham 41 mi – Leicester 48 mi – Coventry 23 mi

🛏 **Chequers Inn**                    `⊞` `⇪` `P` `VISA` `OO`
*91 Banbury Rd* ✉ *CV37 7SR* – ℰ *(01789) 740 387*
– *www.the-chequers-ettington.co.uk* – *Closed Sunday dinner and Monday*
**Rest** – Carte £ 24/34
♦ Chandeliers, brushed velvet furniture and Regency chairs set at chequered tables mean that this is not your typical pub. Menu offers a broad international style, ranging from British classics to Asian-inspired dishes.

---

## EVERSHOT – Dorset – 503 M31 – pop. 225 – ✉ Dorchester                    4 C3
▶ London 149 mi – Bournemouth 39 mi – Dorchester 12 mi – Salisbury 53 mi

🏠 **Summer Lodge** ⌘          `⊞` `⇪` `🗆` `⑩` `⋙` `⼓` `%` `�& rm,` `AK` `☏` `P`
*9 Fore St* ✉ *DT2 0JR* – ℰ *(01935) 482 000*          `VISA` `OO` `AE` `①`
– *www.summerlodgehotel.com*
**20 rm** ⊑ – †£ 235/365 ††£ 330/390 – 4 suites
**Rest** *The Restaurant* – *(booking essential to non residents)* Menu £ 25/40
– Carte dinner £ 48/67 ⑧
♦ Attractive former dower house in mature gardens. Country house style guest areas display heavy fabrics and antiques. Individually designed bedrooms boast quality furnishings and marble bathrooms. Exclusive glass-built wellness centre. Formal dining room and conservatory offer classical cuisine. Smart, effective service.

🏠 **Acorn Inn**                    `⇪` `☏` `P` `VISA` `OO` `AE`
*28 Fore St* ✉ *DT2 0JW* – ℰ *(01935) 83 228* – *www.acorn-inn.co.uk*
**10 rm** ⊑ – †£ 79/109 ††£ 99/189     **Rest** – Carte £ 23/36
♦ Historic inn mentioned in 'Tess of the d'Urbervilles'. Individually styled bedrooms boast fabric-covered walls, good facilities and modern bathrooms. Guest areas include a characterful residents' lounge, a locals bar with skittle alley and a classical restaurant.

🏠 **Wooden Cabbage** ⌘          `<` `⊞` `%` `☏` `P`
*East Chelborough, West : 3.25 mi by Beaminter rd and Chelborough rd on East Chelborough rd* ✉ *DT2 0QA* – ℰ *(01935) 83 362* – *www.woodencabbage.co.uk*
– *Restricted opening in winter*
**3 rm** ⊑ – †£ 75 ††£ 100     **Rest** – Menu £ 30
♦ Attractive former gamekeeper's cottage. Spacious guest areas include a cosy dining room used in winter and an airy conservatory used in summer. Pretty bedrooms boast good facilities and lovely countryside views. Meals (by arrangement) feature home-grown produce.

▶ London 201 mi – Bournemouth 83 mi – Bristol 83 mi – Plymouth 46 mi

✈ Exeter Airport : ✆ (01392) 367433, E : 5 mi by A 30 V

🛈 Princesshay ✆ (01392) 66 57 00, www.discoverexeter.ne

🏌 Downes Crediton Hookway, ✆ (01363) 77 30 25

👁 City★★ - Cathedral★★ Z – Royal Albert Memorial Museum★ Y

🅶 Killerton★★ **AC**, NE : 7 mi by B 3181 V – Ottery St Mary★ (St Mary's★) E : 12 mi by B 3183 - Y - A 30 and B 3174 – Crediton (Holy Cross Church★), NW : 9 mi by A 377

---

🏛 **Abode Exeter**                    🖪 🛎 🛦 👐 🕯 𝒮𝒶 𝗩𝗜𝗦𝗔 ⊙⊙ 𝗔𝗘 ①

*Cathedral Yard ⊠ EX1 1HD – ✆ (01392) 319 955 – www.abodehotels.co.uk*
**52 rm** – ♦£ 95/225, ♦♦£ 95/225, 🍽 £ 13.50 – 1 suite                    **Yz**
**Rest *Michael Caines*** – see restaurant listing

♦ Georgian-style frontage; located on the doorstep of the cathedral. Boutique style hotel with a very modern, stylish interior. Understated bedrooms feature good mod cons.

## Queens Court

*Bystock Terr.* ⊠ *EX4 4HY* – ℰ *(01392) 272 709* – *www.queenscourt-hotel.co.uk* – *Closed 24 December-2 January*                                                              Yn

**18 rm** ⌷ – †£ 115 ††£ 125

**Rest** *Olive Tree* – *(closed Sunday lunch)* Menu £ 20 – Carte £ 32/40

♦ A town house hotel located close to Central train station. Bright public areas decorated in a clean, modern style. Well-equipped, tidily furnished and co-ordinated bedrooms. Brightly painted, clean-lined restaurant.

## Silversprings without rest

*12 Richmond Rd* ⊠ *EX4 4JA* – ℰ *(01392) 494 040* – *www.silversprings.co.uk* – *Closed 19 December-1 January*                                                                        Ya

**10 rm** ⌷ – †£ 58/80 ††£ 85/100

♦ Cream coloured Georgian terraced house in Roman part of town. Warm and friendly, with immaculately kept public areas. Varied palettes and cathedral views distinguish rooms.

## Angela's

*38 New Bridge St* ⊠ *EX4 3AH* – ℰ *(01392) 499 038* – *www.angelasrestaurant.co.uk* – *Closed 2 weeks spring, 1 week autumn, 1 week winter, Sunday, Monday and lunch Tuesday*                                                                                          Za

**Rest** – *(lunch by arrangement)* Carte £ 33/45

♦ Neighbourhood restaurant with welcoming feel. Plain décor with oils and prints; large, well-spaced tables. Extensive menu of local, seasonal fare; plenty of meat, fish and vegetarian choices.

## Michael Caines – at Abode Exeter Hotel

*Cathedral Yard* ⊠ *EX1 1HD* – ℰ *(01392) 223 638* – *www.michaelcaines.com* – *Closed Sunday*                                                                                               Yz

**Rest** – Menu £ 14 (lunch)/17 (early dinner) – Carte £ 47/51

♦ Comfortable, contemporarily stylish restaurant overlooking cathedral. Menu has good choice of well-balanced and confident modern British cooking. Pleasant, efficient service.

**at Rockbeare** East : 7.5 mi by A 30 – V – ⊠ Exeter

🖾    **Jack in the Green Inn**      🚗 🏠 AC P VISA ⓒⓞ
   *London Rd* ⊠ *EX5 2EE* – 𝒞 *(01404) 822 240* – *www.jackinthegreen.uk.com*
   – *Closed 25 December-6 January*
   **Rest** – Menu £ 25 – Carte £ 33/42
   ◆ Unassuming whitewashed pub with warm, welcoming interior. They support local producers and cooking is taken seriously. Extensive menus feature fresh fish specials; and bread, veg and water are satisfyingly free of charge. Jazz evenings take place in summer.

**at Kenton** Southeast : 7 mi by A 3015 - X - on A 379 – ⊠ Exeter

XX    **Rodean**      VISA ⓒⓞ
   *The Triangle* ⊠ *EX6 8LS* – 𝒞 *(01626) 890 195* – *www.rodeanrestaurant.co.uk*
   – *Closed Sunday dinner and Monday*
   **Rest** – *(dinner only and Sunday lunch) (booking advisable)* Menu £ 19
   – Carte £ 28/37
   ◆ Family-run, early-20C butchers shop in pretty spot. Bar area for pre-prandials. Restaurant in two rooms with beams and local photos. Menus employ good use of local ingredients.

---

**EXFORD** – Somerset – 503 J30      **3 A2**
▶ London 193 mi – Exeter 41 mi – Minehead 14 mi – Taunton 33 mi
◉ Church★
ⓖ Exmoor National Park★★

🖾🔒    **Crown**      🚗 🕎 🛜 P VISA ⓒⓞ
   ⊠ *TA24 7PP* – 𝒞 *(01643) 831 554* – *www.crownhotelexmoor.co.uk*
   **16 rm** ⚏ – �£ 69/100 ♙♙£ 119/139
   **Rest** – *(dinner only)* Menu £ 35 – Carte £ 23/33
   ◆ Attractive 17C, family-run coaching inn with delightful terrace and water garden to rear. Relaxed, cosy interior filled with country prints. Comfy, modern bedrooms with bold décor. Large bar serves snacks. Formal dining room offers traditional, seasonal dishes.

---

**EXTON** – Devon – 503 J30      **2 D2**
▶ London 176 mi – Exmouth 4 mi – Topsham 3 mi

🖾    **Puffing Billy**      🕎 AC P VISA ⓒⓞ AE
   *Station Rd* ⊠ *EX3 0PR* – 𝒞 *(01392) 877 888* – *www.thepuffingbilly.co.uk* – *Closed 25 December and Sunday dinner January-15 February*
   **Rest** – Carte £ 25/28
   ◆ Spacious, modern pub with stylish bar, formal dining room and efficient, welcoming service. Menus offer something for everyone, covering the traditional, the regional and the international.

---

**FAIRFORD** – Gloucestershire – 503 O28 – pop. 2 960 📖 Great Britain    **4 D1**
▶ London 88 mi – Cirencester 9 mi – Oxford 29 mi
◉ Church of St Mary★ (Stained glass windows★★)
ⓖ Cirencester★ - Church of St John the Baptist★ - Corinium Museum★ (Mosaic Pavements★), W : 9 mi on A 429, A 435, Spitalgate Lane and Dollar St – Swindon - Great Railway Museum★ **AC** - Railway Village Museum★ **AC**, S : 17 mi on A 419, A 4312, A 4259 and B 4289

XXX    **Allium**      VISA ⓒⓞ AE ⓞ
   *1 London St, Market Pl* ⊠ *GL7 4AH* – 𝒞 *(01285) 712 200*
   – *www.restaurantallium.co.uk* – *Closed 23 December-7 January, Sunday and Monday*
   **Rest** – Menu £ 26/43
   ◆ Unassuming neighbourhood restaurant with stylish lounge and bar. Contemporary, boldly patterned wallpapers and mood lighting. Original, modern set menus showcase seasonal, local produce in complex dishes; excellent presentation.

ENGLAND

▶ London 308 mi – Penzance 26 mi – Plymouth 65 mi – Truro 11 mi

🖪 Prince of Wales Pier  𝒞 (01326) 31 23 00, www.discoverfalmouth.co.uk

📷 Swanpool Rd,  𝒞 (01326) 31 12 62

📷 Budock Vean Hotel Mawnan Smith,  𝒞 (01326) 25 21 02

◉ Town★ – Pendennis Castle★ (≤★★) **AC** B

◎ Glendurgan Garden★★ **AC** – Trebah Garden★, SW : 4.5 mi by Swanpool Rd A – Mawnan Parish Church★ (≤★★) S : 4 mi by Swanpool Rd A – Cruise along Helford River★. Trelissick★★ (≤★★) NW : 13 mi by A 39 and B 3289 A – Carn Brea (≤★★) NW : 10 mi by A 393 A – Gweek (Setting★, Seal Sanctuary★) SW : 8 mi by A 39 and Treverva rd – Wendron (Poldark Mine★) **AC**, SW : 12.5 mi by A 39 - A - and A 394

---

🏠🏠🏠  **Greenbank**          ≤ 🏠 🛎 ✍ ⸙ 🔥 **P** 🚭 VISA ⦿ ᴬᴱ ⓪

*Harbourside* ⌂ TR11 2SR – 𝒞 (01326) 312 440 – www.greenbank-hotel.co.uk
**59 rm** � – †£ 95/165 ††£ 185/235 – 1 suite                              A**a**
**Rest** *Harbourside* – Carte £ 28/34

♦ 17C former coaching inn where flagstone floors and a sweeping staircase contrast with bold, modern colours and contemporary furnishings. Spacious, light wood bedrooms; some overlook the harbour. All day restaurant serves local, seasonal produce and fresh seafood.

---

🏠🏠🏠  **St Michael's H & Spa**          ≤ 🏊 📺 ☽ 🍸 ⿻ ᾱ ✍ ⸙ 🔥 **P** VISA ⦿

*Gyllyngvase Beach* ⌂ TR11 4NB – 𝒞 (01326) 312 707
– www.stmichaelshotel.co.uk                              B**c**
**61 rm** ⊑ – †£ 60/105 ††£ 120/290
**Rest** *Flying Fish* – see restaurant listing

♦ Contemporary hotel with a nautical theme running throughout, from the reception desk 'boat' and portholes in the guest areas to the New England style bedrooms – some of which boast balconies and sea views. Modern leisure club and spa.

---

🏠  **Dolvean House** *without rest*          ⿻ **P** VISA ⦿

*50 Melvill Rd* ⌂ TR11 4DQ – 𝒞 (01326) 313 658 – www.dolvean.co.uk – *Closed first 2 weeks November and 22-28 December*                              B**n**
**10 rm** ⊑ – †£ 39/66 ††£ 77/98

♦ Smart cream property with local books and guides in parlour: exceptionally good detail wherever you look. Elegant, neatly laid breakfast room. Bright, well-kept bedrooms.

---

🏠  **Chelsea House** *without rest*          ≤ 🏠 ✍ ⿻ **P** VISA ⦿

*2 Emslie Rd* ⌂ TR11 4BG – 𝒞 (01326) 212 230 – www.chelseahousehotel.com
**9 rm** ⊑ – †£ 45/50 ††£ 60/110                              B**e**

♦ Large Victorian house in quiet residential area with partial sea-view at front. Neat breakfast room; well-appointed bedrooms, three with their own balconies.

---

🏠  **Prospect House** *without rest*          🏠 ✍ ⿻ **P** VISA ⦿

*1 Church Rd, Penryn, Northwest : 2 mi by A 39 on B 3292* ⌂ TR10 8DA
– 𝒞 (01326) 373 198 – www.prospecthouse-penryn.co.uk
**3 rm** ⊑ – †£ 40/45 ††£ 70/75

♦ Large Georgian guesthouse on Penryn River, set within a walled garden and run by a welcoming owner. Super breakfasts with local produce in abundance. Individually styled bedrooms.

---

🍴  **Bistro de la Mer**          VISA ⦿

*28 Arwenack St* ⌂ TR11 3JB – 𝒞 (01326) 316 509 – www.bistrodelamer.com
– *Closed 2 weeks November, 1 week March, 1 January, 25-26 December, Sunday and Monday except dinner April-September*                              B**r**
**Rest** – Menu £ 18 (lunch) – Carte £ 24/40

♦ Modest bistro with a subtle Mediterranean feel, set over two floors and decorated in sunny seaside colours of yellow and blue. Extensive seafood-oriented menu; honest cooking.

ENGLAND

**ENGLAND**

Glendurgan Garden

❌ **Samphire**  ⟳ 𝚅𝙸𝚂𝙰 ⊛
*36 Arwenack St* ⊠ *TR11 3JF* – ℰ *(01326) 210 759* – *www.samphire-falmouth.co.uk*
**Rest** – Carte £ 27/39  B**x**
◆ Informal restaurant situated in the heart of town, with oversized windows looking onto the street. Appealing seasonal menu includes plenty of fresh local seafood and tasty Sunday roasts. Attentive service.

❌ **Flying Fish** – at St Michael's Hotel & Spa  ≼ 🚗 **P** 𝚅𝙸𝚂𝙰 ⊛
*Gyllyngvase Beach* ⊠ *TR11 4NB* – ℰ *(01326) 312 707*
*– www.stmichaelshotel.co.uk*  B**c**
**Rest** – Menu £ 28 (dinner) – Carte lunch £ 21/29
◆ Glass-fronted hotel restaurant in shades of blue, looking down sloping gardens towards the bay. Snacks served in the daytime; concise à la carte supplemented by daily specials in the evening.

❌ **Rick Stein's Seafood Bar**  𝙰𝙲 𝚅𝙸𝚂𝙰 ⊛ ⓪
*Discovery Quay (1st floor)* ⊠ *TR11 3XA* – ℰ *(01326) 330 053*
*– www.rickstein.com – Closed Monday lunch in winter and Sunday*
**Rest** – Seafood – Carte £ 19/21  B**a**
◆ Head upstairs for keenly priced and very fresh hot or cold 'tapas', which blends British and Spanish influences and uses prime local seafood. Grab a table or watch the kitchen action from a seat at the counter; and don't miss dessert.

**at Maenporth Beach** South : 3.75 mi by Pennance Rd

❌ **Cove**  ≼ 🏠 𝙰𝙲 **P** 𝚅𝙸𝚂𝙰 ⊛
*Maenporth Beach* ⊠ *TR11 5HN* – ℰ *(01326) 251 136* – *www.thecovemaenporth.co.uk*
**Rest** – Carte £ 30/35
◆ Within a modern building overlooking the beach and cove. Concise menu with daily specials; bright, unfussy cooking, with the occasional Asian note. Young, enthusiastic service.

---

**FARNBOROUGH** – Hampshire – **504** R30 – pop. 57 147  **7** C1
▶ London 41 mi – Reading 17 mi – Southampton 44 mi – Winchester 33 mi
🈁 Southwood Ively Rd, ℰ *(01252) 54 87 00*

🏨 **Aviator**  ≼ ♨ 🍴 ♿ 𝙰𝙲 ⚒ ⋯ 🏋 **P** 𝚅𝙸𝚂𝙰 ⊛ 𝙰𝙴 ⓪
*Farnborough Rd, Southwest : 1 mi on A 325* ⊠ *GU14 6EL* – ℰ *(01252) 555 890*
*– www.aviatorfarnborough.co.uk*
**169 rm** – �$£ 205/245 �$�$£ 205/375, ⊇ £ 16
**Rest** *Brasserie* – see restaurant listing
◆ Eye-catching, modern hotel overlooking Farnborough Airport and boasting an unusual circular atrium, a smart first-floor lounge-bar and a small deli. Sleek, good-sized bedrooms feature light wood, modern facilities and fully tiled bathrooms.

❌❌ **Brasserie** – at Aviator Hotel  ≼ ♿ 𝙰𝙲 **P** 𝚅𝙸𝚂𝙰 ⊛ 𝙰𝙴 ⓪
*Farnborough Rd, Southwest : 1 mi on A 325* ⊠ *GU14 6EL* – ℰ *(01252) 555 890*
*– www.aviatorfarnborough.co.uk*
**Rest** – Menu £ 21 (lunch) **s** – Carte £ 30/46 **s**
◆ Stylish brasserie within an eye-catching hotel that overlooks the airport. Contemporary surroundings provide the perfect backdrop for modern, visually appealing dishes of seasonal produce.

---

**FARNHAM** – Dorset – **503** N31 – see Blandford Forum

---

**FARNINGHAM** – Kent – **504** U29  **8** B1
▶ London 22 mi – Dartford 7 mi – Maidstone 20 mi

⌂ **Beesfield Farm** without rest ⬙  🚗 ⏧ ⚒ ⋯ **P**
*Beesfield Lane, off A 225* ⊠ *DA4 0LA* – ℰ *(01322) 863 900*
*– www.beesfieldfarm.co.uk – Closed 25 December*
**3 rm** ⊇ – �$£ 65/70 �$�$£ 80/90
◆ Peaceful valley setting, with attractive garden. Exudes character: oldest part is 400 year-old Kentish longhouse. Comfy sitting room; bedrooms boast beams and garden outlook.

ENGLAND

## FAR SAWREY – Cumbria – 502 L20 – see Hawkshead

## FAVERSHAM – Kent – 504 W30 – pop. 18 222                    9 C1
▶ London 52 mi – Dover 26 mi – Maidstone 21 mi – Margate 25 mi
🛈 13 Preston St ✆ (01795) 53 45 42, www.faversham.org

XXX    **Read's** (David Pitchford) with rm                    🍽 ☆ 📶 P VISA ⓞ AE ①
🏵     *Macknade Manor, Canterbury Rd, East : 1 mi on A 2 ☒ ME13 8XE – ✆ (01795)*
       *535 344 – www.reads.com – Closed 2 weeks early September, 1 week early*
       *January, 25-26 December, Sunday and Monday*
       **6 rm** ☲ – ♥£ 125/185 ♥♥£ 165/195    **Rest** – Menu £ 25/58⁂
       **Spec.** Fillet of smoked eel, new potato salad and crispy bacon. Lamb four ways.
       Rhubarb soufflé with rhubarb ripple ice cream.
       ◆ Elegant red-brick house with beautiful grounds and traditionally furnished din-
       ing rooms. Confident, well-presented, classically based dishes make the best of lo-
       cal produce, including fruit, vegetables and herbs from the walled garden. Com-
       fortable, well-kept bedrooms, tastefully decorated in a country house style.

## at Dargate East : 6 mi by A 2 off A 299 – ☒ Kent

🏠    **Dove**                                                    ☆ P VISA ⓞ AE
      *Plum Pudding Ln ☒ ME13 9HB – ✆ (01227) 751 360*
      *– www.thedoveinndargate.co.uk – Closed 1 week February, Sunday dinner and*
      *Monday*
      **Rest** – *(booking advisable at weekends)* Carte £ 18/34
      ◆ Attractive Victorian pub with well-tended gardens and cosy rooms. Weekday
      menus offer enticing nibbles, pub classics and specials. Concise Friday and Satur-
      day menus are much more ambitious.

## at Oare Northwest : 2.5 mi by A2 off B2045 – ☒ Kent

🏠    **Three Mariners**                                          🍽 ☆ P VISA ⓞ
      *2 Church Rd ☒ ME13 0QA – ✆ (01795) 533 633*
      *– www.thethreemarinersoare.co.uk – Closed Sunday dinner*
      **Rest** – *(closed 25 December)* Menu £ 17 (weekdays) – Carte £ 25/32
      ◆ Welcoming 500 year old pub set by a small marina in a sleepy hamlet, boast-
      ing pleasant marsh views. Constantly evolving menus offer an appealing mix of
      carefully prepared, flavoursome dishes.

## FELIXKIRK – North Yorkshire – 502 Q21 – see Thirsk

## FERMAIN BAY – 503 L33 – see Channel Islands (Guernsey)

## FERNHURST – West Sussex – 504 R30                            7 C2
▶ London 50 mi – Brighton 40 mi – Southampton 46 mi

XX    **Wheeler's at The King's Arms** with rm                  🍽 ☆ ᵹ rm, 📶 P
      *Midhurst Rd, South : 1 mi on A286 ☒ GU27 3HA – ✆ (01428)*    VISA ⓞ AE
      *652 005 – www.wheelerskingsarms.com*
      **6 rm** ☲ – ♥£ 110 ♥♥£ 120    **Rest** – Menu £ 20 – Carte £ 26/36
      ◆ Attractive stone-built former pub with pleasant garden and professional, atten-
      tive service. Spacious, linen-laid restaurant boasts velvet curtains, open fire and
      cartoon prints. Extensive menu offers Marco Pierre White classics. Simple, com-
      pact, modern bedrooms.

## FERRENSBY – North Yorkshire – see Knaresborough

## FLAUNDEN – Hertfordshire – pop. 5 468                        12 A2
▶ London 35 mi – Reading 43 mi – Luton 23 mi – Milton Keynes 42 mi

🏠    **Bricklayers Arms**                                       🍽 ☆ P VISA ⓞ AE
      *Hogpits Bottom ☒ HP3 0PH – ✆ (01442) 833 322 – www.bricklayersarms.com*
      *– Closed 25 December*
      **Rest** – Carte £ 26/39
      ◆ Smart pub tucked away in a small hamlet. There are no snacks, just traditional,
      hearty, French-inspired dishes and old-school puddings. Wine list is a labour of
      love, featuring boutique Australian wines.

## FLETCHING – East Sussex – **504** U30/3 – **pop. 1 722**          **8** A2
▶ London 45 mi – Brighton 20 mi – Eastbourne 24 mi – Maidstone 20 mi

🍴 **Griffin Inn** with rm          🍴 🌳 ⁇ ⁇ **P** 🚗 **VISA** 🅾 **AE** 🅾
✉ TN22 3SS – ✆ (01825) 722 890 – www.thegriffininn.co.uk – Closed 25
December
**13 rm** ⌚ – †£ 60/80 ††£ 145
**Rest** – (meals in bar Sunday dinner) Carte £ 20/27
♦ Hugely characterful brick coaching inn, under the same ownership for over 30
years. Various rooms and sizeable garden/terrace with wood burning oven for
summer BBQs. British and Italian classics. Individually decorated bedrooms accessed via narrow, sloping corridors.

## FOLKESTONE – Kent – **504** X30 – **pop. 45 273** ▌ Great Britain          **9** D2
▶ London 76 mi – Brighton 76 mi – Dover 8 mi – Maidstone 33 mi
**Access** Channel Tunnel : Eurotunnel information and reservations ✆ (08705) 353535
🛈 Bouverie Place Shopping Centre ✆ (01303) 25 85 94, www.discoverfolkestone.co.uk
◎ The Leas ★ (≤ ★) Z

🏠 **Relish** without rest          ⁇ ⁇ **VISA** 🅾 **AE**
4 Augusta Gardens ✉ CT20 2RR – ✆ (01303) 850 952 – www.hotelrelish.co.uk
– Closed 22 December-2 January          **Zn**
**10 rm** ⌚ – †£ 69/95 ††£ 105/145
♦ Large Regency townhouse overlooking private parkland. Stylish black canopy covered entrance; modish furnishings. Handy food and drink area at foot of
stairs. Light, airy bedrooms.

✗✗ **Rocksalt** with rm          ≤ 🌳 **AC** rest, **VISA** 🅾
4-5 Fish Market ✉ CT19 6AA – ✆ (01303) 468 843
– www.rocksaltfolkestone.co.uk – Closed Sunday dinner and Monday
**4 rm** – †£ 75/85 ††£ 85/100          **Zx**
**Rest** – Menu £ 18 (weekday lunch) – Carte £ 22/55
♦ Set within a stylish harbourfront eco-building affording lovely sea views. Smart
cantilevered dining room with full-length windows opening onto a terrace; semi
open air bar upstairs. Menus mix seafood and local meats; veg is from their
farm. Nearby, bedrooms boast antique beds, Egyptian linen and wet rooms.

## FORDINGBRIDGE – Hampshire – **503** O31 – **pop. 5 755**          **6** A2
▶ London 101 mi – Bournemouth 17 mi – Salisbury 11 mi – Southampton 22 mi
🛈 Salisbury St ✆ (01425) 65 45 60, www.visit-hampshire.co.uk

**at Stuckton** Southeast : 1 mi by B 3078 – ✉ Fordingbridge

🏠 **Three Lions** 🍃          🍴 ⁇ **P** **VISA** 🅾
Stuckton Rd ✉ SP6 2HF – ✆ (01425) 652 489
– www.thethreelionsrestaurant.co.uk – Closed last 2 weeks February
**7 rm** – †£ 69/79 ††£ 80/125, ⌚ £ 8.75
**Rest** – (closed Sunday dinner and Monday) Menu £ 25 (weekday lunch)
– Carte £ 35/45
♦ Traditional pine-furnished former farmhouse on quiet rural lane. Pleasant bedrooms are located among various adjoining buildings. Blackboard offers well-presented dishes with classical undertones – which can be more elaborate than descriptions imply.

## FOREST GREEN – Surrey – **pop. 1 843** – ✉ Dorking          **7** D2
▶ London 34 mi – Guildford 13 mi – Horsham 10 mi

🍴 **Parrot Inn**          🍴 🌳 **P** **VISA** 🅾
✉ RH5 5RZ – ✆ (01306) 621 339 – www.theparrot.co.uk – Closed 25 December
and Sunday dinner
**Rest** – Carte £ 20/31
♦ Traditional 17C pub set on the village green. Well-priced, generously proportioned dishes use produce from the pub's own farm. Homemade bread, cheese,
cakes and preserves for sale.

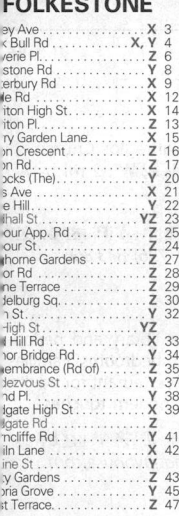

# FOLKESTONE

GIBRALTAR

0 ............ 1 km
0 .... 1/2 mile

PEENE   Pilgrims   Way   Crete   Road   West   Crete Road East

NEWINGTON   CHANNEL TUNNEL (TERMINAL)   Churchill   Av.   Canterbury Hill   Rd

TOLL   M 20   42   15   Park   Farm   Road   Joyes Rd   9

CHERITON   3   15   Cherry Gdn Av.   MOREHALL   4   A 259

14   Cheriton   A 2034   Rd   21

Church Rd   FOLKESTONE WEST   Shorncliffe Rd

33   North Rd   COOLINGE   Coolinge Rd

Blackhouse Hill   Horn Street   SANDGATE   39

HYTHE   Hospital Hill   Sandgate Hill

Seabrook Road   The Esplanade   Lower Sandgate Rd   12

Twiss Rd   Prince's Parade

**X**

**ENGLAND**

# FOLKESTONE

A 259   Pavilion   [16]   A 260   (A 20)   Rd   Bradstone   Rd

RADNOR PARK   Radnor Park Av.   Bournemouth Rd   Ford Rd   Dover   Road   The Tram Road

Radnor Park Rd   Broadmead Rd   38   34   34

CENTRAL   Cheriton   Road   8   16   32   20

A 2034   41   41   23   Tontine   The

A 259   Castle Hill Av.   Cheriton   Road   45   27   CREATIVE QUARTER   Old High St   24

30   BOUVERIE PLACE SHOPPING CENTRE   37

H   J   PDL   West   35   28

Bouverie Rd   AUGUSTA GARDENS   Sandgate   Rd   47   28   25

A 2033   43   17   27   The   Leas   Marine Parade   Marine Prom.

CLIFTON GARDEN   16   LOWER LEAS COASTAL PARK

**CENTRE**

0 ............ 400 m
0 .......... 400 yards

**Y**

**Z**

**X**

**Z**

---

Fancy a last minute break?
Check hotel websites to take advantage of price promotions.

---

**FOREST ROW** – East Sussex – **504** U30 – **pop. 3 623**   **8** A2

▶ London 35 mi – Brighton 26 mi – Eastbourne 30 mi – Maidstone 32 mi

📠 Royal Ashdown Forest Forest Row, Chapel Lane, ☎ (01342) 82 20 18

**Ashdown Park** ♨ ⪡ 🚗 🐕 📺 🏨 🏊 ♨ ✕ 🖼 ⅙ 📶 ♨ 🅿
*Colemans Hatch Rd, South : 3.25 mi by A 22* ✉ *RH18 5JR*   VISA ⓪ AE ⑩
*–* ✆ *(01342) 824 988 – www.ashdownpark.com*
**94 rm** 🛏 – ♦£ 140/160 ♦♦£ 240/300 – 5 suites
**Rest** *Anderida* – Menu £ 25/39 – Carte £ 43/52
♦ Impressive Victorian building in extensive parkland. Luxury country house interior boasts grand staircases, impressive halls and open-fired lounges. Huge bedrooms display antiques and feature beds. Formal restaurant offers classical cooking and good estate views.

---

**FORTON** – Lancashire – **502** M25 ▌ Great Britain                               **20** A1

▶ London 236 mi – Blackpool 18 mi – Manchester 45 mi
◐ Lancaster - Castle★, N : 5.5 mi by A 6

🏠 **Bay Horse Inn** with rm                        🚗 🏯 📶 🅿 VISA ⓪
*Bay Horse Ln, North : 1.25 mi by A 6 on Quernmore rd* ✉ *LA2 0HR –* ✆ *(01524) 791 204 – www.bayhorseinn.com – Closed Sunday dinner and Monday except bank holidays*
**2 rm** 🛏 – ♦£ 75/89 ♦♦£ 75/89   **Rest** – Menu £ 22 (lunch) **s** – Carte £ 22/36 **s**
♦ Cosy pub in a pleasant rural location, with characterful interior and attractive terrace. Seasonal, locally sourced produce is crafted into a mix of classic and modern dishes. Beautifully appointed bedrooms are housed in the nearby corn store.

---

**FOTHERINGHAY** Northants – **504** S26 – see Oundle

---

**FOWEY** – Cornwall – **503** G32 – pop. 2 064                                        **1** B2

▶ London 277 mi – Newquay 24 mi – Plymouth 34 mi – Truro 22 mi
🇮 5 South St ✆ (01726) 83 36 16, www.fowey.co.uk
◉ Town★★
◐ Gribbin Head (⪡★★) 6 mi rtn on foot – Bodinnick (⪡★★) - Lanteglos Church★, E : 5 mi by ferry – Polruan (⪡★★) SE : 6 mi by ferry – Polkerris★, W : 2 mi by A 3082

🏨 **Fowey Hall**                        ⪡ 🚗 🏯 📺 ⚤ 📶 ♨ 🅿 VISA ⓪ AE
*Hanson Drive, West : 0.5 mi off A 3082* ✉ *PL23 1ET –* ✆ *(01726) 833 866 – www.foweyhallhotel.co.uk*
**25 rm** 🛏 – ♦£ 145/230 ♦♦£ 170/245 – 11 suites
**Rest** – *(light lunch Monday-Saturday)* Carte £ 23/43 **s**
♦ Striking 19C manor house overlooking town, with ornate library and period-furnished lounge/billiard room. Mix of traditional and modern bedrooms. Families well-catered for; trendy, informal feel pervades. Oak-panelled restaurant for adults. Conservatory for those with children. Classical à la carte has modern touches.

🏠 **Old Quay House**                        ⪡ 🏯 🍴 📶 VISA ⓪ AE
*28 Fore St* ✉ *PL23 1AQ –* ✆ *(01726) 833 302 – www.theoldquayhouse.com – Closed 7 November-23 December*
**11 rm** 🛏 – ♦£ 120/170 ♦♦£ 140/340
**Rest** – *(closed lunch October-April)* Carte £ 35/52
♦ Friendly boutique hotel, run by experienced owner. Stylish interior has black and white theme; great outlook from terrace. Bedrooms range from small standard to penthouse – some have balconies and water views. Chic, informal bar-cum-restaurant with modern menu.

✕ **Bistro**                        AC VISA ⓪
*24 Fore St.* ✉ *PL23 1AQ –* ✆ *(01726) 832 322 – www.tiffinsbistro.co.uk – Closed 25 December and 1 January*
**Rest** – Menu £ 19 – Carte £ 23/30
♦ Former deli; now a relaxed, cosy, all day eatery. Upstairs restaurant open in evening. Modern European dishes range from sandwiches and pizza to bouillabaisse and beef Bourguignon.

ENGLAND

**at Golant** North : 3 mi by B 3269 – ⊠ Fowey

🏠 **Cormorant** ⊠    ⇐ 🚗 🏠 🖥 💺 📶 **P** VISA ⬤ AE
⊠ PL23 1LL – 𝒞 (01726) 833 426 – www.cormoranthotel.co.uk
**14 rm** ⊇ – ♦£ 80/170 ♦♦£ 160/200
**Rest** – (closed lunch Monday and Tuesday) (booking essential for non residents)
Menu £ 30 (dinner) – Carte (except dinner in winter) £ 29/45
♦ Well-run hotel in superb waterside position. At only one room deep, all its bedrooms overlook the estuary; superior rooms boast balconies. Lounge, bar and formal, linen-laid restaurant. Appealing seasonal menus feature local meats and interesting seafood dishes.

**FREATHY** – **Cornwall** – **see Millbrook**

**FRESSINGFIELD** – **Suffolk** – **504** X26         **15** D2
▶ London 104 mi – Ipswich 34 mi – Lowestoft 27 mi

🍺 **Fox & Goose Inn**    🏠 **P** VISA ⬤
Church Rd ⊠ IP21 5PB – 𝒞 (01379) 586 247 – www.foxandgoose.net – Closed 1
week early January, 25-30 December and Monday
**Rest** – (booking advisable) Menu £ 18 (lunch) – Carte £ 29/36
♦ Attractive 16C pub opposite the duck pond, with wooden beams, open fireplaces and pleasant terrace. Classic pub dishes and local cask ales. More modern,
original dishes in upstairs restaurant.

**FRILSHAM** – **West Berkshire** – **see Yattendon**

**FRISTON** – **Suffolk** – **see Aldeburgh**

**FRITHSDEN** – **Hertfordshire** – **see Hemel Hempstead**

**FRITTON** – **Norfolk**     **15** D2
▶ London 133 mi – Great Yarmouth 8 mi – Norwich 19 mi

🏠 **Fritton House** ⊗    ⇐ 🚗 🏠 ♨ **P** VISA ⬤ ⓞ
Church Ln ⊠ NR31 9HA – 𝒞 (01493) 484 008 – www.adnams.co.uk
**8 rm** ⊇ – ♦£ 120/140 ♦♦£ 120/140 – 1 suite   **Rest** – Carte £ 13/32
♦ Attractive 15C former coaching inn with period features, at the heart of the
Somerleyton Estate. Cosy drawing room. Stylish bedrooms with old beams and
modern bathrooms. Rustic bar and dining area with terrace. Pub dishes at lunch;
restaurant fare at dinner.

**FROGGATT EDGE** – **Derbyshire** – **502** P24     **16** A1
▶ London 167 mi – Bakewell 6 mi – Sheffield 11 mi

🍺 **Chequers Inn** with rm    🏠 💺 📶 **P** VISA ⬤ AE
on A 625 ⊠ S32 3ZJ – 𝒞 (01433) 630 231 – www.chequers-froggatt.com
– Closed 25 December
**5 rm** ⊇ – ♦£ 77/102 ♦♦£ 77/102   **Rest** – Carte £ 24/30
♦ Traditional 16C inn built right into the stone boulders of Froggat Edge and
boasting a direct path up to the peak. Cooking is unfussy, tasty and largely classical, with more imaginative specials. Bedrooms are comfy; the one to the rear is
quietest and best.

**FROME** – **Somerset** – **503** M/N30 – **pop. 24 171**     **4** C2
▶ London 118 mi – Bristol 24 mi – Southampton 52 mi – Swindon 44 mi

🏠 **Babington House** ⊗    🚗 ♨ 🏠 🍴 🖥 ⬤ ♨ ⛳ ❄ ⚒ 📶 ♨ **P**
Babington, Northwest : 6.5 mi by A 362 on Vobster rd    VISA ⬤ AE ⓞ
⊠ BA11 3RW – 𝒞 (01373) 812 266 – www.babingtonhouse.co.uk
**32 rm** – ♦♦£ 190/720, ⊇ £ 16
**Rest Orangery** – Carte £ 27/32
♦ Country house with a vivid difference: Georgian exterior; cool, fashionable inner, with a laid-back, bohemian feel. Good health club, children's play area and
even a cinema. Modern, understated bedrooms. Large conservatory dining room
with solid stone floor; appealing Mediterranean menu.

## FULLER STREET – Essex – **504** V28 – pop. 50

▶ London 52 mi

🍴 **Square & Compasses**      🈺 **P** *VISA* 🅒🅓
✉ CM3 2BB – ☏ (01245) 361 477 – www.thesquareandcompasses.co.uk – Closed
1 January
**Rest** – (closed 25-26 December and Sunday dinner) (booking essential)
Carte £ 20/26
◆ Charming little pub with low beams, wood burning stoves and character
aplenty. Unfussy menus of freshly made pub classics and unashamedly traditional
puddings; daily blackboards offer locally shot game and fish caught nearby.
Friendly team.

## FULMER – **504**

▶ London 21 mi – Croydon 49 mi – Barnet 30 mi – Ealing 13 mi

🍴 **Black Horse**      🈐 🈺 **P** *VISA* 🅒🅓 🅐🅔
*Windmill Rd* ✉ SL3 6HD – ☏ (01753) 663 183 – www.blackhorsefulmer.co.uk
– Closed 25-26 December
**Rest** – Carte £ 23/28
◆ 17C whitewashed inn set in a chocolate box village. Characterful beamed bar
with log fire and dining room overlooking the gardens. Gutsy modern dishes; seasonality and provenance paramount.

## FUNTINGTON – West Sussex – **504** R31 – see Chichester

## FYFIELD – Oxfordshire – see Oxford

## GATESHEAD – Tyne and Wear – **501** P19 – pop. 78 403 ▌ Great Britain

▶ London 282 mi – Durham 16 mi – Middlesbrough 38 mi
– Newcastle upon Tyne 1 mi
**Access** Tyne Tunnel (toll)
🛈 Prince Consort Rd ☏ (0191) 433 84 20, www.newcastlegateshead.com
🏌 Ravensworth Wrekenton Angel View, Long Bank, ☏ (0191) 487 60 14
🏌 Heworth Gingling Gate, ☏ (0191) 469 98 32
◎ Beamish : North of England Open Air Museum★★ **AC**, SW : 6 mi by A 692 and A
6076 BX

Plan : see Newcastle upon Tyne

🏠 **Stables Lodge** without rest      🈐 🈺 📶 **P** *VISA* 🅒🅓 🅐🅔
*South Farm, Lamesley, Southwest : 5 mi by A 167 and Belle Vue Bank on A 692*
✉ NE11 0ET – ☏ (0191) 492 17 56 – www.thestableslodge.co.uk
**4 rm** 🍽 – †£ 65/74 ††£ 85/138
◆ Rustic and cosy former farmhouse, just off the A1. Individually decorated, very
comfortable bedrooms; the Red Room is the most luxurious; the Garden Room
has its own hot tub.

🍴🍴 **Six**      ≼ 🄰🄲 *VISA* 🅒🅓 🅐🅔
*Baltic Centre for Contemporary Art, Gateshead Quays, South Shore Rd*
✉ NE8 3BA – ☏ (0191) 440 49 48 – www.sixbaltic.com – Closed 25 December, 1
January and Sunday dinner      BX**x**
**Rest** – Menu £ 18 (lunch) – Carte £ 32/41
◆ Fantastic location on top floor of Baltic Centre; floor to ceiling windows afford
views of city's skyline, the Tyne and the Millennium Bridge. Modern brasserie,
with a menu to match.

**at Low Fell** South : 2 mi on A 167 - BX – ✉ Gateshead

 **Eslington Villa** 🛋 ⅋ ⁽ⁱ⁾ 🔥 **P** 🆅🅸🆂🅰 ⓒⓞ 🅰🅴
*8 Station Rd, West : 0.75 mi by Belle Vue Bank, turning left at T junction, right at
roundabout then taking first turn right ✉ NE9 6DR – ☎ (0191) 487 60 17
– www.eslingtonvilla.co.uk – Closed 25-26 December*
**18 rm** ⊑ – †£ 80 ††£ 100/120
**Rest** – *(closed Saturday lunch and Sunday dinner)* Menu £ 19/27
♦ Well-run, stylish, privately owned hotel 10 minutes' drive from city centre.
Nicely furnished lounge bar leads from smart reception. Attractively styled, modern bedrooms. Classical dining room and conservatory; wide-ranging, traditional
menu with modern twists.

---

**GEORGE GREEN** – Buckinghamshire                          **11** D3
▶ London 23

 **Pinewood** 🛋 🏠 📶 🔥 rm, 🆔🅲 ⅋ ⁽ⁱ⁾ 🔥 **P** 🆅🅸🆂🅰 ⓒⓞ 🅰🅴
*Wexham Park Ln, Uxbridge Rd, on A 412 ✉ SL3 6AP – ☎ (01753) 896 400
– www.pinewoodhotel.co.uk – Closed 25-28 December*
**49 rm** ⊑ – †£ 65/145 ††£ 95/155
**Rest** *Eden* – Carte £ 24/35 **s**
♦ Located on the A412 close to Slough; ideal for those on business or on a trip
to Legoland. Functional, modern rooms with some flair. Modern dishes with a
twist in Eden.

---

**GERRARDS CROSS** – Buckinghamshire – **504** S29          **11** D3
▶ London 22 mi – Birmingham 106 mi – Bristol 112 mi – Cardiff 145 mi

 **Three Oaks** 🛋 🏠 **P** 🆅🅸🆂🅰 ⓒⓞ 🅰🅴
*Austenwood Rd, Northwest : 0.75 mi by A 413 on Gold Hill rd ✉ SL9 8NL
– ☎ (01753) 899 016 – www.thethreeoaksgx.co.uk – Closed dinner Sunday and
bank holidays*
**Rest** – Menu £ 19 (lunch) – Carte £ 24/38
♦ Revamped pub with reconditioned furniture to add a lived-in look. Two dining
rooms; choose the brighter one overlooking the terrace and garden. Bright young
service and satisfying cooking that sticks to the tried-and-tested.

---

**GILLINGHAM** – Dorset – **503** N30 – pop. 8 630          **4** C3
▶ London 116 mi – Bournemouth 34 mi – Bristol 46 mi – Southampton 52 mi
🄶 Stourhead★★★ **AC**, N : 9 mi by B 3092, B 3095 and B 3092

🏠🏠🏠 **Stock Hill Country House** ☜ 🛋 🕊 📶 ✗ ⅋ ⁽ⁱ⁾ **P** 🆅🅸🆂🅰 ⓒⓞ
*Stock Hill, West : 1.5 mi on B 3081 ✉ SP8 5NR – ☎ (01747) 823 626
– www.stockhillhouse.co.uk*
**8 rm** (dinner included) ⊑ – †£ 130/180 ††£ 260/325
**Rest** – *(booking essential)* Menu £ 30/40 🕮
♦ Well-run Georgian country house with later extensions, in attractive, mature
grounds. Classical lounges boast heavy fabrics and antiques. Bedrooms, in the main
house and stables, are a mix of cottagey and contemporary country house styles; all
have good facilities. Formal, two-roomed restaurant with own kitchen garden.

---

**GITTISHAM** – Devon – **503** K31 – see Honiton

---

**GODSHILL** – Isle of Wight – **504** Q32 – see Wight (Isle of)

---

**GOLANT** Cornwall – Cornwall – **503** G32 – see Fowey

---

**GOLDSBOROUGH** – North Yorkshire – see Whitby

---

**GOREY** – **503** P33 – see Channel Islands (Jersey)

---

**GORING** – Oxfordshire – **503** Q29 – pop. 4 193 ▯ Great Britain     **10** B3
▶ London 56 mi – Oxford 16 mi – Reading 12 mi
🄶 Ridgeway Path★★

ENGLAND

## Leatherne Bottel ⌖ 🏠 P VISA ⦿ AE

*The Bridleway, North : 1.5 mi by B 4009 ⊠ RG8 0HS – ☏ (01491) 872 667
– www.leathernebottel.co.uk – Closed Sunday dinner*

**Rest** – *(booking essential)* Menu £ 20 (lunch) – Carte £ 35/46⚜

◆ Delightful Thameside restaurant with lovely summer terrace. Menus fuse traditional recipes with interesting, modern combinations. Leaves picked fresh from garden. Impressive Chablis selection.

---

## GORRAN HAVEN – Cornwall – 503 F33                                1 B3

▶ London 260 mi – Plymouth 53 mi – Torbay 80 mi – Torquay 83 mi

## Llawnroc ⌖ 🏠 🖥 & rm, 🎦 rm, ⌖ 🎵 ♨ VISA ⦿ AE

*Chute Ln ⊠ PL26 6NU – ☏ (01726) 843 461 – www.thellawnrochotel.co.uk*
**18 rm** ⬚ – †£ 96/208 ††£ 120/260     **Rest** – *(bar lunch)* Menu £ 43

◆ Unpretentious boutique hotel built around The Gwineas pub; enjoy tea on the terrific terrace, fish in the pub or more intimate meals in the main dining room. Plenty of contemporary design touches to the boldly coloured, well-equipped bedrooms. A hotel popular with families.

---

## GOVETON – Devon – 503 I33 – see Kingsbridge

---

## GRANGE-OVER-SANDS – Cumbria – 502 L21 – pop. 4 835          21 A3

▌ Great Britain

▶ London 268 mi – Kendal 13 mi – Lancaster 24 mi

🖪 Main St ☏ (015395) 3 40 26, www.grange-over-sands.com

🛱 Meathop Rd, ☏ (015395) 3 31 80

🄶 Cartmel Priory ★, NW : 3 mi

## Netherwood ⌖ 🚗 🛈 🖥 ♨ 🖥 & 🎦 rest, 🎵 🎵 ♨ P VISA ⦿

*Lindale Rd ⊠ LA11 6ET – ☏ (015395) 32 552 – www.netherwood-hotel.co.uk*
**34 rm** ⬚ – †£ 75/85 ††£ 120/160     **Rest** – Menu £ 18/34

◆ Impressive castellated mansion on the hillside, affording lovely bay views. Traditional guest areas display wood panelling and original features. Simple, well-maintained bedrooms; more contemporary rooms in outbuildings. Formal dining comes with great outlook.

## Clare House ⌖ 🚗 ⌖ 🎵 ♨ P VISA ⦿

*Park Rd ⊠ LA11 7HQ – ☏ (015395) 33 026 – www.clarehousehotel.co.uk – 27
March-9 November*
**18 rm** (dinner included) ⬚ – †£ 86/159 ††£ 172/182
**Rest** – *(dinner only and Sunday lunch) (booking essential for non-residents)*
Menu £ 36

◆ Family-run Victorian house set in lovely gardens, overlooking Morecambe Bay. Two classical sitting rooms. Stylish, boldly coloured bedrooms in main house; smaller, simpler rooms with balconies in wing. Smart, modern dining room offers traditional daily menus.

---

### at Cartmel Northwest : 3 mi – ⊠ Grange-Over-Sands

## L'Enclume (Simon Rogan) with rm 🚗 🎦 rest, VISA ⦿ AE

☖ *Cavendish St ⊠ LA11 6PZ – ☏ (015395) 36 362 – www.lenclume.co.uk*
**12 rm** ⬚ – †£ 69 †††£ 159/199
**Rest** – *(closed lunch Monday-Tuesday) (booking essential)* Menu £ 25 (lunch)
– Carte £ 69/89

**Spec.** Vintage potatoes with onion ashes, lovage and sorrel. Native lobster in pig skin, grilled wild leeks and sea purslane. Coniston oatmeal stout ice cream with apple, sweet bracken and malt.

◆ Stone-built former blacksmiths in an attractive little village, run by a friendly team. Refined, original cooking uses modern techniques and is underpinned by a classical style. Flavours are clean and clear, and home-grown or foraged produce features highly. Choice of 8 or 13 course menu. Smart, traditionally styled bedrooms are spread about the village.

XX **Rogan and Company**                                         *VISA* ⚫⚫
*The Square* ✉ *LA11 6QD* – ✆ *(015395) 35 917* – *www.roganandcompany.co.uk*
*– Closed Monday in low season*
**Rest** – Carte £ 24/39
◆ Converted cottage by lovely stream; informal cousin to L'Enclume. Stylish, split-
level interior with sofas, polished tables and high bar seating. Extensive menus of
locally sourced produce.

---

**GRANTHAM** – Lincolnshire – **502** S25 – **pop. 34 592** 🏛 Great Britain          **17** C2

▶ London 113 mi – Leicester 31 mi – Lincoln 29 mi – Nottingham 24 mi

🛈 St Peter's Hill ✆ (01476) 40 61 66, www.granthamuk.com

🏢 Belton Park Londonthorpe Rd, Belton Lane, ✆ (01476) 56 73 99

🏢 De Vere Belton Woods H., ✆ (01476) 59 32 00

👁 St Wulfram's Church★

🏰 Belton House★ **AC**, N : 2.5 mi by A 607. Belvoir Castle★★ **AC**, W : 6 mi by A 607

**at Hough-on-the-Hill** North : 6.75 mi by A 607 – ✉ Grantham

XX **Brownlow Arms** with rm                      🏠 AC rest, 🛜 P *VISA* ⚫⚫
*High Rd* ✉ *NG32 2AZ* – ✆ *(01400) 250 234*
**4 rm** 🍽 – †£ 65 ††£ 98
**Rest** – *(closed Sunday dinner and Monday) (dinner only and Sunday lunch)*
Carte £ 28/40
◆ Characterful former shooting lodge for the nearby Belton Estate, with wood-pa-
nelled walls and large open fireplaces. Lengthy menu and specials list offer classi-
cally based dishes with modern presentation. Lovely terrace and friendly service.
Delightful bedrooms are furnished with contemporary fabrics and period pieces.

**ENGLAND**

**at Harlaxton** Southwest : 2.5 mi on A 607 – ✉ Grantham

🍴 **Gregory**                                        🏠 P *VISA* ⚫⚫
*The Drift, Southwest : 2 mi by A 607* ✉ *NG32 1AD* – ✆ *(01476) 577 076*
*– www.thegregory.co.uk – Closed dinner 25-26 December and 1 January*
**Rest** – Carte £ 21/33
◆ Roadside community pub with spacious dining room and smaller lounge, both
with very modern feel. Pub classics dominate the menu, with steaks, pies and old-
fashioned puddings.

**at Woolsthorpe-by-Belvoir** West : 7.5 mi by A 607 – ✉ Grantham

🍴 **Chequers** with rm                        🚗 🏠 P *VISA* ⚫⚫ AE
*Main St* ✉ *NG32 1LU* – ✆ *(01476) 870 701* – *www.chequersinn.net – Closed*
*dinner 25-26 December and 1 January*
**4 rm** 🍽 – †£ 50 ††£ 70   **Rest** – Menu £ 17 (weekdays) – Carte £ 21/33
◆ Cosy, open-fired pub in a quaint village owned by the Belvoir Estate, and back-
ing onto the local cricket pitch. Simple homemade and local offerings at lunch,
supplemented by steaks and game at dinner. Crisply furnished, modern bedrooms located in the old stables.

**at Great Gonerby** Northwest : 2 mi on B 1174 – ✉ Grantham

XX **Harry's Place**                                       P *VISA* ⚫⚫
*17 High St* ✉ *NG31 8JS* – ✆ *(01476) 561 780* – *Closed 1 week August, 25-30*
*December, Sunday, Monday and bank holidays*
**Rest** – *(booking essential)* Carte £ 55/66
◆ Long-standing, intimate restaurant consisting of just three tables; run by dedicated and delightful husband and wife team. Warm, welcoming feel, with fresh
flowers, candles and antiques. Classically based, hand-written menus offer two
choices per course.

**at Dry Doddington** Northwest : 11 mi by B 1174 and A 1

🍴 **Wheatsheaf Inn**                                          🛜 **P** VISA ©© ©

*Main St* ✉ *NG23 5HU – ℰ (01400) 281 458 – www.wheatsheaf-pub.co.uk*
*– Closed Monday except bank holidays*
**Rest** – Menu £ 15 (lunch) – Carte £ 23/28
♦ Smartly kept pub overlooking a pretty green, with cosy bar, laid-back restaurant and small courtyard. Simple, unfussy light bites lunch menu; more ambitious à la carte with evening specials.

---

**GRASMERE** – Cumbria – **502** K20 – ✉ **Ambleside** 📗 Great Britain          **21** A2

▶ London 282 mi – Carlisle 43 mi – Kendal 18 mi
👁 Dove Cottage★ **AC** AY **A**
🌀 Lake Windermere★★, SE : by A 591 AZ

Plans : see Ambleside

Plans : see Ambleside

🏠🏠🏠 **Rothay Garden**                        🚗 ⅙ rm, **AC** rest, ¶¶ **P** VISA ©©

*Broadgate* ✉ *LA22 9RJ – ℰ (01539) 435 334 – www.rothaygarden.com*
**30 rm** ☲ – †£ 103/108 ††£ 185/195                                    AY**s**
**Rest** – Menu 40 (dinner) **s** – Carte £ 29/38 **s**
♦ Old Lakeland house with gardens leading to river and stylish, contemporary inner. Boldly coloured lounges. Contemporary bedrooms with good facilities: choose those with patios or the loft suites. Neat, linen-laid dining room has lovely outlook and modern menu.

🏠 **Moss Grove Organic** without rest               ¶¶ **P** VISA ©© **AE**

✉ *LA22 9SW – ℰ (015394) 35 251 – www.mossgrove.com – Closed 25-26*
*December*                                                                BZ**s**
**11 rm** ☲ – †£ 99/114 ††£ 114/129
♦ Large house with stylish, modern interior, which features some reclaimed furnishings. Sizeable bedrooms boast feature walls: several have four-posters; one has a hot tub. Organic breakfasts.

🏠 **Grasmere**                                       🚗 ¶¶ **P** VISA ©©

*Broadgate* ✉ *LA22 9TA – ℰ (015394) 35 277 – www.grasmerehotel.co.uk*
*– Closed January*                                                        BZ**r**
**13 rm** ☲ – †£ 55/63 ††£ 110/126 – 1 suite
**Rest** – (dinner only) (booking essential for non-residents) Menu £ 30 **s**
♦ Small Victorian house close to the village centre, with the River Rothay running through the garden. Traditionally styled lounge and bar. Similarly classical bedrooms, with colourful fabrics adding a modern touch. Pine-roofed dining room overlooks the garden.

🏠 **Oak Bank**                                      ♫ ⅌ ¶¶ **P** VISA ©©

*Broadgate* ✉ *LA22 9TA – ℰ (015394) 35 217 – www.lakedistricthotel.co.uk*
*– Closed 2-26 January and weekdays 12 November-26 December*              BZ**x**
**14 rm** (dinner included) ☲ – †£ 84/102 ††£ 150/192
**Rest** *Restaurant* – see restaurant listing
♦ Victorian house with pretty rear garden, set on the edge of a famous village. Relax beside a converted range in the sitting room or open-fire in the lounge-bar. Stylish, modern bedrooms boast comfortable beds and contemporary furnishings.

🏠 **Lake View Country House** without rest ⌂⅗          ≼ 🚗 ¶¶ **P** VISA ©©

*Lake View Dr* ✉ *LA22 9TD – ℰ (015394) 35 384 – www.lakeview-grasmere.com*
**4 rm** ☲ – ††£ 102/112                                                  BZ**c**
♦ Traditional country house run by an enthusiastic owner. Cosy, homely bedrooms display some antiques; two rooms have spa baths. Linen-laid breakfast room. Yoghurts and compotes are homemade.

ENGLAND

XX **Restaurant** – at Oak Bank Hotel  ⏰ 🅿 VISA ⊕⊙
*Broadgate* ⊠ *LA22 9TA* – ℰ *(015394) 35 217* – *www.lakedistricthotel.co.uk*
*– Closed 2-26 January and weekdays 12 November-26 December*  BZx
**Rest** – *(dinner only)* Menu £ 28
♦ Split-roomed hotel restaurant in a Victorian house, with pleasant conservatory extension overlooking the garden. Concise daily menu features interesting modern dishes crafted from local, seasonal produce. Puddings are classically based.

---

# GRASSINGTON – North Yorkshire – 502 O21 – pop. 1 102    22 A2
– ⊠ Skipton

▶ London 240 mi – Bradford 30 mi – Burnley 28 mi – Leeds 37 mi
ℹ National Park Centre, Colvend, Hebden Rd ℰ (01756) 75 16 90,
www.grassington.uk.com

🏠 **Ashfield House**  🚗 ⚗ 📶 🅿 VISA ⊕⊙ AE
*Summers Fold, off Main St* ⊠ *BD23 5AE* – ℰ *(01756) 752 584*
*– www.ashfieldhouse.co.uk*
**8 rm** ⥮ – ♥£ 85/120 ♥♥£ 96/136
**Rest** – *(closed Sunday in winter) (dinner only) (booking essential for non-residents)* Menu £ 36
♦ Bright, cheery hotel with larger-than-life owner. Cosy beams and flag floors blend well with Mediterranean colours in the bedrooms. Split-level rear cottage boasts spiral staircase and terrace. Modern menus rely on local produce; vegetarian dishes a speciality.

🏠 **Grassington Lodge** without rest  ⚗ 📶 🅿 VISA ⊕⊙
*8 Wood Ln* ⊠ *BD23 5LU* – ℰ *(01756) 752 518* – *www.grassingtonlodge.co.uk*
**12 rm** ⥮ – ♥£ 70/95 ♥♥£ 80/160
♦ Georgian stone house set on a cobbled street close to the square. Fresh, modern inner with comfy lounge, bar and smart terrace. Neat bedrooms: those in the eaves are the best. Good extras.

XX **Grassington House** with rm  🏠 📶 🅿 VISA ⊕⊙
*5 The Square* ⊠ *BD23 5AQ* – ℰ *(01756) 752 406*
*– www.grassingtonhousehotel.co.uk*
**9 rm** ⥮ – ♥£ 90 ♥♥£ 125    **Rest** – Menu £ 17 (lunch) – Carte £ 29/41
♦ Georgian house with large bar-lounge and two-roomed restaurant; one a conservatory with grand piano. Delightful service. Classical menu displays Mediterranean touches and includes home-bred pork. Smart, modern bedrooms. Breakfast offers home-cured bacon/sausages.

---

# GREAT DUNMOW – Essex – 504 V28 – pop. 5 943    13 C2
▶ London 42 mi – Cambridge 27 mi – Chelmsford 13 mi – Colchester 24 mi

XXX **Starr** with rm  📶 🅿 VISA ⊕⊙ AE ⓪
*Market Pl* ⊠ *CM6 1AX* – ℰ *(01371) 874 321* – *www.the-starr.co.uk* – *Closed 27-31 December and 2-5 January*
**8 rm** ⥮ – ♥£ 60/90 ♥♥£ 95/120
**Rest** – *(closed Sunday dinner and Monday)* Menu £ 40 (dinner) – Carte lunch £ 39/49
♦ Former 15C pub with rustic bar and fire. Characterful restaurant has exposed beams and conservatory. Strong, interesting cooking, traditionally inspired. Smart bedrooms.

X **Square 1**  AC VISA ⊕⊙
*15 High St.* ⊠ *CM6 1AB* – ℰ *(01371) 859 922* – *www.square1restaurant.co.uk*
*– Closed 25-26 December and Sunday dinner*
**Rest** – Menu £ 13 (lunch) – Carte £ 23/37
♦ Pretty little whitewashed building; once a 14C monastic reading room. Much original character remains in the form of exposed beams and low ceilings – which contrast with vibrant modern art. Unfussy monthly menu has Mediterranean leanings.

ENGLAND

**at Great Easton** North : 2.75 mi by B 184

🛏  **Green Man**                                             🚗 🏠 **P** VISA ⓪⓪
*Mile End Green, Northeast : 1 mi by B 184 on Mile End Green rd ⊠ CM6 2DN*
*– 𝒞 (01371) 852 285 – www.thegreenmanrestaurant.com – Closed two*
*weeks January, Monday and Tuesday*
**Rest** – *(closed Sunday dinner)* Carte £ 25/38
♦ Contemporary pub, 20 minutes from Stansted Airport. Dishes are more of a
restaurant than pub persuasion, and are coupled with attentive, assured service.
Terrace and garden overlook fields.

## GREAT EASTON – Essex – **504** U28 – see Great Dunmow

## GREAT GONERBY – Lincolnshire – **502** S25 – see Grantham

## GREAT MALVERN – Worcestershire – **503** N27 – pop. 35 588          **18** B3
▶ London 127 mi – Birmingham 34 mi – Cardiff 66 mi – Gloucester 24 mi
🅭 21 Church St 𝒞 (01684) 89 22 89, www.great-malvern.co.uk

🏠  **Bredon House** without rest                         ⩽ 🚗 ⁿ **P** VISA ⓪⓪
*34 Worcester Rd ⊠ WR14 4AA – 𝒞 (01684) 566 990 – www.bredonhouse.co.uk*
**10 rm** ⌂ – ♦£ 55/75 ♦♦£ 90/110                                      B**a**
♦ Elegant, Grade II listed Regency house with spectacular views. Personable owners make breakfast a special event. Most of the individually styled rooms enjoy
the fine vista.

🏠  **Cotford**                                            🚗 ⁿ **P** VISA ⓪⓪
*51 Graham Rd ⊠ WR14 2HU – 𝒞 (01684) 572 427 – www.cotfordhotel.co.uk*
**15 rm** ⌂ – ♦£ 65/79 ♦♦£ 125                                         B**s**
**Rest** *L'Amuse Bouche* – *(dinner only and Sunday lunch)* Menu £ 30
♦ Recently refurbished Victorian gothic stone building in landscaped gardens;
built in 1851 for the Bishop of Worcester. Modern but homely guest areas; cosy
bedrooms. Contemporary dining room with garden views; seasonal menu of local,
organic produce.

**at Guarlford** East : 2.5 mi on B 4211

🛏  **Plough and Harrow**                                  🚗 🏠 **P** VISA ⓪⓪
*Rhydd Rd, East : 0.5 mi on B 4211 ⊠ WR13 6NY – 𝒞 (01684) 310 453*
*– www.theploughandharrow.co.uk – Closed 1 week spring,1 week autumn, 25-26*
*December, 1 January, Sunday dinner and Monday*
**Rest** – Carte £ 21/36
♦ Passionately run pub set off the beaten track. Light lunches; short evening à la
carte; simpler midweek bar snacks. Seasonality is key and much of the fruit/veg
comes from their garden.

**at Malvern Wells** South : 2 mi on A 449 – ⊠ Malvern

🏠🏠  **Cottage in the Wood** ⁑             ⩽ 🚗 🏠 **AC** rest, **P** VISA ⓪⓪ **AE**
*Holywell Rd ⊠ WR14 4LG – 𝒞 (01684) 588 860 – www.cottageinthewood.co.uk*
**30 rm** ⌂ – ♦£ 79/121 ♦♦£ 99/198    **Rest** – Carte £ 22/37 **s** 🍴          A**z**
♦ Three detached properties with woodland behind, superbly set and boasting
amazing views down the valley. Smart, good-sized bedrooms boast modern soft
furnishings; most rooms have views. Cosy bar-lounge. Bright restaurant with full-
length windows and modern menu.

**at Colwall** Southwest : 3 mi on B 4218 – ⊠ Great Malvern

🏠🏠  **Colwall Park**                                🚗 🏋 ⁿ 🕸 **P** VISA ⓪⓪
*⊠ WR13 6QG – 𝒞 (01684) 540 000 – www.colwall.co.uk*                    A**v**
**21 rm** ⌂ – ♦£ 85/100 ♦♦£ 125/135 – 1 suite
**Rest** *Seasons* – *(booking essential at lunch)* Menu £ 25 – Carte £ 22/35
♦ Passionately run, part red-brick, part black and white timbered house with
lovely gardens, nestled in the Malvern Hills. Pleasant lounges. Comfy bedrooms
range from traditional to more contemporary styles. Brasserie menu available in
bar or linen-laid restaurant.

ENGLAND

## GREAT MALVERN

CENTRE

**GREAT MILTON** – Oxfordshire – **503** Q28 – see Oxford

**GREAT MISSENDEN** – Buckinghamshire – **504** R28 – pop. 7 980      **11** C2
▶ London 34 mi – Aylesbury 10 mi – Maidenhead 19 mi – Oxford 35 mi

XX    **La Petite Auberge**                                                        *VISA* ◐◐
      *107 High St ⊠ HP16 0BB – ℰ (01494) 865 370 – www.lapetiteauberge.co.uk
      – Closed 2 weeks Easter, 2 weeks Christmas and Sunday except Mothering
      Sunday*
      **Rest** – French – *(dinner only)* Carte £ 31/39
      ◆ Personally run, neighbourhood restaurant; neat, crisp and candlelit, with an in-
      timate ambience and unhurried style. Bold French menu of carefully prepared,
      flavourful dishes.

🍴    **Nags Head** with rm                                        🚗 🅥 🐾 📶 **P** *VISA* ◐◐ 🆎
      *London Rd, Southeast : 1 mi by A 413. ⊠ HP16 0DG – ℰ (01494) 862 200
      – www.nagsheadbucks.com*
      **5 rm** � – ♦£ 70/130 ♦♦£ 80/140    **Rest** – Carte £ 25/35
      ◆ Traditional 15C inn whose features include original oak beams and thick brick
      walls. Gallic charm mixes with British classics on interesting menus. Cheerful ser-
      vice. Stylish, modern bedrooms; number one is best. Tasty breakfast choice.

**GREAT TOTHAM** – Essex – **504** W28 – pop. 720      **13** C2
▶ London 59 mi – Croydon 64 mi – Barnet 58 mi – Ealing 70 mi

XX    **Willow Room**                                        🚗 🍴 🄰🄺 **P** *VISA* ◐◐ 🆎
      *The Bull Public House, 2 Maldon Rd ⊠ CM9 8NH – ℰ (01621) 894 020
      – www.thewillowroom.co.uk – Closed Monday and Tuesday*
      **Rest** – Menu £ 20/40
      ◆ Luxuriously furnished restaurant with a pleasant designer feel, located within
      'The Bull' pub but with its own front door and dedicated lounge. Elaborate, mod-
      ern cooking relies on local produce and hints at the chef's Scottish heritage.

🍴    **The Bull** with rm                                   🚗 🍴 🅥 📶 **P** *VISA* ◐◐ 🆎
      *2 Maldon Rd ⊠ CM9 8NH – ℰ (01621) 893 385
      – www.thebullatgreattotham.co.uk*
      **4 rm** ⊟ – ♦£ 59/75 ♦♦£ 69/85    **Rest** – Menu £ 16 (lunch) – Carte £ 19/26
      ◆ Dating from the 1500s, this roadside pub has been refurbished and moder-
      nised and comes with a great terrace and garden. Expect pub classics in the bar;
      more ambitious food using local produce in the smart 'Willow Room' restaurant.
      Individually decorated bedrooms are located in the annexe.

**GREAT WOLFORD** – Warwickshire – **503** P27      **19** C3
▶ London 84 mi – Birmingham 37 mi – Cheltenham 26 mi

🍴    **Fox & Hounds Inn** with rm                                   🍴 **P** *VISA* ◐◐
      *⊠ CV36 5NQ – ℰ (01608) 674 220 – www.thefoxandhoundsinn.com
      – Closed first two weeks January, Sunday dinner and Monday*
      **3 rm** ⊟ – ♦£ 60 ♦♦£ 90    **Rest** – Carte £ 17/32
      ◆ Cosy, characterful, family-run country inn with traditional interior, low beams,
      hop bines and a large inglenook. Daily blackboard menus display rustic pub
      dishes of local, seasonal produce. Simple, pine-furnished bedrooms offer pleasant
      country views.

**GREAT YARMOUTH** – Norfolk – **504** Z26 – pop. 58 032      **15** D2
📗 Great Britain
▶ London 126 mi – Cambridge 81 mi – Ipswich 53 mi – Norwich 20 mi
🛈 25 Marine Parade ℰ (01493) 84 63 45, www.great-yarmouth.co.uk
🏌 Gorleston Warren Rd, ℰ (01493) 66 19 11
🏌 Beach House Caister-on-Sea, Great Yarmouth & Caister, ℰ (01493) 72 86 99
◉ Norfolk Broads★

ENGLAND

XX **Andover House** with rm                    ((¹)) VISA ⓒ AE ⓪
*28-30 Camperdown* ⊠ *NR30 3JB* – ℰ *(01493) 843 490*
*– www.andoverhouse.co.uk – Closed 23-30 December and Sunday dinner*
**16 rm** ⌂ – †£ 67/89 ††£ 89/99 – 4 suites
**Rest** – *(dinner only) (residents only Sunday and Monday)* Menu £ 27 **s**
– Carte £ 27/48 **s**
♦ Modernised, listed Victorian property with a crisp, chic style and friendly, well-
drilled service. Constantly evolving à la carte of modern, well-presented and accomplished dishes, with the occasional Asian touch. Simple, modern bedrooms;
some with four-posters, some with large bay windows.

XX **Seafood**                                   AC VISA ⓒ AE ⓪
*85 North Quay* ⊠ *NR30 1JF* – ℰ *(01493) 856 009 – www.theseafood.co.uk*
*– Closed 2 weeks Christmas, last 2 weeks May, Saturday lunch, Sunday and bank
holidays*
**Rest** – Seafood – Menu £ 20 (lunch) – Carte £ 26/49
♦ Long-standing restaurant on the edge of town, run by friendly owners. Traditional interior boasts intimate booths, a lobster tank and fresh fish display. Reliable, classical seafood dishes.

---

**GREAT WHITTINGTON** – Northumberland – **501** O18 – **see Corbridge**

---

**GREEN ISLAND** – **503** P33 – **see Channel Islands (Jersey)**

---

**GREETHAM** – Rutland                                             **17** C2

▶ London 101 mi – Birmingham 86 mi – Liverpool 164 mi – Leeds 98 mi

🏠 **Wheatsheaf Inn**                          🛏 ☆ P VISA ⓒ
*1 Stretton Rd* ⊠ *LE15 7NP* – ℰ *(01572) 812 325*
*– www.wheatsheaf-greetham.co.uk – Closed first 2 weeks January, Monday
except bank holidays and Sunday dinner*
**Rest** – Carte £ 19/30
♦ The aroma of fresh bread is the first thing you notice at this simple, family-
friendly country pub. Robust modern cooking comes with hints of the Med;
cheaper cuts keep prices sensible and desserts are a must. Run by a charming
couple.

---

**GRETA BRIDGE** – Durham – **502** O20 – **see Barnard Castle**

---

**GRIMSTON** – Norfolk – **504** V25 – **see King's Lynn**

---

**GRINDLETON** – Lancashire – **502** M22 – **see Clitheroe**

---

**GRINSHILL** – Shropshire – **503** L25 – **see Shrewsbury**

---

**GROUVILLE** – **503** M33 – pop. 4 658 – **see Channel Islands (Jersey)**

---

**GUARLFORD** – Worcestershire – **see Great Malvern**

---

**GUERNSEY** – Guernsey – **503** O/P33 – pop. 58 867 – **see Channel Islands**

---

**GUILDFORD** – Surrey – **504** S30 – pop. 68 601 ▮ Great Britain      **7** C1

▶ London 33 mi – Brighton 43 mi – Reading 27 mi – Southampton 49 mi
🛈 14 Tunsgate ℰ (01483) 44 43 33, www.guildford.gov.uk
🄲 Clandon Park★★, E : 3 mi by A 246 Z – Hatchlands Park★, E : 6 mi by A 246 Z.
Painshill★★, Cobham, NE : 10 m – Polesden Lacey★, E : 13 mi by A 246 Z and
minor rd

Plan on next page

# GUILDFORD

**ENGLAND**

**at Shere** East : 6.75 mi by A 246 off A 25 - Z - ✉ Guildford

## XX  Kinghams
P VISA ◐◐ AE ①

*Gomshall Ln* ✉ *GU5 9HE* – ☎ *(01483) 202 168*
– *www.kinghams-restaurant.co.uk* – *Closed 25 December-5 January, Sunday dinner and Monday*
**Rest** – *(booking essential)* Menu £ 23 *(weekday lunch)* – Carte £ 26/39
◆ Popular restaurant in 17C cottage, set in an appealing village. Daily blackboard menu and fish specials are particularly good value. Adventurous modern menus feature bold combinations.

**GULVAL** – Cornwall – **503** D33 – see Penzance

## HADLEIGH – Suffolk – **504** W27 – **pop. 7 124**     **15** C3

▶ London 72 mi – Cambridge 49 mi – Colchester 17 mi – Ipswich 10 mi
🛈 29 High St ℰ (01473) 82 37 78, www.suffolktouristguide.com

⚲    **Edge Hall** without rest       🚗 ⁽ʸ⁾ **P**
*2 High St. ⊠ IP7 5AP – ℰ (01473) 822 458 – www.edgehall.co.uk – Closed 23-29 December*
**6 rm** � – †£ 50/60 ††£ 85/99
♦ One of the oldest houses in the town (1590), with a Georgian façade. Spacious, comfy bedrooms are traditionally furnished, as are the communal areas. Very well-kept gardens.

## HADLEY HEATH – Worcestershire – see Droitwich Spa

## HALFORD – Warwickshire – **503** P27 – **pop. 301**     **19** C3

▶ London 94 mi – Oxford 43 mi – Stratford-upon-Avon 8 mi

⚲    **Old Manor House** without rest ⚘      🚗 ⅁ ✗ ⁄ ⁽ʸ⁾ **P** 𝘝𝘐𝘚𝘈 ⚙ 𝖠𝖤
*Queens St ⊠ CV36 5BT – ℰ (01789) 740 264 – www.oldmanor-halford.co.uk – Closed 25-27 December*
**3 rm** �ᵘ – †£ 65 ††£ 90/100
♦ Characterful house in pretty little village, well-located for Stratford and the Cotswolds. Spacious garden next to the River Stour. Well-appointed drawing room and atmospheric bedrooms with rich fabrics.

## HALFWAY BRIDGE – West Sussex – **504** R31 – see Petworth

## HALIFAX – West Yorkshire – **502** O22 – **pop. 83 570**     **22** B2

▶ London 205 mi – Bradford 8 mi – Burnley 21 mi – Leeds 15 mi
🛈 Piece Hall ℰ (01422) 36 87 25, www.visitcalderdale.com
🏌 Halifax Bradley Hall Holywell Green, ℰ (01422) 37 41 08
🏌 Halifax West End Highroad Well Paddock Lane, ℰ (01422) 34 18 78
🏌 Ryburn Sowerby Bridge Norland, ℰ (01422) 83 13 55
🏌 Lightcliffe Knowle Top Rd, ℰ (01422) 20 24 59
🏌 Ogden Union Lane, ℰ (01422) 24 41 71

✗✗    **Design House**        𝖠𝖢 ⟷ **P** 𝘝𝘐𝘚𝘈 ⚙
*Dean Clough (Gate 5) ⊠ HX3 5AX – ℰ (01422) 383 242*
*– www.designhouserestaurant.co.uk – Closed 26 December-8 January, Saturday lunch, Sunday and bank holiday Mondays*
**Rest** – Carte £ 22/37 **s**
♦ Long-standing restaurant in converted mill complex. Striking interior with subtle blue hues; smart team offer warm welcome. Extensive menus of precise, tasty, classical and more modern dishes.

⌂    **Shibden Mill Inn** with rm       🚗 ⌂ ⁽ʸ⁾ **P** 𝘝𝘐𝘚𝘈 ⚙ 𝖠𝖤
*Shibden Mill Fold ⊠ HX3 7UL – ℰ (01422) 365 840 – www.shibdenmillinn.com – Closed 25-26 December and 1 January*
**11 rm** �ᵘ – †£ 105 ††£ 123    **Rest** – Menu £ 13 (lunch) **s** – Carte £ 28/33 **s**
♦ Charming whitewashed country inn – formerly a corn mill – set in the valley. Extensive menu ranges from the traditional to the more modern. Events include fortnightly 'guinea pig' nights. Individually appointed bedrooms are comfy and cosy.

## HALTWHISTLE – Northumberland – **501** M19 – **pop. 3 811**     **24** A2

▌ Great Britain

▶ London 335 mi – Carlisle 22 mi – Newcastle upon Tyne 37 mi
🛈 Station Rd ℰ (01434) 32 20 02, www.visitnorthumberland.com
🏌 Wallend Farm Greenhead, ℰ (01697) 74 73 67
◎ Hadrian's Wall★★, N : 4.5 mi by A 6079 – Housesteads★★ **AC**, NE : 6 mi by B 6318 – Roman Army Museum★ **AC**, NW : 5 mi by A 69 and B 6318 – Vindolanda (Museum★) **AC**, NE : 5 mi by A 69 – Steel Rig (≤★) NE : 5.5 mi by B 6318

🏠 **Centre of Britain**                                    📶 ⚠️ **P** **VISA** 💳 🅾️

*Main St* ✉️ *NE49 0BH –* ☎️ *(01434) 322 422 – www.centre-of-britain.org.uk*
**12 rm** 🛏️ – 🚹£ 59/79 🚹🚹£ 90/110    **Rest** – Menu £ 18/20 – Carte £ 19/30
♦ Attractive hotel on busy main street. The oldest part, a pele tower, dates from the 16C. Comfy modern interior incorporates original architectural features. Bedrooms 3 and 9 boast saunas, while chalet rooms are popular with walkers, cyclists and guests with dogs. Glass-roofed restaurant with light, airy feel.

🏠 **Ashcroft** without rest                          🍽️ 🧏 📶 **P** **VISA** 💳 **AE** 🅾️

*Lantys Lonnen* ✉️ *NE49 0DA –* ☎️ *(01434) 320 213*
*– www.ashcroftguesthouse.co.uk – Closed 25 December*
**9 rm** 🛏️ – 🚹£ 50/90 🚹🚹£ 70/135
♦ Imposing Victorian house, formerly a vicarage, with beautifully kept gardens. Family run and attractively furnished throughout creating a welcoming atmosphere. Large bedrooms.

---

**HAMBLE-LE-RICE** – Hampshire – **503** Q31 – **see Southampton**

---

**HAMBLETON** – Rutland – **see Oakham**

---

**HAMPTON IN ARDEN** – West Midlands – **504** O26 – pop. 1 655        **19** C2

▶ London 113 mi – Birmingham 15 mi – Leicester 39 mi – Coventry 11 mi

🏨 **Hampton Manor**                     🍽️ 🧏 🔥 🆎 📶 ⚠️ **P** **VISA** 💳 **AE**

*Shadowbrook Ln* ✉️ *B92 0EN –* ☎️ *(01675) 446 080 – www.hamptonmanor.eu*
*– Closed 25 December*
**11 rm** – 🚹£ 140 🚹🚹£ 140, 🛏️ £ 15 – 1 suite
**Rest** *Peel's Restaurant by Martyn Pearn* – see restaurant listing
♦ Early Victorian manor house in 45 acres; built for grandson of Sir Robert Peel. Contemporary décor blends with characterful plasterwork and wood panelling; bedrooms boast mod cons.

✕✕ **Peel's Restaurant by Martyn Pearn** – at Hampton Manor Hotel

*Shadowbrook Ln.* ✉️ *B92 0EN –* ☎️ *(01675) 446 080*                 📶 **VISA** 💳 **AE**
*– www.peelsrestaurant.co.uk – Closed 25 December, Sunday dinner and Monday lunch*
**Rest** – Menu £ 19/40
♦ Contemporary dining room situated in former stable courtyard, with slate floor, glass roof and floor-to-ceiling windows. Modern style menus; bold, gutsy flavours. Formal service.

---

**HAMPTON POYLE** – Oxfordshire – pop. 106                          **10** B2

▶ London 68 mi – Birmingham 72 mi – Barnet 71 mi – Ealing 57 mi

🍴 **Bell at Hampton Poyle** with rm                  📶 🧏 📶 **P** **VISA** 💳 **AE** 🅾️

*11 Oxford Rd.* ✉️ *OX5 2QD –* ☎️ *(01865) 376 242*
*– www.thebellathamptonpoyle.co.uk*
**9 rm** 🛏️ – 🚹£ 140 🚹🚹£ 140    **Rest** – Menu £ 18 – Carte £ 23/31
♦ Almost Mediterranean in its style, with a very visual kitchen that includes a wood burning oven. Menu offers everything from mezze and charcuterie boards to pub staples and seafood. Bright, fresh bedrooms are located above the bar and in a cottage.

---

**HARLAXTON** – Lincolnshire – **502** S25 – **see Grantham**

---

**HAROME** – North Yorkshire – **see Helmsley**

London 211 mi – Bradford 18 mi – Leeds 15 mi – Newcastle upon Tyne 76 mi

Crescent Rd ℰ (01423) 53 73 00, www.harrogate.gov.uk

Forest Lane Head, ℰ (01423) 86 31 58

Pannal Follifoot Rd, ℰ (01423) 87 26 28

Oakdale, ℰ (01423) 56 71 62

Crimple Valley Hookstone Wood Rd, ℰ (01423) 88 34 85

Town ★

Fountains Abbey★★★ **AC** :- Studley Royal **AC** (≤★ from Anne Boleyn's Seat)
- Fountains Hall (Fa 0.5ade★), N : 13 mi by A 61 and B 6265 AY – Harewood
House★★ (The Gallery★) **AC**, S : 7.5 mi by A 61 BZ

### HARROGATE

ENGLAND

225

ENGLAND

### Rudding Park

*Rudding Park, Follifoot, Southeast : 3.75 mi by A 661* ✉ *HG3 1JH*
– ℰ *(01423) 871 350* – *www.ruddingpark.co.uk*
**85 rm** �P – ♦£ 105/150 ♦♦£ 126/490 – 5 suites
**Rest** *Clocktower* – see restaurant listing
♦ Grade I listed Georgian manor house and Victorian church, set in 250 acres of mature grounds. Modern lounges and bars are located mainly in the newer extensions. The most luxurious bedrooms boast media hubs and touch lighting. Small spa.

### Hotel du Vin

*Prospect Pl* ✉ *HG1 1LB* – ℰ *(01423) 856 800* – *www.hotelduvin.com*
**48 rm** – ♦£ 85/170 ♦♦£ 125/190, �P £ 14.50                                 BZa
**Rest** *Bistro* – see restaurant listing
♦ Smart, modern hotel set in a terrace of Georgian houses and overlooking a pleasant green. Boutique-style interior with wine-themed décor. Contemporary bedrooms; two run the length of the attic and boast huge bathrooms. Small basement spa.

### Brookfield House without rest

*5 Alexandra Rd* ✉ *HG1 5JS* – ℰ *(01423) 506 646*
– *www.brookfieldhousehotel.co.uk* – *Closed 2 weeks Christmas-New Year*
**6 rm** �P – ♦£ 60/75 ♦♦£ 75/95                                              BYe
♦ Family owned Victorian property in a quiet, residential location close to the town centre. Homely feel in communal areas and comfortable bedrooms with a mix of styles.

### Bijou without rest

*17 Ripon Rd* ✉ *HG1 2JL* – ℰ *(01423) 567 974* – *www.thebijou.co.uk*
**10 rm** �P – ♦£ 55/85 ♦♦£ 95                                                AYa
♦ As the name suggests, a small period house, in the centre of town close to the Convention Centre. Immaculately kept bedrooms; elegantly set breakfast room.

### Van Zeller

*No.8 Montpellier St* ✉ *HG1 2TQ* – ℰ *(01423) 508 762*
– *www.vanzellerrestaurants.co.uk* – *Closed Sunday dinner and Monday*
**Rest** – *(booking advisable)* Menu £ 21 (lunch) – Carte £ 36/52          AZv
♦ Intimate, contemporary show conversion in trendy part of town. Carefully compiled menu, with good value lunch; unfussy, well-crafted and confident cooking. Smart, attentive staff.

### Quantro

*3 Royal Par* ✉ *HG1 2SZ* – ℰ *(01423) 503 034* – *www.quantro.co.uk* – *Closed*
*25-26 December, 1 January and Sunday*                                       AZa
**Rest** – Menu £ 15 (lunch and early dinner) – Carte £ 27/31
♦ Fresh, modern brasserie; popular with all. Keenly priced, seasonal menu with international influences. Some smaller plates at lunch and a choice of dish sizes on à la carte suits local workers.

### Orchid

*28 Swan Rd* ✉ *HG1 2SE* – ℰ *(01423) 560 425* – *www.orchidrestaurant.co.uk*
– *Closed Saturday lunch*                                                    AZc
**Rest** – Asian – Menu £ 14 – Carte £ 25/39
♦ Enter into stylish cocktail bar with comfy lounges. Asian artefacts and wooden screens decorate the downstairs restaurant. Extensive pan-Asian menu has dishes' origins and spiciness marked.

### Bistro – at Hotel du Vin

*Prospect Pl* ✉ *HG1 1LB* – ℰ *(01423) 856 800* – *www.hotelduvin.com*
**Rest** – Carte £ 25/39 ⅏                                                   BZa
♦ Stylish bistro with a buzzy atmosphere and a superb open courtyard to the rear, set inside a contemporary, wine-themed hotel. Brasserie-style menu focuses largely on classical Gallic dishes.

XX **Clocktower** – at Rudding Park Hotel　　　🖫 🕭 AC P VISA ⓒ AE ⓞ
*Rudding Park, Follifoot, Southeast : 3.75 mi by A 661 ⊠ HG3 1JH –* 𝒞 *(01423)*
*871 350 – www.ruddingpark.co.uk*
**Rest** – Menu £ 35 **s** – Carte £ 36/54 **s**
♦ Chic, contemporary hotel dining room with an impressive chandelier at its centre. Set in the old stables, the room is named after a clock that hangs above it. Extensive array of modern dishes.

**at Kettlesing** West : 6.5 mi by A 59 - AY – ⊠ **Harrogate**

⌂ **Knabbs Ash** without rest　　　　　　　 ≼ 🖫 🕭 ⅋ ⁏⁏ P
🖾 *Skipton Rd, on A 59 ⊠ HG3 2LT –* 𝒞 *(01423) 771 040 – www.knabbsash.co.uk*
**3 rm** ⌧ – ♦£ 55/60 ♦♦£ 80/90
♦ Welcoming, stone-built farmhouse set on a smallholding overlooking Knabbs Moor. Comfy, cosy lounge and pine-furnished breakfast room. Light, airy bedrooms have plain walls, modern fabrics and a complimentary decanter of sherry. Spacious gardens and grounds.

---

**HARTINGTON** – Derbyshire – **502** O24 – pop. 1 604 – ⊠ Buxton　　**16** A1
▶ London 168 mi – Derby 36 mi – Manchester 40 mi – Sheffield 34 mi

⌂ **Biggin Hall** ⌧　　　　　　　　 ≼ 🖫 ⁏⁏ P VISA ⓒ
*Biggin, Southeast : 2 mi by B 5054 ⊠ SK17 0DH –* 𝒞 *(01298) 84 451*
*– www.bigginhall.co.uk*
**20 rm** ⌧ – ♦£ 70/126 ♦♦£ 126/136
**Rest** – *(booking essential)* Menu £ 12/20 – Carte £ 16/18
♦ Characterful house with traditional, rustic appeal. Many guests follow the Tissington Trail: bike storage and picnics are offered. Classical, low-beamed bedrooms in main house; brighter rooms in the barns. Pleasant garden views from dining room. Homely cooking.

---

**HARTLAND** – Devon – **503** G31　　　　　　　　　　　　　**1** B1
▶ London 221 mi – Bude 15 mi – Clovelly 4 mi

⌂ **Golden Park** without rest ⌧　　　　　　　 🖫 🕭 ⅋ ⁏⁏ P
🖾 *Southwest : 5 mi following signs for Elmscott and Bude ⊠ EX39 6EP –* 𝒞 *(01237)*
*441 254 – www.goldenpark.co.uk – Closed Christmas-New Year and restricted*
*opening in winter*
**3 rm** ⌧ – ♦£ 65/75 ♦♦£ 75/95
♦ Part-17C farmhouse a stone's throw from the rugged North Devon coastline, in an Area of Outstanding Natural Beauty. Characterful interior with comfy garden room, oak-beamed drawing room and garden/coastal views. Smartly decorated bedrooms, one with a slipper bath.

⌂ **Hart Inn**　　　　　　　　　　　　🖫 🕭 P VISA ⓒ
*The Square ⊠ EX39 6BL –* 𝒞 *(01237) 441 474 – www.thehartinn.com – Closed 1*
*week Spring, Sunday dinner and Monday*
**Rest** – Carte £ 15/24
♦ Part 14 and 16C coaching inn with rustic, homely interior. Regularly changing menu features some Scandinavian influences but produce remains seasonal and local; generous portions.

---

**HARWELL** – Oxfordshire – **503** Q29 – pop. 2 015　　　　　　**10** B3
▶ London 64 mi – Oxford 16 mi – Reading 18 mi – Swindon 22 mi

⌂ **Kingswell**　　　　　　 ⅋ rm, ⁏⁏ ⁏⁏ ⒮ P VISA ⓒ AE ⓞ
*Reading Rd, East : 0.75 mi on A 417 ⊠ OX11 0LZ –* 𝒞 *(01235) 833 043*
*– www.kingswell-hotel.com*
**20 rm** ⌧ – ♦£ 99/103 ♦♦£ 115/130　　**Rest** – Menu £ 15/22 – Carte £ 22/34
♦ Large red-brick hotel located on the south Oxfordshire Downs. Convenient for Didcot rail and Oxford. Spacious, uniform, traditional bedrooms and pubby public areas. Classic menus served in traditional dining room.

ENGLAND

▶ London 78 mi – Chelmsford 41 mi – Colchester 20 mi – Ipswich 23 mi

to Denmark (Esbjerg) (DFDS Seaways A/S) 3-4 weekly (20 h) – to The Netherlands (Hook of Holland) (Stena Line) 2 daily (3 h 30 mn)

🛈 Parkeston 📞 (01255) 50 61 39, www.touruk.co.uk

📍 Parkeston Station Rd, 📞 (01255) 50 36 16

---

🏨🏨 **Pier at Harwich**　　　　　　≤ 🏠 🍽 📶 **P** 𝗩𝗜𝗦𝗔 ⊚ 𝗔𝗘 ⊙
*The Quay* ✉ *CO12 3HH* – 📞 *(01255) 241 212* – *www.milsomhotels.com*
**14 rm** 🛏 – ♦£ 112 ♦♦£ 210
**Rest** *Harbourside* – see restaurant listing
**Rest** *Ha'Penny Pier* – Carte £ 20/35
 ♦ Victorian hotel in a pleasant quayside spot – built to accommodate rail travellers waiting to board their cruise liners and an ideal place to stay if you're catching the ferry. Stylish New England style bedrooms; some boast port views. Smart seafood restaurant or casual all-day dining overlooking the pier.

🍴🍴 **Harbourside** – at Pier at Harwich Hotel　　≤ 𝗔𝗖 **P** 𝗩𝗜𝗦𝗔 ⊚ 𝗔𝗘 ⊙
*The Quay* ✉ *CO12 3HH* – 📞 *(01255) 241 212* – *www.milsomhotels.com*
**Rest** – Seafood – Menu £ 25 (lunch) – Carte £ 31/57 **s**
 ♦ Comfortable hotel dining room boasting crisp linen-laid tables and attractive port and North Sea views. Seafood-orientated menu offers everything from the traditional to the more contemporary.

---

▶ London 65 mi – Brighton 37 mi – Folkestone 37 mi – Maidstone 34 mi

🛈 Town Hall, Queen's Sq, Priory Meadow 📞 (0845) 2 74 10 01, www.hastingschoice.co.uk

📍 Beauport Park Golf Course St Leonards-on-Sea Battle Rd, 📞 (01424) 85 42 45

🏨 **Zanzibar**　　　　　　🚿 🍽 📶 **P** 𝗩𝗜𝗦𝗔 ⊚ 𝗔𝗘
*9 Eversfield Pl* ✉ *TN37 6BY* – 📞 *(01424) 460 109* – *www.zanzibarhotel.co.uk*
**8 rm** 🛏 – ♦£ 89/99 ♦♦£ 155/245　　　　　　　　AZ**c**
**Rest** *Pier Nine* – Menu £ 17 (lunch) – Carte £ 25/32
 ♦ Stylish boutique hotel in a Victorian townhouse, with large lounge and communal breakfast room. Named and themed after places the owner has visited, bedrooms are furnished to a high standard, with intimate lighting, good mod cons and smart bathrooms. Concise seasonal menu of North African inspired dishes.

🏠 **Hastings House** without rest　　　　🍽 📶 𝗩𝗜𝗦𝗔 ⊚ 𝗔𝗘
*9 Warrior Sq.* ✉ *TN37 6BA* – 📞 *(01424) 422 709* – *www.hastingshouse.co.uk*
**8 rm** 🛏 – ♦£ 80/110 ♦♦£ 99/150　　　　　　　　AZ**u**
 ♦ Stylish, modern and very comfortable guesthouse just off the promenade; personally run by hospitable owners. Rooms 3, 5 and 7 are the best choice for their size and sea views.

🍴🍴 **Webbe's Rock-a-Nore**　　　　　🏠 𝗔𝗖 𝗩𝗜𝗦𝗔 ⊚ 𝗔𝗘
*1 Rock-a-Nore* ✉ *TN34 3DW* – 📞 *(01424) 721 650*
*– www.webbesrestaurants.co.uk* – *Closed 24-26 December and 2-16 January*
**Rest** – Seafood – Carte £ 23/46　　　　　　　　BY**x**
 ♦ Bright, contemporary restaurant with horseshoe counter and open kitchen, in an enviable position across the beach from the fishing Stade. Unsurprisingly fresh fish and seafood.

🍴 **St Clements**　　　　　　　　　　𝗩𝗜𝗦𝗔 ⊚ ⊙
☺ *3 Mercatoria, St Leonards on Sea* ✉ *TN38 0EB* – 📞 *(01424) 200 355*
*– www.stclementsrestaurant.co.uk* – *Closed Sunday dinner and Monday*
**Rest** – Menu £ 19/27 – Carte £ 26/34　　　　　　　AZ**a**
 ♦ Pleasant neighbourhood restaurant with striking local artwork hung on plain walls. Comprehensive à la carte and concise, good value lunch and midweek menus. Tasty modern European cooking is unfussy with a rustic edge. Fresh fish from Hastings plays a key role.

ENGLAND

# HASTINGS ST. LEONARDS

Good food at moderate prices? Look for the Bib Gourmand ⊛.

**HATCH BEAUCHAMP** – Somerset – **503** K30 – see Taunton

**HATFIELD HEATH** – Essex – **504** U28 – pop. 1 514          **12** B2
– ⊠ Bishop'S Stortford

▶ London 33 mi – Birmingham 130 mi – Croydon 53 mi – Barnet 31 mi

🏠🏠🏠 **Down Hall Country House** ⊗          ⇐ 🚗 🏊 🛗 🗓 🛌 ☜ ✕ 🎬 ⅙ rm,
*South : 1.5 mi by Matching Ln.*          🅰🅺 rest, ¶¹ 🛌 **P** 𝚅𝙸𝚂𝙰 ⚌ 🅰🅴 ⓪
⊠ CM22 7AS – ℰ (01279) 731 441 – www.downhall.co.uk
**99 rm** ⌷ – ♥£ 69/109 ♥♥£ 99/209
**Rest** *Grill Room* – *(closed Saturday lunch)* Menu £ 30 – Carte £ 36/44
♦ Stunning 19C mansion with formal gardens, fountain and helipad. Classica
guest areas boast ornate plasterwork. Lovely lounge for afternoon tea. Dark
wood furnished bedrooms in wing; characterful feature rooms in main house
Classic grill menu served in informal, parquet-floored dining room.

---

**HATFIELD PEVEREL** – Essex – **504** V28 – pop. 3 258 ▯ Great Britain          **13** C2
▶ London 39 mi – Chelmsford 8 mi – Maldon 12 mi
⬓ Colchester - Castle and Museum★, E : 13 mi by A 12

✕✕ **Blue Strawberry Bistrot**          ⌂ **P** 𝚅𝙸𝚂𝙰 ⚌ 🅰🅴
*The Street* ⊠ CM3 2DW – ℰ (01245) 381 333 – www.bluestrawberrybistrot.co.uk
– *Closed 26 December, Saturday lunch and Sunday dinner*
**Rest** – Menu £ 17/23 – Carte (dinner only Friday-Saturday) £ 24/33
♦ Busy, brick-built former pub, which inside resembles a traditional French neigh-
bourhood brasserie. Keenly priced bistro-style dishes and old-school desserts. Po-
lite service.

---

**HATHERSAGE** – Derbyshire – **502** P24 – pop. 1 582          **16** A1
– ⊠ Sheffield (s. Yorks.)
▶ London 177 mi – Derby 39 mi – Manchester 34 mi – Sheffield 11 mi
⛳ Sickleholme Bamford, ℰ (01433) 65 13 06

🏠🏠 **George**          ⅔ ¶¹ 🛌 **P** 𝚅𝙸𝚂𝙰 ⚌
⊠ S32 1BB – ℰ (01433) 650 436 – www.george-hotel.net
**22 rm** ⌷ – ♥£ 99/125 ♥♥£ 139/175
**Rest** *George's* – see restaurant listing
♦ Keenly run 14C coaching inn where modern furnishings blend nicely with traditional stone, exposed brick walls and wooden beams. Comfy, open-fired
lounge and small cocktail bar. Smart, pastel-hued bedrooms with bright, contemporary fabrics.

✕✕ **George's** – at George Hotel          **P** 𝚅𝙸𝚂𝙰 ⚌ 🅰🅴
⊠ S32 1BB – ℰ (01433) 650 436 – www.george-hotel.net
**Rest** – Menu £ 37
♦ Formally laid hotel restaurant decorated in subtle pastel shades and set within
a keenly run, 14C coaching inn. Modern menus have a largely British base but
display some worldwide influences.

---

**HAWES** – North Yorkshire – **502** N21 – pop. 1 117          **22** A1
▶ London 253 mi – Kendal 27 mi – Leeds 72 mi – Newcastle upon Tyne 76 mi
🄴 Station Yard ℰ (01969) 66 62 10, www.hello-yorkshire.co.uk

🏠🏠 **Stone House** ⊗          ⇐ 🚗 ¶¹ **P** 𝚅𝙸𝚂𝙰 ⚌
*Sedbusk, North : 1 mi by Muker rd* ⊠ DL8 3PT – ℰ (01969) 667 571
– *www.stonehousehotel.com* – *Closed January and mid-week December*
**23 rm** ⌷ – ♥£ 63/150 ♥♥£ 180 – 1 suite          **Rest** – *(Light Lunch)* Menu £ 35
♦ Built in 1908 as a family home. Interior decorated in traditional style; public
areas include billiard room and oak panelled lounge. Some rooms with private
conservatories. Dining room has exposed beams and wooden tables.

---

**HAWKSHEAD** – Cumbria – **502** L20 – pop. 570 – ⊠ Ambleside          **21** A2
▯ Great Britain
▶ London 283 mi – Carlisle 52 mi – Kendal 19 mi
🄴 Main Street ℰ (015394) 3 69 46, www.hawksheadtouristinfo.org.uk
◉ Village ★
⬓ Lake Windermere★★ – Coniston Water★ (Brantwood★, on east side),
SW : by B 5285

230

## at Far Sawrey Southeast : 2.5 mi on B 5285 – ⊠ Ambleside

⩔ **West Vale** without rest ⟜ ✗ ⁎ 🅿 VISA ⊚ AE
⊠ LA22 0LQ – ℰ (015394) 42 817 – www.westvalecountryhouse.co.uk – Closed
25-26 December and restricted opening 3 January-4 February
**7 rm** � – ♦£ 90/130 ♦♦£ 120/175
◆ Welcoming slate house boasting lovely countryside views; run by keen owners.
Two comfy lounges and a smart country house style room for hearty breakfasts.
Good-sized bedrooms with warm, comfy, boutique style. Tea and cake on arrival,
and plenty of extra touches.

## HAWNBY – North Yorkshire – 502 Q21 – ⊠ Helmsley                23 C1

▶ London 245 mi – Middlesbrough 27 mi – Newcastle upon Tyne 69 mi – York 30 mi

⌂ **Inn at Hawnby** ⦚ ⟜ ⩫ ⬟ ⁎ 🅿 VISA ⊚
⊠ YO62 5QS – ℰ (01439) 798 202 – www.innathawnby.co.uk – Closed 25
December
**9 rm** ⊆ – ♦£ 69/79 ♦♦£ 99   **Rest** – Carte £ 24/32
◆ Homely inn set in a very rural spot in prime walking and shooting country.
Classically styled bedrooms are split between the house and barn, and boast
good linens and home comforts. Simplicity is key. Pub-style dishes at lunch;
more substantial, classical dinners.

## at Laskill Northeast : 2.25 mi by Osmotherley rd – ⊠ Hawnby

⩔ **Laskill Country House** ⦚ ⩫ ⩔ ⁎ 🄰 🅿 VISA ⊚
Easterside ⊠ YO62 5NB – ℰ (01439) 798 265 – www.laskillcountryhouse.co.uk
– Closed 24-25 December
**3 rm** ⊆ – ♦£ 45/60 ♦♦£ 120   **Rest** – Menu £ 25
◆ Delightful manor-style house in popular shooting/walking area. Comfy lounge;
small function suite. Good-sized bedrooms with countryside views. Communal
dining; wholesome home-cooked meals, with meat from the family's farms.

## HAWORTH – West Yorkshire – 502 O22 – pop. 6 078 – ⊠ Keighley        22 A2

▮ Great Britain

▶ London 213 mi – Burnley 22 mi – Leeds 22 mi – Manchester 34 mi
▮ 2-4 West Lane ℰ (01535) 64 23 29, www.haworth-village.org.uk
◉ Bront Parsonage Museum**AC**

⩔ **Ashmount Country House** without rest ⩫ ✗ ⁎ 🅿 VISA ⊚ AE
Mytholmes Ln ⊠ BD22 8EZ – ℰ (01535) 645 726
– www.ashmounthaworth.co.uk
**10 rm** ⊆ – ♦£ 50/80 ♦♦£ 75/245
◆ Built in 1870 by the physician to the Brontë sisters, this refurbished guesthouse
has extremely comfortable, period-furnished bedrooms and state-of-the-art bathrooms; some rooms even have their own outdoor hot tubs.

⩔ **Old Registry** without rest ⁎ VISA ⊚ AE
2-6 Main St ⊠ BD22 8DA – ℰ (01535) 646 503
– www.theoldregistryhaworth.co.uk – Closed 24-26 December
**9 rm** ⊆ – ♦£ 55/80 ♦♦£ 100/120
◆ Stone former registrar's office on cobbled main street. Individually themed
bedrooms boast rich fabrics and antiques: 5 are feature rooms; some have four-
posters. Breakfast of local produce.

✗✗ **Weaver's** with rm 🄰 rest, ⁎ VISA ⊚ AE ◔
15 West Ln ⊠ BD22 8DU – ℰ (01535) 643 822 – www.weaverssmallhotel.co.uk
– Closed 21 December-7 January, Saturday lunch, Sunday and Monday
**3 rm** ⊆ – ♦£ 65/75 ♦♦£ 110/120   **Rest** – Menu £ 24 (lunch) – Carte £ 24/35
◆ Charming former weavers' cottages at the top of a cobbled street. Characterful,
cluttered lounge with ornaments, artefacts and informal atmosphere. Wide-ranging menus have a strong northern base. Warm, welcoming bedrooms.

## HAYDON BRIDGE – Northumberland – 501 N19 – see Hexham

ENGLAND

## HAYLING ISLAND – Hampshire – 504 R31 – pop. 14 842

▣ London 77 mi – Brighton 45 mi – Southampton 28 mi
🛈 Seven Seafront, www.hayling.co.uk
🖥 Links Lane, ℰ (023) 9246 44 46

⌂ **Cockle Warren Cottage** without rest     🚗 ⛲ 📶 P̄ VISA ⲟⲟ
*36 Seafront ⊠ PO11 9HL – ℰ (023) 9246 4961 – www.cocklewarren.co.uk*
**6 rm** – †£ 49/59 ††£ 70/89
♦ Pleasant cottage with welcoming owner, set just across the road from the beach. Comfortable, well-kept bedrooms; 1 and 4 have sea views. Conservatory breakfast room and terrace overlook pool.

---

## HAYWARDS HEATH – West Sussex – 504 T31 – pop. 29 110

▮ Great Britain
▣ London 41 mi – Brighton 16 mi
🖥 Lindfield East Mascalls Lane, ℰ (01444) 48 44 67
◪ Sheffield Park Garden★, E : 5 mi on A 272 and A 275

✕✕ **Jeremy's at Borde Hill**     🚗 ⛲ P̄ VISA ⲟⲟ ATE
*Borde Hill Gdns, North : 1.75 mi by B 2028 on Balcombe Rd ⊠ RH16 1XP
– ℰ (01444) 441 102 – www.jeremysrestaurant.com – Closed 1-14 January,
Monday except lunch on bank holidays and Sunday dinner*
**Rest** – Menu £ 18 (weekday lunch) – Carte £ 29/39
♦ Converted 19C stables with delightful views to Victorian walled garden. Contemporary interior with modern art. Confident, vibrant cooking in a light Mediterranean style.

---

## HEADLAM – Durham – 502 O20 – see Darlington

---

## HEBDEN BRIDGE – West Yorkshire – 502 N22 – pop. 4 086
– ⊠ West Yorkshire

▣ London 223 mi – Burnley 13 mi – Leeds 24 mi – Manchester 25 mi
🛈 1 Bridge Gate ℰ (01422) 84 38 31, www.hebdenbridge.co.uk
🖥 Great Mount Wadsworth, ℰ (01422) 84 28 96

⌂ **Holme House** without rest     🚗 📶 P̄ VISA ⲟⲟ
*New Road ⊠ HX7 8AD – ℰ (01422) 847 588
– www.holmehousehebdenbridge.co.uk*
**3 rm** ⌷ – †£ 65 ††£ 78/90
♦ Late Georgian house in town centre with gated parking and neat garden. Smart, comfortable, well furnished rooms. Bedrooms boast excellent facilities and spacious bathrooms.

---

## HEDDON ON THE WALL – Northumberland

▣ London 288 mi – Blaydon 7 mi – Newcastle upon Tyne 8 mi

🏠 **Close House** ⌖     ≤ 🚗 ⓘ 📶 AC rm, 📶 📶 🆚 P̄ VISA ⲟⲟ ATE
*Southwest : 2.25 mi by B 6528 ⊠ NE15 0HT – ℰ (01661) 852 255
– www.closehouse.co.uk*
**31 rm** ⌷ – †£ 150/260 ††£ 150/260
**Rest** *Bewickes* – ℰ (01661) 835 099 – Menu £ 22/33 – Carte dinner £ 30/46
♦ Stunning Georgian mansion in 300 acres of mature grounds that stretch to the river. Original features blend with modern décor; front bedrooms have views, those to rear are more contemporary. Stylish restaurant offers interesting modern cooking and intimate air.

---

## HEDLEY ON THE HILL – Northumberland

▣ London 293 mi – Newcastle upon Tyne 16 mi – Sunderland 26 mi
– South Shields 26 mi

ENGLAND

### 🍸 **Feathers Inn**   🏠 **P** VISA 🐫 **①**

✉ NE43 7SW – 𝒞 (01661) 843 607 – www.thefeathers.net
**Rest** – (closed first 2 weeks in January, Sunday dinner and Mondays except bank holidays) Carte £ 20/29

♦ Traditional stone inn set on a steep hill, offering daily changing menu of hearty British classics, cooked using carefully sourced, regional produce. Relaxed, friendly atmosphere.

---

## HELMSLEY – North Yorkshire – 502 Q21 – pop. 1 559 📗 Great Britain   23 C1

▶ London 239 mi – Leeds 51 mi – Middlesbrough 28 mi – York 24 mi
🄸 Castlegate 𝒞 (01439) 77 01 73, www.yorkshire.com
🄹 Ampleforth College Castle Drive, Gilling East, 𝒞 (01439) 78 82 12
🄶 Rievaulx Abbey ★★ **AC**, NW : 2.5 mi by B 1257

### 🏨 **Black Swan**   🛲 🕍 **P** VISA 🐫 AE

Market Pl ✉ YO62 5BJ – 𝒞 (01439) 770 466 – www.blackswan-helmsley.co.uk
**42 rm** ⌼ – ♦£ 92/182 ♦♦£ 132/197 – 3 suites
**Rest** *The Rutland Room* – see restaurant listing

♦ One of the best known coaching inns in the country, dating back to the 16C and overlooking the historic marketplace. Charming interior with beams, modern lounge-bar and all-day tea shop. Most characterful bedrooms in the original building.

### 🏨 **Feversham Arms**   🛲 🏊 🕥 🕍 🖫🕪 🍴 **P** 🛋 VISA 🐫

on B 1257 ✉ YO62 5AG – 𝒞 (01439) 770 766 – www.fevershamarmshotel.com
**17 rm** (dinner included) ⌼ – ♦£ 193 ♦♦£ 330 – 16 suites
**Rest** *Conservatory* – Menu £ 45 (dinner) – Carte lunch £ 33/41

♦ Former coaching inn; its stone façade concealing a surprisingly modern interior. Muted colours and quality fabrics feature throughout. Comfortable bedrooms have a quiet, restful nature; some overlook the swimming pool. Superb spa facility. Warm, red décor in airy, glass-roofed restaurant; modern brasserie-style menu.

### 🏠 **No.54** without rest   🛲 **P** VISA 🐫

54 Bondgate ✉ YO62 5EZ – 𝒞 (01439) 771 533 – www.no54.co.uk – Closed Christmas and New Year
**3 rm** ⌼ – ♦£ 55 ♦♦£ 110

♦ Victorian terraced cottage, formerly the village vet's. Charming owner. Bedrooms are strong point: set around flagged courtyard, they're airy, bright and very well-equipped.

### 🏠 **Carlton Lodge** without rest   🕪 **P** VISA 🐫

Bondgate ✉ YO62 5EY – 𝒞 (01439) 770 557 – www.carlton-lodge.com
**8 rm** ⌼ – ♦£ 50/70 ♦♦£ 85/95

♦ Late 19C house set just out of town. Homely and traditional air to the décor in the communal areas and the bedrooms, some of which have period features. Cosy breakfast room.

### ✗✗ **The Rutland Room** – at Black Swan Hotel   🛲 **P** VISA 🐫 AE

Market Pl ✉ YO62 5BJ – 𝒞 (01439) 770 466 – www.blackswan-helmsley.co.uk
**Rest** – (dinner only and Sunday lunch) Menu £ 33 – Carte £ 33/52

♦ Fine dining restaurant with a subtle, modern style, set within a historic 16C coaching inn. Concise à la carte and daily specials consist of classically based dishes with some modern twists.

---

## at Harome Southeast : 2.75 mi by A 170 – ✉ York

### 🏨 **Pheasant**   🛲 🏡 ⅙ rm, 🕪 **P** VISA 🐫

✉ YO62 5JG – 𝒞 (01439) 771 241 – www.thepheasanthotel.com
**12 rm** (dinner included) ⌼ – ♦£ 105/145 ♦♦£ 210 – 2 suites
**Rest** – (booking essential for non residents) Menu £ 29/36 – Carte £ 36/44

♦ Ivy-clad hotel in picturesque hamlet with a duck pond and mill stream close by. Under the same ownership as The Star Inn. Charmingly decorated public areas; comfy, up-to-date bedrooms. Formal restaurant and conservatory; choose from array of fresh, modern menus.

**ENGLAND**

**Cross House Lodge**                    🏠 ⌇ 🏊 **P** _VISA_ ⊕

✉ YO62 5JE – 𝒞 (01439) 770 397 – www.thestaratharome.co.uk
**11 rm** ⌷ – ♦£ 150 ♦♦£ 150/240
**Rest** _Star Inn_ – see restaurant listing
♦ Converted farm buildings set opposite a pub, in a pretty village. Open-plan, split-level lounge. Ultra-stylish, super-smart bedrooms in either the main building or local cottages.

**Star Inn**                    🏠 🏠 ⇔ **P** _VISA_ ⊕

High St ✉ YO62 5JE – 𝒞 (01439) 770 397 – www.thestaratharome.co.uk
– Closed Monday lunch, Sunday dinner and bank holidays
**Rest** – (booking essential) Menu £ 25 – Carte £ 35/55 ⅏
♦ Charming 14C thatched pub with cosy bar and two dining rooms: one traditional; one more modern and boasting a chef's table. Pub-style dishes are rooted in tradition but use modern techniques. Herbs and vegetables come straight from the kitchen garden.

**at Ampleforth** Southwest : 4.5 mi by A 170 off B 1257 – ✉ Helmsley

**Shallowdale House** ⌖                    ≼ 🏠 🏊 ⅋ **P** _VISA_ ⊕

West : 0.5 mi ✉ YO62 4DY – 𝒞 (01439) 788 325 – www.shallowdalehouse.co.uk
– Closed Christmas-New Year
**3 rm** ⌷ – ♦£ 80/105 ♦♦£ 100/125   **Rest** – Menu £ 38
♦ Modern guesthouse affording spectacular views of the Howardian Hills; an area of outstanding beauty. Spacious rooms boast large picture windows to make the most of the scenery. A warm, relaxed atmosphere pervades. 4 course, home-cooked evening meals.

**at Scawton** West : 8.5 mi by A 170 – ✉ Helmsley

**Hare Inn**                    🏠 **P** _VISA_ ⊕ **AE**

✉ YO7 2HG – 𝒞 (01845) 597 769 – www.thehareinn.co.uk – Closed 25 December, Sunday dinner and Monday
**Rest** – Carte £ 23/34
♦ Warm, inviting and busy pub, parts of which date from 13C; in a remote setting, close to Rievaulx Abbey. Satisfying local food, with meat from Masham and poultry from Pateley Bridge.

**HELPERBY** – North Yorkshire – **502** Q21                    **22** B2
▶ London 220 mi – Leeds 36 mi – Sheffield 70 mi – Manchester 81 mi

**Oak Tree Inn** with rm                    🏠 ё rm, ⅋ **P** _VISA_ ⊕ **AE**

Raskelf Rd. ✉ YO61 2PH – 𝒞 (01423) 789 189 – www.theoaktreehelperby.com
**6 rm** ⌷ – ♦£ 120 ♦♦£ 150   **Rest** – Carte £ 19/29
♦ A pub of two halves, with a large bar, tap room, two snugs and a smarter dining room. Menus offer hearty, generous dishes using ingredients from small local suppliers. Everything is homemade and combinations are familiar and comforting. Smart, modern bedrooms come with 'Yorkie' bars and Jacuzzi baths.

**HELSTON** – Cornwall – **503** E33 – pop. 10 578                    **1** A3
▶ London 306 mi – Falmouth 13 mi – Penzance 14 mi – Truro 17 mi
◉ The Flora Day Furry Dance★★
◉ Lizard Peninsula★ - Gunwalloe Fishing Cove★, S : 4 mi by A 3083 and minor rd - Culdrose (Flambards Village Theme Park★), SE : 1 mi - Wendron (Poldark Mine★), NE : 2.5 mi by B 3297 – Gweek (Seal Sanctuary★), E : 4 mi by A 394 and minor rd

**Nansloe Manor** ⌖                    ≼ 🏠 🏠 **AC** rest, ⅋ ⅋ 🏊 **P** _VISA_ ⊕ **AE**

Meneage Rd, South : 1.5 mi on A 3083 ✉ TR13 0SB – 𝒞 (01326) 558 400
– www.nansloe-manor.co.uk – Closed 2 weeks January
**15 rm** (dinner included) ⌷ – ♦£ 230/285 ♦♦£ 275/335
**Rest** – (closed Sunday and Monday) Menu £ 19 (lunch) – Carte £ 30/39
♦ Restored Georgian Manor House set in 4 acres. Handmade French furniture, pastel décor and airy, continental feel. Subtly elegant bedrooms; some with balcony/terrace/views. Menus make use of produce from garden; classic combinations are presented in a contemporary style.

**ENGLAND**

HELSTON

**at Trelowarren** Southeast : 4 mi by A 394 and A 3083 on B 3293 – ⊠ Helston

Ⅹ **New Yard**                                          ⌂ P VISA ©©
*Trelowarren Estate ⊠ TR12 6AF – ℰ (01326) 221 595 – www.trelowarren.com
– Closed October-May, Sunday dinner, Monday and Tuesday*
**Rest** – *(booking advisable at dinner)* Menu £ 21/27 – Carte £ 29/44
♦ Converted stable yard adjoining a craft gallery. Large, simply furnished dining
room opens onto a terrace. Dinner offers elaborate seasonal menus of locally in-
spired dishes; lunch is simpler.

**at Cury** South : 5 mi by A394 off A3083

⌂ **Colvennor Farmhouse** without rest ⌂          ⌂ ⌂ ⌂ P VISA ©©
⊠ TR12 7BJ – ℰ (01326) 241 208 – www.colvennorfarmhouse.com
**3 rm** ⌂ – ♦£ 47/48 ♦♦£ 68/70
♦ Part-17C farmhouse in a peaceful location, boasting a lovely mature garden and
vegetable patch to the rear. Homely lounge features a wood burning stove. Simple, wood-furnished bedrooms are of a reasonable size. Linen-laid breakfast room.

**HEMEL HEMPSTEAD** – Hertfordshire – **504** S28 – pop. **83 118**        **12** A2
Great Britain

⊡ London 30 mi – Aylesbury 16 mi – Luton 10 mi – Northampton 46 mi
⊞ Little Hay Golf Complex Bovingdon Box Lane, ℰ (01442) 83 37 98
⊡ Boxmoor 18 Box Lane, ℰ (01442) 24 24 34
⊡ Whipsnade Wild Animal Park★

ENGLAND

Ⅹ **Restaurant 65**                                    P VISA ©© AE
*65 High St (Old Town) ⊠ HP1 3AF – ℰ (01442) 239 010
– www.restaurant65.com – Closed 1 week January, 1 week July, Saturday
lunch, Sunday dinner and Monday*
**Rest** – *(booking advisable)* Menu £ 19/27
♦ Charming 17C building in old part of town; snug restaurant with white walls,
black beams and homely, relaxed feel. Well executed modern British cooking
with a classical base.

**at Frithsden** Northwest : 4.5 mi by A 4146 – ⊠ Hemel Hempstead

⌂ **Alford Arms**                                      ⌂ P VISA ©© AE
⊠ HP1 3DD – ℰ (01442) 864 480 – www.alfordarmsfrithsden.co.uk – Closed
25-26 December
**Rest** – Carte £ 22/28
♦ Attractive Victorian pub overlooking the village green. Traditional British menu
follows the seasons: salads and fish in summer, game and comfort dishes in winter. Good classical desserts.

**HEMINGFORD GREY** – Cambridgeshire – **504** T27 – see Huntingdon

**HENFIELD** – West Sussex – **504** T31 – pop. **4 527**                    **7** D2
⊡ London 47 mi – Brighton 10 mi – Worthing 11 mi

⌂ **Ginger Fox**                               ⌂ ⌂ ⌂ P VISA ©© AE ⓪
⊙ *Albourne, Southwest 3 mi on A281 ⊠ BN6 9EA – ℰ (01273) 857 888
– www.gingermanrestaurants.com – Closed 25 December*
**Rest** – Carte £ 18/30
♦ Characterful 17C inn with thatched roof, wooden beams and open fires. Cooking is skilful, with a real country flavour. Tasty, unfussy dishes and popular vegetarian tasting plate. Favoured by families, with children's menu, spacious garden and slides.

235

**at Wineham** Northeast : 3.5 mi by A 281 and B 2116 on Wineham Lane
– ⊠ Henfield

⋔    **Frylands** without rest ⚓    ⟵ 🛋 🌳 ↰ 🍳 🌹 🛜 **P**

*West : 0.25 mi taking left turn at telephone box* ⊠ BN5 9BP – 𝒞 *(01403) 710 21*
*– www.frylands.co.uk – Closed 20 December-2 January*
**3 rm** ☲ – ♦£ 35/40 ♦♦£ 60/65

◆ Part-Elizabethan farmhouse with outdoor swimming pool and 250 acres o
woods, farmland and fishing ponds. Bedrooms exude charm and character wit
homely furnishings and original features. Fresh home-cooked breakfasts featur
local produce. Very charming owner.

---

**HENLADE** – Somerset – **see Taunton**

---

**HENLEY** – West Sussex – **see Midhurst**

---

**HENLEY-IN-ARDEN** – Warwickshire – **503** O27 – pop. 2 797          **19** C

▶ London 104 mi – Birmingham 15 mi – Stratford-upon-Avon 8 mi – Warwick 8 mi

🍽️    **Crabmill**    🚗 🏠 **P** **VISA** 🆗

*Preston Bagot, Claverdon, East : 1 mi on A 4189* ⊠ B95 5EE – 𝒞 *(01926) 843 34.*
*– www.thecrabmill.co.uk – Closed Sunday dinner*
**Rest** *– (booking essential)* Carte £ 21/33

◆ Characterful timbered pub with various beamed rooms and peaceful terrac
and garden. Good-sized menu offers modern Mediterranean-influenced dishe:
with lighter bites available during the day.

---

**HENLEY-ON-THAMES** – Oxfordshire – **504** R29 – pop. 10 513          **11** C

▶ London 40 mi – Oxford 23 mi – Reading 9 mi

🚢 to Reading (Salter Bros. Ltd) (summer only) daily (2 h 15 mn) – to Marlow (Salter
Bros. Ltd) (summer only) daily (2 h 15 mn)

🅱 Market Place 𝒞 (01491) 57 80 34, www.henley-on-thames.org

🅱 Huntercombe Nuffield, 𝒞 (01491) 64 12 07

🏨    **Hotel du Vin**    🏬 AC 🛜 🕳 **P** **VISA** 🆗 AE

*New St.* ⊠ RG9 2BP – 𝒞 *(01491) 848 400 – www.hotelduvin.com*
**41 rm** – ♦£ 125/205 ♦♦£ 125/205, ☲ £ 14.50 – 2 suites
**Rest** *Bistro* – see restaurant listing

◆ Characterful 1857 building that was formerly the Breakspear Brewery. Stylish
bedrooms include airy doubles and duplex suites: one features two roll-top tub
and a great view of the church; others boast heated balconies and outdoor baths

⋔    **Falaise House** without rest    🌹 🛜 **VISA** 🆗

*37 Market Pl* ⊠ RG9 2AA – 𝒞 *(01491) 573 388 – www.falaisehouse.com – Closec*
*Christmas*
**6 rm** ☲ – ♦£ 85 ♦♦£ 115

◆ Very well located 18C house boasting stylish, luxury bedrooms; some with
chaises longues. Good breakfast choice includes homemade preserves anc
smoked salmon, cooked to order.

🍴🍴    **Bistro** – at Hotel du Vin    **P** **VISA** 🆗 AE

*New St.* ⊠ RG9 2BP – 𝒞 *(01491) 848 400 – www.hotelduvin.com*
**Rest** – Carte £ 28/39 🍴

◆ Classical French bistro in a characterful former brewery building dating back to
1857. Menus are formed around traditional Gallic dishes. Excellent wine list offer:
the choice of over 700 bins.

🍴🍴    **Parisien**    🏠 AC ⇔ **VISA** 🆗

*50 Bell St* ⊠ RG9 2BG – 𝒞 *(01491) 571 115 – www.leparisienrestaurant.co.uk*
*– Closed Sunday dinner*
**Rest** – French *– (booking advisable)* Menu £ 20/23 – Carte £ 33/46

◆ Welcoming French bistro with clothed tables, modern artwork and a private din
ing room overlooking the walled garden terrace. Experienced chef creates seasona
menus of timeless French classics; presentation displays a light, modern touch.

**ENGLAND**

### ✕ Luscombes at The Golden Ball   🚗 🏠 ✿ P VISA ⓒⓑ
*Lower Assendon, Northwest : 0.75 mi by A 4130 on B 480 ✉ RG9 6AH*
*– 𝒞 (01491) 574 157 – www.luscombes.co.uk*
**Rest** – Carte £ 29/45
♦ Cosy restaurant, popular with locals, serving modern menu of tasty, simply cooked dishes. Smiley, attentive service. Lighter lunches, homemade preserves and afternoon cream teas.

## at Lower Shiplake South : 2 mi by A 4155 – ✉ Henley-On-Thames

### ⌂ Crowsley House   🚗 🕯 ⟨⟨ɪ⟩⟩ P VISA ⓒⓑ
*Crowsley Rd ✉ RG9 3JT – 𝒞 (01189) 406 708 – www.crowsleyhouse.co.uk*
**3 rm** – †£ 125 ††£ 150, ⌑ £ 10    **Rest** – Menu £ 30
♦ Discreet guest house in secluded conservation area; two lively cats come as part of the family. Pristine, well-equipped bedrooms boast contemporary bathrooms. Breakfast is an extensive continental affair, with freshly baked pastries. Gourmet meals by arrangement.

## at Shiplake Row South : 3.5mi. by A 4155 by Peppard rd and Binfield Heath rd

### ⎁ Orwells   🏠 P VISA ⓒⓑ ⓞ
*Shiplake Row ✉ RG9 4DP – 𝒞 (01189) 403 673 – www.orwellsatshiplake.co.uk*
*– Closed first 2 weeks January, first 2 weeks September,1 week April, Sunday dinner and Monday except bank holidays*
**Rest** – Menu £ 16 (lunch) – Carte £ 25/53
♦ Dating from the 18C and named after George Orwell, who spent his childhood in the area. Contemporary interior divided into three: the bar, conservatory and 'fine dining' room. Modern cooking, with a 'use local' ethos. More elaborate dishes at dinner in The Room.

---

**HEPWORTH** – West Yorkshire – see Holmfirth

---

**HEREFORD** – Herefordshire – **503** L27 – **pop. 55 213** ▮ Great Britain    **18** B3
▶ London 133 mi – Birmingham 51 mi – Cardiff 56 mi
🛈 1 King St 𝒞 (01432) 26 84 30, www.visitherefordshire.co.uk
⛳ Raven's Causeway Wormsley, 𝒞 (01432) 83 02 19
⛳ Belmont Lodge Belmont Ruckhall Lane, 𝒞 (01432) 35 26 66
⛳ Hereford Municipal Holmer Rd, 𝒞 (01432) 34 43 76
⛳ Burghill Valley Burghill Tillington Rd, 𝒞 (01432) 76 04 56
👁 City★ - Cathedral★★ (Mappa Mundi★) A **A** – Old House★ A **B**
Ⓖ Kilpeck (Church of SS. Mary and David★★) SW : 8 mi by A 465 B

Plan on next page

### ⌂ Brandon Lodge without rest   🚗 🕯 ⟨⟨ɪ⟩⟩ P VISA ⓒⓑ
*Ross Rd, South : 1.75 mi on A 49 ✉ HR2 8BH – 𝒞 (01432) 355 621*
*– www.brandonlodge.co.uk*
**10 rm** ⌑ – †£ 45/50 ††£ 60/68
♦ A good value hotel with 18C origins, charmingly overseen by owner. Bedrooms in main building or adjacent annexe: all are spacious, boasting a cheery warmth and good facilities.

### ✕ Stewing Pot   VISA ⓒⓑ
*17 Church St ✉ HR1 2LR – 𝒞 (01432) 265 233 – www.stewingpot.co.uk – Closed 25-26 December, Sunday and Monday*    A**a**
**Rest** – *(booking essential at dinner)* Menu £ 17 (lunch) – Carte £ 25/36
♦ Neighbourhood eatery tucked away down a narrow street, with plain décor and simple, homely furnishings. Taking on a bistro style, cooking is classical and reliably tasty.

ENGLAND

# HEREFORD

**at Winforton** Northwest : 15 mi on A 438 – ⊠ Hereford

↑ **Winforton Court** without rest                                    ⌨ 🖐 **P**
⊠ HR3 6EA – ℰ (01544) 328 498 – www.winfortoncourt.co.uk – Closed 20-28 December
**3 rm** ⊡ – ♦£ 73/83 ♦♦£ 88/110
• Wonderfully characterful 16C house used as a circuit court by "Hanging" Judge Jeffries. Exudes personality with exposed beams, thick walls and uneven floors. Rustic bedrooms.

---

**HERM** – Herm – **503** P33 – pop. 60 – see Channel Islands

---

**HERNE BAY** – Kent – **504** X29 – pop. 34 747                     **9** D1
▶ London 65 mi – Croydon 68 mi – Bromley 59 mi – Enfield 80 mi

✗ **Le Petit Poisson**                                               ⌨ **VISA** ⓿⓿
*Pier Approach, Central Par.* ⊠ CT6 5JN – ℰ (01227) 361 199
*– www.lepetitpoisson.co.uk – Closed Sunday dinner and Monday except bank holidays when closed Tuesday*
**Rest** – Seafood – Carte £ 23/29
• Sweet whitewashed building with small terrace, overlooking the pier. Split-level interior boasts flag floors, exposed brick and eye-catching mosaic art. Concise, constantly evolving blackboard menus consist of tasty, unfussy seafood dishes.

---

**HERSTMONCEUX** – East Sussex – **504** U31 – pop. 3 898          **8** B3
▶ London 63 mi – Eastbourne 12 mi – Hastings 14 mi – Lewes 16 mi

✗✗✗ **Sundial**                                            ⌨ ✿ **P** **VISA** ⓿⓿ ①
*Gardner St* ⊠ BN27 4LA – ℰ (01323) 832 217 – www.sundialrestaurant.co.uk
*– Closed 2 weeks January, Sunday dinner and Monday*
**Rest** – French – Menu £ 24/40
• Converted 16C cottage retaining leaded windows and beamed ceiling. Comfy dining room. Seasonal menus offer rich, classical French dishes; the chateaubri-and for two must be ordered in advance.

**at Wartling** Southeast : 3.75 mi by A 271 on Wartling rd – ✉ Herstmonceux

⋔ **Wartling Place**　　　🛋 ⚘ 🌐 📶 **P** **VISA** **◎◎** **AE**

✉ BN27 1RY – ℰ (01323) 832 590 – www.wartlingplace.co.uk
**4 rm** ⌨ – ♦£ 75/89 ♦♦£ 145/165　**Rest** – Menu £ 35

♦ Part Georgian house with three acres of gardens, sited in the village. Pleasantly furnished, with some antiques; two of the rooms have four-poster beds. Breakfast is taken communally at an antique table in the dining room. Dinner by arrangement.

---

**HESSLE** – East Riding of Yorkshire – **502** S22 – see Kingston-upon-Hull

---

**HETTON** – North Yorkshire – **502** N21 – see Skipton

---

**HEXHAM** – Northumberland – **501** N19 – pop. 10 682 ▌ Great Britain　　**24** A2

▶ London 304 mi – Carlisle 37 mi – Newcastle upon Tyne 21 mi
🖪 Wentworth Car Park ℰ (01434) 65 22 20, www.visitnorthumberland.com
🏌₁₈ Spital Park, ℰ (01434) 60 30 72
🏌₁₈ De Vere Slaley Hall Slaley, ℰ (01434) 67 31 54
🏌₉ Tynedale Tyne Green, ℰ (01434) 60 81 54
◉ Abbey★ (Saxon Crypt★★, Leschman chantry★)
☒ Hadrian's Wall★★, N : 4.5 mi by A 6079. Housesteads★★, NW : 12.5 mi by A 6079 and B 6318

ENGLAND

⋔ **Hallbank** without rest　　　⚘ 📶 **P** **VISA** **◎◎** **①**

Hallgate ✉ NE46 1XA – ℰ (01434) 605 567 – www.hallbankguesthouse.com
**7 rm** ⌨ – ♦£ 50/80 ♦♦£ 70/120

♦ Set right in the heart of town, in the shadow of the 14C Gaol; formerly two separate houses, now an L-shaped guesthouse with an almost medieval feel. Fair-sized bedrooms offer a good level of comforts and are immaculately kept.

⋔ **West Close House** without rest ⌾　　　🛋 ⚘ **P**

🍽 Hextol Ter, Southwest : 0.5 mi by B 6305 ✉ NE46 2AD – ℰ (01434) 603 307
– Restricted opening December-February
**3 rm** ⌨ – ♦£ 33/49 ♦♦£ 65/66

♦ Detached house hidden down a private road. Immensely peaceful – from the well-maintained, Zen-like garden featuring lots of bamboo, to the cosy, immaculately kept interior boasting plenty of polished wood. Snug breakfast room with window seating and breakfast to order; keenly priced, comfortable bedrooms.

✗✗ **Bouchon**　　　⟺ **VISA** **◎◎**

4-6 Gilesgate ✉ NE46 3NJ – ℰ (01434) 609 943 – www.bouchonbistrot.co.uk
– Closed 24-26 December, Sunday, Monday and bank holidays
**Rest** – French – Menu £ 16 (lunch and early dinner) – Carte £ 22/33

♦ Fiercely French restaurant in the centre of town. Simply styled ground floor with bar and plush intimate first floor dining room with opulent purple furnishings. Tasty, neatly presented, authentic French cooking and a Gallic team.

🍴 **Rat Inn**　　　🍴 **P** **VISA** **◎◎** **AE**

Anick, Northeast : 1.5 mi signposted off A 69 roundabout ✉ NE46 4LN
– ℰ (01434) 602 814 – www.theratinn.com – Closed Sunday dinner and Monday except bank holidays lunch
**Rest** – Carte £ 21/31

♦ Traditional pub with an open range and pleasant Tyne Valley views. Daily changing blackboard menu features wholesome pub classics, as well as some more ambitious dishes – including some for two.

**at Slaley** Southeast : 5.5 mi by B 6306 – ⊠ Hexham

**Slaley Hall** ⌂  ← ⍟ ⏍ ⌖ 🖾 ⌘ ⋒ ⎙ 🖾 🖫 ⌨ rm, ⏍ ⏍ ⌂ ⏍
*Southeast : 2.25 mi* ⊠ *NE47 0BX* – ℰ *(01434) 673 350*  ⓋⒾⓈⒶ ⏍ 🔘
– *www.deverehotels.com*
**135 rm** ⌣ – ♦£ 79/179 ♦♦£ 99/219 – 7 suites
**Rest** *Hadrian's Brasserie* – see restaurant listing
**Rest** *Dukes Grill* – *(dinner only)* Menu £ 26 – Carte £ 28/94
**Rest** *Claret Jug* – Carte £ 24/40
♦ Extended Edwardian manor house set in 1,000 acres and boasting two championship golf courses, a spa and extensive leisure facilities. Spacious, stylish guest areas. Largely classical bedrooms, with 'Double Deluxe' being more contemporary. Classical dishes served in formal, cosy Duke's; Brasserie menu in Hadrian's, British favourites offered in clubby Claret Jug.

XX **Hadrian's Brasserie** – at Slaley Hall Hotel  ⍟ ⌖ ⏍ ⏍ ⌂ ⓋⒾⓈⒶ ⏍ 🔘
*Southeast : 2.25 mi* ⊠ *NE47 0BX* – ℰ *(01434) 673 350* – *www.devere.co.uk*
**Rest** – *(dinner only)* Menu £ 26 – Carte £ 26/48
♦ Large brasserie set within an extended Edwardian manor house in a spacious country leisure resort. À la carte and set menu offer classically based dishes crafted from locally sourced produce.

**at Haydon Bridge** West : 7.5 mi on A 69 – ⊠ Hexham

**Langley Castle** ⌂  ⍟ ⌨ rm, ⏍ ⌂ ⏍ ⓋⒾⓈⒶ ⏍ 🔘
*Langley-on-Tyne, South : 2 mi by A 69 on A 686* ⊠ *NE47 5LU*
– ℰ *(01434) 688 888* – *www.langleycastle.com*
**27 rm** ⌣ – ♦£ 120/210 ♦♦£ 149/275  **Rest** – Menu £ 16/40
♦ Stunning 14C castle in 12 acres. Stone walls, tapestries and heraldic shields give baronial feel. Luxurious bedrooms exhibit period features; some have window seats or four-posters. Stable rooms are simpler. Dining room offers adventurous, seasonally influenced menu.

**HEYTESBURY** – Wiltshire – **503** N30 – see Warminster

**HIGHCLERE** – Hampshire – **503** P29 – pop. 2 409 – ⊠ **Newbury**  **6** B1
◪ London 69 mi – Newbury 5 mi – Reading 25 mi

XX **Yew Tree** with rm  ⌖ ⏍ ⌂ ⓋⒾⓈⒶ ⏍ 🔘
*Hollington Cross, Andover Rd., South : 1 mi on A 343* ⊠ *RG20 9SE* – ℰ *(01635) 253 360* – *www.theyewtree.net* – *Closed dinner 25-26 December*
**7 rm** ⌣ – ♦£ 120 ♦♦£ 120  **Rest** – Menu £ 20 (lunch) – Carte £ 30/41
♦ Characterful 17C whitewashed inn with wood-furnished terrace, rustic beamed interior, three linen-laid dining rooms and a marble-topped bar. Classical cooking mixes pub and restaurant style dishes. Service is structured. Smart, modern bedrooms boast wet rooms.

**HIGHCLIFFE** – Dorset – **503** O31  **4** D3
◪ London 112 mi – Bournemouth 10 mi – Salisbury 21 mi – Southampton 26 mi

**Lord Bute**  ⏍ ⏍ ⌂ ⏍ ⓋⒾⓈⒶ ⏍ 🔘
*179-185 Lymington Rd* ⊠ *BH23 4JS* – ℰ *(01425) 278 884* – *www.lordbute.co.uk*
**11 rm** ⌣ – ♦£ 105 ♦♦£ 115 – 2 suites
**Rest** – *(closed Sunday dinner and Monday)* Menu £ 17/33 – Carte £ 21/36
♦ Modern, purpose-built property with a warm, contemporary style. Light, airy conservatory lounge with terrace. Comfortable, well-appointed bedrooms boast bold colours, safes and spa baths. Smart, formal restaurant hosts occasional cabaret or jazz evenings.

**HIGH CROSBY** – Cumbria – see Carlisle

**HIGHER BURWARDSLEY** – Cheshire West and Chester – see Tattenhall

240

## HINDON – Wiltshire – 503 N30 – pop. 493     4 C2
▶ London 103 mi – Shaftesbury 7 mi – Warminster 10 mi

**Lamb Inn** with rm     🖫 🗊 **P** **VISA** **⬤⬤** **AE**
*High St* ✉ *SP3 6DP –* ℰ *(01747) 820 573 – www.lambathindon.co.uk*
**19 rm –** ♦£ 95/120 ♦♦£ 120/180, � £ 10    **Rest** – Carte £ 20/35
♦ Scottish-themed 13C inn with cosy, characterful rooms featuring deep walls, inglenook fireplaces and antique furniture. Appealing menu blends local produce and traditional Scottish dishes with a few Mediterranean specials. Smart bedrooms; some four-posters.

## HINDRINGHAM – Norfolk     15 C1
▶ London 118 mi – Fakenham 8 mi – Holt 8 mi

⌂ **Field House** without rest     🖫 ৬ 🐾 **P**
*Moorgate Rd* ✉ *NR21 0PT –* ℰ *(01328) 878 726*
*– www.fieldhousehindringham.co.uk – Closed 20 December-1 February*
**3 rm** � *–* ♦£ 70/75 ♦♦£ 90/110
♦ Well-kept flint stone house with pretty garden and summer house. Pristine lounge with books and magazines. Extensive breakfast menus. Carefully co-ordinated rooms with extras.

## HINTLESHAM – Suffolk – 504 X27 – see Ipswich

## HINTON ST GEORGE – Somerset     3 B3
▶ London 138 mi – Taunton 21 mi – Weymouth 41 mi – Yeovil 13 mi

**Lord Poulett Arms** with rm     🗊 **P** **VISA** **⬤⬤**
*High St* ✉ *TA17 8SE –* ℰ *(01460) 73 149 – www.lordpoulettarms.com – Closed 25-26 December and 1 January*
**4 rm** � *–* ♦£ 60/65 ♦♦£ 85/95    **Rest** – Carte £ 20/38
♦ Charming pub with lavender-framed terrace, boules pitch, secret garden and detailed, candlelit country interior. Local, seasonal produce informs an interesting menu that's rooted firmly in the Med. Smart, stylish bedrooms boast roll-top and slipper baths.

## HISTON – Cambridgeshire – 504 U27 – see Cambridge

## HITCHIN – Hertfordshire – 504 T28 – pop. 33 352     12 A2
▶ London 40 mi – Bedford 14 mi – Cambridge 26 mi – Luton 9 mi

**Radcliffe Arms**     🗊 **AC** **P** **VISA** **⬤⬤** **AE**
*31 Walsworth Rd* ✉ *SG4 9ST –* ℰ *(01462) 456 111 – www.radcliffearms.com*
**Rest** – Carte £ 27/42 🍷
♦ True neighbourhood pub with central bar, gravity fed ales and a good spirit and wine selection. Tasty cooking focuses on well-presented, restaurant-style dishes. Breakfast is served from 8am.

## HOCKLEY HEATH – West Midlands – 503 O26 – pop. 1 525     19 C2
– ✉ Solihull
▶ London 117 mi – Birmingham 11 mi – Coventry 17 mi

**Nuthurst Grange Country House**     🖫 🐾 📶 ⅏ **P** **VISA** **⬤⬤** **AE**
*Nuthurst Grange Ln , South : 0.75 mi by A 3400* ✉ *B94 5NL –* ℰ *(01564) 783 972*
*– www.nuthurst-grange.co.uk*
**19 rm** � *–* ♦£ 95/132 ♦♦£ 110/165
**Rest** *Kingswood* – see restaurant listing
♦ Attractive part-Edwardian former farmhouse, next to the M40. Ground and first floor bedrooms boast four-posters; second floor rooms are more modern. Self-contained function suite has two chapels, a minstrel's gallery and walled herb garden.

XXX **Kingswood** – at Nuthurst Grange Country House Hotel     🖫 **P** **VISA** **⬤⬤** **AE**
*Nuthurst Grange Ln, South : 0.75 mi by A 3400* ✉ *B94 5NL –* ℰ *(01564) 783 972*
*– www.nuthurst-grange.co.uk*
**Rest** – *(closed Saturday lunch and Sunday dinner)* Menu £ 25/45
♦ Traditional hotel dining room with formal ambience and country house style décor. Seasonal, classically based menus display innovative modern touches, ranging from 2 courses at lunch to 7 at dinner. Influences come from throughout Europe.

## HOLBEACH – Lincolnshire – **502** U25 – pop. 7 247          **17** D2
▶ London 117 mi – Kingston-upon-Hull 81 mi – Norwich 62 mi – Nottingham 60 mi

⌂  **Pipwell Manor** without rest          ♫ ⅌ **P**
*Washway Rd, Saracen's Head, Northwest : 1.5 mi by A 17 ⌂ PE12 8AY*
*– ℰ (01406) 423 119*
**4 rm** ⌂ – ♦£ 40 ♦♦£ 60
♦ Charming Georgian manor set close to The Wash, on the site of an old Cistercian Grange. Homely guest areas and traditional country bedrooms with fresh, modern touches. A warm welcome is guaranteed, with cake served on arrival. Miniature railway in the garden.

## HOLFORD – Somerset – **503** K30 – pop. 307 – ⌂ Bridgwater          **3** B2
▌ Great Britain
▶ London 171 mi – Bristol 48 mi – Minehead 15 mi – Taunton 22 mi
◉ Stogursey Priory Church★★, W : 4.5 mi

🏠  **Combe House** ♨          ♫ ◎ ♒ ♨ **P** VISA ◐◑
*Southwest : 0.75 mi by Youth Hostel rd ⌂ TA5 1RZ – ℰ (01278) 741 382*
*– www.combehouse.co.uk*
**18 rm** ⌂ – ♦£ 85/115 ♦♦£ 145/165     **Rest** – Carte £ 20/35
♦ Smart country house with lovely garden, in a secluded wooded valley. Stylish, modern interior boasts a pleasant spa. Bright bedrooms feature contemporary fabrics and white furniture. Split-level restaurant offers classical cooking with a modern edge.

## HOLKHAM – Norfolk – **504** W25          **15** C1
▶ London 124 mi – King's Lynn 32 mi – Norwich 39 mi

🏠  **Victoria**          ♫ ⅋ ♚ **P** VISA ◐◑
*Park Rd. ⌂ NR23 1RG – ℰ (01328) 711 008 – www.holkham.co.uk*
**10 rm** ⌂ – ♦£ 90/130 ♦♦£ 130/185
**Rest** *The Restaurant* – see restaurant listing
♦ Extended flint farmhouse boasting country outlook and large lawned gardens. Characterful, shabby-chic interior with individually styled bedrooms; some furniture from Indian sub-continent.

✕✕  **The Restaurant** – at The Victoria Hotel          ♫ ☂ **P** VISA ◐◑
*Park Rd ⌂ NR23 1RG – ℰ (01328) 711 008 – www.holkham.co.uk*
**Rest** – Menu £ 24 (weekend lunch) – Carte £ 30/42
♦ Choice of 2 colonial-style dining rooms, conservatory or wood-furnished terrace. Seasonally evolving menus have unfussy, brasserie style: local produce to the fore. Friendly, attentive service.

## HOLMFIRTH – West Yorkshire – **502** O23 – pop. 21 979          **22** B3
▶ London 187 mi – Leeds 35 mi – Sheffield 32 mi – Manchester 25 mi

⌂  **Sunnybank** ♨          ♫ ⅋ **P** VISA ◐◑
*78 Upperthong Ln, West : 0.5 mi by A 6024 ⌂ HD9 3BQ – ℰ (01484) 684 857*
*– www.sunnybankguesthouse.co.uk*
**5 rm** ⌂ – ♦£ 60 ♦♦£ 70/100     **Rest** – Menu £ 25
♦ Attractive Victorian house with lovely gardens, hidden away down a narrow road. Mix of period and modern furnishings; smart art deco piano in the lounge. Cosy bedrooms have a personal touch – those in the courtyard are slightly more modern. Oak panelled dining room features local produce and valley views.

### at Hepworth Southeast : 2 mi by A 635 off B 6106

🏠  **Butchers Arms**          ♚ **P** VISA ◐◑ AE
*38 Towngate ⌂ HD9 1TE – ℰ (01484) 682 361 – www.thebutchersarms.co.uk*
**Rest** – (booking essential) Menu £ 17 (weekday lunch) – Carte £ 33/45
♦ Stone inn with delightful terraces, hidden on the fringes of a sleepy hamlet. A huge array of menus offer robust, country dishes. All produce is from within 75 miles; most from even closer.

## HOLT – Wiltshire – **503** – see Bradford-on-Avon

## HOLT – Norfolk – 504 X25 – pop. 3 550

▶ London 124 mi – King's Lynn 34 mi – Norwich 22 mi

### 🏠 Byfords
🏤 & ⅍ ♈ **P** *VISA* ⦸ **AE**

*Shirehall Plain* ⌧ *NR25 6BG* – 𝒞 *(01263) 711 400* – *www.byfords.org.uk*
**16 rm** ⌤ – ♦£ 115 ♦♦£ 190  **Rest** – Carte £ 26/36
• Flint-fronted Grade II listed house that boasts something different: a well-stocked deli; rustic cellar café; and stunning rooms, with great bathrooms and under-floor heating.

---

## HOLTON – Somerset – 503 M30 – pop. 225

▶ London 117 mi – Bristol 35 mi – Cardiff 111 mi – Southampton 76 mi

### 🍺 Old Inn
🏤 **P** *VISA* ⦸ ⓪

⌧ *BA9 8AR* – 𝒞 *(01963) 32 002* – *www.theoldinnrestaurant.co.uk*
**Rest** – Carte £ 26/40
• The owner of nearby Clinger Farm always fancied being a chef but instead bought this 400 year old pub, added a large restaurant and now delights in seeing the kitchen make good use of his produce; the Josper grill is the star of the show.

---

## HONITON – Devon – 503 K31 – pop. 11 213

▶ London 186 mi – Exeter 17 mi – Southampton 93 mi – Taunton 18 mi
ℹ️ Lace Walk Car Park 𝒞(01404) 4 37 16, www.honiton.com
◎ All Hallows Museum★ **AC**
◎ Ottery St Mary★ (St Mary's★) SW : 5 mi by A 30 and B 3177. Faraway Countryside Park (⩽★) **AC**, SE : 6.5 mi by A 375 and B 3174

### 🍺 Holt
*VISA* ⦸

*178 High St* ⌧ *EX14 1LA* – 𝒞 *(01404) 47 707* – *www.theholt-honiton.com*
*– Closed 2 January, 25-26 December, Sunday and Monday*
**Rest** – Carte £ 25/29
• Rustic family-run pub providing a 'distinctive and sustainable taste of Devon'. Regularly changing menu of regional and homemade produce; local ales from the family brewery.

### 🍺 Railway
🏤 **P** *VISA* ⦸ ⓪

*Queen St* ⌧ *EX14 1HE* – 𝒞 *(01404) 47 976* – *www.therailwayhoniton.co.uk*
*– Closed 25-26 December, Sunday and Monday*
**Rest** – Carte £ 25/34
• Smart, modern town centre pub offering authentic Italian cooking at affordable prices, including homemade pasta, brick-fired pizzas and steaks. Eclectic wine list. Weekly film club.

### at Gittisham Southwest : 3 mi by A 30 – ⌧ Honiton

### 🏠🏠🏠 Combe House ⌂
⩽ 🚗 ⅍ ♈ ♨ **P** *VISA* ⦸ **AE**

⌧ *EX14 3AD* – 𝒞 *(01404) 540 400* – *www.combehousedevon.com*
*– Closed 3-18 January*
**13 rm** ⌤ – ♦£ 169/179 ♦♦£ 199 – 3 suites
**Rest** – *(booking essential for non-residents)* Menu £ 33/49
• Listed Elizabethan mansion set in glorious Devon countryside. Impressive Great Hall. Individually designed, stylish bedrooms with fine antiques and roaring fires. Unfussy cooking makes good use of local produce. Friendly service.

---

## HOOK – Hampshire – 504 R30 – pop. 6 471 – ⌧ Basingstoke

▶ London 47 mi – Oxford 39 mi – Reading 13 mi – Southampton 31 mi

### 🏠🏠🏠 Tylney Hall ⌂
🚗 ⅍ ⌱ ⌺ ⌛ ♨ ♈ & 🐾 **P** *VISA* ⦸ **AE** ⓪

*Rotherwick , Northwest : 2.5 mi by A30 and Newnham rd on Ridge Ln*
⌧ *RG27 9AZ* – 𝒞 *(01256) 764 881* – *www.tylneyhall.co.uk*
**103 rm** ⌤ – ♦£ 190 ♦♦£ 220 – 9 suites
**Rest** *Oak Room* – Menu £ 25/40 – Carte approx. £ 50
• Grand and beautifully restored 19C mansion in delightful, extensive Gertrude Jekyll gardens. Country house rooms, some with private conservatories or suites over two floors. Classically English dining room with oak panelling and garden views.

ENGLAND

### Old House at Home
*Newnham Green ⊠ RG27 9AH – ℰ (01256) 762 222 – Closed 25 December and dinner Sunday and bank holidays*
**Rest** – *(booking advisable)* Menu £ 18 – Carte £ 26/34
• Mid-19C former post office tucked away in the corner of a lovely green. Main room split in two, with open fires on both sides; the old bar is cosier. Refined, measured, modern seasonal dishes.

### Hogget
*London Rd, (at the junction of A 30 and A 287) ⊠ RG27 9JJ – ℰ (01256) 763 009 – www.hogget.co.uk – Closed 25-26 December and Sunday dinner*
**Rest** – Carte £ 30/36
• Located at junction of A30 and A287. Wholesome, honest cooking; sensibly priced dishes, made using local produce: pie and mash or steak and chips through to crab cake or calves liver.

---

## HOPE – Derbyshire – 502 O23 – ⊠ Sheffield
▶ London 180 mi – Derby 50 mi – Manchester 31 mi – Sheffield 15 mi

**16 A1**

### Losehill House 
*Lose Hill Ln, Edale Rd, North : 1 mi by Edale Rd ⊠ S33 6AF – ℰ (01433) 621 219 – www.losehillhouse.co.uk*
**21 rm** ⊐ – ♥£ 140/160 ♥♥£ 160/265    **Rest** – Menu £ 17/38
• Comfortable, well-kept hotel with a bright, airy, modern feel. Open-plan lounge and bar. Small pool, sauna and outdoor hot tub. Bedrooms all have a view. Formally laid restaurant with superb views up to Win Hill; modern-style dishes, with cheese a speciality.

### Underleigh House without rest 
*Losehill Ln, Hope Valley, North : 1 mi by Edale Rd ⊠ S33 6AF – ℰ (01433) 621 372 – www.underleighhouse.co.uk – Closed 1-25 February, Christmas and New Year*
**5 rm** ⊐ – ♥£ 70 ♥♥£ 90/105
• Converted Victorian property, rurally located and personally run; well situated for the Peak District. Countryside views and a welcoming country ambience.

---

## HORLEY – Surrey – 504 T30 – pop. 22 582
▶ London 27 mi – Brighton 26 mi – Royal Tunbridge Wells 22 mi

**7 D2**

### Langshott Manor
*Langshott, North : 0.5 mi by A 23 turning right at Chequers H. onto Ladbroke Rd ⊠ RH6 9LN – ℰ (01293) 786 680 – www.langshottmanor.com*
**21 rm** ⊐ – ♥£ 150/180 ♥♥£ 180/600 – 1 suite
**Rest** *Mulberry* – see restaurant listing
• Characterful manor house dating back to 1540 and set amidst roses, vines and ponds. Traditional exterior contrasts with contemporary furnishings. Bedrooms are split between the manor and three mews houses: many feature fireplaces or four-posters and one has a patio terrace. Smart marble and granite bathrooms.

### Mulberry – at Langshott Manor Hotel
*Langshott, North : 0.5 mi by A 23 turning right at Chequers H. onto Ladbroke Rd ⊠ RH6 9LN – ℰ (01293) 786 680 – www.langshottmanor.com*
**Rest** – *(booking essential)* Menu £ 20/44 – Carte £ 24/63
• Smart hotel dining room set within a charming manor house, which part-dates back to 1540. Good choice of modern, well-presented dishes from the set menu, à la carte or evening tasting menu.

---

## HORNCASTLE – Lincolnshire – 502 T24 – pop. 6 090
▶ London 143 mi – Lincoln 22 mi – Nottingham 62 mi
🛈 Wharf Rd ℰ (01507) 60 11 11, www.horncastleuk.com

**17 C1**

XX **Magpies** with rm                                          AC rest, VISA ❺
71-75 East St ⊠ LN9 6AA – ℰ (01507) 527 004 – www.magpiesrestaurant.co.uk
– Closed 27 December-11 January, Saturday lunch, Monday and Tuesday
**3 rm** ☟ – ♦♦£ 110 ♦♦♦£ 130
**Rest** – Menu £ 42 (dinner) – Carte (lunch) £ 30/32
♦ Formerly three 18C cottages, now a cosy, family-run restaurant. Hearty, classically based dishes arrive attractively presented, with tasty homemade breads to
start and mini-assiettes to finish. Quarterly wine dinners are a feature. Bedrooms
have floral feature walls and a free-standing bath or double sinks.

---

# HORNDON-ON-THE-HILL – Thurrock – 504 V29 – pop. 1 612          13 C3
▶ London 25 mi – Chelmsford 22 mi – Maidstone 34 mi – Southend-on-Sea 16 mi

🏠 **Bell** with rm                                    🍴 📶 P VISA ❺ AE
High Rd ⊠ SS17 8LD – ℰ (01375) 642 463 – www.bell-inn.co.uk – Closed 25-26
December and bank holiday Mondays
**15 rm** – ♦£ 60 ♦♦£ 85/100, ☟ £ 9.50   **Rest** – Carte £ 22/37
♦ 15C coaching inn, run by the same family for 50 years. Cooking is a step above
your usual pub fare, displaying classically based dishes with some modern
touches. Pub bedrooms are styled after Victorian mistresses; those in Hill House
display thoughtful extras.

---

# HORNINGSEA – Cambridgeshire – see Cambridge

---

# HORNINGSHAM – Wiltshire – 504 N30 – see Warminster

---

# HORN'S CROSS – Devon – 503 H31 – ⊠ Bideford ▌ Great Britain          2 C1
▶ London 222 mi – Barnstaple 15 mi – Exeter 46 mi

◉ Clovelly★★, W : 6.5 mi on A 39 and B 3237 – Bideford : Bridge★★ - Burton Art
Gallery★ **AC** - Lundy Island★★ (by ferry), NE : 7 mi on a 39 and B 3235 – Hartland :
Hartland Church★ - Hartland Quay★ (❋★★) - Hartland Point ≼★★★, W : 9 mi on
A 39 and B 3248 – Great Torrington (Dartington Crystal★ **AC**), SE : 15 mi on A 39
and A 386 – Rosemoor★, SE : 16 mi on A 39, A 386 and B 3220

⌂ **Roundhouse** without rest                          ▱ ✿ P VISA ❺ ⓪
West : 1 mi on A 39 ⊠ EX39 5DN – ℰ (01237) 451 687
– www.the-round-house.co.uk
**3 rm** ☟ – ♦£ 40/50 ♦♦£ 65
♦ Located on site of 13C corn mill, this friendly guesthouse offers cream teas on
arrival. Spacious lounge and good quality breakfasts. Comfy, clean, well-kept
bedrooms.

---

# HORRINGER – Suffolk – 504 W27 – see Bury St Edmunds

---

# HORSHAM – West Sussex – 504 T30 – pop. 47 804          7 D2
▶ London 39 mi – Brighton 23 mi – Guildford 20 mi – Lewes 25 mi
🅇 9 Causeway ℰ (01403) 21 16 61, www.horsham.gov.uk
🏌 Mannings Heath Fullers, Hammerpond Rd, Mannings Heath, ℰ (01403) 21 02 28

🏨 **South Lodge** 🌿          ≼ ▱ ⌂ ᵴ ✕ 📺 🗄 📶 🐾 P VISA ❺ AE ⓪
Brighton Rd, Lower Beeding, Southeast : 5 mi on A 281 ⊠ RH13 6PS – ℰ (01403)
891 711 – www.exclusivehotels.co.uk
**85 rm** ☟ – ♦£ 260 ♦♦£ 260 – 4 suites
**Rest The Pass**❀ – see restaurant listing
**Rest Camellia Country Kitchen** – (booking essential for non-residents)
Menu £ 22/35 – Carte £ 29/47
♦ Victorian mansion set in 93 acres, with period furnishings, heavy panelled walls
and corporate feel. Traditional bedrooms in the main house and more contempo-
rary rooms in the wing; some suites boasts jacuzzis or terraces. Relaxed Camellia
Country Kitchen or live kitchen action in The Pass.

XX **The Pass** – at South Lodge Hotel ❄ ✎ **P** VISA ◑ AE ⓪
❀ *Brighton Rd, Lower Beeding, Southeast : 5 mi on A 281* ✉ *RH13 6PS*
– ✆ *(01403) 891 711 – www.southlodgehotels.co.uk*
**Rest** – *(closed Monday and Tuesday)* Menu £ 25/70
**Spec.** Squab pigeon, orange and parfait. Gigha halibut with baby gem, parsley
and clams. Honey cheesecake, lemon thyme and lavender.
♦ A unique experience and ideal for those for whom a chef's table is not enough.
You sit and watch all the action in the hotel's main kitchen, while the central sta-
tion cooks for you. Expect modern, intricate and balanced dishes, with well-
thought-out combinations.

XX **Restaurant Tristan** VISA ◑
*Stans Way, off East St* ✉ *RH12 1HU* – ✆ *(01403) 255 688*
– *www.restauranttristan.co.uk – Closed 2 weeks late July-early August,*
*25 December-7 January, Sunday and Monday*
**Rest** – Menu £ 18/38
♦ First floor restaurant in characterful 16C beamed house. Cooking is seasonal
but also elaborate in style and the kitchen is a fan of modern techniques. Service
is smooth and effective.

**at Rowhook** Northwest : 4 mi by A 264 and A 281 off A 29 – ✉ Horsham

🍺 **Chequers Inn** ❄ **P** VISA ◑ ⓪
✉ *RH12 3PY* – ✆ *(01403) 790 480 – Closed 25 December and Sunday dinner*
**Rest** – Carte £ 21/35
♦ Part-15C inn with a charming open-fired, stone-floored bar and unusual corru-
gated dining room extension. Chef-owner grows, forages for or shoots the major-
ity of his produce. Classical menus.

---

**HOUGH-ON-THE-HILL** – Lincolnshire – see Grantham

---

**HOVE** – Brighton and Hove – **504** T31 – see Brighton and Hove

---

**HOVERINGHAM** – Nottinghamshire – pop. 308 **16** B2
▶ London 135 mi – Birmingham 77 mi – Leeds 74 mi – Sheffield 57 mi

🍺 **Reindeer Inn** **P** VISA ◑
*Main St* ✉ *NG14 7JR* – ✆ *(01159) 663 629 – www.thereindeerinn.com – Closed 1*
*week May, 1 week October, Tuesday lunch, Sunday dinner and Monday*
**Rest** – Menu £ 10 (lunch) – Carte £ 25/36
♦ Characterful country inn set next to a cricket pitch, with beams, open fire and a
cosy, relaxed atmosphere. Popular with locals. Well-priced menus offer mainly
classical dishes.

---

**HUDDERSFIELD** – West Yorkshire – **502** O23 – pop. 146 234 **22** B3
▶ London 191 mi – Bradford 11 mi – Leeds 15 mi – Manchester 25 mi
🛈 Princes Alexandra Walk ✆ (01484) 22 32 00, www.huddersfieldonline.org.uk
🏌 Bradley Park Bradley Rd, ✆ (01484) 22 37 72
🏌 Woodsome Hall Fenay Bridge, ✆ (01484) 60 29 71
🏌 Outlane Slack Lane, Off New Hey Rd, ✆ (01422) 37 47 62
🏌 Meltham Thick Hollins Hall, ✆ (01484) 85 02 27
🏌 Fixby Hall Lightridge Rd, ✆ (01484) 42 62 03
🏌 Crosland Heath Felks Stile Rd, ✆ (01484) 65 32 16

**at Thunder Bridge** Southeast : 5.75 mi by A 629 – ✉ Huddersfield

🍺 **Woodman Inn** with rm ✍ **P** VISA ◑
✉ *HD8 0PX* – ✆ *(01484) 605 778 – www.woodman-inn.co.uk – Closed 25-26*
*December*
**12 rm** ⌁ – ♦£ 48/68 ♦♦£ 74/85 **Rest** – Carte £ 21/34 **s**
♦ Traditional 19C pub set in a small hamlet in the valley. The classic British menus are extensive and change with the seasons. Lunch is simple and hearty, dinner more ambitious. Nearby cottage bedrooms are simple but well-kept.

**at Shelley** Southeast : 6.25 mi by A 629 – on B 6116 – ⊠ Huddersfield

⌂ **Three Acres**  🚗 🏠 📻 rest, 🛇 📞 **P** **VISA** **ⓒⓓ**
*Roydhouse, Northeast : 1.5 mi on Flockton rd* ⊠ *HD8 8LR –* 𝒞 *(01484) 602 606*
*– www.3acres.com – Closed 1 January*
**14 rm** 🛏 – ✝£ 83/105 ✝✝£ 125 – 2 suites
**Rest** – *(booking essential)* Carte £ 30/43

♦ Well-established stone inn, set in a pleasant rural location. Two smart meeting rooms. Bedrooms are warm, modern and comfortable; those in the annexe are the most spacious. Agreeably busy restaurant with open fires: fish dishes prepared at open seafood bar.

---

# HULLBRIDGE – Essex                                                    13 C2_3
▶ London 40 mi – Croydon 46 mi – Barnet 50 mi – Ealing 63 mi

✗ **Anchor**  ⟨ 🏠 📻 **P** **VISA** **ⓒⓓ**
*Ferry Rd* ⊠ *SS5 6ND –* 𝒞 *(01702) 230 777 – www.theanchorhullbridge.co.uk*
*– Closed 25 December*
**Rest** – Carte £ 21/35

♦ Modern, informal, open-plan restaurant with pleasant terrace, sleek bar and lots of windows to take in the river views. Accessible, seasonal British menu; more adventurous specials at dinner.

---

# HUNNINGHAM – Warwickshire – pop. 190                                   19 D3
▶ London 94 mi – Birmingham 36 mi – Liverpool 129 mi – Leeds 125 mi

🍴 **Red Lion**  🚗 🏠 **P** **VISA** **ⓒⓓ** **AE**
*Main St* ⊠ *CV33 9DY –* 𝒞 *(01926) 632 715 – www.redlionhunningham.co.uk*
**Rest** – Carte £ 19/34

♦ Charming, part-17C timbered inn set by the River Lemm and displaying over 300 framed American comics and a ceiling-mounted air pipe for delivering orders. Daily menu offers well-crafted, unfussy pub fare, with the occasional modern touch.

---

# HUNSDON – Hertfordshire                                                12 B2
▶ London 26 mi – Bishop's Stortford 8 mi – Harlow 7 mi

🍴 **Fox and Hounds**  🚗 🏠 **P** **VISA** **ⓒⓓ** **AE**
*2 High St* ⊠ *SG12 8NH –* 𝒞 *(01279) 843 999*
*– www.foxandhounds-hunsdon.co.uk – Closed 26 December, Sunday dinner and Monday*
**Rest** – Menu £ 17 (weekdays) – Carte £ 26/35

♦ Sizeable pub with rustic bar, cookery book filled dining room, large garden and terrace. Short menus offer unfussy, simply prepared dishes in a range of different styles; portions are generous.

---

# HUNSTANTON – Norfolk – 502 V25 – pop. 4 505                            14 B1
▶ London 120 mi – Cambridge 60 mi – Norwich 45 mi
🛈 The Green 𝒞 (01485) 53 26 10, www.hunstanton-info.com
⛳ Golf Course Rd, 𝒞 (01485) 53 28 11

✗✗ **The Neptune** (Kevin Mangeolles) with rm  🛇 🗣 **P** **VISA** **ⓒⓓ**
✿ *85 Old Hunstanton Rd, Old Hunstanton, Northeast : 1.5 mi on A 149*
⊠ *PE36 6HZ –* 𝒞 *(01485) 532 122 – www.theneptune.co.uk – Closed Monday*
**6 rm** (dinner included) 🛏 – ✝£ 125/150 ✝✝£ 210/225
**Rest** – *(dinner only and Sunday lunch)* Menu £ 30/52
**Spec.** Asparagus with sweetcorn custard and deep-fried hen's egg. Lamb loin with sweetbread and tongue, Epoisses mash. Strawberry parfait, compressed strawberries and Campari jelly

♦ Very personally run, attractive, red-brick former pub. New England style interior boasts rattan-furnished bar and dining room with large nautical photographs. Constantly evolving menu relies on the latest local produce available. Presentation is modern; service is relaxed and efficient. Simple, comfortable bedrooms.

247

ENGLAND

**at Thornham** Northeast : 4.5 mi on A 149

🛏️ **Orange Tree** with rm                                        🍴 🪑 **P** _VISA_ ⊕⊕
*High St* ✉ *PE36 6LY* – ✆ *(01485) 512 213*
*– www.theorangetreethornham.co.uk*
**6 rm** 🛏️ – ❭£ 65/110 ❭❭£ 85/110
**Rest** – Carte £ 25/35 **s**
♦ Gregarious staff ensure a warm welcome at this 17C inn; even your dog will be offered a snack in the bar. Menu in the contemporary restaurant covers all bases and several countries. Compact but modern bedrooms also available.

---

**HUNTINGDON** – Cambridgeshire – **504** T26 – pop. 20 600                    **14** A2

▶ London 69 mi – Bedford 21 mi – Cambridge 16 mi

🛈 St. Mary's St ✆ (01480) 38 85 88, www.visithuntingdonshire.org

⛳ Hemingford Abbots Cambridge Rd, New Farm Lodge, ✆ (01480) 49 50 00

🏨 **Old Bridge**                                               🅐🅒 ☏ ♨ **P** _VISA_ ⊕⊕ 🅐🅔 ⓪
*1 High St* ✉ *PE29 3TQ* – ✆ *(01480) 424 300* – *www.huntsbridge.com*
**24 rm** 🛏️ – ❭£ 99/150 ❭❭£ 150/240
**Rest** *Terrace* – see restaurant listing
♦ Long-standing, family-owned riverside hotel with small wine shop in reception: one owner is a Master of Wine. Contemporary bedrooms feature plenty of fabrics and spacious bathrooms.

🍴🍴 **Terrace** – at Old Bridge Hotel                            🪑 🅐🅒 **P** _VISA_ ⊕⊕ 🅐🅔 ⓪
*1 High St* ✉ *PE29 3TQ* – ✆ *(01480) 424 300* – *www.huntsbridge.com*
**Rest** – Menu £ 20 (lunch) – Carte £ 30/39 **s**♨
♦ Choose between formal wood-panelled dining room and more casual conservatory with terrace. Menus change every two days and feature traditional dishes with some Mediterranean influences.

**at Wyton** East : 2.5 mi by B 1514 off A 1123

🏠 **Magdalene House** without rest                       🍴 ♿ ♨ ☏ **P** _VISA_ ⊕⊕
*Huntingdon Rd* ✉ *PE28 2AD* – ✆ *(01480) 465 011*
*– www.magdalene-house.co.uk*
**3 rm** – ❭£ 78 ❭❭£ 88/98
♦ Modern barn conversion in grounds of attractive 17C thatched house once owned by Magdalene College. Spacious bedrooms with good level of extras. Continental breakfast is taken in your room.

**at Hemingford Grey** Southeast : 5 mi by A 1198 off A 14 – ✉ Huntingdon

🛏️ **Cock**                                                   🍴 🪑 **P** _VISA_ ⊕⊕ 🅐🅔
*47 High St* ✉ *PE28 9BJ* – ✆ *(01480) 463 609* – *www.thecockhemingford.co.uk*
**Rest** – *(booking essential)* Carte £ 26/35
♦ Homely 17C country pub with spacious dining room, run by an experienced team. Tried-and-tested pub cooking offers good value lunches, daily fish specials and a mix and match sausage board.

---

**HUNWORTH** – Norfolk                                                        **15** C1

▶ London 129 mi – Norwich 25 mi – East Dereham 17 mi – Taverham 19 mi

🛏️ **Hunny Bell**                                             🍴 🪑 **P** _VISA_ ⊕⊕ 🅐🅔
*The Green* ✉ *NR24 2AA* – ✆ *(01263) 712 300* – *www.hunnybell.co.uk*
**Rest** – Carte £ 25/34
♦ Sympathetically renovated 18C whitewashed pub with smart country interior. Appealing menu of sophisticated pub classics crafted from local, seasonal produce; even the bar snacks are homemade.

ENGLAND

▶ London 35 mi – Maidenhead 5 mi – Reading 18 mi

🛏️     **Olde Bell Inn**                         🕭 ॐ 🛰️ ♨️ **P** *VISA* ⦿ **AE**
*High St ✉ SL6 5LX – ✆ (01628) 825 881 – www.theoldebell.co.uk – Closed 25-26*
*December*
**47 rm** 🖵 – ♦£ 109/400 – ♦♦£ 109/400 – 1 suite
**Rest** *Restaurant* – see restaurant listing
♦ Part-12C timbered inn close to the Thames. Charming rear gardens with outside
bar, rotisserie and BBQ. Characterful bedrooms in contemporary, minimalist style;
all have rocking chairs, sheepskin rugs and good extras. Lovely open-fired bar.

XX    **Restaurant** – at Olde Bell Inn                        🕭 🕮 **P** *VISA* ⦿ **AE**
*High St ✉ SL6 5LX – ✆ (01628) 825 881 – www.theoldebell.co.uk – Closed 25-26*
*December*
**Rest** – *(closed Sunday dinner and bank holiday Monday dinner)* Menu £ 17
– Carte £ 31/34
♦ Heavily timbered dining room within a part-12C inn, boasting wood-panelling,
tiled floors and shabby-chic furnishings. Interesting seasonal menus with a rustic
base; much of the produce is from the kitchen garden. Pleasant summer terrace.

XX    **Black Boys Inn** with rm                   🕮 🕭 **P** *VISA* ⦿ **AE** ⓪
*Henley Rd, Southwest : 1.5 mi on A 4130 ✉ SL6 5NQ – ✆ (01628) 824 212*
*– www.blackboysinn.co.uk*
**8 rm** 🖵 – ♦£ 75/88 ♦♦£ 120/150
**Rest** – *(closed Sunday dinner)* Menu £ 15 (lunch) – Carte £ 26/42
♦ Rustic restaurant in 16C former pub with exposed beams and wood burning
stove. Experienced owners are avid Francophiles and the concise, traditional
French menu reflects this. Polite service. Clean, unfussy bedrooms with thoughtful
extras such as books.

---

▶ London 77 mi – Bristol 77 mi – Oxford 38 mi – Southampton 33 mi

🛏️     **Esseborne Manor** ॐ               🕭 ॐ 🛰️ ♨️ **P** *VISA* ⦿ **AE** ⓪
*Northeast : 1.5 mi on A 343 ✉ SP11 0ER – ✆ (01264) 736 444*
*– www.esseborne-manor.co.uk*
**19 rm** 🖵 – ♦£ 89/109 ♦♦£ 89/240
**Rest** – Menu £ 17/25 **s** – Carte dinner approx. £ 35 **s**
♦ 100 year old country house in attractive grounds with herb garden. Smart,
well-appointed bedrooms, some in the garden cottages. Ferndown room boasts
a spa bath and private patio. Long, narrow dining room with large windows.

---

▶ London 45 mi – Croydon 35 mi – Barnet 87 mi – Ealing 69 mi

X     **Fig Tree**                                        🕮 *VISA* ⦿
*120 High St ✉ BN6 9PX – ✆ (01273) 832 183 – www.figtreerestaurant.co.uk*
*– Closed 2 weeks January, Tuesday lunch, Sunday dinner and Monday*
**Rest** – Menu £ 19/23 – Carte £ 25/39
♦ Attractive Victorian house in pretty high street, with striking Gothic arched bay
window and small terrace. Carefully priced menus showcase local, seasonal ingredients. Loyal local following.

---

---

▶ London 244 mi – Scarborough 27 mi – York 33 mi

🏠     **Burnley House** without rest                              🕭 **P**
✉ YO62 6UA – ✆ (01751) 417 548 – www.burnleyhouse.co.uk – March-November
**6 rm** 🖵 – ♦£ 60 ♦♦£ 80/95
♦ Attractive part 16C, part Georgian house, Grade II listed in a picturesque Moors
village. Brown trout in beck winding through garden. Simple, individually styled
bedrooms.

**ENGLAND**

**ICKLESHAM** – East Sussex – 504 V/W31                                          **9** C3

▶ London 66 mi – Brighton 42 mi – Hastings 7 mi

↑   **Manor Farm Oast** ॐ                          🍴 🐾 🛜 📶 **P** **VISA** **CO** **AE** **①**
    *Windmill Ln, South : 0.5 mi* ✉ *TN36 4WL* – ✆ *(01424) 813 787*
    *– www.manorfarmoast.co.uk – Closed 26 February-26 March and Christmas-New*
    *Year*
    **3 rm** 🍴 – ♦£ 85/105 ♦♦£ 105   **Rest** – Menu £ 32
    ♦ 19C former oast house retaining original features and surrounded by orchards.
    Welcoming beamed lounge with open fire. One of the comfy bedrooms is
    completely round. Home-cooked menus in circular dining room.

**IDEN GREEN** – Kent – 504 V30                                              **8** B2

▶ London 55 mi – Croydon 49 mi – Barnet 81 mi – Ealing 85 mi

↑   **Waters End Farm** without rest ॐ                    🍴 🐾 🛜 📶 **P** **VISA** **CO**
    *Standen St, Southeast : 1.25 mi* ✉ *TN17 4LA* – ✆ *(01580) 850 731*
    *– www.watersendfarm.co.uk – March-October*
    **5 rm** 🍴 – ♦£ 95/135 ♦♦£ 95/135
    ♦ Characterful part-timbered, part-brick house, set in 43 peaceful acres. Bedrooms
    – in converted barns – boast heavy wood furniture and modern facilities. Huge
    mural of the house in the breakfast room or eat outside on the terrace in summer.

**ILFRACOMBE** – Devon – 503 H30 – pop. 10 490 📗 Great Britain               **2** C1

▶ London 218 mi – Barnstaple 13 mi – Exeter 53 mi

◉ Mortehoe★★ : St Mary's Church - Morte Point★, SW : 5.5 mi on B 3343 – Lundy
Island★★ (by ferry). Braunton : St Brannock's Church★, Braunton Burrows★, S :
8 mi on A 361 – Barnstaple★ : Bridge★, S : 12 mi on A 3123, B 3230, A 39, A 361
and B 3233

🏠   **Hampton's** without rest                          🐾 📶 **P** **VISA** **CO** **AE**
    *Excelsior Villas, Torrs Pk.* ✉ *EX34 8AZ* – ✆ *(01271) 864 246*
    *– www.thehamptonshotel.co.uk*
    **6 rm** 🍴 – ♦£ 75/110 ♦♦£ 80/110
    ♦ Imposing Victorian villa with individual, bohemian style. Open-plan lounge and
    breakfast room with honesty bar and DVDs. Well-equipped, individually styled bed-
    rooms are designed by the friendly owner; those to the front boast rooftop views.

✗   **Gendarmerie**                                              **VISA** **CO**
    *63 Fore St* ✉ *EX34 9ED* – ✆ *(01271) 865 984* – *Closed November,*
    *Tuesday-Wednesday October-March and Monday*
    **Rest** – *(dinner only) (booking advisable)* Menu £ 27
    ♦ Simple little restaurant with intimate, candlelit interior, tucked away on a side
    street and very personally run by a husband and wife team. Concise, daily chang-
    ing menu showcases market produce in precise, skilfully executed combinations.

**ILKLEY** – West Yorkshire – 502 O22 – pop. 13 472                          **22** B2

▶ London 210 mi – Bradford 13 mi – Harrogate 17 mi – Leeds 16 mi

🛈 Station Rd ✆ (01943) 60 23 19, www.visitbradford.com

🟫 Myddleton, ✆ (01943) 60 72 77

✗✗✗  **Box Tree** (Simon Gueller)                          🔳 ⇄ **VISA** **CO**
    ❀ *37 Church St, on A 65* ✉ *LS29 9DR* – ✆ *(01943) 608 484* – *www.theboxtree.co.uk*
    *– Closed 1-6 January, 27-30 December, Sunday dinner and Monday*
    **Rest** – *(dinner only and lunch Friday-Sunday)* Menu £ 25/55 ❀
    **Spec.** Ballotine of salmon with herb fromage blanc. Squab pigeon 'en vessie'
    peas, baby onions and pancetta. Passion fruit soufflé with a hot passion fruit
    sauce.
    ♦ Iconic restaurant in a charming 18C sandstone cottage. Plush sitting area with
    semi-gilded ceiling and fine antiques. Two main dining rooms laid with quality ta-
    bleware. Confident, classical cooking is precise and skilful, with a strong French
    bias. Preparations are straightforward and let the ingredients shine through.

ENGLAND

**ILMINGTON** – **Warwickshire** – **504** O27 📗 Great Britain      **19** C3

▶ London 91 mi – Birmingham 31 mi – Oxford 34 mi – Stratford-upon-Avon 9 mi

◐ Hidcote Manor Garden★★, SW : 2 mi by minor rd – Chipping Campden★★,
SW : 4 mi by minor rd

🏠   **Folly Farm Cottage**         🚗 ⅍ ⁽ᵗ⁾ **P** 𝘝𝘐𝘚𝘈 ◉◉ 𝔸𝔼
*Back St* ✉ *CV36 4LJ* – ℰ *(01608) 682 425* – *www.follyfarm.co.uk*
**3 rm** ⬚ – ♦£65 ♦♦£88   **Rest** – Menu £ 20
◆ Cosy, characterful cottage in small village, with friendly owners and lovely garden. Beams and heavy drapes abound. Bedrooms are named after garden plants;
some have four-posters or whirlpool baths. Simple home-cooked dinners.

🍴   **Howard Arms** with rm      🚗 🛋 𝕂 rest, ⅍ ⁽ᵗ⁾ **P** 𝘝𝘐𝘚𝘈 ◉◉ 𝔸𝔼 ⓪
*Lower Green* ✉ *CV36 4LT* – ℰ *(01608) 682 226* – *www.howardarms.com*
**8 rm** ⬚ – ♦£85 ♦♦£155   **Rest** – Carte £ 21/29
◆ Delightful 17C Cotswold stone inn, on a peaceful village green. Choice of
beamed bar with inglenook fireplace, raised-level dining room and lovely terrace.
Dishes are hearty and British-based. Warm, cosy bedrooms; those in the extension
are more contemporary.

---

**INGHAM** – **Norfolk** – **504** W27 – **pop. 376**      **15** D1

▶ London 139 mi – Norwich 25 mi – Ipswich 65 mi – Lowestoft 30 mi

🍴   **Ingham Swan**        🛋 **P** 𝘝𝘐𝘚𝘈 ◉◉
☺   *Sea Palling Rd* ✉ *NR12 9AB* – ℰ *(01692) 581 099* – *www.theinghamswan.co.uk*
– *Closed 25-26 December*
**Rest** – *(booking essential at dinner)* Menu £ 19/28 **s** – Carte £ 22/41 **s**
◆ Cosy, attractive, thatched 14C pub in the shadow of an 11C church; equally
characterful beamed interior. Quite complex dishes use plenty of ingredients, al-
beit in classic combinations.

---

**INGLETON** – **North Yorkshire** – **502** M21 – **pop. 1 641**
– ✉ **Carnforth (lancs.)**      **22** A2

▶ London 266 mi – Kendal 21 mi – Lancaster 18 mi – Leeds 53 mi

🏠   **Riverside Lodge**      ≤ 🚗 🏠 ⅍ **P** 𝘝𝘐𝘚𝘈 ◉◉
*24 Main St* ✉ *LA6 3HJ* – ℰ *(015242) 41 359* – *www.riversideingleton.co.uk*
– *Closed 24-25 December*
**8 rm** ⬚ – ♦£42 ♦♦£64   **Rest** – Menu £ 17 **s**
◆ Pleasant 19C house close to famous pot-holing caves. Informal gardens. Cosy
sitting room and homely bedrooms. Conservatory dining room with great views
across Yorkshire Dales.

---

**IPSWICH** – **Suffolk** – **504** X27 – **pop. 145 708** 📗 Great Britain   **15** C3

▶ London 76 mi – Norwich 43 mi

🛈 St Stephens Lane ℰ (01473) 25 80 70, www.visit-ipswich.com

⛳ Rushmere Rushmere Heath, ℰ (01473) 72 56 48

⛳ Purdis Heath Bucklesham Rd, ℰ (01473) 72 89 41

⛳ Fynn Valley Witnesham, ℰ (01473) 78 52 67

◐ Sutton Hoo★, NE : 12 mi by A 12 Y and B 1083 from Woodbridge

Plan on next page

🏨   **Salthouse Harbour**      ≤ 🛗 ⅗ ⁽ᵗ⁾ **P** 𝘝𝘐𝘚𝘈 ◉◉ 𝔸𝔼
*1 Neptune Quay* ✉ *IP4 1AX* – ℰ *(01473) 226 789* – *www.salthouseharbour.co.uk*
**68 rm** ⬚ – ♦£125 ♦♦£140/220 – 2 suites      **X a**
**Rest** *Eaterie* – see restaurant listing
◆ Old quayside salt warehouse boasting a modern extension and attractive marina
views. Boutique bedrooms: some with exposed brick walls, others with chaise longues or copper slipper baths; ask for one with a balcony overlooking the marina.

ENGLAND

# IPSWICH

Guesthouses ⚊ don't provide the same level of service as hotels. They are often characterised by a warm welcome and a décor which reflects the owner's personality. Those shown in red ⚊ are particularly pleasant.

ENGLAND

**Kesgrave Hall**   🚗 🅿️ 📶 🔐 📶 🔒 P VISA 💳 AE ⓘ
*Hall Rd, East : 4.75 mi by A 1214 on Bealings rd ⌂ IP5 2PU –* ℘ *(01473) 333 471
– www.kesgravehall.com*
**22 rm –** 🛏£ 184 🛏🛏£ 230/245, ⌂ £ 16 – 1 suite
**Rest** – Carte £ 23/42
♦ White Georgian house with large lawned gardens and impressive terrace. Stylish lounges have relaxed, urban-chic feel. Large, luxurious bedrooms boast quality furnishings, modern facilities and stylish bathrooms. Busy informal dining room offers European menu.

**Eaterie** – at Salthouse Harbour Hotel   ≤ 🔐 P VISA 💳 AE
*1 Neptune Quay ⌂ IP4 1AX –* ℘ *(01473) 226 789 – www.salthouseharbour.co.uk*
**Rest** – Menu £ 18 (lunch) – Carte £ 27/45   **X**a
♦ Informal hotel restaurant within an old salt warehouse. Exposed brick and wood floors contrast with contemporary black booths and a stylish bar. Modern menu displays Mediterranean influences.

**at Hintlesham** West : 5 mi by A 1214 on A 1071 - Y – ⌂ Ipswich

**Hintlesham Hall** ⌂   ≤ 🚗 🅿️ 🍴 📶 🔒 P VISA 💳 AE ⓘ
*⌂ IP8 3NS –* ℘ *(01473) 652 334 – www.hintleshamhall.com*
**30 rm** ⌂ – 🛏£ 150 🛏🛏£ 160 – 3 suites
**Rest** – Menu £ 34/45 **s**
♦ Impressive Georgian manor house with 16C roots; original features such as ornate plasterwork and gold leaf inlaid cornicing remain. Grand bedrooms in main house; cosy courtyard rooms – some with terraces. Vast dining room offers both classical and modern dishes.

**ENGLAND**

**IRBY** – Merseyside – **502** K23   **20** A3
▶ London 212 mi – Liverpool 12 mi – Manchester 46 mi – Stoke-on-Trent 56 mi

**Da Piero**   VISA 💳 ⓘ
*5 Mill Hill Rd ⌂ CH61 4UB –* ℘ *(0151) 648 73 73 – www.dapiero.co.uk – Closed 2 weeks September, 1 week January, Sunday and Monday*
**Rest** – Italian – *(dinner only) (booking essential)* Carte £ 23/49
♦ Family-owned and run restaurant with homely, understated décor and intimate, pleasant feel. Carefully prepared, classical Italian cooking, with lots of rustic Sicilian dishes.

**IRONBRIDGE** – Telford and Wrekin – **503** M26 – pop. 1 560   **18** B2
🏴 Great Britain
▶ London 135 mi – Birmingham 36 mi – Shrewsbury 18 mi
◉ Ironbridge Gorge Museum★★ **AC** (The Iron Bridge★★, Coalport China Museum★★, Blists Hill Open Air Museum★★, Museum of the Gorge and Visitor Centre★)

**Library House** without rest   🚭 📶 VISA 💳
*11 Severn Bank ⌂ TF8 7AN –* ℘ *(01952) 432 299 – www.libraryhouse.com
– Closed 24-30 December*
**4 rm** ⌂ – 🛏£ 70 🛏🛏£ 100
♦ Nicely hidden, albeit tricky to find, guesthouse with rear terrace. Homely sitting room. Cottage style breakfast room. Compact, comfy rooms, with a touch of style about them.

**Restaurant Severn**   VISA 💳 AE
*33 High St. ⌂ TF8 7AG –* ℘ *(01952) 432 233 – www.restaurantsevern.co.uk
– Closed 2 weeks January, 2 weeks August, Sunday dinner, Monday and Tuesday*
**Rest** – *(dinner only and Sunday lunch) (booking essential)* Menu £ 19/29
♦ Close to the Severn and world heritage site 'Ironbridge'. Pleasant, light and airy dining room with a real family feel. Experienced owners cook tasty, classically based dishes.

※ **da Vinci** VISA ⊚⊚
*26 High St ☒ TF8 7AD – ℰ (01952) 432 250*
*– www.davinci-restaurant-ironbridge.co.uk – Closed Christmas-New Year, 1 week spring, 1 week autumn, Sunday and Monday*
**Rest** – Italian – *(dinner only) (booking essential)* Carte £ 17/37
♦ Keenly run osteria in conservation village. Split-level dining with warm décor and simple, rustic style. Italian chef sources produce from his homeland. Authentic cooking; Tuscan specialities.

**ISLE OF MAN** – I.O.M. – **502** G21 – see Man (Isle of)

**ITTERINGHAM** – Norfolk – **504** X25 – ☒ Aylsham **15** C1
▶ London 126 mi – Cromer 11 mi – Norwich 17 mi

🛏 **Walpole Arms** 🚗 🏠 **P** VISA ⊚⊚
😊 *The Common ☒ NR11 7AR – ℰ (01263) 587 258 – www.thewalpolearms.co.uk*
*– Closed 25 December and Sunday dinner*
**Rest** – Carte £ 20/31
♦ 18C inn with characterful beamed bar and more formal restaurant. Interesting, Mediterranean-influenced menu is made up of generous, well-prepared dishes and appealing daily specials. The pork belly with Mediterranean vegetables is a firm favourite with the locals.

**IVYCHURCH** – Kent – **504** W30 ▌Great Britain **9** C2
▶ London 67 mi – Ashford 11 mi – Rye 10 mi
◉ Rye Old Town★★ : Mermaid St★ - St Mary's Church (≤★), SW : 9 mi on A 2070 and A 259

⌂ **Olde Moat House** without rest ⌖ 🚗 ℅ 🖥 **P** VISA ⊚⊚
*Northwest : 0.75 mi on B 2070 ☒ TN29 0AZ – ℰ (01797) 344 700*
*– www.oldemoathouse.co.uk*
**3 rm** ⊡ – ♥£ 50/60 ♥♥£ 70/110
♦ Blissfully characterful guesthouse with 15C origins, set in over three acres, encircled by small moat. Beamed sitting room with inglenook. Individual, homely styled rooms.

**IXWORTH** – Suffolk – **504** W27 – see Bury St Edmunds

**JERSEY** – C.I. – **503** O/P33 – pop. 85 150 – see Channel Islands

**JEVINGTON** – East Sussex – **504** U31 – see Eastbourne

**KEGWORTH** – Leicestershire – **502** Q25 – pop. 3 338 ▌Great Britain **16** B2
▶ London 123 mi – Leicester 18 mi – Loughborough 6 mi – Nottingham 13 mi
◉ Calke Abbey★, SW : 7 mi by A 6 (northbound) and A 453 (southbound) – Derby★ - Museum and Art Gallery★, Royal Crown Derby Museum★, NW : 9 mi by A 50 – Nottingham Castle Museum★, N : 11 mi by A 453 and A 52

🏠 **Kegworth House** without rest 🚗 ℅ 🖥 **P** VISA ⊚⊚ AE
*42 High St ☒ DE74 2DA – ℰ (01509) 672 575 – www.kegworthhouse.co.uk*
*– Closed Christmas and New Year*
**11 rm** ⊡ – ♥£ 90/180 ♥♥£ 140/250
♦ Georgian manor house in village, secluded in walled garden. Fine interior with original decorative features. Individually-decorated bedrooms of charm and character.

**KELSALE** – Suffolk – **504** Y27 – pop. 1 309 – ☒ Saxmundham **15** D3
▶ London 103 mi – Cambridge 68 mi – Ipswich 23 mi – Norwich 37 mi

⌂ **Mile Hill Barn** without rest 🚗 ℅ **P**
*North Green, North : 1.5 mi on A 12 ☒ IP17 2RG – ℰ (01728) 668 519*
*– www.mile-hill-barn.co.uk*
**3 rm** ⊡ – ♥£ 60/75 ♥♥£ 85/95
♦ Traditional 15C Suffolk barn in landscaped gardens. Tea on arrival in impressive raftered lounge. Bedrooms boast feature beds and modern bathrooms. Cosy breakfast room; Aga-cooked breakfasts.

## KELVEDON – Essex – 504 W28 – pop. 4 593

▶ London 56 mi

※※ **George & Dragon**                                   🛜 ⅋ **P** **VISA** ⦿

*Coggleshall Rd, Northwest : 2 mi on B 1024 ⊠ CO5 9PL – ℰ (01376) 561 797
– www.georgeanddragonkelvedon.co.uk – Closed 25 December-2 January,
Sunday and Monday*
**Rest** – Carte £ 25/30
♦ Clean, bright, welcoming restaurant with a sleek, contemporary style, encompassing topiary planters, marble tiled floors, antique mirrors, and art deco pictures and statuettes. Simple, well-priced menu with locally caught fish specials. Pretty terrace.

## KENDAL – Cumbria – 502 L21 – pop. 28 030 ▯ Great Britain

▶ London 270 mi – Bradford 64 mi – Burnley 63 mi – Carlisle 49 mi
🛈 Highgate ℰ (01539) 79 75 16, www.golakes.co.uk
🏌 The Heights, ℰ (01539) 72 34 99
🅖 Levens Hall and Garden★ **AC**, S : 4.5 mi by A 591, A 590 and A 6. Lake
Windermere★★, NW : 8 mi by A 5284 and A 591

⌂ **Beech House** without rest                          🚗 ⅋ ⓦ **P** **VISA** ⦿ ⓞ

*40 Greenside, by All Hallows Lane ⊠ LA9 4LD – ℰ (01539) 720 385
– www.beechhouse-kendal.co.uk – Closed 1 week Christmas*
**6 rm** ⊈ – ♦£ 60/75 ♦♦£ 80/100
♦ Pretty three-storey Georgian house set just out of town. Small honesty bar. Modern, open-plan lounge with comfy sofas and communal breakfast tables. Bright, airy, pine-furnished bedrooms come with complimentary cake and up-to-date bathrooms. Welcoming owners.

※ **Newmoon**                                            **AC** **VISA** ⦿

*129 Highgate ⊠ LA9 4EN – ℰ (01539) 729 254
– www.newmoonrestaurant.co.uk – Closed 1-7 January, 25-26 December,
Sunday and Monday*
**Rest** – *(booking advisable)* Carte £ 23/29
♦ Smart, high street restaurant with ground floor bar, intimate, beamed dining room and a loyal local following. The owner's Turkish heritage is reflected in the menu, which has a strong Mediterranean base; dishes are fresh and colourful.

**at Sizergh** Southwest : 3 mi by A 591 – ⊠ Kendal

🍴 **Strickland Arms**                                    🚗 🛜 **P** **VISA** ⦿

*⊠ LA8 8DZ – ℰ (01539) 561 010 – www.thestricklandarms.com – Closed 25
December*
**Rest** – Carte £ 20/28
♦ Former coach house for next door Sizergh Castle. Sizeable interior with characterful, shabby-chic feel. Menus feature classical pub dishes, with daily specials on the board. Regular events.

**at Crosthwaite** West : 5.25 mi by All Hallows Lane – ⊠ Kendal

🍴 **Punch Bowl Inn** with rm                            ⪡ 🛜 ⅋ ⓦ **P** **VISA** ⦿ **AE**

*⊠ LA8 8HR – ℰ (01539) 568 237 – www.the-punchbowl.co.uk*
**9 rm** ⊈ – ♦£ 120 ♦♦£ 305   **Rest** – Carte £ 21/39
♦ Charming 17C inn set in the picturesque Lyth Valley, boasting cosy fires, exposed wooden beams and trailing hop bines. Choice of rustic bar or formal restaurant, which offer interesting takes on old favourites at lunch and more ambitious dishes at dinner. Luxury bedrooms boast quality linens and roll-top baths.

## KENILWORTH – Warwickshire – 503 P26 – pop. 22 218 ▯ Great Britain

▶ London 102 mi – Birmingham 19 mi – Coventry 5 mi – Leicester 32 mi
🛈 11 Smalley Pl ℰ (01926) 74 89 00, www.kenilworthweb.co.uk
🅞 Castle★ **AC**

**ENGLAND**

⌂ **Victoria Lodge** without rest
🏠 *180 Warwick Rd ⊠ CV8 1HU – ℰ (01926) 512 020*
*– www.victorialodgekenilworth.co.uk – Closed 2 weeks Christmas-New Year*
**10 rm** ⌿ – †£ 50/65 ††£ 82
♦ Keenly and proudly run red-brick house with comfortable lounge and linen-laid breakfast room. Immaculately kept, colourfully decorated bedrooms come with complimentary mineral water and fresh milk; some rooms boast balconies or patios. Excellent breakfasts.

 XX **Bosquet** 🆅🅸🆂🅰 🆎🅴
*97a Warwick Rd ⊠ CV8 1HP – ℰ (01926) 852 463*
*– www.restaurantbosquet.co.uk – Closed 2 weeks July-August, 1 week Christmas, Sunday and Monday*
**Rest** – French – *(dinner only and lunch by arrangement)* Menu £ 33
– Carte £ 36/42
♦ Contemporary feel to this established restaurant with wooden floors, well-spaced tables and stylish leather chairs. Confident, well-informed cooking displays a classical French base.

X **Beef** 🅰🅲 🆅🅸🆂🅰 🆎🅴
*11 Warwick Rd ⊠ CV8 1HD – ℰ (01926) 863 311 – www.beef.uk.com – Closed 1 week Christmas-New Year, 1 week Easter, 22 August-5 September, Sunday dinner and bank holidays*
**Rest** – Beef specialities – Menu £ 20 (lunch) – Carte £ 24/38
♦ Rustic restaurant boasting exposed brickwork, slate floors and quirky cowhide banquettes. Menus offer robust, hearty dishes; mainly Scottish steaks cooked on the charcoal grill and cuts of beef from American, Argentinean or Wagyū cattle.

---

**KENTON** – Devon – **503** J31 – see Exeter

---

**KERNE BRIDGE** – Herefordshire – **503** M28 – see Ross-on-Wye

---

**KESSINGLAND** – Suffolk – pop. 4 211      **15** D2
▶ London 126 mi – Norwich 28 mi – Ipswich 40 mi – Colchester 66 mi

⌂ **Old Rectory**
🏠 *157 Church Rd ⊠ NR33 7SQ – ℰ (01502) 742 188 – www.bandblowestoft.co.uk*
*– Closed 17 December-2 January*
**3 rm** ⌿ – †£ 62 ††£ 94    **Rest** – Menu £ 22 s
♦ 1834 rectory retaining original character, a short walk from the beach. Individually furnished bedrooms boast antique furniture and feature beds. Beautiful gardens. Choice of dishes offered at dinner; locally sourced produce includes their own vegetables and eggs.

---

**KESWICK** – Cumbria – **502** K20 – pop. 4 984 ▯ Great Britain      **21** A2
▶ London 294 mi – Carlisle 31 mi – Kendal 30 mi
ℹ Market Sq. ℰ(017687) 7 26 45, www.keswick.org
🔟 Threlkeld Hall, ℰ(017687) 7 93 24
◉ Derwentwater★ X – Thirlmere (Castlerigg Stone Circle★), E : 1.5 mi X **A**

⌂ **Lairbeck** ⤶
🏠 *Vicarage Hill ⊠ CA12 5QB – ℰ (017687) 73 373*
*– www.lairbeckhotel-keswick.co.uk – Closed Christmas-New Year and restricted opening 9 November-10 March*      X**a**
**14 rm** ⌿ – †£ 61/107 ††£ 126    **Rest** – *(dinner only)* Menu £ 24 s
♦ Attractive Victorian house in the suburbs, its mature garden boasting a huge Sequoia Redwood. Original barley-twist staircase, galleried landing and comfy bar-lounge. Bedrooms come in a mix of styles; some have lovely views. Daily menu in pleasant dining room.

ENGLAND

# KESWICK

ENGLAND

## ✕✕  Morrel's                                    VISA ●● ①

*34 Lake Rd* ⊠ *CA12 5DQ* – ℰ *(017687) 72 666*
– *www.morrels.co.uk*
– *Closed 2 weeks January, 25-26 December and Monday*                Z**x**
**Rest** – *(dinner only)* Carte £ 24/33

♦ Popular local eatery with scrubbed wood flooring, etched glass dividers and
large, colourful canvasses. Seasonally changing dishes have subtle Mediterranean
influences; some come in two sizes.

---

KESWICK

**at Braithwaite** West : 2 mi by A 66 - X - on B 5292 – ⊠ Keswick

**Cottage in the Wood** ⌖
*Magic Hill, Whinlatter Forest, Northwest : 1.75 mi on B 5292 ⊠ CA12 5TW – ℰ (017687) 78 409 – www.thecottageinthewood.co.uk – Closed January*
**10 rm** – ♦£ 80/90 ♦♦£ 110/180
**Rest** – *(closed Sunday dinner and Monday)* Menu £ 32 (dinner) **s** – Carte lunch approx. £ 19
◆ 17C whitewashed property in mountainside forest, affording excellent views down the valley. Beamed lounge filled with books and ornaments. Bedrooms range from simple, cottage-style to smart with large beds, roll-top baths and views. Local, seasonal cooking in restaurant; airy extension offers superb outlook.

**at Portinscale** West : 1.5 mi by A 66 – ⊠ Keswick

**Swinside Lodge** ⌖
*Newlands, South : 1.5 mi on Grange Rd ⊠ CA12 5UE – ℰ (017687) 72 948 – www.swinsidelodge-hotel.co.uk – Restricted opening January & December*
**7 rm** (dinner included) – ♦£ 124/144 ♦♦£ 248/296          X**c**
**Rest** – *(dinner only) (booking essential for non-residents)* Menu £ 45 **s**
◆ Immaculately whitewashed house in countryside location, boasting lovely views over the fells. Local info in reception. Two small, traditional country house lounges filled with books and antiques. Bedrooms are more modern in style. Formal, linen-laid dining room offers classical daily menus and house party atmosphere.

**KETTLESING** – North Yorkshire – **502** P21 – see Harrogate

**KETTLEWELL** – North Yorkshire – **502** N21 – pop. 297          **22** A2
▶ London 246 mi – Darlington 42 mi – Harrogate 30 mi – Lancaster 42 mi

**Littlebeck** without rest
*The Grn., take turning at the Old Smithy shop by the bridge ⊠ BD23 5RD – ℰ (01756) 760 378 – www.little-beck.co.uk*
**3 rm** – ♦£ 50 ♦♦£ 78
◆ Neatly kept house in fresh, neutral tones. Large, book-filled lounge with wood burning stove; rear terrace overlooks stream. Comfy, unfussy bedrooms boast lovely views. Aga-cooked breakfasts.

**KEYSTON** – Cambridgeshire – **504** S26 – pop. 257 – ⊠ Huntingdon          **14** A2
▶ London 75 mi – Cambridge 29 mi – Northampton 24 mi

**Pheasant**
*Village Loop Rd. ⊠ PE28 0RE – ℰ (01832) 710 241 – www.thepheasant-keyston.co.uk*
**Rest** – *(booking essential)* Menu £ 22 (lunch) – Carte £ 28/40 ⌖
◆ Charming thatched 'destination dining' pub set in a sleepy hamlet. Seasonal daily menu features both the classics and some more international flavours – and a good selection of offal.

**KIBWORTH BEAUCHAMP** – Leicestershire – **504** Q/R26          **16** B2
– pop. 3 550 – ⊠ Leicester
▶ London 85 mi – Birmingham 49 mi – Leicester 6 mi – Northampton 17 mi

**Firenze**
*9 Station St ⊠ LE8 0LN – ℰ (0116) 279 62 60 – www.firenze.co.uk – Closed 1 week Christmas-New Year, Sunday, Monday and bank holidays*
**Rest** – Italian – *(booking essential)* Menu £ 23 (weekdays) – Carte £ 23/40
◆ Smart neighbourhood restaurant displaying colourful modern fabrics and Mediterranean artwork. Extensive à la carte and tasting menus offer authentic Italian dishes; good value lunch.

ENGLAND

## KIBWORTH HARCOURT Leics. – Leicestershire – **504** R26      **16** B2

▶ London 101 mi – Leicester 9 mi – Coventry 36 mi – Nottingham 41 mi

X    **Boboli**           ⌂ AC P VISA ⓪
*88 Main St ⊠ LE8 0NQ – ℰ (0116) 279 33 03 – www.bobolirestaurant.co.uk*
*– Closed 25-26 December*
**Rest** – Italian – Menu £ 17 (lunch) – Carte £ 19/35
♦ Stylish Italian restaurant named after gardens in Florence. Fresh, simple and seasonally-changing cooking with bold flavours. Affordable wines and cheery, prompt service.

## KIDDERMINSTER – Worcestershire – **503** N26 – pop. 55 348      **18** B2

▶ London 139 mi – Birmingham 17 mi – Shrewsbury 34 mi – Worcester 15 mi

### at Chaddesley Corbett Southeast : 4.5 mi by A 448 – ⊠ Kidderminster

🏠    **Brockencote Hall** 🌿     ≤ ⇆ ♨ ⌘ & ⚘ ☏ 🔊 P VISA ⓪ AE ⓪
*on A 448 ⊠ DY10 4PY – ℰ (01562) 777 876 – www.brockencotehall.com*
**17 rm** ⌣ – ♥£ 96 ♥♥£ 190
**Rest** *Restaurant* – see restaurant listing
♦ Keenly run, 19C mansion with long driveway leading past a lake, croquet lawn and grazing sheep. Classic guest areas. Spacious, well-equipped bedrooms: some in annexe; some with great park views.

XXX    **Restaurant** – at Brockencote Hall Hotel     ≤ ⇆ P VISA ⓪ AE ⓪
*on A 448 ⊠ DY10 4PY – ℰ (01562) 777 876 – www.brockencotehall.com*
**Rest** – Menu £ 26/40 **s** – Carte £ 45/55 **s**
♦ Well-run restaurant with cocktail bar and conservatory. Large, airy dining room with French windows opening onto a terrace. Skilfully prepared, flavoursome modern dishes have a classical base.

## KILHAM – East Riding of Yorkshire – **502** S21      **23** D2

▶ London 225 mi – Leeds 63 mi – Sheffield 75 mi – Manchester 108 mi

🏠    **Kilham Hall** 🌿        ⇆ ⌘ ⚘ ☏ 🔊 P VISA ⓪ AE
*Driffield Rd, South : 0.25 mi ⊠ YO25 4SP – ℰ (01262) 420 466*
*– www.kilhamhall.co.uk – March-October*
**3 rm** ⌣ – ♥£ 100/110 ♥♥£ 120/170    **Rest** – Menu £ 33
♦ Attractive Victorian house with croquet lawn, tennis court and small heated pool. Stylish guest areas boast heavy fabrics and bespoke furniture; spacious bedrooms mix the modern and classic. Charming owner offers homemade scones on arrival. Substantial communal breakfasts; home-cooked dinners by arrangement.

Don't confuse the couvert rating X with the stars ✿ !
Couverts defines comfort and service, while stars are awarded for the best cuisine across all categories of comfort.

## KINGHAM – Oxfordshire – **503** P28 – pop. 1 434      **10** A1

▶ London 81 mi – Gloucester 32 mi – Oxford 25 mi

🏠    **Mill House** 🌿        ⇆ ⚓ ⌂ ☏ 🔊 P VISA ⓪ AE ⓪
*⊠ OX7 6UH – ℰ (01608) 658 188 – www.millhousehotel.co.uk*
**23 rm** ⌣ – ♥£ 70/80 ♥♥£ 110/130    **Rest** – Menu £ 18/35 – Carte £ 22/30
♦ Privately run house in 10 acres of lawned gardens with a brook flowing through the grounds. Spacious lounge with comfortable armchairs and books. Comfortable, traditionally styled bedrooms. Modern décor suffuses restaurant.

ENGLAND

ENGLAND

⌂ **Moat End** without rest ⌖ ≤ 🚗 🎇 📶 **P**
*The Moat, by West St* ⌧ *OX7 6XZ* – ℰ *(01608) 658 090* – *www.moatend.co.uk*
– *Closed Christmas and New Year*
**3 rm** ⌱ – 🛏£ 60/70 🛏🛏£ 80
♦ Cosy converted barn with garden, ponies and countryside views; luxury breakfasts include eggs from own hens. Neatly kept, compact rooms. Friendly owner has wealth of local knowledge.

🍴 **Kingham Plough** with rm 🏠 **P** *VISA* ◑◐
*The Green* ⌧ *OX7 6YD* – ℰ *(01608) 658 327* – *www.thekinghamplough.co.uk*
– *Closed 25 December*
**7 rm** ⌱ – 🛏£ 75/130 🛏🛏£ 130
**Rest** – Carte £ 27/40
♦ Rustic, laid-back pub and restaurant located on the green in an unspoilt Cotswold village; run by a friendly team and experienced chef-owner. Menus mix modern, gutsy pub dishes with a few more ambitious offerings, and evolve as new ingredients arrive. Comfy bedrooms await: 2 and 4, in the main building, are best.

🍴 **Tollgate Inn** with rm 🏠 📶 **P** *VISA* ◑◐ **AE**
*Church St* ⌧ *OX7 6YA* – ℰ *(01608) 658 389* – *www.thetollgate.com*
– *Closed Sunday dinner and Monday*
**9 rm** ⌱ – 🛏£ 70/75 🛏🛏£ 100
**Rest** – Carte £ 20/35
♦ Grade II listed inn in centre of unspoiled village. Easy-going lunch menu; more ambitious evening à la carte. Comfy seating and inglenooks, plus popular front terrace. Immaculately kept bedrooms have a warm, bright feel.

**KING'S LYNN** – Norfolk – **502** V25 – **pop. 43 119** ▌ Great Britain **14** B1
▶ London 103 mi – Cambridge 45 mi – Leicester 75 mi – Norwich 44 mi
🛈 Purfleet Quay ℰ *(01553) 76 30 44, www.kingslynnonline.com*
📷 Eagles Tilney All Saints School Rd, ℰ *(01553) 82 71 47*
📷 Houghton Hall★★ **AC**, NE : 14.5 mi by A 148 – Four Fenland
Churches★ (Terrington St Clement, Walpole St Peter, West Walton, Walsoken) SW : by A 47

🏨 **Bankhouse** ≤ 🚗 🎇 📶 *VISA* ◑◐
*King's Staithe Sq* ⌧ *PE30 1RD* – ℰ *(01553) 660 492* – *www.thebankhouse.co.uk*
**11 rm** ⌱ – 🛏£ 80/120 🛏🛏£ 100/150
**Rest** – Carte £ 21/29
♦ Grade II listed Georgian house by the River Ouse. Comfortable bedrooms in various shapes and sizes: all have good facilities and excellent bathrooms; some have a pleasant outlook. Stylish, contemporary bar and brasserie.

**at Grimston** East : 6.25 mi by A 148 – ⌧ King'S Lynn

🏨 **Congham Hall** ⌖ ≤ 🚗 🐾 🏠 🖼 🍴 🐾 🎇 🐕 🏋 **P** *VISA* ◑◐ **AE** ◉
*Lynn Rd.* ⌧ *PE32 1AH* – ℰ *(01485) 600 250*
– *www.conghamhallhotel.co.uk*
**13 rm** ⌱ – 🛏£ 106/185 🛏🛏£ 135/395 – 1 suite
**Rest** *Orangery* – Menu £ 22 – Carte £ 41/49
♦ Part-Georgian country house with neat lawns and formal flower garden. Comfy lounges and small bar with terrace. Well-appointed bedrooms offer pleasant views. Currently undergoing an extension project. Good service from smartly attired staff. Restaurant offers classical menu; kitchen and herb garden produce features.

**KINGS MILLS** – see Channel Islands (Guernsey)

**KINGSBRIDGE** – Devon – **503** I33 – **pop. 5 521**                                              2 C3

▣ London 236 mi – Exeter 36 mi – Plymouth 24 mi – Torquay 21 mi
🔝 Thurlestone, ✆(01548) 56 04 05
◉ Town★ – Boat Trip to Salcombe★★ **AC**
◩ Prawle Point (≤★★★) SE : 10 mi around coast by A 379

**at Goveton** Northeast : 2.5 mi by A 381 – ✉ Kingsbridge

🏨       **Buckland-Tout-Saints** ⚲                    ≤ 🚗 🏡 ⁖⁖ ⚒ 𝐏 ᴠɪꜱᴀ ⯑ 🄰🄴
*Goveton, Northeast : 2.5 mi by A 381 ✉ TQ7 2DS – ✆(01548) 853 055*
*– www.tout-saints.co.uk – Closed 3-19 January*
**14 rm** ☐ – †£ 125/205 ††£ 165/205 – 2 suites
**Rest** – Menu £ 20/39
♦ Immaculate, impressive Queen Anne mansion with neat lawned gardens in rural location. Wood panelled lounge; all other areas full of antiques. Well-furnished bedrooms. Accomplished cooking in beautiful wood-panelled country
house restaurant.

---

**KINGSKERSWELL** – Devon – **503** J32 – **pop. 4 624** – ✉ Torquay                 2 C2

▣ London 199 mi – Exeter 18 mi – Torquay 4 mi

🍴       **Bickley Mill Inn** with rm                    🚗 🏡 ⁒ ⁖⁖ ⚒ 𝐏 ᴠɪꜱᴀ ⯑ 🄰🄴
*Stoneycombe, West : 2 mi by Stoneycombe rd. ✉ TQ12 5LN – ✆(01803) 873 201*
*– www.bickleymill.co.uk – Closed 23-30 December*
**12 rm** ☐ – †£ 65/85 ††£ 80/130
**Rest** – Carte £ 18/25
♦ Modern-looking former flour mill with huge decked terrace and gardens built
into the rocks. Menus are simple, traditional and keenly priced; Brixham market
fish features in the specials. Individually designed bedrooms are bold and stylish;
two are in the eaves.

---

**KINGSTON BAGPUIZE** – Oxfordshire – **503** P28 – see Oxford

---

**KINGSTON-UPON-HULL** – Kingston upon Hull – **502** S22                           23 D2
– **pop. 265 615** 📗 Great Britain

▣ London 183 mi – Leeds 61 mi – Nottingham 94 mi – Sheffield 68 mi
**Access** Humber Bridge (toll)
🛫 Humberside Airport : ✆(01652) 688456, S : 19 mi by A 63
🚢 to The Netherlands (Rotterdam) (P & O North Sea Ferries) daily (11 h) – to Belgium
(Zeebrugge) (P & O North Sea Ferries) 3-4 weekly (13 h 45 mn)
🛈 1 Paragon St ✆(01482) 22 35 59, www.hull.touristinformationguide.co.uk
🔝 Springhead Park Willerby Rd, ✆(01482) 65 63 09
🔝 Sutton Park Salthouse Rd, ✆(01482) 37 42 42
◩ Burton Constable★ **AC**, NE : 9 mi by A 165 and B 1238 Z

*Plan on next page*

✗       **Boars Nest**                                                ᴠɪꜱᴀ ⯑ 🄰🄴 ⓞ
*22-24 Princes Ave, Northwest : 1 mi by Ferensway off West Spring Bank Rd*
*✉ HU5 3QA – ✆(01482) 445 577 – www.theboarsnesthull.com*            **Z**x
**Rest** – Menu £ 12/23 – Carte £ 20/28
♦ Rustic restaurant, formerly part-butcher's shop, with tiles/meats hooks still in
situ. 3 main dining areas and upstairs lounge. Simple, classical English dishes use
local, seasonal produce.

**at Hessle** Southwest : 2 mi by A 63 – ✉ Kingston-Upon-Hull

✗✗✗       **Artisan**                                                ᴠɪꜱᴀ ⯑ 🄰🄴
*22 The Weir ✉ HU13 0RU – ✆(01482) 644 906 – www.artisanrestaurant.com*
*– Closed first 2 weeks January, Sunday and bank holiday Mondays*
**Rest** – (dinner only) (booking essential) (lunch by arrangement) Menu £ 50
♦ Intimate restaurant with plush, homely interior, run by a passionate husband
and wife team. Classical French and Italian influenced set menus with local ingredients to the fore.

261

ENGLAND

# KINGSTON-UPON-HULL

**CENTRE**

**BUILT UP AREA**

**KINGSWEAR** – Devon – **503** J32 – see Dartmouth

**KINGTON** – Herefordshire – **503** K27 – pop. 2 597                    **18** A3
▶ London 152 mi – Birmingham 61 mi – Hereford 19 mi – Shrewsbury 54 mi

**at Titley** Northeast : 3.5 mi on B 4355 – ✉ Kington

🕇🗋  **The Stagg Inn** (Steve Reynolds) with rm          🚗 🛆 **P** **VISA** **©©** **AE**
 ✿  ✉ HR5 3RL – 𝒞 (01544) 230 221 – www.thestagg.co.uk – Closed 2 weeks
    between January and February, first 2 weeks in November, 25-26
    December, Sunday dinner and Monday
    **6 rm** ⚏ – 🕇£ 65/70 🕇🕇£ 100/150    **Rest** – (booking essential) Carte £ 29/34
    **Spec.** Scallops and parsnip purée. Fillet of beef with garlic butter. 3 crème brûlées
    of vanilla, elderflower and lemon.
    ♦ Part-medieval, part-Victorian pub with delightfully cosy interior. Straightforward
    cooking uses classically based recipes and relies on careful preparation and top
    quality produce. Menus are short, simple and to the point; dishes are truly satisfy-
    ing. Bedrooms in the pub can be noisy; opt for one in the old vicarage.

**KIRKBY FLEETHAM** – North Yorkshire – **502** P20 – pop. 556          **22** B1
▶ London 234 mi – Liverpool 124 mi – Leeds 53 mi – Sheffield 84 mi

🕇🗋  **Black Horse Inn** with rm          🚗 🛆 ✿ ⑼ **P** **VISA** **©©** **①**
    Lumley Ln ✉ DL7 0SH – 𝒞 (01609) 749 010
    – www.blackhorsekirkbyfleetham.com
    **7 rm** ⚏ – 🕇£ 75 🕇🕇£ 75    **Rest** – (closed Sunday dinner) Carte £ 21/32
    ♦ Subtly modernised 18C pub with original beams, smart new flagged floor, can-
    dlelit bar and rear dining room. Menu ranges from tasty sharing boards to fla-
    voursome British classics that are a step above your usual pub fare. Stylish bed-
    rooms come with good comforts and designer bathrooms.

**KIRKBY LONSDALE** – Cumbria – **502** M21 – pop. 2 076          **21** B3
– ✉ Carnforth (lancs.)
▶ London 259 mi – Carlisle 62 mi – Kendal 13 mi – Lancaster 17 mi
🏌 Scaleber Lane Barbon, 𝒞 (015242) 7 63 66
🏌 Casterton Sedbergh Rd, 𝒞 (015242) 7 15 92

🗙🗙  **Hipping Hall** with rm          🚗 ♿ rm, **P** **VISA** **©©**
    Southeast : 2.5 mi on A 65 ✉ LA6 2JJ – 𝒞 (015242) 71 187
    – www.hippinghall.com – Closed 2-5 January
    **9 rm** (dinner included) ⚏ – 🕇£ 248 🕇🕇£ 330
    **Rest** – (dinner only and lunch Saturday-Sunday) Menu £ 30/50
    ♦ Charming part-15/16C house set in mature grounds; with attractive medieval-
    style restaurant, minstrels gallery and well-spaced tables laid with quality table-
    ware. Concise, modern menus; polite service. Comfy, boldly papered lounges
    and well-appointed, stark white bedrooms featuring thick carpets and modern
    bathrooms.

🕇🗋  **Sun Inn** with rm          **VISA** **©©**
    6 Market St ✉ LA6 2AU – 𝒞 (015242) 71 965 – www.sun-inn.info – Closed
    Monday lunch
    **11 rm** ⚏ – 🕇£ 72/92 🕇🕇£ 102/154
    **Rest** – Menu £ 20 (lunch) – Carte £ 29/34
    ♦ 17C inn in busy market town with lively locals bar and rustically refurbished
    restaurant. Tempting bar nibbles and tasty, seasonal dishes made with locally
    sourced produce. Good quality linen in modern, immaculately kept bedrooms.

**at Lupton** Northwest : 4.75 mi on A 65 – **502** L21

🕇🗋  **Plough** with rm          🛆 **P** **VISA** **©©** **AE**
    Cow Brow ✉ LA6 1PJ – 𝒞 (015395) 67 700 – www.theploughatlupton.co.uk
    **5 rm** – 🕇£ 100/140 🕇🕇£ 115/195, ⚏ £ 7.50    **Rest** – Carte £ 18/29
    ♦ Homely pub with antique tables and comfy sofas, set on the main road from
    the Lake District to North Yorkshire. Choose grills or a selection of small plates
    to mix and match with enticing sides. Smart, individually styled bedrooms com-
    plete the picture.

ENGLAND

**KIRKBY STEPHEN** – Cumbria – **502** M20 – pop. 1 832         **21** B2

▶ London 296 mi – Carlisle 46 mi – Darlington 37 mi – Kendal 28 mi

  🏠    **Augill Castle** ⌖       ≤ 🚗 🐾 ✕ ℅ 🛜 **P** **VISA** ⓪ **AE**
        *Northeast : 4.5 mi by A 685* ✉ *CA17 4DE* – ℰ *(01768) 341 937*
        *– www.stayinacastle.com*
        **12 rm** ⌕ – †£ 80/100 ††£ 180   **Rest** – *(dinner only)* Menu £ 40
        ♦ Carefully restored Victorian folly in neo-Gothic style with extensive gardens; fine antiques and curios abound. Comfy music room and library. Individually decorated bedrooms. Expansive dining room with ornate ceiling and Spode tableware.

**at Ravenstonedale** Southwest : 5 mi by A 685

  🍴    **Black Swan** with rm       🚗 🛋 ✕ & **P** **VISA** ⓪
        ✉ *CA17 4NG* – ℰ *(01539) 623 204 – www.blackswanhotel.com – Closed 25 December*
        **15 rm** ⌕ – †£ 60/125 ††£ 75/125   **Rest** – Carte £ 18/29
        ♦ Set in a remote village, a part-Victorian, family-run pub with a huge garden and babbling beck. Menus feature filling pub classics, supplemented by restaurant-style specials in the evening. Cosy, antique-furnished bedrooms; one is more modern and boasts a four-poster.

**KIRKBYMOORSIDE** – North Yorkshire – **502** R21 – pop. 2 595     **23** C1

▶ London 244 mi – Leeds 61 mi – Scarborough 26 mi – York 33 mi

🏌 Manor Vale, ℰ (01751) 43 15 25

  🏠    **Brickfields Farm** without rest ⌖       🚗 ℅ 🛜 **P** **VISA** ⓪
        *Kirby Mills, East : 0.75 mi by A 170 on Kirby Mills Industrial Estate rd*
        ✉ *YO62 6NS* – ℰ *(01751) 433 074 – www.brickfieldsfarm.co.uk*
        **7 rm** ⌕ – †£ 125 ††£ 125
        ♦ Attractive red-brick farmhouse with most of its bedrooms in converted outbuildings; one boasts a four-poster. Simple, modern comforts and traditional character. Conservatory breakfast room.

  🏠    **Cornmill** without rest       🚗 🐾 & ℅ 🛜 **P** **VISA** ⓪
        *Kirby Mills, East : 0.5 mi by A 170* ✉ *YO62 6NP* – ℰ *(01751) 432 000*
        *– www.kirbymills.co.uk*
        **5 rm** ⌕ – †£ 55/75 ††£ 100/105
        ♦ Charming 18C cornmill with pleasant courtyard. Spacious, rustic bedrooms set in the old farmhouse and stables. Characterful dining room with mill race running beneath a glass panel.

**KIRKWHELPINGTON** – Northumberland – **501** N/O18 – pop. 353     **24** A2
– ✉ **Morpeth** ▌ Great Britain

▶ London 305 mi – Carlisle 46 mi – Newcastle upon Tyne 20 mi

◀ Wallington House★ **AC**, E : 3.5 mi by A 696 and B 6342

  🏠    **Shieldhall** ⌖       🚗 🛋 ✕ 🛜 **P** **VISA** ⓪
  🍴    *Wallington, Southeast : 2.5 mi by A 696 on B 6342* ✉ *NE61 4AQ* – ℰ *(01830) 540 387 – www.shieldhallguesthouse.co.uk – Closed Christmas-New Year*
        **4 rm** ⌕ – †£ 60/78 ††£ 96   **Rest** – Menu £ 28
        ♦ Early 17C farmhouse and outbuildings, where Capability Brown's uncle once lived. Mix of rustic and country house guest areas; library-lounge boasts garden views. Individually styled bedrooms, with furniture handmade by the owner. Beamed, flag-floored dining room offers classical British dishes and Aga-cooked breakfasts.

**KIRTLINGTON** – Oxfordshire – **503** Q28         **10** B2

▶ London 70 mi – Bicester 11 mi – Oxford 16 mi

  🏠    **Dashwood**       & rm, ℅ 📶 **P** **VISA** ⓪ **AE** ⓪
        *South Green, Heyford Rd* ✉ *OX5 3HJ* – ℰ *(01869) 352 707*
        *– www.thedashwood.co.uk*
        **12 rm** ⌕ – †£ 85 ††£ 115/160   **Rest** – *(closed Sunday)* Carte £ 26/38
        ♦ Grade II listed 16C building in local soft stone. Lounge with comfy leather armchairs. Bedrooms, boasting super contemporary décor, divided between main building and barn. Exposed stone dining room: impressive menus with modern European slant.

ENGLAND

▶ London 217 – Bradford 21 – Harrogate 3 – Leeds 18

◪ Market Pl  ℰ (01423) 86 68 86, www.knaresborough.co.uk

🔟 Boroughbridge Rd,  ℰ (01423) 86 26 90

🏠     **Newton House** without rest     (📶) **P** 𝗩𝗜𝗦𝗔 ◍◍
*5-7 York Pl* ✉ *HG5 0AD* – ℰ *(01423) 863 539* – *www.newtonhouseyorkshire.com*
*– Closed 1 week Christmas*
**11 rm** ⬜ – 🛏 £ 55/85  🛏🛏 £ 95/120
♦ Extended mid-18C house boasts homely lounge with soft suites and smart, comfortable, individually decorated bedrooms; those on the first floor and in the annexe are larger.

**at Ferrensby** Northeast : 3 mi on A 6055

🍴🛏     **General Tarleton Inn** with rm     🏂 (📶) 🔥 **P** 𝗩𝗜𝗦𝗔 ◍◍ 𝗔𝗘
(😊)  *Boroughbridge Rd* ✉ *HG5 0PZ* – ℰ *(01423) 340 284* – *www.generaltarleton.co.uk*
**13 rm** ⬜ – 🛏 £ 75/137  🛏🛏 £ 129/150     **Rest** – Carte £ 25/36
♦ This 18C coaching inn has several dining areas inside and out. The menu has a strong seasonal Yorkshire base and features well-priced, tasty dishes and classics aplenty. Bedrooms are comfortable and well-kept.

**at Coneythorpe** Northeast : 4.75 mi by A 59

🍴🛏     **Tiger Inn**     🚲 🛏 **P** 𝗩𝗜𝗦𝗔 ◍◍
✉ *HG5 0RY* – ℰ *(01423) 863 632* – *www.tiger-inn.co.uk* – *Closed 25 December*
**Rest** – *(booking advisable)* Carte £ 20/30
♦ Popular, family-owned pub with bustling atmosphere, particularly in the front bar. Monthly changing menu of pub classics, supplemented by fish specials; hearty, substantial cooking.

**KNOWSTONE** – Devon – see South Molton

▶ London 187 mi – Chester 25 mi – Liverpool 33 mi – Manchester 18 mi

◪ Toft Rd  ℰ (01565) 63 26 11, www.virtual-knutsford.co.uk

🍴🍴     **Belle Epoque Brasserie** with rm     🛏 (📞) 𝗩𝗜𝗦𝗔 ◍◍ 𝗔𝗘 ◐
*60 King St* ✉ *WA16 6DT* – ℰ *(01565) 633 060* – *www.thebelleepoque.com*
**7 rm** ⬜ – 🛏 £ 95  🛏🛏 £ 115
**Rest** – *(closed Sunday dinner)* Menu £ 18 – Carte £ 26/56
♦ Bustling brasserie with art nouveau décor. Traditional and modern dishes with international touches use local produce. Contemporary style bedrooms boast modern facilities.

**at Mobberley** Northeast : 2.5 mi by A 537 on B 5085 – ✉ Knutsford

🏠     **Hinton** without rest     🚲 🏂 (📶) **P** 𝗩𝗜𝗦𝗔 ◍◍ 𝗔𝗘 ◐
*Town Lane, on B 5085* ✉ *WA16 7HH* – ℰ *(01565) 873 484*
*– www.thehinton.co.uk*
**6 rm** ⬜ – 🛏 £ 53  🛏🛏 £ 65
♦ Welcoming cream-washed guesthouse on the main road through the village. Traditional sitting room with velvet sofas. Comfy, well-kept bedrooms have a homely style and offer good facilities.

**at Lower Peover** Southwest : 3.25 mi by A 50 on B 5081

🍴🛏     **Bells of Peover**     🚲 🛏 **P** 𝗩𝗜𝗦𝗔 ◍◍ 𝗔𝗘
*The Cobbles* ✉ *WA16 9PZ* – ℰ *(01565) 722 269*
**Rest** – Carte £ 21/42
♦ Refurbished 16C former coaching inn whose regulars once included Generals Eisenhower and Patton. Offers a range of options: from appealing snacks in the bar, to 'fine dining' upstairs.

ENGLAND

**at Lach Dennis** Southwest : 7 mi by A 50 and B 5081 on B 5082 – ⊠ Knutsforc

⌂ **Duke of Portland**     🚗 🛋 P VISA ⑳ AE ⓪

*Penny's Ln ⊠ CW9 8SY – ℰ (01606) 46 264 – www.dukeofportland.com*
**Rest** – Menu £ 17 – Carte £ 19/30
♦ Village inn on main road; most popular place to dine is smart, contemporary
room housing stag's head. Lengthy menu offers simply prepared dishes of carefully sourced, local produce.

---

**KYNASTON** – Herefordshire – see Ledbury

---

**LACH DENNIS** – Cheshire West and Chester – see Knutsford

---

**LACOCK** – Wiltshire – **503** N29 – pop. 1 068 – ⊠ Chippenham     4 C2
▶ London 109 mi – Bath 16 mi – Bristol 30 mi – Chippenham 3 mi
◉ Village★★ - Lacock Abbey★ **AC** – High St★, St Cyriac★, Fox Talbot Museum of
Photography★ **AC**

⌂ **At The Sign of the Angel**     🚗 🛋 📶 P VISA ⑳ AE

*6 Church St ⊠ SN15 2LB – ℰ (01249) 730 230 – www.lacock.co.uk – Closed
25-28 December*
**11 rm** 🛏 – †£ 85 ††£ 129/159
**Rest** – *(closed Monday lunch except bank holidays)* Menu £ 19/23
– Carte £ 27/35
♦ Delightful 15C inn with beamed ceilings and open fires, located in charming
15C National Trust village. Traditional, antique-furnished bedrooms offer modern
amenities; Room 5 is particularly pleasant and light. Classic country cooking uses
home-grown produce.

---

**LA HAULE** – **503** L33 – see Channel Islands (Jersey)

---

**LAMBOURN WOODLANDS** – West Berkshire     10 A3
▶ London 70 mi – Birmingham 112 mi – Bristol 59 mi – Cardiff 92 mi

✖✖ **Hare**     🛋 ♻ P VISA ⑳ AE

*Ermin St ⊠ RG17 7SD – ℰ (01488) 71 386 – www.theharerestaurant.co.uk*
**Rest** – *(booking essential)* Menu £ 28 *(lunch)* – Carte £ 30/40
♦ Extended red-brick former pub with terrace, gazebo and chicken coop. Small
bar, lounge and three smart dining areas with long banquettes. Daytime snack
menu supplements set menus and an evening à la carte. Classical, country
house cooking.

---

**LANCASTER** – Lancashire – **502** L21 – pop. 45 952 ⃞ Great Britain     20 A1
▶ London 252 mi – Blackpool 26 mi – Bradford 62 mi – Burnley 44 mi
🛈 Meeting House Lane ℰ (01524) 58 23 94, www.visitlancashire.com
🏰 Ashton Hall Ashton-with-Stodday, ℰ (01524) 75 20 90
⛳ Lansil Caton Rd, ℰ (01524) 3 92 69
◉ Castle★ **AC**

⌂ **Ashton**     🚗 🛋 📶 P VISA ⑳

*Wyresdale Rd, Southeast : 1.25 mi by A 6 on Clitheroe rd ⊠ LA1 3JJ – ℰ (01524,
68 460 – www.theashtonlancaster.com*
**5 rm** 🛏 – †£ 98/128 ††£ 128/175     **Rest** – Menu £ 35 **s**
♦ Georgian house in lawned gardens; personally run by friendly owner. Good-
sized bedrooms are decorated in bold colours and feature a blend of modern
and antique furniture. Small, informal dining room; home-cooked comfort food
makes good use of local produce.

⌂ **Borough**     🚗 AC VISA ⑳

*3 Dalton Sq ⊠ LA1 1PP – ℰ (01524) 64 170 – www.theboroughlancaster.co.uk
– Closed 25 December*
**Rest** – Carte £ 19/32
♦ Characterful pub set on cobbled square. Hearty, filling dishes use regional pro-
duce; DIY deli boards are popular. Local bitters and some unusual bottled beers
Regular comedy nights.

ENGLAND

## LANGAR – Nottinghamshire – **502** R25 16 B2

▶ London 132 mi – Boston 45 mi – Leicester 25 mi – Lincoln 37 mi

**Langar Hall** ⌂ ≤ ⌖ ⏚ ⥾ ⌘ ⌾ 🛜 **P** 𝘝𝘐𝘚𝘈 ⓿

✉ NG13 9HG – ☎ (01949) 860 559 – www.langarhall.co.uk
**11 rm** ⚏ – ✝£ 95/140 ✝✝£ 185/195 – 1 suite
**Rest** – Menu £ 25/30 – Carte £ 33/41

◆ Georgian manor in pastoral setting, next to early English church; overlooks park, medieval fishponds. Antique filled rooms named after people featuring in house's history. Elegant, candlelit, pillared dining room.

## LANGHO – Lancashire – **502** M22 – see Blackburn

## LANGPORT – Somerset – **503** L30 – pop. 2 851 3 B3

▶ London 134 mi – Weston-super-Mare 31 mi – Taunton 15 mi – Yeovil 16 mi

**Parsonage** ⏚ ⌾ 🛜 **P** 𝘝𝘐𝘚𝘈 ⓿ 𝘈𝘌

*Mulchelney, South : 2 mi on Muchelney Pottery rd* ✉ TA10 0DL – ☎ (01458) *259 058 – www.parsonagesomerset.co.uk – Closed Christmas and New Year*
**3 rm** ⚏ – ✝£ 53 ✝✝£ 95    **Rest** – Menu £ 30

◆ Traditional Somerset longhouse in charming setting with airy, well-kept country bedrooms and lovely rear garden. Delightful hosts dine with their guests at family style meals crafted from fresh, local ingredients. Al fresco breakfast in summer.

## LANGTHWAITE – North Yorkshire – **502** O20 – see Reeth

## LA PULENTE – **503** P33 – see Channel Islands (Jersey)

## LAPWORTH – Warwickshire – pop. 2 100 19 C2

▶ London 108 mi – Birmingham 23 mi – Leicester 47 mi – Coventry 19 mi

**Boot Inn** ⏚ ⌖ **P** 𝘝𝘐𝘚𝘈 ⓿

*Old Warwick Rd* ✉ B94 6JU – ☎ (01564) 782 464 – www.bootinnlapworth.co.uk *– Closed dinner 25 December and dinner 1 January*
**Rest** – *(booking essential)* Menu £ 16 (weekdays) – Carte £ 26/38

◆ Buzzy large red-brick pub close to the M40, boasting a large terrace, traditional bar and modern first floor restaurant. Dishes vary from simple bar snacks to sophisticated specials and sharing plates.

## LASKILL – North Yorkshire – **502** Q21 – see Hawnby

## LASTINGHAM – North Yorkshire – **502** R21 – pop. 87 – ✉ York 23 C1

▶ London 244 mi – Scarborough 26 mi – York 32 mi

**Lastingham Grange** ⌂ ⏚ ⥾ ⌖ ⌾ **P** 𝘝𝘐𝘚𝘈 ⓿

✉ YO62 6TH – ☎ (01751) 417 345 – www.lastinghamgrange.com *– March-November*
**11 rm** ⚏ – ✝£ 95/135 ✝✝£ 150/200
**Rest** – Menu £ 40 (dinner) – Carte lunch £ 25/34

◆ A delightfully traditional country house atmosphere prevails throughout this extended, pleasantly old-fashioned, 17C farmhouse. Lovely gardens; well-appointed bedrooms. Dining room with rustic fare and rose garden view.

## LAVENHAM – Suffolk – **504** W27 – pop. 1 231 – ✉ Sudbury 15 C3
🏛 Great Britain

▶ London 66 mi – Cambridge 39 mi – Colchester 22 mi – Ipswich 19 mi
🛈 Lady St ☎ (01787) 24 82 07, www.discoverlavenham.co.uk
◉ Town★★ – Church of St Peter and St Paul★

**Swan** ⏚ ⌖ 🄰🄲 rest, 🛜 ⌖🄰 **P** 𝘝𝘐𝘚𝘈 ⓿ 𝘈𝘌

*High St* ✉ CO10 9QA – ☎ (01787) 247 477 – www.theswanatlavenham.co.uk
**42 rm** (dinner included) ⚏ – ✝£ 130/180 ✝✝£ 250 – 3 suites
**Rest** *Gallery* – Menu £ 22/36 **s** – Carte dinner £ 41/50 **s**

◆ Characterful, 15C former coaching inn with superbly atmospheric baronial bar. Beamed, individually decorated bedrooms boast a subtle contemporary style. The Gallery, with its timbered roof and minstrels' gallery, offers a modern British menu. Live piano at weekends.

ENGLAND

⌂ **Lavenham Priory** without rest   ⌚ ☝ ⁅♙ *P* *VISA* ⓪

*Water St. ⊠ CO10 9RW – ℰ (01787) 247 404 – www.lavenhampriory.co.uk*
*– Closed Christmas-New Year*
**6 rm** ⌂ – ♦£ 92 ♦♦£ 166

◆ Part-13C, Grade I listed priory in a historic town, with gorgeous garden and mini parterre. Characterful interior features a vast inglenook fireplace, Elizabethan murals and a Jacobean staircase. Cosy lounge and atmospheric dining room. Heavily beamed bedrooms with feature beds and roll-top or slipper baths.

XXX **Great House** with rm   ⌂ ☝ *VISA* ⓪

*Market Pl. ⊠ CO10 9QZ – ℰ (01787) 247 431 – www.greathouse.co.uk – Closed 3 weeks January, 2 weeks summer, Sunday dinner, Monday and lunch Tuesday*
**3 rm** – ♦£ 95 ♦♦£ 155/195, ⌂ £ 15 – 2 suites
**Rest** – French – Menu £ 21 (weekday lunch) – Carte dinner £ 32/46

◆ Impressive Georgian façade conceals 14C timbered house with eye-catching modern art and heated rear terrace. Classical French cooking displays modern twists. Service is well-paced and attentive. Contemporary, country house bedrooms boast old beams and modern hues.

## LAWHITTON – Cornwall   2 C2

▶ London 221 mi – Bristol 136 mi – Cardiff 156 mi – Plymouth 26 mi

⌂ **Primrose Cottage** without rest ⌰   ⟨ ⌚ ⟩ ☝ ⁅♙ *P* *VISA* ⓪

*Southeast : 1.25 mi on B 3362 ⊠ PL15 9PE – ℰ (01566) 773 645*
*– www.primrosecottagesuites.co.uk – Closed Christmas*
**3 rm** ⌂ – ♦£ 70/90 ♦♦£ 110/130

◆ Part-18C house with friendly owner and lovely gardens leading down to the river. Good-sized bedrooms boast their own entrances, separate sitting rooms and afford great country views. Complimentary wine and homemade cakes; light suppers available in your room.

## LEDBURY – Herefordshire – **503** M27 – pop. 8 491   18 B3

▶ London 119 mi – Hereford 14 mi – Newport 46 mi – Worcester 16 mi

🛏 **Feathers**   ⌂ ▭ ⁅ (◐ ⁅◓ *P* *VISA* ⓪ *AE* ⓪

*High St ⊠ HR8 1DS – ℰ (01531) 635 266 – www.feathers-ledbury.co.uk*
**19 rm** ⌂ – ♦£ 125 ♦♦£ 235 – 3 suites
**Rest** *Quills* – (dinner only Friday-Saturday and lunch Sunday) Menu £ 22 (dinner) – Carte £ 24/36
**Rest** *Fuggles* – Menu £ 22 (dinner) – Carte £ 24/36

◆ Modernised 16C black and white timbered coaching inn; a clever blend of old and new. Comfortable bedrooms; Lanark House suites more contemporary in style. Linen-clad Quills boasts chandeliers. Fuggles is more informal. Modern, seasonally changing menus.

**at Kynaston** West : 6.5 mi by A 449, A 4172 and Aylton rd on Much Marcle rd.
– ⊠ Ledbury

⌂ **Hall End** without rest ⌰   ⟨ ⌚ ⌰ ⟨ ⌚ ⁅♙ *P*

*⊠ HR8 2PD – ℰ (01531) 670 225 – www.hallendhouse.com – Closed Christmas-New Year*
**3 rm** ⌂ – ♦£ 60 ♦♦£ 100

◆ Lovingly restored, personally run, part Georgian home and livery stable in the countryside. Relax in the orangery and, suitably reposed, retire to lavishly furnished bedrooms.

**at Trumpet** Northwest : 3.25 mi on A 438 – ⊠ Ledbury

🛏 **Verzon House**   ⟨ ⌚ ⌂ ⁅ ☝ *P* *VISA* ⓪ *AE*

*Hereford Rd ⊠ HR8 2PZ – ℰ (01531) 670 381 – www.verzonhouse.com – Closed 2-9 January*
**8 rm** ⌂ – ♦£ 90/135 ♦♦£ 125/170   **Rest** – (light lunch) Carte £ 28/42

◆ Pleasantly restored Georgian house with delightful terrace. Modern bedrooms are named after cider apples; most have countryside views. There is a midweek, set price 4 course Italian menu and an à la carte of modern, mostly English dishes. Tapas only at lunchtime.

# LEEDS

See city maps on following pages

ENGLAND

**West Yorkshire** – **pop. 440 954** – **502** P22 – ▮ Great Britain

▶ London 204 – Liverpool 75 – Manchester 43 – Newcastle upon Tyne 95

**🛈 Tourist Information**

City Station ✆ (0113) 242 52 42, www.visitleeds.co.uk

**Airport**

✈ Leeds-Bradford Airport : ✆ (0113) 250 9696, NW : 8 m. by A 65 and A 658 BT

**Golf Courses**

▦ Temple Newsam Halton Temple Newsam Rd, ✆ (0113) 264 56 24
▦ Gotts Park Armley Armley Ridge Rd, ✆ (0113) 234 20 19
▦ Middleton Park Middleton Ring Rd, Beeston Park, ✆ (0113) 270 04 49

**PRACTICAL INFORMATION**

◎ SIGHTS

**In the town :** City★ • Royal Armouries Museum★★★ GZ • City Art Gallery★ **AC** GY**M**

**On the outskirts :** Kirkstall Abbey★ **AC**, NW : 3 mi by A 65 GY • Temple Newsam★ **AC**, E : 5 mi by A 64 and A 63 CU**D**

**In the surrounding area :** Harewood House★★ **AC**, N : 8 mi by A 61 CT • Nostell Priory★, SE : 18 mi by A 61 and A 638 • Yorkshire Sculpture Park★, S : 20 mi by M 1 to junction 38 and 1 mi north off A 637 • Brodsworth Hall★, SE : 25 mi by M 1 to junction 40, A 638 and minor rd (right) in Upton

ENGLAND

LEEDS AND BRADFORD

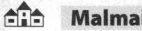

D [A 61] HARROGATE    E

### Malmaison
*1 Swinegate ⊠ LS1 4AG – ℰ (0113) 398 10 00 – www.malmaison.com*
**99 rm** – ✝£ 79/170 ✝✝£ 79/170, � £ 14.50 – 1 suite          GZ**n**
**Rest** – Menu £ 30 (weekdays) – Carte £ 24/38

♦ Relaxed, contemporary hotel hides behind imposing Victorian exterior. Vibrantly and individually decorated rooms are stylishly furnished, with modern facilities to the fore. Dine in modern interpretation of a French brasserie.

### Quebecs without rest
*9 Quebec St ⊠ LS1 2HA – ℰ (0113) 244 89 89 – www.quebechotel.co.uk*
*– Closed 25 December*          FZ**a**
**43 rm** – ✝£ 75/115 ✝✝£ 75/115, ⊆ £ 14.95 – 2 suites

♦ 19C former Liberal Club, now a modish, intimate boutique hotel. Original features include oak staircase and stained glass window depicting Yorkshire cities. Stylish bedrooms.

### 42 The Calls
*42 The Calls ⊠ LS2 7EW – ℰ (0113) 244 00 99 – www.42thecalls.co.uk*
*– Closed 3 days Christmas*          GZ**z**
**38 rm** – ✝£ 85/175 ✝✝£ 125/195, ⊆ £ 15 – 3 suites
**Rest** *Brasserie Forty 4* – see restaurant listing

♦ Converted 18C quayside grain mill retaining many of its original workings. Well-equipped, comfortable bedrooms offer a host of extras; those facing the river are the best.

The sun's out? Then enjoy eating outside on the terrace: 🏡

**LEEDS**

🏠 **New Ellington** 🛗 ⚗ rm, 🅰🄲 ⚗ 🌐 ♨ 𝘝𝘐𝘚𝘈 ⓦ 🄰🄴 ⓓ

*23-25 York Pl.* ⊠ *LS1 2EY –* ℰ *(0113) 204 21 50 – www.thenewellington.com*
*– Closed 25-26 December* **FZx**
**33 rm** – ♦£ 89/125, ♦♦£ 89/125, ☕ £ 11.50 – 1 suite
**Rest** – *(closed Sunday dinner)* Menu £ 19 – Carte dinner £ 29/36

♦ Purpose-built hotel with striking interior. Comfy lounge displays boldly coloured furnishings and is split in two by the cocktail bar. Funky bedrooms boast good facilities and mosaic-tiled bathrooms, and you can borrow ipods and games consoles. Chic, intimate basement brasserie offers modern British cooking.

Prices quoted after the symbol ♦ refer to the lowest rate in low season
followed by the highest rate in high season, for a single room.
The same principle applies to the symbol ♦♦ for a double room.

XXX **Anthony's**                                                    🅰🅲 🆅🅸🆂🅰 ⚙
19 Boar Ln ✉ LS1 6EA – ✆ (0113) 245 59 22 – www.anthonysrestaurant.co.uk
– Closed 25 December-3 January, Sunday and Monday                    GZ**a**
**Rest** – (booking essential) Menu £ 24/45
♦ Family-run, basement restaurant offering immaculately laid tables and formal service from a well-versed team. Creative cooking features modern techniques and some interesting combinations.

XX **Brasserie Forty 4** – at 42 The Calls Hotel      🈂 🅰🅲 🕾 ⇄ 🆅🅸🆂🅰 ⚙ 🅰🅴 ⓪
44 The Calls ✉ LS2 7EW – ✆ (0113) 234 32 32 – www.brasserie44.com – Closed Sunday and bank holidays except Good Friday                         GZ**z**
**Rest** – Carte £ 26/31
♦ Former riverside warehouse with minimalist dining room and stylish bar which exudes atmosphere of buzzy informality. Smokehouse and chargrilled options in an eclectic range of dishes.

XX **Piazza by Anthony**                                          ⇄ 🆅🅸🆂🅰 ⚙
(🈁) The Corn Exchange ✉ LS1 7BR – ✆ (0113) 247 09 95
– www.thefoundrywinebar.co.uk – Closed 25-26 December and 1 January
**Rest** – Carte £ 23/33                                              GZ**b**
♦ Located on the ground floor of the historic former Corn Exchange; large open dining room in the centre, with meeting rooms, private dining areas and artisanal food shops surrounding. Wide-ranging menu of tasty European dishes. Outstanding breads in the bakery.

XX **Foundry**                                                   🈂 🅰🅲 🆅🅸🆂🅰 ⚙
1 Saw Mill Yard, Round Foundry ✉ LS11 5WH – ✆ (0113) 245 03 90
– www.thefoundrywinebar.co.uk – Closed 26 December, Saturday lunch and Sunday
**Rest** – Menu £ 16 (lunch) – Carte £ 20/26                         FZ**b**
♦ Set in a building once joined to the foundry and mills, with vaulted ceiling, ornate bar and French bistro feel. Classical menus feature hearty, robust comfort dishes and extensive daily specials.

XX **Fourth Floor** – at Harvey Nichols            🈂 🅰🅲 🕾 🆅🅸🆂🅰 ⚙ 🅰🅴 ⓪
107-111 Briggate ✉ LS1 6AZ – ✆ (0113) 204 80 00 – www.harveynichols.com
– Closed 25 December, 1 January, Easter Sunday and dinner Sunday-Monday
**Rest** – Menu £ 20 – Carte £ 26/35                                  GZ**s**
♦ Bright, contemporary dining room on the top floor of this chic store; watch the chefs prepare tasty, modern, globally influenced dishes. Pleasant service from a smartly attired team.

---

**LEICESTER** – Leicester – **502** Q26 – **pop. 296 594** ▐ Great Britain      **16** B2
▶ London 107 mi – Birmingham 43 mi – Coventry 24 mi – Nottingham 26 mi
🛫 East Midlands Airport, Castle Donington : ✆ (0871) 9199000 NW : 22 mi by A 50 - AX - and M 1
🇮 7-9 Every St ✆ (0844) 888 51 81, www.goleicestershire.com
🔟 Leicestershire Evington Lane, ✆ (0116) 273 88 25
🔟 Western Park Scudamore Rd, ✆ (0116) 287 52 11
🔟 Humberstone Heights Gipsy Lane, ✆ (0116) 299 55 70
🔟 Oadby Leicester Road Racecourse, ✆ (0116) 270 02 15
🇮9 Blaby Lutterworth Rd, ✆ (0116) 278 48 04
◎ Guildhall ★ BY **B** – Museum and Art Gallery ★ CY **M3** – St Mary de Castro Church ★ BY **D**
🇨 National Space Centre ★ N : 2 mi by A 6 - AX - turning east into Corporation Rd and right into Exploration Drive

Plans on following pages

🏨 **Leicester Marriott**        🖪 🈸 🛌 🈁 🅰🅲 🈺 🕾 🎿 🄿 🆅🅸🆂🅰 ⚙ 🅰🅴 ⓪
Smith Way, Grove Park, Enderby, Southwest : 4 mi by A 5460 off A 563 at junction 21 of M1 ✉ LE19 1SW – ✆ (0116) 282 01 00 – www.leicestermarriott.co.uk
**226 rm** – ♦£ 139 ♦♦£ 139, � £ 15.95 – 1 suite                    AY**z**
**Rest** – (dinner only and Sunday lunch) Menu £ 23 – Carte approx. £ 23
♦ Purpose-built hotel on a suburban business park. Stylish open-plan guest areas include an atrium lounge and informal café in the lobby. Uniform bedrooms boast a good level of facilities. Smart executive lounge and excellent leisure club. East meets West in restaurant; choice of buffet or eclectic à la carte.

## LEICESTER

---

### 🏠 Belmont                    📶 🕭 ⁽ᵗ⁾ 🐕 🅿️ 🚗 VISA ⓜⓞ AE ⓞ

*De Montfort St.* ✉ *LE1 7GR* – ℰ *(0116) 254 47 73* – *www.belmonthotel.co.uk*
– *Closed 26-29 December*                                                    CY**c**
**74 rm** ⬚ – ♦£ 79/99 ♦♦£ 99/109 – 1 suite
**Rest** *Cherry's* – see restaurant listing
♦ Friendly, family-run hotel in a city suburb, made up of a collection of houses
– each with its own classical style. Spacious guest areas and contemporary bar.
Bedrooms vary in shape and size but all are modern and offer good facilities.

### 🏠 Hotel Maiyango                    📶 🕭 AC 🚫 ⁽ᵗ⁾ 🐕 VISA ⓜⓞ AE

*13-21 St. Nicholas Pl* ✉ *LE1 4LD* – ℰ *(0116) 251 88 98* – *www.maiyango.com*
– *Closed 25-26 December*                                                    BY**a**
**13 rm** – ♦£ 163/186 ♦♦£ 163/186, ⬚ £ 7.95 – 1 suite
**Rest** *Maiyango* – see restaurant listing
♦ Privately owned city centre hotel in a 150 year old shoe factory. Stylish interior
with a trendy bar opening onto a terrace overlooking the rooftops. Spacious, individually designed bedrooms boast bespoke wood furniture and a colonial feel.

LEICESTER

## ✗✗ Chutney Ivy

41 Halford Rd ⊠ LE1 1TR – ℰ (0116) 251 1889 – www.chutneyivy.com
– Closed 25-26 December, Saturday lunch and Sunday                    CY**x**

**Rest** – Indian – Menu £ 7/13 – Carte £ 20/39

♦ Keenly run warehouse conversion with smart, industrial feel. Menus mix modern and classical dishes, with influences coming from Hyderabad, Goa and Bengal. Floor-to-ceiling windows open onto the pavement and there's a popular basement bar.

## ✗✗ Maiyango – at Hotel Maiyango

13-21 St. Nicholas Pl ⊠ LE1 4LD – ℰ (0116) 251 88 98 – www.maiyango.com
– Closed 25-26 December                                               BY**a**

**Rest** – (closed Sunday lunch) Menu £ 19/29

♦ Glass-fronted restaurant in a stylish hotel. Dark wood, round booths and silk drapes create a Moorish feel. Refined cooking uses local and allotment produce, and is Mediterranean and Asian-led.

## ✗✗ Cherry's – at Belmont Hotel

De Montfort St. ⊠ LE1 7GR – ℰ (0116) 254 47 73 – www.belmonthotel.co.uk
– Closed 26-29 December, Saturday lunch and Sunday dinner             CY**c**

**Rest** – Menu £ 21 – Carte £ 21/38

♦ Formal restaurant in a friendly, family-run hotel. Wide-ranging menus are classically based; choose from a 3-choice set menu or 4 course à la carte. Seasonal cooking has a Mediterranean edge.

275

X **Boot Room**                                    *VISA* **©©** AE
26-29 Millstone Ln ⊠ LE1 5JN – 𝒞 (0116) 262 25 55
– www.thebootroomeaterie.co.uk – Closed 2 weeks January, 2 weeks
summer, Sunday and Monday                                    BY:
**Rest** – Menu £ 14 (lunch) – Carte £ 20/31
♦ Sizeable restaurant located in former shoe factory, with industrial style, relaxed
ambience and friendly service. Simple, straightforward British cooking with European touches.

## LEIGH-ON-SEA – Southend-on-Sea – 504 W29                    13 C
▶ London 37 mi – Brighton 85 mi – Dover 86 mi – Ipswich 57 mi

XX **Sandbank**                              🛋 AC ⇔ *VISA* ©© AE
1470 London Rd ⊠ SS9 2UR – 𝒞 (01702) 719 000
– www.sandbankrestaurant.co.uk – Closed Sunday dinner and Monday
**Rest** – Menu £ 20 – Carte £ 31/38
♦ Former bank set in parade of shops. Spacious restaurant with small terrace and
bar, high ceilings and intimate lighting. Wide menu of classic '80s cooking displays fresh, neat flavours.

## LETCOMBE REGIS – Oxfordshire – see Wantage

## LEVINGTON – Suffolk                                        15 D.
▶ London 75 mi – Ipswich 5 mi – Woodbridge 8 mi

🏠 **Ship Inn**                                    🛋 P *VISA* ©©
Church Ln ⊠ IP10 0LQ – 𝒞 (01473) 659 573 – www.theshipinnlevington.co.uk
**Rest** – (bookings not accepted) Carte £ 22/31
♦ 14C pub reputedly built from ships' timbers; its small rooms crammed with
nautical memorabilia. Daily changing menu puts its emphasis on local seafood;
rustic, unfussy cooking.

## LEVISHAM – North Yorkshire – 502 R21 – see Pickering

## LEWDOWN – Devon – 503 H32                                  2 C2
▶ London 238 mi – Exeter 37 mi – Plymouth 29 mi
🄲 Lydford★★, E : 4 m. Launceston★ - Castle★ (≤★) St Mary Magdalene★,
W : 8 mi by A 30 and A 388

🏠🏠 **Lewtrenchard Manor** ⑤          🛋 🐾 🌂 🛎 🚶 P *VISA* ©© AE
South : 0.75 mi by Lewtrenchard rd ⊠ EX20 4PN – 𝒞 (01566) 783 222
– www.lewtrenchard.co.uk
**13 rm** 🖃 – ♦£ 175/205 ♦♦£ 275/305 – 1 suite
**Rest** – (booking essential for non-residents) Menu £ 24/51
♦ Historic country house where Jacobean architecture blends with smart, contemporary styling. Characterful main house bedrooms; those in coach house
more modern. Unique private dining concept, Purple Carrot: watch chefs at
work. Traditional dining in formal restaurant; classically based menu utilise
home-grown produce.

## LEWES – East Sussex – 504 U31 – pop. 15 988 ▯ Great Britain     8 A3
▶ London 53 mi – Brighton 8 mi – Hastings 29 mi – Maidstone 43 mi
🅸 187 High St 𝒞 (01273) 48 34 48, www.enjoysussex.info
🅁 Chapel Hill, 𝒞 (01273) 47 32 45
🄾 Town★ (High St★, Keere St★) – Castle (≤★) **AC**
🄲 Sheffield Park Garden★ **AC**, N : 9.5 mi by A 275

🏠🏠 **Shelleys**                              🛋 🛋 📶 🚶 P *VISA* ©©
High St ⊠ BN7 1XS – 𝒞 (01273) 472 361 – www.the-shelleys.co.uk
**18 rm** 🖃 – ♦£ 130/234 ♦♦£ 160/306 – 1 suite
**Rest** – Menu £ 30 (lunch) – Carte £ 36/50
♦ Formerly an inn, and before that, a private house dating back to 1577 – owned
by the great poet's family. Spacious, classically styled bedrooms include a four-
poster and suite with garden views. Smart restaurant overlooks the lawns.

⌂  **Millers** without rest  🚭 ❄ 📶
*134 High St ⊠ BN7 1XS – ☎ (01273) 475 631*
*– www.millersbedandbreakfast.com – Closed 18 December-5 January and*
*4-6 November*
**3 rm** ⚏ – ♦£ 85 ♦♦£ 95
♦ Characterful, small family home in a row of 16C houses that lead to the high street. Appealing personal feel in the individual bedrooms with books, trinkets and knick-knacks.

✗  **Real Eating Company**  🍴 AC VISA ⬤⬤ AE
*18 Cliffe High St ⊠ BN7 2AJ – ☎ (01273) 402 650 – www.real-eating.co.uk*
*– Closed 25 December, Sunday and Monday dinner*
**Rest** – Carte £ 23/34
♦ Light lunches in buzzy atmosphere; more intimate at dinner. Fresh seasonal, local produce cooked in unfussy style to create honest, tasty dishes, including plenty of British favourites.

**at East Chiltington** Northwest : 5.5 mi by A 275 and B 2116 off Novington Lane – ⊠ Lewes

🍴◻  **Jolly Sportsman**  🚭 🍴 AC P VISA ⬤⬤
*Chapel Ln ⊠ BN7 3BA – ☎ (01273) 890 400 – www.thejollysportsman.com*
*– Closed 25-26 December*
**Rest** – *(booking essential)* Menu £ 16 (lunch) – Carte £ 27/35
♦ Set in a small hamlet, a grey clapperboard pub that's popular with the locals. Plenty of choice, including interesting bar bites, good value set menus and a rustic, European-based à la carte.

**LEYBURN** – North Yorkshire – 502 O21 – pop. 1 844          **22 B1**
▶ London 251 mi – Darlington 25 mi – Kendal 43 mi – Leeds 53 mi
🛈 Railway St ☎ (01748) 82 87 47, www.hello-yorkshire.co.uk

⌂  **Clyde House** without rest  ❄ 📶 VISA ⬤⬤
*5 Railway St ⊠ DL8 5AY – ☎ (01969) 623 941 – www.clydehouse.com – Closed*
*8-21 January*
**6 rm** ⚏ – ♦£ 55 ♦♦£ 80
♦ 18C former coaching inn, refurbished to a high standard, with fresh, bright, modern styling. Bedrooms are spacious with high ceilings; those in former stables are smaller but boast exposed beams. Hearty Yorkshire breakfasts served in smart, open-plan kitchen.

🍴◻  **Sandpiper Inn** with rm  🍴 📶 P VISA ⬤⬤ AE
*Market Pl ⊠ DL8 5AT – ☎ (01969) 622 206 – www.sandpiperinn.co.uk – Closed*
*Monday*
**2 rm** ⚏ – ♦£ 75/80 ♦♦£ 85/90   **Rest** – Carte £ 22/35 s
♦ Charming 16C inn just off the square in busy market town. Frequently changing blackboard menus feature fine local produce; simpler dishes and sandwiches at lunchtime. Pleasant bedrooms have a homely feel.

**at Constable Burton** East : 3.5 mi on A 684 – ⊠ Leyburn

🍴◻  **Wyvill Arms** with rm  🚭 🍴 📶 P VISA ⬤⬤ ①
*⊠ DL8 5LH – ☎ (01677) 450 581 – www.thewyvillarms.co.uk – Closed Monday*
*except bank holidays*
**3 rm** ⚏ – ♦£ 60 ♦♦£ 80   **Rest** – Carte £ 20/33 s
♦ Intimate, ivy-clad stone pub with pleasant gardens, formerly an 18C farmhouse. Menus offer plenty of choice and feature local, traceable produce in carefully prepared, classical dishes. Simple, well-kept bedrooms.

**LICHFIELD** – Staffordshire – 502 O25 – pop. 28 435 ▯ Great Britain   **19 C2**
▶ London 128 mi – Birmingham 16 mi – Derby 23 mi – Stoke-on-Trent 30 mi
🛈 Castle Dyke ☎ (01543) 41 21 12, www.visitlichfield.co.uk
▣ Lichfield Golf and Country Club Elmhurst, ☎ (01543) 41 73 33
◉ City★ - Cathedral★★ **AC**

ENGLAND

## ✗ Chandlers Grande Brasserie    🄰🄲 🆅🄸🅂🄰 ⓔ

*Corn Exchange, Conduit St* ✉ *WS13 6JU –* ✆ *(01543) 416 688*
*– www.chandlersrestaurant.co.uk – Closed 26 December, 2-9 January, 1 May and 27 August*
**Rest** – Menu £ 15 (weekday lunch) – Carte £ 25/37
♦ Hexagonal building in heart of the city, with spacious, wood-floored restaurant and mezzanine floor for more intimate dining. Menus offer a mix of classic and Mediterranean dishes.

---

## LIFTON – Devon – **503** H32 – pop. 964    **2** C2

▶ London 238 mi – Bude 24 mi – Exeter 37 mi – Launceston 4 mi

🄶 Launceston ★ - Castle ★ (≤ ★) St Mary Magdalene ★, W : 4.5 mi by A 30 and A 388

### 🛏 Arundell Arms    🖳 🏹 🏞 🍴 🚿 🅿 🆅🄸🅂🄰 ⓔ 🄰🄴

*Fore St* ✉ *PL16 0AA –* ✆ *(01566) 784 666 – www.arundellarms.com*
**23 rm** 🛏 – ♦£ 98/118 ♦♦£ 175/199    **Rest** – Menu £ 20/43
♦ Roadside former coaching inn with access to 20 miles of the Tamar River for fishing. Comfortable, characterful bedrooms. Smart bar and restaurant; the latter with views over the garden and terrace. Light lunches available in bar. Classic menus in restaurant.

---

## LINCOLN – Lincolnshire – **502** S24 – pop. 86 958    📗 Great Britain    **17** C1

▶ London 140 mi – Bradford 81 mi – Cambridge 94 mi – Kingston-upon-Hull 44 mi

✈ Humberside Airport : ✆ (01652) 688456, N : 32 mi by A 15 - Y - M 180 and A 18

ℹ Britain & London Visitor Centre 9 Castle Hill ✆ (01522) 87 32 13, www.lincolntourism.co.uk

🄱 Carholme Carholme Rd, ✆ (01522) 52 37 25

👁 City ★★ - Cathedral and Precincts ★★★ **AC** Y – High Bridge ★★ Z **9** – Usher Gallery ★ **AC** YZ **M1** – Jew's House ★ Y – Castle ★ **AC** Y

🄶 Doddington Hall ★ **AC**, W : 6 mi by B 1003 - Z - and B 1190. Gainsborough Old Hall ★ **AC**, NW : 19 mi by A 57 - Z - and A 156

### 🛏 Charlotte House    🖳 🚿 🍴 🚿 🅿 🆅🄸🅂🄰 ⓔ 🄰🄴 ⓞ

*The Lawns, Union Rd* ✉ *LN1 3BJ –* ✆ *(01522) 541 000*
*– www.charlottehouselincoln.com*    Yv
**14 rm** – ♦£ 175 ♦♦£ 235, 🛏 £ 10 – 6 suites
**Rest** – (dinner only and Sunday lunch) Carte £ 29/42
♦ Set next to a castle, a stylish and contemporary converted Georgian building with 8 acres of grounds, super-cool, comfy bedrooms and luxurious bathrooms. Free town transfers. Dine at linen-laid tables in smart, glass-fronted restaurant.

### 🏠 Bailhouse *without rest*    🖳 🚿 🍴 🅿 🆅🄸🅂🄰 ⓔ ⓞ

*34 Bailgate* ✉ *LN1 3AP –* ✆ *(01522) 541 000 – www.bailhouse.co.uk*
**10 rm** – ♦♦£ 69/225, 🛏 £ 10    Yc
♦ Beautiful 14C building with 19C additions. Intimate, relaxing feel enhanced by unobtrusive service, enclosed garden, and rooms oozing charm, some with 14C exposed beams.

### ⌂ St Clements Lodge *without rest*    🚿 🍴 🅿

*21 Langworthgate* ✉ *LN2 4AD –* ✆ *(01522) 521 532*
*– www.stclementslodge.co.uk*    Yu
**3 rm** 🛏 – ♦£ 50 ♦♦£ 68
♦ A good value house in a convenient location, a short walk from the sights. Run by hospitable owners who keep three large, pleasantly decorated bedrooms.

### 🍽 Wig & Mitre    🄰🄲 🆅🄸🅂🄰 ⓔ 🄰🄴 ⓞ

*30-32 Steep Hill* ✉ *LN2 1LU –* ✆ *(01522) 535 190 – www.wigandmitre.com*
**Rest** – Menu £ 16 – Carte £ 21/30    Yr
♦ Well-established pub with a cosy bar, period dining rooms and an airy beamed restaurant. Classical dishes display some global influences; breakfasts are hearty. Over 50 wines by the glass.

## LINCOLN

**ENGLAND**

---

**LISKEARD** – Cornwall – **503** G32 – pop. 8 478                    **1** B2

▶ London 261 mi – Exeter 59 mi – Plymouth 19 mi – Truro 37 mi

◉ Church★

© Lanhydrock★★, W : 11.5 mi by A 38 and A 390 – NW : Bodmin Moor★★
 - St Endellion Church★★ - Altarnun Church★ - St Breward Church★
 - Blisland★ (church★) - Camelford★ – Cardinham Church★ - Michaelstow
 Church★ - St Kew★ (church★) - St Mabyn Church★ – St Neot★ (Parish
 Church★★) - St Sidwell's, Laneast★ - St Teath Church★ - St Tudy★ – Launceston★
 - Castle★ (≤★) St Mary Magdalene★, NE : 19 mi by A 390 and A 388

**ENGLAND**

🏠 **Pencubitt Country House** 🌿  ⚴ 🍸 📶 **P** **VISA** **⦾**
Station Rd, South : 0.5 mi by B 3254 on Lamellion rd ✉ PL14 4EB
– 𝒞 (01579) 342 694 – www.pencubitt.com – Closed 27 May-11 June and 16
December-6 January
**9 rm** ⌇ – ♦£ 60/80 ♦♦£ 85/120
**Rest** – (closed Saturday and Sunday) (dinner only) (booking essential)
Menu £ 30 **s**
♦ Sympathetically restored Victorian property with delightful views, personally
run by charming owners. Comfortable bedrooms; Room 3 boasts balcony; Room
9 features part-vaulted ceiling and roll-top bath. Simple home-cooked dishes
served in spacious dining room.

**LITTLE BEDWYN** – Wiltshire – **503** P29 – see Marlborough

**LITTLE BOLLINGTON** – Cheshire East – see Altrincham

**LITTLE BUDWORTH** – Cheshire West and Chester – **502** M24 – see Tarporley

**LITTLE ECCLESTON** – Lancashire                                   **20** A2
▶ London 238 mi – Liverpool - 55 mi – Leeds 83 mi – Manchester 51 mi

🍴 **Cartford Inn** with rm   ⿰ 🍸 **P** **VISA** **⦾**
Cartford Ln ✉ PR3 0YP – 𝒞 (01995) 670 166 – www.thecartfordinn.co.uk
– Closed 25 December and Monday lunch
**15 rm** ⌇ – ♦£ 65/120 ♦♦£ 90/190
**Rest** – Carte £ 18/28
♦ 17C coaching inn combining original features with contemporary styling. Menus offer something for everyone; from sandwiches and wood platters of local
produce to gutsy pub favourites. Bedrooms boast feature walls and antique
French furniture.

**LITTLE LANGFORD** – Wiltshire – see Salisbury

**LITTLE MARLOW** – Buckinghamshire – see Marlow

**LITTLE PETHERICK** – Cornwall – **503** F32 – see Padstow

**LITTLE THETFORD** – Cambridgeshire – see Ely

**LITTLE WILBRAHAM** – Cambridgeshire – see Cambridge

**LITTLEHAMPTON** – West Sussex – **504** S31 – pop. 55 716        **7** C3
▶ London 64 mi – Brighton 18 mi – Portsmouth 31 mi
ℹ 63-65 Surrey St 𝒞 (01903) 72 18 66, www.littlehampton.org.uk

🏨 **Bailiffscourt & Spa** 🌿   ⿰ 🍸 🌊 ⛳ 👥 🐾 🔧 ✂ 💬 ♨ **P**
Climping St, Climping, West : 2.75 mi by A 259     **VISA** **⦾** **AE** **①**
✉ BN17 5RW – 𝒞 (01903) 723 511 – www.hshotels.co.uk
**39 rm** (dinner included) ⌇ – ♦£ 248/263 ♦♦£ 450/470
**Rest** – Menu £ 22/50
♦ Charming, reconstructed medieval manor in immaculate gardens. Bedrooms
are split between the house and outbuildings; the newer rooms in the grounds
are more suited to families. Beautiful spa facility. Classic country house cooking
served in formal dining room.

🏠 **Amberley Court** without rest 🌿   ⿰ 🍸 **P**
Crookthorn Ln, Climping, West : 1.75 mi by B 2187 off A 259 ✉ BN17 5SN
– 𝒞 (01903) 725 131 – Closed 25 December
**5 rm** ⌇ – ♦£ 55/79 ♦♦£ 79/89
♦ Converted farm barn with a tidy, homely atmosphere. Exposed beams, flourish-
ing plants and a warm welcome. Clean, modern, simply decorated bedrooms;
some are in the grounds.

# LIVERPOOL

See city maps on following pages

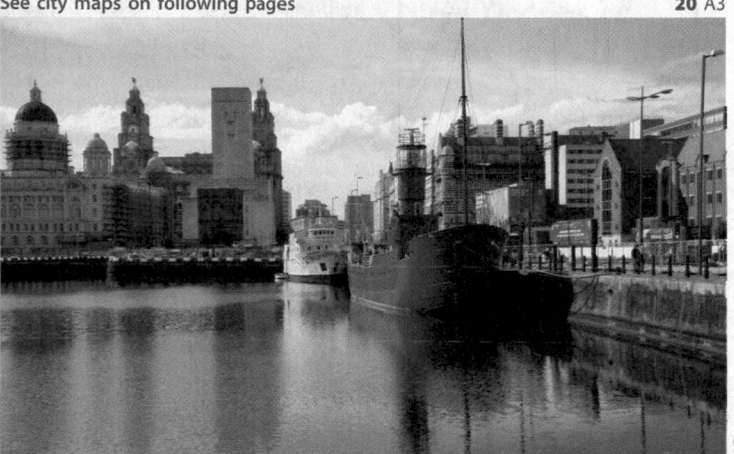

ENGLAND

**Merseyside – pop. 452 773 – 502** L23 **– 503** L23 – ▯ Great Britain

▶ London 219 – Birmingham 103 – Leeds 75 – Manchester 35

**🛈 Tourist Information**

36-38 Whitechapel ✆(0151) 233 24 59, www.visitliverpool.com

**Airport**

✈ Liverpool John Lennon Airport: ✆ (0871) 521 8484, SE: 6 m. by A 561 BX

**Ferries and Shipping Lines**

⛴ to Birkenhead and Wallasey (Mersey Ferries) frequent services daily.

⛴ to Isle of Man (Douglas) (Isle of Man Steam Packet Co. Ltd) 2 daily (2h 30 mn) - to
   Dublin (P & O Irish Sea) 1-2 daily (8h).

**Tunnel**

Mersey Tunnels (toll) AX

**Golf Courses**

🏌 Allerton Municipal Allerton Rd, ✆(0151) 428 10 46

🏌 Liverpool Municipal Kirby Ingoe Lane, ✆(0151) 546 54 35

**◎ SIGHTS**

   **In the town :** City★ • The Walker★★ DY**M3** • Liverpool Cathedral★★ EZ • Metropolitan
Cathedral of Christ the King★★EY • Albert Dock★CZ

   **In the surrounding area :** Speke Hall★ AC, SE : 8 mi by A 561 BX

## LIVERPOOL

ENGLAND

| | | | | | |
|---|---|---|---|---|---|
| Moss Lane | **AV** 85 | Sandhills Lane | **AV** 121 | Walton Vale | **BV** 146 |
| New Chester Rd | **AX** 91 | Scotland Rd | **AX** 125 | Warbreck Moor | **BV** 149 |
| Northfield Rd | **BV** 95 | Seaforth Rd | **AV** 126 | Wellington Rd | **BX** 152 |
| Oakfield Rd | **BV** 95 | Sefton Park Rd | **BX** 127 | West Derby Rd | **BX** 153 |
| Rimrose Rd | **BX** 112 | Stopgate Lane | **BX** 136 | West Derby St | **AX** 154 |
| Rocky Lane | **BX** 113 | Tunnel Rd | **BX** 141 | | |
| St Domingo Rd | **BX** 115 | Walton Breck Rd | **AV** 147 | | |
| St Oswald's St | **BX** 119 | Walton Rd | **ABV** 144 | | |

A 41 CHESTER

A 561 WIDNES   AIRPORT A 561

MERSEY

See following pages

# LIVERPOOL

ENGLAND

# INDEX OF STREET NAMES IN LIVERPOOL

ENGLAND

286

### Hilton
🛏 🗚 📶 🕭 AC 🕯 🕹 🚗 VISA 🜄 AE ⓘ

*3 Thomas Steers Way* ✉ *L1 8LW –* 𝒞 *(0151) 708 42 00*
*– www.hilton.co.uk/liverpool* CZx
**204 rm** – 🛉£ 99/149 🛉🛉£ 109/159, ⌓ £ 14.95 – 11 suites
**Rest** *Exchange* – Menu £ 25 (dinner) – Carte lunch £ 15/27

◆ Spacious, light-filled hotel in waterfront location, with the latest in modern styling and facilities. Floor to ceiling windows in bedrooms. Trendy cocktail bar, good conference facilities and well-equipped gym. Accessible menu of international dishes in Exchange.

### Malmaison
🗚 📶 🕭 AC 🕯 🕹 VISA 🜄 AE ⓘ

*7 William Jessop Way, Princes Dock* ✉ *L3 1QZ –* 𝒞 *(0151) 229 50 00*
*– www.malmaison-liverpool.com* CYn
**130 rm** – 🛉£ 175 🛉🛉£ 175, ⌓ £ 14.50 – 2 suites
**Rest** *Brasserie* – see restaurant listing

◆ Contemporary hotel with striking stone and black glass façade, set overlooking the marina. Stylish bedrooms are decorated in sensuous purple or orange tones and boast sunken baths; two are football-themed suites. Sexy, sophisticated bar.

### Hope Street
📶 🕭 🕯 🕹 VISA AE

*40 Hope St* ✉ *L1 9DA –* 𝒞 *(0151) 709 30 00 – www.hopestreethotel.co.uk*
**80 rm** – 🛉£ 89/180 🛉🛉£ 89/180, ⌓ £ 16.50 – 9 suites EZo
**Rest** *London Carriage Works* – see restaurant listing

◆ Former carriage works; now a modern, boutique hotel. Stylish, minimalist bedrooms boast stark white walls and underfloor heating; top floor loft suites have stunning skyline views. Trendy bar open Thurs-Sat.

### Hard Days Night
📶 🕭 rm, AC 🕯 🕹 🜄 AE

*Central Buildings, North John St* ✉ *L2 6RR –* 𝒞 *(0151) 236 19 64*
*– www.harddaysnighthotel.com* CYi
**110 rm** – 🛉£ 110/275 🛉🛉£ 110/275, ⌓ £ 15.95 – 2 suites
**Rest** *Blakes* – (closed Sunday and Monday) Menu £ 14 (lunch) **s**
– Carte £ 34/49 **s**

◆ Unique Beatles themed hotel; their story recounted in artwork from doorstep to rooftop, with every room featuring original works. Suites styled around Lennon and McCartney. Blakes, named after designer of Sgt. Pepper album cover, features modern brasserie menu.

### Racquet Club
🏊 🗚 📶 VISA 🜄 AE

*Hargreaves Buildings, 5 Chapel St* ✉ *L3 9AG –* 𝒞 *(0151) 236 66 76*
*– www.racquetclub.org – Closed first week January, 25 December and bank holidays* CYe
**8 rm** – 🛉£ 60/100 🛉🛉£ 60/100, ⌓ £ 12
**Rest** *Ziba* – see restaurant listing

◆ Ornate Victorian building, formerly a Shipping Agency office and then a gentleman's club, boasting a grand façade and bohemian style. Bedrooms differ greatly in both layout and décor but most feature antique furniture and eclectic art.

### XXX Panoramic
≼ AC VISA 🜄 AE

*West Tower (34th floor), Brook St.* ✉ *L3 9PJ –* 𝒞 *(0151) 236 55 34*
*– www.panoramicliverpool.com – Closed 25-26 December, Sunday dinner and bank holidays* CYr
**Rest** – Menu £ 20 (lunch) – Carte approx. £ 40

◆ On 34th floor of city's highest building; a stylish glass skyscraper with 360° views. Clothed tables, formal service; intimate dinners. Creative, ambitious cooking; excellent value lunch.

### XX 60 Hope Street
AC 🍸 🖧 VISA 🜄 AE

*60 Hope St* ✉ *L1 9BZ –* 𝒞 *(0151) 707 60 60 – www.60hopestreet.com – Closed Sunday dinner and bank holidays* EZx
**Rest** – Menu £ 27 – Carte £ 41/52

◆ Attractive Grade II listed Georgian house concealing well-established modern brasserie with bold feature walls and informal basement wine bar. Interesting regional dishes provide good value.

ENGLAND

**ENGLAND**

XX **London Carriage Works** – at Hope Street Hotel    AC ☺ VISA ⓪ AE
*40 Hope St* ⊠ *L1 9DA* – 𝒞 *(0151) 705 22 22*
*– www.thelondoncarriageworks.co.uk*    EZo
**Rest** – Menu £ 20 (lunch and early dinner) – Carte £ 23/52
◆ Spacious, open-plan brasserie dominated by impressive glass sculpture, with long bar, squashy sofas and relaxed ambience. Modern European brasserie dishes focus on local ingredients.

XX **Spire**    AC VISA ⓪ AE ①
*1 Church Rd* ⊠ *L15 9EA* – 𝒞 *(0151) 734 50 40* – *www.spirerestaurant.co.uk*
*– Closed first 2 weeks January and lunch Saturday-Monday*    BXa
**Rest** – Menu £ 13 (lunch) – Carte dinner £ 28/37
◆ Simple neighbourhood restaurant set in the Penny Lane area of the city. Good value, understated menus offer regional and modern European dishes. Tasty modern cooking; friendly service.

XX **Ziba** – at Racquet Club Hotel    ⇔ VISA ⓪ AE
*Hargreaves Buildings, 5 Chapel St* ⊠ *L3 9AG* – 𝒞 *(0151) 236 66 76*
*– www.racquetclub.org – Closed first week January, 25 December, Saturday lunch, Sunday and bank holidays*    CYe
**Rest** – Carte £ 18/28 s
◆ Airy, linen-clad restaurant with large arched windows, in a slightly quirky, bohemian-style hotel. Eclectic menu offers British dishes with a twist; many ingredients are from the family farm.

XX **Brasserie** – at Malmaison Hotel    ⇐ AC VISA ⓪ AE ①
*7 William Jessop Way, Princes Dock* ⊠ *L3 1QZ* – 𝒞 *(0151) 229 50 00*
*– www.malmaison-liverpool.com*    CYn
**Rest** – Menu £ 15 (lunch) – Carte £ 26/40
◆ Industrial-style brasserie with exposed ceiling ducts, Liverpool pop art and a stylish chef's table, set in a modern waterfront hotel. Extensive menu offers classic British brasserie dishes.

X **Host**    ☺ AC ☺ VISA ⓪ AE
*31 Hope St* ⊠ *L1 9HX* – 𝒞 *(0151) 708 58 31* – *www.ho-st.co.uk* – *Closed 25 December and 1 January*    EZz
**Rest** – South-East Asian – Carte £ 17/26
◆ Lively place with trendy bar and informal dining area of refectory-style tables. Wide range of Asian-inspired dishes, including Chinese, Japanese, Thai and Vietnamese. Good desserts.

X **Maritime Dining Room**    ⇐ VISA ⓪ AE
*Merseyside Maritime Museum, (4th Floor)* ⊠ *L3 4AQ* – 𝒞 *(0151) 478 40 56*
*– www.liverpoolmuseums.org.uk – Closed 25-26 December*    CZc
**Rest** – (lunch only) Carte £ 17/19
◆ Located on top floor of the superb maritime museum, with views over the famous Albert Dock. Seasonally changing menu of hearty, rustic British classics, with the occasional modern twist.

---

**LIZARD** – Cornwall – **503** E34    **1** A3
▷ London 326 mi – Penzance 24 mi – Truro 29 mi
◎ Lizard Peninsula★ - Mullion Cove★★ (Church★) - Kynance Cove★★ - Cadgwith★ - Coverack★ - Cury★ (Church★) - Gunwalloe Fishing Cove★ - St Keverne (Church★) - Landewednack★ (Church★) – Mawgan-in-Meneage (Church★) - Ruan Minor (Church★) - St Anthony-in-Meneage★

⌂ **Landewednack House** ⌖    🍴 ⅃ 📶 P VISA ⓪
*Church Cove, East : 1 mi by A 3083* ⊠ *TR12 7PQ* – 𝒞 *(01326) 290 877*
*– www.landewednackhouse.com*
**6 rm** ⌷ – †£ 55/85 ††£ 130/190
**Rest** – Menu £ 38 s
◆ Part 17C former rectory and garden, overlooking Church Cove. Smart interiors stylishly furnished with antiques. Diners encouraged to discuss menus: best local produce to hand.

# LONDON

– ▌ Great Britain

## 🛈 Tourist Information

Black Rd ✆ (020) 8846 90 00, www.visitlondon.com

## Airports

✈ **Heathrow** ✆ 0844 335 1801 **12** AX Terminal: Bus and Coach services run regularly, each day from Victoria. By Rail: Heathrow Express and Connect from Paddington Underground, daily every 20 minutes.

✈ **Gatwick** ✆ 0844 335 1802 **13**: by A23 EZ and M23 - Terminal: Coach services from Victoria Coach Station run regularly each day. By Rail: Gatwick Express from Victoria Underground, daily every 15 minutes. Southern Trains every 15 minutes from Victoria, London Bridge and Clapham Junction

✈ **London City Airport** ✆ (020) 7646 0088 **11** HV

✈ **Stansted**, at Bishop's Stortford ✆ 0844 335 1803, NE: 34m **11** by M11 JT and A12O.

**British Airways**, Ticket sales and reservations, Paddington Station London, W2, ✆08700 8509 8500 **36** BX

## Medical Emergencies

To contact a doctor for first aid, emergency medical advice and chemists night service: ✆ 07000 372255.

Accident & Emergency: dial 999 for Ambulance, Police or Fire Services.

## Shopping

Most stores are found in Oxford Street (Selfridges, M & S), Regent Street (Hamleys, Libertys) and Knightsbridge (Harrods, Harvey Nichols). Open usually Monday to Saturday 9 am to 6 pm. Some open later (8 pm) once a week; Knightsbridge Wednesday, Oxford Street and Regent Street Thursday. Other areas worth visiting include Jermyn Street and Savile Row (mens outfitters), Bond Street (jewellers and haute couture).

## Theatres

The "West End" has many major theatre performances and can generally be found around Shaftesbury Avenue. A half-price ticket booth is located in Leicester Square and is open Monday to Saturday 1 pm to 6.30 pm, Sunday and matinée days 12 noon to 6.30 pm. Restrictions apply.

## Tipping

When a service charge is included in a bill it is not necessary to tip extra. If service is not included a discretionary 10% is normal.

## Travel

As driving in London is difficult, it is advisable to take the Underground, a bus or taxi. Taxis can be hailed when the amber light is illuminated.

## Congestion Charging

The congestion charge is £ 10 per day on all vehicles (except motor cycles and exempt vehicles) entering the central zone between 7.00 am and 6.00 pm - Monday to Friday except on Bank Holidays.

Payment can be made in advance, on the day, by post, on the Internet, by telephone (0845 900 1234) or at retail outlets.

A charge of up to £ 100 will be made for non-payment.

Further information is available on the Transport for London website - www.tfl.gov.uk

Localities outside the Greater London limits are listed alphabetically throughout the guide.

## ◙ SIGHTS

### Historical Buildings and Monuments

Palace of Westminster★★★ **39**ALX • Tower of London★★★ • London Eye★★★ ※ **32** AMV •Banqueting House★★ **31**ALV • Buckingham Palace★★ **38**AIX • Kensington Palace★★ **27**ABV • Lincoln's Inn★★ **32**AMT • Lloyds Building★★ **34**ARU • Royal Hospital Chelsea★★ **37**AGZ • St James's Palace★★ **30**AJV • Somerset House★★ **32**AMU • South Bank Arts Centre★★ **32**AMV • Spencer House★★ **30**AIV • The Temple★★ **32**ANU • Tower Bridge★★ **34**ASV • Albert Memorial★★ Gray's Inn★ **32**AMV • Guildhall★ **33**AQT • Shakespeare's Globe★ **33**APV• London Bridge★ **34**ARV • Mansion House★ **33**AQV • The Monument★※ **34**ARU • Old Admiralty★ **31**AKV • Royal Albert Hall★ **36**ADX • Royal Exchange★ **34**ARU • Royal Opera House★ **31**ALU • Theatre Royal★ **31**AKV

### Churches in the City

St Paul's Cathedral★★★ ≼ **33**APU •St Bartholomew the Great★★ **33**APT • Temple Church★★ **32**ANU • All Hallows-by-the-Tower★ **34**ARU • St Giles Cripplegate★ **33**AQT • St Helen Bishopgate★ **34**ART

### Other Churches

Westminster Abbey★★★ **39**ALX • Southwark Cathedral★★ **33**AQV • Queens Chapel★ **39**AJV • St James's★ **30**AJV • St Margaret's★ **39**ALX • St Martin-in-the-Fields★ **31**ALV

### Parks

Regent's Park★★★ **11**QZC • Hyde Park★ **29**AFV • Kensington Gardens★★ **28** ACV • St James's Park★★**31**AKV

### Streets and Squares

The City★★★ **33**AQT •Burlington Arcade★ **30** AIV • Covent Garden★★ **31**ALU • The Mall★★ **31**AKV • Piccadilly★ **30**AIV - Trafalgar Square★★ **31**AKV • Whitehall★★ **31** ALV• Bond Street★ **30** AIU• Jermyn Street★ **30**AJV • Leicester Square★ **31**AKU • Piccadilly Circus★ **31**AJU • Shepherd Market★ **30**AHV • Victoria Embankment Gardens★ **31**ALV

### Museums

British Museum★★★ **31**AKL • Imperial War Museum★★★ **40**ANY • National Gallery★★★ **31**AKV • Science Museum★★★ **36**ADX • Tate Britain★★★ **39**ALY • Victoria and Albert Museum★★★ **36**ADY • Wallace Collection★★★ **29**AGT • Somerset House★★ **32**AMU • Museum of London★★ **33**APT • National Portrait Gallery★ **31**AKU • Natural History Museum★★ **36**ADY • Sir John Soane's Museum★★ **32**AMT • Tate Modern★★ ≼ **33**APV• Madame Tussaud's Waxworks★ **17**QZD

### Outer London

**Brentford 5**BX Syon Park★★

**Chiswick 6**CV Chiswick Mall★★• Chiswick House★ **D** • Hogarth's House★ **E**

**Greenwich 7** and **8** GHV Cutty Sark★★ GV**F** •National Maritime Museum★★ GV**M²** • Royal Naval College★★ GV**G** • The Park and Old Royal Observatory★ HV**K**

**Hampstead** Kenwood House★★ **2** EU**P** •Fenton House★★ **11**PZA

**Kew 6** CX Royal Botanic Gardens★★★

**Kingston upon Thames 5**BY Hampton Court Palace★★★

**Hendon★ 2** Royal Air Force Museum★★ CT**M³**

**Hounslow 5**BV Osterley Park★★

**Richmond 5** and **6** CX Richmond Park★★※CX •Ham House★★ BX**V**

**Twickenham 5**BX Marble Hill House★ **Z** • Strawberry Hill★ **A**

The maps in this section of the Guide are based upon the Ordnance Survey of Great Britain with the permission of the Controller of Her Majesty's Stationery Office. © Crown Copyright 100000247

**Alphabetical index of hotels**

LONDON

LONDON

# Alphabetical index of restaurants

# Starred Restaurants

# Bib Gourmand

Good food at moderate prices

| | | page |
|---|---|---|
| Al Duca | Ⅹ | 453 |
| Anchor and Hope | ⅰ◻ | 421 |
| Azou N | Ⅹ | 388 |
| Barrafina N | Ⅹ | 458 |
| Bar Trattoria Semplice | Ⅹ | 443 |
| Benja Bangkok Table | Ⅹ | 457 |
| Bocca di Lupo | Ⅹ | 457 |
| Bradley's | ⅩⅩ | 377 |
| Brawn N | Ⅹ | 422 |
| Brown Dog | ⅰ◻ | 415 |
| Cafe Spice Namaste | ⅩⅩ | 424 |
| Canton Arms | ⅰ◻ | 413 |
| Chapters | ⅩⅩ | 414 |
| Charlotte's Bistro | ⅩⅩ | 391 |
| Comptoir Gascon | Ⅹ | 394 |
| da Polpo N | Ⅹ | 462 |
| Dehesa | Ⅹ | 458 |
| Drapers Arms | ⅰ◻ | 397 |
| 500 | Ⅹ | 392 |
| Fox and Grapes N | ⅰ◻ | 414 |
| Galvin Café a Vin | Ⅹ | 424 |
| Giaconda Dining Room | Ⅹ | 374 |
| Goldfish City | Ⅹ | 383 |
| Great Queen Street | Ⅹ | 376 |
| Hereford Road | Ⅹ | 429 |
| Iberica | ⅩⅩ | 448 |
| José N | Ⅹ | 419 |
| Kateh N | Ⅹ | 429 |
| Koya N | Ⅹ | 459 |
| Mango and Silk | Ⅹ | 417 |
| Market | Ⅹ | 374 |
| Medcalf | Ⅹ | 395 |
| Morito | Ⅹ | 395 |
| Opera Tavern N | ⅩⅩ | 461 |
| Polpo | Ⅹ | 458 |
| St John Bread and Wine N | Ⅹ | 424 |
| Salt Yard | Ⅹ | 374 |
| Simply Thai | Ⅹ | 416 |
| Sushi-Say N | Ⅹ | 370 |
| Terroirs | Ⅹ | 462 |
| Triphal N | Ⅹ | 427 |
| Trishna N | Ⅹ | 449 |
| Trullo | Ⅹ | 393 |
| 28°-50° | Ⅹ | 383 |
| Zucca | Ⅹ | 418 |

# Particularly pleasant hotels

# Particularly pleasant restaurants

# Restaurants by cuisine type

LONDON

# Outside dining

LONDON

## Restaurants open late

Time of last orders in brackets

☀ **Restaurants open on Sunday**

MAYOR OF LONDON

Transport for London

UNDERGROUND

© Transport for London    Reg. user No. 10/1738/P    Version C 02.2010    Correct at time of going to print

ℹ 24 hour travel information
0843 222 1234*

Website
tfl.gov.uk

*You pay no more than 5p per minute if calling from a BT landline. There may be a connection charge. Charges from mobiles or other landline providers may vary.

Improvement works may affect your journey, please check before you travel

Bakerloo | Central | Circle | District | Hammersmith & City | Jubilee | Metropolitan | Northern | Piccadilly | Victoria | Waterloo & City | Overground | DLR

HERTFORDSHIRE

BARNET

HARROW

HARING

HILLINGDON

BRENT

ISLING

CAMDEN

CITY

EALING

HAMMERSMITH
AND

KENSINGTON
AND
CHELSEA

OF
WESTMINSTER

FULHAM

HEATHROW

HOUNSLOW

RICHMOND
UPON
THAMES

WANDSWORTH

LAMB

THAMES

KINGSTON
UPON
THAMES

MERTON

SUTTON

SURREY

0        6 km
0        4 miles

## GREATER LONDON

- — — — County Boundary
- ············ Borough Boundary

A 10

M 25

ESSEX

M 11

ELD

WALTHAM

FOREST

REDBRIDGE

A 12

HAVERING

HACKNEY

A 406

BARKING

AND

DAGENHAM

NEWHAM

TOWER
HAMLETS

THAMES

A 13

UTHWARK

GREENWICH

A 205

BEXLEY

LEWISHAM

A 20

A 2

BROMLEY

M 20

KENT

ROYDON

M 26

M 25

# GREATER LONDON
## NORTH-WEST

Greater London Boundary
Through route

2

A1 GRANTHAM, BEDFORD

BOREHAMWOOD

HADLEY WOOD

COCKFOSTERS

COCKFOSTERS

OAKWOOD

HIGH BARNET

HIGH BARNET

SOUTHGATE

BARNET

NORTH FINCHLEY

MILL HILL

WOODSIDE PARK

ARNOS GROVE

MILL HILL EAST

WEST FINCHLEY

Road

EDGWARE

Circular

BOUNDS GREEN

BURNT OAK

COLINDALE

HENDON

FINCHLEY CENTRAL

WOOD GREEN

QUEENSBURY

North

KINGSBURY

EAST FINCHLEY

HORNSEY

PRESTON ROAD

HENDON CENTRAL

HARINGEY

BRENT

BRENT CROSS

UPPER HOLLOWAY

WEMBLEY PARK

GOLDERS GREEN

ARCHWAY

WEMBLEY

HAMPSTEAD

CONFERENCE CENTRE

WEMBLEY CENTRAL

STONEBRIDGE PARK

HARLESDEN

NORTH ACTON

PARK ROYAL

WEST ACTON

NORTH EALING

EALING COMMON

ACTON TOWN

CHISWICK PARK

CHISWICK

321

3

E    F    A 10 CAMBRIDGE    G

HADLEY WOOD
COCKFOSTERS
COCKFOSTERS
OAKWOOD
ENFIELD
POL.
H

T
TOTTERIDGE AND WHETSTONE
SOUTHGATE
NORTH FINCHLEY
WOODSIDE PARK
ARNOS GROVE
Road
Circular
North
BOUNDS GREEN
WOOD GREEN
WALTHAM FOREST

A 406
A 111
A 1004
A 105
B 550
A 1000
A 504
A 1080
A 1055

TURNPIKE LANE
TOTTENHAM HALE
A 503
BLACKHORSE ROAD
WALTHAMSTOW CENTRAL

U
EAST FINCHLEY
A 1
HORNSEY
HARINGEY
UPPER HOLLOWAY
HAMPSTEAD
ARCHWAY
SEVEN SISTERS
MANOR HOUSE
FINSBURY PARK
A 105
A 503
A 1201
A 107
A 104
A 1006

(Work in progress)
STRATFORD
PUDDING MILL LANE
A 12
BOW ROAD    A 11
MILE END
BROMLEY-BY-BOW
TOWER HAMLETS

V
CANARY WHARF
BLACK TUNN
ISLE OF DOG
A 200
NEW CROSS GATE
NEW CROSS

E    F    G

# GREATER LONDON
## NORTH-EAST

0        3 km
0      2 miles

Greater London Boundary
Through route

| 1 | 2 | 3 | 4 |
| 5 | 6 | 7 | 8 |

4

LONDON

THEYDON BOIS

EPPING FOREST

A 121

A 1168

DEBDEN

LOUGHTON

A 113

BUCKHURST HILL

A 1069

110

RODING VALLEY

A 113

CHIGWELL

B 173

GRANGE HILL

18

A 1112

WOODFORD

A 123

HAINAULT

M 11

FAIRLOP

18

WOODFORD

A 104

A 11

SOUTH WOODFORD

A 113 North

A 1400

REDBRIDGE

HAVERING

A 12

A 125

J

IPSWICH   A 12   A 127: SOUTHEND-ON-SEA

18.9

18

9

114

SNARESBROOK

REDBRIDGE

BARKINGSIDE

NEWBURY PARK

GANTS HILL

A 118

P

P

P

WANSTEAD

A 12

Circular

A 406

18

LEYTONSTONE

ILFORD

A 1083

A 124

EYTONSTONE

A 116

A 123

Road

BARKING AND DAGENHAM

DAGENHAM EAST

A 11

A 118

A 124

EAST HAM

A 1112

B 1023

A 1240

B 178

A 1112

A 125

NEWHAM

UPTON PARK

BARKING

A 123

UPNEY

BECONTREE

DAGENHAM HEATHWAY

H

PLAISTOW

WEST HAM

A 124

A 13

A 117

CANNING TOWN

P

LONDON CITY AIRPORT

THE O2

N. GREENWICH

THAMES BARRIER

THAMES

A 2016

A 2016

A 2041

A 13 TILBURY

A 206

A 206

A 206

A 102

A 205

GREENWICH

K

H                                    J

**5**

YIEWSLEY

HILLINGDON

EALING

EALING BROAD...

A 312

A 4020

HAYES

A 437

A 408

SOUTHALL

A 3002

SOUTH EALING

HANWELL

NORTHFIELDS

BOSTON MANOR

A 3005

A 4127

OSTERLEY PARK

B 454

A 3044

M 4

A 312

OSTERLEY

A 4

HOUNSLOW EAST

SYON PARK

HEATHROW

TERMINAL 1

HEATHROW AIRPORT

TERMINAL 2

CRANFORD

HOUNSLOW WEST

HOUNSLOW CENTRAL

A 310

TERMINAL 5

TERMINAL 3

HATTON CROSS

HEATHROW 5

HEATHROW 4

TERMINAL 4

A 30

HOUNSLOW

TWICKENHAM

A 375

A 314

A 312

A 305

A 244

A 316

RICHMOND

A 308

UPON THAMES

A 310

A 311

BUSHY PARK

SUNBURY

A 308

A 308

SHEPPERTON

Thames

A 3050

HAMPTON COURT

B 375

**GREATER LONDON**

SOUTH-WEST

0    3 km

0    2 miles

Greater London Boundary

Through route

| 1 | 2 | 3 | 4 |
|---|---|---|---|
| 5 | 6 | 7 | 8 |

WALTON-ON-THAMES

A 307

A 309

Mole

A 244

WEYBRIDGE

A 311

ESHER

A 244

CLAYGATE

CLAREMONT PARK

A 3

A 307

A 244

COBHAM

6

NORTH ACTON
PARK ROYAL
WEST ACTON
NORTH EALING
EALING COMMON
ACTON TOWN
A 315 CHISWICK PARK
GUNNERSBURY
A 4 CHISWICK
A 406
ROYAL BOTANIC GARDENS
KEW GARDENS
A 316
RICHMOND
A 305
EAST SHEEN
PUTNEY
RICHMOND PARK
A 306
SOUTHFIELDS
A 219
A 3
A 308
WIMBLEDON PARK
WIMBLEDON
A 307
A 238
WIMBLEDON
A 238
A 298
B 286
KINGSTON UPON THAMES
A 3
A 240
A 2043
A 24
A 217
A 240
CHESSINGTON
EWELL
A 240
EPSOM
B 280
A 2022

V

CLAPHAM SOUTH
LAMBETH
BALHAM
X
TOOTING BEC
A 23
STREATHAM
TOOTING
A 214
TOOTING BROADWAY
A 216
COLLIERS WOOD
SOUTH WIMBLEDON
MORDEN
MERTON
A 236
A 297
A 217
B 278
A 237
B 2230
A 232
SUTTON
A 2022
A 237
A 23

Y

Z

**7**

V

X

Y

Z

E    F    G

TOWER HAMLETS
MILE END
BROMLEY-BY-BOW
A 102
CANARY WHARF
BLACK TUNN
ISLE OF DOG
A 200
NEW CROSS GATE
NEW CROSS
A 20
DLR
P
LAMBETH
HERNE HILL
M4
Circular
LEWISHAM
A 205
DULWICH
A 2218
CLAPHAM SOUTH
BALHAM
STREATHAM
A 23
A 214
CRYSTAL PALACE PARK
A 212
A 2015
TOOTING BEC
A 234
TOOTING
TOOTING BROADWAY
A 24
A 216
A 212
A 2
COLLIERS WOOD
SOUTH WIMBLEDON
A 215
MORDEN
MERTON
A 236
A 213
A 214
A 297
A 217
B 278
A 237
A 23
CROYDON
A 222
A 232
B 2230
18
SUTTON
18
SOUTH CROYDON
A 212
ADDINGTON
A 2022
18-9
A 235
A 2022
A 237
A 22
SANDERSTEAD
18
18

E    M 23 : GATWICK AIRPORT BRIGHTON    A 23    F    A 22    M 25, EASTBOURNE    G

# GREATER LONDON
## SOUTH-EAST

0         3 km
0         2 miles

Greater London Boundary
Through route
16'2 Low headroom : See map 404

| 1 | 2 | 3 | 4 |
| 5 | 6 | 7 | 8 |

V

8

LONDON

A 124
P
CANNING TOWN
A 13
A 111
LONDON CITY AIRPORT
HE O2
N. GREENWICH
THAMES BARRIER
A 206
A 2016
A 206
THAMES

BEXLEY
A 207
H
A 2 07
A 207

BLACKHEATH
GREENWICH
A 102
A 205
A 207
A 209
P
A 221
A 2

G

X

ELTHAM
A 2
A 2713
A 210
A II
P
18
B 2214
B 2210
A 222
A 205
A 20
A 222

A2 DOVER

A 208
P
P
P
18
A 222 16'3
A 223
Y

FOLKESTONE A 20

CHISLEHURST
18
A 20

Z

P
P
H
P
BROMLEY
A 21
A 224
9
A 208
a
P
P
A 232
A 223
A 224
4

M 25

KESTON
a
FARNBOROUGH
18

A 233
BIGGIN HILL AERODROME

**9** **10** **11** **12** **13** **1**

REGENT'S PARK

**15** **16** **17** **18** **19** **2**

TOWER BRIDGE

HYDE PARK

■ PALACE OF WESTMINSTER

**21** **22** **23** **24** **25** **2**

THAMES

**27** **28** **29** **30** **31** **32** **33** **3**

THAMES

TOWER BRIDGE

HYDE PARK

**35** **36** **37** **38** **39** **40**

■ PALACE OF WESTMINSTER

# INDEX OF STREET NAMES IN LONDON CENTRE

**LONDON**

329

LONDON

333

334

LONDON

K

L

Brent
Reservoir

North Circular Road

A 406

Crest Road

Coles Green Rd

Edgware Rd

A 5

Avenue

Brook Rd

Lane

Cricklewood

NEASDEN
JUNCTION

Tanfield

Dollis Hill

**ZA**

A 4088

Dudden

GLADSTONE PARK

**BRENT**

Mora Rd

Neasden

*Neasden*

Lane

Hill

Kendal Rd

Park Ave North

Anson Road

Sneyd Rd

Burnley Road

Sherrick Green Rd

153

Dollis Hill

Denzil Road

Chapter Road

*Willesden Green*

High Road

Lane

WILLESDEN GREEN

Willesden Green

High Road

A 407

Walm

**ZB**

482

Church Road

Roundwood Road

Pound Lane

WILLESDEN
CEMETERY

357

P

Brondesbury

Peter Ave

KILBURN

Sidmouth

Rd

351

196

ROUNDWOOD
PARK

Donnington Road

Mount

Pleas

Chamberlayne

A 404

352

Manor Park Rd

Harlesden Road

Doyle

Hardinge Rd

480

College

Acton Lane

P

High Street

Wrottesley Road

Furness Road

All Souls Avenue

Bathurst Gdns

Clifford Gdn

Harley Road

Harrow Road

Mortl

**ZC**

Oak Lane

*Willesden
Junction*

A 404

Kensal G

Har

K

15

L

M    N    O

500 m
500 yards

CHILD'S HILL

Vale

Hendon Way

A 41

Cricklewood

475

BARNET

476

Finchley Rd

Hermitage La.

477

West Heath

Road

Lyndale Ave

Platt's La.

FENTON HOUS

Redington

Road

Frognal

Lane

U

Heath

Drive

Finchley

Road

West

End

Lane

CKLEWOOD

Cricklewood

A 407

nson Rd

Lichfield Rd

Westbere Rd

Lane

Up

Mill

Road

Hill

Shoot

Lane

houth Road

Road

Crediton

Lane

a

Hill

Frognal

Finchley

A 41

Arkwrig

FINCHLEY ROAD
AND FROGNAL

WEST
HAMPSTEAD

West
HAMPSTEAD

Rd

West Hampstead

Finchle
Road

tsworth

esden

A 4003

ark

Kilburn

Road

Mapesbury

Avenue

Cavendish

Ave

Iverson

West End

Lane

Broadhurst Gdns

Farhazel

G

14·9

15·9

BRONDESBURY

Dyne Rd

Kilburn

A 5

Gascony Ave

478

Canfield

Greencroft

Christchurch

Rd

Avenue

Willesden

Lane

High

Road

479

Abbey

Priory

Belsize

Road

Road

FINCHLEY ROAD

Road

Bound

BRONDESBURY
PARK

Salusbury

Kingswood

PADDINGTON
CEMETERY

Quex Rd

Road

KILBURN
HIGH ROAD

Greville Pl.

Abb

Carlton

Maida

Vale

Hamilton

erton

Rd

The

Road

Road

Brondesbury

Brondesbury

Villas

335

vening

Milman

QUEEN'S PARK

b

POL

Road

Kilburn
Park

336

Randolph

Vale

Harvist

Road

Queen's
Park

P

Lane

Carlton

Road

Ave

Maida
Vale

ZC

Kilburn

Ave

Avenue

Bravington

Fernhead

Road

Kilburn

Park

Elgin

Randol

erlayne

Rd

x

Shir

16

M    N    O

11

O   P   Q

0   500
0   500 yar

HAMPSTEAD HEATH

Kenwood
Ladies Pond

Vale of
Health Pond

Mixed Bathing
Pond   PARLIAMENT HILL

North End Way   A 502
Spaniards Road

Heath

Lower Ter.

Whitestone
Pond   East Heath   Heath Road

Heath   Road

ZA

FENTON HOUSE   208   305   Well Walk   v   South End Rd   Parliament Hill

171   Heath St   HAMPSTEAD   GOSPE

Frognal   227   Hampstead   209   324   Willow   Rd   236   s   Nassington Rd

Road   479   z   Savernake

139   M   390   106   Rd

HAMPSTEAD   362   Mansfield Rd
HEATH

Fitzjohn's Av.   Rosslyn   Pond St   a   Malden

Lane   Fleet   Lawn Rd

Arkwright   A 502   Rd

Finchley   A 41   Road   Lyndhurst Rd   Hill   Southampton Rd   Parkhill

FINCHLEY ROAD   Frognal Rd   Netherhall   Gdns   Fitzjohns   22   Lane   Oman Rd   a   Belsize Park   Haverstock

AND FROGNAL   Nutley Ter.   n   Belsize Av.   Rd

10   Finchley   Belsize   19   Belsize Park Gardens   x   Hill

Road   oadhurst Gdns   Avenue   CAMDEN   323   Prince

Fairhazel   Gdns   Lancaster   Grove   Chalk

Canfield   Gdns   Eton   Ave.   Primrose   Chalk Farm

Greencroft   Gdns   u   SWISS COTTAGE

CHLEY ROAD   x   Fairfax Road   Swiss Cottage   s   e   Adelaide   Road

SOUTH   Road   Adelaide   Road   a   b   Gloucester

ZB   HAMPSTEAD   297   Elsworthy   s   s

Road   379   Avenue   PRIMROSE HILL   Regent's

Boundary Road   Loudoun   Finchley   Grove   Prince

Abbey   Hill   Ordnance   Rd

reville Pl.   Carlton   Queen's   Hill   Avenue Rd   Prince

b   Marlborough   Place   St John's   Circle   ZOO

Hamilton   Road   Wood   Acacia   Rd   79

Maida Vale   277   Wellington   29   Prince   Albert   REGENT'S

Circus   Allitsen   Rd   Outer   PA

ZC   Ave   REGENT'S PARK   Canal   Boating

Maida   Maida   AND MARYLEBONE   Lake

Randol   Vale   Hall   Terrace   LORD'S CRICKET   Road   QUEEN M

GROUND   17

O   P   Q

Archway
y
s
Holloway
Road
UPPER
HOLLOWAY
A 1
Tollington Way
Tollington
Park
Hornsey
Road
DARTMOUTH
PARK
Dartmouth
Park
Hill
Chetwynd Road
Rd
Highgate
Rd
Tufnell
Park
Tufnell
Park
Road
Junction
Road
Holloway
Road
Seven
Sisters
Hornsey
A 503
ZA
x
a
Lady Margaret Rd
Fortess
Road
Carleton Rd
Dalmeny Ave
Dalmeny Rd
Parkhurst
Road
Caledonian
Road
ISLING
Leighton Rd
Camden
Road
Hillmarton Road
Ho
R
Spring Place
Willes Road
A 400
Kentish
Town
Islip  Street
Gaisford Street
Patshull  Road
16
Road
Torriano Ave
Busby
Place
A 503  Road
Camden
Hungerford Road
North
Road
Road
Market
Road
Brewery
Road
Caledonian
Road
Caledonian Road
Mackenzie
Roman
A 5203
W
CALEDONIAN F
AND BARNSB
13
TISH
WN
16 6
ales
Road
Town
St
Camden
Pancras
Agar
Grove
A 5200
York
Way
15 0
15 6
Offord
a
Road
CAMDEN
ROAD
366
15 0
ZB
Camden
Town
Parkway
x
Rd
Delancey  St
s
Camden
High St
Camden
Camden  St
Royal College St
Pancras Way
Pratt  St
Crowndale Rd
Pancras
Rd
Copenhagen
St
Richmor
York
Road
Casthot St
Outer
Park
Village
East
Albany
Mornington
Crescent
Hampstead
Road
Eversholt
BRITISH
LIBRARY
Midland Rd
Pancras
Rd
Pancras
Rd
KING'S
CROSS
455
M
x
Caledonian
Pentonville
King's
417
ZC
RACES
Circle
REGENT'S
PARK
Robert Street
ester Rd
Road
EUSTON
P
P
18
Euston
Street
b
a
Euston
O
ST
PANCRAS
Judd
d
H
Road
St
Gra
R
S
T

341

LONDON

Finsbury Park

Fonthill Rd

A 503

St

Queen's

Road

Lordship Park

Lordship

Park

Blackstock

Brownswood

Road

Green

CLISSOLD

PARK

Sisters

Road

Road

St Thomas's Rd

Mountgrove Rd

Riverdale

Road

Newington

Seven

Hornsey

Iseldon

Road

Arsenal F.C.

Gillespie

Road

Park

Road

Highbury

Stoke

Cliss old

Cres

ZA

A 503

Caledonian

Road

ARSENAL F.C.

DRAYTON PARK

Benwell Rd

Drayton

Park

Park

Hill

Highbury

b •

333

HIGHBURY

Green

Lanes

Albion

Newington Rd

Ma

Holloway Road

U

Holloway

Drayton

Park

Highbury

New

Petherton

A 105

Caledonian

Road

ISLINGTON

Holloway

Road

Highbury

Grove

Highbury

Grosvenor Av

Mackenzie

Rd

Liverpool

A 1

PARADISE PARK

a •

CANONBURY

Road

CANONBURY

Balls

12

Roman Way

Bride Street

56

Highbury and Islington

A 1

t •

St

Paul's

Road

A 5203

Caledonian

56

Road

CANONBURY SQUARE

Canonbury

CANONBURY

Englefield

CALEDONIAN ROAD AND BARNSBURY

Road

Thornhill

Upper

c •

Essex

Hallford St

a •

15 &

Offord

a •

Road

x •

Barnsbury Street

H

h •

Road

New

Downham

ZB

Hemingford

v •

Road

r •

POL

k •

Essex Road Station

North

Road

A 1200

343

d •

Richmond

Ave

ISLINGTON

St

Essex

O +

St Peter's

Pretend

Street

Eagle Wharf Rd

350

nhagen

St

Barnsbury

Liverpool

St

70

Upper

Street

A 1

Shepherdess

Walk

North

Road

Road

Road

POL P

78

Angel

City

P

Road

Caishot St

345

M

City

478

Pentonville

Road

344

Amwell

John

Gobwell

A 501

City

Road

East

ZC

417

King's

265

T

St

398

U

296

19

Lever

Street

Central

Street

Ba

293

T

U

V

342

Mount Pleasant Hill

500 m
500 yards

STOKE NEWINGTON

Kyverdale Road

Northwold Road

Upper Clapton A 107

Cleveleys Road

Bridge

Chatsworth Road

A 104

'OKE NGTON

Rectory Road

Brooke Road

Maury Road

Kenninghall Road

Lea

Road

ROAD

A 10

High St

Evering

Rd

Evering

POL.

RECTORY ROAD

Clapton Way

Downs Rd

Lower

Millfields Road

Powerscroft Road

Rd

ZA

Nevill

auld

Walford Rd

Amhurst

HACKNEY

Prince George Rd

Barretts Grv

Shacklewell La

Cecilia

Newington Road

HACKNEY DOWNS

Downs Park Road

Amhurst

Pembury Rd

Clapton

378

Lower Clapton Rd A 102

Clifden Rd

Median

Boleyn ad

DALSTON KINGSLAND

337

Sandringham Road

Ridley Rd

Stoke Newington

13·6

Dalston Lane

15·6

HACKNEY DOWNS

HACKNEY CENTRAL

Road

Morning Lane

Homerton High Street

Well Street

Road

Kingsland

A 10

Dalston Lane

DALSTON JUNCTION

Forest Road

Graham Road

c●

Richmond Road

Road

Frampton Park Rd

Cassland Rd

Road

13·9

Richmond Road

Queensbridge Road

Lansdowne Drive

LONDON FIELDS

A 107 Mare Street

Well Street

Middleton Road

13·0

Albion Drive

HAGGERSTON

16·0

DALSTON

Road

Pownall Rd

15·9

a●

Sheep Lane

Mare Street

Victoria Park Road

Park Road

ZB

Nuttall St

Stre

Whiston Road

Queensbridge Road

HAGGERSTON PARK

Road

Pritchard's Rd

VICTORIA PARK

Sewardstone Rd

Bishop's Way

Bonner Rd

Rd

GEFFRYE MUSEUM

HOXTON

Road

Warner Pl

Hackney Road

Green

CAMBRIDGE HEATH

Ford

Road

Hoxton

Kingsland

Hackney

16·0

15·9

Columbia Road

Old Bethnal

a●

Green

Canrobert St

Old Road

●X

M

B 119

Globe Road

ZC

A 1209 Green

Roman Road

Bethnal Green

20

15

K  L

9

ZC

ZD

ZE

ZF

K  21  L

344

ZC

ZD

ZE

ZF

M

N

O

10

22

17

BAYSWATER
AND MAIDA VALE

Royal
Oak

NORTH
KENSINGTON

Notting
Hill Gate

ORANGERY

KENSINGTON
PALACE

KENSINGTON

HOLLAND PARK

LINLEY
SAMBOURNE
HOUSE

High Street
Kensington

KENSINGTON
AND CHELSEA

NAT

LEIGHTON
HOUSE

Edwardes
Square

OLYMPIA

Kensington
Olympia

LONDON

ZC
ZD
ZE
ZF

O
P
Q

REGENT'S PARK AND MARYLEBONE

LORD'S CRICKET GROUND

Canal

Boating Lake

QUEEN

GAR

0     500 m
0     500 yards

TERRACES

U

Outer      TERR.

Maida Vale

Randolph      Avenue

Maida      Hall      Terrace

St      John's      Wood      Road

Regent's      Park      Road

Grove

rdale Rd

Warwick      Ave.

Clifton Gdns

a Ave.

348

n      e

Lisson      St

Rossmore      Rd

Gloucester      Pl

MARYLEBONE

Baker      Street      K

MAD
TUSSA

ZD      P

P

Warwick      Ave.

Maida      Av.

Bloomfield      Edgware      Road

Frampton      St

Church      St

Broadley      St

A 501

Marylebone      Road

WATER
MAIDA VALE

Edgware      Road

Paddin

Baker

WALL
COLLE

Road

Westway

Crawford      St

Bryanston      Square

Shouldan St

PORTMAN
SQUARE

Royal
Oak

PADDINGTON

Praed      Street

Gloucester      Terrace

Sussex      Gardens      Edgware      Road

Kendal      St

Seymour St

Marble Arch

Oxford

16

Queensway

Lancaster      Gate

Bayswater      Road

North      Carriage      Drive

Marble Arch.

Up. Br
Stree

Gros
Squ

Bayswater

Gdns

Broad

The      Long      Water

HYDE      PARK

CITY OF WESTMINSTER

Park

ORANGERY

KENSINGTON
GARDENS

Round
Pond

The      Serpentine

Serpentine      Road

M

ZE

KENSINGTON
PALACE

Walk

ALBERT
MEMORIAL

Kensington

HYDE PARK AND KNIGHTSBRIDGE

Road

Knightsbridge

Hyde
Co

ROYAL
ALBERT
HALL

U

Queen's

Exhibition Rd

MONTPELIER
SQUARE

Knightsbridge      Road

Knightsbridge

BELGR
SQUA

KENSINGTON
AND CHELSEA

SCIENCE
MUSEUM

VICTORIA AND
ALBERT MUSEUM

Brompton

Sloane      Street

Pont      Street

NATURAL HISTORY
MUSEUM

P

Walton Street

Cadogan
Square

Sloane

ZF

Cromwell

Gloucester      Road

South
Kensington

MICHELIN
HOUSE

Pelham St

Gate

Road

23

O
P
Q

LONDON

ZC
ZD
ZE
ZF

T U V

FINSBURY

CHARTERHOUSE

Farringdon

GRAY'S INN

SIR JOHN SOANE'S MUSEUM

STAPLE INN

LINCOLN'S INN

Lincoln's Inn Fields

ST CLEMENT DANES

TEMPLE

Temple

ST BARTHOLOMEW THE GREAT

Holborn Viaduct

New Fetter Lane

Fetter Lane Street

Fleet

ST BRIDE
Tudor St

CITY OF LONDON

Blackfriars

MUSEUM OF LONDON

London

GUILDHALL

ST PAUL'S CATHEDRAL

ROYAL EXCHANGE

ST MARY-LE-BOW

Poultry

Bank

MANSION HOUSE

Cannon Street

MONUMENT

Thames

SOMERSET HOUSE

Victoria Embankment

Temple Pl.

Mansion House

Upper

THAMES

LONDON BRIDGE

SOUTH BANK ARTS CENTRE

Upper Ground

Max Stamford

GLOBE CENTRE

Southwark Bridge

TATE MODERN

SOUTHWARK CATHEDRAL

BRAMAH MUSEUM OF TEA AND COFFEE

Southwark St

Blackfriars

LONDON BRIDGE

LONDON EYE

WATERLOO

The Cut

Southwark

Union Street

Webber Street

Waterloo Rd

Borough

GEORGE INN

Newcomen Street

COUNTY HALL

WESTMINSTER BRIDGE

Belvedere Road

York Road

Lower Marsh

Lambeth North

Bayliss Rd

Suffolk St

Borough

London Rd

Southwark

Long

TRINITY CHURCH SQUARE

MERRICK SQUARE

Trinity St

Harper

Great Dover Street

LAMBETH PALACE

Hercules Rd

Lambeth

Lambeth Palace Rd

Bridge Rd

George's Rd

IMPERIAL WAR MUSEUM

ELEPHANT AND CASTLE SHOPPING CENTRE

New Kent Road

A 201

Lambeth High St

Brook Drive

Kennington

WALWORTH

Heygate St

Rodne

500 m
500 yards

T U V

LONDON

15

RAVENSCOURT PARK

HAMMERSMITH

ZF

Bath Road
Stamford Brook
Goldhawk Road
Ravenscourt Park
Glenthorne Rd
Banim St
Grove
Shepherd's
13
Hammersmith
Turnham Green
14·6
12·0
z
389
a
Chiswick High
e
Road
u
King
a
e
H
A 315
CHISWICK
West
Road
Great
West
Road
Talgarth
Devonshire
Chiswick
Lane
Hammersmith
431
21
HOUNSLOW
402
West
Rd
A 4
CHISWICK MALL
Hammersmith Bridge
Rainville

ZG
Great
HOGARTH'S HOUSE
A 316
Lane
Road
Lonsdale
Verdun
Road
Castelnau
v
CHISWICK HOUSE
Burlington
Road
THAMES
Road
WILDFOWL AND WETLANDS TRUST
Suffolk Road
Ferry Road
A 306
NATURE RESERVE
Lonsdale
Castelnau

a
Church Road
x
Rocks
k
404
The Terrace
13·8
BARNES
Lane
BARNES BRIDGE
Mill Hill Road
RICHMOND UPON THAMES
Station
Road
Road
Mill
Hill
PUTNEY
ZH
White Hart Lane
b
BARNES COMMON
Rocks
Lane
Mill Hill Road
COMMON
v
Rich
Vine
BARNES
B 306
Ride
Lower
Erpingham Rd
Hotham
Upper Richmond Road West
Queen's
Upper
A 205
k
Roehampton Lane
A 306
Dover House Road
Richmond
Road
A 205
PUTNEY
Hertford Ave
Priory Lane
Howards
Lane

0    500 m
0    500 yards

K
L

LONDON

T U V

ZF

ZG

ZH

IMPERIAL WAR MUSEUM
ELEPHANT AND CASTLE SHOPPING CENTRE
19
A 201
WALWO...
Lambeth High St
Lambeth Walk
Fitzalan Street
Brook Drive
Hayles
New Kent Road
163
Heygate St
Rodney
Black...
Chester Way
A 3204
Kennington Lane
Penton Place
Rd
Flint
M
Vauxhall Walk
Prince
Tyers St
Newburn St
Road
Vauxhall
Kennington Road
Kennington Park Road
Braganza St
Manor
POL
East Street
East
Portland
Street
Kennington Lane
KENNINGTON
Kennington Stir.
Clayton St.
A 23
A 3
Chapter Rd
Albany
Harleyford Rd
THE OVAL
Oval
211
Oval
Kennington
KENNINGTON PARK
Ruskin
Street
BURGESS PARK
Rd
Camberwell
Church
New
Edmund St
Southe...
Camberwell
Bethwin Rd
Foxley Rd
John
Road
Dorset Rd
420
Vassall Road
New Wyndham Rd
Comber Gro.
Elmington
Benhil...
Caldwell St
LAMBETH
Lothian Rd
Flodden Rd
A 202
Road
Church Street Camberwell
Calais St.
Warner
Road
Brixton Road
Mostyn Road
Knatchbull Road
Carew St
Denmark Rd
Lane
Grove Lane
Clapham
Stockwell
Groveway
Akerman
Lilford
Minet Rd
Denmark Hill
DENMARK HILL
Park Rd
Stockwell
Sidney Rd
Road
Loughborough Rd
Loughborough
Coldharbour
Champion Park
Way
Angell Dr.
Barrington Rd
Rd
RUSKIN PARK
Ruskin Rd
ZH
A 23
Brixton Road
Wiltshire Road
LOUGHBOROUGH JUNCTION
Road
Herne Hill
Ferndene Rd
Denmark Hill
Brixton
Atlantic Rd
A 2217
Coldharbour
Lane
Road
Acre Lane
Kellett Rd
Elfra Rd
Railton Road
Shakespeare Road
Milkwood Road
Fawnbrake Avenue
Herne Hill
A 215
Red Post Hill
Sunray Avenue

T U V

X  Y

ZF

ZG

ZH

Surrey Quays

Willow Road
Mandela Way
Walk
Southwark Park
Road
Raymouth Rd
Rotherhithe
New Rd
-369
Kent Road
Dunton
Lynton Road
Reverdy Rd
Galleywall
Road
16·0

A 2
Coopers Rd
Rolls Road
St James
Marlborough Gro.
Catlin St
Lynton Road
New Road
Ilderton
Road
15·6
SOUTH BERMONDSEY

Trafalgar Ave
Old
Glengall Road
Kent Road
Rotherhithe
Verney Road
Surrey Canal Rd

BURGESS PARK
Cobourg Rd
Willowbrook Rd
Bird In Bush Road
Road
Old
Kent
Road
Ilderton
Road
Avonley Rd
A 2

George's Way
Street

SOUTHWARK

Summer Road
Peckham Hill St.
Peckham Park Rd
Commercial Way
Naylor Rd
Asylum
Way
House Lane
Carlton Gro.
Clifton Way
Kender Street
Pomeroy
Street

Way
Commercial Way
Road
Meeting House
Road
QUEENS ROAD PECKHAM

Dalwood St
A 202
Peckham High Street
Clayton Rd
Queens
Consort
Road
Queens
Road
Lausanne Rd
Road

H
Shenley Road
Lyndhurst
Hanover Pk
Rye
Consort Rd
Hollydale
Road

Lyndhurst Grove
Way
PECKHAM RYE
15·8

Copeland Rd
NUNHEAD

Avondale Rise
Bellenden
Adys Road
Peck
Heaton Rd
Consort
Road
Evelina
A 2214
Grove

Hill Rd
A 2216
Pytchley Rd
Grove
Oglander Road
Vale
Peckham Rye
East Dulwich Rd
Nunhead Lane
Nunhead Gro.
Linden
Grove

EAST DULWICH
Melbourne Grove
Grove
East Dulwich
Crystal Palace Rd
Peckham
Peckham
Rye
Stuart Rd

Dulwich A 2214
X
Lordship Lane
Barry Rd
Rye
PECKHAM RYE PARK
Cheltenham Rd

500 m
0
0  500 yards

X  Y

LONDON

AC AD AE

Church St.
Edgware Rd.
Bell Street
452
Road
Harrow
Road
Edgware Road
POL
Chapel
Street
Road
Strand
Station Rd
Canal
Harrow
North Wharf Road
Wharf Road
b
Side Place
T
Bishop's
Bridge
PADDINGTON
South Wharf Road
ST MARY'S
Norfolk
Praed
Street
Ter.
Westbourne Terrace
Eastbourne Terrace
London Street
156
Sussex Gardens
156
67
Cleveland
Gloucester
Chilworth Terrace
Craven Terrace
Spring St
Praed Street
Radnor Place
94
Cleveland
Square
Gloucester
Square
Hyde Park
Square
Hyde
136
Queen's
Sussex
Sussex Pl.
Sussex
Gardens
93
U
Gardens
a
Craven Hill
Craven Terrace
x
448
Sussex
Square
29
c Westbourne
158
Hyde Park Gardens
257
P
e
St.
Leinster Ter.
Craven Tce.
Lancaster Gate
Bayswater
Lancaster
Gate
P
Bayswater
Road
FOUNTAIN
GARDEN
The
Ring
Leinster Terrace
The
Long
Water
The
Ring
V
KENSINGTON GARDENS
Round
Pond
PRINCESS DIANA
MEMORIAL FOUNTAIN
The
M
The
Ring
Rotten
AC
36
AD
AE

357

LONDON

AE    AF    AG

Bell Street

Edgware Road

Marylebone
Chapel St
Old Marylebone Rd
Crawford Pl.
Harcourt St
Crawford St
York
Enford St
Upper York St
Montagu St
Montagu Pl.
Dorset St
Gloucester St
Baker Street
Chiltern
Paddington St
Manchester St

T

Sale Place
Sussex Gardens
156
67
332
Norfolk Crescent
Edgware
Shouldham St
Bryanston Pl.
Montagu Pl.
REGENT'S PARK AND MARYLEBONE
14
90
Blandford
George St
Baker St
Harrowby St
Kendal Street
George Street
Street
Street
WALLACE COLLECTION

Hyde Park Square
Connaught St
Connaught Square
Upper Berkeley Street
Great Cumberland Pl.
Seymour St
Bryanston St
Portman St
PORTMAN SQUARE
POL.
Orchard St
476
W

U

93
Albion St
Park St
Marble Arch
Oxford St
North Row
Park Street
Green Street
Lees Pl.
Woods Mews
Upper Brook St
Culross St
Upper Grosvenor St

Gardens
400
The Ring
Bayswater Road
Marble Arch
149

28

HYDE PARK

CITY OF WESTMINSTER

Broad Walk
Park Lane

V

Serpentine
The Serpentine
Road
Princess
Serpentine
Road

0    200 m
0    200 yards

Rotten Row
Rotten Row

AE    AF    37    AG

LONDON

T

U

31

V

FARRINGDON

113

e

a

Street

e

Farringdon

Road

Leather

Hatton

Greville St

15'3

c

Charterhouse

West

b

Smithf

POL

T

Gray's

Inn

Rd

Chancery
Lane

Holborn

Gdn

Holborn

Viaduct

Holborn

POL

PIO

GRAY'S INN

CAMDEN

Row

Bedford

Red

Lion

Lion

St

73

Holborn

STAPLE
INN

Holborn

372

Farringdon

k

a High

SIR JOHN SOANE'S
MUSEUM

HOLBORN

278

LINCOLN'S
INN

n

282

Shoe

298

x

Lincoln's Inn

Fields

a

x

Fetter Lane

New Fetter La.

St

PIO

381

M

New
Sq.

47

DR JOHNSON'S
HOUSE

376

CITY
THAMESLINK

Serle

St

Portugal

Carey

Street

x

St

St

Fleet

St

Ludga

St

New Bridge St

ROYAL
COURTS
OF
JUSTICE

s

c

ST BRIDE

STRAND AND
COVENT GARDEN

Aldwych

ST CLEMENT
DANES

Fleet

St

Bouverie St

Essex

St

TEMPLE

Tudor

St

STRAND

Arundel
St

Temple Ave

17

U

BLACK

33

SOMERSET
HOUSE

175

Temple
Temple

Pl.

Embankment

Blackfriars Bridge

THAMES

OXO
TOWER

a

Ground

LONDON

Upper

SOUTH BANK
ARTS CENTRE

Waterloo
Bridge

Stamford

Street

Blackfriars

P

Ground

Cornwall

Street

Hatfields

Road

a

Upper

Stamford

Street

V

P

IMAX

Roupel

St

Southwark

Union

LONDON EYE

Belvedere

Road

Road

WATERLOO EAST

T

n

Cut

e

Nelson
Sq.

bridges

WATERLOO

40

The

LONDON

AO     AP     AQ

BARBICAN CENTRE

Ropemaker

Barbican

Long Lane

Silk   St

Smithfield

ST BARTHOLOMEW THE GREAT

MUSEUM OF LONDON

ST GILES CRIPPLEGATE

Fore   St

BARBICAN

Aldersgate   St.

London   Wall

ST BARTHOLOMEW'S

CHRIST CHURCH

Newgate

St   St Paul's

GUILDHALL

Gresham

CITY OF LONDON

ST MARGARET LOTHBURY

ST MARTIN LUDGATE

Paternoster Sq.

ST PAUL'S CATHEDRAL

ST VEDAST

Wood   Street

Cheapside

ST MARY-LE-BOW

BANK OF ENGLAND

Ludgate   Hill

New   Change

Cannon   St

Bow   Lane

Victoria   St

Poultry

MANSION HOUSE

ST STEPHEN WALBROOK

304   308

St Paul's   Churchyard

COLE ABBEY PRESBYTERIAN

Queen   St.

Bank

ST MARY ABCHURCH

BLACKFRIARS

Queen

Victoria

Mansion House

ST JAMES GARLICKHYTHE

Cannon   St

Blackfriars Bridge

New Bridge St

Upper   Thames

CANNON STREET

301

Millennium Bridge

Southwark Bridge

INTERNATIONAL SHAKESPEARE GLOBE CENTRE

291

TATE MODERN

Park   St

Southwark   Bridge   Road

SOUTHWARK

SOUTHWARK CATHEDRAL

Blackfriars

Southwark   Street

169

Park   St

Stoney   St

BRAMAH MUSEUM OF TEA AND COFFEE

Great   Guildford   St

London Bridge

Blackfriars Road

Suffolk   St

Ewer   St

Southwark   Street

Southwark   Way

Redcross   Way

High   St

GEORGE INN

GUY'S ST THO

Union   Street

Great   Suffolk   St

Borough

Newcomen   St

Nelson Sq.

AO     AP     AQ

Sun Street
Broadgate
Eldon St
Blomfield
ury
us
Wall
Blomfield St
Broad
472
Old
rdneedle
x
ROYAL
EXCHANGE
L
ELEMENT
CHEAP
nent
319
ENT
V
Lower
T MAGNUS
HE MARTYR
ONDON
RIDGE

Sun Street Passage
LIVERPOOL
STREET
Bishopsgate
Liverpool
St
a
POL
New St
e
c
t

Bishopsgate
Mary
Ave
St HELEN
BISHOPSGATE
SWISS RE
BUILDING
ST ANDREW
UNDERSHAFT
Leadenhall
Street
LLOYD'S
BUILDING
WILLIS
BUILDING
V

Gracechurch St
Fenchurch
St
Lime
ST MARGARET
PATTENS
Eastcheap
ST MARY
AT HILL
ST DUNSTAN-
IN-THE-EAST
Byward St

v
399
a
Brushfield
Street
P
Middlesex
317
Houndsditch
71
34
145
St Botolph St
Aldgate
High St
Aldgate

Street
Bell Lane
Wentworth
Goulston St
Street
Aldgate
East
Branham
Minories
Goodman's
Yd
P
TOWER
GATEWAY
Shorter St

Commercial St
Princelet    St
Brick    Lane

Street
TOWER
HAMLETS
x
Whitechapel High St
St    P
Leman
Mansell    Street
Prescot    St
z
Royal    Mint    Rd

T
U

FENCHURCH STREET
ST OLAVE'S
Pepys    St
318
Tower
Hill
Gt Tower St
Mark Lane
Tower Hill
ALL HALLOWS
BY THE TOWER
P
Lower Thames St
Lower Thames Street

TOWER
HILL
Tower Hill
TOWER
OF LONDON

East    Smithfield
ST KATHARINE
DOCK
P
Tower Bridge Approach

THAMES
H.M.S. BELFAST

St Hill
HAY'S GALLERIA
SHOPPING CENTRE
Tooley
J
r
M
e    Street
LONDON BRIDGE
P
s    Street    St Thomas St
188
a
T
386    125

CITY HALL
Tooley    St
b
Druid St
Tower Bridge Rd

18
TOWER
BRIDGE

0    200 m
0    200 yards

V

Shad
n    c
Thames
u
J    M
Gainford    St
P

LONDON

KENSINGTON

HOLLAND PARK

U

Campden

Horton

Holland

Kensington Church St.

St

Kensington

Green

P Kens

r

c

HOLLAND PARK

Argyll

Phillimore

Holland

Phillimore Gdns

Hill

Road

Road

Street

High

Street

LINLEY SAMBOURNE HOUSE

c

Kensington

High Street Kensington

Young Street

241

Kensington Square

n

242

St Alban's

X

Melbury

Road

High

Street

Earls

Abingdon

a

d

Marloes

Road

LEIGHTON HOUSE

Kensington

c

Edwardes Square

Court

POL

Villas

Scarsdale

Rd

Cornw

Cornwall

Lexham Gdns

Road

Warwick

342

Gardens

Road

Lexham

Gardens

Earls

Court

Cromw

Y

Warwick

P

Pembroke

Logan

Place

Cromwell

Road

b

Kenway

Rd

Knaresborough Pl.

Courtfield

Courtfield Gdns

101

Longridge

119

Nevern

Pl.

Road

s

410

a

c

Road

Kenway

Road

Earls

Court

Earl's Court

Earls Court Gdns

Barkston

Gdns

Courtfield

99

Cromwell

Road

Nevern Square

u

Trebovir

x

Road

Bramham Gdns

Court

Rd

Philbeach

Warwick

Penywern

Rd

EARL'S COURT

Bolton

Gardens

Gardens

Road

Earl's Court Sq.

Redcliffe

Z

North

EARL'S COURT EXHIBITION BLDG

151

Old

Brompton

Road

Road

Finborough

Sq

Gardens

End

WEST KENSINGTON

Road

West Brompton

Redcliffe

Road

Lillie

Road

Seagrave

Rd

P

BROMPTON CEMETERY

Ilfield

Road

27

AA

AB

AA

AB

0 200 m
0 200 yards

LONDON

AE AF 29 AG

X

Y

Z

366

AH · AI · AJ

LONDON

St James's Park Lake
King Charles St
Parliament St
Victoria
WESTMINSTER BRIDGE
31
193
X
Westminster
Birdcage
Walk
Storey's Gate
Parliament Sq.
Bridge
St
PALACE OF WESTMINSTER
Walk
M
52
SUPREME COURT
ST MARGARET'S
QUEEN ANNE'S GATE
Tothill
Street
France
St James's Park
WESTMINSTER ABBEY
X
Petty
Palmer St
a
Great
Great College St
Gate
NEW SCOTLAND YARD
Street
Abingdon St
s e
Caxton St
Victoria
St Anne's St
Smith
Millbank
St
H
Old Pye
Street
c
Tufton
St
Victoria
8
St
Pl.
WESTMINSTER CATHEDRAL
200
Great
Peter
St
416
Greycoat St
Horseferry
Marsham
Street
T
Pl.
Row
Rd
Monck Street
n
J
P
J
Y
Vincent
Square
Horseferry
Road
Lambeth
Bridge
38
Greycoat
Rochester
Page
Street
Thorney Street
Francis
VICTORIA
Vincent Sq.
Regency
z
Marsham
Islip
St
St
Vincent
Vincent
Street
Erasmus
Street
Vauxhall
Douglas St
Tachbrook
Bridge
St
Road
John
Rampayne
TATE BRITAIN
Atterbury St
St
Road
St
Street
Ponsonby Pl.
Millbank
Moreton
Pimlico
Bessborough Gdns
Vauxhall Bridge
THAMES
Albert
Embankment
Street
30
Lupus
Aylesford
Street
14'6
13'3
Chichester St
Z
Claverton
Street
St George's Square
Grosvenor
Road
49
VAUXHALL
14'6
Dolphin Sq.
Vauxhall
341
A 3212
Grosvenor
Nine
Elms
Lane

0       200 m
0       200 yards

## Boroughs and areas

**Greater London** is divided, for administrative purposes, into 32 boroughs plus **the City:** these sub-divide naturally into minor areas, usually grouped around former villages or quarters, which often maintain a distinctive character.

---

### BRENT – Greater London                                    12 A3

#### KENSAL GREEN

🛏 **Paradise by way of Kensal Green**          Ⓐ ✿ 🆅🅸🆂🅰 ⓒⓒ ⓞ
*19 Kilburn Ln. ⊠ W10 4AE ⊖ Kensal Green. – ℰ (020) 8969 0098
– www.theparadise.co.uk*                                      **10**MZC**x**
**Rest** – British – *(dinner only and lunch Saturday and Sunday)* Carte £ 21/36
♦ Great fun, with music, film and comedy nights. Share terrific snacks in the bar; dine on satisfyingly robust British classics in the restaurant or 'host your own roast' with friends.

#### QUEEN'S PARK

🛏 **Salusbury**                                    🆅🅸🆂🅰 ⓒⓒ 🅰🅴 ⓞ
*50-52 Salusbury Rd. ⊠ NW6 6NN ⊖ Queen's Park. – ℰ (020) 7328 3286
– www.thesalusbury.co.uk – Closed 25-26 December and Monday lunch*
**Rest** – Italian – Carte £ 20/30                             **10**MZB**b**
♦ A refitted pub offering a sage green dining room with a slight Edwardian feel on one side and a busy bar on the other. The Italian kitchen prepares dishes as big in flavour as they are in size.

#### WILLESDEN GREEN                                          12 B3

✗ **Sushi-Say**                                          🆅🅸🆂🅰 ⓒⓒ
ⓐ *33B Walm Ln. ⊠ NW2 5SH ⊖ Willesden Green – ℰ (020) 8459 2971 – Closed 2 weeks August, 25-26 December, 1 January, Wednesday after bank holidays, Monday and Tuesday*                                        **9**LZB**a**
**Rest** – Japanese – *(dinner only and lunch Saturday-Sunday)* Menu £ 20/42
– Carte £ 17/42
♦ Very popular with the locals, attracted by sweet service and an extensive selection of Japanese food. Sit at the counter to watch the skill of the owner as he prepares the sushi.

---

### BROMLEY – Greater London                                  12 B3

🔟 Orpington Golf Centre Sandy Lane, St Paul's Cray, ℰ (01689) 83 96 77

🔟 Magpie Hall lane Magpie Hall lane

#### FARNBOROUGH

✗✗✗ **Chapter One**                         Ⓐ ✿ Ⓟ 🆅🅸🆂🅰 ⓒⓒ 🅰🅴 ⓞ
ⓒ *Farnborough Common, Locksbottom ⊠ BR6 8NF – ℰ (01689) 854 848
– www.chaptersrestaurants.com – Closed first week January*        **8**HZ**a**
**Rest** – Modern European – Menu £ 19/35
**Spec.** Pressed terrine of foie gras and smoked duck breast. Slow roast belly of Gloucester Old Spot pork. Iced peanut parfait with raspberry sorbet.
♦ The skilled kitchen produces assured and precisely executed, modern European cooking at a fair price. The mock Tudor exterior belies the contemporary styling of the restaurant and bar within.

#### ORPINGTON

✗✗ **Xian**                                       Ⓐ 🆅🅸🆂🅰 ⓒⓒ 🅰🅴 ⓞ
*324 High St. ⊠ BR6 0NG – ℰ (01689) 871 881 – Closed 2 weeks April, 25-26 December, Sunday lunch and Monday*                              **8**JY**a**
**Rest** – Chinese – Menu £ 10/17 – Carte £ 19/26
♦ Modern, marbled interior with oriental artefacts make this personally run Chinese restaurant a firm favourite with locals. Look out for the Peking specialities.

**BELSIZE PARK**

### XX  XO                                              AC VISA ㏇ AE ①
*29 Belsize Ln.* ⊠ *NW3 5AS* ⊖ *Belsize Park –* ℰ *(020) 7433 0888*
*– www.rickerrestaurants.com/xo – Closed 25-26 December and 1 January*
**Rest** – Asian – Menu £ 15 (lunch) – Carte £ 23/33                **11**PZA**a**
♦ Busy bar behind which is a slick and stylish dining room. Vibrant atmosphere;
popular with all the good-looking locals. Japanese, Korean, Thai and Chinese cooking; dishes are best shared.

### X  Retsina                                          AC VISA ㏇
*48-50 Belsize Ln* ⊠ *NW3 5AR* ⊖ *Belsize Park –* ℰ *(020) 7431 5855*
*– www.retsina-london.com – Closed 25-26 December, 1 January, Monday lunch
and bank holidays*                                              **11**PZA**n**
**Rest** – Greek – Menu £ 20 (lunch) – Carte £ 20/47
♦ Family-run restaurant whose unapologetically traditional menu offers all the
Greek classics but the grill and souvla are the stars of the show. Service and atmosphere are both relaxed and friendly.

### X  Tandis                                           AC VISA ㏇ AE
*73 Haverstock Hill* ⊠ *NW3 4SL* ⊖ *Chalk Farm –* ℰ *(020) 7586 8079*
*– www.tandisrestaurant.com – Closed 25 December*              **11**QZB**a**
**Rest** – Persian – Carte £ 20/30
♦ Enticing Iranian food comes in the form of invigorating 'koresht' stews and
succulent 'kababs', along with specialities such as 'sabzi polo' and 'kashke badem-
jaan'. Contemporary décor.

**BLOOMSBURY**

### 🏠  Covent Garden                  £₅ 🕙 AC 📶 🕸 VISA ㏇ AE ①
*10 Monmouth St.* ⊠ *WC2H 9HB* ⊖ *Covent Garden –* ℰ *(020) 7806 1000*
*– www.coventgardenhotel.co.uk*                                **31**ALU**x**
**56 rm** – ♦£ 300 ♦♦£ 426, ⊑ £ 21 – 2 suites
**Rest** *Brasserie Max* – see restaurant listing
♦ Popular with those of a theatrical bent. Boldly designed, stylish bedrooms, with
technology discreetly concealed. Boasts a very comfortable first floor oak-panelled drawing room with its own honesty bar.

### 🏠  Charlotte Street                £₅ 🕙 🕭 AC 📶 🕸 VISA ㏇ AE ①
*15 Charlotte St.* ⊠ *W1T 1RJ* ⊖ *Goodge Street –* ℰ *(020) 7806 2000*
*– www.charlottestreethotel.co.uk*                             **31**AJT**e**
**48 rm** – ♦£ 288 ♦♦£ 396, ⊑ £ 20 – 4 suites
**Rest** *Oscar* – see restaurant listing
♦ Stylish interior designed with a charming and understated English feel. Impec-
cably kept and individually decorated bedrooms. In-house screening room is popular with the local advertising execs.

### 🏠  Montague on the Gardens        🚗 🕝 🕸 £₅ 🕙 🕭 rm, AC 📶 🕸
*15 Montague St.* ⊠ *WC1B 5BJ* ⊖ *Holborn –* ℰ *(020)*              VISA ㏇ AE ①
*7637 1001 – www.montaguehotel.com*                            **31**ALT**a**
**94 rm** – ♦£ 174/330 ♦♦£ 198/330, ⊑ £ 16.50 – 6 suites
**Rest** *Blue Door Bistro* – English – Menu £ 25 – Carte £ 28/59
♦ A traditional but elegant British feel to this period townhouse; its clubby bar
and conservatory overlook a secluded garden. Individually decorated bedrooms.
Bistro divided between two small, pretty rooms.

### 🏠  Bloomsbury                     🕙 🕭 rm, AC 🕸 📶 🕸 VISA ㏇ AE ①
*16-22 Gt Russell St* ⊠ *WC1B 3NN* ⊖ *Tottenham Court Road –* ℰ *(020)*
*7347 1000 – www.doylecollection.com/bloomsbury*              **31**AKT**n**
**153 rm** – ♦£ 450 ♦♦£ 468, ⊑ £ 21
**Rest** *Landseer* – *(closed lunch Saturday and Sunday )* Menu £ 25 (dinner)
– Carte £ 35/57
♦ Neo-Georgian building by Edward Lutyens, built for YMCA in 1929. Refurbished
in 2009 and now comes with a smart, comfortable interior, from the lobby to the
bedrooms. Restaurant with largely British menu.

LONDON

XXX  **Pied à Terre**                                  AC ⇔ VISA ⊚ AE
⇔  *34 Charlotte St* ⊠ *W1T 2NH* ⊖ *Goodge Street* – ℰ *(020) 7636 1178*
*– www.pied-a-terre.co.uk – Closed last week December, first week January,*
*Saturday lunch and Sunday*                                    **31**AJT**f**
**Rest** – Innovative – Menu £ 30/75🍴
**Spec.** Pressed terrine of foie gras and smoked eel with wasabi vinaigrette. Poached lobster with confit pineapple and pata negra. Millefeuille 'Peach Melba'.
♦ 2011 saw a change at this 20 year veteran of Charlotte Street. Shane Osborn
sailed into the sunset and in his place as head chef came Marcus Eaves from
L'Autre Pied. The menu is an appealing read and the cooking remains ambitious
in its reach and elaborate in its execution.

XX  **Hakkasan Hanway Place**                          AC VISA ⊚ AE
⇔  *8 Hanway Pl.* ⊠ *W1T 1HD* ⊖ *Tottenham Court Road* – ℰ *(020) 7927 7000*
*– www.hakkasan.com – Closed 24-25 December*                   **31**AKT**c**
**Rest** – Chinese – Carte £ 40/89
**Spec.** Peking duck with Royal Beluga caviar. Roasted silver cod. Jivara hazelnut
bomb.
♦ Cool and seductive subterranean restaurant, with an air of exclusivity. Innova-
tion and originality have been added to the Cantonese base to create dishes with
zip and depth. Lunchtime dim sum is a highlight.

XX  **Mon Plaisir**                                    🍷 VISA ⊚ AE
*19-21 Monmouth St.* ⊠ *WC2H 9DD* ⊖ *Covent Garden* – ℰ *(020) 7836 7243*
*– www.monplaisir.co.uk – Closed Christmas-New Year, Sunday and bank*
*holidays*                                                     **31**ALU**g**
**Rest** – French – Menu £ 19 (lunch and early dinner) – Carte £ 30/41
♦ This proud French institution opened in the 1940s. Enjoy satisfyingly authentic
classics in any of the four contrasting rooms, full of Gallic charm; the bar was sal-
vaged from a Lyonnais brothel.

XX  **Incognico**                                      AC 🍷 ⇔ VISA ⊚ AE
*117 Shaftesbury Ave.* ⊠ *WC2H 8AD* ⊖ *Tottenham Court Road* – ℰ *(020)*
*7836 8866 – www.incognico.com – Closed Sunday and bank holidays*
**Rest** – Modern European – Menu £ 25 (lunch) – Carte £ 29/38    **31**AKU**q**
♦ Comfortable, smartly dressed restaurant with dark wood and brown leather
lending a masculine, clubby feel. Influences from France and Italy inform the
cooking from a capable kitchen.

XX  **Roka**                                           AC VISA ⊚ AE ⊙
*37 Charlotte St* ⊠ *W1T 1RR* ⊖ *Goodge Street* – ℰ *(020) 7580 6464*
*– www.rokarestaurant.com – Closed 24-26 December*             **31**AJT**k**
**Rest** – Japanese – Carte £ 35/65
♦ Bright, atmospheric interior of teak and oak; bustling and trendy feel. Contemporary touches added to Japanese dishes; try specialities from the on-view Robata grill. Capable and chatty service.

XX  **Fino**                                           VISA ⊚ AE
*33 Charlotte St. (entrance on Rathbone St.)* ⊠ *W1T 1RR* ⊖ *Goodge Street*
*– ℰ (020) 7813 8010 – www.finorestaurant.com – Closed Saturday lunch, Sunday*
*and bank holidays*                                            **31**AJT**a**
**Rest** – Spanish – Menu £ 18 (lunch) – Carte £ 21/49
♦ Seafood is handled especially well in this lively, quite smart and smoothly run
basement tapas restaurant. Sensibly divided menu, with dishes designed for sharing. Youthful, helpful service.

XX  **Sardo**                                          AC VISA ⊚ AE ⊙
*45 Grafton Way* ⊠ *W1T 5DQ* ⊖ *Warren Street* – ℰ *(020) 7387 2521*
*– www.sardo-restaurant.com – Closed Christmas, Saturday lunch and Sunday*
**Rest** – Italian – Carte £ 26/34                             **18**RZD**c**
♦ Expect a warm and welcoming atmosphere at this simply decorated Italian restaurant, with plenty of regulars and friendly service. Sardinian specialities and seasonal specials are the highlights.

XX **Archipelago**                                              VISA ⦿ AE ⓘ
110 Whitfield St. ⊠ W1T 5ED ⊖ Goodge Street – ℰ (020) 7383 3346
– www.archipelago-restaurant.co.uk – Closed 24-27 December, Saturday
lunch, Sunday and bank holidays                                **18**RZD**c**
**Rest** – Innovative – Carte £ 28/38
♦ Eccentrically decorated in the style of an overflowing bazaar. Asian influence to
the equally exotic and highly unusual menu which could include crocodile, zebra,
wildebeest and even scorpion.

XX **Brasserie Max** – at Covent Garden Hotel          AC ⇔ VISA ⦿ AE ⓘ
10 Monmouth St. ⊠ WC2H 9HB ⊖ Covent Garden – ℰ (020) 7806 1000
– www.firmdalehotels.com                                       **31**ALU**x**
**Rest** – Modern European – (booking essential) Menu £ 24/25 – Carte £ 35/54
♦ It's not just shoppers and theatregoers who appreciate this stylish brasserie. Its
international menu, grilled specialities, Sunday brunches and afternoon teas have
widespread appeal.

XX **Oscar** – at Charlotte Street Hotel                    AC VISA ⦿ AE ⓘ
15 Charlotte St. ⊠ W1T 1RJ ⊖ Goodge Street – ℰ (020) 7907 4005
– www.charlottestreethotel.co.uk                               **31**AJT**e**
**Rest** – Modern European – Menu £ 23/25 – Carte £ 33/56
♦ Its terrace spills out onto Charlotte Street, full of those enjoying cocktails and
sharing platters, while inside is awash with colour. Grilled meats are a highlight of
the large menu.

XX **Rasa Samudra**                                           VISA ⦿ AE
5 Charlotte St. ⊠ W1T 1RE ⊖ Goodge Street – ℰ (020) 7637 0222
– www.rasarestaurants.com – Closed 25 December-1 January, lunch Sunday and
bank holidays                                                  **31**AJT**r**
**Rest** – Indian – Menu £ 23/30 – Carte £ 22/32
♦ Its bright pink hue makes it easy to spot. Specialises in the southwest region of
Kerala so expect fish, vegetarian dishes and plenty of coconut and have the pre-
meal snacks. Well meaning service.

X **Mennula**                                          AC ⇔ VISA ⦿ AE ⓘ
10 Charlotte St. ⊠ W1T 2LT ⊖ Goodge Street – ℰ (020) 7363 2833
– www.mennula.com – Closed 1 week Christmas, Saturday lunch and bank
holidays                                                       **31**AJT**b**
**Rest** – Italian – Menu £ 20 (lunch and early dinner) – Carte approx. £ 30
♦ Sicilian specialities provide the highlights at this enthusiastically run Italian restaurant, whose name means 'almond'. Compact but bright, crisply decorated
room; ask for one of the booths.

X **Paramount**                                      ≤ AC ⇔ VISA ⦿ AE
Centre Point (31st floor) 101-103 New Oxford St. ⊠ WC1A 1DD
⊖ Tottenham Court Road – ℰ (020) 7420 2900 – www.paramount.uk.net
– Closed 25-26 December and Sunday dinner                      **31**AKT**b**
**Rest** – Modern European – Menu £ 24 (lunch and early dinner) – Carte £ 30/46
♦ Worth the palaver of getting into this Grade II listed building: the views are ter-
rific and this is a fun, keenly run restaurant. Ambitious and quite elaborate cook-
ing; champagne bar one floor up.

X **Kopapa**                                          AC ⤦ VISA ⦿ AE
32-34 Monmouth St ⊠ WC2H 9HA ⊖ Covent Garden – ℰ (020) 7240 6076
– www.kopapa.co.uk – Closed 25 December                        **31**ALU**h**
**Rest** – Asian influences – (booking advisable) Menu £ 25 (lunch and early dinner) – Carte £ 24/34
♦ Kopapa, a Maori word for a gathering, is Peter Gordon's just-drop-in-anytime
place. It's cramped but fun, with breakfast morphing into all-day dining. It's the
'fusion'-inspired tapas that will give your taste buds the best workout.

LONDON

✗ **Giaconda Dining Room**   AC VISA ⬤ AE

😊 *9 Denmark St. ⊠ WC2H 8LS ⊖ Tottenham Court Road – ℰ (020) 7240 3334 – www.giacondadining.com – Closed 3 weeks August, 2 weeks Easter, 2 weeks Christmas-New Year, Saturday lunch, Sunday, Monday and bank holidays*
**Rest** – Modern European – *(booking essential)* Carte £ 22/30   **31**AKT**k**
♦ Aussie owners run a small, fun and very busy place in an unpromising location. The very well priced menu offers an appealing mix of gutsy, confident, no-nonsense food, with French and Italian influences.

✗ **Salt Yard**   AC VISA ⬤ AE

😊 *54 Goodge St. ⊠ W1T 4NA ⊖ Goodge Street – ℰ (020) 7637 0657 – www.saltyard.co.uk – Closed 24 December-4 January, Saturday lunch and Sunday*   **31**AJT**d**
**Rest** – Mediterranean – Carte approx. £ 20⊛
♦ Ground floor bar and buzzy basement restaurant specialising in good value plates of tasty Italian and Spanish dishes, ideal for sharing; charcuterie a speciality. Super wine list.

✗ **Cigala**   ☂ AC VISA ⬤ AE ⓪

*54 Lamb's Conduit St. ⊠ WC1N 3LW ⊖ Russell Square – ℰ (020) 7405 1717 – www.cigala.co.uk*   **19**TZD**a**
**Rest** – Spanish – *(booking essential)* Menu £ 18 (lunch) – Carte £ 24/32⊛
♦ Spanish restaurant on corner of attractive street. Simply furnished; open-plan kitchen. Robust Iberian cooking, with some dishes designed for sharing; interesting drinks list.

✗ **Tsunami**   AC VISA ⬤ AE ⓪

*93 Charlotte St. ⊠ W1T 4PY ⊖ Goodge Street – ℰ (020) 7637 0050 – www.tsunamirestaurant.co.uk – Closed Saturday lunch and Sunday*
**Rest** – Japanese – Carte £ 30/38 **s**   **30**AIT**n**
♦ Sister to the original in Clapham. Sweet, pretty place, with lacquered walls, floral motif and moody lighting. Contemporary Japanese cuisine is carefully prepared and sensibly priced.

✗ **Barrica**   AC VISA ⬤ AE

*62 Goodge St ⊠ W1T 4NE ⊖ Goodge Street – ℰ (020) 7436 9448 – www.barrica.co.uk – Closed 25-26 December, 1 January, Sunday and bank holidays*   **31**AJT**x**
**Rest** – Spanish – *(booking essential)* Carte £ 18/20
♦ Lively, noisy and warmly decorated tapas bar. Authentic dishes come with plenty of flavour and are complemented by a thoughtfully compiled Spanish wine list. Busy front bar.

## CAMDEN TOWN

✗✗ **York & Albany** with rm   ☂ 🛏 📶 VISA ⬤ AE ⓪

*127-129 Parkway ⊠ NW1 7PS ⊖ Camden Town – ℰ (020) 7388 3344 – www.gordonramsay.com/yorkandalbany*   **12**RZB**s**
**10 rm** – ♦£ 168/186 ♦♦£ 168/348, ⌴ £ 12
**Rest** – Modern European – *(booking essential)* Carte £ 25/38
♦ 1820s John Nash former coaching inn, now part of Gordon Ramsay's empire. Smart bar and informal dining; lower level offers kitchen views. Cooking is refined without being fussy, and influences are European. Comfortable, individually decorated bedrooms.

✗ **Market**   AC VISA ⬤ AE ⓪

😊 *43 Parkway ⊠ NW1 7PN ⊖ Camden Town – ℰ (020) 7267 9700 – www.marketrestaurant.co.uk – Closed 25 December-3 January ,Sunday dinner and bank holidays*   **12**RZB**x**
**Rest** – British – *(booking essential)* Carte £ 25/34
♦ Market fresh produce used to create satisfying and refreshingly matter of fact British dishes, at excellent prices that entice plenty of passers-by. Appealing décor of exposed brick walls, old school chairs and zinc-topped tables.

## DARTMOUTH PARK

🏠 **Bull and Last**                                                🛋 VISA ☎

*168 Highgate Rd ⊠ NW5 1QS ⊖ Tufnell Park. – ℰ (020) 7267 3641*
*– www.thebullandlast.co.uk – Closed 24- 25 December*          **12**RZA**a**
**Rest** – British – *(booking essential)* Carte £ 27/33
♦ A busy Victorian pub with plenty of charm and character; the upstairs is a little
quieter. Cooking is muscular, satisfying and reflects the time of year; charcuterie is
a speciality.

## EUSTON

🏨 **Novotel London St. Pancras**              🛋 ᴛ 🛋 & rm. 🗚 🕸 ⸙ 🔥

*100-110 Euston Rd. ⊠ NW1 2AJ ⊖ Euston – ℰ (020)*        VISA ☎ AE ①
*7666 9000 – www.novotel.com*                                   **18**SZC**a**
**309 rm** – ♦£ 350 ♦♦£ 350, ⯑ £ 14.95 – 3 suites
**Rest** – *(bar lunch Saturday, Sunday and bank holidays)* Menu £ 19/23
– Carte £ 30/48
♦ Halfway between Euston and Kings Cross, this hotel has good-sized bedrooms
for London and those on the higher floors enjoy views over the city. Good business amenities. International menu and buffet breakfast.

XX **Red n Hot**                                                   ⇔ VISA ☎ AE

*37 Chalton St ⊠ NW1 1JD ⊖ Euston – ℰ (020) 7388 0808*
*– www.rednhotgroup.com – Closed 25 December*                  **12**SZC**b**
**Rest** – Chinese – Carte £ 15/19
♦ The clue is in the name! The fiery pepper dominates the extensive selection of
Sichuan specialities that make good use of freshwater fish and poultry. Simpler
lunchtime menu includes hotpots.

## HAMPSTEAD

X **Goldfish**                                                    ⇔ VISA ☎ AE

*82 Hampstead High St ⊠ NW3 1RE ⊖ Hampstead – ℰ (020) 7794 6666*
*– www.restaurantprivilege.com*                                **11**PZA**z**
**Rest** – Asian – Carte approx. £ 40
♦ Sweet little place, divided into three differently decorated rooms. Mix of Chinese and other Asian countries; chef also adds own creations. Well-priced lunch
menu, including popular weekend dim sum.

X **La Cocotte**                                                  AC VISA ☎ AE

*85b Fleet Rd ⊠ NW3 2QY ⊖ Belsize Park – ℰ (020) 7433 3317*
*– www.la-cocotte.co.uk – Closed Sunday dinner, Monday and lunch*
*Tuesday-Thursday*                                              **11**QZA**a**
**Rest** – French – Menu £ 13 (lunch) – Carte £ 21/31
♦ The decorative clichés are countered by affable, self-deprecating service at this
busy, unpretentious bistro. Expect bourgeois classics, with slow-cooked dishes in
shallow iron pots a highlight.

🏠 **Wells**                                                 🛋 AC VISA ☎ AE

*30 Well Walk ⊠ NW3 1BX ⊖ Hampstead. – ℰ (020) 7794 3785*
*– www.thewellshampstead.co.uk*                                **11**PZA**v**
**Rest** – British – Carte £ 28/38
♦ Part country pub, part city sophisticate; busy ground floor, with more sedate
upstairs restaurant. Cooking is hearty in flavour and sophisticated in look, with a
pleasing British edge.

🏠 **Magdala**                                               🛋 ⇔ VISA ☎

*2A South Hill Park ⊠ NW3 2SB ⊖ Belsize Park. – ℰ (020) 7435 2503*
*– www.the-magdala.com*                                        **11**PZA**s**
**Rest** – Modern European – Carte £ 22/30
♦ Uncomplicated pub food but prepared with care; some dishes designed for
sharing. Relaxed, locals pub on the edge of the Heath, with countryside feel. Upstairs room used at weekends.

## HATTON GARDEN

### Bleeding Heart 🛖 ⇄ VISA ⏀ AE ⊙
*Bleeding Heart Yard, off Greville St.* ✉ *EC1N 8SJ* ⊖ *Farringdon –* ℰ *(020)*
*7242 8238 – www.bleedingheart.co.uk – Closed Christmas-New Year, Saturday*
*and Sunday* **32ANTe**
**Rest** – French – *(booking essential)* Menu £ 25 (lunch) **s** – Carte £ 28/43 **s**⊛
♦ Dickensian yard plays host to this atmospheric, candlelit restaurant; popular
with those from The City. Classic French cuisine is the draw, with service that's
formal but has personality. Wines from owners' New Zealand estate.

## HOLBORN

### Chancery Court 🏨 🛖 🛦 🖃 ⅙ Ⓐ ⅌ ⅙ 🛁 VISA ⏀ AE ⊙
*252 High Holborn* ✉ *WC1V 7EN* ⊖ *Holborn –* ℰ *(020) 7829 9888*
*– www.chancerycourt.com* **32AMTa**
**354 rm** – ⍦£ 264/366 ⍦⍦£ 264/366, ⍯ £ 26 – 2 suites
**Rest** *Pearl* – see restaurant listing
♦ Striking former Pearl Assurance HQ, built in 1914, now an imposing place to
stay. Impressive marbled lobby and grand central courtyard. Decent sized bedrooms with comprehensive modern facilities.

### Pearl – at Chancery Court Hotel Ⓐ ⇄ VISA ⏀ AE ⊙
*252 High Holborn* ✉ *WC1V 7EN* ⊖ *Holborn –* ℰ *(020) 7829 7000*
*– www.pearl-restaurant.com – Closed 2 weeks August, Sunday and bank*
*holidays* **32AMTa**
**Rest** – French – Menu £ 30/60⊛
♦ Impressive former banking hall, with walls clad in Italian marble and Corinthian
columns. Waiters provide efficient service at well-spaced tables; cooking shows
originality.

### Asadal Ⓐ ⇄ VISA ⏀ AE
*227 High Holborn* ✉ *WC1V 7DA* ⊖ *Holborn –* ℰ *(020) 7430 9006*
*– www.asadal.co.uk – Closed 25-26 December, 1 January and Sunday lunch*
**Rest** – Korean – Menu £ 14/20 – Carte £ 17/31 **31ALTn**
♦ Sharing is the key in this busy basement, where you'll be oblivious to its unprepossessing location. Hotpots, dumplings and barbeques are the highlights
from the easy-to-follow menu. Staff cope well with the evening rush.

### Moti Mahal Ⓐ ⇄ VISA ⏀ AE ⊙
*45 Great Queen St.* ✉ *WC2B 5AA* ⊖ *Holborn –* ℰ *(020) 7240 9329*
*– www.motimahal-uk.com – Closed Christmas, Sunday and lunch Saturday and*
*bank holidays* **31ALUk**
**Rest** – Indian – Carte £ 37/46
♦ Restaurant is split between a bright, busy ground floor and more intimate
basement. Specialities follow the Grand Trunk Road, stretching from Bengal to
the North West and the Pakistan border.

### Great Queen Street ⅋ VISA ⏀
*32 Great Queen St* ✉ *WC2B 5AA* ⊖ *Holborn –* ℰ *(020) 7242 0622 – Closed*
*Christmas-New Year and bank holidays* **31ALTd**
**Rest** – British – *(booking essential)* Carte £ 25/30
♦ The menu is a model of British understatement and is dictated by the seasons;
the cooking, confident and satisfying with laudable prices and generous portions.
Lively atmosphere and enthusiastic service.

### French Kitchen 🛖 Ⓐ ⇄ VISA ⏀ AE
*95-97 High Holborn* ✉ *WC1V 6LF* ⊖ *Holborn –* ℰ *(020) 7242 4580*
*– www.french-kitchen.co.uk – Closed 25 December* **32AMTk**
**Rest** – French – Carte £ 20/32
♦ Open all day and offering everything from breakfast and afternoon tea to
pizza, charcuterie and comforting French classics. Large, animated room with a
rustic feel and friendly service.

LONDON

## PRIMROSE HILL

### XX Odette's     🛆 AC ⇄ VISA ⓒ AE
*130 Regent's Park Rd.* ⊠ *NW1 8XL* ⊖ *Chalk Farm* – ℰ *(020) 7586 8569*
*– www.odettesprimrosehill.com – Closed 1 week Christmas*     **11**QZB**b**
**Rest** – Modern European – Menu £ 20 (lunch and early dinner) – Carte £ 31/51
♦ A local institution that has recently lightened up. Warm and inviting interior, with chatty but organised service. Robust and quite elaborate cooking, with chef-owner passionate about his Welsh roots.

### X L'Absinthe     AC ⇄ VISA ⓒ AE
*40 Chalcot Rd* ⊠ *NW1 8LS* ⊖ *Chalk Farm* – ℰ *(020) 7483 4848*
*– www.labsinthe.co.uk – Closed August, Christmas and Monday*     **11**QZB**s**
**Rest** – French – Menu £ 13 (lunch) – Carte £ 22/34⅜
♦ Lively and enthusiastically run French bistro, with tightly packed tables, spread over two floors. All the favourites, from Lyonnais salad to duck confit. Commendably priced French wine list.

### 🏚 Engineer     🛆 P. VISA ⓒ
*65 Gloucester Ave* ⊠ *NW1 8JH* ⊖ *Chalk Farm.* – ℰ *(020) 7722 0950*
*– www.the-engineer.com – Closed 1 week Christmas*     **12**RZB**a**
**Rest** – British – Carte £ 26/44
♦ Grade II listed pub with Italianate façade. Divided between bar and restaurant, with a popular garden terrace at the back. Confident, wholesome cooking; suppliers name-checked on the menu.

## ST PANCRAS

### 🏨 St Pancras Renaissance     🛆 🖾 ⑩ 🕉 Ł₅ ▐❚ & rm, AC ℅ 🎵 🏊
*Euston Rd* ⊠ *NW1 2AR* ⊖ *King's Cross St. Pancras*    VISA ⓒ AE ⓪
*– ℰ (020) 7941 3540 – www.stpancrasrenaissance.co.uk*     **12**SZC**d**
**207 rm** – ❸£ 390 ❸❸£ 390/1140, ⌷ £ 17 – 38 suites
**Rest** *Gilbert Scott* – see restaurant listing
**Rest** *Booking Office* – British – Carte £ 27/40
♦ This Gothic jewel, built in 1873 as the Midland Grand hotel and now finally restored, reopened in 2011 under the Marriott brand. Former taxi rank now the spacious lobby and all-day dining is in the old Booking Office. Corridors and staircases evoke the past; bedrooms are a little more functional.

### XX Gilbert Scott – at St Pancras Renaissance Hotel     AC ⇄ VISA ⓒ AE
*Euston Rd* ⊠ *NW1 2AR* ⊖ *King's Cross St. Pancras* – ℰ *(020) 7278 3888*
*– www.thegilbertscott.co.uk*     **12**SZC**d**
**Rest** – British – Carte £ 32/70
♦ Run under the aegis of Marcus Wareing and named after the architect of this Gothic masterpiece, the restaurant has the look of a Grand Salon but the buzz of a brasserie. It celebrates the UK's many regional and historic specialities.

## SWISS COTTAGE

### XX Bradley's     AC ℅ VISA ⓒ AE
☺   *25 Winchester Rd.* ⊠ *NW3 3NR* ⊖ *Swiss Cottage* – ℰ *(020) 7722 3457*
*– www.bradleysnw3.co.uk – Closed Saturday lunch and Sunday dinner*
**Rest** – Modern European – Menu £ 18/25 – Carte £ 30/40     **11**PZB**e**
♦ A stalwart of the local dining scene and ideal for visitors to the nearby Hampstead Theatre. The thoughtfully compiled and competitively priced set menus of mostly classical cooking draw in plenty of regulars.

### XX Singapore Garden     AC VISA ⓒ AE
*83 Fairfax Rd.* ⊠ *NW6 4DY* ⊖ *Swiss Cottage* – ℰ *(020) 7328 5314*
*– www.singaporegarden.co.uk – Closed 24-28 December*     **11**PZB**x**
**Rest** – Asian – Menu £ 30 (dinner) – Carte £ 31/52
♦ A smart, bright and comfortable room, with endearingly enthusiastic service. Your best bet is to pick vibrant and zesty dishes from the list of Singaporean and Malaysian specialities.

## ✗✗ Eriki    AC VISA ⦿⦿ AE

*4-6 Northways Par, Finchley Rd ✉ NW3 5EN ⊖ Swiss Cottage – ℰ (020)*
*7722 0606 – www.eriki.co.uk – Closed Saturday lunch*    **11**PZB**u**
**Rest** – Indian – Menu £ 20 (dinner) – Carte £ 27/35
◆ The menu offers an invigorating gastronomic tour of all parts of India; vegetarians will be in clover. Vividly coloured, comfortable room with fine tapestries; well-meaning service and lots of regulars.

## TUFNELL PARK

## 🍸 Junction Tavern    🏠 VISA ⦿⦿

*101 Fortess Rd ✉ NW5 1AG ⊖ Tufnell Park. – ℰ (020) 7485 9400*
*– www.junctiontavern.co.uk – Closed 24-26 December and 1 January*
**Rest** – Modern European – Carte £ 23/31    **12**RZA**x**
◆ Sizeable pub with striking matt black façade. Dining room on one side, along with conservatory and busy bar. Well-balanced menu; flavoursome cooking. Interesting and regularly changing guest beers.

## WEST HAMPSTEAD

## ✗ Walnut    AC VISA ⦿⦿ AE ①

*280 West End Ln., Fortune Grn. ✉ NW6 1LJ ⊖ West Hampstead – ℰ (020)*
*7794 7772 – www.walnutwalnut.com – Closed Sunday and Monday*
**Rest** – Traditional – *(dinner only)* Carte £ 24/38    **10**NZA**a**
◆ Eco-aware chef-owner in his raised, open kitchen offers classical cooking, where game and fish are the specialities. Relaxed and informal corner restaurant, with plenty of local regulars.

---

# CITY OF LONDON – Greater London    **12** B3

## 🏨🏨 Andaz Liverpool Street    🛗 🖥 ᰪ rm, AC ⚒ rm, ⁋ 🌊 VISA ⦿⦿ AE ①

*40 Liverpool St. ✉ EC2M 7QN ⊖ Liverpool Street – ℰ (020) 7961 1234*
*– www.andazdining.com*    **34**ART**t**
**264 rm** – †£ 144/516 ††£ 372/600, ⌁ £ 22 – 3 suites
**Rest 1901** – see restaurant listing
**Rest Catch** – see restaurant listing
**Rest Miyako** – Japanese – ℰ (020) 7618 7100 *(closed Saturday lunch and Sunday) (booking essential)* Carte £ 23/52
◆ A contemporary and stylish interior hides behind the classic Victorian façade. Bright and spacious bedrooms with state-of-the-art facilities. Various dining options include Miyako, a compact Japanese restaurant, and a traditional pub.

## 🏨🏨 Threadneedles    🖥 ᰪ AC ⚒ ⁋ 🌊 VISA ⦿⦿ AE ①

*5 Threadneedle St. ✉ EC2R 8AY ⊖ Bank – ℰ (020) 7657 8080*
*– www.theetoncollection.com*    **34**ARU**y**
**68 rm** – †£ 222/414 ††£ 294/546, ⌁ £ 23 – 1 suite
**Rest Bonds** – see restaurant listing
◆ A converted bank, dating from 1856, with a stunning stained-glass cupola in the lounge. Bedrooms are very stylish and individual featuring CD players and Egyptian cotton sheets.

## 🏨🏨 Montcalm London City at The Brewery    🖥 ᰪ AC ⚒ ⁋ 🌊

*52 Chiswell St ✉ EC1Y 4SD ⊖ Moorgate – ℰ (020)*    VISA ⦿⦿ AE ①
*7614 0100 – www.themontcalmlondoncity.co.uk*    **19**VZD**r**
**220 rm** – †£ 300/540 ††£ 300/540, ⌁ £ 20 – 18 suites
**Rest Chiswell Street Dining Rooms** – see restaurant listing
◆ The majority of the contemporary rooms are in the original part of the Whitbread Brewery, built in 1752; ask for a quieter room overlooking the courtyard, or one of the 25 found in one of the 4 restored Georgian townhouses across the road.

XXX **Rhodes Twenty Four**　　　　⟨ AC ⇔ VISA ⑳ AE ⑩
£3
*Tower 42, (24th floor) 25 Old Broad St. ⊠ EC2N 1HQ ⊖ Liverpool Street*
*– ℰ (020) 7877 7703 – www.rhodes24.co.uk – Closed Christmas-New Year,*
*Saturday, Sunday and bank holidays*　　　　　　　　　　**34ARTv**
**Rest** – British – Carte £ 45/65
**Spec.** Scallop raviolo with buttered samphire. Steamed mutton and onion suet
pudding with carrots. Warm chocolate pudding, passion fruit sorbet.
◆ Prepare for security checks at Tower 42 before taking the lift up to its
24th floor; the views will be worth it. The unmistakeable signature of Gary
Rhodes is writ large on the menu: seasonal dishes of a pleasingly British
persuasion.

XXX **Coq d'Argent**　　　　　　　⟨ AC ⟩ VISA ⑳ AE ⑩
*1 Poultry ⊠ EC2R 8EJ ⊖ Bank – ℰ (020) 7395 5000 – www.coqdargent.co.uk*
*– Closed 25-27 December, 1 January, Saturday lunch, Sunday dinner and bank*
*holidays*　　　　　　　　　　　　　　　　　　　　　**33AQUc**
**Rest** – French – *(booking essential)* Menu £ 32 (lunch) – Carte £ 36/45
◆ Resembling the bow of a ship; with a busy bar, terrace and formal garden providing commanding views over the Square Mile. Slick, well run, modern restaurant; appealing shellfish counter.

XXX **1901** – at Andaz Liverpool Street Hotel　　AC ⇔ VISA ⑳ AE ⑩
*Liverpool St. ⊠ EC2M 7QN ⊖ Liverpool Street – ℰ (020) 7618 7000*
*– www.andaz.com – Closed Saturday lunch, Sunday and bank holidays*
**Rest** – French – Menu £ 25 (lunch) – Carte £ 32/52　　　　**34ARTt**
◆ An impressive and imposing room, with an eye-catching cupola, cocktail bar
and cheese and wine room. Kitchen makes proud use of British ingredients in refined and skilled cooking.

XXX **Bonds** – at Threadneedles Hotel　　　　AC ⇔ VISA ⑳ AE ⑩
*5 Threadneedle St. ⊠ EC2R 8AY ⊖ Bank – ℰ (020) 7657 8088*
*– www.theetoncollection.com – Closed Saturday, Sunday and Bank Holidays*
**Rest** – Modern European – Menu £ 23 (lunch and early dinner)　　**34ARUy**
– Carte £ 37/51
◆ Former banking hall from the 1850s, with pillars, marble and panelling. Experienced kitchen produces dishes with bold flavours; fish from Newhaven and slow-
cooked meats the specialities.

XXX **Lutyens**　　　　　　　　　　AC ⇔ VISA ⑳ AE
*85 Fleet St. ⊠ EC4Y 1AE ⊖ St Paul's – ℰ (020) 7583 8385*
*– www.lutyens-restaurant.com – Closed 1 week Christmas, Saturday, Sunday and*
*bank holidays*　　　　　　　　　　　　　　　　　　**32ANUc**
**Rest** – Modern European – Menu £ 40 (dinner) – Carte £ 40/55
◆ The unmistakable hand of Sir Terence Conran: timeless and understated good
looks mixed with functionality and an appealing Anglo-French menu with plenty
of classics that include fruits de mer.

XX **Club Gascon** (Pascal Aussignac)　　　　　AC VISA ⑳ AE
£3
*57 West Smithfield ⊠ EC1A 9DS ⊖ Barbican – ℰ (020) 7796 0600*
*– www.clubgascon.com – Closed Christmas - New Year, Saturday lunch, Sunday*
*and bank holidays*　　　　　　　　　　　　　　　　**33APTz**
**Rest** – French – *(booking essential)* Menu £ 29 (lunch) – Carte £ 50/69 ❀
**Spec.** Line-caught mackerel, pine, abalone and oyster sorbet. Charolais beef varia-
tion, caviar and ox sauce. Turrón, sweet foie gras, Baileys, baby meringues and
passion fruit.
◆ The gastronomy of Gascony and France's southwest are the starting
points but the assured and intensely flavoured cooking also pushes at the
boundaries. Marble and huge floral displays create suitably atmospheric surroundings.

LONDON

379

XX **The Chancery**                                      🅰🅲 𝘝𝘐𝘚𝘈 ⓌⓄ 🅰🅴 ①
*9 Cursitor St ⊠ EC4A 1LL ⊖ Chancery Lane – ℰ (020) 7831 4000*
*– www.thechancery.co.uk – Closed 24 December-4 January, Saturday lunch and*
*Sunday*                                                         **32**ANT**a**
**Rest** – Modern European – Menu £ 35
◆ Cosy restaurant and basement bar, near the Law Courts, with contemporary interior and intimate feel. Quality ingredients put to good use in accomplished, modern dishes.

XX **Mint Leaf Lounge**                                   🅰🅲 𝘝𝘐𝘚𝘈 ⓌⓄ 🅰🅴
*12 Angel Ct., Lothbury ⊠ EC2R 7HB ⊖ Bank – ℰ (020) 7600 0992*
*– www.mintleaflounge.com – Closed 25-26 December, Saturday, Sunday and*
*bank holidays*                                                 **33**AQT**b**
**Rest** – Indian – Menu £ 18 (lunch and early dinner) – Carte £ 38/60
◆ Sister branch to the original in St James's. Slick and stylish, with busy bar. Well paced service of carefully prepared contemporary Indian food, with many of the influences from the south.

XX **Vivat Bacchus**                                      🅰🅲 𝘝𝘐𝘚𝘈 ⓌⓄ 🅰🅴 ①
*47 Farringdon St (basement) ⊠ EC4A 4LL ⊖ Farringdon – ℰ (020) 7353 2648*
*– www.vivatbacchus.co.uk – Closed 25 December, 1 January, Saturday, Sunday*
*and bank holidays*                                             **32**ANT**c**
**Rest** – Traditional – Menu £ 18 – Carte £ 28/60⭑
◆ Platters and tapas served in the large bar; more intimate basement restaurant for meat dishes and South African specialities. Hugely impressive wine list with five cellars of wine.

XX **Vanilla Black**                                      🅰🅲 𝘝𝘐𝘚𝘈 ⓌⓄ 🅰🅴 ①
*17-18 Tooks Ct. ⊠ EC4A 1LB ⊖ Chancery Lane – ℰ (020) 7242 2622*
*– www.vanillablack.co.uk – Closed 2 weeks Christmas-New Year, Saturday lunch*
*and Sunday*                                                    **32**ANT**x**
**Rest** – Vegetarian – Menu £ 24/33
◆ Proving that vegetarian food can be flavoursome and satisfying, with a menu that is varied and imaginative. This is a well run, friendly restaurant with understated décor, run by a husband and wife team.

XX **Cinnamon Kitchen**                            🏠 🅰🅲 ✪ 𝘝𝘐𝘚𝘈 ⓌⓄ 🅰🅴
*9 Devonshire Sq ⊠ EC2M 4YL ⊖ Liverpool Street – ℰ (020) 7626 5000*
*– www.cinnamon-kitchen.com – Closed Saturday lunch, Sunday and bank*
*holidays*                                                      **34**ART**e**
**Rest** – Indian – Menu £ 18/22 – Carte £ 31/56
◆ Sister to The Cinnamon Club. Contemporary Indian cooking, with punchy flavours and arresting presentation. Sprightly service in large, modern surroundings. Watch the action from the Tandoor Bar.

XX **Kenza**                                           🅰🅲 ✪ 𝘝𝘐𝘚𝘈 ⓌⓄ 🅰🅴
*10 Devonshire Sq. ⊠ EC2M 4YP ⊖ Liverpool Street – ℰ (020) 7929 5533*
*– www.kenza-restaurant.com – Closed Saturday lunch, Sunday and bank*
*holidays*                                                      **34**ART**c**
**Rest** – Lebanese – Carte £ 26/33
◆ Exotic basement restaurant, with lamps, carvings, pumping music and nightly belly dancing. Lebanese and Moroccan cooking are the menu influences and the cooking is authentic and accurate.

XX **Sauterelle**                                      🅰🅲 ✪ 𝘝𝘐𝘚𝘈 ⓌⓄ 🅰🅴 ①
*The Royal Exchange ⊠ EC3V 3LR ⊖ Bank – ℰ (020) 7618 2483*
*– www.sauterelle-restaurant.co.uk – Closed Saturday, Sunday and bank holidays,*
**Rest** – French – Menu £ 24 – Carte £ 35/53                    **33**AQU**a**
◆ Impressive location on the mezzanine floor of The Royal Exchange; ask for a table looking down over the Grand Café. A largely French inspired contemporary menu makes good use of luxury ingredients.

XX **Cigalon** 🏧 ⇔ 𝘝𝘐𝘚𝘈 ⓞⓞ 🄰🄴
*115 Chancery Ln* ⊠ *WC2A 1PP* ⊖ *Chancery Lane –* ℰ *(020) 7242 8373*
*– www.cigalon.co.uk – Closed 24 December-3 January, Saturday, Sunday and*
*bank holidays* **32**ANU**x**
**Rest** – French – Menu £ 25 (lunch) – Carte £ 26/31
♦ Pays homage to the food and wine of Provence, in an appropriately bright
space that was a once an auction house. All the classics are here, from bouillabaisse to pieds et paquets. Busy bar in the cellar.

XX **The Mercer** 🏧 ⇔ 𝘝𝘐𝘚𝘈 ⓞⓞ 🄰🄴
*34 Threadneedle St* ⊠ *EC2R 8AY* ⊖ *Bank –* ℰ *(020) 7628 0001*
*– www.themercer.co.uk – Closed 25 December, Saturday, Sunday and bank*
*holidays* **34**ARU**x**
**Rest** – Modern European – Carte £ 28/37 ⅋⅋
♦ Converted bank, with airy feel thanks to high ceilings and large windows. Brasserie style menu with appealing mix of classics and comfort food. Huge choice of
wines available by glass or carafe.

XX **Boisdale of Bishopsgate** 🏧 𝘝𝘐𝘚𝘈 ⓞⓞ 🄰🄴
*Swedeland Crt., 202 Bishopsgate* ⊠ *EC2M 4NR* ⊖ *Liverpool Street*
*–* ℰ *(020) 7283 1763 – www.boisdale.co.uk – Closed 25 December-2 January,*
*Saturday, Sunday and bank holidays* **34**ART**a**
**Rest** – Scottish – Carte £ 28/52
♦ Through ground floor bar, serving oysters and champagne, to brick vaulted
basement with red and tartan décor. Menu featuring Scottish produce. Live jazz
most evenings.

XX **The White Swan** 🏧 𝘝𝘐𝘚𝘈 ⓞⓞ 🄰🄴
*108 Fetter Lane* ⊠ *EC4A 1ES* ⊖ *Chancery Lane –* ℰ *(020) 7242 9696*
*– www.thewhiteswanlondon.com – Closed 25-26 December, Saturday,*
*Sunday and bank holidays* **32**ANT**n**
**Rest** – Modern European – Menu £ 30 (lunch) – Carte £ 28/34
♦ Smart dining room above pub just off Fleet Street: mirrored ceilings, colourful
paintings on walls. Modern, daily changing menus, are good value for the heart
of London.

XX **Manicomio** 🏧 𝘝𝘐𝘚𝘈 ⓞⓞ 🄰🄴
*6 Gutter Ln.* ⊠ *EC2V 8AS* ⊖ *St Paul's –* ℰ *(020) 7726 5010*
*– www.manicomio.co.uk – Closed 1 week Christmas, Saturday, Sunday and bank*
*holidays* **33**APT**s**
**Rest** – Italian – Carte £ 31/54
♦ Second branch to follow the first in Chelsea. Regional Italian fare, with top-
notch ingredients. Bright and fresh first floor restaurant, with deli-café on the
ground floor and bar on top floor.

XX **Luc's Brasserie** 𝘝𝘐𝘚𝘈 ⓞⓞ 🄰🄴
*17-22 Leadenhall Market* ⊠ *EC3V 1LR* ⊖ *Bank –* ℰ *(020) 7621 0666*
*– www.lucsbrasserie.com – Closed 23 December-3 January, Saturday,*
*Sunday and bank holidays* **34**ARU**v**
**Rest** – French – *(lunch only and dinner Tuesday-Thursday) (booking essential at*
*lunch)* Menu £ 20 – Carte £ 27/42
♦ Looks down on the Victorian splendour of Leadenhall Market. First appeared in
1890 but re-invigorated this century. The menu is a paean to all things French
and every classic dish is there.

XX **Barbecoa** 🏧 𝘝𝘐𝘚𝘈 ⓞⓞ 🄰🄴
*20 New Change Passage* ⊠ *EC4M 9AG* ⊖ *St. Paul's –* ℰ *(020) 3005 8555*
*– www.barbecoa.com* **33**APU**v**
**Rest** – Grills – *(booking essential)* Carte £ 28/45
♦ American chef Adam Perry Lane, in collaboration with our own Jamie Oliver,
shows us what barbecuing is all about. The prime meats, butchered in-house, are
cooked to perfection; go for the pulled pork shoulder with cornbread on the side.

LONDON

XX **High Timber**  ⟨⟨ 🛋 AC ⟨⟩ VISA ⬤⬤ AE

*8 High Timber St. ⊠ EC4V 3PA ⊖ Mansion House – 𝒞 (020) 7248 1777*
*– www.hightimber.com – Closed 25 December-4 January, Saturday, Sunday and*
*bank holidays*  **33**APU**b**
**Rest** – Modern European – Menu £ 19 (lunch) – Carte £ 25/55
♦ Rustic look to the room, despite being in a modern block, offering river views.
Great wine cellar, with large choice from South Africa, the owners' homeland.
Cumbrian steaks the speciality.

XX **Goodman City**  AC ⟨⟩ VISA ⬤⬤ AE

*11 Old Jewry ⊠ EC2R 8DU ⊖ Bank – 𝒞 (020) 7600 8220*
*– www.goodmanrestaurants.com – Closed Saturday, Sunday and bank holidays*
**Rest** – Beef specialities – Menu £ 21 (lunch) – Carte £ 48/68  **33**AQU**s**
♦ Steaks, cut to order, are the stars of the show at this sister to the Mayfair original. Choose corn-fed, wet-matured USDA beef or Scottish and Irish grass-fed;
plenty of side dishes available too.

XX **Chiswell Street Dining Rooms** – at Montcalm London City Hotel

*56 Chiswell St ⊠ EC1Y 4SA ⊖ Moorgate – 𝒞 (020)*  AC VISA ⬤⬤ AE
*7614 0177 – www.chiswellstreetdining.com*  **19**VZD**r**
**Rest** – British – Carte £ 30/52
♦ The Martin brothers used their Botanist restaurant as the model for this corner
of the old Whitbread brewery. The cocktail bar comes alive at night. Makes good
use of British produce, especially fish from nearby Billingsgate.

XX **Catch** – at Andaz Liverpool Street Hotel  AC VISA ⬤⬤ AE ⑩

*40 Liverpool St. ⊠ EC2M 7QN ⊖ Liverpool Street – 𝒞 (020) 7618 7200*
*– www.andazdining.com – Closed Saturday and Sunday*  **34**ART**t**
**Rest** – Seafood – Carte £ 34/60
♦ The seafood counter forms the striking centrepiece at Catch, which is located
in what was once the lobby of this Victorian hotel. You decide on the cooking
method for the catch of the day.

X **Amico Bio**  AC VISA ⬤⬤ AE

*44 Cloth Fair ⊠ EC1A 7JQ ⊖ Barbican – 𝒞 (0207) 600 77 78*
*– www.amicobio.co.uk – Closed 25 December, Saturday lunch, Sunday and bank*
*holidays*  **33**APT**v**
**Rest** – Italian vegetarian – Carte £ 21/26
♦ Simple little place owned by an experienced chef and his cousin; the organic
produce comes from the family farm in Capua and the combination of flavours
remain true to their upbringing in Campania.

X **Paternoster Chop House**  🛋 AC VISA ⬤⬤ AE

*Warwick Ct., Paternoster Sq. ⊠ EC4M 7DX ⊖ St Paul's – 𝒞 (020) 7029 9400*
*– www.paternosterchophouse.com – Closed 24 December-1*
*January, Saturday, Sunday dinner and bank holidays*  **33**APT**x**
**Rest** – British – Menu £ 27 – Carte £ 32/57
♦ Appropriately British menu in a restaurant lying in the shadow of St Paul's Cathedral. Large, open room with full-length windows; busy bar attached. Kitchen
uses thoughtfully sourced produce.

X **Cellar Gascon**  AC VISA ⬤⬤ AE

*59 West Smithfield ⊠ EC1A 9DS ⊖ Barbican – 𝒞 (020) 7600 7561*
*– www.cellargascon.com – Closed 22 December-4 January, Saturday, Sunday*
*and bank holidays*  **33**APT**c**
**Rest** – French – *(booking essential at lunch)* Carte £ 14/19🍷
♦ It's not unlike a smart tapas bar and the monthly changing menu has plenty of
treats: pâtés, rillettes, hams, cheeses and even some salads for the virtuous; but
the Toulouse sausages and the Gascony pie stand out.

X
☺ **28°-50°**   `AC` ✦ `VISA` `OO` `AE` `O`
*140 Fetter Ln* ✉ *EC4A 1BT* ⊖ *Temple –* ℰ *(020) 7242 8877 – www.2850.co.uk*
*– Closed Saturday, Sunday and bank holidays*   **32**ANU**s**
**Rest** – French – Menu £ 22 (lunch) – Carte £ 26/30

• Subterranean wine bar and informal restaurant, from the same owners as Texture. Robust, mostly French dishes accompany a thoughtfully assembled wine list, with much choice by the glass.

X
**Restaurant at St Paul's Cathedral**   ✦ `VISA` `OO`
*St Paul's Churchyard* ✉ *EC4M 8AD* ⊖ *St. Paul's –* ℰ *(020) 7248 2469*
*– www.restaurantatstpauls.co.uk – Closed 25 December*   **33**APU**s**
**Rest** – British – *(lunch only) (booking advisable)* Menu £ 26

• Tucked away in a corner of the crypt of Sir Christopher Wren's 17C masterpiece. The kitchen prepares everything from scratch and celebrates all things British, including drinks.

X
**Bar Battu**   `AC` `VISA` `OO` `AE`
*48 Gresham St* ✉ *EC2V 7AY* ⊖ *Bank –* ℰ *(020) 7036 6100*
*– www.barbattu.com – Closed 24 December-2 January, Saturday, Sunday and bank holidays*   **33**AQT**x**
**Rest** – French – Menu £ 20 – Carte £ 24/38

• Captures the zeitgeist with its bare brick interior and appealing menu of small plates and rustic main courses. It is also a self-styled 'natural wine bar' and features unfiltered wines made from organically grown grapes.

X
☺ **Goldfish City**   `AC` `VISA` `OO` `AE`
*46 Gresham St.* ✉ *EC2V 7AY* ⊖ *Bank –* ℰ *(020) 7726 0308*
*– www.goldfish-resaturant.co.uk – Closed Saturday, Sunday and bank holidays*
**Rest** – Asian – *(booking advisable)* Carte £ 19/30   **33**AQU**x**

• Busy at lunch thanks to the selection of well-priced steamed dim sum. Balanced main menu mixes the classic with the modern. Spread over three floors, with discreet décor and helpful service.

---

**CROYDON** – Greater London   **12** B3

**SOUTH CROYDON**

XX **Cassoulet**   `AC` `VISA` `OO` `AE`
*18 Selsdon Rd.* ✉ *CR2 6PA –* ℰ *(020) 8633 1818 – www.lecassoulet.co.uk*
*– Closed 25-26 December*   **7**FZ**v**
**Rest** – French – Menu £ 19/30

• Evolving, seasonal set menus offer a range of traditional and more modern French dishes, with wider choice at dinner. Chic and elegant interior; carefully run, with attentive service.

XX **Albert's Table**   `AC` `VISA` `OO` `AE`
*49b South End* ✉ *CR0 1BF –* ℰ *(020) 8680 2010 – www.albertstable.co.uk*
*– Closed Sunday dinner and Monday*   **7**FZ**x**
**Rest** – Modern European – Menu £ 20/32

• The accomplished cooking defined by its well-judged flavours is somewhat at odds with the decoration, which is a touch sparse. The owner-chef has an impressive pedigree and his restaurant, named after his grandfather, deserves to succeed.

---

**EALING** – Greater London   **12** A3
🖼 West Middlesex Southall Greenford Rd, ℰ (020) 8574 34 50
🖼 Horsenden Hill Woodland Rise

## ACTON GREEN

### Le Vacherin
🏴 🎌 🎌 🎌 🎌 🎌

*76-77 South Par.* ✉ *W4 5LF* ⊖ *Chiswick Park –* ✆ *(020) 8742 2121*
*– www.levacherin.com – Closed 25 December and Sunday dinner*          **6CVo**
**Rest** – French – *(dinner only and lunch Saturday-Sunday)*
Menu £ 20 (weekdays)/35 – Carte £ 20/40
• Authentic feel to this comfortable brasserie, with its brown leather banquette seating, mirrors and belle époque prints. French classics from snails to duck confit; beef is a speciality.

### Bollo
🎌 🎌 🎌 🎌

*13-15 Bollo Ln.* ✉ *W4 5LR* ⊖ *Chiswick Park. –* ✆ *(020) 8994 6037*
*– www.thebollohouse.co.uk*          **6CVz**
**Rest** – Traditional – Carte £ 20/31
• Large Victorian pub with original glass cupola and oak panelling. Menu is a mix of generous pub classics and dishes with a southern Mediterranean influence. Look out for quiz nights and promotions.

### Duke of Sussex
🎌 🎌 🎌

*75 South Par.* ✉ *W4 5LF* ⊖ *Chiswick Park. –* ✆ *(020) 8742 8801*
*– www.realpubs.co.uk – Closed 25 December and Monday lunch*
**Rest** – Mediterranean – Carte £ 23/28          **6CVo**
• Bustling Victorian pub, whose striking dining room was once a variety theatre complete with proscenium arch. Stick to the Spanish dishes; stews and cured meats are the specialities. BYO on Mondays.

## EALING

### Charlotte's Place
🎌 🎌 🎌 🎌 🎌

*16 St Matthew's Rd.* ✉ *W5 3JT* ⊖ *Ealing Common –* ✆ *(020) 8567 7541*
*– www.charlottes.co.uk – Closed 26 December-4 January*          **2CVc**
**Rest** – Modern European – Menu £ 16/26 (early dinner) – Carte £ 28/32
• Warmly run neighbourhood restaurant opposite the Common; divided between bright ground floor room and cosier downstairs. Menu mixes British and Mediterranean influences. Planning to move to another site in Ealing as we went to print.

### Kiraku
🎌 🎌 🎌 🎌

*8 Station Par., Uxbridge Rd.* ✉ *W5 3LD* ⊖ *Ealing Common –* ✆ *(020)*
*8992 2848 – www.kiraku.co.uk – Closed 10 days Christmas-New Year, 10 days*
*August, Tuesday following bank holidays and Monday*          **2CVv**
**Rest** – Japanese – Carte £ 17/33
• The name of this cute little Japanese restaurant means 'relax and enjoy'; easy with such charming service. Extensive menu includes zensai, skewers, noodles, rice dishes and assorted sushi.

## GREENWICH – Greater London          **12 B3**

### Inside
🎌 🎌 🎌 🎌

*19 Greenwich South St.* ✉ *SE10 8NW* ⊖ *Greenwich (DLR) –* ✆ *(020) 8265 5060*
*– www.insiderestaurant.co.uk – Closed 24 December-2 January, Sunday dinner*
*and Monday*          **7GXx**
**Rest** – Modern European – Menu £ 18 (weekday lunch)/23 – Carte dinner £ 21/26
• Inside is tidy, comfortable and uncluttered, although it does take a few diners to generate an atmosphere. On offer is a well-priced set menu, with quite elaborate, largely European cooking.

✗ **Rivington Grill**     AC VISA ◑ AE ⓪
*178 Greenwich High Rd.* ✉ *SE10 8NN* ⊖ *Greenwich (DLR)* – ☏ *(020) 8293 9270*
– *www.rivingtongreenwich.co.uk* – *Closed 25-26 December, Monday and lunch*
*Tuesday-Wednesday*                 **7**GV**s**
**Rest** – British – Carte £ 25/39
♦ Part of the Picturehouse complex; 21C rustic interior with closely set tables.
Firmly English menus in bar and galleried restaurant. Banquets and market break-
fasts on offer.

---

**HACKNEY** – Greater London              **12** B3

**HACKNEY**

🏠 **Cat & Mutton**            VISA ◑
*76 Broadway Mkt.* ✉ *E8 4QJ* ⊖ *Bethnal Green.* – ☏ *(020) 7254 5599*
– *www.catandmutton.co.uk* – *Closed 25-26 December and Sunday dinner*
**Rest** – British – Menu £ 15 (dinner) – Carte £ 24/34     **14**YZB**a**
♦ The pub's lived-in look, music and relaxed vibe attract a young, local crowd.
Satisfying pub food, from a weekly changing menu, delivers on flavour. Regular
quiz nights and art classes.

🏠 **Prince Arthur**          AC VISA ◑ AE
*95 Forest Rd.* ✉ *E8 3BH* ⊖ *Bethnal Green.* – ☏ *(020) 7249 9996*
– *www.theprincearthurlondonfields.com* – *Closed 25-26 December*    **14**XZB**c**
**Rest** – British – *(dinner only and lunch Saturday-Sunday)* Carte £ 26/41
♦ An intimate local pub for local people, with plenty of character. Unpretentious
and heart-warming menu, with classics like a pint of prawns and cottage pie; filling puddings.

**HOXTON**

🏨 **The Hoxton**      🛗 ⅙ AC ℀ ⁽ᵗ⁾ 🛁 VISA ◑ AE ⓪
*81 Great Eastern St.* ✉ *EC2A 3HU* ⊖ *Old Street* – ☏ *(020) 7550 1000*
– *www.hoxtonhotels.com*              **20**XZD**x**
**208 rm** – ✝£ 70/358 ✝✝£ 70/358, ⫯ £ 12
**Rest** *Hoxton Grill* – see restaurant listing
♦ Urban lodge: industrial styled, clean lined modernism. "No rip-offs" mantra:
cheap phone rate, free internet, complimentary 'lite Pret' breakfast. Carefully considered rooms and an appealing laid-back vibe.

✗✗ **Great Eastern Dining Room**        AC VISA ◑ AE ⓪
*54 Great Eastern St* ✉ *EC2A 3QR* ⊖ *Old Street* – ☏ *(020) 7613 4545*
– *www.rickerrestaurants.com* – *Closed Saturday lunch and Sunday*
**Rest** – Asian – Menu £ 20 (lunch and early dinner)     **20**XZD**n**
– Carte £ 22/39
♦ Half the place is a bar that's heaving in the evening. Dining area has candle-lit
tables, contemporary chandeliers, and carefully prepared, seriously tasty pan-
Asian cooking.

✗ **Fifteen London**          AC VISA ◑ AE
*15 Westland Pl.* ✉ *N1 7LP* ⊖ *Old Street* – ☏ *(020) 3375 1515* – *www.fifteen.net*
– *Closed 24-26 December*              **13**VZC**c**
**Rest** – Italian – *(booking essential)* Menu £ 30 (lunch) – Carte dinner £ 29/48
♦ Original branch of Jamie Oliver's charitable restaurants; run by trainees along-
side full-time staff. Buzzy ground floor trattoria; more formal basement restaurant.
Tasty, seasonal Italian food.

✗ **Hoxton Grill** – at The Hoxton Hotel      AC VISA ◑ AE ⓪
*81 Great Eastern St.* ✉ *EC2A 3HU* ⊖ *Old Street* – ☏ *(020) 7550 1000*
– *www.hoxtonhotels.com*              **20**XZD**x**
**Rest** – American – Carte £ 28/44
♦ A young, hip crowd has colonised this large, open-plan space which comes
with a discernible New York feel. Burgers, salads, steaks and smoothies keep the
open kitchen busy all day.

LONDON

**SHOREDITCH**

XXX **Boundary** with rm      AC ((¹)) VISA ☺☺ AE ①
2-4 Boundary St. ⊠ E2 7DD ⊖ Old Street – 𝒞 (020) 7729 1051
– www.theboundary.co.uk – Closed Sunday dinner      20XZD**b**
**12 rm** – †£ 192 ††£ 192, ☑ £ 10 – 5 suites
**Rest** – French – (dinner only and lunch Saturday-Sunday) Menu £ 25 (lunch)
– Carte £ 28/56🏵
• Sir Terence Conran has taken a warehouse and created a 'caff' with a bakery
and shop, a rooftop terrace and a stylish, good-looking French restaurant serving
plenty of cross-Channel classics. Comfy and individual bedrooms.

XXX **L' Anima**      AC VISA ☺☺ AE
1 Snowden St. ⊠ EC2A 2DQ ⊖ Liverpool Street – 𝒞 (0207) 422 70 00
– www.lanima.co.uk – Closed 25 December, Saturday lunch, Sunday and bank
holidays      20XZD**a**
**Rest** – Italian – (booking essential) Menu £ 37 (lunch) – Carte £ 35/63
• Very handsome room, with limestone and leather creating a sophisticated,
glamorous environment. Appealing menu is a mix of Italian classics and less familiar dishes, with the emphasis firmly on flavour. Service is smooth and personable.

XX **Lena**      AC VISA ☺☺ AE ①
66 Great Eastern St. ⊠ EC2A 3JT ⊖ Old Street – 𝒞 (020) 7739 5714
– www.lenarestaurant.com – Closed 25 December, 1 January and Sunday lunch
**Rest** – Italian – Menu £ 14 (lunch) – Carte £ 21/34      20XZD**c**
• Named after the owner's mother and eclectically decorated using leather,
wood, plastic and ceramics. Menu looks to southern Italy for influences. Live jazz
in the stylish bar at weekends.

X **Rivington Grill**      AC VISA ☺☺ AE ①
28-30 Rivington St. ⊠ EC2A 3DZ ⊖ Old Street – 𝒞 (020) 7729 7053
– www.rivingtonshoreditch.co.uk – Closed 25-26 December      20XZD**e**
**Rest** – British – Carte £ 26/48
• Very appealing 'back to basics' British menu, with plenty of comforting classics
including a section 'on toast'. This converted warehouse is popular with the local
community of artists.

🍴 **Princess of Shoreditch**      VISA ☺☺ AE
76-78 Paul St. ⊠ EC2A 4NE ⊖ Old Street. – 𝒞 (020) 7729 9270
– www.theprincessofshoreditch.com – Closed 24-26 December      19VZD**a**
**Rest** – Traditional – Menu £ 18 (lunch) – Carte £ 25/32
• Pies and platters in the busy ground floor bar; more ambitious but still flavoursome European-influenced cooking in the calmer upstairs room. Friendly service
a feature.

---

**HAMMERSMITH and FULHAM** – Greater London      **12** B3

**FULHAM**

XX **Mao Tai**      AC ⟺ VISA ☺☺ AE
58 New Kings Rd., Parsons Green ⊠ SW6 4LS ⊖ Parsons Green
– 𝒞 (020) 7731 2520 – www.maotai.co.uk – Closed 25-27 December
**Rest** – Chinese – (dinner only and Sunday lunch) Carte £ 31/55      22NZH**e**
• Influences from across China inform the modern menu of this stylish, long-
standing Chinese restaurant. Divided into two rooms; the front section with the
cocktail bar is the more animated.

XX **Manson**      🏡 AC VISA ☺☺ AE
676 Fulham Rd. ⊠ SW6 5SA ⊖ Parsons Green – 𝒞 (020) 7384 9559
– www.mansonrestaurant.co.uk – Closed 25-26 December and Sunday dinner
**Rest** – British – (booking advisable) Menu £ 18 (lunch and early      22MZH**x**
dinner) – Carte £ 26/36
• Slight Left Bank aesthetic, with smoked mirrors and 1930s French street lamps.
Pleasant, breezy service. Cooking also has a French bias and displays more sophistication than one expects.

LONDON

## ✕✕ Blue Elephant
4-6 Fulham Broadway ⊠ SW6 1AA ⊖ Fulham Broadway – ✆ (020) 7385 6595
– www.blueelephant.com – Closed 24-27 December and 1 January
**Rest** – Thai – *(booking essential)* Menu £ 20/37 – Carte £ 42/60    **22**NZG**z**
• A London institution, with a gloriously unrestrained décor of plants, streams and bridges. Carefully prepared dishes from across Thailand. Curries are a strength and service is well-meaning.

## ✕ Tendido Cuatro
108-110 New Kings Road ⊠ SW6 4LY ⊖ Parsons Green – ✆ (020) 7371 5147
– www.cambiodetercio.co.uk    **22**NZH**x**
**Rest** – Spanish – Carte £ 21/49
• Along with tapas, the speciality is paella. Designed for a hungry two, they vary from seafood to quail and chorizo; cuttlefish ink to vegetarian. Vivid colours used with abandon deck out the busy room.

## 🍴 Harwood Arms
☺
Walham Grove ⊠ SW6 1QP ⊖ Fulham Broadway. – ✆ (020) 7386 1847
– www.harwoodarms.com – Closed 26-29 August, 25-28 December, 1 January
and Monday lunch    **22**NZG**a**
**Rest** – British – *(booking essential)* Carte £ 30/34 ⌂
**Spec.** Rabbit, prune and bacon faggots with celeriac purée and Horn of Plenty mushrooms. Glazed Aylesbury duck leg and Douglas fir sausage with a beetroot tart. Chilled rice pudding, strawberries and Grasmere gingerbread.
• Its reputation may have spread like wildfire but this remains a proper, down-to-earth pub that just happens to serve really good food. The cooking is very seasonal, proudly British, full of flavour and doesn't seem out of place in this environment. Service is suitably relaxed and friendly.

## 🍴 My dining room
18 Farm Ln ⊠ SW6 1PP ⊖ Fulham Broadway. – ✆ (020) 7381 3331
– www.mydiningroom.net    **22**NZG**r**
**Rest** – French – Menu £ 14/20 – Carte £ 21/37
• A modern bar, a chic dining room and a French owner; this is truly a gastropub of our time. There's plenty of choice from the French rustic menu and lots of wines served by the glass.

## 🍴 Sands End
135-137 Stephendale Rd. ⊠ SW6 2PR ⊖ Fulham Broadway. – ✆ (020)
7731 7823 – www.thesandsend.co.uk – Closed 25-26 December    **22**OZH**r**
**Rest** – British – *(booking advisable)* Carte £ 32/42
• Cosy, warm and welcoming little corner pub, offering appealing bar snacks and a thoughtfully put-together menu with a British bias. Game is handled deftly and ingredients are well-sourced.

## HAMMERSMITH

## ✕✕ River Café (Ruth Rogers)
☺
Thames Wharf, Rainville Rd ⊠ W6 9HA ⊖ Barons Court – ✆ (020) 7386 4200
– www.rivercafe.co.uk – Closed Christmas, Sunday dinner and bank holidays
**Rest** – Italian – *(booking essential)* Carte £ 49/78 ⌂    **21**LZG**v**
**Spec.** Crab linguini. Sea bass baked in salt with salsa verde. Chocolate Nemesis.
• It's all about the natural flavours of some superlative ingredients. The on-view kitchen with its wood-fired oven dominates the stylish riverside room; the contagiously effervescent atmosphere is helped along by very charming service.

## ✕✕ Indian Zing
236 King St. ⊠ W6 0RF ⊖ Ravenscourt Park – ✆ (020) 8748 5959
– www.indianzing.co.uk – Closed dinner 25 December    **21**LZG**a**
**Rest** – Indian – Menu £ 15 (lunch) – Carte £ 25/35
• The enthusiastic chef-owner offers well-judged, flavoursome and quite refined Indian cooking from across all parts of the country. Colourful surroundings; keen, if slightly disorganised, service.

### Azou
AC VISA ©© AE ①

375 King St. ⊠ W6 9NJ ⊖ Stamford Brook – ℰ (020) 8563 7266
– www.azou.co.uk – Closed 25 December, 1 January and bank holidays
**Rest** – North African – *(dinner only and lunch Saturday-Sunday)*   **21**KZG**u**
*(booking essential)* Carte £ 23/35
♦ Silks, lanterns and rugs add to the atmosphere of this personally run, North African restaurant. Most come for the excellent tajines, with triple steamed couscous. Much is designed for sharing.

### Anglesea Arms
AC VISA ©©

35 Wingate Rd. ⊠ W6 0UR ⊖ Ravenscourt Park. – ℰ (020) 8749 1291
– www.anglesea-arms.com – Closed 25-27 December   **15**LZE**c**
**Rest** – British – *(bookings not accepted)* Carte £ 20/52
♦ Busy wood-panelled bar; brighter, calmer rear dining room with part-glass roof and exposed kitchen. Regularly changing blackboard menu; expect robust cooking with a strong British bias.

### Havelock Tavern
AC VISA ©© AE

57 Masbro Rd., Brook Grn. ⊠ W14 0LS ⊖ Kensington Olympia. – ℰ (020)
7603 5374 – www.havelocktavern.com – Closed 25-26 December   **16**MZE**e**
**Rest** – Traditional – *(bookings not accepted)* Carte £ 21/30 **s**
♦ Warm, friendly and atmospheric pub with easygoing service and pleasantly mixed clientele. Blackboard menu offers robust, satisfying pub food. Arrive early if you don't want to wait for a table.

### Dartmouth Castle
VISA ©© AE ①

26 Glenthorne Rd. ⊠ W6 0LS ⊖ Hammersmith. – ℰ (020) 8748 3614
– www.thedartmouthcastle.co.uk – Closed 24 December-2 January and Saturday
lunch   **21**LZF**e**
**Rest** – Mediterranean – Carte £ 18/31
♦ The Mediterranean exerts quite an influence on the large menu at this popular, welcoming and traditional pub. Spread over two levels but the ground floor is the more atmospheric.

### Crabtree
AC VISA ©©

4 Rainville Rd. ⊠ W6 9HA ⊖ Barons Court. – ℰ (020) 7385 3929
– www.thecrabtreeW6.co.uk   **21**LZG**x**
**Rest** – Modern European – Carte £ 24/34
♦ With a beer garden for 200 and a separate dining room terrace, this Victorian pub makes great use of its riverside location. Parfaits and terrines are highlights but Veggies are also considered.

## SHEPHERD'S BUSH

### Princess Victoria
AC P VISA ©© AE

217 Uxbridge Rd. ⊠ W12 9DH ⊖ Shepherd's Bush. – ℰ (020) 8749 5886
– www.princessvictoria.co.uk – Closed 24-28 December   **15**KZE**a**
**Rest** – Traditional – Menu £ 13 (lunch) – Carte £ 21/34 ⌘
♦ Magnificent Victorian gin palace, with original plasterwork. The kitchen knows its butchery; pork board, homemade sausages and terrines all feature. Excellent wine list, with over 350 bottles.

---

## HARINGEY – Greater London   **12** B3

## CROUCH END

### Bistro Aix
AC ⇔ VISA ©© AE ①

54 Topsfield Par., Tottenham Ln. ⊠ N8 8PT – ℰ (020) 8340 6346
– www.bistroaix.co.uk – Closed 1 January   **3**EU**v**
**Rest** – French – *(dinner only and lunch Saturday-Sunday)* Carte £ 23/32
♦ Dressers, cabinets and contemporary artwork lend an authentic Gallic edge to this bustling bistro. Traditionally prepared French classics are the highlights of an extensive menu.

## Queens Pub and Dining Room 🛜 AC VISA ⦿ AE
*26 Broadway Par.* ⊠ *N8 9DE – 𝒞 (020) 8340 2031*
*– www.thequeenscrouchend.co.uk* **3EUc**
**Rest** – British – Carte £ 24/29
• Striking example of a classic Victorian pub, from the original mahogany panelling to the stained glass windows and ornate ceiling. Traditional British comfort dishes are the highlights of the menu.

## FORTIS GREEN

## Clissold Arms 🛜 P VISA ⦿ AE
*105 Fortis Green* ⊠ *N2 9HR* ⊖ *East Finchley. – 𝒞 (020) 8444 4224*
*– www.clissoldarms.co.uk* **3EUa**
**Rest** – Modern European – Carte £ 18/30
• Reputedly the venue for The Kinks' first gig. Now modernised throughout, with a large rear terrace. Interesting menus, with terrines, whole sea bass and 28-day aged steaks the specialities.

## HIGHGATE

## XX Rose and Crown 🛜 VISA ⦿
*86 Highgate High St.* ⊠ *N6 5HX* ⊖ *Archway – 𝒞 (020) 8340 0770*
*– www.roseandcrownhighgate.co.uk – Closed Sunday dinner and Monday lunch*
**Rest** – Modern European – Menu £ 15/18 – Carte £ 26/34 **2EUi**
• Converted pub, smartly kitted out but not overly formal thanks to genial staff. Seasonally changing, European-influenced cooking, with competitively priced weekly-changing set menu.

A restaurant name printed in red denotes a Rising Star - an establishment showing great potential. It is in line for a higher award: a star or an additional star. They are included in the list of starred establishments at the beginning of the guide.

# HARROW – Greater London 12 A3

## HARROW ON THE HILL

## XX Incanto AC VISA ⦿ AE
*41 High St.* ⊠ *HA1 3HT* ⊖ *Harrow on the Hill – 𝒞 (020) 8426 6767*
*– www.incanto.co.uk – Closed 25-26 December, 1 January, Easter*
*Sunday, Monday and dinner Sunday* **1BUz**
**Rest** – Italian – Menu £ 22/24 – Carte £ 29/45
• Within Grade II former post office; split-level restaurant to rear of well stocked deli. Well-paced service; Southern Italian bias to the rustic cooking, with quality produce to the fore.

## PINNER

## XX Friends AC VISA ⦿ AE ⓞ
*11 High St.* ⊠ *HA5 5PJ* ⊖ *Pinner – 𝒞 (020) 8866 0286*
*– www.friendsrestaurant.co.uk – Closed Sunday dinner, Monday and bank*
*holidays* **1BUa**
**Rest** – Modern European – Menu £ 25/33
• Pretty beamed cottage, with some parts dating back 400 years. Inside, a welcoming glow from the log fire; personal service from owners and a fresh, regularly-changing menu.

LONDON

🏨 Haste Hill Northwood The Drive, 𝒞 (01923) 82 52 24

**HEATHROW AIRPORT**

🏨🏨🏨 **Sofitel**      ⊕ ⋒ 🛏 📺 & 🄰🄺 🎿 🎙 🖄 **P** 𝘃𝘪𝘴𝘢 ⚬⚬ 🄰🄴 ⓪
Terminal 5, Heathrow Airport ⊠ TW6 2GD ⊖ Heathrow Terminal 5
– 𝒞 (020) 8757 7777 – www.sofitel.com               **5**AX**a**
**578 rm** – 🛉£ 155/475 🛉🛉£ 155/475, ⌨ £ 21 – 27 suites
**Rest La Belle Époque** – French – Menu £ 26 – Carte £ 27/39
**Rest Vivre** – Menu £ 25 (dinner) – Carte £ 26/50
♦ Smart and well-run contemporary hotel, opened in 2008. Designed around a series of atriums, with direct access to T5. Crisply decorated, comfortable bedrooms with luxurious bathrooms. Choice of restaurant: international or classical French cuisine.

🏨🏨🏨 **Hilton London Heathrow Airport**    🖵 ⋒ 🛏 📺 & rm, 🄰🄺 🎙 🖄 **P**
Terminal 4 ⊠ TW6 3AF ⊖ Heathrow Terminal 4         𝘃𝘪𝘴𝘢 ⚬⚬ 🄰🄴 ⓪
– 𝒞 (020) 8759 7755 – www.hilton.co.uk/heathrow       **5**AX**n**
**355 rm** ⌨ – 🛉£ 197/329 🛉🛉£ 251/395 – 5 suites
**Rest Zen Oriental** – see restaurant listing
**Rest Aromi** – (closed lunch Saturday, Sunday and bank holidays) (buffet lunch) Menu £ 21/29 – Carte £ 29/54
♦ Group hotel with a striking modern exterior and linked to Terminal 4 by a covered walkway. Good-sized bedrooms, with contemporary styled suites. Casual dining in Aromi which occupies part of the vast atrium.

🏨🏨🏨 **London Heathrow Marriott**    🖵 ⋒ 🛏 📺 & rm, 🄰🄺 🎿 🎙 🖄 **P**
Bath Rd., Hayes ⊠ UB3 5AN ⊖ Heathrow Terminal 1,2,3    𝘃𝘪𝘴𝘢 ⚬⚬ 🄰🄴 ⓪
– 𝒞 (020) 8990 1100 – www.londonheathrowmarriott.co.uk    **5**AX**z**
**391 rm** – 🛉£ 202 🛉🛉£ 202, ⌨ £ 17.95 – 2 suites
**Rest Tuscany** – Italian – (dinner only) Carte £ 31/49
**Rest Allie's grille** – Menu £ 13 (lunch) – Carte £ 30/49
♦ Built at the end of 20C, this modern, comfortable hotel is centred around a large atrium, with comprehensive business facilities: there is an exclusive Executive floor. Italian cuisine in bright and convivial Tuscany. Grill favourites in Allie's.

🍴 **Zen Oriental** – at Hilton London Heathrow Airport Hotel      🄰🄺 **P**
Terminal 4 ⊠ TW6 3AF ⊖ Heathrow Terminal 4        𝘃𝘪𝘴𝘢 ⚬⚬ 🄰🄴 ⓪
– 𝒞 (020) 8564 9609 – www.hilton.co.uk/heathrow – Closed 25-26 December
**Rest** – Asian – Menu £ 34/47 – Carte £ 27/50         **5**AX**n**
♦ With its appealing menu of classics and capable service, Zen Oriental has long been a favourite at the Hilton. Popular for business lunches; the atmosphere is more relaxed at dinner.

🄳 High St 𝒞 (0845) 456 29 29, www.hounslow.inuklocal.co.uk
🏨 Wyke Green Isleworth Syon Lane, 𝒞 (020) 8560 87 77
🏨 Airlinks Southall Lane, 𝒞 (020) 8561 14 18
🏨 Hounslow Heath, Staines Rd, 𝒞 (020) 8570 52 71

**BRENTFORD**

🏨🏨🏨 **London Syon Park**    🚂 🕭 ⋑ 🕭 🖵 ⊕ ⋒ 🛏 🍴 & rm, 🄰🄺 🎿 🖄 🖄
Park Rd. ⊠ TW7 6AZ – 𝒞 (020) 7870 777        **P** 𝘃𝘪𝘴𝘢 ⚬⚬ 🄰🄴 ⓪
– www.londonsyonpark.com             **5**BX**x**
**136 rm** – 🛉£ 478 🛉🛉£ 478, ⌨ £ 18.50 – 1 suite
**Rest Capability** – Menu £ 22 (lunch) – Carte £ 32/48
♦ Opened in 2011, no expense was spared with this purpose-built, resort-style hotel. It's in the grounds of Syon House, home to the Duke and Duchess of Northumberland, and run by Hilton under their Waldorf Astoria brand. Ask for a room overlooking the walled garden. British produce features in the restaurant.

# CHISWICK

## Moran 🛱 ♨ |≋| & 🗚 ⅌ ⁽ᵗ⁾ ♨ VISA ☎ AE ⓿

*626 Chiswick High Rd.* ⊠ *W4 5RY* ⊖ *Gunnersbury –* ℰ *(020) 8996 5200*
*– www.moranhotels.com*                                                                          **6**CV**i**
**123 rm** – ♥£ 230 ♥♥£ 230/335, ⌤ £ 10
**Rest *Napa* –** Menu £ 17/25 **s** – Carte £ 30/39 **s**
♦ Converted office block with all-glass exterior, midway between Heathrow and
West End. Decorated in a restrained contemporary style with bright and airy bedrooms. Two-tiered restaurant with terrace and modern menu.

## High Road House |≋| 🗚 ⅌ ⁽ᵗ⁾ VISA ☎ AE ⓿

*162 Chiswick High Rd.* ⊠ *W4 1PR* ⊖ *Turnham Green –* ℰ *(020) 8742 7474*
*– www.highroadhouse.co.uk*                                                          **21**KZG**e**
**14 rm** – ♥♥£ 105/195, ⌤ £ 10.50
**Rest *High Road Brasserie* –** see restaurant listing
♦ Cool, sleek hotel and club, the latter a slick place to lounge around or play
games. Light, bright bedrooms with crisp linen. A carefully appointed, fairly-priced
destination.

## XXX La Trompette 🛱 🗚 VISA ☎ AE

£3

*5-7 Devonshire Rd* ⊠ *W4 2EU* ⊖ *Turnham Green –* ℰ *(020) 8747 1836*
*– www.latrompette.co.uk – Closed 24-26 December*                      **21**KZG**y**
**Rest –** Modern European – *(booking essential)* Menu £ 26/40⅌
**Spec.** Scallops with pea purée, hispi cabbage and bayonne ham. Corn-fed chicken
with morel ragoût, shallots, broad beans and macaroni. Strawberry shortbread and
sorbet with Chantilly cream.
♦ Enthusiastically run and smart neighbourhood restaurant, sister to Chez Bruce.
Small front terrace and light, comfortable interior. Balanced menu and confident
kitchen produce robust, spirited dishes. Wine list varied in price and geography.

## XX Michael Nadra 🗚 VISA ☎ AE

*6-8 Elliott Rd.* ⊠ *W4 1PE* ⊖ *Turnham Green –* ℰ *(020) 8742 0766*
*– www.restaurant-michaelnadra.co.uk – Closed Sunday dinner and Monday*
**Rest –** Modern European – Menu £ 24/35⅌                                  **21**KZG**z**
♦ Enough regulars now appreciate the chef-owner's well-judged cooking for him
to finally put his own name above the door of this intimate, friendly restaurant.
Balanced and sensibly priced menu.

## XX Charlotte's Bistro 🗚 VISA ☎ AE

☺

*6 Turnham Green Terr* ⊠ *W4 1QP* ⊖ *Turnham Green –* ℰ *(020) 8742 3590*
*– www.charlottes.co.uk*                                                          **21**KZG**a**
**Rest –** Modern European – *(booking advisable)* Menu £ 16/26 (early dinner)
– Carte £ 28/31
♦ A pleasant, unpretentious bistro; run by a friendly team, with a well-priced
menu of flavoursome, well prepared dishes of largely European provenance. Little
sister to Charlotte's Place in Ealing.

## X High Road Brasserie – at High Road House Hotel 🛱 🗚 VISA ☎ AE ⓿

*162 Chiswick High Rd.* ⊠ *W4 1PR* ⊖ *Turnham Green –* ℰ *(020) 8742 7474*
*– www.highroadhouse.co.uk*                                                       **21**KZG**e**
**Rest –** Traditional – *(booking essential)* Menu £ 16 (lunch) – Carte £ 20/42
♦ Authentic brasserie, with mirrors, panelling and art deco lighting. Despite the
high volume of customers, the classic dishes are prepared with care and staff
cope well with being busy.

## X Sam's Brasserie 🗚 VISA ☎ AE

*11 Barley Mow Passage* ⊠ *W4 4PH* ⊖ *Turnham Green –* ℰ *(020) 8987 0555*
*– www.samsbrasserie.co.uk – Closed 23-28 December*                      **2**CV**a**
**Rest –** Mediterranean – Menu £ 17 (weekday lunch)/19 (weekday dinner)
– Carte £ 29/35
♦ A former Sanderson wallpaper mill, now a bustling, fun brasserie with Sir Peter
Blake artwork adding to the hip feel. Appealing, modern menu; satisfying dishes
deliver on flavour. Look out for regular Soul and Jazz evenings.

LONDON

### Devonshire Arms
*126 Devonshire Rd ⊠ W4 2JJ ⊖ Turnham Green. – ℰ (020) 8742 2302*
*– www.devonshirearmspub.com*                                    **21**KZG**x**
**Rest** – Modern European – *(booking advisable)* Carte £ 20/25
• Those behind the Drapers Arms in Islington are now at the helm of this characterful local and it's had a makeover true to its Edwardian roots. The menu changes twice daily; dishes are vibrant and appealing, with influences from the Med.

---

## ISLINGTON – Greater London                                    12 B3

### ARCHWAY

### 500
*782 Holloway Rd ⊠ N19 3JH ⊖ Archway – ℰ (020) 7272 3406*
*– www.500restaurant.co.uk – Closed 2 weeks summer, 2 weeks Christmas-New*
*Year and lunch Monday-Thursday*                                **12**SZA**y**
**Rest** – Italian – *(booking essential)* Carte £ 21/25
• Small, fun and well-priced Italian that's always busy. Good pastas and bread; the veal chop and rabbit are specialities. The passion of the ebullient owner and keen chef are evident.

### St John's Tavern
*91 Junction Rd ⊠ N19 5QU ⊖ Archway. – ℰ (020) 7272 1587*
*– www.stjohnstavern.com – Closed 25-26 December and 1 January*
**Rest** – Modern – *(dinner only and lunch Friday-Sunday) (booking*          **12**RZA**s**
*advisable at dinner)* Carte £ 24/33
• Daily changing menu in the dining room at the back of the pub. Cosy atmosphere, with dark colours and fireplace. Rustic cooking from open kitchen and blackboard menu.

### BARNSBURY

### Morgan M
*489 Liverpool Rd. ⊠ N7 8NS ⊖ Highbury & Islington – ℰ (020) 7609 3560*
*– www.morganm.com – Closed 24-30 December, Monday, Sunday dinner*
*and lunch Tuesday and Saturday*                                **13**UZA**a**
**Rest** – French – Menu £ 29/43
• Classic, full flavoured French dishes, seasonal specialities and a separate vegetarian menu ensures a loyal crowd of regulars at this formally run restaurant, set within a converted pub.

### Roots at N1
*115 Hemingford Rd ⊠ N1 1BZ ⊖ Caledonian Road – ℰ (020) 7697 4488*
*– www.rootsatn1.com – Closed 25-26 December and Monday*          **13**UZB**d**
**Rest** – Indian – *(dinner only) (booking essential)* Menu £ 23 – Carte £ 25/39
• Opening their own place was the dream of these three friends from India. Their warm, friendly restaurant is known for its refreshingly short menu; tandoori lamb chops and Rogan Josh are the highlights.

### Fig Bistro
*169 Hemingford Rd. ⊠ N1 1DA ⊖ Caledonian Road – ℰ (020) 7609 3009*
*– www.figbistro.co.uk – Closed 25-26, 31 December, 1 January and Sunday*
*dinner*                                                         **13**UZB**a**
**Rest** – Modern European – *(dinner only and Sunday lunch)* Carte £ 19/31
• Charming service and flavoursome cooking displaying a degree of refinement belie the 'bistro' name. The compact candlelit room is appealingly frayed and the atmosphere very welcoming.

## CANONBURY

### ✗ Trullo

🛦🛈 *AC VISA ◎◎*

300-302 St Paul's Rd. ⊠ N1 2LH ⊖ Highbury & Islington – ☎ (020) 7226 2733
– www.trullorestaurant.com – Closed 23 December-2 January, Sunday dinner
and Monday                                                                                    **13**UZB**t**
**Rest** – Italian – *(dinner only and lunch Saturday-Sunday) (booking essential)*
Carte £ 25/32

• Great value Italian food that delivers on flavour ensures that this friendly and
relaxed restaurant is always full of contented diners. Terrific antipasti and the
charcoal grill dishes are favourites.

### ✗ Canonbury Kitchen

*AC VISA ◎◎ ①*

19 Canonbury Ln ⊠ N1 2AS ⊖ Highbury & Islington – ☎ (0207) 226 97 91
– www.canonburykitchen.com – Closed Monday                                   **13**UZB**c**
**Rest** – Italian – *(dinner only and lunch Saturday-Sunday)* Carte £ 24/31

• A bright, local Italian with seating for just 40; exposed brick walls and painted
floorboards add to the fresh feel. The kitchen keeps things simple and the menu
pricing is prudent.

### 🍴 House

*🛜 VISA ◎◎ AE*

63-69 Canonbury Rd ⊠ N1 2DG ⊖ Highbury & Islington. – ☎ (020) 7704 7410
– www.thehouse.islington.com – Closed Monday except bank holidays
**Rest** – Modern European – Carte £ 20/30                                          **13**UZB**h**

• A smart looking pub with an attractive terrace; but one that still feels like a
genuine local. The cooking is crisp and confident and there's an emphasis on
good quality, organic ingredients.

## CLERKENWELL

### 🏨 Malmaison

*🛌 🕮 ㅕ rm, AC ⟨⟩ 🛎 ◎◎ AE ①*

18-21 Charterhouse Sq ⊠ EC1M 6AH ⊖ Barbican – ☎ (020) 7012 3700
– www.malmaison.com                                                                        **19**UZD**q**
**97 rm** – †£ 282/390 ††£ 318/570, � £ 18.50
**Rest** *Brasserie* – *(closed Saturday lunch)* Carte £ 29/41

• Striking early 20C red-brick building overlooking pleasant square. Stylish,
comfy public areas. Bedrooms in vivid, bold colours, with plenty of extra touches.
Modern brasserie employing meats from Smithfield.

### 🏠 The Rookery without rest

*AC ⟨⟩ ⟨⟩ VISA ◎◎ AE ①*

12 Peters Ln, Cowcross St ⊠ EC1M 6DS ⊖ Barbican – ☎ (020) 7336 0931
– www.rookeryhotel.com – Closed 24-26 December
**32 rm** – †£ 222/282 ††£ 246/282, � £ 11.95 – 1 suite       **33**AOT**p**

• A row of charmingly restored 18C houses. Wood panelling, stone-flagged flooring, open fires and antique furniture. Highly individual bedrooms, with Victorian
bathrooms.

### ✗ Larder

*AC ⇄ VISA ◎◎ AE ①*

91-93 St John St. ⊠ EC1M 4NU ⊖ Farringdon – ☎ (020) 7608 1558
– www.thelarderrestaurant.com – Closed 23 December-3 January, Saturday
lunch, Sunday and bank holidays                                                        **19**UZD**f**
**Rest** – Modern European – Menu £ 15 (lunch) – Carte £ 26/37

• Large, glass-fronted restaurant with stark, noisy, industrial feel and own bakery
selling breads and pastries. Unfussy food has an English accent with some European influences.

### ✗✗ Redhook

*AC ⇄ VISA ◎◎ AE*

89 Turnmill St ⊠ EC1M 5QU ⊖ Farringdon – ☎ (020) 7065 6800
– www.redhooklondon.com – Closed Easter, 25 December, Saturday lunch and
Sunday                                                                                             **19**UZD**a**
**Rest** – Beef specialities – *(booking advisable at dinner)* Menu £ 18 (lunch)
– Carte £ 24/41

• Brooklyn comes to Clerkenwell in the shape of this American-style restaurant
specialising in seafood and steaks. Bare brick walls, booths and a faux industrial
aesthetic add to the New York feel.

LONDON

LONDON

XX **North Road** (Christoffer Hruskova)      `AC` `⇄` `VISA` `OO` `AE`
£3 *69-73 St John St* ✉ *EC1M 4AN* ⊖ *Farringdon* – ✆ *(020) 3217 0033*
*– www.nrrestaurant.com – Closed 23 December- 2 January, Saturday lunch and
Sunday*     **19**UZD**h**
**Rest** – Modern European – Menu £ 20 (lunch) – Carte £ 32/41
**Spec.** Scallops with sea buckthorn, malt bread and wild herbs. Whey-poached
turbot, asparagus and green strawberries. Yoghurt 'in textures and tempera-
tures'.
◆ Owner-chef's Danish roots are evident in his clean, crisp cooking, which
uses sous-vide techniques, little or no butter or cream and is fully respectful
of the seasons. Coolly designed, elegantly understated room provides the
ideal backdrop.

X **St John**     `AC` `⇄` `VISA` `OO` `AE` `O`
£3 *26 St John St* ✉ *EC1M 4AY* ⊖ *Farringdon* – ✆ *(020) 3301 8069*
*– www.stjohnrestaurant.com – Closed Christmas-New Year, Saturday lunch,
Sunday dinner and bank holidays,*     **33**APT**k**
**Rest** – *(booking essential)* Carte £ 26/44
**Spec.** Roast bone marrow and parsley salad with toasted bread and wet salt.
Braised rabbit, peas and bacon. Ginger loaf and butterscotch sauce with vanilla
ice cream.
◆ 'Nose to tail eating' is how they describe their cooking at this busy, bright, converted 19C smokehouse. Strong on offal, game and unusual cuts; gloriously Brit-
ish, highly seasonal, appealingly simple and very satisfying.

X **Comptoir Gascon**     `AC` `VISA` `OO` `AE`
☺ *61-63 Charterhouse St.* ✉ *EC1M 6HJ* ⊖ *Farringdon* – ✆ *(020) 7608 0851*
*– www.comptoirgascon.com – Closed 24 December-4 January, Sunday and
Monday*     **33**AOT**a**
**Rest** – French – *(booking essential)* Carte £ 24/36
◆ Buzzy restaurant; sister to Club Gascon. Rustic and satisfying specialities from
the SW of France include wine, cheese, bread and especially duck. Further produce on display to take home.

X **Bistro du Vin**     `AC` `⇄` `VISA` `OO` `AE` `O`
*40 St John St* ✉ *EC1M 4DL* ⊖ *Farringdon* – ✆ *(020) 7490 9230*
*– www.bistroduvinandbar.com*     **33**APT**t**
**Rest** – Modern European – Carte £ 26/45 ⦸
◆ They've nailed the bistro aesthetic and oenologists will be in clover, so there's
no arguing with the name. Beef dishes are the stand outs – dry-cured in-house
and cooked in a Josper grill.

X **Hix Oyster and Chop House**     `⋔` `VISA` `OO` `AE`
*36-37 Greenhill Rents* ✉ *EC1M 6BN* ⊖ *Farringdon*
*– ✆ (020) 7017 1930 – www.hixoysterandchophouse.co.uk*
*– Closed 25-29 December*     **33**AOT**e**
**Rest** – British – Menu £ 18 (lunch and early dinner) – Carte £ 26/50
◆ Appropriately utilitarian surroundings put the focus on seasonal and often un-
derused British ingredients. Cooking is satisfying and unfussy, with plenty of oysters and aged beef served on the bone.

X **Vinoteca**     `VISA` `OO` `AE`
*7 St John St.* ✉ *EC1M 4AA* ⊖ *Farringdon* – ✆ *(020) 7253 8786*
*– www.vinoteca.co.uk – Closed Christmas-New Year, Sunday and bank holidays*
**Rest** – Modern European – *(bookings not accepted at dinner)*     **33**APT**a**
Carte £ 27/35 ⦸
◆ This cosy and passionately run 'bar and wine shop' is always busy and full of
life. Thrilling wine list is constantly evolving; the classic and vibrant dishes are
the ideal accompaniment.

ISLINGTON

FINSBURY

## Zetter 🏨 🛎 ♿ AC ✗ 📶 🆚 VISA ⊕ AE

St John's Sq., 86-88 Clerkenwell Rd. ✉ EC1M 5RJ ⊖ Farringdon
– ✆ (020) 7324 4444 – www.thezetter.com                    **19**UZD**s**
**72 rm** – ♦£ 222 ♦♦£ 222/480, ☕ £ 9.50
**Rest** *Bistrot Bruno Loubet* – see restaurant listing
♦ A trendy and discreet converted 19C warehouse with well-equipped bedrooms
that come with pleasant touches, such as Penguin paperbacks. The more idiosyncratic Zetter Townhouse across the square is used as an overflow.

## Bistrot Bruno Loubet – at Zetter Hotel 🛎 AC VISA ⊕ AE

St John's Sq., 86-88 Clerkenwell Rd. ✉ EC1M 5RJ ⊖ Farringdon
– ✆ (020) 7324 4455 – www.bistrotbrunoloubet.com – Closed 25-26 December
**Rest** – French – *(booking advisable)* Carte £ 30/40                **19**UZD**s**
♦ Having made his name in the early '90s, Bruno Loubet's London return was
much anticipated. His flavoursome regional French cooking proves a good fit for
this busy, bright restaurant at the Zetter hotel.

## Moro AC VISA ⊕ AE ①

34-36 Exmouth Mkt ✉ EC1R 4QE ⊖ Farringdon – ✆ (020) 7833 8336
– www.moro.co.uk – Closed Christmas-New Year and Sunday       **19**UZD**m**
**Rest** – Mediterranean – *(booking essential)* Carte £ 29/36
♦ Daily changing menu an eclectic mix of Mediterranean, Moroccan and Spanish.
Friendly T-shirted staff. Informal surroundings with bare tables and a large zinc bar.

## Medcalf 🛎 ↔ VISA ⊕

40 Exmouth Mkt. ✉ EC1R 4QE ⊖ Farringdon – ✆ (020) 7833 3533
– www.medcalfbar.co.uk – Closed 31 December-3 January, Sunday dinner and
bank holidays                                                **19**UZD**m**
**Rest** – British – *(booking essential)* Carte £ 24/32
♦ Bustling, no-frills former butcher's shop with lively atmosphere. Satisfying robust cooking, with the emphasis on seasonal, British ingredients. Good range of
beer and wine by the glass.

## Cicada 🛎 ↔ VISA ⊕ AE ①

132-134 St John St. ✉ EC1V 4JT ⊖ Farringdon – ✆ (020) 7608 1550
– www.rickerrestaurants.com – Closed 25 December, 1 January, Saturday lunch
and Sunday                                                   **19**UZD**d**
**Rest** – Asian – Carte £ 24/34
♦ Set in a culinary hotbed, this buzzy restaurant and vibrant bar is spacious, lively
and popular for its south east Asian dishes. You can even just pop in for one
course and a beer.

## The Modern Pantry 🛎 AC ↔ VISA ⊕ AE

47-48 St John's Sq. ✉ EC1V 4JJ ⊖ Farringdon – ✆ (020) 7553 9210
– www.themodernpantry.co.uk – Closed 25-26 December and 29 August
**Rest** – International – *(booking advisable)* Carte £ 35/39        **19**UZD**k**
♦ Fusion cooking that uses complementary flavours to create vibrant, zesty
dishes. The simple, crisp ground floor of this Georgian building has the buzz; upstairs is more intimate. Clued-up service.

## Morito VISA ⊕

32 Exmouth Mkt ✉ EC1R 4QE ⊖ Farringdon – ✆ (020) 7278 7007 – Closed
Christmas-New Year, Sunday and bank holidays                  **19**UZD**b**
**Rest** – Spanish – Carte approx. £ 21
♦ From the owners of next door Moro comes this authentic and appealingly
down to earth little tapas bar. Seven or eight dishes between two should suffice
but over-ordering is easy and won't break the bank.

395

LONDON

✗ **Caravan**                                                    VISA ◐◑ AE ⓪
*11-13 Exmouth Mkt ✉ EC1R 4QD ⊖ Farringdon – ℰ (020) 7833 8115
– www.caravanonexmouth.co.uk – Closed Christmas-New Year and dinner
Sunday*                                                          19UZD◄
**Rest** – International – *(booking advisable)* Carte £ 24/31
• A discernible Antipodean vibe pervades this casual eatery, from the laid-back
charm of the service to the kitchen's confident combining of unusual flavours.
Cooking is influenced by owner's travels – hence the name.

✗ **Clerkenwell Kitchen**                                        🛠 VISA ◐◑
*27-31 Clerkenwell Cl ✉ EC1R 0AT ⊖ Farringdon – ℰ (020) 7101 9959
– www.theclerkenwellkitchen.co.uk – Closed Christmas-New Year, Saturday,
Sunday and bank holidays*                                        19UZD▼
**Rest** – Modern European – *(lunch only) (booking advisable)* Carte approx. £ 19
• The owner of this simple, friendly, tucked away eatery worked with Hugh
Fearnley-Whittingstall and is committed to sustainability. Daily changing, well
sourced produce; fresh, flavoursome cooking.

🍴 **Green**                                                      🛠 AE VISA ◐◑
*29 Clerkenwell Gn ✉ EC1R 0DU ⊖ Farringdon. – ℰ (020) 7490 8010
– www.thegreenec1.co.uk – Closed 25-30 December*                 19UZD►
**Rest** – British – Carte £ 24/34
• The building dates from 1580 and became a tavern in 1720. Appetising and
imaginative bar snacks on the ground floor; intimate upstairs dining room for
fresh, seasonal and unfussy cooking.

🍴 **Peasant**                                                    ⇔ VISA ◐◑ AE
*240 St John St ✉ EC1V 4PH ⊖ Farringdon. – ℰ (020) 7336 7726
– www.thepeasant.co.uk – Closed 25 December-1 January and bank holidays
except Good Friday*                                              19UZD◄
**Rest** – British – *(booking essential)* Carte £ 23/30
• This handsome Victorian pub was at the vanguard of the gastropub move-
ment. Busy bar with its tiles and mosaics; upstairs for a less frantic environment
and wholesome British cooking.

🍴 **Well**                                                       🛠 VISA ◐◑ AE
*180 St John St ✉ EC1V 4JY ⊖ Farringdon. – ℰ (020) 7251 9363
– www.downthewell.com – Closed 25-26 December*                   19UZD►
**Rest** – British – Carte £ 23/33
• Compact pub with sliding glass doors and popular pavement benches. Modern
dishes range from potted shrimps to foie gras and chicken liver parfait. Classic
puddings; splendid cheeses.

## HIGHBURY

✗ **Au Lac**                                                     AE VISA ◐◑
*82 Highbury Park ✉ N5 2XE ⊖ Arsenal – ℰ (020) 7704 9187
– Closed 1-2 January and 24-26 December*                         13UZA▮
**Rest** – Vietnamese – *(dinner only and lunch Thursday-Friday)* Carte £ 10/23
• Cosy Vietnamese restaurant, with brightly coloured walls and painted fans.
Large menus with authentic dishes usefully highlighted. Fresh flavours; good value.

## ISLINGTON

✗✗ **Almeida**                                                   AE 🐕 ⇔ VISA ◐◑ AE
*30 Almeida St. ✉ N1 1AD ⊖ Angel – ℰ (020) 7354 4777
– www.almeida-restaurant.co.uk – Closed Sunday dinner and Monday lunch*
**Rest** – French – Menu £ 19/34 – Carte £ 35/55                 13UZB►
• Crisply decorated restaurant dating from 1891. Classically inspired menus with
plenty of choice; good value lunch. Interesting French regional wines. Over-
whelmingly busy pre/post theatre.

X **Ottolenghi**                                                    AC VISA OO AE
*287 Upper St.* ⊠ *N1 2TZ* ⊖ *Highbury & Islington –* ℰ *(020) 7288 1454*
*– www.ottolenghi.co.uk – Closed 25-26 December, dinner Sunday and bank*
*holidays*                                                      **13**UZB**k**
**Rest** – Mediterranean – *(booking essential)* Carte £ 20/45
♦ This attractive deli morphs into a little restaurant at night, with communal tables and chatty service. Fresh, flavoursome dishes with influences from across all
parts of the Med.

î□ **Drapers Arms**                                              ⛩ ⇄ VISA OO
₍⌂₎ *44 Barnsbury St* ⊠ *N1 1ER* ⊖ *Highbury & Islington. –* ℰ *(020) 7619 0348*
*– www.thedrapersarms.com*                                      **13**UZB**x**
**Rest** – British – *(booking advisable at dinner)* Carte £ 24/32
♦ Expect satisfying and robust British cooking at this handsome Georgian pub.
Prices are kept at reasonable levels for both the appealingly understated menu
and the wine list. The ground floor is more fun than the upstairs room.

î□ **Barnsbury**                                                 ⛩ VISA OO AE
*209-211 Liverpool Rd* ⊠ *N1 1LX* ⊖ *Highbury & Islington. –* ℰ *(020) 7607 5519*
*– www.thebarnsbury.co.uk – Closed 24-26 December*              **13**UZB**v**
**Rest** – Traditional – *(dinner only and lunch Friday-Sunday)* Carte £ 20/35
♦ Expect generous portions of gutsy cooking at this genuine neighbourhood
pub, with friendly and attentive service. Sit in the more atmospheric bar rather
than in the dining area at the back.

î□ **Northgate**                                                 ⛩ VISA OO ①
*113 Southgate Rd* ⊠ *N1 3JS* ⊖ *Dalston Kingsland (rail). –* ℰ *(020) 7359 7392*
*– Closed 1 January*                                            **13**VZB**a**
**Rest** – Mediterranean – *(dinner only and lunch Saturday-Sunday)* Carte £ 20/29
♦ Cavernous corner pub; busy front bar with tables laid for dining at the back.
Large blackboard menu lists mostly Mediterranean-influenced dishes with the
emphasis on flavour. Relaxed service.

## KING'S CROSS

î□ **Fellow**                                                    AC ⇄ VISA OO AE
*24 York Way* ⊠ *N1 9AA* ⊖ *King's Cross St Pancras. –* ℰ *(020) 7833 4395*
*– www.thefellow.co.uk – Closed 25 December and Sunday dinner*  **12**SZB**x**
**Rest** – Modern European – Carte £ 26/33
♦ Busy, atmospheric pub close to the station with a youthful, local clientele. Confident cooking on the ground floor displays a lightness of touch; boisterous upstairs cocktail bar.

## KENSINGTON and CHELSEA (Royal Borough of)               **12** B3
– Greater London

### CHELSEA

🏨🏨🏨 **Jumeirah Carlton Tower**      ← 🚗 🗔 ● 🍴 ℔ ℀ 📶 ㅎ ℀ 📶 ℥ 🚗
*Cadogan Pl.* ⊠ *SW1X 9PY* ⊖ *Knightsbridge –* ℰ *(020)*              VISA OO AE ①
*7235 1234 – www.jumeirahcarltontower.com*                       **37**AGX**r**
**186 rm** – ♦£ 276/900 ♦♦£ 276/900, ⛁ £ 37 – 30 suites
**Rest** *Rib Room* – see restaurant listing
♦ Imposing international hotel overlooking a leafy square and just yards from all
the swanky boutiques. Well-equipped rooftop health club has great views. Generously proportioned bedrooms boast every conceivable facility.

🏨🏨 **Wyndham Grand**                ← ⛩ 🗔 ● 🍴 ℔ 🗎 ℥ rm, AC 📶 ℥ 🚗
*Chelsea Harbour* ⊠ *SW10 0XG* ⊖ *Imperial Wharf (rail)*            VISA OO AE ①
*– ℰ (020) 7823 3000 – www.wyndhamgrandlondon.co.uk*             **23**PZG**k**
**158 suites** – ♦♦£ 192/425, ⛁ £ 23
**Rest** *Chelsea Riverside Brasserie* – Carte £ 25/43
♦ Modern, all-suite hotel within an exclusive marina and retail development.
Many of the spacious and well-appointed rooms have balconies and views across
the Thames. Modern restaurant overlooks the harbour.

**LONDON**

### Sheraton Park Tower  ≤ ⅃₅ ⊜ ᓄ AC 'ᛐ' ♨ ⌂ VISA ⊕ AE ①
*101 Knightsbridge ⊠ SW1X 7RN ⊖ Knightsbridge – ℰ (020) 7235 8050*
*– www.luxurycollection.com/parktowerlondon*  **37**AGX**t**
**275 rm** – ♦£ 516/642 ♦♦£ 516/774, ⊑ £ 26 – 5 suites
**Rest One-O-One** – see restaurant listing
• Built in the 1970s in a unique cylindrical shape. Well-equipped bedrooms are all identical in size. Top floor executive rooms have commanding views of Hyde Park and City.

### The Capital  ⊜ AC ⅍ 'ᛐ' ♨ ⌂ VISA ⊕ AE ①
*22-24 Basil St. ⊠ SW3 1AT ⊖ Knightsbridge – ℰ (020) 7589 5171*
*– www.capitalhotel.co.uk*  **37**AFX**a**
**49 rm** – ♦£ 294/420 ♦♦£ 294/420, ⊑ £ 19.50 – 1 suite
**Rest The Capital Restaurant** – see restaurant listing
• In 2011 this thoroughly British hotel celebrated 40 years under the same private ownership. Immaculately kept bedrooms from a number of different designers, a discreet atmosphere and conscientious, attentive service are the hallmarks.

### Draycott  🚙 ⊜ AC rm, 'ᛐ' VISA ⊕ AE ①
*26 Cadogan Gdns. ⊠ SW3 2RP ⊖ Sloane Square – ℰ (020) 7730 6466*
*– www.draycotthotel.com*  **37**AGY**c**
**24 rm** – ♦£ 168/312 ♦♦£ 282/312, ⊑ £ 20.95 – 11 suites
**Rest** – (room service only)
• Charming 19C house with elegant sitting room overlooking tranquil garden for afternoon tea. Bedrooms are individually decorated in a country house style and are named after writers or actors.

### The Cadogan  🚙 ⅃₅ ⅍ ⊜ AC ⅍ 'ᛐ' ♨ VISA ⊕ AE ①
*75 Sloane St ⊠ SW1X 9SG ⊖ Knightsbridge – ℰ (020) 7235 7141*
*– www.cadogan.com*  **37**AGY**b**
**64 rm** – ♦£ 478 ♦♦£ 538, ⊑ £ 27.50
**Rest Langtry's** – (closed Sunday dinner) Menu £ 20 – Carte £ 28/58
• An Edwardian townhouse, made famous by two former residents – Oscar Wilde and Lillie Langtry. Quiet drawing room for afternoon tea; bedrooms are varied and comfortable. Restaurant offers a traditional menu.

### Knightsbridge  ⊜ ⅍ rm, AC ⅍ 'ᛐ' VISA ⊕ AE ①
*10 Beaufort Gdns ⊠ SW3 1PT ⊖ Knightsbridge – ℰ (020) 7584 6300*
*– www.knightsbridgehotel.com*  **37**AFX**s**
**44 rm** – ♦£ 216/276 ♦♦£ 384/774, ⊑ £ 19   **Rest** – (room service only)
• Attractively furnished townhouse with a very stylish, discreet feel. Every bedroom is immaculately appointed and has an individuality of its own; fine detailing throughout.

### Egerton House  ⊜ AC ⅍ 'ᛐ' VISA ⊕ AE ①
*17-19 Egerton Terr. ⊠ SW3 2BX ⊖ South Kensington – ℰ (020) 7589 2412*
*– www.egertonhousehotel.com*  **37**AFY**e**
**27 rm** – ♦£ 336/408 ♦♦£ 420/732, ⊑ £ 29.50 – 1 suite
**Rest** – (room service only)
• Compact but comfortable townhouse in a very good location, well maintained throughout and owned by the Red Carnation group. High levels of personal service make the hotel stand out.

### The Levin  ⊜ AC ⅍ 'ᛐ' VISA ⊕ AE ①
*28 Basil St. ⊠ SW3 1AS ⊖ Knightsbridge – ℰ (020) 7589 6286*
*– www.thelevinhotel.co.uk*  **37**AFX**c**
**12 rm** – ♦£ 300/384 ♦♦£ 300/384
**Rest Le Metro** – see restaurant listing
• A discreet townhouse and sister to The Capital hotel next door. Impressive façade, contemporary interior and comfortable bedrooms in subtle art deco style, boasting marvellous champagne mini bars.

### Beaufort

🏠 🗚 rm, 🛠 (⦿) 🆅🅸🆂🅰 ☉☉ 🅰🅴 ⓪

*33 Beaufort Gdns* ✉ *SW3 1PP* ⊖ *Knightsbridge –* ✆ *(020) 7584 5252*
*– www.thebeaufort.co.uk*                                                     **37**AFX**n**
**29 rm –** 🛏️£ 216/360 🛏️🛏️£ 288/600, ☕ £ 16    **Rest** *– (room service only)*
♦ A vast collection of English floral watercolours adorn this 19C townhouse in a
useful location. Modern and co-ordinated rooms. Tariff includes all drinks and afternoon tea.

### Sydney House *without rest*

🏠 🗚 🛠 (⦿) 🆅🅸🆂🅰 ☉☉ 🅰🅴 ⓪

*9-11 Sydney St.* ✉ *SW3 6PU* ⊖ *South Kensington –* ✆ *(020) 7376 7711*
*– www.sydneyhousechelsea.com – Closed 25-26 December*                     **36**ADY**s**
**21 rm –** 🛏️£ 125/225 🛏️🛏️£ 155/255, ☕ £ 12.95
♦ Stylish and compact Georgian townhouse made brighter through plenty of
mirrors and light wood. Thoughtfully designed bedrooms; Room 43 has its own
terrace. Part of the Abode group.

### The Sloane Square

🏠 🖔 🗚 🛠 (⦿) 🆅🅸🆂🅰 ☉☉

*7-12 Sloane Sq.* ✉ *SW1W 8EG* ⊖ *Sloane Square –* ✆ *(020) 7896 9988*
*– www.sloanesquarehotel.co.uk*                                               **37**AGY**k**
**102 rm –** 🛏️£ 234/288 🛏️🛏️£ 288/448, ☕ £ 16
**Rest** *Chelsea Brasserie* – see restaurant listing
♦ Well-placed, red-brick hotel boasts bright, contemporary décor. Stylish, co-ordinated bedrooms, with laptops; library of DVDs and games available. Rooms at the
back are slightly quieter.

### Gordon Ramsay

XXXX   🗚 🆅🅸🆂🅰 ☉☉ 🅰🅴 ⓪

❀ ❀ ❀ *68-69 Royal Hospital Rd.* ✉ *SW3 4HP* ⊖ *Sloane Square –* ✆ *(020) 7352 4441*
*– www.gordonramsay.com – Closed Christmas, Saturday and Sunday*
**Rest** – French – *(booking essential)* Menu £ 45/90 ❀❀               **37**AFZ**c**
**Spec.** Ravioli of lobster, langoustine and salmon with a lemongrass and chervil
velouté. Best end of lamb with confit breast, braised shank and a navarin of
spring vegetables. Granny Smith parfait with a blackberry foam, honeycomb and
cider sorbet.
♦ Head Chef Clare Smyth has brought a lighter, more instinctive style to the
cooking while still delivering on the Gordon Ramsay classics. The elegant simplicity of the room exudes calmness; service is equally composed and well-organised.

### Bibendum

XXX   🗚 🆅🅸🆂🅰 ☉☉ 🅰🅴

*Michelin House, 81 Fulham Rd.* ✉ *SW3 6RD* ⊖ *South Kensington –* ✆ *(020)*
*7581 5817 – www.bibendum.co.uk – Closed 24-26 December and 1 January*
**Rest** – French – Menu £ 30 (lunch) – Carte £ 36/63 ❀❀               **37**AEY**s**
♦ Has maintained a loyal following for over 20 years, with its French food that
comes with a British accent. Located on the 1st floor of a London landmark – Michelin's former HQ, dating from 1911.

### The Capital Restaurant – *at The Capital Hotel*

XXX   🗚 ⇄ 🆅🅸🆂🅰 ☉☉ 🅰🅴 ⓪

*22-24 Basil St.* ✉ *SW3 1AT* ⊖ *Knightsbridge –* ✆ *(020) 7591 1202*
*– www.capitalhotel.co.uk*                                                    **37**AFX**a**
**Rest** – French – *(booking essential)* Menu £ 30 (lunch) – Carte £ 46/70 ❀❀
♦ Elegant surroundings, formal service and elaborately presented, classic cuisine
have featured at the family-owned Capital for many years. It is also known for its
superlative wine list.

### Fifth Floor – *at Harvey Nichols*

XXX   🗚 ☕ 🆅🅸🆂🅰 ☉☉ 🅰🅴 ⓪

*109-125 Knightsbridge* ✉ *SW1X 7RJ* ⊖ *Knightsbridge –* ✆ *(020) 7235 5250*
*– www.harveynichols.com – Closed Easter Sunday, 25 December and Sunday*
*dinner*                                                                       **37**AGX**s**
**Rest** – Modern European – Carte £ 35/55 ❀❀
♦ Modern cooking with influences kept mostly from within Europe. Stylish and
elegant, tent-like room with attached bar; reached via its own elevator. Prompt service.

LONDON

LONDON

### XXX Toto's 🛜 VISA ⚫ AE
*Walton House, Walton St.* ⊠ *SW3 2JH* ⊖ *Knightsbridge –* ✆ *(020) 7589 0075*
*– Closed 25-27 December* **37**AFY**x**
**Rest** – Italian – *(booking essential at dinner)* Menu £ 23 (lunch) – Carte £ 35/47
◆ A long standing Chelsea institution, with old school service and plenty of local regulars who add to the discreet atmosphere. Familiar and satisfying dishes, with homemade pasta the highlight.

### XXX Awana AC VISA ⚫ AE ⓞ
*85 Sloane Ave.* ⊠ *SW3 3DX* ⊖ *South Kensington –* ✆ *(020) 7584 8880*
*– www.awana.co.uk – Closed 25-26 December, 1 January and dinner 24 December* **37**AFY**b**
**Rest** – Malaysian – *(booking essential)* Menu £ 15 (lunch) – Carte £ 24/58
◆ Smart and stylish restaurant showcasing Malaysia's rich culinary diversity. The 'Malaysian Journey' menu provides a good introduction. If without a booking, consider sitting at the Satay Bar.

### XXX Chutney Mary AC ⇔ VISA ⚫ AE ⓞ
*535 King's Rd.* ⊠ *SW10 0SZ* ⊖ *Fulham Broadway –* ✆ *(020) 7351 3113*
*– www.realindianfood.com – Closed dinner 25 December* **22**OZG**v**
**Rest** – Indian – *(dinner only and lunch Saturday-Sunday)* Menu £ 22 (week-days) – Carte £ 38/53
◆ Soft lighting and sepia etchings hold sway at this forever popular restaurant. Extensive menu of specialities from all corners of India. Complementary wine list.

### XXX One-O-One – at Sheraton Park Tower Hotel AC VISA ⚫ AE ⓞ
*101 Knightsbridge* ⊠ *SW1X 7RN* ⊖ *Knightsbridge –* ✆ *(020) 7290 7101*
*– www.oneoonerestaurant.com* **37**AGX**t**
**Rest** – Seafood – Menu £ 22 (lunch) – Carte £ 55/75
◆ Smart ground floor restaurant; lacking a little in atmosphere but the seafood is good. Much of the produce from Brittany and Norway; don't miss the King crab legs. Small tasting plates also offered.

### XXX Eleven Park Walk AC ⇔ VISA ⚫ AE
*11 Park Walk* ⊠ *SW10 0AJ* ⊖ *South Kensington –* ✆ *(020) 7352 3449*
*– www.11parkwalk.co.uk – Closed 25 December* **36**ACZ**v**
**Rest** – Italian – Carte £ 34/58
◆ What was Aubergine is now a sophisticated Italian; its menu traverses the country but it is the Sardinian specialities that shine. It attracts an equally smart set who appreciate the polished service.

### XXX Rib Room – at Jumeirah Carlton Tower Hotel ⇐ 🍴 VISA ⚫ AE ⓞ
*Cadogan Pl.* ⊠ *SW1X 9PY* ⊖ *Knightsbridge –* ✆ *(020) 7235 1234*
*– www.jumeirahcarltontower.com* **37**AGX**n**
**Rest** – British – Menu £ 36/50 – Carte £ 61/88
◆ Rib of Aberdeen Angus, steaks and other classic British dishes attract a prosperous, international crowd; few of whom appear to have a beef with the prices at this swish veteran.

### XX Rasoi (Vineet Bhatia) AC ⇔ VISA ⚫ AE
ॐ *10 Lincoln St* ⊠ *SW3 2TS* ⊖ *Sloane Square –* ✆ *(020) 7225 1881*
*– www.rasoirestaurant.co.uk – Closed 25-26 December and Saturday lunch*
**Rest** – Indian – Menu £ 27/59 – Carte £ 59/85 **37**AFY**y**
**Spec.** Tandoori lobster with chilli and wasabi, lentil and lobster soup. Smoked rack of lamb with biryani khichdi. Chocolate craving platter.
◆ Vineet Bhatia proves that Indian food can be just as open to interpretation as other cuisines. You'll find his exotically decorated yet intimate dining room sitting somewhat incongruously within an archetypal Chelsea townhouse.

XX **Le Colombier** ⟺ VISA ⓞⓞ AE
*145 Dovehouse St.* ✉ *SW3 6LB* ⊖ *South Kensington –* ✆ *(020) 7351 1155*
*– www.le-colombier-restaurant.co.uk* **36**ADZ**e**
**Rest** – French – Menu £ 27 (lunch) – Carte £ 32/51
♦ Proudly Gallic corner restaurant in an affluent residential area. Attractive enclosed terrace. Bright and cheerful surroundings and service of traditional French cooking.

XX **Racine** AC ⅋ VISA ⓞⓞ AE
*239 Brompton Rd* ✉ *SW3 2EP* ⊖ *South Kensington –* ✆ *(020) 7584 4477*
*– www.racine-restaurant.com – Closed Christmas* **37**AEY**t**
**Rest** – French – Menu £ 18 (lunch and early dinner) – Carte £ 30/55
♦ An authentic feel to this French brasserie, with dark leather seats, wood floors and mirrors. The menu provides a roll-call of classic regional specialities, from steak tartare to fruits de mer.

XX **Medlar** ⌂ AC ⟺ VISA ⓞⓞ AE
*438 King's Rd* ✉ *SW10 0LJ* ⊖ *Sloane Square –* ✆ *(020) 7349 1900*
*– www.medlarrestaurant.co.uk – Closed Sunday dinner and Monday*
**Rest** – Modern European – Menu £ 25/38 **23**PZG**x**
♦ Two young owners have created a charming local spot; David provides warm but unobtrusive service; Joe, a Chez Bruce alumnus, concentrates on matching flavours. His set menu showcases cooking with a French base but a lighter touch.

XX **Daphne's** AC ⟺ VISA ⓞⓞ AE ⓪
*112 Draycott Ave.* ✉ *SW3 3AE* ⊖ *South Kensington –* ✆ *(020) 7589 4257*
*– www.daphnes-restaurant.co.uk – Closed 25-26 December* **37**AFY**j**
**Rest** – Italian – *(booking essential)* Menu £ 20 (lunch and early dinner)
– Carte £ 30/40
♦ Established over 40 years ago and a Chelsea institution with 'celebrity' following. Reliable formula of tried and tested Italian classics in a room with a warm, Tuscan feel.

XX **Poissonnerie de l'Avenue** AC ⟺ VISA ⓞⓞ AE ⓪
*82 Sloane Ave.* ✉ *SW3 3DZ* ⊖ *South Kensington –* ✆ *(020) 7589 2457*
*– www.poissonneriedelavenue.com – Closed Easter and 25-26 December*
**Rest** – Seafood – Menu £ 30 (lunch) – Carte £ 31/48 **37**AFY**u**
♦ A smart, personally run, wood-panelled Chelsea institution since 1946. Its extensive choice of carefully prepared, traditional seafood dishes attracts a smart and loyal following.

XX **Eight over Eight** AC ⟺ VISA ⓞⓞ AE ⓪
*392 King's Rd* ✉ *SW3 5UZ* ⊖ *Gloucester Road –* ✆ *(020) 7349 9934*
*– www.rickerrestaurants.com – Closed 25-28 December* **23**PZG**n**
**Rest** – Asian – Carte £ 24/50
♦ Reopened in 2010 after a fire, with a slightly plusher feel; still as popular as ever with the fashionable crowds. Influences stretch across South East Asia and dishes are designed for sharing.

XX **Bluebird** AC ⅋ ⟺ VISA ⓞⓞ AE ⓪
*350 King's Rd.* ✉ *SW3 5UU* ⊖ *Sloane Square –* ✆ *(020) 7559 1000*
*– www.bluebird-restaurant.co.uk* **23**PZG**n**
**Rest** – British – Menu £ 25 – Carte £ 26/49
♦ Former industrial space incorporates everything from a wine store to a private members club. Large, buzzy restaurant champions British produce in an appealing menu that has something for everyone.

XX **Le Cercle** AC VISA ⓞⓞ AE ⓪
*1 Wilbraham Pl.* ✉ *SW1X 9AE* ⊖ *Sloane Square –* ✆ *(020) 7901 9999*
*– www.lecercle.co.uk – Closed 25 December, Sunday, Monday and bank holidays*
**Rest** – French – Menu £ 15 (lunch) – Carte £ 28/31 **37**AGY**e**
♦ Deep basement location made into a fashionable spot, with drapes and high ceilings; comes alive more at dinner. Order three or four small plates of the delicate French cooking per person.

LONDON

## XX **Painted Heron**     🖼 AK VISA ⚫⚫ AE

*112 Cheyne Walk* ✉ *SW10 0DJ* ⊖ *Gloucester Road* – ☏ *(020) 7351 5232*
*– www.thepaintedheron.com – Closed 25 December*     **23**PZG**d**
**Rest** – Indian – *(dinner only and lunch Saturday-Sunday)* Menu £ 20/35
– Carte £ 30/38
◆ Well-supported locally and quite formally run Indian restaurant. Nooks and
crannies create an intimate atmosphere. Fish and game dishes are the highlight
of the contemporary Indian cooking.

## XX **Eighty-Six**     AK VISA ⚫⚫ AE ①

*86 Fulham Rd, (1st Floor)* ✉ *SW3 6HR* ⊖ *South Kensington*
*– ☏ (020) 7052 9620 – www.86restaurant.co.uk – Closed Sunday and Monday*
**Rest** – Modern European – *(dinner only)* Menu £ 41     **36**ADZ**x**
◆ A mix of baroque, rococo and bling are used to create a gilded jewel for young
movers and shakers. The menu roams around Europe but the best dishes are the
simpler ones that use British ingredients.

## XX **Ilia**     AK ⇔ VISA ⚫⚫ AE

*96 Draycott Ave.* ✉ *SW3 3AD* ⊖ *South Kensington* – ☏ *(020) 7225 2555*
*– www.ilia-london.com*     **37**AFY**a**
**Rest** – Italian – Carte £ 29/47
◆ Formerly a French restaurant but its owner decided to try Italian. Bewildering
array of dishes but at least there's something for everyone and the cooking is capable. Cool, fresh room; best tables by the French windows.

## XX **Marco**     AK VISA ⚫⚫ AE

*Stamford Bridge, Fulham Rd.* ✉ *SW6 1HS* ⊖ *Fulham Broadway*
*– ☏ (020) 7915 2929 – www.marcorestaurant.org*
*– Closed 2 weeks July-August, 25 December, Sunday and Monday*     **22**OZG**c**
**Rest** – Traditional – *(dinner only) (booking advisable)* Carte £ 31/59
◆ Marco Pierre White's brasserie at Chelsea Football Club offers an appealing
range of classics, from British favourites to satisfying French and Italian fare; puddings are a highlight. Comfortable and well-run room.

## XX **Good Earth**     AK VISA ⚫⚫ AE

*233 Brompton Rd.* ✉ *SW3 2EP* ⊖ *Knightsbridge*
*– ☏ (020) 7584 3658 – www.goodearthgroup.co.uk*
*– Closed 23-31 December*     **37**AFY**h**
**Rest** – Chinese – Menu £ 12/30 – Carte £ 21/36
◆ The basement is busier and more popular than the ground floor. Extensive
menu makes good use of quality ingredients and offers appealing choice between classic and more unusual dishes.

## XX **The Botanist**     AK VISA ⚫⚫ AE

*7 Sloane Sq* ✉ *SW1W 8EE* ⊖ *Sloane Square* – ☏ *(020) 7730 0077*
*– www.thebotanistonsloanesquare.com – Closed 25-26 December*     **37**AGY**r**
**Rest** – Modern European – Carte £ 31/51
◆ Pass through the busy bar to get to the stylish and comfortable restaurant with
its warm and vibrant atmosphere. Appealing and accessible menu delivers unfussy and satisfying dishes.

## XX **Chelsea Brasserie** – at The Sloane Square Hotel     AK 🍴 VISA ⚫⚫

*7-12 Sloane Sq.* ✉ *SW1W 8EG* ⊖ *Sloane Square*
*– ☏ (020) 7896 9988 – www.sloanesquarehotel.co.uk*
*– Closed Sunday dinner*     **37**AGY**k**
**Rest** – French – Menu £ 25 *(lunch and early dinner)* – Carte £ 33/40
◆ You pass through the busy bar to get to the smartly lit brasserie, with exposed
brick, mirrors and tiles. Cooking has a strong French base. Good value theatre
menu and brisk service.

XX **Joe's**  `AC` `VISA` `@O` `AE` `O`
126 Draycott Ave ⊠ SW3 3AH ⊖ South Kensington – ℰ (020) 7225 2217
– www.joseph.co.uk – Closed 25 December, Easter Sunday and dinner
Sunday-Monday                                                    37AFY**f**
**Rest** – Modern European – Menu £ 17 (lunch) – Carte £ 24/37
♦ Back in the '80s when the only thing bigger than the hair were the shoulder
pads, Joe's was the place to be seen. It's now fashionable once again and its appealing, fortnightly changing menu comes with Mediterranean overtones.

XX **Galoupet**  `AC` `VISA` `@O` `AE` `O`
13 Beauchamp Pl ⊠ SW13 1NQ ⊖ Knightsbridge – ℰ (020) 7036 3600
– www.galoupet.co.uk – Closed 25 December                        37AFX**x**
**Rest** – Asian influences – Carte £ 35/50
♦ The 'Enomatic' wine dispensers are a clue that wine plays an important part
here; indeed, the owners have a vineyard in Provence. Dishes fuse the East with
the Med and offer pleasant contrasting textures and a refreshing vitality.

X **Bibendum Oyster Bar**  `VISA` `@O` `AE`
Michelin House, 81 Fulham Rd. ⊠ SW3 6RD ⊖ South Kensington
– ℰ (020) 7589 1480 – www.bibendum.co.uk – Closed 24-26 December and 1 January
**Rest** – Seafood – (bookings not accepted) Carte £ 21/35        37AEY**s**
♦ Oysters, potted shrimps and fruits de mer are the highlights at this continental-
style café, with its mosaic floor and colourful ceramic tiles. Wine list includes
460ml pots.

X **Foxtrot Oscar**  `AC` `VISA` `@O` `AE`
79 Royal Hospital Rd. ⊠ SW3 4HN ⊖ Sloane Square – ℰ (020) 7352 4448
– www.gordonramsay.com – Closed 25 December                      37AFZ**v**
**Rest** – Traditional – (booking essential) Menu £ 22 (lunch) – Carte £ 26/33
♦ Gordon Ramsay's least known restaurant has a relaxed, local feel, with celebrity
photographs adorning its burgundy walls. Bistro cooking, with the Foxtrot Burger
a highlight.

X **Henry Root**  `🛆` `AC` `VISA` `@O` `AE`
9 Park Walk ⊠ SW10 0AJ ⊖ South Kensington – ℰ (020) 7552 7040
– www.thehenryroot.com – Closed 25-27 December                   36ACZ**z**
**Rest** – French – (booking advisable) Menu £ 13 (lunch) – Carte £ 24/34 🍴
♦ William Donaldson satirised many of the good and the great of his day
through the letters of his alter ego, Henry Root. His name lives on in this cheery
local spot, with its appealing menu that includes small plates and charcuterie.

X **Manicomio**  `🛆` `AC` `VISA` `@O` `AE`
85 Duke of York Sq., King's Rd. ⊠ SW3 4LY ⊖ Sloane Square
– ℰ (020) 7730 3366 – www.manicomio.co.uk – Closed 1 January, 24-26 and
31 December                                                      37AGY**x**
**Rest** – Italian – Carte £ 31/43
♦ Modern, busy Italian, popular with shoppers and visitors to the Saatchi Gallery;
the simplest dishes are the best ones. The terrific terrace fills quickly. Next door is
their café and deli.

X **Tom's Kitchen**  `VISA` `@O` `AE`
27 Cale St. ⊠ SW3 3QP ⊖ South Kensington – ℰ (020) 7349 0202
– www.tomskitchen.co.uk                                          37AFZ**b**
**Rest** – French – Carte £ 29/50
♦ A converted pub, whose white tiles and mirrors help to give it an industrial
feel. Appealing and wholesome dishes come in man-sized portions. The eponymous Tom is Tom Aikens.

X **Geales**  `AC` `⇔` `VISA` `@O` `AE`
1 Cale St. ⊠ SW3 3QT ⊖ South Kensington – ℰ (020) 7965 0555
– www.geales.com – Closed 25-26 December, 1 January and Monday lunch
**Rest** – Seafood – Carte £ 28/36                               37AFZ**n**
♦ Fish and chips are the main draw at this cosy, warmly run and sweetly decorated spot. Other choices can include fish pie and soft shell crab tempura, along
with wholesome, homemade puddings.

### Le Metro – at The Levin Hotel
AK VISA ⓌⓄ AE Ⓞ

*28 Basil St. ⊠ SW3 1AS ⊖ Knightsbridge – ℰ (020) 7589 6286*
*– www.thelevinhotel.co.uk – Closed Sunday dinner*  **37**AFX**c**
**Rest** – Mediterranean – Carte £ 25/30

• Open all day and for those in the know, Le Metro is a useful and secretive little spot next to Harrods. Pop in for the pie or pasta of the week or a bellini and a croque monsieur.

### Admiral Codrington
🗧 AK ♻ VISA ⓌⓄ AE

*17 Mossop St ⊠ SW3 2LY ⊖ South Kensington. – ℰ (020) 7581 0005*
*– www.theadmiralcodrington.com – Closed 25-26 December*  **37**AFY**v**
**Rest** – Modern European – Carte £ 23/43

• A Chelsea institution, with popular bar in the evenings and a separate, smart restaurant with retractable roof. The menu covers all bases and mixes British classics with European influences.

### Chelsea Ram
AK VISA ⓌⓄ

*32 Burnaby St. ⊠ SW10 0PL ⊖ Fulham Broadway. – ℰ (020) 7351 4008*
*– Closed Sunday dinner*  **23**PZG**r**
**Rest** – British – Carte £ 22/26 **s**

• A warm, welcoming and relaxed pub surrounded by residential streets, with a loyal local following. Expect proper 'pub grub' where the portions are generous and the prices fair.

### Cadogan Arms
AK VISA ⓌⓄ AE

*298 King's Rd ⊠ SW3 5UG ⊖ South Kensington. – ℰ (020) 7352 6500*
*– www.thecadoganarmschelsea.com – Closed 25-26 December*  **36**ADZ**y**
**Rest** – British – (booking advisable at dinner) Carte £ 24/33

• Part of the Martin Brothers bourgeoning pub group. This is a proper pub, with billiard tables upstairs and a gusty, full-on menu. Stuffed and mounted animals stare down as you eat.

### Builders Arms
AK VISA ⓌⓄ AE

*13 Britten St ⊠ SW3 3TY ⊖ South Kensington. – ℰ (020) 7349 9040*
*– www.geronimo-inns.co.uk*  **37**AFZ**x**
**Rest** – British – (bookings not accepted) Carte £ 22/34

• Smart looking and busy pub for the Chelsea set; drinkers are welcomed as much as diners. Cooking reveals the effort put into sourcing decent ingredients; rib of beef for two is a favourite. Thoughtfully compiled wine list.

### Pig's Ear
VISA ⓌⓄ AE

*35 Old Church St ⊠ SW3 5BS ⊖ Sloane Square. – ℰ (020) 7352 2908*
*– www.thepigsear.com*  **23**PZG**v**
**Rest** – Traditional – Carte £ 15/25

• Honest pub, with rough-and-ready ground floor bar for lunch; more intimate, wood-panelled upstairs dining room for dinner. Robust, confident and satisfying cooking with a classical bent.

### Phoenix
🗧 AK VISA ⓌⓄ AE

*23 Smith St. ⊠ SW3 4EE ⊖ Sloane Square. – ℰ (020) 7730 9182*
*– www.geronimo-inns.co.uk/thepheonix – Closed 25 December*  **37**AFZ**a**
**Rest** – Modern European – Carte £ 21/34

• Friendly, conscientiously run Chelsea local, where satisfying and carefully prepared pub classics are served in the roomy, civilised bar or in the warm, comfortable dining room at the back.

### Lots Road Pub & Dining Room
AK VISA ⓌⓄ AE

*114 Lots Rd ⊠ SW10 0RJ ⊖ Fulham Broadway. – ℰ (020) 7352 6645*
*– www.lotsroadpub.com*  **23**PZG**b**
**Rest** – Traditional – Carte £ 20/30

• Lively semicircular shaped pub, close to Chelsea Harbour. Hearty and satisfying classics, from mussels to Perthshire côte de boeuf and a tart of the day. Staff keep things bright and cheery.

## EARL'S COURT

### K + K George
1-15 Templeton Pl. ⊠ SW5 9NB ⊖ Earl's Court – ☏ (020) 7598 8700
– www.kkhotels.com
**154 rm** ⌂ – ♟£ 140/300 ♟♟£ 150/336    **Rest** – Carte £ 21/42 **s**
♦ Five converted 19C houses overlooking large rear garden. Scandinavian-style
rooms with low beds, white walls and light wood furniture. Breakfast room has
the garden view. Informal dining in the bar.

35AAY**s**

### Twenty Nevern Square without rest
20 Nevern Sq. ⊠ SW5 9PD ⊖ Earl's Court – ☏ (020) 7565 9555
– www.twentynevernsquare.co.uk
**20 rm** – ♟£ 115/180 ♟♟£ 220/250, ⌂ £ 9
♦ In an attractive Victorian garden square, an individually designed, privately
owned townhouse. Original pieces of furniture and some bedrooms with their
own terrace.

35AAY**u**

### Mayflower without rest
26-28 Trebovir Rd. ⊠ SW5 9NJ ⊖ Earl's Court – ☏ (020) 7370 0991
– www.mayflowerhotel.co.uk
**43 rm** – ♟£ 120/130 ♟♟£ 120/130, ⌂ £ 10 – 4 suites
♦ Conveniently placed, friendly establishment with a secluded rear breakfast
terrace and basement breakfast room. Individually styled bedrooms with Asian
influence.

35ABY**x**

### Amsterdam without rest
7-9 Trebovir Rd. ⊠ SW5 9LS ⊖ Earl's Court – ☏ (020) 7370 2814
– www.amsterdam-hotel.com
**19 rm** – ♟£ 86/99 ♟♟♟£ 108/120, ⌂ £ 3 – 8 suites
♦ Basement breakfast room and a small secluded garden. The brightly decorated
bedrooms are light and airy. Some have smart wood floors; some boast their
own balcony.

35ABY**c**

### Rushmore without rest
11 Trebovir Rd. ⊠ SW5 9LS ⊖ Earl's Court – ☏ (020) 7370 3839
– www.rushmore-hotel.co.uk
**22 rm** – ♟£ 89/109 ♟♟£ 129/199
♦ Behind its Victorian façade lies a hotel popular with tourists. Individually decorated bedrooms in a variety of shapes and sizes. Piazza-style conservatory breakfast room.

35ABY**a**

## KENSINGTON

### Royal Garden
2-24 Kensington High St. ⊠ W8 4PT ⊖ High Street Kensington – ☏ (020)
7937 8000 – www.royalgardenhotel.co.uk
**372 rm** – ♟£ 360 ♟♟£ 408, ⌂ £ 23.50 – 22 suites
**Rest** *Min Jiang* – see restaurant listing
**Rest** *Park Terrace* – ☏ (020) 7361 0602 – Menu £ 20/33
♦ A tall, modern hotel with many of its rooms enjoying enviable views over the
adjacent Kensington Gardens. All the modern amenities and services, with well-
drilled staff. Bright, spacious Park Terrace offers British, Asian and modern European cuisine.

35ABX**c**

### The Milestone
1-2 Kensington Ct. ⊠ W8 5DL ⊖ High Street Kensington – ☏ (020) 7917 1000
www.milestonehotel.co.uk
**56 rm** – ♟£ 360/534 ♟♟£ 420/594, ⌂ £ 29.50 – 6 suites
**Rest** *Cheneston's* – see restaurant listing
♦ Elegant hotel with decorative Victorian façade and English feel. Charming oak-
panelled lounge and snug bar. Meticulously decorated bedrooms with period detail. The enthusiasm of the staff also sets it apart.

35ABX**u**

LONDON

### Baglioni

🏗 ⌂ 👁 📶 💪 📶 ♨ 🕒 📶 💳 💳 📶

*60 Hyde Park Gate* ✉ *SW7 5BB* ⊖ *High Street Kensington –* ☏ *(020) 7368 5700*
*– www.baglionihotels.com*                                               **36**ACX**e**
**52 rm** – ♦£ 311/474 ♦♦£ 347/546, ☕ £ 29 – 15 suites
**Rest** *Brunello* – see restaurant listing
♦ Opposite Kensington Palace and no escaping the fact that this is an Italian
owned hotel. The interior is bold and ornate and there's a trendy basement
bar. Stylish bedrooms have a masculine feel and boast impressive facilities.

### Launceston Place

📶 ⇄ 💳 💳 📶 ◑

*1a Launceston Pl.* ✉ *W8 5RL* ⊖ *Gloucester Road –* ☏ *(020) 7937 6912*
*– www.launcestonplace-restaurant.co.uk – Closed 24-30 December, Monday
lunch and dinner bank holiday Mondays*                          **36**ACX**a**
**Rest** – Modern European – Menu £ 22/45
♦ Its most recent reincarnation, with its dark walls and moody lighting, still attracts plenty of locals. Cooking is original, deftly executed and uses ingredients
largely from the British Isles.

### Min Jiang – at Royal Garden Hotel

≤ 📶 ⇄ 💳 💳 📶 ◑

*Royal Garden Hotel (10th Floor), 2-24 Kensington High St.* ✉ *W8 4PT*
⊖ *High Street Kensington –* ☏ *(020) 7361 1988 – www.minjiang.co.uk*
**Rest** – Chinese – Menu £ 17/50 – Carte approx. £ 48           **35**ABX**c**
♦ A comfortable Chinese restaurant looking down over Kensington Gardens from
its 10th floor location. Most provinces of China are represented on the menu but
the main speciality is the Beijing duck.

### Belvedere

🍴 📶 🍷 ⇄ 💳 💳 📶

*Holland House, off Abbotsbury Rd.* ✉ *W8 6LU* ⊖ *Holland Park –* ☏ *(020)
7602 1238 – www.belvedererestaurant.co.uk – Closed Sunday dinner*
**Rest** – Modern European – Menu £ 20 (weekday lunch)           **16**MZE**u**
– Carte £ 28/44
♦ Former 19C orangery in a delightful position in the middle of the park. On two
floors with a bar and balcony terrace and decorated with huge vases of flowers.
Modern take on classic dishes.

### Kitchen W8

📶 💳 💳 📶

*11-13 Abingdon Rd* ✉ *W8 6AH* ⊖ *High Street Kensington –* ☏ *(020) 7937 0120*
*– www.kitchenw8.com – Closed bank holidays*                       **35**AAX**a**
**Rest** – Modern European – Menu £ 20 (lunch) – Carte £ 33/47
**Spec.** Sauté of lamb sweetbreads and tongue with garlic, parsley and morels. Fillet of halibut with wild garlic and meat vinaigrette. Salted chocolate parfait with
malt ice cream.
♦ Smart, comfortable restaurant which is not as casual as its name implies, but
which does have a pleasant, neighbourhood feel. Skilled kitchen produces balanced dishes free of showiness, with the emphasis on flavour.

### Babylon – at The Roof Gardens

≤ 🍴 📶 ⇄ 💳 💳 📶

*99 Kensington High St (entrance on Derry St)* ✉ *W8 5SA*
⊖ *High Street Kensington –* ☏ *(020) 7368 3993 – www.roofgardens.virgin.com*
*– Closed 24-30 December, 1-2 January and Sunday dinner*          **35**ABX**n**
**Rest** – Modern European – Menu £ 23 (lunch) – Carte £ 33/47
♦ Situated on the roof of this pleasant London building affording attractive views
of the London skyline. Stylish modern décor in keeping with the contemporary,
British cooking.

### Clarke's

📶 💳 💳 📶 ◑

*124 Kensington Church St.* ✉ *W8 4BH* ⊖ *Notting Hill Gate –* ☏ *(020) 7221 9225*
*– www.sallyclarke.com – Closed Christmas-New Year, Sunday dinner and bank
holidays*                                                         **27**ABV**c**
**Rest** – Modern European – *(booking advisable)* Menu £ 41 (dinner)
– Carte £ 33/46
♦ Forever popular restaurant, serving a choice of dishes boasting trademark
fresh, seasonal ingredients and Sally Clarke's famed lightness of touch. Has enjoyed a loyal local following for over 25 years.

XX **Yashin**     AC VISA ◌◌ AE
1A Argyll Rd. ⊠ W8 7DB ⊖ High Street Kensington – 𝒞 (020) 7938 1536
– www.yashinsushi.com – Closed first and third Monday in month, 25 and 31
December, and 1 January      **35AAXc**
**Rest** – Japanese – (booking essential) Carte £ 41/90
♦ Ask for a counter seat to watch the chefs prepare the sushi; choose 8, 11 or 15
pieces, to be served together. The quality of fish is clear; tiny garnishes and the
odd bit of searing add originality.

XX **Casa Batavia**     AC ⇔ VISA ◌◌ AE
135 Kensington Church St ⊠ W8 7LP ⊖ Notting Hill Gate – 𝒞 (020) 7221 7348
– www.casabatavia.com      **27AAVx**
**Rest** – Italian – (booking advisable) Menu £ 22 (lunch) – Carte £ 24/37
♦ Intimate restaurant opened in 2011 by an experienced restaurateur and a chef
from Turin. The refined cooking of Piedmont is the main influence; look out for
ricotta crostino, potted rabbit with hazelnuts and, of course, panna cotta.

XX **Zaika**     AC VISA ◌◌ AE ◑
1 Kensington High St. ⊠ W8 5NP ⊖ High Street Kensington – 𝒞 (020)
7795 6533 – www.zaika-restaurant.co.uk – Closed 25-26 December, 1-2 January
and Monday lunch      **35ABXr**
**Rest** – Indian – Menu £ 25 (lunch) – Carte £ 30/45
♦ The smell of incense is one clue that the days of this being a bank are long
gone; bright colours offset the high ceiling and wood panelling. The cooking is
original and sophisticated but at times the spicing can lack a degree of subtlety.

XX **Whits**     AC VISA ◌◌ AE
21 Abingdon Rd. ⊠ W8 6AH ⊖ High Street Kensington – 𝒞 (020) 7938 1122
– www.whits.co.uk – Closed 1 week August, Sunday and Monday    **35AAXd**
**Rest** – Modern European – (dinner only) Menu £ 24 – Carte £ 31/40
♦ Run by friendly owner. Bar runs length of lower level. Most diners migrate upstairs with its modish artwork and intimate tables. Modern cooking with generous portions.

XX **Timo**     AC VISA ◌◌ AE
343 Kensington High St. ⊠ W8 6NW ⊖ High Street Kensington – 𝒞 (020)
7603 3888 – www.timorestaurant.net – Closed Christmas, Sunday and bank
holidays      **35AAYc**
**Rest** – Italian – (booking advisable) Menu £ 18 (lunch and early dinner)
– Carte £ 30/40
♦ Comfortable and comforting neighbourhood Italian restaurant, with careful
and reliable cooking. Service is smart and conscientious and is undertaken under
the watchful eye of the owner.

XX **Seventeen**     AC ⇔ VISA ◌◌ AE ◑
17 Notting Hill Gate ⊠ W11 3JQ ⊖ Notting Hill Gate – 𝒞 (020) 7985 0006
– www.seventeen-london.co.uk      **27ABVx**
**Rest** – Chinese – Menu £ 12/21 – Carte £ 18/45
♦ Stylishly kitted out, intimate and moodily lit Chinese restaurant on two floors.
The kitchen, behind an eye-catching glass wall, specialises in authentic Sichuan
and Shanghainese delicacies.

XX **Cheneston's** – at The Milestone Hotel     AC VISA ◌◌ AE ◑
1-2 Kensington Ct. ⊠ W8 5DL ⊖ High Street Kensington – 𝒞 (020) 7917 1000
– www.milestonehotel.com      **35ABXu**
**Rest** – British – (booking essential for non-residents) Menu £ 30 (lunch)
– Carte £ 51/63 ⌘
♦ The Milestone is an elegant Victorian hotel and her restaurant is equally deco-
rous and includes a charming little oratory. Expect refined British cooking and a
superior wine list.

XX **Brunello** – at Baglioni Hotel    AC VISA ◍◍ AE ◍
60 Hyde Park Gate ⊠ SW7 5BB ⊖ High Street Kensington – ℰ (020) 7368 5900
– www.baglionihotels.com    **36**ACX**e**
**Rest** – Italian – Menu £ 28/33 – Carte £ 45/66
♦ The Baglioni hotel's ground floor bar, lounge and restaurant all merge into one
in a heady mix of grey, gold and glass. The menu traverses all parts of Italy and
uses prime ingredients.

XX **Cibo**    VISA ◍◍ AE
3 Russell Gdns ⊠ W14 8EZ ⊖ Kensington Olympia – ℰ (020) 7371 6271
– www.ciborestaurant.net – Closed 1 week Christmas and bank holidays
**Rest** – Italian – Menu £ 25 – Carte £ 23/37    **16**MZE**b**
♦ Long-standing neighbourhood Italian with local following. More space at the
back of the room. Robust, satisfying cooking; the huge grilled shellfish and seafood platter a speciality.

XX **Malabar**    AC VISA ◍◍ AE
27 Uxbridge St. ⊠ W8 7TQ ⊖ Notting Hill Gate – ℰ (020) 7727 8800
– www.malabar-restaurant.co.uk – Closed 1 week Christmas    **27**AAV**e**
**Rest** – Indian – (buffet lunch Sunday) Menu £ 25 **s** – Carte £ 26/41 **s**
♦ Opened in 1983 in a residential Notting Hill street, but keeps up its appearance, remaining fresh and good-looking. Balanced menu of carefully prepared
and sensibly priced Indian dishes.

X **Kensington Place**    AC ⇔ VISA ◍◍ AE ◍
201-209 Kensington Church St. ⊠ W8 7LX ⊖ Notting Hill Gate – ℰ (020)
7727 3184 – www.kensingtonplace-restaurant.co.uk – Closed Sunday dinner and
Monday lunch    **27**AAV**z**
**Rest** – Modern European – Menu £ 20/25
♦ Opened in 1987 as a big, boisterous, brasserie; these days a little less noisy but
it remains well run. Competitively priced set menu offers a wide choice of modern European dishes.

## NORTH KENSINGTON

🛏 **The Portobello** without rest    ▧ ((¹)) VISA ◍◍ AE
22 Stanley Gdns. ⊠ W11 2NG ⊖ Notting Hill Gate – ℰ (020) 7727 2777
– www.portobellohotel.co.uk – Closed 24-29 December    **16**NZE**n**
**21 rm** – †£ 174/234 ††£ 252/378, � £ 20
♦ An attractive Victorian townhouse in an elegant terrace. Original and theatrical
décor. Circular beds, half-testers, Victorian baths: no two bedrooms are the same.

XXX **Ledbury** (Brett Graham)    ⌂ AC VISA ◍◍ AE
❀❀ 127 Ledbury Rd. ⊠ W11 2AQ ⊖ Notting Hill Gate – ℰ (020) 7792 9090
– www.theledbury.com – Closed 24-26 December, August bank holiday and
Monday lunch    **27**AAT**a**
**Rest** – Modern European – Menu £ 34/70 ❀❀
**Spec.** Buffalo milk curd, truffle toast and grilled onion broth. Loin and shoulder of
lamb, black sugar and garlic glazed aubergine. Whipped ewe's milk yoghurt with
berries, verbena meringues and beignets.
♦ Elegant, understated surroundings with professional, well-organised service but
it still has a neighbourhood feel. Highly skilled kitchen with an inherent understanding of flavour; great ingredients, especially game in season.

XX **Notting Hill Brasserie**    AC ⇔ VISA ◍◍ AE
92 Kensington Park Rd ⊠ W11 2PN ⊖ Notting Hill Gate – ℰ (020) 7229 4481
– www.nottinghillbrasserie.com    **27**AAU**a**
**Rest** – French – Menu £ 20 (weekday lunch) – Carte £ 43/61
♦ More formal than the name suggests and housed within a row of attractive Edwardian townhouses. Menu provides large choice of carefully constructed and
quite elaborate dishes. Nightly live jazz.

LONDON

XX **Edera** `AC` `⟷` `VISA` `OO` `AE`

*148 Holland Park Ave.* ⊠ *W11 4UE* ⊖ *Holland Park* – 𝒞 *(020) 7221 6090*
*– www.edera.co.uk* **16**MZE**n**
**Rest** – Italian – Carte £ 37/54

♦ Warm and comfortable neighbourhood restaurant with plenty of local regulars and efficient, well-marshalled service. Robust cooking has a subtle Sardinian accent and comes in generous portions.

XX **E&O** `AC` `⟷` `VISA` `OO` `AE` `O`

*14 Blenheim Cres.* ⊠ *W11 1NN* ⊖ *Ladbroke Grove* – 𝒞 *(020) 7229 5454*
*– www.rickerrestaurants.com – Closed 25-26 December and 1 January*
**Rest** – Asian – Menu £ 19 (lunch) – Carte £ 23/54 **16**MZD**a**

♦ Mean, moody and cool and that's just the customers. Sophisticated, chic and noisy, thanks to contented groups of diners. Menus scour the Far East, with dishes designed for sharing.

X **Dock Kitchen** `VISA` `OO` `AE`

*Portobello Dock, 342-344 Ladbroke Grove* ⊠ *W10 5BU* ⊖ *Ladbroke Grove*
*– 𝒞 (020) 8962 1610 – www.dockkitchen.co.uk – Closed last week August, 24 December-5 January and Sunday dinner* **16**MZD**k**
**Rest** – Mediterranean – Menu £ 19 (lunch) – Carte £ 26/37

♦ What started as a 'pop-up' became a permanent feature in this open-plan former Victorian goods yard. The chef's peregrinations inform his cooking, which relies on simple, natural flavours.

X **Bumpkin** `AC` `⟷` `VISA` `OO` `AE`

*209 Westbourne Park Rd* ⊠ *W11 1EA* ⊖ *Westbourne Park* – 𝒞 *(020) 7243 9818*
*– www.bumpkinuk.com* **27**AAT**b**
**Rest** – British – Carte £ 29/37

♦ Converted pea-green pub with casual, clubby feel and wholesome philosophy of cooking seasonal, carefully sourced and organic food. The same modern Mediterranean-influenced menu is served on both floors.

## SOUTH KENSINGTON

🏛 **The Pelham** `↳₅` `|♦|` `AC` `⅋` `⌾` `VISA` `OO` `AE` `O`

*15 Cromwell Pl* ⊠ *SW7 2LA* ⊖ *South Kensington* – 𝒞 *(020) 7589 8288*
*– www.pelhamhotel.co.uk* **36**ADY**z**
**51 rm** – ♦£ 216/300 ♦♦£ 324/399, � £ 17.50 – 1 suite
**Rest** *Bistro Fifteen* – see restaurant listing

♦ Immaculately kept, with willing staff and a discreet atmosphere. Decoratively it's a mix of English country house and city town house, with a panelled sitting room and library with honesty bar.

🏛 **Blakes** `⌂` `↳₅` `|♦|` `AC` `rest,` `⌾` `VISA` `OO` `AE` `O`

*33 Roland Gdns.* ⊠ *SW7 3PF* ⊖ *Gloucester Road* – 𝒞 *(020) 7370 6701*
*– www.blakeshotels.com* **36**ACZ**n**
**33 rm** – ♦£ 234/594 ♦♦£ 390/654, � £ 19.50 – 8 suites
**Rest** – Menu £ 23 (lunch) – Carte £ 49/73

♦ Behind the Victorian façade lies one of London's first 'boutique' hotels. Dramatic, bold and eclectic décor, with oriental influences and antiques from around the globe. Fashionable restaurant with bamboo and black walls.

🏛 **Number Sixteen** `⌗` `|♦|` `AC` `rm,` `⌾` `VISA` `OO` `AE` `O`

*16 Sumner Pl.* ⊠ *SW7 3EG* ⊖ *South Kensington* – 𝒞 *(020) 7589 5232*
*– www.numbersixteenhotel.co.uk* **36**ADY**d**
**42 rm** – ♦£ 156/210 ♦♦£ 258, � £ 18.50 **Rest** – *(room service only)*

♦ Enticingly refurbished 19C town houses in smart area. Discreet entrance, comfy sitting room and charming breakfast terrace. Bedrooms in English country house style.

409

## The Cranley

🛗 AC ⚹ ☏ VISA ⦵ AE ⓪

10 Bina Gdns. ✉ SW5 0LA ⊖ Gloucester Road – ℰ (020) 7373 0123
– www.thecranley.com **36**ACYc
**38 rm** – ♦£ 192/300 ♦♦£ 240/312, � £ 17.95 – 1 suite
**Rest** – (room service only)
◆ Delightful Regency townhouse combines charm and period details with modern comforts and technology. Individually styled bedrooms; some with four-posters. Breakfast served in bedrooms.

## The Rockwell

🚠 🛗 AC ⚹ ☏ 🏊 VISA ⦵ AE

181-183 Cromwell Rd. ✉ SW5 0SF ⊖ Earl's Court – ℰ (020) 7244 2000
– www.therockwell.com **35**ABYb
**40 rm** (dinner included) – ♦£ 140/220 ♦♦£ 200/260, ⊒ £ 9.50
**Rest** – Menu £ 48 (dinner) – Carte £ 27/40
◆ Two Victorian houses with open, modern lobby and secluded, south-facing garden terrace. Bedrooms come in bold warm colours; 'Garden Rooms' have their own patios. Small dining room offers easy menu of modern European staples.

## The Gore

🛗 AC ⚹ ☏ 🏊 VISA ⦵ AE ⓪

190 Queen's Gate ✉ SW7 5EX ⊖ Gloucester Road – ℰ (020) 7584 6601
– www.gorehotel.com **36**ACXn
**50 rm** – ♦£ 174/198 ♦♦£ 174/528, ⊒ £ 17.50
**Rest** *190 Queensgate* – see restaurant listing
◆ Idiosyncratic, hip Victorian house whose narrow lobby is covered with pictures and prints. Individually styled bedrooms have plenty of character and charming bathrooms. The closest hotel to Royal Albert Hall.

## Aster House without rest

🚗 AC ⚹ ☏ VISA ⦵

3 Sumner Pl. ✉ SW7 3EE ⊖ South Kensington – ℰ (020) 7581 5888
– www.asterhouse.com **36**ADYt
**13 rm** – ♦£ 96/180 ♦♦£ 162/300
◆ End of terrace Victorian house with a pretty little rear garden and first floor conservatory. Ground floor rooms available. Useful location for visiting many tourist attractions.

## ✕✕✕✕ Bombay Brasserie

AC VISA ⦵ AE ⓪

Courtfield Rd. ✉ SW7 4QH ⊖ Gloucester Road – ℰ (020) 7370 4040
– www.bombaybrasserielondon.com – Closed 25-26 December **36**ACYy
**Rest** – Indian – (booking advisable at dinner) Menu £ 22 (lunch)
– Carte £ 31/43
◆ Plush new look for this well-run, well-known and comfortable Indian restaurant; very smart bar and conservatory with a show kitchen. More creative dishes now sit alongside the more traditional.

## ✕✕ Cassis

AC VISA ⦵ AE ⓪

232-236 Brompton Rd. ✉ SW3 2BB ⊖ South Kensington – ℰ (020) 7581 1101
– www.cassisbistro.co.uk – Closed 25 December **36**AEYx
**Rest** – French – Menu £ 20 (weekday lunch) – Carte £ 26/51 🌺
◆ The colours and aromas of southern France come to south Ken at this crisply stylish Provençal 'bistro'. Start with some 'petites bouchées' such as classic barbajuans or pissaladière; follow up with authentic bouillabaisse or daube of beef.

## ✕✕ L'Etranger

AC ↔ VISA ⦵ AE

36 Gloucester Rd. ✉ SW7 4QT ⊖ Gloucester Road – ℰ (020) 7584 1118
– www.circagroupltd.co.uk **36**ACXc
**Rest** – Innovative – (booking essential) Menu £ 24 (lunch) – Carte dinner £ 41/53 🌺
◆ Eclectic menu mixes French dishes with techniques and flavours from Japanese cooking. Impressive wine and sake lists. Moody and atmospheric room; ask for a corner table.

## XX Pasha     AC ⇔ VISA ◉◉ AE
*1 Gloucester Rd. ⊠ SW7 4PP ⊖ Gloucester Road – ℰ (020) 7589 7969*
*– www.pasha-restaurant.co.uk – Closed 25-26 December*     **36**ACX**r**
**Rest** – Moroccan – Menu £ 20/30 – Carte £ 27/33
♦ Relax over ground floor cocktails, then descend to mosaic floored restaurant where the rose-petal strewn tables are the ideal accompaniment to tasty Moroccan home cooking.

## XX Bistro K     🌣 AC ⇔ VISA ◉◉
*117-119 Old Brompton Rd. ⊠ SW7 3RN ⊖ Gloucester Road – ℰ (020)*
*7373 7774 – www.bistro-k.co.uk – Closed Sunday and Monday*     **36**ACZ**x**
**Rest** – French – Menu £ 15 (lunch) – Carte £ 36/46
♦ More formal than the name would suggest and the cooking is more delicate and sophisticated. The surroundings are bright and contemporary and the front terrace is an appealing spot.

## XX Cambio de Tercio     AC ⇔ VISA ◉◉ AE ◉
*163 Old Brompton Rd. ⊠ SW5 0LJ ⊖ Gloucester Road – ℰ (020) 7244 8970*
*– www.cambiodetercio.co.uk – Closed 25 December*     **36**ACZ**a**
**Rest** – Spanish – Carte £ 30/54 **s** 🥂
♦ Good ingredients and authentic Spanish flavours; desserts are more contemporary. Choose tapas or regular menu. Service improves the more you visit. Owner also has tapas bar across the road.

## XX Bistro Fifteen – at The Pelham Hotel     AC VISA ◉◉ AE ◉
*15 Cromwell Pl ⊠ SW7 2LA ⊖ South Kensington – ℰ (020) 7589 8288*
*– www.pelhamhotel.co.uk*     **36**ADY**z**
**Rest** – Modern European – Menu £ 18 (lunch and early dinner)
– Carte £ 26/41
♦ This concealed little basement bistro offers respite from the plethora of chain restaurants in these parts. It has a sweet, intimate feel and a menu of European and British dishes.

## X Bumpkin     AC ⇔ VISA ◉◉ AE
*102 Old Brompton Rd. ⊠ SW7 3RD ⊖ Gloucester Road – ℰ (020) 7341 0802*
*– www.bumpkinuk.com*     **36**ACY**r**
**Rest** – British – Carte £ 30/37
♦ Sister to the Notting Hill original with the same pub-like informality and friendly service. The kitchen champions British seasonal produce; the simpler dishes are the best ones.

## X Aubaine     AC VISA ◉◉ AE
*260-262 Brompton Rd. ⊠ SW3 2AS ⊖ South Kensington – ℰ (020) 7052 0100*
*– www.aubaine.co.uk*     **37**AEY**c**
**Rest** – French – Carte £ 22/52
♦ 'Boulangerie, patisserie, restaurant'. Pass the bakery aromas to an all-day eatery with 'distressed' country feel. Well-judged menus range from croque monsieur to coq au vin.

## X Bangkok     AC VISA ◉◉
*9 Bute St ⊠ SW7 3EY ⊖ South Kensington – ℰ (020) 7584 8529*
*– www.bankokrestaurant.co.uk – Closed 24 December-2 January and Sunday*
**Rest** – Thai – Carte £ 19/26     **36**ADY**b**
♦ This simple Thai bistro has been a popular local haunt for nearly 40 years. Guests can watch the chefs at work, preparing inexpensive and authentic dishes from the succinct menu.

## X Tendido Cero     AC VISA ◉◉ AE ◉
*174 Old Brompton Rd. ⊠ SW5 0BA ⊖ Gloucester Road – ℰ (020) 7370 3685*
*– www.cambiodetercio.co.uk – Closed 25 December*     **36**ACZ**v**
**Rest** – Spanish – Carte £ 30/34
♦ Highlights at this busy tapas bar include Galician octopus, white bean stew with chorizo and pork cheeks with potato purée. There are also some unusual dishes, like the mini 'hamburger' made with sardines.

LONDON

X **Capote y Toros**                    AC VISA OO AE O
157 Old Brompton Road ⊠ SW5 0LJ ⊖ Gloucester Road – 𝒞 (020) 7373 0567
– www.cambiodetercio.co.uk – Closed Sunday and Monday                **36**ACZ**v**
**Rest** – Spanish – (dinner only) Carte £ 19/32🏶
• Expect to queue at this compact and vividly coloured spot which celebrates
sherry, tapas, ham...and bullfighting. Sherry is the star; those as yet unmoved by
this most underappreciated of wines will be dazzled by the huge variety.

X **190 Queensgate** – at The Gore Hotel             AC VISA OO AE O
190 Queen's Gate ⊠ SW7 5EX ⊖ Gloucester Road – 𝒞 (020) 7584 6601
– www.gorehotel.com                                          **36**ACX**n**
**Rest** – British – (booking essential) Menu £ 20/24 – Carte £ 29/42
• This is the nearest restaurant to the Royal Albert Hall so it's busiest early or late
evening. Bright, bustling bistro atmosphere with an appealing and accessible
menu to match.

## KINGSTON UPON THAMES – Greater London              **12** A3
🔢 Hampton Court Palace Hampton Wick, 𝒞 (020) 8977 24 23

### SURBITON

XX **The French Table**                    AC ✿ VISA OO AE
85 Maple Rd ⊠ KT6 4AW – 𝒞 (020) 8399 2365 – www.thefrenchtable.co.uk
– Closed 2 weeks summer, 25 December, Sunday dinner and Monday
**Rest** – Mediterranean – Menu £ 23 (lunch) – Carte dinner          **6**CY**a**
£ 25/42
• Husband and wife team run this lively local. Expect zesty and satisfying French-
Mediterranean cooking; learn how with Saturday morning cookery lessons. They
also run the bakery next door.

## LAMBETH – Greater London                           **12** B3

### BRIXTON

XX **Upstairs**                                        VISA OO AE
89b Acre Ln. ⊠ SW2 5TN ⊖ Clapham North – 𝒞 (020) 7733 8855
– www.upstairslondon.com – Closed 24 December-9 January, 8-18 April, 19
August-4 September, Sunday and Monday                          **24**SZH**b**
**Rest** – Modern European – (dinner only) Menu £ 32
• Uncomplicated, easy to eat and flavoursome cooking from a concise but balanced and well-priced set menu. First floor bar, second floor dining room – look
for the buzzer next to Opus coffee shop.

### CLAPHAM COMMON

XX **Trinity**                              AC VISA OO AE O
4 The Polygon ⊠ SW4 0JG ⊖ Clapham Common – 𝒞 (020) 7622 1199
– www.trinityrestaurant.co.uk – Closed 24-30 December, Monday lunch and
Sunday dinner                                              **24**RZH**a**
**Rest** – Innovative – Menu £ 20 (lunch) – Carte £ 31/47
• Smartly decorated and smoothly run neighbourhood restaurant; ask for a table
by the windows in summer. Sophisticated cooking displays some innovative combinations. Good value lunch menu.

X **Tsunami**                               AC VISA OO
Unit 3, 5-7 Voltaire Rd ⊠ SW4 6DQ ⊖ Clapham North – 𝒞 (020) 7978 1610
– www.tsunamirestaurant.co.uk – Closed 24-26 December                **24**SZH**a**
**Rest** – Japanese – (dinner only and lunch Saturday-Sunday) Carte £ 23/45
• Stylish and lively surroundings in which to enjoy innovative and original, modern Japanese food. The restaurant enjoys a large, local following and there's
a second branch in Charlotte Street.

🏠 **Bobbin**                                    🛜 VISA ⓒⓞ AE ⓞ
*1-3 Lillieshall Rd* ✉ *SW4 OLN* ⊖ *Clapham Common.* – ℰ *(020) 7738 8953*
*– www.thebobbinclapham.com*                                    **24**RZH**x**
**Rest** – Traditional – Carte £ 19/27
♦ In a quiet residential street which, combined with its warm service, cosy bar
and the Wednesday Quiz night, makes it feel like a proper local. Expect charcuterie boards to share along with wholesome seasonal cooking.

## EAST DULWICH

🏠 **Palmerston**                                    VISA ⓒⓞ AE
*91 Lordship Ln* ✉ *SE22 8EP* ⊖ *East Dulwich (rail).* – ℰ *(020) 8693 1629*
*– www.thepalmerston.net*                                    **26**XZH**x**
**Rest** – Traditional – Menu £ 16 (lunch) – Carte £ 25/32
♦ Full of atmosphere and attracting a range of ages, thanks to the engaging staff
and good food on offer. Menus evolve monthly and mix classics with the more
modern; look out for the well-priced weekday menu.

## KENNINGTON

XX **Kennington Tandoori**                                    AC VISA ⓒⓞ
*313 Kennington Rd* ✉ *SE11 4QE* ⊖ *Kennington* – ℰ *(020) 7735 9247*
*– www.kenningtontandoori.com*                                    **40**ANZ**a**
**Rest** – Indian – *(booking advisable)* Menu £ 18/28 – Carte £ 22/40
♦ Known as KT, the Hoque family's longstanding Indian restaurant was reinvigorated a couple of years ago when their son Kowsar took over. This stylish spot has
a familiar menu of classics but what sets it apart is the skilled execution.

X **Lobster Pot**                                    AC VISA ⓒⓞ AE
*3 Kennington Ln.* ✉ *SE11 4RG* ⊖ *Kennington* – ℰ *(020) 7582 5556*
*– www.lobsterpotrestaurant.co.uk – Closed 24 December-3 January,*
*Sunday and Monday*                                    **40**AOY**e**
**Rest** – French – Carte £ 38/53
♦ Family-run, with exuberant décor of fish tanks, portholes and even the sound
of seagulls. Classic seafood menu with fruits de mer, plenty of oysters and daily
specials. Good crêpes too.

## SOUTHBANK

🏠🏠🏠 **London Marriott H. County Hall**       ≼ 🔲 ☁ 🏠 £⅙ ꒐ 👤 rm, AC ⅀⅍
*Westminster Bridge Rd* ✉ *SE1 7PB* ⊖ *Westminster*       🛜 ⅃ VISA ⓒⓞ AE ⓞ
*– ℰ (020) 7928 5200 – www.marriottcountyhall.com*                  **40**AMX**a**
**195 rm** – ♦£ 448 ♦♦£ 448, ⅀ £ 21 – 5 suites
**Rest** *County Hall* – ℰ (020) 7902 8000 – Carte £ 29/41
♦ Occupying the historic County Hall building. Many of the spacious and com-
fortable bedrooms enjoy river and Parliament outlook. Impressive leisure facilities.
World famous views from restaurant.

XXX **Skylon**                                    ≼ AC VISA ⓒⓞ AE
*1 Southbank Centre, Belvedere Rd* ✉ *SE1 8XX* ⊖ *Waterloo* – ℰ *(020) 7654 7800*
*– www.skylon-restaurant.co.uk – Closed 25 December and Sunday dinner*
**Rest** – Modern European – Menu £ 29/45 ፠                  **32**AMV**a**
♦ Ask for a window table here at the Royal Festival Hall. Informal grill-style operation on one side, a more formal and expensive restaurant on the other, with a
busy cocktail bar in the middle.

## STOCKWELL

🏠 **Canton Arms**                                    🛜 VISA ⓒⓞ ⓞ
🅐 *177 South Lambeth Rd* ✉ *SW8 1XP* ⊖ *Stockwell.* – ℰ *(020) 7582 8710*
*– www.cantonarms.com – Closed Christmas-New Year, Monday lunch, Sunday*
*dinner and bank holidays*                                    **24**SZG**a**
**Rest** – British – Carte £ 19/27
♦ An appreciative crowd of all ages come for the earthy, robust and seasonal
British dishes which suit the relaxed environment of this pub so well. Staff are attentive and knowledgeable.

LONDON

**BLACKHEATH**

❌❌   **Chapters**                                    🈑 🆎 VISA ⏫ 🆑 ⓘ
🈺   *43-45 Montpelier Vale* ✉ *SE3 0TJ* – ✆ *(020) 8333 2666*
      *– www.chaptersrestaurants.com – Closed 2-3 January*            **8**HX**c**
      **Rest** – Modern European – Carte £ 19/35
      • A contemporary and bustling all day brasserie and bar at the top of town.
      Large, appealingly priced menu with British and Mediterranean influences, with
      meats cooked over charcoal a speciality.

**WIMBLEDON**

LONDON

🏠🏠   **Cannizaro House** 🦢                  ⇐ 🚗 🐾 🛎 🆎 🛜 ♨ 🅿 VISA ⏫ 🆑 ⓘ
      *West Side, Wimbledon Common* ✉ *SW19 4UE* ⊖ *Wimbledon*
      *– ✆ (020) 8879 1464 – www.cannizarohouse.com*                **6**DXY**x**
      **44 rm** ⌷ – ❖£ 222/594 ❖❖£ 222/594 – 2 suites
      **Rest** *Cannizaro House* – see restaurant listing
      • Part-Georgian mansion in charming spot overlooking Wimbledon Common.
      Modern bedrooms; funky suites; 'Sophia Johnson' has lovely balcony overlooking
      the park. Local artists' work decorates.

❌❌   **Cannizaro House**                          🚗 🐾 🆎 🅿 VISA ⏫ 🆑 ⓘ
      *West Side, Wimbledon Common* ✉ *SW19 4UE* ⊖ *Wimbledon*
      *– ✆ (020) 8879 1464 – www.cannizarohouse.com*                **6**DXY**x**
      **Rest** – British – Menu £ 30 – Carte £ 33/40
      • London offers a huge choice of dining options, and that includes a Georgian
      mansion in 34 acres of parkland. Here, in the restaurant of the renovated Canni-
      zaro House, British produce is celebrated.

❌   **Light House**                                         VISA ⏫ 🆑
      *75-77 Ridgway* ✉ *SW19 4ST* ⊖ *Wimbledon* – ✆ *(020) 8944 6338*
      *– www.lighthousewimbledon.com – Closed 25-26 December, 1 January and*
      *Sunday dinner*                                                **6**DY**n**
      **Rest** – International – Menu £ 15 (lunch) – Carte £ 23/32
      • The robust and flavoursome Italian dishes provide the highlights of the menu.
      This large, well lit room attracts plenty of locals and the service remains calm
      and cheery.

🛏   **Fox and Grapes** with rm                          🆎 rest, 🍽 VISA ⏫
🈺   *9 Camp Rd.* ✉ *SW19 4UN* ⊖ *Wimbledon.* – ✆ *(020) 8619 1300*
      *– www.foxandgrapeswimbledon.co.uk – Closed 25 December*       **6**DX**v**
      **3 rm** – ❖£ 125 ❖❖£ 125, ⌷ £ 12.50
      **Rest** – British – *(booking advisable)* Menu £ 20 (lunch) – Carte £ 26/38
      • Owned by Claude Bosi, chef-owner of Hibiscus, and run by Cedric, his
      brother. They may be French but they know about 'proper' pub food, from
      Cumberland sausages and prawn cocktail to wild boar scotch egg. Three cosy
      bedrooms also available.

🛈 Whittaker Ave ✆ (020) 8940 91 25, www.visitrichmond.co.uk
🏌 Richmond Park Roehampton Gate, ✆ (020) 8876 32 05
🏌 Sudbrook Park

**BARNES**

❌❌   **Sonny's**                                    🆎 ⇹ VISA ⏫ 🆑
      *94 Church Rd* ✉ *SW13 0DQ* – ✆ *(020) 8748 0393 – www.sonnys.co.uk – Closed*
      *Sunday dinner and bank holidays*                             **21**KZH**x**
      **Rest** – Modern European – Menu £ 17/20 (midweek) – Carte £ 23/35
      • Long-established neighbourhood spot which successfully combines its role as
      deli, café and restaurant. The latter's menus are full of seasonal goodness and
      the service is warm and attentive.

## ✗✗ Indian Zilla     A/C ⇔ VISA ◎◎ AE ◐

*2-3 Rocks Ln.* ✉ *SW13 0DB –* ✆ *(020) 8878 3989 – www.indianzilla.co.uk*
**Rest** – Indian – Menu £ 15 (lunch) – Carte £ 27/36     **21**LZH**k**

♦ Bright, and contemporary restaurant with attentive, friendly service. Modern menu includes a few classics; the authentic, fully-flavoured dishes display a lightness of touch.

## ✗ Riva     A/C VISA ◎◎ AE

*169 Church Rd.* ✉ *SW13 9HR –* ✆ *(020) 8748 0434 – Closed 3 weeks August, 10 days Christmas-New Year, Saturday lunch and bank holidays*    **21**LZH**a**
**Rest** – Italian – Carte £ 32/56

♦ A restaurant built on customer loyalty; the regulars are showered with attention from the eponymous owner. Gutsy, no-nonsense dishes, full of flavour. Interesting all-Italian wine list.

## ⌂ Brown Dog     ⌂ VISA ◎◎ AE

*28 Cross St* ✉ *SW13 0AP* ⊖ *Barnes Bridge (Rail) –* ✆ *(020) 8392 2200*
*– www.thebrowndog.co.uk – Closed 25-26 December*    **21**KZH**b**
**Rest** – Carte £ 20/30

♦ Pretty Victorian pub with a genuine neighbourhood feel; snug bar, intimate dining room and a look that combines the traditional with the modern. Concise, balanced menu delivers commendably priced dishes that display a deft touch.

# KEW

## ✗✗ The Glasshouse     A/C VISA ◎◎ AE

⍟ *14 Station Par.* ✉ *TW9 3PZ* ⊖ *Kew Gardens –* ✆ *(020) 8940 6777*
*– www.glasshouserestaurant.co.uk – Closed 24-26 December and 1 January*
**Rest** – Modern European – Menu £ 26/40 ♨    **6**CX**z**
**Spec.** Sashimi of sea bass, wasabi mayonnaise and shrimp beignet. Roast pollock, wild garlic velouté, morels and leeks. Lemon tart with custard ice cream.

♦ Bright and relaxed interior, with a palpable sense of neighbourhood. Balanced and seasonally informed dishes are full of flavour, from a varied and appealing menu influenced mostly by Europe. Service is pleasant and unflappable.

## ✗✗ Kew Grill     A/C VISA ◎◎ AE

*10b Kew Grn.* ✉ *TW9 3BH* ⊖ *Kew Gardens –* ✆ *(020) 8948 4433*
*– www.awtrestaurants.com – Closed Monday lunch*    **6**CV**u**
**Rest** – Beef specialities – *(booking essential)* Menu £ 15 (weekday lunch)
– Carte £ 29/49

♦ Just off Kew Green, this long, narrow restaurant has a Mediterranean style and feel. Grilled specialities employ top-rate ingredients: the beef is hung for 35 days.

# RICHMOND

## ⌂ Petersham     ⇐ ⇌ ⦿ A/C rest, ✗ ⦿ ⳾ P VISA ◎◎ AE ◐

*Nightingale Ln.* ✉ *TW10 6UZ* ⊖ *Richmond –* ✆ *(020) 8940 7471*
*– www.petershamhotel.co.uk*    **6**CX**c**
**59 rm** ⳨ – ♦£ 135 ♦♦£ 175/185 – 1 suite
**Rest** *Restaurant at The Petersham* – ✆ *(020) 8939 1084* – Menu £ 26/39
– Carte dinner £ 31/52

♦ Extended over the years, a fine example of Victorian Gothic architecture, with Portland stone and self-supporting staircase. The most comfortable bedrooms overlook the Thames. Formal restaurant in which to enjoy a mix of classic and modern cooking; ask for a window table for terrific park and river views.

## ⌂ Bingham     ⇌ A/C ✗ ⦿ ⳾ P VISA ◎◎ AE ◐

*61-63 Petersham Rd.* ✉ *TW10 6UT* ⊖ *Richmond –* ✆ *(020) 8940 0902*
*– www.thebingham.co.uk – Closed first week January*    **6**CX**c**
**15 rm** – ♦£ 215/360 ♦♦£ 240/360, ⳨ £ 15
**Rest** *Bingham Restaurant* – see restaurant listing

♦ A pair of conjoined and restored Georgian townhouses; a short walk from Richmond centre. Ask for a room overlooking the river and garden. Contemporary styled bedrooms; some with four-posters.

LONDON

## Bingham Restaurant – at Bingham Hotel

61-63 Petersham Rd. ✉ TW1O 6UT ⊖ *Richmond* – ℰ (020) 8940 0902
– *www.thebingham.co.uk* – *Closed first week January and Sunday dinner*
**Rest** – Modern European – Menu £ 26/55                                    **6CXc**

• Charming spot, especially if you've arrived on foot from along the river; dine on the balcony overlooking the garden or in the more traditional dining room. There's a modern style to the cooking and dishes are visually impressive.

## Petersham Nurseries Café

Church Ln (off Petersham Rd) ✉ TW10 7AG – ℰ (020) 8605 3627
– *www.petershamnurseries.com* – *Closed 24-29 December and Monday*
**Rest** – Italian influences – *(lunch only) (booking advisable)*          **6CXx**
Carte £ 45/61
**Spec.** Crab salad with nam jim sauce and mixed cress. Sea bass fillet with spinach, fresh chilli and preserved lemon dressing. Chocolate mousse with ginger caramel and Jersey cream.

• The Café is outside on sunny days and in a greenhouse the rest of the time; leave your best shoes at home! The food's all about natural flavours and fresh, vibrant ingredients; its earthiness seems so right when you're eating among plants and flowers.

## Matsuba

10 Red Lion St ✉ TW9 1RW ⊖ *Richmond* – ℰ (020) 8605 3513 – *Closed 25-26 December, 1 January and Sunday*                                    **6CXn**
**Rest** – Japanese – Carte £ 40/45

• Family-run Japanese restaurant with just 11 tables; understated but well-kept appearance. Extensive menu offers wide range of Japanese dishes, along with bulgogi, a Korean barbecue dish.

## Swagat

86 Hill Rise ✉ TW10 6UB ⊖ *Richmond* – ℰ (0208) 940 75 57
– *www.swagatindiancuisine.co.uk* – *Closed 25-26 December, 1 January and Sunday*                                                        **6CXi**
**Rest** – Indian – *(dinner only)* Menu £ 30 – Carte £ 22/34

• Well-meaning service and an appealing menu have made this Indian restaurant popular with locals so it's worth booking. Plenty of classics and vegetarian choices; try the less familiar.

# TEDDINGTON

## Rétro Bistrot

114-116 High St ✉ TW11 8JB – ℰ (0208) 977 22 39 – *www.retrobistrot.co.uk*
– *Closed first 2 weeks August, first 10 days January, Sunday dinner and Monday*
**Rest** – French – Menu £ 14/23 – Carte £ 23/41                              **5BYn**

• There's substance as well as style to this French bistrot. The classic bourgeois cuisine is prepared with innate skill; service is warm and effusive and the slick decoration conductive to merrymaking.

## Al Borgo

3 Church Rd. ✉ TW11 8PF – ℰ (020) 8943 4456 – *www.alborgo.co.uk* – *Closed Sunday and bank holidays*                                          **5BYe**
**Rest** – Italian – Carte approx. £ 35

• A refreshingly unpretentious and keenly run Italian restaurant that exudes warmth and bonhomie. Homemade focaccia and pasta are the highlights. Look out too for seasonal offerings such as the black truffle menu.

## Simply Thai

196 Kingston Rd. ✉ TW11 9JD – ℰ (020) 8943 9747
– *www.simplythai-restaurant.co.uk* – *Closed 25-26 December and Monday*
**Rest** – Thai – *(dinner only)* Menu £ 25 – Carte £ 23/34                     **5BYx**

• Extremely busy local Thai restaurant; the owner does all the cooking and her passion is clear. New creations sit alongside classics on the large menu. Prices are competitive; service can sometimes struggle to keep up.

🍺 **Kings Head**                    🏠 **P** 𝘝𝘐𝘚𝘈 ⊛
*123 High St* ✉ *TW11 8HG* – ℰ *(020) 3166 2900 – www.whitebrasserie.com*
**Rest** – Modern European – Menu £ 14/16 – Carte £ 19/26          **5**BY**c**
◆ Britain has its pubs and France its brasseries; The King's Head does its bit for
the entente cordiale by combining both. Have a drink in the front bar, then enjoy
rustic classics in the rear brasserie.

## TWICKENHAM

XX **A Cena**                    𝘈𝘊 𝘝𝘐𝘚𝘈 ⊛ 𝘈𝘌
*418 Richmond Rd.* ✉ *TW1 2EB* ⊖ *Richmond* – ℰ *(020) 8288 0108*
*– www.acena.co.uk – Closed 25-26 December, Sunday dinner and Monday lunch*
**Rest** – Italian – Carte £ 30/36          **5**BX**e**
◆ Rustic and quite intimate feel to this well-run neighbourhood Italian restaurant.
Appealing, seasonal menu covers most of Italy and the generously sized dishes
are full of flavour.

XX **Brula**                    ⇳ 𝘝𝘐𝘚𝘈 ⊛ 𝘈𝘌
*43 Crown Rd., St Margarets* ✉ *TW1 3EJ* – ℰ *(020) 8892 0602 – www.brula.co.uk*
*– Closed 26-30 December and Sunday dinner*          **5**BX**v**
**Rest** – French – *(booking essential)* Menu £ 18 (lunch) – Carte £ 22/36
◆ Traditional in look, with its mirrors and chandeliers but friendly service and
popular with the locals. They come for the good value, well-crafted cooking,
which is largely French but now comes with a few Spanish and Italian influences.

X **Tangawizi**                    𝘈𝘊 𝘝𝘐𝘚𝘈 ⊛ 𝘈𝘌
*406 Richmond Rd., Richmond Bridge* ✉ *TW1 2EB* ⊖ *Richmond* – ℰ *(020)*
*8891 3737 – www.tangawizi.co.uk – Closed 25-26 December and 1 January*
**Rest** – Indian – *(dinner only and Sunday lunch)* Carte £ 15/31          **5**BX**e**
◆ Name means Ginger in Swahili. Sleek décor in warm purple with subtle Indian
touches. Well-priced, nicely balanced, slowly evolving menus take their influence
from north India.

## EAST SHEEN

X **Mango & Silk**                    𝘝𝘐𝘚𝘈 ⊛ 𝘈𝘌
😋 *199 Upper Richmond Rd. West* ✉ *SW14 8 QT* – ℰ *(020) 8876 6220*
*– www.mangoandsilk.co.uk – Closed 25 December and Monday*          **21**KZH**k**
**Rest** – Indian – *(dinner only and buffet lunch Sunday)* Carte £ 20/23
◆ An air of calm pervades the restaurant, thanks to the charming owner. Udit
Sarkhel is the chef and his cooking is as expertly crafted as ever. The generous
prices make over-ordering the easy option.

🍺 **Victoria** with rm                    🏠 🍽 🐾 **P** 𝘝𝘐𝘚𝘈 ⊛ ⓪
*10 West Temple Sheen* ✉ *SW14 7RT* ⊖ *Mortlake (Rail).* – ℰ *(020) 8876 4238*
*– www.thevictoria.net*          **6**CX**u**
**7 rm** – ♦£ 115 ♦♦£ 125, � £ 8    **Rest** – British – Carte £ 28/30
◆ Beautifully restored pub, eat in the relaxed bar or more formal conservatory
overlooking the terrace; this is a genuine local that plays its part in the community and the kitchen takes its sourcing seriously. Simple bedrooms available.

## SOUTHWARK – Greater London                    **12** B3
🖼 Level 2, Tate Modern, Bankside ℰ (020) 7401 52 66, www.visitlondon.com

## BERMONDSEY

🏨 **Hilton London Tower Bridge**                    🗖 🍽 ᵹ rm, 𝘈𝘊 🐾 🐾 🕶
*5 More London, Tooley St.* ✉ *SE1 2BY* ⊖ *London Bridge*          𝘝𝘐𝘚𝘈 ⊛ 𝘈𝘌 ⓪
*– ℰ (020) 3002 4300 – www.hilton.co.uk/towerbridge*          **34**ARV**e**
**245 rm** – ♦£ 598 ♦♦£ 598, � £ 22.50    **Rest** – Carte £ 35/45
◆ Usefully located new-style Hilton hotel with boldly decorated open-plan lobby.
Contemporary bedrooms boast well-designed features; 4 floors of executive
rooms. Dine on classics and comfort food in restaurant with outdoor seating.

LONDON

**LONDON**

🏨 **Bermondsey Square**  　　　　🛜 📶 🛗 rm, 🆎 🛜 🅢🅐 VISA ⓒ🅐🅔

*Bermondsey Sq, Tower Bridge Rd* ✉ *SE1 3UN* ⊖ *London Bridge*
– ℰ *(020) 7378 2450 – www.bermondseysquarehotel.co.uk*　　　　**20**XZE**n**
**79 rm** – ♚£ 130/250 ♚♚£ 130/600, ☲ £ 11
**Rest *Alfie's*** – English – Carte £ 24/31
◆ Opened in 2009 in hip, regenerated square. Cleverly designed hotel, with subtle '60s influence and fun feel. Well-equipped bedrooms, including four loft suites. English menu in Alfie's makes good use of local food markets.

🏨 **London Bridge**  　　　　🛀 📶 🛗 rm, 🆎 🛜 🛜 🅢🅐 VISA ⓒ🅐🅔 ①

*8-18 London Bridge St* ✉ *SE1 9SG* ⊖ *London Bridge* – ℰ *(020) 7855 2200*
– *www.londonbridgehotel.com*　　　　**33**AQV**a**
**138 rm** – ♚£ 358 ♚♚£ 358, ☲ £ 17 – 3 suites
**Rest *Londinium*** – *(closed Sunday lunch)* Carte £ 28/43
◆ In one of the oldest parts of London, independently owned with an ornate façade dating from 1915. Modern interior with classically decorated bedrooms and an impressive gym. Londinium for brasserie dining.

XXX **Le Pont de la Tour**  　　　　≼ 🛜 ⇔ VISA ⓒ🅐🅔 ①

*36d Shad Thames, Butlers Wharf* ✉ *SE1 2YE* ⊖ *London Bridge*
– ℰ *(020) 7403 8403 – www.lepontdelatour.co.uk*　　　　**34**ASV**c**
**Rest** – French – Menu £ 32/45 ⅙⅙
◆ Providing, since 1991, seasonal French cooking, an urbane atmosphere and a wonderful riverside location, with views of Tower Bridge. Simpler dishes served in the livelier cocktail bar and grill.

XX **Magdalen**  　　　　🆎 VISA ⓒ🅐🅔

*152 Tooley St.* ✉ *SE1 2TU* ⊖ *London Bridge* – ℰ *(020) 7403 1342*
– *www.magdalenrestaurant.co.uk* – *Closed 24 December-5 January, 15-30*
*August, Saturday lunch, Sunday and bank holidays*　　　　**34**ARV**b**
**Rest** – British – Menu £ 19 (lunch) – Carte £ 30/40
◆ The clever sourcing and confident British cooking will leave you satisfied. Add genial service, an affordable lunch menu and a food-friendly wine list and you have the favourite restaurant of many.

X **Zucca**  　　　　🆎 VISA ⓒ①
😊
*184 Bermondsey St* ✉ *SE1 3TQ* ⊖ *Borough* – ℰ *(020) 7378 6809*
– *www.zuccalondon.com* – *Closed 24 December-10 January, Easter, Sunday*
*dinner and Monday*　　　　**20**XZE**s**
**Rest** – Italian – *(booking essential at dinner)* Carte £ 18/25 ⅙⅙
◆ Bright and buzzy modern room, where the informed Italian cooking is driven by the fresh ingredients, the prices are more than generous and the service is sweet and responsive. The appealing antipasti is great for sharing.

X **Blueprint Café**  　　　　≼ VISA ⓒ🅐🅔 ①

*Design Museum, Shad Thames, Butlers Wharf* ✉ *SE1 2YD* ⊖ *London Bridge*
– ℰ *(020) 7378 7031 – www.blueprintcafe.co.uk* – *Closed Sunday dinner*
**Rest** – Modern European – Menu £ 20/22 – Carte £ 24/38　　　　**34**ASV**u**
◆ Champions British produce in dishes using simple, but informed, techniques. Bright, retro feel; located above the Design Museum, with retractable windows and binoculars on each table.

X **Village East**  　　　　🆎 ⇔ VISA ⓒ🅐🅔

*171-173 Bermondsey St.* ✉ *SE1 3UW* ⊖ *London Bridge* – ℰ *(020) 7357 6082*
– *www.villageeast.co.uk* – *Closed 25-27 December*　　　　**20**XZE**a**
**Rest** – Modern European – Carte £ 27/38
◆ In a glass-fronted block sandwiched by Georgian townhouses, this trendy restaurant has two loud, buzzy bars and dining areas serving ample portions of modern British fare.

418

✗ **Cantina Del Ponte**  ≤ 🛋 VISA ⦿ AE
*36c Shad Thames, Butlers Wharf* ⊠ *SE1 2YE* ⊖ *London Bridge*
*– ℰ (020) 7403 5403 – www.cantina.co.uk – Closed 25-27 December*
**Rest** – Italian – Menu £ 18 (lunch) – Carte £ 20/28        **34**ASV**c**
♦ This Italian stalwart offers an appealing mix of classic dishes and reliable favourites from a sensibly priced menu, in pleasant faux-rustic surroundings. Its pleasant terrace takes advantage of its riverside setting.

✗ **Butlers Wharf Chop House**  ≤ 🛋 VISA ⦿ AE ⓪
*36e Shad Thames, Butlers Wharf* ⊠ *SE1 2YE* ⊖ *London Bridge*
*– ℰ (020) 7403 3403 – www.chophouse.co.uk – Closed 1-2 January*
**Rest** – British – Menu £ 27 (lunch) – Carte dinner £ 29/45        **34**ASV**n**
♦ Grab a table on the terrace in summer and dine in the shadow of Tower Bridge. Rustic feel to the interior; noisy and fun. The menu focuses on traditional English ingredients and dishes.

✗ **Champor-Champor**  AC ⇄ VISA ⦿ AE
*62-64 Weston St.* ⊠ *SE1 3QJ* ⊖ *London Bridge – ℰ (020) 7403 4600*
*– www.champor-champor.com – Closed 1 week Christmas, 1 week*
*Easter, Sunday and bank holidays*        **34**ARV**a**
**Rest** – Asian – *(dinner only)* Carte £ 34/43
♦ Choice of two beguiling and colourful rooms: ask for the second as it has even more character, better lighting and a mezzanine. Food is rooted in Malay traditions with a hint of modernity.

✗ **Vivat Bacchus London Bridge**  VISA ⦿ AE
*4 Hays Ln* ⊠ *SE1 2HB* ⊖ *London Bridge – ℰ (0207) 234 08 91*
*– www.vivatbacchus.co.uk – Closed 23 December-2 January, Saturday lunch,*
*Sunday and bank holidays*        **34**ARV**n**
**Rest** – Traditional – Menu £ 17/18 – Carte £ 17/33 🍷
♦ South African element to both the menu and the very impressive wine list. International platters in ground floor wine bar; robust cooking in the basement restaurant, with its great cheese room.

✗ **José**  AC VISA ⦿ AE
😊 *104 Bermondsey St* ⊠ *SE1 3UB* ⊖ *London Bridge – ℰ (020) 7403 4902*
*– www.josepizarro.com – Closed 25-26 December and Sunday dinner*
**Rest** – Spanish – *(bookings not accepted)* Carte approx. £ 25        **20**XZE**v**
♦ Standing up while eating tapas feels so right, especially at this small, fun bar that packs 'em in like boquerones. Five dishes each should suffice; go for the daily fish dishes from the blackboard. There's a great list of sherries too.

🍸 **Garrison**  AC ⇄ VISA ⦿ AE
*99-101 Bermondsey St* ⊠ *SE1 3XB* ⊖ *London Bridge. – ℰ (020) 7089 9355*
*– www.thegarrison.co.uk – Closed 25-27 December*        **20**XZE**z**
**Rest** – *(booking essential at dinner)* Carte £ 23/30
♦ Known for its vintage look, booths and sweet-natured service, The Garrison boasts a warm, relaxed vibe. Open from breakfast until dinner where a Mediterranean-led menu pulls in the crowd.

## SOUTHWARK

🛈 Level 2, Tate Modern, Bankside ℰ (020) 7401 52 66, www.visitlondon.com

✗✗✗ **Oxo Tower**  ≤ 🛋 AC VISA ⦿ AE ⓪
*Oxo Tower Wharf (8th floor), Barge House St* ⊠ *SE1 9PH* ⊖ *Southwark*
*– ℰ (020) 7803 3888 – www.harveynichols.com – Closed 25 December, dinner 24*
*December and lunch 26 December*        **32**ANV**a**
**Rest** – Modern European – Menu £ 35 (lunch) – Carte £ 39/52 🍷
**Rest** *Oxo Tower Brasserie* – see restaurant listing
♦ Top of a converted iconic factory, providing stunning views of the Thames and beyond. Stylish, minimalist interior with huge windows. Expect quite ambitious, mostly European, cuisine.

LONDON

## XX Roast

`AK` `VISA` `AE`

*The Floral Hall, Borough Mkt.* ⊠ *SE1 1TL* ⊖ *London Bridge* – ✆ *(0845) 347 300*
*– www.roast-restaurant.com – Closed 25 December, 1 January and Sunday*
*dinner*
33AQV**e**

**Rest** – British – *(booking essential)* Menu £ 28 (lunch and early dinner)
– Carte £ 37/60
♦ Set into the roof of Borough Market's Floral Hall. Extensive cocktail list in bar;
split-level restaurant has views to St Paul's. Robust English cooking uses market
produce.

## XX Baltic

↔ `VISA` `AE`

*74 Blackfriars Rd* ⊠ *SE1 8HA* ⊖ *Southwark* – ✆ *(020) 7928 1111*
*– www.balticrestaurant.co.uk – Closed 24-25 December, 1 January and bank*
*holidays*
33AOV**e**

**Rest** – Eastern European – *(booking advisable at dinner)* Menu £ 18 (weekday
lunch) – Carte £ 27/37
♦ Enjoy big portions of authentic and hearty east European food, served in a
Grade II listed 18C former coach house. The restaurant, which celebrated 10 years
in 2011, also has some interesting vodkas; live jazz on Sundays.

## X Oxo Tower Brasserie

`AK` `VISA` `AE` `O`

*Oxo Tower Wharf (8th floor), Barge House St* ⊠ *SE1 9PH* ⊖ *Southwark*
*– ✆ (020) 7803 3888 – www.harveynichols.com – Closed 25 December, dinner 24*
*December and lunch 26 December*
32ANV**a**

**Rest** – Modern European – Menu £ 27 (weekday lunch) – Carte £ 33/49
♦ Less formal but more fun than the next-door restaurant. Open-plan kitchen
produces modern, colourful and easy-to-eat dishes with influences from the
Med. Great views too from the bar.

## X Cantina Vinopolis

`AK` `VISA` `AE` `O`

*No.1 Bank End* ⊠ *SE1 9BU* ⊖ *London Bridge* – ✆ *(020) 7940 8333*
*– www.cantinavinopolis.com – Closed bank holidays*
33AQV**z**

**Rest** – Mediterranean – Menu £ 30 – Carte £ 25/39
♦ Beneath vast Victorian arches and next to their wine museum sits this bustling
restaurant, popular with larger parties. Impressive wine choice and carefully prepared food with a Mediterranean slant.

## X Tate Modern (Restaurant)

`VISA` `AE`

*Tate Modern (7th floor), Bankside* ⊠ *SE1 9TG* ⊖ *Southwark*
*– ✆ (020) 7887 8888 – www.tate.org.uk/modern/eatanddrink – Closed 24-26*
*December*
33APV**s**

**Rest** – British – *(lunch only and dinner Friday-Saturday)* Carte £ 28/34
♦ 7th floor restaurant with floor to ceilings windows on two sides and large mural. Appealing mix of light and zesty dishes, with seasonal produce. Good choice
of wines and non-alcoholic drinks.

## X Tapas Brindisa

`VISA` `AE`

*18-20 Southwark St., Borough Market* ⊠ *SE1 1TJ* ⊖ *London Bridge*
*– ✆ (020) 7357 8880 – www.brindisa.com*
33AQV**k**

**Rest** – Spanish – *(bookings not accepted)* Carte £ 12/30
♦ Prime quality Spanish produce sold in owner's shops and this bustling eatery
on edge of Borough Market. Freshly prepared, tasty tapas: waiters will assist with
your choice.

## X Wright Brothers

`VISA` `AE`

*11 Stoney St., Borough Market* ⊠ *SE1 9AD* ⊖ *London Bridge*
*– ✆ (020) 7403 9554 – www.wrightbrothers.co.uk – Closed bank holiday*
*Mondays*
33AQV**m**

**Rest** – Seafood – *(booking advisable)* Carte £ 25/51
♦ Originally an oyster wholesaler; now offers a wide range of oysters along with
porter, as well as fruits de mer, daily specials and assorted pies. It fills quickly and
an air of contentment reigns.

## ✗ Brew Wharf 🕅 AC VISA ◉◉ AE ⓪

*Brew Wharf Yard, Stoney St ⊠ SE1 9AD ⊖ London Bridge*
*– ℰ (020) 7378 6601 – www.brewwharf.com – Closed Sunday dinner and bank*
*holidays* **33**AQV**h**
**Rest** – Traditional – Carte £ 23/35

◆ A busy bar, microbrewery and restaurant; come in a group to enjoy the sports screen and vast selection of beers and ales. The gutsy food and shared platters are the perfect match for the beer.

## 🍴 Anchor & Hope 🕅 VISA ◉◉

⊛ *36 The Cut ⊠ SE1 8LP ⊖ Southwark. – ℰ (020) 7928 9898*
*– Closed Christmas-New Year, Sunday dinner, Monday lunch and bank holidays*
**Rest** – British – *(bookings not accepted)* Carte £ 23/32 **32**ANV**n**

◆ As popular as ever thanks to its congenial feel and lived-in looks but mostly because of the appealingly seasonal menu and the gutsy, bold cooking that delivers on flavour. No reservations so be prepared to wait at the bar.

---

# SUTTON – Greater London 12 B3

## SUTTON

🏊 Oak Sports Centre Carshalton Woodmansterne Rd, ℰ (020) 8643 83 63

## ✗ Brasserie Vacherin AC ☞ VISA ◉◉ AE

*12 High St ⊠ SM1 1HN – ℰ (020) 8722 0180 – www.brasserievacherin.co.uk*
*– Closed 25 December* **7**EZ**x**
**Rest** – French – Menu £ 17 – Carte £ 25/34

◆ Relaxed, modern French brasserie with tiled walls, art nouveau posters and deep red banquettes. Good value midweek set price menu and à la carte of French classics. Diligent service.

## WORCESTER PARK

## ✗ Avventura AC VISA ◉◉ AE

*82-86 Central Rd ⊠ KT4 8HX – ℰ (020) 8335 3355*
*– www.avventura-restaurant.co.uk – Closed 2 weeks July-August, 1 week Easter,*
*24 December-3 January and bank holidays* **6**CZ**x**
**Rest** – Italian – *(dinner only and lunch Saturday-Sunday)* Menu £ 20
*– Carte £ 28/33*

◆ Keenly run, modern day trattoria in a busy suburban high street. Tiled floor, polished tables and informal atmosphere. Experienced owners offer homemade pasta and pizza cooked in a copper, wood-fired oven. Service is engaging and animated.

---

# TOWER HAMLETS – Greater London 12 B3

## BETHNAL GREEN

## 🏠 Town Hall 🖼 ๒ 🖼 ₺ rm, AC ❊ ⁽ᵞ⁾ 🔄 VISA ◉◉ AE

*Patriot Sq ⊠ E2 9NF ⊖ Bethnal Green – ℰ (020) 7871 0460*
*– www.townhallhotel.com* **14**YZB**x**
**97 rm** – ♦£ 174/348 ♦♦£ 207/414, � £ 15 – 1 suite
**Rest** *Viajante* ❀ – see restaurant listing
**Rest** *Corner Room* – *(bookings not accepted)* Carte £ 21/23

◆ Edwardian, former council offices converted into a hotel in 2010. Its period character is balanced with modernity, with individually decorated, understated bedrooms and frequently changing art. 'Corner Room' restaurant merely hints at the superlative cooking found in Viajante.

**LONDON**

XX **Viajante** – at Town Hall Hotel　　　　　　AC VISA ᴐᴏ AE
🕸 *Patriot Sq., (entrance on Cambridge Heath Rd)* ⊠ *E2 9NF* ⊖ *Bethnal Green*
*– ☎ (020) 7871 0461 – www.viajante.co.uk – Closed lunch Monday-Tuesday and*
*bank holidays*　　　　　　　　　　　　　　　　　　**14**YZB**x**
**Rest** – Innovative – *(booking essential)* Menu £ 28/65
**Spec.** Cod and potatoes with egg yolk and saffron. Pork secretos with artichokes
and hot potato gel. White chocolate with grapefruit and lemon.
◆ Highly innovative and original cooking; you choose 6, 9 or 12 delicate courses.
A converted Victorian town hall is the unlikely setting for this creative style of
cooking; ask to sit in the front room if you want to watch the chefs at work.

X **Brawn**　　　　　　　　　　　　　　　　AC VISA ᴐᴏ
😊 *49 Columbia Rd.* ⊠ *E2 7RG* ⊖ *Bethnal Green* – ☎ *(020) 7729 5692*
*– www.brawn.co – Closed Sunday dinner and bank holidays*　　　**20**XZD**z**
**Rest** – Mediterranean – Carte £ 21/28
◆ Unpretentious and simply kitted out baby sister to Terroirs; the name captures
the essence of the cooking perfectly: it is rustic, muscular and makes very good
use of pig. Great local atmosphere and polite, helpful service.

## BOW

🛏 **Morgan Arms**　　　　　　　　　　　　🍴 AC VISA ᴐᴏ AE
*43 Morgan St* ⊠ *E3 5AA* ⊖ *Bow Road* – ☎ *(020) 8980 6389*
*– www.capitalpubcompany.com/The-Morgan-Arms – Closed 25 December*
**Rest** – Carte £ 24/34　　　　　　　　　　　　　　　　　**3**GU**c**
◆ Characterful pub with mismatch of furniture and shabby-chic appeal. Constantly
evolving menu offers robust cooking which occasionally uses some unfamiliar ingredients; simpler food is served in the lively bar.

## CANARY WHARF

🏨🏨 **Four Seasons**　⇐ ▢ 🍴 ⅃🚴 ᔕ AC ⅌ 🕊 🛁 🌐 VISA ᴐᴏ AE ⓪
*Westferry Circus* ⊠ *E14 8RS* ⊖ *Canary Wharf* – ☎ *(020) 7510 1999*
*– www.fourseasons.com/canarywharf*　　　　　　　　　　**3**GV**a**
**128 rm** – †£ 282/312, ††£ 282/312, ☲ £ 26 – 14 suites
**Rest** *Quadrato* – see restaurant listing
◆ Professionally run international hotel geared primarily to the local corporate
market; whose deluxe rooms boast impressive views across the river. Leisure facilities housed in an adjacent club.

XXX **Quadrato** – at Four Seasons Hotel　　　　🍴 AC VISA ᴐᴏ AE ⓪
*Westferry Circus* ⊠ *E14 8RS* ⊖ *Canary Wharf* – ☎ *(020) 7510 1999*
*– www.fourseasons.com/canarywharf*　　　　　　　　　　**3**GV**a**
**Rest** – Italian – Menu £ 39 – Carte £ 37/53
◆ Smart, spacious restaurant on the ground floor of the Four Seasons, with river-
facing terrace. Luxury ingredients used in dishes that cover all parts of Italy.
Knowledgeable service.

XXX **Dockmaster's House**　　　　　　　　　🚗 VISA ᴐᴏ AE
*1 Hertsmere Rd* ⊠ *E14 8JJ* ⊖ *Canary Wharf* – ☎ *(020) 7345 0345*
*– www.dockmastershouse.com – Closed Christmas, Sunday, Saturday lunch and*
*bank holidays*　　　　　　　　　　　　　　　　　　**3**GV**r**
**Rest** – Indian – *(booking advisable)* Menu £ 20 (lunch and early dinner)
*– Carte £ 28/40*
◆ A contemporary overhaul of a three storey Georgian house in the shadow of
Canary Wharf's skyscrapers has created this slick operation. Elaborate Indian cooking, although sometimes a little pretentious.

XX **Plateau**     🍴 AC ♿ VISA ⓪ AE ⓪
*Canada Place (4th floor), Canada Square* ⊠ *E14 5ER* ⊖ *Canary Wharf*
*– 𝒞 (020) 7715 7100 – www.plateaurestaurant.co.uk – Closed 25 December, 1*
*January and Sunday*                                                          **3**GV**n**
**Rest** – Modern European – Menu £ 28 – Carte £ 39/55
♦ Impressive open-plan space with dramatic glass walls and ceilings and striking
1970s design. Rotisserie meats in the Grill; globally-influenced dishes in formal
restaurant.

XX **Roka Canary Wharf**     AC VISA ⓪ AE ⓪
*4 Park Pavilion (1st Floor)* ⊠ *E14 5FW* ⊖ *Canary Wharf* – 𝒞 *(020) 7636 5228*
*– www.rokarestaurant.com – Closed Christmas*                               **3**GV**v**
**Rest** – Japanese – *(booking essential)* Carte £ 35/65
♦ You'll be hit by a wall of sound at this large and perennially busy operation in
the shadow of Canary Wharf Tower. The meats cooked on the robata grill are
highlights of the Japanese menu.

🏠 **Gun**     🍴 ♿ VISA ⓪ AE
*27 Coldharbour* ⊠ *E14 9NS* ⊖ *Blackwall (DLR)* – 𝒞 *(020) 7515 5222*
*– www.thegundocklands.com – Closed 25-26 December*                         **7**GV**x**
**Rest** – Menu £ 18 (lunch) – Carte £ 28/49
♦ Despite its 21C makeover, this 18C pub, with links to Lord Nelson, hasn't for-
gotten its roots. Smart dining room; menu a mix of classic and modern. Always
busy, especially the large decked area.

## LIMEHOUSE

🏠 **Narrow**     🍴 AC ♿ P VISA ⓪ AE ⓪
*44 Narrow St* ⊠ *E14 8DP* ⊖ *Limehouse (DLR).* – 𝒞 *(020) 7592 7950*
*– www.gordonramsay.com*                                                     **3**GV**o**
**Rest** – *(booking essential)* Menu £ 22 (lunch) – Carte £ 24/36
♦ Grade II listed former dockmaster's house on the river; part of Gordon Ramsay's group. Menu specialises in British favourites, from shrimps to sardines,
braised beef to trifle.

## SPITALFIELDS

XXX **Galvin La Chapelle**     🍴 ♿ VISA ⓪ AE ⓪
❀ *35 Spital Sq.* ⊠ *E1 6DY* ⊖ *Liverpool Street* – 𝒞 *(020) 7299 0400*
*– www.galvinrestaurants.com – Closed dinner 24-26 December and 1 January*
**Rest** – French – Menu £ 26 (lunch)/30 (early dinner)                      **34**AST**v**
– Carte £ 32/51
**Spec.** Lasagne of crab with velouté of girolles. Tagine of pigeon with aubergine
purée and harissa sauce. Chilled Valhrona chocolate fondant, banana and yoghurt
ice cream and fresh honeycomb.
♦ The Victorian splendour of St. Botolph's Hall, with its vaulted ceiling, arched win-
dows and marble pillars, lends itself perfectly to its role as a glamorous restaurant.
The food is bourgeois French with a sophisticated edge and is bound to satisfy.

XX **Les Trois Garcons**     AC ♿ VISA ⓪ AE
*1 Club Row* ⊠ *E1 6JX* ⊖ *Shoreditch* – 𝒞 *(020) 7613 1924*
*– www.lestroisgarcons.com – Closed 23 December-3 January, Saturday lunch,*
*Sunday dinner and bank holidays*                                            **20**XZD**r**
**Rest** – French – Menu £ 22/47
♦ Extraordinarily eccentric, with stuffed animals, twinkling beads, assorted chandeliers and ceiling handbags. The French food is more traditional and governed
by the seasons.

X **Hawksmoor**     AC VISA ⓪ AE
*157 Commercial St.* ⊠ *E1 6BJ* ⊖ *Shoreditch* – 𝒞 *(020) 7247 7392*
*– www.thehawksmoor.com – Closed 1 week Christmas and Sunday dinner*
**Rest** – Beef specialities – *(booking essential)* Carte £ 40/60             **20**XZD**s**
♦ Unremarkable surroundings and ordinary starters and puds but no matter: this
is all about great British beef, hung for 35 days, from Longhorn cattle in the heart
of the Yorkshire Moors.

LONDON

LONDON

## Galvin Café a Vin
🛋 VISA ⓴ AE

35 Spital Sq. (entrance on Bishops Sq.) ⊠ E1 6DY ⊖ Liverpool Street
– ℰ (020) 7299 0404 – www.galvinrestaurants.com – Closed 25 December
**Rest** – French – Carte £ 24/30                                    34ASTv
• In the same building as La Chapelle is this simpler but equally worthy opera-
tion from the Galvin brothers. The room may not have the grandeur of next
door but what it does offer is classic French bistro food at very appealing prices.

## St John Bread and Wine
AC VISA ⓴ AE ⓪

94-96 Commercial St ⊠ E1 6LZ ⊖ Shoreditch – ℰ (020) 7251 0848
– www.stjohnbreadandwine.com – Closed Christmas-New Year and bank
holidays                                                             34ASTx
**Rest** – British – Carte £ 23/29
• Part-wine shop/bakery and local restaurant. Highly seasonal and appealing
menu changes twice a day; cooking is British, uncomplicated and very satisfying.
Try the less familiar dishes.

## Owl & Pussycat
VISA ⓴ AE

34 Redchurch St ⊠ E2 7DP ⊖ Shoreditch. – ℰ (020) 3487 0088
– www.owlandpussycatshoreditch.com – Closed 25-26 December, 1 January and
bank holidays                                                        20XZDz
**Rest** – British – Carte £ 25/43
• The former Crown now has a raggedly modish look with ironic touches of Victoriana to match the Edward Lear name. An appealingly stout British menu is offered in the upstairs dining room.

## WAPPING

## Smith's of Wapping
AC VISA ⓴ AE

22 Wapping High St ⊠ E1W 1NJ ⊖ Wapping – ℰ (020) 7488 3456
– www.smithsbrasserie.com – Closed Sunday dinner                     20XZEc
**Rest** – Seafood – (booking advisable) Menu £ 25 (lunch) – Carte £ 33/60
• Having provided seafood to the burghers of Essex for over 50 years, the Smiths
opened this large riverside brasserie in 2011. The kitchen keeps it traditional; the
best dishes are old favourites like dressed crab and Dover sole meunière.

## Wapping Food
🛋 P VISA ⓴ AE

Wapping Wall ⊠ E1W 3SG ⊖ Wapping – ℰ (020) 7680 2080
– www.thewappingproject.com – Closed 24 December-3 January, Sunday dinner
and bank holidays                                                    20YZEn
**Rest** – Modern European – Carte £ 25/41
• This striking Victorian former hydraulic power station houses an atmospheric
restaurant and art gallery. Sit among the old turbines and enjoy robust, straightforward dishes based on what's in season.

## WHITECHAPEL

## Cafe Spice Namaste
AC VISA ⓴ AE ⓪

16 Prescot St. ⊠ E1 8AZ ⊖ Tower Hill – ℰ (020) 7488 9242
– www.cafespice.co.uk – Closed 25 December-2 January, Saturday lunch, Sunday
and bank holidays                                                    34ASUz
**Rest** – Indian – Carte £ 27/33
• Fresh, vibrant and fairly priced Indian cuisine from Cyrus Todiwala, served in a
colourfully decorated room that was once a magistrate's court. Engaging service
from an experienced team.

## Whitechapel Gallery Dining Room
AC ⟷ VISA ⓴ AE ⓪

77-82 Whitechapel High St. ⊠ E1 7QX ⊖ Aldgate East – ℰ (020) 7522 7896
– www.whitechapelgallery.org/dining-room – Closed Christmas-New Year,
Monday and dinner Sunday and Tuesday                                 34ASTx
**Rest** – Italian influences – (booking advisable) Carte £ 24/30
• Founded in 1901 and best known for exhibiting Picasso's 'Guernica', the gallery
underwent a major refit in 2009, which resulted in the creation of this sweet restaurant. Bright, European and Med influenced cooking from an accessible menu.

BALHAM

✗ **Brasserie James**                                    🛆 VISA ◑◉
47 Balham Hill ⊠ SW12 9DR ⊖ Clapham South – ℰ (020) 8772 0057
– www.brasseriejames.com – Closed 23-30 December                **6**EX**x**
**Rest** – Modern European – Carte £ 28/36
♦ Crisp and neat brasserie owned and run by former Conran/D&D chef. Something for everyone on the seasonal menu, from moules to pasta. Weekend brunches; good value set menus; wines by carafe.

✗ **Lamberts**                                       AK VISA ◑◉
2 Station Par. ⊠ SW12 9AZ ⊖ Balham – ℰ (020) 8675 2233
– www.lambertsrestaurant.com – Closed 24-26 December, 1 January, Sunday
dinner and Monday                                          **6**EX**n**
**Rest** – Traditional – (dinner only and lunch Saturday-Sunday) Menu £ 20 (midweek) – Carte £ 27/34
♦ Locals come for the relaxed surroundings, hospitable service and tasty, seasonal food. Sunday lunch is very popular. The enthusiasm of the eponymous owner has rubbed off on his team.

✗ **Harrison's**                                          VISA ◑◉ AE
15-19 Bedford Hill ⊠ SW12 9EX ⊖ Balham – ℰ (020) 8675 6900
– www.harrisonsbalham.co.uk – Closed 24-28 December                **6**EX**a**
**Rest** – Mediterranean – Carte £ 30/39
♦ Sister to Sam's Brasserie in Chiswick. Open all day, with an appealing list of favourites, from fishcakes to Cumberland sausages. Weekend brunches; kids' menu; good value weekday set menus.

🍴 **Avalon**                                    🛆 AK ⟷ VISA ◑◉ AE
16 Balham Hill ⊠ SW12 9EB ⊖ Clapham South. – ℰ (020) 8675 8613
– www.theavalonlondon.com – Closed 25-26 December and 1 January
**Rest** – (booking advisable) Carte £ 25/30                     **6**EX**r**
♦ Large, bustling and atmospheric pub with an appealing summer terrace. Snacks served in the busy, long bar and an appealingly broad menu offered in the tiled and characterful rear dining room.

BATTERSEA

✗✗ **Chada**                                         AK VISA ◑◉ AE
208-210 Battersea Park Rd. ⊠ SW11 4ND – ℰ (020) 7622 2209
– www.chadathai.com – Closed Sunday and bank holidays          **23**QZH**x**
**Rest** – Thai – (dinner only) Carte £ 19/43
♦ Going strong after 20 years; its striking façade stands out in an otherwise unremarkable street. The welcome is warm, the service polite and the Thai food appealing and keenly priced.

✗✗ **Bennett**                                        🛆 VISA ◑◉ AE
7-9 Battersea Sq. ⊠ SW11 3PA ⊖ Clapham Junction (rail) – ℰ (020) 7223 5545
– www.bennettsbrasserie.com – Closed Sunday dinner              **23**PZH**a**
**Rest** – British – Carte £ 29/36
♦ Smart, all-day brasserie with wine shop attached. The menu appeals to a broad constituency by offering everything from brasserie classics and a large seafood selection to traditional British staples and nursery favourites.

✗ **Ransome's Dock**                              🛆 VISA ◑◉ AE ◉
35-37 Parkgate Rd. ⊠ SW11 4NP – ℰ (020) 7223 1611
– www.ransomesdock.co.uk – Closed Christmas, August bank holiday and
Sunday dinner                                            **23**QZG**c**
**Rest** – British – Carte £ 24/37 🍴
♦ Husband and wife team run a brasserie-style operation in a converted warehouse, with a canal-side terrace. Careful sourcing underpins the cooking. Thoughtful, varied and sensibly priced wine list.

LONDON

X **Tom Ilić**    AC VISA ◉◎ AE ◑
123 Queenstown Rd. ⊠ SW8 3RH – 𝒞 (020) 7622 0555 – www.tomilic.com
– Closed Christmas, 1 week summer, Monday, Sunday dinner and Tuesday lunch
**Rest** – Traditional – (booking essential) Menu £ 20/22    **24**RZH
– Carte £ 29/38
♦ Spacious, simply decorated neighbourhood restaurant offering an appealing offal-based menu, with plenty of pork. Skilled, intricate cooking with bold, gutsy flavours to the fore.

X **Entrée**    AC VISA ◉◎ AE
2 Battersea Rise ⊠ SW11 1ED ⊖ Clapham Junction (rail) – 𝒞 (020) 7223 5147
– www.entreebattersea.co.uk – Closed 24-28 December    **23**QZH
**Rest** – Modern European – (dinner only and lunch Saturday-Sunday)
Carte £ 29/36
♦ They've gone for a casual bistro look which, along with a basement bar and weekend pianist, hits the right note with locals. Sensibly priced menu mixes French classic and modern European dishes.

X **Lola Rojo**    🏠 AC VISA ◉◎ ◑
78 Northcote Rd ⊠ SW11 6QL ⊖ Clapham Junction (rail) – 𝒞 (020) 7350 2262
– www.lolarojo.net – Closed 25-26 December    **23**QZH
**Rest** – Spanish – (booking essential) Menu £ 9 (weekday lunch) – Carte £ 22/3
♦ Few spots on Northcote Road are as fun as this lively, if cramped Spanish eatery. The owner-chef comes from Valencia so paella is a sure thing but other Catalan tapas specialities are also worth seeking out.

X **Metrogusto**    AC VISA ◉◎ AE
153 Battersea Park Rd. ⊠ SW8 4BX ⊖ Battersea Park (rail) – 𝒞 (020) 7720 0204
– www.metrogusto.co.uk – Closed 25-26 December, Easter and Sunday dinner
**Rest** – Italian – Carte £ 21/35    **24**RZG
♦ Ambro Ianeselli, one of London's most affable restaurateurs, has moved from Islington back to his original Battersea base, along with his art collection. The Italian food is simple and as heart-warming as Ambro's never-ending hospitality.

🍺 **Bolingbroke**    🏠 AC VISA ◉◎ AE
174 Northcote Rd ⊠ SW11 6RE ⊖ Clapham Junction (rail). – 𝒞 (020)
7228 4040 – www.thebolingbroke.com – Closed 25-28 December    **6**EX
**Rest** – British – Carte £ 21/34
♦ Smart, locally popular pub whose more diminutive size adds extra charm. Glass-roofed dining room sees flavoursome dishes with a mostly British accent, more choice at dinner. Child friendly.

**BATTERSEA HELIPORT**

🏨 **Verta**    ≼ 🏠 ⊛ ⋘ ⅃⅃ 🛗 & rm, AC ⅍ ⁀ ⚒ 🅿 VISA ◉◎ AE ◑
Bridges Wharf ⊠ SW11 3BE – 𝒞 (020) 7801 3500 – www.hotelverta.co.uk
**68 rm** – ♦£ 124/285 ♦♦£ 314/475, ⊑ £ 19.50 – 2 suites    **23**PZH
**Rest** Patrisey – Menu £ 20/25 – Carte £ 32/45
♦ Built in 2010, in a unique riverside location with a heliport. Well-equipped bedrooms; those without views are bigger than those with. Impressive spa facilities. Choose from a wide-ranging menu, while watching the helicopters land.

**PUTNEY**

XX **Enoteca Turi**    AC ⇄ VISA ◉◎ AE ◑
28 Putney High St. ⊠ SW15 1SQ ⊖ Putney Bridge – 𝒞 (020) 8785 4449
– www.enotecaturi.com – Closed 25-26 December, 1 January, Sunday
and lunch bank holiday Mondays    **22**MZH
**Rest** – Italian – Menu £ 20 (lunch) – Carte £ 32/40 🍷
♦ A long-standing owner-run Italian restaurant. Earthy cooking focuses on the northerly regions of Italy. Interesting wine list, with plenty by the glass and carafe

✗ **Cantinetta** 🏠 AC VISA ◍ AE
162-164 Lower Richmond Rd, (Entrance on Pentlow St) ✉ SW15 1LY
⊖ Putney Bridge – ✆ (020) 8780 3131 – www.cantinetta.co.uk
– Closed Sunday dinner and Monday lunch in winter **21**LZH**v**
**Rest** – Italian – Menu £ 16/18 – Carte £ 21/32

♦ A bright and relaxed modern day trattoria, opening onto a popular terrace. Well-priced dishes deliver on flavour, whether that's deep-fried anchovies with carpione dressing or the Ligurian classic 'trofie al pesto'.

🍺 **Prince of Wales** VISA ◍ AE ①
138 Upper Richmond Rd ✉ SW15 2SP ⊖ East Putney. – ✆ (020) 8788 1552
– www.princeofwalesputney.co.uk – Closed 23 December-1 January and Monday
lunch except bank holidays **22**MZH**z**
**Rest** – British – Carte £ 27/43

♦ Warmly run Victorian pub; eat in the busy bar or in lavishly decorated baronial style dining room. Seasonality to the fore, with game a speciality. Spit-roast chickens feature on Sunday lunchtimes.

## SOUTHFIELDS 12 B3

✗ **Triphal** AC VISA ◍
☺ 201 Replingham Rd ✉ SW18 5LY ⊖ Southfields – ✆ (020) 8870 0188 – Closed
25-26 December, 1 January and Monday **6**DX**e**
**Rest** – Indian – Carte £ 15/19

♦ Created on a shoestring by three partners, two of whom are chefs, this is a sweet little place making efforts all round. Fish curries are the stand out dishes from a concise, good value menu of regional Indian cuisine.

## WANDSWORTH

✗✗ **Chez Bruce** (Bruce Poole) AC ✛ VISA ◍ AE
✿ 2 Bellevue Rd ✉ SW17 7EG ⊖ Tooting Bec – ✆ (020) 8672 0114
– www.chezbruce.co.uk – Closed 24-26 December and 1 January **6**EX**e**
**Rest** – French – (booking essential) Menu £ 28 (weekday lunch)/45 ⌘
**Spec.** Rare grilled tuna à la Niçoise, fennel purée and anchovy beignet. Rump and shoulder of lamb with spring vegetables, creamed potato and rosemary. Hot chocolate pudding with praline parfait.

♦ Flavoursome, uncomplicated French cooking with hints of the Mediterranean prepared with innate skill; well-organised, personable service and an easy-going atmosphere - some of the reasons why Chez Bruce remains a favourite of so many.

## WESTMINSTER (City of) – Greater London 12 B3

## BAYSWATER AND MAIDA VALE

🏨 **Lancaster London** ⪕ 🛗 ♿ AC 🍴 🌐 🛎 P VISA ◍ AE ①
Lancaster Ter. ✉ W2 2TY ⊖ Lancaster Gate – ✆ (020) 7262 6737
– www.lancasterlondon.com **28**ADU**e**
**394 rm** – ♦£ 119/372 ♦♦£ 119/372, ⌑ £ 15.50 – 22 suites
**Rest** Island **Rest** Nipa – see restaurant listing

♦ Still known to most people as The Royal Lancaster. Imposing 1960s purpose-built hotel overlooking Hyde Park. Extensive conference facilities. Well-equipped bedrooms are decorated in a traditional style.

🏨 **The Hempel** ⏤ 🛗 ♿ rm, AC 🌐 🛎 🛎 VISA ◍ AE ①
31-35 Craven Hill Gdns. ✉ W2 3EA ⊖ Queensway – ✆ (020) 7298 9000
– www.the-hempel.co.uk – Closed 24-27 December **28**ACU**a**
**44 rm** – ♦£ 214/310 ♦♦£ 241/310, ⌑ £ 22.50 – 6 suites
**Rest** No.35 – (closed Sunday) (dinner only) Carte £ 30/43

♦ A crisp, minimalist environment in a blizzard of white; room 110 has a suspended bed. Basement art gallery also used for private parties. Zen garden in the Square opposite. Bright, ground floor dining room has a British menu.

**LONDON**

🏠 **Colonnade Town House** without rest　🛗 AC ⚡ 📶 VISA ⓐ AE ①
2 Warrington Cres. ⊠ W9 1ER ⊖ Warwick Avenue – ✆ (020) 7286 1052
– www.theetoncollection.co.uk　**17**OZDe
**43 rm** – †£ 125/234 ††£ 138/378, � £ 12.50
♦ Former hospital in quiet yet easily accessible location. Bedrooms range in size according to grade; all are comfortable and classically furnished with good amenities. Lower floor bar.

🏠 **Royal Park** without rest　🛗 AC 📶 P VISA ⓐ AE ①
3 Westbourne Terr ⊠ W2 3UL ⊖ Lancaster Gate – ✆ (020) 7479 6600
– www.theroyalpark.com　**28**ADUx
**45 rm** – †£ 178/378 ††£ 202/390, ⊆ £ 17.95 – 3 suites
♦ Three attractive 19C townhouses set back from the road, in a pleasant location near Hyde Park. Quiet lounges with period furnishings. Breakfast served in the well-appointed bedrooms.

🏠 **New Linden** without rest　🛗 ⚡ 📶 VISA ⓐ AE
59 Leinster Sq. ⊠ W2 4PS ⊖ Bayswater – ✆ (020) 7221 4321
– www.mayflower-group.co.uk　**27**ABUe
**50 rm** – †£ 99/140 ††£ 175/250
♦ Smart four storey white stucco façade. Basement breakfast room opens onto summer courtyard. Bedrooms are its strength: flat screen TVs and wooden floors; two split-level family rooms.

✕✕ **Le Café Anglais**　AC VISA ⓐ AE
8 Porchester Gdns ⊠ W2 4BD ⊖ Bayswater – ✆ (020) 7221 1415
– www.lecafeanglais.co.uk – Closed 25-26 December and 1 January
**Rest** – Modern European – Menu £ 24 (weekday lunch)　**27**ABUr
– Carte £ 25/52
♦ Big, bustling and contemporary brasserie with art deco styling, within Whiteley's shopping centre. Large, appealing selection of classic brasserie food; the rotisserie is the centrepiece. More casual oyster bar by entrance.

✕✕ **Angelus**　AC ⇔ VISA ⓐ AE
4 Bathurst St. ⊠ W2 2SD ⊖ Lancaster Gate – ✆ (020) 7402 0083
– www.angelusrestaurant.co.uk – Closed 24 December-2 January　**28**ADUc
**Rest** – French – Menu £ 32 (lunch) – Carte £ 39/54
♦ Hospitable owner has created an attractive French brasserie within a 19C former pub, with a warm and inclusive feel. Satisfying and honest French cooking uses seasonal British ingredients.

✕✕ **Nipa** – at Lancaster London Hotel　AC P VISA ⓐ AE ①
Lancaster Terr ⊠ W2 2TY ⊖ Lancaster Gate – ✆ (020) 7551 6039
– www.niparestaurant.co.uk – Closed Christmas-NewYear, Saturday lunch and
Sunday　**28**ADUe
**Rest** – Thai – Menu £ 29 – Carte £ 23/32
♦ On the 1st floor and overlooking Hyde Park. Authentic and ornately decorated restaurant offers subtly spiced Thai cuisine. Keen to please staff in traditional silk costumes.

✕✕ **Pearl Liang**　AC ⇔ VISA ⓐ AE
8 Sheldon Sq., Paddington Central ⊠ W2 6EZ ⊖ Paddington
– ✆ (020) 7289 7000 – www.pearlliang.co.uk – Closed 24 and 25 December
**Rest** – Chinese – Menu £ 25 – Carte £ 24/42　**28**ACTb
♦ Spacious, business-orientated Chinese restaurant within a corporate development. Extensive choice from a variety of set menus; try the more unusual dishes like jellyfish or pig's trotter.

✕✕ **Island** – at Lancaster London Hotel　♿ AC P VISA ⓐ AE ①
Lancaster Ter. ⊠ W2 2TY ⊖ Lancaster Gate – ✆ (020) 7551 6070
– www.lancasterlondon.com　**28**ADUe
**Rest** – Modern European – Menu £ 13 (lunch) – Carte £ 17/32
♦ This split-level contemporary looking restaurant is a road-crossing away from Hyde Park. Menu includes jogging-adjourning items like pies and burgers alongside salads and grills.

## Hereford Road
AC VISA ☎ AE

3 Hereford Rd. ⊠ W2 4AB ⊖ Bayswater – ℰ (020) 7727 1144
– www.herefordroad.org – Closed 24 December-3 January and 27-29 August
**Rest** – British – *(booking essential)* Menu £ 16 (weekday lunch)    **27**ABU**s**
– Carte £ 22/27

♦ Converted butcher's shop specialising in tasty British dishes without frills, using first rate, seasonal ingredients; offal a highlight. Booths for six people are the prized seats. Friendly and relaxed feel.

## Assaggi
AC VISA ☎

39 Chepstow Pl, (above Chesterfield pub) ⊠ W2 4TS ⊖ Bayswater – ℰ (020) 7792 5501 – Closed 2 weeks Christmas, Sunday and bank holidays    **27**AAU**c**
**Rest** – Italian – *(booking essential)* Carte £ 37/50

♦ The pared-down simplicity to this room above a pub works well; regulars are given fulsome welcomes and the atmosphere is great. Cooking puts the focus on the quality of the ingredients and the wine list is exclusively Italian.

## Casa Malevo
AC ⇔ VISA ☎ AE

23 Connaught St ⊠ W2 2AY ⊖ Marble Arch – ℰ (020) 7402 1988
– www.casamalevo.com – Closed Sunday dinner    **29**AFU**a**
**Rest** – Argentinian – Menu £ 17 (lunch) – Carte £ 26/36

♦ Carnivores will be in clover at this friendly Argentinian restaurant, with its bare brick walls and intimate lighting. Most come for the grilled Argentine beef, accompanied by a bottle of Malbec.

## El Pirata De Tapas
AC VISA ☎ AE

115 Westbourne Grove ⊠ W2 4UP ⊖ Bayswater – ℰ (020) 7727 5000
– www.elpiratadetapas.co.uk – Closed 24-26 December, 2-3 September and 1 January    **27**ABU**n**
**Rest** – Spanish – Menu £ 10/25 – Carte £ 16/18

♦ Contemporary yet warm Spanish restaurant with a genuine neighbourhood feel. Authentic flavours from a well-priced and appealing selection of tapas, ideal for sharing with friends.

## Kateh
🛋 AC VISA ☎ AE

5 Warwick Pl ⊠ W9 2PX ⊖ Warwick Avenue – ℰ (020) 7289 3393
– www.kateh.net    **28**ACT**a**
**Rest** – Persian – *(dinner only and lunch Friday-Sunday) (booking essential)* Carte £ 17/30

♦ Booking is imperative if you want to join the locals who have already discovered what a little jewel they have in the form of this buzzy, busy Persian restaurant. Authentic stews, expert chargrilling and lovely pastries and teas.

## Prince Alfred & Formosa Dining Room
AC VISA ☎ AE

5A Formosa St ⊠ W9 1EE ⊖ Warwick Avenue. – ℰ (020) 7286 3287
– www.theprincealfred.com    **17**OZD**n**
**Rest** – Modern European – Menu £ 16 (lunch) – Carte £ 25/39

♦ Characterful and classic Victorian pub, with a large, more modern dining room in side extension. Open kitchen and a mix of British specialities and European classics. Friendly service.

## Warrington
AC ⇔ VISA ☎ AE ⓞ

93 Warrington Cres ⊠ W9 1EH ⊖ Maida Vale. – ℰ (020) 7592 7960
– www.gordonramsay.com    **17**OZD**a**
**Rest** – Modern European – Menu £ 22 (lunch and early dinner)
– Carte £ 27/36

♦ Wood panelling, mosaics and friezes add to the atmosphere in the ground floor of this Gordon Ramsay pub. Go upstairs to the restaurant if you want a more sophisticated menu of mostly British produce.

LONDON

**LONDON**

**Waterway** ← 🍴 AC P VISA ⊕ AE ⊙
*54 Formosa St ⊠ W9 2JU ⊖ Warwick Avenue. – ✆ (020) 7266 3557*
*– www.thewaterway.co.uk* **17**OZD**p**
**Rest** – Modern European – Carte £ 26/36
♦ Terrific decked terrace by the canal its most appealing feature. Contemporary interior with busy cocktail bar; menu in separate dining room mixes the classics with more ambitious dishes.

## BELGRAVIA

**Berkeley** 🈺 🍴 ⊕ 🛗 ♨ ⛱ 🛎 AC ⚒ 🍽 ♨ 🚗 VISA ⊕ AE ⊙
*Wilton Pl. ⊠ SW1X 7RL ⊖ Knightsbridge – ✆ (020) 7235 6000*
*– www.the-berkeley.co.uk* **37**AGX**e**
**189 rm** – 🛏£ 588/708 🛏🛏£ 708, � £ 29 – 25 suites
**Rest** *Marcus Wareing at The Berkeley*♧ ♧ **Rest** *Koffmann's* – see restaurant listing
♦ Discreet and rejuvenated hotel with rooftop pool and opulently decorated bedrooms. Relax in the gilded and panelled Caramel Room or have a drink in the cool Blue Bar.

**Lanesborough** ⛱ 🛎 ♨ AC 🍽 ♨ P VISA ⊕ AE ⊙
*Hyde Park Corner ⊠ SW1X 7TA ⊖ Hyde Park Corner – ✆ (020) 7259 5599*
*– www.lanesborough.com* **37**AGX**a**
**83 rm** – 🛏£ 630 🛏🛏£ 738, ⊕ £ 30 – 10 suites
**Rest** *Apsleys*♧ – see restaurant listing
♦ Converted in the 1990s from 18C St George's Hospital. Butler service offered. Regency-era inspired decoration; lavishly appointed rooms with impressive technological extras.

**Halkin** 🛎 AC ⚒ 🍽 VISA ⊕ AE ⊙
*5 Halkin St ⊠ SW1X 7DJ ⊖ Hyde Park Corner – ✆ (020) 7333 1000*
*– www.halkin.como.bz* **38**AHX**b**
**35 rm** – 🛏£ 312/540 🛏🛏£ 312/660, ⊕ £ 28.50 – 6 suites
**Rest** *Nahm* – see restaurant listing
♦ Opened in 1991 as London's first boutique hotel and still looking sharp today. Thoughtfully conceived bedrooms with silk walls and marbled bathrooms; everything at the touch of a button. Abundant Armani-clad staff. Small, discreet bar.

**Jumeirah Lowndes** 🍴 🛎 ♿ rm, AC ⚒ 🍽 ♨ P VISA ⊕ AE
*21 Lowndes St ⊠ SW1X 9ES ⊖ Knightsbridge – ✆ (020) 7823 1234*
*– www.jumeirah.com* **37**AGX**h**
**87 rm** – 🛏£ 354 🛏🛏£ 636, ⊕ £ 30 – 14 suites
**Rest** *Mimosa* – Carte £ 25/44
♦ Compact yet friendly modern corporate hotel within this exclusive residential area. Good levels of personal service offered. Close to the famous shops of Knightsbridge. Modern restaurant opens onto street terrace.

**Marcus Wareing at The Berkeley** AC ⇄ VISA ⊕ AE
♧ ♧ *Wilton Pl. ⊠ SW1X 7RL ⊖ Knightsbridge – ✆ (020) 7235 1200*
*– www.marcus-wareing.com – Closed 1 January, Saturday lunch and Sunday*
**Rest** – French – Menu £ 38/98🍷 **37**AGX**e**
**Spec.** Layered foie gras with prune and Armagnac purée. Best end of lamb with pickled cucumber and pink peppercorn yoghurt. Warm chocolate moelleux with a salted caramel centre and banana ice cream.
♦ Marcus Wareing's cooking is creative, sophisticated and backed by sound classical techniques. The restaurant is sumptuously appointed; service is smooth and well-organised but has personality. The chef's table is one of the best in town.

XXXX **Apsleys** – at Lanesborough Hotel    🏧 ⇔ 🅿 VISA ☺ AE ⓪
£3    *Hyde Park Corner ⊠ SW1X 7TA ⊖ Hyde Park Corner – ℰ (020) 7333 7254*
     *– www.apsleysrestaurant.com*    37AGX**a**
     **Rest** – Italian – Menu £ 35 (lunch) – Carte £ 59/81
     **Spec.** Fish crudo. Carbonara fagotelli. Chocolate soufflé with vanilla and rasp-
     berry.
     ◆ Under the guidance of celebrated chef Heinz Beck from Rome's La Pergola. Ex-
     quisite and precise Italian cooking, in a grand, eye-catching but far from intimi-
     dating room, designed by Adam Tihany. The serving team are polished and the
     atmosphere reassuringly upbeat.

XXX **Pétrus**    🏧 ⇔ VISA ☺ AE
£3    *1 Kinnerton St ⊠ SW1X 8EA ⊖ Knightsbridge – ℰ (020) 7592 1609*
     *– www.gordonramsay.com/petrus – Closed 25 December and Sunday*
     **Rest** – Modern European – Menu £ 30/60 ⅌    37AGX**v**
     **Spec.** Langoustine tails with confit chicken leg, baby artichokes and buttered
     leeks. Best end of lamb with spring vegetables and a thyme jus. Chocolate sphere
     with milk ice cream and honeycomb.
     ◆ Elegant Gordon Ramsay restaurant, opened in 2010, in stylish tones of silver,
     oyster and – as a nod to the name – claret. Experienced team bring personality
     to the service. Elaborate French-based cooking uses top quality ingredients.

XXX **Amaya**    🏧 ⇔ VISA ☺ AE ⓪
£3    *Halkin Arcade, 19 Motcomb St ⊠ SW1X 8JT ⊖ Knightsbridge – ℰ (020)*
     *7823 1166 – www.realindianfood.com – Closed 25 December*    37AGX**k**
     **Rest** – Indian – Menu £ 29/42 – Carte £ 36/70
     **Spec.** Tarragon and turmeric chicken tikka. Duck grilled wtih tamarind glaze.
     Mango brûlée.
     ◆ Order a selection of small dishes from the tawa griddle, tandoor or sigri grill
     and finish with a curry or biryani. Dishes are aromatic and satisfying and the
     cooking skilled and consistent. A stylish, colourful restaurant.

XXX **Zafferano**    🏧 ⇔ VISA ☺ AE
£3    *15 Lowndes St ⊠ SW1X 9EY ⊖ Knightsbridge – ℰ (020) 7235 5800*
     *– www.zafferanorestaurant.co.uk*    37AGX**f**
     **Rest** – Italian – *(booking essential)* Menu £ 26/45 – Carte £ 36/52 ⅌
     **Spec.** Octopus salad with potatoes and olives. Rib of beef with bone marrow. Tir-
     amisu.
     ◆ Pasta is the star of the show at this perennially busy Italian restaurant. The
     cooking is reliable and assured and the menus balanced. The stylish surroundings
     are comfortable but also full of bustle; the bar is an appealing adjunct.

XXX **Koffmann's** – at Berkeley Hotel    🏧 VISA ☺ AE
     *Wilton Pl. ⊠ SW1X 7RL ⊖ Knightsbridge – ℰ (020) 7235 1010*
     *– www.the-berkeley.co.uk*    37AGX**u**
     **Rest** – French – Menu £ 26 (lunch) – Carte £ 51/73
     ◆ Pierre Koffmann, one of London's most fêted chefs, was enticed out of retire-
     ment to open this smart, comfortable and spacious restaurant. Expect plenty of
     gutsy flavours true to his Gascon roots.

XX **Nahm** – at Halkin Hotel    🏧 ⇔ VISA ☺ AE ⓪
     *5 Halkin St. ⊠ SW1X 7DJ ⊖ Hyde Park Corner – ℰ (020) 7333 1234*
     *– www.halkin.como.bz – Closed lunch Saturday and Sunday*    38AHX**b**
     **Rest** – Thai – *(booking advisable)* Menu £ 25/60 – Carte £ 45/60
     ◆ An appealing mix of copper tones, wood and candlelight, along with an under-
     stated hint of Asian design, gives the room a warm feel. The Thai cuisine served
     here is based on Royal Thai traditions.

XX **Noura Brasserie**    🏧 VISA ☺ AE ⓪
     *16 Hobart Pl. ⊠ SW1W 0HH ⊖ Victoria – ℰ (020) 7235 9444*
     *– www.noura.co.uk*    38AHX**n**
     **Rest** – Lebanese – Menu £ 18/45 – Carte £ 24/40
     ◆ Dine in either the bright bar or the comfortable, contemporary restaurant. Au-
     thentic, modern Lebanese cooking specialises in chargrilled meats and meze.

LONDON

🍺 **Pantechnicon**                                                              *VISA* ◎ AE
*10 Motcomb St* ⊠ *SW1X 8LA* ⊖ *Knightsbridge –* ℰ *(020) 7730 6074*
*– www.thepantechnicon.com – Closed 25 December-1 January*          37AGXd
**Rest** – Carte £ 32/46
♦ Urbane, enthusiastically run pub with a busy ground floor and altogether more
formal upstairs dining room. Traditional dishes are given a modern twist; oysters
and Scottish steaks are perennials.

## HYDE PARK AND KNIGHTSBRIDGE

🏨🏨🏨 **Mandarin Oriental Hyde Park**          ⇐ 🏮 🏯 £ẞ 🍴 ₺ 🖭 ᾗ ⑪ 🛁
*66 Knightsbridge* ⊠ *SW1X 7LA* ⊖ *Knightsbridge*                    *VISA* ◎ AE ⓪
*– ℰ (020) 7235 2000 – www.mandarinoriental.com/london*          37AGX⟩
**173 rm** – ♦£ 810 ♦♦£ 900, � £ 19.50 – 25 suites
**Rest** *Dinner by Heston Blumenthal*❀ **Rest** *Bar Boulud* – see restaurant
listing
♦ Built in 1889 this classic international hotel, with its striking façade, remains
one of London's grandest. Many of the luxurious bedrooms, which have a charming English country feel, enjoy views of Hyde Park. Standards of service are extremely high.

XXX **Dinner by Heston Blumenthal** – at Mandarin Oriental Hyde Park Hotel
❀ *66 Knightsbridge* ⊠ *SW1X 7LA* ⊖ *Knightsbridge*          🖭 ⇄ *VISA* ◎ AE ⓪
*– ℰ (020) 7201 3833 – www.dinnerbyheston.com – Closed Christmas*
**Rest** – British – Menu £ 28 (weekday lunch) – Carte £ 45/60🌢          37AGX⟩
**Spec.** Mandarin meat fruit. Spiced pigeon with ale and artichokes. Tipsy cake with
spit roast pineapple.
♦ Was the most eagerly anticipated restaurant opening in 2011. Expect no 'mo-
lecular' alchemy here; this is all about respect for, and an amazing renewal of
British food, with some occasional playfulness thrown in. Each meticulously
crafted dish comes with a date relating to its historical provenance.

XX **Zuma**                                                    🖭 *VISA* ◎ AE ⓪
*5 Raphael St* ⊠ *SW7 1DL* ⊖ *Knightsbridge –* ℰ *(020) 7584 1010*
*– www.zumarestaurant.com – Closed Christmas*                         37AFXm
**Rest** – Japanese – Carte £ 50/70
♦ Eye-catching design that blends East with West. Bustling atmosphere; fashionable clientele; popular sushi bar. Varied and interesting contemporary Japanese
food.

XX **Bar Boulud** – at Mandarin Oriental Hyde Park Hotel              🖭 🐗 ⇄
*66 Knightsbridge* ⊠ *SW1X 7LA* ⊖ *Knightsbridge*                    *VISA* ◎ AE ⓪
*– ℰ (020) 7201 3899 – www.barboulud.com*                          37AGX⟩
**Rest** – French – Menu £ 20 (lunch and early dinner) – Carte £ 25/48
♦ Daniel Boulud's London outpost is fashionable, fun and frantic. His hometown
is Lyon but he built his considerable reputation in New York, so charcuterie, sausages and burgers are the highlights.

XX **Mr Chow**                                                 🖭 *VISA* ◎ AE ⓪
*151 Knightsbridge* ⊠ *SW1X 7PA* ⊖ *Knightsbridge –* ℰ *(020) 7589 7347*
*– www.mrchow.com – Closed 1 January, 24-26 December, Easter Monday
dinner and Monday lunch*                                             37AFXe
**Rest** – Chinese – Carte £ 38/57
♦ Long-standing Chinese restaurant, opened in 1968. Smart clientele, stylish and
comfortable surroundings and prompt service from Italian waiters. Carefully prepared and satisfying food.

X **Chabrot**                                                  🖭 *VISA* ◎ AE
*9 Knightsbridge Grn* ⊠ *SW1X 7QL* ⊖ *Knightsbridge –* ℰ *(020) 7225 2238*
*– www.chabrot.co.uk*                                                37AFXv
**Rest** – French – Carte £ 23/39🌢
♦ In 2011 Thierry Laborde, formerly of Le Gavroche, got together with three
friends to open this fervently French and atmospheric bistro. The kitchen looks
to France's SW and Basque country for most of its influences.

LONDON

# MAYFAIR

## Dorchester
🏠🏠🏠🏠    🛎 ⅃ₒ 🖢 & 🅰🅲 ✗ ⑪ 🕍 ☎ VISA ⑳ 🅰🅴 ⓪

*Park Ln.* ⊠ *W1K 1QA* ⊖ *Hyde Park Corner –* ✆ *(020) 7629 8888*
*– www.thedorchester.com*
                                                      30AHV**a**
**196 rm** – ♦£ 378/798 ♦♦£ 510/798, ⬓ £ 31.50 – 54 suites
**Rest** *Alain Ducasse at The Dorchester*❀❀❀ **Rest** *China Tang* **Rest** *The Grill*
– see restaurant listing
• Luxury hotel on a grand scale offering every possible facility. Striking marbled and pillared promenade provides one of the best backdrops to afternoon tea. Impressive spa and bedrooms quintessentially English in style. Exemplary levels of service.

## Claridge's
🏠🏠🏠🏠    ⅃ₒ 🖢 & 🅰🅲 ✗ ⑪ 🕍 VISA ⑳ 🅰🅴 ⓪

*Brook St* ⊠ *W1K 4HR* ⊖ *Bond Street –* ✆ *(020) 7629 8860*
*– www.claridges.co.uk*
                                                      30AHU**c**
**143 rm** – ♦£ 792 ♦♦£ 792/936, ⬓ £ 31.50 – 60 suites
**Rest** *Gordon Ramsay at Claridge's* – see restaurant listing
• Rightly celebrated for its art deco and one of London's finest hotels. Exceptionally well-appointed and sumptuous bedrooms, all with butler service. Magnificent Foyer for afternoon tea.

## Four Seasons
🏠🏠🏠🏠    🛎 🕊 ⅃ₒ 🖢 & 🅰🅲 ✗ ⑪ 🕍 ☎ VISA ⑳ 🅰🅴

*Hamilton Pl, Park Ln* ⊠ *W1J 7DR* ⊖ *Hyde Park Corner –* ✆ *(020) 7499 0888*
*– www.fourseasons.com*
                                                      30AHV**v**
**148 rm** – ♦£ 690 ♦♦£ 714, ⬓ £ 30 – 45 suites
**Rest** *Amaranto* – see restaurant listing
• Reopened in 2011 after a huge refurbishment project and has raised the bar for luxury hotels. Striking lobby sets the scene; sumptuous bedrooms have a rich, contemporary look and boast every conceivable comfort. Great views from the stunning roof-top spa.

## Connaught
🏠🏠🏠🏠    🖥 🛎 ⅃ₒ 🖢 🅰🅲 ⑪ 🕍 VISA ⑳ 🅰🅴 ⓪

*Carlos Pl.* ⊠ *W1K 2AL* ⊖ *Bond Street –* ✆ *(020) 7499 7070*
*– www.the-connaught.co.uk*
                                                      30AHU**e**
**95 rm** – ♦£ 660 ♦♦£ 780/1104, ⬓ £ 30 – 26 suites
**Rest** *Hélène Darroze at The Connaught*❀❀ – see restaurant listing
**Rest** *Espelette* – ✆ *(020) 3147 7100* – Carte £ 46/84
• One of London's most famous hotels; restored and renovated but still retaining an elegant British feel. All the luxurious bedrooms come with large marble bathrooms and butler service. There's a choice of two stylish bars and Espelette is an all-day venue for classic French and British dishes.

## InterContinental
🏠🏠🏠🏠    ≤ 🛎 🕊 ⅃ₒ 🖢 & 🅰🅲 ✗ ⑪ 🕍 ☎ VISA ⑳ 🅰🅴 ⓪

*1 Hamilton Pl, Park Ln.* ⊠ *W1J 7QY* ⊖ *Hyde Park Corner –* ✆ *(020) 7409 3131*
*– www.london.intercontinental.com*
                                                      30AHV**k**
**399 rm** – ♦£ 287 ♦♦£ 671, ⬓ £ 28 – 48 suites
**Rest** *Theo Randall* **Rest** *Cookbook Café* – see restaurant listing
• International hotel whose position facing the park is an impressive feature. Everything leads off from the large, open-plan lobby. English-style bedrooms with hi-tech equipment; luxurious suites.

## London Hilton
🏠🏠🏠🏠    ≤ 🕊 ⅃ₒ 🖢 & rm, 🅰🅲 ✗ 🕊 🕍 VISA ⑳ 🅰🅴 ⓪

*22 Park Ln.* ⊠ *W1K 1BE* ⊖ *Hyde Park Corner –* ✆ *(020) 7493 8000*
*– www.hilton.co.uk/londonparklane*
                                                      30AHV**e**
**397 rm** – ♦£ 246/449 ♦♦£ 252/660, ⬓ £ 26.50 – 56 suites
**Rest** *Galvin at Windows*❀ – see restaurant listing
**Rest** *Podium* – ✆ *(020) 7208 4022* – Menu £ 23 – Carte £ 28/53
• This 28 storey tower may not be the city's most handsome building but it is certainly one of its tallest hotels, providing impressive views from the upper floors. On-going refurbishment; Club floor bedrooms are particularly comfortable.

**🏨🏨🏨 Grosvenor House**   ⬚ 🛗 🖗 🅰🄲 ♺ 🕻 🚲 🚗 🆅🅸🆂🅰 💳 🄰🄴

*Park Ln* ⊠ *W1K 7TN* ⊖ *Marble Arch* – ☏ *(020) 7499 6363*
– *www.londongrosvenorhouse.co.uk*                                        **29**AGUg
**442 rm** – 🛏£ 263 🛏🛏£ 395, ⬚ £ 29 – 52 suites
**Rest** *JW Steakhouse* – see restaurant listing
♦ A large, landmark property occupying a commanding position by Hyde Park
Uniform, comfortable but well proportioned bedrooms in classic Marriott styling
Busy banqueting department boasts the largest ballroom in Europe.

**🏨🏨🏨 Westbury**   🛗 🖗 🛗 rm, 🅰🄲 ♺ 🕻 🚲 🆅🅸🆂🅰 💳 🄰🄴

*Bond St* ⊠ *W1S 2YF* ⊖ *Bond Street* – ☏ *(020) 7629 7755*
– *www.westburymayfair.com*                                            **30**AIUa
**233 rm** ⬚ – 🛏£ 239/469 🛏🛏£ 239/469 – 13 suites
**Rest** *Gallery* – Italian influences – Menu £ 23 – Carte £ 27/33
**Rest** *Tsukiji* – Japanese (Sushi) – *(booking advisable)* Menu £ 25
– Carte £ 25/32
♦ Caused a commotion with its New York styling when it opened in the 1950s
Designer brands all outside; inside you'll find smart, comfortable bedrooms with art
deco inspired suites. Elegant, well-known Polo bar and a bright, fresh sushi bar.

**🏨🏨🏨 Brown's**   🛗 🖗 🛗 🅰🄲 🖐 🚲 🆅🅸🆂🅰 💳 🄰🄴 🄾

*Albemarle St* ⊠ *W1S 4BP* ⊖ *Green Park* – ☏ *(020) 7493 6020*
– *www.roccofortehotels.com*                                           **30**AIVd
**105 rm** – 🛏£ 264/582 🛏🛏£ 354/858, ⬚ £ 29.50 – 12 suites
**Rest** *HIX at The Albemarle* – see restaurant listing
♦ Opened in 1837 by James Brown, Lord Byron's butler. This urbane and very
British hotel with an illustrious past offers a swish bar with Terence Donovan
prints, bedrooms in neutral hues and a classic English sitting room for afternoon tea.

**🏨🏨🏨 London Marriott H. Park Lane**   📺 🛗 🖗 🛗 rm, 🅰🄲 ♺ 🖐 🚗 🆅🅸🆂🅰 💳 🄰🄴

*140 Park Ln* ⊠ *W1K 7AA* ⊖ *Marble Arch*                                🆅🅸🆂🅰 💳 🄰🄴
– ☏ *(020) 7493 7000* – *www.londonmarriott.parklane.co*                **29**AGUb
**144 rm** – 🛏£ 443 🛏🛏£ 515, ⬚ £ 25 – 9 suites
**Rest** *140 Park Lane* – Menu £ 20 – Carte £ 26/72
♦ Usefully located international hotel, close to the park and shops of Oxford
Street. Basement health club has Park Lane's only pool. Smart, generously sized
bedrooms are well-equipped; the attractive restaurant overlooks Marble Arch.

**🏨🏨 Metropolitan**   ⬅ 🍸 🛗 🛗 🅰🄲 ♺ 🖐 🚗 🆅🅸🆂🅰 💳 🄰🄴 🄾

*Old Park Ln* ⊠ *W1K 1LB* ⊖ *Hyde Park Corner* – ☏ *(020) 7447 1000*
– *www.metropolitan.como.bz*                                           **30**AHVc
**147 rm** – 🛏£ 251/468 🛏🛏£ 287/504, ⬚ £ 28 – 3 suites
**Rest** *Nobu*✿ – see restaurant listing
♦ Minimalist interior and a voguish reputation have made this hotel and its Met
Bar the favoured choice of pop stars and celebrities. Sleek design and fashionably
attired staff set it apart.

**🏨🏨 Athenaeum**   🎬 🛗 🛗 🅰🄲 🖐 🚲 🆅🅸🆂🅰 💳 🄰🄴 🄾

*116 Piccadilly* ⊠ *W1J 7BJ* ⊖ *Hyde Park Corner* – ☏ *(020) 7499 3464*
– *www.athenaeumhotel.com*                                             **30**AHVg
**153 rm** – 🛏£ 240 🛏🛏£ 720, ⬚ £ 27.50 – 11 suites
**Rest** *Restaurant* – Menu £ 19/28 – Carte £ 42/62
♦ Refurbished 1920s building opposite the park; its stylish bedrooms come in
cool pastel shades and have floor to ceiling windows. Bright restaurant and a
bar offering over 270 different whiskies. The hotel also organises events for kids.

**🏨🏨 Chesterfield**   🛗 🛗 rm, 🅰🄲 🖐 🚲 🆅🅸🆂🅰 💳 🄰🄴 🄾

*35 Charles St* ⊠ *W1J 5EB* ⊖ *Green Park* – ☏ *(020) 7491 2622*
– *www.chesterfieldmayfair.com*                                        **30**AHVf
**103 rm** – 🛏£ 263/450 🛏🛏£ 263/450, ⬚ £ 22.50 – 4 suites
**Rest** – Menu £ 23 (lunch) – Carte £ 32/57
♦ An assuredly English feel to this Georgian house. Discreet lobby leads to a
clubby bar and wood panelled library. Individually decorated bedrooms, with
some antique pieces. Intimate and pretty restaurant.

LONDON

## London Marriott H. Grosvenor Square

*Grosvenor Sq.* ⊠ *W1K 6JP* ⊖ *Bond Street*
– ℰ *(020) 7493 1232 – www.marriottgrosvenorsquare.com*
**226 rm** – ♦£ 251 ♦♦£ 491, ⌑ £ 24 – 11 suites
**Rest** *Maze Grill* – see restaurant listing
♦ A well-appointed international group hotel that benefits from an excellent location in the heart of Mayfair. Many of the bedrooms specifically equipped for the business traveller.

30AHUs

## Hilton London Green Park

*Half Moon St* ⊠ *W1J 7BN* ⊖ *Green Park* – ℰ *(020) 7629 7522*
– *www.hilton.co.uk/greenpark*
**162 rm** – ♦£ 191/407 ♦♦£ 203/599, ⌑ £ 20.95
**Rest** – *(bar lunch Saturday and Sunday)* Carte £ 28/37
♦ A row of sympathetically adjoined townhouses in the heart of Mayfair, dating from the 1730s. Bedrooms vary in size and shape; those on the first and fifth floors have been refurbished in a bright, contemporary style. Modern menu served in airy restaurant.

30AIVa

## Alain Ducasse at The Dorchester

*Park Ln.* ⊠ *W1K 1QA* ⊖ *Hyde Park Corner* – ℰ *(020) 7629 8866*
– *www.alainducasse-dorchester.com – Closed Easter, 13 August-4 September,
1-10 January, 26-31 December, dinner 25 December, Saturday lunch, Sunday
and Monday*
**Rest** – French – Menu £ 50/78
**Spec.** Sauté of lobster, truffled chicken quenelles and homemade pasta. Fillet of beef Rossini with 'sacristain' potatoes. 'Baba like in Monte-Carlo'.
♦ Luxury and extravagance are the hallmarks of Alain Ducasse's London outpost. The dining room is elegant without being staid; food is modern and refined yet satisfying and balanced. Service is formal, thoughtful and well-organised.

30AHVa

## Hélène Darroze at The Connaught

*Carlos Pl.* ⊠ *W1K 2AL* ⊖ *Bond Street* – ℰ *(020) 3147 7200*
– *www.the-connaught.co.uk – Closed 2 weeks August, 2-9 January, Sunday and
Monday*
**Rest** – French – *(booking essential)* Menu £ 35/80
**Spec.** Line-caught calamari, ravioli with confit tomatoes. Black pork from Pays Basque, pan-roasted chop larded with black truffle. Manjari chocolate mousse and cumin ice cream.
♦ Landes and the SW of France inform Hélène Darroze's exquisite cooking, although international influences also play a part. The dining room is elegant and comfortable, with original mahogany wood panelling. Service is courteous and professional.

30AHUe

## Le Gavroche (Michel Roux Jnr)

*43 Upper Brook St.* ⊠ *W1K 7QR* ⊖ *Marble Arch* – ℰ *(020) 7408 0881*
– *www.le-gavroche.co.uk – Closed Christmas-New Year, Saturday lunch, Sunday
and bank holidays*
**Rest** – French – *(booking essential)* Menu £ 52 (lunch) – Carte £ 60/128
**Spec.** Soufflé Suissesse. Râble de lapin et galette au parmesan. Palet au chocolat amer et praliné croustillant.
♦ Classical, rich and indulgent French cuisine is the draw at Michel Roux's renowned London institution. The large, smart basement room has a clubby, masculine feel; service is formal and structured but also has charm.

29AGUc

Prices quoted after the symbol ♦ refer to the lowest rate in low season
followed by the highest rate in high season, for a single room.
The same principle applies to the symbol ♦♦ for a double room.

LONDON

**LONDON**

### XXXX  Square (Philip Howard)   [AC] [⟷] [VISA] [MO] [AE]

6-10 Bruton St. ⊠ W1J 6PU ⊖ Green Park – ℰ (020) 7495 7100
– www.squarerestaurant.com – Closed 25 December, 1 January and lunch
Saturday, Sunday and bank holidays                                **30**AIU
**Rest** – French – Menu £ 35/80⊞

**Spec.** Langoustine with parmesan gnocchi and truffle. Loin of lamb, crushe
broad beans, broccoli and mint. Brillat-Savarin cheesecake with pink grapefru
and champagne.
◆ Confident and accomplished kitchen which understands the importance
sound techniques, prime ingredients and clarity of flavour. The room is comfor
able and the buoyant atmosphere prevents things becoming too formal. Goc
cheeseboard.

### XXXX  Sketch (The Lecture Room & Library)   [AC] [VISA] [MO] [AE]

9 Conduit St (1st floor) ⊠ W1S 2XG ⊖ Oxford Street – ℰ (020) 7659 4500
– www.sketch.uk.com – Closed last 2 weeks August, Saturday lunch, Sunday ar
Monday                                                             **30**AIU
**Rest** – French – (booking essential) Menu £ 35 (lunch) – Carte £ 70/129⊞
**Spec.** Scallop, morel and braised veal sweetbreads 'osso buco'. Quercy lamb sac
dle, rack and sweetbreads. Pierre Gagnaire's 'grand dessert'.
◆ Pierre Gagnaire's London operation is within a striking 18C townhouse which
full of colour, energy and vitality. The sophisticated French cooking is ambitiou
and elaborate in conception and execution; dishes arrive artfully presented.

### XXXX  Galvin at Windows – at London Hilton Hotel   [⩽] [AC] [VISA] [MO] [AE] [O]

22 Park Ln (28th floor) ⊠ W1K 1BE ⊖ Hyde Park Corner – ℰ (020) 7208 402
– www.galvinatwindows.com – Closed Saturday lunch, Sunday dinner and ban
holiday Mondays                                                    **30**AHV
**Rest** – French – Menu £ 29/65
**Spec.** Cured salmon, Cornish crab, avocado cream and fennel. Rack, shoulder an
lamb's kidney with anchovy, capers and aubergine. Apple tarte Tatin, vanilla ic
cream and caramel sauce.
◆ Spectacular views from the 28th floor of the Hilton are not the only draw. Th
room is contemporary and cleverly laid out; service is attentive and efficient; cool
ing is confident and detailed and dishes balanced and satisfying.

### XXXX  China Tang – at Dorchester Hotel   [AC] [⟷] [VISA] [MO] [AE] [O]

Park Ln ⊠ W1A 2HJ ⊖ Hyde Park Corner – ℰ (020) 7629 9988
– www.thedorchester.com – Closed 25 December                       **30**AHV
**Rest** – Chinese – Menu £ 15 (lunch) – Carte £ 40/70
◆ Sir David Tang's atmospheric, art deco-inspired Chinese restaurant, downstai
at The Dorchester, is always abuzz with activity. Be sure to see the terrific bar, be
fore sharing the traditional Cantonese specialities.

### XXXX  Gordon Ramsay at Claridge's   [AC] [VISA] [MO] [AE] [O]

Brook St. ⊠ W1K 4HR ⊖ Bond Street – ℰ (020) 7499 0099
– www.gordonramsay.com/claridges                                   **30**AHU
**Rest** – Modern European – (booking essential) Menu £ 30/70⊞
◆ Grand and impressive room within the elegant surroundings of Claridge's h
tel. Service is structured and ceremonial; the cooking is classically based, wit
modern touches. Popular chef's table in the kitchen.

### XXX  Cecconi's   [⌂] [AC] [VISA] [MO] [AE] [O]

5a Burlington Gdns ⊠ W1S 3EP ⊖ Green Park – ℰ (020) 7434 1500
– www.cecconis.com                                                 **30**AIU
**Rest** – Italian – (booking essential) Carte £ 30/44
◆ Branches of this fashionable restaurant are now opening up around the worl
Regulars pop in for a bite at the bar; the restaurant prepares the classic dishe
with care. Open from breakfast onwards; popular for weekend brunches.

XXX **Hibiscus** (Claude Bosi)                    AC ⇄ VISA ◐◐ AE
£3 £3  *29 Maddox St* ⊠ *W1S 2PA* ⊖ *Oxford Circus* – 𝒞 *(020) 7629 2999*
– *www.hibiscusrestaurant.co.uk – Closed 23 December-3 January, Monday lunch,*
*Sunday and bank holidays*                                **30**AIU**s**
**Rest** – Innovative – Menu £ 34/80
**Spec.** Ravioli of spring onion and lime, broad bean and mint purée. Smoked and roasted chicken, onion fondue and liquorice. Chocolate tart with basil ice cream.
♦ The genial Claude Bosi is a 'chef's chef' who brings his own style to the cooking at Hibiscus. That means elaborately constructed dishes with some deft and original touches. The oak walls and formal service create a somewhat sombre feel.

XXX **Benares** (Atul Kochhar)                    AC ⇄ VISA ◐◐ AE ◑
£3  *12a Berkeley Square House* ⊠ *W1J 6BS* ⊖ *Green Park*
– 𝒞 *(020) 7629 8886 – www.benaresrestaurant.com*
– *Closed 25- 26 December and 1 January*                  **30**AIU**q**
**Rest** – Indian – Menu £ 30 (lunch) – Carte £ 55/95
**Spec.** Fennel lamb chop, mustard chicken tikka and king prawn platter. Roasted fillet of roe deer, venison biryani and sesame peanut sauce. Lime mousse, lemon thyme jelly and basil sorbet.
♦ Modern techniques are used to add contemporary touches to the classical base; the inventive Indian food here continues to evolve. The smart first-floor surroundings match the food in their sophistication. Popular and smart Chef's Table.

XXX **Murano** (Angela Hartnett)                    AC VISA ◐◐ AE
£3  *20 Queen St* ⊠ *W1J 5PP* ⊖ *Green Park* – 𝒞 *(020) 7495 1127*
– *www.angela-hartnett.com – Closed Christmas and Sunday*      **30**AHV**b**
**Rest** – Italian influences – Menu £ 30/65
**Spec.** Pumpkin tortellini with sage emulsion. Canon of lamb with courgettes and black olives. Apricot soufflé with biscotti.
♦ Now wholly owned by chef Angela Hartnett, this bright and stylishly decorated restaurant provides a luminous setting for her refined and balanced cooking. The Italian influences are particularly pronounced on the tasting menus.

XXX **Greenhouse**                    AC ⇄ VISA ◐◐ AE ◑
£3  *27a Hay's Mews* ⊠ *W1J 5NY* ⊖ *Hyde Park Corner*
– 𝒞 *(020) 7499 3331 – www.greenhouserestaurant.co.uk*
– *Closed Saturday lunch, Sunday and bank holidays*          **30**AHV**m**
**Rest** – Innovative – Menu £ 29/75🕮
**Spec.** Calves sweetbreads with black garlic and glazed cabbage. Roasted Anjou pigeon breast, pomegranate, turnip purée and a giblet and pancetta jus. "Snix" - chocolate, salted caramel and peanuts.
♦ Discreet and charming mews location for this smart and elegant restaurant. An extensive choice of elaborately presented dishes display plenty of inventive touches but are also underpinned with sound French culinary techniques.

XXX **Umu**                    AC VISA ◐◐ AE
£3  *14-16 Bruton Pl.* ⊠ *W1J 6LX* ⊖ *Bond Street*
– 𝒞 *(020) 7499 8881 – www.umurestaurant.com*
– *Closed Saturday lunch, Sunday and bank holidays*          **30**AIU**k**
**Rest** – Japanese – Menu £ 26 (lunch) – Carte £ 35/151🕮
**Spec.** Tuna tartare salad, Japanese pickles. Wild Scottish lobster, seven pepper shichimi. Japanese tiramisu with macha tea and sake.
♦ Stylish, discreet interior using natural materials, with central sushi bar. Extensive choice of Japanese dishes; choose one of the seasonal kaiseki menus for the full experience. Over 160 different labels of sake.

LONDON

### XXX  Tamarind
⊗

20 Queen St. ⊠ W1J 5PR ⊖ Green Park – ℰ (020) 7629 3561
– www.tamarindrestaurant.com – Closed 25-26 December, 1 January
and Saturday lunch                                                    30AHV

**Rest** – Indian – Menu £ 20/56 – Carte £ 45/68

**Spec.** Grilled scallops, oven roasted peppers and tomato chutney. Fillet of sea
bass, mango and curry leaf sauce. Tandoor grilled pineapple, rose petal ice cream

♦ Makes the best use of its basement location through smoked mirrors, gilded
columns and a somewhat exclusive feel. The appealing and enjoyable Indian
food is mostly traditionally based; kebabs and curries are the specialities, complemented by carefully judged vegetable dishes.

### XXX  Kai
⊗

65 South Audley St. ⊠ W1K 2QU ⊖ Hyde Park Corner – ℰ (020) 7493 8988
– www.kaimayfair.co.uk – Closed 25-26 December and 1 January        30AHVr

**Rest** – Chinese – (booking essential) Menu £ 27 (lunch) – Carte £ 36/84 ✿

**Spec.** Honey-roasted Duke of Berkshire char siew pork. Sea bass with chickpeas,
shallots and ginger. Rice dumplings with honey ice ceam.

♦ Carefully prepared Chinese food, from a menu that mixes the classics with
more innovative dishes; flavours are authentic and assured. Its smart surroundings are spread over two floors - ask for the ground floor; sweet natured service.

### XXX  The Grill – at Dorchester Hotel

Park Ln. ⊠ W1K 1QA ⊖ Hyde Park Corner – ℰ (020) 7629 8888
– www.thedorchester.com                                              30AHVa

**Rest** – British – Menu £ 27 (weekday lunch) – Carte £ 47/75

♦ A bastion of Britishness, where timeless classics are served alongside more
modern creations. The extravagantly kitted out room, bedecked in acres of tar-
tans, is even more memorable.

### XXX  Theo Randall – at Intercontinental Hotel

1 Hamilton Pl, Park Ln. ⊠ W1J 7QY ⊖ Hyde Park Corner – ℰ (020) 7318 8747
– www.theorandall.com – Closed 25-26 December, 1 January, Saturday lunch,
Sunday and bank holidays                                             30AHVk

**Rest** – Italian – Menu £ 29 (lunch) – Carte £ 50/74

♦ Daily changing seasonal menu of comforting Italian dishes, served in the smart
and spacious surroundings of an international hotel. Wood oven a feature; produce imported directly from Italy.

### XXX  HIX at The Albemarle – at Brown's Hotel

Albemarle St ⊠ W1S 4BP ⊖ Green Park – ℰ (020) 7518 4004
– www.roccofortecollection.com                                       30AIVd

**Rest** – British – Menu £ 33 (lunch and early dinner) – Carte £ 29/67

♦ This wood-panelled dining room is lightened with the work of current British
artists. Mark Hix's well-sourced menu of British classics will appeal to the hunter-
gatherer in every man.

### XXX  Amaranto – at Four Seasons Hotel

Hamilton Pl, Park Ln ⊠ W1J 7DR ⊖ Hyde Park Corner – ℰ (020) 7499 0888
– www.fourseasons.com                                                30AHVv

**Rest** – Italian – Menu £ 26 (lunch) – Carte £ 31/51

♦ It's all about flexibility as the Italian influenced menu is served in the stylish bar
or comfortable lounge, on the great terrace or in the restaurant decorated in the
vivid colours of the amaranth plant.

### XXX  Scott's

20 Mount St ⊠ W1K 2HE ⊖ Bond Street – ℰ (020) 7495 7309
– www.scotts-restaurant.com – Closed 25-26 December               30AHUd

**Rest** – Seafood – Carte £ 36/56

♦ Stylish yet traditional and one of London's most fashionable addresses, so getting a table can be tricky. Oak panelling is juxtaposed with vibrant artwork from
young British artists. Enticing choice of top quality fish and shellfish.

XXX **Corrigan's Mayfair**　　　　　　　　　AK ✧ VISA ●● AE

28 Upper Grosvenor St. ⊠ W1K 7EH ⊖ Marble Arch – ✆ (020) 7499 9943
– www.corrigansmayfair.com – Closed 25-26 December, 1 January and Saturday
lunch　　　　　　　　　　　　　　　　　　　　　　　　　**29AGUa**
**Rest** – British – Menu £ 27 (lunch) – Carte £ 39/88
♦ Richard Corrigan's flagship celebrates British and Irish cooking, with game a
speciality. The room is comfortable, clubby and quite glamorous and feels as
though it has been around for years.

XXX **Bentley's (Grill)**　　　　　　　　　　AK ✧ VISA ●● AE

11-15 Swallow St. ⊠ W1B 4DG ⊖ Piccadilly Circus – ✆ (020) 7734 4756
– www.bentleys.org – Closed 25-26 December and 1 January　　　**30AJUc**
**Rest** – British – Carte £ 47/60
♦ Entrance into striking bar; panelled staircase to richly decorated restaurant.
Carefully sourced seafood or meat dishes enhanced by clean, crisp cooking. Un-
ruffled service.

XXX **Sartoria**　　　　　　　　　　　AK ✍ ✧ VISA ●● AE

20 Savile Row ⊠ W1S 3PR ⊖ Green Park – ✆ (020) 7534 7000
– www.sartoriabar.com – Closed 25 December, Saturday lunch, Sunday and
bank holidays　　　　　　　　　　　　　　　　　　　　**30AIUb**
**Rest** – Italian – Menu £ 25 – Carte £ 30/53
♦ In the street renowned for English tailoring, a coolly sophisticated and stylish
restaurant to suit those looking for classic Italian cooking with some modern
touches thrown in. It also comes with confident service.

XXX **Avista**　　　　　　　　　AK ✍ ✧ VISA ●● AE ①

Millennium Mayfair Hotel, 39 Grosvenor Sq ⊠ W1K 2HP ⊖ Bond Street
– ✆ (020) 7596 3399 – www.avistarestaurant.com – Closed Saturday lunch and
Sunday　　　　　　　　　　　　　　　　　　　　　　**30AHUx**
**Rest** – Italian – Menu £ 26 (lunch) – Carte £ 30/66
♦ A large room, softened by neutral shades, within the Millennium Hotel. The
menu traverses Italy and the cooking marries the rustic with the more refined.
Pasta dishes are a highlight.

XX **Wild Honey**　　　　　　　　　AK ✍ VISA ●● AE
⊛
12 St George St. ⊠ W1S 2FB ⊖ Oxford Circus – ✆ (020) 7758 9160
– www.wildhoneyrestaurant.co.uk – Closed 25-26 December and 1 January
**Rest** – Modern European – Menu £ 19 (weekday lunch)　　　**30AIUw**
– Carte £ 29/39
**Spec.** Belly pork with snails and onion purée. Short rib of Wagyu beef and a bone
marrow gratin. Vanilla cheesecake scented with rosewater.
♦ Skilled kitchen uses seasonal ingredients at their peak to create dishes full
of flavour and free from ostentation. Attractive oak-panelled room; ask for
one of the booths. Personable and unobtrusive service adds to the relaxed
feel.

XX **Semplice** (Marco Torri)　　　　　　AK ✧ VISA ●● AE
⊛
9-10 Blenheim St ⊠ W1S 1LJ ⊖ Bond Street – ✆ (020) 7495 1509
– www.ristorantesemplice.com – Closed 2 weeks Christmas, Easter, Saturday
lunch, Sunday and bank holidays　　　　　　　　　　　　**30AHUk**
**Rest** – Italian – (booking essential at dinner) Menu £ 30 (lunch)
– Carte £ 40/51 ⅏
**Spec.** Fassone beef carpaccio. Milk-fed Piedmontese veal with courgettes, sweet
potato sauce. Tiramisu with tiramisu ice cream.
♦ Plenty of regulars are always in evidence in this comfortable and stylish restaurant, decorated with ebony, leather and gold. The enthusiasm of the young
owners is palpable; the kitchen uses small, specialist suppliers in unfussy, flavoursome dishes.

LONDON

LONDON

XX   **Hakkasan Mayfair**                                          AC VISA ◎◎ AE
♔    *17 Bruton St ⊠ W1J 6QB ⊖ Green Park – ℰ (020) 7907 1888*
     *– www.hakkasan.com – Closed 25 December*                        **30**AIU
     **Rest** – Chinese – *(booking essential)* Carte £ 50/100 **s**
     **Spec.** Salt and pepper squid. Stir-fried black pepper rib-eye of beef with Merlot
     Chocolate soufflé with vanilla ice cream and raspberry sauce.
     ● Less a copy, more a sister to the original; a sister who's just as fun but lives in
     nicer part of town. This one has a funky, more casual ground floor to go with the
     downstairs dining room. You can expect the same extensive choice of top quality
     modern Cantonese cuisine; dim sum is a highlight.

XX   **Nobu Berkeley St**                                          AC VISA ◎◎ AE
♔    *15 Berkeley St. ⊠ W1J 8DY ⊖ Green Park – ℰ (020) 7290 9222*
     *– www.noburestaurants.com/berkeley – Closed 25-26 December, Saturday
     and Sunday lunch and bank holiday Mondays*                       **30**AIVE
     **Rest** – Japanese – *(booking essential)* Menu £ 32/90
     **Spec.** King crab claw tempura with butter ponzu. Black cod with miso. Chocolate
     tart with sake kasu ice cream and chocolate sauce.
     ● Offers all the innovative Nobu favourites, along with specialities from the wood
     oven. Large, lively but smoothly run first floor operation with plenty of glamour
     ground floor destination bar. Helpful, well-informed service.

XX   **Bellamy's**                                                 AC VISA ◎◎ AE
     *18 Bruton Pl. ⊠ W1J 6LY ⊖ Bond Street – ℰ (020) 7491 2727*
     *– www.bellamysrestaurant.co.uk – Closed Saturday lunch, Sunday and bank
     holidays*                                                        **30**AIUc
     **Rest** – French – Menu £ 29 – Carte £ 38/54
     ● French deli/brasserie tucked down a smart mews. Go past the caviar and
     cheeses into the restaurant proper for a very traditional, but well-executed, range
     of Gallic classics.

XX   **5 Pollen St**                                               AC VISA ◎◎ AE ◑
     *5 Pollen St ⊠ W1S 1NE ⊖ Oxford Circus – ℰ (020) 7629 1555*
     *– www.5pollenst.com – Closed Sunday*                            **30**AIUz
     **Rest** – Italian – *(booking advisable)* Menu £ 36 (lunch) – Carte dinner £ 50/60
     ● Geared unashamedly to the glamorous Mayfair set untroubled by concepts
     such as value for money. Worth going for the Gary Hume artwork and wallpaper
     alone. Large menu features quality produce and covers all bases.

XX   **Nobu** – at Metropolitan Hotel                       ← AC ⇔ VISA ◎◎ AE ◑
♔    *19 Old Park Ln ⊠ W1Y 1LB ⊖ Hyde Park Corner – ℰ (020) 7447 4747*
     *– www.noburestaurants.com – Closed 25-26 December*              **30**AHVc
     **Rest** – Japanese – *(booking essential)* Menu £ 60/95 – Carte £ 37/68
     **Spec.** Yellowtail jalapeño. Black cod with miso. Chocolate bento box with green
     tea ice cream.
     ● Its celebrity clientele ensure this remains one of London's more glamorous
     spots. Staff are fully conversant in the innovative menu that adds South Ameri-
     can influences to Japanese cooking. Has spawned many imitators around the
     world.

XX   **Maze**                                                AC ⇔ VISA ◎◎ AE ◑
♔    *10-13 Grosvenor Sq ⊠ W1K 6JP ⊖ Bond Street – ℰ (020) 7107 0000*
     *– www.gordonramsay.com*                                         **30**AHUz
     **Rest** – Innovative – Menu £ 25 (lunch) – Carte £ 29/46🏠
     **Spec.** Jasmine and miso cured salmon, ponzu dressing. Devon duck breast, beet-
     root and preserved lemon. Pistachio parfait, cherry sorbet.
     ● Choose a variety of small but expertly formed dishes at this sleek and stylish Da-
     vid Rockwell designed restaurant from the Gordon Ramsay stable. The cooking is
     contemporary and nicely balanced; four dishes per person should suffice.

## ✗✗ Pollen Street Social (Jason Atherton)    🆎 ⇄ VISA ⓒⓑ 🅰🅴
€3
*8-10 Pollen St* ✉ *W1S 1NQ* ⊖ *Oxford Circus* – ℰ *(020) 7290 7606*
*– www.pollenstreetsocial.com – Closed Sunday and bank holidays* **30**AIU**u**
**Rest** – Innovative – *(booking essential)* Menu £ 25 (lunch) – Carte £ 38/55
**Spec.** 'Full English breakfast'. Roasted Dingley Dell pork, beetroot, hops, seeds and
grains. Peanut butter parfait, cherry jam and creamed rice puffs.
♦ Jason Atherton's cooking continues the style he displayed when at Maze; his
restaurant is all about informality and flexibility. His food is exciting, innovative,
delicate in looks but assured in flavour; it is also imaginative and playful.

## ✗✗ Maze Grill – at London Marriott H. Grosvenor Square    🆎 VISA ⓒⓑ 🅰🅴 ⓪
*10-13 Grosvenor Sq.* ✉ *W1K 6JP* ⊖ *Bond Street* – ℰ *(020) 7495 2211*
*– www.gordonramsay.com* **30**AHU**s**
**Rest** – Beef specialities – Menu £ 24 (lunch and early dinner) – Carte £ 27/52
♦ An addendum to Maze, with a menu specialising in steaks, from Hereford
grass-fed to Wagyu 9th grade; all appealingly served on wooden boards, with a
variety of sauces and side dishes.

## ✗✗ Patterson's    🆎 ⇄ VISA ⓒⓑ 🅰🅴 ⓪
*4 Mill St* ✉ *W1S 2AX* ⊖ *Oxford Street* – ℰ *(020) 7499 1308*
*– www.pattersonsrestaurant.com – Closed 25-26 December and Sunday*
**Rest** – Modern European – Menu £ 25/47 – Carte £ 47/55 **30**AIU**p**
♦ Stylish modern interior in black and white. Elegant tables and attentive service.
Modern British cooking with concise wine list and sensible prices.

## ✗✗ Quince    🆎 ⇄ VISA ⓒⓑ 🅰🅴 ⓪
*Stratton St* ✉ *W1J 8LT* ⊖ *Green Park* – ℰ *(020) 7915 3892*
*– www.quincelondon.com – Closed Saturday and Sunday lunch* **30**AIV**s**
**Rest** – Turkish – Menu £ 24 (lunch) – Carte £ 37/53
♦ TV chef Silvena Rowe presents her inimitable Eastern Mediterranean cooking.
Her personality is evident throughout, from personal references on the menu
– "a homage to my grandfather Mehmed" – to the colourful, Ottoman-influenced
decoration.

## ✗✗ Alloro    🆎 ⇄ VISA ⓒⓑ 🅰🅴
*19-20 Dover St* ✉ *W1S 4LU* ⊖ *Green Park* – ℰ *(020) 7495 4768*
*– www.atozrestaurants.com/alloro – Closed 25 December, Saturday lunch and*
*Sunday* **30**AIV**r**
**Rest** – Italian – *(booking essential)* Menu £ 35/39
♦ Confidently run and smartly dressed Italian with an appealing menu of easy-to-
eat dishes; breads and pasta are made in-house. Great atmosphere, especially at
busy lunchtimes. Boisterous adjacent baretto.

## ✗✗ Goodman    🆎 VISA ⓒⓑ 🅰🅴
*26 Maddox St.* ✉ *W1S 1QH* ⊖ *Oxford Circus* – ℰ *(020) 7499 3776*
*– www.goodmanrestaurants.com – Closed Sunday and bank holidays*
**Rest** – Beef specialities – *(booking essential)* Menu £ 20 (lunch) **30**AIU**u**
– Carte £ 42/54
♦ A worthy attempt at recreating a New York steakhouse; all leather and wood
and macho swagger. Beef is dry or wet aged in-house and comes with a choice
of four sauces; rib-eye the speciality.

## ✗✗ Dolada    🆎 ⇄ VISA ⓒⓑ 🅰🅴
*13 Albemarle St.* ✉ *W1S 4HJ* ⊖ *Green Park* – ℰ *(020) 7409 1011*
*– www.dolada.co – Closed 24- December-4 January, Saturday lunch, Sunday and*
*bank holidays* **30**AIV**x**
**Rest** – Italian – Menu £ 30/35 – Carte £ 30/39
♦ Elegant and immaculately kept basement restaurant lightened by confident
and thoughtful service. Expect cooking from across Italy; the deconstructed spa-
ghetti carbonara is a speciality.

LONDON

**LONDON**

XX **Hush** 🛱 🗚 ⇔ 💳 ◑ 🗛 ◉
*8 Lancashire Ct., Brook St.* ⊠ *W1S 1EY* ⊖ *Bond Street*
*– ℰ (020) 7659 1500 – www.hush.co.uk – Closed Easter, 25-26 December,*
*1 January and Sunday*                                                    **30AHUv**
**Rest** – Modern European – *(booking essential)* Carte £ 27/44
♦ Accessible brasserie-style menu served in a large, busy room; smart destination
bar upstairs and plenty of private dining. Tucked away in a charming courtyard
with a summer terrace.

XX **Fakhreldine** 🗚 💳 ◑ 🗛 ◉
*85 Piccadilly* ⊠ *W1J 7NB* ⊖ *Green Park – ℰ (020) 7493 3424*
*– www.fakhreldine.co.uk*                                          **30AIVe**
**Rest** – Lebanese – Menu £ 14/33 – Carte approx. £ 31
♦ Long-standing restaurant with great view of Green Park. Large selection of
classic meze dishes and more modern European-style menu of original Lebanese
dishes.

XX **Tempo** 🗚 💳 ◑ 🗛
*54 Curzon St.* ⊠ *W1J 8PG* ⊖ *Green Park – ℰ (020) 7629 2742*
*– www.tempomayfair.co.uk – Closed 25-27 December, Saturday lunch, Sunday*
*and bank holidays*                                               **30AIVm**
**Rest** – Italian – Menu £ 23 (lunch) – Carte £ 29/52
♦ The hands-on owner is a reassuring presence in this cosy restaurant, which reopened in 2010 after a full revamp. The menu covers all Italian regions and includes cicchetti, or small plates.

XX **Sumosan** 🗚 💳 ◑ 🗛 ◉
*26 Albemarle St.* ⊠ *W1S 4HY* ⊖ *Green Park – ℰ (020) 7495 5999*
*– www.sumosan.com – Closed lunch Saturday-Sunday and bank holidays*
**Rest** – Japanese – Carte £ 29/74                                **30AIUe**
♦ Attracts a young and prosperous crowd with its cocktail list, modern interpretations of Japanese flavours and stylish surroundings. The skilled kitchen deftly
executes a wide-ranging menu.

XX **Mews of Mayfair** ⇔ 💳 ◑ 🗛
*10-11 Lancashire Ct, Brook St, (1st floor)* ⊠ *W1S 1EY* ⊖ *Bond Street – ℰ (020)*
*7518 9388 – www.mewsofmayfair.com – Closed 25-26 December, Sunday dinner*
*and bank holidays*                                               **30AHUa**
**Rest** – Modern European – Carte £ 29/38
♦ This pretty restaurant, bright in summer and warm in winter, is on the first
floor of a mews house, once used as storage rooms for Savile Row. Seasonal menus offer something for everyone.

XX **Sketch (The Gallery)** 🗚 💳 ◑ 🗛
*9 Conduit St* ⊠ *W1S 2XG* ⊖ *Oxford Street – ℰ (020) 7659 4500*
*– www.sketch.uk.com – Closed 25-26 December, Sunday and bank holidays*
**Rest** – International – *(dinner only) (booking essential)*      **30AIUh**
Carte £ 35/63
♦ Unlike anywhere else: an art gallery during the day that morphs into a noisy,
bustling brasserie at night, when aphorisms are projected onto the white walls.
Menu is international in its scope; the cocktail list is equally popular.

XX **JW Steakhouse** – at Lancaster London Hotel 🗚 ⇔ 💳 ◑ 🗛
*Park Ln* ⊠ *W1K 7TN* ⊖ *Marble Arch – ℰ (020) 7399 8460*
*– www.londongrosvenorhouse.co.uk*                                **29AGUg**
**Rest** – Beef specialities – Carte £ 28/69
♦ With Aberdeen Angus or dry-aged American USDA steaks, as well as an impressive choice of bourbon in the bar, there's no guessing as to whom this smart
hotel steakhouse is geared.

XX **Momo**                                                    ☆ AC VISA ⬤⬤ AE ⓞ
*25 Heddon St.* ⌧ *W1B 4BH* ⊖ *Oxford Circus –* ✆ *(020) 7434 4040*
*– www.momoresto.com – Closed Sunday lunch*                    **30**AIU**n**
**Rest** – Moroccan – Menu £ 19/49 – Carte £ 35/40
◆ Lanterns, rugs, trinkets and music contribute to the authentic Moroccan atmosphere; come in a group to better appreciate it. The more traditional dishes are
the kitchen's strength.

XX **Cookbook Café** – at InterContinental Hotel          AC VISA ⬤⬤ AE ⓞ
*1 Hamilton Pl, Park Ln.* ⌧ *W1J 7QY* ⊖ *Hyde Park Corner –* ✆ *(020) 7409 3131*
*– www.london.intercontinental.com*                           **30**AHV**k**
**Rest** – Traditional – Menu £ 18 (lunch) – Carte £ 21/53
◆ Finding a casual spot for a light meal is not easy in Park Lane but the Cookbook Café is one option. Choose salads from the buffet or daily specials from
the central cooking station.

XX **Veeraswamy**                                     AC ▨ ⇔ VISA ⬤⬤ AE ⓞ
*Victory House, 99 Regent St, (entrance on Swallow St.)* ⌧ *W1B 4RS*
⊖ *Piccadilly Circus –* ✆ *(020) 7734 1401 – www.realindianfood.com*
**Rest** – Indian – Menu £ 21 (lunch and early dinner)        **30**AIU**t**
– Carte £ 37/51
◆ May have opened back in 1926 but feels fresh and is awash with vibrant col-
ours and always full of bustle. Skilled kitchen cleverly mixes the traditional with
more contemporary creations.

XX **Cafe at Sotheby's**                                     VISA ⬤⬤ AE ⓞ
*34-35 New Bond St.* ⌧ *W1A 2AA* ⊖ *Bond Street –* ✆ *(020) 7293 5077*
*– www.sothebys.com – Closed 5-31 August, Saturday, Sunday and bank hoildays*
**Rest** – Modern European – *(lunch only) (booking essential)*    **30**AIU**y**
Carte £ 26/32 **s**
◆ Occupying a cosy space just off the foyer of the famous auction house. The
appealing lunch menu changes weekly; the lobster sandwich is a perennial favourite. Service is discreet.

XX **Kiku**                                              AC VISA ⬤⬤ AE ⓞ
*17 Half Moon St.* ⌧ *W1J 7BE* ⊖ *Green Park –* ✆ *(020) 7499 4208*
*– www.kikurestaurant.co.uk – Closed 25-26 December, 1 January, Sunday and*
*lunch on bank holidays*                                       **30**AIV**g**
**Rest** – Japanese – Menu £ 20/50 – Carte £ 25/56
◆ Bright and fresh feel thanks to minimalistic décor of stone and natural
wood. A plethora of menus, a fierce adherence to seasonality and an authentic emphasis on presentation.

X **Bar Trattoria Semplice**                           ☆ AC VISA ⬤⬤ AE
😊 *22 Woodstock St.* ⌧ *W1C 2AR* ⊖ *Bond Street –* ✆ *(020) 7491 8638*
*– www.bartrattoriasemplice.com*                               **30**AHU**m**
**Rest** – Italian – Menu £ 17 (lunch) – Carte £ 22/37
◆ Baby sister to Semplice a few yards away, offering simpler, well-priced cooking
in a relaxed and fun room. Specialities from a different region of Italy are featured
each month. All-day menu in bar.

X **Chisou**                                          AC ⇔ VISA ⬤⬤ AE
*4 Princes St.* ⌧ *W1B 2LE* ⊖ *Oxford Circus –* ✆ *(020) 7629 3931*
*– www.chisourestaurant.com – Closed Christmas-New Year, Sunday and bank*
*holidays*                                                     **30**AIU**m**
**Rest** – Japanese – Menu £ 14 (lunch) – Carte £ 18/43
◆ In Mayfair's Japanese quarter; simple slate flooring and polished wood tables.
Cosy sushi bar to rear. Elaborate menus of both modern and classic Japanese
dishes. Gets very busy.

LONDON

LONDON

✗ **Bentley's (Oyster Bar)**                  ⌂ AC VISA ☺ AE
*11-15 Swallow St.* ✉ *W1B 4DG* ↔ *Piccadilly Circus –* ☏ *(020) 7734 4756*
*– www.bentleys.org – Closed 25 December and 1 January*          **30AJUc**
**Rest** – Seafood – Menu £ 25 (lunch) – Carte £ 35/50
• Sit at the counter to watch white-jacketed staff open oysters by the bucket load. Interesting seafood menus feature tasty fish pies; lots of daily specials on blackboard.

✗ **Aubaine**                               ⌂ AC VISA ☺ AE
*4 Heddon St.* ✉ *W1B 4BS* ↔ *Oxford Circus –* ☏ *(020) 7440 2510*
*– www.aubaine.co.uk – Closed dinner Sunday and bank holidays*      **30AIUo**
**Rest** – French – Carte £ 22/52
• Sister to the Chelsea original but this time without the boulangerie. The look is of a farmhouse as imagined by a townie; the accessible menu wouldn't look out of place in a bistro.

✗ **Automat**                               AC VISA ☺ AE
*33 Dover St.* ✉ *W1S 4NF* ↔ *Green Park –* ☏ *(020) 7499 3033*
*– www.automat-london.com – Closed 25 December and 1 January*
**Rest** – American – Carte £ 24/49                        **30AIVr**
• In contrast to Mayfair's inherent Britishness is this buzzy NYC style brasserie. Stick to the classics – crab cakes, burgers and cheesecakes and don't get palmed off with a table in the first section.

✗ **Le Boudin Blanc**                       ⌂ ☷ ⇔ VISA ☺ AE
*5 Trebeck St.* ✉ *W1J 7LT* ↔ *Green Park –* ☏ *(020) 7499 3292*
*– www.boudinblanc.co.uk – Closed 24-26 December*              **30AHVq**
**Rest** – French – Menu £ 15 (lunch and early dinner) – Carte £ 28/49
• Appealing, lively French bistro in Shepherd Market, spread over two floors. Satisfying French classics and country cooking is the draw, along with authentic Gallic service. Good value lunch menu.

⌂ **Only Running Footman**                  ⇔ VISA ☺ AE
*5 Charles St* ✉ *W1J 5DF* ↔ *Green Park.  –* ☏ *(020) 7499 2988*
*– www.therunningfootmanmayfair.com*                          **30AHVx**
**Rest** – Traditional – Carte £ 21/37
• Busy ground floor bar with its appealing menu of pub classics doesn't take bookings. By contrast, upstairs is formal and its menu more European and ambitious but simpler dishes still the best.

## REGENT'S PARK AND MARYLEBONE

🏠🏠🏠 **The Landmark London**          ▦ ☺ ⌘ ℉ ⅁ ⬯ AC ☆ ⅋ ⅃ ⌂ VISA ☺ AE
*222 Marylebone Rd* ✉ *NW1 6JQ* ↔ *Edgware Rd –* ☏ *(020) 7631 8000*
*– www.landmarklondon.co.uk*                                **29AFTa**
**291 rm** – †£ 239/660 ††£ 239/660, ☲ £ 29 – 9 suites
**Rest** *Winter Garden* – see restaurant listing
• Imposing Victorian Gothic building with a vast glass-enclosed atrium, overlooked by many of the modern, well-equipped bedrooms. Choice of relaxed wood panelled cellar bar or more sophisticated Mirror bar.

🏠🏠🏠 **Langham**                          ▦ ☺ ⌘ ℉ ⅁ ⬯ AC ☆ ⅋ ⅃ VISA ☺ AE ⓘ
*1c Portland Pl., Regent St.* ✉ *W1B 1JA* ↔ *Oxford Circus –* ☏ *(020) 7636 1000*
*– www.langhamhotels.com*                                   **30AITn**
**357 rm** – †£ 239/499 ††£ 239/499, ☲ £ 30 – 21 suites
**Rest** *Roux at the Landau* – see restaurant listing
• Was one of Europe's first purpose-built grand hotels when it opened in 1865. Now back to its best, with its famous Palm Court for afternoon tea, the stylish Artesian bar and bedrooms that are not without personality and elegance.

### Hyatt Regency London-The Churchill

*30 Portman Sq* ⊠ *W1H 7BH* ⊖ *Marble Arch*
– *𝒞 (020) 7486 5800 – www.london.churchill.hyatt.com*

**387 rm** – †£ 240/552 ††£ 264/576, ⊒ £ 27.50 – 47 suites
**Rest** *The Montagu* – see restaurant listing
♦ Smart well-located property whose best bedrooms overlook the attractive square opposite. Elegant marbled lobby with plenty of staff. Well-appointed and refurbished bedrooms have the international traveller in mind.

### Sanderson

*50 Berners St* ⊠ *W1T 3NG* ⊖ *Oxford Circus* – *𝒞 (020) 7300 1400*
– *www.morganshotelgroup.com*

**150 rm** – †£ 270/654 ††£ 270/654, ⊒ £ 23
**Rest** *Suka* – see restaurant listing
♦ Designed by Philippe Starck and still attracting a suitably fashionable crowd. Purple Bar dark and moody; Long Bar bright and stylish. Pure white bedrooms with idiosyncratic design touches such as a framed picture...on the ceiling.

### Arch

*50 Great Cumberland Pl* ⊠ *W1H 7FD* ⊖ *Marble Arch* – *𝒞 (020) 7724 4700*
– *www.thearchlondon.com*

**80 rm** – †£ 258/1020 ††£ 258/1020, ⊒ £ 19.50 – 2 suites
**Rest** *Hunter 486* – *𝒞 (020) 7725 4825* – Menu £ 20 (lunch) – Carte £ 35/60
♦ Fashioned out of a row of seven terrace houses and two mews cottages. Plenty of extras and thoughtful touches are found in the comfortable bedrooms. Interesting pieces of art throughout. Casual restaurant doubles as a bar.

### Montcalm

*34-40 Great Cumberland Pl.* ⊠ *W1H 7TW* ⊖ *Marble Arch* – *𝒞 (020) 7402 4288*
– *www.montcalm.co.uk*

**126 rm** – †£ 420 ††£ 420/1020, ⊒ £ 19.95 – 17 suites
**Rest** *Vetro* – Italian – Menu £ 24 (lunch) – Carte £ 27/41
♦ Named after an 18C French general, The Montcalm forms part of a crescent of townhouses with a Georgian façade. A top-to-toe refurbishment has created smart and contemporary bedrooms in lively colours. Classic Italian dishes in Vetro.

### Durrants

*26-32 George St* ⊠ *W1H 5BJ* ⊖ *Bond Street* – *𝒞 (020) 7935 8131*
– *www.durrantshotel.co.uk*

**89 rm** – †£ 156 ††£ 180, ⊒ £ 22.50 – 3 suites
**Rest** – *(closed dinner 25 December)* Carte £ 32/50
♦ Traditional, privately owned hotel with friendly, long-standing staff. Bedrooms are now brighter in style but still retain a certain English character. Clubby dining room for mix of British classics and lighter, European dishes.

### Mandeville

*Mandeville Pl.* ⊠ *W1U 2BE* ⊖ *Bond Street* – *𝒞 (020) 7935 5599*
– *www.mandeville.co.uk*

**140 rm** – †£ 383/407 ††£ 407, ⊒ £ 22.50 – 2 suites
**Rest** *de Ville* – *(closed Sunday dinner)* Menu £ 23 – Carte dinner £ 34/44
♦ Usefully located hotel with marbled reception leading into a very colourful and comfortable bar. Stylish rooms have flatscreen TVs and make good use of the space available. Modern British cuisine served in bright de Ville restaurant.

### No. Ten Manchester Street

⊠ *W1U 4DG* ⊖ *Baker Street* – *𝒞 (020) 7317 5900*
– *www.tenmanchesterstreethotel.com*

**44 rm** – †£ 179 ††£ 480, ⊒ £ 17.95 – 1 suite **Rest** – *(room service only)*
♦ Converted Edwardian house in an appealing, central location. Discreet entrance leads into stylish little lounge; semi-enclosed cigar bar also a feature. Neat and well-kept bedrooms.

**Sumner** without rest  🕮 🚫 AC ♨ ⁣(¹)⁣ VISA ∞ AE

*54 Upper Berkeley St ⊠ W1H 7QR ⊖ Marble Arch –* ☏ *(020) 7723 2244*
*– www.thesumner.com*  **29**AFU**k**
**19 rm** ⌁ – ♦£ 198/213 ♦♦£ 222/237
♦ Two Georgian terrace houses in central location. Comfy, stylish sitting room;
basement breakfast room. Largest bedrooms, 101 and 201, benefit from having full-length windows.

**Marble Arch by Montcalm** without rest  🕮 AC ♨ ⁣(¹)⁣ VISA ∞ AE ①

*31 Great Cumberland Pl. ⊠ W1H 7TA ⊖ Marble Arch –* ☏ *(020) 7258 0777*
*– www.themarblearch.co.uk*  **29**AGU**s**
**42 rm** – ♦£ 290/350 ♦♦£ 290/350, ⌁ £ 19.50
♦ Bedrooms at this 5-storey Georgian townhouse come with the same high standards of stylish, contemporary design as its parent hotel opposite, the Montcalm,
but are just a little more compact.

**Hart House** without rest  ♨ ⁣(¹)⁣ VISA ∞

*51 Gloucester Pl ⊠ W1U 8JF ⊖ Marble Arch –* ☏ *(020) 7935 2288*
*– www.harthouse.co.uk*  **29**AGT**d**
**15 rm** ⌁ – ♦£ 98/115 ♦♦£ 150/175
♦ Within an attractive Georgian terrace and run by the same family for over 35
years. Warm and welcoming service; well-kept, competitively priced bedrooms
over three floors.

**Rhodes W1 (Restaurant)**  VISA ∞ AE
£3

*Cumberland Hotel, Great Cumberland Pl. ⊠ W1H 7DL ⊖ Marble Arch*
*–* ☏ *(020) 7616 5930 – www.rhodesw1.com – Closed 2 weeks January, 2 weeks*
*August, Saturday lunch, Sunday, Monday and bank holidays*  **29**AGU**z**
**Rest** – French – *(booking advisable)* Menu £ 26/50 ✦✦
**Spec.** Fillet of mackerel, honey and sesame caramel and sea purslane. Pigeon
with foie gras, chicory and pickled blackberries. Prune and Armagnac soufflé, va-
nilla bean ice cream.
♦ Just 12 tables in a formal but warm and textured room designed by Kelly Hop-
pen. Influences are more European and cooking more elaborate than usual for a
Gary Rhodes restaurant, but you'll find the same emphasis on uncluttered flavours.

**Locanda Locatelli**  AC VISA ∞ AE ①
£3

*8 Seymour St. ⊠ W1H 7JZ ⊖ Marble Arch –* ☏ *(020) 7935 9088*
*– www.locandalocatelli.com*  **29**AGU**r**
**Rest** – Italian – Carte £ 32/62 ✦✦
**Spec.** Pan-fried scallops with celeriac purée and saffron vinaigrette. Homemade
pasta ribbons with broad beans and rocket. Tasting of Amedei chocolate.
♦ Slick and dapper-looking Italian with a celebrity following and a sophisticated
atmosphere. Plenty of interest on the extensive menu, with cooking that is confident, balanced and expertly rendered; pastas and desserts are the stand-out
courses.

**Roux at the Landau** – at Langham Hotel  AC ✧ VISA ∞ AE ①

*1c Portland Pl., Regent St. ⊠ W1B 1JA ⊖ Oxford Circus –* ☏ *(020) 7965 0165*
*– www.thelandau.com – Closed Saturday lunch and Sunday*  **30**AIT**n**
**Rest** – French – Menu £ 48 (lunch and early dinner) – Carte £ 37/67
♦ Grand, oval-shaped hotel restaurant run under the aegis of the Roux organisa-
tion. Classical, French-influenced cooking is the order of the day, but a lighter
style of cuisine using the occasional twist is also emerging.

**Latium**  AC VISA ∞ AE

*21 Berners St. ⊠ W1T 3LP ⊖ Oxford Circus –* ☏ *(020) 7323 9123*
*– www.latiumrestaurant.com – Closed 25-26 December, 1 January, Saturday*
*lunch, Sunday and bank holidays*  **31**AJT**n**
**Rest** – Italian – Menu £ 23/36
♦ Bright and contemporary surroundings but with warm and welcoming service.
Owner-chef from Lazio but dishes come from across Italy, often using British produce. Ravioli is the house speciality.

XXX **Orrery** ⬚ AC ⬚ VISA ⬚ AE ⬚
*55 Marylebone High St* ⬚ *W1U 5RB* ⬚ *Regent's Park* – ℰ *(020) 7616 8000*
*– www.orrery-restaurant.co.uk*                                    **18**RZD**a**
**Rest** – Modern European – *(booking essential)* Menu £ 25 (lunch)
– Carte £ 37/48
♦ These are actually converted stables from the 19C but, such is the elegance and
style of the building, you'd never know. Featured is elaborate, modern European
cooking; dishes are strong on presentation and come with the occasional twist.

XX **Texture** (Agnar Sverrisson) AC ⬚ VISA ⬚ AE
❀ *34 Portman St.* ⬚ *W1H 7BY* ⬚ *Marble Arch* – ℰ *(020) 7224 0028*
*– www.texture-restaurant.co.uk* – *Closed Christmas-New Year, 2 weeks August,*
*Sunday and Monday*                                    **29**AGU**p**
**Rest** – Innovative – Menu £ 24 (lunch) – Carte £ 50/64 ⑳
**Spec.** Organic Scottish salmon, horseradish and cucumber. Icelandic salted cod,
barley risotto and prawns. Skyr ice cream, strawberry and muesli.
♦ Technically skilled but light and invigorating cooking from Icelandic chef-owner,
who uses ingredients from home. Bright restaurant with high ceiling and popular
adjoining champagne bar. Pleasant service from keen staff, ready with a smile.

XX **L'Autre Pied** AC VISA ⬚ AE
❀ *5-7 Blandford St.* ⬚ *W1U 3DB* ⬚ *Bond Street* – ℰ *(020) 7486 9696*
*– www.lautrepied.co.uk* – *Closed 23 December-5 January and Sunday dinner*
**Rest** – Modern European – Menu £ 23 (lunch and early dinner)        **30**AHT**k**
– Carte £ 39/47
**Spec.** Cauliflower risotto, scallops and toasted almonds with lemongrass sauce.
Pan-fried cod with carrot and star anise purée and tarragon sauce. Ginger
mousse, vanilla poached apricots and honey ice cream.
♦ This more casual sibling to Pied à Terre is a lively, hospitable spot in the even-
ing. The cooking may be slightly simpler but it's still carefully prepared and
makes good use of classic combinations of ingredients.

XX **Galvin Bistrot de Luxe** AC ⬚ VISA ⬚ AE
*66 Baker St.* ⬚ *W1U 7DJ* ⬚ *Baker Street* – ℰ *(020) 7935 4007*
*– www.galvinrestaurants.com* – *Closed 25-26 December, 1 January and dinner*
*24 December*                                    **29**AGT**b**
**Rest** – French – Menu £ 20 (lunch and early dinner) – Carte £ 35/41
♦ Firmly established modern Gallic bistro with ceiling fans, globe lights and
wood panelled walls. Satisfying and precisely cooked classic French dishes from
the Galvin brothers.

XX **Zayna** AC VISA ⬚ AE
*25 New Quebec St.* ⬚ *W1H 7SF* ⬚ *Marble Arch* – ℰ *(020) 7723 2229*
*– www.zaynarestaurant.co.uk*                                    **29**AGU**x**
**Rest** – Indian – Menu £ 15 (lunch) – Carte £ 30/39
♦ Enthusiastically run, elegant restaurant spread over two floors, with keen
owner. Interesting north Indian and Pakistani delicacies; kitchen only uses halal
meat and free-range chicken.

XX **Ozer** AC ⬚ VISA ⬚ AE
*5 Langham Pl., Regent St.* ⬚ *W1B 3DG* ⬚ *Oxford Circus* – ℰ *(020) 7323 0505*
*– www.ozer.co.uk*                                    **30**AIT**z**
**Rest** – Turkish – Menu £ 21/24
♦ The large front bar is always busy but go through to the equally popular but
comfortable restaurant to enjoy authentic Turkish food. Wide range of appealing
meze is the draw, along with succulent lamb dishes.

XX **Rhodes W1 Brasserie** AC VISA ⬚ AE
*Cumberland Hotel, Great Cumberland Pl.* ⬚ *W1H 7DL* ⬚ *Marble Arch*
*– ℰ (020) 7616 5930 – www.rhodesw1.com*                        **29**AGU**z**
**Rest** – Modern European – Menu £ 21 (lunch) – Carte £ 24/43
♦ Large brasserie on the ground floor of the Cumberland hotel, with keen, help-
ful service and equally big bar. Expect Gary Rhodes' signature dishes, alongside
others of a more European persuasion.

LONDON

XX **Royal China**　　　　　　　　　　　　　AC VISA OO AE
24-26 Baker St ✉ W1U 7AB ⊖ Baker Street – ✆ (020) 7487 4688
– www.royalchinagroup.co.uk　　　　　　　　　　　　　29AGT**h**
**Rest** – Chinese – Menu £ 30 – Carte £ 31/42
♦ Barbeque meats, assorted soups and stir-fries attract plenty of large groups to this smart and always bustling Cantonese restaurant. Over 40 different types of dim sum served during the day.

XX **Colony**　　　　　　　　　　　　AC ⇌ VISA OO AE
8 Paddington St ✉ W1U 5QH ⊖ Baker Street – ✆ (020) 7935 3353
– www.colonybarandgrill.com　　　　　　　　　　　　30AHT**d**
**Rest** – Indian – Menu £ 17 (lunch) – Carte dinner £ 23/33
♦ Small tasting plates making good use of the grill and tandoor, lunchtime thalis and grazing menus with mostly Indian influences are served at this relaxed lounge bar, with chilled music and an extensive cocktail list.

XX **Iberica**　　　　　　　　　　　　AC ⇌ VISA OO AE ①
⊛ 195 Great Portland St ✉ W1W 5PS ⊖ Great Portland St – ✆ (020) 7636 8650
– www.ibericalondon.co.uk – Closed 1 January, Sunday dinner and bank holidays　　　　　　　　　　　　　　　　　　　　18RZD**x**
**Rest** – Spanish – (booking advisable at dinner) Carte £ 20/36
♦ These large premises pay homage to Spain's food and culture. Punchy flavoured tapas in the ground floor bar; more intimate upstairs. Wander through the deli to appreciate the quality of ingredients.

XX **Verru**　　　　　　　　　　　　　　VISA OO AE ①
69 Marylebone Ln ✉ W1U 2PH ⊖ Bond Street – ✆ (020) 7935 0858
– www.verru.co.uk　　　　　　　　　　　　　　30AHT**a**
**Rest** – Modern European – Menu £ 17 (lunch) – Carte £ 35/42
♦ Chef-owner is Estonian so his cooking not only displays a Baltic boldness of flavour but also makes good use of northern European influences. The restaurant is tiny and tucked away but warmly run and smartly dressed.

XX **Roganic**　　　　　　　　　　　　AC VISA OO AE
19 Blandford St ✉ W1U 3DH ⊖ Baker Street – ✆ (020) 7486 0380
– www.roganic.co.uk – Closed Sunday and Monday　　　29AGT**r**
**Rest** – Innovative – (booking advisable) Menu £ 29 (lunch and early dinner)/80
♦ Simon Rogan of L'Enclume in the Lake District created this "extended pop-up restaurant" by taking on the last 2 years of an existing lease. From the tasting menus come dishes of invention and originality, using produce from their own farm.

XX **The Providores**　　　　　　　　　　AC VISA OO AE
109 Marylebone High St. ✉ W1U 4RX ⊖ Bond Street – ✆ (020) 7935 6175
– www.theprovidores.co.uk – Closed 24 December-4 January　　30AHT**y**
**Rest** – Innovative – Menu £ 46 – Carte £ 34/49
♦ Packed ground floor for tapas; upstairs for innovative fusion cooking, with spices and ingredients from around the world, including Australasia. Starter-sized dishes at dinner allow for greater choice.

XX **Cafe Luc**　　　　　　　　　　　　AC ⓥ VISA OO AE
50 Marylebone High St ✉ W1U 5HN ⊖ Regent's Park – ✆ (020) 7258 9878
– www.cafeluc.com – Closed 25 December　　　　　30AHT**b**
**Rest** – Modern European – Menu £ 16 (lunch) – Carte £ 29/41
♦ Spacious, grand and keenly run brasserie with smart leather banquette seating and clusters of lights. The menu offers a host of brasserie and continental classics to suit all tastes.

XX **Levant**　　　　　　　　　　　　AC VISA OO AE
Jason Ct., 76 Wigmore St. ✉ W1U 2SJ ⊖ Bond Street – ✆ (020) 7224 1111
– www.levant.co.uk – Closed 25-26 December　　　　30AHT**c**
**Rest** – Lebanese – (dinner only and lunch Saturday-Sunday) Menu £ 22/28 – Carte £ 30/45
♦ Belly dancing, lanterns and a low-slung bar all add up to an exotic dining experience. The Lebanese food is satisfying and authentic, carefully prepared and ideal for sharing in groups.

LONDON

XX **L'Aventure**                                                    🖼 VISA ⊙⊙ AE

3 Blenheim Terr ⊠ NW8 0EH ⊖ St John's Wood – ℰ (020) 7624 6232
– *Closed first week January, Saturday lunch, Sunday and bank holidays*
**Rest** – French – Menu £ 21/39                                    **11**PZB**b**
◆ Behind the pretty tree-lined entrance you'll find a charming neighbourhood restaurant. Relaxed atmosphere and service by personable owner. Authentic French cuisine.

XX **The Montagu** – at Hyatt Regency London-The Churchill        🅰🅲 VISA ⊙⊙ AE ⓞ

30 Portman Sq ⊠ W1H 7BH ⊖ Marble Arch – ℰ (020) 7299 2037
– www.london.churchill.hyatt.com                                   **29**AGT**x**
**Rest** – British – Menu £ 24/26 – Carte £ 37/57
◆ Offering sanctuary from Oxford Street, The Montagu is a light, spacious affair within the discreet Hyatt Regency hotel. Open all day; its afternoon teas are particularly popular.

XX **Winter Garden** – at The Landmark London Hotel              🅰🅲 VISA ⊙⊙ AE

222 Marylebone Rd ⊠ NW1 6JQ ⊖ Edgware Rd – ℰ (020) 7631 8000
– www.landmarklondon.co.uk                                         **29**AFT**a**
**Rest** – Mediterranean – Menu £ 35 (lunch) – Carte £ 41/64
◆ Impressive glass atrium in an international hotel, of the sort more commonly found in Asia. Ideal for an informal lunch, when the Mediterranean dishes come into their own.

XX **Suka** – at Sanderson Hotel                                  🅰🅲 VISA ⊙⊙ AE ⓞ

50 Berners St ⊠ W1T 3NG ⊖ Oxford Circus – ℰ (020) 7300 1400
– www.morganshotelgroup.com                                        **31**AJT**c**
**Rest** – Asian influences – Carte £ 26/51
◆ Beyond the Sanderson hotel's trendy Long Bar is Suka, a casual eatery that extends into the garden terrace. Expect British ingredients and Asian influences, with Malaysia dominating.

XX **Phoenix Palace**                                        ₺ 🅰🅲 ⇔ VISA ⊙⊙ AE

5 Glentworth St. ⊠ NW1 5PG ⊖ Baker Street – ℰ (020) 7486 3515
– www.phoenixpalace.co.uk – *Closed 25 December*                   **17**QZD**x**
**Rest** – Chinese – *(booking advisable at dinner)* Menu £ 28 (dinner) – Carte approx. £ 24
◆ Huge restaurant offering a plethora of menus but the cooking is still good. Dim sum during the day and Cantonese dishes and rotisserie meats at night draw in the groups of families and friends.

X **Trishna**                                                🅰🅲 ⇔ VISA ⊙⊙ AE
☺
15-17 Blandford St. ⊠ W1U 3DG ⊖ Baker Street – ℰ (020) 7935 5624
– www.trishnalondon.com – *Closed 25-28 December and 1-3 January*
**Rest** – Indian – Menu £ 18 (lunch) – Carte £ 24/37               **29**AGT**r**
◆ A franchise of the celebrated Mumbai restaurant. Specialises in fish and seafood dishes; the rich Cornish brown crab with butter garlic is certainly a highlight. Bright surroundings allow the focus to stay on the food.

X **Riding House Café**                                      🅰🅲 ⇔ VISA ⊙⊙ AE

43-51 Great Titchfield St ⊠ W1W 7PQ ⊖ Oxford Circus – ℰ (020) 7927 0840
– www.ridinghousecafe.co.uk – *Closed 25-26 December*              **30**AIT**k**
**Rest** – Modern European – Carte £ 24/42
◆ It's less a café, more a large, quirkily designed, all-day New York style brasserie and cocktail bar. The 'small plates' have more zing than the main courses. The unbookable side of the restaurant is the more fun part.

X **The Wallace**                                                       VISA ⊙⊙

Hertford House, Manchester Sq ⊠ W1U 3BN ⊖ Bond Street – ℰ (020) 7563 9505 – www.thewallacerestaurant.com – *Closed 24-26 December*
**Rest** – French – *(lunch only and dinner Friday-Saturday)*      **29**AGT**k**
Carte £ 30/39
◆ Large glass-roofed courtyard on the ground floor of Hertford House, home to the splendid Wallace Collection. French-influenced menu, with fruits de mer section; terrines are the house speciality.

449

LONDON

### Hix (Selfridges)

AC VISA ◑◐ AE ◑

*Mezzanine Fl, Selfridges, 400 Oxford St ⊠ W1A 1AB ⊖ Bond St – ℰ (020)*
*7499 5400 – www.hixatselfridges.co.uk – Closed 25 December and Sunday dinner*
**Rest** – Modern European – Menu £ 23 (lunch) – Carte £ 25/113      **30**AHU**p**
◆ On the mezzanine floor of the famous store; open from breakfast onwards, with a popular champagne bar to refuel shoppers. Menu is lighter and more European than at the other Hix restaurants.

### Caffé Caldesi

AC VISA ◑◐

*118 Marylebone Ln. (1st floor) ⊠ W1U 2QF ⊖ Bond Street – ℰ (020) 7487 0754*
*– www.caldesi.com*      **30**AHT**s**
**Rest** – Italian – Menu £ 20 (lunch) – Carte £ 28/44
◆ Head upstairs at this converted corner pub for generously proportioned, big flavoured classics from across Italy. Stay on the ground floor for a simpler and more accessibly priced menu.

### Dinings

VISA ◑◐ AE ◑

*22 Harcourt St. ⊠ W1H 4HH ⊖ Marylebone – ℰ (020) 7723 0666*
*– www.dinings.co.uk – Closed Christmas, Saturday lunch and Sunday*
**Rest** – Japanese – (booking essential)      **29**AFT**c**
◆ Resembles an after-work Japanese izakaya, or pub, with chummy atmosphere and loud music. Food is a mix of small plates of delicate dishes, a blend of modern and the more traditional.

### Il Baretto

AC VISA ◑◐ AE

*43 Blandford St. ⊠ W1U 7HF ⊖ Baker Street – ℰ (020) 7486 7340*
*– www.ilbaretto.co.uk – Closed 25-26 December and lunch 1 January*
**Rest** – Italian – Carte £ 40/53      **29**AGT**n**
◆ The wood-fired oven is the star of the show at this neighbourhood Italian. Extensive and variably priced menu has something for everyone. The basement room has a lively atmosphere, with frantic service to match.

### Vinoteca

AC VISA ◑◐ AE

*15 Seymour Pl. ⊠ W1H 5BD ⊖ Marble Arch – ℰ (020) 7724 7288*
*– www.vinoteca.co.uk – Closed 25-26 December, 1 January and Sunday dinner*
**Rest** – Modern European – (booking advisable) Carte £ 24/30 ⅋      **29**AFU**x**
◆ Follows the formula of the original: great fun, great wines, gutsy and wholesome food, enthusiastic staff and almost certainly a wait for a table. Influences from sunnier parts of Europe, along with some British dishes.

### Yalla Yalla

AC VISA ◑◐ ◑

*12 Winsley St. ⊠ W1W 8HQ ⊖ Oxford Circus – ℰ (020) 7637 4748*
*– www.yalla-yalla.co.uk – Closed 27-29 August and Sunday*      **30**ALT**v**
**Rest** – Lebanese – Carte £ 18/22
◆ Queues form for the Beirut street food which includes zesty mezze and succulent charcoal-grilled lamb dishes. Desserts come from the enticing pastry corner and wines from the Bekaa Valley. Takeaway also available.

### Chada Chada

AC VISA ◑◐ AE

*16-17 Picton Pl. ⊠ W1U 1BP ⊖ Bond Street – ℰ (020) 7935 8212*
*– www.chadathai.com – Closed 25 December and lunch Sunday-Monday*
**Rest** – Thai – Carte £ 14/38      **30**AHU**b**
◆ Authentic and fragrant Thai cooking; the good value menu offers some interesting departures from the norm. Service is eager to please in the compact and cosy rooms.

### Grazing Goat with rm

⌖ ⦿ VISA ◑◐ AE

*6 New Quebec St ⊠ W1H 7RQ ⊖ Marble Arch. – ℰ (020) 7724 7243*
*– www.thegrazinggoat.co.uk*      **29**AGU**d**
**8 rm** – �$ £ 195/225 �$�$ £ 195/225, � £ 11
**Rest** – Traditional – (booking essential at dinner) Carte £ 30/45
◆ A smart city facsimile of a country pub; it's first-come-first-served in the bar but you can book in the upstairs dining room. Proper pub classics such as pies and Castle of Mey steaks are on offer. Bedrooms with Nordic style bathrooms.

## Larrik                                    VISA ⓒⓞ AE ①
*32 Crawford Pl ⊠ W1H 5NN ⊖ Edgware Road. – ℰ (020) 7723 0066*
*– www.thelarrik.com – Closed 25 December*                      **29**AFT**x**
**Rest** – Traditional – Menu £ 13 (dinner) – Carte £ 25/37
♦ The front section of this traditional looking pub is brighter and more fun. The kitchen is well-grounded in the basics and reliable, whether making a salad or burger. Regularly changing real ales.

## Portman                                   VISA ⓒⓞ AE
*51 Upper Berkeley St ⊠ W1H 7QW ⊖ Marble Arch. – ℰ (020) 7723 8996*
*– www.theportmanmarylebone.com*                              **29**AFU**n**
**Rest** – Modern European – Carte £ 22/31
♦ The condemned on their way to Tyburn Tree gallows would take their last drink here. Now it's an urbane pub with a formal upstairs dining room. The ground floor is more fun for enjoying the down-to-earth menu.

# ST JAMES'S

**LONDON**

## 🏨🏨🏨🏨 Ritz                          *Ⅰ-₆* 🕴 AC 🛇 🇼 🛅 VISA ⓒⓞ AE ①
*150 Piccadilly ⊠ W1J 9BR ⊖ Green Park – ℰ (020) 7493 8181*
*– www.theritzlondon.com*                                      **30**AIV**c**
**116 rm** – †£ 360/696 ††£ 426/822, � £ 35 – 20 suites
**Rest** *Ritz Restaurant* – see restaurant listing
♦ World famous hotel, opened 1906 as a fine example of Louis XVI architecture and decoration. Elegant Palm Court famed for its afternoon tea. Many of the lavishly appointed and luxurious rooms and suites overlook the park.

## 🏨🏨🏨 Haymarket              🖼 *Ⅰ-₆* 🕴 🅶 AC 🛇 🛅 🕭 VISA ⓒⓞ AE ①
*1 Suffolk Pl. ⊠ SW1Y 4HX ⊖ Piccadilly Circus – ℰ (020) 7470 4000*
*– www.haymarkethotel.com*                                     **31**AKV**x**
**47 rm** – †£ 312 ††£ 564, ⊷ £ 20 – 3 suites
**Rest** *Brumus* – see restaurant listing
♦ Smart, spacious hotel in John Nash Regency building, with stylish blend of modern and antique furnishings. Large, comfortable bedrooms in soothing colours. Impressive basement pool often used in photo-shoots.

## 🏨🏨 Dukes ☜                          *Ⅰ-₆* 🕴 AC 🛇 🇼 🛅 VISA ⓒⓞ AE ①
*35 St James's Pl. ⊠ SW1A 1NY ⊖ Green Park – ℰ (020) 7491 4840*
*– www.dukeshotel.com*                                         **30**AIV**f**
**84 rm** – †£ 270 ††£ 420, ⊷ £ 24 – 6 suites
**Rest** *Thirty Six by Nigel Mendham* – 36 St James's Pl. – Menu £ 22 (lunch)
– Carte £ 32/43
♦ The most recent redecoration retained the discreet, traditionally British feel of this hotel in a central but quiet location. Dukes bar famous for its martinis. Elegant bedrooms with country house feel. Calm, comfortable dining room offers seasonal British menu.

## 🏨🏨 Stafford ☜                        *Ⅰ-₆* 🕴 AC 🛇 🇼 🛅 VISA ⓒⓞ AE ①
*16-18 St James's Pl. ⊠ SW1A 1NJ ⊖ Green Park – ℰ (020) 7493 0111*
*– www.kempinski.com/london*                                   **30**AIV**u**
**73 rm** – †£ 330/492 ††£ 443/660, ⊷ £ 25 – 15 suites
**Rest** – Menu £ 28 (lunch) – Carte £ 34/55
♦ Currently being refurbished, the bedrooms of this 'country house in the city' are divided between the main house, converted 18C stables and more modern mews. Legendary American bar a feature; British food served in the restaurant.

## 🏨🏨 St James's Hotel and Club ☜           🕴 AC 🛇 🇼 🛅 VISA ⓒⓞ AE ①
*7-8 Park Pl. ⊠ SW1A 1LS ⊖ Green Park – ℰ (020) 7316 1600*
*– www.stjameshotelandclub.com*                                **30**AIV**k**
**50 rm** – †£ 282/414 ††£ 282/414, ⊷ £ 22 – 10 suites
**Rest** *Seven Park Place*❀ – see restaurant listing
♦ 1890s house in cul-de-sac, formerly a private club, reopened as a hotel in 2008. Modern, boutique–style interior with over 200 mostly German works of art from the '30s and '40s. Fine finish to compact, but well-equipped bedrooms.

451

**LONDON**

### Cavendish    🛗 ♿ rm, 🄰🄲 🛇 ⁽ᵗ⁾ ♨ 🍴 🚗 🆅🅸🆂🅰 🅾🅾 🄰🄴 🄾

*81 Jermyn St ✉ SW1Y 6JF ⊖ Piccadilly Circus – 𝒞 (020) 7930 2111*
*– www.thecavendishlondon.com*    **30**AIV**p**
**228 rm** – ♦£ 179/372, ♦♦£ 179/372, ⚏ £ 21 – 2 suites
**Rest** – British – *(closed 25 December, lunch Saturday-Sunday and bank holidays)* Menu £ 21 (dinner) – Carte £ 30/45
◆ There's been a hotel on this site since the 18C; this one was built in the '60s but is smart and contemporary inside. Great location, bistro-style dining with British menu and good views across London from the top 5 floors; a parking space for every room too!

### ✕✕✕✕✕ Ritz Restaurant – at The Ritz Hotel    🈸 🄰🄲 🆅🅸🆂🅰 🅾🅾 🄰🄴 🄾

*150 Piccadilly ✉ W1J 9BR ⊖ Green Park – 𝒞 (020) 7493 8181*
*– www.theritzlondon.com*    **30**AIV**c**
**Rest** – Traditional – Menu £ 39/48 **s** – Carte £ 71/94 **s**
◆ Grand and lavish restaurant, with Louis XVI decoration, trompe l'oeil and ornate gilding. Delightful terrace over Green Park. Structured, formal service. Classic, traditional dishes are the highlight of the menu. Jacket and tie required.

### ✕✕✕ Seven Park Place – at St James's Hotel and Club    🄰🄲 ♿ 🆅🅸🆂🅰 🅾🅾 🄰🄴 🄾
❀

*7-8 Park Pl ✉ SW1A 1LS ⊖ Green Park – 𝒞 (020) 7316 1614*
*– www.stjameshotelandclub.com – Closed Sunday and Monday*    **30**AIV**k**
**Rest** – Modern European – *(booking essential)* Menu £ 30/55
**Spec.** Lobster tail with asparagus, pea shoots and truffle dressing. Saddle of lamb with peas, lettuce and onions. Piña colada bavarois with poached pineapple.
◆ Small restaurant concealed somewhat within St James's Hotel and divided between two rooms; ask for the gilded back room. The accomplished food has a French base, displays confidence and clarity and uses quality British ingredients.

### ✕✕✕ The Wolseley    🄰🄲 🆅🅸🆂🅰 🅾🅾 🄰🄴 🄾

*160 Piccadilly ✉ W1J 9EB ⊖ Green Park – 𝒞 (020) 7499 6996*
*– www.thewolseley.com – Closed 25 December,*
*dinner 24 and 31 December and August bank holiday*    **30**AIV**q**
**Rest** – Modern European – *(booking essential)* Carte £ 24/48
◆ Feels like a grand European coffee house, with pillars and high vaulted ceiling. Appealing menus range from caviar to a hot dog. Open from breakfast and boasts a celebrity following.

### ✕✕ Sake No Hana    🄰🄲 🆅🅸🆂🅰 🅾🅾 🄰🄴

*23 St James's St ✉ SW1A 1HA ⊖ Green Park – 𝒞 (020) 7925 8988*
*– www.sakenohana.com – Closed Saturday lunch and Sunday*    **30**AIV**n**
**Rest** – Japanese – Carte £ 38/50
◆ Ground floor sushi bar; first floor restaurant reached by elevator, where cedar wood goes some way to disguising an ugly, if iconic, '60s building. The Japanese menu has been simplified somewhat; service can also be a little lacklustre.

### ✕✕ Le Caprice    🄰🄲 ♿ 🆅🅸🆂🅰 🅾🅾 🄰🄴 🄾

*Arlington House, Arlington St. ✉ SW1A 1RJ ⊖ Green Park – 𝒞 (020) 7629 2239*
*– www.le-caprice.co.uk – Closed 25-26 December*    **30**AIV**h**
**Rest** – Modern European – Carte £ 21/46
◆ Its clubby atmosphere, pianist, slick monochrome decoration and catch-all menu have been attracting a shiny, self assured clientele since 1981. Little wonder that a New York outpost opened in 2009.

### ✕✕ Franco's    🄰🄲 ♿ 🆅🅸🆂🅰 🅾🅾 🄰🄴

*61 Jermyn St. ✉ SW1Y 6LX ⊖ Green Park – 𝒞 (020) 7499 2211*
*– www.francoslondon.com – Closed Sunday and bank holidays*    **30**AIV**i**
**Rest** – Italian – *(booking essential)* Menu £ 26 (lunch) – Carte £ 35/55
◆ Open from breakfast until late, with café at the front leading into smart, clubby restaurant. Menu covers all parts of Italy and includes popular grill section and plenty of classics.

XX **Avenue**  🏧 ▨ 𝘝𝘐𝘚𝘈 ◉◉ 🄰🄴

*7-9 St James's St.* ✉ *SW1A 1EE* ⊖ *Green Park* – ✆ *(020) 7321 2111*
– *www.avenue-restaurant.co.uk* – *Closed 25-26 December,*
*Saturday lunch and Sunday*                                    30AIV**y**
**Rest** – Modern European – Menu £ 24 (lunch) – Carte £ 25/55
♦ Large, brash restaurant, with sheer white décor and a very popular bar. All-encompassing menu, with everything from caviar to burgers. Service comes with an urgency not always required.

XX **Matsuri - St James's**  🏧 ▨ ⇔ 𝘝𝘐𝘚𝘈 ◉◉ 🄰🄴 ◍

*15 Bury St.* ✉ *SW1Y 6AL* ⊖ *Green Park* – ✆ *(020) 7839 1101*
– *www.matsuri-restaurant.com* – *Closed 25 December and 1 January*
**Rest** – Japanese – Menu £ 35 (dinner) – Carte £ 28/39         30AIV**w**
♦ Sweet natured service at this traditional Japanese stalwart. Teppan-yaki is their speciality, with Scottish beef the highlight; sushi counter also available. Good value lunch menus.

XX **Quaglino's**  🏧 ▨ ⇔ 𝘝𝘐𝘚𝘈 ◉◉ 🄰🄴

*16 Bury St* ✉ *SW1Y 6AJ* ⊖ *Green Park* – ✆ *(020) 7930 6767*
– *www.quaglinos.co.uk* – *Closed Sunday*                      30AIV**j**
**Rest** – Modern European – *(booking essential)* Menu £ 25 (lunch)
– Carte £ 43/59
♦ This big, bold restaurant achieved iconic status on reopening in the early '90s. No longer quite so glamorous but it still offers a good night out and a easy menu, with fruits de mer the highlight.

XX **Mint Leaf**  🏧 ▨ 𝘝𝘐𝘚𝘈 ◉◉ 🄰🄴

*Suffolk Pl.* ✉ *SW1Y 4HX* ⊖ *Piccadilly Circus* – ✆ *(020) 7930 9020*
– *www.mintleafrestaurant.com* – *Closed 25 December,*
*1 January, lunch Saturday and Sunday*                        31AKV**k**
**Rest** – Indian – Menu £ 18 (lunch and early dinner) – Carte £ 38/60
♦ Cavernous and moodily lit basement restaurant incorporating trendy bar with lounge music and extensive cocktail list. Contemporary Indian cooking with curries the highlight.

XX **Brumus** – at Haymarket Hotel  🏧 ▨ 𝘝𝘐𝘚𝘈 ◉◉ 🄰🄴 ◍

*1 Suffolk Pl* ✉ *SW1Y 4HX* ⊖ *Piccadilly Circus* – ✆ *(020) 7470 4000*
– *www.haymarkethotel.com*                                    31AKV**x**
**Rest** – Modern European – Menu £ 19/23 – Carte £ 34/56
♦ Ideally positioned for pre or post theatre dining, when a good value menu is offered. Energetic room, with busy bar attached, and an unthreatening menu of Mediterranean favourites.

X **Al Duca**  🏧 ▨ 𝘝𝘐𝘚𝘈 ◉◉ 🄰🄴
☺

*4-5 Duke of York St.* ✉ *SW1Y 6LA* ⊖ *Piccadilly Circus* – ✆ *(020) 7839 3090*
– *www.alduca-restaurant.co.uk* – *Closed Easter, 25 December, Sunday and bank*
*holidays*                                                     31AJV**r**
**Rest** – Italian – Menu £ 28
♦ Cooking which focuses on flavour continues to draw in the regulars at this warm and spirited Italian restaurant. Prices are keen when one considers the central location and service is brisk and confident.

X **Inn the Park**  ⋚ 🏠 𝘝𝘐𝘚𝘈 ◉◉

*St James's Park* ✉ *SW1A 2BJ* ⊖ *Charing Cross* – ✆ *(020) 7451 9999*
– *www.innthepark.com* – *Closed 26 December and 1 January*   31AKV**n**
**Rest** – British – Carte £ 25/39
♦ Oliver Peyton's eco-friendly restaurant in the middle of the park, with a terrific terrace. British menu uses many small suppliers. Cooking is straightforward and wholesome.

453

LONDON

### Portrait ⟨⟨ AK VISA ☺☺ AE

*National Portrait Gallery, (3rd floor), St Martin's Pl.* ✉ *WC2H 0HE*
⊖ *Charing Cross –* ✆ *(020) 7312 2490 – www.searcys.co.uk*
*– Closed 24-26 December* **31**AL**V**n
**Rest** – Modern European – *(lunch only and dinner Thursday-Saturday) (booking essential)* Menu £ 25 – Carte £ 32/40
• On the top floor of National Portrait Gallery with rooftop local landmark views: a charming spot for lunch. Modern British/European dishes; weekend brunch.

### The National Dining Rooms AK VISA ☺☺

*Sainsbury Wing, The National Gallery, Trafalgar Sq* ✉ *WC2N 5DN*
⊖ *Charing Cross –* ✆ *(020) 7747 2525 – www.peytonandbyrne.co.uk – Closed 24-26 December* **31**AK**V**b
**Rest** – British – *(lunch only)* Carte £ 27/37
• Set on the East Wing's first floor, you can tuck into cakes in the bakery or grab a prime corner table in the restaurant for great views and proudly seasonal British menus.

## SOHO

### Soho 🛋 📶 ৬ AK ⅏ 🔧 VISA ☺☺ AE ⓪

*4 Richmond Mews* ✉ *W1D 3DH* ⊖ *Tottenham Court Road –* ✆ *(020) 7559 3000 – www.sohohotel.com* **31**AJ**U**n
**85 rm** – ♦£ 354 ♦♦£ 570, ⬚ £ 20 – 2 suites
**Rest** *Refuel* – see restaurant listing
• Stylish and very fashionable hotel that mirrors the vibrancy of the neighbourhood. Boasts two screening rooms, a comfortable drawing room and up-to-the-minute bedrooms, some vivid, others more muted but all boasting hi-tech extras.

### W London ☺☺ 🛋 📶 ৬ AK ⅏ 🔧 VISA ☺☺ AE ⓪

*10 Wardour St* ✉ *W1D 6QF* ⊖ *Leicester Square –* ✆ *(020) 7758 1000 – www.wlondon.co.uk* **31**AK**U**b
**177 rm** – ♦£ 503 ♦♦£ 503, ⬚ £ 25 – 15 suites
**Rest** *Spice Market* – see restaurant listing
• Achingly trendy hotel, opened in 2011. A DJ in the lobby lounge, low slung tables in the bar and slick, über cool bedrooms in categories called 'Fantastic' or 'Spectacular'. Anyone over 40 will be lost.

### Sanctum Soho 📶 AK 🔧 ⅏ 🔧 VISA ☺☺ AE ⓪

*20 Warwick St.* ✉ *W1B 5NF* ⊖ *Piccadilly Circus –* ✆ *(020) 7292 6100 – www.sanctumsoho.com* **30**AI**U**g
**30 rm** – ♦£ 240/276 ♦♦£ 360/660, ⬚ £ 21
**Rest** *No. 20* – Modern – *(closed Sunday dinner)* Menu £ 18/21 – Carte £ 25/41
• Plenty of glitz and bling at this funky, self-styled rock 'n' roll hotel, with some innovative touches such as TVs behind mirrors. Rooftop lounge and hot tub. Relaxed and comfortable dining with plenty of classic dishes.

### Dean Street Townhouse 📶 AK ⅏ 🔧 VISA ☺☺ AE ⓪

*69-71 Dean St.* ✉ *W1D 3SE* ⊖ *Tottenham Court Road –* ✆ *(020) 7434 1775 – www.deanstreettownhouse.com* **31**AK**U**t
**39 rm** – ♦£ 90 ♦♦£ 370, ⬚ £ 10
**Rest** *Dean Street Townhouse Restaurant* – see restaurant listing
• In the heart of Soho where bedrooms range from tiny to bigger; the latter have roll-top baths in the room. All are well designed and come with a good range of extras. Cosy ground floor lounge.

### Hazlitt's AK 🔧 ⅏ 🔧 VISA ☺☺ AE ⓪

*6 Frith St* ✉ *W1D 3JA* ⊖ *Tottenham Court Road –* ✆ *(020) 7434 1771 – www.hazlittshotel.com* **31**AK**U**u
**27 rm** – ♦£ 222 ♦♦£ 282 – 3 suites **Rest** – *(room service only)*
• Three adjoining early 18C townhouses and former home of the eponymous essayist. Idiosyncratic bedrooms, many with antique furniture and Victorian baths; ask for one of the newer ones.

## Gauthier - Soho
83

XXX

AC 🕸 ⇄ VISA ☎ AE

*21 Romilly St ⊠ W1D 5AF ⊖ Leicester Square – ℰ (020) 7494 3111*
*– www.gauthiersoho.co.uk – Closed Saturday lunch, Sunday and bank holidays*
**Rest** – French – Menu £ 25/35                                          **31**AKU**k**
**Spec.** Warm lobster salad with lemon balm and peach. Cuts of roe deer with truffle and celeriac. Orange blossom soufflé with warm madeleines.
♦ Professionally run restaurant with an intimate and somewhat secretive feel, spread over three floors of a bright 18C townhouse. The refined, elegant cooking emphasises the natural flavours and seasonal freshness of the quality ingredients.

## Quo Vadis

XXX

AC ⇄ VISA ☎ AE

*26-29 Dean St. ⊠ W1D 3LL ⊖ Tottenham Court Road – ℰ (020) 7437 9585*
*– www.quovadis.co.uk – Closed Christmas, Sunday and bank holidays*
**Rest** – British – Menu £ 20 (lunch) – Carte £ 31/46                    **31**AKU**v**
♦ Dating from the 1920s and renewed in 2008; a veritable Soho institution with an art deco feel. Instantly appealing menu of carefully prepared classics, from grilled Longhorn beef to assorted seafood.

## Aqua Nueva

XXX

AC 🕸 ⇄ VISA ☎ AE

*240 Regent St., (entrance on Argyll St.) ⊠ W1B 3BR ⊖ Oxford Circus – ℰ (020)*
*7478 0540 – www.aqua-london.com – Closed 25 December and 1 January*
**Rest** – Spanish – Carte £ 45/74                                         **30**AIU**x**
♦ Large operation on the 5th floor of a former department store. Choose between the elegant main dining room or the more buzzy but equally stylish tapas bar. Spanish food interpreted in a modern style.

## Red Fort

XXX

AC 🕸 VISA ☎ AE

*77 Dean St. ⊠ W1D 3SH ⊖ Tottenham Court Road – ℰ (020) 7437 2525*
*– www.redfort.co.uk – Closed 25 December, lunch Saturday, Sunday and bank*
*holidays*                                                                **31**AKU**x**
**Rest** – Indian – (booking advisable at dinner) Menu £ 20/35 – Carte £ 35/41
♦ A feature in Soho since 1983 but the last makeover gave it a stylish, contemporary look. Balanced cooking uses much UK produce such as Herdwick lamb; look out for more unusual choices like rabbit.

## Imperial China

XXX

AC ⇄ VISA ☎ AE

*White Bear Yard, 25a Lisle Street ⊠ WC2H 7BA ⊖ Leicester Square – ℰ (020)*
*7734 3388 – www.imperial-china.co.uk – Closed 24-25 December*            **31**AKU**l**
**Rest** – Chinese – (booking advisable) Menu £ 19 – Carte £ 30/50
♦ Sharp service and comfortable surroundings are not the only things that set this restaurant apart: the Cantonese cooking exudes freshness and vitality, whether that's the steamed dumplings or the XO minced pork with fine beans.

## Dean Street Townhouse Restaurant

XX

🍴 AC VISA ☎ AE ⓞ

*69-71 Dean St. ⊠ W1D 3SE ⊖ Tottenham Court Road – ℰ (020) 7434 1775*
*– www.deanstreettownhouse.com*                                          **31**AKU**t**
**Rest** – British – (booking essential) Menu £ 20 (lunch) – Carte £ 23/31
♦ Georgian house now home to a fashionable and very busy bar and restaurant; the Parlour is the less hectic area. Appealingly classic British food includes some retro dishes and satisfying puddings.

## Yauatcha
83

XX

AC VISA ☎ AE

*15 Broadwick St ⊠ W1F 0DL ⊖ Tottenham Court Road – ℰ (020) 7494 8888*
*– www.yauatcha.com – Closed 24-25 December and*
*lunch 26 December and 1 January*                                        **31**AJU**k**
**Rest** – Chinese – Carte £ 30/50
**Spec.** Scallop shui mai. Jasmine tea smoked ribs. Milk chocolate praline cake with kalamansi sorbet.
♦ Refined, delicate and delicious dim sum; ideal for sharing in a group. Stylish surroundings spread over two floors: the lighter, brighter ground floor or the darker, more atmospheric basement. Afternoon teas also a speciality.

LONDON

## XX Aqua Kyoto · 🗚 🕾 ⇔ �@ 🆎

*240 Regent St., (entrance on Argyll St.)* ✉ *W1F 7EB* ⊖ *Oxford Circus* – ✆ *(020) 7478 0540* – *www.aqua-london.com* – *Closed 25 December and 1 January*
**Rest** – Japanese – Carte £ 45/65 **s** **30**AIU**x**

• The more boisterous of the two large restaurants on the 5th floor of Aqua London, along with a busy bar. Ideally suited to larger groups, as the contemporary Japanese food is designed for sharing.

## XX Bob Bob Ricard · 🗚 �@ 🆎

*1 Upper James St* ✉ *W1F 9DF* ⊖ *Oxford Circus* – ✆ *(020) 3145 1000* – *www.bobbobricard.com* – *Closed 25-26 December, 1 January, Sunday and Monday* **31**AJU**a**
**Rest** – Traditional – Menu £ 24 (lunch) – Carte £ 29/70

• Enigmatically decorated and flamboyant grand café, with a menu that offers everything from caviar and jelly, to beef Wellington or a bowl of cornflakes. Open from early to very late.

## XX Spice Market – at W London Hotel · 🗚 ⇔ �@ 🆎 ⓘ

*10 Wardour St* ✉ *W1D 6QF* ⊖ *Leicester Square* – ✆ *(020) 7758 1000* – *www.spicemarketlondon.co.uk* **31**AKU**b**
**Rest** – Asian – Menu £ 18/24 – Carte £ 29/51

• Over two floors and as strikingly decorated and as fun as Jean-Georges Vongerichten's original in Manhattan's Meatpacking district. Influences from across Asia in dishes designed for sharing; curries a highlight.

## XX Floridita · 🗚 ⇔ �@ 🆎 ⓘ

*100 Wardour St.* ✉ *W1F 0TN* ⊖ *Tottenham Court Road* – ✆ *(020) 7314 4000* – *www.floriditalondon.com* – *Closed Sunday, Monday and bank holidays*
**Rest** – Latin American – *(dinner only and lunch in December)* **31**AJU**z**
Menu £ 28 – Carte £ 24/56

• Mediterranean tapas on the ground floor; the huge downstairs for live music, dancing and Latin American specialities, from Cuban spice to Argentinean beef. Great cocktails and a party atmosphere.

## XX Vasco and Piero's Pavilion · 🗚 🕾 ⇔ �@ 🆎

*15 Poland St* ✉ *W1F 8QE* ⊖ *Oxford Circus* – ✆ *(020) 7437 8774* – *www.vascosfood.com* – *Closed Saturday lunch, Sunday and bank holidays*
**Rest** – Italian – *(booking essential at lunch)* Menu £ 20 (lunch and **31**AJU**b**
early dinner) – Carte £ 30/38

• Celebrated forty years in 2011; its longevity down to its twice-daily changing menu and the simple but effective Umbrian-influenced cooking. The bright room attracts a high proportion of regulars.

## XX Plum Valley · ⇔ �@ 🆎

*20 Gerrard St.* ✉ *W1D 6JQ* ⊖ *Leicester Square* – ✆ *(020) 7494 4366* – *Closed 24-25 December* **31**AKU**i**
**Rest** – Chinese – Menu £ 38 – Carte £ 23/44

• Its striking black façade make this modern Chinese restaurant easy to spot in Chinatown. Mostly Cantonese cooking, with occasional forays into Vietnam and Thailand; dim sum is the strength.

## XX Haozhan · 🗚 �@ 🆎 ⓘ

*8 Gerrard St* ✉ *W1D 5PJ* ⊖ *Leicester Square* – ✆ *(020) 7434 3838* – *www.haozhan.co.uk* – *Closed 24-26 December* **31**AKU**n**
**Rest** – Chinese – Carte £ 21/41

• Interesting dishes in a fusion style, with mostly Cantonese but other Asian influences too. Specialities like jasmine ribs or wasabi prawns reveal a freshness that marks this restaurant out from the plethora of Chinatown mediocrity.

**Refuel** – at Soho Hotel      AC VISA ◯◯ AE ◯

*4 Richmond Mews ⊠ W1D 3DH ⊖ Tottenham Court Road – 𝒞 (020)*
*7559 3007 – www.sohohotel.com*      **31**AJU**n**

**Rest** – Modern European – Menu £ 25 – Carte £ 34/56

♦ At the heart of the cool Soho hotel is their aptly named bar and restaurant. With a menu to suit all moods and a cocktail list to lift all spirits, it's a fun and frantic spot.

**Bistro du Vin**      AC ⇔ VISA ◯◯ AE ◯

*36 Dean St ⊠ W1D 4PS ⊖ Tottenham Court Road – 𝒞 (020) 7432 4800*
*– www.bistroduvin.co.uk – Closed 25 December*      **31**AKU**e**

**Rest** – Modern European – Carte £ 25/48 ஃ

♦ Followed hot on the heels of their first bistro in Clerkenwell; this one's slightly bigger but otherwise adopts the same formula, by offering an appealing selection of brasserie classics and a decent selection of well-priced wines.

**Arbutus**      AC ஃ VISA ◯◯ AE

ఘ
*63-64 Frith St. ⊠ W1D 3JW ⊖ Tottenham Court Road – 𝒞 (020) 7734 4545*
*– www.arbutusrestaurant.co.uk – Closed 25-26 December and 1 January*

**Rest** – Modern European – *(booking advisable)* Menu £ 17      **31**AKU**h**
(lunch) – Carte £ 27/38 ஃ

**Spec.** Squid and mackerel 'burger', razor clams and sea purslane. Saddle of rabbit, shoulder cottage pie. Cold chocolate fondant, salted caramel ice cream.

♦ It takes a lot of work and experience to make it all look so easy. Bubbly and enthusiastic service; relaxed, sociable surroundings and bistro-style dishes packed with flavour from a highly skilled kitchen. Terrific, affordable wine list.

**Nopi**      AC VISA ◯◯ AE

*21-22 Warwick St. ⊠ W1B 5NE ⊖ Piccadilly Circus – 𝒞 (020) 7494 9584*
*– www.nopi-restaurant.com*      **30**AIU**g**

**Rest** – International – Carte £ 32/40

♦ The bright, clean look of Yotam Ottolenghi's restaurant matches the fresh, invigorating food. The sharing plates take in the Mediterranean, Middle East and Asia and the veg dishes stand out.

**St John** with rm      ⬢ AC ⁽¹⁾ VISA ◯◯ AE ◯

*1 Leicester St. ⊠ WC2H 7BL ⊖ Leicester Square – 𝒞 (020) 3301 8069*
*– www.stjohnhotellondon.com*      **31**AKU**s**

**15 rm** – †£ 330 ††£ 330, ⊑ £ 15

**Rest** – British – *(booking advisable)* Carte £ 28/46

♦ There's a Nordic lucidity to the bedrooms but it is the restaurant that's the heart of the hotel. It follows the Clerkenwell original with its terse menu descriptions, fiercely seasonal, no-nonsense "nose to tail" cooking, municipal-white surroundings and clued-up staff. Dinner is served until 2am.

**Bocca di Lupo**      AC ஃ ⇔ VISA ◯◯ AE

☺
*12 Archer St ⊠ WID 7BB ⊖ Piccadilly Circus – 𝒞 (020) 7734 2223*
*– www.boccadilupo.com – Closed 24 December-4 January and Sunday dinner*

**Rest** – Italian – *(booking essential)* Carte £ 24/35      **31**AJU**e**

♦ Atmosphere, food and service are all best when sitting at the marble counter, watching the chefs at work. Specialities from across Italy come in large or small sizes and are full of flavour and vitality. Try also their Gelato shop opposite.

**Benja Bangkok Table**      AC VISA ◯◯ AE ◯

☺
*17 Beak St. ⊠ W1F 9RW ⊖ Oxford Circus – 𝒞 (020) 7287 0555*
*– www.benja-bankoktable.com*      **30**AIU**j**

**Rest** – Thai – Menu £ 10/15 – Carte £ 18/22

♦ A recent makeover left this Thai restaurant on the edge of Soho with a simpler look that is more typical of a Bangkok eatery. The colourful mix of dishes is authentic and the set menus represent excellent value.

**LONDON**

X
☺ **Polpo**                                    `AC` ⇄ `VISA` ⊙⊙ `AE` ⊙
41 Beak St. ⊠ W1F 9SB ⊖ Oxford Circus – ℰ (0207) 734 44 79
– www.polpo.co.uk – Closed 25 December-1 January, Sunday dinner and bank
holidays                                                        **30**AJU**d**
**Rest** – Italian – (bookings not accepted at dinner) Carte £ 15/25
♦ A fun and lively Venetian bacaro, with a stripped-down, faux-industrial look.
The small plates, from arancini and prosciutto to fritto misto and Cotechino sausage, are so well priced that waiting for a table is worth it.

X
☺ **Dehesa**                                🏠 `AC` ⇄ `VISA` ⊙⊙ `AE`
25 Ganton St ⊠ W1F 9BP ⊖ Oxford Circus – ℰ (020) 7494 4170
– www.dehesa.co.uk – Closed Sunday dinner                       **30**AlU**i**
**Rest** – Mediterranean – Carte £ 20/29 ⌾
♦ Repeats the success of its sister restaurant, Salt Yard, by offering tasty, good
value Spanish and Italian tapas. Unhurried atmosphere in appealing corner location. Terrific drinks list too.

X **Wright Brothers Soho**                      🏠 `AC` `VISA` ⊙⊙ `AE`
13 Kingly St. ⊠ W1B 5PW ⊖ Oxford Circus – ℰ (020) 7434 3611
– www.thewrightbrothers.co.uk – Closed 25-27 December and bank holidays
**Rest** – Seafood – Carte £ 24/35                              **30**AlU**z**
♦ Bigger than the original in Borough Market, this branch is spread over three
levels but the best spot is at the counter on the lower floor. Oysters a speciality
but all seafood is handled deftly.

X **Hix**                                        `AC` ⇄ `VISA` ⊙⊙ `AE` ⊙
66-70 Brewer St. ⊠ WIF 9UP ⊖ Piccadilly Circus – ℰ (020) 7292 3518
– www.hixsoho.co.uk – Closed 25-26 December                     **30**AJU**z**
**Rest** – British – Menu £ 23 (lunch) – Carte £ 29/61
♦ The exterior hints at exclusivity but the enormous interior is fun and sociable
and comes decorated with the works of eminent British artists. Expect classic British dishes and ingredients.

X **Tapas Brindisa**                                      `VISA` ⊙⊙ `AE`
46 Broadwick St. ⊠ W1F 7AF ⊖ Oxford Circus – ℰ (020) 7534 1690
– www.brindisa.com – Closed 25 December                         **31**AJU**f**
**Rest** – Spanish – (bookings not accepted) Carte £ 18/44
♦ A few changes in 2011 to this sister of Tapas Brindisa in Borough Market. They
moved the bar to the front, changed the name and no longer take bookings; but
expect the same quality of tapas from these importers of Spanish produce.

X
☺ **Barrafina**                                  `AC` `VISA` ⊙⊙ `AE` ⊙
54 Frith St. ⊠ W1D 3SL ⊖ Tottenham Court Road – ℰ (020) 7813 8016
– www.barrafina.co.uk – Closed 24 December and 1 January        **31**AKU**c**
**Rest** – Spanish – (bookings not accepted) Carte £ 17/26
♦ Centred around a counter with seating for 20, come here if you want authentic
Spanish tapas served in a buzzy atmosphere. Seafood is a speciality and the Ja-
bugo ham a must.

X **Barshu**                                     `AC` ⇄ `VISA` ⊙⊙ `AE`
28 Frith St. ⊠ W1D 5LF ⊖ Leicester Square – ℰ (020) 7287 8822
– www.bar-shu.co.uk – Closed 24-25 December                     **31**AKU**g**
**Rest** – Chinese – (booking advisable) Carte £ 19/47
♦ The fiery and authentic flavours of China's Sichuan Province are the draw here;
help is at hand as menu has pictures. It's decorated with carved wood and lanterns; downstairs is better for groups.

X **Polpetto**                                          `VISA` ⊙⊙ `AE`
46 Dean St. (1st floor) ⊠ W1D 5BG ⊖ Leicester Square – ℰ (020) 7734 1969
– www.polpetto.co.uk – Closed 24 December-2 January, Sunday and bank
holidays                                                        **31**AKU**d**
**Rest** – Italian – Carte £ 18/20
♦ Baby sister to Polpo is located, incongruously, above the iconic French House
pub. It's just one small but thoughtfully designed room; order a number of the
small, keenly priced plates.

X **Spuntino**    AC VISA ⓄⓄ AE

*61 Rupert St.* ⊠ *W1D 7PW* ⊖ *Piccadilly Circus*
*– www.spuntino.co.uk – Closed 25 December-2 January and dinner*
*24 December*                                                          **31**AJU**j**
**Rest** – American – *(bookings not accepted)* Carte £ 12/22
• Influenced by Downtown New York, with its no-booking policy and industrial look. Sit at the counter and order classics like Mac 'n' cheese or mini burgers. The staff, who look like they could also fix your car, really add to the fun.

X **Ba Shan**    AC ⇄ VISA ⓄⓄ AE

*24 Romilly St.* ⊠ *W1D 5AH* ⊖ *Leicester Square* – ✆ *(020) 7287 3266*
*– Closed 24-25 December*                                              **31**AKU**f**
**Rest** – Chinese – *(booking advisable)* Carte £ 17/30
• 3-4 tables in each of the five rooms. Open all day, serving a mix of 'snack' and 'home-style' dishes, some with Sichuan leanings, others from northern areas and Henan province.

X **Imli**    AC VISA ⓄⓄ AE Ⓞ

*167-169 Wardour St* ⊠ *W1F 8WR* ⊖ *Tottenham Court Road*
*– ✆ (020) 7287 4243 – www.imli.co.uk – Closed 25-26 December and 1 January*
**Rest** – Indian – Menu £ 20 (dinner) – Carte £ 16/20              **31**AJU**w**
• Diffusion line from the people behind Tamarind restaurant, where good value, fresh and tasty Indian tapas-style dishes prove a popular currency. The long, spacious interior is a busy, buzzy place.

X **Cây Tre**    AC VISA ⓄⓄ AE

*42-43 Dean St* ⊠ *W1D 4PZ* ⊖ *Tottenham Court Road* – ✆ *(020) 7317 9118*
*– www.caytreesoho.co.uk*                                             **31**AKU**m**
**Rest** – Vietnamese – *(booking advisable)* Menu £ 14/21 – Carte £ 20/40
• Bright, sleek and bustling surroundings where Vietnamese standouts include Cha La lot (spicy ground pork wrapped in betel leaves), slow-cooked Mekong catfish with a well-judged sweet and spicy sauce, and 6 versions of Pho (noodle soup).

X **Baozi Inn**    AC VISA ⓄⓄ AE

*25 Newport Court* ⊠ *WC2H 7JS* ⊖ *Leicester Square* – ✆ *(020) 7287 6877*
*– Closed 24-25 December*                                             **31**AKU**o**
**Rest** – Chinese – Carte approx. £ 14
• Baozi, or steamed filled buns, are a good way to start, followed by some fiery Sichuan specialities. Simple, honest and friendly restaurant, just off the main strip of Chinatown.

X **Koya**    AC VISA ⓄⓄ AE
☺
*49 Frith St.* ⊠ *W1D 4SG* ⊖ *Tottenham Court Road* – ✆ *(020) 7434 4463*
*– www.koya.co.uk – Closed Christmas*                                 **31**AKU**y**
**Rest** – Japanese – *(bookings not accepted)* Carte £ 14/18
• Come for authentic udon noodles, made with wheat kneaded by foot, at this sweetly run, simply adorned place. The dashi base stock is freshly made every day. Be respectful by slurping with abandon.

X **Beijing Dumpling**    AC VISA ⓄⓄ AE

*23 Lisle St.* ⊠ *WC2H 7BA* ⊖ *Leicester Square* – ✆ *(020) 7287 6888*
*– Closed 24-25 December*                                             **31**AKU**l**
**Rest** – Chinese – Carte £ 15/25
• This relaxed little place serves freshly prepared dumplings of both Beijing and Shanghai styles. Although the range is not as comprehensive as the name suggests, they do stand out, especially varieties of the famed Siu Lung Bao.

## STRAND AND COVENT GARDEN

### Savoy 🔲 🖪 🎽 🔥 🕮 📶 🚵 🗺 📵 🌚 🌚 🌚

*Strand* ✉ *WC2R 0EU* ⊖ *Charing Cross –* ✆ *(020) 7836 4343*
*– www.fairmont.com/savoy*                                  **31**ALU**s**
**221 rm –** ♦£ 678 ♦♦£ 750, � £ 30 – 47 suites
**Rest** *Savoy Grill* **Rest** *River Room* – see restaurant listing
• The grande dame of London hotels dazzles once again! Reopened in 2010 following a 3 year restoration, its luxurious bedrooms and stunning suites come in an Edwardian or art deco style. Thames Foyer is the hotel's heart; choose the famous American Bar or new Beaufort Bar.

### One Aldwych 🔲 🕮 🖪 🕮 🎽 rm, 🕮 🕌 📶 🚵 🅿 🗺 🌚 🌚 🌚

*1 Aldwych* ✉ *WC2B 4RH* ⊖ *Temple –* ✆ *(020) 7300 1000*
*– www.onealdwych.com*                                      **32**AMU**r**
**93 rm –** ♦£ 288/415 ♦♦£ 288/498, � £ 24 – 12 suites
**Rest** *Axis* – see restaurant listing
**Rest** *Indigo –* ✆ *(020) 7300 0000* – Menu £ 20 (lunch) – Carte £ 39/52
• Former 19C bank, now a stylish hotel with lots of artwork; the lobby changes its look seasonally and doubles as a bar. Stylish, contemporary bedrooms with the latest mod cons; the deluxe rooms and suites are particularly desirable. Impressive leisure facilities. Light, accessible menu at Indigo.

### St Martins Lane 🖪 🖪 🕮 🎽 🚵 🗺 🌚 🌚 🌚

*45 St Martin's Ln* ✉ *WC2N 3HX* ⊖ *Charing Cross –* ✆ *(020) 7300 5500*
*– www.stmartinslane.com*                                   **31**ALU**e**
**202 rm –** ♦£ 258/594 ♦♦£ 258/594, � £ 25 – 2 suites
**Rest** *Asia de Cuba* – see restaurant listing
• The unmistakable hand of Philippe Starck evident at this most contemporary of hotels. Unique and stylish, from the starkly modern lobby to the state-of-the-art rooms. 350 varieties of rum and tasty Asian dishes at fashionable Asia de Cuba.

### XXX Savoy Grill – at Savoy Hotel 🕮 🍽 ⇄ 🗺 🌚 🌚 🌚

*Strand* ✉ *WC2R 0EU* ⊖ *Charing Cross –* ✆ *(020) 7592 1600*
*– www.gordonramsay.com/thesavoygrill*                      **31**ALU**s**
**Rest** – British – Carte £ 30/56
• Archives were explored, designers briefed and much money spent, with the result that The Savoy Grill has returned to the traditions that made it famous. As befits the name, it is the charcoal grilling of meats that takes centre stage.

### XXX The Ivy 🕮 🍽 ⇄ 🗺 🌚 🌚

*1-5 West St* ✉ *WC2H 9NQ* ⊖ *Leicester Square –* ✆ *(020) 7836 4751*
*– www.the-ivy.co.uk – Closed 25-26 December*                **31**AKU**p**
**Rest** – International – Carte £ 38/50
• One of the original celebrity hang-out restaurants; still pulling them in. Appealing menu, from shepherd's pie to fishcakes and nursery puddings. Staff go about their business with alacrity.

### XXX Axis – at One Aldwych Hotel 🕮 🍽 ⇄ 🗺 🌚 🌚 🌚

*1 Aldwych* ✉ *WC2B 4RH* ⊖ *Temple –* ✆ *(020) 7300 0300*
*– www.onealdwych.com – Closed Sunday and Monday*            **31**AMU**r**
**Rest** – Modern European – Menu £ 20 (lunch and early dinner) – Carte £ 34/39

• A spiral marble staircase leading down to this impressively high-ceilinged restaurant adds to the expectation. The menu is a combination of British classics and lighter European choices.

### XXX River Room – at Savoy Hotel 🍽 🕮 🗺 🌚 🌚 🌚

*Strand* ✉ *WC2R 0EU* ⊖ *Charing Cross –* ✆ *(020) 7836 4343*
*– www.fairmont.com/savoy*                                   **31**ALU**s**
**Rest** – Modern European – Menu £ 35 (lunch) – Carte £ 24/67
• Few restaurants have boasted such an illustrious guest list. Its look has been rejuvenated and the menu updated but the formality, grandeur and river views are as impressive as ever.

LONDON

XX **J. Sheekey**  ⒶⒸ ☜ 🆅🅸🆂🅰 ⊛ 🅰🅴 ⓪
28-34 St Martin's Ct. ✉ WC2 4AL ⊖ Leicester Square – ✆ (020) 7240 2565
– www.j-sheekey.co.uk – Closed 25-26 December  **31**ALU**v**
**Rest** – Seafood – (booking essential) Menu £ 28 (weekends) – Carte £ 30/72
♦ Festooned with photographs of actors and linked to the theatrical world since opening in 1890. Wood panels and alcove tables add famed intimacy. Accomplished seafood cooking.

XX **Rules**  ⒶⒸ ☜ ⇔ 🆅🅸🆂🅰 ⊛ 🅰🅴
35 Maiden Ln ✉ WC2E 7LB ⊖ Leicester Square – ✆ (020) 7836 5314
– www.rules.co.uk – Closed Christmas  **31**ALU**n**
**Rest** – British – (booking essential) Carte £ 34/47
♦ London's oldest restaurant boasts a fine collection of antique cartoons, drawings and paintings. Tradition continues in the menu, specialising in game from its own estate.

XX **Clos Maggiore**  ⒶⒸ ☜ ⇔ 🆅🅸🆂🅰 ⊛ 🅰🅴 ⓪
33 King St ✉ WC2E 8JD ⊖ Leicester Square – ✆ (020) 7379 9696
– www.closmaggiore.com – Closed 25 December and 1 January  **31**ALU**z**
**Rest** – French – Menu £ 20 (lunch and early dinner) – Carte £ 32/36 ⌂
♦ Well-dressed restaurant with poised service; ask for a table in the enchanting little rear conservatory, whose roof opens in summer. Sophisticated cooking from a largely French repertoire. Exceptional value lunch and pre-theatre menus.

XX **Forge**  ⒶⒸ ☜ 🆅🅸🆂🅰 ⊛ 🅰🅴
14 Garrick St ✉ WC2E 9BJ ⊖ Leicester Square – ✆ (020) 7379 1432
– www.theforgerestaurant.co.uk – Closed 24-26 December
**Rest** – Modern European – Menu £ 17/30 – Carte £ 29/38  **31**ALU**a**
♦ Décor mixes the old with the new; the front area is more intimate, the back more fun. Extensive menu offers something for everyone, from pasta to Dover sole, tournedos Rossini to a hamburger.

XX **Le Deuxième**  ⒶⒸ ☜ 🆅🅸🆂🅰 ⊛ 🅰🅴
65a Long Acre ✉ WC2E 9JH ⊖ Covent Garden – ✆ (020) 7379 0033
– www.ledeuxieme.com – Closed 24-25 December  **31**ALU**b**
**Rest** – Modern European – Menu £ 17 (lunch) – Carte £ 29/38
♦ Caters well for theatregoers: opens early, closes late. Buzzy eatery, simply decorated in white with subtle lighting. International menu but emphasis within Europe.

XX **Les Deux Salons**  ⒶⒸ ☜ ⇔ 🆅🅸🆂🅰 ⊛ 🅰🅴
40-42 William IV St ✉ WC2N 4DD ⊖ Charing Cross – ✆ (020) 7420 2050
– www.lesdeuxsalons.co.uk – Closed 25-26 December and 1 January
**Rest** – French – Menu £ 16 (lunch) – Carte £ 28/40 ⌂  **31**ALU**m**
♦ Authentic Parisian brasserie complete with smoked mirrors, globe lights and striking mosaic floor. Ground floor is the better salon for atmosphere. Appealing menu mixes French classics, chargrilled meats and the odd British interloper.

XX **Opera Tavern**  ⒶⒸ 🆅🅸🆂🅰 ⊛ 🅰🅴
🙂 23 Catherine St. ✉ WC2B 5JS ⊖ Covent Garden – ✆ (020) 7836 3680
– www.operatavern.co.uk – Closed 24 December-2 January and dinner
Sunday and bank holidays  **31**ALU**y**
**Rest** – Mediterranean – Carte £ 22/39 ⌂
♦ Shares the same appealing concept of small plates of Spanish and Italian delicacies as its sisters, Salt Yard and Dehesa. All done in a smartly converted old boozer which dates from 1879; ground floor bar and upstairs dining room.

XX **Kyashii**  ⒶⒸ ⇔ 🆅🅸🆂🅰 ⊛ 🅰🅴
4a Upper St Martin's Lane ✉ WC2H 9NY ⊖ Leicester Square – ✆ (020)
7836 5211 – www.kyashii.co.uk – Closed 25 December  **31**ALU**w**
**Rest** – Japanese – Carte £ 25/43
♦ Bright young things come for contemporary Japanese food at this eye-catching restaurant, with its mix of cream leather, mirrors, fish tanks and long marble sushi bar; trendy Shaker bar upstairs.

LONDON

LONDON

XX **Asia de Cuba** – at St Martins Lane Hotel    AC VISA ◎◎ AE ①
*45 St Martin's Ln ⊠ WC2N 3HX ⊖ Charing Cross – ℰ (020) 7300 5500
– www.morganshotelgroup.com*    31ALUe
**Rest** – Asian – Carte £ 49/74
♦ The striking Philippe Starck designed room and the Asian and Cuban inspired
cooking appeal to a young, hip crowd. Sharing is the key and that should also
include the bill.

X **L'Atelier de Joël Robuchon**    AC ❄❄ VISA ◎◎ AE
❀❀ *13-15 West St. ⊠ WC2H 9NE ⊖ Leicester Square – ℰ (020) 7010 8600
– www.joelrobuchon.co.uk – Closed 25-26 December,1 January, Sunday and
bank holiday Mondays*    31AKUa
**Rest** – French – Menu £ 29/125 – Carte £ 45/83
**Spec.** Chicken broth with foie gras ravioli and zesty whipped cream. Free-range
quail stuffed with foie gras and truffled mashed potatoes. Warm yuzu soufflé
with vanilla infused raspberry sorbet.
♦ Wonderfully precise, creative and occasionally playful cooking; dishes may look
delicate but pack a punch. Ground floor Atelier with counter seating and chefs on
view. More structured La Cuisine. Cool top floor bar.

X **J. Sheekey Oyster Bar**    ❄❄ VISA ◎◎ AE ①
*33-34 St Martin's Ct. ⊠ WC2 4AL ⊖ Leicester Square – ℰ (020) 7240 2565
– www.j-sheekey.co.uk – Closed 25-26 December*    31ALUv
**Rest** – Seafood – Carte £ 24/57
♦ An addendum to J. Sheekey restaurant. Sit at the bar to watch the chefs prepare the same quality seafood as next door but at slightly lower prices; fish pie
and fruits de mer are the popular choices. Open all day.

X **Terroirs**    VISA ◎◎ AE
☺ *5 William IV St ⊠ WC2N 4DW ⊖ Charing Cross – ℰ (020) 7036 0660
– www.terroirswinebar.com – Closed 25-26 December, 1 January, Sunday and
bank holidays*    31ALUh
**Rest** – French – Carte £ 19/31❄
♦ Eat in the ground floor bistro/wine bar or two floors below at 'Downstairs at
Terroirs' where the menu is a little more substantial. Flavoursome French cooking
with extra Italian and Spanish influences. Thoughtfully compiled wine list.

X **Hawksmoor**    AC ❄❄ ⇔ VISA ◎◎ AE
*11 Langley St ⊠ WC2H 9GJ ⊖ Covent Garden – ℰ (020) 7856 2154
– www.thehawksmoor.com – Closed 2-4 January , 24-30 December and Sunday
dinner*    31ALUz
**Rest** – Beef specialities – Menu £ 23 (lunch and early dinner) – Carte £ 36/55
♦ Steaks from Longhorn cattle lovingly reared in North Yorkshire and dry-aged
for at least 35 days are the stars of the show. Atmospheric, bustling basement
restaurant in former brewery cellars.

X **da Polpo**    AC VISA ◎◎ AE
☺ *6 Maiden Ln. ⊠ WC2E 7NA ⊖ Leicester Square – ℰ (020) 7836 8448
– www.dapolpo.co.uk – Closed dinner 24 December-1 January*    31ALUp
**Rest** – Italian – (bookings not accepted at dinner) Carte £ 15/25
♦ First Soho, now Covent Garden gets a fun Venetian bacaro. The small plates are
surprisingly filling, with delights such as pizzette of white anchovy vying with fennel and almond salad, fritto misto competing with spaghettini and meatballs.

X **Bedford & Strand**    VISA ◎◎ AE
*1a Bedford St ⊠ WC2E 9HH ⊖ Charing Cross – ℰ (020) 7836 3033
– www.bedford-strand.com – Closed 24 December-2 January, Sunday and bank
holidays*    31ALUc
**Rest** – British – (booking essential) Menu £ 18 (dinner) – Carte £ 26/35
♦ They call themselves a 'wine room and bistro' which neatly sums up both the
philosophy and the style of the place – interesting wines, reassuringly familiar
food and relaxed basement surroundings.

**VICTORIA**

### Corinthia 🔲 🏵 🏠 ℆ 🖼 ⚫ 🗚 ✗ ⚟ 🆒 🚗 VISA ⓪ AE ①
*Whitehall Pl.* ⊠ *SW1A 2BD* ⊖ *Embankment* – ℘ *(020) 7930 8181*
*– www.corinthia.com/london*                                              **31**ALV**x**
**271 rm** – ♦£ 346/594 ♦♦£ 370/900, � £ 33 – 23 suites
**Rest *Northall* Rest *Massimo*** – see restaurant listing
♦ London's latest grand hotel opened in 2011; its restored Victorian splendour cannot fail to impress. Tasteful, immaculately finished bedrooms are some of the largest in town; suites come with butlers. The stunning spa is over four floors.

### Goring 🚗 🖼 AC ✗ ⚟ 🆒 VISA ⓪ AE ①
*15 Beeston Pl, Grosvenor Gdns* ⊠ *SW1W 0JW* ⊖ *Victoria* – ℘ *(020) 7396 9000*
*– www.thegoring.com*                                                      **38**AIX**a**
**62 rm** – ♦£ 492/570 ♦♦£ 550, ⊠ £ 25 – 7 suites
**Rest *Goring*** – see restaurant listing
♦ Celebrated its centenary in 2010; this very English hotel is still owned, invested in and run by the Goring family who built it – the fourth generation now at the helm. Many of the attractive rooms overlook a peaceful garden.

### Crowne Plaza London - St James 🏠 🖼 ⚫ 🗚 AC ✗ ⚟ 🆒
*45 Buckingham Gate* ⊠ *SW1E 6AF* ⊖ *St James's Park*              VISA ⓪ AE ①
*– ℘ (020) 7834 6655 – www.london.crowneplaza.com*                        **39**AJX**e**
**323 rm** – ♦£ 142/546 ♦♦£ 390/546, ⊠ £ 22.50 – 19 suites
**Rest *Quilon*❀** – see restaurant listing
♦ Built in 1897 as serviced accommodation for visiting aristocrats. Behind the impressive Edwardian façade lies an equally elegant interior. Quietest rooms overlook courtyard.

### 51 Buckingham Gate without rest 🏵 🏠 🖼 ⚫ AC ✗ ⚟ VISA ⓪ AE ①
*51 Buckingham Gate* ⊠ *SW1E 6AF* ⊖ *St James's Park* – ℘ *(020) 7769 7766*
*– www.51-buckinghamgate.com*                                             **39**AJX**s**
**86 suites** – ♦♦£ 600, ⊠ £ 22.50
♦ In the courtyard of the Crowne Plaza but offering greater levels of comfort and service. Contemporary in style, suites range from one to nine bedrooms. Butler service available. Restaurants located in adjacent hotel.

### St Ermin's 🏠 🖼 ⚫ 🗚 & rm, AC ⚟ 🆒 🚗 VISA ⓪ AE ①
*2 Caxton St.* ⊠ *SW1H 0QW* ⊖ *St James's Park* – ℘ *(020) 7222 7888*
*– www.sterminshotel.co.uk*                                                **39**AKX**a**
**290 rm** – ♦£ 412 ♦♦£ 412, ⊠ £ 24 – 41 suites – ♦♦£ 625/875
**Rest *Caxton Grill*** – Menu £ 25 (lunch) – Carte £ 35/50
♦ Built as an apartment block in 1897 but it has spent most of its life as a hotel and has been a favoured spot for many a politician. A comprehensive 2011 refurbishment restored many of its original features; the public areas are the strength. The restaurant specialises in meat cooked on the Josper grill.

### 41 without rest ⚫ AC ⚟ VISA ⓪ AE ①
*41 Buckingham Palace Rd.* ⊠ *SW1W 0PS* ⊖ *Victoria* – ℘ *(020) 7300 0041*
*– www.41hotel.com*                                                        **38**AIX**n**
**29 rm** – ♦£ 299 ♦♦£ 443, ⊠ £ 25 – 1 suite
♦ Smart and discreet addendum to The Rubens hotel next door. Attractively decorated and quiet lounge where breakfast is served; comfortable bedrooms boast fireplaces and plenty of extras.

### The Rubens at The Palace ⚫ AC ⚟ 🆒 VISA ⓪ AE ①
*39 Buckingham Palace Rd* ⊠ *SW1W 0PS* ⊖ *Victoria* – ℘ *(020) 7834 6600*
*– www.rubenshotel.com*                                                    **38**AIX**n**
**160 rm** – ♦£ 167/311 ♦♦£ 179/671, ⊠ £ 18.50 – 1 suite
**Rest *Old Masters*** – (closed lunch Saturday and Sunday) Menu £ 30
**Rest *Library*** – (dinner only) Menu £ 40 – Carte £ 45/58
**Rest *bbar*** – ℘ (020) 7958 7000 (closed Sunday) Menu £ 21 – Carte £ 27/45
♦ Discreet, comfortable hotel in great location for visitors to London. Constant reinvestment ensures bright and contemporary bedrooms. Old Masters for grills., Fine dining in cosy Library. Casual dining in bbar.

**Tophams** without rest     📶 🕸 📵 🚩 VISA ⓒ AE

*24-32 Ebury St ⊠ SW1W 0LU ⊖ Victoria – ℰ (020) 7730 3313*
*– www.tophamshotel.com*     **38**AHY**d**
**50 rm** – †£ 180/225 ††£ 195/275, � £ 14.95

• A row of five pretty terraced houses, in a good spot for tourists and recently refurbished. Neat bedrooms with large bathrooms and good mod cons. Comfortable breakfast room.

**B + B Belgravia** without rest     🚗 ຮ 🚩 VISA ⓒ AE

*64-66 Ebury St ⊠ SW1W 9QD ⊖ Victoria – ℰ (020) 7259 8570*
*– www.bb-belgravia.com*     **38**AHY**x**
**17 rm** ⊠ – †£ 99 ††£ 150/275

• Two houses, three floors, and, considering the location, representing good value accommodation. Sleek, clean-lined bedrooms. Breakfast overlooking little garden terrace.

**Lord Milner** without rest     📶 AC 🕸 🚩 VISA ⓒ AE

*111 Ebury St ⊠ SW1W 9QU ⊖ Victoria – ℰ (020) 7881 9880*
*– www.lordmilner.com*     **38**AHY**k**
**10 rm** – †£ 125/175 ††£ 155/175, ⊠ £ 14 – 1 suite

• A four storey terraced house, with individually decorated bedrooms, three with four-poster beds and all with marble bathrooms. Garden Suite the best room, with its own patio. No public areas.

XXX    **Quilon** – at Crowne Plaza London - St James Hotel     AC VISA ⓒ AE ⓪
ⓔ3   *41 Buckingham Gate ⊠ SW1E 6AF ⊖ St James's Park – ℰ (020) 7821 1899*
*– www.quilon.co.uk – Closed 25 December and Saturday lunch*     **39**AJX**e**
**Rest** – Indian – Menu £ 24/41 – Carte dinner £ 45/60
**Spec.** Crab cakes with curry leaves, ginger and green chillies. Seared fillet of monkfish in a shrimp, scallop and mustard sauce. Rice pudding with rose ice cream.

• Vibrant and well-balanced Indian dishes, many of which originate from the south west coast of India but are given a 'Western' twist. Skilled use of spices, appealing seafood specialities and well-organised service.

XXX    **Roux at Parliament Square**     AC 🔄 VISA ⓒ AE ⓪

*RICS, Parliament Sq. ⊠ SW1P 3AD ⊖ Westminster – ℰ (020) 7334 3737*
*– www.rouxatparliamentsquare.co.uk – Closed 23 December-3 January,*
*Saturday, Sunday and bank holidays*     **39**ALX**x**
**Rest** – French – Menu £ 25 (lunch) – Carte £ 39/55
• Light floods through the Georgian windows of this comfortable Westminster restaurant, popular with MPs and surveyors. French base to the food, which is intricate but also light and contemporary.

XXX    **Roussillon**     AC VISA ⓒ AE

*16 St Barnabas St ⊠ SW1W 8PE ⊖ Sloane Square – ℰ (020) 7730 5550*
*– www.roussillon.co.uk – Closed 25 December, Saturday lunch*
*and Sunday, restricted opening on Bank Holidays*     **38**AHZ**c**
**Rest** – French – Menu £ 35/65 ⊛
• A longstanding neighbourhood restaurant, with a comfortable, discreet and grown up feel. Expect quite formal service and a menu offering plenty of choice and a creative style of cooking.

XXX    **The Cinnamon Club**     AC 🕸 🔄 P VISA ⓒ AE ⓪

*30-32 Great Smith St ⊠ SW1P 3BU ⊖ St James's Park – ℰ (020) 7222 2555*
*– www.cinnamonclub.com – Closed 26 December, 1 January and Sunday*
**Rest** – Indian – Menu £ 22 (lunch) – Carte £ 40/75     **39**AKX**c**
• Housed in former Westminster Library: exterior has ornate detail, interior is stylish and modern. Walls are lined with books. New Wave Indian cooking with plenty of choice.

XXX **Santini**                                    🛝 AC 🕼 VISA ⚫ AE

*29 Ebury St ⊠ SW1W 0NZ ⊖ Victoria – ℰ (020) 7730 4094
– www.santini-restaurant.com – Closed Easter, 24-26 December, 1 January and
lunch Saturday-Sunday*                                    **38**AHY**v**
**Rest** – Italian – Menu £ 25 (dinner) – Carte £ 32/54
♦ Smart, crisp and cool Italian restaurant, with a large, impressive terrace and
old-school service. Menu has subtle Venetian accent but is not inexpensive; pastas and desserts are good.

XXX **Shepherd's**                                AC ⇄ VISA ⚫ AE ⓘ

*Marsham Ct., Marsham St. ⊠ SW1P 4LA ⊖ Pimlico – ℰ (020) 7834 9552
– www.langansrestaurants.co.uk – Closed Saturday, Sunday and bank holidays*
**Rest** – British – (booking essential) Carte £ 22/26              **39**AKY**z**
♦ A thoroughly British and enjoyably old-school restaurant where the menu
reads like a UKIP manifesto; game and traditional puddings are a highlight. Popular with those from Westminster – the booths offer a degree of privacy.

XXX **Goring** – at Goring Hotel                🚗 AC VISA ⚫ AE ⓘ

*15 Beeston Pl, Grosvenor Gdns ⊠ SW1W 0JW ⊖ Victoria – ℰ (020) 7396 9000
– www.thegoring.com – Closed Saturday lunch*                **38**AIX**a**
**Rest** – British – Menu £ 36/49 ⅏
♦ Designed by David Linley, this is a refined and grown-up restaurant as befits a
hotel as charming as The Goring. The menu celebrates British cooking; the roast
from the trolley is always popular.

XXX **Northall** – at Corinthia Hotel            AC VISA ⚫ AE ⓘ

*Whitehall Pl. ⊠ SW1A 2BD ⊖ Embankment – ℰ (020) 7930 8181
– www.corinthia.com/london*                                **31**ALV**x**
**Rest** – British – Menu £ 28 – Carte £ 28/56
♦ The menu champions British produce and producers and you can get a choice
of room, linked by a display of meats and cheeses: a modern bistro-style room or
a more formal dining room set over two levels.

XXX **Massimo** – at Corinthia Hotel            AC 🕼 ⇄ VISA ⚫ AE ⓘ

*Whitehall Pl. ⊠ SW1A 2BD ⊖ Embankment – ℰ (020) 7930 8181
– www.corinthia.com/london*                                **31**ALV**x**
**Rest** – Italian – Menu £ 28 – Carte £ 35/75
♦ Opulent, visually impressive room with an oyster bar on one side. On offer are
traditional dishes true to the regions; fish and seafood dishes stand out. Impressive private dining room comes with its own chef.

XX **Il Convivio**                               AC ⇄ VISA ⚫ AE

*143 Ebury St ⊠ SW1W 9QN ⊖ Sloane Square – ℰ (020) 7730 4099
– www.ilconvivio.co.uk – Closed Christmas-New Year and Sunday*    **38**AHY**a**
**Rest** – Italian – Carte £ 32/51
♦ Handsome Georgian house, with a retractable roof and Dante's poetry embossed on the walls. All pasta is made on the top floor of the house. Dishes are
artfully presented and flavoursome.

XX **Tinello**                                        VISA ⚫ AE

*87 Pimlico Rd ⊠ SW1W 8PH ⊖ Sloane Square – ℰ (020) 7730 3663
– www.tinello.co.uk – Closed Sunday and bank hoildays*          **37**AGZ**s**
**Rest** – Italian – (booking essential at dinner) Carte £ 38/44
♦ Sleekly designed Italian restaurant run by two brothers, both alumni of Locanda Locatelli. Their native Tuscany informs the cooking; the antipasti or 'small
eats' section is very appealing.

XX **Boisdale**                                  🛝 AC ⇄ VISA ⚫ AE ⓘ

*15 Eccleston St ⊠ SW1W 9LX ⊖ Victoria – ℰ (020) 7730 6922
– www.boisdale.co.uk – Closed 1 week Christmas, Saturday lunch and Sunday*
**Rest** – Scottish – Carte £ 29/77                          **38**AHY**c**
♦ A proudly Scottish restaurant with acres of tartan and a charmingly higgledy-
piggledy layout. Stand-outs are the smoked salmon and the 28-day aged Aberdeenshire cuts of beef. Live nightly jazz.

LONDON

**LONDON**

XX **Bank** – at Crowne Plaza London-St James Hotel  〔icons〕
*45 Buckingham Gate* ⊠ *SW1E 6BS* ⊖ *St James's Park –* 𝒞 *(020) 7630 6644*
*– www.bankrestaurants.com – Closed Sunday and bank holidays*  **39**AJX
**Rest** – Modern European – *(booking essential at lunch)* Menu £ 38 – Carte £ 35/8
♦ Behind the understated entrance lies a vibrant and busy interior. Pass throug
one of Europe's longest bars to reach the conservatory restaurant, where you'
find a varied, accessible menu.

XX **Ebury Wine Bar**  〔icons〕
*139 Ebury St.* ⊠ *SW1W 9QU* ⊖ *Victoria –* 𝒞 *(020) 7730 5447*
*– www.eburyrestaurant.co.uk – Closed 22 December-2 January*  **38**AHY
**Rest** – Modern European – Menu £ 22 (lunch and early dinner) – Carte £ 31/39
♦ Going strong for over 50 years and as likeable as ever. Some imaginativ
touches but generally quite classic cooking. Dairy and gluten free menus offere
along with a keenly-priced wine list.

XX **Osteria Dell' Angolo**  〔icons〕
*47 Marsham St.* ⊠ *SW1P 3DR* ⊖ *St. James's Park –* 𝒞 *(020) 3268 1077*
*– www.osteriadellangolo.co.uk – Closed Easter, 20 August-2 September,*
*24 December-3 January, Saturday lunch, Sunday and bank holidays*
**Rest** – Italian – Menu £ 21 (lunch) – Carte £ 32/39  **39**AKY
♦ Expert restaurateur Claudio Pulze opened this sunny Italian restaurant opposi
the Home Office in 2009. Tuscan element to the cooking, along with some crea
tivity; service is keen and friendly.

X **Olivo**  〔icons〕
*21 Eccleston St* ⊠ *SW1W 9LX* ⊖ *Victoria –* 𝒞 *(020) 7730 2505*
*– www.olivorestaurant.com – Closed lunch Saturday-Sunday and bank holiday*
**Rest** – Italian – Menu £ 28 (lunch) – Carte dinner £ 25/32  **38**AHY
♦ Carefully prepared, authentic Sardinian specialities are the highlight at th
popular Italian restaurant. Simply decorated in blues and yellows, with an atmo
sphere of bonhomie.

X **Olivomare**  〔icons〕
*10 Lower Belgrave St* ⊠ *SW1W 0LJ* ⊖ *Victoria –* 𝒞 *(020) 7730 9022*
*– www.olivorestaurants.com – Closed bank holidays*  **38**AHY
**Rest** – Seafood – Carte £ 29/38
♦ Expect understated and stylish piscatorial decoration and seafood with a Sa
dinian base. Fortnightly changing menu, with high quality produce, much o
which is available in shop next door.

🍴 **Ebury**  〔icons〕
*11 Pimlico Rd* ⊠ *SW1W 8NA* ⊖ *Sloane Square. –* 𝒞 *(020) 7730 6784*
*– www.theebury.co.uk*  **38**AHZ
**Rest** – Modern European – Carte £ 30/39
♦ Smart and stylish room, with an appealing menu ranging from burgers to blac
bream. Low-slung tables around popular central bar; efficient service. Upstairs
used for private parties.

🍴 **Thomas Cubitt**  〔icons〕
*44 Elizabeth St* ⊠ *SW1W 9PA* ⊖ *Sloane Square. –* 𝒞 *(020) 7730 6060*
*– www.thethomascubitt.co.uk – Closed Christmas and New Year*  **38**AHY
**Rest** – Modern European – *(booking essential)* Carte £ 29/49
♦ A pub of two halves: choose the busy ground floor bar with its accessibl
menu or upstairs for more ambitious, quite elaborate cooking with courteous se
vice and a less frenetic environment.

🍴 **Orange** with rm  〔icons〕
*37 Pimlico Rd* ⊠ *SW1W 8NE* ⊖ *Sloane Square. –* 𝒞 *(020) 7881 9844*
*– www.theorange.co.uk*  **38**AHZ
**4 rm** – ♛£ 185/205 ♛♛£ 185/205, ☲ £ 12
**Rest** – Modern European – Carte £ 24/41
♦ Family-friendly pub with laid-back atmosphere and slight colonial feel. Pizz
from the wood-fired oven in the bar or rustic cooking in the upstairs dinin
room. Film nights on Monday. Bedrooms named after local streets.

**LONDON HEATHROW AIRPORT** – Greater London – **504** S29 – see Hillingdon (London)

---

**LONG COMPTON** – Warwickshire – pop. 705 – ⊠ Shipston-On-Stour    **19** C3

▶ London 81 mi – Birmingham 53 mi – Liverpool 147 mi – Bristol 72 mi

🍴 **Red Lion** with rm    🚗 🛜 ⁽ᵗᵖ⁾ 🅿 VISA ⚈ AE ①
⊠ CV36 5JS – ℰ (01608) 684 221 – www.redlion-longcompton.co.uk
**5 rm** ⊆ – ♦£ 55 ♦♦£ 85/115
**Rest** – Menu £ 15 (lunch and early dinner) – Carte £ 26/36
◆ 18C former coaching inn with flag floors, log fires and a warm, modern feel. Seasonal menu of tasty, home-cooked pub classics, with more adventurous daily specials. Stylish, contemporary bedrooms.

---

**LONG CRENDON** – Buckinghamshire – **504** Q/R28 – pop. 2 383    **11** C2
– ⊠ Aylesbury

▶ London 50 mi – Aylesbury 11 mi – Oxford 15 mi

🍴🍴 **Angel** with rm    🛜 ⁽ᵗᵖ⁾ 🅿 VISA ⚈
47 Bicester Rd ⊠ HP18 9EE – ℰ (01844) 208 268 – www.angelrestaurant.co.uk
– Closed Sunday dinner
**4 rm** ⊆ – ♦£ 75 ♦♦£ 100
**Rest** – Menu £ 15 (weekday lunch) – Carte £ 27/44 ⅏
◆ Comfortable, characterful former pub with low ceilings, leather-furnished lounge/bar and airy conservatory. Wide-ranging menus offer tasty, globally influenced dishes. Well-chosen wine list. Stylish bedrooms, all individually decorated; Room 4 is the biggest.

---

**LONG MELFORD** – Suffolk – **504** W27 – pop. 2 734 ▮ Great Britain    **15** C3

▶ London 62 mi – Cambridge 34 mi – Colchester 18 mi – Ipswich 24 mi

◉ Melford Hall ★ **AC**

🏠 **Black Lion**    🛜 ⁽ᵗᵖ⁾ 🅿 VISA ⚈ AE
Church Walk, The Green ⊠ CO10 9DN – ℰ (01787) 312 356
– www.blacklionhotel.net
**9 rm** ⊆ – ♦£ 102/150 ♦♦£ 150 – 1 suite    **Rest** – Menu £ 18/38
◆ 17C Georgian inn overlooking village green. Named after wines, bedrooms are smart, stylish and individually designed; good facilities and traditional bathrooms. Formal restaurant with enclosed rear terrace features extensive, popular menu.

🍴 **Scutchers**    AC VISA ⚈ AE
Westgate St, on A 1092 ⊠ CO10 9DP – ℰ (01787) 310 200 – www.scutchers.com
– Closed 2 weeks Christmas
**Rest** – Carte £ 27/47
◆ Former medieval hall house set in pleasant rural village: now a smart, split-level, personally run restaurant. Traditional dishes use quality ingredients and feature tried-and-tested combinations.

---

**LONG SUTTON** – Somerset – **503** L30 – ⊠ Langport    **3** B3

▶ London 132 mi – Bridgwater 16 mi – Yeovil 10 mi

🍴 **Devonshire Arms** with rm    🚗 🛜 ⁽ᵗᵖ⁾ 🅿 VISA ⚈
⊠ TA10 9LP – ℰ (01458) 241 271 – www.thedevonshirearms.com – Closed 25-26 December and 1 January
**9 rm** ⊆ – ♦£ 78/130 ♦♦£ 88/130    **Rest** – Carte £ 25/39
◆ Spacious Grade II listed hunting lodge set on village green; contemporary interior, with relaxing, open-plan bar and formal dining room. Locally sourced produce used in seasonal European dishes. Comfortable bedrooms boast excellent quality linen and toiletries.

---

**LONGHORSLEY** – Northumberland – **501** O18 – see Morpeth

ENGLAND

**LONGRIDGE** – Lancashire – **502** M22 – pop. 7 491      **20 A2**

▶ London 241 mi – Blackburn 12 mi – Burnley 18 mi

XX   **Longridge Restaurant**     🗚 ⇄ 𝚅𝚂𝙰 ⓿ 🄰🄴
*104-106 Higher Rd, Northeast : 0.5 mi by B 5269 following signs for Jeffrey Hill*
✉ *PR3 3SY* – ✆ *(01772) 784 969 – www.heathcotes.co.uk – Closed January,*
*Monday and Tuesday*
**Rest** – Carte £ 34/50
♦ Stylish, subtly hued restaurant with changing character: bright by day and intimate at night. Seasonal, regional cooking uses quality ingredients to create appealing, flavoursome dishes.

**LONGSTOCK** – Hampshire – **503** P30 – see Stockbridge

**LONGTOWN** – Cumbria – **502** L18      **21 A1**

▶ London 326 mi – Carlisle 9 mi – Newcastle upon Tyne 61 mi

↑   **Bessiestown Farm** ⌖      🖼 📺 🖥 🍴 🐾 📶 🅿 𝚅𝚂𝙰 ⓿ 🄰🄴 ⓘ
*Catlowdy, Northeast : 8 mi by Netherby St on B 6318* ✉ *CA6 5QP*
– ✆ *(01228) 577 219 – www.bessiestown.co.uk – Closed 25 December*
**6 rm** ⛌ – ♦£ 57 ♦♦£ 89   **Rest** – Menu £ 20 **s**
♦ Immaculately kept converted farmhouse in rural location. Traditional, homely lounge with pleasant conservatory overlooking garden. Friendly owner. Spacious bedrooms; Dovecote is the largest. Bright, airy dining room; home-cooked meals available Monday-Saturday.

**LOOE** – Cornwall – **503** G32 – pop. 5 280      **1 B2**

▶ London 264 mi – Plymouth 23 mi – Truro 39 mi

🛈 Fore St ✆ (01503) 26 20 72, www.visit-southeastcornwall.co.uk

🏌 Bin Down, ✆ (01503) 24 02 39

🏌 Whitsand Bay Hotel Torpoint Portwrinkle, ✆ (01503) 23 02 76

◎ Town★ – Monkey Sanctuary★ **AC**

🏨   **Barclay House**      ≤ 🚘 ⅃ 🏠 ⅃🏊 ⅃ & 🍴 🅿 𝚅𝚂𝙰 ⓿
*St Martins Rd, East Looe, East : 0.5 mi by A 387 on B 3253* ✉ *PL13 1LP*
– ✆ *(01503) 262 929 – www.barclayhouse.co.uk*
**11 rm** ⛌ – ♦£ 55/118 ♦♦£ 150/200 – 1 suite
**Rest** *Restaurant* – see restaurant listing
♦ Imposing, whitewashed Victorian house in elevated position; most bedrooms come with a view. Room 7 is contemporary with superb estuary vista; 9 boasts a balcony and whirlpool bath.

XX   **Restaurant** – at Barclay House Hotel      ≤ 🚘 🏠 🅿 𝚅𝚂𝙰 ⓿
*St Martins Rd, East Looe, East : 0.5 mi by A 387 on B 3253* ✉ *PL13 1LP*
– ✆ *(01503) 262 929 – www.barclayhouse.co.uk*
**Rest** – *(closed Sunday dinner) (dinner only and Sunday lunch June-October)*
Menu £ 29
♦ Light, modern restaurant featuring abstract local art and with extensive views of the estuary. Dishes make use of local, seasonal produce, including seafood from the day boats.

X   **Trawlers on the Quay**      𝚅𝚂𝙰 ⓿ 🄰🄴 ⓘ
*The Quay, East Looe* ✉ *PL13 1AH* – ✆ *(01503) 263 593*
*– www.trawlers-restaurant.co.uk – Closed Monday in winter*
**Rest** – Seafood – Carte £ 20/31
♦ Bright, contemporary restaurant, perched on the edge of the quay; ask for a window table. The menu focuses on seafood and ranges from light lunches up to the full three courses.

**LORTON** – Cumbria – **502** K20 – see Cockermouth

**LOUGHBOROUGH** – Leicestershire – **502** Q25 – pop. 55 258          **16** B2

▶ London 117 mi – Birmingham 41 mi – Leicester 11 mi – Nottingham 15 mi

🛈 Market Pl ℰ (01509) 23 19 14, www.loughboroughuk.co.uk

🔢 Lingdale Woodhouse Eaves Joe Moore's Lane, ℰ (01509) 89 07 03

**at Woodhouse Eaves** South : 4.5 mi by A 6 via Woodhouse – ✉ Loughborough

XX     **Woodhouse**                               ⇔ 🅿 𝖵𝖨𝖲𝖠 ⓪ 𝖠𝖤
*43 Maplewell Rd ✉ LE12 8RG – ℰ (01509) 890 318 – www.thewoodhouse.co.uk
– Closed Sunday dinner and Monday*
**Rest** – Menu £ 15 (lunch)/19 (midweek dinner) – Carte approx. £ 35
♦ Smart village restaurant with comfy lounge, bold modern colours and eye-
catching art. Concise, understated menu relies on quality local produce: classical
combinations have a personal twist.

---

**LOUTH** – Lincolnshire – **502** T/U23 – pop. 15 930          **17** D1

▶ London 156 mi – Boston 34 mi – Great Grimsby 17 mi – Lincoln 26 mi

🛈 Cannon St. ℰ (01507) 60 11 11, www.louthuk.com

🏨     **Brackenborough**          𝗄ⁿ 𝖠𝖪 rest, ⅍ ⁽ᵗ⁾ 𝗌𝐀 🅿 𝖵𝖨𝖲𝖠 ⓪ 𝖠𝖤
*Cordeaux Corner, Brackenborough, North : 2 mi by A 16 ✉ LN11 0SZ
– ℰ (01507) 609 169 – www.oakridgehotels.co.uk*
**24 rm** ⌑ – ♥£ 85/158 ♥♥£ 100/158     **Rest** – Carte £ 19/38
♦ Contemporary, family-owned hotel with relaxed feel and warm, personal style.
Spacious, individually designed bedrooms boast all mod cons; executive rooms
include jacuzzi baths. Sexy cocktail bar. Lounge/bar and conservatory for all-day
dining. Formal restaurant.

---

**LOVINGTON** – Somerset – **503** M30 – see Castle Cary

---

**LOW FELL** – Tyne and Wear – see Gateshead

---

**LOW ROW** – North Yorkshire – **502** N20 – see Reeth

---

**LOWER FROYLE** – Hampshire – see Alton

---

**LOWER HARDRES** – Kent – **504** X30 – see Canterbury

---

**LOWER ODDINGTON** – Gloucestershire – see Stow-on-the-Wold

---

**LOWER PEOVER** – Cheshire East – see Knutsford

---

**LOWER SHIPLAKE** – Oxfordshire – **504** R29 – see Henley-on-Thames

---

**LOWER SLAUGHTER** – Gloucestershire – **503** – see Bourton-on-the-Water

---

**LOWER SWELL** – Gloucestershire – see Stow-on-the-Wold

---

**LOWER VOBSTER** – Somerset – pop. 2 222 – ✉ Radstock          **4** C2

▶ London 119 mi – Bath 16 mi – Frome 5 mi

🍴     **Vobster Inn** with rm                    ⬚ ⅍ ⁽ᵗ⁾ 🅿 𝖵𝖨𝖲𝖠 ⓪ ⓪
*✉ BA3 5RJ – ℰ (01373) 812 920 – www.vobsterinn.co.uk – Closed Sunday dinner
and Monday*
**3 rm** ⌑ – ♥£ 55/75 ♥♥£ 68/95     **Rest** – Carte £ 19/31 **s**
♦ Solid stone pub with homely, traditional inner, featuring exposed beams and
open fires. Seasonal, Mediterranean-inspired menu reflects owners' Spanish heritage. Popular theme evenings. Cosy, well-equipped bedrooms; the family room
overlooks the garden.

ENGLAND

**LOWESTOFT** – Suffolk – **504** Z26 – **pop. 68 340** ▮ Great Britain          **15** D2

▶ London 116 mi – Ipswich 43 mi – Norwich 30 mi

🛈 Royal Plain ℰ (01502) 53 36 00, www.visit-sunrisecoast.co.uk

🏌 Rookery Park Carlton Colville, ℰ (01502) 50 91 90

ⓖ Norfolk Broads★

⛫ **Britten House** without rest          ≤ 🚗 ❄ ⓦ 🅿 🚾
21 Kirkley Cliff Rd ⊠ NR33 0DB – ℰ (01502) 573 950 – www.brittenhouse.co.uk
**8 rm** � – †£ 60/70 ††£ 75/95 – 1 suite
♦ Fine brick-built Victorian house overlooking the promenade; birthplace of Benjamin Britten in 1913. Classically furnished bedrooms named after composers; choose a front-facing room with sea view.

**LUDFORD** – Lincolnshire          **17** C1

▶ London 174 mi – Sheffield 74 mi – Kingston upon Hull 43 mi – Nottingham 59 mi

🍴 **Black Horse Inn**          ⓦ 🅿 🚾 ⓒⓞ
*Magna Mile ⊠ LN8 6AJ – ℰ (01507) 313 645 – www.blackhorseludford.co.uk
– Closed 2 weeks January, 25 December, Sunday dinner, Monday and bank
holidays*
**Rest** – Menu £ 14 (lunch) – Carte £ 20/28
♦ Slightly worn but well-loved pub with homely décor, simple furnishings and welcoming open fires. Concise menus feature good old-fashioned classics, including game, pies and stews in winter.

**LUDLOW** – Shropshire – **503** L26 – **pop. 9 870** ▮ Great Britain          **18** B2

▶ London 162 mi – Birmingham 39 mi – Hereford 24 mi – Shrewsbury 29 mi

🛈 Castle St ℰ (01584) 87 50 53, www.virtual-shropshire.co.uk

◎ Town★ Z – Castle★ **AC** – Feathers Hotel★ – St Laurence's Parish
Church★ (Misericords★) **S**

ⓖ Stokesay Castle★ **AC**, NW : 6.5 mi by A 49

🏨 **Overton Grange**          ≤ 🚗 📺 🐾 ❄ ⓦ 🛁 🅿 🚾 ⓒⓞ
*Old Hereford Rd, South : 1.75 mi by B 4361 ⊠ SY8 4AD – ℰ (01584) 873 500
– www.overtongrangehotel.com*
**14 rm** � – †£ 115/145 ††£ 145/245
**Rest** – (booking essential for non-residents) Menu £ 33/43
♦ Well-maintained Edwardian country house boasting subtle modern touches alongside original features. Bedrooms feature modern facilities and smart bathrooms. Superb pool. Dining rooms offer immaculately laid tables and countryside views; cooking has a French base.

🏨 **Dinham Hall**          🚗 ❄ ⓦ 🛁 🅿 🚾 ⓒⓞ
*Dinham ⊠ SY8 1EJ – ℰ (01584) 876 464 – www.dinhamhall.com*          Z**b**
**13 rm** ⊵ – †£ 110/145 ††£ 145/246     **Rest** – Menu £ 18/40
♦ 18C manor house, with pretty walled garden, situated by Ludlow Castle in the heart of charming medieval town. Period furnishings and individual rooms. Informal dining with crisp, bright décor.

🏨 **Fishmore Hall**          🚗 🛗 🅰ⓒ rest, ❄ ⓦ 🚾 ⓒⓞ 🅰🅴
*Fishmore Rd, North : 1.5 mi off A 4117 ⊠ SY8 3DP – ℰ (01584) 875 148
– www.fishmorehall.co.uk*
**15 rm** ⊵ – †£ 75/100 ††£ 89/220     **Rest** – Menu £ 25/49
♦ Elegantly restored Georgian house – a former boys' school – set out of town in half an acre of land. Very modern, designer bedrooms, boasting bold wallpaper and flat screen TVs. Two smart dining rooms serve modern British menus.

# LUDLOW

Stokesay Castle [B 4361] SHREWSBURY, (A 49)

B 4364 KINDDERMINSTER

0    200 m
0    200 yards

Coronation Av.

Burway Bridge

Corve

River

Corve

Linney

Linney

Linney

Hillside

Quarry Hill

Gardens

Gravel

Station

Drive

H

Upper Linney

e

Corve Street

Castle Street

CASTLE

f

Dinham

Dinham Bridge

Addle Wood Rd

Camp Lane

Mill Street

Dinham

b

8 S

6 M

4

M

M

14 X

20

Bell Lane

18   22

FEATHERS HOTEL

2

Lower Galdeford

Tower Street

Broad St.

Brand Lane

Old Street

POL

Jockey Field

9'

e

St. John's La.

Lower Broad St.

Teme Av. Temeside

Z

Whitcliffe Road

WHITCLIFFE

River Teme

Ludford Bridge

Overton Rd.

Park Rd

LUDFORD

HEREFORD [B 4361] (A 49)

ENGLAND

🏠 **De Grey's Town House** without rest    ⚅ ❧ ⟨⟨⟩⟩ VISA ◎◎ AE

*Broad St ⊠ SY8 1NG – ℰ (01584) 872 764 – www.degreys.co.uk*    Z**x**
**9 rm** ☐ – †£ 115 ††£ 145/165

♦ Dating back to 1570 this building retains all its good old English style and charm. Bedrooms are spacious, very individual and feature quality hand made oak furniture.

🏠 **Bromley Court** without rest    ❧ VISA ◎◎

*18-20 Lower Broad St ⊠ SY8 1PQ – ℰ (01584) 876 996 – www.ludlowhotels.com – Closed January*    Z**e**
**3 rm** – †£ 80/120 ††£ 100/120

♦ Delightful Tudor cottage with three self-contained units, traditionally furnished in keeping with the style of the house. Pleasant walled rear garden. Continental breakfasts.

471

ENGLAND

XXX **La Bécasse**  VISA ⓪
*17 Corve St ⊠ SY8 1DA – ℰ (01584) 872 325 – www.labecasse.co.uk – Closed 2*
*weeks Christmas-New Year, Sunday dinner, Tuesday lunch and Monday*
**Rest** – Menu £ 30/60 – Carte £ 30/60                                                    Y●
♦ 17C former coaching inn; its characterful dining room split into three intimate
areas, with smartly laid tables and attractive listed wood panelling. Expect classically based cooking and attentive, formal service.

XX **Mr Underhill's at Dinham Weir** (Chris Bradley) with rm   ≤ ⌂ ↺
🏵 *Dinham ⊠ SY8 1EH – ℰ (01584) 874 431*            🛏 🌱 🐾 P VISA ⓪
*– www.mr-underhills.co.uk – Closed 2 weeks June, 2 weeks October, 25-26 and*
*31 December, 1 January, Monday and Tuesday*                                          Z●
**4 rm** ⌂ – †£ 135/160 ††£ 145/175 – 2 suites
**Rest** – *(dinner only) (booking essential) (set menu only)* Menu £ 60🍃
**Spec.** Hake with lemon crumb on couscous and a ras el hanout dressing. Slow
roasted breast of duck with a coffee vinaigrette. Oakly Park rarebit with mustard
ice cream and an anchovy and miso dressing.
♦ Yellow painted riverside house, away from town centre. Daily set menu with
classical base makes particularly good use of local meats and cheeses. Comfortable and stylishly decorated bedrooms.

X **Koo**  VISA ⓪ AE ⓪
*127 Old St ⊠ SY8 1NU – ℰ (01584) 878 462 – www.koo-ook.co.uk – Closed 25*
*December, 1 January, Sunday, Monday and restricted opening in winter*
**Rest** – Japanese – *(dinner only)* Carte £ 18/23                                  Za
♦ Friendly atmosphere in a simply styled interior decorated with banners and ar-
tefacts. Good value meals from a regularly changing menu of authentic and tasty
Japanese dishes.

X **Green Café**  ⌂
*Mill on the Green ⊠ SY8 1EG – ℰ (01584) 879 872 – Closed 3 January-13*
*February, 24-25 December and Monday*                                                Z●
**Rest** – *(lunch only) (booking advisable)* Carte £ 19/24
♦ Simple little eatery with delightful waterside terrace, set in a charming 14C
watermill on the banks of the River Teme. Concise menu of unfussy, daily
changing dishes that showcase British ingredients in simple, flavoursome
combinations.

**at Woofferton** South : 4 mi by B 4361 - Z - on A 49 – ⊠ Ludlow

↟ **Ravenscourt Manor** without rest   ⌂ 🌱 🐾 P
*on A 49 ⊠ SY8 4AL – ℰ (01584) 711 905 – March-October*
**3 rm** ⌂ – †£ 55 ††£ 80/85
♦ Characterful black and white timbered 16C manor house in two and a half
acres of lawned gardens. Friendly welcome; comfy lounge. Individually decorated
period style rooms.

**at Bromfield** Northwest : 2.5 mi on A 49 - Y - ⊠ Ludlow

XX **Clive** with rm   ⌂ ⓰ 🐾 🄰 P VISA ⓪ AE
*⊠ SY8 2JR – ℰ (01584) 856 565 – www.theclive.co.uk – Closed 25-26 December*
**15 rm** ⌂ – †£ 65/90 ††£ 90/115
**Rest** – *(booking essential at dinner)* Carte £ 23/33
♦ Large converted pub with modern décor in vivid colours. Restaurant, bar, café
and bistro areas. Menu of internationally inspired traditional dishes. Very good
modern bedrooms.

**LUPTON** – Cumbria – **502** L21 – see Kirkby Lonsdale

**LUTON** – Luton – **504** S28 – **pop. 185 543** ▯ Great Britain    **12** A2

▶ London 35 mi – Cambridge 36 mi – Ipswich 93 mi – Oxford 45 mi

🛪 Luton International Airport : ✆ (01582) 405100, E : 1.5 mi X

🅸 St George's Sq ✆ (01582) 40 15 79,
www.visitorinformationcentre.luton.towntalk.co.uk

🔟 Stockwood Park London Rd, ✆ (01582) 41 37 04

🄶 Whipsnade Wild Animal Park★, West : 8 mi by B 489, signed from M 1 (junction 9)
and M 25 (junction 21) X

🏨🏨🏨 **Luton Hoo** ⌂    ≼ ⬚ 🐾 🛜 🖵 ⑨ 🎐 🗲 ※ 📻 🕅 ₺ 🕻 ⏢ 🄿
*The Mansion House, Southeast : 2.5 mi by A 505 on A*    🆅🆂🅰 ⓪ 🄰🄴 ⓪
*1081* ✉ *LU1 3TQ* – ✆ *(01582) 734 437* – *www.lutonhoo.com*
**135 rm** ⌶ – ✝£ 230 ✝✝£ 230 – 9 suites
**Rest *Wernher*** – *(closed Monday and Tuesday)* Menu £ 30/43 – Carte £ 53/71
**Rest *Adam's Brasserie*** – *(closed Sunday dinner)* Carte £ 25/37
♦ Stunning 18C house set in over 1,000 acres of gardens, some designed by
Capability Brown. Main mansion boasts numerous comfortable sitting rooms
and characterful bedrooms. Formal, marble-filled Wernher restaurant offers
sophisticated modern cuisine. Contemporary brasserie classics in more casual Adam's.

---

**LUXBOROUGH** – Somerset – **503** J30 – ✉ Watchet    **3** A2

▶ London 205 mi – Exeter 42 mi – Minehead 9 mi – Taunton 25 mi

🏠 **Royal Oak Inn of Luxborough** with rm    🛜 🄿 🆅🆂🅰 ⓪
*Exmoor National Park* ✉ *TA23 0SH* – ✆ *(01984) 640 319*
– *www.theroyaloakinnluxborough.co.uk* – *Closed 25 December*
**11 rm** ⌶ – ✝£ 55/75 ✝✝£ 100    **Rest** – Carte £ 18/32
♦ Red sandstone pub in an extremely beautiful location; well used by the community. Seasonal menu offers substantial dishes of classically prepared, boldly flavoured foods, with an international edge. Bedrooms are compact but charming;
Room 14 has its own terrace.

---

**LYDDINGTON** – Rutland – see Uppingham

---

**LYDFORD** – Devon – **503** H32 – **pop. 1 734** – ✉ Okehampton    **2** C2

▶ London 234 mi – Exeter 33 mi – Plymouth 25 mi

🄾 Village★★

🄶 Dartmoor National Park★★

🏠 **Dartmoor Inn** with rm    🛜 🍴 🄿 🆅🆂🅰 ⓪ 🄰🄴
*Moorside, East : 1 mi on A 386* ✉ *EX20 4AY* – ✆ *(01822) 820 221*
– *www.dartmoorinn.com* – *Closed Sunday dinner and Monday lunch*
**3 rm** ⌶ – ✝£ 80/95 ✝✝£ 105/130    **Rest** – Menu £ 24 (lunch) – Carte £ 26/39
♦ Lovely pub on the edge of Dartmoor National Park, close to Lydford Gorge and
the White Lady waterfall. Shabby-chic, French farmhouse styling. Set, easy dining
and à la carte menus feature tasty modern dishes; the mixed grill of sea fish is
popular. Spacious bedrooms and some unusual, yet appealing, breakfast choices.

---

**LYME REGIS** – Dorset – **503** L31 – **pop. 4 406**    **3** B3

▶ London 160 mi – Dorchester 25 mi – Exeter 31 mi – Taunton 27 mi

🅸 Church St ✆ (01297) 44 21 38, www.lymeregis.org

🔟 Timber Hill, ✆ (01297) 44 29 63

🄾 Town★ – The Cobb★

ENGLAND

### Alexandra
⪯ 🚗 🎄 ♨ **P** **VISA** ⊚

*Pound St* ✉ *DT7 3HZ* – *ℰ (01297) 442 010* – *www.hotelalexandra.co.uk* – *Closed Christmas-New Year*

**24 rm** ⊑ – †£ 80/220 ††£ 220    **Rest** – Menu £ 42 (dinner) – Carte £ 27/42

♦ Smart, extended 18C house in lawned gardens, superbly located with magnificent views out to sea. Family-run, the hotel features a comfortable lounge, a south-facing conservatory and modern bedrooms. Room 12 has a large bow window. Tasty, home-cooked menus.

### Hix Oyster and Fish House
⪯ 🎄 **VISA** ⊚ **AE**

*Lister Gdns, Cobb Rd* ✉ *DT7 3JP* – *ℰ (01297) 446 910*
*– www.hixoysterandfishhouse.co.uk* – *Closed first 2 weeks January and Monday-Tuesday October-March*

**Rest** – Seafood – *(booking essential)* Menu £ 21 (weekday lunch) – Carte £ 28/66

♦ Small restaurant in a terrace by the new gardens; superb views over the bay and Cobb. Rustic, simple and understated. Daily seafood menu with a real understanding of less is more.

### Mill Tea & Dining Room
🎄 **VISA** ⊚

*The Town Mill* ✉ *DT7 3PU* – *ℰ (01297) 445 757* – *www.teaanddiningroom.co.uk* *– Closed January, Tuesday lunch and Monday*

**Rest** – British – *(booking essential)* Carte £ 25/41

♦ Sweet little restaurant with quirky, vintage interior, in a listed mill building on the banks of the River Lym. Menus offer fresh, local, often foraged ingredients, in traditional, unadorned combinations. Even the soft drinks are homemade.

---

## LYMINGTON – Hampshire – 504 P31 – pop. 14 227    6 A3

▶ London 103 mi – Bournemouth 18 mi – Southampton 19 mi – Winchester 32 mi
▬ to the Isle of Wight (Yarmouth) (Wightlink Ltd) frequent services daily (30 mn)
🅸 New St ℰ (01590) 68 90 00, www.lymington.org

### Stanwell House
🚗 ⑴ **P** **VISA** ⊚ **AE**

*14-15 High St* ✉ *SO41 9AA* – *ℰ (01590) 677 123* – *www.stanwellhouse.com*
**24 rm** ⊑ – †£ 75/99 ††£ 89/140 – 6 suites
**Rest** *Seafood at Stanwells* – see restaurant listing
**Rest** *Bistro* – *(dinner only)* Carte £ 31/41

♦ Neatly painted former coaching inn, set in the town centre and run by a friendly owner. Comfy, well-equipped bedrooms: those in the original house are more characterful, those in the extension, more contemporary. Trendy wine bar, smart restaurant and wood-furnished bistro with covered courtyard and terrace.

### Mill at Gordleton
🎄 **AC** rest, ♨ ⑴ **P** **VISA** ⊚ **AE**

*Silver St, Hordle, Northwest : 3.5 mi by A 337 off Sway Rd* ✉ *SO41 6DJ*
*– ℰ (01590) 682 219* – *www.themillatgordleton.co.uk* – *Closed 25 December*
**7 rm** ⊑ – †£ 100/125 ††£ 140 – 1 suite
**Rest** – Menu £ 18/28 – Carte £ 32/48

♦ Delightfully located part-17C water mill in well-kept gardens. Comfortable, traditional interior with a pubby bar and country house lounge. Homely, individually styled bedrooms. Formal restaurant offers classic British cooking, with terrace for alfresco dining.

### Seafood at Stanwells – at Stanwell House Hotel
🚗 **P** **VISA** ⊚ **AE**

*14-15 High St* ✉ *SO41 9AA* – *ℰ (01590) 677 123* – *www.stanwellhouse.com*
**Rest** – Carte £ 31/42

♦ Smart hotel restaurant in a centrally located and keenly run former coaching inn. Trendy adjoining wine bar and wood-furnished bistro with terrace. Fresh seafood menu and attentive service.

**⚓ East End** East : 3 mi by B3054

🗗 **East End Arms** with rm       🛜 **P** 🆅🆂🅰 ⓪⓪
*Lymington Rd* ✉ *SO41 5SY –* ✆ *(01590) 626 223 – www.eastendarms.co.uk*
*– Closed Sunday dinner*
**5 rm** 🛏 **–** 🛏†£ 68 🛏🛏†£ 95/115    **Rest** – Carte £ 19/27
◆ Traditional country pub owned by John Illsley of Dire Straits. Shabby locals bar and classical pine-furnished dining room; great display of music-based photos. Concise menus of satisfying British dishes. Modern, cottage-style bedrooms provide a smart contrast.

**⚓ Downton** West : 3 mi on A 337 – ✉ **Lymington**

🏠 **The Olde Barn** without rest       🚳 📶 🛜 **P** 🆅🆂🅰 ⓪⓪
*Christchurch Rd, East : 0.5 mi on A 337* ✉ *SO41 0LA –* ✆ *(01590) 644 939*
*– www.theoldebarn.co.uk*
**3 rm** 🛏 **–** 🛏†£ 50/70 🛏🛏†£ 70/80
◆ Converted 17C barn with small, traditional lounge and communal breakfast room. Bedrooms in the barn annexe – a converted dairy – are spotlessly kept, with a homely, cottagey style.

---

**YMM** – Warrington – **502** M23 – **pop. 9 554**       **20** B3
🚗 London 190 mi – Liverpool 26 mi – Leeds 62 mi – Sheffield 68 mi

🗗 **Church Green**       🚳 🛜 **P** 🆅🆂🅰 ⓪⓪ 🅰🅴
*Higher Ln, on A 56* ✉ *WA13 0AP –* ✆ *(01925) 752 068*
*– www.thechurchgreen.co.uk*
**Rest** – *(booking essential)* Menu £ 40 – Carte £ 24/40
◆ Double gable-fronted Victorian pub beside Lymm Dam. Smart, modern interior with conservatory, attractive terrace and kitchen garden. Simple pub-style bar dishes; more ambitious evening menu.

---

**YNDHURST** – Hampshire – **503** – **pop. 2 281** ▌ Great Britain       **6** A2
🚗 London 95 mi – Bournemouth 20 mi – Southampton 10 mi – Winchester 23 mi
🅿 Main Car Park ✆ (023) 8028 22 69, www.new-forest-uk.co.uk
🏌 Dibden Golf Centre Main Rd, ✆ (023) 8020 75 08
🅱 New Forest Southampton Rd, ✆ (023) 8028 27 52
🌲 New Forest★★ (Bolderwood Ornamental Drive★★, Rhinefield Ornamental Drive★★)

🏨 **Lime Wood** 🌿    ⇐ 🚳 🐾 🍸 🛁 🖥 🌐 🕸 🏋 🧖 🛗 ⛱ 📶 **P** 🆅🆂🅰 ⓪⓪ 🅰🅴 ⓪
*Beaulieu Rd, Southeast : 1 mi by A 35 on B 3056* ✉ *SO43 7FZ –* ✆ *(023)*
*8028 7177 – www.limewoodhotel.co.uk*
**15 rm** – 🛏†£ 445 🛏🛏†£ 445, 🛏 £ 18 – 14 suites – 🛏🛏†£ 445/775
**Rest** *Dining Room* – ✆ (023) 8028 7167 *(closed Monday except lunch bank holidays)* Menu £ 23/50
**Rest** *Scullery* – ✆ (023) 8028 7168 – Carte £ 28/42
◆ Impressive extended Georgian mansion with stunning spa. Various stylish guest lounges with quality fabrics and furnishings; one set around a courtyard and boasting a retractable glass roof. Beautifully furnished bedrooms boast luxurious marble-tiled bathrooms; many have New Forest views. Refined restaurant or classic home favourites in relaxed, all-day Scullery.

---

**YNMOUTH** – Devon – **503** I30 – see Lynton

---

**YNTON** – Devon – **503** I30 – **pop. 1 870**       **2** C1
🚗 London 206 mi – Exeter 59 mi – Taunton 44 mi
🅿 Lee Rd ✆ (01598) 75 22 25, www.lynton-lynmouth-tourism.co.uk
🏛 Town★ (⇐★)
🌲 Valley of the Rocks★, W : 1 mi – Watersmeet★, E : 1.5 mi by A 39. Exmoor National Park★★ – Doone Valley★, SE : 7.5 mi by A 39 (access from Oare on foot)

ENGLAND

ENGLAND

⌂ **Hewitt's - Villa Spaldi** without rest ⅏ 🅕 ⌂ 🛈 📠 Ⓟ ᴠɪ̄sᴀ ⓒⓞ 🄰🄴 ⓪
*North Walk ⊠ EX35 6HJ – 𝒞 (01598) 752 293 – www.hewittshotel.com*
*– April-September*
**7 rm** ⌂ – †£ 85/95 ††£ 130/190 – 1 suite
♦ Splendid 19C Arts and Crafts house in tranquil wooded cliffside setting. Staine
glass window by Burne Jones and library filled with antiques. Stylish rooms wit
sea views.

⌂ **Victoria Lodge** without rest 📠 🕬 ⌂ Ⓟ ᴠɪ̄sᴀ ⓒⓞ
*30-31 Lee Rd ⊠ EX35 6BS – 𝒞 (01598) 753 203 – www.victorialodge.co.uk*
*– 22 March-October*
**8 rm** ⌂ – †£ 119 ††£ 140
♦ Large 19C house decorated with period photographs, prints and Victorian
Traditional décor in communal areas and bedrooms which are comfortable an
inviting.

⌂ **St Vincent** without rest 📠 🕬 ⌂ ᴠɪ̄sᴀ ⓒⓞ
*Market St, Castle Hill ⊠ EX35 6JA – 𝒞 (01598) 752 244*
*– www.st-vincent-hotel.co.uk – Easter-October*
**5 rm** ⌂ – †£ 70/75 ††£ 80
♦ Grade II listed Georgian House with charming Belgian owners, set 200 metre
from the coastal path. Lovely fire-lit lounge and fresh, uncluttered bedrooms wit
smart bathrooms.

**at Lynmouth** East : 1 mi

⌂ **Shelley's** without rest ⅏ 🕬 ⌂ ᴠɪ̄sᴀ ⓒⓞ
*8 Watersmeet Rd ⊠ EX35 6EP – 𝒞 (01598) 753 219 – www.shelleyshotel.co.uk*
*– March-October*
**11 rm** ⌂ – †£ 75/95 ††£ 75/110
♦ Centrally located hotel named after eponymous poet who honeymooned her
in 1812. Stylish public areas. Very comfortable bedrooms with good views of pi
turesque locale.

⌂ **Heatherville** ⅏ ⅏ 🕬 Ⓟ ᴠɪ̄sᴀ ⓒⓞ
*Tors Park, by Tors Rd ⊠ EX35 6NB – 𝒞 (01598) 752 327 – www.heatherville.co.u*
*– April-October*
**6 rm** ⌂ – †£ 110 ††£ 110 **Rest** – Menu £ 25
♦ Victorian house perched above the town. Well kept throughout with brigh
warm décor. Rooms with bold fabrics and woodland views: room 6 has the be
outlook. Home-cooked meals employ fresh, local produce.

**at Martinhoe** West : 4.25 mi via Coast rd (toll) – ⊠ Barnstaple

⌂ **Old Rectory** ⅏ 📠 🕬 ⌂ Ⓟ ᴠɪ̄sᴀ ⓒⓞ 🄰🄸
*⊠ EX31 4QT – 𝒞 (01598) 763 368 – www.oldrectoryhotel.co.uk – April-October*
**10 rm** (dinner included) ⌂ – †£ 165/180 ††£ 210/245
**Rest** – *(dinner only)* Menu £ 36
♦ Built in 19C for rector of Martinhoe's 11C church, this quiet country retreat is se
in a charming spot, with a well-tended three acre garden and cascading broo
Fresh, bright bedrooms are modern, yet retain period touches: Heddon and Pad
dock are two of the best. Comfortable dining room; simple home-cooking.

**LYTHAM** – Lancashire – **502** L22 – see Lytham St Annes

**LYTHAM ST ANNE'S** – Lancashire – **502** L22 – pop. 41 327    **20 A**
▶ London 237 mi – Blackpool 7 mi – Liverpool 44 mi – Preston 13 mi
🄸 St Annes Rd West 𝒞 (01253) 72 56 10, www.visitlythamstannes.co.uk
🄸🄸 Fairhaven Ansdell, Oakwood Avenue, 𝒞 (01253) 73 67 41
🄸🄸 St Annes Old Links Highbury Rd, 𝒞 (01253) 72 35 97

## at Lytham

�␣ **Rooms** without rest ⊘ 🖓 📶 VISA ☺ AE
*35 Church Rd* ⊠ *FY8 5LL –* ℰ *(01253) 736 000 – www.theroomslytham.com*
**5 rm** ⊆ – †£ 105 ††£ 130
♦ Boutique-style guesthouse with striking, contemporary décor. Good-sized bedrooms boast modern facilities, including iPod docks and large flat screen TVs. Extensive breakfasts.

XX **Hastings** 🕮 AC ⇔ VISA ☺ AE
*26 Hastings Pl.* ⊠ *FY8 5LZ –* ℰ *(01253) 732 400 – www.hastingslytham.com*
*– Closed Sunday dinner and Monday*
**Rest** – Menu £ 14 (lunch)/18 (midweek dinner) – Carte £ 23/35
♦ Red-brick restaurant with modern bar, intimate ground floor dining room and brighter mezzanine, featuring exposed rafters and glass skylight. Wide-ranging menu with a regional slant.

## at St Anne's

🏨 **Grand** ≤ 🕮 ▦ 🎿 ᒲ ᕓ 占 ⊘ 🖓 ⅍ ℙ VISA ☺ AE
*South Promenade* ⊠ *FY8 1NB –* ℰ *(01253) 721 288 – www.the-grand.co.uk*
*– Closed 24-26 December*
**54 rm** – †£ 111 ††£ 188, ⊆ £ 6.50
**Rest** *Café Grand* – ℰ *(01253) 643 409* – Carte £ 29/47
♦ Impressive, turreted Victorian hotel on promenade. Stylish, contemporary guest areas. Variously sized bedrooms, most with good views; turret rooms are the most spacious, and have particularly good aspects. Laid-back, stylish Café Grand offers accessible menu.

**MADINGLEY** – Cambridgeshire – **504** U27 – see Cambridge

**MAENPORTH** – Cornwall – see Falmouth

**MAIDEN BRADLEY** – Wiltshire – **503** N30 – pop. 335     **4** C2
▣ London 114 mi – Bristol 36 mi – Cardiff 77 mi – Southampton 75 mi

🏠 **Somerset Arms** with rm ⇒ 🕮 🖓 ℙ VISA ☺ AE
*Church St* ⊠ *BA12 7HW –* ℰ *(01985) 844 207 – www.thesomersetarms.org*
**5 rm** ⊆ – †£ 70 ††£ 110    **Rest** – Carte £ 18/37
♦ Proudly run pub, with polite, well-paced service; popular with locals. Oft-changing menu uses local produce, including eggs from their own hens and veg from the garden. Flavourful, rustic cooking; steaks a speciality. Contemporary bedrooms; one with free-standing bath.

**MAIDENCOMBE** – Torbay – **503** J32 – see Torquay

**MAIDENHEAD** – Windsor and Maidenhead – **504** R29 – pop. 58 848   **11** C3
▣ London 33 mi – Oxford 32 mi – Reading 13 mi
⛴ to Marlow, Cookham and Windsor (Salter Bros. Ltd) (summer only) (3 h 45 mn)
🛈 St Ives Rd ℰ (01628) 79 65 02, www.windsor.gov.uk
🔟 Bird Hills Hawthorn Hill Drift Rd, ℰ (01628) 77 10 30
🔟 Shoppenhangers Rd, ℰ (01628) 62 46 93

Plan on next page

ENGLAND

## MAIDENHEAD

ENGLAND

478

**Fredrick's**
*Shoppenhangers Rd* ⊠ *SL6 2PZ* – ℰ *(01628) 581 000* – *www.fredricks-hotel.co.uk*
*– Closed 24-25 December* **Xc**
**36 rm** – †£ 225/275 ††£ 275, ⊒ £ 23.50 – 1 suite
**Rest** *Fredrick's* – *(closed Saturday lunch)* Menu £ 25/40 – Carte £ 41/57
♦ Red-brick former inn with very stylish, well-equipped spa. Ornate, marble reception with smoked mirrors; wicker-furnished conservatory and comfortable, individually styled bedrooms. Large restaurant boasts chandeliers, full-length windows and elaborate British menus.

XX **Boulters Riverside Brasserie** ≤ 斎 AC P VISA ⚈ AE
*Boulters Lock Island* ⊠ *SL6 8PE* – ℰ *(01628) 621 291*
*– www.boultersrestaurant.co.uk – Closed Sunday dinner and Monday*
**Rest** – Menu £ 20 (lunch) – Carte £ 25/46 **Vx**
♦ Stylish modern eatery beside a lock, on a small island in the Thames. Full-length windows open onto terrace; excellent river views. Hearty yet refined brasserie classics use quality produce.

---

**MAIDENSGROVE** – Oxfordshire – pop. 1 572 – ⊠ Henley-On-Thames 11 C3

▶ London 43 mi – Oxford 23 mi – Reading 15 mi

ENGLAND

🍴 **Five Horseshoes** 斎 斎 P VISA ⚈
⊠ *RG9 6EX* – ℰ *(01491) 641 282* – *www.thefivehorseshoes.co.uk*
**Rest** – Carte approx. £ 25
♦ Walkers' paradise: a charming part-17C inn boasting characterful beamed bar and suntrap restaurant with countryside views. Doorstop sandwiches, comforting classics and homely desserts.

---

**MAIDSTONE** – Kent – **504** V30 – pop. 89 684 📗 Great Britain 8 B2

▶ London 36 mi – Brighton 64 mi – Cambridge 84 mi – Colchester 72 mi
🔢 High St ℰ (01622) 60 21 69, www.visitmaidstone.com
🏌 Tudor Park Hotel Bearsted Ashford Rd, ℰ (01622) 73 43 34
🏌 Cobtree Manor Park Boxley Chatham Rd, ℰ (01622) 75 32 76
🏰 Leeds Castle ★ **AC**, SE : 4.5 mi by A 20 and B 2163

**at Bearsted** East : 3 mi by A 249 off A 20 – ⊠ Maidstone

XX **Fish On The Green** 斎 AC P VISA ⚈ AE
*Church Ln.* ⊠ *ME14 4EJ* – ℰ *(01622) 738 300*
*– www.fishonthegreen.com – Closed 25 December-26 January, Sunday dinner
and Monday*
**Rest** – Seafood – Menu £ 18 (lunch) – Carte £ 30/44
♦ Well-run, contemporary restaurant with pleasant terrace, tucked away in corner of the green. Focus on fresh fish, with a few local meat dishes. Good value lunch menu; friendly service.

---

**MALMESBURY** – Wiltshire – **503** N29 – pop. 5 094 4 C2

▶ London 108 mi – Bristol 28 mi – Gloucester 24 mi – Swindon 19 mi
🔢 Cross Hayes ℰ (01666) 82 37 48, www.malmesbury.gov.uk
🎡 Town ★ – Market Cross ★★ – Abbey ★

ENGLAND

**Whatley Manor** ⌂  ≪ ⬚ ◷ ⓦ ☍ ⌷ ✦ & ↑ ⚒ Ⓟ VISA ◉ AE
❀❀ *Easton Grey, West : 2.25 mi on B 4040 ⊠ SN16 0RB – ℰ (01666) 822 888*
*– www.whatleymanor.com*
**15 rm** ⌑ – ♦£ 305/515 ♦♦£ 305/515 – 8 suites
**Rest *Le Mazot*** – see restaurant listing
**Rest *The Dining Room*** – *(closed Monday and Tuesday) (dinner only) (booking essential for non-residents)* Menu £ 76/96 **s**🌢
**Spec.** Poached and roasted squab pigeon with pan-fried foie gras, Pedro Ximenez reduction. Fillets of Dover sole with glazed shrimps, confit salt cod and onion cassonade. Prune and Armagnac soufflé, Ceylon tea granité.
♦ Cotswold stone buildings set in beautiful gardens. Chic, contemporary, luxurious bedrooms; sumptuous bathrooms. Stunning spa, top class business centre and cinema. The Dining Room offers comfortable surroundings in which to enjoy technically-skilled and innovative cooking, with charming service.

**Old Bell** ⬚ ↑ ⚒ Ⓟ VISA ◉ AE
*Abbey Row ⊠ SN16 0BW – ℰ (01666) 822 344*
*– www.oldbellhotel.com*
**33 rm** ⌑ – ♦£ 90/99 ♦♦£ 115/275
**Rest *The Restaurant*** – see restaurant listing
♦ Hugely characterful part-13C former abbots' hostel in pleasant gardens, set next to the abbey. Intimate bar. Mix of bedroom styles: bold and fashionable in main house, more classical in annexe.

✕✕ **Le Mazot** – at Whatley Manor Hotel AC Ⓟ VISA ◉ AE
*Easton Grey, West : 2.25 mi on B 4040 ⊠ SN16 0RB – ℰ (01666) 822 888*
*– www.whatleymanor.com*
**Rest** – Menu £ 24 (lunch) **s** – Carte £ 33/37 **s**
♦ Unusual gold wood Swiss chalet restaurant within delightful country house, offering casual dining on comfy banquettes. Cooking is refined, light and skilled. Polite, careful service.

✕✕ **The Restaurant** – at The Old Bell Hotel ⌂ Ⓟ VISA ◉ AE
*Abbey Row ⊠ SN16 0BW – ℰ (01666) 822 344*
*– www.oldbellhotel.com – Closed dinner Sunday and Monday*
**Rest** – *(booking essential at dinner)* Menu £ 40 (dinner) – Carte £ 28/40
♦ Imposing, richly coloured dining room displaying old portraits and fine china. Skilled kitchen offers brasserie-style lunch and fine dining in evening. Refined, artful dishes; attentive service.

**at Crudwell** North : 4 mi on A 429 – ⊠ Malmesbury

**Rectory** ⬚ ⌂ ⟰ ↑ Ⓟ VISA ◉
*⊠ SN16 9EP – ℰ (01666) 577 194*
*– www.therectoryhotel.com*
**12 rm** ⌑ – ♦£ 105 ♦♦£ 195 **Rest** – *(dinner only)* Menu £ 29
♦ 17C stone-built former Rectory with formal garden. A little quirky but personally run. Comfortable, individually-styled bedrooms with many modern extras, some with spa baths. Airy oak-panelled dining room; modern seasonal cooking.

**Potting Shed** ⬌ Ⓟ VISA ◉ AE
*The Street ⊠ SN16 9EW – ℰ (01666) 577 833*
*– www.thepottingshedpub.com*
**Rest** – Carte £ 23/33
♦ Spacious, light-filled pub with contemporary décor, exposed beams and a relaxing feel. Monthly changing menus offer wholesome, satisfying dishes, with vegetables and herbs from their garden.

## MALPAS – Cheshire West and Chester – 502 L24 – pop. 3 684      20 A3

▶ London 177 mi – Birmingham 60 mi – Chester 15 mi – Shrewsbury 26 mi

**at Tilston** Northwest : 3 mi on Tilston Rd – ⊠ Malpas

⌂    **Tilston Lodge** without rest      🚗 🐾 🌿 🛜 **P**
     ⊠ SY14 7DR – ℰ (01829) 250 223
     **3 rm** ⊑ – †£ 50 ††£ 100
     ♦ Large, red-brick former Victorian hunting lodge with neat gardens and mature grounds. Homely bedrooms boast good facilities and country views. Charming owner is Lord Mayor of Chester.

## MALTBY – Stockton-on-Tees – 502 Q23      24 B3

▶ London 251 mi – Liverpool 141 mi – Leeds 69 mi – Sheffield 101 mi

🍴    **Chadwicks Inn**      🚗 🍽 **P** 𝘝𝘐𝘚𝘈 ⬤⬤
     High Ln ⊠ TS8 0B9 – ℰ (01642) 590 300 – www.chadwicksinnmaltby.co.uk
     – Closed 25 December, 1 January and Monday
     **Rest** – (booking advisable) Menu £ 16 (lunch) – Carte £ 26/40
     ♦ Dating back over 200 years and a favourite haunt of the Spitfire pilots before their missions. Open-fired bar and two smart dining rooms. Ambitious à la carte offers intricate dishes, supplemented by a set lunch and tapas in the afternoons.

## MALVERN WELLS – Worcestershire – 503 N27 – see Great Malvern

ENGLAND

## MAN (Isle of) – I.O.M. – 502 G21 – pop. 80 058 📗 Great Britain      20 B1

⛴ from Douglas to Belfast (Isle of Man Steam Packet Co. Ltd) (summer only) (2 h 45 mn) – from Douglas to Republic of Ireland (Dublin) (Isle of Man Steam Packet Co. Ltd) (2 h 45 mn/4 h) – from Douglas to Heysham (Isle of Man Steam Packet Co.) (2 h/3 h 30 mn) – from Douglas to Liverpool (Isle of Man Steam Packet Co. Ltd) (2 h 30 mn/4 h)

◉ Laxey Wheel★★ – Snaefell★ (🌲★★★) – Cregneash Folk Museum★

### DOUGLAS – Douglas – pop. 26 218      20 B1

🛫 Ronaldsway Airport : ℰ (01624) 821600, SW : 7 mi
ℹ Sea Terminal Buildings ℰ (01624) 68 67 66, www.iomguide.com
🏌 Douglas Pulrose Park, ℰ (01624) 67 59 52
🏌 King Edward Bay Onchan Groudle Rd, ℰ (01624) 62 04 30

🏨    **Sefton**      🖥 🏄 🛁 🛗 🛗 rm, 🌿 🛜 🚴 **P** 𝘝𝘐𝘚𝘈 ⬤⬤ 𝔸𝔼
     Harris Promenade ⊠ IM1 2RW – ℰ (01624) 645 500 – www.seftonhotel.co.im
     **90 rm** ⊑ – ††£ 110/130 – 12 suites
     **Rest The Gallery** – (closed Sunday in winter) (bar lunch) Menu £ 30
     – Carte approx. £ 35 **s**
     ♦ Victorian-fronted promenade hotel, built around unique atrium water garden. Bedrooms may have balconies, look out to sea or have water garden views. Impressive apartment suites. The Gallery, with its boldly coloured Manx art, offers speciality flambé dishes.

🏨    **Regency**      ⇐ 🛗 🌿 🛜 🚴 𝘝𝘐𝘚𝘈 ⬤⬤ 𝔸𝔼 ⓞ
     Queens Promenade ⊠ IM2 4NN – ℰ (01624) 680 680 – www.regency.im
     **34 rm** ⊑ – †£ 80/145 ††£ 125/165 – 4 suites
     **Rest Five Continents** – (dinner only) Menu £ 26 – Carte £ 26/43 🍷
     ♦ Perfect for business travellers: mobile phone loan, PCs with free internet in every bedroom and special office suites, combined with traditional seaside styling and Douglas Bay views. Oak panelled restaurant boasts original collection of Island pictures.

🏠 **Penta** without rest 🛗 ℅ 📶 VISA ◉◉ AE ①
*Queens Promenade* ✉ *IM9 4NE* – ℅ *(01624) 680 680* – *www.regency.im*
**22 rm** – 🛏£ 49/90 🛏🛏£ 59/100
♦ Set on the promenade, with views over Douglas Bay. Large, functional, well-equipped bedrooms feature computers with free internet access. Wine-themed, Mediterranean-style breakfast room.

ℜℜℜ **JAR** VISA ◉◉ AE
*Admirals House, 11-12 Loch Promenade* ✉ *IM1 2LX* – ℅ *(01624) 663 553*
– *www.jar.co.im* – *Closed 25 December*
**Rest** – Menu £ 25 (lunch) – Carte £ 32/51
♦ Set on ground floor of hotel, with comfy, leather-furnished lounge and pleasant coastal outlook from front tables. Italian-influenced menus; clean, unfussy, flavoursome cooking.

ℜℜ **Macfarlane's** VISA ◉◉
*24 Duke St* ✉ *IM1 2AY* – ℅ *(01624) 624 777* – *www.macfarlanes.im* – *Closed 1 week Spring, 2 weeks early August,1 week Christmas-New Year, Sunday and Monday*
**Rest** – *(dinner only and lunch Thursday and Friday)* *(booking essential)*
Carte £ 27/47
♦ Small, simple restaurant in heart of town, with leather-topped tables and high-sided booths. Unfussy, regularly changing menu relies on fresh local produce, with fish to the fore.

**PORT ERIN** – Port Erin – pop. 3 575                                   **20** B1

🏠 **Rowany Cottier** without rest ≤ 🚗 ℅ 🅿
*Spaldrick* ✉ *IM9 6PE* – ℅ *(01624) 832 287* – *www.rowanycottier.com*
**5 rm** ⬜ – 🛏£ 50/65 🛏🛏£ 80/96
♦ Large, purpose-built house set by Bradda Glen. Pleasant guest areas with views over Port Erin and Calf of Man. Simple, well-kept bedrooms. Locally sourced breakfast; homemade bread.

**PORT ST MARY** – Port Saint Mary – pop. 1 913                         **20** B1

🏠 **Aaron House** without rest ℅ 📶
*The Promenade* ✉ *IM9 5DE* – ℅ *(01624) 835 702* – *www.aaronhouse.co.uk*
– *Closed Christmas-New Year*
**6 rm** ⬜ – 🛏£ 98/108 🛏🛏£ 118/138
♦ Charming, antique-furnished guesthouse with bay/harbour views and strong Victorian feel. Comfy, traditional bedrooms. Afternoon tea on arrival. Interesting breakfast choices.

**RAMSEY** – Ramsey – pop. 7 309                                       **20** B1

🏠 **River House** without rest 🐾 🚗 📶 🅿
*North : 0.25 mi by A 9 turning left immediately after bridge* ✉ *IM8 3DA*
– ℅ *(01624) 816 412*
**3 rm** ⬜ – 🛏£ 70 🛏🛏£ 120
♦ Attractive Georgian country house with pleasant gardens. Tastefully furnished throughout, with comfy drawing room, antiques and objets d'art. Traditional, cottage-style bedrooms.

ENGLAND

# MANCHESTER

See city maps on following pages

**Greater Manchester** – pop. 396 322 – **502** N23 – **503** N23 – **504** N23 – ▯ Great Britain

▶ London 202 – Birmingham 86 – Glasgow 221 – Leeds 43

**🗓 Tourist Information**

Manchester Visitor Centre, Town Hall Extension, Lloyd St *(0871) 222 82 23, www.visitmanchester.com

**Airport**

✈ Manchester International Airport : *(08712) 710 711, S : 10 m. by A 5103 - AX - and M 56

**Golf Courses**

🏌 Heaton Park Prestwich, *(0161) 654 98 99
🏌 Houldsworth Park Stockport Houldsworth St, Reddish, *(0161) 442 17 12

**◎ SIGHTS**

**In the town :** City★ • Castlefield Urban Heritage Park★ CZ • Town Hall★ CZ • Manchester Art Gallery★ CZ**M2** • Cathedral★ CY • Museum of Science and Industry★ CZ**M** • Imperial War Museum North★, Trafford Park AX**M**

**On the outskirts :** Whitworth Art Gallery★, S : 1.5 m

**In the surrounding area :** Quarry Bank Mill★, S : 10 mi off B 5166, exit 5 from M 56

ENGLAND

ENGLAND

485

# MANCHESTER

ENGLAND

## Lowry 🕙 🕙 ⫶⫶ ⫶ ⫶ 🅰🅺 ⫶ ⫶ 🅿 VISA ⬤ AE ①
*50 Dearmans Pl, Chapel Wharf, Salford* ✉ *M3 5LH* – ℰ *(0161) 827 40 00*
*– www.roccofortehotels.com* CYn
**158 rm** – ♦£ 387 ♦♦£ 453, ⌇ £ 18.50 – 7 suites
**Rest** *River* – see restaurant listing
♦ Modern and hugely spacious, with excellent facilities, impressive spa and mini-malist feel: art displays and exhibitions feature throughout. Stylish bedrooms with oversized windows; some river views.

## Hilton ≤ 🔲 🕙 ⫶⫶ ⫶ ⫶ 🅰 ⫶ ⫶ 🅰 VISA ⬤ AE ①
*303 Deansgate* ✉ *M3 4LQ* – ℰ *(0161) 870 16 00*
*– www.hilton.co.uk/manchesterdeansgate* CZe
**275 rm** – ♦£ 169/369 ♦♦£ 169/369, ⌇ £ 17.95 – 5 suites
**Rest** *Podium* – Menu £ 20/27 – Carte £ 28/41
♦ 23 floors of a striking glass skyscraper. Smart atrium lobby with elevated walk-ways; glass bottomed pool above. Comfortable, contemporary bedrooms with views. Superb 360° outlook from Cloud bar. Stylish Podium restaurant offers mod-ern brasserie menu of European dishes.

## Malmaison 🕙 🕙 ⫶⫶ ⫶ ⫶ 🅰🅺 ⫶ ⫶ 🅰 VISA ⬤ AE
*Piccadilly* ✉ *M1 3AQ* – ℰ *(0161) 278 10 00* – *www.malmaison-manchester.com*
**166 rm** – ♦£ 99/170 ♦♦£ 99/170, ⌇ £ 14.50 – 1 suite CZu
**Rest** *Brasserie* – see restaurant listing
♦ Old cotton warehouse and dolls hospital joined by a striking granite exten-sion. Seductive red and black Moulin Rouge style décor and sensuous spa. Styl-ish bedrooms: uniquely designed suites include a Man Utd theme and mini cin-ema dark room.

## Abode 🔲 ⫶ 🅰🅺 ⫶ ⫶ 🅰 VISA ⬤ AE ①
*107 Piccadilly* ✉ *M1 2DB* – ℰ *(0161) 247 77 44* – *www.abodehotels.co.uk*
**61 rm** – ♦£ 79/170 ♦♦£ 79/170, ⌇ £ 14 CZc
**Rest** *Michael Caines* – see restaurant listing
♦ Late Victorian cotton merchant's former head office with iron columns and gir-ders still in situ. Relaxed boutique ambience with modern, trendy open-plan rooms and stylish bathrooms.

## Mint 🔲 ⫶⫶ ⫶ ⫶ 🅰 ⫶ ⫶ 🅰 🔲 VISA ⬤ AE
*One Piccadilly Place, 1 Auburn Street* ✉ *M1 3DG* – ℰ *(0161) 242 10 00*
*– www.minthotel.com* CZt
**284 rm** – ♦£ 245 ♦♦£ 245, ⌇ £ 16 – 1 suite
**Rest** *Elements* – ℰ *(0161) 242 10 20* – Menu £ 16/20 – Carte £ 24/34
♦ Contemporary glass building with spacious, airy interior and local art on dis-play. Modern bedrooms boast pale hues, iMac computers and excellent entertain-ment facilities. Showers only. Smart, stylish restaurant with appealing, wide rang-ing menu.

## River – at The Lowry Hotel 🔲 🅰 ⇔ 🅿 VISA ⬤ AE ①
*50 Dearmans Pl, Chapel Wharf, Salford* ✉ *M3 5LH* – ℰ *(0161) 827 40 00*
*– www.roccofortehotels.com* CYn
**Rest** – Menu £ 20 – Carte £ 44/50
♦ Airy first-floor restaurant with river views; vast mirrors, modern artwork and decorative plates fill the walls. Modern presentation of classic combinations with regional ingredients to the fore.

## Wings 🅰 VISA ⬤ AE
*1 Lincoln Sq* ✉ *M2 5LN* – ℰ *(0161) 834 90 00* – *www.wingsrestaurant.co.uk*
**Rest** – Chinese – Menu £ 33 – Carte £ 19/56 CZd
♦ Well-run restaurant off busy square. Narrow room with linen-clad tables, comfy booths, terracotta army replicas and Hong Kong skyline murals. Extensive menu of authentic Cantonese dim sum.

ENGLAND

ENGLAND

XX **Second Floor - Restaurant** – at Harvey Nichols          AC VISA ⓞⓞ AE
*21 New Cathedral St ⊠ M1 1AD – ℰ (0161) 828 88 98 – www.harveynichols.com*
*– Closed 25-26 December, 1 January, Sunday and dinner Monday*          CYk
**Rest** – Menu £ 40
♦ Smart restaurant with stylish, colour-changing lighting and oversized windows offering big wheel and city views. Elaborate modern European menu with interesting twists; good presentation.

XX **Michael Caines** – at Abode Hotel          AC ⇔ VISA ⓞⓞ AE ⓞ
*107 Piccadilly ⊠ M1 2DB – ℰ (0161) 247 77 44 – www.michaelcaines.co.uk*
*– Closed first 2 weeks January and Sunday*          CZc
**Rest** – Menu £ 14 (lunch) – Carte approx. £ 43
♦ Modern restaurant in hotel basement, featuring subdued lighting and a sophisticated style. Contemporary British cooking, with some Mediterranean influences. Tasting menu and matching wines.

XX **Brasserie** – at Malmaison Hotel          & AC VISA ⓞⓞ AE
*Piccadilly ⊠ M1 3AQ – ℰ (0161) 278 10 01 – www.malmaison-manchester.com*
**Rest** – Menu £ 30 – Carte £ 25/30          CZu
♦ Richly decorated, two-roomed brasserie with intimate candlelit booths, set in a stylish hotel that was once an old cotton warehouse and dolls hospital. Menu offers unfussy British classics.

X **Second Floor - Brasserie** – at Harvey Nichols          ⇐ AC VISA ⓞⓞ AE
*21 New Cathedral St ⊠ M1 1AD – ℰ (0161) 828 88 98 – www.harveynichols.com*
*– Closed 25 December, 1 January and dinner Sunday-Monday*          CYk
**Rest** – Menu £ 20 (dinner) – Carte £ 21/31
♦ Relaxed, minimalist brasserie and bar, with colour-changing strip lighting and buzzy atmosphere. Extensive menu of modern British dishes, with some lighter meals available. Popular with shoppers.

X **Northern Quarter**          VISA ⓞⓞ AE
*108 High St ⊠ M4 1HQ – ℰ (0161) 832 71 15 – www.tnq.co.uk – Closed 25*
*December, 1-2 January and Sunday dinner*          CYz
**Rest** – *(booking essential at dinner)* Menu £ 14 (lunch and early dinner)
– Carte £ 24/37
♦ Friendly, modern restaurant with floor to ceiling windows. Keenly priced, seasonal menus offer classic dishes presented in a modern style. Popular, bi-monthly themed evenings.

**at Didsbury** South : 5.5 mi by 5103 - AX - on A 5145 – ⊠ Manchester

🏠🏠 **Didsbury House**          ℹ ⁛ P VISA ⓞⓞ AE ⓞ
*Didsbury Pk, South : 1.5 mi on A 5145 ⊠ M20 5LJ – ℰ (0161) 448 22 00*
*– www.didsburyhouse.com*
**23 rm** – ♦£ 143 ♦♦£ 143, � £ 15.50 – 4 suites    **Rest** – Carte £ 19/30 s
♦ Cream-washed Victorian villa – now a boutique townhouse; original features include an impressive stained glass window. Bedrooms are comfortable and stylish with a contemporary edge; some boast hot tubs. Small basement dining room; accessible, all-day menu.

🏠 **Eleven Didsbury Park**          🚗 ⁛ P VISA ⓞⓞ AE ⓞ
*11 Didsbury Pk, South : 1.5 mi by A 5145 ⊠ M20 5LH – ℰ (0161) 448 77 11*
*– www.elevendidsburypark.com*
**19 rm** – ♦£ 143 ♦♦£ 143, ⊑ £ 15.50 – 1 suite
**Rest** – *(room service only)* Carte £ 19/30 s
♦ Comfortable, boutique-style townhouse in pleasant residential setting, with simply furnished breakfast room overlooking delightful garden. Stylish, contemporary bedrooms with warm décor and good facilities; many have tubs in the rooms. Informal all-day menu.

X **Jem&I** 🖼 VISA ⦿ AE
*1c School Ln ⊠ M20 6RD – ℰ (0161) 445 39 96 – jemandirestaurant.co.uk*
**Rest** – Carte £ 20/34
♦ Simple, unpretentious cream-coloured building tucked away off the high street. Open-plan kitchen; homely, bistro feel. Good value, modern European menus. Polite, friendly service.

**at West Didsbury** South : 5.5 mi by A 5103 - AX - on A 5145 – ⊠ Manchester

X **Rhubarb** 🍴 AC VISA ⦿ AE
*167 Burton Rd ⊠ M20 2LN – ℰ (0161) 448 88 87 – www.rhubarbrestaurant.co.uk*
*– Closed 25 December and 1 January*
**Rest** – *(dinner only and Sunday lunch)* – Carte £ 22/31
♦ Suburban eatery with small pavement terrace, where neutral hues are offset by large canvasses and a colourful feature wall. Large, seasonally changing menus display an eclectic mix of dishes.

**at Chorlton-Cum-Hardy** Southwest : 4 mi . by A 5103 - AX - on A 6010
– ⊠ Manchester

⛫ **Abbey Lodge** without rest 🚗 📶 P VISA ⦿ AE
*501 Wilbraham Rd ⊠ M21 0UJ – ℰ (0161) 862 92 66 – www.abbey-lodge.co.uk*
**4 rm** – ♦£ 50/60 ♦♦£ 70, � £ 7.50                                                      AXz
♦ Attractive Edwardian house boasting many original features including stained glass windows. Owner provides charming hospitality and pine fitted rooms are immaculately kept.

**at Prestwich** Northwest : 5 mi on A 56

XX **Aumbry** VISA ⦿
*2 Church Ln ⊠ M25 1AJ – ℰ (0161) 798 58 41 – www.aumbryrestaurant.co.uk*
*– Closed first 2 weeks January, 25 December, Sunday dinner, Monday and Tuesday*                                                                                     AVx
**Rest** – *(booking essential)* Menu £ 22 (weekday lunch) – Carte £ 30/44
♦ Intimate neighbourhood restaurant offering small à la carte or 9 course tasting menu. Precise cooking with a good combination of flavours; local, seasonal produce well used.

---

**MANSFIELD** – Nottinghamshire – **502** Q24 – pop. 69 987                    **16** B1
▶ London 143 mi – Chesterfield 12 mi – Worksop 14 mi

XX **No.4 Wood Street** AC ⇔ P VISA ⦿ AE
*4 Wood St ⊠ NG18 1QA – ℰ (01623) 424 824 – www.4woodstreet.co.uk*
*– Closed 26 December, 1 January, Saturday lunch, Sunday dinner and Monday*
**Rest** – Menu £ 18 (weekdays) – Carte £ 21/36
♦ Solid brick restaurant hidden away in town centre. Relax in lounge bar with comfy armchairs before enjoying well-executed, modern, seasonal dishes in rustic dining room.

XX **Lambs at the Market** VISA ⦿
*Cattle Market House, Nottingham Rd ⊠ NG18 1BD – ℰ (01623) 424 880*
*– www.lambsatthemarket.co.uk – Closed first week January and Monday*
**Rest** – *(dinner only and Sunday lunch)* Menu £ 18 (lunch) – Carte dinner £ 24/43
♦ Family-run restaurant in attractive Victorian building, with a more contemporary interior. Modern European cooking has a British bias; portions are generous and flavours, clear.

ENGLAND

**MARAZION** – Cornwall – **503** D33 – pop. 1 381 – ⊠ Penzance    **1** A3

▶ London 318 mi – Penzance 3 mi – Truro 26 mi

◉ Praa Sands Penzance, ℰ (01736) 76 34 45

◐ St Michael's Mount★★ (⩽★★) – Ludgvan★ (Church★) N : 2 mi by A 30
– Chysauster Village★, N : 2 mi by A 30 – Gulval★ (Church★) W : 2.5 m – Prussia
Cove★, SE : 5.5 mi by A 30 and minor rd

⌂ **Mount Haven**    ⩽ 🖼 😤 ℅ ⑩ **P** 𝚅𝙸𝚂𝙰 ⓪ ①
Turnpike Rd, East : 0.25 mi ⊠ TR17 0DQ – ℰ (01736) 710 249
– www.mounthaven.co.uk – Closed mid-December-early-February
**18 rm** ⌷ – ♦£ 90/120 ♦♦£ 160/190
**Rest** – (bar lunch Monday-Saturday) Menu £ 30 – Carte £ 20/32
♦ Small hotel overlooking St Michael's Bay. Spacious bar and lounge featuring
Indian crafts and fabrics. Contemporary rooms with modern amenities, most
with balcony and view. Bright attractive dining room; menu mixes modern and
traditional.

**at Perranuthnoe** Southeast : 1.75 mi by A 394 – ⊠ Penzance

⌂ **Ednovean Farm** without rest 🌿    ⩽ 🖼 🕓 ℅ ⑩ **P** 𝚅𝙸𝚂𝙰 ⓪
⊠ TR20 9LZ – ℰ (01736) 711 883 – www.ednoveanfarm.co.uk – Closed
Christmas
**3 rm** ⌷ – ♦£ 100/115 ♦♦£ 105/120
♦ Very spacious, characterful converted 17C granite barn offering peace, tranquil-
lity and Mounts Bay views. Fine choice at breakfast on oak table. Charming, individual rooms.

📖 **Victoria Inn** with rm    🖼 ⑩ **P** 𝚅𝙸𝚂𝙰 ⓪
⊠ TR20 9NP – ℰ (01736) 710 309 – www.victoriainn-penzance.co.uk – Closed
25-26 December, 1 January, Monday in winter and Sunday dinner
**2 rm** ⌷ – ♦£ 50/75 ♦♦£ 75    **Rest** – Carte £ 27/34
♦ Characterful, pink-washed pub in the heart of the village, with a cosy, homely
feel and a suntrap terrace. Short menu of wholesome dishes showcases local produce and is supplemented by blackboard of seafood specials. Simple, nautically
themed bedrooms.

**at St Hilary** East : 2.5 mi by Turnpike Rd on B 3280 – ⊠ Penzance

⌂ **Ennys** without rest 🌿    🖼 ⑩ ⌁ 🍽 ℅ ⑩ **P** 𝚅𝙸𝚂𝙰 ⓪
Trewhella Ln ⊠ TR20 9BZ – ℰ (01736) 740 262 – www.ennys.co.uk
– April-October
**5 rm** ⌷ – ♦£ 85/135 ♦♦£ 105/150
♦ A beautiful and delightfully remote guesthouse, its lovingly restored interior
simply furnished in light colours, with Indian artefacts from the charming owner's
travels. Grass tennis court and pool set in secluded part of the garden. Complimentary afternoon tea.

---

**MARCHAM** – Oxfordshire – **503** P29 – see Abingdon

---

**MARGATE** – Kent – **504** Y29 – pop. 58 465    **9** D1

▶ London 74 mi – Canterbury 17 mi – Dover 21 mi – Maidstone 43 mi

ℹ 12-13 The Parade ℰ (0872) 64 61 11, www.visitthanet.co.uk

⌂ **Reading Rooms** without rest    ℅ ⑩ 𝚅𝙸𝚂𝙰 ⓪ 𝙰𝙴
31 Hawley Sq ⊠ CT9 1PH – ℰ (01843) 225 166
– www.thereadingroomsmargate.co.uk
**3 rm** ⌷ – ♦£ 135/165 ♦♦£ 170/180
♦ Passionately run guesthouse with stripped plaster, worn woodwork and unique
shabby-chic style. Eclectic bedrooms – one per floor – boast distressed furniture,
super comfy beds and huge bathrooms. Extensive breakfasts served in your room.

## ✗ Ambrette     AK P VISA ◐◉ AE

*44 King St ✉ CT9 1QE – ℰ (01843) 231 504 – www.theambrette.co.uk – Closed 25-26 December and Monday*
**Rest** – Indian – Menu £ 20 (lunch) – Carte £ 17/31

♦ Quirky Indian restaurant in modest surroundings. Concise, seasonal menu showcases Kentish produce in an original style; freshly prepared dishes offer well-balanced flavours and subtle spicing.

---

## MARKET DRAYTON – Shropshire – 502 M25 – pop. 10 407     18 B1

▶ London 159 mi – Nantwich 13 mi – Shrewsbury 21 mi

## ☆ Goldstone Hall ⌂     ≼ ⇏ ℀ ⸙ P VISA ◐◉ AE

*Goldstone, South : 4.5 mi by A 529 ✉ TF9 2NA – ℰ (01630) 661 202 – www.goldstonehall.com*
**12 rm** ☲ – †£ 82 ††£ 120    **Rest** – Menu £ 22 (lunch) **s** – Carte £ 31/49 **s**

♦ 16C red-brick country house that's been extensively added to over the ages. Five acres of formal garden: PG Wodehouse enjoyed its shade! Modern rooms with huge beds. Contemporary twists on daily changing menus.

---

## MARLBOROUGH – Wiltshire – 503 O29 – pop. 7 713     4 D2

▶ London 84 mi – Bristol 47 mi – Southampton 40 mi – Swindon 12 mi
ℹ High St ℰ (01225) 774 2 22, www.visitwiltshire.co.uk
⛳ The Common, ℰ (01672) 51 21 47
◎ Town ★
Ⓖ Savernake Forest★★ (Grand Avenue★★★), SE : 2 mi by A 4 – Whitehorse (≼★), NW : 5 m – West Kennett Long Barrow★, Silbury Hill★, W : 6 mi by A 4. Ridgeway Path★★ – Avebury★★ (The Stones★, Church★), W : 7 mi by A 4 – Crofton Beam Engines★ **AC**, SE : 9 mi by A 346 – Wilton Windmill★ **AC**, SE : 9 mi by A 346, A 338 and minor rd

ENGLAND

## ✗ Coles     �🍴 AK VISA ◐◉ AE

*27 Kingsbury Hill ✉ SN8 1JA – ℰ (01672) 515 004 – www.colesrestaurant.co.uk – Closed 25 December, Sunday and bank holidays, except Good Friday*
**Rest** – Carte £ 25/32

♦ Shots of 70s film stars adorn a busy, bay-windowed former pub which retains its firelit bar. Friendly staff and elaborate but robust cuisine with an array of daily specials.

---

**at Little Bedwyn** East : 9.5 mi by A 4 – ✉ Marlborough

## ✗✗ Harrow at Little Bedwyn (Roger Jones)     ⍝ VISA ◐◉
☙

*✉ SN8 3JP – ℰ (01672) 870 871 – www.theharrowatlittlebedwyn.co.uk – Closed 2 weeks August, 2 weeks Christmas, and Sunday-Tuesday*
**Rest** – Menu £ 30/40 – Carte approx. £ 47 ⌓

**Spec.** Lobster fish finger. Line caught turbot, chicken and morel broth. Chocolate, pistachio, golden raisin and praline torte.

♦ Former pub with smartly laid tables and an intimate atmosphere. Flavourful, seasonal cooking is presented in a modern style, whilst retaining its classical base. Top quality produce; fish plays an important role. Comprehensive wine list and regular wine evenings.

---

**at East Kennett** West : 5.25 mi by A4

## ⌂ Old Forge without rest     ⇏ ℀ P VISA ◐◉

*✉ SN8 4EY – ℰ (01672) 861 686 – www.theoldforge-avebury.co.uk*
**4 rm** ☲ – †£ 70 ††£ 80

♦ Converted former smithy with a relaxing, homely feel. Comfortable bedrooms have classic country house style; the family room has pleasant countryside views. Communal breakfast.

▶ London 193 mi – Newton Abbott 7 mi – Paignton 3 mi

🏠 **Church House Inn**                              🗚 🛎 **P** 𝖵𝖨𝖲𝖠 ⓾

*Village Rd* ✉ *TQ3 1SL* – *𝒞 (01803) 558 279 – www.churchhousemarldon.com*
*– Closed 25 December and dinner 26 December*
**Rest** – Carte £ 22/35
• Charming inn of huge character displaying original Georgian windows. Fresh and simple décor. Menu leans towards the Mediterranean with some North African and Asian influences.

▶ London 35 mi – Aylesbury 22 mi – Oxford 29 mi – Reading 14 mi
🚢 to Henley-on-Thames (Salter Bros. Ltd) (summer only) (2 h 15 mn) – to Maidenhead, Cookham and Windsor (Salter Bros. Ltd) (summer only)
🛈 31 High St 𝒞 (01628) 48 35 97, www.visitbuckinghamshire.org

**ENGLAND**

🏨 **Danesfield House** ⌂        ⪅ 🗚 🐾 🛎 🗔 ⓾ 🚿 🎧 ⅋ 🛗 𝖠𝖢 rest, ⅋ 🎙

*Henley Rd, Southwest : 2.5 mi on A 4155* ✉ *SL7 2EY*        ⅍ **P** 𝖵𝖨𝖲𝖠 ⓾ 𝖠𝖤 ⓪
*– 𝒞 (01628) 891 010 – www.danesfieldhouse.co.uk*
**86 rm** – ♦£ 134/249 ♦♦£ 249/299, ⬓ £ 10.50
**Rest** *Adam Simmonds at Danesfield House*⌘ – see restaurant listing
**Rest** *Orangery* – Menu £ 24 (lunch) – Carte £ 32/37
• Stunning house and gardens in Italian Renaissance style, with breathtaking views of the Thames. Grand lounge with country house feel, comfy bedrooms, cocktail bar and state-of-art health spa. Charming, informal terrace brasserie.

🏨 **Compleat Angler**                  ⪅ 🗚 🦢 🛗 𝖠𝖢 🎙 ⅍ **P** 𝖵𝖨𝖲𝖠 ⓾ 𝖠𝖤

*Marlow Bridge, Bisham Rd* ✉ *SL7 1RG* – *𝒞 (0844) 879 91 28*
*– www.macdonaldhotels.co.uk/compleatangler*
**61 rm** ⬓ – ♦£ 125/205 ♦♦£ 125/215 – 3 suites
**Rest** *Aubergine at the Compleat Angler* – 𝒞 (01628) 405 405 *(closed Monday and Tuesday) (booking essential)* Menu £ 29/50
**Rest** *Bowaters* – 𝒞 (01628) 405 406 *(closed Sunday dinner)* Menu £ 23 (weekday lunch) – Carte £ 39/43
• Smart riverside hotel boasting superb views, in enviable location between the bridge and weir. Bedrooms mix classical furnishings with contemporary fabrics: some have waterfront balconies; feature rooms are the best. Ambitious French menu in Aubergine. More traditional British fare in contemporary Bowaters.

🍽🍽🍽🍽 **Adam Simmonds at Danesfield House**        🗚 🕯 **P** 𝖵𝖨𝖲𝖠 ⓾ 𝖠𝖤 ⓪

⌘        *Henley Rd, Southwest : 2.5 mi on A 4155* ✉ *SL7 2EY* – *𝒞 (01628) 891 010*
*– www.danesfieldhouse.co.uk – Closed Sunday and Monday*
**Rest** – *(dinner only and lunch Thursday-Saturday)* Menu £ 62
**Spec.** Crab salad, tartare of mackerel, cucumber and avocado purée. Slow cooked loin of lamb, lamb sweetbreads, carrot purée and cumin croquettes. Lemon parfait and mousse with fennel pollen ice cream and olive oil jelly.
• Elegant, very intimate fine dining restaurant with a huge fireplace, panelled walls, linen-laid tables and a relaxed air. Creative, flavourful, intricate cooking uses modern techniques, making skilful use of excellent quality, seasonal ingredients. Formal service.

🍽🍽 **Vanilla Pod**                           🛎 𝖠𝖢 ⇕ 𝖵𝖨𝖲𝖠 ⓾ 𝖠𝖤

*31 West St* ✉ *SL7 2LS* – *𝒞 (01628) 898 101 – www.thevanillapod.co.uk*
*– Closed 24 December-8 January, Sunday, Monday and bank holidays*
**Rest** – *(booking essential)* Menu £ 20 (lunch) **s** – Carte £ 20/40
• Discreet, well-established address with plush furnishings and just a few tables; formerly home to T. S. Elliot. Ambitious cooking boasts French foundations, original touches and artistic flair.

🛏 **Hand and Flowers** (Tom Kerridge) with rm    🚗 🍴 **P** **VISA** **©**
❀❀ *126 West St.* ⊠ *SL7 2BP* – ℰ *(01628) 482 277* – *www.thehandandflowers.co.uk*
*– Closed 24-26 December and Sunday dinner*
**4 rm** ⊿ – **†**£ 140 **††**£ 190
**Rest** – *(booking essential)* Menu £ 17 *(weekday lunch)* – Carte £ 37/48
**Spec.** Parsley soup with smoked eel, bacon and parmesan tortellini. Fillet of
Cornish plaice with English asparagus, morels and razor clams. Vanilla crème
brûlée.
♦ Softly lit pub with low beamed ceilings, flagstone floors and a characterful
dining area. Friendly, young team serve refined, flavoursome dishes created
using classical techniques. Ingredients marry perfectly and the simple is
turned into the sublime. Charming cottage bedrooms; some boasting outdoor jacuzzis.

🛏 **Royal Oak**    🚗 🍴 **P** **VISA** **©** **AE**
*Frieth Rd, Bovingdon Green, West : 1.25 mi by A 4155* ⊠ *SL7 2JF* – ℰ *(01628)*
*488 611* – *www.royaloakmarlow.co.uk* – *Closed 25-26 December*
**Rest** – Carte £ 22/29
♦ Part-17C, country-chic pub with herb garden, petanque pitch and pleasant terrace. Set close to the M40 and M4: an ideal London getaway. Largely British
menu with the odd Asian influence.

**at Little Marlow** East : 3 mi on A 4155

🛏 **Queens Head**    🚗 **P** **VISA** **©**
*Pound Ln* ⊠ *SL7 3SR* – ℰ *(01628) 482 927* – *www.marlowslittlesecret.co.uk*
*– Closed 25-26 December*
**Rest** – Carte £ 20/25
♦ 16C pub popular with walkers. Lunch menu ranges from ploughman's and fish
& chips to refined dishes from the à la carte, such as scallops with black pudding.
Poised, friendly service.

---

**MARPLE** – Greater Manchester – **502** N23 – pop. 23 480    **20** B3
▶ London 190 mi – Chesterfield 35 mi – Manchester 11 mi

🏠 **Springfield** without rest    🚗 ⚒ 📶 **P** **VISA** **©** **AE** **①**
*99 Station Rd* ⊠ *SK6 6PA* – ℰ *(0161) 449 07 21*
*– www.springfieldhotelmarple.co.uk*
**8 rm** ⊿ – **†**£ 60 **††**£ 80
♦ Personally run, part-Victorian house with sympathetic extensions and pleasant
rural views. Bright breakfast room; individually styled bedrooms. Useful for visits
to the Peak District.

---

**MARSDEN** – West Yorkshire – **502** O23 – pop. 3 499 – ⊠ **Huddersfield**    **22** A3
▶ London 195 mi – Leeds 22 mi – Manchester 18 mi – Sheffield 30 mi

🛏 **Olive Branch** with rm    🍴 ⚒ 📶 **P** **VISA** **©**
⊠ *HD7 6LU* – ℰ *(01484) 844 487* – *www.olivebranch.uk.com* – *Closed first 2*
*weeks January*
**3 rm** – **†**£ 65 **††**£ 80, ⊿ £ 12.50
**Rest** – *(dinner only and Sunday lunch)* Carte £ 26/41
♦ Characterful drovers' inn with stone floors, rustic walls, secluded garden and
pleasant views from terrace. Classical, French-influenced menu supplemented by
fish specials. Good choice of wines by the glass. Bedrooms are modern, cosy and
individually themed.

---

**MARSTON MEYSEY** – Wiltshire    **4** D1
▶ London 91 mi – Birmingham 82 mi – Bristol 56 mi – Coventry 85 mi

🛏 **Old Spotted Cow** with rm    🚗 📞 **P** **VISA** **©**
*The Street* ⊠ *SN6 6LQ* – ℰ *(01285) 810 264* – *www.theoldspottedcow.co.uk*
*– Closed Sunday dinner*
**1 rm** ⊿ – **†**£ 45/55 **††**£ 75/95    **Rest** – Carte £ 19/28
♦ Enthusiastically run country pub serving seasonal, rustic cooking, which combines hearty British classics with worldly spices. Sunday roasts, summer barbecues
and monthly spice nights. One comfortable, contemporary bedroom.

**ENGLAND**

**MARTINHOE** – Devon – see Lynton

**MARTON** – Shropshire ▌ Great Britain                                    **18** A1
▶ London 174 mi – Birmingham 57 mi – Shrewsbury 16 mi
◉ Powis Castle★★★, NW : 7 mi by B 4386 and A 490

🏠   **Sun Inn**                                               ☆ **P** _VISA_ ◉◉
    ✉ SY21 8JP – ℰ (01938) 561 211 – www.suninn.org.uk – Closed lunch
Monday-Tuesday and dinner Sunday
**Rest** – Carte £ 22/30
    ♦ Welcoming, family-run country pub on the English-Welsh border. Pub snacks in
the cosy fire-lit bar; regularly changing à la carte of classic dishes in the bright
restaurant.

**MASHAM** – North Yorkshire – **502** P21 – pop. 1 171 – ✉ Ripon        **22** B1
▶ London 231 mi – Leeds 38 mi – Middlesbrough 37 mi – York 32 mi

🏨🏨🏨   **Swinton Park** ⌖          ← ⛳ 🐾 🞄 🖻 🛗 ᇰ rm, 🍴 🛎 **P** _VISA_ ◉◉
Swinton, Southwest : 1 mi ✉ HG4 4JH – ℰ (01765) 680 900
– www.swintonpark.com
**26 rm** � – †£ 105/180 ††£ 105/180 – 4 suites
**Rest** Samuels – Menu £ 25/48
    ♦ 17C castle with Georgian and Victorian additions, on a 20,000 acre estate and
deer park. Luxurious, antique filled lounges. Very comfortable, individually styled
bedrooms. Grand dining room with ornate gold leaf ceiling and garden views.

🏠   **Bank Villa**                                     ⛳ 🐾 🍴 **P** _VISA_ ◉◉
on A 6108 ✉ HG4 4DB – ℰ (01765) 689 605 – www.bankvilla.com
**6 rm** ⊑ – †£ 50/60 ††£ 70/105   **Rest** – Menu £ 22 **s**
    ♦ Stone-built Georgian villa with Victorian additions. Two lounges and conserva-
tory; delightful, sun-trap stepped garden. Cosy, cottagey rooms: some are in the
eaves. Home-cooked menus in pastel dining room/tea room.

🍴🍴   **Vennell's**                                             _VISA_ ◉◉ **AE**
😊   7 Silver St ✉ HG4 4DX – ℰ (01765) 689 000 – www.vennellsrestaurant.co.uk
– Closed first 2 weeks January, 1 week June, 1 week September, 26-30
December, Sunday dinner and Monday
**Rest** – (dinner only and Sunday lunch) (booking essential) Menu £ 28 **s**
    ♦ Local art for sale at this personally run local eatery with comfy basement
bar. Bold, confident cooking executed with care and precision. Popular annual
'lobster week'.

**MATFEN** – Northumberland – **501** O18 – pop. 500                      **24** A2
▶ London 309 mi – Carlisle 42 mi – Newcastle upon Tyne 24 mi

🏨🏨🏨   **Matfen Hall** ⌖          ← ⛳ 🐾 🖻 ⊕ 🞄 ᛤ 🖻 🛗 ᇰ rm, 🕭 🛎 **P** _VISA_ ◉◉ **AE**
✉ NE20 0RH – ℰ (01661) 886 500 – www.matfenhall.com
**53 rm** ⊑ – †£ 190 ††£ 190
**Rest** **Library and Print Room** – (dinner only) Menu £ 32 – Carte £ 45/60
    ♦ 19C country mansion built by Thomas Ruckman, master of Gothic design. Set
in 500 acres with superb Grand Hall, fine paintings, plush drawing room and mix
of bedroom styles. Characterful Library dining room has display of original books.

**MAWGAN PORTH** – Cornwall – **503** E32 – see Newquay

**MEDBOURNE** – Leicestershire – **504** R26                             **16** B2
▶ London 93 mi – Corby 9 mi – Leicester 16 mi

🏠   **Homestead House** without rest                      ⛳ 🍴 🍴 **P** _VISA_ ◉◉
Ashley Rd ✉ LE16 8DL – ℰ (01858) 565 724 – www.homesteadhouse.co.uk
**3 rm** ⊑ – †£ 36 ††£ 56
    ♦ Personally run, spotlessly kept guest house with comfortable, leather-furnished
lounge and traditionally styled, homely bedrooms; two with a pleasant countryside outlook.

**MELLOR** – Lancashire – see Blackburn

**MELTON MOWBRAY** – Leicestershire – **502** R25 – pop. 25 554　　**16** B2

▸ London 113 mi – Leicester 15 mi – Northampton 45 mi – Nottingham 18 mi

ℹ️ Nottingham Rd ✆ (01664) 48 09 92, www.goleicestershire.com

🏌 Thorpe Arnold Waltham Rd, ✆ (01664) 56 21 18

🏨 **Stapleford Park** ◆　　⟨ 🚲 🐎 🐕 📺 ⊛ 🛏 ⛷ ℉ 🍽 🏌 📶 ⸆ ⚓ 📎 **P**.
*East : 5 mi by B 676 on Stapleford rd ⊠ LE14 2EF*　　*VISA* **☺** **AE** **①**
*– ✆ (01572) 787 000 – www.staplefordpark.com*
**52 rm** ⬜ – **†**£ 140/288 **††**£ 140/288 – 3 suites
**Rest *Grinling Gibbons Dining Room*** – *(closed dinner Sunday-Tuesday)*
*(booking essential)* Menu £ 24/47
◆ Astoundingly beautiful stately home in 500 glorious acres, exuding a grandeur rarely surpassed. Extensive leisure facilities; uniquely designed rooms of sumptuous elegance. Ornate rococo dining room a superb example of master craftsman's work.

**at Stathern** North : 8 mi by A 607 – ⊠ Melton Mowbray

🏠 **Red Lion Inn**　　🛏 **P**. *VISA* **☺**
🐷 *2 Red Lion St ⊠ LE14 4HS – ✆ (01949) 860 868 – www.theredlioninn.co.uk*
*– Closed Sunday dinner*
**Rest** – *(booking essential)* Menu £ 17 (lunch) – Carte £ 19/28
◆ Large, whitewashed village pub. Menus offer straightforward cooking and refined pub classics with the odd international twist. Produce is sourced from their allotment and local suppliers.

**MEVAGISSEY** – Cornwall – **503** F33 – pop. 2 221　　**1** B3

▸ London 287 mi – Newquay 21 mi – Plymouth 44 mi – Truro 20 mi

👁 Town ★★

🏛 NW : Lost Gardens of Heligan ★

🏨 **Trevalsa Court**　　⟨ 🚲 📶 **P**. *VISA* **☺** **AE**
*School Hill, East : 0.5 mi on B 3273 (St Austell rd) ⊠ PL26 6TH – ✆ (01726)*
*842 468 – www.trevalsa-hotel.co.uk – Closed January and December*
**14 rm** ⬜ – **†**£ 80/95 **††**£ 215/235　**Rest** – *(dinner only)* Carte £ 25/36
◆ Charming Arts and Crafts style house combines dark wood panelling with bright modern art and bold soft furnishings. Well-appointed bedrooms; most with coastal views. Oak-panelled dining room looks onto terrace and garden; short, set price dinner menu.

**MICKLETON** – Gloucestershire – **503** O27 – see Chipping Campden

**MIDDLEHAM** – North Yorkshire – **502** O21 – pop. 754　　**22** B1

▸ London 233 mi – Kendal 45 mi – Leeds 47 mi – Newcastle upon Tyne 63 mi

**at Carlton-in-Coverdale** Southwest : 4.5 mi by Coverham rd – ⊠ Leyburn

🏠 **Abbots Thorn** without rest ◆　　⟨ 📶
⊠ *DL8 4AY – ✆ (01969) 640 620 – www.abbotsthorn.co.uk*
*– February-November*
**3 rm** ⬜ – **†**£ 60 **††**£ 75
◆ Well priced, comfortable, quiet guesthouse in attractive rural village. Handy for visits to Moors. Cosy sitting room. Sizeable bedrooms which are homely and well-kept.

**MIDDLETON-IN-TEESDALE** – Durham – **502** N20 – pop. 1 143　　**24** A3

▸ London 447 mi – Carlisle 91 mi – Leeds 124 mi – Middlesbrough 70 mi

ℹ️ 10 Market Pl ✆ (01833) 64 10 01, www.middletonplus.org.uk

🏠 **Grove Lodge**　　⟨ 🚲 **P**.
*Hude, Northwest : 0.5 mi on B 6277 ⊠ DL12 0QW – ✆ (01833) 640 798*
*– www.grovelodgeteesdale.co.uk*
**6 rm** ⬜ – **†**£ 52 **††**£ 82　**Rest** – Carte £ 16/32
◆ Victorian former shooting lodge perched on a hill where the two front facing rooms have the best views. Neat and friendly house, traditionally decorated. Home-cooked dinners are proudly served.

**MIDHURST** – West Sussex – **504** R31 – pop. 6 120        **7** C2

▶ London 57 mi – Brighton 38 mi – Chichester 12 mi – Southampton 41 mi
ℹ️ North St ✆ (01730) 81 73 22, www.visitmidhurst.com

🏨   **Spread Eagle**      🛁 📺 ⊚ ♨ ⅃♠ ‰ 🛂 **P** **VISA** ◎ **AE** ⓪
South St ✉ GU29 9NH – ✆ (01730) 816 911 – www.hshotels.co.uk
**37 rm** ⬜ – †£ 95 ††£ 160 – 2 suites   **Rest** – Menu £ 22/44 **s**
♦ 15C hotel retaining plenty of character in the form of antiques, gleaming brass and inglenook fireplaces. Traditional bedrooms; good leisure facilities. Formally laid restaurant offers good value set price menus; classic dishes presented in a modern style.

**at Henley** North : 4.5 mi by A286

🍴   **Duke of Cumberland**      ⌇ 🛁 **P** **VISA** ◎ **AE**
✉ GU27 3HQ – ✆ (01428) 652 280 – www.dukeofcumberland.com – Closed Sunday and Monday dinner
**Rest** – Carte £ 31/41
♦ Hidden gem with delightful, low-beamed interior, huge fireplace and tiered gardens with babbling brooks. Appealing, daily changing menu of carefully prepared, seasonal dishes. Charming service.

**at Bepton** Southwest : 2.5 mi by A 286 on Bepton rd – ✉ Midhurst

🏨   **Park House** ⚘      ⌇ 🛁 🏊 📺 ⊚ ♨ ⅃♠ ✕ 🖽 🗲 ‰ rm, ⚑ 🛂 **P** **VISA** ◎ **AE**
✉ GU29 0JB – ✆ (01730) 819 000 – www.parkhousehotel.com – Closed 24-26 December
**20 rm** ⬜ – †£ 102/116 ††£ 208/224 – 1 suite
**Rest** – (booking essential at lunch) Menu £ 27/38
♦ Comfortable country house with light, modern style and smart spa and leisure facilities. Spacious bedrooms in neutral shades; most have views of well-tended gardens and golf course; some in separate two-storey house. Stylish restaurant/conservatory offers modern menus.

**at Redford** West : 3 mi by A272 then following signs for Redford

🏠   **Redford Cottage** without rest      ⌇ **P**
✉ GU29 0QF – ✆ (01428) 741 242 – Closed Christmas and New Year
**3 rm** ⬜ – †£ 65/125 ††£ 95/125
♦ Charming 15C cottage in delightful gardens. Uniquely styled, attractively furnished bedrooms; china, books and pictures abound. Hearty breakfast from the Aga can be taken on the terrace.

**at Trotton** West : 3.25 mi on A 272

🍴   **Keepers Arms**      ⌇ 🛁 **P** **VISA** ◎ **AE** ⓪
✉ GU31 5ER – ✆ (01730) 813 724 – www.keepersarms.co.uk – Closed 25 December, Monday in winter and Sunday dinner
**Rest** – Carte £ 21/32
♦ Cheery, welcoming neighbourhood inn with many regular diners and a family feel. Low ceilings, an open fire and a host of quirky tables. Good value, honest cooking and an oft-changing wine list.

---

**MID LAVANT** – West Sussex – **504** R31 – see Chichester

---

**MIDSOMER NORTON** – Bath and North East Somerset – **503** M30     **4** C2

▶ London 125 mi – Bath 11 mi – Wells 12 mi

✕✕   **Moody Goose at the Old Priory** with rm      ⌇ ⚑ **P** **VISA** ◎ **AE**
Church Sq ✉ BA3 2HX – ✆ (01761) 416 784 – www.theoldpriory.co.uk
– Closed Christmas-New Year, Sunday and bank holiday Monday
**6 rm** ⬜ – †£ 75/85 ††£ 120/145   **Rest** – Menu £ 40
♦ 12C former priory, by a church, with an enviable walled garden. Impressive interior with open bar and smart dining room, featuring solid stone floors, beams and vast fireplaces. Classical French cooking utilises quality seasonal ingredients. Warm, comfy bedrooms.

## MILFIELD – Northumberland                                    24 A1

▶ London 336 mi – Glasgow 118 mi – Edinburgh 72 mi – Aberdeen 204 mi

⌂ **Red Lion Inn** with rm                    🖨 🛜 🍴 P VISA ⌾
*Main Rd ⊠ NE71 6JD – ℰ (01668) 216 224 – www.redlioninn-milfield.co.uk*
**2 rm – †£ 25 ††£ 50   Rest** – *(booking advisable)* Carte £ 18/25
♦ Close to the border, a former coaching inn that plays a large part in the local community. Inside it has a traditional look matched by a classic menu which makes good use of the larders of both Scotland and England – you won't leave hungry. Simple, functional bedrooms.

## MILFORD-ON-SEA – Hampshire – 503 P31 – pop. 4 229           6 A3
– ⊠ Lymington

▶ London 109 mi – Bournemouth 15 mi – Southampton 24 mi – Winchester 37 mi

⌂⌂ **Westover Hall** ⌖          ⪡ 🖨 🛜 ⑨ P VISA ⌾ AE ⓪
*Park Ln ⊠ SO41 0PT – ℰ (01590) 643 044 – www.westoverhallhotel.com*
**11 rm ⌷ – †£ 99/135 ††£ 120/280 – 4 suites**
**Rest *Vista Bistro*** – Menu £ 15/25 – Carte £ 29/38
**Rest *One Park Lane*** – *(closed Monday-Wednesday October-May) (dinner only)*
Menu £ 42
♦ Characterful 19C mansion in delightful spot overlooking the coast. Impressive hall and minstrels gallery, comfortable sitting room and contemporary bedrooms. Informal Vista offers classic bistro menus. Wood-panelled One Park Lane has a formal, elegant feel.

## MILLBROOK – Cornwall – 503 H32                                2 C2

▶ London 235 mi – Liskeard 16 mi – Plymouth 23 mi

**at Freathy** West : 3 mi by B 3247, Whitsand Bay Rd on Treninnow Cliff Rd
– ⊠ Millbrook

🍴 **View**                              ⪡ 🛜 P VISA ⌾ AE
ⓘ  *East : 1 mi ⊠ PL10 1JY – ℰ (01752) 822 345 – www.theview-restaurant.co.uk*
   *– Closed February, Monday, Tuesday and restricted opening November-January*
   **Rest** – Menu £ 15 (lunch) – Carte £ 26/33
   ♦ Charming and informal converted café perched on a cliff, with coastal views. Relaxed daytime vibe; more atmospheric in the evening. Assured, confident cooking and friendly service. Plenty of seafood; generous portions. Try the rustic homemade bread.

## MILSTEAD – Kent – pop. 264                                    9 C1

▶ London 46 mi – Croydon 48 mi – Barnet 68 mi – Ealing 84 mi

⌂ **Red Lion**                            🖨 🛜 P VISA ⌾
*Rawling St ⊠ ME9 0RT – ℰ (01795) 830 279 – www.theredlionmilstead.co.uk*
*– Closed Sunday and Monday*
**Rest** – *(booking advisable at weekends)* Carte £ 24/32
♦ Simple, cosy country pub, personally run by an experienced couple. Ever-changing blackboard menu offers French-influenced country cooking. Dishes are honest, wholesome and richly flavoured.

## MILTON ABBOT – Devon – 503 H32 – see Tavistock

## MILTON KEYNES – Milton Keynes – 504 R27 – pop. 156 148       11 C1

▶ London 56 mi – Bedford 16 mi – Birmingham 72 mi – Northampton 18 mi

🛈 The Chapel, The Knoll, Newport Pagnell ℰ (01908) 614 6 38,
www.destinationmiltonkeynes.co.uk

⛳ Abbey Hill Two Mile Ash Monks Way, ℰ (01908) 56 38 45

⛳ Tattenhoe Bletchley Tattenhoe Lane, ℰ (01908) 63 11 13

⛳ Wavendon Golf Centre Wavendon Lower End Rd, ℰ (01908) 28 18 11

                        Plans on following pages

ENGLAND

497

## HORIZONTAL ROADS

Bletcham Way (H10) . . . . . . . . **CX**
Chaffron Way (H7) . . . . . . . **BX, CV**
Childs Way (H6) . . . . . . . . **BX, CV**
Dansteed Way (H4) . . . . . . . . **ABV**
Groveway (H9) . . . . . . . . . **CVX**
Millers Way (H2) . . . . . . . . . . **AV**
Monks Way (H3) . . . . . . . . . **ABV**
Portway (H5) . . . . . . . . . . **BCV**
Ridgeway (H1) . . . . . . . . . . **AV**
Standing Way (H8) . . . . . . **BX, CV**

## MILTON KEYNES

Buckingham Rd . . . . . . . . . . **BX**
London Rd . . . . . . . . . . . **CUV**
Manor Rd . . . . . . . . . . . . **CX**
Marsh End Rd . . . . . . . . . . **CU**
Newport Rd . . . . . . . . . . . **BV**
Northampton Rd . . . . . . . . . **AU**
Stoke Rd . . . . . . . . . . . . **CX**
Stratford Rd . . . . . . . . . . . **AV**
Whaddon Way . . . . . . . . . . **BX**
Wolverton Rd. . . . . . . . . . . **BU**

## VERTICAL ROADS

Brickhill St (V10) . . . . . . **BU, CX**
Fulmer St (V3) . . . . . . . . . **ABX**
Grafton St (V6) . . . . . . . . . **BVX**
Great Monks St (V5) . . . . . . . **AV**
Marlborough St (V8) . . . . **BV, CX**
Overstreet (V9) . . . . . . . . . **BV**
Saxon St (V7) . . . . . . . . . . **BVX**
Snelshall St (V1) . . . . . . . . . **BX**
Tattenhoe St (V2) . . . . . . . **ABX**
Tongwell St (V11) . . . . . . . **CVX**
Watling St (V4) . . . . . . . . **AV, BX**

# MILTON KEYNES

## XX Brasserie Blanc

*Chelsea House, 301 Avebury Blvd* ⊠ *MK9 2GA –* ☏ *(01908) 546 590*
*– www.brasserieblanc.com*                                                        EZc
**Rest** – French – *(booking essential)* Menu £ 14/16 – Carte £ 22/47
♦ Striking modern building with a bustling trade – part of the Raymond Blanc
chain. Menu features refined French brasserie dishes, mainly classics, with some
house specialities.

Don't confuse the couvert rating X with the stars ❀!
Couverts defines comfort and service, while stars are awarded
for the best cuisine across all categories of comfort.

ENGLAND

**MINEHEAD** – Somerset – **503** J30 – pop. 11 699       **3 A2**

▶ London 187 mi – Bristol 64 mi – Exeter 43 mi – Taunton 25 mi

🛈 Warren Rd ✆ (01643) 70 26 24, www.visitsomerset.co.uk

⛳ The Warren Warren Rd, ✆ (01643) 70 20 57

◉ Town★ - Higher Town (Church Steps★, St Michael's★)

◉ Dunster★★ - Castle★★ **AC** (upper rooms ⩔★) Water Mill★ **AC**,
St George's Church★, Dovecote★, SE : 2.5 mi by A 39
– Selworthy★ (Church★, ⩔★★) W : 4.5 mi by A 39. Exmoor National Park★★
– Cleeve Abbey★★ **AC**, SE : 6.5 mi by A 39

501

**Channel House** 🐾

*Church Path, off Northfield Dr* ✉ *TA24 5QG –* ☎ *(01643) 703 229*
*– www.channelhouse.co.uk – March-October*
**8 rm** (dinner included) ☕ – ♦£ 82/85 ♦♦£ 164/170
**Rest** – *(dinner only)* Menu £ 30 **s** – Carte £ 40/60 **s**

♦ Pleasantly located Edwardian hotel in rural location surrounded by mature ye
carefully manicured gardens. Small, homely style lounge and fair sized, immacu
late bedrooms. Home-cooked meals using local ingredients.

**Glendower House** without rest

*30-32 Tregonwell Rd* ✉ *TA24 5DU –* ☎ *(01643) 707 144*
*– www.glendower-house.co.uk – February to November*
**11 rm** ☕ – ♦£ 45/60 ♦♦£ 80

♦ Good value, warmly run guesthouse, convenient for seafront and town; boasts
original Victorian features. Immaculately kept bedrooms with a homely feel.

---

## MINSTER LOVELL – Oxfordshire – **503** P28                           **10** A2

▶ London 74 mi – Birmingham 87 mi – Bristol 67 mi – Sheffield 151 mi

**Minster Mill**

✉ *OX29 ORN –* ☎ *(01993) 774 441 – www.oldswanandminstermill.com*
**44 rm** ☕ – ♦£ 125/145 ♦♦♦£ 165/325
**Rest** *see Old Swan below* –

♦ Old Cotswold stone mill set on the riverbank in a small hamlet. Comfy lounge
and minstrels' gallery. Corporate-style bedrooms with contemporary furnishings
the best boast riverside terraces. Meals taken at sister establishment, the Old
Swan pub.

**Old Swan** with rm

✉ *OX29 ORN –* ☎ *(01993) 774 441 – www.oldswanandminstermill.com*
**16 rm** ☕ – ♦£ 125/145 ♦♦£ 165/325
**Rest** – *(booking essential)* Carte £ 29/41

♦ Smart pub with parquet floors, roaring open fires and garden games. Large
herb plots contribute to unfussy pub classics; tasty daily specials feature fish
from the Brixham day boats. Bedrooms boast period furnishings, mod cons and
some have feature bathrooms.

---

## MISTLEY – Essex – **504** X28 – pop. 1 684                           **13** D2

▶ London 69 mi – Colchester 11 mi – Ipswich 14 mi

**Mistley Thorn** with rm

*High St* ✉ *CO11 1HE –* ☎ *(01206) 392 821 – www.mistleythorn.com – Closed 25*
*December*
**8 rm** ☕ – ♦£ 75/85 ♦♦£ 90/130
**Rest** – Menu £ 15 (weekday lunch) – Carte £ 19/33

♦ Passionately run pub by the river in a small coastal village. Traditional, flavoursome cooking displays American and Italian influences – a reference to the owner's childhood; fish and game frequently feature on the tempting specials list. Spacious, wood-furnished bedrooms boast modern bathrooms; two have river views.

**at Bradfield** East : 2 mi by B 1352

**Curlews** without rest

*Station Rd* ✉ *CO11 2UP –* ☎ *(01255) 870 890*
*– www.curlewsaccommodation.co.uk*
**5 rm** ☕ – ♦£ 60 ♦♦£ 95

♦ Homely guest house where traditional bedrooms boast modern bathrooms;
one is self contained disabled suite; others have balconies with splendid views
over farmland and the Stour Estuary.

ENGLAND

**MITTON** – Lancs. – **502** M22 – see Whalley

**MOBBERLEY** – Cheshire East – **502** N24 – see Knutsford

**MONKS ELEIGH** – Suffolk – **504** W27                                   **15** C3
▶ London 72 mi – Cambridge 47 mi – Colchester 17 mi – Ipswich 16 mi

#### Swan                                         ⛩ ⇔ **P** **VISA** ⊛
*The Street* ✉ *IP7 7AU – ℰ (01449) 741 391 – www.monkseleigh.com – Closed 2
weeks July, 25-26 December, Sunday dinner and Monday*
**Rest** – *(booking essential in summer)* Menu £ 18 – Carte £ 21/35
♦ Thatched pub with fresh, bright interior. Frequently changing, seasonal menu
of generous, flavourful dishes, with the occasional Italian influence; all homemade
from local produce.

**MONKTON COMBE** – Bath and North East Somerset – see Bath

**MORECAMBE** – Lancashire – **502** L21 – pop. 49 569                      **20** A1
▶ London 247 mi – Preston 27 mi – Blackpool 39 mi – Blackburn 34 mi

#### Midland         ≤ ⇌ ⛩ 🛁 🛎 ♿ ¶ ♨ **P** **VISA** ⊛
*Marine Road West* ✉ *LA4 4BU – ℰ (01524) 424 000 – www.englishlakes.co.uk*
**43 rm** ⊡ – †£ 94 ††£ 128/348 – 1 suite   **Rest** – Carte £ 27/42
♦ Iconic 1933 hotel set in a stunning location, with views of Morecambe Bay and
the mountains. Art deco styling; original features include a listed staircase. Variously sized, starkly decorated, contemporary bedrooms. Modern restaurant offers
superb outlook.

**MORETONHAMPSTEAD** – Devon – **503** I32 – pop. 1 380                     **2** C2
– ✉ **Newton Abbot**
▶ London 213 mi – Exeter 13 mi – Plymouth 30 mi
🏌 Bovey Castle North Bovey, ℰ (01647) 44 50 09
◎ Dartmoor National Park★★

#### White Hart                                   ⛩ ¶ ♨ **VISA** ⊛ **AE**
*The Square* ✉ *TQ13 8NF – ℰ (01647) 441 340 – www.whitehartdartmoor.co.uk*
**28 rm** ⊡ – †£ 70/79 ††£ 99/109   **Rest** – Menu £ 23 – Carte £ 29/40
♦ 17C Grade II listed former coaching inn in the town; bright and comfortable,
with a cosy lounge and pleasant locals bar. Simply furnished bedrooms have
modern touches; the newer ones are in the annexe. Open-style, wood-floored
dining room offers classic dishes.

#### Higher Westcott Farm ⌖                       ≤ ⇌ ♯ ¶ **P**
*Westcott, East : 4 mi by B 3212 on Westcott rd* ✉ *TQ13 8SU – ℰ (01647)
441 205 – www.higherwestcottfarm.com*
**3 rm** ⊡ – †£ 110/120 ††£ 110/120   **Rest** – Menu £ 30
♦ Part-thatched former longhouse, up a steep, leafy lane in a tiny hamlet. Mod-
ern, boutique interior with large lounge, honesty bar and communal dining room.
Bedrooms offer good facilities, smart, natural stone bathrooms and country views.
Home-cooked dinners feature local, organic produce and biodynamic wines.

#### White Horse Inn                              ⛩ **VISA** ⊛ **AE** ①
*7 George St* ✉ *TQ13 8PG – ℰ (01647) 440 267 – www.whitehorsedevon.co.uk
– Closed Sunday except bank holidays and restricted opening in winter*
**Rest** – Carte £ 18/30
♦ Pub with rustic, flag-floored rooms and a sunny, Mediterranean-style courtyard.
Tasty, unfussy dishes offer more than a hint of Italy. Thin crust pizzas baked in a
custom-built oven.

ENGLAND

📗 Great Britain
▶ London 86 mi – Birmingham 40 mi – Gloucester 31 mi – Oxford 29 mi
🔲 Chastleton House★★, SE : 5 mi by A 44

🏠🏠🏠 **Manor House**        🖼 🖵 📶 ⅙ rm, 🔠 rm, ℡ 🏊 P. VISA ⦿ AE
*High St ✉ GL56 0LJ – 𝒞 (01608) 650 501*
*– www.cotswold-inns.co.uk/manor*
**34 rm** ⬚ – ♦£ 120/160 ♦♦£ 175/215 – 1 suite
**Rest** *Mulberry* – see restaurant listing
**Rest** *Brasserie* – Menu £ 16 (lunch) – Carte £ 29/35
♦ Part-16C manor house in an attractive town. Smart, modern interior features various lounge and bar areas; the latter being popular for cocktails. Chic, stylish bedrooms boast bold décor and feature walls; those in the main house are largest. Sophisticated restaurant or brasserie serving classical dishes.

🏠 **Old School** without rest        🖼 🍴 ℡ P. VISA ⦿
*Little Compton, East : 4 mi on A 44 ✉ GL56 0SL – 𝒞 (01608) 674 588*
*– www.theoldschoolbedandbreakfast.com*
**4 rm** ⬚ – ♦£ 96/120 ♦♦£ 120/150
♦ Attractive stone-built former school with large monkey puzzle tree and chickens in the garden. Leather-furnished sitting room with communal dining table; upstairs lounge displays exposed beams and A-frame ceiling. Bright, modern bedrooms offer a high level of facilities. Homemade cakes served on arrival.

✂✂✂ **Mulberry** – at Manor House Hotel        🖼 ⅙ 🔠 P. VISA ⦿ AE
*High St ✉ GL56 0LJ – 𝒞 (01608) 650 501*
*– www.cotswold-inns.co.uk/manor*
**Rest** – *(dinner only and Sunday lunch)* Menu £ 39 – Carte £ 39/55
♦ Formal restaurant with enclosed walled garden, in a part-16C manor house. French-influenced 4 course set or 8 course tasting menus. Seasonal tasting menus offers some challenging combinations.

**at Bourton-on-the-Hill** West : 2 mi on A 44 – ✉ Moreton-In-Marsh

🍴 **Horse & Groom** with rm        🖼 🖵 🍴 ℡ P. VISA ⦿
*✉ GL56 9AQ – 𝒞 (01386) 700 413 – www.horseandgroom.info – Closed 1 week early January, 25 December and Sunday dinner*
**5 rm** ⬚ – ♦£ 80 ♦♦£ 175    **Rest** – *(booking essential)* Carte £ 21/33
♦ Charterful Grade II listed yellow-stone building with a friendly atmosphere, set in a remote Cotswold village. Menus feature classic pub dishes; cooking is hearty, unfussy and flavoursome. Modern bedrooms, each one individually styled.

▶ London 301 mi – Edinburgh 93 mi – Newcastle upon Tyne 15 mi
ℹ Bridge St 𝒞 (01670) 50 07 00, www.visitnorthumberland.com
⛳ The Clubhouse, 𝒞 (01670) 50 49 42

**at Longhorsley** Northwest : 6.5 mi by A 192 on A 697 – ✉ Morpeth

🏠 **Thistleyhaugh Farm** 🌿        🖼 🍷 🍴 ℡ P. VISA ⦿
🍴 *Northwest : 3.75 mi by A 697 and Todburn rd taking first right turn ✉ NE65 8RG – 𝒞 (01665) 570 629 – www.thistleyhaugh.co.uk – Closed 19 December-31 January*
**5 rm** ⬚ – ♦£ 70/85 ♦♦£ 90    **Rest** – Menu £ 25
♦ Attractive Georgian farmhouse set off the beaten track on an organic farm, with the River Coquet flowing through its grounds. Many of the bedrooms boast carved wood, sleigh or cast iron beds and most have luxurious bathrooms with feature baths. Charming, welcoming owner. Beef and lamb from the farm feature at dinner.

**MORSTON** – Norfolk – see Blakeney

ENGLAND

## MORTON – Nottinghamshire – 504 S25
**16** B1

▶ London 149 mi – Birmingham 89 mi – Liverpool 117 mi – Leeds 51 mi

🍴 **Full Moon**   🚗 🍴 **P** VISA ⦿

*Main St ⊠ NG25 0UT – ℰ (01636) 830 251 – www.themoonatmorton.co.uk
– Closed Sunday dinner*
**Rest** – Carte £ 20/30 **s**

• This modernised, child-friendly pub fashioned from 3 cottages is at the heart of village life; it even holds civil ceremonies. Cooking sticks to their motto of 'big flavours and no frills'. Open for breakfast and they even do takeaway.

---

## MOULSFORD – Oxfordshire – pop. 491
**10** B3

▶ London 53 mi – Newbury 16 mi – Reading 13 mi

🍴🍴 **Beetle & Wedge Boathouse** with rm   ≤ 🍴 ⁿ **P** VISA ⦿ AE

*Ferry Ln. ⊠ OX10 9JF – ℰ (01491) 651 381 – www.beetleandwedge.co.uk
– Closed 1 week January*
**3 rm** ⊡ – ♦£ 75 ♦♦£ 90
**Rest** – *(booking essential)* Menu £ 23 (weekdays) – Carte £ 27/38

• Busy Thameside restaurant with charming terrace; dine in the light conservatory or more rustic char grill. Classic menu with plenty of choice, including dishes from the grill. Comfortable bedrooms in Ferryman's Cottage; some boast roll-top baths.

---

## MOULTON – North Yorkshire – 502 P20 – pop. 197 – ⊠ Richmond
**22** B1

▶ London 243 mi – Leeds 53 mi – Middlesbrough 25 mi
– Newcastle upon Tyne 43 mi

🍴🍴 **Black Bull Inn**   ⇔ **P** VISA ⦿ AE

*⊠ DL10 6QJ – ℰ (01325) 377 289 – www.blackbullmoulton.com – Closed
Sunday dinner*
**Rest** – Seafood – Carte £ 32/55

• Set in heart of rural village; dine in bar, conservatory, beamed dining room or Brighton Belle Pullman carriage from 1932. Seafood based menu and traditional desserts.

---

## MOUSEHOLE – Cornwall – 503 D33 – ⊠ Penzance
**1** A3

▶ London 321 mi – Penzance 3 mi – Truro 29 mi
◎ Village ★
Ⓖ Penwith ★★ – Lamorna (The Merry Maidens and The Pipers Standing Stone ★) SW : 3 mi by B 3315. Land's End ★ (cliff scenery ★★★) W : 9 mi by B 3315

🏠 **Old Coastguard**   ≤ 🚗 ⁿ **P** VISA ⦿ AE

*The Parade ⊠ TR19 6PR – ℰ (01736) 731 222 – www.oldcoastguardhotel.co.uk
– Closed 9 January-10 February and 24-26 December*
**14 rm** ⊡ – ♦£ 150/165 ♦♦£ 200/220   **Rest** – Carte £ 22/32 **s**

• Creamwash hotel in unspoilt village with good views of Mounts Bay. Spacious lounge has sun terrace overlooking water. Modern rooms: Premier variety are best for the vista. Gutsy, unfussy dishes of local produce served in modern, open-plan restaurant.

🍴 **Cornish Range** with rm   ⁿ VISA ⦿ ⓪

*6 Chapel St ⊠ TR19 6SB – ℰ (01736) 731 488 – www.cornishrange.co.uk
– Closed 2 weeks January-February*
**3 rm** ⊡ – ♦♦£ 80/110   **Rest** – Seafood – *(booking essential)* Carte £ 23/35

• Converted 18C pilchard processing cottage hidden away in narrow street. Cottagey inner filled with Cornish artwork. Excellent local seafood dishes. Very comfortable bedrooms.

**ENGLAND**

## ✗ 2 Fore Street  ⏦ ⓦ 🆚 ⓐ ⓔ ⓞ

*2 Fore St ☒ TR19 6PF – ☎ (01736) 731 164 – www.2forestreet.co.uk – Closed Monday November-early December and restricted opening in winter*
**Rest** – Seafood – *(booking essential at dinner)* Carte £ 24/28
♦ Cosy, bright bistro in pretty harbourside setting; popular with locals and tourists. Menu based on the best of the day's catch; simple, unfussy preparation. Casual, friendly service.

## MUCH HADHAM – Hertfordshire  12 B2

▶ London 44 mi – Birmingham 130 mi – Bristol 152 mi – Croydon 64 mi

### 🍴 Hoops Inn  ⏦ ⓦ Ⓟ 🆚 ⓐ

*Perry Green, Southeast : 2.75 mi by B1004 and Perry Green rd ☒ SG10 6EF – ☎ (01279) 843 568 – www.hoops-inn.co.uk – Closed Sunday dinner and Monday*
**Rest** – Carte £ 18/27
♦ Smart 19C pub in a pretty hamlet, opposite the old home of Henry Moore. Compact interior is full of character. Fresh, tasty dishes from a concise, thoughtfully compiled menu; a tasting plate of all starters is offered and pudding is a must.

## MUCH WENLOCK – Shropshire – 502 M26 – pop. 1 959  18 B2

▌ Great Britain

▶ London 154 mi – Birmingham 34 mi – Shrewsbury 12 mi – Worcester 37 mi
🅸 High St ☎ (01952) 72 76 79, www.muchwenlockguide.info
◉ Priory★ **AC**
Ⓖ Ironbridge Gorge Museum★★ **AC** (The Iron Bridge★★ - Coalport China Museum★★ - Blists Hill Open Air Museum★★ – Museum of the Gorge and Visitor Centre★) NE : 4.5 mi by A 4169 and B 4380

### at Brockton Southwest : 5 mi on B 4378 – ☒ Much Wenlock

### 🍴 Feathers at Brockton  ⏦ Ⓟ 🆚 ⓐ

*☒ TF13 6JR – ☎ (01746) 785 202 – www.feathersatbrockton.co.uk – Closed 26 December, 1 January, Monday and lunch Tuesday*
**Rest** – Menu £ 13/15 – Carte £ 24/30
♦ Rustic 16C pub set in prime walking country, with a snug, characterful inner and relaxing atmosphere. Traditional dishes display some Mediterranean influences and are made using locally sourced produce.

## MURCOTT – Oxfordshire – pop. 1 293 – ☒ Kidlington  10 B2

▶ London 70 mi – Oxford 14 mi – Witney 20 mi

### 🍴 Nut Tree (Mike North)  ⏦ Ⓟ 🆚 ⓐ ⓔ
ⓢ
*Main St ☒ OX5 2RE – ☎ (01865) 331 253 – www.nuttreeinn.co.uk – Closed Sunday dinner and Monday*
**Rest** – Menu £ 22 (weekday lunch) – Carte £ 32/49
**Spec.** Pan-fried terrine of pig's head and black pudding. Olive oil poached fillet of halibut with green herb risotto. Sticky toffee pudding and praline ice cream.
♦ Traditional thatched village pub owned by a local and his wife; its unassuming interior a real contrast to the quality cuisine. Menus change constantly, relying on seasonal ingredients that arrive at the door: produce is organic, free range or wild where possible. Rare breed pigs and Dexter cattle are raised out back.

**NAILSWORTH** – Gloucestershire – **503** N28 – pop. 5 276      **4** C1

▶ London 110 mi – Bristol 30 mi – Swindon 28 mi

XX **Wild Garlic**      🛱 AK VISA ⚫ AE ⓿
*3 Cossack Sq ⊠ GL6 0DB – ℰ (01453) 832 615 – www.wild-garlic.co.uk – Closed first week January, Sunday dinner, Tuesday lunch and Monday*
**Rest** – Carte £ 27/39
♦ Relaxed, friendly restaurant decorated with foodie photos. Produce sourced from within 30 miles where possible. Everything made in-house, including excellent garlic-infused bread.

---

**NANTWICH** – Cheshire East – **502** M24 – pop. 13 447      **20** A3

▶ London 176 mi – Chester 20 mi – Liverpool 45 mi – Manchester 40 mi

ℹ Market St ℰ (01270) 61 09 83, www.nantwich.ivisitorguide.com

🏌 Alvaston Hall Middlewich Rd, ℰ (01270) 62 84 73

🏨 **Rookery Hall** �---    ← 🚗 🐾 🐕 🛱 🖥 🏊 🏋 🖎 🎧 ⅙ 🏊 ♨ 🏌 ⛳ P
*Worleston, North : 2.5 mi by A 51 on B 5074 ⊠ CW5 6DQ*    VISA ⚫ AE ⓿
*– ℰ (01270) 610 016 – www.handpicked.co.uk*
**68 rm** � – †£ 99/140 ††£ 136/172 – 2 suites
**Rest** – *(dinner only and Sunday lunch) (booking essential)* Carte £ 30/50 **s**
♦ 19C property set in pleasant grounds, with considerable extensions. Main building offers characterful, country house bedrooms. More modern bedrooms in purpose-built rear wing. Smart impressive spa. Formal, two-roomed, wood-panelled dining room overlooking gardens.

---

**NETHER BURROW** – ⊠ **Kirkby Lonsdale**      **20** B1

▶ London 257 mi – Liverpool 73 mi – Leeds 101 mi – Manchester 68 mi

🍽 **Highwayman**      🛱 P VISA ⚫ AE
*⊠ LA6 2RJ – ℰ (01524) 273 338 – www.highwaymaninn.co.uk – Closed 25 December*
**Rest** – Carte £ 19/38
♦ Sizeable 18C coaching inn with open-fired, stone-floored bar and lovely terrace. Extensive menu offers hearty, rustic cooking with a familiar, comforting feel. Very seasonal, local ethos.

---

**NETHER WESTCOTE** – Gloucestershire – see Stow-on-the-Wold

---

**NETLEY MARSH** – Hampshire – **503** P31 – see Southampton

---

**NEW MILTON** – Hampshire – **503** P31 – pop. 24 324      **6** A3

▶ London 106 mi – Bournemouth 12 mi – Southampton 21 mi – Winchester 34 mi

🏌 Barton-on-Sea Milford Rd, ℰ (01425) 61 53 08

🏨 **Chewton Glen** 🌿    ← 🚗 🐾 🛱 🏊 🖥 🏊 🏋 🖎 ⅙ 🍴 🖳 🎧 ⅙ rm, AK 🏊
*Christchurch Rd, West : 2 mi by A 337 and*    🏊 ⅙ P VISA ⚫ AE ⓿
*Ringwood Rd on Chewton Farm Rd ⊠ BH25 6QS – ℰ (01425) 275 341*
*– www.chewtonglen.com*
**48 rm** – †£ 299/625 ††£ 299/625, � £ 26 – 10 suites
**Rest Vetiver** – Menu £ 25 **s** – Carte £ 35/80 **s**🏵
♦ 19C country house in 130 acres of New Forest parkland. Luxurious bedrooms and grand suites blend the classic with the contemporary; most have terraces or balconies. Impressive leisure facilities include croquet, archery and clay pigeon shooting. Restaurant offers a choice of rooms and accomplished cooking.

ENGLAND

507

## NEW ROMNEY – Kent – **504** W31

9 C2

▶ London 71 mi – Brighton 60 mi – Folkestone 17 mi – Maidstone 36 mi

**Romney Bay House** ⟋     ⟨ ◱ ⁒ ⁏ ⁑ **P** VISA ◍ AE
*Coast Rd, Littlestone, East : 2.25 mi by B 2071* ✉ *TN28 8QY –* ✆ *(01797) 364 747*
*– www.romneybayhousehotel.co.uk – Closed 1 week Christmas*
**10 rm** ⌑ – ♦£ 70/95 ♦♦£ 164
**Rest** – *(closed Sunday, Monday and Thursday) (dinner only) (booking essential for non-residents) (set menu only)* Menu £ 45
♦ Beach panorama for late actress Hedda Hopper's house, built by Portmeirion architect Clough Williams-Ellis. Individual rooms; sitting room with telescope and bookcases. Enjoy drinks on terrace before conservatory dining.

---

## NEWARK-ON-TRENT – Nottinghamshire – **502** R24 – pop. 35 454

17 C1

▮ Great Britain
▶ London 127 mi – Lincoln 16 mi – Nottingham 20 mi – Sheffield 42 mi
🔟 Coddington, Newark, ✆ (01636) 62 62 82
◉ St Mary Magdalene ★

**Grange**     ◱ ⌂ ⁒ ⁑ **P** VISA ◍ AE ①
*73 London Rd, South : 0.5 mi on Grantham rd (B 6326)* ✉ *NG24 1RZ*
*–* ✆ *(01636) 703 399 – www.grangenewark.co.uk – Closed 23 December-4 January*
**19 rm** ⌑ – ♦£ 85/110 ♦♦£ 125/170
**Rest Cutlers** – *(closed Sunday dinner) (dinner only and Sunday lunch)*
Carte £ 25/30
♦ Small, personally run hotel with tranquil landscaped garden, set in residential area not far from the town. Traditional bedrooms vary in size but all are cosy and comfy; some have four-posters. Classical menu served in restaurant, amongst antique china and cutlery.

**at Caunton** Northwest : 7 mi by A 616 – ✉ Newark-On-Trent

**Caunton Beck**     ⌂ **P** VISA ◍ AE ①
*Main St* ✉ *NG23 6AB –* ✆ *(01636) 636 793 – www.wigandmitre.com*
**Rest** – Menu £ 16 – Carte £ 23/33
♦ Modern looking pub with tan coloured bricks, a wrought iron pergola and large front terrace. Menus offer gutsy masculine cooking, with the odd global influence. Open from 8am for breakfast.

---

## NEWBIGGIN – Cumbria – **502** L19 – see Penrith

---

## NEWBURY – West Berkshire – **503** Q29 – pop. 32 675

10 B3

▶ London 67 mi – Bristol 66 mi – Oxford 28 mi – Reading 17 mi
🔟 Newbury and Crookham Greenham Common Bury's Bank Rd, ✆ (01635) 4 00 35
🔟 Donnington Valley Donnington Snelsmore House, Snelsmore Common, ✆ (01635) 56 81 40

Plans on following pages

**Vineyard at Stockcross**     ◱ ▦ ⌂ ⌾ ⁘ ▥ ⁒ ⁑ 🛁 **P** VISA ◍ AE ①
*Stockcross, Northwest : 2 mi by A 4 on B 4000* ✉ *RG20 8JU –* ✆ *(01635) 528 770*
*– www.the-vineyard.co.uk*
AV**b**
**34 rm** – ♦♦£ 140/325, ⌑ £ 20.50 – 15 suites    **Rest** – Menu £ 29/72 ⊛
♦ Extended, bay-windowed former hunting lodge with striking fire and water feature. Some bedrooms have a country house style; others are more contemporary – all boast marble bathrooms. Smart, split-level restaurant with immaculately dressed tables and professional service. French-rooted menus; intricate, detailed cooking.

**ENGLAND**

# NEWBURY

**ENGLAND**

---

🏠🏠🏠 **Donnington Valley H. & Spa**      🚗 🐾 📺 ⊙ ℘ ⅃♨ 📶 ⬦ ♿ AC ⚡ 🌐
*Old Oxford Rd, Donnington, North : 1.75 mi by A 4*      ♨ 🅿 VISA ◎◎ AE ①
*off B 4494 ⊠ RG14 3AG – 𝒞 (01635) 551 199 – www.donningtonvalley.co.uk*
**113 rm** – †£ 99/200 ††£ 99/280, ⊑ £ 14.85      AV**a**
**Rest** *Winepress* – see restaurant listing
♦ Modern, business-orientated hotel with golf club and 18 hole course. Spacious,
stylishly furnished guest areas and wine-themed bar. Smart bedrooms offer a
high level of facilities; opt for 'Executive'. Excellent leisure and wellness centre.

XX **Winepress** – at Donnington Valley Hotel & Spa      🚗 🐾 AC 🅿
*Old Oxford Rd, Donnington, North : 1.75 mi by A 4 off B*      VISA ◎◎ AE ①
*4494 ⊠ RG14 3AG – 𝒞 (01635) 551 199 – www.donningtonvalley.co.uk*
**Rest** – Menu £ 23/28 **s** – Carte £ 33/45 **s** 🏵      AV**a**
♦ Intimate wine-themed restaurant in a business-led hotel. Local, seasonal pro-
duce features in both classically based and more modern dishes. Lighter 'Bar +
Mezz' menu available during the day.

To make the most of your guide, look up the section 'How to use this guide'
in the introduction: symbols, classification, abbreviations and other signs
are explained to help you make an informed choice!

509

▶ London 270 mi – Kendal 16 mi – Lancaster 27 mi
◎ Lake Windermere★★

## Lakeside    ≤ ⊿ ➘ ▯ ⊕ ⋔ ⅃₆ ▮ & rm, ⅍ ⁀ ⅍ **P.** **VISA** ◉◎ **AE** ⓪
*Lakeside, Northeast : 1 mi on Hawkshead rd* ⊠ *LA12 8AT* – ⌂ *(015395) 30 001*
*– www.lakesidehotel.co.uk – Closed 3-22 January*
**72 rm** ⌤ – ♦£ 120/190 ♦♦£ 280/380 – 3 suites
**Rest** *John Ruskins Brasserie* – see restaurant listing
**Rest** *Lakeview* – *(dinner only)* Menu £ 38
• Superbly situated on the water's edge, with great lake views from the conservatory. Very comfy, traditional guest areas. Smart, modern bedrooms; some with four-posters, feature walls or great views. Contemporary spa, leisure club and good-sized pool. Refined, formal dining room and stylish, modern brasserie.

## Knoll    ⊿ ⅍ ⁀ **P.** **VISA** ◉◎
*Lakeside, Northeast : 1.25 mi on Hawkshead rd* ⊠ *LA12 8AU* – ⌂ *(015395)*
*31 347 – www.theknoll-lakeside.co.uk – Closed 24-26 December, 31 December and 1 January*
**9 rm** ⌤ – ♦£ 75/98 ♦♦£ 90/140
**Rest** – *(closed Sunday and Monday) (dinner only) (booking essential for non-residents)* Menu £ 26 **s**
• Keenly run, late Victorian house opposite the lake, with smart interior that successfully blends classic and modern styles. Comfy, leather-furnished lounge. Good-sized bedrooms with bold décor and modern bathrooms. Simple dining room displays heart-themed art.

## ⅍⅍ John Ruskins Brasserie – at Lakeside Hotel    ≤ ⊿ **P.** **VISA** ◉◎ **AE** ⓪
*Lakeside, Northeast : 1 mi on Hawkshead rd* ⊠ *LA12 8AT* – ⌂ *(015395) 30 001*
*– www.lakesidehotel.co.uk – Closed 3-22 January*
**Rest** – *(dinner only)* Menu £ 38
• Stylish brasserie in a superbly situated hotel on the shore of Lake Windermere. Classical brasserie menu. Have a drink in the conservatory or on the terrace to fully appreciate the view.

**ENGLAND**

# NEWCASTLE UPON TYNE

See city maps on following pages

24 B2

**Tyne and Wear – pop. 168 075 – 501** O19 – **502** O19 – ▌ Great Britain

▶ London 276 – Edinburgh 105 – Leeds 95

**🛈 Tourist Information**

8-9 Central Arcade ✆(0191) 277 80 00, www.newcastlegateshead.com

**Airport**

✈ Newcastle Airport : ✆ (0871) 882 1121, NW : 5 m. by A 696 AV

**Ferries and Shipping Lines**

⛴ to Norway (Bergen, Haugesund and Stavanger) (Fjord Line) (approx 26 h) – to The Netherlands (Amsterdam) (DFDS Seaways A/S) daily (15 h)

**Tunnel**

**Tyne Tunnel (toll)**

**Golf Courses**

🛆 Broadway East Gosforth, ✆(0191) 285 05 53

🛆 City of Newcastle Gosforth Three Mill Bridge, ✆(0191) 285 17 75

**◉ SIGHTS**

**In the town :** City★• Quayside★ CZ : Composition★, All Saints Church★ • Castle Keep★ **AC** CZ • Laing Art Gallery and Museum★ **AC** CY**M1** • Great North Museum★ CY**M2** • LIFE Interactive World★ CZ • Gateshead Millennium Bridge★ CZ

**On the outskirts :** Hadrian's Wall★★, W : by A 69 AV

**In the surrounding area :** Beamish : North of England Open-Air Museum★★ **AC**, SW : 7 mi by A 692 and A 6076 AX

**NEWCASTLE UPON TYNE**

ENGLAND

513

# NEWCASTLE-UPON-TYNE

**ENGLAND**

LONGBENTON

BENTON

FOUR LANE ENDS

LONGBENTON

Benton Park Road

Benton Lane

Front Street A 191

Whitley Road

Coach Lane

Station Road

North Road

Coast Road

JESMOND

Newcastle — Tynemouth

WALLSEND

WALLSEND

SEGENDUM

Chillingham Road

HEATON PARK

Jesmond Rd

Benfield

Road

WALKERGATE

CHILLINGHAM ROAD

Shields Fossway A 187

A 193

Scrogg Road

A 186

Road

BYKER

BYKER A 193 Rd.

Shields

WALKER

Welbeck

WALKER PARK

Walker Road

City Rd

BALTIC ARTS CENTRE

Gateshead Millennium Bridge

South Shore Rd

Hawks Rd Saltmeadows Rd

Park Road

A 186 Walker

GATESHEAD

Prince Consort Rd

GATESHEAD STADIUM

Felling A 184

FELLING

Shields Road

PELAW

ESHEAD

SALTWELL PARK

Sunderland Road

Split Crow Road B 1296

FELLING

HEWORTH

The Drive

By-Pass

Durham Road

Lingey Lane

A 195

## BUILT UP AREA

0   1 km
0   1 mile

ENGLAND

TYNEMOUTH A 1058 CONTINENT

A 187 TYNEMOUTH

SOUTH SHIELDS A 185

SUNDERLAND (A 19)

A 184 (A 1 (M))

ENGLAND

### Jesmond Dene House 🍃    🚗 🏠 🛋 ⭐ rm, 🗲 📶 🕭 🅿 VISA ⚫ AE ⓞ
*Jesmond Dene Rd, Northeast : 1.5 mi by B 1318 off A 189* ✉ *NE2 2EY* – ✆ *(0191, 212 30 00 – www.jesmonddenehouse.co.uk*      BV**x**
**40 rm** – ✝£ 115/163 ✝✝£ 115/163, ☕ £ 16
**Rest** – Menu £ 23/27 – Carte £ 36/61
• 19C house attractively located in a tranquil dene. Subtle modern touches blend with period features to create a cosy, arts and crafts feel; fantastic inner hall complete with open fire. Well-appointed bedrooms differ in décor and outlook. Carefully judged modern cooking is crafted from regional ingredients.

### Hotel du Vin      🛋 & 🗚 🕭 VISA ⚫ AE
*Allan House, City Rd* ✉ *NE1 2BE* – ✆ *(0191) 229 22 00 – www.hotelduvin.com*
**42 rm** – ✝✝£ 105/495, ☕ £ 15      BX**a**
**Rest** *Bistro* – see restaurant listing
• Extended red-brick building overlooking the river – formerly home to the Tyne Tees Steam Shipping Company. Characterful lounge with gas fire and zinc-topped bar. Chic, stylish, wine-themed bedrooms; some boast feature baths or terraces.

### Malmaison      ⚫ 🏠 🖍 📶 🛋 & 🗚 🕭 🕭 🅿 VISA ⚫ AE ⓞ
*104 Quayside* ✉ *NE1 3DX* – ✆ *(0191) 245 50 00 – www.malmaison.com*
**122 rm** – ✝£ 99/160 ✝✝£ 99/345, ☕ £ 15      BX**e**
**Rest** *Brasserie* – see restaurant listing
• Well-run, former co-operative building on the quayside. Trendy bar-lounge looks out over the Tyne towards Millennium Bridge. Stylish, modern bedrooms are well-equipped; one suite boasts a four-poster bed and twin bathtubs set side-by-side.

### ✗✗ Café 21      🗚 ⟷ VISA ⚫ AE ⓞ
*Trinity Gardens* ✉ *NE1 2HH* – ✆ *(0191) 222 07 55 – www.cafetwentyone.co.uk* – *Closed Easter Monday, 25-26 December and 1 January*      CZ**a**
**Rest** – Menu £ 20 (lunch and early dinner) – Carte £ 27/52
• Stylish, open-plan brasserie where subtle greys contrast with bold floral fabrics. Appealing classics display French undertones; best value menus at lunch/early dinner. Efficient service.

### ✗✗ David Kennedy's Food Social      ⟷ VISA ⚫ AE
*The Biscuit Factory, 16 Stoddart St* ✉ *NE2 1AN* – ✆ *(0191) 260 54 11* – *www.foodsocial.co.uk* – *Closed 25-26 December, 1 January and Sunday dinner*
**Rest** – Menu £ 16 (weekday lunch) – Carte £ 21/33      BV**c**
• Art gallery restaurant set in a 1930s former biscuit factory. Pass through modish lounge to airy dining space with industrial ambience, wall art and recognisable brasserie dishes; grill section features tasty mature steaks.

### ✗✗ Rasa      🗚 VISA ⚫ AE
*27 Queen St* ✉ *NE1 3UG* – ✆ *(0191) 232 77 99 – www.rasarestaurants.com* – *Closed 1 January, 24-27 December, Sunday lunch and bank holiday lunch*
**Rest** – Indian – Carte £ 16/23      CZ**g**
• Extensive menu of authentic Keralan cooking; friendly, knowledgeable staff are happy to explain dishes. Vegetarians particularly well catered for. Very good value lunch menus.

### ✗✗ Brasserie – at Malmaison Hotel      🗚 🅿 VISA ⚫ AE
*104 Quayside* ✉ *NE1 3DX* – ✆ *(0191) 245 50 00 – www.malmaison.com*
**Rest** – *(dinner only and Sunday lunch)* Carte £ 27/43      BX**e**
• Richly decorated brasserie in a trendy quayside hotel overlooking the Tyne and Millennium Bridge. French-influenced bistro menu is in keeping with the surroundings; local ingredients feature.

### ✗✗ Bistro – at Hotel du Vin      🗚 VISA ⚫ AE
*Allan House, City Rd* ✉ *NE1 2BE* – ✆ *(0191) 229 22 00 – www.hotelduvin.com*
**Rest** – Carte £ 21/35 🌿      BX**a**
• Bistro-style restaurant in a stylish wine-themed hotel overlooking the river. Classical brasserie menu name-checks suppliers on the rear. Impressive wine list and glass-fronted tasting room.

X **Pan Haggerty**  AK VISA ⓒⓢ AE ①

*21 Queen St ⊠ NE1 3UG – ℰ (0191) 221 09 04 – www.panhaggerty.com*
*– Closed 25 December and Sunday dinner*  CZz
**Rest** – Menu £ 16 (lunch) – Carte £ 27/32

♦ Stylish, modern restaurant situated on the quayside, which appeals to both young and old alike. Mix of regional and British dishes made with locally sourced ingredients; well presented, with precise flavours.

X **Caffé Vivo**  AK ⓒⓨ VISA AE

*29 Broad Chare ⊠ NE1 3DQ – ℰ (0191) 232 13 31 – www.caffevivo.co.uk*
*– Closed Sunday, Monday and bank holidays*  CZd
**Rest** – Italian – Menu £ 18 – Carte £ 20/36

♦ Housed within a quayside warehouse, along with a theatre. Much of the produce is imported from Italy and the Italian chefs ensure authenticity. Cooking is simple and satisfying, with dishes from Abbruzzi featuring heavily.

X **Barn Asia**  ⓐ VISA ⓒⓢ AE

*Waterloo Square, St James's Boulevard ⊠ NE1 4DN – ℰ (0191) 221 10 00*
*– www.barnasia.com – Closed Sunday and Monday*  CZr
**Rest** – South-East Asian – *(dinner only and Friday lunch)* Carte £ 25/33

♦ Stark furnishings vibrantly decorated with interesting artwork and bright lanterns. Wide-ranging SE Asian menu offers dishes from Vietnamese classics to some Thai and Japanese.

X **Blackfriars**  ⓐ AK ⓓ VISA ⓒⓢ AE ①

*Friars St ⊠ NE1 4XN – ℰ (0191) 261 59 45 – www.blackfriarsrestaurant.co.uk*
*– Closed Sunday dinner and bank holidays*  CZh
**Rest** – Menu £ 15 (lunch) – Carte dinner £ 22/30

♦ Late 13C stone-built monks' refectory; the split-level beamed restaurant overlooking the courtyard. Relaxed atmosphere with medieval feel and friendly service. Interesting, original menu of gutsy dishes that are firmly rooted in the region.

ⒾⒹ **Broad Chare**  AK ⓓ VISA ⓒⓢ

*25 Broad Chare ⊠ NE1 3DQ – ℰ (0191) 211 2144 – www.thebroadchare.co.uk*
*– Closed 25 December and Sunday dinner*  CZc
**Rest** – *(booking advisable)* Carte £ 19/34

♦ Owned by Terry Laybourne and next to its sister, Caffé Vivo. Snug ground floor bar offers over 24 beers and a snack menu of 'Geordie Tapas'. Dine upstairs where the dish of the day is often the highlight, like steak and kidney pudding.

**at Ponteland** Northwest : 8.25 mi by A 167 on A 696 - AV

– ⊠ Newcastle Upon Tyne

X **Cafe Lowrey**  AK VISA ⓒⓢ AE

*33-35 Broadway, Darras Hall Estate, Southwest : 1.5 mi by B 6323 off Darras Hall*
*Estate rd ⊠ NE20 9PW – ℰ (01661) 820 357 – www.cafelowrey.co.uk*
*– Closed Monday and bank holidays*
**Rest** – *(dinner only and lunch Saturday and Sunday)* *(booking essential)*
Menu £ 19 (lunch) – Carte £ 26/36

♦ Small restaurant in shopping parade with wooden chairs and cloth-laid tables. Blackboard menus offering modern British cooking using local produce.

**NEWICK** – East Sussex – **504** U31 – pop. 2 129  8 A2

🖪 London 57 mi – Brighton 14 mi – Eastbourne 20 mi – Hastings 34 mi

🏠 **Newick Park** ⓢ  ≤ 🚗 🐎 🐟 🎾 ⓖ rm, ⓨ ⓐ Ⓟ VISA ⓒⓢ AE

*Southeast : 1.5 mi following signs for Newick Park ⊠ BN8 4SB – ℰ (01825)*
*723 633 – www.newickpark.co.uk – Closed 31 December-6 January*
**15 rm** ⌂ – †£ 125/215 ††£ 165/285 – 1 suite
**Rest** – *(booking essential for non-residents)* Carte £ 26/39

♦ Georgian manor in 200 acres; views of Longford river and South Downs. Stately hallway and lounge. Unique rooms, some with original fireplaces, all with Egyptian cotton sheets. Dine in relaxed formality on high-back crimson chairs.

517

▶ London 57 mi – Bedford 13 mi – Luton 21 mi – Northampton 15 mi

Plan : see Milton Keynes

XX **Robinsons**                                             🍴 *VISA* ◉◉ AE ①
18-20 St John St ✉ MK16 8HJ – ℰ *(01908) 611 400*
– www.robinsonsrestaurant.co.uk – Closed 25 December, Easter, Saturday lunch
Sunday and bank holidays                                                     CU
**Rest** – Menu £ 14/20 – Carte £ 35/40
♦ Smart restaurant combining exposed brick and wood floors with neutral hue
and contemporary furnishings. Great value, seasonal menus display an interesting
mix of British/European dishes.

▶ London 291 mi – Exeter 83 mi – Penzance 34 mi – Plymouth 48 mi
✈ Newquay Airport : ℰ *(01637) 860600* Y
🛈 Marcus Hill ℰ *(01637) 85 40 20, www.visitnewquay.org*
🏌 Tower Rd, ℰ *(01637) 87 20 91*
🏌 Treloy, ℰ *(01637) 87 85 54*
🏌 Merlin Mawgan Porth, ℰ *(01841) 54 02 22*
Ⓖ Penhale Point and Kelsey Head★ (≼★★), SW : by A 3075 Y – Trerice★ **AC**, SE :
3.5 mi by A 392 - Y - and A 3058. St Agnes - St Agnes Beacon★★ (⁂★★), SW :
12.5 mi by A 3075 - Y - and B 3285

**at Watergate Bay** Northeast : 3 mi by A 3059 on B 3276 – ✉ Newquay

XX **Fifteen Cornwall**                                  ≼ AK ✿ *VISA* ◉◉ AE
On The Beach ✉ TR8 4AA – ℰ *(01637) 861 000 – www.fifteencornwall.co.uk*
**Rest** – Italian – *(booking essential)* Menu £ 27/58 – Carte lunch £ 31/42
♦ Lively restaurant boasting fabulous bay views – a registered charity as well
as Jamie Oliver's training academy. Unfussy Italian menus feature homemade
bread and pasta, olives and oils imported from Italy and other ingredients
sourced nearby. 5 course tasting menu offered at dinner; opens early for
breakfast.

**at Mawgan Porth** Northeast : 6 mi by A 3059 on B 3276

🔼 **Scarlet** ⌖                          ≼ 🖥 ◉ 🖺 & ⚡ ♨ 🄿 *VISA* ◉◉ AE
Tredragon Rd ✉ TR8 4DQ – ℰ *(01637) 861 800 – www.scarlethotel.co.uk*
– Closed 2 January-2 February
**37 rm** ⌕ – ✚£ 165/415 ✚✚£ 180/430
**Rest** *Restaurant* – see restaurant listing
♦ Eco-centric hotel set high on the cliff and boasting stunning coastal views.
Modern bar or lounges for relaxing and great spa offering extensive treatments.
Bedrooms range from 'Just Right' to 'Indulgent' and have a cool, Scandic style
and unusual open-plan bathrooms – every room has a terrace and sea view.

XX **Restaurant** – at Scarlet Hotel                        ≼ 🍴 & 🄿 *VISA* ◉◉ AE
Tredragon Rd ✉ TR8 4DQ – ℰ *(01637) 861 800 – www.scarlethotel.co.uk*
– Closed 2 January-2 February
**Rest** – Menu £ 20/43
♦ Airy hotel restaurant with neutral hues, wood panelling and plush banquettes.
Concise daily menu showcases local, seasonal ingredients and promotes small
suppliers. Stunning coastal views.

▶ London 52 mi – Birmingham 77 mi – Bristol 110 mi – Sheffield 126 mi

🏠 **Crooked Billet**                                    🍽 🍴 🄿 *VISA* ◉◉ AE
2 Westbrook End ✉ MK17 0DF – ℰ *(01908) 373 936 – www.thebillet.co.uk*
– Closed 27-28 December, Sunday dinner and Monday lunch
**Rest** – *(booking advisable)* Menu £ 20/24 – Carte £ 24/41 ❀
♦ Charming 17C thatched pub with smart yet informal interior. Modern, seasonal
dishes are crafted from local produce and a 7 course tasting menu is available at
dinner. Excellent wine list.

**ENGLAND**

---

**NEWTON POPPLEFORD** – Devon – **503** K31 – see Sidmouth

**NEWTON-ON-OUSE** – North Yorkshire – **502** Q22 – see York

**NITON** – Isle of Wight – **504** Q32 – see Wight (Isle of)

**NOMANSLAND** – Hampshire – **503** P31                                          **4** D3
▶ London 96 mi – Bournemouth 26 mi – Salisbury 13 mi – Southampton 14 mi

XX    **Mirabelles**                                            🏡 AK VISA ⓞⓞ AE
*Forest Edge Rd* ⊠ SP5 2BN – ℰ (01794) 390 205 – www.lesmirabelles.co.uk
*– Closed 1 week May, 22 December-13 January, Sunday and Monday*
**Rest** – French – Menu £ 20 (except dinner Friday-Saturday) – Carte £ 28/43 🕸
♦ Bright, modern restaurant overlooking the common, enthusiastically run by a
welcoming Frenchman. Well-balanced menu of classic Gallic dishes; superb wine
list. Friendly atmosphere.

**NORTH BOVEY** – Devon – **503** I32 – pop. 254 – ⊠ Newton Abbot         **2** C2
▶ London 214 mi – Exeter 13 mi – Plymouth 34 mi – Torquay 21 mi
ⓖ Dartmoor National Park★★

NORTH BOVEY

🏨 **Bovey Castle** ♨  ⟨ ⟩
Northwest : 2 mi by un-marked single track road.       VISA ⓶ AE
✉ TQ13 8RE – ✆ (01647) 445 000 – www.boveycastle.com
**60 rm** – ♦£ 179/279 ♦♦£ 249/279, � £ 14.95 – 4 suites
**Rest** *Castle Bistro* – see restaurant listing
**Rest** *The Edwardian* – (dinner only and Sunday lunch) Menu £ 36
– Carte £ 38/54
♦ Opulent castle with extensive sporting estate, beautifully set in Dartmoor National Park. Relaxed, homely feel and a high degree of comfort throughout. Bedrooms come in pastel hues and with contemporary touches but retain a classic edge. Modern grill-style menu in The Edwardian or pub dishes in Castle bistro.

🏠 **Gate House** without rest ♨       ⟨ ⟩
just off village green, past "Ring of Bells" public house ✉ TQ13 8RB – ✆ (01647) 440 479 – www.gatehouseondartmoor.com – Closed 24-26 December
**3 rm** ⊑ – ♦£ 55 ♦♦£ 84
♦ Charming 15C medieval hallhouse set in the heart of an attractive village and boasting a characterful thatched roof, large oak door and lovely country garden. Simple, spotlessly kept bedrooms; some with moor views. Amiable owners serve breakfast beside the AGA.

🍴 **Castle Bistro** – at Bovey Castle Hotel       VISA ⓶ AE
Northwest : 2 mi by un-marked single track road. ✉ TQ13 8RE – ✆ (01647) 445 000 – www.boveycastle.com
**Rest** – Carte £ 25/33
♦ All-day bistro with open-plan kitchen and superb decked terrace, set in an opulent castle in Dartmoor National Park. All-encompassing modern menu offers everything from pastries to pub dishes.

**NORTH CHARLTON** – Northumberland – **501** O17 – see Alnwick

**NORTH HINKSEY** – Oxfordshire – **504** Q28 – see Oxford

**NORTH KILWORTH** – Leicestershire – **502** Q26       **16 B3**
▶ London 95 mi – Leicester 20 mi – Market Harborough 9 mi

🏨 **Kilworth House** ♨       VISA ⓶ AE ⓵
Lutterworth Rd, West : 0.5 mi on A 4304 ✉ LE17 6JE – ✆ (01858) 880 058 – www.kilworthhouse.co.uk
**41 rm** ⊑ – ♦£ 110/150 ♦♦£ 120/165 – 3 suites
**Rest** *Orangery* – see restaurant listing
**Rest** *Wordsworth* – (dinner only) Carte £ 35/46
♦ Impressively restored and extended Victorian mansion in 38 acres of tranquil grounds, with popular open-air theatre. Spacious, classical drawing rooms. Immaculately kept bedrooms boast luxurious bathrooms; the largest are in the main house. Traditional menus in ornate restaurant. Attractive bar and brasserie.

🍴🍴 **Orangery** – at Kilworth House Hotel       VISA ⓶ AE ⓵
Lutterworth Rd, West : 0.5 mi on A 4304 ✉ LE17 6JE – ✆ (01858) 880 058 – www.kilworthhouse.co.uk
**Rest** – Carte £ 26/39
♦ Charming orangery in an impressively restored Victorian mansion. Ornate wrought iron and plenty of glass make it light and airy by day and more intimate at night. Light, brasserie-style menu.

**NORTH LOPHAM** – Norfolk – **504** W26       **15 C2**
▶ London 98 mi – Norwich 34 mi – Ipswich 31 mi – Bury Saint Edmunds 20 mi

🏠 **Church Farm House**       ⟨ ⟩
Church Rd ✉ IP22 2LP – ✆ (01379) 687 270 – www.churchfarmhouse.org – Closed January
**3 rm** ⊑ – ♦£ 50/60 ♦♦£ 100   **Rest** – Menu £ 30
♦ Characterful thatched farmhouse with lovely garden, simple facilities, homely feel and personal touches. Individually styled bedrooms look to the church. Home cooked meals use local produce, with breakfast served outside in summer.

520

▶ London 192 mi – Cardiff 118 mi – Plymouth 87 mi – Swansea 153 mi

🏠 **Heasley House**                                    ⚞ ⁽ᵗ⁾ **P** 🆅🅸🆂🅰 ⓪ⓑ
*Heasley Mill, Northwest : 1.25 mi by Heasley Mill rd.* ⊠ *EX36 3LE –* ℰ *(01598)*
*740 213 – www.heasley-house.co.uk – Closed February and Christmas-New Year*
**7 rm** 🖵 – ♦£ 115 ♦♦£ 150/170
**Rest** – *(dinner only) (booking essential for non residents)* Menu £ 32
• Former Georgian Dower House in remote Devon village bordering Exmoor
National Park. Clean, fresh style with whitewashed walls, rush matting and
quirky modern artwork. Hands-on owners. Tea and cakes on arrival. Simple,
wholesome cooking.

---

**NORTH WALSHAM** – Norfolk – **503** Y25 – pop. 11 845                    **15** D1
🏴 Great Britain

▶ London 125 mi – Norwich 16 mi

🅶 Blicking Hall★★ **AC**, W : 8.5 mi by B 1145, A 140 and B 1354

🏨 **Beechwood**                                        ⚞ ⁽ᵗ⁾ **P** 🆅🅸🆂🅰 ⓪ⓑ
*20 Cromer Rd* ⊠ *NR28 0HD –* ℰ *(01692) 403 231 – www.beechwood-hotel.co.uk*
**17 rm** 🖵 – ♦£ 82 ♦♦£ 90/160
**Rest** – *(dinner only and Sunday lunch)* Menu £ 23/36
• Privately owned, peacefully set, part 19C hotel where Agatha Christie once
stayed. Thoughtfully appointed bedrooms; newer ones are larger. Attentive service. Handsome dining room with flowers.

---

**NORTHALLERTON** – North Yorkshire – **502** P20 – pop. 15 517            **22** B1

▶ London 238 mi – Leeds 48 mi – Middlesbrough 24 mi
– Newcastle upon Tyne 56 mi

🅸 Applegarth ℰ (01609) 77 68 64, www.visit-northallerton.com

**at Staddlebridge** Northeast : 7.5 mi by A 684 on A 19 at junction with A 172
– ⊠ **Northallerton**

✗✗ **McCoys Bistro at The Tontine** with rm        🄰🄲 rm, ⁽ᵗ⁾ **P** 🆅🅸🆂🅰 ⓪ⓑ 🄰🄴 ⑩
*on southbound carriageway (A 19)* ⊠ *DL6 3JB –* ℰ *(01609) 882 671*
*– www.mccoystontine.co.uk – Closed 25-26 December and 1-2 January*
**7 rm** 🖵 – ♦£ 100/115 ♦♦£ 130/140
**Rest** – *(booking essential)* Menu £ 20 (lunch) – Carte £ 33/53
• Established basement bistro with Parisian-themed décor, long wooden bar and
conservatory bedecked with Indian-style parasols. Yorkshire meets France on the
constantly evolving, classically based menus and steaks remain a firm favourite.
Quirky modern bedrooms boast bold wallpapers and free-standing baths.

---

**NORTHAMPTON** – Northamptonshire – **504** R27 – pop. 185 255            **16** B3
🏴 Great Britain

▶ London 69 mi – Cambridge 53 mi – Coventry 34 mi – Leicester 42 mi
🅸 Guildhall Rd ℰ 62 26 77, www.explorenorthamptonshire.co.uk
🅱 Delapre Nene Valley Way, Eagle Drive, ℰ (01604) 76 40 36
🅸🄸 Collingtree Park Windingbrook Lane, ℰ (01604) 70 00 00
🅶 All Saints, Brixworth★, N : 7 mi on A 508 Y

Plan on next page

✗ **Dang's**                                                    🄰🄲 🆅🅸🆂🅰
*205 Wellingborough Rd* ⊠ *NN1 4ED –* ℰ *(01604) 607 060 – www.dangs.ws*
*– Closed 1 January, 25-26 December and Monday*                          **Z n**
**Rest** – Vietnamese – *(dinner only)* Carte £ 15/40 **s**
• Immaculately furnished, contemporary Vietnamese restaurant. Passionately
run, food is fresh, tasty, good value and mostly homemade. Noodle bowls are a
speciality.

ENGLAND

# NORTHAMPTON

ENGLAND

## NORTHAW – Hertfordshire – 504 T28 · 12 B2

▶ London 22 mi – Birmingham 110 mi – Bristol 134 mi – Croydon 57 mi

🍴 **Sun at Northaw** 🛋 🍽 **P** VISA ⓒ ①
*1 Judges Hill ⊠ EN6 4NL – ℰ (01707) 655 507 – www.thesunatnorthaw.co.uk*
*– Closed Sunday dinner and Monday*
**Rest** – Menu £ 18 (weekday lunch) – Carte £ 27/37
♦ Whitewashed 16C inn by village green; dine in the bar or either dining room. Hearty, traditional, flavoursome cooking uses East of England produce, and beers and ciders are equally local.

## NORTHLEACH – Gloucestershire – pop. 1 923 · 4 D1

▶ London 87 mi – Birmingham 73 mi – Bristol 54 mi – Coventry 47 mi

🍴 **Wheatsheaf Inn** with rm 🛋 🍽 «¶» **P** VISA ⓒ AE ①
*West End ⊠ GL50 3EZ – ℰ (01451) 860 244 – www.cotswoldswheatsheaf.com*
**14 rm** – ♦£ 120 ♦♦£ 120/180, ☲ £ 12
**Rest** – Menu £ 15 (lunch) – Carte £ 26/33
♦ Characterful 17C former coaching inn set in historic village, with stone-floored bar and open fires. Daily changing menus offer mostly pub classics; refined, flavoursome cooking.

## NORTON ST PHILIP – Somerset – 503 N30 – pop. 820 – ⊠ Bath · 4 C2

▶ London 113 mi – Bristol 22 mi – Southampton 55 mi – Swindon 40 mi

🏠 **Plaine** without rest «¶» **P** VISA ⓒ ①
*⊠ BA2 7LT – ℰ (01373) 834 723 – www.theplaine.co.uk*
**3 rm** ☲ – ♦£ 50/90 ♦♦£ 120/140
♦ Charming 16C stone cottages in a delightful village, on the site of the original market place. Snug, beamed interior with small lounge and airy breakfast room. Simple bedrooms feature fresh, colour-themed linens. Bubbly owner.

## NORWICH – Norfolk – 504 Y26 – pop. 171 243 📗 Great Britain · 15 D2

▶ London 109 mi – Kingston-upon-Hull 148 mi – Leicester 117 mi
 – Nottingham 120 mi

🛩 Norwich Airport : ℰ (0844) 748 0112, N : 3.5 mi by A 140 V
🛈 Millennium Plain ℰ (01603) 21 39 99, www.visitnorwich.co.uk
🏌 Royal Norwich Hellesdon Drayton High Rd, ℰ (01603) 42 57 12
🏌 Marriott Sprowston Manor Hotel Wroxham Rd, ℰ (0870) 4 00 72 29
🏌 Costessy Park Costessey, ℰ (01603) 74 63 33
🏌 Bawburgh Marlingford Rd, Glen Lodge, ℰ (01603) 74 04 04
◎ City★★ - Cathedral★★ Y – Castle (Museum and Art Gallery★ **AC**) Z – Market Place★ Z
◎ Sainsbury Centre for Visual Arts★ **AC**, W : 3 mi by B 1108 X. Blicking Hall★★ **AC**, N : 11 mi by A 140 - V - and B 1354 – NE : Norfolk Broads★

Plans on following pages

🏨 **St Giles House** 🍽 📶 ⅙ rm, 🅰 rest, 🛁 «¶» 🕍 **P** VISA ⓒ AE
*41-45 St Giles St ⊠ NR2 1JR – ℰ (01603) 275 180 – www.stgileshousehotel.com*
**23 rm** ☲ – ♦£ 120 ♦♦£ 130 – 1 suite **Rest** – Carte £ 25/38 YZ**o**
♦ Stylish, centrally located hotel with impressive façade, columns and wood panelling. Luxurious 'Deluxe' front suites. Rear bedrooms are quieter and more contemporary. Open-plan lounge/bar/dining room with pleasant terrace serves modern brasserie classics.

🏠 **Catton Old Hall** without rest 🛋 🛁 «¶» **P** VISA ⓒ
*Lodge Ln., Old Catton, North : 3.5 mi by Catton Grove Rd. off St Faiths Rd.*
*⊠ NR6 7HG – ℰ (01603) 419 379 – www.catton-hall.co.uk*
**7 rm** ☲ – ♦♦£ 95/150
♦ Attractive 17C house with characterful interior. Individually designed bedrooms include 5 feature rooms; Anna Sewell, with exposed rafters and a vast four-poster, is the best.

## ✗✗ Roger Hickman's

AC VISA ◉◎ AE

*79 Upper St Giles St* ⊠ *NR2 1AB* – ℰ *(01603) 633 522*
– *www.rogerhickmansrestaurant.com* – Closed 1 week August, 1 week Christmas,
Sunday and Monday
**Rest** – Menu £ 20/39

Z

♦ Traditionally styled restaurant with plenty of romantic corners. Classic combinations of ingredients presented in a distinctly contemporary style. Tasting menu available at dinner.

## ✗ Mackintosh's Canteen

⌂ AC VISA ◉◎ AE

*Unit 410, Chapelfield Plain* ⊠ *NR2 1SZ* – ℰ *(01603) 305 280*
– *www.mackintoshscanteen.co.uk*
**Rest** – Menu £ 20 – Carte £ 25/33

Z

♦ Smart modern brasserie boasting full length windows, combined with an all day terraced café: a shoppers' haven. Friendly, efficient team serve tasty, freshly prepared modern dishes.

**NORWICH**
BUILT UP AREA

0 _____ 1 km
0 _____ 1/2 mile

MOUSEHOLD HEATH

THORPE ST-ANDREW

EATON PARK

TROWSE

| A 11 | THETFORD | A 140 | IPSWICH | LOWESTOFT | A 146 |

### 103

*103 Unthank Rd ⊠ NR2 2PE – ℰ (01603) 610 047 – www.103unthank.com
– Closed 25 December and Sunday dinner*                                    X**r**

**Rest** – *(bookings not accepted)* Carte £ 28/30

♦ Popular deli/restaurant in the heart of the Golden Triangle, with open-plan kitchen, deli counter and heated pavement terrace. Daily changing menus; Mediterranean and Asian influences.

### Mad Moose Arms

*2 Warwick St., off Dover St. ⊠ NR2 3LD – ℰ (01603) 627 687
– www.madmoose.co.uk – Closed 25 December*                                X**n**

**Rest** – Carte £ 21/30

♦ Attractive neighbourhood pub with busy, buzzy atmosphere and blackboard of pub favourites. More formal upstairs restaurant offers ambitious, classically based dishes with modern presentation.

**at Stoke Holy Cross** South : 5.75 mi by A 140 - X – ⊠ Norwich

### Wildebeest Arms

*82-86 Norwich Rd ⊠ NR14 8QJ – ℰ (01508) 492 497 – www.thewildebeest.co.uk
– Closed 25 December*

**Rest** – *(booking essential)* Menu £ 17/22 – Carte £ 25/35

♦ Attractive pub with tree trunk tables, wild animal artefacts, a smartly furnished front terrace and a warm, friendly feel. Good value set menus and daily changing à la carte with a strong Mediterranean slant; accomplished, seasonal cooking. Well-organised service.

525

## NOSS MAYO – Devon – **503** H33

**2** C3

▶ London 242 mi – Plymouth 12 mi – Yealmpton 3 mi

☑ Saltram House★★, NW : 7 mi by B 3186 and A 379 – Plymouth★, NW : 9 mi by B 3186 and A 379

### 🍷 Ship Inn

☐ 🅿 VISA ⓒⓒ AE

✉ PL8 1EW – ℰ (01752) 872 387 – www.nossmayo.com

**Rest** – Carte £ 26/31

♦ Large, busy, well run pub with wonderful waterside views from its peaceful spot on the Yealm Estuary. Appealing menu of pub classics, with desserts from the tried-and-tested stable.

---

## NOTTINGHAM – Nottingham – **502** Q25 – pop. 249 584

**16** B2

▌ Great Britain

▶ London 135 mi – Birmingham 50 mi – Leeds 74 mi – Leicester 27 mi

✈ Nottingham East Midlands Airport, Castle Donington : ℰ (0871) 9199000 SW : 15 mi by A 453 AZ

🅵 1-4 Smithy Row ℰ (08444) 77 56 78, www.visitnottingham.com

🏌 Bulwell Forest Hucknall Rd, ℰ (0115) 977 05 76

🏌 Wollaton Park, ℰ (0115) 978 75 74

🏌 Mapperley Central Ave, Plains Rd, ℰ (0115) 955 66 72

🏌 Nottingham City Bulwell Norwich Gardens, ℰ (0115) 927 27 67

🏌 Beeston Fields Beeston, ℰ (0115) 925 70 62

🏌 Ruddington Grange Ruddington Wilford Rd, ℰ (0115) 984 61 41

🏌 Edwalton Wellin Lane, ℰ (0115) 923 47 75

🏌 Cotgrave Place G. & C.C. Stragglethorpe Cotgrave, Nr Cotgrave Village, ℰ (0115) 933 33 44

👁 Castle Museum★ (alabasters★) **AC**, CZ **M**

☑ Wollaton Hall★ **AC**, W : 2.5 mi by Ilkeston Rd, A 609 AZ **M**. Southwell Minster★★, NE : 14 mi by A 612 BZ - Newstead Abbey★ **AC**, N : 11 mi by A 60, A 611 - AY - and B 683 – Mr Straw's House★, Worksop, N : 20 mi signed from B 6045 (past Bassetlaw Hospital) – St Mary Magdalene★, Newark-on-Trent, NE : 20 mi by A 612 BZ

Plans on following pages

### 🏨 Hart's

≤ 🚗 📶 ♿ 🛎 🛜 🅿 VISA ⓒⓒ AE

Standard Hill, Park Row ✉ NG1 6FN – ℰ (0115) 988 19 00

– www.hartsnottingham.co.uk

CZ**e**

**30 rm** – ♦£ 125 ♦♦£ 175, ⌑ £ 14 – 2 suites

**Rest** Hart's – see restaurant listing

♦ Sophisticated, boutique-style hotel built on the ramparts of a medieval castle. Bedrooms boast superb linen and modern bathrooms; Garden Rooms come with a view. Small bar/lounge.

### 🏨 Lace Market

🛎 🛜 ♿ VISA ⓒⓒ AE ⓪

29-31 High Pavement ✉ NG1 1HE – ℰ (0115) 852 32 32

– www.thefinessecollection.com – Closed 1 week Christmas

DZ**a**

**42 rm** ⌑ – ♦£ 89/109 ♦♦£ 119/249

**Rest** Merchants – (closed Sunday and Monday) Menu £ 15 (lunch)

– Carte dinner £ 32/41

♦ Boutique hotel situated in the old lacemaking quarter. Bedrooms are furnished in a contemporary style; those at the front, with their large windows, are the best. Minimalist, David Collins designed Merchants offers traditional dishes presented in a modern style.

526

## NOTTINGHAM

**ENGLAND**

527

NOTTINGHAM
BUILT UP AREA

XXX **Restaurant Sat Bains** with rm     🚗 AC rest, "¶" P VISA ⦿⦿

&#x2318; &#x2318; *Trentside, Old Lenton Ln ⊠ NG7 2SA – ℰ (0115) 986 65 66*
*– www.restaurantsatbains.com – Closed 3 weeks August, 2 weeks*
*December-January, Sunday and Monday*       **AZn**
**5 rm** ⏁ – ♥£ 114 ♥♥£ 129/175 – 3 suites   **Rest** – *(dinner only)* Menu £ 75/89
**Spec.** Pork belly with pearl barley, parsley and pickled turnip. Braised mutton with
shallot textures, wild garlic and capers. Chocolate, yoghurt, cumin caramel and
coriander.

♦ Restored farm buildings housing an intimate stone-floored dining room and
conservatory. Formal atmosphere with smartly laid round tables and smooth,
knowledgeable service. 7 and 10 course menus offer highly original, intricate
and visually impressive dishes; bespoke lunches served for groups of 4 and
more. Modern, individually furnished bedrooms.

XXX **Anoki**         AC VISA ⦿⦿ AE ⓪

*Barkergate ⊠ NG1 1JU – ℰ (0115) 948 38 88 – www.anoki.co.uk – Closed 25-26*
*December*       **DYs**
**Rest** – Indian – *(dinner only)* Menu £ 28 – Carte £ 24/34

♦ Elegant, modern Indian restaurant in city centre serving full flavoured, satisfying dishes cooked with vibrancy and skill. Smartly dressed staff delighted to give
advice – or even a taster.

XX **Hart's**        🏠 AC 🐱 ⇔ VISA ⦿⦿ AE

*Standard Ct., Park Row ⊠ NG1 6GN – ℰ (0115) 988 19 00*
*– www.hartsnottingham.co.uk – Closed dinner 25-26 December, lunch 31*
*December and 1 January*       **CZe**
**Rest** – Menu £ 18/26 *(except Friday-Saturday)* – Carte £ 24/50

♦ Light, contemporary restaurant in former A&E dept. of the old city hospital; sit
in one of the central booths. Well-priced, flavourful, modern British dishes. Professional service.

XX **World Service**       🏠 ⇔ VISA ⦿⦿ AE

*Newdigate House, Castlegate ⊠ NG1 6AF – ℰ (0115) 847 55 87*
*– www.worldservicerestaurant.com – Closed 1-13 January and Sunday dinner*
**Rest** – Menu £ 19 *(lunch)* – Carte £ 31/38       **CZn**

♦ Double-fronted Georgian property with modern extension; enter via Indone-
sian-inspired courtyard garden. Modern, visually appealing British dishes; excellent set price lunch. Formal service.

XX **MemSaab**        AC ⇔ VISA ⦿⦿ AE

*12-14 Maid Marian Way ⊠ NG1 6HS – ℰ (0115) 957 00 09*
*– www.mem-saab.co.uk – Closed 25 December*       **CYn**
**Rest** – Indian – *(dinner only)* Carte approx. £ 27

♦ Spacious restaurant dominated by a wooden copy of the Gateway of India,
with some striking portraits on the walls. Authentic Indian cooking: dishes might
include locally farmed ostrich.

XX **1877**         AC ⇔ VISA ⦿⦿ ⓪

*128 Derby Rd ⊠ NG1 5FB – ℰ (0115) 958 80 08 – www.restaurant1877.com*
*– Closed Sunday dinner and Monday*       **CYa**
**Rest** – *(dinner only and lunch Saturday-Sunday)* Carte £ 20/40

♦ Keenly run, contemporary restaurant set on corner site, with elegant private
first floor dining room. Wholesome, tasty, modern English dishes made from seasonal, local produce.

X **Iberico World Tapas**       VISA ⦿⦿ ⓪

*High Pavement ⊠ NG1 1HN – ℰ (0115) 941 04 10 – www.ibericotapas.com*
*– Closed Sunday*       **DZe**
**Rest** – Menu £ 12 *(lunch)* **s** – Carte £ 25/38 **s**

♦ Lively restaurant in basement of former city jail and law courts, with vaulted
ceiling and colourful Moorish tiles and fretwork. Tasty tapas menu with 'Spanish'
and 'World' sections.

**ENGLAND**

**at Plumtree** Southeast : 5.75 mi by A 60 - BZ - off A 606 – ✉ Nottingham

XX  **Perkins**                                     ⌂ 🅰🅲 🅿 🆅🅸🆂🅰 ⓒⓒ 🅰🅴
*Old Railway Station, Station Rd ✉ NG12 5NA – ℰ (0115) 937 36 95*
*– www.perkinsrestaurant.co.uk – Closed Sunday dinner*
**Rest** – Menu £ 16 (lunch and early dinner) – Carte £ 28/34
♦ Former railway station; now a light, modern, airy restaurant; sit in the conserva
tory and watch the trains. Classically based menus include sharing boards and tu
reens; local produce features.

**at Stapleford** Southwest : 5.5 mi by A 52 - AZ - ✉ Nottingham

XX  **Crème**                                            🅰🅲 🆅🅸🆂🅰 ⓒⓒ 🅰🅴
*12 Toton Ln ✉ NG9 7HA – ℰ (0115) 939 74 22 – www.cremerestaurant.co.uk*
*– Closed 26 December-2 January, Saturday lunch, Sunday dinner and Monday*
**Rest** – Menu £ 15/18
♦ Smart, well run restaurant offering well-presented, modern British cookin
served by friendly staff. Long lounge area with comfy sofas; airy, formally-laid din
ing room.

**at Sherwood Business Park** Northwest : 10 mi by A 611 - AY - off A 608
– ✉ Nottingham

🏨  **Holiday Inn**           ⌂ ⅙ 🛏 ⅙ rm, 🅰🅲 ⓒ 🛁 🅿 🆅🅸🆂🅰 ⓒⓒ 🅰🅴
*Lake View Dr. ✉ NG15 0DA – ℰ (01623) 727 670 – www.holidayinn.com*
**92 rm** – ♥£ 129 ♥♥£ 129, ⌹ £ 13.50
**Rest** *Grill* – Carte £ 25/43
♦ Situated close to the M1, in the heart of the business park. Spacious bedroom
feature exposed brickwork, king-sized beds and all mod cons; bathrooms have
walk-in showers. Spacious restaurant with bar/lounge. Seasonal classics on grill
style menu.

---

**NUNEATON** – Warwickshire – **503** P26 – pop. 70 721                    **19** D2
▶ London 102 mi – Birmingham 25 mi – Coventry 17 mi

🏠  **Leathermill Grange** without rest ⅊              ⌂ ⅗ ⓒ 🅿
*Leathermill Lane, Caldecote, Northwest : 3.5 mi by B 4114 on B 4111*
*✉ CV10 0RX – ℰ (01827) 714 637 – www.leathermillgrange.co.uk – Closed 2*
*weeks Christmas-New Year and 8-14 May*
**5 rm** ⌹ – ♥£ 70 ♥♥£ 90
♦ Imposing Victorian farmhouse in peaceful rural spot. Spacious, spotless bed
rooms - one four poster. Homebaking and tea on arrival. Guest lounge and con
servatory with garden view.

---

**OAKHAM** – Rutland – **502** R25 – pop. 9 620 ▯ Great Britain            **17** C2
▶ London 103 mi – Leicester 26 mi – Northampton 35 mi – Nottingham 28 mi
🛈 Catmose St ℰ (01572) 75 84 41, www.discover-rutland.co.uk
◉ Oakham Castle ★
◙ Rutland Water ★, E : by A 606 – Normanton Church ★ **AC**, SE : 5 mi by A 603 and
minor road East

🏨  **Barnsdale Lodge**                      ⌂ ⅙ ⓒ 🛁 🅿 🆅🅸🆂🅰 ⓒⓒ 🅰🅴 ⓞ
*The Avenue, Rutland Water, East : 2.5 mi on A 606 ✉ LE15 8AH – ℰ (01572)*
*724 678 – www.barnsdalelodge.co.uk*
**45 rm** ⌹ – ♥£ 90/105 ♥♥£ 105/130
**Rest** *Restaurant* – see restaurant listing
♦ Collection of converted, interconnecting farm buildings set in neatly lawned
gardens. Characterful guest areas with York stone flooring in lounge and bar. In
dividually designed bedrooms boast good facilities and a pleasant cottagey style.

ENGLAND

XX **Restaurant** – at Barnsdale Lodge Hotel 🚗 ㅎ 🅿 𝘝𝘐𝘚𝘈 ⓒⓞ 🄰🄴 ⓞ
*The Avenue, Rutland Water, East : 2.5 mi on A 606* ⊠ *LE15 8AH –* ℰ *(01572)*
*724 678 – www.barnsdalelodge.co.uk*
**Rest** – Menu £ 15 (lunch) – Carte £ 27/35
♦ Formal dining room with casual conservatory and large enclosed courtyard, set
in a personally run hotel close to Rutland Water. Keen owners grow their own veg
and raise their own chickens.

**at Hambleton** East : 3 mi by A 606 – ⊠ Oakham

🏠🏠 **Hambleton Hall** ⅋ ＜ 🚗 🕭 🏊 �料 🛋 ⓥ 🅿 𝘝𝘐𝘚𝘈 ⓒⓞ 🄰🄴
✿ ⊠ *LE15 8TH –* ℰ *(01572) 756 991 – www.hambletonhall.com*
**16 rm** � – ♦£ 195/215 ♦♦£ 360/420 – 1 suite
**Rest** – Menu £ 37/39 – Carte £ 63/80 ஃ
**Spec.** Poached langoustine tails with asparagus. Whissendine veal with sweetbread raviolo and morel mushrooms. Pavé of chocolate and honeycomb.
♦ Beautiful red-brick Victorian manor house with mature grounds, in a peaceful
location overlooking Rutland Water. Classical country house lounges and drawing
rooms boast heavy drapes, open fires and antiques. Good-sized bedrooms are designed by the owner herself – who is part of the original founding family. Highly
skilled cooking uses gutsy, seasonal ingredients in classic combinations.

🛏 **Finch's Arms** with rm ＜ 🚗 🏠 🅿 𝘝𝘐𝘚𝘈 ⓒⓞ 🄰🄴 ⓞ
*Oakham Rd* ⊠ *LE15 8TL –* ℰ *(01572) 756 575 – www.finchsarms.co.uk*
**10 rm** ⊠byeuro – ♦£ 75/95 ♦♦£ 115/125 **Rest** – Menu £ 16/20 – Carte £ 21/27
♦ Attractive 17C sandstone inn boasting contemporary Mediterranean-style
rooms and a large terrace with beautiful Rutland Water views. Menus feature
both classic and modern British dishes. Smart, stylish bedrooms.

**OAKSEY** – Wiltshire – **503** N29                                                  **4** C1
▶ London 98 mi – Cirencester 8 mi – Stroud 20 mi

🛏 **Wheatsheaf at Oaksey** 🏠 🅿 𝘝𝘐𝘚𝘈 ⓒⓞ 🄰🄴
*Wheatsheaf Ln* ⊠ *SN16 9TB –* ℰ *(01666) 577 348*
*– www.thewheatsheafatoaksey.co.uk – Closed Sunday dinner and Monday*
**Rest** – Carte £ 25/36
♦ Community pub with traditional fire-lit bar and more modern dining room.
Blackboard menu of wholesome dishes with the occasional Thai influence. Ap-
pealing nursery puddings.

**OARE** – Kent – **504** W30 – **see Faversham**

**OBORNE** – Dorset – **503** M31 – **see Sherborne**

**OCKLEY** – Surrey – **504** S30                                                      **7** D2
▶ London 31 mi – Brighton 32 mi – Guildford 23 mi – Lewes 36 mi
🖼 Gatton Manor Hotel G. & C.C. Standon Lane, ℰ (01306) 62 75 55

🛏 **Bryce's** 🏠 🅿 𝘝𝘐𝘚𝘈 ⓒⓞ
*Old School House, Stane St, on A 29* ⊠ *RH5 5TH –* ℰ *(01306) 627 430*
*– www.bryces.co.uk – Closed 25-26 December, 1 January and Sunday dinner*
*January, February and November*
**Rest** – Seafood – Menu £ 16 (weekdays) – Carte £ 29/34
♦ Smart dining pub offering fresh seafood from the South Coast day boats.
Choice of cheaper, simpler bar menu or more adventurous offerings and black-
board specials in the linen-laid dining room.

**OFFCHURCH** – Warwickshire – **see Royal Leamington Spa**

ENGLAND

**OLD BURGHCLERE** – Hampshire – **504** Q29 – ✉ **Newbury**       **6** B1

▶ London 77 mi – Bristol 76 mi – Newbury 10 mi – Reading 27 mi

XX    **Dew Pond**               ⟨ P VISA ⚫⚫
✉ *RG20 9LH – ✆ (01635) 278 408 – www.dewpond.co.uk – Closed 2 weeks Christmas-New Year, Sunday and Monday*
**Rest** – *(dinner only)* Menu £ 34
♦ Long-standing, personally run restaurant with attractive country views. Homely lounge; two dining rooms display local art for sale. Classical cooking with French influences. Friendly service.

**OLD WARDEN** – Central Bedfordshire – **504** S27 – **pop. 275**      **12** A1

▶ London 51 mi – Birmingham 89 mi – Bristol 164 mi – Sheffield 134 mi

🏠    **Hare & Hounds**          🚗 🏠 P VISA ⚫⚫ ①
*The Village ✉ SG18 9HQ – ✆ (01767) 627 225*
*– www.hareandhoundsoldwarden.co.uk – Closed 26 December, 1 January, Sunday dinner and Monday except bank holidays*
**Rest** – Carte £ 22/28
♦ Charming picture postcard pub in an idyllic village, boasting ornate barge-boards and manicured shrubs. Monthly changing à la carte offers hearty, flavoursome dishes; blackboard menu presents choices of a classic pub persuasion. Tasty homemade bread and pasta.

**OLDHAM** – Greater Manchester – **502** N23 – **pop. 103 544**      **20** B2

▶ London 212 mi – Leeds 36 mi – Manchester 7 mi – Sheffield 38 mi

🏌 Crompton and Royton Royton High Barn, ✆ (0161) 624 21 54

🏌 Werneth Garden Suburb Green Lane, ✆ (0161) 624 11 90

🏌 Lees New Rd, ✆ (0161) 624 49 86

Plan : see Manchester

🏠    **White Hart Inn** with rm        📶 ♿ P VISA ⚫⚫ AE
(☺)   *51 Stockport Rd, Lydgate ✉ OL4 4JJ – ✆ (01457) 872 566*
*– www.thewhitehart.co.uk – Closed 26 December*
**12 rm** �br – †£ 95 ††£ 128
**Rest** – Menu £ 20 (Sunday lunch) – Carte £ 26/35
♦ Stone-built inn overlooking Saddleworth Moor, boasting a large dark wood bar, exposed beams, open fires and photos of the owner's mountain travels. Good-sized menus display modern, brasserie-style dishes and a few pub classics – and at very reasonable prices. Individually styled bedrooms are furnished with antiques.

**OLDSTEAD** – North Yorkshire – **502** Q21             **23** C2

▶ London 235 mi – Liverpool 125 mi – Leeds 54 mi – Sheffield 86 mi

🏠    **Black Swan** with rm 🌿       🚗 🏠 ♻ 📶 P VISA ⚫⚫
❀   ✉ *YO61 4BL – ✆ (01347) 868 387 – www.blackswanoldstead.co.uk – Closed 2 weeks in January and lunch Monday-Wednesday*
**4 rm** (dinner included) �br – †£ 165 ††£ 190/310
**Rest** – Menu £ 25 (lunch) – Carte £ 35/48
**Spec.** Scallops with cauliflower purée, raisins, curry and coriander. Lamb '4 ways' with Anna potatoes and baby gem lettuce. Set lemon custard with elderflower ice cream.
♦ Owned by a family who've lived and farmed here for generations. Top-rate bar meals in characterful beamed bar; more ambitious dishes in upstairs restaurant. Cooking is modern and highly skilled but satisfyingly unpretentious. Bedrooms boast modern fabrics, antiques, luxurious bathrooms and private patios.

**OLTON** – West Midlands – **502** O26 – **see Solihull**

**OMBERSLEY** – Worcestershire – **503** N27 – pop. 2 089      **18** B3

▶ London 148 mi – Birmingham 42 mi – Leominster 33 mi

🔟 Bishopswood Rd, ℰ (01905) 62 07 47

XX    **Venture In**               AC P VISA ◉◉
Main St ⊠ WR9 0EW – ℰ (01905) 620 552 – Closed 2 weeks February, 2 weeks
August, 1 week Christmas, Sunday dinner and Monday
**Rest** – Menu £ 28/38
♦ Charming, restored Tudor inn, traditional from its broad inglenook to its
fringed Victorian lights. Modern, flavourful menu, well judged and locally sourced.
Friendly staff.

---

**ORFORD** – Suffolk – **504** Y27 – pop. 1 153 – ⊠ Woodbridge     **15** D3

▶ London 103 mi – Ipswich 22 mi – Norwich 52 mi

🏨    **Crown and Castle**          🚗 ⁽ᵗ⁾ P VISA ◉◉
⊠ IP12 2LJ – ℰ (01394) 450 205 – www.crownandcastle.co.uk
**18 rm** ☕ – ♦£ 104 ♦♦£ 220 – 1 suite
**Rest Trinity** – see restaurant listing
♦ Refreshingly well-run, mock-Tudor style house with relaxed yet professional
service; set next to the 12C castle. Smart guest areas. Modern, individually designed bedrooms with good comforts and stylish bathrooms; some have terraces,
others boast distant sea views.

XX    **Trinity** – at Crown and Castle Hotel         🚗 P VISA ◉◉
⊠ IP12 2LJ – ℰ (01394) 450 205 – www.crownandcastle.co.uk
**Rest** – (closed lunch 31 December) (booking essential at dinner) Carte £ 27/39 🏵
♦ Relaxed dining room with red banquettes, eclectic art and chic, modern bar-
lounge. Wide-ranging lunches and more sophisticated dinners; classical British
puddings. Simple yet precise cooking relies on quality, seasonal ingredients.
Friendly, efficient service.

---

**OSMOTHERLEY** – North Yorkshire – **502** Q20 – pop. 1 217     **22** B1
– ⊠ Northallerton

▶ London 245 mi – Darlington 25 mi – Leeds 49 mi – Middlesbrough 20 mi

🏠    **Golden Lion** with rm                ⁽ᵗ⁾ VISA ◉◉
6 West End ⊠ DL6 3AA – ℰ (01609) 883 526
– www.goldenlionosmotherley.co.uk – Closed 25 December, lunch Monday and
Tuesday except bank holidays
**5 rm** ☕ – ♦£ 65/75 ♦♦£ 90    **Rest** – Carte £ 24/33
♦ Set in a delightful village, with a warm, rustic, fire-lit interior. Staff make you
feel instantly at ease; unpretentious, classic cooking leaves you relaxed, sated
and satisfied. Modern bedrooms have good showers.

---

**OSWESTRY** – Shropshire – **502** K25 – pop. 16 660     **18** A1

▶ London 182 mi – Chester 28 mi – Shrewsbury 18 mi

ℹ️ Mile End Services ℰ (01691) 66 24 88, www.oswestry-welshborders.org.uk

🔟 Aston Park, ℰ (01691) 61 05 35

🔟 Llanymynech Pant, ℰ (01691) 83 09 83

X    **Walls**               🍴 ⇧ P VISA ◉◉ AE
Welsh Walls ⊠ SY11 1AW – ℰ (01691) 670 970 – www.the-walls.co.uk – Closed
26 December and 1 January
**Rest** – Menu £ 15 – Carte £ 21/33
♦ Built in 1841 as a school; now a buzzy restaurant. High ceiling with wooden
rafters; original wood flooring. Friendly atmosphere. Varied menu offers some adventurous options.

**at Rhydycroesau** West : 3.25 mi on B 4580 – ⊠ Oswestry

🏠   **Pen-Y-Dyffryn Country H.** ⍒      ⪡ 🛋 🕯 ⒯⒯ **P** _VISA_ ⦿
⊠ SY10 7JD – ℰ (01691) 653 700 – www.peny.co.uk
**12 rm** ⊻ – ♥£ 85/110 ♥♥£ 136/164
**Rest** – (dinner only) (booking essential for non-residents) Menu £ 36
◆ Peaceful 19C listed rectory in five-acre informal gardens near Offa's Dyke. Cosy
lounge, friendly ambience; good-sized, individually styled rooms, four in the
coach house. Home-cooked dishes utilising organic ingredients.

---

**OUNDLE** – Northamptonshire – **504** S26 – pop. 5 219                **17** C3
– ⊠ Peterborough

▶ London 89 mi – Leicester 37 mi – Northampton 30 mi
🛈 14 West St ℰ (01832) 27 43 33, www.northamptonshiretouristguide.com
🛅 Benefield Rd, ℰ (01832) 27 32 67

XX   **Oundle Mill** with rm         🚗 🕮 ⒯⒯ **P** _VISA_ ⦿
Barnwell Rd, South : 1 mi by West St and Mill Rd ⊠ PE8 5PB – ℰ (01832)
272 621 – www.oundlemill.co.uk
**2 rm** ⊻ – ♥£ 320 ♥♥£ 320    **Rest** – Menu £ 17/21 – Carte £ 22/47
◆ 17C limestone watermill on the banks of the Nene. Interior fuses original features with strikingly modern new designs, including glass floors looking down to
the water. Detailed modern British cooking; locally and ethically sourced produce.
Well-appointed bedrooms boasts low beams and original mill workings.

**at Fotheringhay** North : 3.75 mi by A 427 off A 605 – ⊠ Peterborough (cambs.)

🏠   **Castle Farm** without rest          🚗 🕯 ⚿ ⒯⒯ **P**
⊠ PE8 5HZ – ℰ (01832) 226 200 – www.castlefarm-guesthouse.co.uk
**5 rm** ⊻ – ♥£ 45/50 ♥♥£ 80/90
◆ Large 19C wisteria-clad former farmhouse, with lawned gardens leading down
to the river. Comfy open-fired lounge with country views and traditionally styled
bedrooms; two are in the wing.

🍴   **Falcon Inn**           🚗 🕮 ⇔ **P** _VISA_ ⦿ AE ①
⊠ PE8 5HZ – ℰ (01832) 226 254 – www.thefalcon-inn.co.uk
**Rest** – Menu £ 16 (lunch) – Carte £ 23/32 ⍒
◆ Attractive ivy-clad inn with neat garden and terrace, set in a pretty village.
Good-sized menus include unusual combinations and some interesting modern
takes on traditional dishes.

---

**OXFORD** – Oxfordshire – **503** Q28 – pop. 146 692 ▯ Great Britain     **10** B2
▶ London 59 mi – Birmingham 63 mi – Brighton 105 mi – Bristol 73 mi
**Access** Swinford Bridge (toll)
⛴ to Abingdon Bridge (Salter Bros. Ltd) (summer only) daily (2 h)
🛈 15-16 Broad St ℰ (01865) 25 22 00, www.visitoxfordandoxfordshire.com
◎ City★★★ - Christ Church★★ (Hall★★ **AC**, Tom Quad★, Tom Tower★, Cathedral★
**AC** - Choir Roof★) BZ – Merton College★★ **AC** BZ - Magdalen College★★ BZ
– Ashmolean Museum★★ BY **M1** - Bodleian Library★★ (Ceiling★★, Lierne
Vaulting★) **AC** BZ **A1** – St John's College★ BY - The Queen's College★ BZ
– Lincoln College★ BZ - Trinity College (Chapel★) BY – New College (Chapel★) **AC**,
BZ – Radcliffe Camera★ BZ **P1** – Sheldonian Theatre★ **AC**, BZ **T** – University
Museum of National History★ BY **M4** – Pitt Rivers Museum★ BY **M3**
◎ Iffley Church★ AZ **A**. Woodstock : Blenheim Palace★★★ (Park★★★) **AC**, NW : 8 mi
by A 4144 and A 34 AY

Plans on following pages

## OXFORD

ENGLAND

### Randolph

Beaumont St. ⊠ OX1 2LN – 𝒞 (0844) 879 91 32
– www.macdonaldhotels.co.uk                                    BY**n**
**142 rm** – ♺£ 134/294 ♺♺£ 174/324, ⊇ £ 17.50 – 9 suites
**Rest Restaurant at the Randolph** – 𝒞 (01865) 256 410 *(dinner only and lunch Saturday-Sunday)* Menu £ 30 – Carte £ 39/58

♦ Grand Victorian edifice. Lounge bar: deep burgundy, polished wood and chandeliers. Handsome rooms in a blend of rich fabrics; some, more spacious, have half-tester beds. Spacious, linen-clad Restaurant.

535

# OXFORD

## COLLEGES

## 🏠 Malmaison                                         🛏 ⌖ 🅰 🕿 🔏 🚗 VISA ⚌ AE
*3 Oxford Castle* ⊠ *OX1 1AY* – ℰ *(01865) 268 400* – *www.malmaison.com*
**92 rm** – †£ 155/265, ††£ 155/265, �)☌ £ 15 – 3 suites                         BZ**a**
**Rest** *Brasserie* – see restaurant listing
◆ Unique hotel in an old 13C prison not far from the castle. Pleasant rooftop terrace contrasts with moody interior: the most characterful bedrooms are in the old A Wing Cells; feature rooms are in the Governors House and House of Correction.

## 🏠 Old Bank                                          🛏 ⌖ 🅰 ⌖ 🕪 🔏 P VISA ⚌ AE
*92-94 High St.* ⊠ *OX1 4BN* – ℰ *(01865) 799 599* – *www.oldbank-hotel.co.uk*
**41 rm** – †£ 132/255, ††£ 132/305, ☌ £ 13.95 – 1 suite                         BZ**s**
**Rest** *Quod* – see restaurant listing
◆ Warm, welcoming hotel in the heart of the city, with smart neo-classical façade – formerly the area's first bank. Sleek, elegant bedrooms display modern furnishings and eclectic artwork; those higher up boast great views. Personable team.

## 🏠 Old Parsonage                                     ⌂ 🅰 🕪 VISA ⚌ AE
*1 Banbury Rd.* ⊠ *OX2 6NN* – ℰ *(01865) 310 210*
– *www.oldparsonage-hotel.co.uk*                                                 BY**e**
**30 rm** – †£ 105/198, ††£ 133/295, ☌ £ 14
**Rest** – Menu £ 18 (weekday lunch) – Carte £ 33/42
◆ Discreet address with airy, minimalist feel. Characterful guest areas include a library, richly coloured bar-lounge and terrace. Some of the bedrooms boast balconies or gardens. Afternoon tea is followed by contemporary Mediterranean dinner, with jazz on Fridays.

## 🏠 Remont *without rest*                             🚗 🛏 ⌖ ⌖ 🕪 P VISA ⚌ AE
*367 Banbury Rd.* ⊠ *OX2 7PL* – ℰ *(01865) 311 020* – *www.remont-oxford.co.uk*
– *Closed 17 December-5 January*                                                 AY**c**
**25 rm** ☌ – †£ 75/139, ††£ 89/139
◆ Stylish hotel on outskirts of city. Crisp, contemporary bedrooms; superior rooms have sofas; rear room quietest. Light, airy breakfast room with buffet counter overlooks garden.

## 🏠 Burlington House *without rest*                    ⌖ ⌖ P VISA ⚌ AE
*374 Banbury Rd* ⊠ *OX2 7PP* – ℰ *(01865) 513 513* – *www.burlington-house.co.uk*
– *Closed 20 December-6 January*                                                 AY**a**
**12 rm** ☌ – †£ 66/96, ††£ 86/116
◆ Handsome former merchant's house dating from 1889, with smart lounge, Japanese courtyard and modern bedrooms (compact singles). Breakfast includes homemade bread and granola, served on blue china.

## 🍴🍴 4550 Miles from Delhi                            VISA ⚌ AE
*40-41 Park End St* ⊠ *OX1 1JD* – ℰ *(01865) 244 922*
– *www.milesfromdelhi.com/oxford*                                                BZ**v**
**Rest** – Indian – Carte £ 18/30
◆ Capacious restaurant with open kitchen and friendly staff. Fantastic choice includes sizzling Tandoori specialities, Tawa dishes from the Punjab and good vegetarian selection.

## 🍴🍴 Shanghai 30's                                    VISA ⚌ AE ⓪
*82 St Aldates* ⊠ *OX1 1RA* – ℰ *(01865) 242 230* – *www.shanghai30s.com*
– *Closed 19 December-4 January and Monday lunch*                                BZ**n**
**Rest** – Chinese – Menu £ 11/23 – Carte £ 14/27
◆ Colonial-style restaurant in characterful 15C building; sit in more intimate wood panelled room. Menu focuses on fiery Sichuan and Shanghainese cooking. Friendly, eager staff.

## 🍴🍴 Brasserie Blanc                                  🅰 ⌖ VISA ⚌ AE
*71-72 Walton St.* ⊠ *OX2 6AG* – ℰ *(01865) 510 999* – *www.brasserieblanc.com*
– *Closed 25 December*                                                           AY**z**
**Rest** – French – Menu £ 14/16 – Carte £ 21/42
◆ Busy, informal brasserie; striking interior and sharp service; French regional recipes with the new-wave touch: John Dory with coriander or ribeye steak in béarnaise.

ENGLAND

ENGLAND

XX **Brasserie** – at Malmaison Hotel    AC VISA ⊙⊙ AE ①

*3 Oxford Castle* ⊠ *OX1 1AY* – ℰ *(01865) 268 400* – *www.malmaison.com*
**Rest** – Carte £ 24/45    BZ**a**

• Basement brasserie in a unique hotel that was once a prison. Private dining rooms are in the old cells and original metal staircases remain. Modern British cooking displays French influences.

XX **Quod** – at Old Bank Hotel    ⌂ AC P VISA ⊙⊙ AE

*92-94 High St.* ⊠ *OX1 4BN* – ℰ *(01865) 202 505* – *www.oldbank-hotel.co.uk*
**Rest** – Menu £ 15 (lunch) – Carte £ 20/33    BZ**s**

• Lively Italian-influenced brasserie with busy, buzzy vibe, set within a city centre hotel and once the banking hall of the area's first bank. Accessible menu and twice-daily blackboard specials.

X **Branca**    AC VISA ⊙⊙ ①

*111 Walton St.* ⊠ *OX2 6AJ* – ℰ *(01865) 556 111* – *www.branca-restaurants.com*
*– Closed 25-26 December*    BY**a**
**Rest** – Italian – Carte £ 19/31

• Modern restaurant with casual, friendly feel and minimalist décor. Vibrant, simple, fresh Italian influenced dishes: antipasti taster plates, pasta and pizza are specialities.

X **Fishers**    AC VISA ⊙⊙ AE

*36-37 St Clements* ⊠ *OX4 1AB* – ℰ *(01865) 243 003*
*– www.fishers-restaurant.com* *– Closed 25-26 Decmber and 1 January*
**Rest** – Seafood – Menu £ 20 (lunch) – Carte £ 26/33    AZ**a**

• Well-established seafood restaurant on eastern side of city, with paper-topped tables, rustic décor and lively, informal atmosphere. Daily changing menus; friendly service.

🏠 **Magdalen Arms**    🍴 VISA ⊙⊙

⊛ *243 Iffley Rd* ⊠ *OX4 1SJ* – ℰ *(01865) 243 159* – *Closed 2 weeks August, 24-26 December, 1 January, Sunday dinner, Tuesday lunch, Monday and bank holidays*
**Rest** – Carte £ 26/38    AZ**s**

• Battleship-grey pub that's a hit with the locals, boasting quirky standard lamps, eclectic 1920s posters, board games and a bar billiards table. Tasty, good value dishes rely on seasonal local produce. Delicious fresh juices and homemade lemonade.

🏠 **Anchor**    ⌂ ⇔ P VISA ⊙⊙

⊛ *2 Hayfield Rd, Walton Manor* ⊠ *OX2 6TT* – ℰ *(01865) 510 282*
*– www.theanchoroxford.com* *– Closed 25-26 December*    AY**u**
**Rest** – Carte £ 24/29

• Striking art deco pub with real community feel: host to a breakfast club and regular quiz nights. Chef promotes local, seasonal ingredients and creates tasty, gutsy, carefully presented dishes.

🏠 **Black Boy**    🍴 P VISA ⊙⊙ AE

*91 Old High St, Headington* ⊠ *OX3 9HT* – ℰ *(01865) 741 137*
*– www.theblackboy.uk.com*    AY**v**
**Rest** – Carte £ 19/28

• Sizeable pub just off Headington village serving sensibly priced pub classics with a French edge. Homemade breads and pizzas; popular Sunday roasts. Thursday jazz night.

---

Symbols shown in red indicate particularly charming establishments 🏠 XxX.

OXFORD

at **Sandford-on-Thames** Southeast : 5 mi by A 4158 – ⊠ Oxford

### Oxford Thames Four Pillars
Henley Rd ⊠ OX4 4GX – ℰ (01865) 334 444
– www.four-pillars.co.uk
62 rm ⊑ – ♦£ 95/185 ♦♦£ 120/240                          AZv
**Rest** *River Room* – (closed Saturday lunch) Menu £ 18 (lunch) – Carte dinner £ 23/34
♦ Contemporary sandstone hotel set in 30 acres of peaceful parkland leading to the Thames. Bright Connoisseur rooms are the best; some have garden views and balconies. Lovely pool. Great outlook from The River Room, which has a formal air and serves old classics with a modern edge.

at **Toot Baldon** Southeast : 5.5 mi by B 480 - AZ – ⊠ Oxford

### Mole Inn
⊠ OX44 9NG – ℰ (01865) 340 001 – www.themoleinn.com – Closed 25 December
**Rest** – (booking advisable) Carte £ 27/29
♦ Popular pub with pleasant terrace and beautiful landscaped gardens. Appealing menu suits all tastes and appetites. Sourcing is taken seriously, so when ingredients are gone, they're gone.

at **Great Milton** Southeast : 12 mi by A 40 off A 329 - AY – ⊠ Oxford

### Le Manoir aux Quat' Saisons (Raymond Blanc)
Church Rd ⊠ OX44 7PD – ℰ (01844) 278 881
– www.manoir.com – Closed 3-13 January
25 rm – ♦£ 495/635 ♦♦£ 635, ⊑ £ 16 – 7 suites   **Rest** – French – Carte £ 95/125
**Spec.** Warm salmon fillet with elderflower, garden radish and yuzu cream. Wild sea bass fillet, langoustine, smoked potato mash and star anis jus. 100% chocolate textures.
♦ Majestic property providing the ultimate guest experience: service levels are unparalleled. Sumptuous, open-fired lounges and lovely terrace. Luxurious bedrooms. Cosy restaurant and conservatory offer French-inspired cuisine using seasonal garden produce. Dishes are prepared with skill, clarity and a lightness of touch.

ENGLAND

at **North Hinksey** Southwest : 3.5 mi by A 420 – ⊠ Oxford

### Gables without rest
6 Cumnor Hill ⊠ OX2 9HA – ℰ (01865) 862 153 – www.gables-guesthouse.co.uk
– Closed 25-26 December                                  AZr
5 rm ⊑ – ♦£ 50/70 ♦♦£ 75/90
♦ Proudly run guest house with welcoming owner and thoughtful touches in its immaculately kept rooms. Relaxing conservatory looks out onto pretty garden. Flexible arrival times.

### Fishes
⊠ OX2 0NA – ℰ (01865) 249 796 – www.fishesoxford.co.uk – Closed 25 December
**Rest** – Carte £ 20/40                                  AZn
♦ Lively, family-friendly pub with pretty riverside garden, perfect for picnics. Food is fresh, free range and available all day. Wednesday is steak night; Sunday means a roast.

at **Fyfield** Southwest : 9.5 mi by A 420 AZ – ⊠ Abingdon

### White Hart
Main Rd ⊠ OX13 5LW – ℰ (01865) 390 585 – www.whitehart-fyfield.com
**Rest** – (closed Monday except bank holidays) Menu £ 19 (lunch) – Carte £ 25/35
♦ 15C former chantry house with cosy, open-fired bar and impressive flag-floored, vaulted dining room. Honest British cooking relies on produce from the vegetable plot; excellent desserts.

at **Kingston Bagpuize** Southwest : 7 mi by A 420 AZ – ⊠ Oxford

### Fallowfields Country House
Faringdon Rd. ⊠ OX13 5BH – ℰ (01865) 820 416 – www.fallowfields.com
10 rm ⊑ – ♦£ 108 ♦♦£ 175   **Rest** – Menu £ 18/49
♦ 19C manor house with lawned garden and fire-lit lounge. Spacious, individually styled bedrooms boast lovely views; most have spa baths. The elephant emblem appears throughout. Modern menus feature locally sourced produce; much is home-grown.

539

**at Wolvercote** Northwest : 2.5 mi by A 4144 (Woodstock Rd) on Godstow Rd

### Trout Inn  🏠 P VISA ⓸ AE
*195 Godstow Rd ⊠ OX2 8PN – ℰ (01865) 510 930 – www.thetroutoxford.co.uk*
**Rest** – *(booking advisable)* Carte £ 22/30  AYs
• Idyllically set Cotswold stone inn with delightful riverside terrace. Menus display strong Italian influences, as well as more international dishes. Popular in summer, when booking is a must.

---

**OXHILL** – Warwickshire – **503** P27 – **pop. 303**  **19** C3
▣ London 90 mi – Banbury 11 mi – Birmingham 37 mi

### Oxbourne House ⌂  ≤ 🚗 ✕ ♈ P
⊠ CV35 0RA – ℰ (01295) 688 202 – www.oxbournehouse.com
**3 rm** ⊡ – †£ 65 ††£ 90  **Rest** – Menu £ 30
• Large brick house in a quiet village, with lovely mature garden and tennis court to the rear. Elegant, antique-furnished lounge features a wood burning stove. Comfy, immaculately kept bedrooms offer good facilities and extras; one room is split-level. Traditionally styled communal dining room offers tasty home-cooking.

---

**PADSTOW** – Cornwall – **503** F32 – **pop. 2 449**  **1** B2
▣ London 288 mi – Exeter 78 mi – Plymouth 45 mi – Truro 23 mi
🛈 North Quay ℰ (01841) 53 34 49, www.padstowlive.com
🏌 Trevose Constantine Bay, ℰ (01841) 52 02 08
◉ Town★ - Prideaux Place★
◉ Trevone (Cornwall Coast Path★★) W : 3 mi by B 3276 – Trevose Head★ (≤★★) W : 6 mi by B 3276. Bedruthan Steps★, SW : 7 mi by B 3276 – Pencarrow★, SE : 11 mi by A 389

### Metropole  ≤ 🚗 🏊 📶 ♈ P VISA ⓸ AE
*Station Rd ⊠ PL28 8DB – ℰ (01841) 532 486 – www.the-metropole.co.uk*
**58 rm** ⊡ – †£ 118/203 ††£ 152/236  BYa
**Rest** – *(bar lunch Monday-Saturday)* Menu £ 16/30
• Grand 19C hotel perched on a cliff above the old railway station, just a short walk from town. Characterful, well-appointed guest areas. Smart, contemporary bedrooms; No.6 boasts great harbour and estuary views. Simply prepared lunches; more elaborate dinners.

### Old Custom House Inn  ≤ AC rest, ✕ ♈ VISA ⓸ AE
*South Quay ⊠ PL28 8BL – ℰ (01841) 532 359 – oldcustomhousepadstow.co.uk*
**21 rm** – †£ 105/125 ††£ 120/180  BYc
**Rest Pescadou** – Seafood – *(booking essential)* Carte £ 18/31 s
• Well-run, slate hotel; formerly a grain store and exciseman's house. Smart beauty studio and ice cream parlour. Nautically themed bedrooms feature good mod cons – some have roll-top baths or harbour/estuary views. Traditional bar and open-plan seafood restaurant.

### Treverbyn House without rest  ≤ 🚗 ✕ 📞 P
*Station Rd ⊠ PL28 8DA – ℰ (01841) 532 855 – www.treverbynhouse.com*
*– Closed 25 December-13 February*  BYe
**5 rm** ⊡ – †£ 108 ††£ 120
• Charming Edwardian house built for a wine merchant. Comfortable bedrooms boast polished floors and interesting furniture from local sale rooms – one has a huge roll-top bath; some have harbour views. Breakfast in the garden or lovely dining room. Delightful owner.

### Woodlands Country House without rest  ≤ 🚗 & ♈ P VISA ⓸ AE
*Treator, West : 1.25 mi on B 3276 ⊠ PL28 8RU*
*– ℰ (01841) 532 426 – www.woodlands-padstow.co.uk*
*– Closed 20 December-1 February*
**8 rm** ⊡ – †£ 88/94 ††£ 126/138
• Characterful Victorian country house with great coastal outlook to rear. Tastefully furnished lounge, breakfast room and honesty bar; pictures, books and objets d'art abound. Comfy, homely bedrooms; Beach is the largest and best. Homemade muesli and hot specials at breakfast.

ENGLAND

PADSTOW

ENGLAND

⌂ **Treann** without rest  ← 🚄 🤚 📶 📱 P̄ VISA ⬤⬤
24 Dennis Rd ⊠ PL28 8DE – ℰ (01841) 533 855 – www.treannhouse.com
– Closed Christmas-February   BZ**n**
**3 rm** ⌴ – ♦£ 85/95 ♦♦£ 125
♦ Edwardian house set in an elevated position, with first floor views over the Camel Estuary. Chic breakfast room, cool lounge and superb bedrooms which mix antiques with contemporary furnishings to create an understated, elegant style.

⌂ **Althea Library** without rest  📶 📶 📱 P̄ VISA ⬤⬤
27 High St, (access via Church St.) ⊠ PL28 8BB – ℰ (01841) 532 717
– www.althealibrary.co.uk – Closed 30 April-1 May and 22-26 December
**3 rm** ⌴ – ♦£ 80/96 ♦♦£ 96   AY**g**
♦ Grade II listed former school library, just 5min from the harbour. Homely lounge and breakfast room. Beamed bedrooms boast sitting areas and smart bathrooms. Lovely terraced garden with pond.

Guesthouses ⌂ don't provide the same level of service as hotels. They are often characterised by a warm welcome and a décor which reflects the owner's personality. Those shown in red ⌂ are particularly pleasant.

541

ENGLAND

XX **Seafood** with rm       AC rest, ⁽¹⁾ **P** *VISA* ◑◑
*Riverside ⊠ PL28 8BY – ℰ (01841) 532 700 – www.rickstein.com*
*– Closed dinner 24-26 December and 1 May*     BY**k**
**20 rm** � – †£ 97 ††£ 280
**Rest** – Seafood – *(booking essential)* Menu £ 37 – Carte £ 40/81
♦ Relaxed, stylish seafood restaurant dominated by large stainless steel topped bar. Daily menu of fresh local fish and shellfish, ranging from three types of simply prepared oysters to chilli crab or monkfish vindaloo. New England style bedrooms boast quality furnishings; some have terraces or balconies and bay views.

XX **Paul Ainsworth at No.6**        *VISA* ◑◑ ◑
*6 Middle St ⊠ PL28 8AP – ℰ (01841) 532 093 – www.number6inpadstow.co.uk*
*– Closed 10 January-1 February, 24-26 December, Sunday-Monday October-May and Monday June-November (except bank holidays)*     BY**n**
**Rest** – Menu £ 20 (lunch) **s** – Carte £ 34/39 **s**
♦ Delightful bright yellow Georgian townhouse on a harbour backwater. L-shaped bar and restaurant with black & white floor tiles. Relaxed air and friendly, enthusiastic service. Precise, modern, seasonal cooking with artistic presentation.

XX **St Petroc's** with rm        ⛲ 🚗 *VISA* ◑◑
*4 New St ⊠ PL28 8EA – ℰ (01841) 532 700 – www.rickstein.com*
*– Closed 24-26 December and 1 May*     BY**m**
**10 rm** ⊠ – †£ 145/220 ††£ 145/220 – 2 suites
**Rest** – Seafood – *(booking essential)* Carte £ 26/42
♦ Attractive house on a steep hill, with pine-furnished bistro and terrace running down one side. Unfussy, largely seafood-based menu offers simply prepared, old-fashioned favourites. Smart, well-appointed bedrooms in house/annexe; small lounge and quiet library.

X **Rick Stein's Café** with rm       ⛲ ⁽¹⁾ *VISA* ◑◑
(☺) *10 Middle St ⊠ PL28 8AP – ℰ (01841) 532 700 – www.rickstein.com*
*– Closed dinner 25-26 December and 2 May*     BY**p**
**3 rm** ⊠ – †£ 97/105 ††£ 105/145
**Rest** – *(booking essential at dinner)* Menu £ 22 – Carte £ 23/29
♦ Deceptively large café hidden behind a tiny shop front on a small side street. Concise, seasonally changing menu of tasty, unfussy cooking with influences from Thailand, Morocco and the Med. Homemade bread to start; great value set menus. Comfy, simply furnished bedrooms. Breakfast in café or small courtyard garden.

X **Margot's**        *VISA* ◑◑ AE ◑
*11 Duke St ⊠ PL28 8AB – ℰ (01841) 533 441 – Closed January, 24-31 December, Sunday and Monday*     BY**r**
**Rest** – *(booking essential at dinner)* Menu £ 23/30
♦ Small yellow and blue bistro with relaxed atmosphere and loyal local following. Daily menu features the latest seasonal produce. Dinner also offers a good value set selection and tasting menu.

**at Little Petherick** South : 3 mi on A 389 – ⊠ Wadebridge

🏠 **Molesworth Manor** without rest       ≤ 🚗 🍴 **P**
*⊠ PL27 7QT – ℰ (01841) 540 292 – www.molesworth.co.uk*
*– February-October*
**9 rm** ⊠ – †£ 75/80 ††£ 115
♦ Part 17C and 19C former rectory. Charming individual establishment with inviting country house atmosphere amid antique furniture and curios. Rooms furnished in period style.

**at St Merryn** West : 2.5 mi by A 389 on B 3276  – **503** F32 – ⊠ Padstow

🍴 **Rosel & Co.**                                                                    VISA ◍ AE
*The Dog House* ⊠ PL28 8NF – 𝒞 (01841) 521 289 – www.roselandco.co.uk
*– Closed November-March, Sunday and Monday*
**Rest** – *(dinner only)* Menu £ 35
♦ Simply styled restaurant with chunky wooden tables, open kitchen and warm,
relaxed ambience. Concise menu of precise, flavourful cooking: well-sourced ingredients used to create classic combinations with interesting modern twists.

🍺 **Cornish Arms**                                                          ⌂ P VISA ◍
*Churchtown* ⊠ PL28 8ND – 𝒞 (01841) 532 700 – www.rickstein.com
**Rest** – Carte £ 18/27
♦ A real locals pub, surprisingly leased by Rick Stein. Sound, sensibly priced cooking offer typical pub dishes and a few fish specials; and doesn't exclude the regulars. Smart terrace.

**at Constantine Bay** West : 4 mi by B 3276 – ⊠ Padstow

🏨 **Treglos** ✆                        ⇐ 🚗 ⌂ 🖥 🕌 & rm, AC rest, P 🏮 VISA ◍
⊠ PL28 8JH – 𝒞 (01841) 520 727 – www.tregloshotel.com – March-November
**38 rm** 🖵 – � £ 70/177 ♦♦£ 140/236 – 4 suites
**Rest** – *(bar lunch Monday-Saturday)* Menu £ 30 – Carte £ 30/50
♦ An extensive, family run building surrounded by garden. Facilities include
games rooms, children's play area and a lounge bar. Consistently decorated,
bright, neat bedrooms. Smart attire the code in very comfortable dining room.

**at St Issey** South : 3.5 mi on A 389 – ⊠ Wadebridge

🏠 **Higher Trevorrick Country House** ✆               ⇐ 🚗 📶 P VISA ◍
*Northwest : 0.75 mi by Burgois rd on Sea Mills and Trevorrick rd.* ⊠ PL27 7QH
*– 𝒞 (01841) 540 943 – www.higher-trevorrick.co.uk – Closed January*
**3 rm** 🖵 – ♦£ 156/201 ♦♦£ 108/138   **Rest** – *(closed Tuesday)* Menu £ 28
♦ Restored property with spectacular first floor views out over Camel Estuary
and towards Rock. Spacious, well-kept bedrooms. Experienced, personable owners. No children policy. Daily changing menu served in pleasant conservatory
overlooking garden.

---

**PAINSWICK** – Gloucestershire – **503** N28 – **pop. 1 666** ▌ Great Britain        **4** C1
▶ London 107 mi – Bristol 35 mi – Cheltenham 10 mi – Gloucester 7 mi
◉ Town ★

🏨 **Cotswolds 88**                                       🚗 ⌂ ❄ 📞 P VISA ◍
*Kemps Ln* ⊠ GL6 6YB – 𝒞 (01452) 813 688 – www.cotswolds88hotel.com
**17 rm** 🖵 – ♦£ 88/95 ♦♦£ 95/395   **Rest** – Menu £ 18/45 – Carte £ 22/33
♦ Stone-built, Regency-style house with attractive garden and terrace. Bold stylish colours, quirky furnishings and striking fixtures abound. Eclectic bedrooms
and modern bathrooms. Restaurant offers modern menu of organic produce.

---

**PATELEY BRIDGE** – North Yorkshire – **502** O21 – **pop. 2 504**                **22** B2
– ⊠ **Harrogate** ▌ Great Britain
▶ London 225 mi – Leeds 28 mi – Middlesbrough 46 mi – York 32 mi
🛈 18 High St 𝒞 (01423) 71 11 47, www.aboutbritain.com
◉ Fountains Abbey ★★★ AC - Studley Royal AC (⇐ ★ from Anne Boleyn's Seat)
- Fountains Hall (Fa 0.5ade★), NE : 8.5 mi by B 6265

ENGLAND

PATELEY BRIDGE

**at Ramsgill-in-Nidderdale** Northwest : 5 mi by Low Wath Rd – ⊠ Harrogate

XXX   **Yorke Arms** (Frances Atkins) with rm      🚗 🛜 ✝ P VISA ⊛
✿     ⊠ HG3 5RL – ☏ (01423) 755 243 – www.yorke-arms.co.uk
**15 rm** (dinner included) ☕ – ♦£ 150/250 ♦♦£ 340/399 – 1 suite
**Rest** – (closed Sunday dinner to non-residents) Menu £ 35 (lunch)
– Carte (dinner) £ 51/63 ⊛
**Spec.** Stuffed oxtail pastry, celery and truffle cream. Grouse with bilberries, roots
and a heather scented jus. Tarragon parfait, pistachio brûlée, lemon and roasted fig
◆ Charming, part-17C former shooting lodge overlooking a small village green
and run in a friendly, professional manner. Traditional, antique-furnished restaurant with beamed ceiling and open fires. Measured and accomplished classical
cooking demonstrates a good understanding for flavours; modern presentation.
Bedrooms have a subtle modern style and offer good comforts.

**PATRICK BROMPTON** – North Yorkshire – **502** P21 – ⊠ Bedale    **22** B1
▶ London 242 mi – Newcastle upon Tyne 58 mi – York 43 mi

⌂   **Elmfield House**   🚗 🐕 🏊 ✝ P VISA ⊛ AE
Arrathorne, Northwest : 2.25 mi by A 684 on Richmond rd ⊠ DL8 1NE
– ☏ (01677) 450 558 – www.elmfieldhouse.co.uk
**4 rm** ☕ – ♦£ 65/70 ♦♦£ 86    **Rest** – Menu £ 15
◆ Spacious, uncluttered guest house set in peaceful farmland, with nearby fishing lake and 14 acre forest. Neat, classically styled bedrooms with modern
touches; some four-posters.

⌂   **Mill Close Farm** without rest   🚗 ✝ P VISA ⊛
Patrick Brompton ⊠ DL8 1JY – ☏ (01677) 450 257 – www.millclose.co.uk
– Closed January and December
**3 rm** ☕ – ♦£ 50/65 ♦♦£ 80/100
◆ Modernised farmhouse with walled garden and summerhouse. Bedrooms
blend contemporary furnishings with traditional features and have an uncluttered, homely feel; two boast whirlpool baths.

**PATTISWICK** – Essex – see Coggeshall

**PAULERSPURY** – Northamptonshire – **503** R27 – see Towcester

**PAXFORD** – Gloucestershire – **504** O27 – see Chipping Camden

**PENN** – Buckinghamshire – **504** R/S29 – pop. 3 779    **11** D2
▶ London 31 mi – High Wycombe 4 mi – Oxford 36 mi

🍴   **Old Queens Head**   🚗 🛜 P VISA ⊛ AE
Hammersley Ln ⊠ HP10 8EY – ☏ (01494) 813 371
– www.oldqueensheadpenn.co.uk – Closed 25-26 December
**Rest** – Carte £ 22/29
◆ Lively pub with characterful rustic feel, part-dating back to 1666; head for the
old barn. Menus offer generous, hearty dishes and some appealing sides. Homemade puddings are a must.

**PENRITH** – Cumbria – **501** L19 – pop. 14 471    **21** B2
▶ London 290 mi – Carlisle 24 mi – Kendal 31 mi – Lancaster 48 mi
🛈 Middlegate ☏ (01768) 86 74 66, www.penrithtown.co.uk
🔟 Salkeld Rd, ☏ (01768) 89 19 19
544

↑ **Brooklands** without rest                          ⚛ ⁽¹⁾ VISA ⦿ ⓘ

⊠ 2 Portland Pl ⊠ CA11 7QN – ℰ (01768) 863 395
– www.brooklandsguesthouse.com – Closed Christmas and New Year
**6 rm** ⌂ – ♦£ 40/60 ♦♦£ 85

◆ Victorian terraced house located close to the town centre; run by warm, welcoming owners. Traditional, antique-furnished hall and smart breakfast room with marble-topped tables. Homely, pine-furnished bedrooms boast good modern facilities; one has a four-poster.

**at Temple Sowerby** East : 6.75 mi by A 66 – ⊠ Penrith

🏠 **Temple Sowerby House**                    ⚛ ⁽¹⁾ ⚙ P VISA ⦿

⊠ CA10 1RZ – ℰ (01768) 361 578 – www.templesowerby.com – Closed Christmas-New Year
**12 rm** ⌂ – ♦£ 90/110 ♦♦£ 125/160
**Rest** – (dinner only) (booking essential to non residents) Menu £ 40

◆ Attractive, red-brick Georgian mansion with spacious, classically styled guest areas. Traditional country house bedrooms boast antique furnishings and contemporary facilities. Modern menus of local, seasonal produce served overlooking enclosed, lawned gardens.

**at Clifton** Southeast : 3 mi on A 6

🏠 **George and Dragon** with rm                  🏠 ⁽¹⁾ P VISA ⦿ ⒜Ⓔ

⊠ CA10 2ER – ℰ (01768) 865 381 – www.georgeanddragonclifton.co.uk – closed 26 December
**10 rm** ⌂ – ♦£ 75 ♦♦£ 145   **Rest** – Carte £ 22/39

◆ 18C coaching inn belonging to local landowners, the Lowther family. Simple, effective cooking; organic meats, seasonal game and vegetables come fresh from the surrounding estate. Comfortable, modern bedrooms are decorated in bold colours.

**at Newbiggin** West : 3.5 mi by A 66 – ⊠ Penrith

↑ **Old School**                              ⚛ ⚛ ⁽¹⁾ P VISA ⦿

⊠ CA11 0HT – ℰ (01768) 483 709 – www.theold-school.com – Closed 23 December-1 January
**3 rm** ⌂ – ♦£ 38/55 ♦♦£ 75/80   **Rest** – Carte approx. £ 20

◆ Grey-stone Victorian schoolhouse in a small village. Compact, traditionally styled guest areas. Classical bedrooms are named after the colour of their décor – red, green and blue – the latter is the largest and has the best outlook. Home-cooked meals.

**PENZANCE** – Cornwall – **503** D33 – pop. 20 255                 **1** A3

🚹 London 319 mi – Exeter 113 mi – Plymouth 77 mi – Taunton 155 mi

**Access** Access to the Isles of Scilly by helicopter, British International Heliport (01736) 364296, Fax (01736) 363871

🚢 to the Isles of Scilly (Hugh Town) (Isles of Scilly Steamship Co. Ltd) (summer only) (approx. 2 h 40 mn)

🛈 Station Rd ℰ (01736) 362 2 07, www.purelypenzance.co.uk

◉ Town★ - Outlook★★★ – Western Promenade (≼★★★) YZ – National Lighthouse Centre★ **AC** Y – Chapel St★ Y – Maritime Museum★ **AC** Y **M1** – Penlee House Gallery and Museum★, **AC**

◉ St Buryan★★ (church tower★★), SW : 5 mi by A 30 and B 3283 - Penwith★★ – Trengwainton Garden★★, NW : 2 mi – Sancreed - Church★★ (Celtic Crosses★★) - Carn Euny★, W : 3.5 mi by A 30 Z – St Michael's Mount★★ (≼★★), E : 4 mi by B 3311 - Y - and A 30 – Gulval★ (Church★), NE : 1 mi – Ludgvan★ (Church★), NE : 3.5 mi by A 30 - Chysauster Village★, N : 3.5 mi by A 30, B 3311 and minor rd – Newlyn★ - Pilchard Works★, SW : 1.5 mi by B 3315 Z - Lanyon Quoit★, NW : 3.5 mi by St Clare Street – Men-an-Tol★, NW : 5 mi by B 3312 - Madron Church★, NW : 1.5 mi by St Clare Street Y. Morvah (≼★★), NW : 6.5 mi by St Clare Street Y – Zennor (Church★), NW : 6 mi by B 3311 Y – Prussia Cove★, E : 8 mi by B 3311 - Y - and A 394 – Land's End★ (cliff scenery★★★), SW : 10 mi by A 30 Z – Porthcurno★, SW : 8.5 mi by A 30, B 3283 and minor rd

Plan on next page

ENGLAND

## Hotel Penzance

⟨ 🚗 🍽 📶 📶 🅿 VISA ⑩ AE

*Britons Hill ⊠ TR18 3AE – ℰ (01736) 363 117 – www.hotelpenzance.com*
*– Closed first 2 weeks January*
**25 rm** ☐ – †£ 85/125 ††£ 190/195                                    **Yc**
**Rest** *Bay* – see restaurant listing
♦ Adjoining Edwardian merchants' houses, overlooking the bay and St Michael's Mount. Several lounges, pleasant garden terrace and outdoor pool. Mix of classic and contemporary bedrooms.

## Abbey

🚗 📶 🅿 VISA ⑩ AE

*Abbey St ⊠ TR18 4AR – ℰ (01736) 366 906 – www.theabbeyonline.co.uk*
*– Closed January-February and December except 20 December-4 January*
**6 rm** ☐ – †£ 75/90 ††£ 150/200 – 2 suites                          **Yu**
**Rest** *Untitled by Robert Wright* 😊 – see restaurant listing
♦ 17C country house in powder blue, with tranquil walled gardens. Relaxed, slightly quirky atmosphere with shabby-chic charm. Lovely antique-filled sitting room and bright, well-kept bedrooms.

🏠 **Beachfield** ← �🅟 _VISA_ ⓒⓞ ⒜⒠
_The Promenade ⊠ TR18 4NW – ℘ (01736) 362 067 – www.beachfield.co.uk_
_– Closed 2 weeks Christmas-New Year_ **Za**
**18 rm** ⌁ – †£ 58/93 ††£ 125/160   **Rest** – _(dinner only)_ Carte £ 20/33
♦ Classic seaside hotel with good views. Well-kept public areas include traditional lounge. Comfy bedrooms are well maintained and have a neat, bright feel. Traditional, varied menus, featuring fish specials.

🏠 **Chy-An-Mor** without rest ← ⌁ ⅍ ⅏ ⅌ ℗ _VISA_ ⓒⓞ ⓞ
_15 Regent Terr ⊠ TR18 4DW – ℘ (01736) 363 441 – www.chyanmor.co.uk – 16_
_March-14 November_ **Ye**
**9 rm** ⌁ – †£ 40/70 ††£ 80/90
♦ Terraced guesthouse overlooking the promenade. Lounge displays various artefacts from the charming owners' travels. Bedrooms boast lovely soft furnishings; some have 6ft iron beds.

🏠 **Summer House** ⌁ ℞ ⅍ ⅏ ℗ _VISA_ ⓒⓞ
_Cornwall Ter ⊠ TR18 4HL – ℘ (01736) 363 744_
_– www.summerhouse-cornwall.com – Closed 1 April to 30 September_
**5 rm** ⌁ – †£ 95/120 ††£ 120/150   **Rest** – Menu £ 39 **Zs**
♦ There's a friendly atmosphere to this listed Regency House in bright blues and yellows. Pleasant patio garden. Residents can enjoy Mediterranean influenced cooking.

✗✗ **Untitled by Robert Wright** – at Abbey Hotel ⒜⒞ _VISA_ ⓒⓞ ⓞ
☺ _Abbey St ⊠ TR18 4AR – ℘ (01736) 448 022 – www.untitledbyrobertwright.com_
_– Closed Sunday-Monday_ **Yc**
**Rest** – _(booking essential at dinner)_ Carte £ 26/28
♦ The chef credits Alistair Little for instilling in him the philosophy of simplicity and keeping flavours honest. A slight French edge runs through the menu, where the focus is on fish. Alternatively, you can order tapas on the ground floor.

✗✗ **Bay** – at Hotel Penzance ← ⌁ ℞ ⒜⒦ ℗ _VISA_ ⓒⓞ ⒜⒠
_Britons Hill ⊠ TR18 3AE – ℘ (01736) 366 890 – www.bay-penzance.co.uk_
_– Closed first 2 weeks January_ **Yc**
**Rest** – _(closed Saturday lunch) (booking essential for non-residents)_
Menu £ 16/30 – Carte £ 20/45
♦ Large, contemporary hotel restaurant with lovely terrace boasting harbour views. Adventurous modern menus showcase local produce. Every third Sunday, lunch comes from within a 25 mile radius.

✗✗ **Harris's** _VISA_ ⓒⓞ
_46 New St ⊠ TR18 2LZ – ℘ (01736) 364 408 – www.harrissrestaurant.co.uk_
_– Closed 3 weeks winter, 25-26 December, Sunday and Monday except Monday_
_dinner June-September_ **Ya**
**Rest** – Carte £ 27/46
♦ Long-standing, split-level restaurant with spiral staircase and unusual metal ceiling; run by keen husband and wife. Classical cooking uses seasonal Cornish produce – everything is homemade.

**at Gulval** Northeast : 1.25 mi by A 30

🍴 **Coldstreamer** with rm _VISA_ ⓒⓞ ⓞ
⊠ _TR18 3BB – ℘ (01736) 362 072 – www.coldstreamer-penzance.co.uk – Closed_
_25 December_
**3 rm** ⌁ – †£ 60/75 ††£ 70/85
**Rest** – Menu £ 17 (weekday lunch) – Carte £ 20/28
♦ Handsome pub in the heart of Gulval with large bar and bright dining room. Concise menus feature local, seasonal produce; cooking is clean, generous and modern, with more elaborate dishes in the evening. Popular wine dinners. Fresh, well-appointed bedrooms.

**PERRANUTHNOE** – Cornwall – **503** D33 – see Marazion

ENGLAND

## PERSHORE – Worcestershire – **503** N27 – pop. 7 104

▶ London 106 mi – Birmingham 33 mi – Worcester 8 mi

↑ **Barn** without rest ⇐ 🚗 ✗ ⌖ **P**
*Pensham Hill House, Pensham, Southeast : 1 mi by B 4084* ✉ *WR10 3HA*
*– 𝒞 (01386) 555 270 – www.pensham-barn.co.uk*
**3 rm** ☑ – ♦£ 55 ♦♦£ 90
♦ Stylish barn renovation in enviable hillside location. Attractive open-plan lounge and breakfast area with exposed roof timbers. Rooms individually styled to a high standard.

✗✗ **Belle House** 🅰🅲 ⇔ 𝗩𝗜𝗦𝗔 ⓿⓿ 🅰🅴
*Bridge St* ✉ *WR10 1AJ – 𝒞 (01386) 555 055 – www.belle-house.co.uk*
*– Closed first 2 weeks January, 24-25 December, Sunday and Monday*
**Rest** – Menu £ 21/32 **s**
♦ 16C and 18C high street building with some very characterful parts, including heavily beamed bar. Accomplished cooking on modern menus using carefully sourced ingredients.

**at Eckington** South : 4 mi by A 4104 on B 4080

↑ **Eckington Manor** 🚗 �"" **P** 𝗩𝗜𝗦𝗔 ⓿⓿
*Manor Farm, Hammock Rd, (by Drakesbridge Rd.)* ✉ *WR10 3BH*
*– 𝒞 (01386) 751 600 – www.eckingtonmanor.co.uk*
**14 rm** ☑ – ♦£ 65/150 ♦♦£ 110/275    **Rest** – Menu £ 32
♦ Characterful converted 13C manor house with popular cookery school, set on a 260 acre working farm. Comfortable, contemporary bedrooms and stylish bathrooms with underfloor heating. Dinner served Friday and Saturday in the cookery school.

## PETERBOROUGH – Peterborough – **502** T26 – pop. 136 292

▌ Great Britain

▶ London 85 mi – Cambridge 35 mi – Leicester 41 mi – Lincoln 51 mi
ℹ Bridge St 𝒞 (01733) 45 23 36, www.visitpeterborough.com
⛳ Thorpe Wood Nene Parkway, 𝒞 (01733) 26 77 01
⛳ Peterborough Milton Milton Ferry, 𝒞 (01733) 38 04 89
⛳ Orton Meadows Ham Lane, 𝒞 (01733) 23 74 78
◎ Cathedral ★★ **AC** Y

✗ **Jim's Bistro** 🅰🅲 𝗩𝗜𝗦𝗔 ⓿⓿
*52 Broadway* ✉ *PE1 1SB – 𝒞 (01733) 341 122 – www.jimsyard.biz*
*– Closed 24 December-6 January, last week July, first week August, Sunday and Monday*                                                                                      **Y a**
**Rest** – Carte £ 20/37 **s**
♦ Bright room with quirky mural, bar and open-plan kitchen; choose banquette seating under the mirror. Daily changing menu of tasty, wholesome, seasonal dishes. Friendly service.

🍴 **Beehive** 🍴 🅰🅲 𝗩𝗜𝗦𝗔 ⓿⓿
*62 Albert Pl.* ✉ *PE1 1DD – 𝒞 (01733) 310 600 – www.jimsyard.biz – Closed 1
January and Sunday dinner*                                                                                 **Z x**
**Rest** – Carte £ 20/29
♦ Just off the city centre ring road, with smart, modern interior, stripped floorboards, zinc-topped bar and range of seating options. Light lunches and well-presented, satisfying dinner menu.

ENGLAND

ENGLAND

# PETERBOROUGH

549

▶ London 60 mi – Brighton 45 mi – Portsmouth 21 mi – Southampton 34 mi

🏠 **Langrish House** ⬙      ≤ 🛋 🕭 ⚑ 🖳 VISA ⬤⬤ AE
*Langrish, West : 3.5 mi by A 272 ✉ GU32 1RN – ℰ (01730) 266 941*
*– www.langrishhouse.co.uk – Closed 2 weeks early January*
**13 rm** ⬚ – ♦£ 80/90 ♦♦£ 130/170    **Rest** – Menu £ 21/38
♦ Unassuming mid-17C house in lovely grounds; run by charming owners. Spacious country house lounges – one in the old Civil War cellars. Traditional bedrooms have individual themes and good modern facilities. Small formal dining room offers classically based menus.

ⓧⓧⓧ **JSW** (Jake Watkins) with rm      🕭 ⚑ 🖳 VISA ⬤⬤ AE
⁣⁣ ⬡ *20 Dragon St ✉ GU31 4JJ – ℰ (01730) 262 030 – www.jswrestaurant.com*
*– Closed 2 weeks January, 2 weeks July, Sunday and Monday*
**3 rm** – ♦£ 70 ♦♦£ 85/110    **Rest** – Menu £ 28/48 s⬙
**Spec.** Fricassee of quail with chestnut and truffle custard. Three textures of lamb with bergamot. Dark chocolate and chicory délice.
♦ 17C former coaching inn, in pleasant town. Spacious beamed restaurant with linen-laid tables, wood-furnished terrace and rustic feel. Technically accomplished, refined, flavoursome cooking relies on quality ingredients. Choice of classical market menu, tasting menu and à la carte. Modern bedrooms boast good facilities.

ⓧⓧ **Annie Jones**      🕭 VISA ⬤⬤
*10 Lavant St ✉ GU32 3EW – ℰ (01730) 262 728 – www.anniejones.co.uk*
*– Closed Sunday dinner, Tuesday lunch and Monday*
**Rest** – Menu £ 19/35 s – Carte £ 28/36 s
♦ Relaxed neighbourhood restaurant on a busy street, with deep red décor and a bohemian feel. Refined bistro-style cooking uses quality seasonal produce. Wicker-furnished terrace.

▶ London 54 mi – Brighton 31 mi – Portsmouth 33 mi
🏌 Osiers Farm Petworth London Rd, ℰ (01798) 34 40 97
◉ Petworth House★★ AC

🏠 **Old Railway Station** without rest      🛋 ⚸ ⚑ 🖳 VISA ⬤⬤ AE
*South : 1.5 mi by A 285 ✉ GU28 0JF – ℰ (01798) 342 346*
*– www.old-station.co.uk – Closed 24-26 December*
**10 rm** ⬚ – ♦£ 70/83 ♦♦£ 174/198
♦ As the name suggests. Waiting room with vaulted ceiling and ticket office now a lounge, Pullman carriages with marquetry now bedrooms; original features abound. Cake on arrival; breakfast on platform.

ⓧⓧ **Leconfield**      🕭 AC ⬌ VISA ⬤⬤
*New St ✉ GU28 0AS – ℰ (01798) 345 111 – www.theleconfield.co.uk – Closed Sunday dinner and Monday*
**Rest** – Carte £ 28/38
♦ Old 18C antique shop in a charming town, with modern bar, vaulted dining room, conservatory and terrace. Modern British menu relies on seasonal and foraged produce and there's always a dish for two; some original and global touches feature.

🏠 **Badgers**      🕭 🖳 VISA ⬤⬤
*Coultershaw Bridge, South : 1.5 mi on A 285 ✉ GU28 0JF – ℰ (01798) 342 651*
*– www.badgerspetworth.co.uk – Closed Sunday dinner in winter*
**Rest** – Carte £ 25/36
♦ Homely pub close to the river, boasting log fires, fresh flowers and candles. Eclectic menus offer robust, flavoursome cooking with international influences. In summer, lobster is a speciality.

**at Halfway Bridge** West : 3 mi on A 272 – ⊠ Petworth

🛏️ **Halfway Bridge Inn** with rm      🚗 🛜 ⁽ᵖ⁾ P VISA ⚹⚹ AE
⊠ GU28 9BP – ℰ (01798) 861 281 – www.halfwaybridge.co.uk – Closed 25
December
**6 rm** ☑ – †£ 75/95 ††£ 100/130    **Rest** – Carte £ 25/31
♦ 17C pub with several cosy, fire-lit rooms, set on the edge of Cowdray Park.
Lunchtime baguettes, traditional pub dishes and nursery puddings. Bedrooms
are set in converted stables and, like the pub, blend rustic charm with modern
fittings and facilities.

**at Tillington** West : 1 mi on A272 – **504** S31

🛏️ **Horse Guards Inn** with rm      🚗 🛜 ⁽ᵖ⁾ VISA ⚹⚹
Upperton Rd ⊠ GU28 9AF – ℰ (01798) 342 332 – www.thehorseguardsinn.co.uk
**3 rm** ☑ – †£ 80/105 ††£ 80/105    **Rest** – Carte £ 22/36
♦ In an elevated spot in the heart of a quiet village sits this pretty mid-17C inn;
which is equally charming on the inside as it is out. Local seafood stands out and
some of the vegetables come from their own patch. Young, friendly service. Simple, rustic bedrooms, with a family room in the cottage opposite.

---

**PICKERING** – North Yorkshire – **502** R21 – pop. 6 616       **23** C1
🚊 London 237 mi – Middlesbrough 43 mi – Scarborough 19 mi – York 25 mi

🏨 **White Swan Inn**      P VISA ⚹⚹ AE
Market Pl ⊠ YO18 7AA – ℰ (01751) 472 288 – www.white-swan.co.uk
**20 rm** ☑ – †£ 115/135 ††£ 150/180 – 1 suite    **Rest** – Carte £ 26/46
♦ Well-run former coaching inn, with bar and lounges in modern hues. Appealing bedrooms boast good mod cons and smart bathrooms: those in the outbuildings have heated stone floors; one has a bath in the lounge. Brasserie-style restaurant offers classical menus.

🏠 **17 Burgate** without rest      🚗 ⁽ᵖ⁾ P VISA ⚹⚹
17 Burgate ⊠ YO18 7AU – ℰ (01751) 473 463 – www.17burgate.co.uk
– Restricted opening in winter
**5 rm** ☑ – †£ 70/100 ††£ 110
♦ Restored 17C townhouse with colourful gardens; run by charming, experienced
couple. Lounge boasts honesty bar and large inglenook; breakfast room has
Mackintosh-style chairs. Spacious bedrooms furnished in comfy, modern style:
two have a subtle oriental theme.

🏠 **Bramwood** without rest      🚗 🍴 ⁽ᵖ⁾ P VISA ⚹⚹
19 Hall Garth ⊠ YO18 7AW – ℰ (01751) 474 066
– www.bramwoodguesthouse.co.uk
**8 rm** ☑ – †£ 50/70 ††£ 80/90
♦ Georgian townhouse with pretty gardens, set close to town. Cosy, homely interior with fire-lit lounge and tea on arrival. Breakfast in large kitchen, beside china-
filled dressers, or in more formal dining room. Comfy, cottagey bedrooms. Owners go the extra mile.

**at Levisham** Northeast : 6.5 mi by A 169 – ⊠ Pickering

🏠 **Moorlands Country House** 🌿      ≤ 🚗 🍴 ⁽ᵖ⁾ P VISA ⚹⚹
⊠ YO18 7NL – ℰ (01751) 460 229 – www.moorlandslevisham.co.uk – March-19
November, minimum 2 night stay
**4 rm** ☑ – †£ 70/90 ††£ 130/150    **Rest** – Menu £ 25
♦ 19C restored vicarage in the heart of the national park, boasting superb views
down the valley. Spacious, well-maintained interior with a classically decorated
lounge and flowery wallpapers. Comfortable bedrooms boast rich colour
schemes; one has a four-poster bed. Traditional three course dinners. Menu
changes daily.

ENGLAND

**at Sinnington** Northwest : 4 mi by A 170 – ✉ York

🛏 **Fox and Hounds** with rm 　　　　　　🍴 **P** 𝘝𝘐𝘚𝘈 ⓸
*Main St ✉ YO62 6SQ – ℰ (01751) 431 577 – www.thefoxandhoundsinn.co.uk*
*– Closed 25-26 December*
**10 rm** ⬜ – ♦£ 59/89 ♦♦£ 100/130　**Rest** – Carte £ 22/37
♦ Handsome and sturdy 18C coaching inn in pretty village; substantial interior
has plenty of charm. Flexible menus, with local specialities the popular choice.
Comfortable, cottagey bedrooms are popular at weekends.

**PICKHILL** – North Yorkshire – **502** P21 – pop. 412 – ✉ Thirsk　　**22** B1
▶ London 229 mi – Leeds 41 mi – Middlesbrough 30 mi – York 34 mi

🏠 **Nags Head Country Inn** 　　　🍴 🍽 📞 🛎 **P** 𝘝𝘐𝘚𝘈 ⓸
✉ YO7 4JG – ℰ (01845) 567 391 – www.nagsheadpickhill.co.uk – Closed 25
*December*
**14 rm** ⬜ – ♦£ 50/67 ♦♦£ 80/95　**Rest** – Carte £ 20/29
♦ Atmospheric 300 year old inn in an ancient hamlet, an easy drive to Thirsk and
Ripon races. Neat rooms in soft floral fabrics. Over 800 ties on display in the rustic
bar. Rural restaurant adorned with bookshelves and patterned rugs.

**PILLERTON PRIORS** – Warwickshire – **503** P27 – pop. 123　　　**19** C3
– ✉ Stratford-Upon-Avon
▶ London 93 mi – Birmingham 43 mi – Liverpool 137 mi – Leeds 141 mi

🏠 **Fulready Manor** without rest 🌿 　　　≤ 🍴 🍸 🎾 🍴 **P**
*South : 0.75 mi on Halford rd ✉ CV37 7PE – ℰ (01789) 740 152*
*– www.fulreadymanor.co.uk*
**3 rm** ⬜ – ♦£ 100 ♦♦£ 125/140
♦ Delightfully run manor house next to a lake, in 125 acres of peaceful arable
farmland. Spacious lounge. Elegant bedrooms with feature beds, smart bathrooms and extras. Excellent views.

**PLUMTREE** – Nottinghamshire – see Nottingham

**PLYMOUTH** – Plymouth – **503** H32 – pop. 253 188　　　　　**2** C2
▶ London 242 mi – Bristol 124 mi – Southampton 161 mi
**Access** Tamar Bridge (toll) AY
🛫 Plymouth City (Roborough) Airport : ℰ (01752) 204090, N : 3.5 mi by A 386 ABY
🚢 to France (Roscoff) (Brittany Ferries) 1-3 daily (6 h) – to Spain (Santander) (Brittany
Ferries) 2 weekly (approx 24 h)
ℹ 3-5 The Barbican ℰ (01752) 30 63 30, www.visitplymouth.co.uk
🏌 Plymouth Mayflower
🏌 Staddon Heights Plymstock, ℰ (01752) 40 24 75
🏌 Elfordleigh Hotel G. & C.C. Plympton Colebrook, ℰ (01752) 34 84 25
👁 Town★ - Smeaton's Tower (≤★★) **AC** BZ **T1** – Royal Citadel (ramparts ≤★★) **AC**
BZ – City Museum and Art Gallery★ BZ **M1**
🖼 Saltram House★★ **AC**, E : 3.5 mi BY **A** - Tamar River★★ – Anthony House★ **AC**, W :
5 mi by A 374 – Mount Edgcumbe (≤★) **AC**, SW : 2 mi by passenger ferry from
Stonehouse AZ. NE : Dartmoor National Park★★ – Buckland Abbey★★ **AC**, N :
7.5 mi by A 386 ABY

Plans on following pages

🏠 **Bowling Green** without rest 　　　　　　🍸 🍴 𝘝𝘐𝘚𝘈 ⓸ ⓪
*9-10 Osborne Pl, Lockyer St, The Hoe ✉ PL1 2PU – ℰ (01752) 209 090*
*– www.thebowlinggreenplymouth.com*　　　　　　　　　　BZ**r**
**12 rm** ⬜ – ♦£ 50/60 ♦♦£ 75
♦ Georgian house, half overlooking Hoe, near site of Drake's legendary game.
High-ceilinged rooms in pine and modern fabrics; some have power showers.
Stroll to promenade.

# PLYMOUTH

ENGLAND

ROSCOFF SANTANDER

ENGLAND

## PLYMOUTH

See following page

XXX **Tanners** ✿ 🚳 ☎ 🆎 ⓞ
*Prysten House, Finewell St ⊠ PL1 2AE – ℰ (01752) 252 001*
*– www.tannersrestaurant.com – Closed 24 December-10 January, Sunday and*
*Monday* BZ**n**
**Rest** – *(booking essential) Menu £ 20 (lunch)* **s** – *Carte £ 39/45* **s**
♦ Characterful 15C house, reputedly Plymouth's oldest building: mullioned windows, tapestries, exposed stone and an illuminated water well. Modern, interesting cooking.

XX **Artillery Tower** ≤ ✿ 🚳 ☎
*Firestone Bay ⊠ PL1 3QR – ℰ (01752) 257 610 – www.artillerytower.co.uk*
*– Closed Saturday lunch, Sunday and Monday* AZ**a**
**Rest** – *(booking essential at lunch) Menu £ 37*
♦ Uniquely located in 500 year-old circular tower, built to defend the city. Courteous service of mostly well executed local dishes: blackboard fish specialities.

XX **Barbican Kitchen** 🍴 🚳 ☎ 🆎 ⓞ
*Black Friars Distillery, 60 Southside St ⊠ PL1 2LQ – ℰ (01752) 604 448*
*– www.barbicankitchen.com – Closed 25-26 December and dinner 31 December*
**Rest** – *(booking advisable) Carte £ 21/33* **s** BZ**u**
♦ Fun, informal eatery set in the Plymouth Gin Distillery. Two long, industrial style rooms decorated in vibrant fuschia and lime. Brasserie menus offer a good selection of simply cooked dishes.

XX **Chloe's** 🍴 🚳 ☎ 🆎
*Gill Akaster House, Princess St ⊠ PL1 2EX – ℰ (01752) 201 523 – www.*
*chloesrestaurant .co.uk – Closed 3-5 January, 25-31 December, Sunday and*
*Monday* BZ**a**
**Rest** – *Menu £ 19/40*
♦ Airy, open plan restaurant with simple neighbourhood feel, neutral décor and hanging Hessian lights. Tasty dishes display a classical French base. Live pianist every night.

**at Plympton St Maurice** East : 6 mi by A 374 on B 3416 - BY - ⊠ Plymouth

🏨 **St Elizabeth's House** 🛏 📶 ㊑ rm, 🍴 🛜 🧖 🅿 🚳
*Longbrook St ⊠ PL7 1NJ – ℰ (01752) 344 840 – www.stelizabeths.co.uk – Closed*
*25-26 December*
**13 rm** 🍽 – ♦£ 139 ♦♦£ 159 – 1 suite
**Rest** – *Menu £ 11 (lunch) – Carte £ 21/36*
♦ Immaculate cream-washed former convent, now a stylish boutique hotel; lounge is dressed in period décor while light bedrooms are contemporary, with up-to-date facilities. Formal dining room offers classically based cooking with a modern twist.

**PLYMPTON SAINT MAURICE** Devon – Plymouth – **503** H32 – see Plymouth

**POLPERRO** – Cornwall – **503** G33 – ⊠ Looe **1** B2
▶ London 271 mi – Plymouth 28 mi
◎ Village ★

⌂ **Trenderway Farm** without rest 🌿 ≤ 🚗 🐶 🍴 🛜 🅿 🚳 ☎
*Northeast : 2 mi by A 387 ⊠ PL13 2LY – ℰ (01503) 272 214*
*– www.trenderwayfarm.co.uk*
**8 rm** 🍽 – ♦£ 125/175 ♦♦£ 125/175
♦ 16C farmhouse and outbuildings in 206 acres of working farmland. Well-appointed bedrooms in mix of styles; some with seating areas and kitchenettes. Cream tea on arrival; Aga-cooked breakfasts.

**PONTELAND** – Northumberland – **501** O19 – see Newcastle upon Tyne

ENGLAND

## POOLE – Poole – 503 O31 – pop. 144 800

▶ London 116 mi – Bournemouth 4 mi – Dorchester 23 mi – Southampton 36 mi

🚢 to France (Cherbourg) (Brittany Ferries) 1-2 daily May-October (4 h 15 mn) day (5 h 45 mn) night – to France (St Malo) (Brittany Ferries) daily (8 h) – to France (St Malo) (Condor Ferries Ltd)

🛈 Poole Quay ℰ (01202) 25 32 53, www.pooletourism.com

🏌 Parkstone Links Rd, ℰ (01202) 70 71 38

🏌 Bulbury Woods Lytchett Minster Bulberry Lane, ℰ (01929) 45 95 74

◎ Town★ (Waterfront M1 , Scaplen's Court M2 )

◎ Compton Acres★★, (English Garden ⩽★★★) AC, SE : 3 mi by B 3369 BX (on Bournemouth town plan) – Brownsea Island★ (Baden-Powell Stone ⩽★★) AC, by boat from Poole Quay or Sandbanks BX (on Bournemouth town plan)

Plan of Built up Area : see Bournemouth BX

---

🏨 **Hotel du Vin**      AK 🛜 🖧 P VISA ⓸ AE

*7-11 Thames St.* ✉ *BH15 1JN –* ℰ *(01202) 785 570 – www.hotelduvin.com*
**38 rm** 🛏 – ✝£ 170/190 ✝✝£ 245/400     **a**
**Rest Bistro** – see restaurant listing

◆ Strikingly extended Queen Anne property in the heart of the old town. Smart guest areas with eye-catching, wine-themed murals. Stylish, modern bedrooms are named after wine or champagne houses; one boasts an 8ft bed and twin roll-top baths.

**ENGLAND**

**Harbour Heights** ≤ 🚗 🛜 🎬 🅰️ 🎾 🎵 🛗 **P** 𝒱𝒾𝒮𝒜 ⚌ 🅰️🅴
*Haven Rd, Sandbanks, Southeast : 3 mi by B 3369* ⊠ *BH13 7LW* – ℰ *(01202)
707 272* – *www.harbourheights.com* **BXn**
**38 rm** ⊡ – †£ 135/230 ††£ 200/390
**Rest** *Habar Bistro* – Menu £ 27/30 – Carte £ 32/45
♦ Refurbished 1920s whitewashed hotel perched on the hillside; overlooking the
bay and Brownsea Island. Modern lounge-bar boasts superb three-tiered terrace.
Contemporary bedrooms come with good mod cons and smart bathrooms.
Open-plan restaurant serves modern menu.

**Cranborne House** without rest 🎾 🎵 **P**
*45 Shaftesbury Rd* ⊠ *BH15 2LU* – ℰ *(01202) 685 200*
– *www.cranborne-house.co.uk* **c**
**5 rm** ⊡ – †£ 49/69 ††£ 69/89
♦ Victorian house on the main road; run by friendly owners. Small, homely
lounge-cum-breakfast room. Bedrooms – in modern extension – boast quality
handmade furniture and good modern facilities.

**Bistro** – at Hotel du Vin 🅰️🅲 **P** 𝒱𝒾𝒮𝒜 ⚌ 🅰️🅴
*7-11 Thames St.* ⊠ *BH15 1JN* – ℰ *(01202) 785 570* – *www.hotelduvin.com*
**Rest** – Carte £ 30/45 🍷 **a**
♦ Large hotel bistro in a striking Queen Anne property set in the heart of the old
town. Local produce appears in dishes with a classical French base. 300 bin wine
list and superb tasting room.

**Cow** 🛜 🅰️🅲 ⇔ **P** 𝒱𝒾𝒮𝒜 ⚌ 🅰️🅴
*58 Station Rd, Ashley Cross* ⊠ *BH14 8UD* – ℰ *(01202) 749 569*
– *www.thecowpub.co.uk* – *Closed 25 December and Sunday dinner*
**Rest** – Menu £ 25 – Carte £ 27/40 **BXa**
♦ Smart, modern pub next to the railway station. Light lunch menu of pub favourites. Evening à la carte steps things up a gear, but is only available in the
French-style bistro.

**POOLEY BRIDGE** – Cumbria – **501** L20 – see Ullswater

**PORLOCK** – Somerset – **503** J30 – pop. 1 395 – ⊠ **Minehead** **3** A2
▶ London 190 mi – Bristol 67 mi – Exeter 46 mi – Taunton 28 mi
◉ Village★ - Porlock Hill (≤★★) – St Dubricius Church★
◪ Dunkery Beacon★★★ (≤★★★), S : 5.5 mi – Exmoor National Park★★
  - Selworthy★ (≤★★, Church★), E : 2 mi by A 39 and minor rd
  - Luccombe★ (Church★), E : 3 mi by A 39 – Culbone★ (St Beuno), W : 3.5 mi by B
3225, 1.5 mi on foot – Doone Valley★, W : 6 mi by A 39, access from Oare on foot

**Oaks** ≤ 🚗 🎾 🎵 **P** 𝒱𝒾𝒮𝒜 ⚌
⊠ *TA24 8ES* – ℰ *(01643) 862 265* – *www.oakshotel.co.uk* – *April-October*
**7 rm** (dinner included) ⊡ – †£ 145 ††£ 210/220
**Rest** – *(dinner only) (booking essential for non-residents)* Menu £ 38 **s**
♦ Imposing Edwardian house boasting great views over the weir and Porlock
Bay. Antique-filled entrance hall with beautiful parquet floor. Cake on arrival in
snug lounge. Large, comfy bedrooms come with fresh fruit bowls, good mod
cons and smart bathrooms. Dining room offers classical daily menu and views
from every table.

**PORT ERIN** – Port Erin – **502** F21 – see Man (Isle of)

**PORT ST MARY** – Port Saint Mary – **502** F/G21 – see Man (Isle of)

## PORT SUNLIGHT – Merseyside – 502 L23     20 A3

▶ London 206 mi – Liverpool 6 mi – Bolton 42 mi – St Helens 20 mi

🏠 **Leverhulme H. & Spa**    🚗 ⅙ ❄ ¶ 🛁 🅿 VISA ◉ AE
Lodge Ln, Central Rd ⊠ CH62 5EZ – ℰ (0151) 644 55 55
– www.leverhulmehotel.co.uk
**15 rm** ☷ – †£ 160 ††£ 395
**Rest** *Richard Fox at Leverhulme* – ℰ (0151) 644 66 55 – Menu £ 15 (lunch)
– Carte £ 29/40
♦ Originally the cottage hospital for a Victorian conservation village. Now a hotel with personality, whose bright interior mixes contemporary design with art deco. Retro restaurant with vivid purple carpet, glass-topped tables and classic British menu.

## PORTGATE – Devon – pop. 1 453     2 C2

▶ London 211 mi – Launceston 8 mi – Plymouth 34 mi

🍴 **Harris Arms**    ⚋ 🅿 VISA ◉ AE
⊠ EX20 4PZ – ℰ (01566) 783 331 – www.theharrisarms.co.uk – Closed Sunday
dinner and Monday
**Rest** – Carte £ 20/33 ₰
♦ Simple exterior hides classical rooms, a large terrace and lovely rear views. Concise menus offer fresh, tried-and-tested dishes, supplemented by tasty daily specials. Excellent wine list.

## PORTHLEVEN – Cornwall – pop. 3 190     1 A3

▶ London 284 mi – Helston 3 mi – Penzance 12 mi

🍴🍴 **Kota** with rm    ❄ ¶ VISA ◉
Harbour Head ⊠ TR13 9JA – ℰ (01326) 562 407 – www.kotarestaurant.co.uk
– Closed 1 January-12 February, 25-26 December, Monday in low season and
Sunday except bank holiday weekends
**2 rm** ☷ – †£ 50/80 ††£ 80/95
**Rest** – (dinner only and lunch Friday-Saturday) Menu £ 15 (lunch and early
dinner) – Carte £ 23/34
♦ Cottagey converted 18C harbourside granary. Characterful restaurant - thick walls, tiled floors - serves modern Asian inspired dishes with local fish specials. Simple rooms.

## PORTINSCALE – Cumbria – see Keswick

## PORTSCATHO – Cornwall – 503 F33 – ⊠ Truro     1 B3

▶ London 298 mi – Plymouth 55 mi – Truro 16 mi

◉ St Just-in-Roseland Church★★, W : 4 mi by A 3078 – St Anthony-in-Roseland
(≤★★) S : 3.5 m

🏠 **Driftwood** ॐ    ≤ 🚗 ❄ ¶ 🅿 VISA ◉ AE
🍃 Rosevine, North : 2 mi by A 3078 ⊠ TR2 5EW – ℰ (01872) 580 644
– www.driftwoodhotel.co.uk – Closed 10 December-4 February
**14 rm** (dinner included) ☷ – †£ 210/251 ††£ 270/357
**Rest** – (dinner only) (booking essential) Menu £ 46
**Spec.** Spider crab and dill risotto with seaweed and samphire. Crisp shoulder of spring lamb, broad beans and onion purée. Strawberries with toasted marshmallow and clotted cream jelly.
♦ Charming and delightfully run house whose stylish décor and contemporary feel make it a lovely spot to lay one's head. Terrific sea views, mature gardens and smart powder-blue bedrooms; some have their own terrace. Seasonally pertinent food displays excellent combinations of flavours and textures.

ENGLAND

**⌂Ⓗ** **Rosevine**      ≤ 🚗 🏠 🖼 🕸 📶 **P.** 𝘝𝘐𝘚𝘈 ☎
*Rosevine, North : 2 mi by A 3078* ⊠ *TR2 5EW* – ℰ *(01872) 580 206*
*– www.rosevine.co.uk – Closed January*
**15 suites** – **♟♟**£ 155/250, 🍽 £ 7
**Rest** – *(closed Sunday dinner) (bar lunch)* Carte £ 27/35
♦ Dramatically refurbished and extended country house overlooking the sea. Cool, contemporary, neutrally hued inner. Stylish, modern bedrooms boast kitchenettes. Strongly family orientated services; kids have their own lounge. All-day brasserie uses local produce.

---

**PORTSMOUTH and SOUTHSEA** – Portsmouth – **503** Q31     **6** B3
– pop. 203 646 ▌ Great Britain

▶ London 78 mi – Brighton 48 mi – Salisbury 44 mi – Southampton 21 mi

▬ to the Isle of Wight (Ryde) (Wightlink Ltd) frequent services daily (15 mn) – from Southsea to the Isle of Wight (Ryde) (Hovertravel Ltd) frequent services daily (10 mn)

▬ to France (St Malo) (Brittany Ferries) daily (8 h 45 mn) day (10 h 45 mn) night – to France (Caen) (Brittany Ferries) 2-4 daily (6 h) day (6 h 45 mn) night – to France (Cherbourg) (Brittany Ferries) 2 daily (5 h) day, (7 h) night – to France (Le Havre) (LD Lines) daily (5 h 30 mn/7 h 30 mn) – to France (Cherbourg) (Brittany Ferries) 1-2 daily (2 h 45 mn) – to France (Caen) (Brittany Ferries) 2-4 daily (3 h 45 mn) – to Spain (Bilbao) (P & O European Ferries Ltd) 1-2 weekly (35 h) – to Guernsey (St Peter Port) and Jersey (St Helier) (Condor Ferries Ltd) daily except Sunday (10 hrs) – to the Isle of Wight (Fishbourne) (Wightlink Ltd) frequent services daily (35 mn)

🛈 Southsea ℰ (023) 9282 67 22, www.visitportsmouth.co.uk

🏌 Southsea Burrfields Rd, ℰ (023) 9266 86 67

🏌 Crookhorn Lane Waterlooville Widley, ℰ (023) 9237 22 10

🏌 Southwick Park Southwick Pinsley Drive, ℰ (023) 9238 01 31

◉ City★ – Naval Portsmouth BY : H.M.S. Victory★★★ **AC**, The Mary Rose★★, National Museum of the Royal Navy★★ **AC** – Old Portsmouth★ BYZ : The Point (≤★★) - St Thomas Cathedral★ – Southsea (Castle★ **AC**) AZ – Royal Marines Museum, Eastney★ **AC**, AZ **M1**

◎ Portchester Castle★ **AC**, NW : 5.5 mi by A 3 and A 27 AY

Plans pages 560, 561

ENGLAND

---

**⌂** **Clarence** without rest      🆎 🕸 📶 **P.** 𝘝𝘐𝘚𝘈 ☎ 𝘈𝘌
*Clarence Rd.* ⊠ *PO5 2LQ* – ℰ *(023) 9287 6348 – www.theclarencehotel.co.uk*
*– Closed 24 December-2 January*          AZ**c**
**8 rm** 🍽 – **♟**£ 95/135 **♟♟**£ 99/225
♦ Red-brick, bay windowed house a short walk from the sea. Variously sized bedrooms feature contemporary décor, a good level of facilities, superb modern bathrooms and pleasing extra touches.

**⌂** **Retreat** without rest      🕸 📶 𝘝𝘐𝘚𝘈 ☎
*35 Grove Rd South, Southsea* ⊠ *PO5 3QS* – ℰ *(023) 9235 3701*
*– www.theretreatguesthouse.co.uk*          CZ**e**
**4 rm** 🍽 – **♟**£ 80 **♟♟**£ 105
♦ Grade II listed Arts and Crafts house; originally built for the mayor. Original terrazzo floors and stained glass. Relaxed, spacious inner with stylish, understated décor. One four-poster room.

**✕✕** **Restaurant 27**      𝘝𝘐𝘚𝘈 ☎ 𝘈𝘌
*27a South Par, Southsea* ⊠ *PO5 2JF* – ℰ *(023) 9287 6272*
*– www.restaurant27.com – Closed 25-31 December, Sunday dinner, Monday and Tuesday*          AZ**x**
**Rest** – *(dinner only and Sunday lunch) (booking advisable)* Menu £ 40
♦ Keenly run, open-plan restaurant with lounge area for aperitifs and canapés. Cooking is skilful with creative touches. Attentive, knowledgeable service from smart young team.

# PORTSMOUTH AND SOUTHSEA

0 — 1 km
0 — 1/2 mile

M 27 SOUTHAMPTON

Southwick

Hill Road

Portsdown

Hill Road

B 2177

M 27

PAULSGROVE

WYMERING

Road

London

Road

Southampton

A 3

COSHAM

Western

Road

Northern Rd

A 387

Havant

Road

DRAYTON

A 2030

PORT SOLENT

A 27

M 27

Northern

Road

South Coast Road

A 3

M 275

Y

HORSEA ISLAND

Parade

15 B

HILSEA

Norway Rd

INDUSTRIAL ESTATES

LANGSTONE HARBOUR

PORTSMOUTH HARBOUR

Northern

Road

A 2047

Copnor Road

Anchorage Road

INDUSTRIAL ESTATES

Eastern Road

A 2030

WHALE ISLAND

Twyford Av.

14

46

London Road

NORTH END

Stubbington Av.

A 288

OCEAN RETAIL PARK

Burrfields

Road

18

POL

24

Kingston Rd

COPNOR

New Road

Tangier Road

Eastern Road

DOCKS

A 3

LANDPORT

Lake Rd

St. Mary's Rd

Langstone Rd

Holbrook

Road

A 2047

Fratton Rd

FRATTON

Milton Road

POMPEY CENTRE

Velder Av.

A 2030

EASTNEY

Z

See following page

50

13

A 2030

Goldsmith

Avenue

Eastney

Elm Grove

27

Winter Rd

Highland Rd

52

Albert Rd

38

9

M 1

28

56

40

Eastern Par.

A 288

42

C

M P

BLUE REEF AQUARIUM

M P

CASTLE

PYRAMIDS CENTRE

HOVERCRAFT

CHERBOURG, ST. MALO, CAEN

ISLE OF WIGHT

ENGLAND

For names of numbered streets, see following page.

**CENTRE**

0 ————— 300 m
0 ————— 300 yards

**ENGLAND**

PORTSMOUTH and SOUTHSEA

## ❌❌ Montparnasse　　　　　　　　　⇌ VISA ⊛ AE
*103 Palmerston Rd, Southsea ⊠ PO5 3PS – ℰ (023) 9281 6754*
*– www.bistromontparnasse.co.uk – Closed 25-26 December, 1 January, Sunday*
*and Monday*　　　　　　　　　　　　　　　　　　　　　　　CZa
**Rest** – Menu £ 37
• Keenly run, suburban restaurant with shabby-chic styling. Set lunch and dinner
menus. Ambitious cooking features original, sometimes unusual, combinations.
Refined appearance but hearty to eat.

## ❌❌ Brasserie Blanc　　　　　　　　　　　 VISA ⊛ AE
*1 Gunwharf Quays ⊠ PO1 3FR – ℰ (023) 9289 1320 – www.brasserieblanc.com*
**Rest** – French – Menu £ 14/16 – Carte £ 21/45　　　　　　　　BY
• Bustling brasserie on ground floor of 'The Lipstick', serving well-priced, tasty
classics prepared with care. Comfy seating, well-spaced tables, open kitchen and
super terrace.

## POSTBRIDGE – Devon – 503 I32　　　　　　　　　　　　　　2 C2
▶ London 207 mi – Exeter 21 mi – Plymouth 21 mi

### 🏠 Lydgate House ⌂　　　　　　　 ≤ ♨ ⅋ ♚ P VISA ⊛ AE
⊠ PL20 6TJ – ℰ (01822) 880 209 – www.lydgatehouse.co.uk
**7 rm** ⌿ – ♦£ 55/80 ♦♦£ 120
**Rest** – *(closed Sunday and Monday) (dinner only)* Menu £ 30
• In an idyllic secluded location high up on the moors within woodland and
overlooking the East Dart River. Comfortable sitting room with log fires and neat,
snug bedrooms. Candlelit conservatory dining room.

## POTTERNE – Wiltshire – 503 O29 – see Devizes

## POWERSTOCK – Dorset　　　　　　　　　　　　　　　　　3 B3
▶ London 144 mi – Bristol 92 mi – Cardiff 113 mi – Plymouth 87 mi

### 🍴 Three Horseshoes with rm　　　　　　　 ☎ ♚ P VISA ⊛
⊠ DT6 3TF – ℰ (01308) 485 328 – Closed dinner 25 December, Monday in
winter and Sunday dinner
**3 rm** ⌿ – ♦£ 45/70 ♦♦£ 50/70　**Rest** – Carte £ 21/36
• Looks-wise, it's nothing special, despite the lovely setting – it's simply all about
the food at the 'Shoes. They make their own breads, ice creams, chutneys and
pickles; try the wild boar Scotch egg or veal and bone marrow burger.

## PRESTBURY – Cheshire East – 502 N24 – pop. 3 269　　　20 B3
▶ London 184 mi – Liverpool 43 mi – Manchester 17 mi – Stoke-on-Trent 25 mi
🏌 Mottram Hall Hotel Mottram St Andrews Wilmslow Rd, ℰ (01625) 82 00 64

### 🏠 White House Manor without rest　　　　 ♨ ⅋ ♚ P VISA ⊛ AE
*New Road ⊠ SK10 4HP – ℰ (01625) 829 376 – www.thewhitehousemanor.co.uk*
*– Closed 25-26 December*
**12 rm** – ♦£ 60/115 ♦♦£ 130/150, ⌿ £ 11.95
• Attractive Georgian house with mature lawned garden and sheltered terrace.
Nicely furnished lounge boasts an honesty bar. Beautifully appointed bedrooms
display quality furnishings and extras.

## PRESTON – Lancashire – 502 L22　　　　　　　　　　　　20 A2
▶ London 226 mi – Blackpool 18 mi – Burnley 22 mi – Liverpool 30 mi
ℹ Lancaster Rd ℰ (01772) 25 37 31, www.visitpreston.com
🏌 Fulwood Fulwood Hall Lane, ℰ (01772) 70 00 11
🏌 Ingol Tanterton Hall Rd, ℰ (01772) 73 45 56
🏌 Ashton & Lea Lea Tudor Ave, Blackpool Rd, ℰ (01772) 73 52 82
🏌 Penwortham Blundell Lane, ℰ (01772) 74 46 30

ENGLAND

✗✗ **Inside Out**  🚗 🎍 **P** **VISA** **⚫** **AE** **⊙**
*100 Higher Walton Rd, Walton-le-Dale, Southeast : 1.75 mi by A 6 on A 675*
✉ *PR5 4HR* – ✆ *(01772) 251 366* – *www.insideoutrestaurant.co.uk* – *Closed first week January and Monday*
**Rest** – Menu £ 16/18 **s** – Carte £ 28/33 **s**
♦ Inside - a chic and stylish restaurant; 'out' - a lovely decked terrace with heaters overlooking a garden. Well sourced, quality ingredients assembled with love and flair.

---

**PRESTON CANDOVER** – Hampshire – **504** Q30                                                      **6 B2**
▶ London 59 mi – Croydon 67 mi – Barnet 72 mi – Ealing 54 mi

🍺 **Purefoy Arms**  🎍 **P** **VISA** **⚫** **AE**
😊 ✉ *RG25 2EJ* – ✆ *(01256) 389 777* – *www.thepurefoyarms.co.uk* – *Closed 1 January*
**Rest** – *(closed Sunday dinner and Monday except bank holidays)* Carte £ 20/35
♦ Dating from the 1860s, this once crumbling pub was thoughtfully restored and is run by a charming, young but experienced couple. There are hints of Spain on the menu, especially in the bar nibbles; prices are very competitive and the focus is on flavour.

---

**PRESTWICH** – Greater Manchester – **503** N23 – see Manchester

---

**PULHAM MARKET** – Norfolk – **504** X26 – pop. 919 – ✉ Diss                              **15 C2**
▶ London 106 mi – Cambridge 58 mi – Ipswich 29 mi – Norwich 16 mi

⌂ **Old Bakery** without rest  🚗 🕸 📶 **P** **VISA** **⚫**
*Church Walk* ✉ *IP21 4SL* – ✆ *(01379) 676 492* – *www.theoldbakery.net* – *Closed Christmas-New Year*
**4 rm** ⌷ – ♦£ 80 ♦♦£ 95
♦ Pretty 16C former bakery just off the village green. Characterful interior features exposed beams and inglenooks: homely lounge and breakfast room; good-sized bedrooms with modern facilities.

---

**PURTON** – Wiltshire – **503** O29 – pop. 3 328 – ✉ Swindon                                 **4 D2**
▶ London 94 mi – Bristol 41 mi – Gloucester 31 mi – Oxford 38 mi

🏠 **Pear Tree at Purton**  🚗 📶 🧖 **P** **VISA** **⚫** **AE** **⊙**
*Church End, South : 0.5 mi by Church St on Lydiard Millicent rd* ✉ *SN5 4ED*
– ✆ *(01793) 772 100* – *www.peartreepurton.co.uk* – *Closed 26 December*
**15 rm** ⌷ – ♦£ 114 ♦♦£ 144 – 2 suites   **Rest** – Menu £ 21/36 **s**
♦ Personally run, extended 16C sandstone vicarage in mature seven-acre garden. Spacious flower-filled lounge. Rooms with traditional comforts and thoughtful extras. Conservatory restaurant overlooks wild flower borders.

---

**RADNAGE** – Buckinghamshire – see Stokenchurch

---

**RAINHAM** – Medway – **504** U29                                                                          **9 C1**
▶ London 14 mi – Basildon 16 mi – Dartford 9 mi

✗✗ **Barn**  **AK** **P** **VISA** **⚫** **AE**
*507 Lower Rainham Rd, North : 1.75 mi by Station Rd* ✉ *ME8 7TN* – ✆ *(01634) 361 363* – *www.thebarnrestaurantrainham.co.uk* – *Closed 2 weeks January, 25 December, Saturday lunch, Sunday dinner and Monday*
**Rest** – Menu £ 18/24 **s** – Carte £ 24/43 **s**
♦ Black and white timbered, 18C Essex barn, reconstructed on this site. Heavily beamed, rustic dining room and upstairs lounge. Good choice of menus. Elaborate cooking comes in generous portions.

ENGLAND

## RAMSBOTTOM – Greater Manchester – 502 N23 – pop. 17 352          20 B

▶ London 223 mi – Blackpool 39 mi – Burnley 12 mi – Leeds 46 mi

XX **ramsons**          VISA ©©
*18 Market Pl* ⊠ *BL0 9HT* – *ℰ (01706) 825 070* – *www.ramsons-restaurant.com*
*– Closed 26 December, 1 January, Sunday dinner, Monday and Tuesday lunch*
**Rest** – Italian influences – *(booking essential)* Menu £ 18/23 – Carte £ 30/39 ₰
♦ Intimate, two-roomed restaurant run by passionate owner. Array of menus in cludes 6/10 course tasting options. Clean, refined, Italian-influenced cookin mixes quality local/imported produce.

XX **Sanmini's**          VISA ©©
*7 Carrbank Lodge, Ramsbottom Ln.* ⊠ *BL0 9DJ* – *ℰ (01706) 821 831*
*– www.sanminis.com – Closed Monday*
**Rest** – Indian – *(booking essential)* Menu £ 10 (lunch) – Carte £ 19/30
♦ Charming little restaurant in Victorian gatehouse. Neatly presented, authenti south Indian dishes with gentle spicing; every one is made from scratch. Famil are doctors, so it's healthy too.

## RAMSEY – Ramsey – 502 G21 – see Man (Isle of)

## RAMSGATE – Kent – 504 Y30 – pop. 37 967          9 D

▶ London 77 mi – Southend-on-Sea 89 mi – Ipswich 128 mi

XX **Age & Sons**          🛖 VISA ©© AE
(㉒) *Charlotte Ct* ⊠ *CT11 8HE* – *ℰ (01843) 851 515* – *www.ageandsons.co.uk*
*– Closed 1-24 January, Sunday dinner and Monday*
**Rest** – Menu £ 13/16 (weekdays) – Carte £ 20/28
♦ Attractive converted wine warehouse in centre of town. Sexy basement bar rustic ground floor café; more formal 1st floor restaurant and lovely terrace. Inter esting modern menu of gutsy, flavourful cooking. Charming service.

X **Eddie Gilberts**          VISA ©© AE ①
*32 King St.* ⊠ *CT11 8NT* – *ℰ (01843) 852 123* – *www.eddiegilberts.com – Closec*
*Sunday dinner*
**Rest** – Seafood – Carte £ 19/31
♦ High street fish shop; head upstairs to light, airy restaurant, with fishing net and piscatorial pictures. Extensive array of fresh fish; well presented in generou portions.

## RAMSGILL-IN-NIDDERDALE – North Yorkshire – 502 021 – see Pateley Bridge

## RAVENSTONEDALE – Cumbria – 502 M20 – see Kirkby Stephen

## RAYLEIGH – Essex – 504 V29 – pop. 30 629          13 C3

▶ London 35 mi – Chelmsford 13 mi – Southend-on-Sea 6 mi

**at Thundersley** South : 1.25 mi on A 129 – ⊠ Rayleigh

🍽 **Woodmans Arms**          🛖 P VISA ©© AE ①
*Rayleigh Rd* ⊠ *SS7 3TA* – *ℰ (01268) 775 799* – *www.thewoodmans.co.uk*
**Rest** – Carte £ 25/35
♦ Comfy sofas for drinkers; neatly laid tables for diners. Seasonal cooking is hearty and flavourful; traditional in the main with lighter choices at lunch. Service from a cheerful young team.

## READING – Reading – 503 Q29 – pop. 232 662          11 C3

▶ London 43 mi – Brighton 79 mi – Bristol 78 mi – Croydon 47 mi
**Access** Whitchurch Bridge (toll)
🚢 to Henley-on-Thames (Salter Bros. Ltd) (summer only)
🏌 Calcot Park Calcot Bath Rd, *ℰ (0118) 942 71 24*

# READING
## BUILT UP AREA

A 4074 OXFORD    A 4155 HENLEY

THAMES

Henley   Rd

CAVERSHAM

0   1 km
0   1 mile

RIVERMEAD LEISURE COMPLEX

Richfield   Av.

THAMES VALLEY PARK

Portman Road

THAMES

A 4 MAIDENHEAD

Oxford

Rd

London   Rd

14   Bath's   Lane

Tilehurst Rd

Wokingham

LONDON (M 4)

PROSPECT PARK

Rd

Whiteknights

Church   Rd

A 3290

Bath   Rd

Berkeley   Av.

A 329 WOKINGHAM

Rose

Kennet

Kiln

Pepper   Lane

Wilderness

X

Lane

Cressingham   Rd

Shinfield   Road

Elm   Rd

ENGLAND

MADEJSKI STADIUM

WHITLEY

Hartland   Rd

Whitley   Wood   Rd

B 3360

Basingstoke   Road

A 33   M 4, BASINGSTOKE

A 327   ALDERSHOT

## CENTRE

A 4155    B 3345 (A 4155)

THAMES

Vastern   Rd

0   300 m
0   300 yards

Caversham   Road

Great Knollys St.

George St.

Bedford

Chatham

St.

Friar   St.

Forbury

Kennet

Y

Broad   St

King's

Oxford   Road

BROAD ST MALL

Queen's

A 329 (A 329 (M))

HEXAGON THEATRE

CIVIC CENTRE

ORACLE SHOPPING CENTRE

Rd

Eldon   Road

Russell   Street

Inner   Distribution

London   Road

London

U

Castle   Hill

Kennet

Southampton   St.

Silver   St.

Kendrick   Road

Redlands   Rd

Craven   Road

N

Bath   Rd

Coley   Av.

Berkeley   Av.

Pell   St.

Addington   Rd

A 33    (A 33)   A 327

565

## Forbury    🛜 📶 ♿ rm, Ⓐ rest, 🍽 📶 ⚗ 🅿 🆅🆂🅰 ◐◐ 🅰🅴

26 The Forbury ⊠ RG1 3EJ – ℰ (0118) 952 77 70 – www.theforburyhotel.co.uk
**23 rm** ☷ – ♦£ 252 ♦♦£ 264    Y•
**Rest** *Cerise* – ℰ (0800) 789 789 – Menu £ 20 (lunch) – Carte £ 30/47
♦ Former civic hall overlooking Forbury Square Gardens; now a very stylish town house hotel. Eye-catching artwork features in all the stunningly individualistic bedrooms. Stylish basement cocktail bar/restaurant where clean, crisp, modern cooking holds sway.

## Malmaison    🛗 📶 ♿ Ⓐ 📶 ⚗ 🆅🆂🅰 ◐◐ 🅰🅴

Great Western House, 18-20 Station Rd ⊠ RG1 1JX – ℰ (0118) 956 23 00
– www.malmaison.com    Y•
**75 rm** – ♦£ 120/195 ♦♦£ 120/195, ☷ £ 14.50
**Rest** *Brasserie* – see restaurant listing
♦ Converted Victorian railway hotel with stylish lounges, rich, contemporary décor and funky feel. Named after famous trains, smart bedrooms display bold colours, a high level of facilities and quirky touches; one even has a train set in it.

## Holiday Inn    🛜 📺 📶 🛗 ♿ rm, Ⓐ 📶 ⚗ 🏊 🆅🆂🅰 ◐◐ 🅰🅴 ⓪

Wharfedale Rd., Winnersh Triangle, Southeast : 4.5 mi by A 4, A 3290 off
Winnersh rd ⊠ RG41 5TS – ℰ (0118) 944 42 33
– www.meridianleisurehotels.com/reading
**174 rm** – ♦£ 59/149 ♦♦£ 59/149, ☷ £ 10
**Rest** *Caprice* – Menu £ 21 – Carte £ 29/32
♦ Modern, purpose-built hotel set on a business park close to the M4. Spacious, open-plan guest areas and well-equipped leisure club. Uniform bedrooms offer good facilities, including 32 inch flat-screen TVs. Compact, up-to-date bathrooms.

## 🏠 Beech House without rest    🚐 ♿ 📶 🅿 🆅🆂🅰 ◐◐ 🅰🅴

60 Bath Rd ⊠ RG30 2AY – ℰ (0118) 959 19 01 – www.beechhousehotel.com
**15 rm** ☷ – ♦£ 75/95 ♦♦£ 95/105    X**a**
♦ Red-brick Victorian house with slightly Gothic exterior. Neat garden, terrace and summer house. Traditionally furnished throughout, with antiques and period ornaments. Pleasant, well-equipped bedrooms.

## ✗✗ Forbury's    🛜 Ⓐ ⇄ 🆅🆂🅰 ◐◐ 🅰🅴

1 Forbury Sq ⊠ RG1 3BB – ℰ (0118) 957 40 44 – www.forburys.com – Closed
26-27 December, 1-2 January and Sunday    Y**a**
**Rest** – French – Menu £ 17/23 – Carte £ 36/42 ⊗
♦ Well-established eatery near law courts. Relaxing area of comfy leather seats. Spacious dining room enhanced by bold prints of wine labels. Eclectic menus with Gallic starting point.

## ✗✗ Brasserie – at Malmaison Hotel    Ⓐ 🆅🆂🅰 ◐◐ 🅰🅴

Great Western House, 18-20 Station Rd ⊠ RG1 1JX – ℰ (0118) 956 23 00
– www.malmaison.com – Closed Saturday lunch    Y•
**Rest** – Carte £ 27/38
♦ Informal brasserie in a modernised Victorian railway hotel. Industrial-feel room with exposed pipes and a glass-fronted wine cellar. Classic brasserie menu mixes French and British dishes.

## ✗ Mya Lacarte    ⇄ 🆅🆂🅰 ◐◐ 🅰🅴

5 Prospect St, Caversham ⊠ RG4 8JB – ℰ (0118) 946 34 00
– www.myalacarte.co.uk – Closed 25-26 December, 1 January and Sunday
dinner    X**c**
**Rest** – Menu £ 18 (lunch) – Carte £ 27/37
♦ Buzzy, well-run neighbourhood restaurant. Friendly team serve modern British cooking with a twist. Produce is from nearby farms and allotments; 10kg of produce from local growers = a free meal.

ENGLAND

X **London Street Brasserie**                    🔗 VISA ⦾ AE ⓘ
*2-4 London St ✉ RG1 4PN – ✆ (0118) 950 50 36 – www.londonstbrasserie.co.uk*
*– Closed 25 December*                                            Zc
**Rest** – *(booking essential)* Menu £ 20 (lunch) – Carte £ 30/37
♦ Lively and modern: a polite, friendly team serve appetising British classics and
international dishes. Deck terrace and first-floor window tables overlook the river
Kennett.

**at Shinfield** South : 4.25 mi on A 327 - X – ✉ **Reading**

XXX **L'Ortolan**                               🏗 ⇔ P VISA ⦾ AE
⭐ *Church Lane ✉ RG2 9BY – ✆ (0118) 988 85 00 – www.lortolan.com – Closed 25*
*December-6 January, Sunday and Monday*
**Rest** – Menu £ 30/67
**Spec.** Marinated terrine and pan-fried foie gras with rhubarb chutney and sloe
gin jelly. Shoulder, loin and lamb sweetbreads with peas, anchovies and capers.
Raspberry soufflé, peach salad and vanilla cheesecake.
♦ Red brick former vicarage with lawned gardens and stylish lounge and conser-
vatory. Bright, comfortable dining room; classically based cooking with some orig-
inal touches and pretty presentation. Smart, busy private dining rooms.

**at Sonning-on-Thames** Northeast : 4.25 mi by A 4 on B 4446

XXX **French Horn** with rm          ≤ 🏗 ᴊ rm, ᴷ ᵗ P VISA ⦾ AE ⓘ
✉ *RG4 6TN – ✆ (0118) 969 22 04 – www.thefrenchhorn.co.uk – Closed 25-30*
*December*
**17 rm** ☕ – ♥£ 135 ♥♥£ 170 – 4 suites
**Rest** – *(booking essential)* Menu £ 26 (lunch) – Carte £ 36/72 **s**
♦ Long-standing, family-owned restaurant in pretty riverside setting. Bay windowed dining room overlooks lovely garden and offers French-influenced menus
crafted from seasonal ingredients. Comfy, traditional bedrooms; some in annexe, some with views.

**REDDITCH** – Worcestershire – **503** O27 – pop. 74 803            **19** C2
▶ London 111 mi – Birmingham 15 mi – Cheltenham 33 mi
– Stratford-upon-Avon 15 mi
🄳 Alcester St ✆ (01527) 6 08 06, www.ukinformationcentre.com
🖸 Abbey Hotel G. & C.C. Dagnell End Rd, ✆ (01527) 40 66 00
🖸 Lower Grinsty Callow Hill Green Lane, ✆ (01527) 54 30 79
🖸 Pitcheroak Plymouth Rd, ✆ (01527) 54 10 54

🏠 **Old Rectory** ⌖              🏗 ᵗ ᴊᴬ P VISA ⦾ AE
*Ipsley Lane, Ipsley ✉ B98 0AP – ✆ (01527) 523 000*
*– www.theoldrectory-hotel.co.uk – Closed 25-31 December*
**10 rm** ☕ – ♥£ 168 ♥♥£ 175
**Rest** – *(closed Friday-Sunday) (booking essential for non-residents)*
Menu £ 20/25 – Carte £ 25/33
♦ Converted early Georgian rectory surrounded by pleasant mature gardens creating a quiet and secluded haven. Smart, traditional interior décor and individually styled rooms. Charming Georgian style conservatory restaurant.

**REDFORD** – West Sussex – see Midhurst

**REED** – Hertfordshire – pop. 273                              **12** B2
▶ London 51 mi – Birmingham 115 mi – Sheffield 148 mi – Croydon 75 mi

🄳 **Cabinet at Reed**                        🏗 🔗 P VISA ⦾
*High St ✉ SG8 8AH – ✆ (01763) 848 366 – www.thecabinetatreed.co.uk – Closed*
*25 December, 1 January and Monday lunch*
**Rest** – Menu £ 16/26 – Carte £ 23/35
♦ White clapperboard pub with pleasant restaurant and delightful snug. Cooking
is flavoursome but not always what it seems, as traditional dishes are given a
more modern twist.

**ENGLAND**

▶ London 253 mi – Leeds 53 mi – Middlesbrough 36 mi
 – Newcastle upon Tyne 61 mi
🛈 The Green ℰ (01748) 88 40 59, www.reeth.org

🏨 **Burgoyne**    ≼ ⇌ & rm, ⁙ **P** ᴠᴵˢᴬ ⓐⓞ
*On The Green ⊠ DL11 6SN – ℰ (01748) 884 292 – www.theburgoyne.co.uk
– Closed 2 January-10 February*
**8 rm** ⌷ – †£ 111/121 ††£ 151/161 – 1 suite
**Rest** – *(dinner only) (booking essential for non-residents)* Menu £ 36
• Late Georgian hotel overlooking the green with views of the Dales. A charming, personally run, traditionally furnished house with well-appointed, individually styled rooms. Deep green dining room complements surrounding fells.

**at Low Row** West : 4 mi on B 6270

🏠 **Punch Bowl Inn** with rm    🏠 **P** ᴠᴵˢᴬ ⓐⓞ
⊠ *DL11 6PF – ℰ (01748) 886 233 – www.pbinn.co.uk – Closed 25 December*
**11 rm** ⌷ – †£ 102/105 ††£ 123/129 **Rest** – Carte £ 22/32
• Popular with walkers, this traditional 17C stone-built inn has a modernised shabby-chic interior. Classic dishes are listed on mirrors above the fireplace. Supremely comfortable bedrooms, decorated in a fresh, modern style; all with views over Swaledale.

**at Langthwaite** Northwest : 3.25 mi on Langthwaite rd – ⊠ Reeth

🏠 **Charles Bathurst Inn** with rm ⌘    ≼ 🏠 ⌕ ⁙ **P** ᴠᴵˢᴬ ⓐⓞ
⊠ *DL11 6EN – ℰ (01748) 884 567 – www.cbinn.co.uk*
**19 rm** ⌷ – †£ 77/105 ††£ 131/137 **Rest** – Carte £ 20/27
• Characterful 18C hostelry set in a peaceful hillside village, boasting commanding rural views. The daily menu, inscribed on a mirror, offers refined yet hearty classical British dishes. Bedrooms are spacious and extremely comfy.

▶ London 26 mi – Brighton 33 mi – Guildford 20 mi – Maidstone 38 mi

ⅩⅩ **Tony Tobin @ The Dining Room**    ᴬᴷ ᴠᴵˢᴬ ⓐⓞ ᴬᴱ
*59a High St ⊠ RH2 9AE – ℰ (01737) 226 650 – www.tonytobinsrestaurants.co.uk
– Closed 23 December-3 January, Saturday lunch, Sunday dinner and bank holidays*
**Rest** – Menu £ 21 (lunch) – Carte £ 40/50
• Contemporary first floor restaurant with pale hues and comfy lounge/bar above. Classical set lunch, more modern à la carte and 5 course tasting menu; the latter with wine recommendations.

Ⅹ **Westerly**    ✿ ᴠᴵˢᴬ ⓐⓞ
⊠ *RH2 9AN – ℰ (01737) 222 733 – www.thewesterly.co.uk – Closed 24
December-6 January, 1 week August, Sunday, Monday and lunch Tuesday
and Saturday*
**Rest** – *(booking essential at dinner)* Menu £ 22 (lunch) – Carte dinner £ 29/37
• Popular, two-roomed restaurant on the corner of a busy road. Concise menus follow the seasons; well-executed dishes are a mix of traditional preparations and modern interpretations of classics.

Ⅹ **Barbe**    ᴬᴷ ᴠᴵˢᴬ ⓐⓞ ᴬᴱ
*71 Bell St ⊠ RH2 7AN – ℰ (01737) 241 966 – www.labarbe.co.uk – Closed 2-3
January, 26-28 December, Saturday lunch, Sunday dinner and bank holiday
Mondays*
**Rest** – French – Menu £ 25/35
• Long-standing French bistro with cheery owner and huge local following. Two main dining areas strewn with Gallic memorabilia. Simply laid, tightly packed tables. Classical, bi-monthly menu.

ENGLAND

**RETFORD** – Nottinghamshire – **502** R24 – **pop. 20 679**                    **16** B1

🄳 London 148 mi – Lincoln 23 mi – Nottingham 31 mi – Sheffield 27 mi

🄸 40 Grove St ℰ (01777) 86 07 80, www.visitnottingham.com

⌂     **Barns** without rest ☜                                  🚗 🕸 **P** 𝚅𝙸𝚂𝙰 ◍◍
       *Morton Farm, Babworth, Southwest : 2.25 mi by A 6420 ⊠ DN22 8HA*
       *– ℰ (01777) 706 336 – www.thebarns.co.uk – Closed Christmas-New Year*
       **6 rm** � – †£ 42/68 ††£ 75
       ♦ Privately owned and run converted part 18C farmhouse on a quiet country
       road. Informal, old-fashioned, cottage décor throughout. Beams within and
       lawned gardens without.

---

**RHYDYCROESAU** – Shropshire – **502** K25 – **see Oswestry**

---

**RICHMOND** – North Yorkshire – **502** O20 – **pop. 8 178** 🛈 Great Britain     **22** B1

🄳 London 243 mi – Leeds 53 mi – Middlesbrough 26 mi
  – Newcastle upon Tyne 44 mi

🄸 Victoria Rd ℰ (01748) 828 7 42, www.guide2richmond.com

🄸🄰 Bend Hagg, ℰ (01748) 82 53 19

🄸🄰 Catterick Leyburn Rd, ℰ (01748) 83 32 68

◉ Town★ - Castle★ **AC** – Georgian Theatre Royal and Museum★

◉ The Bowes Museum★, Barnard Castle, NW : 15 mi by B 6274, A 66 and minor rd
  (right) – Raby Castle★, NE : 6 mi of Barnard Castle by A 688

⌂     **Millgate House** without rest                              ⪕ 🚗 🕪 **P**
       *3 Millgate ⊠ DL10 4JN – ℰ (01748) 823 571 – www.millgatehouse.com*
       **4 rm** ⊆ – †£ 95/145 ††£ 145
       ♦ Georgian townhouse with fine elevated views of river Swale and Richmond
       Castle. Award winning terraced garden. Antique furnished interior. Bedrooms are
       tastefully restrained.

---

**RINGWOOD** – Hampshire – **503** O31 – **pop. 13 387**                    **6** A2

🄳 London 102 mi – Bournemouth 11 mi – Salisbury 17 mi – Southampton 20 mi

🄸 Visitor Information Point ℰ (01425) 47 08 96, www.ringwood.inuklocal.co.uk

⌂     **Moortown Lodge** without rest                              🕪 **P** 𝚅𝙸𝚂𝙰 ◍◍
       *244 Christchurch Rd, South : 1 mi on B 3347 ⊠ BH24 3AS – ℰ (01425) 471 404*
       *– www.moortownlodge.co.uk*
       **7 rm** ⊆ – †£ 73 ††£ 96
       ♦ Welcoming Georgian hunting lodge, on a busy road at the edge of the forest.
       Large room with soft seating and neatly laid breakfast tables. Comfy bedrooms;
       some larger, with feature beds.

---

**RIPLEY** – North Yorkshire – **502** P21 – **pop. 193** – ⊠ Harrogate     **22** B2

🄳 London 213 mi – Bradford 21 mi – Leeds 18 mi – Newcastle upon Tyne 79 mi

🏠🏠   **Boar's Head**                                  🕸 **P** 𝚅𝙸𝚂𝙰 ◍◍ 𝙰𝙴 ◍
       *⊠ HG3 3AY – ℰ (01423) 771 888 – www.boarsheadripley.co.uk*
       **25 rm** ⊆ – †£ 85 ††£ 150
       **Rest** *Restaurant* – Carte £ 20/32
       **Rest** *Bistro* – Carte £ 20/32
       ♦ 18C coaching inn within estate village of Ripley Castle, reputedly furnished
       from castle's attics. Comfy, stylish, unique rooms are individually furnished; some
       in courtyard or adjacent house. Classically based, seasonal dishes in The Restau-
       rant. More informal dining in The Bistro.

ENGLAND

▶ London 28 mi – Guildford 6 mi

🏨 **Talbot Inn**                                          ⌂ 📶 ⚒ 🅿 VISA ⦿ AE
*High St. ✉ GU23 6BB – ℰ (01483) 225 188 – www.thetalbotinn.com*
**39 rm** – ♦£ 90/125 ♦♦£ 110/125, ☲ £ 7.95
**Rest** – *(closed Sunday dinner)* Carte £ 26/37
• Historic coaching inn dating back to the 15C. Characterful bedrooms in the main house; more uniform rooms in the courtyard. Charming lounge and bar with low beams and open fires. Brasserie-style dining room offers a mix of classic pub and more modern dishes.

XXX **Drake's** (Steve Drake)                                    ⧉ VISA ⦿
🏵 *The Clock House, High St ✉ GU23 6AQ – ℰ (01483) 224 777*
*– www.drakesrestaurant.co.uk – Closed 2 weeks August, 10 days January, 2 days Christmas, Tuesday lunch, Sunday and Monday*
**Rest** – Menu £ 28/55
**Spec.** Grilled mackerel, burnt aubergine and cucumber ceviche. Lamb, anchovy, pickled rhubarb and ceps. Raspberry and pineapple ravioli with white pepper.
• Georgian restaurant's red brick façade dominated by large clock. Intimate lounges and relaxing, open plan dining room with local gallery art on walls. Simple, seasonal menu; kitchen makes use of modern techniques and interesting combinations. Well-established team provide formal service.

▶ London 222 mi – Leeds 26 mi – Middlesbrough 35 mi – York 23 mi
ℹ Minster Rd ℰ (01765) 60 46 25, www.visitripon.org
🛈 Ripon City Palace Rd, ℰ (01765) 60 36 40
👁 Town★ - Cathedral★ (Saxon Crypt) **AC**
🄖 Fountains Abbey★★★ **AC** :- Studley Royal **AC** (≼★ from Anne Boleyn's Seat) - Fountains Hall (Fa 0.5ade★), SW : 2.5 mi by B 6265 – Newby Hall (Tapestries★) **AC**, SE : 3.5 mi by B 6265

🏨 **Old Deanery**                                        ⧉ ⚒ 🅿 VISA ⦿ AE
*Minster Rd ✉ HG4 1QS – ℰ (01765) 600 003 – www.theolddeanery.co.uk*
*– Closed first week January*
**11 rm** ☲ – ♦£ 80/105 ♦♦£ 130/155
**Rest** – *(closed Sunday dinner)* Menu £ 17 (lunch) – Carte dinner £ 26/38
• Eponymously named hotel opposite cathedral. Stylish interior blends seamlessly with older charms. Afternoon tea in secluded garden. 18C oak staircase leads to modern rooms. Appealing seasonal cooking in spacious dining room.

⌂ **Sharow Cross House**                                  ⧉ 🏡 📶 🅿
🔲 *Dishforth Rd, Sharow, Northeast : 1.75 mi by A 61 on Sharow rd ✉ HG4 5BQ*
*– ℰ (01765) 609 866 – www.sharowcrosshouse.co.uk – Closed Christmas-New Year*
**3 rm** ☲ – ♦£ 60/70 ♦♦£ 90/100   **Rest** – Menu £ 25
• Late Victorian villa, originally a country residence for a soap manufacturer. Characterful interior with spacious, light-filled rooms; tea serving in comfy lounge on arrival. Tastefully furnished bedrooms with thoughtful extras; master room offers cathedral views. Set dinners – choose in advance from a series of seven.

**at Aldfield** Southwest : 3.75 mi by B 6265 – ✉ Ripon

⌂ **Bay Tree Farm** 🌿                                ⧉ 👍 rm, 🏡 📶 🅿 VISA ⦿
✉ *HG4 3BE – ℰ (01765) 620 394 – www.baytreefarm.co.uk*
**6 rm** ☲ – ♦£ 50/60 ♦♦£ 85   **Rest** – *(closed Sunday dinner)* Menu £ 18
• 18C sandstone barn with rural views, set on a working farm. Lounge with wood burning stove and French windows opening into garden; bright, spacious bedrooms with modern bathrooms. Homely food could include beef from the farm.

**RISHWORTH** – West Yorkshire – see Sowerby Bridge

– **Northamptonshire** – **504** R27 – **pop. 2 254**                    **16** B3
London 66 mi – Coventry 36 mi – Leicester 42 mi – Northampton 5 mi

XX     **Roade House** with rm                           🄰🄲 rest, 🟊 P VISA 🆖 AE
16 High St ⊠ NN7 2NW – ℰ (01604) 863 372 – www.roadehousehotel.co.uk
– Closed 26-30 December, Sunday dinner and bank holiday Mondays
**10 rm** ⌷ – ♦£ 85/150 ♦♦£ 90/150
**Rest** – Menu £ 25 (lunch) – Carte dinner £ 26/38
♦ Personally run, former village pub and schoolhouse, with open-fired lounge
and simple linen-laid dining room. Crafted from local produce, set lunch and à la
carte dinner menus offer classical cooking with modern touches. Pleasant bedrooms are furnished in pine.

ROCHDALE – **Greater Manchester** – **502** N23 – **pop. 95 796**              **20** B2
London 224 mi – Blackpool 40 mi – Burnley 11 mi – Leeds 45 mi
🄸 The Esplanade ℰ (01706) 92 49 28, www.manchesterscountryside.com
🄸🄸 Bagslate Edenfield Rd, ℰ (01706) 64 38 18
🄸🄸 Marland Bolton Rd, Springfield Park, ℰ (01706) 64 98 01
🄸🄸 Castle Hawk Castleton Chadwick Lane, ℰ (01706) 64 08 41

XX     **Peacock Room at The Crimble**              🍽 🄰🄲 P VISA 🆖 AE ⓘ
Crimble Ln, Bamford , West : 2 mi on B 6222 ⊠ OL11 4AD – ℰ (01706) 368 591
– www.thedeackersgroup.com – Closed Saturday lunch, Sunday dinner, Monday
and Tuesday
**Rest** – Menu £ 16 (lunch and early dinner)/19 – Carte £ 30/41
♦ Large, mirror-ceilinged dining room with vast chandeliers, candelabras, crisp
linen and an elegant lounge, set in a landmark Victorian house. Constantly evolving menus and modern presentation.

XX     **Nutters**                                    ≼ 🄰🄲 ⇆ P VISA 🆖 AE
Edenfield Rd, Norden, West : 3.5 mi on A 680 ⊠ OL12 7TT – ℰ (01706) 650 167
– www.nuttersrestaurant.com – Closed 27-28 December, 2-3 January and
Monday
**Rest** – Menu £ 17/40 – Carte £ 26/40
♦ Views of the lyrical gardens contrast with a menu of often complex modern
British dishes with international twists and influences. Best views at either end of
the room.

ROCK – **Cornwall** – **503** F32 – **pop. 4 593** – ⊠ Wadebridge              **1** B2
London 266 mi – Newquay 24 mi – Tintagel 14 mi – Truro 32 mi
🄶 Pencarrow★, SE : 8.5 mi by B 3314 and A 389

🏨     **St Enodoc**                            ≼ 🍽 🏊 🐾 🌢 🟊 P VISA 🆖 AE ⓘ
⊠ PL27 6LA – ℰ (01208) 863 394 – www.enodoc-hotel.co.uk – Closed 10
December-10 February
**16 rm** ⌷ – ♦£ 115/185 ♦♦£ 170/235 – 4 suites
**Rest** Restaurant Nathan Outlaw ✿ ✿ **Rest** Seafood and Grill – see restaurant
listing
♦ Beautifully located hotel boasting stunning bay views. Strong New England
theme throughout with pastel painted woodwork and stripy sofas. Comfy guest
areas and modern, well-appointed bedrooms.

XXX    **Restaurant Nathan Outlaw** – at the St Enodoc Hotel           ≼ P
✿✿    ⊠ PL27 6LA – ℰ (01208) 863 394 – www.nathan-outlaw.com           VISA 🆖 ⓘ
– Closed 18 December-1February, Sunday and Monday
**Rest** – Seafood – (dinner only) (booking essential) (set menu only) Menu £ 75
**Spec.** John Dory with parsley dumpling, bacon and hazelnut dressing and aspara-
gus. Roasted turbot with slow cooked lamb belly, beetroot and rosemary. Rhu-
barb jelly with vanilla cream, rhubarb compote and ginger sorbet.
♦ Intimate fine dining restaurant consisting of just 9 tables, featuring pale colours
and modern art. Clean, precise cooking uses the finest quality, seasonal ingredients. Frequently changing set menu showcases fresh, locally caught seafood.

**ENGLAND**

ENGLAND

## ✗✗ **Dining Room** 🖼 VISA ⓪

*Pavilion Buildings, Rock Rd* ✉ *PL27 6JS –* ✆ *(01208) 862 622*
*– www.thediningroomrock.co.uk – Closed 2 weeks January-February, 2 weeks*
*November, Monday and Tuesday*
**Rest** – Menu £ 20 (lunch) – Carte dinner £ 30/36
♦ Immaculately kept restaurant with small terrace and friendly team. Flavoursome
classically based cooking features local, seasonal produce: good value set lunches;
dinner is more of an event. Everything is homemade, including the butter.

## ✗ **Seafood and Grill** – at the St Enodoc Hotel ← 🖼 P VISA ⓪ AE

✉ *PL27 6LA –* ✆ *(01208) 863 394 – www.nathan-outlaw.com – Closed 10*
*December-10 February*
**Rest** – Carte £ 23/38
♦ All day, split-level restaurant and bar overlooking the Camel Estuary and open-
ing out onto a lovely rear terrace. Menus feature light offerings and simply exe-
cuted steak and seafood dishes.

## at **Trebetherick** North : 1 mi by Trewint Lane

## ⛪ **St Moritz** ← 🚗 🏊 🏊 🧖 🐶 ₤ 🏋 🍴 🛜 P VISA ⓪

✉ *PL27 6SD –* ✆ *(01208) 862 242 – www.stmoritzhotel.co.uk*
**30 rm** 🛏 – †£ 85/150 ††£ 140/230 – 15 suites
**Rest** – *(dinner only)* Carte £ 31/43
♦ Art deco style hotel with leisure club, indoor and outdoor swimming pools and
a 6 room spa. Smartly furnished bedrooms; spacious bathrooms. Suites have a
lounge, kitchen and estuary views. Restaurant displays a simple, flavoursome
menu of unfussy dishes.

---

**ROCKBEARE** – Devon – see Exeter

---

**ROECLIFFE** – North Yorkshire – see Boroughbridge

---

**ROGATE** – West Sussex – **504** R30 – pop. 1 785 – ✉ Petersfield (hants.)  **7** C2
▶ London 63 mi – Brighton 42 mi – Guildford 29 mi – Portsmouth 23 mi

## ⛪ **Mizzards Farm** without rest ⟨ ← 🚗 🦆 🏊 🥘 🛜 P

*Southwest : 1 mi by Harting rd* ✉ *GU31 5HS –* ✆ *(01730) 821 656 – Closed*
*Christmas and New Year*
**3 rm** 🛏 – †£ 55/60 ††£ 90
♦ 17C farmhouse with delightful landscaped gardens, which include a lake, bor-
dered by river Rother. Views of woods and farmland. Fine fabrics and antiques in
appealing rooms.

---

**ROMALDKIRK** – Durham – **502** N20 – see Barnard Castle

---

**ROMSEY** – Hampshire – **503** P31 – pop. 17 386 📗 Great Britain  **6** A2
▶ London 82 mi – Bournemouth 28 mi – Salisbury 16 mi – Southampton 8 mi
🅸 13 Church St ✆ (01794) 51 29 87, www.manchesterscountryside.com
🔟 Dunwood Manor Awbridge Danes Rd, ✆ (01794) 34 05 49
🔟 Nursling, ✆ (023) 8073 46 37
🔟 Wellow East Wellow Ryedown Lane, ✆ (01794) 32 28 72
👁 Abbey★ (interior★★)
🌳 Broadlands★ **AC**, S : 1 m

## ⛪ **Ranvilles Farm House** without rest 🚗 🛜 P

*Ower, Southwest : 2 mi on A 3090 (southbound carriageway)* ✉ *SO51 6AA*
*–* ✆ *(023) 8081 4481 – www.ranvilles.com – Closed 25 December*
**5 rm** 🛏 – †£ 30/40 ††£ 60/90
♦ Attractive part-16C former farmhouse in mature grounds. Spacious beamed interior has a cottagey, country house feel. Comfy lounge with antique breakfast table and good-sized, homely bedrooms.

### 🍴 **Three Tuns** 🦽 P VISA ◉◎ AE

*58 Middlebridge St ⊠ SO51 8HL – ℰ (01794) 512 639*
*– www.the3tunsromsey.co.uk – Closed Sunday dinner in winter*
**Rest** – Carte £ 15/26
♦ This delightful pub, dating back to the 1720s, now has the tenants it deserves.
It oozes charm, with a beamed bar for great nibbles. Expect a proper pub menu
with steak and kidney pie, honey-glazed ham and Hampshire rhubarb crumble.

---

## ROSS-ON-WYE – Herefordshire – **503** M28 – **pop. 10 085**     **18** B3
📗 Great Britain

▶ London 118 mi – Gloucester 15 mi – Hereford 15 mi – Newport 35 mi
🛈 Edde Cross St ℰ (01989) 56 27 68, www.wyenot.com
👁 Market House★ – Yat Rock (⩽★)
🌀 SW : Wye Valley★ – Goodrich Castle★ AC, SW : 3.5 mi by A 40

### 🏠 **Wilton Court** 🦽 🛁 🌐 P VISA ◉◎ AE

*Wilton Ln, Wilton, West : 0.75 mi by B 4260 (A 49 Hereford) ⊠ HR9 6AQ*
*– ℰ (01989) 562 569 – www.wiltoncourthotel.com – Closed 2-15 January*
**10 rm** ⌷ – †£ 100/155 ††£ 125/175
**Rest** *Mulberry* – Menu £ 18/33 – Carte £ 32/39
♦ Attractive, part-Elizabethan house on the banks of the river Wye. 16C wood pa-
nelling in situ in bar and two of the bedrooms: others have a distinctly William
Morris influence. Light, airy conservatory restaurant boasts Lloyd Loom furniture
and garden views.

### 🍴🍴 **Orles Barn** with rm 🦽 P VISA ◉◎ AE ①

*Wilton ⊠ HR9 6AE – ℰ (01989) 562 155 – www.orles-barn.co.uk*
**6 rm** ⌷ – †£ 75/135 ††£ 145/175    **Rest** – *(booking essential)* Menu £ 22/35
♦ Lovely period house with parts dating from the 14C, 16C and 18C. Spacious
dining room and cosy open-fired bar with sage green panelling; cooking is flavoursome and seasonal. Chatty owner provides the service. Smart, comfortable
bedrooms boast designer fabrics.

## at Kerne Bridge South : 3.75 mi on B 4234 – ⊠ Ross-On-Wye

### 🏠 **Lumleys** without rest 🦽 P

*⊠ HR9 5QT – ℰ (01600) 890 040 – www.thelumleys.co.uk*
**3 rm** ⌷ – †£ 65 ††£ 65/75
♦ Double-fronted brick house with colourful gardens; formerly the village pub,
now a cosy, characterful guesthouse run with love and care. Cluttered, homely
bedrooms, comfy lounge, and drying room for walkers. Well-located for the Wye
Valley and Forest of Dean.

## at Walford South: 3.75 mi on B 4234

### 🍴 **Mill Race** 🛁 P VISA ◉◎ ①

*⊠ HR9 5QS – ℰ (01989) 562 891 – www.millrace.info*
**Rest** – Carte £ 21/34
♦ Surprisingly modern-looking pub in a small country village. Regulars gather at
the bar and families are welcome. Cooking is simple and lets the locally sourced
ingredients speak for themselves.

---

## ROTHBURY – Northumberland – **501** O18 – **pop. 1 963** – ⊠ Morpeth   **24** A2
📗 Great Britain

▶ London 311 mi – Edinburgh 84 mi – Newcastle upon Tyne 29 mi
🛈 Church St ℰ (01669) 62 08 87, www.visitnorthumberland.com
👁 Cragside House★ (interior★) AC

ENGLAND

↑ **Farm Cottage** without rest
*Thropton, West : 2.25 mi on B 6341* ✉ *NE65 7NA* – ✆ *(01669) 620 831*
– *www.farmcottageguesthouse.co.uk* – *Closed 1 week Christmas*
**5 rm** ⬛ – †£ 55/65 ††£ 75/100
• 18C stone cottage and gardens; the owner was actually born here. Two comfy lounges filled with family prints and curios. Individually styled rbedoom with plenty of extra touches; the Garden Room is located outside and is the most modern.

↑ **Thropton Demesne Farmhouse** without rest
*Thropton, West : 2.25 mi on B 6341* ✉ *NE65 7LT* – ✆ *(01669) 620 196*
– *www.throptondemesne.co.uk* – *March-October*
**4 rm** ⬛ – †£ 50 ††£ 75
• Early 19C stone-built former farmhouse; unbroken Coquet Valley views. Lounge defined by quality décor. Artwork on walls by owner. Individually styled rooms with lovely vistas.

---

**ROWDE** – Wiltshire – **503** N29 – **see Devizes**

---

 **ROWHOOK** – West Sussex – **see Horsham**

---

**ROWSLEY** – Derbyshire – **502** P24 – pop. 451 – ✉ Matlock     **16** A1
▌ Great Britain
▶ London 157 mi – Derby 23 mi – Manchester 40 mi – Nottingham 30 mi
◪ Chatsworth ★★★ (Park and Garden ★★★) **AC**, N : by B 6012

🏠 **East Lodge**
✉ DE4 2EF – ✆ (01629) 734 474 – www.eastlodge.com
**12 rm** ⬛ – †£ 80/150 ††£ 80/150
**Rest** – Menu £ 40 (dinner) – Carte £ 27/39
• 17C hunting lodge in 10 acres of landscaped gardens. Elegant, well-appointed guest areas. Smart bedrooms – several with four-posters – have good views and state-of-the-art bathrooms, some with TVs. Fresh cooking: everything made in-house; simpler dishes at lunch.

🏠 **Peacock**
*Bakewell Rd* ✉ DE4 2EB – ✆ (01629) 733 518 – www.thepeacockatrowsley.com
– *Closed 24-26 December*
**16 rm** – †£ 105/215 ††£ 190/250, ⬛ £ 7.25
**Rest** – (closed dinner 24-26 December and Sunday) Menu £ 26 (lunch)
– Carte £ 41/55
• Characterful 17C house with gardens leading down to the river. Bold modern colours sit alongside fine art and period furnishings in both the guest areas and bedrooms. Charming bar boasts stone walls, large fireplace and snack menu. Restaurant offers modern dishes.

---

**ROYAL LEAMINGTON SPA** – Warwickshire – **503** P27     **19** D3
– pop. 61 595
▶ London 99 mi – Birmingham 23 mi – Coventry 9 mi – Leicester 33 mi
�894 The Parade ✆ (01926) 74 27 62, www.royal-leamington-spa.co.uk
🄳8 Leamington and County Whitnash Golf Lane, ✆ (01926) 42 59 61

# ROYAL
# LEAMINGTON SPA

KENILWORTH A 452  A 445  RUGBY

CENTRE

ENGLAND

---

### 🏠 Mallory Court ☻  🎇 ⅃ ※ 🛎 ᶑ ※ rm, ⁽ᵗⁱ⁾ ⳻ 🄿 VISA ⚙ AE ①
☆☆

*Harbury Lane, Bishop's Tachbrook, South : 2.25 mi by B 4087 (Tachbrook Rd)*
✉ CV33 9QB – ℰ (01926) 453 939 – www.mallory.co.uk
**30 rm** ⌧ – †£ 105/395 ††£ 159/495
**Rest** *Brasserie at Mallory* – see restaurant listing
**Rest** *The Dining Room* – (closed Saturday lunch) (booking essential)
Menu £ 33/60
**Spec.** Salad of blue lobster, compressed melon and Parma ham. Chump of lamb,
tagine style spring roll and tahini. 'K' lime pie with chocolate ice cream and meringues.
♦ Charming part-Edwardian country house in Lutyens style, with delightful gardens. Classical lounges display fine antiques and quality furnishings; more modern extension houses the function room. Smart bedrooms are in keeping with
the age of the building and come with fresh flowers and fruit. Excellent service.
Smart brasserie or elegant, wood-panelled dining room offering daily set menu
and elaborate à la carte.

---

### 🏠 Adams *without rest*  🎇 ※ ⁽ᵗⁱ⁾ 🄿 VISA ⚙

*22 Avenue Rd ✉ CV31 3PQ – ℰ (01926) 450 742 – www.adams-hotel.co.uk*
*– Closed 23 December-2 January*  **Vn**
**12 rm** ⌧ – †£ 68/88 ††£ 88/115
♦ Delightful house of the Regency period with plenty of charm and character:
original features include ceiling mouldings. Immaculate and similarly attractive
bedrooms.

---

### ※※ Restaurant 23  AC VISA ⚙ AE ①

*23 Dormer Pl. ✉ CV32 5AA – ℰ (01926) 422 422 – www.restaurant23.co.uk*
*– Closed 1-14 January, last 2 weeks August, 25-26 December, Sunday and*
*Monday*  **Va**
**Rest** – Menu £ 20/25 – Carte £ 38/55 ⅜
♦ Intimate restaurant with open kitchen and elegantly appointed surroundings.
Classically based, seasonal, modern dishes are created by the owner. Interesting
wine list features some rarely seen 'esoteric' wines.

575

ENGLAND

XX **Oscar's**                                              VISA ✪ AE

*39 Chandos St* ✉ *CV32 4RL* – ✆ *(01926) 452 807* – *www.oscarsfrenchbistro.co.uk*
*– Closed Sunday and Monday*                                          U✕
**Rest** – French – *(booking essential)* Menu £ 11/28
• Two-floored, classical French bistro close to the main shopping street. Three
dining rooms with closely set linen-laid tables, busy walls and plenty of atmo-
sphere. Good value menus and friendly service.

XX **Emperors**                                        AK VISA ✪ AE ①

*Bath Pl.* ✉ *CV31 3BP* – ✆ *(01926) 313 030* – *Closed 1 January, 25-26 December*
*and Sunday*                                                          Vi
**Rest** – Chinese – Carte £ 21/30 **s**
• Former warehouse, now a spacious Chinese restaurant with smart red, gold
and black décor. Emperors' jackets hang on the walls. Large menus mix popular
and authentic dishes with seasonal specials.

XX **Brasserie at Mallory** – at Mallory Court Hotel       ⌂ AK ✿ P

*Harbury Lane, Bishop's Tachbrook, South : 2.25 mi by B*            VISA ✪ AE ①
*4087 (Tachbrook Rd)* ✉ *CV33 9QB* – ✆ *(01926) 453 939* – *www.mallory.co.uk*
*– Closed Sunday dinner*
**Rest** – *(booking essential)* Carte £ 25/42
• Smart brasserie in a part-Edwardian country house. Striking bar with black art
deco features; pleasant restaurant with airy, conservatory style. Wide-ranging modern British menu follows the seasons. Lovely views of the pretty walled garden.

**at Weston under Wetherley** Northeast : 4.5 mi by A 445 on B 4453
– ✉ Royal Leamington Spa

⌂ **Wethele Manor** without rest ⌖          ⌂ ♨ ✾ ⌆ P VISA ✪ ①

✉ *CV33 9BZ* – ✆ *(01926) 831 772* – *www.wethelemanor.com*
**9 rm** ⌕ – †£ 70 ††£ 70/95
• 16C farmhouse with large garden, patio and water feature, set in 250 acres of
working farm. Comfy lounge in old dairy; wood-furnished breakfast room complete with well. Classical bedrooms.

**at Offchurch** East : 3.5 mi by A 425

⌂ **Stag**                                          ⌂ ⌂ AK VISA ✪ AE ①

*Welsh Rd* ✉ *CV33 9AQ* – ✆ *(01926) 425 801* – *www.thestagatoffchurch.com*
**Rest** – Carte £ 22/40
• 16C thatched pub with boldly coloured bar and 2 modern dining rooms. Extensive menu changes with the seasons, offering generous, classically based
dishes and sharing plates. Efficient service.

---

**ROYAL TUNBRIDGE WELLS** – Kent – **504** U30 – pop. 59 371          **8** B2
⌷ Great Britain

▶ London 36 mi – Brighton 33 mi – Folkestone 46 mi – Hastings 27 mi
🛈 The Pantiles ✆ (01892) 51 56 75, www.visittunbridgewells.com
🏌 Langton Rd, ✆ (01892) 52 30 34
👁 The Pantiles ★ B **26** – Calverley Park ★ B

🏨 **Hotel du Vin**                          ⌂ ⌷ AK ⌖ ⌂ P VISA ✪ AE ①

*Crescent Rd* ✉ *TN1 2LY* – ✆ *(01892) 526 455* – *www.hotelduvin.com*
**34 rm** ⌕ – †£ 130/290 ††£ 130/290                                Bc
**Rest** *Bistro* – see restaurant listing
• Attractive 18C property in the town centre, boasting southerly views over the
park. Wine-themed throughout, with comfy lounge, clubby bar and even its own
vineyard. Contemporary bedrooms; some have baths in the room and emperor-
sized beds.

# OYAL TUNBRIDGE WELLS

ENGLAND

## Brew House
*1 Warwick Pk.* ⊠ *TN2 5TA* – *ℰ (01892) 520 587* – *www.brewhousehotel.com*
**15 rm** ⬜ – ✝£155 ✝✝£199                                                                 B**x**
**Rest *One*** – Carte £18/37
♦ Former brewhouse and Subbuteo factory; now a boutique hotel. Bedrooms – 3 of which have balconies – boast a clean, minimalist style; bathrooms have glass walls which turn opaque at the touch of a button. Stylish restaurant decorated in vivid pinks and stark whites.

## Danehurst without rest
*41 Lower Green Rd, Rusthall, West : 1.75 mi by A 264* ⊠ *TN4 8TW* – *ℰ (01892) 527 739* – *www.danehurst.net* – *Closed Christmas and New Year*                        A**e**
**4 rm** ⬜ – ✝£70/95 ✝✝£99/139
♦ Quiet Victorian house with terrace and koi carp pond. Quality furnishings and good attention to detail in bedrooms. Comfy lounge, library and conservatory breakfast room with homemade bread/jam.

## Thackeray's
*85 London Rd* ⊠ *TN1 1EA* – *ℰ (01892) 511 921*
*– www.thackerays-restaurant.co.uk* – *Closed Sunday dinner and Monday*
**Rest** – Menu £19/27 – Carte £42/53                                                        B**n**
♦ Attractive clapperboard house; former residence of the author Thackeray. Lovely terrace, lounge and two dining rooms with bold art. Classical cooking uses good ingredients; modern presentation.

## Bistro – at Hotel du Vin
*Crescent Rd* ⊠ *TN1 2LY* – *ℰ (01892) 526 455* – *www.hotelduvin.com*
**Rest** – (booking essential) Carte £25/36                                                   B**c**
♦ Popular bistro in an attractive 18C town centre hotel. Walls are covered with wine-themed pictures and hops hang from the ceiling. Concise menu offers classic British and international dishes.

**at Speldhurst** Northwest : 3.5 mi by A 26 - A

🏠 **George & Dragon**  🕽 P VISA ⊛⊛
*Speldhurst Hill* ✉ TN3 0NN – ☎ *(01892) 863 125 – www.speldhurst.com – Closed 1 January, Sunday dinner and bank holiday Monday dinner*
**Rest** – Carte £ 23/31
♦ Impressive and hugely characterful Wealden Hall house dating back to 1212. Generous cooking uses local, organic produce. Lunch offers pub classics; the evening menu is more elaborate.

---

**ROZEL BAY** – Saint Martin – **503** P33 – see Channel Islands (Jersey)

---

**RUNSWICK BAY** – North Yorkshire – ✉ Whitby                                      23 C1
▶ London 285 mi – Middlesbrough 24 mi – Whitby 9 mi

🏠 **Cliffemount**  ⩽ ⇙ P VISA ⊛⊛
✉ TS13 5HU – ☎ *(01947) 840 103 – www.cliffemounthotel.co.uk*
**20 rm** ⌓ – ♦£ 70/110 ♦♦£ 175
**Rest** – *(dinner only and light lunch)* Menu £ 33 – Carte £ 28/43
♦ Enviably located hotel which has benefitted hugely from refurbishment. Cosy bar with blackboard menu. Balanced mix of luxurious or cosy bedrooms, 10 of which have balconies. Light, airy dining room boasts fantastic views of bay. Strong seafood base.

---

**RUSHLAKE GREEN** – East Sussex – **504** U31 – ✉ Heathfield                    8 B2
▶ London 54 mi – Brighton 26 mi – Eastbourne 13 mi

🏠 **Stone House** ⌂  ⇙ 🕮 🔇 👘 P VISA ⊛⊛
*(Northeast corner of the green.)* ✉ TN21 9QJ – ☎ *(01435) 830 553*
*– www.stonehousesussex.co.uk – Closed 20 February-16 March, Christmas and New Year*
**5 rm** ⌓ – ♦£ 102/138 ♦♦£ 204/275 – 2 suites
**Rest** – *(dinner only and lunch May-August) (residents only)* Menu £ 29 (dinner) **s** – Carte lunch approx. £ 19 **s**
♦ Impressive gates and beautiful gardens lead to charming, part-15C house; personally run and still in the same family. Country house interior with original staircases, wood-panelling and antiques. Individually decorated bedrooms feature period furnishings and some four-posters. Classical menus use kitchen garden produce.

---

**RYE** – East Sussex – **504** W31 – pop. 3 708 ▊ Great Britain                   9 C2
▶ London 61 mi – Brighton 49 mi – Folkestone 27 mi – Maidstone 33 mi
🛈 4/5 Lion St ☎ (01797) 22 90 49, www.visitrye.co.uk
👁 Old Town★★ : Mermaid Street★, St Mary's Church (⩽★)

🏠 **George in Rye**  🕽 👘 👘 ⅍ VISA ⊛⊛
*98 High St.* ✉ TN31 7JT – ☎ *(01797) 222 114 – www.thegeorgeinrye.com*
**24 rm** ⌓ – ♦♦£ 195  **Rest** – Carte £ 16/34
♦ Part 16C coaching inn; appealing mix of contemporary design and original features. Variously-sized bedrooms have state-of-the-art TVs and quality linen. Pleasant courtyard. Trendy restaurant offers Mediterranean dishes made with locally sourced produce and good choice of wines by glass.

🏠 **Mermaid Inn**  👘 👘 P VISA ⊛⊛ AE
*Mermaid St.* ✉ TN31 7EY – ☎ *(01797) 223 065 – www.mermaidinn.com*
**31 rm** ⌓ – ♦£ 90/260 ♦♦£ 220/260  **Rest** – Menu £ 25/38 – Carte £ 27/61
♦ Historic inn dating from 15C. Immense character from the timbered exterior on a cobbled street to the heavily beamed, antique furnished interior warmed by roaring log fires. Two dining options: both exude age and character.

🏠 **Jeake's House** without rest  👘 P VISA ⊛⊛
*Mermaid St.* ✉ TN31 7ET – ☎ *(01797) 222 828 – www.jeakeshouse.com*
**11 rm** ⌓ – ♦£ 69/79 ♦♦£ 138
♦ Down a cobbled lane, a part 17C house, once a wool store and a Quaker meeting place. Welcoming atmosphere amid antiques, sloping floors and beams. Pretty, traditional rooms.

↑ **Oaklands** without rest ⤴    ≤ 🚗 ⅌ 🛰 🅿 🆅🆂🅰 🆔
*Udimore Rd, Southwest : 1.25 mi on B 2089* ⊠ *TN31 6AB* – ℰ *(01797) 229 734*
*– www.oaklands-rye.co.uk*
**3 rm** ⌷ – ♦£ 70/80 ♦♦£ 100/120
♦ Friendly Edwardian house with town/coast/white cliff views. Guest areas feature souvenirs from owner's time abroad – breakfast table is an Omani front door. Well-kept bedrooms; 2 four-posters.

↑ **Willow Tree House** without rest    🚗 ⅌ 🛰 🅿 🆅🆂🅰 🆔 🆎
*113 Winchelsea Rd., South : 0.5 mi on A 259* ⊠ *TN31 7EL* – ℰ *(01797) 227 820*
*– www.willow-tree-house.com*
**6 rm** ⌷ – ♦£ 75/95 ♦♦£ 90/130
♦ Lovingly restored 18C house close to harbour. Light colours and modern fabrics sit beside exposed brickwork and original fireplaces. Bedrooms boast excellent bathrooms with power showers. Good breakfasts.

✗ **Webbe's at The Fish Café**    🅰🅲 ⇔ 🆅🆂🅰 🆔 🆎
*17 Tower St.* ⊠ *TN31 7AT* – ℰ *(01797) 222 226* – *www.webbesrestaurants.co.uk*
*– Closed 24 December-2 January*
**Rest** – Seafood – Carte £ 21/42
♦ Relaxed café in former antiques warehouse, with terracotta-coloured brick walls, open-plan kitchen and small counter. Extensive menu of simply prepared seafood from Rye/Hastings day boats.

🛏 **Ship Inn** with rm    🛋 🆅🆂🅰 🆔
*The Strand* ⊠ *TN31 7DB* – ℰ *(01797) 222 233* – *www.theshipinnrye.co.uk*
**10 rm** ⌷ – ♦£ 80 ♦♦£ 100   **Rest** – Carte £ 23/28
♦ 16C former warehouse with shabby, slightly wacky styling and extremely laidback feel. Carefully prepared, rustic dishes arrive in generous, flavoursome portions and ingredients are well-sourced. Compact bedrooms boast unusual feature walls and bold styling.

**at Camber** Southeast : 4.25 mi by A 259 – ⊠ Rye

🏨 **Gallivant**    🅰🅲 🛰 🅿 🆅🆂🅰 🆔 🅾
*New Lydd Rd.* ⊠ *TN31 7RB* – ℰ *(01797) 225 057* – *www.thegallivanthotel.com*
**18 rm** ⌷ – ♦£ 85/125 ♦♦£ 95/135
**Rest** *Beach Bistro* – see restaurant listing
♦ Laid-back hotel opposite Camber Sands, run by a keen, friendly team. Small lounge and terrace with slightly bohemian feel. Bedrooms come in blues and whites, with distressed wood furniture and good modern facilities; four are studio-style.

✗✗ **Beach Bistro** – at Gallivant Hotel    🛋 🅰🅲 🅿 🆅🆂🅰 🆔 🅾
*New Lydd Rd.* ⊠ *TN31 7RB* – ℰ *(01797) 225 057* – *www.thegallivanthotel.com*
**Rest** – Carte £ 23/36
♦ Informal hotel restaurant displaying distressed wood furniture and white and blue hues, set opposite Camber Sands. All-day menus have local seafood to the fore. Pleasant covered terrace.

**SAFFRON WALDEN** – Essex – **504** U27 – pop. 14 313    **12** B1
🚇 London 43 mi – Bishop's Stortford 12 mi – Cambridge 18 mi

✗ **the restaurant**    🆅🆂🅰 🆔 🆎
*Victoria House, 2 Church St* ⊠ *CB10 1JW* – ℰ *(01799) 526 444* – *www.trocs.co.uk*
*– Closed 2 weeks summer, 26 December-2 January, Easter, Sunday and Monday*
**Rest** – *(dinner only)* Menu £ 18 (weekdays) – Carte £ 24/35 **s**
♦ Cosy basement restaurant in town centre, displaying stone floors, exposed brick and modern art. Stylishly presented dishes boast well-defined flavours and some interesting Mediterranean touches.

ENGLAND

### ✗ Dish
AC VISA ⑩⓪

*13a King St ⊠ CB10 1HE – ℰ (01799) 513 300 – www.dishrestaurant.co.uk
– Closed 25-26 December, 1 January, Sunday dinner and bank holiday Mondays*
**Rest** – Menu £ 20/25

• First floor restaurant within characterful beamed house in town centre. Modern oil paintings exude jazzy theme. Classically based dishes take on adventurous note at dinner.

---

## ST ALBANS – Hertfordshire – 504 T28 – pop. 80 664 ▌ Great Britain    12 A2

▶ London 27 mi – Cambridge 41 mi – Luton 10 mi

🛈 Market Pl ℰ (01727) 86 45 11, www.allaboutstalbans.com

🏌18 Batchwood Hall Batchwood Drive, ℰ (01727) 83 33 49

🏌27 Redbourn Kinsbourne Green Lane, ℰ (01582) 79 34 93

◉ City★ - Cathedral★ BZ – Verulamium★ (Museum★ **AC** AY)

🅖 Hatfield House★★ **AC**, E : 6 mi by A 1057

**St Michael's Manor** 🚗 ⚖ 🛁 ☎ ⚒ **P** VISA ⦿ 🆎 ①

*St Michael's Village, Fishpool St* ⊠ *AL3 4RY* – ☎ *(01727) 864 444*
*– www.stmichaelsmanor.com*                                                        AY**d**
**29 rm** ⌂ – †£ 125/180 ††£ 260 – 1 suite
**Rest** *The Lake* – see restaurant listing
◆ Part-16C William and Mary manor house boasting well-tended gardens and
lake views. Characterful guest areas display contemporary touches. Well-appointed, traditionally styled bedrooms; annexe rooms are more modern and
some have terraces.

XX **Cibo DiVino** 🆎 VISA ⦿

*4-5 Waddington Rd* ⊠ *AL3 5EX* – ☎ *(01727) 899 189* – *www.cibodivino.co.uk*
*– Closed Sunday dinner and Monday*                                          BY**x**
**Rest** – Italian – Menu £ 14 (lunch) – Carte £ 28/37
◆ Keenly run restaurant hidden down a side street; a partnership between an
Italian and an experienced English chef. Authentic Italian cooking displays fresh,
clear flavours. Pasta is homemade and many ingredients are imported from Italy.

**1081** *HARPENDEN, LUTON*

ENGLAND

*( M25 ) POTTERS BAR* A 1081

ENGLAND

XX **The Lake** – at St Michael's Manor Hotel    ⪡ ⪤ P̲ VISA ⬤ AE ⓘ
*St Michael's Village, Fishpool St* ⊠ *AL3 4RY –* ℰ *(01727) 864 444*
*– www.stmichaelsmanor.com*    AYd
**Rest** *– (closed dinner 25 December)* Menu £ 17/21 *(weekday dinner)*
– Carte £ 34/43
♦ Light, airy conservatory restaurant in a family owned, part-16C William and
Mary manor house; set to the rear, it looks out over well-tended gardens. Modern
menu has a largely classical base.

X **Sukiyaki**    VISA ⬤ AE ⓘ
*6 Spencer St* ⊠ *AL3 5EG –* ℰ *(01727) 865 009 – Closed 2 weeks in summer, 1
week Christmas, Sunday, Monday and Tuesday lunch*    BYe
**Rest** *– Japanese –* Menu £ 9/22 – Carte £ 17/20
♦ A pared-down style, minimally decorated restaurant with simple, precise help-
ings of Japanese food. No noodles or sushi, expect instead sukiyaki (a beef dish),
and tempura.

🍺 **Blue Anchor**    ⪢ P̲ VISA ⬤ ⓘ
*145 Fishpool St* ⊠ *AL3 4RY –* ℰ *(01727) 855 038*
*– www.theblueanchorstalbans.co.uk – Closed Sunday dinner*    AYx
**Rest** – Menu £ 17 *(lunch)* – Carte £ 22/30
♦ Smart pub with bistro-style interior and riverside garden. The chef is passionate
about local, seasonal produce; menus display top notch ingredients, homemade
and home-smoked products.

**ST ANNE'S** – Lancashire – **502** K22 – see Lytham St Anne's

**ST AUBIN** – **503** P33 – see Channel Islands (Jersey)

**ST AUSTELL** – Cornwall – **503** F32 – pop. 22 658    1 B2
▶ London 281 mi – Newquay 16 mi – Plymouth 38 mi – Truro 14 mi
🏬 Carlyon Bay, ℰ(01726) 81 42 50
◉ Holy Trinity Church★
◢ St Austell Bay★★ (Gribbin Head★★) E : by A 390 and A 3082 – Carthew : Wheal
Martyn China Clay Heritage Centre★★ **AC**, N : 2 mi by A 391 – Mevagissey★★
- Lost Gardens of Heligan★, S : 5 mi by B 3273 – Charlestown★, SE : 2 mi by A 390
– Eden Project★★, NE : 3 mi by A 390 at St Blazey Gate. Trewithen★★★ **AC**, NE :
7 mi by A 390 – Lanhydrock★★, NE : 11 mi by A 390 and B 3269 – Polkerris★, E :
7 mi by A 390 and A 3082

⌂ **Poltarrow Farm** without rest    ⪤ 🖐 📺 💈 ☝ P̲ VISA ⬤
*St Mewan, Southwest : 1.75 mi by A 390* ⊠ *PL26 7DR –* ℰ *(01726) 67 111*
*– www.poltarrow.co.uk – Closed Christmas-New Year*
**5 rm** � – ♦£ 60 ♦♦£ 80
♦ Appealing 19C house on working farm. Homely bedrooms. Facilities include a
snooker table, badminton court, pool and bowling alley. Cosy lounge; lovely conservatory for Aga-cooked breakfasts.

**at Tregrehan** East : 2.5 mi by A 390 – ⊠ St Austell

⌂ **Anchorage House**    ⪤ 📺 🏠 💈 💇 ☝ P̲ VISA ⬤ AE
*Nettles Corner, Boscundle* ⊠ *PL25 3RH –* ℰ *(01726) 814 071*
*– www.anchoragehouse.co.uk – 15 March-15 November*
**5 rm** ⊡ – ♦£ 70/75 ♦♦£ 105/135   **Rest** – Carte approx. £ 22
♦ Modern guesthouse owned by ex-Canadian Naval Commander. Afternoon tea
served in comfy lounge. Charming, antique-filled bedrooms boast modern fabrics, state-of-the-art bathrooms and plenty of extras. Indoor pool, gym, sauna
and chill out lounge. Conservatory dining room offers simple, home-cooked
dishes. Lovely owners.

**at Carlyon Bay** East : 2.5 mi by A 3601 – ⊠ St Austell

🏨 **Carlyon Bay** ≤ 🚇 ♨ ⌇ ⊠ 🚗 🛜 🏄 ♨ ⚓ 🏊 🛎 ⚔ 🎦 rest, 🐾 🛜 🕭 **P** VISA ⓪ AE
⊠ PL25 3RD – ✆ (01726) 812 304 – www.carlyonbay.com
**86 rm** (dinner included) ⌇ – ♦£ 95/300 ♦♦£ 280/400
**Rest** *Bay View* – Menu £ 22/38 – Carte £ 38/53
**Rest** *Taste* – (dinner only) Carte £ 33/59
♦ Imposing 1920s hotel boasting original art deco features and superb bay views. Large, traditionally furnished guest areas. Modern bedrooms feature lightly hued fabrics: rear rooms are bright; front rooms have views. Bay View serves unfussy classics. Taste offers modern brasserie fare.

🍴 **Austell's** VISA ⓪
10 Beach Rd. ⊠ PL25 3PH – ✆ (01726) 813 888 – www.austells.net – Closed 1-14 January, 25-26 December and Monday
**Rest** – (dinner only) Menu £ 20/33
♦ Keenly run restaurant with relaxed, stylish interior. Small bar and open-plan kitchen. Modern, seasonal menu showcases local produce and features original touches. More casual weekend lunches.

**ST BLAZEY** – Cornwall – **503** F32 – pop. 8 837 **1** B2
🚗 London 276 mi – Newquay 21 mi – Plymouth 33 mi – Truro 19 mi
🎦 Eden Project★★, NW; 1.5 mi by A 390 and minor roads

🏠 **Penarwyn House** without rest ♨ 🚇 🐾 🛜 **P** VISA ⓪ AE
West : 0.75 mi by A 390 turning left at Doubletree School ⊠ PL24 2DS
– ✆ (01726) 814 224 – www.penarwyn.co.uk – Closed 1 week Christmas
**3 rm** ⌇ – ♦£ 65/85 ♦♦£ 80/150
♦ Whitewashed former gentleman's residence, surrounded by mature gardens and run by welcoming owners. Spacious lounge, clubby snooker room and formal breakfast room. Bedrooms boast bold features walls, antique furniture and modern facilities.

**ST BRELADE'S BAY** – **503** P33 – see Channel Islands (Jersey)

**ST HELIER** – **503** P33 – see Channel Islands (Jersey)

**ST HILARY** – Cornwall – see Marazion

**ST ISSEY** – Cornwall – **503** F32 – see Padstow

**ST IVES** – Cornwall – **503** D33 – pop. 9 866 **1** A3
🚗 London 319 mi – Penzance 10 mi – Truro 25 mi
🛈 Street-an-Pol ✆ (01736) 79 62 97, www.stives-cornwall.co.uk
🔼 Tregenna Castle H., ✆ (01736) 79 52 54
🔼 West Cornwall Lelant, ✆ (01736) 75 34 01
◉ Town★★ - Barbara Hepworth Museum★★ **AC** Y **M1** – Tate St Ives★★ (≤★★) - St Nicholas Chapel (≤★★) Y – Parish Church★ Y **A**
🎦 S : Penwith★★ Y. St Michael's Mount★★ (≤★★) S : 10 mi by B 3306 - Y - B 3311, B 3309 and A 30

Plan on next page

🏠 **Blue Hayes** without rest ≤ 🚇 🐾 🛜 **P** VISA ⓪ AE
Trelyon Ave ⊠ TR26 2AD – ✆ (01736) 797 129 – www.bluehayes.co.uk
– March-October **Yu**
**6 rm** ⌇ – ♦£ 100/140 ♦♦£ 210/230
♦ 19C house with super view from terrace over the harbour; access to coast path from garden. Hi-tech interior. Single course supper available. Well-appointed bedrooms.

ENGLAND

Traffic restrictions apply in town centre during summer months.

ST. IVES

0 — 300 m
0 — 300 yards

TATE GALLERY

Y

ST. IVES BAY

ENGLAND

ZENNOR
(B 3311) B 3306 LAND'S END

CARBIS BAY

Z

600 Yards

(A 30) A 3074 HAYLE (A 3074)

🏠 **Primrose Valley** without rest ⟨≤ ⚘ ⟨⟩ P VISA ⑩ AE

*Porthminster Beach* ⊠ *TR26 2ED –* ☎ *(01736) 794 939*
*– www.primroseonline.co.uk – Closed 21-26 December and 3-31 January*
**9 rm** � *–* 🛏£ 130/160 🛏🛏£ 140/240 – 1 suite    Y**r**
♦ Edwardian villa with unrivalled proximity to beach. Stylish café bar and lounge; relaxing front patio. Local suppliers ensure good breakfast choice. Individually styled rooms.

🏠 **abode st ives** without rest 🚅 ⚘ ⟨⟩ P VISA ⑩ AE

*1 Fern Glen* ⊠ *TR26 1QP –* ☎ *(01736) 799 047 – www.abodestives.co.uk*
**4 rm** ⊏ *–* 🛏£ 100/120 🛏🛏£ 110/130    Y**x**
♦ Chic, contemporary guesthouse offering stylish, immaculately kept bedrooms; two with sea views. Cosy minimal sitting room. Open-plan kitchen/breakfast room. Laid-back owners.

XX **Alba**  ≤ AC VISA ⓜ AE
*Old Lifeboat House, The Wharf* ⊠ *TR26 1LF –* ℰ *(01736) 797 222*
*– www.thealbarestaurant.com – closed 25-26 December*  **Yd**
**Rest** – Menu £ 19 (lunch and early dinner) – Carte £ 26/33
◆ Ideally situated in centre of town, on both floors of Old Lifeboat House; good
harbour views. Modern feel; artwork on walls. Tasty, extensive menus with a
modern slant.

X **Porthminster Beach Cafe**  ≤ �苗 VISA ⓜ ①
*Porthminster Beach* ⊠ *TR26 2EB –* ℰ *(01736) 795 352*
*– www.porthminstercafe.co.uk – Closed January and December 25*  **Yp**
**Rest** – Seafood – *(booking advisable)* Carte £ 24/36
◆ 1930s beach house on Porthminster sands. Super views: large terrace for al
fresco dining. Colourful local artwork on walls. Seafood oriented dishes plus eclectic dinner menus.

X **Loft**  ≤ �苗 VISA ⓜ
*Norway Ln* ⊠ *TR26 1LZ –* ℰ *(01736) 794 204*
*– www.theloftrestaurantandterrace.co.uk – March-November, closed Sunday and
Monday during November*  **Ys**
**Rest** – Menu £ 16 (lunch and early dinner) – Carte £ 24/48
◆ Long, narrow first floor restaurant; choose a table on the roof terrace with
views out towards the harbour and beaches. Generous portions; plenty of local
seafood. Relaxed, friendly service.

X **Black Rock**  🍴 VISA ⓜ
☺ *Market Pl* ⊠ *TR26 1RZ –* ℰ *(01736) 791 911 – www.theblackrockstives.co.uk*
*– Closed January, November, Sunday and restricted opening in winter*
**Rest** – *(dinner only)* *(booking advisable)* Carte £ 23/30  **Yv**
◆ Relaxed, modern bistro, featuring contemporary artworks and a minimalist
style; well run, with attentive, friendly service. Menu of fresh local produce with
the emphasis on seafood.

**at Carbis Bay** South : 1.75 mi on A 3074 – ⊠ St Ives

🏠 **Boskerris**  ≤ 🚗 🌠 🎱 ℗ VISA ⓜ
*Boskerris Rd* ⊠ *TR26 2NQ –* ℰ *(01736) 795 295 – www.boskerrishotel.co.uk*
*– mid-February-mid-November*  **Zx**
**15 rm** ⊆ – †£ 128/154 ††£ 170/240
**Rest** – *(closed Sunday)* *(dinner only)* Carte £ 24/31
◆ Ever-improving, contemporary hotel with panoramic views of Carbis Bay and
coastline. Tastefully appointed bedrooms; relaxing lounge. Enthusiastic young
owners. Good, honest home-cooking.

**ST KEVERNE** – Cornwall – **503** E33 – pop. 1 843  **1** A3
🖸 London 302 mi – Penzance 26 mi – Truro 28 mi

🏠 **Old Temperance House** without rest  🌠 🎱 ℗
*The Square* ⊠ *TR12 6NA –* ℰ *(01326) 280 986 – www.oldtemperancehouse.co.uk*
**4 rm** ⊆ – †£ 55 ††£ 84
◆ Pretty pink-washed cottage framed by olive trees. Immaculately kept, contemporary interior; bright bedrooms display thoughtful touches. Fresh fruit and produce from local butcher for breakfast.

X **Greenhouse**  VISA ⓜ
*6 High St.* ⊠ *TR12 6NN –* ℰ *(01326) 280 800 – www.tgor.co.uk – Closed last 2
weeks January, Sunday lunch at bank holidays and Mother's Day*
**Rest** – *(dinner only and Sunday lunch)* Carte £ 20/34
◆ Simply furnished eatery with open kitchen, set in a sleepy little village. Daily
blackboard menu is centred around local, organic and gluten free produce. Cooking is unfussy and flavoursome.

**ST KEW** – Cornwall – see Wadebridge

**ST LAWRENCE** – Saint Lawrence – **503** P33 – see Channel Islands (Jersey)

ENGLAND

**ST MARGARET'S AT CLIFFE** – Kent – **504** Y30 – see Dover

**ST MARTIN** – **503** P33 – see Channel Islands (Guernsey)

**ST MARTIN'S** – **503** B34 – see Scilly (Isles of)

**ST MARY'S** – **503** B34 – see Scilly (Isles of)

**ST MAWES** – Cornwall – **503** E33 – ✉ Truro                                                         **1** B3
▶ London 299 mi – Plymouth 56 mi – Truro 18 mi
◉ Town★ - Castle★ **AC** (≤★)
◉ St Just-in-Roseland Church★★, N : 2.5 mi by A 3078

🏨 **Hotel Tresanton** ⚑                                         ≤ ⚓ ⁽ᵖ⁾ 🛁 **P** 𝘝𝘐𝘚𝘈 ⦿ 𝘈𝘌
*27 Lower Castle Rd* ✉ *TR2 5DR* – *𝒞 (01326) 270 055* – *www.tresanton.com*
*– Closed 2 weeks January*
**30 rm** ⌂ – †£ 230/365 ††£ 230/365 – 1 suite
**Rest** *Restaurant Tresanton* – see restaurant listing
♦ Collection of old fishermen's cottages, a yacht club and cinema. Elegant, nautically themed guest areas include an intimate bar and a movie room. Understated
bedrooms, some in cottages, have a high level of facilities and afford superb sea
views. Lovely split-level terrace shares the outlook. Delightful team.

⌂ **Nearwater** without rest                                    ⚑ ⁝ ⁽ᵖ⁾ **P** 𝘝𝘐𝘚𝘈 ⦿ 𝘈𝘌
*Polvarth Rd., East : 0.5 mi on A 3078* ✉ *TR2 5AY* – *𝒞 (01326) 279 278*
*– www.nearwaterstmawes.co.uk*
**3 rm** ⌂ – †£ 85/90 ††£ 90/100
♦ Modern, purpose-built guesthouse with small lawned garden, set on the main
road of a popular coastal town. Open-plan lounge and breakfast room with real
fires and subtle nautical theme. Smart, New England style bedrooms offer good
mod cons.

⚔⚔ **Restaurant Tresanton** – at Hotel Tresanton                    ≤ ⚐ **P** 𝘝𝘐𝘚𝘈 ⦿ 𝘈𝘌
*27 Lower Castle Rd* ✉ *TR2 5DR* – *𝒞 (01326) 270 055* – *www.tresanton.com*
*– Closed 2 weeks January*
**Rest** – *(booking essential)* Menu £ 35/44
♦ Appealing hotel restaurant boasting a large terrace and superb bay views; popular for its Sunday BBQs and live jazz band. Bright interior with nautical theme
and attractive mosaic flooring. Daily menus offer unfussy dishes crafted from
quality local produce; seafood is a feature. Polite, efficient service.

**ST MERRYN** – Cornwall – **503** F32 – see Padstow

**ST OSYTH** – Essex – **504** X28 – pop. 4 119                                                          **13** D2
▶ London 83 mi – Croydon 88 mi – Barnet 81 mi – Ealing 94 mi

⌂ **Park Hall** without rest ⚑                                  ⚑ ⌂ ⁝ ⁽ᵖ⁾ **P** 𝘝𝘐𝘚𝘈 ⦿ 𝘈𝘌
*Park Hall, East : 1.5 mi on B 1027* ✉ *CO16 8HG* – *𝒞 (01255) 820 922*
*– www.parkhall.info – Closed first two weeks January*
**3 rm** ⌂ – †£ 75/110 ††£ 130/190
♦ 14C antique-filled former monastery in 600 acres of arable farmland, with 5
acres of grounds, where peacocks roam free. Traditionally styled rooms come
with many thoughtful extras.

**ST PETER PORT** – **503** P33 – see Channel Islands (Guernsey)

**ST SAVIOUR** – **503** P33 – see Channel Islands (Jersey)

**ST SAVIOUR** – **503** P33 – see Channel Islands (Guernsey)

**ENGLAND**

**SALCOMBE** – Devon – **503** I33 – pop. 1 893                    **2** C3

 London 243 mi – Exeter 43 mi – Plymouth 27 mi – Torquay 28 mi

 Market St *C* (01548) 84 39 27, www.salcombeinformation.co.uk

G Sharpitor (Overbecks Museum and Garden★) (≤★★) **AC**, S : 2 mi by South Sands
Z. Prawle Point (≤★★★) E : 16 mi around coast by A 381 - Y - and A 379

---

🏨 **South Sands**                    ≤ 命 ㅎ rm, ⁽ᵗ⁾ **P** *VISA* **⬤⬤**
   *Bolt Head* ⊠ TQ8 8LL – *C* (01548) 859 000 – www.southsands.com
   **22 rm** � – †£ 135/190 ††£ 250/350 – 5 suites                    **Z**x
   **Rest** – Carte £ 28/42
   ◆ Stylish hotel by the water's edge, with subtle New England theme and stunning spiral staircase. Subtle, tasteful bedrooms; go for one at the front with a balcony. Large, airy restaurant with delightful decked terrace; menus place their emphasis on fresh seafood.

**at Soar Mill Cove** Southwest : 4.25 mi by A 381 - Y - via Malborough village
– ⊠ Salcombe

🏨 **Soar Mill Cove** ⑤                    ≤ 命 ⌂ ⌘ ⌥ 㿟 ※ **P** *VISA* **⬤⬤**
   ⊠ TQ7 3DS – *C* (01548) 561 566 – www.soarmillcove.co.uk – mid
   February-October
   **22 rm** ⊕ – †£ 115/215 ††£ 190/240    **Rest** – Menu £ 29
   ◆ Family-run hotel built from local slate and stone; delightfully set by the water's
   edge in a secluded cove. Good range of leisure facilities. Spacious bedrooms in
   bright, contemporary styles; half have sea views. Smart champagne bar. Classically based modern menu.

ENGLAND

**SALCOMBE**

587

**SALE** – Greater Manchester – **502** N23 – pop. 55 234 – ⊠ **Manchester**    **20** B3
▶ London 212 mi – Liverpool 36 mi – Manchester 6 mi – Sheffield 43 mi
🖫 Sale Lodge Golf Rd, ✆ (0161) 973 16 38

⌂    **Cornerstones** without rest    🖫 🕯 📶 **P** VISA ⊛ ①
     *230 Washway Rd, (on A 56)* ⊠ *M33 4RA* – ✆ *(0161) 283 69 09*
     *– www.cornerstonesguesthouse.com – Closed 25 December-1 January*
     **9 rm** – ♦£ 30/55 ♦♦£ 60/68, ⌸ £ 6.50
     ◆ Substantial red-brick Victorian house with neat garden, in leafy suburban loca-
     tion. Slightly wacky interior with bohemian-style lounge and breakfast room. Bed-
     rooms range from retro to modern.

**SALISBURY** – Wiltshire – **503** O30 – pop. 42 940    **4** D3
▶ London 91 mi – Bournemouth 28 mi – Bristol 53 mi – Southampton 23 mi
🛈 Fish Row ✆ (01722) 33 49 56, www.visitwiltshire.co.uk
🖫 Salisbury & South Wilts. Netherhampton, ✆ (01722) 74 26 45
🖫 High Post Great Durnford, ✆ (01722) 78 23 56
👁 City★★ - Cathedral★★★ **AC** Z – Salisbury and South Wiltshire Museum★ **AC** Z **M2**
– Close★ Z : Mompesson House★ **AC** Z **A** – Sarum St Thomas Church★ Y **B**
– Redcoats in the Wardrobe★ Z **M1**
🌀 Wilton Village★ (Wilton House★★ **AC**, Wilton Carpet Factory★ **AC**), W : 3 mi by A
30 Y – Old Sarum★ **AC**, N : 2 mi by A 345 Y – Woodford (Heale House Garden★)
**AC**, NW : 4.5 mi by Stratford Rd Y. Stonehenge★★★ **AC**, NW : 10 mi by A 345 - Y
- and A 303 – Wardour Castle★ **AC**, W : 15 mi by A 30 Y

🏠    **Cricket Field House** without rest    🖫 ♿ 🕯 📶 🏊 **P** VISA ⊛
     *Wilton Rd, West : 1.25 mi on A 36* ⊠ *SP2 9NS* – ✆ *(01722) 322 595*
     *– www.cricketfieldhouse.co.uk*
     **14 rm** – ♦£ 50/85 ♦♦£ 65/105
     ◆ Personally run extended house overlooking the County Cricket Ground. Bed-
     rooms are prettily decorated with pictures and floral touches; majority of rooms
     are in the annex.

⌂    **2 Park Lane** without rest    🖫 🕯 📶 **P** VISA ⊛
     *2 Park Lane, North : 1.25 mi by A 345* ⊠ *SP1 3NP* – ✆ *(01722) 321 001*
     *– www.2parklane.co.uk – Closed 25-26 December and 1 January*
     **6 rm** ⌸ – ♦£ 60/65 ♦♦£ 70/80
     ◆ Fine Victorian house hidden away on a private road. Pleasant entranceway
     with original tiled floor; smart period breakfast room. Comfortable, modern bed-
     rooms come in light, understated hues.

⌂    **St Anns House** without rest    📶 VISA ⊛ AE
     *32-34 St Ann St* ⊠ *SP1 2DP* – ✆ *(01722) 335 657* – *www.stannshouse.co.uk*
     *– Closed Christmas-New Year*    Z**e**
     **8 rm** – ♦£ 54/79 ♦♦£ 79/89, ⌸ £ 8.50
     ◆ Traditional Georgian townhouse with immaculate bedrooms, sash windows
     and original fireplaces. Large breakfast menu offers well sourced options. Honesty
     bar and private dining available.

✗✗    **Anokaa**    AC VISA ⊛ AE
     *60 Fisherton St* ⊠ *SP2 7RB* – ✆ *(01722) 414 142* – *www.anokaa.com*
     **Rest** – Indian – *(buffet lunch)* Menu £ 9/24 – Carte £ 19/24    Y**e**
     ◆ Lives up to being "something out of the ordinary", with eye-catching interior
     and staff in silky full-length gowns. Indian dishes mix modern and classical styles
     with aplomb.

**at Burcombe** West : 5.25 mi by A 36 - Y - off A 30 – ⊠ **Salisbury**

🏠    **Ship Inn**    🖫 🍴 **P** VISA ⊛ AE
     *Burcombe Ln* ⊠ *SP2 0EJ* – ✆ *(01722) 743 182* – *www.theshipburcombe.co.uk*
     **Rest** – Carte £ 24/35
     ◆ Charming 17C pub with open fire, low ceilings and oak beams. Seasonal à la
     carte and twice-daily changing specials offer satisfying portions of traditional
     dishes. Delightful riverside garden.

ENGLAND

## SALISBURY

Stonehenge, AMESBURY **A 345**  LONDON (A 303), MARLBOROUGH **A 30**

**at Teffont** West : 10.25 mi by A 36 - Y - and A 30 on B 3089 – ⊠ Salisbury

🏠 **Howard's House** ⊱  🚗 🌐 **P** *VISA* 🏧 **AE**
*Teffont Evias* ⊠ *SP3 5RJ* – ℰ *(01722) 716 392* – *www.howardshousehotel.co.uk*
*– Closed 1 week Christmas*
**9 rm** ⊒ – 🛏£ 120 🛏🛏£ 210  **Rest** – Menu £ 20 (lunch) – Carte £ 30/45
♦ Personally run, part 17C dower house boasting fine gardens in a quaint, quiet
village. Comfortable lounge and pleasant bedrooms with village or garden vistas.
Garden herbs and vegetables grace accomplished cooking.

**at Little Langford** Northwest : 8 mi by A 36 - Y - and Great Wishford rd – ⊠ Salisbury

⋔   **Little Langford Farmhouse** without rest    ⬳ 🐾 🕭 🦚 🍴 **P** **VISA** **⦿**
  ⊠ SP3 4NP – ℰ (01722) 790 205 – www.littlelangford.co.uk – Restricted opening in winter
**3 rm** ⌷ – ⅋£ 60/75 ⅋⅋£ 80/85
◆ Unusual Victorian gothic farmhouse boasting a turret, crenellations and lancet windows; set amidst rolling farmland. Original features include a fine tile-floored entranceway and stripped oak furnishings. Spacious, double aspect bedrooms have a classical style.

**at Upper Woodford** North : 6.75 mi by A 360

🍴   **Bridge Inn**    🐾 🕭 **P** **VISA** **⦿** **AE**
⊠ SP4 6NU – ℰ (01722) 782 323 – www.thebridgewoodford.co.uk – Closed 25 December and Sunday dinner January-February
**Rest** – Carte £ 24/35
◆ Light, airy pub on banks of the River Avon, its garden an alfresco delight. Light bites lunch menu and classic à la carte; fresh, tasty dishes neatly presented on wood or slate.

---

**SANDFORD-ON-THAMES** – Oxfordshire – see Oxford

**SANDIWAY** – Cheshire West and Chester – **502** M24 – pop. 4 299    **20** A3
– ⊠ Northwich
▶ London 191 mi – Liverpool 34 mi – Manchester 22 mi – Stoke-on-Trent 26 mi

🏣   **Nunsmere Hall**    🐾 🕭 🕭 📺 ⅋ 🍴 ⅃ **P** **VISA** **⦿** **AE** **①**
Tarporley Rd, Southwest : 1.5 mi A 556 on A 49 ⊠ CW8 2ES – ℰ (01606) 889 100 – www.nunsmere.co.uk
**36 rm** ⌷ – ⅋£ 135 ⅋⅋£ 135
**Rest** *The Crystal* – Menu £ 22/30 – Carte dinner £ 41/51
◆ Secluded, on a wooded peninsular, originally built in 1900. Deep-seated sofas and sumptuous drawing rooms. Tasteful, individually furnished bedrooms exude quality and comfort. Dine in the classical style on imaginative and accomplished cuisine.

---

**SANDSEND** – North Yorkshire – **502** R/S20 – see Whitby

**SANDWICH** – Kent – **504** Y30 – pop. 4 398 ▌ Great Britain    **9** D2
▶ London 72 mi – Canterbury 13 mi – Dover 12 mi
🄳 Guildhall ℰ (01304) 61 35 65, www.discoversandwich.co.uk
◉ Town ★

🏨   **Bell at Sandwich**    ⅋ 🍴 ⅃ **VISA** **⦿** **AE**
The Quay ⊠ CT13 9EF – ℰ (01304) 613 388 – www.bellhotelsandwich.co.uk
**37 rm** ⌷ – ⅋£ 80/115 ⅋⅋£ 105/115
**Rest** *Old Dining Room* – see restaurant listing
◆ Substantial Victorian property with a cool modern interior, located next to the River Stour. Clubby, intimate bar; airy conservatory for coffee and light meals. Stylish, modern bedrooms come in cool pastel shades; some overlook the river.

🍴🍴   **Old Dining Room** – at Bell Hotel at Sandwich    **VISA** **⦿** **AE**
The Quay ⊠ CT13 9EF – ℰ (01304) 626 992 – www.bellhotelsandwich.co.uk
**Rest** – Menu £ 16 (lunch) – Carte £ 25/34
◆ Hotel dining room of grand proportions, set within a coolly modernised Victorian property overlooking the River Stour. Modern menu relies on seasonal ingredients sourced from local suppliers.

---

**SANDYPARK** – Devon – **503** I31 – see Chagford

**SAPPERTON** – Gloucestershire – see Cirencester

**SCARBOROUGH** – North Yorkshire – **502** S21 – pop. 38 364    **23** D1

📗 Great Britain

▶ London 253 mi – Kingston-upon-Hull 47 mi – Leeds 67 mi – Middlesbrough 52 mi

🛈 Brunswick, Westborough- Harbourside, Sandside ✆ (01723) 38 36 36, www.discoveryorkshirecoast.co.uk

🏊 Scarborough North Cliff North Cliff Ave, Burniston Rd, NW : 2 mi. by A 165, ✆ (01723) 35 53 97

🏊 Scarborough South Cliff Deepdale Ave, S : 1 mi. by A 165, off Filey Rd, ✆ (01723) 37 47 37

🅖 Robin Hood's Bay★, N : 16 mi on A 171 and minor rd to the right (signposted) – Whitby Abbey★, N : 21 mi on A 171 – Sledmere House★, S : 21 mi on A 645, B 1249 and B 1253 (right)

ENGLAND

ENGLAND

### Crown Spa ⟨icons⟩ rm, rest, P VISA AE

8-10 Esplanade ✉ YO11 2AG – ☎ (01723) 357 400 – www.crownspahotel.com
**114 rm** ⌷ – †£ 104/154 ††£ 178/248 – 1 suite                                   Zi
Rest *Taste* – ☎ (01723) 357 439 – Menu £ 30 **s** – Carte £ 27/36 **s**
• Refurbished 19C landmark hotel, in a prime position on the headland. Contemporary guest areas and good leisure facilities. Smart bedrooms with bespoke furnishings and latest mod cons. Four-roomed restaurant: 2 in bistro style, 2 more informal with a TV and bar.

### Beiderbecke's ⟨icons⟩ rest, VISA AE

1-3 The Cres ✉ YO11 2PW – ☎ (01723) 365 766 – www.beiderbeckes.com
**26 rm** ⌷ – †£ 85/90 ††£ 120/130 – 1 suite                                     Zs
Rest *Marmalade's* – ☎ (01723) 350 349 – Menu £ 22 (dinner) – Carte £ 27/35
• Named after the jazz musician. Although housed in a restored Georgian building, the rooms' décor is balanced between period style and contemporary feel with bright colours. Colourful, contemporary brasserie.

### Ox Pasture Hall ⟨icons⟩ P VISA AE

Lady Edith's Dr., Raincliffe Woods, West : 3.25 mi by A 171 following signs for
Raincliffe Woods ✉ YO12 5TD – ☎ (01723) 365 295 – www.oxpasturehall.com
**20 rm** ⌷ – †£ 79/125 ††£ 89/165
Rest *Courtyard* – (closed Monday and Tuesday) Carte £ 31/38 **s**
Rest *Brasserie* – Menu £ 18 **s** – Carte £ 22/30 **s**
• Charming, creeper-clad part-17C farmhouse, in 17 acres of landscaped gardens and grounds. Stylish, contemporary guest areas. Characterful bedrooms in main house; smarter rooms in rear courtyard. Linen-laid restaurant offers concise, modern à la carte. Brasserie serves simpler menu.

### Alexander ⟨icons⟩ P VISA

33 Burniston Rd ✉ YO12 6PG – ☎ (01723) 363 178
– www.alexanderhotelscarborough.co.uk – April-October                         Ya
**8 rm** ⌷ – †£ 65/75 ††£ 80/90
Rest – (closed Sunday) (dinner only) Menu £ 19 **s**
• 1930s red-brick house at the popular North Beach end of town. Well-kept, classically styled lounge. Contemporary bedrooms with flat-screen TVs, good comforts and clean, uncluttered style; some boast feature walls. Traditional cocktail bar and linen-laid dining room offering 3 choice set menu. Local seafood a feature.

### ✗✗ Lanterna VISA

33 Queen St ✉ YO11 1HQ – ☎ (01723) 363 616 – www.lanterna-ristorante.co.uk
– Closed last 2 weeks October, 25-26 December, 1 January and Sunday
Rest – Italian – (dinner only) Carte £ 30/94                                     Yc
• Scarborough's best known restaurant: a landmark for decades. Endearing trattoria style "clutter". Classic Italian menu, plus a renowned selection of truffle dishes.

### ✗ Green Room VISA

138 Victoria Rd ✉ YO11 1SL – ☎ (01723) 501 801
– www.thegreenroomrestaurant.com – Closed 26 December, Sunday, Monday
and Tuesday                                                                     Ze
Rest – (dinner only) Menu £ 19 – Carte £ 32/41
• Pleasant family run bistro; son cooks and mum is out front serving. Great care is taken to use only locally sourced produce and ingredients. Cooking is modern and imaginative.

**at Sawdon** Southwest : 9.75 mi by A 170 - Z – ✉ Scarborough

### Anvil Inn ⟨icons⟩ P VISA

Main St ✉ YO13 9DY – ☎ (01723) 859 896 – www.theanvilinnsawdon.co.uk
– Closed 25-26 December, 1 January, Monday and Tuesday
Rest – Carte £ 21/30
• Formerly a smithy, with bellows, tools, forge and anvil still in situ. Classical cooking features locally sourced produce and the odd international influence. Intimate restaurant.

**SCAWTON** – North Yorkshire – **502** Q21 – see Helmsley

## SCILLY (Isles of) – Cornwall – 503 A/B34       1 A3

↔ London 295 mi – Camborne 23 mi – Saint Austell 52 mi – Falmouth 36 mi

**Access** Helicopter service from St Mary's and Tresco to Penzance : ℰ (01736) 363871

✈ St Mary's Airport : ℰ (01720) 422677, E : 1.5 mi from Hugh Town

⛴ from Hugh Town to Penzance (Isles of Scilly Steamship Co. Ltd) (summer only) (2 h 40 mn)

🛈 St Mary's ℰ (01720) 42 40 31, www.simplyscilly.co.uk

◉ Islands★ - The Archipelago (≤★★★)

◎ St Agnes : Horsepoint★

## BRYHER – Cornwall – pop. 78 – ✉ New Grimsby       1 A3

🛈 St Mary's ℰ (01720) 42 40 31, www.simplyscilly.co.uk

◉ Watch Hill (≤★) – Hell Bay★

### 🛏️   **Hell Bay** 🌿       ≤ 🚗 🛜 🏊 🍽 🖈 VISA ⓐ
✉ TR23 0PR – ℰ (01720) 422 947 – www.hellbay.co.uk – 17 March-October
**11 rm** (dinner included) ☕ – ♦£ 169/600 ♦♦£ 169/300 – 14 suites –
♦♦£ 270/600
**Rest** – *(booking essential for non-residents)* Menu £ 35 – Carte approx. £ 30
• Several charming New England style buildings set around a central courtyard. Fabulous coastal location with far-reaching views. Contemporary inner has nautical edge and impressive modern art collection. Immaculately kept bedrooms come with good extras. Informal lunches in bar/courtyard/terrace; elaborate daily dinners.

### ↟   **Bank Cottage** without rest 🌿       ≤ 🚗 🌾
✉ TR23 0PR – ℰ (01720) 422 612 – www.bank-cottage.com – May-October
**4 rm** ☕ – ♦£ 54 ♦♦£ 110
• Friendly guesthouse with bright sub-tropical garden, koi carp pond and rowing boat. Breakfast room, lounge and honesty bar; free use of kitchen. Simple, compact bedrooms; one with roof terrace.

## ST MARTIN'S – Cornwall – pop. 113       1 A3

🛈 St Mary's ℰ (01720) 42 40 31, www.simplyscilly.co.uk

◉ St Martin's Head (≤★★)

### 🏨   **St Martin's on the Isle**       ≤ 🚗 🛜 🖳 🍽 🖈 🏊 VISA ⓐ AE ①
✉ TR25 0QW – ℰ (01720) 422 092 – www.stmartinshotel.co.uk
– April-September
**27 rm** (dinner included) ☕ – ♦£ 125/150 ♦♦£ 250/350 – 3 suites
**Rest** *Teän* – see restaurant listing
**Rest** *Bistro* – Menu £ 40
• Contemporary hotel in stunning location, with unrivalled views of white beaches and blue sea. Comfortable bedrooms: most overlook the water; some look onto the garden. The best is 'Volunteer'; a large first floor suite with views to the lighthouse. Lively ground floor bistro with terrace; simple dishes, ideal for lunch.

### XXX   **Teän** – St Martin's on the Isle       ≤ 🚗 🛜 🍽 VISA ⓐ AE ①
✉ TR25 0QW – ℰ (01720) 422 092 – www.stmartinshotel.co.uk
– April-September
**Rest** – *(Closed Monday evenings) (booking essential)* Carte £ 28/35 **s**
• First floor restaurant with fantastic views. Short menu of classically based dishes; cooking is precise, with hearty portions making the best of local produce. Professional service.

## ST MARY'S – Cornwall – pop. 1 607       1 A3

🛈 St Mary's ℰ (01720) 42 40 31, www.simplyscilly.co.uk

🏌 Carn Morval, ℰ (01720) 42 26 92

◉ Gig racing★★ - Garrison Walk★ (≤★★) – Peninnis Head★ – Hugh Town
- Museum★

**Star Castle** ⌖      < ⚎ 🏡 📶 🍴 <u>VISA</u> ⦾ AE

*The Garrison* ✉ *TR21 0JA –* ℰ *(01720) 422 317 – www.star-castle.co.uk*
*– Closed 2 January-10 February*
**34 rm** (dinner included) ⌑ – †£ 96/250 ††£ 190/324 – 4 suites
**Rest *Castle Dining Room*** *– (dinner only)* Menu £ 33
**Rest *Conservatory*** – Seafood *– (closed November-March) (dinner only)*
Menu £ 33
♦ Elizabethan castle in the shape of an 8-pointed star. Well-appointed, classical bedrooms; brighter garden suites – some harbour/island views. 17C staircase leads from stone ramparts to charming Dungeon bar. Fabulous fireplace and kitchen garden produce in dining room. Seafood menus in Conservatory.

**Atlantic**      < ⅙ rm, <u>VISA</u> ⦾

*Hugh St, Hugh Town* ✉ *TR21 0PL –* ℰ *(01720) 422 417*
*– www.atlantichotelscilly.co.uk – 7 February-19 November*
**25 rm** (dinner included) ⌑ – †£ 89/135 ††£ 170/270
**Rest** *– (bar lunch)* Menu £ 25 – Carte £ 26/31
♦ Former Customs Office in a charming bay setting, affording lovely views across the harbour. Bedrooms – accessed through twisty passages – are well-equipped; many share the view. Comfortable lounge and small bar. Wicker-furnished restaurant offers accessible menu.

**Evergreen Cottage** without rest      (ꞏ)

*Parade, Hugh Town* ✉ *TR21 0LP –* ℰ *(01720) 422 711*
*– www.evergreencottageguesthouse.co.uk – Closed 1 week February and*
*Christmas-New Year*
**5 rm** ⌑ – †£ 38/60 ††£ 76/82
♦ 300 year old captain's cottage in the heart of town. Welcoming window boxes. Cosy inner with small, low-ceilinged lounge and breakfast room. Compact, spotlessly kept, pine-furnished bedrooms.

**TRESCO** – Cornwall – pop. 167 – ✉ **New Grimsby**      **1** A3

🛈 St Mary's ℰ *(01720) 42 40 31, www.simplyscilly.co.uk*
◉ Island★ - Abbey Gardens★★ **AC** (Lighthouse Way < ★★)

**New Inn**      < 🏡 ⅃ ⅍ <u>VISA</u> ⦾

*New Grimsby* ✉ *TR24 0QQ –* ℰ *(01720) 423 006 – www.tresco.co.uk*
**16 rm** ⌑ – †£ 75/180 ††£ 150/240
**Rest** *– (booking essential for non-residents)* Carte £ 21/34
♦ Stone-built inn boasting a large terrace, an appealing outdoor pool and pleasant coastal views. Bedrooms are bright, fresh and very comfy. Regular live music events attract guests from near and far. Hugely characterful bar and restaurant offer accessible menu.

**SCUNTHORPE** – North Lincolnshire – **502** S23 – pop. 72 660      **23** C3
▶ London 167 mi – Leeds 54 mi – Lincoln 30 mi – Sheffield 45 mi
✈ Humberside Airport : ℰ (01652) 688456, E : 15 mi by A 18
🏌 Ashby Decoy Burringham Rd, ℰ (01724) 84 29 13
🏌 Kingsway, ℰ (01724) 84 09 45
🏌 Grange Park Messingham Butterwick Rd, ℰ (01724) 76 29 45

**San Pietro**      ⇔ 🅿 <u>VISA</u> ⦾ AE ⓞ

*11 High St East* ✉ *DN15 6UH –* ℰ *(01724) 277 774 – www.sanpietro.uk.com*
*– Closed first week January, 25-26 December, Monday lunch, Sunday and bank*
*holiday Mondays*
**Rest** – Menu £ 17/23 – Carte £ 29/53
♦ Characterful former pub with private dining room, housed in 19C listed windmill. Seasonal menus offer skilfully cooked Mediterranean dishes. Professional service from smartly attired staff.

**SEAHAM** – Durham – **501** P/Q19 – **pop. 21 153**                    **24** B2

◘ London 284 mi – Carlisle 77 mi – Leeds 84 mi – Middlesbrough 24 mi

🏠🏠🏠   **Seaham Hall** ॐ                    ≤ 🚗 🕭 🔲 🌐 🏖 🐾 & rm, 🄺 ½ ¶ ¼ 🄿
*Lord Byron's Walk, North : 1.25 mi by B 1287* ✉ *SR7 7AG*          𝑽𝑰𝑺𝑨 ⚪⚪ 🄰🄴 ⓪
*– ℰ (0191) 516 14 00 – www.seaham-hall.co.uk*
**18 rm** ☲ – †£ 175/375 ††£ 225/425 – 2 suites
**Rest** *White Room* – (dinner only and Sunday lunch) (booking essential for non-residents) Menu £ 32/55
**Rest** *Ozone* – Menu £ 23
♦ Impressive extended coastal mansion with portico entrance, modern styling, spacious sitting room and superb oriental spa, complete with impressive indoor pool and outdoor hot-tubs. Large bedrooms boast luxury bathrooms and impressive technology. Well-presented, modern dishes in the White Room. A blend of Asian and European food in Ozone.

---

**SEAHOUSES** – Northumberland – **501** P17 ▌ Great Britain          **24** B1

◘ London 328 mi – Edinburgh 80 mi – Newcastle upon Tyne 46 mi

🄸 Seafield Rd ℰ (01665) 72 08 84, www.seahouses.org

🔟 Beadnell Rd, ℰ (01665) 72 07 94

🄖 Farne Islands★ (by boat from harbour)

🏠   **Olde Ship**                    ≤ ½ ¶ ¼ 🄿 𝑽𝑰𝑺𝑨 ⚪⚪ ⓪
*9 Main St* ✉ *NE68 7RD* – ℰ *(01665) 720 200 – www.seahouses.co.uk*
*– February-November*
**13 rm** ☲ – †£ 51/118 ††£ 102/130 – 5 suites
**Rest** – (bar lunch Monday-Saturday) Menu £ 10 (weekday dinner)
– Carte £ 17/31 **s**
♦ Cosy, part-18C, family-run inn, close to the thriving harbour – boasting old ships' decking floors, nautical bric-a-brac and great harbour views from the wardroom. Comfortable, individually designed bedrooms. Characterful bar and classical dining room.

---

**SEASALTER** – Kent – **504** X29 – **see Whitstable**

---

**SEAVIEW** – Isle of Wight – **503** Q31 – **see Wight (Isle of)**

---

**SEER GREEN** – Buckinghamshire – **see Beaconsfield**

---

**SETTLE** – North Yorkshire – **502** N21 – **pop. 3 621**          **22** A2

◘ London 238 mi – Bradford 34 mi – Kendal 30 mi – Leeds 41 mi

🄸 Cheapside ℰ (01729) 82 51 92, www.settle.org.uk

🔟 Giggleswick, ℰ (01729) 82 52 88

✗   **Little House**                    𝑽𝑰𝑺𝑨 ⚪⚪
*17 Duke St* ✉ *BD24 9DJ* – ℰ *(01729) 823 963 – www.littlehouserestaurant.co.uk*
*– Closed 2 weeks January, 1 week spring, 1 week September, Monday, Tuesday and Sunday in winter*
**Rest** – (dinner only) (booking essential) Carte £ 23/30
♦ Former 19C gate house, a 'little house' of stone that was once a cobblers. Well-kept, rustic style within a compact space. Traditional and classic styles of cooking prevail.

---

**SHAFTESBURY** – Dorset – **503** N30 – **pop. 6 665**          **4** C3

◘ London 115 mi – Bournemouth 31 mi – Bristol 47 mi – Dorchester 29 mi

🄸 8 Bell St ℰ (01747) 85 35 14, www.shaftesburydorset.com

🄖 Gold Hill★ (≤★) – Local History Museum★ **AC**

🄖 Wardour Castle★ **AC**, NE : 5 m

ENGLAND

## 🏨 Hotel Grosvenor                    🎐 & ❦ ⚙ P ▥ ⊕

*The Commons* ✉ *SP7 8JA* – ℰ *(01747) 850 580* – *www.hotelgrosvenor.com*
**16 rm** ⌷ – ♦£ 175 ♦♦£ 175
**Rest** *Greenhouse* – see restaurant listing
♦ Stylish former coaching inn with Georgian-style façade and spacious, trendy
bar. Bedrooms feature stark décor and modern facilities including flat screen TVs
and espresso machines.

## 🏠 Fleur de Lys                        & rm, ❦ ❦ P ▥ ⊕ AE

*Bleke St* ✉ *SP7 8AW* – ℰ *(01747) 853 717* – *www.lafleurdelys.co.uk* – *Closed 2
weeks January*
**7 rm** ⌷ – ♦£ 80/100 ♦♦£ 135/175
**Rest** – *(closed lunch Monday-Tuesday and Sunday dinner)* Menu £ 33
– Carte approx. £ 32
♦ Keenly run, ivy-clad stone house in lovely market town. Comfortable, well-kept
bedrooms named after grape varieties; each comes with its own laptop. Cosy
lounge with mahogany bar. Dine from traditional menus in L-shaped restaurant
or on wood-furnished terrace.

## 🏠 Retreat without rest                & ❦ P ▥ ⊕

*47 Bell St* ✉ *SP7 8AE* – ℰ *(01747) 850 372* – *www.the-retreat.co.uk* – *Closed 25
December and 1 January*
**10 rm** ⌷ – ♦£ 55/70 ♦♦£ 85/90
♦ Pretty Georgian house on narrow street in delightful market town – once a
school for poor boys. Wood-furnished breakfast room; immaculately kept bedrooms with good facilities. Charming owner.

## ✕✕ Greenhouse – at Hotel Grosvenor        ❦ ▥ ⊕ AE

*The Commons* ✉ *SP7 8JA* – ℰ *(01747) 850 580* – *www.hotelgrosvenor.com*
**Rest** – Menu £ 25 – Carte £ 27/44
♦ Ground floor restaurant enlivened by boldly coloured abstract art. Enjoy aperi-
tifs in the enclosed courtyard. Refined brasserie cooking; good value set menus.
Excellent service.

---

**SHALDON** – Devon – **503** J32 – pop. 1 628                    **2** D2
▶ London 188 mi – Exeter 16 mi – Torquay 7 mi – Paignton 13 mi

## ✕ ODE                                    ▥ ⊕ AE ⊙

*21 Fore St* ✉ *TQ14 0DE* – ℰ *(01626) 873 977* – *www.odetruefood.co.uk*
*– Closed 2 weeks February, 2 weeks October, 25-26 December,
Sunday-Tuesday and bank holidays*
**Rest** – *Organic* – *(dinner only and lunch Thursday-Friday) (booking essential)*
Menu £ 22 (lunch) – Carte dinner £ 30/40
♦ Intimate neighbourhood restaurant in glass-fronted Georgian house – leave
time to park. Cooking has a strong seafaring base and often involves water baths.
Produce is local and 100% organic.

---

**SHANKLIN** – Isle of Wight – **503** Q32 – see Wight (Isle of)

---

**SHEDFIELD** – Hampshire – **503** Q31 – pop. 3 558 – ✉ Southampton    **6** B2
▶ London 75 mi – Portsmouth 13 mi – Southampton 10 mi
🏌 Meon Valley Shedfield Sandy Lane, off A 334, ℰ (01329) 83 34 55

## ✕✕ Vatika                            < 🏠 Ⓚ P ▥ ⊕ AE ⊙

*Botley Rd, Wickham Vineyard, on A334* ✉ *SO32 2HL* – ℰ *(01329) 830 405*
*– www.vatikarestaurant.co.uk – Closed November-February, Monday, Tuesday,
Sunday dinner and lunch Wednesday and Thursday*
**Rest** – *(dinner only and lunch Friday-Sunday) (booking advisable at dinner)*
Menu £ 40
♦ Sleek, contemporary restaurant overlooking delightful vineyard. Refined fusion
cooking uses modern techniques to create unusual, highly artistic British and In-
dian combinations.

🏛 Great Britain

▶ London 174 mi – Leeds 36 mi – Liverpool 80 mi – Manchester 41 mi

ℹ 14 Norfolk Row ℰ (0114) 221 19 00, www.spinsheffield.com

🏌 Tinsley Park Darnall High Hazel Park, ℰ (0114) 203 74 35

🏌 Beauchief Abbey Lane, ℰ (0114) 236 72 74

🏌 Birley Wood Birley Lane, ℰ (0114) 264 72 62

🏌 Concord Park Shiregreen Lane, ℰ (0114) 257 73 78

🏌 Abbeydale Dore Twentywell Lane, ℰ (0114) 236 07 63

🏌 Lees Hall Norton Hemsworth Rd, ℰ (0114) 255 44 02

👁 Cutlers' Hall★ CZ **A** – Cathedral Church of SS. Peter and Paul CZ **B** : Shrewsbury Chapel (Tomb★)

🎦 Magna★ **AC**, NE : 3 mi by A 6178 - BY - and Bessemer Way

Plans pages 598, 599

---

🏨 **Leopold**    🛗 ♿ AC ⚡ 🐾 🏋 VISA ◉◉ AE
*Leopold Sq ⊠ S1 1GZ – ℰ (0114) 252 40 00 – www.leopoldhotelssheffield.com*
*– Closed 23 December-2 January*    CZ**a**
**76 rm** 🛏 – ♥♥£ 120/140 – 14 suites   **Rest** – *(bar meals)* Carte approx. £ 34
♦ Former Boys Grammar School, now an elegant boutique townhouse with stylish, contemporary bedrooms, state-of-the-art facilities and old school photos on the walls. Light meals served in the bar.

🏠 **Westbourne House** without rest    🍴 ♿ 🛜 P VISA ◉◉
*25 Westbourne Rd ⊠ S10 2QQ – ℰ (0114) 266 01 09*
*– www.westbournehousehotel.com*    AZ**c**
**8 rm** 🛏 – ♥£ 49/65 ♥♥£ 75/80
♦ Red brick Victorian house in residential area; lovely breakfast room and rear bedrooms overlook mature gardens. Individually styled bedrooms boast original features and good facilities.

🍴🍴🍴 **Old Vicarage** (Tessa Bramley)    🍴 P VISA ◉◉
✿ *Ridgeway Moor, Southeast : 6.75 mi by A 6135 (signed Hyde Park) and B 6054 turning right at Ridgeway Arms ⊠ S12 3XW – ℰ (0114) 247 58 14*
*– www.theoldvicarage.co.uk – Closed 26 December-6 January, first two weeks August, Saturday lunch, Sunday, Monday and Tuesday after bank holidays*
**Rest** – *(lunch by arrangement)* Menu £ 40/65 ⅜
**Spec.** Langoustine tails on wild garlic risotto. Roast fillet of local beef with truffles and thyme-roasted beetroot. Strawberry and vanilla millefeuille, violet ice cream.
♦ Long-standing, family-run restaurant in an old Victorian vicarage just outside the city. Traditional, homely lounge. Two dining rooms – one a wood-floored, bay-windowed room, the other, an airy conservatory. Refined, classical cooking uses sophisticated techniques and top quality ingredients. Formal service.

🍴🍴 **Rafters**    AC VISA ◉◉ AE
*220 Oakbrook Rd, Nether Green, Southwest : 2.5 mi by A 625 and Fulwood rd, turning left at mini roundabout, on right at traffic lights ⊠ S11 7ED – ℰ (0114) 230 48 19 – www.raftersrestaurant.co.uk – Closed first week January, 2 weeks August, 25-26 December, Sunday and Tuesday*
**Rest** – *(dinner only)* Menu £ 36
♦ Small first floor restaurant above residential parade of shops, displaying exposed brickwork and vibrant decor. Classical menu with some Asian influences; produce sourced from within 100 miles.

🍴🍴 **Artisan**    VISA ◉◉
☺ *32-34 Sandygate Rd, West : 2.25 mi by A 57, turning left at Crosspool Tavern ⊠ S10 5RY – ℰ (0114) 266 60 96 – www.relaxeatanddrink.co.uk – Closed 26 December and bank holidays*
**Rest** – Menu £ 16/27 **s** – Carte £ 22/39 **s**
♦ Smart brasserie with roomy bar and dark, clubby dining room. Careful, honest cooking is fiercely British and very seasonal. Choice of menus to suit all tastes, including a daily ladies' menu, good value set selections and largely fish-based blackboard specials.

ENGLAND

ENGLAND

SHEFFIELD

0 ___ 1 km
0 ___ 1 mile

A · A 61 CHESTERFIELD · (A 61) A 6102 · B

✂

## Nonnas

🚄 VISA ⓜⓞ

535-541 Ecclesall Rd ✉ S11 8PR – ✆ (0114) 268 61 66 – www.nonnas.co.uk
– Closed 25 December and 1 January

AZe

**Rest** – Italian – Menu £ 13/24 – Carte £ 19/29

♦ Long-standing Italian restaurant with rustic, bistro-style; run by friendly family team. Coffee and cakes in bar. Classical menu of generous, full-flavoured dishes; lighter options available.

SHEFFIELD

300 m
300 yards

ENGLAND

## Milestone

VISA ◯◯ AE ◯

84 Green Ln ⊠ S3 8SE – ℰ (0114) 272 83 27 – www.the-milestone.co.uk – Closed
25-26 December and 1 January                                                                  CYe

**Rest** – Carte £ 26/30

♦ Spacious 18C pub in industrial area of the city. Emphasis firmly on seasonal,
organic, locally sourced produce. Hearty gastro menu downstairs; more formal
first floor dining.

**at Totley** Southwest : 5.5 mi on A 621 - AZ – ⊠ South Yorkshire

🏠 **Cricket Inn**   ☆ **P** VISA ⓿⓿
*Penny Ln ⊠ S17 3AZ – ℰ (0114) 236 52 56 – www.relaxeatanddrink.co.uk*
**Rest** – Menu £ 25 – Carte £ 21/39
♦ Hidden away next to cricket pitch, with open fires and rustic wood floors
Wide-ranging, Yorkshire-based menu offers bar snacks through to grills and
roasts. Hearty, wholesome cooking.

**SHEFFORD** – Central Bedfordshire – **504** S27 – **pop. 3 319**   **12** A1
▶ London 48 mi – Bedford 10 mi – Luton 16 mi – Northampton 37 mi

🏠 **Black Horse** with rm   ⌖ ☆ **Ⓚ** rest, ⅍ rm, **P** VISA ⓿⓿ ﾑﾃ
*Ireland, Northwest : 1.5 mi by Northbridge St and B 658 on Ireland rd*
⊠ SG17 5QL – ℰ (01462) 811 398 – www.blackhorseireland.com – Closed
25-26 December, 1 January and Sunday dinner
**2 rm** ⌁ – ♦£ 55 ♦♦£ 55   **Rest** – Carte £ 23/38
♦ Traditional façade masks a stylish, contemporary interior with marble floors
granite bar and hi-tech fittings. Eclectic menu ranges from pies to confit of duck
and sea bass. Delightfully cosy bedrooms.

**SHELLEY** – West Yorkshire – **502** O23 – see Huddersfield

**SHERBORNE** – Dorset – **503** M31 – **pop. 9 835**   **4** C3
▶ London 128 mi – Bournemouth 39 mi – Dorchester 19 mi – Salisbury 36 mi
🛈 Digby Rd ℰ (01935) 81 53 41, www.sherbornetown.com
🏗 Higher Clatcombe, ℰ (01935) 81 22 74
◎ Town★ - Abbey★★ – Castle★ **AC**
◎ Sandford Orcas Manor House★ **AC**, NW : 4 mi by B 3148 – Purse Caundle Manor★
**AC**, NE : 5 mi by A 30. Cadbury Castle (≼★★) N : 8 mi by A 30 – Parish Church★
Crewkerne, W : 14 mi on A 30

**at Oborne** Northeast : 2 mi by A 30 – ⊠ Sherborne

🏢 **Grange** ⌂   ⌖ ♿ rm, ⅍ ⌖ ☆ **P** VISA ⓿⓿ ﾑﾃ ⓿
⊠ DT9 4LA – ℰ (01935) 813 463 – www.thegrangeatoborne.co.uk
**18 rm** ⌁ – ♦£ 125/135 ♦♦£ 159/165   **Rest** – Menu £ 26/35
♦ Family-run, stone-built country house in pretty village; dating back 200 years.
Comfy guest areas overlook attractive mature gardens. Spacious bedrooms boast
good facilities; some have balconies or patios. Menus showcase the latest local,
seasonal ingredients.

**SHERE** – Surrey – **504** S30 – see Guildford

**SHERINGHAM** – Norfolk – **504** X25 – **pop. 7 143**   **15** C1
▶ London 136 mi – Cromer 5 mi – Norwich 27 mi

🏠 **Ashbourne House** without rest   ⌖ ⅍ ⌖
*1 Nelson Rd ⊠ NR26 8BT – ℰ (01263) 821 555*
*– www.ashbournehousesheringham.co.uk*
**3 rm** ⌁ – ♦£ 45/50 ♦♦£ 65/75
♦ Well-appointed guesthouse in elevated position, with large, landscaped garden. Comfortable bedrooms: two with coastal views. Impressive fireplace in
wood-panelled breakfast room.

**SHERWOOD BUSINESS PARK** – Nottinghamshire – see Nottingham

**SHILTON** – Warwickshire – **503** P26 – see Coventry

**SHINFIELD** – Wokingham – **504** R29 – see Reading

---

**SHIPLAKE ROW** – Oxfordshire – see Henley-on-Thames

---

**SHIPLEY** – West Yorkshire – **502** O22 – pop. 28 162                    **22** B2
- London 216 mi – Bradford 4 mi – Leeds 12 mi
- Northcliffe High Bank Lane, ℰ (01274) 58 40 85
- Bingley Beckfoot Lane, Cottingley Bridge, ℰ (01274) 56 86 52

X    **Zaara's**                                                    AC VISA ⦿ ⓘ
     34-38 Bradford Rd ⊠ BD18 3NT – ℰ (01274) 588 114 – www.zaaras.com
     **Rest** – Indian – *(dinner only)* Carte £ 15/22                      ATa
     ◆ Funky, modern restaurant with bright décor and lots of neon. Tasty, authentic
     Indian cooking, with an emphasis on Punjabi dishes. Efficient service from smartly
     dressed team.

---

**SHOTTLE** – Derbyshire – see Belper

---

**SHREWSBURY** – Shropshire – **502** L25 – pop. 65 326 ▯ Great Britain    **18** B2
- London 164 mi – Birmingham 48 mi – Chester 43 mi – Derby 67 mi
- Barker St ℰ (01743) 28 12 00, www.visitshrewsbury.com
- Condover, ℰ (01743) 87 29 77
- Meole Brace, ℰ (01743) 36 40 50
- Abbey★ **D**
- Ironbridge Gorge Museum★★ **AC** (The Iron Bridge★★ - Coalport China
  Museum★★ - Blists Hill Open Air Museum★★ – Museum of the Gorge and Visitor
  Centre★) SE : 12 mi by A 5 and B 4380

ENGLAND

Plan on next page

🏠🏠  **Lion and Pheasant**                          ⚒ ⎙ **P** VISA ⦿ AE
     49-50 Wyle Cop ⊠ SY1 1XJ – ℰ (01743) 770 345 – www.lionandpheasant.co.uk
     – Closed 25 December                                                     s
     **22 rm** ⊡ – †£ 75/95 ††£ 130/175    **Rest** – Carte £ 29/38
     ◆ Collection of adjoining 16C and 18C townhouses, located on a famous medie-
     val street towards the edge of town. Modern, minimalist décor throughout: bed-
     rooms, designed by the owners daughter, vary in shape and size and have a Scan-
     dic feel. Bistro-style menu offered at wooden tables in a choice of dining rooms.

🏠  **Pinewood House** without rest                              ⇋ **P**
     Shelton Park, The Mount, Northwest : 1.5 mi on A 458 ⊠ SY3 8BL – ℰ (01743)
     364 200 – Closed 1 week Christmas
     **3 rm** ⊡ – †£ 45/48 ††£ 58/60
     ◆ Lovely Edwardian property on the edge of town, converted from three coach
     houses. Fresh, uncluttered feel throughout, with large, light-filled drawing room
     and flowers all around. One split-level bedroom with bathroom in the old dove-
     cote. Communal breakfasts.

XXX  **Hayward**                                             **P** VISA ⦿ AE
     The Lion Hotel, Wyle Cop ⊠ SY1 1UY – ℰ (01743) 353 107
     – www.thelionhotelshrewsbury.co.uk – Closed Monday                       x
     **Rest** – Menu £ 20/38
     ◆ Spacious, modern restaurant set within the historic Lion hotel, boasting ele-
     gant furnishings and formally laid tables. Ambitious, modern cooking and refined
     presentation; huge polished carving trolley is a feature. Simpler dishes at lunch.

SHREWSBURY

XX **Mad Jack's** with rm                    🛜 🎧 VISA 🅾️ AE ①

15 St. Mary's St. ⊠ SY1 1EQ – 𝒞 (01743) 358 870 – www.madjacks.uk.com
– Closed 25 December                                                    a

**4 rm** 🛏 – †£70/100 ††£80/145   **Rest** – Carte £21/33

◆ Centrally located in the heart of a busy market town. Spacious main dining area, snug and hidden courtyard, with plain décor and marble tables. Good service, slightly eclectic menu. Modern, comfy bedrooms.

**at Grinshill** North : 7.5 mi by A 49 – ⊠ Shrewsbury

X **Inn at Grinshill** with rm                    🛜 🎧 P VISA 🅾️

The High St ⊠ SY4 3BL – 𝒞 (01939) 220 410 – www.theinnatgrinshill.co.uk
– Closed Sunday dinner and Monday

**6 rm** 🛏 – †£60/90 ††£120   **Rest** – Menu £33 (dinner) **s** – Carte £25/32 **s**

◆ 18C former stable block in small village. Rustic bar and light, airy restaurant boasting an open kitchen, grand piano and wine bar. À la carte offers mix of old classics and more modern tasting boards; simpler bar menu. Up-to-date bedrooms provide good comforts.

**at Atcham** Southeast : 3 mi by A 5064 on B 4380

🏠 **Mytton and Mermaid**    🚗 🎣 ⁽ᵖ⁾ 🦮 P̄ VISA 🐄 AE ⓪
✉ SY5 6QG – ℰ (01743) 761 220 – www.myttonandmermaid.co.uk – Closed 25
December
**16 rm** ⌒ – ♦£ 85/110 ♦♦£ 110/185
**Rest** *Restaurant* – see restaurant listing
• Impressive Georgian riverside house with neat lawned gardens. Characterful,
traditionally styled bedrooms in main house, some with views; smaller, more con-
temporary rooms in old stables.

✗ **Restaurant** – at The Mytton and Mermaid Hotel    🚗 🏠 P̄ VISA 🐄 AE ⓪
✉ SY5 6QG – ℰ (01743) 761 220 – www.myttonandmermaid.co.uk – Closed 25
December
**Rest** – Carte £ 24/28
• Choice of three dining areas: casual bar, more formal dining room or pleasant
outside terraces. Same menu served throughout, offering tasty classically based
dishes and daily specials.

**SHREWTON** – Wiltshire – **503** O30 – pop. 1 648      **4 D2**

▶ London 91 mi – Bristol 53 mi – Southampton 52 mi – Reading 69 mi

🏠 **Manor**    🚗 🌿 ⁽ᵖ⁾ P̄ VISA 🐄 ⓪
Southeast : 0.5 mi on A 360 ✉ SP3 4HF – ℰ (01980) 620 216
– www.rollestonemanor.com
**7 rm** ⌒ – ♦£ 80 ♦♦£ 130
**Rest** – (dinner only and Sunday lunch) Carte £ 24/32
• Grade II listed former farmhouse set on main road, just out of the village.
Good-sized, antique-furnished bedrooms offer modern facilities. Traditional
lounge. Two-roomed restaurant for classic dishes at linen-laid tables.

**SHURDINGTON** – Gloucestershire – **503** N28 – see Cheltenham

**SIBFORD GOWER** – Oxfordshire – see Banbury

**SIDFORD** – Devon – **503** K31 – see Sidmouth

**SIDLESHAM** – West Sussex – see Chicester

**SIDMOUTH** – Devon – **503** K31 – pop. 12 066      **2 D2**

▶ London 176 mi – Exeter 14 mi – Taunton 27 mi – Weymouth 45 mi
ℹ Ham Lane ℰ (01395) 51 64 41, www.visitsidmouth.co.uk
🏌 Cotmaton Rd, ℰ (01395) 51 34 51
🄶 Bicton★ (Gardens★) **AC**, SW : 5 m

🏨 **Riviera**    ≤ 🏠 🛎 AC rest, ⁽ᵖ⁾ 🦮 🚗 VISA 🐄 AE ⓪
The Esplanade ✉ EX10 8AY – ℰ (01395) 515 201 – www.hotelriviera.co.uk
**26 rm** (dinner included) ⌒ – ♦£ 132/194 ♦♦£ 264/368
**Rest** – Menu £ 30/42 – Carte £ 42/50
• Long-standing, family-run hotel with characterful Regency façade. Superbly
kept classical guest areas; fresh flowers and friendly staff abound. Smart bedrooms in rich blues and gold, some with a view. Traditional menus have a modern edge. Cream teas a speciality.

**ENGLAND**

603

**at Sidford** North : 2 mi – ⊠ Sidmouth

XX **Salty Monk** with rm   🗔 🏠 **P** **VISA** 🐼
*Church St, on A 3052* ⊠ *EX10 9QP* – 𝒞 *(01395) 513 174* – *www.saltymonk.co.u*
– *Closed January, 2 weeks November and lunch Monday-Wednesday*
**6 rm** ⌑ – ✝£ 70/75 ✝✝£ 120/180
**Rest** – *(booking essential)* Menu £ 43 (dinner) – Carte lunch £ 24/34
♦ Former 16C salt house, where monks stayed en route to Exeter Cathedral
Characterful beamed lounge and conservatory dining room. Extensive modern
menus feature fresh fish and local produce; tasting option available weekends.
Smart bedrooms and mini spa facility.

**at Newton Poppleford** Northwest : 4 mi by B 3176 on A 3052 – ⊠ Sidmouth

XX **Moores'**   🏠 **VISA** 🐼 **AE** ①
*6 Greenbank, High St* ⊠ *EX10 0EB* – 𝒞 *(01395) 568 100*
– *www.mooresrestaurant.co.uk* – *Closed first two weeks January, Sunday dinner
and Monday*
**Rest** – Menu £ 21/29 **s**
♦ Two pretty 18C cottages set back from the main road are the setting for this
busy, personally run restaurant with conservatory extension. Modern, locally
sourced dishes.

**SINNINGTON** – North Yorkshire – **502** R21 – see Pickering

**SISSINGHURST** – Kent – **504** V30 – see Cranbrook

**SITTINGBOURNE** – Kent – **504** W29 – pop. 39 974   9 C1
▶ London 44 mi – Canterbury 18 mi – Maidstone 15 mi – Sheerness 9 mi

🏠🏠🏠 **Hempstead House**   🗔 ⊛ 🏠 🕭 🕭 ⟨ℙ⟩ 🕼 **P** **VISA** 🐼 **AE** ①
*London Rd, Bapchild, East : 2 mi on A 2* ⊠ *ME9 9PP* – 𝒞 *(01795) 428 020*
– *www.hempsteadhouse.co.uk*
**27 rm** ⌑ – ✝£ 85 ✝✝£ 160
**Rest** *Lakes* – see restaurant listing
♦ Privately run, red-brick Victorian house with extensions, set in pleasant landscaped gardens. Cosy, wood-panelled lounges. Classical bedrooms in the main
house; more contemporary rooms boasting the latest mod cons above the luxurious spa.

XX **Lakes** – at Hempstead House Hotel   🗔 🏠 **P** **VISA** 🐼 **AE** ①
*London Rd, Bapchild, East : 2 mi on A 2* ⊠ *ME9 9PP* – 𝒞 *(01795) 428 020*
– *www.hempsteadhouse.co.uk*
**Rest** – *(residents only Sunday dinner)* Menu £ 19/28 – Carte £ 28/40
♦ Formal conservatory restaurant featuring Georgian columns, crystal chandeliers
and linen-laid tables, set within a red-brick Victorian house in pleasant landscaped gardens. Classical menus.

**SIZERGH** – Cumbria – see Kendal

**SKIPTON** – North Yorkshire – **502** N22 – pop. 14 313 ▮ Great Britain   22 A2
▶ London 217 mi – Kendal 45 mi – Leeds 26 mi – Preston 36 mi
🄵 35 Coach St 𝒞 (01756) 79 28 09, www.skiptonweb.co.uk
🖼 Short Lee Lane, off NW Bypass, 𝒞 (01756) 79 39 22
◎ Castle ★ **AC**

🏠 **Bull**   🏠 **P** **VISA** 🐼 **AE**
*West : 3 mi on A 59* ⊠ *BD23 3AE* – 𝒞 *(01756) 792 065*
– *www.thebullatbroughton.co.uk* – *Closed 25 December*
**Rest** – Carte £ 19/33
♦ Part of Ribble Valley Inns, a burgeoning pub company which proudly promotes
local and very British ingredients and dishes. This solid, sizeable pub boasts log
fires, beams and stone floors.

**Hetton** North : 5.75 mi by B 6265 – ⊠ Skipton

XXX **Angel Inn and Barn Lodgings** with rm    AC 🛜 P VISA ◎ AE
⊠ BD23 6LT – 𝒞 (01756) 730 263 – www.angelhetton.co.uk – Closed 4 days
January
**9 rm** ⌂ – ♦£ 140 ♦♦£ 190
**Rest** *Angel Inn* – see restaurant listing
**Rest** – (booking essential) Carte £ 22/36 ⅋
• Well regarded restaurant with stone walls, beams and roaring log fire. Fine
quality, locally sourced produce. Bedrooms with antique furniture and modern
appointments.

🍴 **Angel Inn**    🛜 P VISA ◎ AE
⊠ BD23 6LT – 𝒞 (01756) 730 263 – www.angelhetton.co.uk – Closed 4 days
January
**Rest** – (booking essential) Menu £ 15 (lunch and weekday dinner)
– Carte £ 19/34 ⅋
• Remotely set 18C stone inn that's become a Yorkshire institution: the wine
cave is worth a visit. Menus offer something for everyone, featuring local produce
in tasty, satisfying dishes.

**SLALEY** – Northumberland – see Hexham

**SLAPTON** – Devon – **503** J33    **2** C3
London 223 mi – Dartmouth 7 mi – Plymouth 29 mi
Dartmouth ★★, N : 7 mi by A 379 – Kingsbridge ★, W : 7 mi by A 379

🍴 **Tower Inn** with rm    🛏 🛜 🛜 P VISA ◎
Church Rd ⊠ TQ7 2PN – 𝒞 (01548) 580 216 – www.thetowerinn.com – Closed
first 2 weeks January and Sunday in winter
**3 rm** ⌂ – ♦£ 65 ♦♦£ 85    **Rest** – Carte £ 24/33
• Charming pub overlooked by the ruins of a chantry tower. Menus differ between services and offer pub food with a twist: maybe venison sausages with
sauerkraut or fish and chips in vodka batter. Simple bedrooms await.

**SNAINTON** – North Yorkshire – **502** S21    **23** C2
London 241 mi – Pickering 8 mi – Scarborough 10 mi

🍴 **Coachman Inn** with rm    🛏 🛜 🛜 P VISA ◎ AE ①
Pickering Rd West, West : 0.5 mi by A 170 on B 1258 ⊠ YO13 9PL – 𝒞 (01723)
859 231 – www.coachmaninn.co.uk
**5 rm** ⌂ – ♦£ 60 ♦♦£ 85    **Rest** – Carte £ 19/30
• Grade II listed coaching inn with a rustic bar and spacious linen-laid restaurant
– which is run with some formality. Cooking is classical but presentation is modern and refined. Simpler pub favourites offered at lunch. Bedrooms are smart
and spacious.

**SNAPE** – Suffolk – **504** Y27 – pop. 1 509    **15** D3
London 113 mi – Ipswich 19 mi – Norwich 50 mi

🍴 **Crown Inn**    🛏 🛜 VISA ◎ AE ①
Bridge Rd ⊠ IP17 1SL – 𝒞 (01728) 688 324 – www.snape-crown.co.uk
**Rest** – Carte £ 19/29
• Charming 15C former smugglers' inn on village outskirts. Constantly evolving
menu offers highly seasonal dishes, light bites and appealing specials. Produce is
local, home-grown or home-reared.

ENGLAND

**SNETTISHAM** – Norfolk – **504** V25 – **pop. 2 145**                    **14 B**

▶ London 113 mi – King's Lynn 13 mi – Norwich 44 mi

🛏  **Rose and Crown** with rm                    🖳 🏡 ⅙ rm, ᵗᵀ¹ **P** 💳 ⚫

*Old Church Rd* ✉ *PE31 7LX* – ℰ *(01485) 541 382*
– *www.roseandcrownsnettisham.co.uk*
**16 rm** ⌂ – **†**£ 70/85 **††**£ 90/110   **Rest** – Carte £ 21/29
♦ A warren of rooms with uneven floors and low beamed ceilings. Gutsy cookin
uses locally sourced produce, with globally influenced dishes alongside trus
pub classics. Modern bedrooms are decorated in sunny colours, with a good lev
of facilities.

---

**SOAR MILL COVE** – Devon – **503** i33 – **see Salcombe**

---

**SOLIHULL** – West Midlands – **503** O26 – **pop. 94 753**                    **19 C**

▶ London 109 mi – Birmingham 7 mi – Coventry 13 mi – Warwick 13 mi

🔼 Homer Rd ℰ (0121) 704 61 30, www.solihull.gov.uk

ХХ  **Town House**                    🏠 🆔 ⇔ **P** 💳 ⚫ 🆔

*727 Warwick Rd* ✉ *B91 3DA* – ℰ *(0121) 704 15 67* – *www.thetown-house.com*
– *Closed Monday from 1 April-30 August and Sunday*
**Rest** – Menu £ 17 (lunch) – Carte £ 26/41
♦ Smart, keenly run eatery with bright interior and spacious bar-lounge for cock
tails. Keenly priced, international menu ranges from small plates and mini des
serts to a 5 course tasting selection.

**at Olton** Northwest : 2.5 mi on A 41 – ✉ Solihull

ХХ  **Rajnagar**                    🆔 💳 ⚫ 🆔 🅾

*256 Lyndon Rd., Northeast : 1 mi by Richmond rd.* ✉ *B92 7QW* – ℰ *(0121)*
*742 81 40* – *www.rajnagar.com*
**Rest** – Indian – *(dinner only)* Menu £ 16 – Carte £ 22/33
♦ A busy, modern neighbourhood favourite, privately owned, offering authenti
regional specialities of Indian cuisine. Service is flexible and friendly.

---

**SOMERTON** – Somerset – **503** L30 – **pop. 4 133**                    **3 B.**

▶ London 138 mi – Bristol 32 mi – Taunton 17 mi

🔲 Town★ - Market Place★ (cross★) – St Michael's Church★

🔲 Long Sutton★ (Church★★) SW : 2.5 mi by B 3165 – Huish Episcopi (St Mary's
Church Tower★★) SW : 4.5 mi by B 3153 – Lytes Cary★, SE : 3.5 mi by B 3151
– Street - The Shoe Museum★, N : 5 mi by B 3151. Muchelney★★ (Parish
Church★★) SW : 6.5 mi by B 3153 and A 372 – High Ham (≤★★, St Andrew's
Church★), NW : 9 mi by B 3153, A 372 and minor rd – Midelney Manor★ **AC**, SW
9 mi by B 3153 and A 378

🏠  **Lynch Country House** without rest                    ≤ 🖳 🐕 ᵗᵀ¹ **P** 💳 ⚫ 🆔 🅾

*4 Behind Berry* ✉ *TA11 7PD* – ℰ *(01458) 272 316*
– *www.thelynchcountryhouse.co.uk*
**9 rm** ⌂ – **†**£ 65/80 **††**£ 80/115
♦ Stands on a crest overlooking the Cary Valley. The grounds of this Regency
house are equally rich with unusual shrubs, trees and lake. Coach house room
more modern.

---

**SONNING-ON-THAMES** – Wokingham – **504** R29 – **see Reading**

## SOUTH BRENT – 503 I32 – pop. 2 847 – ⊠ Devon
2 C2

▶ London 201 – Plymouth 17 – Torbay 15 – Exeter 29

🍴🛏 **Oak Inn** with rm       🎇 🅰️🅲 rest, 💳 ⓪⓪
*Station Rd ⊠ TQ10 9BE – ℰ (01364) 72 133 – www.oakonline.net*
**5 rm** 🖵 – ♥£ 65/95 ♥♥£ 90/130    **Rest** – Carte £ 15/29
◆ This pub boasts a traditional bar and a more modern restaurant with an attractive courtyard. Lunch offers a simple bar menu and a fish and a dish 'of the day', while dinner is more complex. The cheesecakes are worth saving room for. Modern, spacious bedrooms.

## SOUTH DALTON – East Riding of Yorkshire – see Beverley

## SOUTH MOLTON – Devon – 503 I30 – pop. 4 093
2 C1

▶ London 197 mi – Barnstaple 11 mi – Bristol 81 mi

**at Knowstone** Southeast : 9.5 mi by A 361 – ⊠ South Molton

🍴 **Masons Arms** (Mark Dodson)       🚗 🎇 🅿️ 💳 ⓪⓪ 🅰🅴
❀ ⊠ EX36 4RY – ℰ (01398) 341 231 – www.masonsarmsdevon.co.uk – *Closed first
2 weeks January, 1 week spring and August, Sunday dinner and Monday*
**Rest** – *(booking essential)* Carte £ 34/46
**Spec.** Salted cod with crushed potatoes and chorizo, tomato and thyme vinaigrette. Beef fillet and oxtail, parsnip purée and red wine jus. Mango parfait with coconut sorbet.
◆ Pretty 13C thatched inn set in Exmoor's foothills, with cosy bar and bright dining room featuring celestial ceiling mural. Sophisticated cooking of French and British classics using local produce. Pronounced, assured flavours.

## SOUTH RAUCEBY – Lincolnshire – 502 S24/2 – pop. 335
17 C2

▶ London 131 – Sheffield 68 – Leicester 54 – Kingston upon Hull 69

🍴 **Bustard Inn**       🎇 🅿️ 💳 ⓪⓪ 🅰🅴
*44 Main St ⊠ NG34 8QG – ℰ (01529) 488 250 – www.thebustardinn.co.uk
– Closed 1 January, Sunday dinner and Monday*
**Rest** – Menu £ 19 (lunch) – Carte £ 24/43
◆ Grade II listed inn set in a peaceful hamlet. Traditional pub favourites served in flag-floored bar. Modern-style English dishes and old-fashioned puddings in the spacious beamed restaurant.

## SOUTHAMPTON – Southampton – 503 P31 – pop. 236 895
6 B2
📗 Great Britain

▶ London 87 mi – Bristol 79 mi – Plymouth 161 mi

**Access** Itchen Bridge (toll) AZ

🛫 Southampton/Eastleigh Airport : ℰ (0844) 481 7777, N : 4 mi BY

🚢 to Hythe (White Horse Ferries Ltd) frequent services daily (12 mn) – to the Isle of Wight (Cowes) (Red Funnel Ferries) frequent services daily (approx. 22 mn)

🚢 to the Isle of Wight (East Cowes) (Red Funnel Ferries) frequent services daily (55 mn)

🛈 9 Civic Centre Rd ℰ (023) 8083 33 33, www.visit-southampton.co.uk

🏌 Southampton Municipal Bassett Golf Course Rd, ℰ (023) 8076 05 46

🏌 Stoneham Bassett Monks Wood Close, ℰ (023) 8076 92 72

🏌 Chilworth Main Rd, ℰ (023) 8074 05 44

◎ Old Southampton AZ : Bargate ★ **B** - Tudor House Museum ★ **M1**

Plans on following pages

## ✗ Oxfords
☐ 🅥🅘🅢🅐 ⚫⚫ 🅐🅔

35-36 Oxford St ⊠ SO14 3DS – ℰ (023) 8022 4444
– www.oxfordsrestaurant.com

AZx

**Rest** – Menu £ 16/18 (except Saturday dinner) – Carte £ 26/30
• Double-fronted restaurant in lively area. Wood-furnished bar and semi open-plan dining room with brushed velvet banquettes. Good choice of classic brasserie dishes with an international edge.

## ⊓ White Star Tavern, Dining and Rooms with rm
☐ 🅐🅒 rest, ⁹⁰

28 Oxford Street ⊠ SO14 3DJ – ℰ (023) 8082 1990
🅥🅘🅢🅐 ⚫⚫ 🅐🅔
– www.whitestartavern.co.uk – Closed 25-26 December

AZx

**13 rm** – †£ 79/99 ††£ 129/149, ☐ £ 8  **Rest** – Carte £ 21/34
• Eye-catching black pub with vast windows and smart pavement terrace, set in the lively maritime district. Choice of all day tapas-style small plates or modern British à la carte of meaty dishes. Smart, modern bedrooms boast good facilities and extra touches.

**at Hamble-le-Rice** Southeast : 5 mi by A 3025 - A - on B 3397
– ⊠ Southampton

## ⊓ Bugle
☐ ⇔ 🅥🅘🅢🅐 ⚫⚫ 🅐🅔

High St ⊠ SO31 4HA – ℰ (023) 8045 3000 – www.buglehamble.co.uk
**Rest** – (booking essential) Carte £ 20/28 **s**
• Attractive pub down a cobbled street, its terrace overlooking the marina. Bar menu offers sandwiches, small plates and pub classics. More ambitious à la carte available in the dining room.

**SOUTHAMPTON**

**ENGLAND**

**at Netley Marsh** West : 6.5 mi by A 33 off A 336

**Hotel TerraVina**

174 Woodlands Rd ⊠ SO40 7GL – ℰ (023) 8029 3784
– *www.hotelterravina.co.uk*

**11 rm** – ✝£ 160 ✝✝£ 265, � £ 14.50
**Rest** – Menu £ 29 (lunch) – Carte dinner £ 33/48 ⊛

◆ Neat Victorian red-brick house with wood-clad extensions, set in a peaceful New Forest location. Comfy lounge and good-sized bar. Brown and orange hues create a relaxed Mediterranean atmosphere. Bedrooms boast good facilities and extras; some have roof terraces. Menus mix modern British and Mediterranean influences.

*Good food and accommodation at moderate prices? Look for the Bib symbols: red Bib Gourmand ⊛ for food, blue Bib Hotel 🏠 for accommodation.*

609

## SOUTHEND-ON-SEA – Southend-on-Sea – **504** W29 – pop. 160 257    13 C3

▶ London 39 mi – Cambridge 69 mi – Croydon 46 mi – Dover 85 mi

🛧 Southend-on-Sea Airport : ℰ (01702) 608100, N : 2 m

🛈 Western Esplanade ℰ (01702) 21 51 20, www.visitsouthend.co.uk

🏌 Belfairs Leigh-on-Sea Eastwood Road North, ℰ (01702) 52 53 45

🏌 Ballards Gore G. & C.C. Gore Rd, Canewdon, ℰ (01702) 25 89 17

🏌 Garon Park Golf Complex Garon Park, Eastern Ave, ℰ (01702) 60 17 01

---

⌂ **Beaches** without rest                                     ≤ 🕸 ¶⁰ 🚾 🟦 AE
    192 Eastern Esplanade, Thorpe Bay ⊠ SS1 3AA – ℰ (01702) 586 124
    – www.beachesguesthouse.co.uk
    **7 rm** – ♦£ 40/70 ♦♦£ 80
    ◆ Attractive terraced guesthouse on the promenade, boasting fine views over
    Thorpe Bay and the Thames Estuary. Individually decorated bedrooms are com-
    fortable and well-furnished; those to the front have balconies and afford the
    best views. Good buffet breakfasts.

⌂ **Pier View** without rest                                   ≤ 🚗 🕸 ¶⁰ 🚾 🟦
    5 Royal Terr. ⊠ SS1 1DY – ℰ (01702) 437 900
    – www.pierviewguesthouse.co.uk
    **8 rm** – ♦£ 60/100 ♦♦£ 130
    ◆ Set in Georgian terrace close to centre of town, with superb views of cliffs, pier
    and estuary. Bedrooms decorated in pastel shades, with flat screen TVs and Egyp-
    tian bedding.

---

## SOUTHPORT – Merseyside – **502** K23 – pop. 91 404           20 A2

▶ London 221 mi – Liverpool 25 mi – Manchester 38 mi – Preston 19 mi

🛈 112 Lord St ℰ (01704) 53 33 33, www.visitsouthport.com

🏌 Southport Golf Links Park Road West, ℰ (01704) 53 52 86

---

🏨 **Vincent**                              🛗 🖫 ಓ 🗚 🕸 ¶⁰ 🛦 🚗 🚾 🟦 AE
    98 Lord St. ⊠ PR8 1JR – ℰ (01704) 883 800
    – www.thevincenthotel.com
    **59 rm** ⊡ – ♦£ 140 ♦♦£ 180 – 3 suites
    Rest **V-Cafe** – see restaurant listing
    ◆ Striking glass, steel and stone hotel beside the gardens and bandstand. Styl-
    ish, boutique interior with chic bar, fitness room and spa. Sleek, modern bed-
    rooms come in dark colours, boasting Nespresso machines and deep Japanese
    soaking tubs.

✗ **Bistrot Vérité**                                           🗚 🚾 🟦
    7 Liverpool Rd, Birkdale, South : 1.5 mi by A 565 ⊠ PR8 4AR
    – ℰ (01704) 564 199 – www.bistrotverite.co.uk
    – Closed 1 week summer, 1 week winter, 25-26 December, 1 January, Sunday
    and Monday
    Rest – French – (booking essential) Carte £ 21/35
    ◆ Simple bistro with tiled floor and panelled walls; sit on the red banquette
    which runs down one side. Rustic, hearty French cooking; desserts a speciality.
    Friendly, efficient service.

✗ **V-Cafe** – at Vincent Hotel                                🗚 🚾 🟦 AE
    98 Lord St. ⊠ PR8 1JR – ℰ (01704) 883 800
    – www.thevincenthotel.com
    Rest – Carte £ 24/34
    ◆ Relaxed café in a striking modern hotel, its glass façade overlooking the street.
    Open all-day and offering everything from sushi at the counter to 3 courses of
    globally influenced dishes.

ENGLAND

## SOUTHROP – Gloucestershire – **503** O28

4 D1

▶ London 87 mi – Birmingham 77 mi – Bristol 60 mi – Sheffield 146 mi

### ⁱ⃞ Swan
VISA ◐◯ AE

✉ GL7 3NU – ℰ (01367) 850 205 – www.theswanatsouthrop.co.uk – *Closed 25 December and Sunday dinner*
**Rest** – Menu £ 19 (weekdays) – Carte £ 30/37

♦ Ex-London restaurateur combines Italian-influenced cooking with pub classics at this delightful creeper-clad inn, set in a picture perfect Cotswold village. Charming service.

## SOUTHWOLD – Suffolk – **504** Z27 – pop. 3 858

15 D2

▶ London 108 mi – Great Yarmouth 24 mi – Ipswich 35 mi – Norwich 34 mi
ℹ 69 High St ℰ (01502) 72 47 29, www.exploresouthwold.co.uk
◫ The Common, ℰ (01502) 72 32 34

### ⌂⌂⌂ Swan
⤗ ⌂ ⌆ & rm, ⌂ P VISA ◐◯ AE ①

Market Pl. ✉ IP18 6EG – ℰ (01502) 722 186 – www.adnams.co.uk
**40 rm** ⌂ – †£ 95/137 ††£ 170/284 – 2 suites
**Rest** – Menu £ 22/39 – Carte £ 25/41⌂

♦ Attractive 18C coaching inn set in the town centre. Subtle modernisations and stylish touches in cosy lounge and bar. Mix of bedrooms: some traditional, some boldly coloured, some charming. Grand dining room with portraits and chandeliers; modern European menu.

### ⁱ⃞ Crown with rm
⌂ P VISA ◐◯ AE

90 High St ✉ IP18 6DP – ℰ (01502) 722 275 – www.adnams.co.uk
**14 rm** ⌂ – †£ 100/118 ††£ 184/195 – 1 suite   **Rest** – Carte £ 22/37⌂

♦ 17C Georgian-fronted former coaching inn with appealing, relaxed style, buzzing atmosphere and nautically themed locals bar. Modern, seasonal menu served in all areas. Contemporary, individually styled bedrooms; those at the rear are the quietest.

## SOWERBY BRIDGE – West Yorkshire – **502** O22 – pop. 9 901 – ✉ Halifax

22 A2

▶ London 211 mi – Bradford 10 mi – Burnley 35 mi – Manchester 32 mi

### ✕ El Gato Negro
AC VISA ◐◯

Oldham Rd ✉ HX6 4DN – ℰ (01422) 823 070 – www.elgatonegrotapas.co.uk – *Closed first 2 weeks June, 24 December-7 January, Monday and Tuesday*
**Rest** – Spanish – *(dinner only and lunch Friday-Sunday) (booking advisable)* Carte £ 25/36

♦ Fun, relaxed former pub with solid stone walls and open fires, serving tasty, authentic tapas. Menus printed on placemats: choose 5 or 6 dishes between 2 people. Staff give sound advice.

**at Rishworth** Southwest : 4 mi by A 58 on A 672 – ✉ Sowerby Bridge

### ⁱ⃞ Old Bore
⌂ ⟳ P VISA ◐◯

Oldham Rd, South : 0.5 mi on A 672 ✉ HX6 4QU – ℰ (01422) 822 291 – www.oldbore.co.uk – *Closed 2 weeks January, Monday and Tuesday*
**Rest** – Carte £ 30/38

♦ 19C stone coaching inn hidden away in a charming rural area. Cosy, characterful interior crammed with knick-knacks and memorabilia. Appealingly robust cooking often features local game.

## SPARSHOLT – Hampshire – **503** P30 – see Winchester

ENGLAND

**SPEEN** – Buckinghamshire – **504** R28 – ✉ **Princes Risborough**     **11** C2
▶ London 41 mi – Aylesbury 15 mi – Oxford 33 mi – Reading 25 mi

XX   **Old Plow**     🚗 🏠 **P** 𝘝𝘐𝘚𝘈 ⓩ 𝖠𝖤
*Flowers Bottom, West : 0.5 mi by Chapel Hill and Highwood Bottom*
✉ HP27 0PZ – 𝒞 (01494) 488 300 – www.yeoldplough.co.uk – Closed August, 1
week late May, Christmas, Sunday and Monday
**Rest** – Carte £ 29/42

♦ Characterful 17C building with beams and log fires, in a peaceful hamlet. Restaurant has extensive set menu of traditional French dishes. Cosy bistro offers several different menus, including a blackboard selection and tapas Saturday lunch.

---

**SPELDHURST** – Kent – **504** U30 – see Royal Tunbridge Wells

---

**SPRIGG'S ALLEY** – Oxfordshire – see Chinnor

---

**STADDLE BRIDGE** – North Yorkshire – see Northallerton

---

**STADHAMPTON** – Oxfordshire – **503** Q28 – pop. 718     **10** B2
▶ London 53 mi – Aylesbury 18 mi – Oxford 10 mi

XX   **Crazy Bear** with rm     🚗 🏠 ℀ rest, ⁋ 🐕 **P** 𝘝𝘐𝘚𝘈 ⓩ 𝖠𝖤
*Bear Ln., off Wallingford rd* ✉ OX44 7UR – 𝒞 (01865) 890 714
– www.crazybeargroup.co.uk
**17 rm** – ♦£ 90 ♦♦£ 340, ⬷ £ 19
**Rest** – Menu £ 19 (lunch) – Carte £ 29/46
**Rest *Thai Thai*** – Thai – *(booking essential)* Menu £ 30 (dinner)/40
– Carte £ 20/42

♦ Wacky eatery with red London bus reception, smart glasshouse and huge toy bear in trendy bar. Flamboyant English restaurant serves British and French brasserie dishes. More intimate room offers authentic Thai cuisine. Glamorous, individually styled bedrooms boast chic designer furnishings; some have infinity baths.

---

**STAFFORD** – Staffordshire – **502** N25 – pop. 63 681     **19** C1
▶ London 142 mi – Birmingham 26 mi – Derby 32 mi – Shrewsbury 31 mi
🛈 Eastgate St 𝒞 (0871) 7 16 19 32, www.enjoystaffordshire.com
🏰 Stafford Castle Newport Rd, 𝒞 (01785) 22 38 21

🏠   **Moat House**     🚗 🛎 �, 🆔 rest, ℀ ⁋ 🐕 **P** 𝘝𝘐𝘚𝘈 ⓩ 𝖠𝖤
*Lower Penkridge Rd, Acton Trussell, South : 3.75 mi by A 449* ✉ ST17 0RJ
– 𝒞 (01785) 712 217 – www.moathouse.co.uk – Closed 25 December
**40 rm** ⬷ – ♦£ 135 ♦♦£ 155/195 – 1 suite
**Rest *The Conservatory*** – Menu £ 20/30 – Carte dinner £ 23/38

♦ Timbered 15C moated manor house with modern extensions and lawned gardens, within sight of the M6. Characterful rustic bar. Colourful rooms with individual style. Bright, airy conservatory restaurant overlooks canal.

---

**STAINES** – Surrey – **504** S29 – pop. 50 538     **7** C1
▶ London 26 mi – Reading 25 mi

🍴   **Three Horseshoes**     🚗 **P** 𝘝𝘐𝘚𝘈 ⓩ 𝖠𝖤
*25 Shepperton Rd, South : 2 mi on B 376* ✉ TW18 1SE – 𝒞 (01784) 455 014
– www.3horseshoeslaleham.co.uk
**Rest** – Carte £ 21/35

♦ A sturdy 17C inn which has had a sympathetic makeover. Pretty enclosed garden and inviting interior divided into three dining areas with charm and character. Traditional food, done well.

▶ London 92 mi – Leicester 31 mi – Lincoln 50 mi – Nottingham 45 mi

🛈 27 St Mary's St ℰ (01780) 75 56 11, www.stamford.co.uk

◉ Town★★ - St Martin's Church★ – Lord Burghley's Hospital★ – Browne's Hospital★
AC

◐ Burghley House★★ **AC**, SE : 1.5 mi by B 1443

🏨 **George of Stamford**                     🚗 🛋 📶 ♨ **P** 🆅 🆅 AE ①
*71 St Martin's ✉ PE9 2LB – ℰ (01780) 750 750*
*– www.georgehotelofstamford.com*
**46 rm** 🍽 – †£ 95/115 ††£ 280 – 1 suite
**Rest** *Garden Room* – see restaurant listing
**Rest** – Carte £ 43/65
♦ Historic coaching inn dating back over 900 years and still offering good, old-
fashioned hospitality. Plenty of seating options in various bars, lounges, the courtyard and walled garden. Bedrooms have a surprisingly contemporary feel. Formal
oak-panelled restaurant requires smart dress; menu has a modern edge.

🏨 **Crown**                                    🛋 AK rest, 🍽 📶 **P** 🆅 🆅 AE
*All Saints Pl. ✉ PE9 2AG – ℰ (01780) 763 136*
*– www.thecrownhotelstamford.co.uk*
**28 rm** 🍽 – †£ 160/180 ††£ 180/210     **Rest** – Carte £ 21/34
♦ Former coaching inn set in historic market town. Main house bedrooms have a
funky, boutique style; those in the Town House are larger with a more classical
feel. Dine in the modern cocktail bar, in one of the cosy lounges or in the quieter
rear dining room.

🏠 **Rock Lodge** without rest                🚗 🍽 📶 **P** 🆅 🆅 AE
*1 Empingham Rd ✉ PE9 2RH – ℰ (01780) 481 758 – www.rock-lodge.co.uk*
*– Closed 25 December-5 January*
**7 rm** 🍽 – †£ 72/82 ††£ 110/115
♦ Victorian house built in 1900 by the town's mayor. Displays a mix of influences,
with mullioned windows, mock-Tudor gables, gargoyles and stones from old
churches in the garden walls. Comfy lounge and breakfast room; well-equipped
bedrooms.

XX **Jim's Yard**                                🛋 🆅 🆅
ⓒ *3 Ironmonger St, off Broad St ✉ PE9 1PL – ℰ (01780) 756 080*
*– www.jimsyard.biz – Closed last week July, first week August, 25 December-10
January, Sunday and Monday*
**Rest** – Menu £ 17 (lunch) – Carte £ 22/33
♦ Two 18C houses in a courtyard: conservatory or first-floor dining options. Smart
tableware enhances enjoyment of great value menus employing well-executed,
classic cooking.

X **Garden Room** – at George of Stamford       🚗 **P** 🆅 🆅 AE ①
*71 St Martin's ✉ PE9 2LB – ℰ (01780) 750 750*
*– www.georgehotelofstamford.com*
**Rest** – Carte £ 28/48
♦ Relaxed all-day restaurant within a 900 year old coaching inn. Extensive menu
is accompanied by a steak counter in winter and salad bar in summer. The enclosed courtyard is a popular spot.

🍴 **Bull & Swan** with rm                      🛋 📶 🆅 🆅 AE
*St Martins ✉ PE9 2LJ – ℰ (01780) 766 412 – www.thebullandswan.co.uk*
**7 rm** 🍽 – †£ 90 ††£ 110     **Rest** – Carte £ 22/34
♦ Stone-built former hall house converted to an inn during the 1600s and still
the only pub south of the river. Characterful beamed bar and smarter dining
room. Menu ranges from sharing slates to regional classics and locally sourced
steaks. Stylish, individually designed bedrooms boast Egyptian cotton sheets.

**ENGLAND**

**STANDISH** – Greater Manchester – **502** M23 – **pop. 14 350** – ⊠ Wigan     **20** A2

▶ London 210 mi – Liverpool 25 mi – Manchester 21 mi – Preston 15 mi

**at Wrightington Bar** Northwest : 3.5 mi by A 5209 on B 5250 – ⊠ Wigan

🍴 **Mulberry Tree**                                              **P** VISA ⓒⓞ
*9 Wood Ln ⊠ WN6 9SE – ℰ (01257) 451 400 – www.themulberrytree.info*
**Rest** – Carte £ 27/40
◆ Spacious 19C pub with laid-back bar and more formal, linen-laid dining room.
Wide-ranging menus of good value, generously proportioned dishes, with plenty
of pub favourites.

---

**STANSTED MOUNTFITCHET** – Essex – **504** U28 – **pop. 5 311**     **12** B2

▶ London 38 mi – Birmingham 125 mi – Croydon 59 mi – Barnet 37 mi

↑ **Chimneys** without rest                                  ᵗₚ⁾ **P** VISA ⓒⓞ
*44 Lower St, on B 1351 ⊠ CM24 8LR – ℰ (01279) 813 388*
*– www.chimneysguesthouse.co.uk*
**4 rm** ⊇ – ♦£ 58/62 ♦♦£ 80
◆ Charming 17C house with low-beamed ceilings, a cosy lounge and snug breakfast room. Bedrooms have a modern, cottagey style, displaying pine furnishings
and homely touches. Tasty breakfast offerings might include Manx kippers or
smoked haddock with poached eggs.

---

**STANTON** – Suffolk – **504** W27 – **pop. 2 073**     **15** C2

▶ London 88 mi – Cambridge 38 mi – Ipswich 40 mi – King's Lynn 38 mi

✕✕ **Leaping Hare**                           🍴 🏡 **P** VISA ⓒⓞ AE ①
ⓐ  *Wyken Vineyards, South : 1.25 mi by Wyken Rd ⊠ IP31 2DW – ℰ (01359)*
*250 287 – www.wykenvineyards.co.uk – Closed 25 December-5 January*
**Rest** – *(lunch only and dinner Friday-Saturday) (booking essential)* Menu £ 19
(lunch) – Carte £ 26/29 ❀
◆ Beautiful 17C barn with lovely terrace; at the centre of a vineyard. Interesting
all-day light bites or accomplished weekly menu. Well-sourced, seasonal ingredients; many from their own farm. Carefully judged cooking relies on quality produce and natural flavours.

---

**STANTON ST QUINTIN** – Wiltshire – **503** N29 – see Chippenham

---

**STAPLEFORD** – Nottinghamshire – **504** Q25 – see Nottingham

---

**STATHERN** – Leicestershire – see Melton Mowbray

---

**STAVERTON** – Northants. – **504** Q27 – see Daventry

---

**STAVERTON** – Northamptonshire – **503** I32 – **pop. 468** – ⊠ Daventry     **16** B3

▶ London 220 mi – Exeter 20 mi – Torquay 33 mi

🏠 **Kingston House** ⑳         ⟨ 🏡 🕭 🐱 ♨ ⅍ ℭ⟩ 𝄞 **P** VISA ⓒⓞ
*Northwest : 1 mi on Kingston rd ⊠ TQ9 6AR – ℰ (01803) 762 235*
*– www.kingston-estate.com – Closed Christmas-New Year*
**3 rm** ⊇ – ♦£ 110/120 ♦♦£ 180/200
**Rest** – *(dinner only) (residents only, set menu only)* Menu £ 38 **s**
◆ Attractive Georgian mansion in a stunning location. Original features and antiques abound. Spacious bedrooms boast feature beds and good views over the
parterre garden; some have original baths. Vaulted basement dining room serves
classical, home-cooked dishes.

ENGLAND

🖸 London 76 mi – Cambridge 30 mi – Northampton 43 mi – Peterborough 6 mi

🖬🖬    **Bell Inn**    🚗 ₤ rm, ⅍ ⁽ᵢ⁾ 🗄 **P** 𝗩𝗜𝗦𝗔 ⊕ 𝗔𝗘 ⓘ
*Great North Rd* ⊠ *PE7 3RA* – *ℰ (01733) 241 066* – *www.thebellstilton.co.uk*
*– Closed 25 December*
**22 rm** ☲ – ♦£ 76 ♦♦£ 115
**Rest** *Village Bar* – see restaurant listing
**Rest** *Galleried Restaurant* – *(dinner only and Sunday lunch)* Menu £ 25
♦ Historic coaching inn with hospitable, hands-on owner. Comfortable bedrooms
have traditional feel: some have four-posters; the three newest are in the former
smithy, overlooking the garden. First floor restaurant offers seasonal menu with
strong classical base.

🍴    **Village Bar** – at Bell Inn    🚗 🍴 **P** 𝗩𝗜𝗦𝗔 ⊕ 𝗔𝗘 ⓘ
*Great North Rd* ⊠ *PE7 3RA* – *ℰ (01733) 241 066* – *www.thebellstilton.co.uk*
*– Closed 25 December*
**Rest** – Carte £ 20/30 **s**
♦ 17C coaching inn where Stilton cheese was born. Choose from a characterful
bar or more modern bistro area. Served throughout, the classical menu is a step
above your usual pub fare.

---

🖸 London 75 mi – Salisbury 14 mi – Southampton 19 mi – Winchester 9 mi

🍴    **Greyhound** with rm    🚗 ⅍ ⁽ᵢ⁾ **P** 𝗩𝗜𝗦𝗔 ⊕
*31 High St* ⊠ *SO20 6EY* – *ℰ (01264) 810 833* – *www.thegreyhound.info* – *Closed
24-26 December and Sunday dinner*
**7 rm** ☲ – ♦£ 70 ♦♦£ 95/125    **Rest** – Carte £ 23/35
♦ Unassuming pub with low-beamed bar and comfy lounge. Lunch mainly aimed
at one course; concise evening à la carte features pub dishes with restaurant-style
touches and refined presentation. Picnic by the river in the garden. Spacious bedrooms with huge showers.

**at Longstock** North : 1.5 mi on A 3057 – ⊠ Stockbridge

🍴    **Peat Spade Inn** with rm    🍴 🍴 ⁽ᵢ⁾ **P** 𝗩𝗜𝗦𝗔 ⊕ 𝗔𝗘 ⓘ
⑬    *Village St* ⊠ *SO20 6DR* – *ℰ (01264) 810 612* – *www.peatspadeinn.co.uk*
**6 rm** ☲ – ♦£ 145 ♦♦£ 145    **Rest** – *(booking essential)* Carte £ 20/30
♦ Charming 19C inn with country pursuits theme, period furnishings and welcoming candlelight. Menus offer classically based dishes that have been brought
up-to-date. Stylish bedrooms are split between the inn and annexe. Shooting/-
fishing trips can be arranged.

---

🖸 London 201 mi – Liverpool 42 mi – Leeds 50 mi – Sheffield 52 mi

✗✗    **Damson**    🍴 𝗔𝗖 𝗩𝗜𝗦𝗔 ⊕ 𝗔𝗘
*113 Heaton Moor Rd, Northwest : 2.25 mi by A 6, Heaton Rd, A 5145 and Bank
Hall Rd* ⊠ *SK4 4HY* – *ℰ (0161) 432 46 66* – *www.damsonrestaurant.co.uk*
*– Closed 25-26 December and 1 January*
**Rest** – Menu £ 17 (lunch) – Carte £ 28/45
♦ Smart, modern, glass-fronted restaurant with damson walls, velvet chairs and
rustic tables. Appealing menu of traditional dishes with modern touches. Atten-
tive, formal service.

ENGLAND

## STOKE BY NAYLAND – Suffolk – 504 W28                                    15 C

▶ London 70 mi – Bury St Edmunds 24 mi – Cambridge 54 mi – Colchester 11 mi

**Crown** with rm                    🍴 🏡 ⅙ rm, ⅞ rest, ⁇ 🄿 *VISA* ⓪ 🄰🄴
⊠ CO6 4SE – ℰ (01206) 262 001 – www.crowninn.net – Closed 25-26 December
**11 rm** ⌷ – ♦£ 80 ♦♦£ 135/200   **Rest** – Carte £ 23/38 🕸
♦ Spacious 16C pub with smart wood-furnished patio; set in a hillside village
overlooking the valley. Menus feature locally sourced, seasonal produce, a daily
catch and seafood specials. Spacious bedrooms boast country views; some have
French windows and a terrace.

## STOKE HOLY CROSS – Norfolk – 504 X26 – see Norwich

## STOKE-ON-TRENT – Stoke-on-Trent – 502 N24 – pop. 259 252              19 C
📗 Great Britain

▶ London 162 – Birmingham 46 – Leicester 59 – Liverpool 58
🄸 City Centre ℰ (01782) 23 60 00, www.visitstoke.co.uk
🄸🄸 Greenway Hall Stockton Brook, ℰ (01782) 50 31 58
🄸🄸 Parkhall Weston Coyney Hulme Rd, ℰ (01782) 59 95 84
👁 The Potteries Museum and Art Gallery★ Y **M** – Gladstone Pottery Museum★ **AC**
🅖 The Wedgwood Story★ **AC**, S : 7 mi on A 500, A 34 and minor rd V. Little Moreton
Hall★★ **AC**, N : 10 mi by A 500 on A 34 U – Biddulph Grange Garden★, N : 7 mi by
A 52, A 50 and A 527 U

ENGLAND

# STOKE-ON-TRENT NEWCASTLE-UNDER-LYME

ENGLAND

---

## STOKE POGES – Buckinghamshire – **504** S29 – pop. 4 112  11 D3

▶ London 30 mi – Aylesbury 28 mi – Oxford 44 mi

🗺 Stoke Park Park Rd, ℰ (01753) 71 71 71

---

**Stoke Park** 🐾  
Park Rd ⊠ SL2 4PG – ℰ (01753) 717 171  
– www.stokepark.com – Closed 25-26 December        VISA ◑◑ AE ◑  
**49 rm** – ♦£ 265/675, ♦♦£ 495/675, ⌁ £ 22  
**Rest *Dining Room*** – Menu £ 30/48 – Carte lunch £ 43/59  
♦ Grand, palatial hotel in huge grounds, with golf course, extensive sporting activities and impressive spa. Choice of smart classical or stunning contemporary bedrooms. Lounge offers all day brasserie menu. Stylish restaurant displays classical à la carte.

**Stoke Place** 🍴 🕭 ⌐ 🍽 ㄴ rm, % ⊤⌐ ♨ 🅿 VISA ⚙ AE
*Stoke Green, South : 0.5 mi by B 416* ✉ *SL2 4HT –* ✆ *(01753) 534 790*
*– www.stokeplace.co.uk – Closed 24 December-8 January*
**39 rm** ⌐ – ♥£ 130/225 ♥♥£ 155/285
**Rest** *Garden Room – (closed Sunday lunch)* Menu £ 25/40
♦ 17C Queen Anne mansion, by a lake, in 22 acres of grounds. Chic, quirky guest areas display bold print wallpapers and original furnishings; sleek, modern bedrooms boast clean lines and stylish beds. Contemporary menu served in the Garden Room.

---

**STOKENCHURCH** – Buckinghamshire – **504** R29 – pop. 3 949        **11** C2
◘ London 42 mi – High Wycombe 10 mi – Oxford 18 mi

**at Radnage** Northeast : 1.75 mi by A 40 – ✉ Stokenchurch

**Three Horseshoes Inn** with rm        🍴 ⌐ ⊤⌐ 🅿 VISA ⚙
*Bennett End, North : 1.25 mi by Town End rd.* ✉ *HP14 4EB –* ✆ *(01494) 483 273*
*– www.thethreehorseshoes.net – Closed Sunday dinner and Monday lunch*
**6 rm** ⌐ – ♥£ 85/100 ♥♥£ 95/125      **Rest** – Menu £ 17/20 – Carte £ 26/37
♦ Attractive pub with lovely terrace, in a fantastic hillside location. Classically prepared dishes display French touches. Lighter offerings at lunch; à la carte or tapas at dinner. Good choice for Sunday lunch. Comfortable yet minimalistic bedrooms have character beds and modern bathrooms; Molières is best.

---

**STOKESLEY** – North Yorkshire – **502** Q20 – pop. 4 725        **23** C1
– ✉ **Middlesbrough** ▮ Great Britain
◘ London 239 mi – Leeds 59 mi – Middlesbrough 8 mi – Newcastle upon Tyne 49 mi
◩ Great Ayton (Captain Cook Birthplace Museum ★ **AC**), NE : 2.5 mi on A 173

**Chapter's** with rm        ⌐ AC rest, ⊤⌐ VISA ⚙ AE
*27 High St* ✉ *TS9 5AD –* ✆ *(01642) 711 888 – www.chaptershotel.co.uk – Closed 25-26 December, 1 January and Sunday dinner*
**13 rm** ⌐ – ♥£ 74/89 ♥♥£ 89/99
**Rest** – Menu £ 15 (lunch) – Carte dinner £ 29/42
♦ Solid, mellow brick Victorian house with colour washed rooms. Bistro style dining with strong Mediterranean colour scheme. Eclectic menu: classics and more modern dishes.

---

**STON EASTON** – Somerset – **503** M30 – pop. 579        **4** C2
– ✉ **Bath (bath And North East Somerset)**
◘ London 131 mi – Bath 12 mi – Bristol 11 mi – Wells 7 mi

**Ston Easton Park** 🌳        ≤ 🍴 🕭 % ✆ 🅿 VISA ⚙ AE
✉ *BA3 4DF –* ✆ *(01761) 241 631 – www.stoneaston.co.uk*
**20 rm** ⌐ – ♥£ 150/210 ♥♥£ 170/230 – 2 suites
**Rest** *Sorrel* – see restaurant listing
♦ Striking aristocratic Palladian mansion, in 36 acres of attractive grounds designed by Humphrey Repton. Fine rooms of epic proportions are filled with antiques, curios and impressive floral arrangements. Stylish, individually designed bedrooms – many with coronet or four-poster beds – one is set in a cottage.

**Sorrel** – at Ston Easton Park Hotel        ≤ 🍴 🕭 🅿 VISA ⚙ AE ⊙
✉ *BA3 4DF –* ✆ *(01761) 241 631 – www.stoneaston.co.uk*
**Rest** – *(booking essential for non-residents)* Menu £ 23 (lunch) – Carte £ 40/51
♦ Formal country house dining room in a striking Palladian mansion, surrounded by 36 acres of parkland. Classical menus offer luxurious ingredients and produce from the Victorian kitchen garden.

---

**STONEHALL COMMON** – Worcestershire – **see Worcester**

**STORRINGTON** – West Sussex – **504** S31 – **pop. 7 727**

▶ London 54 mi – Brighton 20 mi – Portsmouth 36 mi

XX **Old Forge**  VISA ©© AE ①
*6 Church St ⊠ RH20 4LA – 𝒞 (01903) 743 402 – www.oldforge.co.uk – Closed 2 weeks spring, 1 week autumn, Christmas-New Year, Saturday lunch, Sunday and Wednesday dinner, Monday and Tuesday*
**Rest** – Menu £ 19/35 🍸
◆ Appealing whitewashed and brick cottages with three dining rooms bearing all hallmarks of flavoursome traditional cuisine. Array of cheeses; fine wine from small producers.

---

**STOWMARKET** – Suffolk – **504** W27 – **pop. 15 059**     15 C3

▶ London 95 mi – Ipswich 14 mi – Colchester 35 mi – Clacton-on-Sea 40 mi

**at Buxhall** West : 3.75 mi by B 115 – ⊠ Stowmarket

🍺 **Buxhall Crown**  🍽 P VISA ©©
*Mill Rd ⊠ IP14 3DW – 𝒞 (01449) 736 521 – www.thebuxhallcrown.co.uk – Closed 25 December and Sunday dinner*
**Rest** – Menu £ 16 (lunch) – Carte £ 19/31
◆ Part-16C country pub set off the beaten track, with bright dining room and cosy, low-beamed bar. Classic dishes offered on seasonal menu. Good value set 2 course menu and fun retro puds.

---

**STOW-ON-THE-WOLD** – Gloucestershire – **503** O28 – **pop. 2 074**     4 D1

▌ Great Britain

▶ London 86 mi – Birmingham 44 mi – Gloucester 27 mi – Oxford 30 mi

🔢 12 Talbot Court 𝒞 (01451) 87 01 50, www.stowonthewold.info

🄲 Chastleton House ★★, NE : 6.5 mi by A 436 and A 44

🏨 **Number Four at Stow**  🚗 🍽 AK ✂ rm, ¶¶ 🛁 P VISA ©©
*Fosseway, South : 1.25 mi by A 429 on A 424 ⊠ GL54 1JX – 𝒞 (01451) 830 297 – www.hotelnumberfour.co.uk – Closed 24-29 December*
**14 rm** � – †£ 100/120 ††£ 130/145 – 4 suites
**Rest *Cutlers at Number Four*** – (closed Sunday dinner except bank holiday weekends) Carte £ 25/36
◆ Contemporary, open-plan hotel with small bar and comfy lounge boasting bold brushed velvet and white leather seating. Bright, compact bedrooms feature smart leather headboards, cream furniture and modern facilities. Informal brasserie offers modern British menu.

🏨 **Grapevine**  🍽 ¶¶ 🛁 P VISA ©© AE
*Sheep St ⊠ GL54 1AU – 𝒞 (01451) 830 344 – www.thegrapevinehotel.com*
**22 rm** ⊠ – †£ 72/88 ††£ 113/164
**Rest *La Vigna*** – see restaurant listing
**Rest *Conservatory*** – Menu £ 35
◆ Two extended 17C houses, nestled in amongst the local antique shops. The bar, guest areas and bedrooms that are set in the main house have a traditional feel; bedrooms in the annexe are boldly coloured, more modern in style and quieter. Classical dishes served in conservatory; Mediterranean menu in La Vigna.

🏨 **Royalist**  ¶¶ P VISA ©© AE
*Digbeth St ⊠ GL56 1BN – 𝒞 (01451) 830 670 – www.theroyalisthotel.com*
**14 rm** ⊠ – †£ 68/120 ††£ 103/185
**Rest *Eagle & Child*** – Carte £ 19/25
**Rest *947 AD*** – Menu £ 37 (dinner) – Carte lunch £ 24/29
◆ Historic high street inn - reputedly England's oldest. Comfortable, stylish rooms, individual in shape and décor and quieter at the rear. Two-room bar in exposed stone. Robust cooking in the attached stone pub. Fine dining in the intimate, beamed restaurant with inglenook fireplace.

ENGLAND

**ENGLAND**

⌂ **Number Nine** without rest  🏵 ⁽ᵗ⁾ 𝑉𝐼𝑆𝐴 ⓪
*9 Park St ⊠ GL54 1AQ – 𝒞 (01451) 870 333 – www.number-nine.info*
**3 rm** ⌂ – ♦£ 45/65 ♦♦£ 65/89
♦ Ivy-clad, 18C Cotswold stone house set on the high street of a historic market town, close to the square. Comfy lounge and breakfast room boast exposed stone, open fires and dark beams. Winding staircase leads to simple, neutrally-hued, wood-furnished bedrooms.

✗✗ **Old Butchers**  🏠 𝐴𝐶 𝑉𝐼𝑆𝐴 ⓪ 𝐴𝐸 ⓪
*Park St ⊠ GL54 1AQ – 𝒞 (01451) 831 700 – www.theoldbutchers.com – Closed 1 week May and 1 week October*
**Rest** – Carte £ 24/30
♦ Former butcher's, now a smart, modern restaurant with welcoming ambience and flower-filled terrace. Brightly painted bar with food-themed prints, church candles, cushions and display of fresh bread. Well-priced menus evolve from service to service, featuring hearty, flavoursome dishes and comforting desserts.

✗ **La Vigna** – at Grapevine Hotel  𝑃 𝑉𝐼𝑆𝐴 ⓪ 𝐴𝐸
*Sheep St ⊠ GL54 1AU – 𝒞 (01451) 830 344 – www.thegrapevinehotel.com*
**Rest** – Carte £ 18/23
♦ Informal, brasserie-style, hotel restaurant in a traditional 17C extended house. Menu offers plenty of choice and displays Mediterranean-influences; most produce is sourced from within 20 miles.

🛏 **White Hart Inn** with rm  🏠 🏵 rm, ⁽ᵗ⁾ 𝑃 𝑉𝐼𝑆𝐴 ⓪ 𝐴𝐸 ⓪
*The Square ⊠ GL54 1AF – 𝒞 (01451) 830 674 – www.whiteheartstow.com – Closed 1 week October and 1 week May*
**5 rm** ⌂ – ♦£ 70 ♦♦£ 80/100  **Rest** – Carte £ 21/28
♦ 13C former coaching inn with contemporary, individual style. Small, open-fired bar, leather-furnished lounge and slightly kitsch dining room. Light dishes or soup and sandwich combos at lunch; classic British offerings at dinner. Antique-furnished bedrooms.

**at Upper Oddington** East : 2 mi by A 436 – ⊠ Stow-On-The-Wold

🛏 **Horse & Groom Village Inn** with rm  🚗 🏠 𝑃 𝑉𝐼𝑆𝐴 ⓪
*⊠ GL56 0XH – 𝒞 (01451) 830 584 – www.horseandgroom.uk.com*
**7 rm** ⌂ – ♦£ 65/79 ♦♦£ 89/110  **Rest** – Carte £ 21/33
♦ Part-16C mellow-stone inn in a village designated an AONB. Seasonal menus feature strictly homemade and local produce, with consideration given to ethical production and sustainable sourcing. Cosy bedrooms; serious breakfasts include local eggs and sausages.

**at Lower Oddington** East : 3 mi by A 436 – ⊠ Stow-On-The-Wold

🛏 **Fox Inn** with rm  🚗 🏠 𝑃 𝑉𝐼𝑆𝐴 ⓪
*⊠ GL56 0UR – 𝒞 (01451) 870 555 – www.foxinn.net*
**3 rm** – ♦£ 75/95 ♦♦£ 75/95  **Rest** – (booking essential) Carte £ 24/32
♦ Quintessentially English, creeper-clad inn with cosy, characterful bar, charming garden and heated terrace. Cooking is hearty and satisfying; produce is sourced from local markets. Uniquely designed bedrooms display lovely antiques; some boast feature beds.

**at Daylesford** East : 3.5 mi by A 436 – ⊠ Stow-On-The-Wold

✗ **Café at Daylesford Organic**  🏠 𝑃 𝑉𝐼𝑆𝐴 ⓪ 𝐴𝐸
*⊠ GL56 0YG – 𝒞 (01608) 731 700 – www.daylesfordorganic.com – Closed 25-26 December and 1 January*
**Rest** – Organic – (lunch only) (bookings not accepted) Carte £ 23/32
♦ Stylish café attached to the rear of a farm shop, its rustic interior boasting an open charcoal grill and wood-fired oven. Menus showcase an interesting array of home-cooked dishes. Everything is organic, with much of the produce coming from the farm itself.

**at Bledington** Southeast : 4 mi by A 436 on B 4450 – ⊠ Kingham

🍴 **Kings Head Inn** with rm      🕍 **P** 𝘃𝘪𝘴𝘢 ⊚⊚
*The Green ⊠ OX7 6XQ – 𝒞 (01608) 658 365 – www.kingsheadinn.net – Closed 25-26 December*
**12 rm** ⌱ – 🛏£ 50/70 🛏🛏£ 100/125    **Rest** – Carte £ 21/35
♦ 15C stone inn with low-ceilinged, beamed bar and comfortable dining room. Traditional dishes with odd international influence; robust, rustic cooking. Smart bedrooms; those in pub more characterful; those in annex more stylish.

**at Nether Westcote** Southeast : 4.75 mi by A 429 and A 424

🍴 **Feathered Nest** with rm     ← 🍴 🕍 🍽 rest, 🛜 **P** 𝘃𝘪𝘴𝘢 ⊚⊚ 𝐀𝐄
⊠ *OX7 6SD – 𝒞 (01993) 833 030 – www.thefeatherednestinn.co.uk – Closed 25 December*
**4 rm** ⌱ – 🛏£ 110 🛏🛏£ 185
**Rest** – *(closed Monday except bank holidays) (booking advisable)*
Carte £ 25/34 🍴
♦ With its laid-back bar, rustic snug, casual conservatory and formal dining room, this pub offers something for everyone. Sit on quirky stools made from horse saddles and choose from the simple bar menu or try more complex dishes while sitting at elegant antique tables. Wine list features over 200 bins. Comfy bedrooms boasts antiques, quality linens and roll-top baths.

**at Lower Swell** West : 1.25 mi on B 4068 – ⊠ Stow-On-The-Wold

🏠 **Rectory Farmhouse** without rest      🍴 🍽 **P**
🔲 *by Rectory Barns Rd ⊠ GL54 1LH – 𝒞 (01451) 832 351 – Closed Christmas-New Year*
**3 rm** ⌱ – 🛏£ 60/70 🛏🛏£ 93/100
♦ 17C former farmhouse of Cotswold stone. Bedrooms are very comfortable and decorated in distinctive cottage style. Breakfast in kitchen, conservatory or, in summer, on the terrace.

---

**STRATFORD-UPON-AVON** – Warwickshire – **503** P27      **19** C3
– **pop. 23 085** ▌ Great Britain

▶ London 96 mi – Birmingham 23 mi – Coventry 18 mi – Leicester 44 mi

🛈 Bridgefoot 𝒞 (0870) 160 79 30, www.shakespeare-country.co.uk

🏌 Tiddington Rd, 𝒞 (01789) 20 57 49

🏌 Menzies Welcombe Hotel & GC Warwick Rd, 𝒞 (01789) 41 38 00

🏌 Stratford Oaks Snitterfield Bearley Rd, 𝒞 (01789) 73 19 80

👁 Town★★ - Shakespeare's Birthplace★ **AC**, AB

Ⓖ Mary Arden's House★ **AC**, NW : 4 mi by A 3400 A. Ragley Hall★ **AC**, W : 9 mi by A 422 A

*Plan on next page*

🏨🏨 **Ettington Park** 🍴     🍴 🏛 🖅 🏠 🍽 🍽 ✐ & 🆎 🍽 🐕 🚣 **P** 𝘃𝘪𝘴𝘢 ⊚⊚ 𝐀𝐄 ⓞ
*Alderminster, Southeast : 6.5 mi on A 3400 ⊠ CV37 8BU – 𝒞 (0845) 072 74 54 – www.handpicked.co.uk*
**48 rm** ⌱ – 🛏£ 105/205 🛏🛏£ 145/225
**Rest** *Oak Room* – see restaurant listing
♦ Impressive Gothic mansion surrounded by lovely gardens. Characterful guest areas display ornate plasterwork, marble fireplaces and vast portraits. Feature bedrooms boast original fires and grand beds; others bedrooms are more contemporary.

ENGLAND

# STRATFORD-UPON-AVON

---

🏠🏠🏠 **Welcombe H. Spa and Golf Club**   ⟨ 🚗 ◯ 🏊♨ 🐾 ♨ ✕ 📷 ♿

*Warwick Rd, Northeast : 1.5 mi on A 439*   📶 🔊 **P** 🅟 *VISA* ⓜ 🅐🅔
✉ *CV37 0NR* – ✆ *(01789) 295 252* – www.menzieshotels.co.uk
**73 rm** ⬜ – †£ 92/205 ††£ 112/215 – 5 suites
**Rest** *Trevelyan* – Menu £ 25/30 **s** – Carte £ 29/50 **s**
◆ Imposing Jacobean-style house built in 1866, with attractive grounds, superb
spa/leisure club and classical guest areas. Choose from corporate, or traditional,
antique-filled bedrooms. Formal dining room overlooks the gardens and water
features.

---

🏠🏠 **Arden**   🚗 🛎 ♿ ✕ 📶 **P** *VISA* ⓜ 🅐🅔

*Waterside* ✉ *CV37 6BA* – ✆ *(01789) 298 682* – www.theardenhotelstratford.com
**45 rm** ⬜ – †£ 213/228 ††£ 325/355   **B**x
**Rest** *Waterside Brasserie* – see restaurant listing
◆ Great location opposite the RSC Theatre. Plush interior with smart, modern sitting rooms. Twisty corridors lead to stylish, sage green bedrooms. Large terrace
and gardens overlook the Avon.

---

🏠 **Cherry Trees** without rest   🚗 ✕ 📶 **P** *VISA* ⓜ

*Swan's Nest Ln* ✉ *CV37 7LS* – ✆ *(01789) 292 989*
– www.cherrytrees-stratford.co.uk
**3 rm** ⬜ – †£ 75 ††£ 120   **B**e
◆ Smart, proudly run guesthouse with town just a short stroll away over the River
Avon. Spacious bedrooms boast quality furnishings, state-of-the-art showers, conservatory seating areas and thoughtful extras. Cake served on arrival.

---

🏠 **White Sails** without rest   🚗 🅐🅚 ✕ 📶 **P** *VISA* ⓜ

*85 Evesham Rd, Southwest : 1 mi on B 439* ✉ *CV37 9BE* – ✆ *(01789) 550 469*
– www.white-sails.co.uk
**5 rm** ⬜ – †£ 125 ††£ 125/132
◆ Friendly guest house boasting excellent bedrooms; all individually furnished
and with a high level of facilities, including superb bathrooms. Leather furnished
lounge with local info.

ХХХ **Oak Room** – at Ettington Park Hotel          📠 🕭 ċ. **P** *VISA* ☻ AE ➊
*Alderminster, Southeast : 6.5 mi on A 3400* ⊠ *CV37 8BU* – 𝒞 *(0845) 727 454*
*– www.handpicked.co.uk*
**Rest** – Menu £ 35 **s** – Carte £ 33/45 **s**
♦ Named after its smart wood panelling, an intimate hotel dining room in an impressive Gothic mansion with beautiful façade. Modern menu has classical undertones. Private room in the old chapel.

ХХ **Waterside Brasserie** – at Arden Hotel          🛜 AC ☻ **P** *VISA* ☻ AE
*Waterside* ⊠ *CV37 6BA* – 𝒞 *(01789) 298 682* – *www.theardenhotelstratford.com*
**Rest** – Menu £ 19 (lunch) – Carte £ 36/44 🕮                                 B**x**
♦ Large, contemporary hotel brasserie with lovely outlook courtesy of multi-
paned, Georgian-style doors. Appealing modern British menu; tasty, well-prepared
dishes follow the seasons closely.

ХХ **Church Street Town House** with rm          *VISA* ☻
*16 Church St* ⊠ *CV37 6HB* – 𝒞 *(01789) 262 222*
*– www.churchstreettownhouse.com*                                              A**n**
**12 rm** ⌂ – ♥£ 100 ♥♥£ 160     **Rest** – Carte £ 22/32
♦ Handsome, part-17C property run by an experienced local team. Series of
charming dining rooms display rich fabrics and a mix of furniture. Contemporary
menu offers an extensive choice of globally influenced dishes and sharing platters. Beautiful bedrooms display bold colours, smart bathrooms and great extras.

ХХ **Rooftop**          ≼ 🛜 AC ☻ ⇔ *VISA* ☻
*Royal Shakespeare Theatre, Waterside* ⊠ *CV37 6BB* – 𝒞 *(01789) 403 449*
*– www.rsc.org.uk/eat* – *Closed Sunday dinner*                                 B**a**
**Rest** – Menu £ 19 (lunch) – Carte dinner £ 26/38
♦ Modern, open-plan restaurant with lovely terrace, set on top of the Royal Shakespeare Theatre and boasting views over the canal basin, river and gardens. Interesting modern menu with classical British undertones; attractive presentation.

ХХ **No 9 Church St.**          ☻ ⇔ *VISA* ☻ AE
*9 Church St* ⊠ *CV37 6HB* – 𝒞 *(01789) 415 522* – *www.no9churchst.com* – *Closed*
*25 December-3 January, Sunday dinner and Monday*                               A**a**
**Rest** – Menu £ 16 (lunch) – Carte £ 24/33 **s**
♦ Cosy little restaurant set within a 400 year old townhouse, a little off the main
streets. Experienced chef-owner has returned home to offer honest, flavoursome
British cooking with a modern twist. Classical puddings and friendly service.

Х **Lambs**          ☻ *VISA* ☻
*12 Sheep St* ⊠ *CV37 6EF* – 𝒞 *(01789) 292 554* – *www.lambsrestaurant.co.uk*
*– Closed 25-26 December and Monday lunch*                                      B**c**
**Rest** – Menu £ 12/15 – Carte £ 22/38
♦ Attractive 16C timbered house, with characterful beams, original features and
split-level dining rooms. Concise menu offers refined modern dishes and fish specials, with good value pre-theatre options.

**at Alveston** *East : 2 mi by B 4086 - B -* ⊠ *Stratford-Upon-Avon*

Х **Baraset Barn**          🛜 AC ⇔ **P** *VISA* ☻
*1 Pimlico Ln, on B 4086* ⊠ *CV37 7RJ* – 𝒞 *(01789) 295 510*
*– www.barasetbarn.co.uk* – *Closed 1 January and Sunday dinner*
**Rest** – Menu £ 16 (lunch and early dinner) – Carte £ 21/38
♦ Modernised barn offering something for everyone: original features, contemporary furnishings and large terraces. Good-sized menu caters for all and includes
daily fish specials and tasty rotisserie selection.

**STRETE** – Devon – see Dartmouth

**STRETTON** – Staffordshire – **502** P25 – see Burton-upon-Trent

**STUCKTON** – Hampshire – see Fordingbridge

## STUDLAND – Dorset – 503 O32 – pop. 471
4 C3

▶ London 135 mi – Bournemouth 25 mi – Southampton 53 mi – Weymouth 29 mi

⋇ **Shell Bay**  ∈ 🏡 VISA ⬤⬤ AE ⓞ
Ferry Rd, North : 3 mi or via car ferry from Sandbanks ✉ BH19 3BA – 𝒞 (01929)
450 363 – www.shellbay.net – March-October
**Rest** – Seafood – *(booking essential)* Carte £ 24/32
♦ Airy, simply furnished seafood restaurant with decked terrace; superbly set on
the waterfront and boasting views over the harbour to Brownsea Island – all tables have a view. Choose between an informal lunch/early evening menu or classically based daily menu.

## SUMMERCOURT – Cornwall – 503 F32 – ✉ Newquay
1 B2

▶ London 263 mi – Newquay 9 mi – Plymouth 45 mi

⋇ **Viners**  🏡 ⇔ P VISA ⬤⬤ AE
Carvynick, 1.5 mi Northwest off the junction of A 30 and A 3058. ✉ TR8 5AF
– 𝒞 (01872) 510 544 – www.vinersrestaurant.co.uk – Closed 2 weeks early
January, and Sunday dinner and Monday out of season
**Rest** – Menu £ 14 (lunch)/19 – Carte £ 24/39 **s**
♦ Rustic, stone-built former farmhouse. Snacks available amongst roaring log
fires and low slung beams in the bar. Relaxed first floor restaurant offers seasonal
menu of old classics, a few more ambitious dishes and tasty daily specials. Keen,
friendly service.

## SUMMERHOUSE – Darlington – see Darlington

## SUNBURY ON THAMES – Surrey – 504 S29 – pop. 27 415
7 C1

▶ London 16 mi – Croydon 38 mi – Barnet 44 mi – Ealing 10 mi

⋇⋇ **Indian Zest**  🏡 P VISA ⬤⬤ AE
21 Thames St ✉ TW16 5QF – 𝒞 (01932) 765 000 – www.indianzest.co.uk
**Rest** – Indian – Carte £ 21/25
♦ Original in its decoration and food. 450 year old building; a series of small
rooms set around a bar; subtle colonial feel. Interesting mix of modern Indian
and traditional regional cuisine.

## SUNNINGDALE – Windsor and Maidenhead – 504 S29
11 D3

▶ London 33 mi – Croydon 39 mi – Barnet 46 mi – Ealing 22 mi

⋇⋇⋇ **Bluebells**  🚗 🏡 AC ⇔ P VISA ⬤⬤ AE
Shrubbs Hill, London Rd, Northeast : 0.75 mi on A 30 ✉ SL5 0LE – 𝒞 (01344)
622 722 – www.bluebells-restaurant.com – Closed 1-12 January, 25-26
December, Sunday dinner and Monday
**Rest** – Menu £ 17/25 – Carte dinner £ 33/59
♦ Smart, well-manicured façade matched by sophisticated interior of deep
green. Large rear terrace, deck and garden. Modern British cooking with original
starting point.

## SUNNISIDE – Tyne and Wear
24 B2

▶ London 283 mi – Newcastle upon Tyne 6 mi – Sunderland 16 mi
– Middlesbrough 41 mi

⌂ **Hedley Hall** without rest ⌂  🚗 🕭 🖤 🏡 P VISA ⬤⬤
Hedley Lane, South : 2 mi by A 6076 ✉ NE16 5EH – 𝒞 (01207) 231 835
– www.hedleyhall.com – Closed Christmas-New Year
**4 rm** ⌂ – ♦£ 55/65 ♦♦£ 86
♦ Pleasant former farmhouse in quiet rural location close to Beamish, with spacious conservatory and sitting room. Rooms are large, with good levels of comfort
and country views.

**SUTTON COLDFIELD** – West Midlands – **503** O26 – pop. 105 452    **19** C2

▶ London 124 mi – Birmingham 8 mi – Coventry 29 mi – Nottingham 47 mi

🏌 Pype Hayes Walmley Eachelhurst Rd, ℰ (0121) 351 10 14

🏌 Boldmere Monmouth Dr., ℰ (0121) 354 33 79

🏌 110 Thornhill Rd, ℰ (0121) 580 78 78

🏌 The Belfry Wishaw Lichfield Rd, ℰ (01675) 47 03 01

Plan : see Birmingham pp. 2 and 3

XX   **Mint**         🔐 AC VISA ⓪

*52 Thornhill Rd, Little Aston, Northwest : 3.5 mi by A 5127, A 454 and B 4151 on B 4138. ✉ B74 3EN – ℰ (0121) 353 04 88 – www.mint-restaurant.com – Closed first week January, one week Easter, last week August, Monday and Tuesday*
**Rest** – Menu £ 19/37                             DT**x**
♦ Bright, modern, brasserie-style restaurant set in a smart residential area. Short menu of flavoursome, visually appealing British dishes. Good value lunch menu. Hands-on owner.

---

**SUTTON COURTENAY** – Oxfordshire – **504** Q29 – pop. 2 413    **10** B2

▶ London 72 mi – Bristol 77 mi – Coventry 70 mi

🏠   **Fish**         🚗 P̲ VISA AE

*4 Appleford Rd ✉ OX14 4NQ – ℰ (01235) 848 242*
*– www.thefishatsuttoncourtenay.co.uk – Closed Monday except bank holidays and Sunday dinner*
**Rest** – Menu £ 17 (lunch) – Carte £ 24/34
♦ Robust, seasonal country cuisine: escargots and crème brûlée meet steak and kidney pie and profiteroles on Franco-Anglo menu. Neat garden and bright conservatory. Charming service.

---

**SUTTON GAULT** – Cambridgeshire – **504** U26 – see Ely

---

**SUTTON-ON-THE-FOREST** – North Yorkshire – **502** P21 – pop. 281    **23** C2

▶ London 230 mi – Kingston-upon-Hull 50 mi – Leeds 52 mi – Scarborough 40 mi

🏠   **Rose & Crown**         🚗 P̲ VISA ⓪ AE
😊

*Main St ✉ YO61 1DP – ℰ (01347) 811 333 – www.rosecrown.co.uk – Closed Sunday dinner and Monday*
**Rest** – (booking essential) Menu £ 18 (lunch) **s** – Carte £ 26/30 **s**
♦ Always a welcoming atmosphere at this village pub, with its cosy bar and busy dining room. Variety of menus ensures something for everyone; good food and local specialities. Large terrace and gazebo.

🏠   **Blackwell Ox Inn** with rm         🔐 ▮ ❄ rest, P̲ VISA ⓪

*Huby Rd ✉ YO61 1DT – ℰ (01347) 810 328 – www.blackwelloxinn.co.uk*
**7 rm** ⌂ – †£ 65 ††£ 110
**Rest** – (closed Sunday dinner) Menu £ 15 (lunch) **s** – Carte £ 20/30 **s**
♦ Smart, contemporary inn with homely bar/lounge and formal, linen-clad dining room. Blackboard snacks and daily changing à la carte; dishes range from the down-to-earth to more ambitious. Spacious, stylish bedrooms; some boast four-posters and Room 2 has a roll-top bath.

---

**SWETTENHAM** – Cheshire East – pop. 248    **20** B3

▶ London 177 mi – Birmingham 63 mi – Liverpool 43 mi – Leeds 79 mi

🏠   **Swettenham Arms**         🚗 🔐 P̲ VISA ⓪ AE

*✉ CW12 2LF – ℰ (01477) 571 284 – www.swettenhamarms.co.uk*
**Rest** – Carte £ 17/40
♦ Traditional pub with beaten copper bar, open fires, horse brasses and lavender meadow. Seasonal menu provides plenty of choice, ranging from sharing platters and pub classics to carefully prepared, well-presented restaurant-style dishes.

---

**SWINBROOK** – Oxfordshire – **503** P28 – see Burford

ENGLAND

**SWINDON** – Swindon – **503** O29 – **pop. 155 432**                          **4** D2

▶ London 83 mi – Bournemouth 69 mi – Bristol 40 mi – Coventry 66 mi

🚺 37 Regent St ✆ (01793) 53 03 28, www.visitwiltshire.co.uk

🚗 Broome Manor Pipers Way, ✆ (01793) 53 24 03

🏌 Shrivenham Park Shrivenham Penny Hooks, ✆ (01793) 78 38 53

🏌 The Wiltshire G & CC Wootton Bassett Vastern, ✆ (01793) 84 99 99

🏌 Wrag Barn G & C.C. Highworth Shrivenham Rd, ✆ (01793) 86 13 27

👁 Great Western Railway Museum★ **AC** – Railway Village Museum★ **AC** Y **M**

🅖 Lydiard Park (St Mary's★) W : 4 mi U. Ridgeway Path★★, S : 8.5 mi by A 4361
  – Whitehorse (≤★)E : 7.5 mi by A 4312, A 420 and B 400 off B 4057

**at Bishopstone** East : 5.5 mi by A 4312 off A 420

🍺 **Royal Oak**                                          🍴 **P** 📧 ⓒⓞ ⓘ
   *Cues Ln ⊠ SN6 8PP* – ✆ *(01793) 790 481* – *www.royaloakbishopstone.co.uk*
   **Rest** – Carte £ 24/35
   ♦ Relaxing country pub with open fires and rustic décor. Menu changes accord-
   ing to what's fresh, local and seasonal, with much of the produce coming from
   the owner's organic farm.

**TADCASTER** – North Yorkshire – **502** Q22 – **pop. 6 548**            **22** B2

▶ London 206 mi – Harrogate 16 mi – Leeds 14 mi – York 11 mi

**at Wighill** North : 3 mi by A 659 – ⊠

🍺 **White Swan**                                       🍴 🍴 **P** 📧 ⓒⓞ
   *Main St ⊠ LS24 8BQ* – ✆ *(01937) 832 217* – *www.whiteswanwighill.co.uk*
   **Rest** – Carte £ 19/24
   ♦ Warm, welcoming pub with a cosy snug, several comfy dining rooms and a
   small shop. Blackboard specials supplement the main monthly menu, which features pub classics, some more ambitious dishes and a popular selection of 'Yorkshire Tapas'.

**at Colton** Northeast : 3 mi by A 659 off A 64 – ⊠ Tadcaster

🍺 **Ye Old Sun Inn** with rm                          🍴 🍴 ⓣⓟ **P** 📧 ⓒⓞ ⒜Ⓔ
   *Main St ⊠ LS24 8EP* – ✆ *(01904) 744 261* – *www.yeoldsuninn.co.uk* – *Closed 26
   December*
   **3 rm** ⊒ – ♦£ 75 ♦♦£ 100   **Rest** – Carte £ 23/30
   ♦ Rustic, family-run pub with warming open fires and a small deli. Owners are
   great ambassadors of local suppliers and seasonal produce, and give regular
   cookery demonstrations. Smart bedrooms are located in the house next door.

**TANGMERE** – West Sussex – **504** R31 – **see Chichester**

**TAPLOW** – Buckinghamshire – **504** R29                                 **11** C3

▶ London 33 mi – Maidenhead 2 mi – Oxford 36 mi – Reading 12 mi

🏨 **Cliveden** 🌳              ≤ 🍴 🏊 🛥 🎾 🌐 🐎 🎬 🔧 ⓣⓟ 🅿 **P** 📧 ⓒⓞ ⒜Ⓔ ⓘ
   *North : 2 mi by Berry Hill ⊠ SL6 0JF* – ✆ *(01628) 668 561*
   – *www.clivedenhouse.co.uk*
   **31 rm** ⊒ – ♦£ 210/590 ♦♦£ 210/590 – 8 suites
   **Rest** *Waldo's* – Modern – *(dinner only) (booking essential)* Menu £ 79
   **Rest** *Terrace* – Modern – Menu £ 39/60
   ♦ Stunning 19C stately home in a superb location, boasting views over the parterre and National Trust gardens to the Thames. Opulent interior with sumptuous,
   antique-filled lounges and luxuriously appointed bedrooms; choose one in the
   main house. Journey in style in their classic cars, vintage launches or helicopters.
   Modern classics in Waldo's; simpler menu in Terrace.

**Taplow House**  ⬛ 🔊 AC rm, 🍴 📶 🔥 **P** **VISA** ⦿ **AE**
*Berry Hill* ⊠ SL6 0DA – ✆ *(01628) 670 056 – www.taplowhouse.com*
**32 rm** 🛏 – †£ 95/205 ††£ 95/205
**Rest** *Berry's* – Menu £ 18/30 – Carte £ 29/35
♦ Georgian house built in 1751, its expansive gardens boasting Europe's tallest tulip tree, which was reputedly planted by Elizabeth I. Characterful guest areas; mix of modern furnishings and period furniture in the well-equipped bedrooms. Formal restaurant overlooks the grounds – menu offers modern classics.

---

**TARPORLEY** – Cheshire West and Chester – **502** L/M24 – pop. 2 634        **20** A3
▶ London 186 mi – Chester 11 mi – Liverpool 27 mi – Shrewsbury 36 mi
🏌 Portal G & C.C. Cobblers Cross Lane, ✆(01829) 73 39 33
🏌 Portal Premier Forest Rd, ✆(01829) 73 38 84

**at Cotebrook** Northeast : 2.5 mi on A 49 – ⊠ Tarporley

🍴 **Fox and Barrel**   ⬛ 🔊 **P** **VISA** ⦿
*Foxbank* ⊠ CW6 9DZ – ✆ *(01829) 760 529 – www.foxandbarrel.co.uk – Closed dinner 25-26 December and 1 January*
**Rest** – Carte £ 23/30
♦ Well-run pub with wood-panelled walls, heaving bookshelves and smart terrace. Constantly evolving menu offers originality and interest. Sensibly priced dishes are generous and neatly presented.

**at Little Budworth** Northeast : 3.5 mi on A 49 – ⊠ Tarporley

🍴🍴 **Cabbage Hall**   ⬛ 🔊 **P** **VISA** ⦿
*Forest Rd.* ⊠ CW6 9ES – ✆ *(01829) 760 292 – www.cabbagehallrestaurant.com – Closed 2-16 January, 24-25 December, Tuesday and dinner Sunday*
**Rest** – Menu £ 22 – Carte £ 32/38
♦ Unassuming former pub in 11 acres; run by experienced chef. Bold, modern inner with comfy lounge, laminated tables and low-backed dining chairs. Several classical menus from which to choose.

---

**TARR STEPS** – Somerset – **503** J30        **3** A2
▶ London 191 mi – Taunton 31 mi – Tiverton 20 mi
👁 Tarr Steps ★★ (Clapper Bridge ★★)

🍴 **Tarr Farm Inn** with rm   ⬛ 🔊 🍴 📶 **P** **VISA** ⦿ **AE**
⊠ TA22 9PY – ✆ *(01643) 851 507 – www.tarrfarm.co.uk – Closed 1-13 February*
**9 rm** 🛏 – †£ 95/120 ††£ 150    **Rest** – Carte £ 18/36
♦ Beside a river, in idyllic countryside, this is a true destination pub. Food ranges from cream teas and sandwiches to three courses at lunch, with more ambitious dishes at dinner. Bedrooms are elegant, luxurious and extremely well-equipped.

---

**TATTENHALL** – Cheshire West and Chester – **502** L24 – pop. 1 860        **20** A3
▶ London 200 mi – Birmingham 71 mi – Chester 10 mi – Liverpool 29 mi

🏠 **Higher Huxley Hall** without rest 🌿   ⬅ ⬛ 🍴 📶 **P** **VISA** ⦿ **AE**
*North : 2.25 mi on Huxley rd* ⊠ CH3 9BZ – ✆ *(01829) 781 484*
*– www.huxleyhall.co.uk – Closed Christmas*
**4 rm** 🛏 – †£ 55/75 ††£ 90/95
♦ Attractive part-13C farmhouse boasting field and castle views. Classical, open-fired lounge and linen-laid breakfast room. Original Elizabethan staircase. Homely bedrooms have good facilities.

**ENGLAND**

**at Higher Burwardsley** Southeast : 1 mi – ✉ Tattenhall

🏠 **Pheasant Inn** with rm 🐾    🛋 🛜 📶 **P** **VISA** 🆚 **AE**
✉ CH3 9PF – 𝒞 (01829) 770 434 – www.thepheasantinn.co.uk
**12 rm** 🛏 – 🛏£ 75/95 🛏🛏£ 95/150   **Rest** – Carte £ 17/30
♦ Characterful stone pub boasting reclaimed beams, stone columns and great views over the Cheshire Plains. Extensive daily menus offer refined pub dishes and Mediterranean influences. Bedrooms are compact, stylish and comfortable; most have views.

---

**TAUNTON** – Somerset – **503** K30 – pop. 58 241      **3** B3
▶ London 168 mi – Bournemouth 69 mi – Bristol 50 mi – Exeter 37 mi
ℹ Paul St 𝒞 (01823) 33 63 44, www.visitsomerset.co.uk
🚆 Taunton Vale Creech Heathfield, 𝒞 (01823) 41 22 20
⛳ Vivary Vivary Park, 𝒞 (01823) 28 92 74
⛳ Taunton and Pickeridge Corfe, 𝒞 (01823) 42 15 37
👁 Town★ - St Mary Magdalene★ V – Somerset County Museum★ **AC** V **M** – St James'★ U – Hammett St★ V **25** – The Crescent★ V – Bath Place★ V **3**
🅖 Trull (Church★), S : 2.5 mi by A 38 – Hestercombe Gardens★, N : 5 mi by A 3259 BY and minor roads to Cheddon Fitzpaine. Bishops Lydeard★ (Church★), NW : 6 mi – Wellington : Church★, Wellington Monument (< ★★), SW : 7.5 mi by A 38 – Combe Florey★, NW : 8 mi – Gaulden Manor★ **AC**, NW : 10 mi by A 358 and B 3227

🏰 **Castle**    🛋 🎿 📶 🛎 **P** **VISA** 🆚 **AE** ①
Castle Green ✉ TA1 1NF – 𝒞 (01823) 272 671 – www.the-castle-hotel.com
**44 rm** 🛏 – 🛏£ 145/175 🛏🛏£ 225/325      V**a**
**Rest** *Brazz* – see restaurant listing
♦ Part-12C Norman castle boasting impressive gardens, a keep and two wells. Traditional furnished throughout and run by the same family for three generations. Well-kept, individually decorated bedrooms; great views from the penthouse suite.

🏠 **Meryan House**    🛋 📶 **P** **VISA** 🆚
Bishop's Hull Rd, West : 0.75 mi by A 38 ✉ TA1 5EG – 𝒞 (01823) 337 445
– www.meryanhouse.co.uk      AZ**c**
**12 rm** 🛏 – 🛏£ 65/70 🛏🛏£ 75/90
**Rest** – *(dinner only) (booking essential for non-residents)* Menu £ 22/26 **s**
♦ Spacious house; well-run run by charming owner. Open sitting room features fantastic juke box. Highly individual bedrooms boast quality wallpapers and beautiful feature beds – many are antiques. Cosy bar. Traditional, open-fired dining room with classical menu.

🍴 **Willow Tree**    📶 ♻ **VISA** 🆚
3 Tower Ln ✉ TA1 4AR – 𝒞 (01823) 352 835
– www.thewillowtreerestaurant.com – Closed January, August, Sunday, Monday and Thursday      V**c**
**Rest** – *(dinner only) (booking essential)* Menu £ 28/34
♦ Converted 17C townhouse with intimate dining rooms, exposed beams and large inglenook. Bi-monthly menu blends a classical base with artful, innovative ideas. Friendly, efficient service.

🍴 **Augustus**    📶 **VISA** 🆚
3 The Courtyard, St James St. ✉ TA1 1JR – 𝒞 (01823) 324 354
– www.augustustaunton.co.uk – Closed 23 December-2 January, Sunday and Monday      V**x**
**Rest** – Menu £ 18 – Carte £ 26/34
♦ Simple little bistro set in a small courtyard and run by an experienced chef. Good-sized menu of hearty, unfussy dishes which mix French, British and some Asian influences. Good value 3 course blackboard menu. Bright and breezy service.

# TAUNTON

ENGLAND

☒ **Brazz** – at Castle Hotel     🚗 **P** *VISA* **◯◯** AE **①**
*Castle Green ☒ TA1 1NF – 𝒞 (01823) 252 000 – www.the-castle-hotel.com*
**Rest** – Carte £ 25/35        **Va**
• Relaxed brasserie located in a part-12C, wisteria-clad Norman castle. Accessible à la carte and good value set menu. Produce is sourced locally, with fruits, herbs and veg from within 5 miles.

**at Henlade** East : 3.5 mi on A 358 - BZ – ☒ Taunton

🏨 **Mount Somerset** ⌂     ≼ 🚗 🐾 🔥 🛁 📶 🍴 ⛳ **P** *VISA* **◯◯** AE **①**
*Lower Henlade, South : 0.5 mi by Stoke Rd ☒ TA3 5NB – 𝒞 (01823) 442 500*
*– www.mountsomersethotel.co.uk*
**19 rm** ⌂ – ♦£ 130/230 ♦♦£ 145/305
**Rest** – (booking advisable) Menu £ 18/50 – Carte £ 35/50 **s**
• Fine Regency country house with formal gardens, set in four acres. Elegant bedrooms, excellent bathrooms and spacious, modern sitting rooms. Capacious dining room with immaculately set tables. Menus offer a mix of traditional and modern dishes.

**at Hatch Beauchamp** Southeast : 6 mi by A 358 - BZ – ☒ Taunton

🏠 **Farthings**     🚗 🍴 **P** *VISA* **◯◯** AE
*Village Rd ☒ TA3 6SG – 𝒞 (01823) 480 664 – www.farthingshotel.co.uk*
**12 rm** ⌂ – ♦£ 70/120 ♦♦£ 80/130   **Rest** – Menu £ 24/29 **s** – Carte £ 32/41 **s**
• Fine Georgian house in mature, well-tended gardens. Small bar and open lounge; many original features remain. Immaculately kept, antique-filled bedrooms – master rooms are particularly comfortable. Two-roomed restaurant offers constantly evolving, seasonal menu.

**at West Bagborough** Northwest : 10.5 mi by A 358 - AY – ☒ Taunton

🍴☒ **Rising Sun Inn** with rm     *VISA* **◯◯**
*☒ TA4 3EF – 𝒞 (01823) 432 575 – www.risingsuninn.info*
**2 rm** – ♦£ 65 ♦♦£ 95   **Rest** – Carte £ 24/34
• Warm, intimate inn with a lovely 'village pub' atmosphere. Locally sourced ingredients contribute to a well-balanced mix of modern and traditional dishes – with plenty of care taken in the kitchen. Two very comfortable bedrooms; one boasts a four-poster.

**at Triscombe** Northwest : 11 mi by A 358 - AY – ☒ Taunton

🍴☒ **Blue Ball Inn** with rm     🚗 🌳 **P** *VISA* **◯◯**
*☒ TA4 3HE – 𝒞 (01984) 618 242 – www.theblueballinn.com – Closed 25-26*
*December, dinner 1 January, Monday and Sunday dinner in autumn and winter*
**3 rm** ⌂ – ♦£ 65/80 ♦♦£ 80/95   **Rest** – Carte £ 22/30
• 15C thatched and stone-built former stables in the Quantock Hills. Rustic beamed inner with country pursuits memorabilia and lovely tiered garden. Fresh soup, homemade terrines, warm salads and interesting sandwiches at lunch. Hearty, tasty offerings on the à la carte. Plush, stylish bedrooms boast quality furnishings.

---

**TAVISTOCK** – Devon – **503** H32 – pop. 11 018      **2 C2**
▶ London 239 mi – Exeter 38 mi – Plymouth 16 mi
🗐 Bedford Sq 𝒞 (01822) 61 29 38, www.tavistockpeople.co.uk
🏴 Down Rd, 𝒞 (01822) 61 23 44
🏴 Hurdwick Tavistock Hamlets, 𝒞 (01822) 61 27 46
◩ Morwellham★ **AC**, SW : 4.5 m. E : Dartmoor National Park★★ – Buckland Abbey★★ **AC**, S : 7 mi by A 386 – Lydford★★, N : 8.5 mi by A 386

### 🏠🛏 **Horn of Plenty** ⌂     ⩗ 🍴 🌲 🆔 **P** **VISA** ⓸
*Gulworthy, West : 4 mi by A 390 off B 3362* ✉ *PL19 8JD* – ☎ *(01822) 832 528*
*– www.thehornofplenty.co.uk*
**10 rm** 🍽 – ✝£ 185/215 ✝✝£ 195/225   **Rest** – Menu £ 20/50
♦ Attractive creeper-clad house in a peaceful countryside location, boasting
lovely Tamar Valley and Bodmin Moor views. Comfy, contemporary guest areas.
Well-equipped, modern bedrooms in the house and annexe; some with balconies
or terraces. Linen-laid dining room offers classical menu and impressive outlook.

### 🏠🛏 **Browns**     🌲 🛎 🖐 👘 **P** **VISA** ⓸ 🆎 ⓪
*80 West St* ✉ *PL19 8AQ* – ☎ *(01822) 618 686* – *www.brownsdevon.co.uk*
**20 rm** – ✝£ 55/99 ✝✝£ 119/209, 🍽 £ 9   **Rest** – Menu £ 24/40 – Carte £ 27/54
♦ Smart hotel in former coaching inn – the oldest licensed premises in town.
Bedrooms take on a modern style while still retaining original features; those in
the old coach house are best. Open-plan bar and lounge. Simple, all-day brasserie
offering modern menu.

## at Milton Abbot *Northwest : 6 mi on B 3362* – ✉ **Tavistock**

### 🏠🛏 **Hotel Endsleigh** ⌂     ⩗ 🍴 👗 🌲 👘 **P** **VISA** ⓸ 🆎
*Southwest : 1 mi* ✉ *PL19 0PQ* – ☎ *(01822) 870 000* – *www.hotelendsleigh.com*
*– Closed 2 weeks January*
**14 rm** 🍽 – ✝£ 162/198 ✝✝£ 220/260 – 2 suites   **Rest** – Menu £ 25/40
♦ Painstakingly restored Regency lodge in magnificent Devonian gardens and
grounds. Stylish lounge and refined bedrooms are imbued with an engaging, understated elegance. Interesting, classically based dishes served in two minimalist
dining rooms.

## at Chillaton *Northwest : 6.25 mi by Chillaton rd* – ✉ **Tavistock**

### 🏠 **Tor Cottage** without rest ⌂     ⩗ 🍴 👗 🍵 👗 👘 **P** **VISA** ⓸
*Southwest : 0.75 mi by Tavistock rd, turning right at bridle path sign, down
unmarked track for 0.5 mi* ✉ *PL16 0JE* – ☎ *(01822) 860 248*
*– www.torcottage.co.uk – Closed mid-December-1 February*
**5 rm** 🍽 – ✝£ 98 ✝✝£ 140
♦ Remotely set cottage set in 28 hillside acres, with peaceful gardens and lovely
outdoor pool. Bedrooms, most in converted outhouses, boast small kitchenettes
and wood burning stoves. Breakfast is taken on the terrace or in the conservatory.
Charming owner.

---

**TEFFONT** – Wiltshire – **see Salisbury**

---

**TEIGNMOUTH** – Devon – **503** J32 – pop. 14 799     **2** D2
▶ London 216 mi – Exeter 16 mi – Torquay 8 mi
🛈 Sea Front ☎ (01626) 21 56 66, www.visitsouthdevon.co.uk

### 🏠 **Thomas Luny House** without rest     🌲 👗 👘 **P** **VISA** ⓸
*Teign St, follow signs for the Quays, off the A 381* ✉ *TQ14 8EG* – ☎ *(01626)
772 976 – www.thomas-luny-house.co.uk – Closed January-mid-February*
**4 rm** 🍽 – ✝£ 68/75 ✝✝£ 90/102
♦ Georgian merchant's house with attractive walled garden. Classical lounge and
antique-filled breakfast room; tea and cake on arrival. One bedroom with hand-
painted oriental furniture, another with a four-poster. Quality breakfasts and
home-grown figs in season.

---

**TEMPLE SOWERBY** – Cumbria – **502** M20 – **see Penrith**

---

**TENTERDEN** – Kent – **504** W30 – pop. 6 977     **9** C2
▶ London 57 mi – Folkestone 26 mi – Hastings 21 mi – Maidstone 19 mi
🛈 High St ☎ (01580) 76 35 72, www.tenterdentown.co.uk

ENGLAND

XX **Richard Phillips at Chapel Down**  ⟨ 🛱 🖭 ⇔ 🅿 🚾 ⮾ 🖭
*Tenterden Vineyard, Small Hythe, South: 2.5 mi on B 2082* ⊠ *TN30 7NG*
*– ℰ (01580) 761 616 – www.richardphillipsatchapeldown.co.uk – Closed Monday*
**Rest** *– (lunch only and dinner Thursday-Saturday)* Menu £ 16 (lunch)
*– Carte £ 28/50*

♦ Spacious modern restaurant and casual bar on 1st floor of a barn conversion;
terrace has countryside views. Good value lunch menu and more elaborate à la
carte showcase seasonal produce.

---

**TETBURY** – Gloucestershire – **503** N29 – pop. 5 250 ▌ Great Britain  **4** C1

▶ London 113 mi – Bristol 27 mi – Gloucester 19 mi – Swindon 24 mi

🄳 33 Church St ℰ (01666) 50 35 52, www.visittetbury.co.uk

🄵 Westonbirt, ℰ (01666) 88 02 42

🄶 Westonbirt Arboretum ★ **AC**, SW : 2.5 mi by A 433

🏠🏠 **Calcot Manor** 🦢  🛋 🕪 🛱 ⌇ 🗕 🕭 🔉 ⌂ %% ⋇⋇ 🕪 🛁 🅿
*Calcot, West : 3.5 mi on A 4135* ⊠ *GL8 8YJ – ℰ (01666)*  🚾 ⮾ 🖭 ⓪
*890 391 – www.calcotmanor.co.uk*
**34 rm** ⌑ – †£ 234 ††£ 460 – 1 suite
**Rest** *Gumstool Inn* 🙂 *– see restaurant listing*
**Rest** *Conservatory* *– (booking essential)* Menu £ 27 (lunch) – Carte £ 39/52
♦ Impressive Cotswold farmhouse, gardens and meadows with converted ancient
barns and stables. Superb spa. Variety of luxuriously appointed rooms with contemporary flourishes. Stylish Conservatory serves interesting modern dishes.

X **Chef's Table**  🚾 ⮾
*49 Long St* ⊠ *GL8 8AA – ℰ (01666) 504 466 – www.thechefstable.co.uk – Closed*
*25-26 December, 1 January, Sunday, bank holidays and dinner Monday-Tuesday*
**Rest** *–* Carte £ 30/37
♦ Glass-fronted deli shop with busy, informal restaurant to the rear; mix of tables
and high stools. Daily blackboard menu displays rustic, generous dishes of local,
organic produce.

🍴 **Gumstool Inn** – at Calcot Manor Hotel  🛋 🕪 🛱 🅿 🚾 ⮾ 🖭 ⓪
😊 *West : 3.5 mi on A 4135* ⊠ *GL8 8YJ – ℰ (01666) 890 391*
*– www.calcotmanor.co.uk*
**Rest** *– (booking essential)* Carte £ 24/32
♦ Converted farm out-building on the Calcot Estate, which dates back to the 14C.
Cooking is seasonal, rustic and hearty, with a wide-ranging menu and extensive
daily specials.

🍴 **Trouble House**  🛱 🅿 🚾 ⮾
*Cirencester Rd, Northeast : 2 mi on A 433* ⊠ *GL8 8SG – ℰ (01666) 502 206*
*– www.troublehousetetbury.co.uk – Closed 2 weeks January, 25*
*December, Sunday dinner and Monday except bank holidays*
**Rest** *–* Menu £ 15 (weekday lunch) – Carte £ 23/36
♦ Unassuming roadside pub with shabby, homely style, where you'll discover a
warm welcome and tasty food. Dishes range from sardines on toast to rib of
beef for two. Daily specials usually feature fish.

---

**TEWKESBURY** – Gloucestershire – **503** N28 – pop. 9 978  **4** C1
▌ Great Britain

▶ London 108 mi – Birmingham 39 mi – Gloucester 11 mi

🄳 100 Church St ℰ (01684) 85 50 40, www.visitcotswoldsandsevernvale.gov.uk

🄵 Tewkesbury Park Hotel Lincoln Green Lane, ℰ (01684) 29 54 05

🄾 Town ★ – Abbey ★★ (Nave ★★, vault ★)

🄶 St Mary's, Deerhurst ★, SW : 4 mi by A 38 and B 4213

X **Owens**  ⟳ *VISA* ⓩ
73 Church St ⊠ GL20 5RX – *ℰ* (01684) 292 703 – www.eatatowens.co.uk
– *Closed Monday lunch*
**Rest** – Menu £ 15 (lunch and early dinner) – Carte £ 19/35
• Simple restaurant set behind the Cathedral, with characterful beamed interior
and just 10 tables. Concise, good value menu of French and British dishes. Clean,
unfussy, flavoursome cooking.

**at Corse Lawn** Southwest : 6 mi by A 38 and A 438 on B 4211 – ⊠ Gloucester

🏠 **Corse Lawn House**  🚗 📺 ⚒ 📶 ⚓ **P** *VISA* ⓩ ᴁ ①
⊠ GL19 4LZ – *ℰ* (01452) 780 771 – www.corselawn.com – *Closed 24-26*
*December*
**15 rm** 🛏 – ♦£ 100 ♦♦£ 160 – 3 suites
**Rest** *Restaurant* – see restaurant listing
**Rest** *Bistro* – Menu £ 20 **s** – Carte £ 25/34 **s**
• Elegant Grade II listed Queen Anne house, with a pond in front, just off the
village green. Traditionally appointed lounges boast open fires and antiques; spa-
cious bedrooms have a cottage style. Large pool in glass-enclosed outbuilding.
Formal restaurant and characterful bistro-cum-bar with simpler menu.

XXX **Restaurant** – at Corse Lawn House Hotel  🚗 **P** *VISA* ⓩ ᴁ ①
⊠ GL19 4LZ – *ℰ* (01452) 780 771 – www.corselawn.com – *Closed 24-26*
*December*
**Rest** – Menu £ 26/34 **s** – Carte £ 27/41 **s**🍴
• Formally laid restaurant set within an elegant Grade II listed Queen Anne
house, affording pleasant views over the rear gardens. Good-sized menus offer
classically based dishes. Helpful team.

**THIRSK** – North Yorkshire – **502** P21 – **pop. 9 099**  **22 B1**
▶ London 227 mi – Leeds 37 mi – Middlesbrough 24 mi – York 24 mi
🛈 49 Market Pl *ℰ* (01845) 52 27 55, www.visit-thirsk.com
🖥 Thirsk & Northallerton Thornton-Le-Street, *ℰ* (01845) 52 51 15

**at Felixkirk** Northeast : 3 mi by A 170

🍽 **Carpenter's Arms**  🚗 🏠 **P** *VISA* ⓩ ᴁ
⊠ YO7 2DP – *ℰ* (01845) 537 369 – www.thecarpentersarmsfelixkirk.com
**Rest** – Carte £ 21/29
• Proper village pub with one long, open-fired room and 18C origins, set in a
village mentioned in the Domesday Book. Choose from blackboard specials or a
wide-ranging menu of seasonal dishes that offers everything from gammon to
sea bass.

**at Asenby** Southwest : 5.25 mi by A 168 – ⊠ Thirsk

🏠 **Crab Manor**  🚗 🏠 ⚒ 📶 ⚓ **P** *VISA* ⓩ ᴁ
Dishforth Rd ⊠ YO7 3QL – *ℰ* (01845) 577 286 – www.crabandlobster.co.uk
**14 rm** 🛏 – ♦£ 120 ♦♦£ 240
**Rest** *Crab and Lobster* – see restaurant listing
• Split between an 18C Georgian Manor and individual Scandinavian log cabins,
the stylish bedrooms are themed around famous hotels of the world. All have
sharing or private hot tubs.

🍽 **Crab and Lobster** – at Crab Manor Hotel  🚗 🏠 **P** *VISA* ⓩ ᴁ ①
Dishforth Rd ⊠ YO7 3QL – *ℰ* (01845) 577 286 – www.crabandlobster.com
**Rest** – Seafood – Carte £ 20/42
• Charming thatched pub with characterful, quirky interior. Extensive menu fea-
tures plenty of seafood – from fish soup to whole lobster – as well as traditional
British dishes.

**THORNBURY** – South Gloucestershire – **503** M29 – **pop. 11 969**  **4 C1**
– ⊠ Bristol
▶ London 128 mi – Bristol 12 mi – Gloucester 23 mi – Swindon 43 mi

**🏠🏠🏠 Thornbury Castle** ⚓     ⚓ 🕭 🕯 ⚙ **P** VISA ⚫ AE ①

*Castle St* ⊠ *BS35 1HH – 𝒞 (01454) 281 182 – www.thornburycastle.co.uk*
**24 rm** ⊑ – **♦**£ 120/180 **♦♦**£ 175/535 – 3 suites    **Rest** – Menu £ 30/50
♦ 16C castle built by Henry VIII with gardens and vineyard. Two lounges boast
plenty of antiques. Rooms of stately comfort; several bathrooms resplendent in
marble. Restaurant exudes formal aura.

---

**THORNHAM** – Norfolk – **504** V25 – see Hunstanton

---

**THORNTON** – Lancashire – **502** K22 – see Blackpool

---

**THUNDER BRIDGE** – West Yorkshire – see Huddersfield

---

**THUNDERSLEY** – Essex – **504** V29 – see Rayleigh

---

**THURSFORD GREEN** – Norfolk        **15** C1
◗ London 120 mi – Fakenham 7 mi – Norwich 29 mi

**🏠 Holly Lodge** ⚓       ⚓ 🕏 🕯 **P** VISA ⚫

*The Street* ⊠ *NR21 0AS – 𝒞 (01328) 878 465 – www.hollylodgeguesthouse.co.uk*
**3 rm** ⊑ – **♦**£ 90 **♦♦**£ 120    **Rest** – Menu £ 20
♦ Remotely set 18C house with delightful gardens and nice pond. Individually
themed bedrooms are located in the old stable block and boast exposed beams,
feature beds and numerous extra touches. Communal breakfasts, in smart conservatory, use local and homemade produce. Home-cooked dinners from daily
changing set menu.

---

**TICKTON** – East Riding of Yorkshire – **502** S22 – see Beverley

---

**TILLINGTON** – West Sussex – **504** S31 – see Petworth

---

**TILSTON** – Cheshire West and Chester – **502** L24 – see Malpas

---

**TINTINHULL** – Somerset – **503** L31 – pop. 956      **3** B3
◗ London 131 mi – Bristol 39 mi – Cardiff 97 mi – Southampton 92 mi

**🍴 Crown and Victoria Inn** with rm     ⚓ 🕭 🕯 **P** VISA ⚫
*14 Farm St* ⊠ *BA22 8PZ – 𝒞 (01935) 823 341 – www.thecrownandvictoria.co.uk*
*– Closed Sunday dinner*
**5 rm** ⊑ – **♦**£ 75/85 **♦♦**£ 95    **Rest** – Carte £ 19/32
♦ Enthusiastically run, solid stone pub boasting mature grounds – set next to
award winning National Trust gardens. Flavoursome cooking has an honest,
homemade, classical base and produce is local, organic and ethically sourced.
Bedrooms are cosy and welcoming.

---

**TITCHWELL** – Norfolk – **504** V25 – pop. 99      **15** C1
◗ London 128 mi – King's Lynn 25 mi – Boston 56 mi – Wisbech 36 mi

**🏠🏠 Titchwell Manor**        ⚓ 🕭 ⚙ rm, **P** VISA ⚫
⊠ *PE31 8BB – 𝒞 (01485) 210 221 – www.titchwellmanor.com*
**27 rm** ⊑ – **♦**£ 65/125 **♦♦**£ 110/250    **Rest** – Carte £ 26/35 s
♦ Attractive red-brick former farmhouse. Stylish inner with bare floorboards,
leather sofas and seaside photos. Classical bedrooms in main house; stylish rooms
in grounds. Informal bar and terrace. Smart, conservatory restaurant with modern
7 course tasting menu.

---

**TITLEY** – Herefordshire – **503** L27 – see Kington

**TOLLARD ROYAL** – Wiltshire                                                                          **4** C3

▶ London 118 mi – Bristol 63 mi – Southampton 40 mi – Portsmouth 59 mi

🛏  **King John Inn** with rm                                    ⏚ 🛋 📶 🅿 VISA ⊕ AE
⊠ SP5 5PS – ℰ (01725) 516 207 – www.kingjohninn.co.uk – Closed 25 December
**8 rm** ⊡ – ✚£ 145 ✚✚£ 195  **Rest** – Carte £ 29/41
• Red-brick Victorian pub in pretty village; smart, spacious and open-plan. Daily
changing, classically based menus, with game a speciality. Comfortable, contemporary bedrooms mix modern facilities with antique furniture; some are in the
coach house opposite.

---

**TOOT BALDON** – Oxfordshire – see Oxford

---

**TOPSHAM** – Devon – **503** J31 – pop. 3 545 – ⊠ Exeter                                  **2** D2

▶ London 175 mi – Torbay 26 mi – Exeter 4 mi – Torquay 24 mi

✗  **Petite Maison**                                                                          VISA ⊕
35 Fore St ⊠ EX3 0HR – ℰ (01392) 873 660 – www.lapetitemaison.co.uk
– Closed 2 weeks autumn, 1 week April, 26-30 December, Sunday and Monday
**Rest** – (booking essential at lunch) Menu £ 37
• Cosy two-roomed restaurant in charming village by River Clyst. Flavourful, clas-
sic dishes are presented in a modern style and come in generous portions.
Friendly, welcoming owners.

---

**TORQUAY** – Torbay – **503** J32 – pop. 62 968                                            **2** C-D2

▶ London 223 mi – Exeter 23 mi – Plymouth 32 mi
🛈 5 Vaughan Parade ℰ (01803) 21 12 11, www.torquay.com
🔝 St Marychurch Petitor Rd, ℰ (01803) 32 74 71
👁 Torbay★ – Kent's Cavern★ **AC** CX **A**
🅖 Paignton Zoo★★ **AC**, SE : 3 mi by A 3022 - Cockington★, W : 1 mi AX

Plans on following pages

🏨  **Osborne**                            ≤ ⏚ 🛋 ☄ 🗦 ♨ 🛠 ✗ 🖥 ✂ 📶 🅫 🅿 VISA ⊕ AE
Hesketh Cres, Meadfoot ⊠ TQ1 2LL – ℰ (01803) 213 311
– www.osborne-torquay.co.uk                                                                  CX**n**
**32 rm** ⊡ – ✚£ 65/125 ✚✚£ 69/230
**Rest** Langtry's – (dinner only) Menu £ 19/23 **s**
**Rest** Brasserie – (closed Sunday dinner, Monday and Tuesday October-April)
Carte £ 19/30 **s**
• Smart hotel in stunning Regency crescent, with lovely gardens and Torbay
views. Modern lounge. Stylish bedrooms with light wood furniture, dark leather
chairs and good mod cons; some have balconies. Traditional Langtry's offers British classics. Informal dining in split-level Brasserie.

🏠  **Marstan** without rest                                   ⏚ ☄ ✂ 📶 🅿 VISA ⊕ AE
Meadfoot Sea Rd ⊠ TQ1 2LQ – ℰ (01803) 292 837 – www.marstanhotel.co.uk
– Closed 1 November-23 December and 4 January-28 February                          CX**a**
**9 rm** ⊡ – ✚£ 55/120 ✚✚£ 120/148
• Substantial 19C house in quiet area; given a 21C edge with hot tub, sun deck
and pool. Opulent interior with gold coloured furniture and antiques. Room décor
of high standard.

🏠  **Somerville** without rest                                  ⏚ ✂ 📶 🅿 VISA ⊕ AE
515 Babbacombe Rd. ⊠ TQ1 1HJ – ℰ (01803) 294 755
– www.somervillehotel.co.uk                                                                  CX**u**
**9 rm** ⊡ – ✚£ 70/98 ✚✚£ 105/125
• Comfortable hotel, an easy walk down the hill into town. Modern, opulently
decorated bedrooms boast all mod cons. One has a small private courtyard;
Room 4 is the largest.

ENGLAND

636

TORBAY

TORQUAY-PAIGNTON

Y

N

Church Rd

Windsor

Ellacombe

Hoxton

32

Putlands Pl.

16

St. Marychurch Rd

Rd

UNION SQUARE

Market St.

23

33

39

41

LIVING COASTS

Fleet

PRINCESS GARDENS

UPTON

Road

38

UPTON PARK

St. Luke's Rd North

34

37

Warren

Abbey

Rd

Warren

Road

Rd

BRIXHAM

Lymington

13

Belgrave

36

37

Croft

Road

26

Road

Road

C

TORRE

28

20

6

RIVIERA CENTRE

ABBEY GARDENS

A 3022 Torbay Rd

Newton

Road

Avenue

Mill

Lane

The

King's

M

A 3022

Drive

Rd

Rrathmore

Falkland

Road

TORQUAY

CENTRE

400 m

400 yards

0

TORRE

14

PIO

Mill

CHELSTON

Rd

Walnut Road

Seaway

Lane

Rd

PIO

N

Y

A 3022

B

TORQUAY

**ENGLAND**

A 3022

A 3022 BRIXHAM DARTMOUTH

A 379

Southfield

Avenue

Torquay

Road

Kelly End

Penwill

Way

STEAM RAILWAY

Dartmouth

Road

Road

Goodington Rd

A

Ash

Road

Colley

ZOO

Totnes

TWEENAWAYS CROSS

A 380

Brixham

15

Road

Long

Road

Road

A 385 PLYMOUTH

N

Y

## Colindale

🚫 P VISA ᴆ
*20 Rathmore Rd, Chelston ✉ TQ2 6NY – ℰ (01803) 293 947*
*– www.colindalehotel.co.uk*                                          BZa
**6 rm** ☕ – ♦£ 45/55 ♦♦£ 60/75   **Rest** – Menu £ 25 **s**
• 19C terraced house with pretty front garden and neatly designed bedrooms displaying colour co-ordinated furnishings. Sit in the cosy rear bar or in deep sofas in the lounge, amongst shelves crammed with books. Sunny yellow breakfast room boasts a smart Welsh dresser. Tasty, home-cooked dinners are served by arrangement.

## Kingston House without rest

🚫 🛈 P VISA ᴆ
*75 Avenue Rd ✉ TQ2 5LL – ℰ (01803) 212 760 – www.kingstonhousehotel.co.uk*
*– Closed 23 December-2 January*                                     BYn
**5 rm** ☕ – ♦£ 68 ♦♦£ 75/95
• Sunny yellow Victorian house enhanced by vivid summer floral displays; run by friendly husband and wife. Convivial sitting room; bedrooms of individual character.

## Room in the Elephant (Simon Hulstone)

≤ VISA ᴆ
*3-4 Beacon Terr, (1st Floor) ✉ TQ1 2BH – ℰ (01803) 200 044*
*– www.elephantrestaurant.co.uk – Closed October-Easter, Sunday and Monday*
**Rest** – (dinner only) Menu £ 50                                   CZe
**Spec.** Scallops with a lemon and cabbage risotto. Sea bass with clams, cod cheeks, morels and pickled shallots. Treacle tart, marmalade and clotted cream.
• First floor restaurant in elegant Georgian terrace overlooking Torbay and the marina. Modern cocktail bar and simply decorated dining room. Concise à la carte and tasting menu offer appealing, flavoursome, classical combinations with no unnecessary elaboration.

## Brasserie

VISA ᴆ
*3-4 Beacon Terr, (Ground Floor) ✉ TQ1 2BH – ℰ (01803) 200 044*
*– www.elephantrestaurant.co.uk – Closed 3 weeks January, Sunday and Monday*
**Rest** – Menu £ 20/25 – Carte £ 27/38                              CZe
• Light, airy brasserie run by pleasant team. Appealing, set price menus revolve around the seasons; cooking is fresh and simple. Good value wine selection – or visit the upstairs cocktail bar.

## Number 7

AC VISA ᴆ AE
*Beacon Terr. ✉ TQ1 2BH – ℰ (01803) 295 055 – www.no7-fish.com – Closed 2 weeks February, 1 week November, Christmas-New*
*Year, Monday November-May and Sunday June-October*                  CZe
**Rest** – Seafood – (dinner only and lunch Wednesday-Saturday) (booking advisable) Carte £ 33/41
• On harbour front in centre of town: modest, friendly, family run restaurant specialising in simply prepared fresh fish, mostly from Brixham. Fishing themes enhance ambience.

## Orange Tree

VISA ᴆ
*14-16 Parkhill Rd ✉ TQ1 2AL – ℰ (01803) 213 936*
*– www.orangetreerestaurant.co.uk – Closed 2 weeks January, 2 weeks November, Sunday and bank holiday Mondays*                                         CZu
**Rest** – (dinner only) (booking essential) Carte £ 27/41
• Intimate neighbourhood eatery hidden away from the town, with homely décor and a modern, comfortable feel. Classical cooking displays a French base and uses local, seasonal produce.

Undecided between two equivalent establishments in the same town?
Within each category, establishments are classified in our order of
preference: the best first.

ENGLAND

## at Babbacombe Northeast : 2 mi on A 379

🍴 **Cary Arms** with rm  ⇐ 🏠 🛱 ⁿ P VISA ☺☺
*Babbacombe Beach, East : 0.25 mi by Beach Rd.* ⊠ TQ1 3LX – ☎ (01803)
327 110 – www.caryarms.co.uk                                             CXi
**8 rm** 🖵 – †£ 105/210 ††£ 205/260   **Rest** – Carte £ 24/31
◆ Idyllic location built into the rocks, with terraces down to the shore. Stone/-slate-floored bar serving traditional pub dishes. Nautically styled residents lounge and modern, boutique-chic bedrooms in New England style, with roll-top baths looking out to sea.

## at Maidencombe North : 3.5 mi by A 379 - BX – ⊠ Torquay

🏠 **Orestone Manor** 🕭  ⇐ 🚗 🏠 ⌁ ⁿ 🖧 P VISA ☺☺
*Rockhouse Ln* ⊠ TQ1 4SX – ☎ (01803) 328 098 – www.orestonemanor.com
– *Closed 3-30 January*
**12 rm** 🖵 – †£ 99 ††£ 150/225   **Rest** – Menu £ 32 – Carte £ 17/32
◆ Characterful house set among thick shrubbery and mature trees. Colonial feel throughout with dark wood furniture, Oriental/African artefacts and recurring elephant motif. Individually designed bedrooms – some with feature beds; most have sea/country views. Classical menus; dine in restaurant, conservatory or on terrace.

---

## TOTFORD – Hampshire                                           6 B2
▶ London 104 mi – Birmingham 210 mi – Bristol 149 mi – Cardiff 202 mi

🍴 **Woolpack Inn** with rm  🚗 🏠 ⁿ P VISA ☺☺ AE
⊠ SO24 9TJ – ☎ (0845) 293 8066 – www.thewoolpackinn.co.uk – *Closed dinner
25 December and bank holiday Mondays*
**7 rm** 🖵 – †£ 85/100 ††£ 85/100   **Rest** – Carte £ 22/32
◆ Grade II listed pub, popular with walkers and shooters. Two menus for the rustic bar and dining room – one of pub classics, the other more ambitious – and two wine lists; one for quaffing, one for sipping. They smoke their own salmon and game is a highlight. Bedrooms are housed in the former skittle alley.

---

## TOTLEY – South Yorkshire – 502 P24 – see Sheffield

---

## TOTNES – Devon – 503 I32 – pop. 7 929                        2 C2
▶ London 224 mi – Exeter 24 mi – Plymouth 23 mi – Torquay 9 mi
🛈 Coronation Rd ☎ (01803) 86 31 68, www.totnesinformation.co.uk
🏌 Dartmouth G & C.C. Blackawton, ☎ (01803) 71 26 86
◉ Town★ – Elizabethan Museum★ - St Mary's★ – Butterwalk★ – Castle (⇐★★★)
AC
🎠 Paignton Zoo★★ AC, E : 4.5 mi by A 385 and A 3022 – British Photographic
Museum, Bowden House★ AC, S : 1 mi by A 381 – Dartington Hall (High Cross
House★), NW : 2 mi on A 385 and A 384. Dartmouth★★ (Castle ⇐★★★), SE :
12 mi by A 381 and A 3122

🏠 **Royal Seven Stars**  🏠 ⁿ 🖧 P VISA ☺☺ AE
*The Plains* ⊠ TQ9 5DD – ☎ (01803) 862 125 – www.royalsevenstars.co.uk
**21 rm** 🖵 – †£ 85/95 ††£ 149
**Rest** *TQ9* – *(dinner only and Sunday lunch and Sunday lunch)* Carte £ 20/29
◆ 17C former coaching inn in centre of town. Lounge with smart colonial edge, contemporary, light and fresh bedrooms; some have jacuzzi baths, Agatha Christie has a four poster. TQ9 a dining room in converted stables.

🍴 **Steam Packet Inn** with rm  🏠 🍽 rm, P VISA ☺☺ AE ①
*St Peter's Quay* ⊠ TQ9 5EW – ☎ (01803) 863 880 – www.steampacketinn.co.uk
**4 rm** 🖵 – †£ 60 ††£ 80   **Rest** – Carte £ 21/26
◆ Deservedly popular pub with vast terrace; set on the River Dart, in a slightly bohemian market town. Traditional bar and light, airy conservatory. Eclectic, wide-ranging menu, with fresh fish a speciality. Bedrooms are comfortable, cosy and have a modern feel.

**at Ashprington** South : 3.5mi by A 381 – ⊠ Devon

X **Vineyard Café** ⇐ 🈺 **P** 𝚅𝙸𝚂𝙰 ⓪⓪
*Sharpham Estate ⊠ TQ9 7UT – ℰ (01803) 732 178 – www.thevineyardcafe.co.uk*
*– Easter-September*
**Rest** – *(lunch only)* Carte £ 15/25
♦ Simple, teak-furnished café on an estate famed for its wines and cheeses; located in a lovely chocolate box village and offering far-reaching country views. Fresh, unfussy dishes are packed with flavour and feature local, organic produce.

**TOWCESTER** – Northamptonshire – **503** R27 – pop. 8 073          **16** B3
🛇 London 70 mi – Birmingham 50 mi – Northampton 9 mi – Oxford 36 mi
🔟 Whittelbury Park G. & C.C. Whittlebury, ℰ (01327) 85 00 00
🔟 Farthingstone Hotel Farthingstone, ℰ (01327) 36 12 91

**at Paulerspury** Southeast : 3.25 mi by A 5 – ⊠ Towcester

XX **Vine House** with rm 🈺 **P** 𝚅𝙸𝚂𝙰 ⓪⓪
*100 High St ⊠ NN12 7NA – ℰ (01327) 811 267 – www.vinehousehotel.com*
*– Closed 1 week Christmas, Monday lunch and Sunday*
**6 rm** ⊑ – †£ 69/85 ††£ 95   **Rest** – Menu £ 31
♦ Keenly run 17C stone cottage with lovely garden, traditional lounges and split-level dining room. Concise set menus feature refined, flavoursome dishes with a classical base and modern edge. Individually styled, period bedrooms are named after grape vines.

**TREBETHERICK** – Cornwall – see Rock

**TREGREHAN** – Cornwall – **503** F32 – see St Austell

**TRELOWARREN** – Cornwall – see Helston

**TRESCO** – **503** B34 – see Scilly (Isles of)

**TRISCOMBE** – Somerset – **503** K30 – see Taunton

**TROTTON** – West Sussex – see Midhurst

**TROUTBECK** – Cumbria – **502** L20 – see Windermere

**TROWBRIDGE** – Wiltshire – **503** N30 – pop. 34 401          **4** C2
🛇 London 115 mi – Bristol 27 mi – Southampton 55 mi – Swindon 32 mi
🛈 St Stephen's Pl ℰ (01225) 71 05 35, www.visitwiltshire.co.uk
🛇 Westwood Manor★, NW : 3 mi by A 363 – Farleigh Hungerford★ (St Leonard's Chapel★) **AC**, W : 4 m. Longleat House★★★ **AC**, SW : 12 mi by A 363, A 350 and A 362 - Bratton Castle (⇐★★) SE : 7.5 mi by A 363 and B 3098 – Steeple Ashton★ (The Green★) E : 6 mi – Edington (St Mary, St Katherine and All Saints★) SE : 7.5 m

🏠 **Old Manor** 🈺 & rm, ⁎ 🎙 **P** 𝚅𝙸𝚂𝙰 ⓪⓪
*Trowle, Northwest : 1 mi on A 363 ⊠ BA14 9BL – ℰ (01225) 777 393*
*– www.oldmanorhotel.com*
**21 rm** ⊑ – †£ 99/130 ††£ 99/175
**Rest** – *(dinner only)* Menu £ 26 – Carte £ 20/26
♦ Attractive Grade II listed Queen Anne house with 15C origins, French château styling and lovely gardens; run by an eccentric owner. Quirky interior filled with antiques and curios. Uniquely designed bedrooms, some with feature beds or wet rooms. Traditional menu served in the open-fired dining room.

ENGLAND

## XX Red or White 🛐 🖽 ⟷ 🅿 VISA ⚫ ⓞ
*Evolution House, 46 Castle St ⊠ BA14 8AY – ℰ (01225) 781 666*
*– www.redorwhite.biz – Closed 15 August-1 September, 25-26 December, Sunday and bank holidays*
**Rest** – Italian – Menu £ 16/23 – Carte £ 27/31
♦ Spacious restaurant whose names indicates its owners' passion for wine. Frequently changing Sicilian-based menu and regular theme nights. Impressive coloured-glass dome and small food shop.

---

**TRUMPET** – Herefordshire – see Ledbury

---

**TRURO** – Cornwall – **503** E33 – pop. 20 920                    **1** B3
🚇 London 295 mi – Exeter 87 mi – Penzance 26 mi – Plymouth 52 mi
🛈 Boscawen St ℰ (01872) 27 45 55, www.tourism.truro.gov.uk
🛅 Treliske, ℰ (01872) 27 26 40
🛅 Killiow Kea Killiow, ℰ (01872) 27 02 46
👁 Royal Cornwall Museum★★ AC
🅖 Trelissick Garden★★ (≤★★) AC, S : 4 mi by A 39 – Feock (Church★) S : 5 mi by A 39 and B 3289. Trewithen★★★, NE : 7.5 mi by A 39 and A 390 – Probus★ (tower★ - garden★) NE : 9 mi by A 39 and A 390

**ENGLAND**

## 🏨 Mannings 🕭 🕸 ⟨ℙ⟩ 🅿 VISA ⚫ 🆑 ⓞ
*Lemon St ⊠ TR1 2QB – ℰ (01872) 270 345 – www.manningshotels.co.uk*
*– Closed 1 week Christmas*
**34 rm** – ♦£ 79/99 ♦♦£ 99/129, � £ 7.50
**Rest** *Mannings* – see restaurant listing
♦ Imposing hotel located in the city centre, close to the cathedral. Boutique bedrooms are bright, modern and stylish; spacious apartment-style rooms in the neighbouring mews boast over-sized beds and galley kitchens. Chic cocktail bar.

## XX Tabb's VISA ⚫ 🆑
*85 Kenwyn St ⊠ TR1 3BZ – ℰ (01872) 262 110 – www.tabbs.co.uk – Closed 1 week January, 1 week October, Saturday lunch, Sunday and Monday*
**Rest** – Menu £ 25 (lunch) – Carte £ 29/37
♦ Series of pleasant slate-floored rooms in a small cottage conversion. Appealing menu of refined dishes, where quality produce shines through. Chef is a passionate chocolatier and duck is a speciality.

## X Saffron VISA ⚫ 🆑
*5 Quay St ⊠ TR1 2HB – ℰ (01872) 263 771 – www.saffronrestauranttruro.co.uk*
*– Closed 25-26 December, Monday dinner January-June, Sunday and bank holidays*
**Rest** – Menu £ 20 – Carte £ 26/34
♦ Keenly run restaurant in the heart of town, close to the cathedral. Simply appointed, rustic inner with hearty, flavoursome cooking to match. Extensive menus showcase seasonal Cornish produce.

## X Mannings – at Mannings Hotel 🅿 VISA ⚫ 🆑 ⓞ
*Lemon St ⊠ TR1 2QB – ℰ (01872) 247 900 – www.manningshotels.co.uk*
*– Closed 1 week Christmas*
**Rest** – *(closed Sunday lunch)* Carte £ 21/40
♦ Stylish restaurant in an imposing boutique hotel, close to the cathedral. Extensive, all-day menu follows the seasons, relying on locally sourced produce and displaying some Asian influences.

**TUDDENHAM** – Suffolk – **504** V27 – **pop. 400**　　　　　　**14** B2

▶ London 76 mi – Birmingham 120 mi – Sheffield 152 mi – Croydon 96 mi

X X　　**Tuddenham Mill** with rm　　　　　　　🖫 ⸢🏠⸣ **P** 𝗩𝗜𝗦𝗔 ⬤⬤
High St ⊠ IP28 6SQ – 𝒞 (01638) 713 552 – www.tuddenhammill.co.uk
**15 rm** � – ♦£ 275 ♦♦£ 395　**Rest** – Carte £ 31/42
◆ Delightful 18C watermill overlooking the millpond. Stylish bar with mill workings in situ; beamed restaurant with black furnishings above. Cooking uses innovative techniques and showcases quality seasonal produce in unusual combinations. Trendy bedrooms are located in attractive, timber-faced outbuildings.

---

**TURNERS HILL** – West Sussex – **504** T30 – **pop. 1 534**　　　　　**7** D2

▶ London 33 mi – Brighton 24 mi – Crawley 7 mi

🏠🏠🏠🏠　**Alexander House** ⹋　　⟨ 🖫 🐾 ⬤⬤ 🐾 🏠 🐾 ⸢🏠⸣ 🎗 **P** 𝗩𝗜𝗦𝗔 ⬤⬤ 𝗔𝗘
East St, East : 1 mi on B 2110 ⊠ RH10 4QD – 𝒞 (01342) 714 914
– www.alexanderhouse.co.uk
**36 rm** ⊏ – ♦£ 185/225 ♦♦£ 220/410 – 2 suites
**Rest** *Reflections Brasserie* – Menu £ 16 (weekday lunch) – Carte £ 42/58
**Rest** *AG's Grill Room* – (booking essential) Carte £ 32/54
◆ Stunning country house in extensive grounds; once owned by Percy Shelley's
family. Comfy guest areas; superb spa with 25 treatment rooms. Spacious, well
equipped bedrooms – some with four-posters, claw-foot baths or double
showers. Light, seasonal dishes in brasserie. Grill menu in AG's.

---

**TWO BRIDGES** – Devon – **503** I32 – ⊠ Yelverton　　　　　　**2** C2

▶ London 226 mi – Exeter 25 mi – Plymouth 17 mi
🄶 Dartmoor National Park★★

🏠🏠　**Prince Hall** ⹋　　　　　　⟨ 🖫 🐾 **P** 𝗩𝗜𝗦𝗔 ⬤⬤
East : 1 mi on B 3357 ⊠ PL20 6SA – 𝒞 (01822) 890 403 – www.princehall.co.uk
**8 rm** ⊏ – ♦£ 70/170 ♦♦£ 120/190
**Rest** – (booking essential for non-residents) Menu £ 15/40 s
◆ Remotely set hotel with welcoming interior. Cosy lounges boast real fires and
eclectic art. Comfy, homely bedrooms display subtle modern touches and smart
bathrooms; some overlook the moor. Small bar. Bright restaurant with wood
burning stove and classical menus.

---

**TYNEMOUTH** – Tyne and Wear – **501** P18 – **pop. 17 056**　　　　**24** B2

▶ London 290 mi – Newcastle upon Tyne 8 mi – Sunderland 7 mi

🏠🏠　**Grand**　　　　　　　　　　⟨ 🏠 🐾 🎗 𝗩𝗜𝗦𝗔 ⬤⬤ 𝗔𝗘
Grand Par ⊠ NE30 4ER – 𝒞 (0191) 293 66 66 – www.grandhotel-uk.com
**45 rm** ⊏ – ♦£ 85/95 ♦♦£ 119/125
**Rest** *Victoria* – (closed Sunday dinner) Menu £ 22 (dinner) – Carte lunch
£ 21/34
◆ Victorian hotel with superb sea views, once the Duchess of Northumberland's
holiday home. Impressive carved staircase and sizeable guest areas boasting ornate coving and pillars. Mix of simply furnished and more comfortable bedrooms;
222 has a four-poster and jacuzzi. Classical dining room with menu to match.

↑　**Martineau** without rest　　　　　　🖫 🐾 ⸢🏠⸣ 𝗩𝗜𝗦𝗔 ⬤⬤ ⓞ
　57 Front St ⊠ NE30 4BX – 𝒞 (0191) 257 90 38 – www.martineau-house.co.uk
**4 rm** ⊏ – ♦£ 60/80 ♦♦£ 85/95
◆ Attractive 18C stone guesthouse located down a narrow alleyway and named
after Harriet Martineau. Cosy, individually furnished bedrooms come with thoughtful extras; two boast pleasant Tyne views. Communal breakfasts feature award-
winning sausages and are also accompanied by a river and South Shields outlook.

ENGLAND

## JCKFIELD – East Sussex – 504 U31 – pop. 15 374      8 A2
▶ London 45 mi – Brighton 17 mi – Eastbourne 20 mi – Maidstone 34 mi

🏠🏠    **Horsted Place** ⅋    ≤ 🚗 🕭 🎣 ☒ 🖼 🕭 🕭 🎣 📶 🏌 **P** **VISA** ◉ **AE** ①
*Little Horsted, South : 2.5 mi by B 2102 and A 22 on A 26 ☒ TN22 5TS*
*– ℰ (01825) 750 581 – www.horstedplace.co.uk – Closed first week January*
**15 rm** ☐ – ♦£ 145/180 ♦♦£ 145/180 – 3 suites
**Rest** – *(closed Saturday lunch)* Menu £ 21 (lunch) – Carte approx. £ 38
• Imposing country house from the height of the Victorian Gothic revival; handsome Pugin-inspired drawing rooms and luxurious bedrooms overlook formal gardens and parkland. Pristine restaurant with tall 19C archways and windows.

## UFFORD – Peterborough – pop. 163      14 A2
▶ London 90 mi – Leicester 38 mi – Coventry 69 mi – Nottingham 50 mi

🍺    **White Hart** with rm    🚗 🕭 ₺ rm, 🕭 🏌 **P** **VISA** ◉ **AE**
*Main St ☒ PE9 3BH – ℰ (01780) 740 250 – www.whitehartufford.co.uk – Closed Sunday dinner*
**6 rm** ☐ – ♦£ 70/90 ♦♦£ 80/110    **Rest** – Carte £ 21/38
• Delightful 17C inn with superb sun-trap of a terrace and garden. Eat in the cosy bar, rustic restaurant or conservatory. Menus offer a broad range of dishes, with much of the meat coming from their own farm. They have a brewery on-site and the sweet, individually styled bedrooms are named after their beers.

## ULLSWATER – Cumbria – 502 L20 – pop. 1 199 – ☒ Penrith      21 B2
▶ London 296 mi – Carlisle 25 mi – Kendal 31 mi – Penrith 6 mi
🛈 Beckside Car Park, Glenridding, Penrith ℰ (017684) 8 24 14, www.ullswater.co.uk

### at Pooley Bridge on B 5320 – ☒ Penrith

🏠🏠    **Sharrow Bay Country House** ⅋    ≤ 🚗 🔧 🖾 rest, 🕭 **P**
🌸    *South : 2 mi on Howtown rd ☒ CA10 2LZ – ℰ (017684)*    **VISA** ◉ **AE**
     *86 301 – www.sharrowbay.co.uk*
     **21 rm** (dinner included) ☐ – ♦£ 160/340 ♦♦£ 280/600 – 3 suites
     **Rest** – *(booking essential)* Menu £ 25/75 ⅋
     **Spec.** Suissesse soufflé of spinach and stilton. Fillet of beef, fricassee of wild mushrooms and roasted shallots. Francis Coulson's icky sticky toffee pudding with cream.
     • Celebrated Victorian villa in mature gardens, beautifully located on the shores of Ullswater. Traditional country house style throughout, with very charming drawing rooms. Bedrooms come with a cottagey feel. Expect classical cooking in the delightful dining rooms; dinner is particularly special.

### at Watermillock on A 592 – ☒ Penrith

🏠🏠    **Rampsbeck Country House** ⅋    ≤ 🚗 🕭 🕭 **P** **VISA** ◉
     *☒ CA11 0LP – ℰ (017684) 86 442 – www.rampsbeck.co.uk*
     **18 rm** ☐ – ♦£ 98/200 ♦♦£ 145/300 – 1 suite
     **Rest** *Restaurant* – see restaurant listing
     • Immaculately whitewashed country house in mature grounds, affording lovely views over Ullswater and the fells. Spacious guest areas boast heavy fabrics and antique furniture. Contemporary country house bedrooms display up-to-date facilities and marble bathrooms.

XXX    **Restaurant** – at Rampsbeck Country House Hotel    ≤ 🚗 🕭 **P** **VISA** ◉
     *☒ CA11 0LP – ℰ (017684) 86 442 – www.rampsbeck.co.uk*
     **Rest** – *(booking essential)* Menu £ 32/50 **s**
     • Elegant restaurant with good-sized tables, high-backed chairs and beautiful lake/fell views. Oft-changing set menu of well-prepared, refined, classical dishes. Canapés and coffee in the lounge.

## ULVERSTON – Cumbria – 502 K21 – pop. 11 210      21 A3
▶ London 278 mi – Kendal 25 mi – Lancaster 36 mi
🛈 County Sq ℰ (01229) 58 71 40, www.cumbria-the-lake-district.co.uk

🏠 **Eden Lodge**      🚗 ఉ 🌿 📶 *VISA* 🅫 🅰🅴
*Coast Rd, Bardsea, South : 2 mi on A 5087* ✉ *LA12 9QZ* – ✆ *(01229) 587 067*
*– www.eden-lodge.com*
**11 rm** (dinner included) ⚏ – ♦£ 80/99 ♦♦£ 105/210
**Rest** – Menu £ 12/20 – Carte £ 28/49
• Large, bay-windowed Victorian house with pleasant gardens. Variously sized
modern bathrooms boast excellent bathrooms; superior rooms are larger, with a
view out to Morecambe Bay. Therapies and treatments available. Good value
weekend rates. Traditional menus.

---

**UPPER ODDINGTON** – Gloucestershire – **503** O28 – see Stow-on-the-Wold

---

**UPPER SLAUGHTER** – Gloucestershire – **503** O28 – see Bourton-on-the-Water

---

**UPPER WOODFORD** – Wiltshire – **503** O30 – see Salisbury

---

**UPPINGHAM** – Rutland – **504** R26 – pop. 3 947      **17** C2
▶ London 101 mi – Leicester 19 mi – Northampton 28 mi – Nottingham 35 mi

XX **Lake Isle** with rm      🅰🅲 rest, 📶 🄿 *VISA* 🅫
*16 High St East* ✉ *LE15 9PZ* – ✆ *(01572) 822 951* – *www.lakeisle.co.uk* – *Closed
26 December-2 January, Sunday dinner and Monday lunch*
**12 rm** ⚏ – ♦£ 58/80 ♦♦£ 110
**Rest** – *(light lunch)* Menu £ 19 (weekdays) – Carte £ 27/35 🕸
• Pleasant town centre property accessed via a narrow passageway, with small
characterful lounge and heavy wood furnishings. Light lunches and much more
elaborate dinners with modern influences and the odd Asian touch. Bedrooms
boast good facilities and extras: superior are the largest, with whirlpool baths.

**at Lyddington** South : 2 mi by A 6003 – ✉ Uppingham

🛏 **Marquess of Exeter** with rm      🚗 🌣 📶 🄿 *VISA* 🅫
*52 Main St* ✉ *LE15 9LT* – ✆ *(01572) 822 477* – *www.marquessexeter.co.uk*
**17 rm** ⚏ – ♦£ 70/80 ♦♦£ 90/115    **Rest** – Menu £ 15 (lunch) – Carte £ 26/31
• Attractive 16C thatched pub with cosy bar, characterful exposed beams, inglenook fireplaces and a rustic dining room. Daily menu offers tasty, classical combinations of local, home-grown and home-reared produce. Comfy bedrooms are located across the car park.

🛏 **Old White Hart** with rm      🚗 🌣 🌿 📶 🄿 *VISA* 🅫
*51 Main St* ✉ *LE15 9LR* – ✆ *(01572) 821 703* – *www.oldwhitehart.co.uk*
*– Closed 25 December*
**10 rm** ⚏ – ♦£ 60/70 ♦♦£ 85/95
**Rest** – *(closed Sunday dinner in winter)* Menu £ 14 (lunch and early dinner)
– Carte £ 20/31
• Traditional coaching inn with neat garden and canopy covered terrace.
Monthly changing menus display simple, unfussy pub classics. Regular petanque
evenings offer game play and dinner. Stylish, modern bedrooms boast smart
bathrooms.

---

**UPTON SCUDAMORE** – Wiltshire – **503** N30 – see Warminster

---

**URMSTON** – Greater Manchester – **502** M23 – pop. 40 964     **20** B2
▶ London 204 mi – Manchester 9 mi – Sale 4 mi

X **Isinglass**      *VISA* 🅫 🅰🅴 🅾
*46 Flixton Rd* ✉ *M41 5AB* – ✆ *(0161) 749 84 00* – *www.isinglassrestaurant.com*
**Rest** – English – *(dinner only and lunch Friday-Sunday)* Menu £ 20
– Carte £ 24/37
• Rustic neighbourhood eatery with simple, almost bohemian atmosphere.
Hearty, flavourful cooking features generously proportioned, homemade British
dishes. Only seasonal English produce used.

**UTTOXETER** – Staffordshire – **503** O25 – pop. 12 023          **19** C1

London 150 mi – Birmingham 41 mi – Stafford 16 mi

**at Beamhurst** Northwest : 3 mi on A 522 – ✉ Uttoxeter

XX  **Gilmore at Strine's Farm**                    🖪 **P** **VISA** **⬤**
✉ ST14 5DZ – ℰ (01889) 507 100 – www.restaurantgilmore.com – Closed 1
week January, 1 week Easter, 1 week July-August, 1 week October-November,
Monday, Tuesday, and dinner Sunday.
**Rest** – (dinner only and lunch Thursday, Friday and Sunday) (booking essential)
Menu £ 30/43
♦ Personally run converted farmhouse in classic rural setting. Three separate,
beamed, cottage style dining rooms. New approach to classic dishes: fine local in-
gredients used.

---

**VENTNOR** – Isle of Wight – **503** Q32 – see Wight (Isle of)

---

**VERYAN** – Cornwall – **503** F33 – pop. 877 – ✉ Truro          **1** B3

London 291 mi – St Austell 13 mi – Truro 13 mi

Village ★

🏨  **Nare** ॐ              ≼ 🖪 🛱 🏊 🖫 ⋔ 𝕃ᵦ ℋ 📶 🔢 rest, ⓦ **P** **VISA** **⬤** **AE**
Carne Beach, Southwest : 1.25 mi ✉ TR2 5PF – ℰ (01872) 501 111
– www.narehotel.co.uk
**30 rm** ☲ – ♦£ 136/325 ♦♦£ 396/488 – 7 suites
**Rest Quarterdeck** – see restaurant listing
**Rest The Dining Room** – (dinner only and Sunday lunch) (booking essential to
non-residents) Menu £ 50 – Carte £ 25/38
♦ Personally run country house hotel boasting a stunning bay outlook. Classical
bedrooms: some with patios/balconies; most with a view. Have afternoon tea in
the drawing room and canapés in the bar in the evening. Outdoor pool and hot
tub. Classical daily menu in dining room or lighter dishes in Quarterdeck.

X  **Quarterdeck** – at Nare Hotel              ≼ 🖪 🔢 **P** **VISA** **⬤** **AE**
Carne Beach, Southwest : 1.25 mi ✉ TR2 5PF – ℰ (01872) 500 000
– www.narehotel.co.uk
**Rest** – (booking essential to non-residents) Carte £ 25/38
♦ Informal restaurant in a personally run country house, with large black and
white prints on the walls and a nautical theme. The fish platter and roast rib of
beef to share are specialities.

---

**VIRGINSTOW** – Devon – **503** H31          **2** C2

London 227 mi – Bideford 25 mi – Exeter 41 mi – Launceston 11 mi

🏠  **Percy's**              ≼ 🖪 🕭 ⓦ ⓦ **P** **VISA** **⬤** **AE**
Coombeshead Estate, Southwest : 1.75 mi on Tower Hill rd ✉ EX21 5EA
– ℰ (01409) 211 236 – www.percys.co.uk
**7 rm** ☲ – ♦£ 110/150 ♦♦£ 150/250
**Rest** – (dinner only) (booking essential for non residents) (set menu only)
Menu £ 40
♦ Stone hotel in 130 acres of fields and woodland; where the owners grow veg,
rear pigs and sheep, breed racehorses and sell wool, skins and produce. Spacious,
comfy bedrooms in the former barn; one has a jacuzzi bath. Set menu uses ingre-
dients from the estate.

---

**WADDESDON** – Buckinghamshire – **504** R28 – pop. 1 865          **11** C2
– ✉ Aylesbury ▌ Great Britain

London 51 mi – Aylesbury 5 mi – Northampton 32 mi – Oxford 31 mi

Chiltern Hills ★

Waddesdon Manor ★★, S : 0.5 mi by a 41 and minor rd – Claydon House ★,
N : by minor rd

XX **Five Arrows** with rm          🛲 🕼 📶 P̄ VISA ⚙ AE
*High St ⊠ HP18 0JE – ℰ (01296) 651 727 – www.thefivearrows.com*
**10 rm** 🖵 – ♦£ 69/99 ♦♦£ 129 – 1 suite
**Rest** – Menu £ 18 (lunch) – Carte £ 26/39
♦ Beautiful 19C inn on the Rothschild estate, an influence apparent in the pu
crest and wine cellar. Striking architecture, stylish dining, relaxed ambience an
classical menu. Individually decorated bedrooms – some four posters – divide
between main house and courtyard; the latter being smaller but quieter.

---

**WADEBRIDGE** – Cornwall – **503** F32 – pop. 6 222          **1** B
🖪 London 245 mi – Plymouth 41 mi – Torbay 68 mi – Torquay 88 mi

**at St Kew** Northeast : 4.5 mi by A 39

🗈 **St Kew Inn**          🛲 🕼 P̄ VISA ⚙
⊠ PL30 3HB – ℰ (01208) 841 259 – www.stkewinn.co.uk
**Rest** – Carte £ 23/34
♦ Characterful country pub in quintessentially English location. Wide-rangin
menu of fresh, tasty dishes and St Austell beer in wooden casks. Attractive ga
den with picnic tables and heaters.

---

**WALBERSWICK** – Suffolk – **504** Y27 – pop. 1 648          **15** D
🖪 London 115 mi – Norwich 31 mi – Ipswich 31 mi – Lowestoft 16 mi

🗈 **Anchor** with rm          🛲 🕼 P̄ VISA ⚙ AE
*Main St ⊠ IP18 6UA – ℰ (01502) 722 112 – www.anchoratwalberswick.com*
**8 rm** 🖵 – ♦£ 95/115 ♦♦£ 110/150
**Rest** – (closed 25 December) Carte £ 23/33 ⊛
♦ An Arts and Crafts building with a sizeable garden and seaward views. Globa
flavours alongside British classics on interesting menu; careful cooking uses loca
seasonal produce. Excellent beers and wines. Simple chalet bedrooms; impressive
breakfasts.

---

**WALFORD** – Herefordshire – see Ross-on-Wye

---

**WALLINGFORD** – Oxfordshire – **503** Q29 – pop. 8 019 📗 Great Britain          **10** B3
🖪 London 54 mi – Oxford 12 mi – Reading 16 mi
🖬 Market Pl ℰ (01491) 82 69 72, www.wallingford.co.uk
ⓖ Ridgeway Path★★

⌂ **North Moreton House** without rest          🛲 ⌱ ※ 📶 P̄
🏠 *North Moreton, West : 4 mi by A 4130 ⊠ OX11 9AT – ℰ (01235) 813 283*
– www.northmoretonhouse.co.uk
**3 rm** 🖵 – ♦£ 50/60 ♦♦£ 70/80
♦ Grade II listed former rectory and 17C barn, set in a picture postcard village
Two spacious, classical drawing rooms and traditional bedrooms. Have breakfas
on a vast antique oak table beside an inglenook fireplace or in the conservatory
try the daily special.

XX **Partridge**          🕼 VISA ⚙ AE
*32 St Mary's St ⊠ OX10 0ET – ℰ (01491) 825 005 – www.partridge-inn.com*
– Closed Sunday dinner
**Rest** – Menu £ 16/20 **s** – Carte £ 24/37 **s**
♦ Former pub, now a stylish, contemporary restaurant, with separate lounge, gar
den and raised rear terrace. Well-priced market menu offered alongside interest
ing à la carte of European dishes: cooking is flavourful, confident and accom
plished. Efficient service.

---

**WANTAGE** – Oxfordshire – **504** P29 – pop. 9 452          **10** B3
🖪 London 71 mi – Oxford 16 mi – Reading 24 mi – Swindon 21 mi
🖬 19 Church St ℰ (01235) 76 01 76, www.wantage.com

**at East Hendred** West : 4.5 mi by A 417 – ⊠ Oxfordshire

🗔 **Eyston Arms**                    🏠 **P** VISA ☯ AE ①
*High St. ⊠ OX12 8JY – ℰ (01235) 833 320 – www.eystonarms.co.uk – Closed 25 December and Sunday dinner*
**Rest** – Carte £ 21/32
♦ Set in a characterful, largely estate-owned village, a modern dining pub with scrubbed tables, original tiled floors and exposed brick. Tasty, unfussy dishes include popular antipasti boards and desserts with a twist. Warm, welcoming team.

**at Letcombe Regis** South : 1.5 mi by B 4507

⛮ **Brook Barn** ☜                    🛏 🌿 ☏ **P** VISA ☯ AE
⊠ OX12 9JD – ℰ (01235) 766 502 – www.brookbarn.com
*– Closed Christmas-New Year*
**5 rm** ⌿ – ♦£ 85/225 ♦♦£ 180/225
**Rest** – Carte £ 27/39
♦ Converted barns with welcoming beamed lounge – complete with inglenook – and small library on mezzanine. Spacious, stylish bedrooms boast modern comforts; some have terraces out to the garden, croquet lawn and chalk stream. Afternoon tea and set dinners offered.

---

**WAREHAM** – Dorset – **503** N31 – pop. 2 568                    **4** C3
🔁 London 123 mi – Bournemouth 13 mi – Weymouth 19 mi
🛈 South St ℰ (01929) 55 27 40, www.visit-dorset.com
👁 Town ★ – St Martin's ★★
🏴 Blue Pool ★ **AC**, S : 3.5 mi by A 351 – Bovington Tank Museum ★ **AC**, Woolbridge Manor ★, W : 5 mi by A 352. Moreton Church ★★, W : 9.5 mi by A 352 – Corfe Castle ★ (⩽ ★★) **AC**, SE : 6 mi by A 351 – Lulworth Cove ★, SW : 10 mi by A 352 and B 3070 – Bere Regis ★ (St John the Baptist Church ★), NW : 6.5 mi by minor rd

🛗 **Priory** ☜                    ⩽ 🛏 ⟍ 🏠 🌿 ☏ **P** VISA ☯ AE ①
*Church Green ⊠ BH20 4ND – ℰ (01929) 551 666 – www.theprioryhotel.co.uk*
**16 rm** ⌿ – ♦£ 164/236 ♦♦£ 205/295 – 2 suites
**Rest** – Menu £ 43 (dinner) – Carte lunch £ 32/40
♦ Charming, privately run part 16C priory, friendly and discreetly cosy. Well-equipped rooms. Manicured four-acre gardens lead down to River Frome: luxury suites in boathouse. Charming restaurant beneath stone vaults of undercroft.

⛮ **Gold Court House** without rest                    🛏 🌿 ☏ **P**
*St John's Hill ⊠ BH20 4LZ – ℰ (01929) 553 320 – www.goldcourthouse.co.uk*
**3 rm** ⌿ – ♦£ 55 ♦♦£ 80
♦ Attractive Georgian house in small square off the high street. Built in 1762 it was once a goldsmith's and next to the mint. Antique-furnished lounge and traditionally styled bedrooms with private bathrooms. Communal breakfasts. Cellar dates from Saxon times.

---

**WAREN MILL** – Northumberland – **501** O17 – see Bamburgh

---

**WARKWORTH** – Northumberland – **502** P17                    **24** B2
🔁 London 316 mi – Alnwick 7 mi – Morpeth 24 mi

⛮ **Roxbro House** without rest                    ☏ **P** VISA ☯
*5 Castle Terr ⊠ NE65 0UP – ℰ (01665) 711 416 – www.roxbrohouse.co.uk*
*– Closed 24-28 December*
**6 rm** ⌿ – ♦£ 60 ♦♦£ 150/180
♦ A discreet style enhances this 19C stone house in the shadow of Warkworth Castle. Well-appointed lounge. Very smart boutique bedrooms with elegant wallpapers and opulent styling; two face the castle.

ENGLAND

**WARMINSTER** – Wiltshire – **503** N30 – pop. 17 486      4 C:

▶ London 111 mi – Bristol 29 mi – Exeter 74 mi – Southampton 47 mi

ℹ Central Car Park ℘ (01985) 21 85 48, www.visitwiltshire.co.uk

◉ Longleat House ★★★ **AC**, SW : 3 m. Stonehenge ★★★ **AC**, E : 18 mi by A 36 and A 303 – Bratton Castle (≤ ★★) NE : 6 mi by A 350 and B 3098

**at Upton Scudamore** North : 2.5 mi by A 350 – ✉ Warminster

🍴    **Angel Inn** with rm      🛜 ⌑ ⁽ᵗ⁾ **P** 𝐕𝐈𝐒𝐀 ⓒⓞ
     ✉ BA12 0AG – ℘ (01985) 213 225 – www.theangelinn.co.uk
     **10 rm** ⌑ – ♦£ 80 ♦♦£ 80/98    **Rest** – Carte £ 18/28
     ♦ Dependable village local with cottagey dining room and lovely terrace. Menus are fairly formal and classical, offering the likes of home-cured gravadlax, roast duck, venison steak and old-fashioned puddings. Individually themed bedrooms are cosy and well-kept.

**at Heytesbury** Southeast : 3.75 mi by B 3414 – ✉ Warminster

🏠    **Resting Post** without rest      ⌑ ⁽ᵗ⁾ 𝐕𝐈𝐒𝐀 ⓒⓞ
     67 High St ✉ BA12 OED – ℘ (01985) 840 204 – www.therestingpost.co.uk
     **3 rm** ⌑ – ♦£ 50/60 ♦♦£ 75
     ♦ Immaculately kept Grade II listed building dating back to 17C – originally a post office and general store run by the same couple. Individually styled bedrooms, one with a 6ft bed.

🍴    **Angel Inn**      🛜 **P** 𝐕𝐈𝐒𝐀 ⓒⓞ **AE**
     High St ✉ BA12 0ED – ℘ (01985) 840 330 – www.theangelheytesbury.co.uk
     **Rest** – Carte £ 20/35
     ♦ Pretty 16C pub with open fires and wooden beams; boasts a typically English feel emphasized by the locals and their dogs. Dishes make good use of fresh, local produce; steaks are a speciality.

**at Crockerton** South : 2 mi by A 350

🍴    **Bath Arms** with rm      🚗 ⌑ **P** 𝐕𝐈𝐒𝐀 ⓒⓞ
     Clay St, on Shearwater rd ✉ BA12 8AJ – ℘ (01985) 212 262
     – www.batharmscrockerton.co.uk
     **2 rm** ⌑ – ♦£ 80/110 ♦♦£ 80/110    **Rest** – Carte £ 21/31
     ♦ Down-to-earth pub with big ambitions, situated on Longleat Estate. Daily changing menu features classic pub dishes, snacks and grills alongside more modern fare. Two ultra-spacious, contemporary bedrooms.

**at Horningsham** Southwest : 5 mi by A 362 – ✉ Wiltshire

🍴    **Bath Arms** with rm      🚗 🛜 **P** 𝐕𝐈𝐒𝐀 ⓒⓞ
     Longleat ✉ BA12 7LY – ℘ (01985) 844 308 – www.batharms.co.uk
     **15 rm** ⌑ – ♦£ 95/135 ♦♦£ 155/175
     **Rest** – Menu £ 30 (dinner) – Carte £ 25/30
     ♦ Charming pub within the Longleat estate, with open fire in bar, grand dining room and delightful terrace. Appealing menus offer something for everyone; produce is locally sourced, much of it from the estate. Quirky, comfortable, individually themed bedrooms.

---

**WARTLING** – East Sussex – **504** V31 – see Herstmonceux

---

**WARWICK** – Warwickshire – **503** P27 – pop. 23 350 ▮ Great Britain      19 C3

▶ London 96 mi – Birmingham 20 mi – Coventry 11 mi – Leicester 34 mi

ℹ Jury St ℘ (01926) 49 22 12, www.visitwarwick.co.uk

🏇 Warwick Racecourse, ℘ (01926) 49 43 16

◉ Town ★ - Castle ★★ **AC** Y – Leycester Hospital ★ **AC** Y **B** – Collegiate Church of St Mary ★ (Tomb ★) Y **A**

# WARWICK-ROYAL LEAMINGTON SPA

ENGLAND

---

⌂ **Charter House** without rest    🚗 AC ✂ 📶 P VISA ☻ ⓪

87 West St ⊠ CV34 6AH – ℰ (01926) 496 965 – Closed 1 week Christmas

**3 rm** ⌷ – †£ 65/69 ††£ 85/95    **Yc**

♦ Timbered 15C house not far from the castle. Comfortable, delicately ordered rooms with a personal touch: pretty counterpanes and posies of dried flowers. Tasty breakfasts.

---

⌂ **Park Cottage** without rest    ✂ 📶 P VISA ☻ AE

113 West St ⊠ CV34 6AH – ℰ (01926) 410 319 – www.parkcottagewarwick.co.uk
– Closed 23-30 December    **Ye**

**7 rm** ⌷ – †£ 55/65 ††£ 70/85

♦ 15C cross wing house with wattle and daub walls, originally belonging to the Earl and sited within the grounds of Warwick Castle; the 300 year old yew tree behind was used to make longbows. Small lounge, cottagey breakfast room and spacious bedrooms with lots of extras.

649

ENGLAND

## ✗✗ Saffron Gold     🔠 VISA ⓸ AE ⓪

*Unit 1, Westgate House, Market St* ✉ *CV34 4DE –* ✆ *(01926) 402 061
– www.saffrongoldwarwick.co.uk*                                                    Yr
**Rest** – Indian – *(dinner only)* Carte £ 17/32

◆ Modern Indian restaurant with split-level dining room hung with contemporary
artwork. Extensive menus of interesting, authentic cooking, with Goan fish dishes
a highlight and a daily changing special chalked on the board. Friendly owner.

---

## WATERGATE BAY – Cornwall – **503** E32 – **see Newquay**

---

## WATERMILLOCK – Cumbria – **502** L20 – **see Ullswater**

---

## WATFORD – Hertfordshire – **504** S29 – pop. 120 960                12 A2

▶ London 21 mi – Aylesbury 23 mi

▣ West Herts. Cassiobury Park, ✆ (01923) 23 64 84

▣ Oxhey Park South Oxhey Prestwick Rd, ✆ (01923) 24 82 13

Plan : see Greater London (North-West) 2

## 🏨🏨 Grove     🚗 🖐 🛋 🏊 🏞 🌅 🍴 ☕ 🏋 ✗ 🖼 🛎 🚪 rm, ✦✦ 🖈 ✗ 🛜 🔒 🅿

*Chandler's Cross, Northwest : 2 mi on A 411* ✉ *WD3 4TG*          VISA ⓸ AE ⓪
*–* ✆ *(01923) 807 807 – www.thegrove.co.uk*
**215 rm** ☐ – ♦£ 285/390 ♦♦£ 310/776 – 12 suites
**Rest** *Colette's*
**Rest** *Stables* – see restaurant listing
**Rest** *Glasshouse* – *(buffet)* Menu £ 33/49

◆ Impressive Grade II listed country house in 300 acres of pretty grounds. Mix of
period and contemporary bedrooms and suites. Leisure facilities include a spa,
outdoor pool and urban beach; as well as tennis, croquet, golf and volleyball.
Fine dining in Colette's; casual meals in Stables; buffet in Glasshouse.

## ✗✗✗ Colette's – at Grove Hotel     🖈 🅿 VISA ⓸ AE

*Chandler's Cross, Northwest : 2 mi on A 411* ✉ *WD3 4TG –* ✆ *(01923) 296 010
– www.thegrove.co.uk – Closed Sunday dinner except bank holiday weekends
and Monday*
**Rest** – *(dinner only)* Menu £ 45/65

◆ Sleek, stylish, hotel restaurant with high ceilings and large windows overlooking
the grounds. Complex, modern dishes feature imaginative combinations; choose
from an extensive à la carte, 7 course tasting menu or simpler market selection.

## ✗✗ Clarendon     🍴 🖈 🅿 VISA ⓸ AE

*Redhall Ln, Chandlers Cross, West : 5 mi by A 412, Baldwins Lane and Sarratt Rd*
✉ *WD3 4LU –* ✆ *(01923) 270 009 – www.theclarendon.co.uk – Closed 25
December*
**Rest** – Menu £ 16 (lunch) – Carte £ 22/45

◆ Former pub deep in country lanes; now a vibrantly decorated, modern restaurant with bar and open kitchen. Tasty British classics and good old-fashioned
puds. Attentive service.

## ✗✗ Stables – at Grove Hotel     🚗 🖐 🖈 🅿 VISA ⓸ AE ⓪

*Chandler's Cross, Northwest : 2 mi on A 411* ✉ *WD3 4TG –* ✆ *(01923) 296 015
– www.thegrove.co.uk*
**Rest** – Carte £ 35/50

◆ Informal, New England style restaurant in the clubhouse of an impressive
Grade II listed country house. It boasts its own sports bar and pleasant views
over the course, and offers a grill menu.

## WATTON – Norfolk – 504 W26 – pop. 7 435

▶ London 95 mi – Norwich 22 mi – Swaffham 10 mi

✗✗ **Café at Brovey Lair** with rm ⌂     🚗 🏠 ☰ AC rest, ☏ P VISA ©© AE
Carbrooke Rd., Ovington, Northeast : 1.75 mi by A 1075 ⌂ IP25 6SD – 🕾 (01953) 882 706 – www.broveylair.com
**3 rm** ☲ – †£ 120 ††£ 135
**Rest** – Seafood – (booking essential 2 days in advance) (set menu only)
Menu £ 48/53
◆ Keenly run restaurant with integral kitchen. Unique dinner party style dining from single-choice seafood menu, where ambitious dishes display largely Asian and Mediterranean influences. Well-appointed bedrooms sit beside a pool and terrace in lovely gardens.

## WELLINGHAM – Norfolk – 504 W25

▶ London 120 mi – King's Lynn 29 mi – Norwich 28 mi

⌂ **Manor House Farm** without rest ⌂     🚗 🏠 ☏ P
⌂ PE32 2TH – 🕾 (01328) 838 227 – www.manor-house-farm.co.uk
**3 rm** ☲ – †£ 65/75 ††£ 90/100
◆ Attractive, wisteria-clad farmhouse with large gardens, set by a church in a beautifully peaceful spot. Spacious, airy bedrooms in former stables. Home-grown/home-reared produce at breakfast.

## WELLINGTON – Herefordshire – 503 L27

▶ London 161 mi – Gloucester 38 mi – Worcester 31 mi – Hereford 6 mi

🍺 **Wellington**     🚗 🏠 P VISA ©© AE
⌂ HR4 8AT – 🕾 (01432) 830 367 – www.wellingtonpub.co.uk – Closed 25 December, Sunday dinner and Monday
**Rest** – Carte £ 25/30
◆ Bright and airy neighbourhood pub where locals gather fireside in the spacious bar. Enjoy flavourful dishes from the daily changing menu in the more formal conservatory dining room.

## WELLS – Somerset – 503 M30 – pop. 11 148

▶ London 132 mi – Bristol 20 mi – Southampton 68 mi – Taunton 28 mi
ℹ Market Pl 🕾 (01749) 67 25 52, www.wellssomerset.com
🏌 East Horrington Rd, 🕾 (01749) 67 50 05
◎ City★★ – Cathedral★★★ – Bishop's Palace★ (≤★★) AC – St Cuthbert★
◎ Glastonbury★★ - Abbey★★ (Abbot's Kitchen★) AC, St John the Baptist★★, Somerset Rural Life Museum★ AC, Glastonbury Tor★ (≤★★★), SW : 5.5 mi by A 39 – Wookey Hole★ (Caves★ AC, Papermill★), NW : 2 m. Cheddar Gorge★★ (Gorge★★, Caves★, Jacob's Ladder ✳★) - St Andrew's Church★, NW : 7 mi by A 371 – Axbridge★★ (King John's Hunting Lodge★, St John the Baptist Church★), NW : 8.5 mi by A 371

🏨 **Swan**     🏠 & rm, ✗ ☏ ⚒ P VISA ©© AE ①
11 Sadler St ⌂ BA5 2RX – 🕾 (01749) 836 300 – www.swanhotelwells.co.uk
**48 rm** ☲ – †£ 98/118 ††£ 120/198 – 1 suite    **Rest** – Carte £ 27/40
◆ Refurbished to a very good standard, this friendly former posting inn faces the Cathedral's west front. Two firelit lounges; stylish, individually decorated rooms. Stunning Cathedral suite. Restaurant boasts framed antique clothing and oak panelling.

🏠 **Beryl** without rest ⌂     ≤ 🚗 ☏ ☰ ☏ P VISA AE
East : 1.25 mi by B 3139 off Hawkers Lane ⌂ BA5 3JP – 🕾 (01749) 678 738 – www.beryl-wells.co.uk – Closed 23-26 December
**10 rm** ☲ – †£ 75/95 ††£ 95/140
◆ Neo-gothic former hunting lodge in formal gardens run in idiosyncratic style. Impeccable antique-filled drawing room. Traditional rooms, larger on first floor. Charming hosts.

 X **Old Spot** `VISA` `OO` `AE`

*12 Sadler St ⊠ BA5 2SE – ℰ (01749) 689 099 – www.theoldspot.co.uk – Closed 1 week Christmas, Monday, Sunday dinner and Tuesday lunch*
**Rest** – Menu £ 16 (lunch) – Carte dinner £ 28/31
• Simple, understated, city centre restaurant run by a husband and wife team; its plain walls hung with framed menus and opening out to boast stunning cathedral views at the rear. Well-executed, classical dishes rely on flavoursome English produce. Preparation is kept simple.

**at Easton** Northwest : 3 mi on A 371 – ⊠ Wells

⤊ **Beaconsfield Farm** without rest `⇆` `⅘` `🛈` `P`

*on A 371 ⊠ BA5 1DU – ℰ (01749) 870 308 – www.beaconsfieldfarm.co.uk – Closed 23 December-2 January*
**3 rm** ⊆ – †£ 70/80 ††£ 70/90
• Former farmhouse hidden away in the foothills of the Mendips and run by a personable owner. Snug, homely interior with comfy lounge and pleasant breakfast room overlooking the grounds. Well-kept, cottage-style bedrooms; ask for the one with the four-poster bed.

**WELLS-NEXT-THE-SEA** – Norfolk – **504** W25 – pop. 2 451 **15** C1
🄳 London 122 mi – Cromer 22 mi – Norwich 38 mi

⌂ **Crown** `⇆` `🛈` `VISA` `OO`

*The Buttlands ⊠ NR23 1EX – ℰ (01328) 710 209 – www.flyingkiwisiinns.co.uk*
**12 rm** ⊆ – †£ 70/155 ††£ 90/175
**Rest** *Crown* – Carte £ 21/37
• Characterful 16C former coaching inn located in the centre of town, overlooking the green. Individually styled bedrooms blend classical furniture with more modern décor and facilities. Dine from an accessible menu in the charming bar, orangery or dining room.

⤊ **Machrimore** without rest `⇆` `⅘` `🛈` `P`

*Burnt St., on A 149 ⊠ NR23 1HS – ℰ (01328) 711 653 – www.machrimore.co.uk*
**4 rm** ⊆ – †£ 70 ††£ 84
• Converted farm buildings with delightful gardens and illuminated water features. Accessed via the garden, bedrooms have quality furniture, good facilities, their own patio and seating.

**at Wighton** Southeast : 2.5 mi by A 149

⤊ **Meadowview** without rest `⇆` `⅘` `🛈` `P` `VISA` `OO` `AE`

*53 High St ⊠ NR23 1PF – ℰ (01328) 821 527 – www.meadow-view.net*
**5 rm** ⊆ – †£ 65 ††£ 90/105
• Set in peaceful village, with neat garden, hot tub, comfy furniture and gazebo overlooking meadow. Smart, modern interior with comfy furnishings; good facilities. Breakfast cooked on Aga.

**WELWYN** – Hertfordshire – **504** T28 – pop. 10 512 **12** B2
🄳 London 31 mi – Bedford 31 mi – Cambridge 31 mi

🄷🄷 **Tewin Bury Farm** `⇆` `🛈` `&` `M` `⅘` `🛈` `sA` `P` `VISA` `OO` `AE`

*Southeast : 3.5 mi by A 1000 on B 1000 ⊠ AL6 0JB – ℰ (01438) 717 793 – www.tewinbury.co.uk*
**29 rm** ⊆ – †£ 123 ††£ 138
**Rest** *Tewin Bury Farm* – see restaurant listing
• Collection of converted farm buildings on a 400 acre working farm, next to a nature reserve. Rustic interior with comfortable, oak-furnished bedrooms in various wings. Function room is in an impressive tithe barn beside the old mill race.

✗ **Tewin Bury Farm** – at Tewin Bury Farm Hotel    🚗 🏷 AC P VISA ⚫⚫ AE
*Southeast : 3.5 mi by A 1000 on B 1000 ⌧ AL6 0JB –* ✆ *(01438) 717 793*
*– www.tewinbury.co.uk*
**Rest** – Carte approx. £ 25
♦ Hotel restaurant in an old timber granary, set among converted farm buildings
on a 400 acre farm. Contemporary interior with open kitchen and smart bar. Classical menu displays modern touches.

**at Ayot St Lawrence** West : 2.75 mi by B 656

🍴 **Brocket Arms** with rm    🚗 🏷 ⁙⁙ P VISA ⚫⚫
⌧ *AL6 9BT –* ✆ *(01438) 820 250 – www.brocketarms.com – Closed Sunday*
*dinner*
**6 rm** ⌷ – ✚£ 95/125 ✚✚£ 95/125    **Rest** – Menu £ 25 – Carte lunch £ 23/28
♦ Characterful 14C inn boasting leaded windows, a wood-furnished restaurant and
a cosy beamed bar with huge inglenook and monk's hole. Good value bar menu
and more ambitious 'menu du jour' offering original, flavoursome combinations;
regular BBQs in summer. Simple, comfortable bedrooms, some in the courtyard.

---

# WELWYN GARDEN CITY – Hertfordshire – 504 T28 – pop. 43 512    12 B2
▶ London 22 mi – Luton 21 mi
🏌 Panshanger Golf Complex Old Herns Lane, ✆ (01707) 33 33 12

✗✗✗ **Auberge du Lac**    🏷 🏷 AC ⇔ P VISA ⚫⚫ AE ⓞ
✿ *Brocket Hall, West : 3 mi by A 6129 on B 653 ⌧ AL8 7XG –* ✆ *(01707) 368 888*
*– www.brocket-hall.co.uk – Closed 27 December-14 January, Sunday and*
*Monday*
**Rest** – Menu £ 33/55⅜⅜
**Spec.** Sandalwood-smoked sea trout, pickled winkles, honeycomb and watercress.
Rump of lamb, salt-baked goat's cheese, pomme dauphine and rosemary. Rhu-
barb and custard soufflé, crisp gingerbread and rose petal.
♦ You get buzzed in at the gates to reach this part-18C former hunting lodge in
the grounds of Brocket Hall; a charming setting with its lakeside terrace. Cooking
is technically adept, elaborate and complicated, with ambitious flavour combina-
tions. Excellent cheeseboard.

ENGLAND

---

# WENTBRIDGE – West Yorkshire – 502 Q23 – ⌧ Pontefract    22 B3
▶ London 183 mi – Leeds 19 mi – Nottingham 55 mi – Sheffield 28 mi

🏠 **Wentbridge House**    🚗 🏷 📶 ⅙ rm, ⁙ ⁙⁙ 🛁 P VISA ⚫⚫ AE ⓞ
*Old Great North Rd. ⌧ WF8 3JJ –* ✆ *(01977) 620 444*
*– www.wentbridgehouse.co.uk*
**41 rm** ⌷ – ✚£ 110 ✚✚£ 170/220
**Rest** *Fleur de Lys* – see restaurant listing
**Rest** *Wentbridge Brasserie* – Carte £ 24/37
♦ Personally run, bay-windowed house, dating back to 18C and surrounded by
20 acres of immaculately kept gardens. Bedrooms are a mix of characterful,
wood-panelled, period styles and spacious, modern designs boasting up-to-date
facilities. Modern restaurant or smart brasserie offering classics and newer dishes.

✗✗ **Fleur de Lys** – at Wentbridge House Hotel    🚗 🏷 P VISA ⚫⚫ AE ⓞ
*Old Great North Rd. ⌧ WF8 3JJ –* ✆ *(01977) 620 444*
*– www.wentbridgehouse.co.uk – Closed Sunday dinner*
**Rest** – (dinner only and Sunday lunch) Carte £ 34/54
♦ Formal hotel dining room boasting contemporary fabrics, etched fleur mirrors
and Italian chandeliers; set in a personally run, Victorian house. Appealing menu
offers creative modern dishes.

---

# WEST BAGBOROUGH – Somerset – 503 K30 – see Taunton

---

# WEST DIDSBURY – Greater Manchester – see Manchester

**WEST END** – Surrey – **504** S29 – pop. 4 135 – ⊠ Guildford                    7 C1

▶ London 37 mi – Bracknell 7 mi – Camberley 5 mi – Guildford 8 mi

🛏️ **The Inn @ West End**                                      🖪 P. VISA ☎ AE
*42 Guildford Rd, on A 322 ⊠ GU24 9PW – ℰ (01276) 858 652*
*– www.the-inn.co.uk*
**Rest** – Carte £ 28/40
◆ A snug and friendly village pub with a roaring fire and a country feel. An array
of menus offer something for everyone. Interesting selection of wines and a
pleasant garden/terrace.

---

**WEST HOATHLY** – West Sussex – pop. 2 121                         7 D2

▶ London 36 mi

🛏️ **Cat Inn** with rm                                 ⇔ ⅍ (ϡ) P. VISA ☎
😊 *Queen's Sq ⊠ RH19 4PP – ℰ (01342) 810 369 – www.catinn.co.uk*
*– Closed Sunday dinner*
**4 rm** ☑ – ♥£ 80 ♥♥£ 100/140   **Rest** – *(closed 25 December)* Carte £ 25/32
◆ Charming 17C pub in a pleasant hamlet, run by experienced owners and a
bubbly team. A myriad of rooms range from rustic and intimate, to larger and
more formally laid. Menus feature satisfying country classics. Bedrooms are modern and extremely comfortable.

---

**WEST KIRBY** – Merseyside – **502** K23 ▐ Great Britain                  20 A3

▶ London 219 mi – Chester 19 mi – Liverpool 12 mi

◎ Liverpool★ - Cathedrals★★, The Walker★★, Merseyside Maritime Museum★ and
Albert Dock★, E : 13.5 mi by A 553

🏠 **Peel Hey** without rest                             🖨 ₺ (ϡ) P. VISA ☎
*Frankby Rd, Frankby, East : 2.25 mi by A 540 on B 5139 ⊠ CH48 1PP – ℰ (0151)*
*677 90 77 – www.peelhey.com*
**10 rm** ☑ – ♥£ 75/95 ♥♥£ 95/120
◆ Personally run, 19C house with attractive bedrooms; those to the rear are quieter, with countryside views. Comfortable conservatory and pleasant lawned garden. Pubs for dinner close by.

XX **Collingwood**                                   🖨 🖨 P. VISA ☎ AE ①
*19 Black Horse Hill, East : 0.5 mi by A 540 on B 5139 ⊠ CH48 6DS – ℰ (0151)*
*625 45 25 – www.thecollingwood.co.uk – Closed 25 December*
**Rest** – Menu £ 15/35
◆ Contemporary restaurant in an old pub, boasting a huge central bar and tables
and sofas scattered about. Tasty pub classics at lunch; accomplished, modern, restaurant-style dishes at dinner.

---

**WEST MALLING** – Kent – **504** V30 – pop. 2 144                        8 B1

▶ London 35 mi – Maidstone 7 mi – Royal Tunbridge Wells 14 mi

🏰 Addington Maidstone, ℰ (01732) 84 47 85

X **Swan**                                           🖨 ⇔ VISA ☎ AE
*35 Swan St. ⊠ ME19 6JU – ℰ (01732) 521 910 – www.theswanwestmalling.co.uk*
**Rest** – *(booking essential)* Carte £ 26/37 ⅜
◆ Informal 15C former coaching inn where original beams blend with stylish,
contemporary furnishings. Nicely appointed bar and comfy lounge are located
upstairs. Modern European menus offer cleanly presented, flavoursome combinations; side dishes are required.

ENGLAND

## WEST MEON – Hampshire – **504** Q30

**6** B2

▷ London 74 mi – Southampton 27 mi – Portsmouth 21 mi – Basingstoke 32 mi

🏠 **Thomas Lord** 　　　　　　　　　　　　🍴 🛋 **P** 🆅🅸🆂🅰 ⁑
*High St ⊠ GU32 1LN – ℰ (01730) 829 244 – www.thethomaslord.co.uk – Closed 1 January, 25 December and Monday*
**Rest** – Menu £ 20 (weekdays) – Carte £ 26/36
♦ Named after the founder of Lord's Cricket Ground; memorabilia abounds among the shabby-chic styling. Locally sourced produce informs oft-changing menu of tasty British dishes.

## WEST OVERTON – Wiltshire – **503** O29

**4** D2

▷ London 82 mi – Bristol 54 mi – Cardiff 87 mi – Southampton 62 mi

🏠 **Bell at West Overton** 　　　　　　　　　🛋 **P** 🆅🅸🆂🅰 ⁑
*Bath Rd ⊠ SN8 1QD – ℰ (01672) 861 099 – www.thebellwestoverton.co.uk*
**Rest** – *(closed dinner Sunday and Monday)* Menu £ 21 – Carte £ 23/43
♦ A simple, friendly pub, rescued from oblivion by a local couple who were sensible enough to hire an experienced pair to run it. Menu mixes pub classics with Med-influenced dishes; fish from Cornish day boats a highlight.

## WEST TANFIELD – North Yorkshire – **502** P21 – pop. 551 – ⊠ Ripon

**22** B2

▷ London 237 mi – Darlington 29 mi – Leeds 32 mi – Middlesbrough 39 mi

🏠 **Old Coach House** without rest 　　　　🍴 🛇 ⁕ **P** 🆅🅸🆂🅰 ⁑ 🅰🅴
*2 Stable Cottage, Southeast : 1 mi on A 6108 ⊠ HG4 3HT – ℰ (01765) 634 900 – www.oldcoachhouse.info*
**8 rm** 🍽 – ♦£ 55/75 ♦♦£ 99
♦ Smart 18C former coach house, nestled between the dales and moors. Bedrooms – in two main buildings – differ in size, but all have a bright, modern style and are furnished by local craftsmen. Breakfast room overlooks the pleasant courtyard garden and fountain.

## WEST WITTON – North Yorkshire – **502** O21 – ⊠ Leyburn

**22** B1

▷ London 241 mi – Kendal 39 mi – Leeds 60 mi – Newcastle upon Tyne 65 mi

🏠 **Wensleydale Heifer** 　　　　　　　　　🛋 **P** 🆅🅸🆂🅰 ⁑ 🅰🅴
*⊠ DL8 4LS – ℰ (01969) 622 322 – www.wensleydaleheifer.co.uk*
**13 rm** 🍽 – ♦£ 110/130 ♦♦£ 130/210
**Rest** – Seafood – Menu £ 18/20 – Carte £ 30/41
♦ Pretty whitewashed former pub on main street of village. Quirky, themed bedrooms boast quality linen and all mod cons. Characterful lounge with roaring fire. Dine in the fish bar or at clothed tables in the beamed restaurant; cooking has strong seafood base.

## WESTFIELD – East Sussex – **504** V31 – pop. 1 509

**8** B3

▷ London 66 mi – Brighton 38 mi – Folkestone 45 mi – Maidstone 30 mi

🍴🍴 **Wild Mushroom** 　　　　　　　　　　🍴 **P** 🆅🅸🆂🅰 ⁑ 🅰🅴
*Woodgate House, Westfield Ln., Southwest : 0.5 mi on A 28 ⊠ TN35 4SB – ℰ (01424) 751 137 – www.webbesrestaurants.co.uk – Closed Sunday dinner and Monday*
**Rest** – *(booking essential)* Menu £ 20 (weekday lunch) – Carte £ 25/34
♦ Rural roadside house with classical dining room and intimate conservatory bar. Good value French/European menus feature well-presented, tried-and-tested combinations. Tasting menu available.

## WESTLETON – Suffolk – **504** Y27 – pop. 1 317 – ⊠ Saxmundham

**15** D2

▷ London 97 mi – Cambridge 72 mi – Ipswich 28 mi – Norwich 31 mi

🏠 **Westleton Crown** with rm 　　　　　🍴 🛋 � rm, ⁕ **P** 🆅🅸🆂🅰 ⁑ 🅰🅴
*The Street ⊠ IP17 3AD – ℰ (01728) 648 777 – www.westletoncrown.co.uk*
**34 rm** 🍽 – ♦£ 80/110 ♦♦£ 105/120 　**Rest** – Carte £ 28/38
♦ Good-looking, red-brick 17C former coaching inn, set in a pretty little village. Welcoming beamed bar with open fires – venture further in for the more modern conservatory. The same appealing menu is served throughout. Uncluttered bedrooms boast smart bathrooms.

ENGLAND

655

**WESTON-SUPER-MARE** – North Somerset – **503** K29 – pop. 78 044     3 B2

▶ London 147 mi – Bristol 24 mi – Taunton 32 mi

ℹ️ Beach Lawns ℰ (01934) 88 88 00, www.visitsomerset.co.uk

🏌 Worlebury Monks Hill, ℰ (01934) 62 57 89

◉ Seafront (≤ ★★) BZ

◎ Axbridge ★★ (King John's Hunting Lodge ★, St John the Baptist Church ★) SE : 9 m
by A 371 - BY - and A 38 – Cheddar Gorge ★★ (Gorge ★★, Caves ★, Jacob's Ladde
❋★) – Clevedon ★ (≤ ★★, Clevedon Court ★), NE : 10 mi by A 370 and M 5 –
St Andrew's Church ★, SE : 10.5 mi by A 371

| | | | |
|---|---|---|---|
| Albert Quadrant .... **BZ** 2 | | Royal Parade ....... **BZ** 11 | |
| Flowerdown | | Sovereign Centre ... **BZ** | |
| Bridge .......... **BY** 4 | | Upper Bristol Rd .... **BY** 12 | |
| High St. ........... **BZ** 7 | | Upper Church Rd ... **AY** 13 | |
| Meadow St. ........ **BZ** 8 | | Walliscote Rd ...... **BZ** 14 | |
| Oxford St. ......... **BZ** 9 | | Waterloo St. ....... **BZ** 15 | |
| Regent St. ......... **BZ** 10 | | Windwhistle Rd .... **AZ** 16 | |

## ✗✗ Duets                                                                    VISA ◉◉

*103 Upper Bristol Rd.* ⊠ *BS22 8ND –* ℰ *(01934) 413 428 – www.duets.co.uk*
*– Closed 1 week spring, 1 week summer, 1 week winter, Sunday dinner, Monday*
*and Tuesday*                                                                  BY**a**
**Rest** – Menu £ 17/30 – Carte £ 32/36
♦ Diligent and unfussy service sets the tone in this traditionally styled restaurant, deservedly a neighbourhood favourite. Ably judged cooking on a tasty classical base.

## ✗ Cove                                                          ⇐ 🐚 VISA ◉◉ AE

*Birnbeck Rd* ⊠ *BS23 2BX –* ℰ *(01934) 418 217 – www.the-cove.co.uk – Closed 25*
*December, Sunday dinner and Monday except bank holidays*                      AY**e**
**Rest** – Menu £ 17 (lunch) – Carte £ 22/32
♦ Seafront eatery with striking lines, contemporary styling and bay views. Modern, seasonal menu displays European flair and seafood slant; most produce from within 20 miles. Tapas 3-9pm.

---

# WESTON UNDER WETHERLEY – Warwickshire – 503 P27 – see Royal
Leamington Spa

---

# WEYBRIDGE – Surrey – 504 S29 – pop. 19 463                          7 C1

▶ London 23 mi – Crawley 27 mi – Guildford 17 mi – Reading 33 mi

## 🏨 Brooklands                    ◉◉ 🎾 🖫 🕭 🐍 AC 🎾 ♤ 🛆 ℙ VISA ◉◉ AE

*Brooklands Dr, Southwest : 1.5 mi by B 374 and A 318* ⊠ *KT13 0SL –* ℰ *(01937)*
*355 700 – www.brooklandshotelsurrey.com*
**105 rm** – ♦£ 120/240 ♦♦£ 120/240, ⊡ £ 15.95 – 15 suites
**Rest** *Brasserie* – see restaurant listing
♦ Contemporary hotel with art deco feel, situated next to Mercedes Benz World on what was Brooklands racetrack. Buzzy bar; great spa. Stylish, comfortable, good-sized bedrooms.

## ✗✗ Brasserie – at Brooklands Hotel                          AC ℙ VISA ◉◉ AE

*Brooklands Dr, Southwest : 1.5 mi by B 374 and A 318* ⊠ *KT13 0SL –* ℰ *(01932)*
*355 700 – www.brooklandshotelsurrey.com*
**Rest** – Italian influences – Carte £ 23/48
♦ Bright, modern dining room, with black décor and a funky feel. Choose a traditional 3 course meal or a number of tasting plates. Tasty, authentic Italian cooking; effective service.

## 🍴 Queen's Head                                              🐚 ℙ VISA ◉◉

*1 Bridge Rd* ⊠ *KT13 8XS –* ℰ *(01932) 839 820 – www.whitebrasserie.com*
*– Closed 25 December*
**Rest** – Menu £ 14/16 – Carte £ 22/30
♦ Lovingly restored 18C coach house with a series of snug little rooms, warming open fires and a pewter bar, that can't fail to impress. Menus mix British pub dishes with French brasserie classics. Spacious restaurant boasts an open-kitchen.

---

# WEYMOUTH – Dorset – 503 M32 – pop. 48 279                          4 C3

▶ London 142 mi – Bournemouth 35 mi – Bristol 68 mi – Exeter 59 mi
⛴ to Guernsey (St Peter Port) and Jersey (St Helier) (Condor Ferries Ltd)
🛈 The Esplanade ℰ (01305) 78 57 47, www.visitweymouth.co.uk
🏌 Links Rd, ℰ (0844) 980 99 09
◉ Town★ – Timewalk★ **AC** – Nothe Fort (⇐★) **AC** – Boat Trip★ (Weymouth Bay and Portland Harbour) **AC**
◻ Chesil Beach★★ – Portland★ – Portland Bill (❅★★) S : 2.5 mi by A 354. Maiden Castle★★ (⇐★) N : 6.5 mi by A 354 – Sub-Tropical Gardens★ **AC**, St Catherine's Chapel★) NW : 9 mi by B 3157

ENGLAND

### 🏠 Chandlers without rest     🛜 🐾 P VISA ⬤⬤
*4 Westerhall Rd ⊠ DT4 7SZ – ℰ (01305) 771 341 – www.chandlershotel.com*
*– Closed Christmas and New Year*
**10 rm** 🛏 – ♦£ 62/125 ♦♦£ 155
♦ Substantial Victorian house near the promenade, run by friendly owners. Stylish, modern interior with comfy lounge and airy breakfast room. Bedrooms have plain walls and colour-themed fabrics.

---

## WHALLEY – Lancashire – 502 M22 – pop. 3 230 – ⊠ Blackburn    20 B2
▶ London 233 mi – Blackpool 32 mi – Burnley 12 mi – Manchester 28 mi
🏌 Long Leese Barn Clerkhill, ℰ (01254) 82 22 36

### ✗ Food by Breda Murphy     🛜 P VISA ⬤⬤
*Abbots Ct, 41 Station Rd ⊠ BB7 9RH – ℰ (01254) 823 446*
*– www.foodbybredamurphy.com – Closed 24 December-4 January, Sunday and Monday*
**Rest** – *(lunch only)* Carte £ 22/29
♦ Bright, modern restaurant with popular deli. Extensive menu of tasty, traditional, home-cooked dishes – from salads and sandwiches to the full three courses. Charming service.

**at Mitton** Northwest : 2.5 mi on B 6246 – ⊠ Whalley

### 🍴 Three Fishes     🛜 P VISA ⬤⬤ AE
*Mitton Rd ⊠ BB7 9PQ – ℰ (01254) 826 888 – www.thethreefishes.com – Closed 25 December*
**Rest** – *(bookings not accepted)* Carte £ 21/33
♦ Spacious, modern country inn offering extensive, seasonally changing menu which celebrates Lancastrian produce. Family-friendly, with a children's menu and popular Sunday roast.

---

## WHEPSTEAD – Suffolk – 504 W27 – see Bury St Edmunds

---

## WHITBY – North Yorkshire – 502 S20 – pop. 13 594 ▯ Great Britain    23 C1
▶ London 257 mi – Middlesbrough 31 mi – Scarborough 21 mi – York 45 mi
ℹ Langborne Rd ℰ (01723) 38 36 37, www.visitwhitby.com
🏌 Low Straggleton Sandsend Rd, ℰ (01947) 60 06 60
👁 Abbey ★

### 🏨 Bagdale Hall     🛜 🐾 P VISA ⬤⬤ AE ⓞ
*1 Bagdale ⊠ YO21 1QL – ℰ (01947) 602 958 – www.bagdale.co.uk*
**14 rm** 🛏 – ♦£ 60/130 ♦♦£ 80/220
**Rest** – *(dinner only)* Menu £ 15 – Carte £ 20/29
♦ Tudor manor with fine fireplaces in carved wood and 19C Delft tiles; panelled rooms with mullioned windows; four-posters in period style bedrooms. Annexe for more modern rooms. Dining room boasts timbered ceiling and massive wooden fireplace.

### ✗✗ Green's     AC VISA ⬤⬤
*13 Bridge St ⊠ YO22 4BG – ℰ (01947) 600 284 – www.greensofwhitby.com*
*– Closed 25-26 December and 1 January*
**Rest** – Seafood – *(booking essential)* Menu £ 43 (dinner) – Carte £ 27/43
♦ Established eatery near the quay. Formal dining room offers 3 course menu. Lively bistro serves concise à la carte and daily specials – mainly market fish. Influences range from Italian to Thai.

### ✗ Red Chard Lounge and Grill     🗩 VISA ⬤⬤
*22-23 Flowergate ⊠ YO21 3BA – ℰ (01947) 606 660 – www.redchard.com*
*– Closed first week January, Sunday lunch and dinner Monday-Tuesday*
**Rest** – Beef specialities – Carte £ 28/35
♦ Modern town centre bar/lounge/dining room in one; funky and relaxing, with art-covered walls. Wide ranging menu with local produce to the fore; quality 21 day hung beef.

ENGLAND

**at Briggswath** Southwest : 3.5 mi by A 171 (Teesdale Rd), A 169 on B 1410
– ✉ Whitby

⌂ **Lawns** without rest ⇐ ⇌ 🖏 📶 **P**
73 Carr Hill Ln. ✉ YO21 1RS – 𝒞 (01947) 810 310
– www.thelawnsbedandbreakfastwhitby.co.uk – Closed 22 December-1 January
**3 rm** ⌑ – 🛉£ 38 🛉🛉£ 76
♦ Large converted house with south-facing garden, set in an elevated position
3 miles from the coast. Comfortable lounge and well-kept bedrooms with understated décor. Delightful views over the Esk Valley to the North York Moors. Tea
and cake served on arrival.

**at Sandsend** Northwest : 3 mi on A 174 – ✉ Whitby

⌂ **Woodlands** 🌿 ⇐ ⇌ 🖏 📶 **P** 𝓥𝓘𝓢𝓐 ⊛
The Valley ✉ YO21 3TE – 𝒞 (01947) 893 438
– www.thewoodlands-sandsend.com – Closed January and restricted opening in
winter
**5 rm** ⌑ – 🛉£ 125 🛉🛉£ 135
**Rest** – (booking essential) Carte approx. £ 22 **s**
♦ Laid-back country house in a peaceful valley, set back from the sea. Small
lounge with honesty bar; individually designed bedrooms in colourful, contemporary style. Breakfast on the terrace in summer or in your room from a
hamper in winter. All-day café offers cakes and home-cooked local produce
at dinner.

✕✕ **Estbek House** with rm 📶 𝓥𝓘𝓢𝓐 ⊛
East Row ✉ YO21 3SU – 𝒞 (01947) 893 424 – www.estbekhouse.co.uk – Closed
January-10 February
**4 rm** ⌑ – 🛉£ 80/125 🛉🛉£ 100/190
**Rest** – Seafood – (dinner only) Carte £ 36/50
♦ This personally run Regency house, adjacent to beach, boasts delightful ter-
race, basement bar, smart restaurant serving local, wild seafood, and utterly
charming rooms.

**at Goldsborough** Northwest : 6 mi by A 174

✕ **Fox & Hounds** ⇔ **P** 𝓥𝓘𝓢𝓐 ⊛ ⓪
✉ YO21 3RX – 𝒞 (01947) 893 372 – www.foxandhoundsgoldsborough.co.uk
– Closed Christmas and Sunday-Tuesday
**Rest** – (dinner only) Carte £ 29/40
♦ Former village pub with homely, cottagey style, set in tiny coastal hamlet. Con-
stantly evolving menu features local produce and unfussy cooking, with emphasis
on fresh fish and seafood.

**WHITEHAVEN** – Cumbria – **502** J20 – pop. 24 978 **21** A2
◧ London 332 mi – Carlisle 39 mi – Keswick 28 mi – Penrith 47 mi

✕✕ **Zest** **P** 𝓥𝓘𝓢𝓐 ⊛ ⓪
Low Rd, South : 0.5 mi on B 5345 (St Bees) ✉ CA28 9HS – 𝒞 (01946) 692 848
– www.zestwhitehaven.com – Closed 25 December, 1 January and
Sunday-Tuesday
**Rest** – (dinner only) Carte £ 21/41
♦ Unassuming exterior conceals stylish, red-hued room with brushed velvet
chairs and leather banquettes. Large, modern menu with Asian edge and black-
board specials. Unfussy, flavoursome cooking.

ENGLAND

**WHITEWELL** – Lancashire – **502** M22 – pop. 5 617 – ⊠ Clitheroe          **20** B2
▶ London 281 mi – Lancaster 31 mi – Leeds 55 mi – Manchester 41 mi

🛏 **Inn at Whitewell** with rm          ⟨ 🚗 🔗 📶 🛜 **P** 𝖵𝖨𝖲𝖠 ⏻⏻
Forest of Bowland ⊠ BB7 3AT – ℰ (01200) 448 222 – www.innatwhitewell.com
**23 rm** ⬚ – ♦£ 88/158 ♦♦£ 120/200 – 1 suite    **Rest** – Carte £ 16/43
♦ 14C creeper-clad inn, high on the banks of the River Hodder, with panoramic
valley views. Atmospheric bar and more formal restaurant. Classic menus of regionally inspired dishes. Spacious bedrooms; some traditional in style, with four-
posters and antique baths.

---

**WHITSTABLE** – Kent – **504** X29 – pop. 30 195          **9** C1
▶ London 68 mi – Dover 24 mi – Maidstone 37 mi – Margate 12 mi
🛈 7 Oxford St ℰ (0871) 7 16 24 49, www.canterbury.co.uk

✕ **Whitstable Oyster Fishery Co.**          ⟨ 𝖵𝖨𝖲𝖠 ⏻⏻ 𝖠𝖤 ⏻
Royal Native Oyster Stores, The Horsebridge ⊠ CT5 1BU – ℰ (01227) 276 856
– www.whitstableoystercompany.com – Closed 25-26 December and Monday
dinner
**Rest** – Seafood – (booking essential) Carte £ 35/50
♦ Former oyster warehouse right by the sea. Large, rough, wood-furnished interior with great informal atmosphere. Blackboard displays simply prepared seafood
dishes. Fresh oysters at the counter.

🛏 **Pearson's Arms**          ⟨ 𝖠𝖢 ✂ 𝖵𝖨𝖲𝖠 ⏻⏻
The Horsebridge, Sea Wall ⊠ CT5 1BT – ℰ (01227) 773 133
– www.pearsonsarmsbyrichardphillips.co.uk – Closed Sunday-Tuesday dinner
**Rest** – Menu £ 13 (lunch) – Carte £ 23/37
♦ Characterful refurbished pub in a great spot, with the Thames Estuary
stretched out in front. Busy ground floor bar for nibbles like jellied eels; top floor
dining room serves reassuringly familiar dishes, with Kentish produce to the fore.

**at Seasalter** Southwest : 2 mi by B 2205 – ⊠ Whitstable

🛏 **The Sportsman** (Steve Harris)          🚗 **P** 𝖵𝖨𝖲𝖠 ⏻⏻
✿ Faversham Rd, Southwest : 2 mi following coast rd ⊠ CT5 4BP – ℰ (01227)
273 370 – www.thesportsmanseasalter.co.uk – Closed 25-26 December, Sunday
dinner and Monday
**Rest** – (booking advisable) Carte £ 32/41
**Spec.** Slip sole grilled in seaweed butter. Roast pork belly, crackling and apple
sauce. Warm chocolate mousse, salted caramel and milk sorbet.
♦ Unassuming pub set by the sea wall, with a modest, open-plan interior. Concise daily blackboard menu offers simple-sounding dishes, which are rarely as
straightforward as they seem. Preparation is precise; flavours, well-judged; and
presentation, original.

---

**WICKHAM** – Hampshire – **503** – pop. 1 915          **6** B2
▶ London 74 mi – Portsmouth 12 mi – Southampton 11 mi – Winchester 16 mi

🏨 **Old House**          🚗 🛜 ✂ 📶 **P** 𝖵𝖨𝖲𝖠 ⏻⏻ 𝖠𝖤
The Square ⊠ PO17 5JG – ℰ (01329) 833 049 – www.oldhousehotel.co.uk
– Closed 19-20 May
**12 rm** ⬚ – ♦£ 110 ♦♦£ 110/150
**Rest** – (closed Sunday dinner) Menu £ 18/25 – Carte £ 35/46
♦ Lovely, creeper-clad, Queen Anne townhouse built in 1707. Characterful bedrooms; some with original fireplaces, all with modern furnishings. Those in the
garden have a slightly Mediterranean feel, boasting tiled floors and large bathrooms. Small restaurant and airy conservatory offer modern takes on classics.

---

**WIGHILL** – North Yorkshire – **502** Q22 – **see Tadcaster**

## WIGHT (Isle of) – Isle of Wight – 503 P/Q31 – pop. 138 500     6 A/B 3

📗 Great Britain

🚤 from Ryde to Portsmouth (Hovertravel Ltd) frequent services daily (10 mn) – from Ryde to Portsmouth (Wightlink Ltd) frequent services daily (15 mn) – from East Cowes to Southampton (Red Funnel Ferries) frequent services daily (22 mn)

🚢 from East Cowes to Southampton (Red Funnel Ferries) frequent services daily (1 h) – from Yarmouth to Lymington (Wightlink Ltd) frequent services daily (30 mn) – from Fishbourne to Portsmouth (Wightlink Ltd) frequent services daily (35 mn)

👁 Island★★

📷 Osborne House, East Cowes★★ **AC** – Carisbrooke Castle, Newport★★ **AC** (Keep ≤★) – Brading★ (Roman Villa★ **AC**, St Mary's Church★, Nunwell House★ **AC**) – Shorwell : St Peter's Church★ (wall paintings★)

---

### BONCHURCH – Isle of Wight     6 B3

🍴 **Pond Café**     🕌 VISA ⬤⬤
✉ PO38 1RG – 𝒞 (01983) 855 666 – www.robert-thompson.com – Closed 1-26 January
**Rest** – Menu £ 18 (lunch) – Carte £ 23/36
♦ Intimate neighbourhood restaurant with candlelit, bistro-style interior. Attractive terrace with fairy lights overlooks duck pond. Generously proportioned, flavoursome dishes use island produce.

---

### GODSHILL – Isle of Wight     6 B3

🏠 **Taverners**     🚗 **P** VISA ⬤⬤
High St ✉ PO38 3HZ – 𝒞 (01983) 840 707 – www.thetavernersgodshill.co.uk – Closed first 3 weeks January
**Rest** – Carte £ 21/24
♦ Whitewashed pub with cosy bar and two large dining rooms. Cooking is fresh and tasty, mixing traditional pub classics with more ambitious daily specials. Local island produce is a feature.

---

### NITON – Isle of Wight     6 B3

🏠 **Hermitage** ⬥     🚗 🐾 🖧 🐕 **P** VISA ⬤⬤ AE
North : 3 mi by Newport rd (A 3020) ✉ PO38 2PD – 𝒞 (01983) 730 010 – www.hermitage-iow.co.uk – Closed 22 December-9 January
**10 rm** ⌓ – †£ 100/120 ††£ 125/145    **Rest** – (dinner only) Carte £ 19/31
♦ Large 19C country house with 12 acres of gardens/woodland; set in pleasant rural location. Traditionally styled drawing room and peaceful lounge. Individually designed, well-equipped bedrooms. Elegant dining room displays a contemporary edge; classical menus.

---

### SEAVIEW – Isle of Wight – pop. 2 286     6 B3

🏨 **Priory Bay** ⬥     🚗 🐾 🏊 🍽 🐕 **P** VISA ⬤⬤ AE
Priory Dr., Southeast : 1.5 mi by B 3330 ✉ PO34 5BU – 𝒞 (01983) 613 146 – www.priorybay.co.uk
**18 rm** ⌓ – †£ 105/225 ††£ 200/300 – 2 suites
**Rest** *The Restaurant* – Menu £ 20/35 – Carte £ 25/49
♦ Peacefully located medieval priory overlooking the water. Romantic shabby-chic interior, spacious guest areas and relaxed vibe. Bedrooms range in style from classical country house to nautical, boasting good facilities and modern bathrooms.

🏨 **Seaview**     🕌 📶 ⅗ VISA ⬤⬤ AE ①
High St ✉ PO34 5EX – 𝒞 (01983) 612 711 – www.seaviewhotel.co.uk – Closed 1 week Christmas
**25 rm** ⌓ – †£ 115/210 ††£ 170/210 – 3 suites
**Rest** *The Restaurant and Sunshine Room* – (dinner only and lunch during summer) (booking essential) Carte £ 27/31
♦ Long-standing, bay-windowed hotel covered in foliage. Interesting nautical-themed décor with paintings/model ships throughout. Smart, modern bedrooms in various styles; some in outbuildings. One bright and one more intimate room in restaurant; classical cooking.

661

ENGLAND

## SHANKLIN – Isle of Wight – pop. 8 055      6 B3

▶ Newport 9 mi

🛈 67 High St ℰ (01983) 81 38 13, www.visitshanklin.co.uk

🏌 The Fairway Lake Sandown, ℰ (01983) 40 32 17

---

🏠 **Rylstone Manor** ⏎      🚗 ⁑ ⁙ **P** 𝗩𝗜𝗦𝗔 ⊙ ⓪

Rylstone Gdns ✉ PO37 6RG – ℰ (01983) 862 806 – www.rylstone-manor.co.uk
– Closed 28 November-10 February

**9 rm** ⌷ – ♦£ 70/75 ♦♦£ 170/180   **Rest** – (dinner only) Menu £ 32

• Originally a gift from the Queen to one of her physicians: an attractive part-Victorian house close to the historic gardens. Classical interior boasts heavy fabrics and warm, cosy feel. Bedrooms combine antique furniture and modern facilities. Formal dining room.

---

🏠 **Foxhills** without rest      🚗 ⁑ ⁙ **P** 𝗩𝗜𝗦𝗔 ⊙

30 Victoria Ave ✉ PO37 6LS – ℰ (01983) 862 329 – www.foxhillsofshanklin.co.uk
**8 rm** ⌷ – ♦£ 59/96 ♦♦£ 96/106

• Large, stone-built house in leafy residential avenue. Spacious, Victorian-styled lounge and modern breakfast room; comfy bedrooms in pastel hues. Jacuzzi, spa and beauty treatments available.

---

## VENTNOR – Isle of Wight – pop. 6 257      6 B3

▶ Newport 10 mi

🛈 Steephill Down Rd, ℰ (01983) 85 33 26

---

🏨 **Royal**      🚗 ⟏ 🛗 ♿ ⚹ **P** 𝗩𝗜𝗦𝗔 ⊙ 𝖠𝖤 ⓪

Belgrave Rd ✉ PO38 1JJ – ℰ (01983) 852 186 – www.royalhoteliow.co.uk
– Closed 2 weeks January

**53 rm** ⌷ – ♦£ 125/190 ♦♦£ 235/275

**Rest** – (closed Sunday lunch July and August) (dinner only and Sunday lunch) Menu £ 20/40

• Large Victorian building with mature lawned gardens and heated outdoor pool. Modern touches in lounge and bar. Traditionally styled bedrooms with good facilities: premier rooms are larger; some have lovely sea views. Classical menu served in formal dining room.

---

🍴🍴 **Hambrough** with rm      ⟨ 🚗 𝖠𝖢 rest, ⁙ 𝗩𝗜𝗦𝗔 ⊙
🕸

Hambrough Rd ✉ PO38 1SQ – ℰ (01983) 856 333 – www.robert-thompson.com
– Closed January, November, 10 days April, Sunday and Monday

**7 rm** ⌷ – ♦£ 210 ♦♦£ 300

**Rest** – (booking essential) Menu £ 28/55

Spec. Lemon sole with clam and cockle risotto. Rose veal with bone marrow sauce and white asparagus. Chocolate delice with Earl Grey tea and walnut.

• Eye-catching clifftop villa with leather-furnished lounge and two warm, stylish dining rooms boasting excellent sea views. Skilful, confident chef uses top quality ingredients to create refined, modern dishes. Service is polite and knowledgeable. Smart, comfortable bedrooms feature quality linens and espresso machines.

---

## WOOTTON BRIDGE – IOW – pop. 3 618      6 B3

🏨 **Lakeside Park**      ⟨ 🚗 🐾 🍽 🔲 🛁 🌀 🛗 ♿ 𝖠𝖢 ⁑ ⁙ ♨ **P** 𝗩𝗜𝗦𝗔 ⊙ 𝖠𝖤

High St. ✉ PO33 4LJ – ℰ (01983) 882 266 – www.lakesideparkhotel.com
**44 rm** ⌷ – ♦£ 120/175 ♦♦£ 120/175

**Rest** *Oyster Room* – (closed Sunday, Monday and Tuesday) (booking essential) Menu £ 25/59

**Rest** *Brasserie* – Menu £ 15 (lunch) – Carte £ 21/30

• Purpose-built hotel with lawned gardens. Stylish, comfortable, modern bedrooms offer a high level of facilities. Smart, fine dining restaurant with lounge and private terrace. Open-plan split-level bar, lounge and brassiere with large decked terrace and view over lake.

**YARMOUTH** – Isle of Wight – pop. 855                     **6** A3

▶ Newport 10 mi

🏨 **George**                                   ⟨ 🚗 ⚓ 🍽 VISA ⓪ AE
   *Quay St* ✉ *PO41 0PE* – ℰ *(01983) 760 331* – *www.thegeorge.co.uk*
   **19 rm** ⬜ – †£ 99/140 ††£ 290
   **Rest** *Brasserie* – see restaurant listing
   ♦ Smart 17C townhouse that blends subtle modern touches with characterful
   period features. Bedrooms boast up-to-date facilities: one has a large wet room
   and opens onto the garden; another boasts a sizeable balcony and excellent Solent views.

🍴🍴 **Brasserie** – at George Hotel              ⟨ 🚗 🛖 ⚓ AC ⇔ VISA ⓪ AE
   *Quay St* ✉ *PO41 0PE* – ℰ *(01983) 760 331* – *www.thegeorge.co.uk*
   **Rest** – Carte £ 35/48
   ♦ Contemporary hotel restaurant with pewter bar and small heated terrace. Modern menu offers some interesting combinations, with a tasting option in the
   evening. Tasty homemade bread and daily fish specials, with local game dishes
   in season.

---

**WIGHTON** – Norfolk – **504** W25 – see Wells-Next-The-Sea

---

**WILLIAN** – Hertfordshire – **504** T28 – pop. 326                     **12** B2

▶ London 39 mi – Birmingham 107 mi

🍴 **Fox**                                      🚗 🛖 P VISA ⓪
   ✉ *SG6 2AE* – ℰ *(01462) 480 233* – *www.foxatwillian.co.uk* – *Closed Sunday dinner*
   **Rest** – Carte £ 21/33
   ♦ Bright, airy pub that's always bustling. Lunch served throughout; dinner in the
   dining room only. Menu offers modern dishes with game in season and plenty of
   seafood; some Asian influences.

---

**WIMBORNE MINSTER** – Dorset – **503** O31 – pop. 14 844                     **4** C3

▶ London 112 mi – Bournemouth 10 mi – Dorchester 23 mi – Salisbury 27 mi

🛈 29 High St ℰ (01202) 88 61 16, www.visit-dorset.org.uk

◉ Town ★ - Minster ★ – Priest's House Museum ★ AC

◉ Kingston Lacy ★★ AC, NW : 3 mi by B 3082

🍴🍴🍴 **Les Bouviers** with rm             🚗 🛖 🎵 🔊 P VISA ⓪ AE ⓪
   *Arrowsmith Rd, Canford Magna, Southeast : 2.25 mi by A 349 on A 341*
   ✉ *BH21 3BD* – ℰ *(01202) 889 555* – *www.lesbouviers.co.uk*
   **6 rm** – ††£ 175/225, ⬜ £ 5   **Rest** – (closed Sunday dinner) Menu £ 20/34
   ♦ Formerly a private residence, now a two-roomed restaurant overlooking a terrace and large lawned grounds. Small leather-furnished lounge; large rear function room. Formal team serve complex dishes from traditional menus. Smart,
   comfy, slightly kitsch bedrooms.

---

**WIMBORNE ST GILES** – Dorset – **504** O31 – pop. 366                     **4** C3

▶ London 107 mi – Bristol 72 mi – Southampton 32 mi – Reading 75 mi

🍴 **Bull Inn** with rm                          🚗 🛖 🎵 P VISA ⓪
😊 *Coach Rd* ✉ *BH21 5NF* – ℰ *(01725) 517 300* – *www.bullwsg.com*
   **5 rm** ⬜ – †£ 65/100 ††£ 110/130
   **Rest** – Carte £ 25/34
   ♦ Smart, modern, olive green pub with neutrally hued interior. Menus change
   daily and sometimes between services. Produce is sourced from their farm and
   within the county. Refined dishes use interesting ingredients and unusual cuts.
   Smart, stylish bedrooms.

ENGLAND

**WINCHCOMBE** – Gloucestershire – **503** O28 – **pop. 3 682**                    **4** D1

▶ London 100 mi – Birmingham 43 mi – Gloucester 26 mi – Oxford 43 mi

🄳 High St 𝒞 (01242) 60 29 25, www.winchcombewelcomeswalkers.com

⌂    **Westward** without rest ⌖          ≤ 🖭 🕪 ⸙ℙ 𝑽𝑰𝑺𝑨 ⓪⓪
   *Sudeley Lodge, East : 1.5 mi by Castle St on Sudeley Lodge rd* ✉ *GL54 5JB*
   *– 𝒞 (01242) 604 372 – www.westward-sudeley.co.uk – Closed December-January*
   **3 rm** ⌸ – ♦£ 65/95 ♦♦£ 100/110
   ♦ Secluded, personally run, 18C former hunting lodge to nearby Studeley Castle.
   Elegant wood-floored drawing room and charming sitting room; bedrooms share
   fine views of the 550 acre estate and mature gardens.

✕✕   **5 North St** (Marcus Ashenford)              𝑽𝑰𝑺𝑨 ⓪⓪ 𝔸𝔼
✿   *5 North St* ✉ *GL54 5LH* – 𝒞 *(01242) 604 566*
   *– www.5northstreetrestaurant.co.uk – Closed 2 weeks January, 1 week August,*
   *Monday, Tuesday lunch and Sunday dinner*
   **Rest** – Menu £ 26/48
   **Spec.** Lobster and crab terrine with shellfish dressing. Belly pork and roasted scallop, artichoke purée and sage jus. Presentation of British desserts
   ♦ Long-standing neighbourhood restaurant that's very personally run by a husband and wife team. Characterful low-beamed ceilings and burgundy walls create
   an intimate feel. Menus change with the seasons and feature British ingredients in
   tried-and-tested combinations. Dishes are precise, well-crafted and full of flavour.

✕✕   **Wesley House** with rm              𝔸ℂ ⸙ ⸙⸫ ℙ 𝑽𝑰𝑺𝑨 ⓪⓪ 𝔸𝔼
   *High St* ✉ *GL54 5LJ* – 𝒞 *(01242) 602 366* – *www.wesleyhouse.co.uk*
   **5 rm** ⌸ – ♦£ 65 ♦♦£ 75/110
   **Rest** – *(closed Sunday dinner)* Menu £ 16/25 – Carte £ 24/46
   ♦ Hugely characterful part 15C house: dine amongst the beams or in the stylish
   glass-roofed extension. Tasty modern British cooking with original twists. Smil-
   ingly quaint rooms.

---

**WINCHELSEA** – East Sussex – **504** W31 🎫 Great Britain                    **9** C3

▶ London 64 mi – Brighton 46 mi – Folkestone 30 mi

🄾 Town★ – St Thomas Church (effigies★)

⌂   **Strand House**              🖭 ⸙ ℙ 𝑽𝑰𝑺𝑨 ⓪⓪
   *Tanyard's Ln., East : 0.25 mi on A 259* ✉ *TN36 4JT* – 𝒞 *(01797) 226 276*
   *– www.thestrandhouse.co.uk*
   **10 rm** ⌸ – ♦£ 95/140 ♦♦£ 115/165
   **Rest** – *(closed Monday and Tuesday)* Menu £ 30 **s**
   ♦ 14C and 15C half-timbered house of low beams and inglenook fireplaces: carefully tended rear garden shaded by tall trees, snug lounge; well-kept rooms in traditional style. Simple homecooking.

---

**WINCHESTER** – Hampshire – **503** P30 – **pop. 44 144** 🎫 Great Britain          **6** B2

▶ London 72 mi – Bristol 76 mi – Oxford 52 mi – Southampton 12 mi

🄳 High Street 𝒞 (01962) 84 05 00, www.visitwinchester.co.uk

🄾 City★★ - Cathedral★★★ **AC** B – Winchester College★ **AC** B **B** – Castle Great Hall★
   B **D** – God Begot House★ B **A**

🄶 St Cross Hospital★★ **AC** A

🏨   **Hotel du Vin**             🖭 𝔸ℂ ⸙ ♨ ℙ 𝑽𝑰𝑺𝑨 ⓪⓪ 𝔸𝔼
   *14 Southgate St* ✉ *SO23 9EF* – 𝒞 *(01962) 841 414* – *www.hotelduvin.com*
   **24 rm** – ♦£ 125/165 ♦♦£ 140/295, ⌸ £ 14.50            B**i**
   **Rest** *Bistro* – see restaurant listing
   ♦ Attractive Georgian house dating from 1715; the first ever Hotel du Vin.
   Shabby-chic lounge and characterful champagne bar. Split between the house
   and garden, stylish, minimalist bedrooms are well-equipped; some have baths in
   the room.

**ENGLAND** *(vertical side text)*

---

### Giffard House without rest
*50 Christchurch Rd ⊠ SO23 9SU – ℰ (01962) 852 628*
*– www.giffardhotel.co.uk – Closed 24 December-2 January*  **Bs**
**13 rm** 🛏 – ♦£ 71/85 ♦♦£ 91/128
• Imposing red-brick house. Spacious, classically styled guest areas with comfy drawing room and formal breakfast room. Individually styled bedrooms boast quality furnishings and good facilities.

### 29 Christchurch Road without rest
*29 Christchurch Rd. ⊠ SO23 9SU – ℰ (01962) 868 661*
*– www.fetherstondilke.com*  **Bv**
**3 rm** 🛏 – ♦£ 55/100 ♦♦£ 85/100
• Modern, Regency style guesthouse in attractive residential area close to town. Comfortable lounge and communal, linen-laid breakfast room. Simple bedrooms with plain walls and floral drapes.

### XX Chesil Rectory
*Chesil St. ⊠ SO23 0HU – ℰ (01962) 851 555*
*– www.chesilrectory.co.uk – Closed 25-26 December and bank holidays except Good Friday*  **Br**
**Rest** – Menu £ 20 (lunch and early dinner Monday-Friday) – Carte £ 28/33
• Timbered 15C house on edge of the town centre; its characterful interior taking in beamed ceilings and a large inglenook fireplace. Appealing menu of classically based dishes.

A red **Rest** mention denotes an establishment with an award for culinary excellence, ✿ (star) or ⊕ (Bib Gourmand).

XX **Brasserie Blanc**                    ☂ AC ⇔ VISA ⓒ AE
*19-20 Jewry St* ✉ *SO23 8RZ* – ✆ *(01962) 810 870*
*– www.brasserieblanc.com – Closed 25 December*                     B**x**
**Rest** – French – *(booking advisable)* Menu £ 14/16 – Carte £ 25/34
♦ Bustling informal brasserie in city centre. Spacious, split-level dining with 2 small terraces; open-plan kitchen on first-floor. Extensive menus of classical French dishes and local specials.

X **The Black Rat**                         ☂ ⇔ VISA ⓒ AE
ⵙ *88 Chesil St.* ✉ *SO23 0HX* – ✆ *(01962) 844 465*
*– www.theblackrat.co.uk – Closed 2 weeks December-January, 1 week spring and 1 week autumn*                     B**a**
**Rest** – British – *(dinner only and lunch Saturday-Sunday)* Carte £ 32/38
**Spec.** Octopus carpaccio, wasabi whitebait, compressed cucumber and mandarin dressing. Lamb rump, tongue and shoulder boulangère with baby gem lettuce and peas. Honey baked madeleines and butterscotch sauce.
♦ Unassuming exterior conceals quirky, bohemian-style inner with small bar, lounge and two-roomed restaurant. Refined, classically based cooking with Mediterranean influences and modern twists; local, seasonal produce. Four wicker-roofed booths on rear terrace.

X **Bistro** – at Hotel du Vin               ☀ P VISA ⓒ AE
*14 Southgate St* ✉ *SO23 9EF* – ✆ *(01962) 841 414*
*– www.hotelduvin.com*                     B**i**
**Rest** – *(booking essential)* Carte £ 28/42 ☕
♦ Characterful hotel bistro set within the original Hotel du Vin, in an attractive Georgian house dating from 1715. Wine-related pictures and memorabilia adorn the walls. French-inspired menu.

🍺 **Wykeham Arms** with rm            ☀ ☂ P VISA ⓒ AE
*75 Kingsgate St* ✉ *SO23 9PE* – ✆ *(01962) 853 834*
*– www.wykehamarmswinchester.co.uk*                     B**u**
**14 rm** ☕ – ♦£ 72/112 ♦♦£ 145
**Rest** – *(booking essential)* Menu £ 15/21 – Carte £ 29/44
♦ Appealingly shabby, 18C red-brick inn tucked away on a cobbled street and packed with memorabilia. Dishes range from simple soups, pies and pastas to more elaborate lobster. Bedrooms have good facilities: those upstairs are characterful; those opposite, quieter.

**at Sparsholt** Northwest : 3.5 mi by B 3049 - A – ✉ Winchester

🏛 **Lainston House** ॐ           ≤ ☀ ☝ ⊃ ♨ ✗ 🎵 ⅄ P VISA ⓒ AE
*Woodman Lane* ✉ *SO21 2LT* – ✆ *(01962) 776 088*
*– www.exclusivehotels.co.uk*
**49 rm** – ♦£ 150/245 ♦♦£ 170/245, ☕ £ 21 – 1 suite
**Rest** *Avenue* – see restaurant listing
♦ Impressive 17C William and Mary manor house with attractive gardens and a striking Avenue of lime trees in the grounds. Guest areas include a clubby, wood-panelled drawing room, a modern country house lounge and a small gym. Spacious bedrooms vary from classical to contemporary; all boast good facilities.

XXX **Avenue** – at Lainston House Hotel      ≤ ☀ ☝ P VISA ⓒ AE
*Woodman Lane* ✉ *SO21 2LT* – ✆ *(01962) 776 088*
*– www.exclusivehotels.co.uk*
**Rest** – Menu £ 33/55
♦ Hotel restaurant in an impressive 17C manor house, named after the striking Avenue of lime trees it overlooks. One traditional and one contemporary room. Modern menus include a tasting option.

▶ London 274 mi – Blackpool 55 mi – Carlisle 46 mi – Kendal 10 mi

ℹ Victoria St 𝒞 (015394) 4 64 99, www.golakes.co.uk

◐ Lake Windermere★★ – Brockhole National Park Centre★ **AC**,
NW : 2 mi by A 591

Plan on next page

---

🏨   **Holbeck Ghyll** 🌿      ≤ 🚗 🐾 ⋔ ℔ ⚒ ⁋ 🎿 **P** **VISA** **◯◯** **AE**

𝔖   *Holbeck Ln., Northwest : 3.25 mi by A 591* ✉ *LA23 1LU*
– 𝒞 *(015394) 32 375*
– *www.holbeckghyll.com*
**20 rm** (dinner included) ☕ – 🛏£ 263 🛏🛏£ 301/450
– 3 suites
**Rest** – *(booking advisable at lunch)* Menu £ 30/60 ⅍
**Spec.** Honey glazed pork belly with spiced carrot. Best end of lamb, confit peppers, aubergine and black olive gnocchi. Vanilla poached pineapple, coconut sorbet and banana beignets
♦ Victorian hunting lodge in mature grounds, boasting excellent lake/country views. Traditional guest areas display antiques and heavy fabrics. Similarly styled bedrooms, some in annexes, have good facilities. Two-roomed restaurant; one room with a view. Precise, confident, classical cooking employs quality local produce.

---

🏨   **Miller Howe**      ≤ 🚗 **AC** **P** **VISA** **◯◯**

*Rayrigg Rd* ✉ *LA23 1EY* – 𝒞 *(015394) 42 536* – *www.millerhowe.com* – *Closed 2 weeks January*    **Ys**
**13 rm** (dinner included) ☕ – 🛏£ 120/160 🛏🛏£ 240
– 2 suites
**Rest** – *(booking essential)* Menu £ 25/45
– Carte £ 29/48 ⅍
♦ Superbly situated Victorian villa in mature gardens, looking down the lake to the mountains. Spacious, comfortable bedrooms display a classical style and contemporary edge. Fabulous views from conservatory. Split-level dining room offers traditional cooking.

---

🏠   **Windermere Suites** without rest      ⚒ ⁋ **P** **VISA** **◯◯**

*New Rd* ✉ *LA23 2LA* – 𝒞 *(01539) 444 739*
– *www.windermeresuites.co.uk*    **Yo**
**7 rm** ☕ – 🛏🛏£ 146/180 – 1 suite
♦ Spacious Victorian house with seductive interior. Luxurious bedrooms boast bold modern décor, designer furniture and walk-in wardrobes. Huge bathrooms feature TVs and colour-changing lights. Breakfast served in your room.

---

🏠   **Cedar Manor**      🚗 ⚒ ⁋ **P** **VISA** **◯◯** **AE**

*Ambleside Rd* ✉ *LA23 1AX* – 𝒞 *(015394) 43 192* – *www.cedarmanor.co.uk*
– *Closed 3-23 January and 14-26 December*    **Yi**
**10 rm** ☕ – 🛏£ 100/120 🛏🛏£ 160/180 – 1 suite
**Rest** – *(dinner only)* Menu £ 40
♦ Attractive slate house complete with cedar tree. Modern guest areas boast smart furnishings. Contemporary country house bedrooms display locally made furniture, feature walls and up-to-date facilities; some have lovely views. Appealing menus of local produce.

---

🏠   **Howbeck** without rest      ⚒ ⁋ **P** **VISA** **◯◯**

*New Rd* ✉ *LA23 2LA* – 𝒞 *(015394) 44 739*
– *www.howbeck.co.uk*    **Yo**
**11 rm** ☕ – 🛏🛏£ 78/135
♦ Smart slate house 5min from town. Comfy leather-furnished lounge with honesty bar; black-themed breakfast room with interesting menu. Plain, modern décor in bedrooms; some feature four-posters.

**ENGLAND**

## WINDERMERE

⟨⟩ **Newstead** without rest ⚅ 🛜 ⁽¹⁾ **P** VISA ⊙⊙

*New Rd* ⊠ *LA23 2EE –* 𝒞 *(015394) 44 485 – www.newstead-guesthouse.co.uk*
*– Closed 1-28 December* **Ya**
**9 rm** ⟳ – ✦£ 60/85 ✦✦£ 70/95

◆ Imposing Victorian house with spacious, classical interior; original features include servants' bells and ornate coving. Traditional bedrooms have sinks in the
rooms; some boast four-posters.

⟨⟩ **Fir Trees** without rest 🚗 ⚅ 🛜 ⁽¹⁾ **P** VISA ⊙⊙ AE ⓪

*Lake Rd* ⊠ *LA23 2EQ –* 𝒞 *(015394) 42 272 – www.fir-trees.co.uk* **Zx**
**9 rm** ⟳ – ✦£ 55/60 ✦✦£ 64/72

◆ Welcoming guesthouse boasting original Victorian staircase and lovely tile-
floored hallway. Surprisingly spacious interior includes simple, comfy bedrooms
and wood-furnished breakfast room.

⌂ **1 Park Rd**   ⚒ 🌐 P VISA ☺☺ AE ①
*1 Park Rd ⊠ LA23 2AW – ℰ (015394) 42 107 – www.1parkroad.com*
**6 rm** ⊑ – ♦£ 56/64 ♦♦£ 96/104   **Rest** – Menu £ 25   Y**r**
 • Larger corner property in residential part of town; run by friendly owners. Comfy lounge complete with piano. Good-sized, homely bedrooms with modern facilities and locally made toiletries. Simple, linen-laid dining room serving home-cooked meals by arrangement.

ХХ **Jerichos** with rm   🌐 P VISA ☺☺ AE
*College Rd ⊠ LA23 1BX – ℰ (015394) 42 522 – www.jerichos.co.uk – Closed last 3 weeks January, last 2 weeks November, first week December, 24-26 December, 1 January and Thursday*   Y**z**
**10 rm** ⊑ – ♦£ 40/85 ♦♦£ 85/125   **Rest** – *(dinner only)* Carte £ 27/45
 • Traditional Victorian house in town centre. Two-roomed restaurant with modern, understated styling. Concise, constantly evolving menus of ambitious dishes crafted from quality produce. Smart, contemporary bedrooms boast bold feature walls and good facilities.

Х **Francine's**   VISA ☺☺
*27 Main Rd ⊠ LA23 1DX – ℰ (015394) 44 088
– www.francinesrestaurantwindermere.co.uk – Closed last 2 weeks January, first week December, 25-26 December, 1 January, Monday and dinner Sunday and Tuesday*   Y**c**
**Rest** – *(booking essential at dinner)* Menu £ 16/20 – Carte £ 19/30
 • Intimate neighbourhood restaurant decorated in red and cream. Simple, homely feel and friendly service. Straightforward classical cooking has French influences; chef is passionate about game.

**at Bowness-on-Windermere** South : 1 mi - Z – ⊠ Windermere

🏨 **Gilpin H. & Lake House** ⌂   ≤ 🚗 🕭 🍷 🛎 📺 🏠 ⚒ P VISA ☺☺ AE ①
*Crook Rd, Southeast : 2.5 mi by A 5074 on B 5284
⊠ LA23 3NE – ℰ (015394) 88 818 – www.gilpinlodge.co.uk*
**26 rm** (dinner included) ⊑ – ♦£ 200 ♦♦£ 380/400
**Rest** – *(booking essential for non-residents)* Menu £ 30/58 – Carte £ 31/34 ⌂
 • Family-run, country house hotel in appealing rural location, with comfy lounge, retro bar and landscaped terrace. Individually themed bedrooms, most in contemporary styles: vast Garden Suites boast hot-tubs; Lake House Suites are the most peaceful and luxurious. Slick service. Four differently styled dining rooms, where classical cooking displays modern touches.

🏨 **Linthwaite House** ⌂   ≤ 🚗 🕭 🍷 🛎 P VISA ☺☺ AE
*Crook Rd, South : 0.75 mi by A 5074 on B 5284 ⊠ LA23 3JA – ℰ (015394) 88 600 – www.linthwaite.com*
**31 rm** (dinner included) ⊑ – ♦£ 172/204 ♦♦£ 274/564
**Rest** – Menu £ 20/52
 • Traditional country house in peaceful setting, overlooking the lake/fells. Stylish, modern lounges; funky bar with fish tank in wall. Smart bedrooms boast feature walls, mood lighting, double showers and views from the front. Contemporary, three-roomed restaurant.

🏨 **Lindeth Howe** ⌂   ≤ 🚗 📺 🏠 👪 rm, ⚒ 🛎 P VISA ☺☺ AE ①
*Lindeth Dr., Longtail Hill, South : 1.25 mi by A 5074 on B 5284 ⊠ LA23 3JF – ℰ (015394) 45 759 – www.lindeth-howe.co.uk – Closed 3-12 January*
**33 rm** ⊑ – ♦£ 95/160 ♦♦£ 360 – 1 suite
**Rest** *The Dining Room* – Menu £ 18/43 – Carte dinner £ 32/44
 • Attractive country house once owned by Beatrix Potter. Homely, clubby bar and lounge; pleasant views from drawing room. Traditional bedrooms – top floor boasts the best views; suites are more contemporary. Large, classically styled restaurant has menus to match.

### Storrs Hall ⊗ ≤ 🚗 🌙 🐟 📶 🛜 🖪 P 🚹 VISA ⚫ AE
✉ LA23 3LG – ℰ (015394) 47 111 – www.englishlakes.co.uk
**29 rm** ⌸ – ♦£ 129/149 ♦♦£ 286 – 1 suite
**Rest** *The Terrace* – Menu £ 20/44 – Carte £ 42/57
◆ Part-Georgian mansion in 17 acres, with gardens leading to the lakeside. Variety of spacious, country house guest areas. Comfy, well-equipped bedrooms range from classical to bold, modern styles; some have lake views. Formal restaurant offers traditional menus.

### Fayrer Garden House ⊗ ≤ 🚗 AC rest, P VISA ⚫
*Lyth Valley Rd, South : 1 mi on A 5074* ✉ LA23 3JP – ℰ (015394) 88 195
– www.fayrergarden.com
**28 rm** (dinner included) ⌸ – ♦£ 72/150 ♦♦£ 144/300
**Rest** *The Terrace* – (dinner only) (booking essential for non-residents)
Menu £ 43
◆ Edwardian slate house on the hillside, affording lovely views over the lake and mountains. Comfy lounges with quality, cottagey furniture. Cosy, classical bedrooms with floral themes; some have whirlpool baths. Two-roomed restaurant offers traditional menus.

### Angel Inn 🚗 🌳 AC rm, 🛜 P VISA ⚫ AE
*Helm Rd* ✉ LA23 3BU – ℰ (015394) 44 080 – www.the-angelinn.com – Closed
24-25 December                                                         Zv
**13 rm** ⌸ – ♦£ 75/90 ♦♦£ 170/180    **Rest** – Carte £ 21/33
◆ Cream-washed pub off the main street, boasting smart, contemporary bedrooms with iPod docks, flat screen TVs and modern bathrooms; the largest in an annexed 18C cottage. Large, semi-open-plan bar and wood-furnished, terraced garden offer classic pub-style dishes.

### Fair Rigg without rest ≤ 🛜 P VISA ⚫
*Ferry View, South : 0.5 mi on A 5074* ✉ LA23 3JB – ℰ (015394) 43 941
– www.fairrigg.co.uk – April to late December
**6 rm** ⌸ – ♦£ 50/55 ♦♦£ 72/90
◆ Late 19C detached house affording distant lake and hill views; run by friendly owners. Neat, linen-laid breakfast room. Immaculately kept bedrooms with quality furniture and good facilities.

Prices quoted after the symbol ♦ refer to the lowest rate in low season
followed by the highest rate in high season, for a single room.
The same principle applies to the symbol ♦♦ for a double room.

## at Troutbeck North : 4 mi by A 592 - Y – ✉ Windermere

### Queen's Head with rm ≤ 🌳 🛜 P VISA ⚫ AE
*North : 0.75 mi on A 592* ✉ LA23 1PW – ℰ (01539) 432 174
– www.queensheadtroutbeck.co.uk
**15 rm** ⌸ – ♦£ 75 ♦♦£ 150    **Rest** – Menu £ 20 – Carte £ 24/42
◆ Amazingly characterful, memorabilia-filled pub in delightful Lakeland setting, with several interlinking rooms and unique four-poster bar counter. Extensive menu offers something for everyone. Smart bedrooms have strong comforts; 10 and 11 have the best views.

## at Winster South : 4 mi on A 5074 – ✉ Windermere

### Brown Horse Inn with rm 🌳 P VISA ⚫ ⓞ
*on A 5074* ✉ LA23 3NR – ℰ (01539) 443 443 – www.thebrownhorseinn.co.uk
**9 rm** ⌸ – ♦£ 50/75 ♦♦£ 65/100    **Rest** – Carte £ 22/33
◆ Shabby-chic coaching inn with lovely split-level terrace. Seasonal menus feature unfussy, generous dishes and more adventurous specials. Much of the produce is from their fields out the back. Bedrooms are a mix of classic and boutique styles; some have terraces.

▶ London 40 mi – Reading 18 mi – Southampton 53 mi

ⓘ **The Bee**                              🚗 🛋 **P** *VISA* ⊕

*School Rd ⊠ GU20 6PD – ℰ (01276) 479 244 – www.thebeepub.co.uk – Closed Sunday dinner*
**Rest** – Menu £ 16 (lunch) – Carte £ 26/38
♦ Stylish, modern pub with buzzing atmosphere. Daily changing menus showcase seasonal, local produce in precisely cooked dishes. Good value two course lunch. Summer barbecues.

ⓘ **Brickmakers**                          🚗 **P** *VISA* ⊕ **AE**

*Chertsey Rd, East : 1 mi on B 386 ⊠ GU20 6HT – ℰ (01276) 472 267 – www.thebrickmakerswindlesham.co.uk*
**Rest** – Menu £ 24 – Carte £ 23/30
♦ Red-brick pub in pretty location; its immaculately kept garden is quite a feature in summer. Simple bar menu and more interesting à la carte; dishes are good value and full of flavour.

---

▯ Great Britain

▶ London 28 mi – Reading 19 mi – Southampton 59 mi
▬ to Marlow, Maidenhead and Cookham (Salter Bros. Ltd) (summer only)
ⓩ The Old Booking Hall, Central Station, Thames St ℰ (01753) 74 39 00, www.windsor.gov.uk
◉ Town★ – Castle★★★ : St George's Chapel★★★ **AC** (stalls★★★), State Apartments★★ **AC**, North Terrace (≼★★) Z – Eton College★★ **AC** (College Chapel★★, Wall paintings★) Z
◔ Windsor Park★ **AC** Y

**ENGLAND**

Plan on next page

🏨 **Macdonald Windsor**           📶 ᴄ rm, **AC** ⟨ɣ⟩ ㏒ 🚗 *VISA* ⊕ **AE**

*23 High St. ⊠ SL4 1LH – ℰ (0844) 879 91 01 – www.macdonaldhotels.co.uk/windsor*                                   **Z**r
**118 rm** – ♦£ 195/245 ♦♦£ 295/345, ⊇ £ 15.50 – 2 suites
**Rest Caleys** – Menu £ 20/25 – Carte £ 20/38
♦ Opened in 2010 in a former department store. Attractive open-plan guest areas in striking grey, cream and silver; small but state-of-the-art meeting rooms. Contemporary bedrooms with warm hues and high level of facilities. Modern brasserie with menus to match.

🏨 **Sir Christopher Wren's House**     🛋 ㏒ ⟨ɣ⟩ ㏒ *VISA* ⊕ **AE**

*Thames St ⊠ SL4 1PX – ℰ (01753) 442 400 – www.sirchristopherwren.co.uk*
**94 rm** ⊇ – ♦£ 100/235 ♦♦£ 140/245 – 1 suite                        **Z**e
**Rest Strok's** – see restaurant listing
♦ Built by Wren in 1676 as his family home, this characterful house sits on the riverbank by Windsor bridge. Traditional guest areas; smart gym. Bedrooms, some in annexes, range from classical to modern – some boast balconies and river views.

🏨 **Royal Adelaide**                **AC** ⟨ɣ⟩ ㏒ **P** *VISA* ⊕ **AE**

*46 Kings Rd, Eton ⊠ SL4 2AG – ℰ (01753) 863 916 – www.theroyaladelaide.com*
**42 rm** ⊇ – ♦£ 99/220 ♦♦£ 145/220   **Rest** – Carte £ 20/40      **Z**v
♦ Three adjoining Georgian houses with light blue painted façade, built for Queen Adelaide. Bedooms vary in shape and size, and all are decorated in an individual, traditional style. Dining room offers international, brasserie-style menu.

🏨 **Christopher**                  🛋 ᴄ rm, **AC** rm, ⟨ɣ⟩ **P** *VISA* ⊕ **AE**

*110 High St, Eton ⊠ SL4 6AN – ℰ (01753) 852 359 – www.thechristopher.co.uk*
**34 rm** – ♦£ 127/141 ♦♦£ 186, ⊇ £ 12.50   **Rest** – Carte £ 22/31    **Z**a
♦ 17C former coaching inn close to Eton College and perfect for walking to the castle. Contemporary bedrooms are split between main building and a mews annexe. International menus display North African influences.

# WINDSOR

**ENGLAND**

## XX **Windsor Grill**  AC ⟷ VISA ◎ AE
*65 St Leonards Rd* ⊠ *SL4 3BX –* ℰ *(01753) 859 658 – www.awtrestaurants.com*
*– Closed 25-26 December and Sunday* Zx
**Rest** – Beef specialities – *(dinner only)* Carte £ 32/46
♦ Rustic Victorian property owned by Antony Worrall Thompson. Wide menu displays classic comfort dishes, including well flavoured hung beef and pork/chicken from his farm.

## XX **Strok's** – at Sir Christopher Wren's House Hotel  AC VISA ◎ AE
*Thames St* ⊠ *SL4 1PX –* ℰ *(01753) 442 400 – www.sarova.com* Ze
**Rest** – Menu £ 28 **s** – Carte £ 30/46 **s**
♦ Classical hotel restaurant in a characterful 17C house, built by Wren as his family home. Wood-furnished terrace and lovely Thames views. Accessible menu displays international influences.

## ⅼⅅ **Greene Oak**  🍴 P VISA ◎ AE
*Oakley Grn, West : 3 mi by A 308 on B 3024* ⊠ *SL4 5UW –* ℰ *(01753) 864 294*
*– www.thegreeneoak.co.uk – Closed Sunday dinner*
**Rest** – *(booking advisable)* Menu £ 15 *(lunch except Friday and Sunday)*
*– Carte £ 25/36*
♦ Set on the west side of Windsor, with appealing green-hued décor and contemporary soft furnishings. Seasonal menu of tasty European dishes. Popular terrace for alfresco dining.

---

**WINEHAM** – West Sussex – **504** T31 – see Henfield

**WINFORTON** – Herefordshire – **503** L27 – see Hereford

**WINSFORD** – Somerset – **503** J30 – pop. 270 – ⊠ Minehead    3 A2
▶ London 194 mi – Exeter 31 mi – Minehead 10 mi – Taunton 32 mi
👁 Village ★
Ⓖ Exmoor National Park ★★

## ⅼⅅ **Royal Oak Inn** with rm  🛏 🍴 P VISA ◎ AE
*Exmoor National Park* ⊠ *TA24 7JE –* ℰ *(01643) 851 455*
*– www.royaloakexmoor.co.uk*
**8 rm** ⊇ – ♥£ 55 ♥♥£ 100/120
**Rest** – Carte £ 20/27
♦ Delightful 12C thatched pub set by a ford in a picturesque Exmoor village. Arriving exactly as described, British dishes use homemade, local and seasonal produce. Smart, individually styled bedrooms; private in-room therapy treatments available.

---

**WINSTER** – Cumbria – **502** L20 – see Windermere

**WINSTON** – Durham    24 A3
▶ London 252 mi – Leeds 71 mi

## ⅼⅅ **Bridgewater Arms**  🛏 🍴 P VISA ◎ AE
⊠ *DL2 3RN –* ℰ *(01325) 730 302 – www.thebridgewaterarms.com*
*– Closed 25-26 December, Sunday and Monday*
**Rest** – Carte £ 22/36
♦ Originally located by the bridge but moved into the old school in the 1950s; look for the copperplate alphabet and old school programme. Seafood is the highlight here, from Dover Sole to langoustines, but the steaks are also good.

---

**WINTERBOURNE STEEPLETON** – Dorset – **503** M31 – see Dorchester

**WINTERINGHAM** – North Lincolnshire – **502** S22 – pop. 4 714    23 C3
– ⊠ Scunthorpe
▶ London 176 mi – Kingston-upon-Hull 16 mi – Sheffield 67 mi

ENGLAND

ENGLAND

XXX **Winteringham Fields** with rm     P. VISA ©© AE
*1 Silver St* ⊠ *DN15 9ND –* ℰ *(01724) 733 096 – www.winteringhamfields.co.uk*
*– Closed first week January and 25 December*
**10 rm** – †£ 145 ††£ 180/220, ☲ £ 20 – 1 suite
**Rest** – *(closed Sunday-Monday) (booking essential for non-residents)*
Menu £ 40/75
♦ Characterful 16C house with pleasant garden, elegant dining room and severa
antique-filled private rooms. Self-taught chef adopts a complex, modern ap
proach to cooking, offering a concise à la carte and daily 6 course 'Menu Sur
prise'. Comfortable, antique-furnished bedrooms, with breakfast in spacious rea
dining room.

The symbol ॐ guarantees a good night's sleep. In red ॐ ? The very essence
of peace: only the sound of birdsong in the early morning…

---

**WISWELL** – Lancashire – **502** M22 – *see Clitheroe*

---

**WITHERSLACK** – Cumbria – **502** L21      **21** A3
▶ London 266 mi – Liverpool 83 mi – Manchester 78 mi

🏠 **Derby Arms** with rm     🖚 「∥」 P. VISA ©© ①
⊠ *LA11 6RH –* ℰ *(015395) 52 207 – www.thederbyarms.co.uk*
**6 rm** – †£ 50/65 ††£ 55/85
**Rest** – Menu £ 10 (lunch and early dinner)/16
– Carte £ 22/32
♦ Substantial 19C coaching inn with characterful shabby-chic interior, beams
open fires and a small community shop. Cooking is rustic yet refined and pud
dings are suitably old-fashioned. Classical bedrooms display antiques; some boas
views or roll-top baths.

---

**WIVETON** – Norfolk – *see Blakeney*

---

**WOBURN** – **504** S28 – pop. 1 534 – ⊠ **Milton Keynes** ▌ Great Britain    **12** A2
▶ London 49 mi – Bedford 13 mi – Luton 13 mi
– Northampton 24 mi
◉ Woburn Abbey★★

🏨 **Inn at Woburn**     & rm, 🅺 rest, ⅌ 「∥」 ⛵ P. VISA ©© AE
*George St* ⊠ *MK17 9PX –* ℰ *(01525) 290 441 – www.woburn.co.uk/inn*
**51 rm** – †£ 90/140 ††£ 90/140, ☲ £ 12.25 – 4 suites
**Rest** *Olivier's* – Menu £ 16 (lunch) – Carte dinner £ 26/36
♦ 18C coaching inn, part of Woburn Estate with its abbey and 3000 acre park.
Pleasant modern furnishings and interior décor. Tastefully decorated rooms:
book a Cottage suite. Classic dishes in contemporary Olivier's.

XXX **Paris House**     🍽 🛏 🖙 ⇔ P. VISA ©© AE
ॐ *Woburn Park, Southeast : 2.25 mi on A 4012* ⊠ *MK17 9QP –* ℰ *(01525) 290 692*
*– www.parishouse.co.uk – Closed dinner 24 December-7 January, Sunday dinner,*
*Tuesday lunch and Monday*
**Rest** – *(booking essential)* Menu £ 30/67
**Spec.** Confit sea trout, pickled cucumber, guacamole and wasabi mayonnaise. Rabbit saddle stuffed with chorizo and prawn, saffron braised rice
and Gewürztraminer sauce. Jaffa orange soufflé, orange sponge and chocolate sorbet.
♦ Striking black and white timbered house, originally built in Paris and reas-
sembled in this charming location, where deer wander freely. Classic dishes are
given an imaginative modern makeover, with confident flavours and artistic presentation. Polished, unobtrusive service.

✗ **Birch**                          🏠 AC P VISA ⊕ AE
*20 Newport Rd, North : 0.5 mi on A 5130 ✉ MK17 9HX*
*– ℰ (01525) 290 295 – www.birchwoburn.com*
*– Closed 25-26 December, 1 January and Sunday dinner*
**Rest** – *(booking essential)* Carte £ 22/33
♦ Smart, well-run former pub, whose traditional façade masks a bright, modern interior with contemporary furnishings. Menu offers old favourites, daily specials and grills by the ounce.

---

**WOKING** – Surrey – **504** S30                          **7** C1
▶ London 34 mi – Farnborough 14 mi – Guildford 7 mi

🍸 **Red Lion**                    🚗 🏠 AC P VISA ⊕ AE ①
*High St, Horsell, Northwest : 1.5 mi by A 324 ✉ GU21 4SS*
*– ℰ (01483) 768 497 – www.redlionhorsell.co.uk*
**Rest** – *(booking advisable)* Carte £ 23/36
♦ A modern take on the traditional pub, with all-day dining, plenty of outside seating and occasional live music. Traditional pub food, with sharing plates and fish dishes the highlights.

---

**WOLD NEWTON** – East Riding of Yorkshire                          **23** D2
▶ London 229 mi – Bridlington 25 mi – Scarborough 13 mi

🏠 **Wold Cottage** ✍          ← 🚗 ⏀ ⸙ 🐾 P VISA ⊕
*South : 0.5 mi on Thwing rd ✉ YO25 3HL*
*– ℰ (01262) 470 696 – www.woldcottage.com*
**5 rm** ⌷ – ♦£ 65/75 ♦♦£ 110/150
**Rest** – Menu 25
♦ Fine Georgian house and extensive collection of outbuildings, at the centre of 300 acres of rolling farmland. Welcoming owner. Homely interior where personal items abound; snug lounge displays large oils. Sizeable bedrooms boast quality soft furnishings and antiques; the two in the courtyard are more simply furnished. Formal dining room offers hearty British dishes.

---

**WOLVERCOTE** – Oxfordshire – **504** Q28 – see Oxford

---

**WOLVERHAMPTON** – Staffordshire – **502** N26 – pop. 251 462                          **19** C2
▶ London 132 mi – Birmingham 15 mi – Liverpool 89 mi – Shrewsbury 30 mi
ℹ 18 Queen Sq ℰ (01902) 31 20 51, www.wolverhampton.co.uk

Plan of Enlarged Area : see Birmingham pp. 4 and 5

Plan on next page

✗✗ **Bilash**                          AC ⧖ ⇄ VISA ⊕ AE
*No 2 Cheapside ✉ WV1 1TU – ℰ (01902) 427 762*
*– www.thebilash@co.uk – Closed 25-26 December and Sunday*          **B**c
**Rest** – Indian – Menu £ 16/19
*– Carte £ 28/55*
♦ Long-standing, personally-run restaurant with several family generations involved. Appealing menu of freshly cooked Indian dishes and tempting specials. Strictly local and homemade produce.

---

**WOOBURN COMMON** – Bucks. – **504** S29 – see Beaconsfield

WOLVERHAMPTON

## WOODBRIDGE – Suffolk – 504 X27 – pop. 10 956                    15 D3

▶ London 81 mi – Great Yarmouth 45 mi – Ipswich 8 mi
  – Norwich 47 mi

▣ Cretingham Grove Farm, ℰ (01728) 68 52 75

▣ Seckford Great Bealings Seckford Hall Rd,
  ℰ (01394) 38 80 00

676

**Seckford Hall** 🕭 　　　🔊 🕭 📺 📠 ₤ ৳ 🖶 🗐 & rm, AK rest, ⁇ ⁇ P
Southwest : 1.25 mi by A 12 ⊠ IP13 6NU – ℰ (01394)　　VISA ⚬⚬ AE ①
385 678 – www.seckford.co.uk – Closed 25 December
**25 rm** – ♥£ 85/150 ♥♥£ 150/230, � £ 13.95 – 7 suites
**Rest** – (closed lunch Monday) Menu £ 17 (weekday lunch)/33 **s**
◆ Reputedly once visited by Elizabeth I, a part Tudor country house set in attractive gardens. Charming traditionally panelled public areas. Comfortable bedrooms. Local lobster proudly served in smart dining room.

**Riverside** 　　　　　　　　　　　🖙 AK VISA ⚬⚬ AE
Quayside ⊠ IP12 1BH – ℰ (01394) 382 587 – www.theriverside.co.uk – Closed
25-26 December, 1 January and Sunday dinner
**Rest** – (booking essential) Menu £ 30 (dinner) – Carte £ 25/36
◆ Not just a restaurant, but a cinema too! Floor to ceiling windows and busy terrace. Appealing menus offer modern, well-presented cooking. Set menu includes ticket for film.

**Crown** with rm 　　　　　　　　🖙 ⁇ P VISA ⚬⚬ AE
Thoroughfare ⊠ IP12 1AD – ℰ (01394) 384 242
– www.thecrownatwoodbridge.co.uk
**10 rm** – ♥£ 110/180 ♥♥£ 125/180　**Rest** – Menu £ 20 – Carte £ 24/32
◆ Modern dining pub in town centre, with smart granite-floored bar and four different dining areas. Extensive menu makes good use of local produce. Well presented, rustic cooking and polite, friendly service. Stylish, contemporary bedrooms boast good facilities.

**at Bromeswell** Northeast : 2.5 mi by B 1438 off A 1152 – ⊠

**British Larder** 　　　　　　　　🔊 🖙 P VISA ⚬⚬
Orford Rd, on A 1152 ⊠ IP12 2PU – ℰ (01394) 460 310
– www.britishlardersuffolk.co.uk – Closed Sunday dinner and Monday in
winter except December
**Rest** – Carte £ 28/40
◆ Once down-at-heel, this 17C pub has been modernised in looks and transformed into a beacon for local Suffolk produce. Skilled cooking uses ingredients thoughtfully; wine events and cookery classes held regularly.

**WOODHOUSE EAVES** – Leicestershire – **503** Q25 – see Loughborough

**WOODSTOCK** – Oxfordshire – **503** P28 – pop. 2 389 🏷 Great Britain　　**10** B2
🚩 London 65 mi – Gloucester 47 mi – Oxford 8 mi
🛈 Park St ℰ (01993) 81 32 76, www.woodstock-oxfordshire.co.uk
👁 Blenheim Palace★★★ (Park★★★) **AC**

**Bear** 　　　　　　　　　　& rm, ⁇ P VISA ⚬⚬ AE ①
Park St. ⊠ OX20 1SZ – ℰ (0844) 879 91 43 – www.macdonald-hotels.co.uk/bear
**47 rm** ⊇ – ♥£ 120 ♥♥£ 120/250 – 7 suites
**Rest** – Menu £ 32
◆ Characterful part 16C inn. Original personality and charm; oak beams, open fires and stone walls. Particularly comfortable contemporarily furnished rooms. Dining room exudes an elegant air.

**Feathers** 　　　　　　　　　　🖙 ⁇ VISA ⚬⚬ AE ①
Market St ⊠ OX20 1SX – ℰ (01993) 812 291 – www.feathers.co.uk
**17 rm** – ♥£ 104/194 ♥♥£ 229/459 – 4 suites
**Rest** – (booking essential) Carte £ 40/50
◆ Stylish 17C house boasting individually styled bedrooms with boutique twists: some have feature walls; others, modern art and bold fabrics. Bar-lounge and terrace offer casual menu. Formal dining room serves classically based dishes with a creative, original edge.

ENGLAND

### Kings Arms                                    ⚑ ⬲ ᵞⁱ VISA ⬤⬤ AE

*19 Market St. ✉ OX20 1SU –* ℰ *(01993) 813 636*
*– www.kings-hotel-woodstock.co.uk*
**15 rm** ⏚ – ♥£ 75 ♥♥£ 140
**Rest** *Atrium* – Menu £ 25 (dinner) – Carte £ 22/29
◆ Keenly run, contemporary hotel in heart of a busy market town. Immaculately kept, with sleek bedrooms – named after Kings – displaying golden wood starched linen and plump cushions. Informal bar-restaurant offers local, seasonal British dishes.

---

**WOOFFERTON** – Shropshire – **503** L26 – **see Ludlow**

---

**WOOLACOMBE** – Devon – **503** H30                                   **2** C1

▶ London 237 mi – Barnstaple 15 mi – Exeter 55 mi

◉ Exmoor National Park★★ - Mortehoe★★ (St Mary's Church★, Morte Point - vantage point★) N : 0.5 mi – Ilfracombe : Hillsborough (⬉★★) **AC**, Capstone Hill★ (⬉★), St Nicholas' Chapel (⬉★) **AC**, NE : 5.5 mi by B 3343 and A 361. Braunton★ (St Brannock's Church★, Braunton Burrows★), S : 8 mi by B 3343 and A 361

### Cleeve House                       ⚘ ⬲ rm, ᵞⁱ ᵞⁱ ℙ VISA ⬤⬤

*North Morte Rd, Mortehoe, North : 0.5 mi ✉ EX34 7ED –* ℰ *(01271) 870 719*
*– www.cleevehouse.co.uk – April-September*
**6 rm** ⏚ – ♥£ 59/62 ♥♥£ 90/94
**Rest** – *(closed 21 July-31 August and Wednesday) (dinner only)* Menu £ 29 – Carte £ 26/31
◆ Bright and welcoming feel in décor and atmosphere. Very comfortable lounge and individually styled bedrooms with co-ordinated fabrics. Rear rooms with great country views. Neat dining room; walls hung with local artwork.

---

**WOOLER** – Northumberland – **502** N17 – **pop. 1 857**          **24** A1

▶ London 330 mi – Alnwick 17 mi – Berwick-on-Tweed 17 mi

### Firwood without rest ⌂              ⬚ ⚘ ℙ VISA ⬤⬤

*Middleton Hall, South : 1.75 mi by Earle rd on Middleton Hall rd ✉ NE71 6RD*
*–* ℰ *(01668) 283 699 – www.firwoodhouse.co.uk – February-November*
**3 rm** ⏚ – ♥£ 60 ♥♥£ 90
◆ 19C former hunting lodge with beautiful original tiled hall, set in tranquil spot overlooking the Cheviots. Comfy bay-windowed guest areas great for sighting red squirrels/wild birds. Spacious bedrooms.

---

**WOOLHOPE** – Herefordshire                                      **18** B3

▶ London 138 mi – Birmingham 70 mi

### Butchers Arms                          ⬚ ⬚ ℙ VISA ⬤⬤

✉ HR1 4RF – ℰ *(01432) 860 281 – www.butchersarmswoolhope.co.uk – Closed 25 December, Sunday dinner and Monday except bank holidays*
**Rest** – Menu £ 22 (Sunday lunch) – Carte £ 21/28
◆ Stephen Bull's third pub is an attractive, half-timbered 16C inn, with a pretty garden by a babbling brook and charming bars with low-slung beams and open fires. Daily changing menu of honest, well-priced, regional dishes; local lamb and cheese the highlights.

---

**WOOLSTHORPE BY BELVOIR** – Lincolnshire – **502** R25 – **see Grantham**

---

**WOOTTON BRIDGE** – **503** P31 – **see WIGHT (Isle of)**

ENGLAND

18 B3

> London 124 mi – Birmingham 26 mi – Bristol 61 mi – Cardiff 74 mi

> High St ℰ (01905) 72 63 11, www.visitworcestershire.org

> Perdiswell Park Bilford Rd, ℰ (01905) 75 46 68

> City★ – Cathedral★★ – Royal Worcester Porcelain Works★ (Museum of Worcester Porcelain★) **M**

> The Elgar Trail★

## ✗✗ Glasshouse
🛒 AC VISA ⦿ AE

*Sidbury ⊠ WR1 2HU – ℰ (01905) 611 120 – www.theglasshouse.co.uk*
*– Closed 25-26 December, Sunday and bank holidays*
**c**
**Rest** – Menu £ 20 (lunch)
– Carte £ 27/39

♦ Leather furnished lounge. Stylish chocolate and blue hued dining areas; the first floor has glass wall and views of city. Brasserie style menu offers modern British dishes.

## ✗✗ Brown's
VISA ⦿

*24 Quay St ⊠ WR1 2JJ – ℰ (01905) 26 263 – www.brownsrestaurant.co.uk*
**Rest** – Carte £ 23/33
**x**

♦ Converted riverside corn mill. Spacious, open interior as befits the building's origins. Impressive collection of modern artwork. Mainly British dishes are renowned locally.

ENGLAND

**at Stonehall Common** Southeast : 5.75 mi by A 38 and Norton rd.

🏠 **Inn at Stonehall**     🚗 🛋 P VISA ⑩ AE
✉ WR5 3QG – ℰ (01905) 820 462 – www.theinnatstonehall.com – *Closed first week January, Sunday dinner and Monday*
**Rest** – Carte £ 22/29
♦ Smart, modern dining pub in a peaceful hamlet, with comfy lounge, airy dining room and lovely views. Concise menus feature well-prepared, flavoursome, seasonal dishes; desserts a speciality.

---

**WORFIELD** – Shropshire – see Bridgnorth

---

**WORKSOP** – Nottinghamshire – **502** Q24 – pop. 39 072     **16** B
▶ London 160 mi – Sheffield 20 mi – Nottingham 37 mi – Rotherham 17 mi

🏠 **Browns** without rest ≫     🚗 🛋 P
The Old Orchard Cottage, Holbeck, Southwest : 4.5 mi by A 60 ✉ S80 3NF
– ℰ (01909) 720 659 – www.brownsholbeck.co.uk – *Closed 24-26 December*
**3 rm** ⊑ – ♦£ 59/68 ♦♦£ 79/89
♦ Cosy, comfortable, individually-decorated bedrooms in cottage dating from 1730 and named after the owners. Mature orchard and tranquil garden. Comprehensive breakfast.

---

**WORTH** – Kent – **504** Y30 – see Deal

---

**WRIGHTINGTON BAR** – Lancashire – **502** L23 – see Standish

---

**WYE** – Kent – **504** W30 – pop. 2 066 – ✉ Ashford     **9** C2
▶ London 60 mi – Canterbury 10 mi – Dover 28 mi – Hastings 34 mi

✕✕ **Wife of Bath** with rm     🚗 🛏 P VISA ⑩ AE
4 Upper Bridge St ✉ TN25 5AF – ℰ (01233) 812 232 – www.thewifeofbath.com
**5 rm** ⊑ – ♦£ 75 ♦♦£ 115
**Rest** – (closed Sunday dinner, Tuesday lunch and Monday) (booking advisable)
Menu £ 18 (weekday lunch) – Carte £ 28/35
♦ A lovely timber-framed house built in 1760. Fine cloth tables. Well chosen menu of satisfying dishes. Full or Continental breakfast after staying in comfy soft-toned rooms.

---

**WYMONDHAM** – Leicestershire – **504** R25 – pop. 600     **17** C2
▶ London 107 mi – Birmingham 70 mi – Liverpool 138 mi – Leeds 100 mi

🏠 **Berkeley Arms**     🚗 ⇔ P VISA ⑩
⑤ 59 Main St ✉ LE14 2AG – ℰ (01572) 787 587 – www.theberkeleyarms.co.uk
– *Closed first 2 weeks January, 10 days summer, Sunday dinner and Monday lunch*
**Rest** – Menu £ 18 (lunch) – Carte £ 21/32
♦ Attractive 16C village pub run by an enthusiastic, experienced local couple. Low-beamed bar and slightly more formal dining room. Gutsy, satisfying dishes rely on local produce. Choose from daily changing bar snacks or the more adventurous à la carte. Relaxed, personable service.

---

**WYTON** – Cambridgeshire – See Huntingdon

▶ London 242 mi – Middlesbrough 8 mi – Newcastle upon Tyne 47 mi

---

**Judges Country House** ⬧    🝆 🕭 🕭 📶 👫 🏊 P. VISA 🐟 ΑΕ ①
*Kirklevington Hall, Kirklevington, South : 1.5 mi on A 67 ⊠ TS15 9LW*
– ☏ *(01642) 789 000 – www.judgeshotel.co.uk*
**21 rm** – ♦£ 90/180 ♦♦£ 130/210, � £ 15
**Rest** – Menu £ 28 (lunch) – Carte £ 49/68
♦ Former Victorian judge's residence surrounded by gardens. Welcoming panelled bar and spacious lounge filled with antiques and curios. Attractive rooms
with a host of extras. Conservatory dining room overlooks the gardens.

---

---

▶ London 61 mi – Oxford 23 mi – Reading 12 mi

---

**Royal Oak** with rm    🝆 🕭 🕪 VISA 🐟
*The Square ⊠ RG18 0UF – ☏ (01635) 201 325 – www.royaloakyattendon.com*
**5 rm** ⊇ – ♦£ 85 ♦♦£ 85
**Rest** – *(booking advisable)* Menu £ 15 (lunch) – Carte £ 27/34
♦ Eye-catching red-brick pub with attractive gardens, in picture postcard village
close to the M4; a beamed bar with roaring fire at its hub. Honest British dishes
and traditional puddings; Sunday roast of 28-day aged rib of beef. Comfy bedrooms in country house style.

**at Frilsham** South : 1 mi by Frilsham rd on Bucklebury rd – ⊠ Yattendon

---

**Pot Kiln**    🝆 🕭 P. VISA 🐟
⊠ *RG18 0XX – ☏ (01635) 201 366 – www.potkiln.org – Closed 25 December and*
*Tuesday*
**Rest** – Menu £ 16 (weekday lunch) – Carte £ 28/33 ⌘
♦ Pleasant pub in prime game country. Flavoursome British dishes arrive in un-
ashamedly gutsy portions. Chef-owner stalks or gathers much of the produce
himself. Fish is from Looe or local rivers.

---

▶ London 136 mi – Exeter 48 mi – Southampton 72 mi – Taunton 26 mi
ℹ Hendford ☏ (01935) 84 59 46, www.yeoviltown.com
🏌 Sherborne Rd, ☏ (01935) 42 29 65
◉ St John the Baptist★
🅖 Monacute House★★ **AC**, W : 4 mi on A 3088 – Fleet Air Arm Museum,
Yeovilton★★ **AC**, NW : 5 mi by A 37 – Tintinhull House Garden★ **AC**, NW: 5.5 mi
– Ham Hill (≤★★) W : 5.5 mi by A 3088 – Stoke sub Hamdon (parish church★) W :
5.25 mi by A 3088. Muchelney★★ (parish church★★) NW : 14 mi by A 3088, A 303
and B 3165 – Lytes Cary★, N : 7.5 mi by A 37, B 3151 and A 372 – Sandford Orcas
Manor House★, NW : 8 mi by A 359 – Cadbury Castle (≤★★) NE : 10.5 mi by A
359 – East Lambrook Manor★ **AC**, W : 12 mi by A 3088 and A 303

---

**Lanes**    🝆 🕭 👫 🕭 🖹 🕭 rm, 📶 👫 P. VISA 🐟
*West Coker, Southwest : 3 mi on A 30 ⊠ BA22 9AJ – ☏ (01935) 862 555*
*– www.laneshotel.net*
**29 rm** ⊇ – ♦£ 90 ♦♦£ 130    **Rest** – Menu £ 17 (lunch) – Carte £ 19/30
♦ 18C former rectory in pleasant walled grounds. Airy interior boasts modern
meeting rooms, laid-back lounge and large bar. Relax in smart leisure suite or on
croquet lawn. Stylish bedrooms with up-to-date bathrooms. Modern bistro dishes
in striking dining room.

ENGLAND

## at Barwick South : 2 mi by A 30 off A 37 – ⊠ Yeovil

### XX  Little Barwick House with rm 🕭  🚗 🗚 rest, 🄿 🐵 🄰🄴

⊠ BA22 9TD – ℰ (01935) 423 902 – www.littlebarwickhouse.co.uk – Closed 3
weeks Christmas, 1 week August, Sunday dinner, Monday and lunch Tuesday
**6 rm** ⌴ – ♦£ 85/100 ♦♦£ 230/260
**Rest** – (booking essential) Menu £ 28/44
♦ Charming Georgian dower house in a secluded spot, run by a delightful and
hospitable couple. The cooking is robust, gutsy and visually bold but without
gimmicks. Comfortable, stylish and immaculately kept bedrooms.

---

## YORK – York – 502 Q22 – pop. 198 900 📗 Great Britain                    23 C2

▶ London 203 mi – Kingston-upon-Hull 38 mi – Leeds 26 mi – Middlesbrough 51 mi
ℹ Museum St ℰ (01904) 55 00 99, www.visityork.org
🏌 Strensall Lords Moor Lane, ℰ (01904) 49 18 40
🏌 Heworth Muncastergate Muncaster House, ℰ (01904) 42 46 18
👁 City★★★ – Minster★★★ (Stained Glass★★★, Chapter House★★, Choir Screen★★)
CDY – National Railway Museum★★★ CY – The Walls★★ CDXYZ – Castle
Museum★ **AC** DZ **M2** – Jorvik Viking Centre★ **AC** DY **M1** – Fairfax House★ **AC** DY A
– The Shambles★ DY **54**

### 🏨  Cedar Court Grand H. & Spa           🔲 🐵 🕸 🎧 🛗 🏋 & rm, 🗚 📶 🍴 🄿

Station Rise ⊠ YO1 6HT – ℰ (01904) 380 038           🆅🅸🆂🅰 🐵 🄰🄴
– www.cedarcourtgrand.co.uk                                CYv
**94 rm** – ♦£ 125/295 ♦♦£ 125/295, ⌴ £ 20 – 13 suites
**Rest HQ** – ℰ (01904) 655 554 – Menu £ 25 (lunch) – Carte £ 35/48
♦ Early 20C building – the former offices of the North Eastern Railway Co. – where
original features blend with contemporary décor. Impressive spa and leisure facilities in cellar. Spacious bedrooms. Modern menu served in HQ, with views of the
castle walls.

### 🏤  Middlethorpe Hall          ← 🚗 🏊 🔲 🐵 🕸 🏋 🛗 & rm, 🍴 🍴 📶 🄿 🆅🅸🆂🅰 🐵 🄰🄴

Bishopthorpe Rd, South : 1.75 mi ⊠ YO23 2GB – ℰ (01904) 641 241
– www.middlethorpe.com
**20 rm** – ♦£ 99/189 ♦♦£ 199/269, ⌴ £ 7 – 9 suites
**Rest** – (booking essential for non-residents) Menu £ 24 (lunch) **s**
– Carte £ 35/54 **s**
♦ Impressive William and Mary country house dating from 1699. Elegantly and
carefully restored; abundantly furnished with antiques. Most characterful rooms
in main house. Wood-panelled, three-roomed restaurant with period feel.

### 🏤  Grange                        🍴 📶 🄿 🆅🅸🆂🅰 🐵 🄰🄴

1 Clifton ⊠ YO30 6AA – ℰ (01904) 644 744 – www.grangehotel.co.uk
**35 rm** ⌴ – ♦£ 123/180 ♦♦£ 168/208 – 1 suite           CXu
**Rest Ivy Brasserie** – see restaurant listing
**Rest New York Grill** – (closed Sunday lunch) Carte £ 26/38
♦ Well-run, classical Grade II listed hotel: floral decorations (by the owner) and
horse racing memorabilia abound. Choose between traditionally styled bedrooms
– some with four-posters – or more contemporary rooms with TVs in the bathrooms. Modern brasserie or informal grill with classical American à la carte.

### 🏤  Hotel du Vin                     🚗 🛗 & 🍴 📶 🄿 🆅🅸🆂🅰 🐵 🄰🄴 🅞

89 The Mount ⊠ YO24 1AX – ℰ (01904) 557 350 – www.hotelduvin.com
**44 rm** – ♦£ 210 ♦♦£ 210, ⌴ £ 14.50                     CZa
**Rest Bistro** – see restaurant listing
♦ Georgian house close to Knavesmire racecourse and just outside of city centre.
As part of a 'wine-orientated' group, the contemporary bedrooms boast smart,
wine-coloured themes.

| | | |
|---|---|---|
| Bishopgate St. | | |
| Bishophill Senior | CZ 3 | |
| Blake St. | CZ 4 | |
| Campleshon Rd. | CY 5 | |
| Church St. | AZ 7 | |
| Clifford St. | DY 8 | |
| Colliergate | DY 10 | |
| Coney St. | DY 12 | |
| Cromwell Rd. | DY 13 | |
| Davygate | CY 15 | |
| Deangate | CY 16 | |
| | DY 18 | |

| | | |
|---|---|---|
| Fawcett St. | DZ 21 | |
| Fetter Lane | CY 22 | |
| Goodramgate | DY 25 | |
| High Ousegate | CY 26 | |
| High Petergate | CY 28 | |
| Knavesmire Rd. | AZ 29 | |
| Leeman Rd. | AY, CY 30 | |
| Lendal | CY 32 | |
| Lord Mayor's Walk | DX 33 | |
| Low Petergate | DY 35 | |
| Melrosegate | BY 36 | |
| Museum St. | CY 39 | |
| Parliament St. | DY 42 | |

| | | |
|---|---|---|
| Peasholme Green | DY 45 | |
| Penley's Grove | | |
| St. | DX 46 | |
| Queen St. | CZ 49 | |
| St Helen's Rd. | AZ 50 | |
| St Leonard's Pl. | CY 52 | |
| St Maurice's Rd. | DXY 53 | |
| Shambles (The) | DY 54 | |
| Station Rd. | CY 55 | |
| Stonebow (The) | DY 56 | |
| Stonegate | CY 58 | |
| Tower St. | DZ 59 | |
| University Rd. | BZ 60 | |

A 1036 X      Y      A 1079  N

A 1079 (A 166) BRIDLINGTON
KINGSTON- UPON- HULL

ENGLAND

ENGLAND

### 🛏️ York Pavilion
🛜 ও rm, ⁽¹⁾ ♨ **P** **VISA** **⊕** **AE** **①**

*45 Main St, Fulford, South : 1.5 mi on A 19* ✉ *YO10 4PJ* – ℰ *(01904) 622 099*
*– www.yorkpavilionhotel.com*
**63 rm** ⚏ – **†**£ 79/135 **††**£ 99/135
**Rest** *Langtons Brasserie* – Carte £ 24/30
• Georgian house on main road in suburbs. Wood panelled reception and period-style lounge. Older, more individual rooms in main house and uniform chintzy style in extension. Informal dining.

### 🛏️ Dean Court
🛗 🄰 rest, ⅏ ⁽¹⁾ ♨ **P** **VISA** **⊕** **AE** **①**

*Duncombe Pl* ✉ *YO1 7EF* – ℰ *(01904) 625 082* – *www.deancourt-york.co.uk*
**37 rm** ⚏ – **†**£ 75/145 **††**£ 99/240                            CY
**Rest** *D.C.H* – *(dinner only and lunch Saturday-Sunday)* Menu £ 23 *(lunch)*
– Carte £ 30/40
• Built in the 1950s to house clerics visiting next door York Minster. Contemporary guest areas include a lounge-bar serving all day snacks. Bedrooms mix modern and classical styles; those with the best views are larger and smarter. Modern menu served in D.C.H.

### ⌂ Alexander House without rest
⅏ ⁽¹⁾ **P** **VISA** **⊕**

*94 Bishopthorpe Rd* ✉ *Y023 1JS* – ℰ *(01904) 625 016*
*– www.alexanderhouseyork.co.uk* – *Closed 11 December-13 January*
**4 rm** ⚏ – **†**£ 59/75 **††**£ 69/85                               CZ
• Classic Victorian terraced house, well run by particularly personable owners. Small lounge and brightly painted breakfast room displaying a collection of smart blue and white china. Clean, simply decorated bedrooms are named after different streets in the city.

### ⌂ Hazelwood without rest
⅏ ⁽¹⁾ **P** **VISA** **⊕**

*24-25 Portland St* ✉ *Y031 7EH* – ℰ *(01904) 626 548*
*– www.thehazelwoodyork.com* – *Restricted opening in January*          CX
**14 rm** ⚏ – **†**£ 65/120 **††**£ 125
• Two 19C town houses with characterful basement sitting room featuring original cooking range. Welcoming breakfast room in blue. Individual bedrooms, some with four posters.

### ⌂ Crook Lodge without rest
⅏ ⁽¹⁾ **P** **VISA** **⊕**

*26 St Mary's, Bootham* ✉ *YO30 7DD* – ℰ *(01904) 655 614*
*– www.crooklodge.co.uk*                                               CZ
**6 rm** ⚏ – **†**£ 60/80 **††**£ 75/85
• Privately owned, attractive Victorian redbrick house in quiet location. Basement breakfast room with original cooking range. Some rooms compact, all pleasantly decorated.

### ✕✕ Ivy Brasserie – at Grange Hotel
⇔ **P** **VISA** **⊕** **AE**

*1 Clifton* ✉ *YO30 6AA* – ℰ *(01904) 644 744* – *www.grangehotel.co.uk*
**Rest** – *(dinner only and Sunday lunch)* Carte £ 30/43                 CX
• Bright, leather-furnished brasserie with bold artwork and colourful murals, set in a keenly run hotel. Classically based British menu relies on local produce and displays touches of modernity.

### ✕✕ Melton's
🄰🄲 ⇔ **VISA** **⊕**

*7 Scarcroft Rd* ✉ *YO23 1ND* – ℰ *(01904) 634 341*
*– www.meltonsrestaurant.co.uk* – *Closed 3 weeks Christmas, Sunday and*
*Monday*                                                                CZ
**Rest** – *(booking essential)* Menu £ 25 *(lunch)* – Carte £ 30/35
• Glass fronted restaurant with mural decorated walls and neighbourhood feel. Smart, crisp tone in both service and table cover. Good modern British food with some originality.

ENGLAND

XX **J. Baker's**                                    AC VISA ◐◐ AE ◑

*7 Fossgate ⊠ YO1 9TA – ℰ (01904) 622 688 – www.jbakers.co.uk*
*– Closed first week January, Sunday and Monday*                    DYc
**Rest** – Menu £ 12/30 – Carte lunch £ 20/40
♦ Lively, double-fronted bistro on cobbled street, with simple, up-to-date interior.
Interesting modern dishes on the à la carte and grazing menus. Chocolate dessert
menu also served in the bar.

XX **Bistro** – at Hotel du Vin                          VISA ◐◐ AE ◑

*89 The Mount ⊠ YO24 1AX – ℰ (01904) 567 350 – www.hotelduvin.com*
**Rest** – French – Carte £ 27/41 ❀                              CZa
♦ Typical bustling Bistro offering modern French dishes as well as all the old fa-
vourites. Set in Hotel du Vin, it offers a good selection of wines by the glass.

X **Blue Bicycle** with rm                                   VISA ◐◐

*34 Fossgate ⊠ YO1 9TA – ℰ (01904) 673 990 – www.thebluebicycle.com*
*– Closed 25-26 December and lunch 27 and 31 December*
**6 rm** ⌓ – ♥£ 175 ♥♥£ 175                                       DYe
**Rest** – *(dinner only and lunch Thursday-Sunday and December) (booking
essential)* Carte £ 31/48
♦ Split-level restaurant with Mediterranean-style dining room and cosy bar. Menus offer modern classics: some simple, some more elaborate in style. Smart, studio style bedrooms in rear mews, each with a kitchen; create your own breakfast
from ingredients provided.

X **31 Castlegate**                                   ❀ VISA ◐◐ AE ◑

*31 Castlegate ⊠ YO1 9RN – ℰ (01904) 621 404 – www.31castlegate.co.uk*
*– Closed 25-26 December, 1 January and Monday*                    DYr
**Rest** – Menu £ 16 – Carte £ 27/31
♦ Former Georgian architect's house boasting original fireplaces and plasterwork.
Café atmosphere by day; more intimate restaurant by night. Classical cooking is
presented in a modern manner.

X **Melton's Too**                                    AC VISA ◐◐

*25 Walmgate ⊠ YO1 9TX – ℰ (01904) 629 222 – www.meltonstoo.co.uk*
*– Closed dinner 24 December-26 December and dinner 31 December-2 January*
**Rest** – Carte £ 20/24                                         DYa
♦ Café-bistro 'descendant' of Melton's restaurant. Located in former saddlers
shop with oak beams and exposed brick walls. Good value eclectic dishes, with
tapas a speciality.

**at Newton-on-Ouse** Northwest : 8 mi by A 19

🏠 **Dawnay Arms**                               🍴 🔥 P VISA ◐◐

*⊠ YO30 2BR – ℰ (01347) 848 345 – www.thedawnayatnewton.co.uk*
*– Closed 1 January, Sunday dinner and Monday except bank holidays*
**Rest** – Menu £ 15 (lunch) – Carte £ 23/34
♦ Spacious 18C inn boasting handsome rustic style, with beamed ceilings and
roaring fires. Tasty, good value dishes on seasonal menus. Dining room looks out
over River Ouse.

**ZENNOR** – Cornwall – 503 D33                                   **1** A3
🔺 London 305 mi – Penzance 11 mi – St Ives 5 mi

🏠 **Gurnard's Head** with rm                         🍴 P VISA ◐◐

*Treen, West : 1.5 mi on B 3306 ⊠ TR26 3DE – ℰ (01736) 796 928*
*– www.gurnardshead.co.uk – Closed 24 and 25 December*
**7 rm** ⌓ – ♥£ 70/85 ♥♥£ 90/110
**Rest** – Menu £ 17 (lunch) – Carte £ 25/29
♦ Remotely located and dog-friendly, with stone floors, shabby-chic décor, blaz-
ing fires and a relaxed, cosy feel. Simple menu relies on regional produce. Traditional puddings; interesting wine list. Comfy beds feature good quality linen;
communal breakfasts.

▶ Edinburgh 130 mi – Dundee 67 mi

🛧 Aberdeen Airport, Dyce : 𝒞 (0844) 481 6666, NW : 7 mi by A 96 X

🚢 to Shetland Islands (Lerwick) and via Orkney Islands (Stromness) (P and O Scottish Ferries) 1-2 daily

ℹ 23 Union St 𝒞 (01224) 28 88 28, www.aberdeen-grampian.com

🏌 Hazelhead Hazelhead Park, 𝒞 (01224) 32 18 30

🏌 Royal Aberdeen Bridge of Don Links Rd, 𝒞 (01224) 70 25 71

🏌 Balnagask St Fitticks Rd, 𝒞 (01224) 87 12 86

🏌 King's Links Golf Rd, 𝒞 (01224) 63 22 69

🏌 Portlethen Badentoy Rd, 𝒞 (01224) 78 10 90

🏌 Murcar Links Bridge of Don, 𝒞 (01224) 70 43 54

🏌 Auchmill West Heatheryfold Bonnyview Rd, 𝒞 (01224) 71 52 14

◉ City★★ - Old Aberdeen★★ X – St Machar's Cathedral★★ (West Front★★★, Heraldic Ceiling★★★) X **A** – Art Gallery★★ (Macdonald Collection★★) Y **M** – Mercat Cross★★ Y **B** – King's College Chapel★ (Crown Spire★★★, medieval fittings★★★) X **D** – Provost Skene's House★ (painted ceilings★★) Y **E** – Maritime Museum★ Z **M1** – Marischal College★ Y **U**

◎ Brig o' Balgownie★, by Don St X. SW : Deeside★★ - Crathes Castle★★ (Gardens★★★) **AC**, SW : 16 mi by A 93 X – Dunnottar Castle★★ **AC** (site★★★), S : 18 mi by A 90 X – Pitmedden Garden★★, N : 14 mi by A 90 on B 999 X – Castle Fraser★ (exterior★★) **AC**, W : 16 mi by A 944 X – Fyvie Castle★, NW : 26.5 mi on A 947

**SCOTLAND**

🏨🏨🏨 **Marcliffe H. and Spa**     🚗 🕪 🐶 ⅃ᵇ 📶 ⅙ 🎇 🎱 **P** 📧 VISA ⊕ 🄰🄴 ⊙
North Deeside Rd ⊠ AB15 9YA – 𝒞 (01224) 861 000 – www.marcliffe.com
**40 rm** ⊒ – †£ 165/229 ††£ 185/249 – 2 suites    Xr
**Rest Conservatory** – see restaurant listing
♦ Spacious, professionally run, modern country house; popular with business travellers. Eleven acres of pleasant grounds. Individually decorated rooms with antique furniture. Small spa and hairdressing salon.

🏨🏨 **Malmaison**     ⅃ᵇ 📶 ⅙ 🎇 🎱 **P** VISA ⊕ 🄰🄴
49-53 Queens Rd ⊠ AB15 4YP – 𝒞 (01224) 327 370 – www.malmaison.com
**79 rm** – †£ 195 ††£ 215, ⊒ £ 14.50    Xv
**Rest Brasserie** – see restaurant listing
♦ Located in a smart city suburb and built around a period property; now the height of urban chic. Black slate floored reception adorned with bagpipes and kilts; stylish bar with whisky cellar. Luxurious tartan bedrooms boast smart bathrooms.

🏨 **bauhaus**     📶 ⅙ rm, 🄰🄲 rest, 🎇 🎇 🎱 VISA ⊕ 🄰🄴
52-60 Langstane Pl. ⊠ AB11 6EN – 𝒞 (01224) 212 122 – www.thebauhaus.co.uk
**38 rm** ⊒ – †£ 90/115 ††£ 70/115 – 1 suite    Zr
**Rest** – Menu £ 28 – Carte £ 20/38
♦ Modern hotel just off the main street; its functional, minimalist style in keeping with the Bauhaus school of design. Trendy lounge. Stylish, colour-coded bedrooms with sharp, clean lines and uncluttered feel; Gropius and Kandinsky are the best. First-floor restaurant offers accessible menu of modern classics.

🏨 **Atholl**     ⅙ rm, 🎇 🕪 🎱 **P** VISA ⊕ 🄰🄴
54 King's Gate ⊠ AB15 4YN – 𝒞 (01224) 323 505 – www.atholl-aberdeen.com – Closed 1 January
**34 rm** ⊒ – †£ 95/110 ††£ 145    **Rest** – Carte £ 18/32    Xs
♦ Baronial style hotel set in leafy suburbs; well run by friendly staff. Traditional lounge bar; well-priced, up-to-date rooms. A useful address for visitors to the city. Dining room specialises in tried-and-tested Scottish cooking.

🍴🍴🍴 **Conservatory** – at Marcliffe Hotel and Spa     🚗 🍴 🄰🄲 **P** VISA ⊕ 🄰🄴 ⊙
North Deeside Rd ⊠ AB15 9YA – 𝒞 (01224) 861 000 – www.marcliffe.com
**Rest** – Carte £ 37/50 s 🕸    Xr
♦ Spacious conservatory dining room with large open kitchen. Good-sized classical menu offers hearty tasty dishes, including superbly flavourful steaks; king crab is a speciality. Warm service and a relaxing atmosphere.

FRASERBURGH    Brig o' Balgownie    A 956    FRASERBURGH (A 90)

**ABERDEEN**
BUILT UP AREA

0 — 1 km
0 — 1/2 mile

SCOTLAND

SHETLAND ISLANDS / ORKNEY ISLANDS

XX **Fusion**                                    AC ⇆ VISA ⦿ AE

*10 North Silver St* ⊠ *AB10 1RL* – ℰ *(01224) 652 959* – *www.fusionbarbistro.com*
– *Closed 2 weeks January, 2 weeks July, 25 December, Sunday and Monday*
**Rest** – *(dinner only)* Menu £ 28                                    **Zc**
♦ Very stylish, modernised townhouse with cavernous, stark white room, neatly laid tables and designer touches. Concise monthly menu offers creative modern dishes in well-presented, interesting combinations. The bar is the place to be seen.

XX **Silver Darling**                          ⇆ ⇆ VISA ⦿ AE ⓞ

*Pocra Quay, North Pier* ⊠ *AB11 5DQ* – ℰ *(01224) 576 229*
– *www.thesilverdarlingrestaurant.co.uk* – *Closed 2 weeks Christmas-New Year,*
*Saturday lunch, Sunday dinner and Sunday lunch in winter*                **Xa**
**Rest** – Seafood – Menu £ 22 (lunch) – Carte £ 33/50
♦ Former customs house attractively set at port entrance; panoramic views across harbour and coastline. Attentive service of superb quality seafood prepared in imaginative ways.

XX **Brasserie** – at Malmaison Hotel          ⌂ AC P VISA ⦿ AE

*49-53 Queens Rd* ⊠ *AB15 4YP* – ℰ *(01224) 327 370* – *www.malmaison.com*
**Rest** – Beef specialities – Menu £ 20 (early dinner Friday & Saturday)      **Xv**
– Carte £ 22/54
♦ Vast hotel brasserie with high ceiling, tartan and red leather banquettes and huge photos of foodstuffs on the walls. Accessible menu of classics; speciality steaks can be viewed in the meat room and are then cooked on the Josper grill.

## ✗✗ Courtyard ⇆ VISA 𝟎𝟎 AE

*1 Alford Pl ⊠ AB10 1YD – 𝒞 (01224) 589 109 – www.thecourtyardaberdeen.co.uk
– Closed first week January and Sunday* **Zx**

**Rest** – Menu £ 16/37

◆ Contemporary restaurant with modern bar, linen-clad tables and efficient service. Menus feature up-to-date classics: lunch offers simple dishes and a set menu;
dinner is more elaborate and includes a blackboard of local seafood specials.

## ✗✗ Stella 𝟘𝟫 VISA 𝟎𝟎

*28 Adelphi ⊠ AB11 5BL – 𝒞 (01224) 211 414 – www.lastella.co.uk – Closed Sunday*

**Rest** – Menu £ 16/37 **Zs**

◆ Snug bistro hidden away down a side street, with simple, bright décor and a
neighbourhood feel. Seasonally changing menus focus on quality ingredients,
with fish a speciality.

SCOTLAND

XX **Nargile**　　　　　　　　　　　AC VISA ©© AE ©

*77-79 Skene St ⊠ AB10 1QD – ℰ (01224) 636 093 – closed 25-26 December,*
*1 January, Monday lunch and Sunday*　　　　　　　**Y**a
**Rest** – Turkish – Menu £ 25 – Carte £ 20/34

♦ Traditionally decorated Turkish restaurant with subdued lighting from Turkish lamps. Open-plan kitchen allows the diner to watch the chefs prepare the authentic dishes.

X **Rendezvous at Nargile**　　　　　　　AC VISA ©© AE

*106-108 Forest Ave ⊠ AB15 4UP – ℰ (01224) 323 700*
*– www.rendezvousatnargile.co.uk – Closed 1-2 January and 25-26 December*
**Rest** – Turkish – Menu £ 19 – Carte £ 23/28　　　　　**X**i

♦ Bright, refreshing neighbourhood restaurant set opposite the Rendezvous Gallery. All day menus offer plenty of choice, with cooking influenced by the Mediterranean, and in particular, Turkey.

---

**ABERFELDY** – Perth and Kinross – **501** I14 – pop. 1 895　　**28** C2

▶ Edinburgh 75 mi – Dunkeld 17 mi – Pitlochry 14 mi

**at Fortingall** West : 8 mi by B 846 on Fortingall rd

🏠 **Fortingall**　　　　　　＜ ⇊ ⏸ ⤳ ᴾ VISA ©©

⊠ PH15 2NQ – ℰ (01887) 830 367 – www.fortingall.com
**10 rm** ⌷ – ♥♥£ 150/250
**Rest** – Carte £ 20/46

♦ Arts and Crafts style house on tranquil private estate, boasting lovely country views. Stylish interior with contemporary country fabrics. Modern bedrooms remain in keeping with the building's age. Light snacks in cosy bar; contemporary cooking in restaurant.

---

**ABRIACHAN** – Highland – **501** G11 – pop. 120　　　　**30** C2

▶ London 573 mi – Edinburgh 168 mi – Inverness 11 mi – Elgin 50 mi

🏨 **Loch Ness Lodge**　　　＜ ⇊ ⏸ ⤳ ⧉ ⚡ ᴾ VISA ©© AE

*Brachla, on A 82 ⊠ IV3 8LA – ℰ (01456) 459 469 – www.loch-ness-lodge.com*
*– Closed first 3 weeks January and 23-27 December*
**7 rm** (dinner included) ⌷ – ♥£ 224/269 ♥♥£ 334/379
**Rest** – (dinner only) (booking essential to non residents) Carte approx. £ 55

♦ Comfortable, modern country house overlooking Loch Ness; warmly decorated, spacious bedrooms boast a high level of facilities. Sauna and hot tub for guests. Daily changing 5 course menu uses Scottish produce; cooking is flavourful and classically based. Linen laid dining room with excellent views; attentive service.

---

**ACHILTIBUIE** – Highland – **501** D9　　　　　　　**30** C1

▶ Edinburgh 243 mi – Inverness 84 mi – Ullapool 25 mi

🏨 **Summer Isles** ⌂　　　　　＜ ⇊ ⤳ ⚡ ᴾ VISA ©©

⊠ IV26 2YG – ℰ (01854) 622 282 – www.summerisleshotel.com – April to
October
**10 rm** ⌷ – ♥£ 115/155 ♥♥£ 155/190 – 3 suites
**Rest Summer Isles (Bar)** – see restaurant listing
**Rest** – (booking essential) (set menu only at dinner, light seafood lunch)
Menu £ 58

♦ Remotely located hotel, with magnificent views over the eponymous islands. Individually styled, comfortable bedrooms split between main house and various converted outbuildings. Pleasant restaurant, with polished, well-set tables. Daily set menu of traditional dishes, with emphasis on seafood.

SCOTLAND

🏠 **Summer Isles (Bar)** – at Summer Isles Hotel    🏠 P VISA 💳
✉ IV26 2YG – ℰ (01854) 622 282 – www.summerisleshotel.com
– April-October
**Rest** – Seafood – (bookings not accepted) Carte £ 14/30
♦ 19C former crofters' bar boasting two snug rooms, a large garden and a small terrace with glorious views. Daily changing menus feature local ingredients and have a strong seafood base.

---

**ALYTH** – Perth and Kinross – **501** J14 – pop. 2 301     **28** C2
▶ Edinburgh 63 mi – Aberdeen 69 mi – Dundee 16 mi – Perth 21 mi
🏠 Pitcrocknie, ℰ (01828) 63 22 68

🏠 **Tigh Na Leigh**    🏊 📶 P VISA 💳 AE
22-24 Airlie St ✉ PH11 8AJ – ℰ (01828) 632 372 – www.tighnaleigh.co.uk
– Closed 24 December-4 February
**5 rm** 🍽 – †£ 43/75 ††£ 107/125   **Rest** – (residents only) Menu £ 28
♦ Imposing Victorian house, once owned by a doctor, run in a professional yet relaxed manner. Surprisingly modern interior with spacious, inviting guest areas. Contemporary bedrooms boast feature beds and great bathrooms; some have spa baths. Superb kitchen garden informs unfussy modern menu; great garden view.

---

**ANNBANK** – South Ayrshire – **501** G17 – pop. 854     **25** B2
▶ Edinburgh 84 mi – Ayr 6 mi – Dumfries 54 mi – Paisley 34 mi

🏠 **Enterkine** 🌳    ⇐ 🏊 🐾 🐕 📶 🔒 P VISA 💳
Southeast : 0.5 mi on B 742 (Coylton rd) ✉ KA6 5AL – ℰ (01292) 520 580
– www.enterkine.com
**13 rm** 🍽 – †£ 60/85 ††£ 100/150 – 1 suite
**Rest** – (booking essential) Menu £ 19 (lunch) – Carte £ 29/47
♦ 1930s country house surrounded by extensive gardens and woodlands. Spacious, comfortable lounges. Luxurious bedrooms; one with large roof terrace. Charming library. Formal restaurant with views over River Ayr serves modern cooking; popular with non-residents.

---

**ANSTRUTHER** – Fife – **501** L15 – pop. 3 442 📖 Scotland     **28** D2
▶ Edinburgh 46 mi – Dundee 23 mi – Dunfermline 34 mi
ℹ Harbourhead ℰ (01333) 31 10 73, www.visitscotland.com
🏠 Marsfield Shore Rd, ℰ (01333) 31 09 56
◉ Scottish Fisheries Museum★★ AC
🟢 The East Neuk★★ – Crail★★ (Old Centre★★, Upper Crail★) NE : 4 mi by A 917. Kellie Castle★ AC, NW : 7 mi by B 9171, B 942 and A 917

🏠 **Spindrift**    📶 P VISA 💳 AE
Pittenweem Rd ✉ KY10 3DT – ℰ (01333) 310 573 – www.thespindrift.co.uk
– Closed January and 24-26 December
**8 rm** 🍽 – †£ 45/65 ††£ 60/80   **Rest** – Menu £ 23
♦ Detached Victorian house on the edge of the village, originally owned by a tea clipper captain. Comfortable lounge with honesty bar. Cosy, individually furnished bedrooms, some with distant sea views – opt for the top floor Captain's Cabin. Homely cooking relies on local produce, with seafood from East Neuk to the fore.

✕✕ **Cellar**    VISA 💳 AE ①
24 East Green ✉ KY10 3AA – ℰ (01333) 310 378 – www.cellaranstruther.co.uk
– Closed 24-26 December, Monday in winter and Sunday
**Rest** – Seafood – (booking essential) Menu £ 25/40
♦ Long-standing restaurant hidden behind the Fisheries Museum. Atmospheric beamed room with flickering candlelight and open fire. Simply prepared, fresh, quality seafood from Scottish waters.

SCOTLAND

▶ London 639 mi – Edinburgh 234 mi – Gairloch 56 mi – Portree 76 mi

---

X     **Applecross Walled Garden**                     🚗 🏠 **P** **VISA** **①** **AE** **①**
*Northeast : 0.5 mi ⊠ IV54 8ND – ℰ (01520) 744 440*
*– www.applecrossgarden.co.uk – February-October*
**Rest** – Menu £ 22 (dinner) – Carte £ 17/29
♦ Lovely 17C walled kitchen garden whose restaurant has grown from a tea-room. Its simple structure belies its tasty dishes, fresh from owner's fishing boat or the garden itself.

---

🏠     **Applecross Inn** with rm                        ← 🚗 🏠 ও **P** **VISA** **①**
*Shore St ⊠ IV54 8LR – ℰ (01520) 744 262 – www.applecross.uk.com – Closed 25 December and 1 January*
**7 rm** ☞ – ♦£ 70/80 ♦♦£ 100/120   **Rest** – *(booking essential)* Carte £ 18/27
♦ Charming Highland inn set in an extremely remote location, boasting stunning water and hill views. Menus feature local, seasonal produce from the nearby estate and bay; seafood a speciality. Set in old fishermen's cottages, smart, comfy bedrooms boast sea views.

---

**ARBROATH** – Angus – **501** M14 – pop. 22 785                      **28** D2

▶ Edinburgh 72 mi – Dundee 17 mi – Montrose 12 mi

↑     **Old Vicarage** without rest                     🚗 ও ⁕ ⁖ **P** **VISA** **①** **AE**
*2 Seaton Rd, Northeast : 0.75 mi by A 92 and Hayshead Rd ⊠ DD11 5DX*
*– ℰ (01241) 430 475 – www.theoldvicaragebandb.co.uk*
**3 rm** ☞ – ♦♦£ 80/90
♦ Detached 19C house, of large proportions, clothed in Victorian style throughout. Antique furnished bedrooms: ask for view of Arbroath Abbey.

---

**ARCHIESTOWN** – Moray – **501** K11 – ⊠ Aberlour (aberdeenshire)   **28** C1

▶ Edinburgh 194 mi – Aberdeen 62 mi – Inverness 49 mi

🏠     **Archiestown**                          🚗 ⁖ 🏠 ⁕ ⁖ **P** **VISA** **①** **AE**
*The Square ⊠ AB38 7QL – ℰ (01340) 810 218 – www.archiestownhotel.co.uk*
*– Closed 2 January-10 February and 22-29 December*
**11 rm** ☞ – ♦£ 60/100 ♦♦£ 130/160
**Rest** *Bistro* – Menu £ 17/30
♦ Welcoming hotel hidden away in a small hamlet; ideally located for shooters/-fishermen. Spacious, comfy sitting rooms with warming open fires. Cosy bedrooms, many boasting country views. Daily changing dishes in laid-back bistro.

---

**ARDHASAIG** – Western Isles – **501** Z10 – see Lewis and Harris (Isle of)

---

**ARDUAINE** – Argyll and Bute – **501** D15 – ⊠ Oban ▌ Scotland    **27** B2

▶ Edinburgh 142 mi – Oban 20 mi

🄶 Loch Awe★★, E : 12 mi by A 816 and B 840

🏠     **Loch Melfort** ☞                          ← 🚗 ⏏ 🏠 **P** **VISA** **①**
*⊠ PA34 4XG – ℰ (01852) 200 233 – www.lochmelfort.co.uk*
*– Closed 2 weeks January*
**25 rm** (dinner included) ☞ – ♦£ 128 ♦♦£ 196/306
**Rest** *Asknish Bay* – see restaurant listing
**Rest** *Chartroom II* – Carte £ 20/35
♦ Large hotel next to the beautiful Arduaine Gardens, affording superb views out over the bay and Sound of Jura. Modern lounges with tartan/nautical themes. Bigger bedrooms in the main house; great outlook from private terraces in the wing. Simple, largely seafood menu in Chartroom II; more formal Asknish Bay.

XX **Asknish Bay** – at Loch Melfort Hotel  ≤ ⊜ ⠪ 🄿 ⦿ ⦿
✉ PA34 4XG – 𝒞 (01852) 200 233 – www.lochmelfort.co.uk – Closed 2 weeks January
**Rest** – Seafood – (dinner only) Menu £ 37 – Carte £ 26/38
♦ Formal hotel restaurant boasting fantastic bay views. Daily 5 course menu and à la carte showcase local produce; everything from bread to ice cream is home-made. Sunday seafood buffet in July/Aug.

**ARRAN (Isle of)** – North Ayrshire – **501** E17 – pop. 5 058 🗓 Scotland   **25** A2
▶ London 449 mi – Edinburgh 95 mi – Glasgow 45 mi – Paisley 31 mi
⛴ from Brodick to Ardrossan (Caledonian MacBrayne Ltd) 4-6 daily (55 mn) – from Lochranza to Kintyre Peninsula (Claonaig) (Caledonian MacBrayne Ltd) frequent services daily (30 mn) – from Brodick to Isle of Bute (Rothesay) (Caledonian MacBrayne Ltd) 3 weekly (2 h 5 mn)
◉ Island★★ - Brodick Castle★★ **AC**

**BRODICK** – North Ayrshire – pop. 621   **25** A2
🄹 Welcome Centre 𝒞 (01770) 30 37 76, www.visitscotland.com
🄸 Brodick, 𝒞 (01770) 30 23 49
🄹 Machrie Bay, 𝒞 (01770) 85 02 32

🏨 **Auchrannie**   ⊜ ⠪ ➘ 🏞 🗔 🐾 ⛱ 🛏 🍴 rm, ⚹⚹ ❡ 🏋 🄿 ⦿ ⦿ ⧄
Northwest : 0.75 mi by Shore Rd. ✉ KA27 8BZ – 𝒞 (01770) 302 234 – www.auchrannie.co.uk
**64 rm** – ♦£ 80/115 ♦♦£ 109/204, ⌷ £ 12.95
**Rest Eighteen69** – (closed November-March except Christmas, Sunday and Monday) (dinner only) Menu £ 33 – Carte £ 32/48
**Rest Brambles** – Carte £ 26/45
**Rest Cruize** – Carte £ 21/33
♦ Mini resort hotel set in 96 acres and offering a good range of family orientated leisure facilities. Built in 1869, the old dower house boasts well-equipped, classical and contemporary bedrooms; family rooms are located in the spa house. Smart conservatory restaurant offers fine dining menu; Brambles serves seafood and grills; all-day Cruize is ideal for families.

🏨 **Kilmichael Country House** ⌾   ⊜ 🄿 ⦿ ⦿
Glen Cloy, West : 1 mi by Shore Rd, taking left turn opposite Golf Club
✉ KA27 8BY – 𝒞 (01770) 302 219 – www.kilmichael.com – Easter-October
**5 rm** ⌷ – ♦£ 78/98 ♦♦£ 130/163 – 3 suites
**Rest** – (Closed Monday and Tuesday) (dinner only) (booking essential) Menu £ 45
♦ Reputedly the oldest house on the Isle of Arran, in peaceful location with im-maculate lawned grounds. Comfortable country house style and individually dec-orated bedrooms. Welcoming owners. Restaurant housed in extension. Daily-changing menus.

🏨 **Douglas**   ≤ ⊜ 🏞 🖪 ⛱ rm, ⌖ ❡ 🄿 ⦿ ⦿
✉ KA27 8AW – 𝒞 (01770) 302 968 – www.thedouglashotel.co.uk
**21 rm** ⌷ – ♦£ 90/135 ♦♦£ 90/250
**Rest Bistro** – Carte £ 25/34
♦ Set just past the ferry terminal and thought to have been built in 1830 by the occupants of the nearby castle to accommodate their guests. Spacious, light-filled bedrooms are decorated in a contemporary style; one has a large roof terrace. Large bistro offers classical French dishes with slight modern twists.

🏠 **Alltan** without rest   ⊜ ⌖ ❡ 🄿
Knowe Rd, West : 0.5 mi by Shore Rd taking left at Golf Club ✉ KA27 8BY
– 𝒞 (01770) 302 937 – www.alltanarran.co.uk – March-October
**3 rm** ⌷ – ♦£ 72 ♦♦£ 80
♦ Friendly, modern guesthouse built into the hillside, not far from the ferry termi-nal; an ideal base for exploring the island. Communal breakfast room, decked bal-cony and comfy lounge overlooking the garden and river. Bright, fresh bedrooms.

SCOTLAND

**LAMLASH** – North Ayrshire – pop. 1 010 – ⊠ Brodick
 Lamlash, ✆ (01770) 60 02 96

| ⌂ | **Glenisle** | ⟨ 🚗 🈂 🐾 🍴 P VISA ⓒⓑ |

*Shore Rd.* ⊠ *KA27 8LY* – ✆ *(01770) 600 559* – *www.glenislehotel.com*
**13 rm** ⊇ – ♦£ 75/100 ♦♦£ 168/184
**Rest** – Carte £ 19/31
♦ Attractive whitewashed Victorian property, formerly an inn, boasting views over the bay to Holy Island. Open-plan bar-lounge and small snug. Bright, airy bedrooms come in natural hues; one covers the whole top floor and has a roll-top bath. Rustic dining room with terrace offers fresh, simple, homely cooking.

**LOCHRANZA**

| ⌃ | **Apple Lodge** | ⟨ 🚗 🐾 P |

⊠ *KA27 8HJ* – ✆ *(01770) 830 229* – *Closed 15 December-15 January,minimum 3 night stay in high season*
**4 rm** ⊇ – ♦£ 54 ♦♦£ 78    **Rest** – *(closed July-August and Tuesday)* Menu £ 25
♦ Extended period house with small garden and pleasing views, in centre of quiet village. Homely cottage-style decor with antique furniture and a welcoming atmosphere. Food is home-cooked and uses island and home produce in good, hearty, varied dishes.

**ASCOG** – Argyll and Bute – **501** E16 – see Bute (Isle of)

**AUCHENCAIRN** – Dumfries and Galloway – **501** I19        **25** B3
– ⊠ Castle Douglas
▶ Edinburgh 94 mi – Dumfries 21 mi – Stranraer 60 mi

| ⌃ | **Balcary Mews** without rest ⌂ | ⟨ 🚗 🐾 🍴 P |

*Balcary Bay, Southeast : 2 mi on Balcary rd* ⊠ *DG7 1QZ* – ✆ *(01556) 640 270* – *www.balcarymews.co.uk* – *Closed mid December to mid January*
**3 rm** ⊇ – ♦£ 55 ♦♦£ 80
♦ Former mews for the neighbouring country house, boasting superb views over Balcary Bay and the Solway Firth. Lovely garden with a gate down to the shore. Neat sun lounge and traditional bedrooms; all have views. Homemade bread and jam feature at breakfast.

**AUCHTERARDER** – Perth and Kinross – **501** I15 – pop. 3 945        **28** C2
▮ Scotland
▶ Edinburgh 55 mi – Glasgow 45 mi – Perth 14 mi
 Ochil Rd, ✆ (01764) 66 28 04
▮ Dunning Rollo Park, ✆ (01764) 68 47 47
▮ Tullibardine Chapel★, NW : 2 m

| ⌂⌂⌂⌂ | **Gleneagles** | ⟨ 🚗 🐕 🎣 🈂 🖥 ⓢ ♨ ⅙ 🍴 🎬 🛎 ᵹ rm, ✶ 🍴 💆 P |
| | | VISA ⓒⓑ AE ⓞ |

*Southwest : 2 mi by A 824 on A 823* ⊠ *PH3 1NF*
– ✆ *(01764) 662 231* – *www.gleneagles.com*
**216 rm** ⊇ – ♦♦£ 315/435 – 16 suites
**Rest** *Andrew Fairlie at Gleneagles*❀❀ – see restaurant listing
**Rest** *Strathearn* – ✆ *(01764) 694 270 (dinner only and Sunday lunch)*
Menu £ 58
**Rest** *Deseo* – ✆ *(01764) 694 270* – Carte £ 25/58
♦ World-famous resort hotel with renowned championship golf course. Excellent leisure facilities include state-of-the-art spa, popular equestrian centre and gun-dog school. Majestic, art deco styling, elegant interior and luxurious bedrooms. Strathearn offers classical menu and superb estate views. All-day Deseo serves Mediterranean-influenced dishes, including tapas.

XXXX **Andrew Fairlie at Gleneagles**     AK P VISA OO AE O

✿✿ *Southwest : 2 mi by A 824 on A 823* ✉ *PH3 1NF* – ✆ *(01764) 694 267*
*– www.andrewfairlie.co.uk – Closed 3 weeks January, 24-25 December and
Sunday*
**Rest** – *(dinner only)* Menu £ 85/95
**Spec.** Home smoked lobster, lime and herb butter. Slow cooked rump and shoulder of beef, soy and balsamic. Hot mango soufflé, piña colada sorbet and exotic
fruit sauce.
♦ Elegant, understated restaurant where reserved yet passionate chef creates
precise, balanced, flavourful dishes with a refined French style and Scottish
edge. Concise à la carte includes signature smoked lobster. Dégustation
menu showcases dishes 'en miniature'. Menu du Marché offers latest seasonal
produce.

---

# AVIEMORE – Highland – **501** I12 – pop. 2 397 ▌ Scotland     30 D3

▶ Edinburgh 129 mi – Inverness 29 mi – Perth 85 mi

🛈 Grampian Rd ✆ (08452) 25 51 21, www.visitcairngorms.com

◎ Town ★

◎ The Cairngorms ★★ ( ≤ ★★★) - ✳ ★★★ from Cairn Gorm, SE : 11 mi by B 970
– Landmark Visitor Centre (The Highlander ★) **AC**, N : 7 mi by A 9 – Highland
Wildlife Park ★ **AC**, SW : 7 mi by A 9

⌂ **Old Minister's Guest House** without rest    ⛻ ⅍ 🛜 P VISA OO AE
*Rothiemurchus, Southeast : 1 mi on B 970* ✉ *PH22 1QH* – ✆ *(01479) 812 181*
*– www.theoldministershouse.co.uk*
**4 rm** ⌑ – †£ 45/65 ††£ 90/96
♦ Early 20C house on outskirts of town, with a river at the bottom of its pretty
garden. Nicely-laid breakfast room. Spacious bedrooms, finished to high standard.

---

# AYR – South Ayrshire – **501** G17 – pop. 46 431 ▌ Scotland     25 A2

▶ Edinburgh 81 mi – Glasgow 35 mi

🛈 22 Sandgate ✆ (01292) 29 03 00, www.visitscotland.com

🔞 Seafield Doonfoot Rd, Belleisle Park, ✆ (01292) 44 12 58

🔞 Dalmilling Westwood Ave, ✆ (01292) 26 38 93

🔞 Doon Valley Patna Hillside, ✆ (01292) 53 16 07

◎ Alloway ★ (Burns Cottage and Museum ★ **AC**) S : 3 mi by B 7024 BZ. Culzean
Castle ★ **AC** (setting ★★★, Oval Staircase ★★) SW : 13 mi by A 719 BZ

⌂ **No.26 The Crescent** without rest    ⅍ 🛜 VISA OO O
🏠 *26 Bellevue Cres* ✉ *KA7 2DR* – ✆ *(01292) 287 329 – www.26crescent.co.uk*
**5 rm** ⌑ – †£ 45/70 ††£ 70/80      BZc
♦ Well-run Georgian terraced guesthouse, displaying a pleasing mix of traditional
features – such as original fireplaces – and smart, modern décor. Comfortable
throughout, boasting cosy, individually furnished bedrooms; the best one, at the
front, has a four-poster.

⌂ **Coila** without rest    ⅍ 🛜 P VISA OO AE
🏠 *10 Holmston Rd* ✉ *KA7 3BB* – ✆ *(01292) 262 642 – www.coila.co.uk*
**4 rm** ⌑ – †£ 35/50 ††£ 55/80      AYu
♦ Spotlessly kept Georgian guesthouse on the edge of town, proudly decorated
with the owners' personal ornaments and family photos. Warm, homely lounge
and small breakfast room. Well-kept bedrooms with king-sized beds and modern
facilities. Very warm welcome.

SCOTLAND

## AYR AND PRESTWICK

**SCOTLAND**

---

**BALLACHULISH** – Highland – **501** E13 – pop. 615 🏴 Scotland    **30** C3

🇩 Edinburgh 117 mi – Inverness 80 mi – Kyle of Lochalsh 90 mi
   – Oban 38 mi

🇮 Loan sern ℰ (01855) 81 18 66, www.glencoetourism.co.uk

🇬 Glen Coe★★, E : 6 mi by A 82

---

⌂ **Ardno House** without rest    ⪻ 🛋 ⅋ ⁽ᵗ⁾ 🅿
Lettermore, Glencoe, West : 3.5 mi by A 82 on A 828 ⊠ PH49 4JD
– ℰ (01855) 811 830 – www.ardnohouse.co.uk
– February-October
**4 rm** ⌹ – ♦£ 48/56 ♦♦£ 76/86
♦ Purpose-built guesthouse with fine view of Loch Linnhe and the Morven Hills.
Personally run and providing good value, comfortable accommodation. Spacious
bedrooms.

---

Guesthouses ⌂ don't provide the same level of service as hotels.
They are often characterised by a warm welcome and a décor
which reflects the owner's personality. Those shown in red ⌂
are particularly pleasant.

▶ Edinburgh 115 mi – Ayr 33 mi – Stranraer 18 mi

**SCOTLAND**

### 🏨 Glenapp Castle ⌂ ← 🚗 ⌄ ⌙ ⌖ ✗ 📶 📞 P VISA ⓒ AE

❀ South : 1 mi by A 77 taking first right turn after bridge ✉ KA26 0NZ – ℰ (01465) 831 212 – www.glenappcastle.com – Closed 2 January to mid-March and 1 week Christmas

**14 rm** (dinner included) ☲ – ♦£ 265/285 ♦♦£ 415/620 – 3 suites
**Rest** – (booking essential for non-residents) Menu £ 38/60
**Spec.** Wild halibut with smoked haddock brandade, garlic and lemon purée. Milk-fed pork, trotter cromesquis, rhubarb and crackling. Cranachan soufflé with oat-meal and whisky.

♦ Long wooded drive leads to beautifully manicured gardens and stunning baro-nial castle. Grand antique-filled interior boasts oak-panelled hallways, impressively proportioned lounges, handsomely appointed bedrooms and Ailsa Craig views. Intimate formal dining room, where confident, focused cooking employs a wealth of local ingredients, including herbs from the garden.

### 🏠 Cosses Country House ⌂ 🚗 ⌙ 📶 P VISA ⓒ

East : 2.25 mi by A 77 (South) taking first turn left after bridge ✉ KA26 0LR – ℰ (01465) 831 363 – www.cossescountryhouse.com – Restricted opening in winter

**3 rm** ☲ – ♦£ 75 ♦♦£ 90/110 **Rest** – Menu £ 35

♦ 17C shooting lodge with lovely gardens, in idyllic rural location. Immaculately kept bedrooms – some in the old stables and byre – boast iPod docks, fresh flowers and underfloor heated bathrooms. Homemade cake on arrival in the kitchen, dining room or garden. 4 course, single-choice set dinner uses local/gar-den produce.

▶ Edinburgh 111 mi – Aberdeen 41 mi – Inverness 70 mi – Perth 67 mi
🛈 Station Square ℰ (013397) 5 53 06, www.visitballater.com
🏌 Victoria Rd, ℰ (013397) 5 55 67

### 🏨 Darroch Learg ← 🚗 P VISA ⓒ

Braemar Rd ✉ AB35 5UX – ℰ (013397) 55 443 – www.darrochlearg.co.uk – Closed last 3 weeks January and Christmas
**12 rm** (dinner included) ☲ – ♦£ 130/195 ♦♦£ 210/330
**Rest** *Conservatory* – see restaurant listing

♦ Late Victorian country house affording superb views over the Dee Valley and Grampians. Personally run by the second family generation, it boasts comfy, open-fired, antique-furnished lounges and traditional, individually designed bed-rooms.

### 🏠 Moorside House without rest 🚗 ⌇ 📶 P VISA ⓒ

26 Braemar Rd ✉ AB35 5RL – ℰ (013397) 55 492 – www.moorsidehouse.co.uk – April-October
**9 rm** ☲ – ♦£ 45 ♦♦£ 65

♦ 19C former manse with large garden, simple, homely bedrooms and comfy lounge filled with books about the local area. Original Victorian features include ornate cornicing and an attractive pine staircase. Hearty breakfasts feature home-made bread and preserves.

### ✗✗ Conservatory – at Darroch Learg Hotel ← 🚗 P VISA ⓒ ⓞ

Braemar Rd ✉ AB35 5UX – ℰ (013397) 55 443 – www.darrochlearg.co.uk – Closed last 3 weeks January and Christmas
**Rest** – (dinner only and Sunday lunch) Menu £ 45

♦ Conservatory dining room in a Victorian country house, boasting attractive mountain views from majority of its smartly laid tables. Concise menu with quality seasonal ingredients to the fore; carefully judged, well-crafted modern cooking.

XX **Green Inn** with rm                    (¶) VISA ⓒⓑ
*9 Victoria Rd ⊠ AB35 5QQ – ℰ (013397) 55 701 – www.green-inn.com*
*– Closed December, Sunday in winter and Tuesday*
**2 rm** – †£ 80 ††£ 80, ⌁ £ 12.50
**Rest** – *(dinner only) (booking essential)* Menu £ 45
♦ Former temperance hall, opposite the green, boasting comfy lounges and pleasant conservatory. Interesting, well sourced and accomplished modern British cooking. Cosy rooms.

XX **Auld Kirk** with rm                    (¶) P VISA ⓒⓑ
*Braemar Rd ⊠ AB35 5RQ – ℰ (013397) 55 762 – www.theauldkirk.com – Closed January, 25-26 December and Monday*
**6 rm** ⌁ – †£ 65/73 ††£ 110/140
**Rest** – *(dinner only and Sunday lunch)* Menu £ 38
♦ Built in 1870 and operating as a church until 1938. The stylish modern bar and lounge contrast with original windows and a pine panelled ceiling in the elegant dining room. Concise menu offers elaborate dishes in well-matched combinations. Pleasant, comfortable bedrooms come with smart, fully tiled bathrooms.

---

**BALLOCH** – West Dunbartonshire – **501** G15 – ⊠ Alexandria          **25** B1
▮ Scotland
▶ Edinburgh 72 mi – Glasgow 20 mi – Stirling 30 mi
ℹ Balloch Rd ℰ (08707) 20 06 07, www.explore-callander.com
◨ N : Loch Lomond★★

SCOTLAND

🏠🏠🏠 **Cameron House** ⊱        ≤ 🚗 🔌 🖥 🕾 ⊕ 🐎 ♨ ≷ 🖼 🍴 🕿 ⛷ 🎖 🔞 📞 🐕
*Loch Lomond, Northwest : 1.5 mi by A 811 on A 82*          P VISA ⓒⓑ AE ①
*⊠ G83 8QZ – ℰ (01389) 755 565 – www.cameronhouse.co.uk*
**121 rm** ⌁ – †£ 145/355 ††£ 145/355 – 7 suites
**Rest** *Martin Wishart at Loch Lomond*❀ **Rest** *Camerons Grill* **Rest** *Boat House* – see restaurant listing
♦ Extensive Victorian house and timeshare lodges, set in 250 acres on the shore of Loch Lomond. Excellent leisure facilities include a health club, spa, golf course and use of a launch and seaplane. Moody, modern bedrooms; traditional suites.

XXX **Martin Wishart at Loch Lomond** – at Cameron House Hotel          ≤
❀   *Loch Lomond, Northwest : 1.5 mi by A 811 on A*        🚗 🔌 🔞 P VISA ⓒⓑ AE
*82 ⊠ G83 8QZ – ℰ (01389) 722 504 – www.martinwishartlochlomond.co.uk*
*– Closed 1-18 January, Monday and Tuesday*
**Rest** – *(dinner only and Saturday-Sunday lunch) (booking essential)*
Menu £ 25/65
**Spec.** Tortellini of roe deer, cauliflower cream and grand veneur sauce. Fillets of Dover sole, baby artichoke, parsley and lemon. Valrhona chocolate mousse with hazelnuts and exotic fruits.
♦ Formal restaurant within the grounds of a resort hotel, superbly situated on the banks of Loch Lomond and boasting water and mountain views. Seasonal, modern menus showcase Scottish ingredients in complementary combinations. Haggis bon bons have become a signature dish. Professional yet personable service.

XXX **Camerons Grill** – at Cameron House Hotel          ≤ 🚗 🔌 🔞 P
*Loch Lomond, Northwest : 1.5 mi by A 811 on A 82*          VISA ⓒⓑ AE ①
*⊠ G83 8QZ – ℰ (01389) 755 565 – www.cameronhouseco.uk*
**Rest** – *(dinner only)* Carte £ 42/54
♦ Contemporary, leather-furnished grill restaurant located within an extensive Victorian house, where 250 acres of grounds lead down to Loch Lomond. Concise menu of dishes from the Josper grill.

XX **Boat House** – at Cameron House Hotel          ≤ 🚗 🔌 P VISA ⓒⓑ AE ①
*Loch Lomond, Northwest : 1.5 mi by A 811 on A 82 ⊠ G83 8QZ – ℰ (01389) 755 565 – www.cameronhouse.co.uk*
**Rest** – Carte £ 26/36
♦ Set in the grounds of Cameron House, on the loch shore, this casual restaurant has a true New England feel. The Mediterranean menu offers unfussy dishes, including pizzas from the wood-oven.

**BALLYGRANT** – Argyll and Bute – **501** B16 – see Islay (Isle of)

**BALMACARA** – ⌧ Highland                                              **29** B2
▶ London 582 mi – Edinburgh 198 mi – Inverness 75 mi

⌂  **Balmacara Mains** without rest ⌂          ≤ ⬛ ⬛ ⬛ ⬛ ⬛ **P** _VISA_ ⬤⬤
  Glaick, West : 0.75 mi by A 87 ⌧ IV40 8DN – ℰ (01599) 566 240
  – www.ontheloch.com
  **8 rm** ⌓ – ♦£ 60/75 ♦♦£ 105/120
  ◆ Superb lochside location, between Eilean Donan Castle and Skye Bridge. Stylish
  bedrooms vary in size, some cosy, some huge; most have loch views. Large
  lounge with open fire.

**BALMEDIE** – Aberdeenshire – **501** N12 – pop. 1 653                  **28** D1
▶ Edinburgh 137 mi – Aberdeen 7 mi – Peterhead 24 mi

⌂  **Cock and Bull** with rm              ⬛ ⬛ ⬛ **P** _VISA_ ⬤⬤ AE ⓞ
  Ellon Rd, Blairton, North : 1 mi on A 90 ⌧ AB23 8XY – ℰ (01358) 743 249
  – www.thecockandbull.co.uk
  **3 rm** ⌓ – ♦£ 85 ♦♦£ 85    **Rest** – Carte £ 26/48
  ◆ Quirky pub with a profusion of knick-knacks; dine in the cosy, open-
  fired lounge, formal dining room or airy conservatory. Menu offers classic pub
  fare and well-presented, restaurant style dishes. Bedrooms boast striking modern
  black and white designs.

**BALQUHIDDER** – Stirling – **501** G14 – see Lochearnhead

**BANCHORY** – Aberdeenshire – **501** M12 – pop. 6 034 ▌ Scotland       **28** D2
▶ Edinburgh 118 mi – Aberdeen 17 mi – Dundee 55 mi – Inverness 94 mi
ℹ Bridge St ℰ (01330) 82 20 00, www.aberdeen-grampian.com
▸ Kinneskie Kinneskie Rd, ℰ (01330) 82 23 65
▸ Torphins Bog Rd, ℰ (013398) 8 21 15
◉ Crathes Castle★★ (Gardens★★★) **AC**, E : 3 mi by A 93 – Cairn o'Mount
Road★ (≤★★), S : by B 974. Dunnottar Castle★★ (site★★★) **AC**, SW : 15.5 mi by A
93 and A 957 – Aberdeen★★, NE : 17 mi by A 93

🏠  **Raemoir House** ⌂              ≤ ⬛ ⬛ ⬛ ⬛ **P** _VISA_ ⬤⬤ AE
  North : 2.5 mi by A 980 ⌧ AB31 4ED – ℰ (01330) 824 884 – www.raemoir.com
  **20 rm** ⌓ – ♦£ 120 ♦♦£ 160/200
  **Rest** Raemoir House – see restaurant listing
  ◆ One of the best-known Scottish estate country houses, in an idyllic rural spot
  and surrounded by mature grounds. Original features include an intricately
  carved bar and charming drawing room with flock wallpaper. Subtly modernised
  bedrooms.

🏠  **Banchory Lodge** ⌂              ≤ ⬛ ⬛ ⬛ ⬛ **P** _VISA_ ⬤⬤ AE ⓞ
  Dee St ⌧ AB31 5HS – ℰ (01330) 822 625 – www.banchorylodge.co.uk
  **22 rm** ⌓ – ♦£ 70/95 ♦♦£ 130/160
  **Rest** – Menu £ 23/30 s – Carte £ 17/44 s
  ◆ Part 16C former coaching inn delightfully situated on River Dee. Country house
  style accentuated by antiques and china. Individually decorated bedrooms. Dee
  views and floral displays enhance the attraction of the dining room.

🍴  **Raemoir House**              ≤ ⬛ ⬛ **P** _VISA_ ⬤⬤ AE
  North : 2.5 mi by A 980 ⌧ AB31 4ED – ℰ (01330) 824 884 – www.raemoir.com
  **Rest** – (bar lunch Monday-Saturday) Menu £ 40
  ◆ Formal dining room in a well-known Georgian country house, boasting grand
  dimensions and pitch pine panelling on both the walls and ceiling. Set dinner
  menu offers classically based dishes.

**BARCALDINE** – Argyll and Bute – **501** D14                                     **27** B2

➡ London 504 mi – Edinburgh 150 mi – Glasgow 100 mi – Dundee 122 mi

🏠 **Barcaldine House** ⌂                        ⟨ 🚗 ﾉ 🄿 VISA ⌾
✉ PA37 1SG – ✆ (01631) 720 219 – www.barcaldinehouse.co.uk
**10 rm** ⌙ – ♦£ 135 ♦♦£ 195 – 1 suite
**Rest** – (light lunch) (booking advisable) Menu £ 50 (dinner)
♦ Charming grey-stone country house built in 1709 by 'Red Patrick'. Lovely guest
areas include a comfy lounge, well-stocked bar and baronial-style billiard room.
Well-appointed bedrooms with heavy drapes, quality beds and antique furnish-
ings. Delightful dining room serves precise, well-crafted 6 course dinners.

**BARRA (Isle of)** – Western Isles – **501** X12/1 – ✉ **Castlebay**          **29** A3

➡ London 506 mi – Edinburgh 132 mi

**CASTLEBAY** – Western Isles                                                    **29** A3

🏠 **Castlebay**                              ⟨ & rm, ⁇ 🄿 VISA ⌾
✉ HS9 5XD – ✆ (01871) 810 223 – www.castlebayhotel.com – Closed 22
December-6 January
**15 rm** ⌙ – ♦£ 49/105 ♦♦£ 95/160    **Rest** – (bar lunch) Carte £ 20/32
♦ Homely hotel boasting excellent castle and island views – the hub of the island
community. Bedrooms mix styles: newer rooms feature subtle tartan fabrics; Mac-
Neil has harbour views. Cosy lounge and busy locals bar. Linen-clad dining room
serves seafood specials.

🏡 **Grianamul** without rest                    ⟨ 🚗 ⁇ ⁇ 🄿 VISA ⌾
✉ HS9 5XD – ✆ (01871) 810 416 – www.isleofbarraaccommodation.com
– April-September
**3 rm** ⌙ – ♦♦£ 70
♦ Set at the heart of a small hamlet; a homely guesthouse run by caring owners.
Bright, clean, spacious bedrooms. Comfortable lounge and sunny breakfast room,
where huge breakfasts are served.

**NORTH BAY** – Western Isles                                                    **29** A3

🏠 **Heathbank**                              ⟨ 🚗 🍽 ⁇ 🄿 VISA ⌾ ①
✉ HS9 5YQ – ✆ (01871) 890 266 – www.barrahotel.co.uk – Easter-October
**5 rm** ⌙ – ♦£ 60/80 ♦♦£ 90
**Rest** – (bar lunch) (booking essential) Carte £ 18/31
♦ Former Presbyterian Church, now a smart, modern hotel that's popular with locals and visitors alike. Fresh, up-to-date bedrooms. Bright, airy bar that forms the
hotel's hub and, along with the dining room, serves straightforward, local seafood
orientated menus.

**BENDERLOCH** – Argyll and Bute – **501** D14 – see Connel

**BERNISDALE** – Highland – **501** A/B11 – see Skye (Isle of)

**BISHOPTON** – Renfrewshire – **501** G16                                       **25** B1

➡ Edinburgh 59 mi – Dumbarton 9 mi – Glasgow 13 mi

🏰 **Mar Hall** ⌂       ⟨ 🚗 ﾉ 🖥 🌐 🌀 ᒪ₃ 🖼 ᕢ & rm, ⁇ 🎿 🄿 VISA ⌾ AE ①
Earl of Mar Dr., Northeast : 1 mi on B 815 ✉ PA7 5NW – ✆ (0141) 812 99 99
– www.marhall.com
**50 rm** ⌙ – ♦£ 129/219 ♦♦£ 245/295 – 3 suites
**Rest Cristal** – (closed Sunday-Monday) (dinner only) Carte £ 30/65
♦ Stunning Gothic mansion with period charm, well-equipped gym, impressive
spa and championship golf course. Great Hall displays ornate plaster ceiling. Spacious bedrooms; those by the spa have golf course views. 250 acres of parkland
stretch to the Clyde. High-ceilinged Cristal offers accessible menu.

SCOTLAND

**BLAIRGOWRIE** – Perth and Kinross – **501** J14 – **pop. 7 965** ▮ Scotland    **28** C2

▶ Edinburgh 60 mi – Dundee 19 mi – Perth 16 mi

🗓 26 Wellmeadow 𝒞 (01250) 87 29 60, www.perthshire.co.uk

ⓖ Scone Palace★★ **AC**, S : 12 mi by A 93

🏨🏨🏨 **Kinloch House** ⊛    ← 🍴 🕭 🎇 🕪 **P** 🆅🆂🅰 ㏇
*West : 3 mi on A 923* ✉ *PH10 6SG* – 𝒞 *(01250) 884 237*
*– www.kinlochhouse.com – Closed 14-29 December*
**16 rm** � – 🛉£ 110/225 🛉🛉£ 215/305 – 1 suite    **Rest** – Menu £ 28/55
♦ Imposing ivy-clad country house in a tranquil, elevated setting, with beautiful walled gardens to the rear and 25 acres of grounds. Smart oak-panelled hall and vast array of welcoming guest areas complete with log fires and antiques. Classical bedrooms are individually styled and well-appointed. Formal restaurant offers concise daily menu of traditional dishes.

🏠 **Heathpark House** without rest    🍴 🎇 🕪 **P** 🆅🆂🅰 ㏇
*Coupar Angus Rd, Rosemount, Southeast : 0.75 mi on A 923* ✉ *PH10 6JT*
*– 𝒞 (01250) 870 700 – www.heathparkhouse.com – Closed 24-26 December and 1 January*
**3 rm** � – 🛉£ 45/50 🛉🛉£ 75
♦ Substantial Victorian guesthouse in a quiet residential spot with mature gardens. Spacious lounge; breakfasts taken in welcoming dining room. Large, individually styled rooms.

🏠 **Gilmore House** without rest    🕪 **P** 🆅🆂🅰 ㏇
🍽 *Perth Rd, Southwest : 0.5 mi on A 93* ✉ *PH10 6EJ* – 𝒞 *(01250) 872 791*
*– www.gilmorehouse.co.uk*
**3 rm** � – 🛉£ 70/80 🛉🛉£ 70/80
♦ Traditional stone-built house with flower-filled entrance, only a few minutes walk from town. Quaint, comfortable lounge complete with bottles of whisky and sherry. Cosy, up-to-date bedrooms with little extras. Extensive buffet and cooked options at breakfast.

**BOWMORE** – Argyll and Bute – **501** B16 – see Islay (Isle of)

**BRAEMAR** – Aberdeenshire – **501** J12 – **pop. 500** ▮ Scotland    **28** C2

▶ Edinburgh 85 mi – Aberdeen 58 mi – Dundee 51 mi – Perth 51 mi

🗓 Mar Rd 𝒞 (013397) 4 16 00, www.braemarscotland.co.uk

🔞 Cluniebank Rd, 𝒞 (013397) 4 16 18

ⓖ Lin O'Dee★, W : 5 m

🏠 **Callater Lodge** without rest    🍴 🎇 🕪 **P** 🆅🆂🅰 ㏇ 🅰🅴
*9 Glenshee Rd* ✉ *AB35 5YQ* – 𝒞 *(013397) 41 275 – www.callaterlodge.co.uk*
*– Closed 1 week Christmas*
**6 rm** � – 🛉£ 40/65 🛉🛉£ 80
♦ Victorian granite house on the village outskirts. Classically furnished interior with tartan carpets and stag's heads. Bright breakfast room and comfy lounge with local info. Fresh, individually styled bedrooms; some with valley views.

**BREASCLETE** – Western Isles – **501** Z9 – see Lewis and Harris (Isle of)

**BROADFORD** – Highland – **501** C12 – see Skye (Isle of)

**BRODICK** – North Ayrshire – **501** E17 – see Arran (Isle of)

**BRORA** – Highland – **501** I9 – **pop. 1 140**    **30** D2

▶ Edinburgh 234 mi – Inverness 78 mi – Wick 49 mi

🔞 Golf Rd, 𝒞 (01408) 62 14 17

**Royal Marine** 🚗 🔌 🗺 🕭 ⚿ ⛗ 🏊 P VISA ☎ AE ⊙
*Golf Rd* ⊠ KW9 6QS – ℰ (01408) 621 252 – www.royalmarinebrora.com
**21 rm** ☐ – †£ 95/135 ††£ 140/200
**Rest** – Carte £ 17/40
• Cream-washed former laird's house set next to a top golf course. Leather-furnished lounges and wood-floored bar. Smart, modern, country house bedrooms with warm fabrics and good level of facilities. Formal linen-laid restaurant offers traditional Scottish menus.

**BROUGHTY FERRY** – Dundee City – 501 L14 – see Dundee

**BUNCHREW** – Highland – see Inverness

**BURRAY** – 501 L7 – see Orkney Islands (Mainland)

**BUTE (Isle of)** – Argyll and Bute – 501 E16 – pop. 7 354         27 B3
▨ from Rothesay to Wemyss Bay (Mainland) (Caledonian MacBrayne Ltd) frequent services daily (35 mn) – from Rhubodach to Colintraive (Mainland) (Caledonian MacBrayne Ltd) frequent services daily (5 mn)

**ASCOG** – Argyll and Bute                                            27 B3

**Balmory Hall** without rest 🌣 ≤ 🚗 🔌 ⚿ ⛗ P ☎
*Balmory Rd* ⊠ PA20 9LL – ℰ (01700) 500 669 – www.balmoryhall.com – Closed 25 December and 1 January
**4 rm** ☐ – †£ 170 ††£ 170/200
• 19C Italianate mansion with boules pitch and croquet lawn. Impressive original features include ornate plaster ceilings, gilt cornicing, Doric columns and a grand cantilevered staircase. Dramatic photos and family artwork abound. Homemade bread/jam at breakfast.

**CADBOLL** – Highland – see Tain

**CALLANDER** – Stirling – 501 H15 – pop. 2 754 ▍ Scotland         28 C2
▣ Edinburgh 52 mi – Glasgow 43 mi – Oban 71 mi – Perth 41 mi
🎗 Ancaster Sq ℰ (08707) 20 06 28, www.explore-callander.com
🔞 Aveland Rd, ℰ (01877) 33 00 90
◉ Town★
◉ The Trossachs★★★ (Loch Katrine★★) – Hilltop Viewpoint★★★ (⌖★★★)
W : 10 mi by A 821

**Roman Camp** 🌣 🚗 🔌 🔌 ⚿ ⛗ P VISA ☎ AE ⊙
*Main St* ⊠ FK17 8BG – ℰ (01877) 330 003 – www.romancamphotel.co.uk
**12 rm** ☐ – †£ 95/150 †††£ 195/200 – 3 suites
**Rest** *Restaurant* – see restaurant listing
• Attractive 17C former hunting lodge next to a Roman settlement. Charming interior with beautiful drawing room, antique-filled library and chapel. Classical bedrooms have a subtle contemporay edge.

**Lubnaig** without rest 🚗 ⚿ ⛗ P VISA ☎
*Leny Feus* ⊠ FK17 8AS – ℰ (01877) 330 376 – www.lubnaighouse.co.uk – Mid April to October
**8 rm** ☐ – †£ 45/55 ††£ 65/80
• Built in 1864, a characterful Victorian house on the outskirts of town. Well-kept mature gardens visible from communal rooms. Homely bedrooms, two in converted stables.

**Restaurant** – at Roman Camp Hotel 🚗 🔌 P VISA ☎ AE ⊙
*Main St* ⊠ FK17 8BG – ℰ (01877) 330 003 – www.romancamphotel.co.uk
**Rest** – Menu £ 27/50 – Carte dinner £ 47/71
• Spacious country house restaurant with unique ceiling and impressive flower displays. Daily changing set menu and concise à la carte offer ambitious modern dishes of local, seasonal produce.

SCOTLAND

※ **Mhor Fish**                                                    *VISA* ◉◉
*75-77 Main St ⊠ FK17 8DX – ℰ (01877) 330 213 – www.mhor.net – Closed 1
January, 25-26 December and Monday except bank holidays*
**Rest** – Seafood – Menu £ 25 – Carte £ 18/30
• Simple, busy, well-run eatery on main street; popular with locals. Great variety
of fish, homemade pies and chips cooked in beef dripping. All-day menu and
more ambitious specials.

**CARINISH** – Western Isles – **501** Y11 – see Uist (Isles of)

**CARNOUSTIE** – Angus – **501** L14 – pop. 10 561                    **28** D2
▶ Edinburgh 68 mi – Aberdeen 59 mi – Dundee 12 mi
🖪 21 High St ℰ (01241) 85 96 20, www.angusanddundee.co.uk
🖪 Monifieth Golf Links Princes St, Medal Starter's Box, ℰ (01382) 53 27 67
🖪 Burnside Links Par, ℰ (01241) 80 22 90
🖪 Panmure Barry, ℰ (01241) 85 51 20
🖪 Buddon Links Links Par, ℰ (01241) 80 22 80

⌂ **Old Manor** without rest 🕭          ⇐ 🚗 ⅏ 🐾 **P** *VISA* ◉◉
🔄 *Panbride, Northeast : 1.25 mi by A 930 on Panbride Rd ⊠ DD7 6JP – ℰ (01241)
854 804 – www.oldmanorcarnoustie.com – Closed 2 weeks October and
Christmas-New Year*
**5 rm** ⌹ – ♦£ 55/60 ♦♦£ 70/80
• Sizeable house built in 1765, commanding great views over patchwork fields to
the sea beyond. Comfy lounge and good-sized breakfast room. Spotlessly kept
bedrooms come with quality bedding, chocolates and biscuits; Balmoral and Du-
notter boast superb outlooks.

**CARRADALE** – Argyll and Bute – **501** D17 – see Kintyre (Peninsula)

**CASTLEBAY** – Western Isles – **501** X12/1 – see Barra (Isle of)

**CASTLE DOUGLAS** – Dumfries and Galloway – **501** I19 – pop. 3 671    **25** B3
▮ Scotland
▶ Edinburgh 98 mi – Ayr 49 mi – Dumfries 18 mi – Stranraer 57 mi
🖪 Market Hill ℰ (01556) 50 26 11, www.visitscotland.com
🖪 Abercromby Rd, ℰ (01556) 50 28 01
🖪 Threave Garden★★ **AC**, SW : 2.5 mi by A 75 – Threave Castle★ **AC**, W : 1 m

⌂ **Douglas House** without rest            ⅏ 🐾 **P** *VISA* ◉◉
*63 Queen St ⊠ DG7 1HS – ℰ (01556) 503 262 – www.douglas-house.com
– Closed Christmas*
**4 rm** ⌹ – ♦£ 36/65 ♦♦£ 74/90
• Attractive 19C stone-built house, set close to the high street. Open-plan lounge
and breakfast room. Comfy, individually decorated bedrooms with contemporary
feel. Extensive breakfast menu.

**CAWDOR** – Highland – **501** I11 – pop. 812 – ⊠ Inverness          **30** D2
▶ Edinburgh 170 mi – Aberdeen 100 mi – Inverness 14 mi

🍴 **Cawdor Tavern**                              🏠 **P** *VISA* ◉◉ **AE**
*The Lane ⊠ IV12 5XP – ℰ (01667) 404 777 – www.cawdortavern.co.uk – Closed
2 weeks January, 25 December and 1 January*
**Rest** – (booking essential) Carte £ 18/27
• Charming, personally run whitewashed pub – formerly the joiners' workshop of
Cawdor Castle. Wide-ranging menu offers a good selection of frequently chang-
ing, classically based dishes.

**CHIRNSIDE** – The Scottish Borders – **501** N16 – pop. 1 204 – ⊠ Duns    **26** D1
▶ Edinburgh 52 mi – Berwick-upon-Tweed 8 mi – Glasgow 95 mi
– Newcastle upon Tyne 70 mi

SCOTLAND

**Chirnside Hall** ⌂     ≤ 🚗 🎣 ⅃₆ ⁾⁾ **P** 𝚅𝙸𝚂𝙰 ⓒⓓ 𝙰𝙴
*East : 1.75 mi on A 6105* ✉ *TD11 3LD –* 𝒞 *(01890) 818 219*
*– www.chirnsidehallhotel.com – Closed March*
**10 rm** ⌷ – ♦£ 90/160 ♦♦£ 160/175
**Rest** – *(dinner only) (booking essential for non-residents)* Menu £ 35
♦ Sizeable 1834 country house with lovely revolving door; boasting beautiful views over the Cheviots. Grand lounges with original cornicing and huge fireplaces. Cosy, classical bedrooms, some have four-posters. Local, seasonal dishes in traditional dining room.

---

**CLEAT** – **501** K/L6 – see Orkney Islands (Island of Westray)

---

**COLONSAY (Isle of)** – Argyll and Bute – **501** B15 – pop. 106     **27** A2

▶ London 502 mi – Edinburgh 129 mi – Greenock 98 mi

⛴ from Scalasaig to Oban (Caledonian MacBrayne Ltd) 3 weekly (2 h) – from Scalasaig to Kintyre Peninsula (Kennacraig) via Isle of Islay (Port Askaig) (Caledonian MacBrayne Ltd) weekly

🏌 Colonsay, 𝒞 (01951) 20 02 90

**SCALASAIG** – Argyll and Bute – ✉ **Colonsay**     **27** A2

**Colonsay** ⌂     ≤ 🚗 ⅋⁾ **P** 𝚅𝙸𝚂𝙰 ⓒⓓ 𝙰𝙴
✉ *PA61 7YP –* 𝒞 *(01951) 200 316 – www.colonsayestate.co.uk – March-October, Christmas and New Year*
**9 rm** – ♦£ 70 ♦♦£ 90/145, ⌷ £ 6.50     **Rest** – *(bar lunch)* Carte £ 21/29
♦ Listed building from mid-18C; a thoroughly rural, remote setting. Public areas include excellent photos of local scenes and the only bar on the island. Bright, modern rooms. Welcoming, informal dining room.

SCOTLAND

---

**COMRIE** – Perth and Kinross – **501** I14 – pop. 1 926     **28** C2

▶ Edinburgh 66 mi – Glasgow 56 mi – Oban 70 mi – Perth 24 mi

🏌 Comrie Laggan Braes, 𝒞 (01764) 67 00 55

**Royal** 🏨     🚗 ⅋⁾ **P** 𝚅𝙸𝚂𝙰 ⓒⓓ 𝙰𝙴 ⓞ
*Melville Sq* ✉ *PH6 2DN –* 𝒞 *(01764) 679 200 – www.royalhotel.co.uk – Closed 25-26 December*
**11 rm** ⌷ – ♦£ 85 ♦♦£ 140/180
**Rest** *Royal* – see restaurant listing
♦ Charming coaching inn dating back to the 18C and set at the heart of a riverside town. Cosy bar and lovely open-fired library with squashy sofas. Well-appointed bedrooms; some with four-posters and antiques. Relaxed, personable service.

**Royal** – at Royal Hotel     🚗 **P** 𝚅𝙸𝚂𝙰 ⓒⓓ 𝙰𝙴
*Melville Sq* ✉ *PH6 2DN –* 𝒞 *(01764) 679 200 – www.royalhotel.co.uk – Closed 25-26 December*
**Rest** – Menu £ 30 – Carte £ 21/28
♦ Intimate dining room and bright conservatory, set within a stylishly decorated coaching inn. Concise menu of locally sourced, seasonal produce; classically based dishes display modern touches.

---

**CONNEL** – Argyll and Bute – **501** D14 – ✉ **Oban**     **27** B2

▶ Edinburgh 118 mi – Glasgow 88 mi – Inverness 113 mi – Oban 5 mi

**Ards House** without rest     ≤ 🚗 ⅋⁾ **P** 𝚅𝙸𝚂𝙰 ⓒⓓ ⓞ
*on A 85* ✉ *PA37 1PT –* 𝒞 *(01631) 710 255 – www.ardshouse.com – Closed mid December-mid January*
**4 rm** ⌷ – ♦£ 50/65 ♦♦£ 80/100
♦ Attractive house with equally welcoming, hospitable owner. Large, homely, open-fired lounge packed with books and antiques. Cosy, personally decorated bedrooms show good attention to detail; small bathrooms boast locally made toiletries. Excellent breakfasts.

📠 **Oyster Inn** with rm  ⟨ 🏠 P VISA ⦿ AE
✉ PA37 1PJ – ℰ (01631) 710 666 – www.oysterinn.co.uk – Closed 25-26 December
**11 rm** ⬙ – ⫶£ 55/75 ⫶⫶£ 100/130
**Rest** – Seafood – (dinner only) Carte £ 27/57
♦ Cosy 18C pub looking over the Falls or Lora and the bay. Rustic bar serves pub classics. Smarter, nautically themed restaurant offers a regularly changing seafood menu and views of the sunset. Bedrooms are modern and colourful; budget bunk rooms are available.

---

**CRIEFF** – Perth and Kinross – **501** I14 – **pop. 6 579** ▮ Scotland  **28** C2
▶ Edinburgh 60 mi – Glasgow 50 mi – Oban 76 mi – Perth 18 mi
🛈 High St ℰ (01764) 65 25 78, www.crieffandstrathearn.co.uk
🖭 Perth Rd, ℰ (01764) 65 29 09
🏌 Muthill Peat Rd, ℰ (01764) 68 15 23
◉ Town★
🗗 Drummond Castle Gardens★ AC, S : 2 mi by A 822. Scone Palace★★ AC, E : 16 mi by A 85 and A 93

↑ **Merlindale** without rest  📠 ⣏ ⟨⟨ P VISA ⦿ ①
Perth Rd, on A 85 ✉ PH7 3EQ – ℰ (01764) 655 205 – www.merlindale.co.uk
– Closed mid December-mid January
**3 rm** ⬙ – ⫶£ 50/80 ⫶⫶£ 70/90
♦ Spacious manor house with comfy lounge, well-stocked library and dark wood furnished dining room. Immaculate bedrooms have classical furnishings, heavy floral drapes and large bathrooms; some boast roll-top baths. Family style breakfasts.

✕✕ **Yann's at Glenearn House** with rm  📠 ⟨⟨ P VISA ⦿ AE
Perth Rd, on A 85 ✉ PH7 3EQ – ℰ (01764) 650 111
– www.yannsatglenearnhouse.com
**5 rm** – ⫶£ 55 ⫶⫶£ 80
**Rest** – French – (closed Monday and Tuesday) (dinner only and lunch Saturday & Sunday) Carte £ 25/30
♦ Busy, keenly run, bistro-style restaurant with informal lounge. Well-priced, French cooking makes good use of Scottish produce; Savoyard sharing dishes a speciality. Polite, swift service. Comfortable bedrooms with good facilities and a relaxed, bohemian style.

**at Muthill** South : 3mi. by A 822

✕ **Barley Bree** with rm  P VISA ⦿
6 Willoughby St ✉ PH5 2AB – ℰ (01764) 681 451 – www.barleybree.com
– Closed 2 weeks February, 2 weeks October, Christmas, Monday and Tuesday
**6 rm** ⬙ – ⫶£ 70 ⫶⫶£ 130/140  **Rest** – (booking advisable) Carte £ 19/37 s
♦ Converted coaching inn, in the centre of a busy village, with spacious, fire-lit sitting room and dining room hung with angling memorabilia. Generous portions of rustic, classical cooking; dishes utilise local ingredients. Friendly service. Comfortable, well-thought-out bedrooms.

---

**CRINAN** – Argyll and Bute – **501** D15 – ✉ **Lochgilphead** ▮ Scotland  **27** B2
▶ Edinburgh 137 mi – Glasgow 91 mi – Oban 36 mi
◉ Hamlet★
🗗 Kilmory Knap (Macmillan's Cross★) SW : 14 m

🏨 **Crinan**  ⟨ 📠 ⧉ P VISA ⦿ ①
✉ PA31 8SR – ℰ (01546) 830 261 – www.crinanhotel.com – Closed Christmas
**20 rm** (dinner included) ⬙ – ⫶£ 130/155 ⫶⫶£ 290/360
**Rest** *Westward* – see restaurant listing
**Rest** *Seafood Bar* – Carte £ 19/33
♦ Built in the 19C to accommodate the Laird of Jura's business associates and boasting lovely Sound views. Simply furnished bedrooms – some with balconies and views. Small coffee shop sells homemade cakes; superb 3rd floor bar with terrace. Larger, wood-panelled bar offers an appealing menu of seafood dishes.

SCOTLAND

XX **Westward** – at Crinan Hotel ⟨ ⚞ **P** ̄VISĀ ⚬⚬
☒ PA31 8SR – ℰ (01546) 830 261 – www.crinanhotel.com – *Closed Christmas*
**Rest** – *(dinner only)* Menu £ 45
♦ Set within a welcoming, family-run hotel and boasting lovely views over the loch and Sound of Jura. Concise seafood-based menus rely on local and island produce. Homemade chocolates to finish.

**CULLODEN** – Highland – **501** H11 – see Inverness

**CUPAR** – Fife – **501** K15 – pop. 8 506                                 **28** C2
▶ Edinburgh 45 mi – Dundee 15 mi – Perth 23 mi

XX **Ostler's Close** ̄VISĀ ⚬⚬ ̄AĒ
25 Bonnygate ☒ KY15 4BU – ℰ (01334) 655 574 – www.ostlerclose.co.uk
– *Closed 1-2 January, 2 weeks April, 2 weeks October, 25-26 December, Sunday and Monday*
**Rest** – *(dinner only and Saturday lunch)* Carte £ 25/44
♦ Long-standing, personally run restaurant down a narrow alley just off the main street. Three cosy rooms decorated in warm reds; friendly, chatty service. Concise, traditional menus with beef and seafood to the fore and a Mediterranean edge.

**CURRIE** – City of Edinburgh – **501** K16 – see Edinburgh

**DALKEITH** – Midlothian – **501** K16 – pop. 11 566                      **26** C1
▶ London 402 mi – Edinburgh 7 mi – Glasgow 52 mi – Aberdeen 138 mi

🛏 **Sun Inn** with rm ☆ ⁽⁾ **P** ̄VISĀ ⚬⚬ ̄AĒ ⓪
*Lothian Bridge, Southwest : 2 mi by A 6094, B 6392 on A 7* ☒ EH22 4TR
– ℰ (0131) 663 24 56 – www.thesuninnedinburgh.co.uk
**5 rm** ⌂ – †£ 70/125 ††£ 90/175
**Rest** – Menu £ 14 (lunch and early dinner) – Carte £ 13/28
♦ Former 17C blacksmith's with two large, open-fired rooms, wood and stone-faced walls and modern black and white photos. Extensive menus feature good quality local produce; dinner is more ambitious. Smart bedrooms boast hand-made furniture and Egyptian cotton.

**DALRY** – North Ayrshire – **501** F16                                      **25** A1
▶ Edinburgh 70 mi – Ayr 21 mi – Glasgow 25 mi

⌂ **Lochwood Farm Steading** without rest ☞ ⟨ ⚙ **P** ̄VISĀ ⚬⚬
*Southwest : 5 mi by A 737 and Saltcoats rd* ☒ KA21 6NG – ℰ (01294) 552 529
– www.lochwoodfarm.co.uk – *Closed Christmas and New Year*
**3 rm** ⌂ – †£ 55 ††£ 75
♦ Remote farmhouse on a 100 acre working dairy farm. Bedrooms are split between a converted barn and Scandinavian-style wood house complete with hot tub; the best are luxuriously appointed suites with fine linens and Isle of Arran toiletries.

XX **Braidwoods** (Keith Braidwood) **P** ̄VISĀ ⚬⚬ ̄AĒ
❀ *Drumastle Mill Cottage, Southwest : 1.5 mi by A 737 on Saltcoats rd*
☒ KA24 4LN – ℰ (01294) 833 544 – www.braidwoods.co.uk – *Closed 25 December-23 January, 2 weeks September, Sunday dinner, Monday, Tuesday lunch and Sunday from May-mid September*
**Rest** – *(booking essential)* Menu £ 28/48
**Spec.** Timbale of Arbroath smokies with leeks and horseradish hollandaise. West coast turbot with braised fennel and langoustine jus. Valrhona chocolate truffle cake with salted caramel ice cream.
♦ Well-established crofter's cottage in remote location; very personally run by husband and wife team. Two-part dining room with homely feel. Seasonal, regional produce is the cornerstone of the flavoursome classical dishes. Smooth service.

SCOTLAND

**DINGWALL** – Highland – **501** G11 – pop. 5 026                    30 C2

▶ Edinburgh 172 mi – Inverness 14 mi

XX **Cafe India Brasserie**                    AC VISA ⑳ AE
*Lockhart House, Tulloch St* ⊠ *IV15 9JZ* – ℰ *(01349) 862 552*
– *www.cafeindiadingwall.co.uk*
– *Closed 25 December*
**Rest** – Indian – Carte £ 24/38
♦ Bustling, locally regarded Indian restaurant, handily located in town centre. Updated décor is fresh and modern. Authentically prepared, tasty regional Indian food.

---

**DORNOCH** – Highland – **501** H10 – pop. 1 206 ▯ Scotland                    30 D2

▶ Edinburgh 219 mi – Inverness 63 mi – Wick 65 mi

🄳 Castle St ℰ (08452) 25 51 21, www.visitdornoch.com

🄳 Royal Dornoch Golf Rd, ℰ (01862) 81 02 19

👁 Town ★

⌂ **Highfield House** without rest                    ≤ ⇱ ⁑ ⁐ P̂
*Evelix Rd* ⊠ *IV25 3HR* – ℰ *(01862) 810 909*
– *www.highfieldhouse.co.uk*
**4 rm** ⌷ – ♦£ 55 ♦♦£ 85
♦ Welcoming guesthouse with immaculately kept gardens and pleasant summer house. Spacious interior boasts conservatory style lounge and smart breakfast room. Comfy bedrooms have good facilities.

---

**DOUNBY** – **501** K16 – see Orkney Islands (Mainland)

---

**DRUMBEG** – Highland – **501** E9 – ⊠ Highland                    30 C1

▶ Edinburgh 262 mi – Inverness 105 mi – Ullapool 48 mi

⌂ **Blar na Leisg at Drumbeg House** ⌾                    ≤ ⇱ ⁑ ⁐ P̂ VISA
*take first right on entering village from Kylesku direction* ⊠ *IV27 4NW*
– ℰ *(01571) 833 325* – *www.blarnaleisg.com*
**4 rm** ⌷ – ♦£ 100/160 ♦♦£ 160
**Rest** – Menu £ 50
♦ Remotely set Edwardian house, affording lovely loch views. Large, open-fired sitting room filled with a vast array of books; spacious, luxuriously appointed bedrooms. Impressive modern art collection includes lots of Bauhaus works. Smart, contemporary dining room; fresh, local fish and shellfish are a speciality.

---

**DRUMNADROCHIT** – Highland – **501** G11 – pop. 813 – ⊠ Milton                    30 C2
▯ Scotland

▶ Edinburgh 172 mi – Inverness 16 mi – Kyle of Lochalsh 66 mi

🄶 Loch Ness ★★ – Loch Ness Monster Exhibition ★ **AC** – The Great Glen ★

⌂ **Drumbuie Farm** without rest                    ≤ ⥾ ⁑ P̂ VISA
*Drumbuie, East : 0.75 mi by A 82* ⊠ *IV63 6XP* – ℰ *(01456) 450 634*
– *www.loch-ness-farm.co.uk* – *February-November*
**3 rm** – ♦£ 45/48 ♦♦£ 66/70
♦ Immaculate purpose-built guesthouse on working farm with Highland cattle. Pleasant breakfast room has Loch Ness views. Good collection of malt whiskies. Spacious bedrooms.

---

**DUISDALEMORE** – Highland – see Skye (Isle of)

SCOTLAND

▶ Edinburgh 80 mi – Ayr 59 mi – Carlisle 34 mi – Glasgow 79 mi

🛈 64 Whitesands 𝒞 (01387) 25 38 62, www.visitdumfriesandgalloway.co.uk

🏌 Dumfries & Galloway Maxwelltown 2 Laurieston Ave,
𝒞 (01387) 25 35 82

🏌 Dumfries & County Edinburgh Rd, Nunfield, 𝒞 (01387) 25 35 85

🏌 Crichton Bankend Rd, 𝒞 (01387) 24 78 94

👁 Town★ – Midsteeple★ A **A**

🅒 Lincluden College (Tomb★) **AC**, N : 1.5 mi by College St A.
Drumlanrig Castle★★ (cabinets★) **AC**, NW : 16.5 mi by A 76 A – Shambellie
House Museum of Costume (Costume Collection★) S : 7.25 mi by A 710 A -
Sweetheart Abbey★ **AC**, S : 8 mi by A 710 A – Caerlaverock Castle★ (Renaissance
fa 0.5ade★★) **AC**, SE : 9 mi by B 725 B – Glenkiln (Sculptures★) W : 9 mi by A 780
- A - and A 75

## DUMFRIES

**SCOTLAND**

⛰ **Hazeldean House** without rest    🚗 🕸 **P** VISA ◍ ◑
*4 Moffat Rd ⊠ DG1 1NJ – 𝒞 (01387) 266 178 – www.hazeldeanhouse.com*
**6 rm** ⌱ – ♦£ 35/45 ♦♦£ 60                        Bu
♦ Victorian villa built in 1898. Lovely garden; curio-filled lounge and conservatory breakfast room. Victorian-themed bedrooms, 3 with four-posters; basement room has a nautical cabin style.

⛰ **Hamilton House** without rest    🕸 🛜 **P** VISA ◍ AE
*12 Moffat Rd ⊠ DG1 1NJ – 𝒞 (01387) 266 606*
*– www.hamiltonhousedumfries.co.uk – Closed 24 December-3 January*
**7 rm** ⌱ – ♦£ 35/45 ♦♦£ 58/65                   Bc
♦ Converted Victorian townhouse next to the bowls club. Large conservatory lounge; neat breakfast tables overlook the tennis courts. Large bedrooms combine the classical and the contemporary.

---

**DUNBAR** – East Lothian – **501** M15 – pop. 6 354      **26** D1
▶ London 377 mi – Edinburgh 31 mi – Glasgow 77 mi – Aberdeen 162 mi

🍴 **Creel**              VISA ◍ AE
*The Harbour, 25 Lamer St ⊠ EH42 1HG – 𝒞 (01368) 863 279*
*– www.creelrestaurant.co.uk – Closed Sunday dinner, Monday and Tuesday*
**Rest** – Menu £ 18/25
♦ Unassuming former pub in a working harbour. Wood panelled walls and polished tables are brightened by a welcoming team. Experienced chef uses lesser known cuts from local suppliers and transforms them into good value, full-flavoured dishes.

---

**DUNBLANE** – Stirling – **501** I15 – pop. 7 911 ▯ Scotland     **28** C2
▶ Edinburgh 42 mi – Glasgow 33 mi – Perth 29 mi
◉ Town★ – Cathedral★★ (west front★★)
◔ Doune★ (castle★ **AC**) W : 4.5 mi by A 820

🏠 **Cromlix House** 🦌     ≤ 🚗 ⏸ 🐦 🕸 🛜 **P** VISA ◍ AE
*Kinbuck, North : 3.5 mi on B 8033 ⊠ FK15 9JT – 𝒞 (01786) 822 125*
*– www.cromlixhouse.com*
**6 rm** ⌱ – ♦£ 95/140 ♦♦£ 195/285 – 8 suites – ♦♦£ 235/285
**Rest** – (booking essential) Menu £ 27/54
♦ Effortlessly relaxing 19C mansion in extensive grounds with ornate private chapel. Charming morning room; spacious conservatory with plants. Definitive country house rooms. Two elegant, richly furnished dining rooms.

🏠 **Doubletree by Hilton Dunblane Hydro**   ≤ 🚗 🏠 ♨ 🛗 ♿ 🛜
*Perth Rd, North : .0.75 mi on B 8033 ⊠ FK15 0HG*     🅰 **P** VISA ◍ AE ◑
*– 𝒞 (01786) 826 600 – www.doubletreedunblane.com*
**194 rm** ⌱ – ♦£ 110/140 ♦♦£ 120/150 – 6 suites
**Rest** *Kailyard by Nick Nairn* – see restaurant listing
♦ 'Grand old lady' originally built in 1800s; rejuvenated and given a modern, corporate style. Set in ten acres, it boasts a family orientated spa and smart, up-to-date bedrooms.

🍴🍴 **Kailyard by Nick Nairn** – at Doubletree by Hilton Dunblane Hydro Hotel
*Perth Rd ⊠ FK15 0HG – 𝒞 (01786) 822 551*   ≤ 🚗 ⏸ **P** VISA ◍ AE ◑
*– www.doubletreedunblane.com/the_kailyard*
**Rest** – Carte £ 28/45
♦ Large, contemporary restaurant set within characterful, grand hotel; its name means 'small Scottish vegetable garden'. Rustic menus feature simple, well-prepared, flavourful dishes.

**DUNDEE** – Dundee City – **501** L14 – pop. 154 674                    **28** C2

Scotland

▶ Edinburgh 63 mi – Aberdeen 67 mi
– Glasgow 83 mi

**Access** Tay Road Bridge (toll) Y

Dundee Airport : ℰ (01382) 662200, SW : 1.5 mi Z

Discovery Quay ℰ (01382) 52 75 27, www.angusanddundee.co.uk

Caird Park Mains Loan, ℰ (01382) 45 36 06

Camperdown Camperdown Park, ℰ (01382) 62 33 98

Downfield Turnberry Ave, ℰ (01382) 82 55 95

Town★ - The Frigate Unicorn★ **AC** Y **A** – Discovery Point★ **AC** Y **B**
– Verdant Works★ Z **D** – McManus Galleries★ Y **M**

SCOTLAND

🏨 **Apex City Quay**  ≤ 🔲 🐾 🕸 ⅙ 🖧 ⅙ ⅘ 🕊 🔊 🅿 VISA ⚙ 🆎 ⓪
*1 West Victoria Dock Rd* ⊠ *DD1 3JP –* ℰ *(01382) 202 404*
*– www.apexhotels.co.uk*                                                                Ya
**150 rm –** ♦£ 80/230 ♦♦£ 80/230, ⊑ £ 13.50 – 2 suites
**Rest** *Metro Brasserie* – see restaurant listing
♦ Modern waterfront hotel in an up-and-coming area. Vast bar-lounge and
good business facilities. Spacious, contemporary bedrooms boast king-sized
beds and large windows looking over the city or marina. Atmospheric spa and
treatment rooms.

🏨 **Landmark**  ☞ 🔲 🕸 ⅙ ⅙ ⅘ 🕊 🔊 🅿 VISA ⚙ 🆎 ⓪
*Kingsway West, West 4.5mi by A85 at junction with A90* ⊠ *DD2 5JT –* ℰ *(01382,*
*641 122 – www.thelandmarkdundee.co.uk*
**95 rm –** ♦£ 59/129 ♦♦£ 79/139, ⊑ £ 13.95
**Rest** *Garden Room* – see restaurant listing
♦ Imposing granite country house – formerly a private residence – dating back to
1870. Welcoming bar-lounge and good leisure facilities. Dark wood furnished
bedrooms with good mod cons and smart bathrooms; Executive rooms are worth
the extra.

XX **Playwright**  🆎 🐾 VISA ⚙
*11 Tay Sq, South Tay St.* ⊠ *DD1 1PB –* ℰ *(01382) 223 113*
*– www.theplaywright.co.uk – Closed 1 January and 25-26 December*
**Rest** *– (closed Sunday)* Menu £ 18 (lunch) – Carte £ 30/46          Yx
♦ Smart, modern bar and restaurant in an imposing grey-stone building dating
back to the 1800s. Seasonal menus offer modern interpretations of classical
dishes and everything from the bread to ice cream is made in-house. Great value
lunch.

XX **Garden Room** – at Landmark Hotel  ☞ 🅿 VISA ⚙ 🆎
*Kingsway West, West 4.5mi by A85 at junction with A90* ⊠ *DD2 5JT –* ℰ *(01382)*
*641 122 – www.thelandmarkdundee.co.uk*
**Rest** *– (dinner only and bar lunch)* Menu £ 25 – Carte £ 26/40
♦ Boasting pleasant rural views, a light, bright conservatory in a well-located
country house. Menus mix simple comfort food and skilfully prepared, more adventurous dishes. Carvery on Sundays.

X **Metro Brasserie** – at Apex City Quay Hotel  ≤ 🆎 🅿 VISA ⚙ 🆎 ⓪
*1 West Victoria Dock Rd* ⊠ *DD1 3JP –* ℰ *(01382) 202 404*
*– www.apexhotels.co.uk*                                                                Ya
**Rest** – Menu £ 14/22 – Carte £ 24/35
♦ Popular brasserie set in a contemporary waterfront hotel, boasting comfy banquette booths and pleasant views across the quay. Long-standing chef offers a
modern, seasonal, grill-based menu.

**at Broughty Ferry** East : 4.5 mi by A 930 - Z – ⊠ Dundee

🏨 **Broughty Ferry**  🔲 🕸 ⅙ ⅘ 🕊 🅿 VISA ⚙ 🆎
*16 West Queen St* ⊠ *DD5 1AR –* ℰ *(01382) 480 027*
*– www.hotelbroughtyferry.co.uk*
**15 rm** ⊑ **–** ♦£ 70/82 ♦♦£ 90   **Rest** – Indian – Carte £ 16/29 **s**
♦ Friendly, family-run hotel, located on the roadside in a small village outside
Dundee. Traditionally decorated interior and spacious, individually decorated bedrooms with complimentary mini bottles of wine. High tea features homemade
cakes. Restaurant offers classic European dishes and extensive Indian menu.

---

**DUNKELD** – Perth and Kinross – 501 J14 – pop. 1 005 ▮ Scotland          **28** C2
▶ Edinburgh 58 mi – Aberdeen 88 mi – Inverness 98 mi – Perth 14 mi
🛈 The Cross ℰ (01350) 72 76 88, www.dunkeldandbirnam.co.uk
⛳ Dunkeld & Birnam Fungarth, ℰ (01350) 72 75 24
◉ Village ★ - Cathedral Street ★

**Letter Farm** without rest ॐ     🚗 🍴 **P** **VISA** 🌐
*Loch of the Lowes, Northeast : 3 mi by A 923 on Loch of Lowes rd* ✉ PH8 0HH
– 𝒞 (01350) 724 254 – www.letterfarm.co.uk – May-November
**3 rm** ☷ – ♦£ 50 ♦♦£ 80
• Traditional farmhouse on a family-run stock farm, nestled between Butterstone
Loch and the Loch of Lowes Nature Reserve. Open-fired lounge with TV/DVD
player; homely communal breakfast room. Comfortable, simply furnished bed-
rooms boast king-sized beds; no TVs.

---

**DUNOON** – Argyll and Bute – **501** F16 – pop. 8 251 ▌ Scotland    **27** B3
▶ Edinburgh 73 mi – Glasgow 27 mi – Oban 77 mi
🛳 from Dunoon Pier to Gourock Railway Pier (Caledonian MacBrayne Ltd) frequent
services daily (20 mn) – from Hunters Quay to McInroy's Point, Gourock (Western
Ferries (Clyde) Ltd) frequent services daily (20 mn)
🛈 7 Alexandra Parade 𝒞 (08707) 20 06 29, www.visitcowal.co.uk
🏌 Cowal Ardenslate Rd, 𝒞 (01369) 70 56 73
🏌 Innellan Knockamillie Rd, 𝒞 (01369) 83 02 42
◐ The Clyde Estuary★

**Dhailling Lodge**     🚗 ▤ & rm, 🍴 🛖 **P** **VISA** 🌐
*155 Alexandra Par, North : 0.75 mi on A 815* ✉ PA23 8AW – 𝒞 (01369) 701 253
– www.dhaillinglodge.com
**7 rm** ☷ – ♦£ 40/76 ♦♦£ 81
**Rest** – *(dinner only) (booking essential)* Menu £ 20
• Proudly run Victorian villa on main seafront, with pleasant gardens and nice
bay views. Snug, homely lounge; cosy, individually decorated bedrooms with
good extras. Smart dining room with period fireplace; classical daily menu of unfussy pies, roasts and fish.

---

**DUNVEGAN** – Highland – **501** A11 – see Skye (Isle of)

---

**DURNESS** – Highland – **501** F8 – ✉ Highland    **30** C1
▶ Edinburgh 266 mi – Thurso 78 mi – Ullapool 71 mi
🛈 Durine 𝒞 (0845) 2 25 51 21, www.durness.org
🏌 Durness Balnakeil, 𝒞 (01971) 51 13 64

**Mackay's**     🍴 rm, 🛖 **P** **VISA** 🌐 **AE**
✉ IV27 4PN – 𝒞 (01971) 511 202 – www.visitmackays.com – May-October
**7 rm** ☷ – ♦£ 110/125 ♦♦♦£ 125
**Rest** – Carte £ 23/38
• Smart grey house at most north westerly point of mainland – the family own a
number of places in the village. Two nicely furnished, oak-clad lounges. Lovely
bedrooms with exposed wood floors, plasma screens and iPod docks. Formal dining room offers ambitious menu.

---

**DUROR** – Highland – **501** E14    **29** B3
▶ Edinburgh 131 mi – Ballachulish 7 mi – Oban 26 mi

**Bealach House** ॐ     🚗 🍴 🛖 **P** **VISA** 🌐 **AE**
*Salachan Glen, Southeast : 4.5 mi by A 828* ✉ PA38 4BW – 𝒞 (01631) 740 298
– www.bealach-house.co.uk – March-October
**3 rm** ☷ – ♦£ 70/80 ♦♦£ 100/120    **Rest** – Menu £ 30
• Superbly set, former crofter's house with impressive 1.5 mile driveway lined
with mature, deer-filled forest: the scenery is breathtaking. Snug conservatory
and cosy bedrooms; homely guest areas are hung with Lowry tapestries. Classical,
daily changing menu.

---

**DYKE** – Moray – **501** J11 – see Forres

---

**EDDLESTON** – The Scottish Borders – **501** K16 – see Peebles

---

**EDINBANE** – Highland – **501** A11 – see Skye (Isle of)

SCOTLAND

# EDINBURGH

See city maps on following pages

**SCOTLAND**

**City of Edinburgh** – pop. 430 082 – 501 K16 –  Scotland

▶ Glasgow 46 – Newcastle upon Tyne 105

🛈 **Tourist Information**

3 Princes St ℰ (08452) 255 1 21, www.edinburgh.org

**Airport**

✈ Edinburgh Airport : ℰ (0844) 481 8989, W : 6 m. by A 8 AV

**Golf Courses**

🏌 Braid Hills Braid Hills Rd, ℰ (0131) 447 66 66
🏌 Carrick Knowe Glendevon Park, ℰ (0131) 3 37 10 96
🏌 Duddingston Duddingston Road West, ℰ (0131) 661 76 88
🏌 Silverknowes Parkway, ℰ (0131) 336 38 43

◎ SIGHTS

**In the town :** City★★★ • Edinburgh International Festival★★★ (August) • Royal Museum of Scotland★★★ EZ**M2** • National Gallery of Scotland★★ DY**M4** • Royal Botanic Garden★★★ AV • The Castle★★★ **AC** DYZ • Abbey and Palace of Holyroodhouse★★ **AC** BV • New Town★★ CY**14** • The Georgian House★ **AC** CY**D** • Scottish National Portrait Gallery★ EY**M6** • Dundas House★ EY**E)** • Scottish National Gallery of Modern Art★ AV**M1** • Scott Monument★ ≤**AC** EY**F** • Craigmillar Castle★ **AC**, SE : 3 mi by A 7 BX • Dean Gallery★ AV opposite **M1** • Royal Yacht Britannia★ BV

**On the outskirts :** Edinburgh Zoo★★ **AC** AV • The Royal Observatory ≤★ **AC** BX

**In the surrounding area :** Rosslyn Chapel★★ **AC** S : 7.5 mi by A 701 - BX - and B 7006 • Forth Bridges★★, NW : 9.5 mi by A 90 AV • Hopetoun House★★ **AC**, NW : 11.5 mi by A 90 - AV - and A 904

714

SCOTLAND

715

# EDINBURGH

FIRTH

0 ___ 1 km
0 ___ 1 mile

Traffic subject to disruption
due to tram construction

SCOTLAND

**V**

CRAMOND

Marine
Silverknowes

FORTH-ROAD-BRIDGE

West Shore Rd    West Harbour Rd    Lower Gran

West    Drive    West    Granton    Rd    Granton

Cramond    Road    South

Road

Ferry    Road

Queensferry    Road    A 90

Drum Brae North    B 9085    Ferry    Road    POL    Road    Crewe    Road    South    ROYAL BOT
GARD

Main    St.

Hillhouse    Telford    Road    Road    902

Craigcrook    Road    BLACKHALL    CRAIGLEITH
SHOPPING CENTRE

Craigleith Road

**(A 8)**    **A 902**    Drum Brae South

Clermiston    Rd    Road    A 90    Queensferry    Road

Ravelston    Dykes

Ravelston    Dykes Rd    Ravelston    Dykes    **M¹**

(M 9) STIRLING

EDINBURGH
ZOO    58    MURRAYFIELD

43    Road    A 8    **W**    Coates

Glasgow Road    St. John's    Corstorphine    MURRAYFIELD    12.9

**A 8**    GLASGOW (M 8)    POL    Meadow    Pl. Rd    Rd    Balgreen    Road    18    HEARTS F.C.    15.6    Road

SOUTH GYLE    Broomhouse Rd    SIGHTHILL    Road    Gorgie    Slateford    Road

B 701    Calder    Road    Longstone Rd    14.9    Union Canal

**A 71** KILMARNOCK    **A 720** AIRPORT    Calder    Wester    Road    41    Colinton    Comiston

B 701    Leith    54

Hailes    Water    Road    Colinton    Road    Comiston

**X**    A 720    Road    Road    Colinton    Mains    Dri.    POL.    Comiston

Gillespie Rd    Colinton    Redford    Oxgangs    Road

**A 70** LANARK    JUNIPER    GREEN    Lanark    B 701    Road

18    A 720    18    18

**A**

716

SCOTLAND

## Balmoral

*1 Princes St* ⊠ *EH2 2EQ* – ℰ *(0131) 556 24 14* – *www.roccofortehotels.com*
**168 rm** – †£ 165/415 ††£ 165/415, � £ 21 – 20 suites                    EY**n**
**Rest** *Number One* ♢ **Rest** *Hadrian's* – see restaurant listing
♦ Deluxe Edwardian hotel boasting classically styled bedrooms with rich fabrics
and a subtle contemporary edge. Have traditional afternoon tea to the accompaniment of live harp music or try out the cocktails in the bar. Highly detailed service.

## Sheraton Grand H. & Spa

*1 Festival Sq* ⊠ *EH3 9SR* – ℰ *(0131) 229 91 31*
– *www.sheratonedinburgh.co.uk*                                                   CDZ**v**
**258 rm** – †£ 265/305 ††£ 285/325, ⊠ £ 20 – 11 suites
**Rest** *Santini* – see restaurant listing
♦ Spacious, modern hotel with two entrances. Sleek, stylish bedrooms boast
strong comforts, the latest mod cons and smart bathrooms complete with mood
lighting. Impressive four-storey glass cube houses a stunning spa.

## Prestonfield ⌖

*Priestfield Rd* ⊠ *EH16 5UT* – ℰ *(0131) 225 78 00* – *www.prestonfield.com*
**18 rm** ⊠ – †£ 295 ††£ 295 – 5 suites                                          BX**r**
**Rest** *Rhubarb* – see restaurant listing
♦ 17C country house in a pleasant rural spot, with dimly lit, opulent interior displaying warm colours, fine furnishings and old tapestries – one of the most romantic hotels around. Various elegant lounges and a whisky room. Unique, luxurious bedrooms boast a high level of modern facilities. Excellent service.

## Howard

*34 Great King St* ⊠ *EH3 6QH* – ℰ *(0131) 557 35 00* – *www.thehoward.com*
**17 rm** ⊠ – †£ 115/210 ††£ 210/260 – 1 suite                                   DY**s**
**Rest** *Atholl* – *(booking essential for non-residents)* Menu £ 32
♦ Series of 3 Georgian townhouses displaying characterful original features and
plenty of charm. Comfy period lounges. Spacious, luxurious bedrooms with classic
furnishings and a contemporary edge; each room is assigned a butler. Fine dining
in elegant restaurant.

## Scotsman

*20 North Bridge* ⊠ *EH3 1TR* – ℰ *(0131) 556 55 65*
– *www.thescotsmanhotel.co.uk*                                                   EY**x**
**67 rm** – †£ 320/350 ††£ 320/350, ⊠ £ 16.95 – 2 suites
**Rest** *North Bridge Brasserie* – see restaurant listing
♦ Characterful Victorian hotel set within the old 'Scotsman' newspaper offices.
Lovely period guest areas with wood panelling, stained glass and marble staircase. Good business facilities and large leisure club. Traditionally styled bedrooms.

## Hotel Missoni

*1 George IV Bridge* ⊠ *EH1 1AD* – ℰ *(0131) 220 66 66* – *www.hotelmissoni.com*
**134 rm** – †£ 190/400 ††£ 205/415, ⊠ £ 18.50 – 2 suites                        EZ**v**
**Rest** *Cucina* – see restaurant listing
♦ Striking, modern hotel; the first from this Milan fashion house, whose trademark
stripes feature throughout. Funky bar; boldly coloured bedrooms with clever design features, complimentary mini bar and smart, black mosaic floored bathrooms.

## Channings

*15 South Learmonth Gdns* ⊠ *EH4 1EZ* – ℰ *(0131) 274 74 01*
– *www.channings.co.uk*                                                          CY**e**
**38 rm** ⊠ – †£ 95/250 ††£ 125/250 – 3 suites   **Rest** – Carte £ 14/30 **s**
♦ Cosy Edwardian townhouse, tastefully furnished and run by a friendly team. Individually appointed bedrooms: the newer rooms are spacious, contemporary and
themed after Shackleton, who lived in one of the four houses that now make up
the hotel. Formal basement restaurant serves Gallic dishes.

**Hotel du Vin**  🛗 ⑇ 🅰🄺 ℅ ⑇ 🏋 💳 ⊛ 🄰🄴

*11 Bristo Pl ⊠ EH1 1EZ – ℰ (0131) 247 49 00 – www.hotelduvin.com/edinburgh*
**47 rm** – ♦£ 195/250, ♦♦£ 195/250, ⌑ £ 14.95    **EZn**
**Rest** *Bistro* – see restaurant listing
♦ Boutique hotel boasting unique modern murals, not far from the Royal Mile.
Guest areas include a whisky snug offering 300 spirits and mezzanine bar with
wine tasting room and glass-fronted cellars. Dark wood furnished, wine-themed
bedrooms.

 **Tigerlily**  🛗 ⑇ rm, 🅰🄺 ℅ ⑇ 💳 ⊛ 🄰🄴

*125 George St ⊠ EH2 4JN – ℰ (0131) 225 50 05 – www.tigerlilyedinburgh.co.uk*
*– Closed 25 December*    **DYa**
**33 rm** ⌑ – ♦£ 165/195, ♦♦£ 165/195    **Rest** – Carte £ 25/50
♦ Classic Georgian townhouse concealing a funky, boutique interior. Large, individually designed bedrooms are luxurious, boasting seductive lighting, quality furnishings and superb wet rooms. Busy open-plan bar and dining room have similarly stylish, modern décor.

 **Glasshouse** without rest  🚙 🛗 ⑇ 🅰🄺 ℅ ⑇ 🏋 💳 ⊛ 🄰🄴 ⓘ

*2 Greenside Pl ⊠ EH1 3AA – ℰ (0131) 525 82 00 – www.theetoncollection.com*
*– Closed 24-26 December*    **EYo**
**65 rm** – ♦£ 150/325, ♦♦£ 190/325, ⌑ £ 18.50
♦ Contemporary glass hotel with 150 year old church façade. Stylish bedrooms
have floor to ceiling windows and some balconies. Impressive two acre roof garden; honesty bar and 3 course room service.

 **Number Ten**  ℅ ⑇ 💳 ⊛ 🄰🄴 ⓘ

*6-10 Gloucester Pl ⊠ EH3 6EF – ℰ (0131) 225 27 20*
*– www.numbertenedinburgh.com*    **DYu**
**28 rm** – ♦£ 99/190, ♦♦£ 135/250, ⌑ £ 12.50
**Rest** – *(closed Saturday) (dinner only)* Carte £ 23/34
♦ Luxurious adjoining townhouses with romantic interiors and stunningly restored staircases. Decorated in gold, black and silver colour schemes, bedrooms
boast top class furnishings and jacuzzis. Sleek, modern dining room – set in
the original house – offers simple, Scottish-based menu.

 **Rutland**  🛗 ⑇ rm, 🅰🄺 ℅ ⑇ 💳 ⊛ 🄰🄴

*1-3 Rutland St. ⊠ EH1 2AE – ℰ (0131) 229 34 02 – www.therutland.com*
*– Closed 25 December*    **CZa**
**12 rm** – ♦£ 135/250, ♦♦£ 135/250, ⌑ £ 7.95
**Rest** – Menu £ 13 – Carte £ 26/44
♦ Boutique hotel with commanding position at top of Princes Street. Stylish,
modern bedrooms have bold décor, flat screen TVs and large, slate-floored
shower rooms; ask for one with a castle view. Contemporary restaurant uses
plenty of Scottish produce in its classic dishes.

 **Chester Residence** without rest  ℅ ⑇ 💳 ⊛ 🄰🄴

*9 Rothesay Pl ⊠ EH3 7SL – ℰ (0131) 226 2075 – www.chester-residence.com*
**25 suites** – ♦♦£ 165/275, ⌑ £ 9    **CZc**
♦ Collection of townhouses boasting one or two bedrooms suites. State-of-the-
art facilities include video entry and sounds systems wired throughout. Fully
equipped kitchens: the owners provide breakfast items or deliver a continental
option. Concise selection of pre-prepared dishes available at dinner.

**Dunstane City** without rest  ℅ ⑇ 🅿 💳 ⊛ 🄰🄴

*5 Hampton Terr, Haymarket ⊠ EH12 5JD – ℰ (0131) 337 61 69*
*– www.dunstanehotels.co.uk*    **AVe**
**16 rm** – ♦£ 79/169, ♦♦£ 89/179 – 1 suite
♦ Victorian house with modern feature wallpapers, black granite tiled floors and
large chandeliers in guest areas. Stylish, wood-furnished bedrooms offer good facilities; some boast jacuzzis.

SCOTLAND

SCOTLAND

🏠 **Kingsburgh House** without rest     🚗 ⁽𝕪⁾ P̄ VISA ⦿

2 Corstorphine Rd ⊠ EH12 6HN – ℰ (0131) 313 16 79
– www.thekingsburgh.co.uk     AV
**6 rm** ⬚ – †† £ 120/145

• Attractive Victorian villa with hands-on owners. Comfy lounge and formally laid breakfast room; ornate coving features throughout. Warm, classically styled bedrooms feature antiques, modern facilities and good extras; some are four-posters.

🏠 **Kildonan Lodge**     ⅍ ⁽𝕪⁾ P̄ VISA ⦿ AE

27 Craigmillar Pk. ⊠ EH16 5PE – ℰ (0131) 667 27 93
– www.kildonanlodgehotel.co.uk – Closed 25-26 December     BXa
**12 rm** ⬚ – † £ 69/129 †† £ 89/159

**Rest** – (closed Sunday) (dinner only, booking essential) Carte £ 18/24

• Well-managed detached Victorian house on main road into city. Spacious and traditionally furnished, with cosy fire-lit drawing room and comfy bedrooms some with four-posters and jacuzzis. Mathew's offers classical dining and plenty of Scottish produce.

🏠 **One Royal Circus** without rest     ⁽𝕪⁾ VISA ⦿ AE

1 Royal Circus ⊠ EH3 6SU – ℰ (0131) 625 6669 – www.oneroyalcircus.com
**5 rm** ⬚ – † £ 139/199 †† £ 178/258     DYw

• Stunning Georgian house at the end of a crescent; designed by William Playfair in 1823. Spacious interior with billiard room and 2 lounges boasting ornate plasterwork, a grand piano and bar. Stylish, understated bedrooms; marble bathrooms.

🏠 **94 DR** without rest     ⅍ ⁽𝕪⁾ P̄ VISA ⦿ ①

94 Dalkeith Rd ⊠ EH16 5AF – ℰ (0131) 662 92 65 – www.94dr.com – Closed
5-26 January and 25-26 December     BXn
**6 rm** ⬚ – † £ 80/120 †† £ 95/125

• Victorian terraced house on the main road into the city. Brightly tiled hallway leads to retro-style lounge with honesty bar. Lovely breakfast conservatory opens onto a decked terrace. Stylish, well-equipped bedrooms boast Scottish touches.

🏠 **Millers64** without rest     ⅍ ⁽𝕪⁾

64 Pilrig St ⊠ EH6 5AS – ℰ (0131) 454 3666 – www.millers64.co.uk
**3 rm** ⬚ – † £ 80/90 †† £ 90/140     BVe

• Modernised Victorian house in a renovated terrace, in an up and coming part of town. Smart, spacious bedrooms are all suites and boast good quality linen and extras. Communal breakfasts include a hot special and homemade pastries and jams.

🏠 **Kew House** without rest     ⅍ ⁽𝕪⁾ P̄ VISA ⦿

1 Kew Terr, Murrayfield ⊠ EH12 5JE – ℰ (0131) 313 07 00 – www.kewhouse.com
– Closed January and 25-26 December     AVa
**7 rm** ⬚ – † £ 79/130 †† £ 99/195

• Personally run stone-built house, close to Murrayfield Stadium. Larger than it looks from the outside. Neat lounge and wood furnished breakfast room. Immaculately kept bedrooms are up-to-date, of a decent size and come with good extras.

🏠 **Ardmor House** without rest     ⁽𝕪⁾ VISA ⦿ AE ①

74 Pilrig St ⊠ EH6 5AS – ℰ (0131) 554 4944 – www.ardmorhouse.com
**5 rm** ⬚ – † £ 55/90 †† £ 85/145     BVn

• Comfortable, laid-back guesthouse on a quiet residential street. Bedrooms range in size and boast bright, fresh décor, original plaster ceilings and granite fireplaces. Homemade bread, preserves and cakes at breakfast. Good local knowledge.

🏠 **Davenport House** without rest     ⅍ ⁽𝕪⁾ VISA ⦿ ①

58 Great King St ⊠ EH3 6QY – ℰ (0131) 558 84 95 – www.davenport-house.com
– Closed 1 week Christmas     DYv
**6 rm** ⬚ – † £ 65/110 †† £ 75/110

• Traditional Georgian townhouse restored to its former glory; set on an attractive cobbled street. Cosy sitting room and spacious breakfast room. Bedrooms are at the top of the house and furnished in individual styles.

720

↑ **Elmview** without rest     🛇 ⁽ᵗᵖ⁾ VISA ⓪
15 Glengyle Terr ⊠ EH3 9LN – 𝒞 (0131) 228 19 73 – www.elmview.co.uk
– April-November          DZ**e**
**5 rm** ⬛ – †£ 75/115 ††£ 90/140
♦ Occupies the basement of a Victorian house in pretty terrace overlooking The
Meadows. Bedrooms are spotlessly kept and are very large, with modern bathrooms. Owners are very welcoming.

XXXX **Number One** – at Balmoral Hotel     AC 🛇 VISA ⓪ AE ⓪
❀ 1 Princes St ⊠ EH2 2EQ – 𝒞 (0131) 557 67 27 – www.restaurantnumberone.com
**Rest** – Modern – (dinner only) Menu £ 62 ꧁      EY**n**
**Spec.** Scallops with apple purée, Iberico ham and chorizo crumb. Fillet of beef
with Anna potato, sweetbreads and Madeira jus. Slow-cooked cherries, goat's
cheese sorbet and honey and fennel mousse.
♦ Stylish restaurant in a grand hotel, displaying bold red walls hung with fine
art, well-spaced tables and deep corner banquettes. Ambitious cooking uses
quality Scottish produce to create elaborate, precisely executed dishes. Assured,
attentive service.

XXX **21212** (Paul Kitching) with rm     AC ⁽ᵗᵖ⁾ VISA ⓪ AE
❀ 3 Royal Terr ⊠ EH7 5AB – 𝒞 (0845) 222 12 12 – www.21212restaurant.co.uk
– Closed 10 days January and 10 days summer      EY**c**
**4 rm** ⬛ – †£ 325 ††£ 325
**Rest** – Inventive – (closed Sunday and Monday) Menu £ 26/67 s
**Spec.** Nugget of smoked salmon with chickpeas, pimento, aubergine, yoghurt, kidney
bean and thyme cream sauce. Baby halibut with golden beetroot, smoked chicken
wafers, sweet ginger butter sauce and piccalilli mayonnaise. Layered trifle of Granny
Smith, Williams pear and Victoria plum purée, crushed 'Weetabix' crumble.
♦ Smart Georgian townhouse with high-ceilinged dining room, contemporary décor and an open kitchen. The restaurant's name reflects the number of dishes per
course; skilful and innovative cooking offers some quirky combinations. Opulent
1st floor sitting room and luxurious bedrooms.

XXX **Castle Terrace** (Dominic Jack)     AC VISA ⓪ AE
❀ 33-35 Castle Terr ⊠ EH1 2EL – 𝒞 (0131) 229 12 22
– www.castleterracerestaurant.com – Closed Christmas, New Year, Sunday and
Monday      DZ**a**
**Rest** – Modern European – Menu £ 20 (lunch) – Carte £ 34/53
**Spec.** Spelt risotto with crispy ox tongue and veal heart confit. Seared hampe of
beef with potato millefeuille and beef jus. Ravioli of lemongrass with poached
rhubarb.
♦ Set in the shadows of the castle, an understatedly stylish restaurant with gilded
ceiling and attractive bar-lounge. Refined cooking showcases seasonal, local produce in an assured, unfussy manner, following a 'nature to plate' philosophy.

XXX **Hadrian's** – at Balmoral Hotel     AC VISA ⓪ AE ⓪
2 North Bridge ⊠ EH1 1TR – 𝒞 (0131) 557 50 00 – www.roccofortehotels.com
**Rest** – Brasserie – Menu £ 23/27 – Carte £ 31/50      EY**n**
♦ Delightful restaurant where a light, bright interior offsets dark floors and brown
leather chairs. Brasserie classics display plenty of Scottish produce; excellent value
3 course set menu.

XXX **Oloroso**     ⇐ �ております AC ⇕ VISA ⓪ AE
33 Castle St ⊠ EH2 3DN – 𝒞 (0131) 226 76 14 – www.oloroso.co.uk – Closed
25-26 December      DY**o**
**Rest** – Modern European – Menu £ 25/40 s – Carte £ 31/43 s
♦ Contemporary rooftop restaurant with buzzy atmosphere and good service.
Huge glass windows and superb terrace boast city, river and castle views. Bar
and grill menus display modern cooking.

SCOTLAND

XXX **Rhubarb** – at Prestonfield Hotel

*Priestfield Rd ⊠ EH16 5UT – ℰ (0131) 225 13 33 – www.prestonfield.com*
**Rest** – Modern – Menu £ 30 – Carte £ 37/59                                                    BX
♦ Richly decorated dining room set within a romantic 17C country house; s
named, as this was the first place in Scotland where rhubarb was grown. Concis
menu of both classic and modern dishes.

XX **The Honours**

*58A North Castle St. ⊠ EH2 3LU – ℰ (0131) 220 2513 – www.thehonours.co.uk
– Closed first 2 weeks January, Sunday dinner and Monday*                          DY
**Rest** – Modern European – Menu £ 18 (weekday lunch)/20 (early dinner)
– Carte £ 26/38
♦ Owned by a well-established chef, a bustling brasserie with a smart, stylish in
terior and pleasingly informal atmosphere. Menus take their influences from
throughout Europe but have a French leaning and always offer some Scottish
dishes.

XX **Santini** – at Sheraton Grand Hotel & Spa.

*8 Conference Sq ⊠ EH3 8AN – ℰ (0131) 221 77 88
– www.santiniedinburgh.co.uk*                                                         CDZ
**Rest** – Italian – *(Closed Saturday lunch and all day Sunday)* Menu 19
– Carte £ 22/49
♦ Smart hotel restaurant; the more relaxed sister to Santini in London. Dining
room split in two: the right side is more relaxed with a pleasant terrace. Wide
ranging menu of Italian classics; good value set selection.

XX **Ondine**

*2 George IV Bridge (first floor) ⊠ EH1 1AD – ℰ (0131) 226 18 88
– www.ondinerestaurant.co.uk – Closed 1 week early January and
24-26 December*                                                                      EZs
**Rest** – Seafood – Menu £ 20 (lunch and early dinner) – Carte £ 32/61
♦ Smart, lively restaurant dominated by granite-topped bar and crustacean
counter. Classic menus showcase prime Scottish seafood. Straightforward, tasty
cooking. Well-structured service.

XX **Mark Greenaway**

*12 Picardy Pl. ⊠ EH1 3JT – ℰ (0131) 557 09 52 – www.no12picardyplace.com
– Closed 25 December, 1 January, Sunday and Monday*                         EYe
**Rest** – Modern – Menu £ 20 (lunch and early dinner) – Carte £ 29/41
♦ Modern restaurant set within a Georgian house in the heart of the city. Cooking
is original, innovative and very visual, with Scottish produce arriving in unusual
flavour and texture combinations. Good value set lunch and pre-theatre menus.

XX **Angels with Bagpipes**

*343 High St., Royal Mile ⊠ EH1 1PW – ℰ (0131) 220 1111
– www.angelswithbagpipes.co.uk – Closed 24-26 December*                     EZa
**Rest** – Modern – Menu £ 20 (lunch) – Carte £ 26/42
♦ Small, split-level restaurant, just across from St Giles Cathedral on the Royal Mile.
Simple interior; some tables overlook a rear courtyard. Seasonal menus change ev-
ery six weeks, offering a mix of unfussy classics and more modern dishes.

XX **Forth Floor - Restaurant (at Harvey Nichols)**

*30-34 St Andrew Sq ⊠ EH2 2AD – ℰ (0131) 524 83 50
– www.harveynichols.com – Closed 1 January, 25 December, Sunday and
Monday dinner*                                                                       EYz
**Rest** – Modern European – Menu £ 28/35 – Carte £ 33/44
♦ Wonderful skyline views from huge room-length window; great sunsets. Bar di-
vides it into formal area with pricier modern European menu, and more casual
brasserie; good Scottish ingredients.

XX **Cucina** – at Hotel Missoni     AK VISA ⓒⓞ AE ⓞ
*1 George IV Bridge* ⊠ *EH1 1AD* – 𝒞 *(0131) 220 66 66* – *www.hotelmissoni.com*
**Rest** – Italian – *(closed dinner 25 December, and lunch 31 De-*     EZ**v**
*cember and 1 January)* Menu £ 20 (lunch) – Carte £ 32/58
♦ Stylish mezzanine restaurant with buzzy atmosphere, set amongst the trade-mark stripes of this fashion house hotel. Classic Italian dishes served on boldly patterned china; some sharing plates.

XX **North Bridge Brasserie** – at Scotsman Hotel     VISA ⓒⓞ AE ⓞ
*20 North Bridge* ⊠ *EH1 1TR* – 𝒞 *(0131) 622 29 00*
– *www.northbridgebrasserie.com*     EY**x**
**Rest** – Scottish – Carte £ 25/48
♦ Stylish brasserie in a characterful Victorian hotel; once home to 'The Scotsman' newspaper. Beautiful room with ornate ceiling, dark wood panelling and minstrels gallery. Scottish cuisine.

XX **Bistro** – at Hotel du Vin     AK VISA ⓒⓞ AE
*11 Bristo Pl* ⊠ *EH1 1EZ* – 𝒞 *(0131) 247 49 00* – *www.hotelduvin.com/edinburgh*
**Rest** – French – Carte £ 21/29 ✿✿     EZ**n**
♦ Located within a boutique hotel, a classical French bistro which plays host to regular themed lunches. Main menu offers traditional European choices and is ac-companied by a superb wine list.

X **Café St Honoré**     VISA ⓒⓞ AE
*34 North West Thistle Street Ln.* ⊠ *EH2 1EA* – 𝒞 *(0131) 226 22 11*
– *www.cafesthonore.com* – *Closed 1 January and 24-26 December*
**Rest** – French – *(booking essential)* Menu £ 20/23 – Carte £ 26/41     DY**r**
♦ Long-standing classical French bistro, hidden away down a side street. Simple interior crammed full of mirrors and bric-a-brac. Affordable daily menu with Gallic touch. Friendly service.

X **Cafe Fish**     VISA ⓒⓞ AE
*15 North West Circus Pl.* ⊠ *EH3 6SX* – 𝒞 *(0131) 538 61 31* – *www.cafefish.net*
– *Closed 25 December*     DY**x**
**Rest** – Seafood – Menu £ 25 (dinner) – Carte £ 19/29
♦ Well-established, family-run restaurant, previously located in Leith. Set in the city centre in a converted 1930s bank, it boasts characterful original features and excellent quality seafood. Menus are classically based with modern hints.

X **L'Escargot Bleu**     VISA ⓒⓞ AE ⓞ
*56-56a Broughton St* ⊠ *EH1 3SA* – 𝒞 *(0131) 557 16 00*
– *www.lescargotbleu.co.uk* – *Closed 25 December, 1 January and Sundays*
**Rest** – French – Carte £ 15/30     EY**u**
♦ Authentic French bistro with basement épicerie; sit in the front room, with its large windows, gingham tablecloths and buzzy atmosphere. Keenly priced menus offer classic French dishes.

X **Zucca**     🏠 AK 🍸 VISA ⓒⓞ AE
*15-17 Grindlay St* ⊠ *EH3 9AX* – 𝒞 *(0131) 221 93 23*
– *www.zuccarestaurant.co.uk* – *Closed 1 January, 25-26 December, Sunday and Monday*     DZ**s**
**Rest** – Italian – *(booking essential)* Menu £ 12/18 – Carte £ 18/29
♦ Friendly, well-run restaurant adjacent to Lyceum Theatre. Head upstairs for classic Italian dishes and all-Italian wine list, with great value pre-theatre menus. Book or come after 8pm.

X **Bia Bistrot**     🍸 VISA ⓒⓞ AE ⓞ
*19 Colinton Rd* ⊠ *EH10 5DP* – 𝒞 *(0131) 452 84 53* – *www.biabistrot.co.uk*
– *Closed first week January, second week July, Sunday and Monday*
**Rest** – Bistro – Menu £ 11 (lunch and early dinner)     AX**a**
– Carte £ 20/31
♦ Good value neighbourhood bistro with buzzy vibe and shabby chic style. Un-fussy, flavoursome dishes range in influence due to the friendly owners' Irish-Scottish and French-Spanish heritages.

**SCOTLAND**

✗ **Wedgwood**                                                    _VISA_ ⓦ AE

*267 Canongate ⊠ EH8 8BQ – ℰ (0131) 558 87 37*
*– www.wedgwoodtherestaurant.co.uk – Closed 3-20 January and*
*25-26 December*                                                        EY

**Rest** – Bistro – Menu £ 14 (lunch) – Carte £ 28/42

♦ Popular, atmospheric, split-level bistro with bold white and crimson décor, hidden away at bottom of Royal Mile. Personally run, with friendly staff. Well-presented, seasonal dishes.

✗ **Seadogs**                                               AC _VISA_ ⓦ AE ①

*43 Rose St ⊠ EH2 2NH – ℰ (0131) 225 80 28 – www.seadogsonline.co.uk*
*– Closed 1 January and 25 December*                                     DY

**Rest** – Seafood – Carte £ 18/21

♦ Lively seafood restaurant with canine motif, funky wallpaper and fast, friendly service. Well-priced menus offer sustainable fish and chips, plus a choice of tasty lighter dishes.

✗ **Amore Dogs**                                              _VISA_ ⓦ AE ①

*104 Hanover St ⊠ EH2 1DR – ℰ (0131) 220 51 55 – www.amoredogs.co.uk*
*– Closed 25 December and 1 January*                                     DY

**Rest** – Italian – Carte £ 14/24

♦ Sister to 'The Dogs' next door, with similar canine-themed décor. Simple, spacious and open-plan, with a buzzy atmosphere and friendly service. Good value rustic Italian dishes.

✗ **Dogs**                                                    _VISA_ ⓦ AE
☺
*110 Hanover St ⊠ EH2 1DR – ℰ (0131) 220 12 08 – www.thedogsonline.co.uk*
*– Closed 1 January and 25 December*                                     DY

**Rest** – British – Carte £ 12/23

♦ Simple eatery set on the first floor of a classic Georgian mid-terraced property; the original opening in the 'Dogs' group. Two high-ceilinged, shabby chic dining rooms and appealing bar area. Robust, good value comfort food is crafted from fresh, local, seasonal produce.

## at Leith

🏠 **Malmaison**                      ♨ 🖻 㐅 🍴 ㏿ P _VISA_ ⓦ AE ①

*1 Tower Pl ⊠ EH6 7DB – ℰ (0131) 468 50 00 – www.malmaison-edinburgh.com*
**100 rm** – †£ 100/205, ††£ 100/205, ☕ £ 14.50                          BV

**Rest** *Brasserie* – see restaurant listing

♦ Impressive former seamen's mission, set on the quayside; the first of the Malmaison hotels. Mix of bold stripes and black and white décor. Imitate bar and comfortable, well-equipped bedrooms; one with a four-poster and tartan roll-top bath.

✗✗✗ **Martin Wishart**                                        _VISA_ ⓦ ①
❀❀
*54 The Shore ⊠ EH6 6RA – ℰ (0131) 553 35 57 – www.martin-wishart.co.uk*
*– Closed 25-26 December, 1-19 January, Sunday and Monday*               BVu

**Rest** – Innovative – (booking essential) Menu £ 29/65

**Spec.** Roasted Kilbrannan langoustines with parsnip and white chocolate purée. Loin of Borders roe deer with goat's cheese gnocchi. Jivara dark chocolate, milk chocolate mousse and Earl Grey ice cream.

♦ Discrete façade leads to tastefully decorated room with bold, modern designs. Underpinned by a classical base, well presented dishes display carefully judged modern touches and excellent ingredients. Two tasting menus available.

✗✗✗ **Kitchin** (Tom Kitchin)                               🍴 AC _VISA_ ⓦ ①
❀❀
*78 Commercial Quay ⊠ EH6 6LX – ℰ (0131) 555 17 55 – www.thekitchin.com*
*– Closed Christmas, New Year, Sunday and Monday*                        BVz

**Rest** – Modern European – (booking essential) Menu £ 25 (lunch)
– Carte £ 53/64

**Spec.** Razor clams with chorizo and lemon confit. Saddle of Highland lamb, cooked on local hay. Rhubarb and crème fraîche tart with rhubarb sorbet.

♦ Converted dockside warehouse overlooking the quay. Expect refreshingly honest, very flavoursome and unfussy cooking from menus offering considerable choice. Seasonality, freshness and provenance are at the heart of the chef's philosophy.

XX **Plumed Horse**                                                   ⇦ VISA ◉ AE

*50-54 Henderson St* ⊠ *EH6 6DE* – ℰ *(0131) 554 55 56* – *www.plumedhorse.co.uk*
*– Closed 2 weeks summer, 1 week Easter, autumn and Christmas, Sunday and Monday*
**Rest** – Modern – Menu £ 26/55                                              BV**a**
◆ Personally run restaurant with ornate ceiling, vivid paintings, an intimate feel
and formal service. Well-crafted, classical cooking with strong, bold flavours and
good use of Scottish ingredients.

XX **Vintners Rooms**                                                    VISA ◉ AE

*The Vaults, 87 Giles St* ⊠ *EH6 6BZ* – ℰ *(0131) 554 67 67*
*– www.vintersrooms.com – Closed Sunday and Monday*                          BV**r**
**Rest** – Mediterranean – Menu £ 24 (lunch) – Carte £ 38/51
◆ Hugely atmospheric former wine merchants. Characterful, flag-floored room
displays over 1,300 whiskies. More intimate, candlelit room with superb 1739
stucco ceiling is used for dining. Wide-ranging Mediterranean menu.

XX **Brasserie** – at Malmaison Hotel                          🛱 P VISA ◉ AE ◉

*1 Tower Pl* ⊠ *EH6 7DB* – ℰ *(0131) 468 50 00* – *www.malmaison-edinburgh.com*
**Rest** – French – Carte £ 28/50                                             BV**i**
◆ Popular French brasserie in what was the first of the Malmaison hotels. Menus
offers a choice of classically based Gallic dishes. Dine outside in the summer,
overlooking the Port of Leith.

🛏 **Ship on the Shore**                                        🛱 ℅ VISA ◉ AE ◉

*24-26 The Shore* ⊠ *EH6 6QN* – ℰ *(0131) 555 04 09*
*– www.theshipontheshore.co.uk – Closed 24-26 December*                      BV**x**
**Rest** – Seafood – Menu £ 17 – Carte £ 29/41
◆ Smart period building on the quayside, modelled on the Royal Yacht Britannia
and filled with nautical memorabilia. Seafood menu offers fresh, simply prepared,
classical dishes.

**t Currie** Southwest : 5 m on A 70

↑ **Violet Bank House** without rest                      🚃 ℅ ⸨ℹ⸩ P VISA ◉

*167 Lanark Rd West* ⊠ *EH14 5NZ* – ℰ *(0131) 451 51 03* – *www.violetbankhouse.co.uk*
**3 rm** ⌑ – ♦£ 65/85 ♦♦£ 136
◆ Comfortable, well-run cottage with charming, individually decorated bedrooms
and attractive garden running down to river. Impressive Scottish breakfast features lots of choice.

**t Kirknewton** Southwest : 7 mi on A 71 - AX – ⊠ Edinburgh

🏨🏨 **Dalmahoy H. & Country Club** 🕭         ≤ 🚃 🐾 ⊠ 🕅 ⥮ ⅄ ℅ 📷 🔋
⊠ *EH27 8EB* – ℰ *(0131) 333 18 45*                🕭 rm, AC rest, ℅ ⸨ℹ⸩ ⥰ P VISA ◉ AE
*– www.marriottdalmahoy.co.uk*
**213 rm** ⌑ – ♦£ 90/120 ♦♦£ 100/130 – 2 suites
**Rest** *Pentland* – (dinner only) Carte £ 32/40
**Rest** *Long Weekend* – Carte £ 21/30
◆ Extended Georgian mansion boasting 2 championship golf courses and extensive leisure facilities. Country house style guest areas and well-equipped, uniformly styled bedrooms. Fine dining and good views over the 1,000 acre
grounds in Pentland. Laid-back dining in The Long Weekend.

**t Ingliston** West : 7 mi on A 8 – ⊠ EH28 8

🏨🏨 **Norton House**              🚃 🐾 ⊠ ⓓ 🕅 ⅄ ℅ 🕭 rm, AC rest, ℅ ℡ ⥰ P
*West : 6 mi on A 89* ⊠ *EH28 8LX* – ℰ *(0131) 333 12 75*                    VISA ◉ AE
*– www.handpicked.co.uk/nortonhouse*
**79 rm** ⌑ – ♦£ 120/220 ♦♦£ 122/230 – 4 suites
**Rest** *Ushers* – (closed Sunday-Tuesday) (dinner only) Carte £ 37/45
**Rest** *Brasserie* – Carte £ 21/38
◆ 19C country house in mature grounds, with impressive oak staircase and superb spa. Classic bedrooms in original house. Large, luxurious junior suites in extension; most have balconies. Classic cooking with seasonal Scottish produce in
intimate Ushers. Stylish, modern Brasserie.

SCOTLAND

---

**ELGIN** – Moray – **501** K11 – pop. 20 829    28 C

🏴 Scotland

▶ Edinburgh 198 mi – Aberdeen 68 mi – Fraserburgh 61 mi – Inverness 39 mi

🛈 Cooper Park ℰ (01343) 562 6 08, www.visitscotland.com

🏌 Moray Lossiemouth Stotfield Rd, ℰ (01343) 81 20 18

🏌 Hardhillock Birnie Rd, ℰ (01343) 54 23 38

🏌 Hopeman Moray, ℰ (01343) 83 05 78

👁 Town ★ - Cathedral ★ (Chapter house ★★) **AC**

🅖 Glenfiddich Distillery ★, SE : 10 mi by A 941

### 🏠 **Mansion House**    ⊟ ⊠ 🐾 🖫 🕸 🌡 🎿 **P** VISA ⬤⬤ 🅰

*The Haugh, via Haugh Rd* ⊠ *IV30 1AW*
– ℰ *(01343) 548 811 – www.mansionhousehotel.co.uk*
– *Closed 25 December*
**23 rm** ⊆ – ♦£ 102/120 ♦♦£ 161/192
**Rest** *Mansion House* – see restaurant listing
◆ Sizeable Victorian country house in attractive gardens. Grand inner wi[th]
beautiful Georgian-style drawing room featuring a grand piano; snooker tab[le]
in the 'wee bar'. Luxurious bedrooms – some with sleigh beds, four-posters o[r]
river views.

### 🏠 **Pines** without rest    ⊟ 🕸 **P** VISA ⬤⬤

*East Rd, East : 0.5 mi on A 96* ⊠ *IV30 1XG*
– ℰ *(01343) 552 495 – www.thepinesguesthouse.com*
**6 rm** ⊆ – ♦£ 45/55 ♦♦£ 60/74
◆ Charming Victorian house featuring original tiled floors and stained glass windows. Homely lounge and comfortable bedrooms; one with an antique fou[r]
poster bed. Highland products at breakfast.

### ✕✕ **Mansion House** – at Mansion House Hotel    ⊟ **P** VISA ⬤⬤ 🅰🅴

*The Haugh, via Haugh Rd* ⊠ *IV30 1AW*
– ℰ *(01343) 548 811 – www.mansionhousehotel.co.uk*
– *Closed 25 December*
**Rest** – Menu £ 24/35 – Carte £ 28/40
◆ Classically furnished formal dining room with linen-laid tables, set within a sub[-]
stantial 19C baronial mansion. À la carte offers traditional dishes and relies on lo[-]
cally sourced ingredients.

---

**ELIE** – Fife – **501** L15 – pop. 942    28 D

▶ Edinburgh 44 mi – Dundee 24 mi – St Andrews 13 mi

### ✕✕ **Sangster's** (Bruce Sangster)    VISA ⬤⬤ 🅰🅴 🅞

❀ *51 High St* ⊠ *KY9 1BZ*
– ℰ *(01333) 331 001 – www.sangsters.co.uk*
– *Closed January-mid February, 1 week November,*
*25-26 December, Sunday dinner, Monday and Tuesday*
*November-March*
**Rest** – *(dinner only and Sunday lunch) (booking essential)*
Menu £ 40
**Spec.** Scallop tempura on gingered lentils and wasabi dressing. Fillet of turbo[t]
shallots, mushrooms and red wine sauce. Lemon and raspberry tart, lemon posse[t]
and lemon and poppy seed sorbet.
◆ This sweet little restaurant is run by a husband and wife team. The understate[d]
decoration includes a collection of local artwork on the walls. The cooking is de[-]
tailed, finely tuned and informed by the seasons.

## ERISKA (Isle of) – Argyll and Bute – **501** D14 – ✉ Oban

27 B2

▶ Edinburgh 127 mi – Glasgow 104 mi – Oban 12 mi

### Isle of Eriska ⚜    ≼ 🖗 🔞 🖻 🌐 🏖 ♨ ⚒ ※ 🖸 ⅃ rm, 🆉 rest, ⅋ 🛎 ▣
*Benderloch* ✉ *PA37 1SD* – ✆ *(01631) 720 371*   🆅🆂🅰 ⓿ 🅰🅴
*– www.eriska-hotel.co.uk – Closed 3-20 January*
**23 rm** ⌑ – ♦£ 170/250 ♦♦£ 340/400 – 7 suites
**Rest** – *(light lunch residents only) (booking essential)* Menu £ 44 *(dinner)*
♦ 19C baronial mansion on private island, boasting fantastic views over Lismore and the mountains. Classically styled, open-fired guest areas display modern touches. Comfy bedrooms feature bright fabrics and hi-tech equipment. Superb spa and leisure facilities. Contemporary dining room offers daily menu of local produce.

---

## EUROCENTRAL – Glasgow – **see Glasgow**

---

## FAIRLIE – North Ayrshire – **501** F16 – pop. 1 510

25 A1

▶ Edinburgh 75 mi – Ayr 50 mi – Glasgow 36 mi

### ※ Fins   ▣ 🆅🆂🅰 ⓿
*Fencebay Fisheries, Fencefoot Farm, South : 1.5 mi on A 78* ✉ *KA29 0EG*
*– ✆ (01475) 568 989 – www.fencebay.co.uk – Closed 1-2 January, 25-26 December, Sunday dinner and Monday*
**Rest** – *Seafood* – *(booking essential)* Carte £ 30/49
♦ Sweet, simply furnished little restaurant and conservatory, set on a trout and oyster farm, complete with smokery and farm shop. Menus offer straightforward dishes of fresh fish and shellfish, alongside their own beech-smoked products.

SCOTLAND

---

## FIONNPHORT – Argyll and Bute – **501** A15 – **see MULL (Isle of)**

---

## FLODIGARRY – Highland – **501** B11 – **see Skye (Isle of)**

---

## FORGANDENNY – Perth and Kinross – **501** J14 – **see Perth**

---

## FORRES – Moray – **501** J11 – pop. 8 967

28 C1

▌ Scotland

▶ Edinburgh 165 mi – Aberdeen 80 mi – Inverness 27 mi

ℹ 116 High St ✆ (01309) 67 29 38, www.forresweb.net

🏌 Muiryshade, ✆ (01309) 67 29 49

◉ Sueno's Stone★★, N : 0.5 mi by A 940 – Brodie Castle★ **AC**, W : 3 mi by A 96. Elgin★ (Cathedral★, chapter house★★ **AC**), E : 10.25 mi by A 96

### 🏠 Knockomie ⚜   🖾 🖗 ⅋ 🛎 ▣ 🆅🆂🅰 ⓿ 🅰🅴 ⓪
*Grantown Rd., South : 1.5 mi on A 940* ✉ *IV36 2SG* – ✆ *(01309) 673 146*
*– www.knockomie.co.uk – Closed 2 weeks January and 24-27 December*
**15 rm** ⌑ – ♦£ 100/145 ♦♦£ 120/180
**Rest** *Grill Room* – see restaurant listing
♦ Personally run, extended Arts and Crafts house, which resembles an old hunting lodge. Relaxed lounge and pubby bar. Individually styled bedrooms: those in the original house are classical; those in the extension are more modern in style.

### ※※ Grill Room – at Knockomie Hotel   🖾 🖗 ▣ 🆅🆂🅰 ⓿ 🅰🅴 ⓪
*Grantown Rd., South : 1.5 mi on A 940* ✉ *IV36 2SG* – ✆ *(01309) 673 146*
*– www.knockomie.co.uk – Closed 23-28 December*
**Rest** – Carte £ 26/39
♦ Contemporary hotel restaurant with formal atmosphere, located in a charming, rurally set Arts and Crafts house. Seasonally changing Scottish-based menu showcases locally sourced produce.

727

**at Dyke** West : 3.75 mi by A 96 – ⊠ Forres

⋔   **Old Kirk** without rest 🌿        📠 ⅍ **P** 𝗩𝗜𝗦𝗔 ⊗ 𝗔𝗘

*Northeast : 0.5 mi ⊠ IV36 2TL – ℰ (01309) 641 414 – www.oldkirk.co.uk*
**3 rm** ⌛ – ♦£ 50/53 ♦♦£ 70/76

◆ Peacefully set, converted 1856 church, surrounded by grain fields. Airy inner with open-fired lounge displaying an original stained glass window. Charming bedrooms boast original stonework and arched windows; one has a carved four-poster.

---

# FORT AUGUSTUS – Highland – 501 F12 – pop. 508 – ⊠ PH32    30 C3

▶ London 543 mi – Edinburgh 159 mi – Inverness 34 mi – Fort William 32 mi

🏨   **The Lovat**        📠 🛎 ⅖ ℅ 🌙 **P** 𝗩𝗜𝗦𝗔 ⊗ 𝗔𝗘

⊠ PH32 4DU – ℰ (01456) 459 250 – www.thelovat.com
**28 rm** ⌛ – ♦£ 85/185 ♦♦£ 180/280
**Rest** – Carte £ 22/39

◆ Professionally run Victorian house with traditional lounge and lawned gardens set in pleasant village at southern end of Loch Ness. Variously sized bedrooms have a contemporary feel and good facilities. Smart, modern brasserie offers classic cooking.

---

# FORT WILLIAM – Highland – 501 E13 – pop. 9 908 ▯ Scotland    30 C3

▶ Edinburgh 133 mi – Glasgow 104 mi – Inverness 68 mi – Oban 50 mi

🖪 15 High St ℰ (0845) 2 25 51 21, www.visit-fortwilliam.co.uk

🖪 North Rd, ℰ (01397) 70 44 64

👁 Town★

🖾 The Road to the Isles★★ (Neptune's Staircase (≼★★), Glenfinnan★ ≼★, Arisaig★, Silver Sands of Morar★, Mallaig★), NW : 46 mi by A 830 – Ardnamurchan Peninsula★★ - Ardnamurchan Point (≼★★), NW : 65 mi by A 830, A 861 and B 8007 - SE : Ben Nevis★★ (≼★★) - Glen Nevis★

🏨🏨   **Inverlochy Castle** 🌿        ≼ 📠 🕓 🗞 ℅ 🌙 **P** 𝗩𝗜𝗦𝗔 ⊗ 𝗔𝗘

❀  *Torlundy, Northeast : 3 mi on A 82 ⊠ PH33 6SN – ℰ (01397) 702 177*
*– www.inverlochycastlehotel.com*
**17 rm** ⌛ – ♦£ 265/525 ♦♦£ 420/525 – 1 suite
**Rest** – *(booking essential for non-residents)* Menu £ 38/67 🌿
**Spec.** Blue lobster with melon, sesame biscuit and herb salad. Smoked pigeon with roasted foie gras, dandelion salad and morels. Pineapple tarte Tatin with pineapple sorbet and spiced syrup.

◆ Striking castellated house in beautiful grounds, boasting stunning loch/mountain views. Classical country house interior with sumptuous open-fired lounges. Elegant bedrooms offer the height of luxury Choice of smart dining rooms serving traditional dishes executed with care and precision. Top quality Scottish produce.

🏠   **Distillery Guesthouse** without rest        📠 ⅍ 🌙 **P** 𝗩𝗜𝗦𝗔 ⊗ 𝗔𝗘

*North Rd. ⊠ PH33 6LR – ℰ (01397) 700 103 – www.stayinfortwilliam.co.uk*
*– Closed 1 week Christmas*
**10 rm** ⌛ – ♦£ 55/75 ♦♦£ 76/89

◆ Smart hotel – formerly 3 distillery workers' cottages – at the foot of Ben Nevis. Comfy lounge with shortbread, whisky and books about the area. Landscaped gardens; terrace boasts lovely views.

⋔   **Grange** without rest 🌿        ≼ 📠 🌙 **P**

*Grange Rd., South : 0.75 mi by A 82 and Ashburn Lane ⊠ PH33 6JF – ℰ (01397)*
*705 516 – www.thegrange-scotland.co.uk – April-October*
**4 rm** ⌛ – ♦£ 108 ♦♦£ 120

◆ Delightful Victorian house with attractive garden and immaculate interior, set in a quiet residential area. Beautiful lounge displays fine fabrics; lovely breakfast room boasts Queen Anne style chairs. Bedrooms are extremely well appointed, with smart bathrooms.

↑ **Ashburn House** without rest      🚗 ❧ 📶 **P** 💳 ⊙⊙
*18 Achintore Rd., South : 0.5 mi on A 82* ⊠ *PH33 6RQ –* ✆ *(01397) 706 000*
*– www.highland5star.co.uk*
**7 rm** ☕ – 👤£ 45/55 👤👤£ 90/120
♦ Attractive Victorian house with comfy lounge and conservatory breakfast room.
Bright, modern pine-furnished bedrooms; Room 2 is largest and has the best
view. Homemade shortbread on arrival.

↑ **The Gantocks** without rest      ≤ 🚗 ❧ 📶 **P**
*Achintore Rd., South : 1 mi on A 82* ⊠ *PE33 6RN –* ✆ *(01397) 702 050*
*– www.fortwilliam5star.co.uk – March-October*
**3 rm** ☕ – 👤£ 70/90 👤👤£ 100/120
♦ Whitewashed bungalow with loch views; run by experienced owners. Spacious,
modern bedrooms boast king-sized beds, large baths and nice toiletries. Unusual
offerings and water views at breakfast.

✕ **Crannog**      ≤ 💳 ⊙⊙ ⓪
*Town Pier* ⊠ *PH33 6DB –* ✆ *(01397) 705 589 – www.crannog.net – Closed 25*
*December, 1 January and dinner 24 and 31 December*
**Rest** – Seafood – *(booking essential)* Menu £ 16 (lunch) – Carte £ 31/38
♦ Brightly painted eatery set on the pier over Loch Eil. Good value set lunch. À la
carte and daily blackboard menu of local fish and shellfish; try the mussels. Own-
ers also have a seafood shop.

---

**FORTINGALL** – Perth and Kinross – **501** H14 – **see Aberfeldy**

---

**FORTROSE** – Highland – **501** H11 – **pop. 1 174**      **30** C2
▶ London 574 mi – Edinburgh 168 mi – Inverness 14 mi – Nairn 27 mi

↑ **Water's Edge** without rest      ≤ 🚗 ❧ 📶 **P** 💳 ⊙⊙ 🅰🅴
*Canonbury Ter., on A 832* ⊠ *IV10 8TT –* ✆ *(01381) 621 202*
*– www.watersedge.uk.com – April-October*
**3 rm** ☕ – 👤£ 80 👤👤£ 120
♦ Personally run guest house with attractive gardens and superb views over the
Moray Firth. Immaculately kept guest areas. Three 1st floor rooms have French
windows onto terrace.

---

**GALSON** – Western Isles – **501** A8 – **see Lewis and Harris (Isle of)**

---

**GATTONSIDE** – The Scottish Borders – **see Melrose**

# GLASGOW

See city maps on following pages

**Glasgow City – pop. 629 501 – 501 H16 – 502 H16 – ▌ Scotland**

▶ Edinburgh 46 – Manchester 221

**🛈 Tourist Information**

11 George Sq ☎ (0141) 204 44 00, www.visitscotland.com

**Airports**

🛫 Glasgow Airport : ☎ (0844) 481 5555, W : 8 m. by M 8, AV
Access to Oban by helicopter

**Golf courses**

🏌 Littlehill Auchinairn Rd, ☎ (0141) 2 76 07 04
🏌 Rouken Glen Thornliebank Stewarton Rd, ☎ (0141) 638 70 44
🏌 Linn Park Simshill Rd, ☎ (0141) 633 03 77

**◎ SIGHTS**

**In the town :** City★★★ • Cathedral★★★ ⩽ DZ • The Burrell Collection★★★ AXM1 • Hunterian Art Gallery★★ AC CYM4 • Museum of Transport★★ AVM6 • Art Gallery and Museum Kelvingrove★★ CY • Pollok House★ AXD • Tolbooth Steeple★ DZ • Hunterian Museum★ CYM5 • City Chambers★ DZC • Glasgow School of Art★ AC CYM3 • Necropolis ⩽★ DYZ • Gallery of Modern Art★

**On the outskirts :** Paisley Museum and Art Gallery★, W : 4 mi by M 8 AV

**In the surrounding area :** The Trossachs★★★, N : 31 mi by A 879 - BV -, A 81 and A 821 • Loch Lomond★★, NW : 19 mi by A 82 AV

# INDEX OF STREET NAMES IN GLASGOW

SCOTLAND

# GLASGOW

SCOTLAND

SCOTLAND

### Blythswood Square
🔲 🍽 🐾 ↳ 🛐 ↹ 🗚 🎵 🆒

*11 Blythswood Sq* ✉ *G2 4AD –* ℰ *(0141) 248 88 88*
*– www.blythswoodsquare.com*
CY
**99 rm** 🍽 *–* **†**£ 195/245 **††**£ 245 *– 1 suite*
**Rest** *Restaurant –* see restaurant listing
◆ Stunning property on delightful Georgian square; formerly the Scottish RA
HQ. Modern décor contrasts with original fittings. Dark, moody bedrooms an
marble bathrooms; Penthouse Suite displays a bed adapted from a snooker tabl
Smart spa.

### Hotel du Vin at One Devonshire Gardens
↳ ↹ 🎵 🆒

*1 Devonshire Gdns* ✉ *G12 0UX –* ℰ *(0141) 339 20 01*
🆅🆂🅰 🆘 🆎
*– www.hotelduvin.com*
AV
**45 rm** 🍽 *–* **†**£ 125/165 **††**£ 125/165 *– 4 suites*
**Rest** *Bistro –* see restaurant listing
◆ Collection of adjoining 19C townhouses boasting original stained glass, woo
panelling and a labyrinth of corridors. Furnished in dark, moody shades but wit
a modern, country house air. Stylish bedrooms; one with a small gym and sauna

### Radisson Blu Glasgow
🔲 ↹ ↳ 🛐 ↹ rm, 🗚 ❄ 🎵 🆒 🅿

*301 Argyle St.* ✉ *G2 8DL –* ℰ *(0141) 204 33 33*
🆅🆂🅰 🆘 🆎 🅾
*– www.radissonblu.co.uk/hotel-glasgow*
DZ
**246 rm** *–* **†**£ 99/205 **††**£ 99/205, 🍽 £ 16 *– 1 suite*
**Rest** *Collage –* Modern *– (closed Sunday lunch)* Menu £ 20 *–* Carte £ 27/43
◆ Stylish, modern, commercial hotel with impressive open-plan interior; set i
central location close to the station. Three styles of bedroom – all offering goo
levels of comfort. Spacious dining room with central buffet area and all-encom
passing menu.

### Malmaison
↳ 🛐 ↳ 📞 🆒 🆅🆂🅰 🆘 🆎

*278 West George St* ✉ *G2 4LL –* ℰ *(0141) 572 10 00 – www.malmaison.com*
**68 rm** *–* **††**£ 160, 🍽 £ 14.50 *– 4 suites*
CY
**Rest** *Brasserie –* see restaurant listing
◆ Impressive-looking, former Masonic chapel with moody, masculine décor. Styl
ish, boldly coloured bedrooms offer good facilities. Named after Billy Connolly, th
Big Yin Suite has a roll-top bath in the room. Chic, glass-roofed champagne bar.

### Abode Glasgow
🛐 ↳ rm, 🗚 ❄ 📞 🆒 🆅🆂🅰 🆘 🆎 🅾

*129 Bath St.* ✉ *G2 2SZ –* ℰ *(0141) 221 67 89 – www.abodehotels.co.uk*
**59 rm** *–* **†**£ 99/175 **††**£ 99/175, 🍽 £ 14
DY
**Rest** *Bar MC & Grill – (Closed Sunday lunch and Monday)* Menu £ 14 (lunch)
*–* Carte approx. £ 35
◆ 20C former offices for the education authority. Original brass lift runs up th
centre of a spiral staircase. Small art exhibition; pictures of city landmarks on ev
ery headboard – the best room boasts wood panelling and a feature fireplace
Sizeable bar and restaurant with buzzy atmosphere and grill menu.

### Grand Central
🛐 ↳ rm, 🗚 rest, ❄ 📞 🆒 🆅🆂🅰 🆘 🆎

*99 Gordon St* ✉ *G1 3SF –* ℰ *(0141) 240 37 00*
*– www.principal-hayley.com/grandcentralhotel*
DZa
**183 rm** *–* **†**£ 79/199 **††**£ 89/199, 🍽 £ 17 *– 3 suites*
**Rest** *Tempus –* Modern *– (dinner only)* Carte £ 28/45
◆ Renowned hotel built into the main station; the first TV signal broadcast from
London was to this hotel. Smart bedrooms aimed at corporate market. Origina
plasterwork in ballroom; marble floors in champagne bar. Contemporary restau
rant boasts Murano chandeliers.

### Sherbrooke Castle
🚗 ↳ rm, 🗚 rest, ❄ 🎵 🆒 🅿 🆅🆂🅰 🆘 🆎 🅾

*11 Sherbrooke Ave, Pollokshields* ✉ *G41 4PG –* ℰ *(0141) 427 42 27*
*– www.sherbrooke.co.uk*
AX
**16 rm** 🍽 *–* **†**£ 90/150 **††**£ 95/175 *– 1 suite*
**Rest** *Morrisons –* Menu £ 14 *–* Carte £ 23/39
◆ Late 19C baronial Romanticism given free rein inside and out. The hall is richly
furnished and imposing; rooms in the old castle have a comfortable country
house refinement. Panelled Victorian dining room with open fire.

介↑ **15 Glasgow** without rest ⬤ P VISA ⬤ AE
*15 Woodside Pl.* ✉ *G3 7QL* – ℰ *(0141) 332 12 63* – *www.15glasgow.com*
– *Closed 25 December and 1 January*  CY**s**
**5 rm** ☵ – ✝£ 110/120 – ✝✝£ 120/150
♦ Charming Georgian townhouse on quiet square. Extremely spacious bedrooms with quality furnishings and some original mosaic and parquet floors. Cooked breakfast trays delivered to your door.

XXX **Brian Maule at Chardon d'Or** AC 🍴 VISA ⬤ AE
*176 West Regent St.* ✉ *G2 4RL* – ℰ *(0141) 248 38 01* – *www.brianmaule.com*
– *Closed 1 January, 25 December, Sunday and bank holidays*  CY**i**
**Rest** – Modern – Menu £ 21 (lunch) – Carte £ 42/53
♦ Georgian house in the heart of the city, boasting original pillars, ornate carved ceiling and modern art. Well-spaced, linen-clad tables; friendly, formal service from well-versed team. Classically based cooking presented in a modern style.

XXX **Rogano** 🍴 AC 🍴 VISA ⬤ AE
*11 Exchange Pl.* ✉ *G1 3AN* – ℰ *(0141) 248 40 55* – *www.roganoglasgow.com*
– *Closed 1 January*  DZ**c**
**Rest** – Seafood – Menu £ 17 (lunch) – Carte £ 34/61
♦ City institution established over 75 years ago. Charming art deco interior with marquetry reputedly from the craftsmen who fitted the Queen Mary. Formal service and largely seafood-based menu. More keenly priced dishes in basement bistro.

XXX **Two Fat Ladies at The Buttery** 🍴 ⇔ P VISA ⬤ AE
*652 Argyle St* ✉ *G3 8UF* – ℰ *(0141) 221 81 88*
– *www.twofatladiesrestaurant.com* – *Closed 26 December and 1 January*
**Rest** – Traditional – Menu £ 19 (lunch) – Carte £ 29/45  CZ**v**
♦ Wood-panelled restaurant with banquette seating and tartan furnishings; an old classic revived. Tasty, seasonal cooking; charming, attentive service and a great range of whiskies.

XXX **Bistro** – at Hotel du Vin at One Devonshire Gardens VISA ⬤ AE
*1 Devonshire Gdns* ✉ *G12 0UX* – ℰ *(0141) 339 20 01* – *www.hotelduvin.com*
**Rest** – Modern – *(Closed Saturday lunch)* Menu £ 18 (weekday  AV**a**
lunch) – Carte £ 35/53 🍷
♦ Elegant oak-panelled hotel restaurant in a terraced Georgian townhouse. Dark, moody feel, with modern wine-themed canvases on the walls. Menu offers classically based Gallic dishes and steaks.

XX **La Vallée Blanche** VISA ⬤ AE ⓞ
*360 Byres Rd., (1st floor)* ✉ *G12 8AY* – ℰ *(0141) 334 33 33*
– *www.lavalleeblanche.com* – *Closed 1 January, 25 December and Monday*
**Rest** – French – Menu £ 17 (lunch) – Carte dinner £ 28/39  CY**v**
♦ First floor restaurant-cum-ski-lodge, with wood-clad walls, stag antler lights and myriad candles. Classical cooking with a seasonal French base. Formal service from a jolly team.

XX **Grill Room at The Square** VISA ⬤ AE ⓞ
*29 Royal Exchange Sq (2nd Floor)* ✉ *G1 3AJ* – ℰ *(0141) 225 56 15*
– *www.grillroomglasgow.com*  DZ**r**
**Rest** – Steakhouse – *(booking advisable)* Menu £ 21 (lunch) – Carte £ 24/55
♦ Second floor of impressive Georgian building on Royal Exchange Square. Appealing menu focuses on seafood and 28-day hung Scottish steak, with choice of sauce and chunky chips.

XX **Urban** AC ⇔ VISA ⬤ AE
*23-25 St Vincent Pl.* ✉ *G1 2DT* – ℰ *(0141) 248 56 36* – *www.urbanbrasserie.co.uk*
– *Closed 1-2 January and 25-26 December*  DZ**i**
**Rest** – Modern – Menu £ 20 – Carte £ 26/46
♦ Imposing 19C building in heart of city centre. Stylish, modern interior with individual booths and illuminated glass ceiling. Modern English cooking. Live piano at weekends.

SCOTLAND

SCOTLAND

## XX Gamba
🍴 VISA ⦿ AE
*225a West George St. ✉ G2 2ND – ℰ (0141) 572 08 99 – www.gamba.co.uk*
*– Closed 1 January, 25-26 December and Sunday lunch* DZx
**Rest** – Seafood – Menu £ 20 (lunch) – Carte £ 27/69
♦ Extensive and appealing seafood menu; simple and effective cooking from chef-owner, with lemon sole a speciality. Comfortable dining room with good service from well-versed team.

## XX Parmigiana
AC VISA ⦿ AE ⓞ
*447 Great Western Rd, Kelvinbridge ✉ G12 8HH – ℰ (0141) 334 06 86*
*– www.laparmigiana.co.uk – Closed 1 January, 25-26 December and Sunday dinner* CYr
**Rest** – Italian – *(booking essential)* Menu £ 16 (lunch and early dinner)/19 – Carte £ 28/43
♦ Compact, pleasantly decorated traditional eatery with a lively atmosphere and good local reputation. Obliging, professional service and a sound, authentic Italian repertoire.

## XX Ubiquitous Chip
AC VISA ⦿ AE ⓞ
*12 Ashton Ln ✉ G12 8SJ – ℰ (0141) 334 5007 – www.ubiquitouschip.co.uk*
*– Closed 1 January and 25 December* AVe
**Rest** – Modern European – *(booking advisable at dinner)* Menu £ 30/40
♦ Iconic Glaswegian restaurant on a cobbled street close to Byres Road. Brasserie on the mezzanine level serves traditional Scottish dishes, while the restaurant – in a glass-roofed former courtyard – offers set selections of modern classics.

## XX Brasserie – at Malmaison Hotel
VISA ⦿ AE
*278 West George St ✉ G2 4LL – ℰ (0141) 572 10 00 – www.malmaison.com*
**Rest** – French – Menu £ 17 (weekday lunch) – Carte £ 20/36 CYc
♦ Characterful hotel brasserie set in the vaults of a former Masonic chapel, with informal, intimate atmosphere, booth seating and adjoining champagne bar. Classical menus have a French edge.

## XX Restaurant – at Blythswood Square Hotel
AC VISA ⦿ AE ⓞ
*11 Blythswood Sq ✉ G2 4AD – ℰ (0141) 248 88 88*
*– www.blythswoodsquare.com* CYn
**Rest** – Modern – Menu £ 20 (lunch) – Carte £ 31/61
♦ Stylish hotel restaurant in the old ballroom of the stunning former RAC building. Menus divide each course into 'classic' and 'contemporary' dishes, and there's a dedicated steak selection.

## X Balthassar
VISA ⦿ AE ⓞ
*33 Ingham St ✉ G1 1HA – ℰ (0141) 552 57 36 – www.balthassar.co.uk – Closed 1 January, 25 December and Monday* DZs
**Rest** – French – Menu £ 12/20 – Carte £ 19/43
♦ Former fire station in merchant city area. Brasserie styling with range of seating options, floor-to-ceiling windows and buzzy atmosphere. Offers snacks, brunch and unfussy French classics.

## X Dhabba
VISA ⦿ AE
*44 Candleriggs ✉ G1 1LE – ℰ (0141) 553 12 49 – www.thedhabba.com*
**Rest** – Indian – Menu £ 10 (lunch) – Carte £ 20/35 DZu
♦ In the heart of the Merchant City, this large, modern restaurant boasts bold colours and huge wall photos. Concentrates on authentic, accomplished North Indian cooking.

## X Stravaigin
VISA ⦿ AE ⓞ
🙂
*28 Gibson St, ✉ G12 8NX – ℰ (0141) 334 26 65 – www.stravaigin.com*
*– Closed 25 December and 1 January* CYz
**Rest** – Modern – Menu £ 15 (lunch) – Carte £ 23/38
♦ Well-run, long-standing restaurant with shabby-chic style and relaxed feel. Bustling bar and choice of dining areas on 3 levels. Their motto is 'think global, eat local', with interesting menus ranging from old favourites to Asian-inspired dishes. Cooking is careful and full flavoured. Monthly 'thali' nights.

✗ **Stravaigin 2**    `AC` `VISA` `AE` `OO`
*8 Ruthven Ln. , off Byres Rd* ⊠ *G12 9BG* – ℰ *(0141) 334 71 65*
*– www.stravaigin.com – Closed 1 January and 25 December*    AV**s**
**Rest** – Modern – Menu £ 13 (lunch) – Carte £ 18/37
♦ Simple neighbourhood eatery set back from the main road. Cosy split-level interior and warm, friendly service. Eclectic menu offers old favourites alongside Asian and fusion dishes. Clean, fresh flavours and well-thought-out combinations.

✗ **Cail Bruich West**    `AC` `VISA` `OO` `AE`
*725 Great Western Rd.* ⊠ *G12 8QX* – ℰ *(0141) 334 62 65* – *www.cailbruich.co.uk*
*– Closed 1 January, 26 December, 1 week spring, 1 week winter and Monday*
**Rest** – Modern – Menu £ 17 (lunch) – Carte £ 25/43    CY**a**
♦ Friendly, brasserie-style eatery – a real family-run affair – set opposite the botanic gardens. Extensive menu of tasty dishes that respect their ingredients. It's name means 'to eat well'.

✗ **Dakhin**    `VISA` `OO` `AE`
*89 Candleriggs, (1st Floor)* ⊠ *G1 1NP* – ℰ *(0141) 553 25 85* – *www.dakhin.com*
**Rest** – South Indian – Menu £ 10 (lunch) – Carte £ 18/35    DZ**n**
♦ Large open-plan first floor restaurant in redeveloped area of city, serving authentic, flavoursome south Indian cooking. Friendly, informal atmosphere; knowledgeable service.

✗ **Shandon Belles**    `P` `VISA` `OO` `AE` `OO`
*652 Argyle St* ⊠ *G3 8UF* – ℰ *(0141) 221 81 88*
*– www.twofatladiesrestaurant.com – Closed 25-26 December and 1-2 January*
**Rest** – Traditional – *(booking advisable)* Menu £ 15    CZ**v**
♦ Rustic restaurant in the basement of The Buttery, with exposed brick walls, church pews and formally laid tables. Tasty, unfussy dishes with a hearty base. Friendly service.

ᵗⁱᵈ **Babbity Bowster**    `WC` `VISA` `OO` `AE` `OO`
*16-18 Blackfriars St* ⊠ *G1 1PE* – ℰ *(0141) 552 50 55* – *www.babbitybowster.com*
*– Closed 25 December and 1 January*    DZ**e**
**Rest** – Traditional – *(closed Sunday)* Carte £ 25/34
♦ Double-fronted Georgian pub with fiercely Scottish interior; close to the Merchant City. Honest, seasonal cooking features traditional Scottish favourites; restaurant menu is more elaborate.

**at Eurocentral** East : 12 mi by M 8 off A 8 – ⊠ Glasgow

🏨 **Dakota**    `&` `⇄` `&` rm, `AC` `⁽¹⁾` `&` `P` `VISA` `OO` `AE`
⊠ *ML1 4WJ* – ℰ *(01698) 835 444* – *www.dakotahotels.co.uk*
**92 rm** – †£ 99 ††£ 99, � £ 11.95
**Rest Grill** – Menu £ 17/30 – Carte £ 16/37
♦ Stylish, modern hotel with sleek, masculine feel. Well-thought out bedrooms have king-sized beds and plasma TVs. Comfortable lounge popular for afternoon tea. Open plan bar and grill offers good selection of modern cooking.

---

**GLENDEVON** – Perth and Kinross – **501** I/J15    **28** C2
▶ Edinburgh 37 mi – Perth 26 mi – Stirling 19 mi

ᵗⁱᵈ **Tormaukin Inn** with rm    `⇄` `WC` `P` `VISA` `OO`
⊠ *FK14 7JY* – ℰ *(01259) 781 252* – *www.tormaukinhotel.co.uk*
**13 rm** ⊒ – †£ 55 ††£ 80    **Rest** – Carte £ 18/35
♦ Characterful inn run by truly welcoming team. Huge granite fireplace, dark, beamed bar and spacious, traditional dining room. Carefully executed dishes are largely traditional, with the odd contemporary offering; tasty homemade bread and ice cream. Tartan-floored bedrooms spread between the inn, stable block and chalet.

SCOTLAND

## GLENKINDIE – Aberdeenshire – 501 L12      28 D1

▶ London 537 mi – Edinburgh 125 mi – Aberdeen 41 mi – Dundee 85 mi

**Glenkindie Arms** with rm      🛋 🖁 P VISA ⚈

✉ AB33 8SX – ✆ (01975) 641 288 – www.theglenkindiearms.co.uk – Closed
25-26 December, restricted opening in winter
**3 rm** ⊊ – ♦£ 40/57 ♦♦£ 75/90
**Rest** – (booking essential) Menu £ 28 – Carte £ 24/44
♦ Remotely set, 400 year old, rustic Highland inn. Charming bar with an open fire
and a huge collection of malt whiskies. Concise, daily changing blackboard menu
of unfussy, seasonal dishes crafted from local produce. Simple bedrooms complete the picture.

## GLENROTHES – Fife – 501 K15 – pop. 38 679 ▌ Scotland      28 C2

▶ Edinburgh 33 mi – Dundee 25 mi – Stirling 36 mi

🔟 Thornton Station Rd, ✆ (01592) 77 11 73

🔟 Golf Course Rd, ✆ (01592) 75 86 86

🔟 Balbirnie Park Markinch, ✆ (01592) 61 20 95

🔟 Auchterderran Cardenden Woodend Rd, ✆ (01592) 72 15 79

🔟 Leslie Balsillie Laws, ✆ (01592) 62 00 40

🔟 Falkland ★ (Palace of Falkland ★ **AC**, Gardens ★ **AC**) N : 5.5 mi by A 92 and A 912

**Balbirnie House** ⑤      🗲 🕭 🔟 🕭 🕭 P VISA ⚈ AE ①

Balbirnie Park, Markinch, Northeast : 1.75 mi by A 911 and A 92 on B 9130
✉ KY7 6NE – ✆ (01592) 610 066 – www.balbirnie.co.uk
**30 rm** ⊊ – ♦£ 95/125 ♦♦£ 210
**Rest Orangery** – (closed Monday and Tuesday) Menu £ 18 (lunch)/35
– Carte lunch £ 26/32
**Rest Bistro** – Menu £ 13 – Carte £ 17/31
♦ Stunning Palladian mansion with formal gardens and extensive parkland. Large,
well-furnished drawing rooms in country house style; period features abound.
Luxurious, comfortable bedrooms come in varying sizes. Elegant glass-roofed Or-
angery serves classics with a twist. Basement Bistro offers French favourites.

## GRANTOWN-ON-SPEY – Highland – 501 J12 – pop. 2 166      30 D2

▶ Edinburgh 143 mi – Inverness 34 mi – Perth 99 mi

🄳 54 High St ✆ (01479) 87 27 73, www.visitgrantown.co.uk

🔟 Golf Course Rd, ✆ (01479) 87 20 79

🔟 Abernethy Nethy Bridge, ✆ (01479) 82 13 05

**Culdearn House**      🗲 🕭 🖁 P VISA ⚈

Woodlands Terrace ✉ PH26 3JU – ✆ (01479) 872 106 – www.culdearn.com
**6 rm** (dinner included) ⊊ – ♦£ 92/110 ♦♦£ 220/260
**Rest** – (booking essential for non-residents) Menu £ 37
♦ Personally run Victorian granite stone hotel offering a high degree of luxury,
including beautifully furnished drawing room and very tastefully furnished bedrooms. Formally attired dining room; good Scottish home cooking.

**Dulaig** without rest      🗲 🕭 🖁 P VISA ⚈ AE

Seafield Ave ✉ PH26 3JF – ✆ (01479) 872 065 – www.thedulaig.com
– Closed 20 December-7 January
**3 rm** ⊊ – ♦£ 100/110 ♦♦£ 140/150
♦ Small, detached, personally run guest house, built in 1910 and tastefully furnished with original Arts and Crafts pieces. Modern fabrics and uncluttered feel in
comfortable bedrooms. Tea on arrival. Communal breakfast includes homemade
muffins and bread.

## GRULINE – Argyll and Bute – see Mull (Isle of)

## GUILDTOWN – Perth and Kinross – 501 J14 – see Perth

SCOTLAND

**GULLANE** – East Lothian – **501** L15 – **pop. 2 172** ▯ Scotland     **26** C1

▶ Edinburgh 19 mi – North Berwick 5 mi
ⓖ Dirleton ★ (Castle ★) NE : 2 mi by A 198

🏠🏠🏠  **Greywalls** ☜                    ← 🥢 ✵ 🛰 🕸 **P.** 🚐 ⓒⓞ **AE**
*Duncur Rd, Muirfield, Northeast : 0.75 mi by A 198* ✉ *EH31 2EG –* ℰ *(01620)*
*842 144 – www.greywalls.co.uk*
**23 rm** ⌷ – ♦£ 80/105 ♦♦£ 260/320
**Rest** *Chez Roux* – see restaurant listing
♦ Classic Edwardian country house by Lutyens, in superb location adjoining the
famous Muirfield golf course. Spacious, antique-furnished bedrooms. Delightful
formal gardens by Jekyll.

🍴🍴  **La Potinière**                              **P.** 🚐 ⓒⓞ
*Main St* ✉ *EH31 2AA –* ℰ *(01620) 843 214 – www.la-potiniere.co.uk – Closed*
*January, 25-26 December, Sunday dinner October-May, Monday, Tuesday and*
*bank holidays*
**Rest** – *(booking essential)* Menu £ 23/42
♦ Intimate restaurant dressed in pink and white, serving fresh, seasonal cooking.
Regularly changing menus of traditional dishes, with ingredients from the owner's
vegetable plot and herb greenhouse, as well as local suppliers. Good value lunch.

🍴🍴  **Chez Roux** – at Greywalls Hotel            ← 🥢 **P.** 🚐 ⓒⓞ **AE**
*Duncur Rd, Muirfield, Northeast : 0.75 mi by A 198* ✉ *EH31 2EG –* ℰ *(01620)*
*842 144 – www.greywalls.co.uk*
**Rest** – French – *(booking essential for non-residents)* Menu £ 25/28
– Carte £ 31/42
♦ Country house style dining room with a modern edge; sit on high-backed
chairs at well-spaced tables, overlooking the golf course. Classical French menus
with a Roux signature style.

**HARRAY** – **501** K6 – see Orkney Islands (Mainland)

**HARRIS** – Highland – **501** Z10 – see Lewis and Harris (Isle of)

**INGLISTON** – City of Edinburgh – **501** J16 – see Edinburgh

**INNERLEITHEN** – The Scottish Borders – **501** K17 – **pop. 2 586**     **26** C2
– ✉ Scottish Borders
▶ Edinburgh 31 mi – Dumfries 57 mi – Glasgow 60 mi

🏠  **Caddon View**                                🥢 **P.** 🚐 ⓒⓞ
*14 Pirn Rd.* ✉ *EH44 6HH –* ℰ *(01896) 830 208 – www.caddonview.co.uk*
**8 rm** ⌷ – ♦£ 55/95 ♦♦£ 94/115
**Rest** – *(closed Sunday and Monday) (dinner only)* Carte £ 18/27 **s**
♦ Substantial Victorian house run by hospitable couple. Individually decorated
bedrooms with modern touches; spacious Yarrow, and Moorfoot with its view,
are the best. Bright, airy dining room; regularly changing menu of local produce
from the Tweed Valley.

**INVERGARRY** – Highland – **501** F12 – ✉ **Inverness** ▯ Scotland     **30** C3
▶ Edinburgh 159 mi – Fort William 25 mi – Inverness 43 mi – Kyle of Lochalsh 50 mi
ⓖ The Great Glen ★

🏠🏠🏠  **Glengarry Castle** ☜          ← 🥢 🐾 🐿 ✵ 🛰 **P.** 🚐 ⓒⓞ
*on A 82* ✉ *PH35 4HW –* ℰ *(01809) 501 254 – www.glengarry.net*
*– 23 March-4 November*
**26 rm** ⌷ – ♦£ 67/97 ♦♦£ 160/180
**Rest** – *(light lunch Monday-Saturday)* Menu £ 29 **s**
♦ Family-run Victorian house, named after the ruined castle in its 60 acre
grounds. 2 large, open-fired sitting rooms; stuffed wild animals abound. Classical,
individually styled bedrooms, some with original art deco baths. Formal dining
from 4 course Scottish menu.

SCOTLAND

**Invergarry** 　　　🚗 📶 📶 P VISA ⬤⬤ ⬤

*on A 87 – ☎ (01809) 501 206 – www.invergarryhotel.co.uk – Closed 2 January to mid-February*

**12 rm** 🛏 – †£ 55/90 ††£ 80/150   **Rest** – Carte £ 25/37

◆ Welcoming hotel in the style of a traditional inn. Smaller, quirky bedrooms in the eaves; first floor superior rooms offer more space and luxury. Comfy lounge featuring shotguns, open fires and tartan carpets. Simple cooking focuses on fresh Highland produce.

**INVERKEILOR** – Angus – **501** M14 – pop. 902 – ✉ Arbroath　　　**28** D2
▶ Edinburgh 85 mi – Aberdeen 32 mi – Dundee 22 mi

XX **Gordon's** with rm 　　　🚗 P VISA ⬤⬤

*32 Main St ✉ DD11 5RN – ☎ (01241) 830 364 – www.gordonsrestaurant.co.uk – Closed 2 weeks January*

**5 rm** 🛏 – †£ 50/80 ††£ 100/130

**Rest** – *(closed Tuesday and Saturday lunch) (booking essential)* Menu £ 28/48

◆ Long-standing, passionately run restaurant; wife oversees service, husband and son are in the kitchen. Charming interior with stone walls, open fires and exposed beams. Concise menu of classical dishes, well-crafted from local, seasonal produce. Well-kept bedrooms; the courtyard suite is the biggest and best.

**INVERMORISTON** – Highland – **501** G12　　　**30** C2
▶ London 550 mi – Edinburgh 166 mi – Inverness 28 mi – Dingwall 42 mi

↑ **Tigh na Bruach** without rest 　　　⬕ 🚗 📶 📶 P VISA ⬤⬤

*Southwest : 0.5 mi on A 82 ✉ IV63 7YE – ☎ (01320) 351 349 – www.tighnabruach.com – Restricted opening in winter*

**3 rm** 🛏 – †£ 87/96 ††£ 116/128

◆ Name means 'house on the bank'. Located by Loch Ness, it boasts splendid loch/mountain views and beautiful gardens. Very comfy bedrooms have pleasant terraces which overlook the lake.

**INVERNESS** – Highland – **501** H11 – pop. 40 949 ▌Scotland　　　**30** C2
▶ Edinburgh 156 mi – Aberdeen 107 mi – Dundee 134 mi
✈ Inverness Airport, Dalcross : ☎ (01667) 464000, NE : 8 mi by A 96 Y
ℹ Castle Wynd ☎ (01463) 23 43 53, www.visithighlands.com
🏌 Culcabock Rd, ☎ (01463) 23 98 82
🏌 Torvean Glenurquhart Rd, ☎ (01463) 22 56 51
◉ Town★ – Museum and Art Gallery★ Y **M**
◉ Loch Ness★★, SW : by A 82 Z – Clava Cairns★, E : 9 mi by Culcabock Rd, B 9006 and B 851 Z – Cawdor Castle★ **AC**, NE : 14 mi by A 96 and B 9090 Y

**Rocpool Reserve** 　　　♿ AC 📶 📶 P VISA ⬤⬤ AE

*14 Culduthel Rd ✉ IV2 4AG – ☎ (01463) 240 089 – www.rocpool.com*

**11 rm** 🛏 – †£ 150/175 ††£ 320/395　　　Z**r**

**Rest** *Chez Roux* – see restaurant listing

◆ Ultra-stylish boutique hotel with elegant, modern furnishings and sexy bar. Chic, comfortable bedrooms; some with their own terrace and hot tub. Attentive, professional service.

**Glenmoriston Town House** 　　　📶 📶 P VISA ⬤⬤ AE ⬤

*20 Ness Bank ✉ IV2 4SF – ☎ (01463) 223 777 – www.glenmoristontownhouse.com – Closed 8-9 January*　　　Z**x**

**30 rm** 🛏 – †£ 100/170 ††£ 140/170

**Rest** *Abstract* – see restaurant listing

**Rest** *Contrast* – Menu £ 12/15 – Carte £ 24/35

◆ Chic, stylish town house. Modern cocktail bar a trendy meeting point. Bedrooms are individualistic, those on the front enjoying river views; those at the rear are quieter. Locally sourced cooking at Contrast.

A 82 · A 9 : WICK, PERTH, A 96 : ABERDEEN

# INVERNESS

0    400 m
0    400 yards

B 865

EASTGATE SHOPPING CENTRE

Y

Z

SCOTLAND

HAUGH

NORTHERN MEETING PARK

BELLFIELD PARK

TOMNAHURICH CEMETERY

BALLIFEARY

BUGHT PARK

A 82 | LOCH-NESS, FORT-AUGUSTUS

B 862 | FORT-AUGUSTUS

## ⌂ Ballifeary Guest House without rest    🕭 ((•)) P VISA ⑩

*10 Ballifeary Rd* ⊠ *IV3 5PJ –* ℰ *(01463) 235 572*
*– www.ballifearyguesthouse.co.uk*
*– Closed 24-28 December*        **Zn**

**7 rm** ⌷ – ♦£ 40/70 ♦♦£ 70/85

• Pleasant house set away from town centre, with homely sitting room and comfortable, immaculately kept bedrooms. Smart breakfast room with crisp linen and polished glassware.

## ⌂ Moyness House without rest    🚗 🕭 P VISA ⑩

*6 Bruce Gdns* ⊠ *IV3 5EN –* ℰ *(01463) 233 836 – www.moyness.co.uk*
*– Closed 24-26 December*        **Zc**

**6 rm** ⌷ – ♦£ 65/85 ♦♦£ 94/110

• Immaculately clipped hedges frame this attractive Victorian villa. Bedrooms vary in shape and size but all are comfortable, individually decorated and fully en suite.

XXX **Abstract** – at Glenmoriston Town House Hotel     P VISA ◐◐ AE ◑

*20 Ness Bank* ⊠ *IV2 4SF* – ☏ *(01463) 223 777* – *www.abstractrestaurant.com*
*– Closed Sunday and Monday*     **Zx**
**Rest** – *(dinner only)* Carte £ 44/52

♦ Restaurant, bar and conservatory with considerable style. Vast wall mirror off-sets abstract ink pictures. Accomplished cooking with Gallic accent is impres-sively original.

XX **Rocpool**     AC VISA ◐◐ AE

*1 Ness Walk* ⊠ *IV3 5NE* – ☏ *(01463) 717 274* – *www.rocpoolrestaurant.com*
*– Closed 1-3 January, 25-26 December and Sunday except dinner*
*July-September*     **Yi**
**Rest** – Menu £ 18 (lunch and early dinner)/20 – Carte £ 22/38

♦ On the banks of the river Ness, this modern, cosmopolitan restaurant has a stylish ambience, popular with business diners. Modern cooking with a British/-Mediterranean axis.

XX **Chez Roux** – at Rocpool Reserve Hotel     🛏 AC P VISA ◐◐ AE

*14 Culduthel Rd* ⊠ *IV2 4AG* – ☏ *(01463) 240 089* – *www.rocpool.com*
**Rest** – Menu £ 25 – Carte £ 28/39     **Zr**

♦ Smart, stylish restaurant; its walls filled with photos of the Roux brothers' early days. Classic flavourful French cooking; smooth, attentive service from a profes-sional team.

X **Café 1**     VISA ◐◐ AE

*Castle St* ⊠ *IV2 3EA* – ☏ *(01463) 226 200* – *www.cafe1.net* – *Closed 1-2 January,*
*25-26 December and Sunday*     **Ye**
**Rest** – Carte £ 24/33

♦ Personally run bistro opposite the castle with an informal touch, enhanced by tiled flooring and modish chairs. Local ingredients feature in regularly changing modern menus.

**at Culloden** East : 3 mi by A 96 - Y – ⊠ Inverness

🏠 **Culloden House** 🐾     ⩽ 🚗 🐾 🕪 ⁙ P VISA ◐◐ AE

⊠ *IV2 7BZ* – ☏ *(01463) 790 461* – *www.cullodenhouse.co.uk* – *Closed 25-26*
*December*
**25 rm** ⊑ – †£ 95/270 – ††£ 135/270 – 3 suites
**Rest** *Adams Dining Room* – Menu £ 45 (dinner) – Carte £ 33/54

♦ Imposing Georgian country house in 40 acres, requisitioned by Bonnie Prince Charlie in 1746. Drawing rooms boast ornate wall-hung plaster friezes. Antique-furnished rooms. Adam's plaster reliefs adorn walls and ceiling of grand dining room; traditional menu.

**at Bunchrew** West : 3 mi on A 862 - Y – ⊠ Inverness

🏠 **Bunchrew House** 🐾     ⩽ 🚗 🐾 ⅏ rm, 🍴 P VISA ◐◐

⊠ *IV3 8TA* – ☏ *(01463) 234 917* – *www.bunchrewhousehotel.com*
**16 rm** ⊑ – †£ 170/185 ††£ 178/270     **Rest** – Menu £ 24/40

♦ Unhurried relaxation is assured at this 17C Scottish mansion nestling in a tran-quil spot on the shores of Bealy Firth. Drawing room is wood panelled; bedrooms restful. Gardens seen through the windows provide a pleasant backdrop to spa-cious dining room.

---

**ISLAY (Isle of)** – Argyll and Bute – 501 B16     **27** A3

🛫 Port Ellen Airport : ☏ (01496) 302361

🚢 from Port Askaig to Isle of Jura (Feolin) (Caledonian MacBrayne Ltd) frequent services daily (approx. 4 mn) – from Port Ellen or Port Askaig to Kintyre Peninsula (Kennacraig) (Caledonian MacBrayne Ltd) 1-2 daily – from Port Askaig to Oban via Isle of Colonsay (Scalasaig) (Caledonian MacBrayne Ltd) weekly – from Port Askaig to Isle of Colonsay (Scalasaig) and Kintyre Peninsula (Kennacraig) (Caledonian MacBrayne Ltd) weekly

ℹ The Square, Main St, Bowmore ☏ (01496) 81 02 54, www.islayinfo.com

🏨 Port Ellen 25 Charlotte St, ☏ (01496) 30 00 94

**BALLYGRANT** – Argyll and Bute                                    **27** A3

⌂  **Kilmeny** ℅                                    ≤ 🛏 🔊 🏊 ⚅ **P**
*Southwest : 0.5 mi on A 846* ⊠ *PA45 7QW* – 𝒞 *(01496) 840 668*
*– www.kilmeny.co.uk – Closed Christmas and New Year*
**5 rm** ⚏ – **†**£ 90/95 **††**£ 130/150   **Rest** – Menu £ 38 **s**
♦ Delightful house in over 350 acres of working farmland. Large lounge with
mock open fire and fine array of books about Islay. Superb bedrooms with beautiful feature beds, lovely tartans/tweeds/woollens woven on the island and
thoughtful extras. Spacious dining room serves garden/island produce. Truly welcoming owner.

**BOWMORE** – Argyll and Bute                                    **27** A3

ХХ  **Harbour Inn** with rm                                    ≤ 𝑉𝐼𝑆𝐴 ⚏
*The Square* ⊠ *PA43 7JR* – 𝒞 *(01496) 810 330* – *www.harbour-inn.com*
**7 rm** ⚏ – **†**£ 135 **††**£ 160   **Rest** – Carte £ 25/40
♦ Traditional restaurant with pleasant bar and chunky wooden tea tables covered in deep blue cloths. Classical cooking uses fresh local seafood and island
meats. Bedrooms are brightly decorated. Two cosy residents' lounges afford fantastic bay and island views.

**PORT CHARLOTTE** – Argyll and Bute                                    **27** A3

🏨  **Port Charlotte**                                    ≤ 🛏 ⚙ **P** 𝑉𝐼𝑆𝐴 ⚏
*Main St* ⊠ *PA48 7TU* – 𝒞 *(01496) 850 360* – *www.portcharlottehotel.co.uk*
*– Closed 24-26 December*
**10 rm** ⚏ – **†**£ 95 **††**£ 170   **Rest** – *(bar lunch)* Carte £ 21/33
♦ Waterside hotel packed full of modern art. Large lounge with wood burning
stove; cosy bar hung with old island photos. Bedrooms display traditional furniture and modern colour schemes; most have a sea view. Good mix of meat and
fish dishes in the restaurant.

**PORT ELLEN** – Argyll and Bute                                    **27** A3

🏠  **Glenegedale House**                                    🛏 ⚙ **P**
*Northwest : 4.75 mi on A 846* ⊠ *PA42 7AS* – 𝒞 *(01496) 300 400*
*– www.glenegedalehouse.co.uk – March-October*
**8 rm** ⚏ – **†**£ 90 **††**£ 115   **Rest** – Menu £ 35
♦ Well-run hotel opposite the airport. Immaculately kept bedrooms feature designer fabrics. Choice of two sitting rooms, both displaying leather sofas, coffee
tables and an array of curios. Traditional menu of island produce served in
smartly laid dining rooms.

⌂  **Glenmachrie Farmhouse** without rest                                    🛏 🔊 ⤳ ⚙ **P**
*Northwest : 4.5 mi on A 846* ⊠ *PA42 7AQ* – 𝒞 *(01496) 302 560*
*– www.glenmachrie.com – Closed Christmas and New Year*
**5 rm** ⚏ – **†**£ 90 **††**£ 100
♦ Homely tartan-themed guesthouse where antiques and curious abound. Exclusive access to private loch; catch a fish and they will prepare and even smoke it
for you. Breakfast at Glenegedale House.

**JEDBURGH** – The Scottish Borders – **501** M17 – **pop. 4 090** 📗 Scotland   **26** D2
▶ Edinburgh 48 mi – Carlisle 54 mi – Newcastle upon Tyne 57 mi
ℹ Murray's Green 𝒞 (01835) 86 31 70, www.visitscotland.com
📓 Jedburgh Dunion Rd, 𝒞 (01835) 86 35 87
◉ Town★ - Abbey★★ **AC** – Mary Queen of Scots House Visitor Centre★ **AC** –
The Canongate Bridge★
◐ Waterloo Monument (❄★★) N : 4 mi by A 68 and B 6400

SCOTLAND

## Willow Court without rest 🛋 📶 P.

*The Friars* ✉ TD8 6BN – ☎ *(01835) 863 702 – www.willowcourtjedburgh.co.uk*
**3 rm** 🍽 – ♦£ 70/75 ♦♦£ 75/85
 ◆ Contemporary guesthouse looking out over the town's rooftops. Comfortable ground floor bedrooms offer a light, stylish space, with flat screen TVs, iPod docks and DVD players, as well as smart, modern bathrooms. Communal breakfasts, with eggs from their own hens.

## KELSO – The Scottish Borders – 501 M17 – pop. 5 116 ◗ Scotland    26 D2

▶ Edinburgh 44 mi – Hawick 21 mi – Newcastle upon Tyne 68 mi
ℹ The Square ☎ (01835) 86 31 70, www.kelso.bordernet.co.uk
🏌 Golf Course Rd, ☎ (01573) 22 30 09
👁 Town★ - The Square★★ - ≼★ from Kelso Bridge
🌄 Tweed Valley★★ - Floors Castle★ **AC**, NW : 1.5 mi by A 6089.
Mellerstain★★ (Ceilings★★★, Library★★★) **AC**, NW : 6 mi by A 6089 – Waterloo Monument (❄★★), SW : 7 mi by A 698 and B 6400 – Jedburgh Abbey★★ **AC**, SW : 8.5 mi by A 698 - Dryburgh Abbey★★ **AC** (setting★★★), SW : 10.5 mi by A 6089, B 6397 and B 6404 – Scott's View★★, W : 11 mi by A 6089, B 6397, B 6404 and B 6356 – Smailholm Tower★ (❄★★), NW : 6 mi by A 6089 and B 6397 - Lady Kirk (Kirk o'Steil★), NE : 16 mi by A 698, A 697, A 6112 and B 6437

## Roxburghe 🌳    ≼ 🛋 🐕 🏌 🖥 ⚘ 📶 🖢 P. VISA ⊕ AE ①

*Heiton, Southwest : 3.5 mi by A 698* ✉ TD5 8JZ – ☎ *(01573) 450 331
– www.roxburghe-hotel.com*
**20 rm** 🍽 – ♦£ 99/190 ♦♦£ 159/250 – 2 suites
**Rest** – Carte £ 23/41 **s**
 ◆ Characterful Jacobean style mansion in extensive parkland, owned by the Duke of Roxburghe. Plush lounge and cosy library bar boating antiques/heirlooms. Feature bedrooms the most luxurious; courtyard rooms, more modern. Formal dining – local produce to the fore.

## Ednam House    ≼ 🛋 🐕 🖢 P. VISA ⊕

*Bridge St.* ✉ TD5 7HT – ☎ *(01573) 224 168 – www.ednamhouse.com*
– Closed 24 December-9 January
**32 rm** 🍽 – ♦£ 91/138 ♦♦£ 119/167
**Rest** – Menu £ 14/33
 ◆ Longstanding sports hotel on the Tweed; in the family since 1928. Original features, grand drawing rooms and classically styled bedrooms boasting a timeless elegance. Fishing-themed bar displays mural of the Tweed. 4 course classical dinner overlooking the river.

**at Ednam** North : 2.25 mi on B 6461 – ✉ Kelso

## Edenwater House 🌳    ≼ 🛋 ⚘ 📶 P. VISA ⊕

*off Stichill rd* ✉ TD5 7QL – ☎ *(01573) 224 070 – www.edenwaterhouse.co.uk*
– March-November
**5 rm** 🍽 – ♦£ 85 ♦♦£ 120
**Rest** – (Closed Sunday-Monday) (dinner only) Menu £ 38
 ◆ Delightful house run by charming couple, boasting a lovely garden and stream. Antique-filled lounges and comfy, classical bedrooms with tasteful décor and antique furniture. Pleasant dining room overlooks a meadow and offers a traditional, daily changing set menu.

## KENMORE – Perth and Kinross – 501 I14 – pop. 596 ◗ Scotland    28 C2

▶ Edinburgh 82 mi – Dundee 60 mi – Oban 71 mi – Perth 38 mi
🏌 Taymouth Castle Aberfeldy, ☎ (01887) 83 02 28
🏞 Mains of Taymouth, ☎ (01887) 83 02 26
👁 Village★
🌄 Loch Tay★★. Ben Lawers★★, SW : 8 mi by A 827

SCOTLAND

### Kenmore
    🖼 🌂 ⬛ 🅐🅒 rest, �🍴 ♨ 🅿 VISA ⑩ AE

*The Square* ✉ PH15 2NU – ✆ (01887) 830 205 – www.kenmorehotel.com
**40 rm** (dinner included) ⌂ – ✝£ 100/110 ✝✝£ 167/230
**Rest** – Carte £ 21/35
♦ Scotland's oldest inn. Standing on the Tay, it is now a smart, white-fronted hotel with Poet's Parlour featuring original pencilled verse by Burns. Cosy, well-kept rooms. Restaurant with panoramic river views.

---

**KILBERRY** – Argyll and Bute – **501** D16 – see Kintyre (Peninsula)

---

**KILCHRENAN** – Argyll and Bute – **501** E14 – ✉ **Taynuilt** 📗 Scotland    **27** B2

▶ Edinburgh 117 mi – Glasgow 87 mi – Oban 18 mi
◉ Loch Awe★★, E : 1.25 m

### Ardanaiseig ⌛
    ⩽ 🖼 🕭 🌂 ⅍ 🅿 VISA ⑩ AE ⑩

*Northeast : 4 mi* ✉ PA35 1HE – ✆ (01866) 833 333 – www.ardanaiseig.com
– Closed 2 January-1 February
**17 rm** ⌂ – ✝£ 69/108 ✝✝£ 138/218 – 1 suite
**Rest** – (booking essential for non-residents) Menu £ 30/50
♦ Stunningly located, laid-back country house boasting a vast azalea-filled estate and lovely views down the loch. Large sitting room with impressive columns; bedrooms mix styles – the Lake Suite is best. Elegant formal dining room; daily set menu of local produce.

⌂ **Roineabhal** without rest ⌛
    🖼 ⅍ �🍴 🅿 VISA ⑩ AE

✉ PA35 1HD – ✆ (01866) 833 207 – www.roineabhal.com – Easter-October
**3 rm** ⌂ – ✝£ 70/90 ✝✝£ 100
♦ Purpose-built, log cabin style guesthouse; jolly owner serves tea and homemade biscuits on arrival. Cosy bedrooms reached via spiral staircase: all have showers; roll-top bath is shared. Bluebell-lined walk in garden.

---

**KILDRUMMY** – Aberdeenshire – **501** L12 – ✉ **Alford** 📗 Scotland    **28** D1

▶ Edinburgh 137 mi – Aberdeen 35 mi
◉ Castle★ **AC**
◉ Huntly Castle (Heraldic carvings★★★) N : 15 mi by A 97 – Craigievar Castle★, SE : 13 mi by A 97, A 944 and A 980

### Kildrummy Castle ⌛
    ⩽ 🖼 🕭 🌂 ⅍ 🅿 VISA ⑩ AE

*South : 1.5 mi on A 97* ✉ AB33 8RA – ✆ (019755) 71 288
– www.kildrummycastlehotel.co.uk – Closed January
**16 rm** ⌂ – ✝£ 98/120 ✝✝£ 175/217
**Rest** *Dining Room* – see restaurant listing
♦ Imposing stone mansion in beautiful grounds, overlooking a 13C castle. Impressive gallery corridor hung with tapestries; lovely lounge, library and drawing room with attractive Georgian plasterwork. Traditional bedrooms; one with a terrace.

XXX **Dining Room** – at Kildrummy Castle Hotel
    ⩽ 🖼 🕭 🅿 VISA ⑩ AE

*South : 1.5 mi on A 97* ✉ AB33 8RA – ✆ (019755) 71 288
– www.kildrummycastlehotel.co.uk – Closed January and lunch Monday
**Rest** – Menu £ 21/37
♦ Grand dining room with linen-laid tables, imposing wooden ceiling and original fireplace, set in a stone-built baronial mansion dating back to 1900. Classical dishes display some modern twists.

---

**KILLIECRANKIE** – Perth and Kinross – **501** I13 – see Pitlochry

**KINCLAVEN** – Perth and Kinross – **501** J14 – pop. 394 – ⊠ Stanley      **28** C2

▶ Edinburgh 56 mi – Perth 12 mi

### Ballathie House ⌂      ⟨ 🚗 🐾 🐟 & rm, ⸌¹⸍ 🍴 P VISA ☎ AE ⓞ

*Stanley ⊠ PH1 4QN – ℰ (01250) 883 268 – www.ballathiehousehotel.com*
**39 rm** (dinner included) ☐ – ♦£ 105/165 ♦♦£ 290/370 – 3 suites
**Rest** – Menu £ 27/44 **s**
♦ Well-established, mid-19C former shooting lodge, set on a peaceful estate of several hundred acres, on the banks of the River Tay. Comfortable guest areas and individually furnished bedrooms: some with floral themes, some more contemporary. Concise country house menu showcases seasonal, regional produce.

**KINGAIRLOCH** – HLD Highland – **501** D14      **29** B3

▶ London 521 mi – Edinburgh 147 mi – Greenock 116 mi

### ✕ Boathouse and Steadings with rm      🐟 🛖 & rm, P VISA ☎ AE

*Ardgour ⊠ PH33 7AE – ℰ (01967) 411 232 – www.kingairloch.co.uk*
*– 23 March-27 October*
**5 rm** ☐ – ♦£ 80 ♦♦£ 80
**Rest** – (closed Monday-Wednesday and Sunday dinner) (booking advisable)
Carte £ 17/31
♦ A converted Victorian boathouse on the shore of Loch a'Choire in the heart of the Kingairloch Estate. Appealing dishes use estate produce, including full-flavoured venison, and seasonal herbs and vegetables from the kitchen garden. Spacious, immaculately maintained bedrooms in The Steadings. Dramatic mountain views.

**KINGUSSIE** – Highland – **501** H12 – pop. 1 410 ▌ Scotland      **30** C3

▶ Edinburgh 117 mi – Inverness 41 mi – Perth 73 mi

🔟 Gynack Rd, ℰ (01540) 66 16 00

🟢 Highland Wildlife Park★ **AC**, NE : 4 mi by A 9. Aviemore★, NE : 11 mi by A 9 – The Cairngorms★★ (⟨★★★) - ❄★★★ from Cairn Gorm, NE : 18 mi by B 970

### ⌂ Hermitage      🚗 & rm, ⸌¹⸍ ⸌¹⸍ P VISA ☎

*Spey St ⊠ PH21 1HN – ℰ (01540) 662 137 – www.thehermitage-scotland.com*
*– Closed 20 December-4 January*
**5 rm** ☐ – ♦£ 32/55 ♦♦£ 60/100
**Rest** – Menu £ 24 **s**
♦ Traditional Victorian house built from stone and slate; formerly a doctor's surgery. Spacious garden affords great views of the Cairngorm Mountains and Ruthven Barracks. Warm, cosy lounge and comfy bedrooms; one has a super-king-sized bed and wet room. Simple dining room offers daily menu of home-cooked local produce.

### ✕✕ Cross at Kingussie with rm ⌂      ⸌¹⸍ P VISA ☎ AE

*Tweed Mill Brae, Ardbroilach Rd ⊠ PH21 1LB – ℰ (01540) 661 166*
*– www.thecross.co.uk – Closed 3 January-9 January, 25 December,*
*Sunday and Monday*
**8 rm** (dinner included) ☐ – ♦£ 150/185 ♦♦£ 230/250
**Rest** – (dinner only) (booking essential) Menu £ 50 **s**🍷
♦ Personally run converted tweed mill restaurant in four acres of waterside grounds with beamed ceilings and modern artwork. Modish Scottish cuisine. Comfortable rooms.

**KINTILLO** – Perth and Kinross – see Perth

## KINTYRE (Peninsula) – Argyll and Bute – 501 D16 📓 Scotland    27 B3

🛧 Campbeltown Airport : 𝒞 (01586) 553797

🚢 from Claonaig to Isle of Arran (Lochranza) (Caledonian MacBrayne Ltd) frequent services daily (30 mn) – from Kennacraig to Isle of Islay (Port Ellen or Port Askaig) (Caledonian MacBrayne Ltd) 1-3 daily – from Kennacraig to Oban via Isle of Colonsay (Scalasaig) and Isle of Islay (Port Askaig) 3 weekly

🏌️ Machrihanish Campbeltown, 𝒞 (01586) 81 02 13

🏌️ Dunaverty Campbeltown Southend, 𝒞 (01586) 83 06 77

🏌️ Gigha Isle of Gigha, 𝒞 (01583) 50 52 42

👁 Carradale ★ – Saddell (Collection of grave slabs ★)

## CARRADALE – Argyll and Bute    27 B3

🏠 **Dunvalanree** ⌾    ≤ 🖼 & rm, **P** 𝘝𝘐𝘚𝘈 ⓿
*Port Righ Bay* ⊠ *PA28 6SE* – 𝒞 *(01583) 431 226* – *www.dunvalanree.com*
**5 rm** (dinner included) 🛏 – 🛉£ 95 🛉🛉£ 175
**Rest** – *(dinner only)* Menu £ 23/28

♦ 1930s house in its own bay, with gardens and terrace overlooking the beach and Sound. Charming interior with many original Arts and Crafts features. Individually furnished bedrooms – one in Mackintosh style; some with views. Homely cooking with a seafood base.

## KILBERRY – Argyll and Bute    27 A3

🍴 **Kilberry Inn** with rm ⌾    **P** 𝘝𝘐𝘚𝘈 ⓿
😊 ⊠ *PA29 6YD* – 𝒞 *(01880) 770 223* – *www.kilberryinn.com* – *Closed January-February and Christmas*
**5 rm** (dinner included) 🛏 – 🛉£ 110 🛉🛉£ 195
**Rest** – *(closed Monday and lunch November to mid-March) (booking essential at dinner)* Carte £ 25/36

♦ Remotely set, rustic country inn with wooden beams, stone walls, open fires and mix of bare and linen-laid tables. Classical dishes are crafted from carefully sourced local produce; meat and fish are smoked in-house. Well-stocked bar. Comfy, modern bedrooms are named after nearby islands; one has an outdoor hot tub.

## KIRKBEAN – Dumfries and Galloway – 501 J19 📓 Scotland    26 C3

▶ Edinburgh 92 mi – Dumfries 13 mi – Kirkcudbright 29 mi

👁 Sweetheart Abbey ★, N : 5 mi by A 710. Threave Garden ★★ and Threave Castle ★, W : 20 mi by A 710 and A 745

🏠 **Cavens** ⌾    ≤ 🖼 & rm, 🄌 **P** 𝘝𝘐𝘚𝘈 ⓿
⊠ *DG2 8AA* – 𝒞 *(01387) 880 234* – *www.cavens.com* – *Closed January-February and 25 December*
**8 rm** 🛏 – 🛉🛉£ 150/190
**Rest** – *(dinner only)* Menu £ 35

♦ Attractive 18C country house in mature grounds. Elegant drawing room with grand piano and cosy, book-filled 'Green Room'. Luxurious 'Estate' bedrooms boast views over the Solway Firth; comfy 'Country' rooms are simpler. Linen-clad dining room offers unfussy 3 course menu of local produce. Complimentary afternoon tea.

## KIRKCUDBRIGHT – Dumfries and Galloway – 501 H19 – pop. 3 447    25 B3
📓 Scotland

▶ Edinburgh 108 mi – Dumfries 28 mi – Stranraer 50 mi

ℹ Harbour Sq 𝒞 (01557) 33 04 94, www.kirkcudbright.co.uk

🏌️ Stirling Crescent, 𝒞 (01557) 33 03 14

👁 Town ★

👁 Dundrennan Abbey ★ **AC**, SE : 5 mi by A 711

**🔒 Selkirk Arms**     🚗 ⁽ᵗ⁾ 🅿 VISA ◎ AE
*High St ⊠ DG6 4JG – ℰ (01557) 330 402 – www.selkirkarmshotel.co.uk*
**17 rm** ☑ – ♦£ 70/150 ♦♦£ 90/116 – 2 suites
**Rest** *Artistas* – see restaurant listing
• Well-run 18C former coaching inn where Robert Burns reputedly wrote the Selkirk Grace. Spacious, comfortable bedrooms; some recently refurbished. Light lunches in the cosy sports bar, which displays caricatures of famous sporting figures.

**Gladstone House**     🚗 ⁒ ⁽ᵗ⁾ VISA ◎
*48 High St ⊠ DG6 4JX – ℰ (01557) 331 734 – www.kirkcudbrightgladstone.com – Closed 2 weeks January-February and Christmas*
**3 rm** ☑ – ♦£ 55 ♦♦£ 75
**Rest** – Menu £ 26
• Attractive 18C former merchant's house with friendly owners. Comfy, antique-furnished lounge. Simple, pastel-hued bedrooms with seating areas by the windows and views over the rooftops. 3 course dinner of local produce, tailored around guests' preferences.

**Ⓧ Artistas** – at Selkirk Arms Hotel     🚗 🅿 VISA ◎ AE
*High St ⊠ DG6 4JG – ℰ (01557) 330 402 – www.selkirkarmshotel.co.uk*
**Rest** – Menu £ 29 – Carte £ 24/38
• Formal hotel restaurant in an 18C former coaching inn. Extensive set menu offers traditional dishes crafted from regional ingredients. Galloway Beef and Kirkcudbright scallops are a feature.

---

## KIRKMICHAEL – Perth and Kinross – 501 J13     28 C2
▶ Edinburgh 73 mi – Aberdeen 85 mi – Inverness 102 mi – Perth 29 mi

**🍺 Strathardle Inn** with rm     🚗 🅿 VISA ◎
*on A 924 ⊠ PH10 7NS – ℰ (01250) 881 224 – www.strathardleinn.co.uk – Closed Monday lunch and Tuesday-Friday lunch November-March*
**8 rm** ☑ – ♦£ 45/50 ♦♦£ 70/80
**Rest** – *(dinner only and lunch Saturday-Sunday)* Carte £ 21/31
• 18C drover's inn serving robust cooking with a Scottish twist. Concise lunch menu of pub favourites. Dinner menu might feature smoked salmon or local venison. Simple, modern bedrooms.

---

## KIRKNEWTON – West Lothian – 501 J16 – see Edinburgh

---

## KIRKWALL – 501 L7 – see Orkney Islands (Mainland)

---

## KIRK YETHOLM – The Scottish Borders     26 D2
▶ London 346 mi – Edinburgh 57 mi – Hawick 26 mi – Galashiels 27 mi

**Mill House** without rest     🚗 ⁒ ⁽ᵗ⁾ 🅿
*Main St ⊠ TD5 8PE – ℰ (01573) 420 604 – www.millhouseyetholm.co.uk*
**3 rm** ☑ – ♦£ 50/60 ♦♦£ 90
• Charming former grain mill set on the edge of the village, looking down the valley. Spacious interior with vast lounge. Comfy bedrooms are simply furnished, with modern bathrooms. Indoor hot tub. Extensive offerings at breakfast.

---

## KYLESKU – Highland – 501 E9 ▮ Scotland     30 C1
▶ Edinburgh 256 mi – Inverness 100 mi – Ullapool 34 mi
◉ Loch Assynt★★, S : 6 mi by A 894

## ⌂ Kylesku  ≤ ≋ ⁙ 𝐕𝐈𝐒𝐀 ⊙⊙
✉ IV27 4HW – ℰ (01971) 502 231 – www.kyleskuhotel.co.uk – March-October
**8 rm** ⌑ – †£ 69 ††£ 99/104
**Rest** *Kylesku (Bar)* – see restaurant listing
**Rest** – *(dinner only)* Menu £ 33 – Carte £ 20/35
♦ Delightfully located 17C coaching inn, set beside 2 sea-lochs in a peaceful village. Spectacular panoramic views from cosy lounge, restaurant and most of the homely bedrooms. Cooking centres around fresh Highland game and locally landed seafood.

## ⌑ Kylesku (Bar) – at Kylesku Hotel  𝐕𝐈𝐒𝐀 ⊙⊙
✉ IV27 4HW – ℰ (01971) 502 231 – www.kyleskuhotel.co.uk – March-October
**Rest** – Carte £ 22/38
♦ Friendly staff and relaxed atmosphere, with breathtaking views of Loch Glendhu and the spectacular surrounding scenery. Menu focuses on fresh seafood landed daily in front of the inn.

---

## LAIRG – Highland – 501 G9 – pop. 857  30 C2
▶ Edinburgh 218 mi – Inverness 61 mi – Wick 72 mi
ℹ Sutherland ℰ (01549) 40 21 60, www.visitscotland.com

## ⌂ Park House  ≤ ≋ ⁙ 𝐏 𝐕𝐈𝐒𝐀 ⊙⊙
✉ IV27 4AU – ℰ (01549) 402 208 – www.parkhousesporting.com – Closed 20 December-2 January
**4 rm** ⌑ – †£ 50/60 ††£ 80/90
**Rest** – Menu £ 25
♦ Victorian sporting lodge offering fishing and field sports, its walls fittingly hung with rods and hunting prints. Cosy, open-fired sitting room and good-sized, homely bedrooms. Dining room offers loch views and a classical menu. Game and seafood feature highly.

---

## LANGASS – Western Isles – see Uist (Isles of)

## LEITH – City of Edinburgh – 501 K16 – see Edinburgh

## LERWICK – 501 Q3 – see Shetland Islands (Mainland)

---

# LEWIS and HARRIS (Isle of) – 501 A9 ▌ Scotland

⛴ from Stornoway to Ullapool (Mainland) (Caledonian MacBrayne Ltd) 2/3 daily (2 h 40 mn) – from Kyles Scalpay to the Isle of Scalpay (Caledonian MacBrayne Ltd) (10 mn) – from Tarbert to Isle of Skye (Uig) (Caledonian MacBrayne Ltd) 1-2 daily (1 h 45 mn) – from Tarbert to Portavadie (Caledonian MacBrayne Ltd) (summer only) frequent services daily (25 mn) – from Leverburgh to North Uist (Otternish) (Caledonian MacBrayne Ltd) (3-4 daily) (1 h 10 mn)

◉ Callanish Standing Stones★★ – Carloway Broch★ – St Clement's Church, Rodel (tomb★)

---

## LEWIS – Western Isles  29 A1
▶ London 618 mi – Edinburgh 212 mi

## BREASCLETE – Western Isles  29 B1

## ⌂ Eshcol ⌖  ≤ ≋ ⁙ ⁙ 𝐏
21 Breasclete ✉ HS2 9ED – ℰ (01851) 621 357 – www.eshcol.com – March-October
**3 rm** ⌑ – †£ 55 ††£ 80/90
**Rest** – Menu £ 22 (dinner)
♦ Immaculately kept guesthouse set on a small croft, in a former weaving village. Lovely loch and island views from the lounge and conservatory. Simple, homely bedrooms also share the view. Breakfast and dinner served in next door sister guesthouse 'Loch Roag'.

↑ **Loch Roag** ⌂      🖨 ⁑ ⸮ Ⓟ
*22A Breasclete* ✉ *HS2 9EF* – ✆ *(01851) 621 771* – *www.lochroag.com*
*– April-September*
**4 rm** �里 – 🛉£ 40/55 🛉🛉£ 80/90
**Rest** – ✆ *(01851) 621 357 (by arrangement)* Menu £ 22
• Run in conjunction with sister guesthouse 'Eshcol'. Simple, well-maintained bedrooms are a little larger than next door. Comfy lounge and dining room; big windows take in the view. Local specialities to start the day – home-cooked regional produce to finish it.

**GALSON** – Western Isles       **29 B1**

↑ **Galson Farm** ⌂      < 🖨 🕭 ⸮ Ⓟ 𝗩𝗜𝗦𝗔 ⓪
*South Galson* ✉ *HS2 0SH* – ✆ *(01851) 850 492* – *www.galsonfarm.co.uk*
**4 rm** �里 – 🛉£ 48 🛉🛉£ 96
**Rest** – Menu £ 25
• Welcoming guesthouse in a wonderfully remote location, boasting views out across the Atlantic. Traditional, homely guest areas and cosy bedrooms. The owner also operates the village post office from just inside the porch. Freshly prepared, home-cooked meals.

**STORNOWAY** – Western Isles       **29 B1**
🛈 26 Cromwell St ✆ (01851) 70 30 88, www.visitscotland.com
🔞 Lady Lever Park, ✆ (01851) 70 22 40

↑ **Braighe House** without rest       < 🖨 ⁑ ⸮ Ⓟ 𝗩𝗜𝗦𝗔 ⓪
*20 Braighe Rd, Southeast : 3 mi on A 866* ✉ *HS2 0BQ*
*– ✆ (01851) 705 287* – *www.braighehouse.co.uk*
*– March-November*
**5 rm** �里 – 🛉£ 75/105 🛉🛉£ 95/125
• Smart dormer bungalow with relaxed, modern interior. Deluxe rooms have sleigh beds and sea outlooks. Complimentary port and use of fishing rods. Car-/golf club hire arranged. Diverse breakfasts.

**HARRIS** – Western Isles       **29 A1**
▶ London 638 mi – Edinburgh 254 mi

**ARDHASAIG** – Western Isles       **29 A1**

✕✕ **Ardhasaig House** with rm ⌂      < ⸮ Ⓟ 𝗩𝗜𝗦𝗔 ⓪ 𝗔𝗘 ⓪
✉ *HS3 3AJ* – ✆ *(01859) 502 500* – *www.ardhasaig.co.uk*
**6 rm** �里 – 🛉£ 45/120 🛉🛉£ 120/200
**Rest** – *(dinner only)* Menu £ 35
• Purpose-built house that's been in the family for over 100 years. Modern, airy bar-lounge; flag-floored dining room with antique tables and dramatic bay/mountain views. Set menu offers local meats and seafood. Cosy bedrooms; the one in the stone lodge is the best.

**SCALPAY** – Western Isles       **29 B2**

↑ **Hirta House** without rest       < ⁑ ⸮ Ⓟ
✉ *HS4 3XZ* – ✆ *(01859) 540 394*
*– www.hirtahouse.co.uk*
**3 rm** �里 – 🛉£ 60/65 🛉🛉£ 70
• Simple, characterful guesthouse in a small fishing village. Harbour views from lounge and conservatory. One traditional four-poster bedroom; two more modern rooms, one with a queen-sized bed.

SCOTLAND

**SCARISTA** – Western Isles                                                              29 A2

 **Scarista House** 🌦                                          ⟵ 🚏 **P** 𝚟𝚒𝚜𝚊 ⊚⊚
✉ HS3 3HX – ℰ (01859) 550 238 – www.scaristahouse.com
– Closed 18 December-29 February
**6 rm** ⬜ – ♦£ 155 ♦♦£ 200/220
**Rest** – (dinner only) (booking essential for non-residents) (set menu only)
Menu £ 45
• Simple whitewashed house boasting amazing bay and mountain views. Caring
owners; cosy, homely interior with open-fired library and drawing room. Tradi-
tional bedrooms, those at the rear are best. Set dinners use garden produce and
offer the choice of meat or fish.

**TARBERT** – Western Isles – pop. 1 338 – ✉ Harris                          29 A2

🏨 **Hotel Hebrides**                                             🕉 (ᵖ) 𝚟𝚒𝚜𝚊 ⊚⊚ ⊙
Pier Rd ✉ HS3 3DG – ℰ (01859) 502 364 – www.hotel-hebrides.com
**21 rm** ⬜ – ♦£ 50/150 ♦♦£ 120/180
**Rest** Pier House – see restaurant listing
• Keenly run boutique hotel situated on the harbourside, next to the ferry terminal. Bedrooms are stylish, well-thought-out and come in bold designs; good
facilities, they even have hair straighteners available to borrow. Smart, friendly
bar.

🏠 **Ceol na Mara** without rest 🌦                                   🚏 🕉 **P** 𝚟𝚒𝚜𝚊 ⊚⊚ ⊙
7 Direcleit, South : 1 mi by A 859 ✉ HS3 3DP – ℰ (01859) 502 464
– www.ceolnamara.com
**3 rm** ⬜ – ♦£ 90/100 ♦♦£ 90/100
• Former crofter's cottage – one of only three on the island with three storeys.
Spacious, homely interior. Various well-kept lounges and good-sized, comfy bedrooms. Stunning lochside location.

✕✕ **Pier House** – at Hotel Hebrides                                        𝚟𝚒𝚜𝚊 ⊚⊚ ⊙
Pier Rd ✉ HS3 3DG – ℰ (01859) 502 364 – www.hotel-hebrides.com
**Rest** – Carte £ 21/41 **s**
• Well-run restaurant in a stylish harbourside hotel close to the ferry terminal.
Modern à la carte menu showcases local island produce, which appears in some
original, unexpected combinations.

**LEWISTON** – Highland – 501 G12 📗 Scotland                              30 C2
▶ Edinburgh 173 mi – Inverness 17 mi
🌀 Loch Ness★★ – The Great Glen★

🏠 **Woodlands** without rest                                    🚏 ᕃ 🕉 **P** 𝚟𝚒𝚜𝚊 ⊚⊚
East Lewiston ✉ IV63 6UJ – ℰ (01456) 450 356
– www.woodlands-lochness.co.uk – April-October
**3 rm** ⬜ – ♦£ 43 ♦♦£ 65
• Spacious, purpose-built guesthouse with large garden and decked terrace; situated just away from the village centre. Bedrooms are airy, comfortable and immaculately kept.

 **Loch Ness Inn** with rm                          ⌂ 🕉 (ᵖ) **P** 𝚟𝚒𝚜𝚊 ⊚⊚
✉ IV63 6UW – ℰ (01456) 450 991 – www.staylochness.co.uk
**12 rm** ⬜ – ♦£ 69/89 ♦♦£ 89/112
**Rest** – Carte £ 19/32
• Honest local pub with traditional bar, contemporary dining room and
smart wood-furnished rear terrace. Pub classics on the blackboard at lunch,
more restaurant-style dishes at dinner. Individually styled bedrooms have a
country feel.

**LINLITHGOW** – West Lothian – **501** J16 – pop. 13 370 ▮ Scotland          **26** C1

▶ Edinburgh 19 mi – Falkirk 9 mi – Glasgow 35 mi

🛈 High St 𝒞 (01506) 77 53 20, www.visitscotland.com

🛝 Braehead, 𝒞 (01506) 84 25 85

🛝 West Lothian Airngath Hill, 𝒞 (01506) 82 60 30

👁 Town★★ – Palace★★ **AC** : Courtyard (fountain★★), Great Hall (Hooded Fireplace★★), Gateway★ – Old Town★ – St Michaels★

🄶 Cairnpapple Hill★ **AC**, SW : 5 mi by A 706 – House of the Binns (plasterwork ceilings★) **AC**, NE : 4.5 mi by A 803 and A 904. Hopetoun House★★ **AC**, E : 7 mi by A 706 and A 904 – Abercorn Parish Church (Hopetoun Loft★★) NE : 7 mi by A 803 and A 904

---

⤒  **Arden House** without rest ⏸          🚗 ⚙ **P** **VISA** **◎◎**

Belsyde, Southwest : 2.25 mi on A 706 ✉ EH49 6QE – 𝒞 (01506) 670 172
– www.ardencountryhouse.com – Closed 25 December
**3 rm** ⌧ – ♱£ 58/100 ♱♱£ 86/104

♦ Purpose built guesthouse set in 105 acres of sheep farming land. Spacious, tastefully styled bedrooms boast modern, slate-floored bathrooms and plenty of extras. Tasty, wide-ranging breakfasts are a highlight. Welcoming owner pays great attention to detail.

---

XXX  **Champany Inn** with rm          ♿ rm, 🎇 **P** **VISA** **◎◎** **AE** **◎**

Northeast : 2 mi on A 803 at junction with A 904 ✉ EH49 7LU
– 𝒞 (01506) 834 532 – www.champany.com
– Closed 1-2 January, 25-26 December, Saturday lunch and Sunday
**16 rm** ⌧ – ♱£ 99/110 ♱♱£ 125/140
**Rest** Chop and Ale House – see restaurant listing
**Rest** – Beef specialities – Menu £ 29/43 – Carte £ 58/73 ☙☙

♦ Collection of buildings that create a 'mini-village'. Polished tables, smart silverware and formal service in restaurant. Classically based dishes, with top quality 21-day aged Aberdeen Angus beef their speciality. Excellent wine list with extensive South African selection. Smart, spacious, tartan-themed bedrooms.

---

XX  **Livingston's**          🚗 � **VISA** **◎◎** **AE** **◎**

52 High St ✉ EH49 7AE – 𝒞 (01506) 846 565 – www.livingstons-restaurant.co.uk
– Closed 2 weeks January, 1 week June, 1 week October, Sunday and Monday
**Rest** – Menu £ 20/39

♦ Long-standing, family-run restaurant. Conservatory-like dining room with large garden and terrace; friendly, efficient service. Set menus feature Scottish produce and Mediterranean touches.

---

X  **Chop and Ale House** – at Champany Inn          🌿 **P** **VISA** **◎◎** **AE** **◎**

Northeast : 2 mi on A 803 at junction with A 904 ✉ EH49 7LU
– 𝒞 (01506) 834 532 – www.champany.com
– Closed 1 January and 25-26 December
**Rest** – Carte £ 24/40

♦ Cosy restaurant with stone walls and beamed ceilings hung with animal traps and hunting prints. Menu offers quality steaks, speciality burgers, South African Boerewors and seafood classics.

---

**LOANS** – South Ayrshire – **501** G17 – see Troon

---

**LOCHALINE** – Highland – **501** C14          **29** B3

▶ Edinburgh 162 mi – Craignure 6 mi – Oban 7 mi

---

X  **Whitehouse**          **P** **VISA** **◎◎**

✉ PA34 5XT – 𝒞 (01967) 421 777 – www.thewhitehouserestaurant.co.uk
– Closed November-Easter, Monday and Sunday
**Rest** – Menu £ 25/30 – Carte £ 28/38

♦ Understated, wood-panelled restaurant in remote headland village. Constantly evolving blackboard menu of local seafood, game and garden produce. Unfussy, flavoursome cooking. Hands-on owners.

SCOTLAND

**LOCHEARNHEAD** – Stirling – **501** H14 ▮ Scotland                28 C2

▶ Edinburgh 65 mi – Glasgow 56 mi – Oban 57 mi – Perth 36 mi

**at Balquhidder** Southwest : 5 mi by A84 – ⊠ Stirling

🏨   **Monachyle Mhor** ⌂                              ≤ 🚗 🕭 🕾 **P** 𝖵𝖨𝖲𝖠 ⓒⓒ 𝖠𝖤 ⓪
West : 4 mi ⊠ FK19 8PQ – ℰ (01877) 384 622 – www.mhor.net – Closed 3-31
January
**16 rm** (dinner included) 🍽 – ♥£ 235/303 ♥♥£ 235/359
**Rest** – (booking essential for non residents) Menu £ 47 (dinner)
– Carte lunch £ 28/32
♦ Eye-catching pink former farmhouse, located in a beautiful, very remote valley.
Contemporary furnishings blend with original features in the reception, lounge
and bar. Smart, modern bedrooms boast slate-tiled bathrooms; those in the
main house are smaller but afford great views over the Braes of Balquhidder.

**LOCHINVER** – Highland – **501** E9 – pop. 470 – ⊠ Lairg ▮ Scotland       30 C1

▶ Edinburgh 251 mi – Inverness 95 mi – Wick 105 mi

🛈 Kirk Lane ℰ (01506) 832 2 22, www.visitscotland.com

◉ Village ★

🅖 Loch Assynt ★★, E : 6 mi by A 837

🏨🏨   **Inver Lodge**                              ≤ 🚗 ⌇ 🕭 🕾 **P** 𝖵𝖨𝖲𝖠 ⓒⓒ 𝖠𝖤
Iolaire Rd ⊠ IV27 4LU – ℰ (01571) 844 496 – www.inverlodge.com
– April-October
**20 rm** 🍽 – ♥£ 115 ♥♥£ 215/220
**Rest** *Chez Roux* – see restaurant listing
♦ Well-run hotel on the hillside, overlooking a quiet fishing village. Spacious
open-fired lounge, elegant bar and billiard room. Smart bedrooms with good
mod cons and great bay/island views.

⌂   **Ruddyglow Park Country House** ⌂                   ≤ 🚗 ⌇ 🕭 🕾 **P**
Loch Assynt, Northeast : 6.75 mi on A 837 ⊠ IV27 4HB                 𝖵𝖨𝖲𝖠 ⓒⓒ 𝖠𝖤
– ℰ (01571) 822 216 – www.ruddyglowpark.com – March-November
**3 rm** 🍽 – ♥£ 120/140 ♥♥£ 120/200   **Rest** – Menu £ 30/45 **s**
♦ Yellow-washed house in superb location, boasting fantastic loch and mountain
views. Spacious guest areas filled with antiques, paintings and silverware. High
level of facilities and extras in classically styled bedrooms; modern log cabin room
offers extra privacy. Communal, home dining; local seafood and game feature.

🍴🍴   **Albannach** (Colin Craig and Lesley Crosfield) with rm ⌂      ≤ 🚗 🕾 **P**
£3   Baddidarroch, West : 1 mi by Baddidarroch rd ⊠ IV27 4LP          𝖵𝖨𝖲𝖠 ⓒⓒ
– ℰ (01571) 844 407 – www.thealbannach.co.uk – Closed 12 December-
22 March and Monday to Wednesday November to 11 December
**5 rm** (dinner included) 🍽 – ♥£ 180/210 ♥♥£ 257/365
**Rest** – (Closed Monday to non residents) (dinner only) (booking essential for
non-residents) (set menu only) Menu £ 58
**Spec.** Seared monkfish with Parma ham and red pepper essence. Roast wild turbot, black potatoes and red wine sauce. Lime soufflé, chocolate ice cream and
brambles.
♦ Substantial 19C Scottish house in remote location, boasting exceptional bay/-
mountain views from the conservatory, terrace and garden. Strong focus on the
food. Traditional daily 5 course set menu of local, seasonal produce. Well-appointed bedrooms are spread about the building; one boasts a private terrace
and hot tub.

🍴🍴   **Chez Roux** – at Inver Lodge Hotel              ≤ 🚗 **P** 𝖵𝖨𝖲𝖠 ⓒⓒ 𝖠𝖤
Iolaire Rd ⊠ IV27 4LU – ℰ (01571) 844 496 – www.inverlodge.com
– April-October
**Rest** – Menu £ 44
♦ Romantic restaurant hung with photos of the eponymous brothers and boast-
ing well-spaced tables that take in fantastic bay and mountain views. Regularly
changing, classical French menus.

SCOTLAND

755

**LOCHMADDY** – Western Isles – **501** Y11 – see Uist (Isles of)

**LOCHRANZA** – North Ayrshire – **501** E16 – see Arran (Isle of)

**MELROSE** – The Scottish Borders – **501** L17 – pop. 1 656 ▊ Scotland    **26** D2

▶ Edinburgh 38 mi – Hawick 19 mi – Newcastle upon Tyne 70 mi

🔎 Abbey St 𝒞 (01835) 86 31 70, www.visitscotland.com

🔟 Melrose Dingleton Dingleton Rd, 𝒞 (01896) 82 28 55

◉ Town★ - Abbey★★ (decorative sculpture★★★) **AC**

🔲 Eildon Hills (❄★★★) – Scott's View★★ – Abbotsford★★ **AC**, W : 4.5 mi by A 6091
and B 6360 – Dryburgh Abbey★★ **AC** (setting★★★), SE : 4 mi by A 6091 – Tweed
Valley★★. Bowhill★★ **AC**, SW : 11.5 mi by A 6091, A 7 and A 708 – Thirlestane
Castle (plasterwork ceilings★★) **AC**, NE : 21 mi by A 6091 and A 68

🏨 **Burts**    🚗 🔐 🛜 **P** **VISA** 🅒🅞
Market Sq. ⊠ TD6 9PL – 𝒞 (01896) 822 285 – www.burtshotel.co.uk – Closed 2-9
January and 26 December
**20 rm** ⬚ – ♦£ 70/130 ♦♦£ 100/133
**Rest** – Menu £ 28/36
◆ Characterful coaching inn on the main square; run by the same family for two
generations. Appealing bedrooms blend contemporary furnishings with original
features. Cosy bar serves old classics; formal dining room offers a mix of modern
and traditional dishes.

🏨 **Townhouse**    🔐 🛜 🕪 🕍 **P** **VISA** 🅒🅞
Market Sq. ⊠ TD6 9PQ – 𝒞 (01896) 822 645 – www.thetownhousemelrose.co.uk
– Closed 2-9 January and 26 December
**11 rm** ⬚ – ♦£ 90/136 ♦♦£ 124/136
**Rest** – Menu £ 26/34 – Carte £ 20/35
◆ Former home of Catherine Spence and contemporary sister to nearby Burts.
Stylish bedrooms are decorated in black and purple and display bold feature
walls; standards are shower only. Trendy all day café-cum-bar; dining room offers
the best Border ingredients.

**at Gattonside** North : 2 mi by B 6374 on B 6360 – ⊠ Melrose

🏠 **Fauhope House** without rest ⌂    ≤ 🚗 🕭 🛜 🕪 **P** **VISA** 🅒🅞
East : 0.25 mi by B 6360 taking unmarked lane to the right of Monkswood Rd at
edge of village ⊠ TD6 9LU – 𝒞 (01896) 823 184 – www.fauhopehouse.com
**3 rm** ⬚ – ♦£ 70/100 ♦♦£ 100/110
◆ Charming 19C house by the Tweed, overlooking Melrose. Quirky interior displays an eclectic mix of art and antiques. Bedrooms are all very different; some
boast stylish bold colour schemes.

**MEMUS** – Angus    **28** D2

▶ London 497 mi – Edinburgh 86 mi – Aberdeen 52 mi – Dundee 25 mi

🍸 **Drovers Inn**    🚗 🔐 **P** **VISA** 🅒🅞 **AE**
⊠ DD8 3TY – 𝒞 (01307) 860 322 – www.the-drovers.com
**Rest** – Carte £ 15/26
◆ Attractive Highland inn with immaculately kept lawned garden, set in an extremely remote spot. Wide-ranging menu represents good value for money and
showcases local, seasonal produce, with game and vegetables coming from the
estate.

**MOFFAT** – Dumfries and Galloway – **501** J17 – pop. 2 135 ▊ Scotland    **26** C2

▶ Edinburgh 61 mi – Carlisle 43 mi – Dumfries 22 mi – Glasgow 60 mi

🔎 Churchgate 𝒞 (01683) 22 06 20, www.visitmoffat.co.uk

🔟 Coatshill, 𝒞 (01683) 22 00 20

🔲 Grey Mare's Tail★★, NE : 9 mi by A 708

🏠 **Hartfell House**                            🍴 🌃 **P** **VISA** **◎** **①**
*Hartfell Cres.* ⊠ *DG10 9AL –* 𝒞 *(01683) 220 153 – www.hartfellhouse.co.uk*
*– Closed 1 week January, spring, autumn and Christmas*
**7 rm** ⌿ – ♦£ 35/50 ♦♦£ 60/70
**Rest** *Lime Tree* – see restaurant listing
◆ Keenly run Victorian house in quiet crescent. Original features include parquet
floors and ornate cornicing. Comfy lounge boasts nice southerly aspect. Large,
traditionally decorated bedrooms.

🏠 **Bridge House**                                🍴 🌃 **P** **VISA** **◎**
*Well Rd., East : 0.75 mi by Selkirk rd (A 708) taking left hand turn before bridge*
⊠ *DG10 9JT –* 𝒞 *(01683) 220 558 – www.bridgehousemoffat.co.uk – Closed 25
December-February*
**7 rm** ⌿ – ♦£ 55 ♦♦£ 70    **Rest** – Menu £ 24
◆ Large Victorian house on quiet residential road, run by experienced owners.
Comfy lounge with deep sofas. Individually decorated bedrooms – those to the
front are biggest. Beautiful valley views. Lovely cornicing in dining room; exten-
sive menu has Asian twists.

🏠 **Well View**                            🍴 🌃 rest, **P** **VISA** **◎** **AE**
*Ballplay Rd., East : 0.75 mi by Selkirk rd (A 708)* ⊠ *DG10 9JU –* 𝒞 *(01683)
220 184 – www.wellview.co.uk*
**3 rm** ⌿ – ♦£ 60/75 ♦♦£ 90/110    **Rest** – Menu £ 22/35
◆ Substantial 19C house located in a peaceful suburb, boasting spacious, traditionally styled bedrooms and good comforts. Formerly a restaurant, dinner is still
a key focus here. The daily changing 4 course set menu is taken at a communal
table; wine is included.

❌❌ **Lime Tree** – at Hartfell House Hotel              **P** **VISA** **◎** **①**
*Hartfell Cres.* ⊠ *DG10 9AL –* 𝒞 *(01683) 220 153 – www.hartfellhouse.co.uk
– Closed 1 week January, spring, autumn and Christmas, Sunday dinner and
Monday*
**Rest** – *(dinner only and Sunday lunch) (booking essential)* Menu £ 20/28
◆ Small hotel restaurant with smartly laid tables, open fire and attractive marque-
try. Large bay window looks down the valley. Good value weekly menu features
tasty, well-presented classics.

**MONTROSE** – **Angus** – **501** M13 – **pop. 10 845** 🏴 Scotland            **28** D2
▶ Edinburgh 92 mi – Aberdeen 39 mi – Dundee 29 mi
🅭 Panmure Place 𝒞 (01674) 67 32 32, www.visitmontrose.co.uk
🅵₃₆ Traill Drive, 𝒞 (01674) 67 29 32
🅖 Edzell Castle★ (The Pleasance★★★) **AC**, NW : 17 mi by A 935 and B 966 – Cairn
O'Mount Road★ (≤★★) N : 17 mi by B 966 and B 974 – Brechin (Round Tower★)
W : 7 mi by A 935 – Aberlemno (Aberlemno Stones★, Pictish sculptured stones★)
W : 13 mi by A 935 and B 9134

🏠 **36 The Mall** without rest            🍴 🌃 🛜 **VISA** **◎** **AE**
*36 The Mall, North : 0.5 mi by A 92 at junction with North Esk Road*
⊠ *DD10 8SS –* 𝒞 *(01674) 673 646 – www.36themall.co.uk*
**3 rm** ⌿ – ♦£ 48/65 ♦♦£ 60/80
◆ Lovely bay-windowed, 19C former manse with pleasant conservatory lounge
overlooking the garden. Immaculately kept, high-ceilinged bedrooms with tasteful styling and handy extras. Impressive plate collection is the talking point of
the communal breakfast room.

❌❌ **Quay**                                        **VISA** **◎** **AE**
*1-4 Wharf St* ⊠ *DD10 8BD –* 𝒞 *(01674) 672 821 – www.thequaymontrose.co.uk
– Closed 1-18 January, 25-26 December and Monday*
**Rest** – Menu £ 29 (dinner) – Carte lunch £ 17/21
◆ Set on the quayside and run by a bubbly local couple. Large bar and smart columned dining room with bold wallpaper. Accessible lunch menu is stepped up at
dinner; local, seasonal dishes are precisely executed, tasty and full of flavour.

**SCOTLAND**

**MUIR OF ORD** – Highland – **501** G11 – pop. 1 812    30 C2

▶ Edinburgh 173 mi – Inverness 10 mi – Wick 121 mi

🔢 Great North Rd, ✆ (01463) 87 08 25

⌂ **Dower House** ॐ    ⊞ ⁱⁱ Ⓟ 💳 ⚫⚫
*Highfield, North : 1 mi on A 862* ⊠ *IV6 7XN* – ✆ *(01463) 870 090*
– *www.thedowerhouse.co.uk – Closed 1 week November and 25 December*
**3 rm** ⊆ – 🛉£ 75/95 🛉🛉£ 120/175
**Rest** – *(dinner only) (residents only)* Menu £ 22/42
♦ Personally run, part 17C house in mature garden. Stacked bookshelves, soft fireside armchairs, cosy bedrooms and fresh flowers: a relaxed but well-ordered country home. Dining room offers careful cooking of fine fresh ingredients.

---

**MULL (Isle of)** – Argyll and Bute – **501** B/C14 – pop. 1 841 ▋ Scotland    27 A2

🚢 from Fionnphort to Isle of Iona (Caledonian MacBrayne Ltd) frequent services daily (10 mn) – from Pierowall to Papa Westray (Orkney Ferries Ltd) (summer only) (25 mn)

🚢 from Craignure to Oban (Caledonian MacBrayne Ltd) frequent services daily (45 mn) – from Fishnish to Lochaline (Mainland) (Caledonian MacBrayne Ltd) frequent services daily (15 mn) – from Tobermory to Isle of Tiree (Scarinish) via Isle of Coll (Arinagour) (Caledonian MacBrayne Ltd) 3 weekly (2 h 30 mn) – from Tobermory to Kilchoan (Caledonian MacBrayne Ltd) 4 daily (summer only) (35 mn)

ℹ Craignure ✆ (08707) 20 06 10, www.holidaymull.co.uk

🏌 Craignure Scallastle, ✆ (01688) 30 25 17

◉ Island★ - Calgary Bay★★ – Torosay Castle **AC** (Gardens★ ≼★)

🏛 Isle of Iona★ (Maclean's Cross★, St Oran's Chapel★, St Martin's High Cross★, Infirmary Museum★ **AC** (Cross of St John★))

**FIONNPHORT** – Argyll and Bute

✕✕ **Ninth Wave**    Ⓟ 💳 ⚫⚫ AE
*Bruach Mhor, East : 0.75 mi by A 849* ⊠ *PA66 6BL* – ✆ *(01681) 700 757*
– *www.ninthwaverestaurant.co.uk – Restricted opening in winter*
**Rest** – Seafood – *(dinner only) (booking essential)* Menu £ 40
♦ Converted farm building featuring stylish, modern décor, with trinkets from the owner's travels. Daily changing menu focuses on local seafood, with strong Asian flavours. Try the lobster.

**GRULINE** – Argyll and Bute    27 A2

⌂ **Gruline Home Farm** ॐ    ≼ ⊞ ⁱⁱ Ⓟ
⊠ *PA71 6HR* – ✆ *(01680) 300 581 – www.gruline.com – Closed Christmas-New Year*
**3 rm** (dinner included) ⊆ – 🛉£ 148 🛉🛉£ 200
**Rest** – Menu £ 40
♦ Very rurally set, in 3 acres of land, with colourful gardens and lovely mountain views. Relax in the large lounges or spot sea eagles from the telescope in the spacious conservatory. Good-sized, antique-furnished bedrooms. Mousey Thompson pieces in the traditionally styled dining room. Classical, daily changing menu.

**TIRORAN** – Argyll and Bute    27 A2

⌂ **Tiroran House** ॐ    ≼ ⊞ ⌖ ⁱⁱ Ⓟ 💳 ⚫⚫
⊠ *PA69 6ES* – ✆ *(01681) 705 232 – www.tiroran.com – mid-March to mid-November*
**9 rm** ⊆ – 🛉£ 100/120 🛉🛉£ 195/210
**Rest** – *(dinner only)* Menu £ 48
♦ Stunning 19C whitewashed house, set in 17 acres of parkland that run down to the water's edge. Charming, antique-filled interior with two open-fired lounges and immaculate, highly individual bedrooms. Welcoming owner. Dining room split into conservatory area and darker, more clubby area. Concise, daily changing menus.

SCOTLAND

**TOBERMORY** – Argyll and Bute – pop. 980                                    27 A2

🔟 Erray Rd, ✆ (01688) 30 23 87

🏠 **Tobermory**                                    ⩽ ⅃ rm, ⑪ 𝗩𝗜𝗦𝗔 ⦿⦿
53 Main St ⊠ PA75 6NT – ✆ (01688) 302 091 – www.thetobermoryhotel.com
– Closed 7 January-7 February and 1 week Christmas
**16 rm** ⬛ – ✝£ 40/70 ✝✝£ 78/132
**Rest Waters Edge** – (dinner only) Menu £ 32
♦ Converted fishermen's cottages right on the quayside, close to the local distillery. Bedrooms vary in size but most have a pleasant harbour view. Small lounge;
popular dining room with seafaring feel. Concise, classical menu of island produce. Plenty of seafood.

🏠 **Sonas House** without rest 🐟                    ⩽ 🖨 🖥 🌿 ⑪ 🄿 𝗩𝗜𝗦𝗔 ⦿⦿ 𝗔𝗘 ⓪
The Fairways, North : 0.5 mi by Black Brae and Erray Rd following signs for the
golf club ⊠ PA75 6PS – ✆ (01688) 302 304 – www.sonashouse.co.uk
– March-October
**3 rm** ⬛ – ✝£ 50/80 ✝✝£ 90/125
♦ In elevated position above Tobermory, with views over the Sound of Mull.
Choose a room in the house or the annexe studio; all come with a host of extras
and superb views. Luxury swimming pool.

🏠 **Brockville** without rest                         ⩽ 🖨 🌿 ⓦ 🄿
Raeric Rd, by Back Brae ⊠ PA75 6RS – ✆ (01688) 302 741
– www.brockville-tobermory.co.uk
**3 rm** ⬛ – ✝£ 40/65 ✝✝£ 70/80
♦ Welcoming guesthouse with warm, homely feel. Good-sized bedrooms offer
everything you could want. Communal breakfast room boasts nice sea views.
Friendly owner has plenty of local knowledge.

XX **Highland Cottage** with rm                       ⑪ 🄿 𝗩𝗜𝗦𝗔 ⦿⦿
Breadalbane St, via B 8073 ⊠ PA75 6PD – ✆ (01688) 302 030
– www.highlandcottage.co.uk – March-October
**6 rm** ⬛ – ✝£ 125/140 ✝✝£ 150/190
**Rest** – (dinner only) (booking essential for non-residents) Menu £ 48
♦ Long-standing, personally run restaurant in intimate cottage; family antiques
and knick-knacks abound. Classical linen-laid dining room and homely lounge.
Traditional daily menu with a seafood base and plenty of local produce. Snug, individually styled bedrooms.

---

**MUTHILL** – Perth and Kinross – **501** I15 – pop. 675 – see Crieff

---

**NAIRN** – Highland – **501** I11 – pop. 8 418 ▯ Scotland              30 D2
▶ Edinburgh 172 mi – Aberdeen 91 mi – Inverness 16 mi
🔢 Seabank Rd, ✆ (01667) 45 32 08
🔢 Nairn Dunbar Lochloy Rd, ✆ (01667) 45 27 41
◎ Forres (Sueno's Stone★★) E : 11 mi by A 96 and B 9011 - Cawdor Castle★ **AC**, S :
5.5 mi by B 9090 – Brodie Castle★ **AC**, E : 6 mi by A 96. Fort George★, W : 8 mi by
A 96, B 9092 and B 9006

🏨 **Golf View**        ⩽ 🖨 🖥 🐟 ⅃ 🌿 🎐 ⚡ 🄰🄲 rest, ⑪ 🄪 🄿 𝗩𝗜𝗦𝗔 ⦿⦿ 𝗔𝗘
The Seafront ⊠ IV12 4HD – ✆ (01667) 452 301 – www.golfviewhotel.com
**41 rm** ⬛ – ✝£ 95/190 ✝✝£ 130/250 – 1 suite
**Rest Restaurant** – (dinner only and Sunday lunch) Menu £ 34 – Carte £ 20/39
**Rest Conservatory** – Carte £ 23/33
♦ Non-golfers may prefer the vista of the Moray Firth from one of the sea-view
rooms or a poolside lounger. Smart, traditional accommodation, up-to-date gym
and beauty salon. Half-panelled dining room. Stylish, spacious conservatory restaurant.

SCOTLAND

SCOTLAND

### Boath House  ≤ 🚗 🐕 🦢 🀄 ᵭ rm, ⁇ **P** **VISA** 🕩
⊛ *Auldearn, East : 2 mi on A 96* ⊠ *IV12 5TE* – ✆ *(01667) 454 896*
*– www.boath-house.com*
**8 rm** (dinner included) 🍴 – **†**£ 260 **††**£ 450
**Rest** – *(booking essential)* Menu £ 30/70 **s**
**Spec.** Mackerel, cauliflower, capers and sorrel. Lamb shoulder, onions and asparagus. Rhubarb, parkin parfait and ginger jelly.
♦ 1820s neo-classical mansion, owned by a charming couple, hosts modern
Highland art collections. Intimate, elegant bedrooms; some have half-tester
beds/views of the trout lake. Smart, contemporary bathrooms. Formally laid
dining room has garden views; accomplished cooking, with vivid presentation
and subtle flavours.

### Bracadale House without rest 🚗 🌾 ⁇ **P** **VISA** 🕩
 *Albert St* ⊠ *IV12 4HF* – ✆ *(01667) 452 547* – *www.bracadalehouse.com*
*– Closed Christmas-New Year*
**3 rm** 🍴 – **†**£ 40/50 **††**£ 60
♦ Elegant Victorian guesthouse close to a championship golf course and the
beach, and run by a friendly, enthusiastic owner. Enjoy complimentary sherry beside the open fire in the cosy, intimate first floor lounge. Traditionally styled bedrooms boast huge windows.

### Cawdor House 🚗 🌾 ⁇ **VISA** 🕩 ⓪
*7 Cawdor St* ⊠ *IV12 4QD* – ✆ *(01667) 455 855* – *www.cawdorhousenairn.co.uk*
*– Closed 21 December-14 January*
**5 rm** – **†**£ 50/90 **††**£ 70/90
**Rest** – Menu £ 28
♦ Comfortable house whose original features blend with contemporary styling;
friendly owners are a font of local knowledge. Variously sized bedrooms are clean
and uncluttered. Cosy lounge with log fire. Simple dining room; set menu dinner
by arrangement.

---

## NEWTON STEWART – Dumfries and Galloway – **501** G19    **25** B3
*– pop. 3 573* 📖 Scotland

▶ Edinburgh 131 mi – Dumfries 51 mi – Glasgow 87 mi – Stranraer 24 mi

🄳 Dashwood Sq ✆ *(01671) 40 24 31, www.newtonstewart.org*

🏠 Minnigaff Kirroughtree Ave, ✆ *(01671) 40 21 72*

🏠 Wigtownshire County Glenluce Mains of Park, ✆ *(01581) 30 04 20*

🄶 Galloway Forest Park★, Queen's Way★ (Newton Stewart to New Galloway)
N : 19 mi by A 712

### Kirroughtree House 🍃 ≤ 🚗 🔊 ⁇ **P** **VISA** 🕩 **AE**
*Northeast : 1.5 mi by A 75 on A 712* ⊠ *DG8 6AN* – ✆ *(01671) 402 141*
*– www.kirroughtreehouse.co.uk – Closed 2 January-mid February*
**15 rm** 🍴 – **†**£ 115/150 **††**£ 230/250 – 2 suites
**Rest** – *(booking essential for non-residents)* Menu £ 18/35 **s** – Carte lunch
Monday-Saturday £ 24/35 **s**
♦ Impressive 1719 mansion in landscaped gardens, overlooking the woods and
bay. Grand interior with vast open-fired hall and impressive staircase. Traditionally
styled bedrooms with plenty of extras. Concise 4 course menu of quality produce
in classic combinations.

---

## NIGG – **501** H10 – see Tain

---

## NORTH BAY – Western Isles – see Barra (Isle of)

## NORTH BERWICK – East Lothian – **501** L15 – pop. 6 223 ▯ Scotland  **26** D1

▰ Edinburgh 24 mi – Newcastle upon Tyne 102 mi

▰ 1 Quality St ℰ (01620) 89 21 97, www.northberwickuk.com

▰ North Berwick Beach Rd, West Links, ℰ (01620) 89 03 12

▰ Glen East Links, Tantallon Terrace, ℰ (01620) 89 27 26

▰ North Berwick Law (✴★★★) S : 1 mi - Tantallon Castle★★ (clifftop site★★★) **AC**, E : 3.5 mi by A 198 – Dirleton★ (Castle★ **AC**) SW : 2.5 mi by A 198. Museum of Flight★, S : 6 mi by B 1347 – Preston Mill★, S : 8.5 mi by A 198 and B 1047 – Tyninghame★, S : 7 mi by A 198 – Coastal road from North Berwick to Portseton★, SW : 13 mi by A 198 and B 1348

⌂     **Glebe House** without rest ⌖                          ▱ ⌘ **P**
*Law Rd* ⌂ *EH39 4PL* – ℰ *(01620) 892 608* – *www.glebehouse-nb.co.uk*
– *Closed Christmas*
**3 rm** ⌷ – ♦£ 75 ♦♦£ 100/110
♦ Spacious, welcoming Georgian house with walled gardens and views over the town and sea. Classical, country house drawing room and antique communal breakfast table. Comfortable, well-furnished bedrooms.

---

## NORTH QUEENSFERRY – Fife – **501** J15 – pop. 1 102  **28** C3

▰ Edinburgh 13 mi – Dunfermline 6 mi – Glasgow 45 mi

✗     **Wee Restaurant**                              **VISA** **⊙⊙** **AE** **①**
*17 Main St* ⌂ *KY11 1JT* – ℰ *(01383) 616 263* – *www.theweerestaurant.co.uk*
– *Closed 25-26 December*
**Rest** – Menu £ 20/32 **s**
♦ Simple, quarry-floored restaurant in the shadow of the Forth Rail Bridge. Fresh Scottish ingredients are served in neatly presented, classical combinations. Lunch represents the best value.

---

## NORTH UIST – Western Isles – **501** X/Y10 – see Uist (Isles of)

---

## OBAN – Argyll and Bute – **501** D14 – pop. 8 120 ▯ Scotland  **27** B2

▰ Edinburgh 123 mi – Dundee 116 mi – Glasgow 93 mi – Inverness 118 mi

**Access** Access to Glasgow by helicopter

⎈ to Isle of Mull (Craignure) (Caledonian MacBrayne Ltd) (45 mn) – to Isle of Tiree (Scarinish) via Isle of Mull (Tobermory) and Isle of Coll (Arinagour) (Caledonian MacBrayne Ltd) – to Isle of Islay (Port Askaig) and Kintyre Peninsula (Kennacraig) via Isle of Colonsay (Scalasaig) (Caledonian MacBrayne Ltd) (summer only) – to Isle of Lismore (Achnacroish) (Caledonian MacBrayne Ltd) 2-3 daily (except Sunday) (55 mn) – to Isle of Colonsay (Scalasaig) (Caledonian MacBrayne Ltd) 3 weekly (2 h)

▰ Argyll Sq ℰ (08707) 20 06 30, www.oban.org.uk

▰ Glencruitten Glencruitten Rd, ℰ (01631) 56 28 68

▰ Loch Awe★★, SE : 17 mi by A 85 – Bonawe Furnace★, E : 12 mi by A 85 – Cruachan Power Station★ **AC**, E : 16 mi by A 85 – Seal and Marine Centre★ **AC**, N : 14 mi by A 828

🏠     **Manor House**                          ⪕ ▱ ⸙ **P** **VISA** **⊙⊙** **AE** **①**
*Gallanach Rd.* ⌂ *PA34 4LS* – ℰ *(01631) 562 087* – *www.manorhouseoban.com*
– *Closed 25-26 December*
**11 rm** ⌷ – ♦£ 99/199 ♦♦£ 120/210
**Rest** – *(lunch by arrangement)* Menu £ 24/38
♦ 18C dower house, formerly part of the Argyll Estate. Country house style interior offers traditional comforts; spacious lounge and rustic bar boast delightful bay and harbour views. Individually styled bedrooms. Classical daily menu served in formal dining room.

### Glenburnie House without rest
*Corran Esplanade ⊠ PA34 5AQ – ℰ (01631) 562 089 – www.glenburnie.co.uk*
*– April-November*
**12 rm** 🖵 – ♦£ 50/100 – ♦♦£ 80/110
• Bay-windowed house on main esplanade, affording great bay and island view. Period features include a delightful staircase and etched glass widows; antique abound. Comfy, good-sized bedrooms.

### Alltavona without rest
*Corran Esplanade ⊠ PA34 5AQ – ℰ (01631) 565 067 – www.alltavona.co.uk*
*– March-November*
**10 rm** 🖵 – ♦£ 35/85 ♦♦£ 70/95
• Commanding bay and island views from this charming 19C villa on the main esplanade. Fresh, tasty breakfasts in stylish black, white and red room. Striking modern bedrooms boast feature beds.

### Coast
*104 George St ⊠ PA34 5NT – ℰ (01631) 569 900 – www.coastoban.com*
*– Closed 25-26 December, Sunday lunch and Sunday October-March*
**Rest** – Menu £ 16 (lunch) – Carte £ 25/39
• Busy high street restaurant with wooden floor and khaki fabric strips on the walls. Unfussy, modern cooking with good seasoning; local produce is key. Plenty of shellfish and steaks on offer.

### Waterfront
*No 1, The Pier ⊠ PA34 4LW – ℰ (01631) 563 110 – www.waterfrontoban.co.uk*
*– Closed 25 December*
**Rest** – Seafood – Carte £ 24/33
• Former seaman's mission boasting harbour/bay views. Extensive menu features local produce and mixes modern and classical cooking. Lots of daily specials; fish a strength. Relaxed bistro feel.

### Ee-usk
*The North Pier ⊠ PA34 5QD – ℰ (01631) 565 666 – www.eeusk.com*
*– Closed 1 January, 25-26 December and restricted opening in January*
**Rest** – Seafood – Carte £ 26/38
• Long-standing local seafood restaurant on the harbour, run by experienced owners. Stylish modern building with brasserie feel and great bay views. Large in-depth menu with good value specials.

Undecided between two equivalent establishments in the same town? Within each category, establishments are classified in our order of preference: the best first.

---

## ONICH – Highland – 501 E13 – ⊠ Fort William
**29 B3**
▶ Edinburgh 123 mi – Glasgow 93 mi – Inverness 79 mi – Oban 39 mi

### Lochleven Seafood Café
*Lochleven, Southeast : 6.5 mi by A 82 on B 863 ⊠ PH33 6SA – ℰ (01855) 821 048 – www.lochlevenseafoodcafe.co.uk – Restricted opening in winter*
**Rest** – Seafood – (booking advisable at dinner) Carte £ 19/50 **s**
• Stunning Lochside location looking toward Glencoe Mountains. Extremely fresh, simply prepared seafood; shellfish platter and razor clams a speciality. Themed evenings in winter.

# ORKNEY ISLANDS – 501 K/L7 – pop. 19 800 🏛 Scotland

🚇 see Kirkwall

🚢 from Burwick (South Ronaldsay) to John O'Groats (John O'Groats Ferries) 2-4 daily (40 mn) (summer only)

🚢 service between Isle of Hoy (Longhope), Isle of Hoy (Lyness), Isle of Flotta and Houton (Orkney Ferries Ltd) – from Stromness to Scrabster (P & O Scottish Ferries) (1-3 daily) (2 h) – from Stromness to Shetland Islands (Lerwick) and Aberdeen (Northlink Ferries) 1-2 daily – from Kirkwall to Westray, Stronsay via Eday and Sanday (Orkney Ferries Ltd) – from Tingwall to Wyre via Egilsay and Rousay (Orkney Ferries Ltd) – from Kirkwall to Shapinsay (Orkney Ferries Ltd) (25 mn) – from Stromness to Isle of Hoy (Moness) and Graemsay (Orkney Ferries Ltd) – from Kirkwall to North Ronaldsay (Orkney Ferries Ltd) weekly (2 h 40 mn) - from Kirkwall to Invergordon (Orcargo Ltd) daily (8 h 30 mn) – from Houton to Isle of Hoy (Lyness), Flotta and Longhope (Orkney Ferries Ltd)

🔲 Old Man of Hoy★★★ – Islands★★ – Maes Howe★★ **AC** – Skara Brae★★ **AC** – Kirkbuster Museum and Corrigal Farm Museum★ **AC** – Brough of Birsay★ **AC** – Birsay (`◁≼★`) – Ring of Brodgar★ – Unstan Cairn★

---

## MAINLAND – Orkney Islands                                        31 A3

▶ London 683 mi – Edinburgh 278 mi

## BURRAY – Orkney Islands                                          31 A3

🏠 **Sands**                                      ≼ 🕭 📶 **P** VISA ⚏ AE ⓪
   ✉ KW17 2SS – ℰ (01856) 731 298 – www.thesandshotel.co.uk
   – Closed 1-3 January and 25-26 December
   **6 rm** 🛏 – ♦£ 60/90 ♦♦£ 95/115 – 2 suites
   **Rest** – Carte £ 17/28
   ♦ Converted 19C herring packing store in small hamlet overlooking Scapa Flow. Pleasant bedrooms boast smart bathrooms. Bar with pool table and dartboard offers traditional menu. Dining room serves more refined dishes, featuring island produce and lots of shellfish.

## DOUNBY – Orkney Islands                                          31 A3

🏠 **Ashleigh** without rest 🌿                    ≼ 🖀 📶 **P**
   Howaback Rd, South : 0.75 mi by A986 ✉ KW17 2JA – ℰ (01856) 771 378
   – www.ashleigh-orkney.com – Closed 20 December-10 January
   **4 rm** 🛏 – ♦£ 38/40 ♦♦£ 80
   ♦ Purpose-built house in the heart of the island's countryside, boasting loch-/mountain views. Large breakfast room and lounge filled with guidebooks. Good-sized bedrooms with modern facilities.

## HARRAY – Orkney Islands                                          31 A3

🏠🏠 **Merkister** 🌿                            ≼ 🖀 🔧 ਗ rm, 📶 **P** VISA ⚏ AE ⓪
   off A 986 ✉ KW17 2LF – ℰ (01856) 771 366 – www.merkister.com – Closed 23 December-4 January
   **16 rm** 🛏 – ♦£ 55/95 ♦♦£ 75/175
   **Rest** – (bar lunch) Menu £ 24 **s**
   – Carte £ 19/40 **s**
   ♦ Family-run, lochside hotel affording wonderful water and mountain views. Comfortable, well-kept bedrooms; those outside have their own terraces and gardens. Snug, open-fired bar serves snacks. Dining room offers strictly Orkney-based produce and a scenic backdrop.

**SCOTLAND**

↑ **Holland House** without rest ⅏ ← 🚗 ℅ ⁽ᵖ⁾ P VISA ⓧ AE
*on St Michael's Church rd* ✉ *KW17 2LQ* – ℰ *(01856) 771 400*
*– www.hollandhouseorkney.co.uk – Closed 7 December-12 January and restricted opening in winter*
**3 rm** ⚏ – ♦£ 48/60 ♦♦£ 96
♦ Converted manse run by a welcoming owner, with commanding view throughout. Open-fired lounge – packed with local art and handmade furnitur – stone-floored breakfast room and conservatory. Spotless bedrooms with a hos of extras and great attention to detail.

**KIRKWALL** – Orkney Islands ▌ Scotland **31 A**
🛬 Kirkwall Airport : ℰ (01856) 886210, S : 3.5 mi
🛈 West Castle St ℰ (01856) 87 28 56, www.visitorkney.com
🏴 Grainbank, ℰ (01856) 87 24 57
👁 Kirkwall★★ - St Magnus Cathedral★★ – Western Mainland★★, Eastern Mainland (Italian Chapel★) - Earl's Palace★ **AC** – Tankerness House Museum★ **AC** – Orkney Farm and Folk Museum★

🏨 **Ayre** 🛆 P VISA ⓧ AE
*Ayre Rd.* ✉ *KW15 1QX* – ℰ *(01856) 873 001* – *www.ayrehotel.co.uk – Closed 25 December and 1 January*
**51 rm** ⚏ – ♦£ 70/90 ♦♦£ 113/130 **Rest** – *(bar lunch)* Carte £ 20/37
♦ Well-run hotel close to the harbour. Formerly 3 Victorian houses, now a tradi tionally styled hotel with comfortable bedrooms – the newer extension rooms are biggest and best. Spacious bar filled with locals. Dining room offers sizeable menu of Orcadian produce.

🏨 **Lynnfield** 🚗 ₺ rm, ⁽ᵖ⁾ P VISA ⓧ
*Holm Rd* ✉ *KW15 1SU* – ℰ *(01856) 872 505* – *www.lynnfieldhotel.com – Closec 1-7 January and 25-26 December*
**7 rm** ⚏ – ♦£ 70/95 ♦♦£ 110/135 – 3 suites **Rest** – Carte £ 20/37
♦ Spacious hotel with cosy sitting rooms, Orcadian furniture and a fine range o Scotch whiskies. Supremely comfortable bedrooms; two with four-posters. Forma dining room with large conservatory affording great views of the countryside Seasonal menus.

↑ **Avalon House** without rest 🚗 ℅ ⁽ᵖ⁾ P VISA ⓧ ⓞ
*Carness Rd, Northeast : 1.5 mi by Shore St.* ✉ *KW15 1UE* – ℰ *(01856) 876 665* – *www.avalon-house.co.uk – Closed 2 weeks Christmas*
**5 rm** ⚏ – ♦£ 50/55 ♦♦£ 60/70
♦ Modern, purpose-built guesthouse in a pleasant residential area. Lounge fillec with maps and books about the islands. Good-sized bedrooms with simple, homely feel. Nice coastal outlook.

XX **Foveran** with rm ⅏ ← 🚗 ℅ ⁽ᵖ⁾ P VISA ⓧ
*St Ola, Southwest : 3 mi on A 964* ✉ *KW15 1SF* – ℰ *(01856) 872 389* – *www.foveranhotel.co.uk – Restricted opening October-April*
**8 rm** ⚏ – ♦£ 78/95 ♦♦£ 116 **Rest** – *(dinner only)* Carte £ 26/36
♦ Spacious restaurant boasting superb panoramic views over Scapa Flow and the south islands. Traditional menu features local, seasonal produce, including Orca dian lamb/beef and plenty of fresh seafood. Homely, well-kept bedrooms display simple colour schemes.

**ST MARGARET'S HOPE** – Orkney Islands **31 A3**

XX **Creel** with rm ← P VISA ⓧ
*Front Rd* ✉ *KW17 2SL* – ℰ *(01856) 831 311* – *www.thecreel.co.uk* – *May-September*
**3 rm** ⚏ – ♦£ 75 ♦♦£ 110 **Rest** – Seafood – *(dinner only)* Menu £ 38
♦ Long-standing, family-run restaurant in seafront village. Spacious dining room is hung with local oils and prints. Daily changing menu displays a fresh, tradi tional seafood base. Comfortable, cosy bedrooms boast modern, co-ordinated fur nishings and bay views.

**TROMNESS** – **Orkney Islands** ▯ Scotland                                  **31 A3**

▯ Town★ - Pier Gallery (collection of abstract art★)

---

X   **Hamnavoe**                                                        _VISA_ **OO** **(I)**
35 Graham Pl, off Victoria St ⊠ KW16 3BY – ⨍ (01856) 850 606 – restricted
opening in winter
**Rest** – (closed Monday) (dinner only) Carte £ 28/35
♦ Homely restaurant in a sleepy harbourside town. Plain walls are dotted with
local oils and open fires. Unfussy home cooking uses fresh market produce; local,
where possible. Booking essential.

---

**SLE OF WESTRAY** – **Orkney Islands**                                       **31 A2**

▯ London 696 mi – Edinburgh 290 mi

---

**LEAT** – ⊠ **Orkney Islands**                                              **31 A3**

---

▯   **Cleaton House** ⌂           ⩽ ⇆ ⟍ ⟨ rm, ⟨⟩ **P** _VISA_ **OO**
⊠ KW17 2DB – ⨍ (01857) 677 508 – www.cleatonhouse.com
**6 rm** � – ♦£ 65 ♦♦£ 95/120
**Rest** – (bar lunch) (booking essential for non-residents) Menu £ 35
♦ Victorian former laird's mansion, set on a peninsula and boasting panoramic
views over the bay and Papa Westray. Original tiled floors, antique-filled lounge
and rear bar. Spacious, classically styled bedrooms. Formal set menu relies on local island produce.

---

**IEROWALL** – **Orkney Islands**                                            **31 A2**

↑   **No 1 Broughton** without rest ⌂     ⩽ ⍲ ⟨⟩ ⟨⟩ **P** _VISA_ **OO** **AE** **(I)**
⊠ KW17 2DA – ⨍ (01857) 677 726 – www.no1broughton.co.uk – Closed 24-25
December
**3 rm** ⊵ – ♦£ 35/60 ♦♦£ 60
♦ 19C pink-washed house boasting views over Pierowall Bay and out to Papa
Westray. Comfy lounge and conservatory. Simple, homely bedrooms with modern
bathrooms. Sauna on request. Home-cooked meals showcase local meats/sea-
food; homemade bread and shortcake feature.

---

**EAT INN** – **Fife**                                                        **28 D2**

▯ London 462 mi – Edinburgh 45 mi – Dundee 17 mi – Kirkcaldy 19 mi

---

XXX  **Peat Inn** (Geoffrey Smeddle) with rm     ⇆ ⟨⟩ ⟨⟩ **P** _VISA_ **OO** **AE**
❀   ⊠ KY15 5LH – ⨍ (01334) 840 206 – www.thepeatinn.co.uk – Closed 2 weeks
January, Christmas, Sunday and Monday
**8 rm** – ♦£ 120/150 ♦♦£ 180/195
**Rest** – (booking essential) Menu £ 18/35 – Carte £ 27/54 ⬚
**Spec.** Poached langoustines, braised squid and asparagus. Roast loin and confit
flank of lamb with wild garlic. Amedei chocolate ganache with caramel ice cream
and macadamia nut brownie.
♦ Passionately run, former inn found in the heart of the Fife countryside. Roaring
fire in the lounge; three cosy dining rooms with beams. The accomplished, classically based cooking – with just a hint of the modern – uses fine Scottish produce.
Stylish, split-level bedrooms with good facilities, set in an annexe and overlooking
the lovely back garden and surrounding countryside.

---

**EEBLES** – **The Scottish Borders** – **501** K17 – pop. 8 065 ▯ Scotland   **26 C2**

▣ Edinburgh 24 mi – Glasgow 53 mi – Hawick 31 mi

High St ⨍ (01835) 86 31 70, www.peebles.info

⒅ Kirkland St, ⨍ (01721) 72 01 97

▱ Tweed Valley★★. Traquair House★★ **AC**, SE : 7 mi by B 7062 – Rosslyn Chapel★★
**AC**, N : 16.5 mi by A 703, A 6094, B 7026 and B 7003

SCOTLAND

### Cringletie House ⬧    ≼ ⚭ ⊕ ⛾ ⛟ P VISA ⲟⲟ ⲁ

*Edinburgh Rd., North : 3 mi on A 703 ⊠ EH45 8PL – ℰ (01721) 725 750
– www.cringletie.com – Closed 8-27 January*
**12 rm** ⌷ – **✝**£ 110/160 **✝✝**£ 140/190 – 1 suite
**Rest** *Sutherland Room* – Menu £ 15/33 **s** – Carte £ 33/45 **s**
• Handsome Victorian house boasting far-reaching Tweed Valley views. Luxurious interior with library, drawing room and cosy bar. Tastefully furnished bedrooms have subtle contemporary style. Formal restaurant offers elaborate dining beneath stunning 1902 mural.

### Rowanbrae without rest    ⚓ ⛟

*103 Northgate ⊠ EH45 8BU – ℰ (01721) 721 630 – February-November*
**3 rm** ⌷ – **✝**£ 40/50 **✝✝**£ 60/65
• Tiny cottage close to the town, with pretty front terrace and surprisingly spacious interior. Long-standing owners provide a warm welcome and a cosy, homely atmosphere reigns. Pleasant, well-kept bedrooms have a modern edge courtesy of their soft furnishings.

### ✗✗ Osso    VISA ⲟⲟ ⲁ

*Innerleithen Rd ⊠ EH45 8BA – ℰ (01721) 724 477 – www.ossorestaurant.com
– Closed 1 January, 25 December, dinner Sunday and Monday*
**Rest** – Menu £ 24 (dinner) – Carte £ 17/33
• By day, a coffee shop serving light snacks, tapas and daily specials. By night, much more sophisticated restaurant offering a regularly changing, great value menu of tasty, well-presented dishes, with the occasional Asian influence. Friendly, attentive service.

## at Eddleston North : 4.5 mi on A 703

### ✗✗ Horseshoe Inn with rm    ⚓ rm, ⛟ P VISA ⲟⲟ

*Edinburgh Rd. ⊠ EH45 8QP – ℰ (01721) 730 225 – www.horseshoeinn.co.uk
– Closed 2 weeks January and Monday except bank holidays*
**8 rm** ⌷ – **✝**£ 70 **✝✝**£ 100
**Rest** – (closed Sunday) Menu £ 20/40
**Rest** *Bistro* – Carte £ 19/33
• Former roadside inn; now a smart, columned restaurant with elegant tableware and formal, white-gloved service. Sophisticated à la carte and tasting menu offer ambitious, well-presented, European-influenced dishes. Old classics served in the bistro. Chic, modern bedrooms are in the annexe.

---

## PERTH – Perth and Kinross – 501 J14 – pop. 43 450 ▮ Scotland    28 C

▶ Edinburgh 44 mi – Aberdeen 86 mi – Dundee 22 mi – Dunfermline 29 mi
🛈 West Mill St ℰ (01738) 45 06 00, www.perthshire.co.uk
🔞 Craigie Hill Cherrybank, ℰ (01738) 62 08 29
🔞 King James VI Moncreiffe Island, ℰ (01738) 62 51 70
🔞 Murrayshall New Scone, ℰ (01738) 55 48 04
🔞 North Inch, c/o Perth & Kinross Council 35 Kinncoll St, ℰ (01738) 63 64 81
◉ City★ – Black Watch Regimental Museum★ Y **M1** – Georgian Terraces★ Y
– Museum and Art Gallery★ Y **M2**
◳ Scone Palace★★ **AC**, N : 2 mi by A 93 Y – Branklyn Garden★ **AC**, SE : 1 mi by A 85
Z – Kinnoull Hill (≼★) SE : 1.25 mi by A 85 Z – Huntingtower Castle★ **AC**, NW :
3 mi by A 85 Y – Elcho Castle★ **AC**, SE : 4 mi by A 912 - Z - and Rhynd rd.
Abernethy (11C Round Tower★), SE : 8 mi by A 912 - Z - and A 913

### Parklands    ⚭ ⛟ P VISA ⲟⲟ AE

*2 St Leonard's Bank ⊠ PH2 8EB – ℰ (01738) 622 451
– www.theparklandshotel.com – Closed 25 December-5 January*    Z▶
**15 rm** ⌷ – **✝**£ 93/129 **✝✝**£ 129/169
**Rest** *No.1 The Bank* **Rest** *63@Parklands* – see restaurant listing
• Personally run, extended Georgian house by the railway station, with contemporary interior. Spacious, modern bedrooms boast good facilities and sizeable bathrooms; those to the front are quietest and afford pleasant views over the park.

## ⌂ **Taythorpe** without rest
*Isla Rd, North : 1 mi on A 93* ✉ *PH2 7HQ –* ✆ *(01738) 447 994*
*– www.taythorpe.co.uk*

**3 rm** ⬛ – ♦£ 40/50 ♦♦£ 70/80

Ya

♦ Modern, stone-built house close to Scone Palace, run by a bubbly owner. Immaculately kept interior with fresh flower displays. Homely lounge and cosy breakfast room – order in advance from a vast menu. Warm, well-kept bedrooms display good attention to detail.

## ⅩⅩ **63 Tay Street**
*63 Tay St* ✉ *PH2 8NN –* ✆ *(01738) 441 451 – www.63taystreet.co.uk*
*– Closed 1-9 January, 2-8 July, 26-31 December, Sunday and Monday*

**Rest** – Menu £ 35 (dinner)

Zr

*– Carte £ 33/44* ⅁

♦ Well-established riverside restaurant with fresh décor, bold modern artwork and attentive team. Good value lunches and choice of grill or gourmet dinners, the latter where the cooking really comes into its own. Wine list of over 250 bins.

SCOTLAND

## ✗✗ Deans @ Let's Eat     _VISA_ 🅐 🅞

*77-79 Kinnoull St ⊠ PH1 5EZ – ℰ (01738) 643 377 – www.letseatperth.co.uk*
*– Closed 2 weeks January, Sunday and Monday*                          Y
**Rest** – Menu £ 18/20 – Carte £ 24/38
♦ Bottle-green corner restaurant close to the theatre and concert hall. Comfy
lounge and friendly, chatty team. All-encompassing menus feature seasonal
deals and special events. Passionate, classically based cooking with an ambitious edge.

## ✗✗ 63@Parklands – at Parklands Hotel     🚗 🛋 ✿ P _VISA_ 🅐 AE

*2 St Leonard's Bank ⊠ PH2 8EB – ℰ (01738) 622 451 – www.63atparklands.com*
*– Closed 25 December-6 January*                                       Zn
**Rest** – (dinner only Thursday-Monday) Menu £ 35
♦ Located within a privately run hotel, an intimate conservatory restaurant and
relaxed lounge. Gourmet-style 5 course menu offers one or two choices per
course and changes weekly. Cooking is modern and features some interesting
combinations.

## ✗ No.1 The Bank – at Parklands Hotel     🚗 🛋 P _VISA_ 🅐 AE

*2 St Leonard's Bank ⊠ PH2 8EB – ℰ (01738) 622 451*
*– www.theparklandshotel.com – Closed 26 December-5 January*           Zn
**Rest** – Carte £ 24/38
♦ Informal restaurant set within a personally run Georgian house. Small bar leads
into a bright conservatory with marble tables and garden views. Seasonal à la
carte uses superb local produce; grill menu offers quality Aberdeen Angus beef.

### at Guildtown North : 5 mi on A 93 - Y – ⊠ Perth And Kinross

## ✗✗ Anglers with rm     P _VISA_ 🅐 AE 🅞

*Main Rd ⊠ PH2 6BS – ℰ (01821) 640 329 – www.theanglersinn.co.uk – Closed*
*25-26 December and Monday*
**5 rm** ⌑ – ♥£ 70/100 ♥♥£ 70/100
**Rest** – Carte £ 22/28
♦ Unassuming whitewashed building, formerly an inn, located in a tiny hamlet;
now a spacious, linen-laid restaurant with formal service. Good value lunch menu
and more elaborate, modern British dishes cooked with skill and care in the evening. Comfortable, simply furnished bedrooms offer pleasant country views.

### at Kintillo Southeast : 4.5 mi off A912

## ✗ Roost     P _VISA_ 🅐 AE

*Forgandenny Rd ⊠ PH2 9AZ – ℰ (01738) 812 111*
*– www.theroostrestaurant.co.uk – Closed 1-16 January, 25-26 December,*
*Monday and dinner Sunday, Tuesday and Wednesday*
**Rest** – Carte £ 20/36
♦ Converted former hen house in the heart of the village. Restaurant-cum-
coffee shop by day, serving homemade cakes and light, Italian-influenced
dishes. Dinner steps up a gear, offering well-crafted, classically based plates.
Pleasant team.

### at Forgandenny Southwest : 6.5 mi by A 912 - Z - on B 935 – ⊠ Perth

## ⌂ Battledown without rest ⌁     🚗 ᕮ ୩ P _VISA_ 🅐 🅞

*by Station Rd on Church and School rd ⊠ PH2 9EL – ℰ (01738) 812 471*
*– www.accommodationperthshire.com*
**3 rm** ⌑ – ♥£ 35/40 ♥♥£ 65/70
♦ Immaculately whitewashed, part 18C cottage in quiet village. Lovely garden;
owner's paintings on show. Cosy, pine-furnished breakfast room. Neat, tidy
rooms, all on ground level.

**at Stanley** North :7 mi off A9 (Inverness)

✗ **Apron Stage**        *VISA* **⚫⚫** AE
5 King St ⌂ PH1 4ND – ✆ (01738) 828 888 – www.apronstagerestaurant.co.uk
– Closed one week May, one week September, and Sunday-Tuesday
**Rest** – *(dinner only and Friday lunch)* Menu £ 16 (lunch) – Carte £ 22/33
 ◆ Lovely little restaurant in a small village, consisting of a cosy room with for-
mally laid tables and an open-kitchen to the rear. Appealing, weekly menu mixes
Scottish, French and Asian influences in generous, flavoursome portions.

**PIEROWALL** – **501** K6 – see Orkney Islands (Isle of Westray)

**PITLOCHRY** – Perth and Kinross – **501** I13 – pop. 2 564 ▯ Scotland     **28** C2
▶ Edinburgh 71 mi – Inverness 85 mi – Perth 27 mi
*ℹ* 22 Atholl Rd ✆ (01796) 47 22 15, www.pitlochry.org
▦ Pitlochry Estate Office, ✆ (01796) 47 27 92
◉ Town★
◎ Blair Castle★★ **AC**, NW : 7 mi by A 9 A – Queen's View★★, W : 7 mi by B 8019 A
– Falls of Bruar★, NW : 11 mi by A 9 A

**SCOTLAND**

**Green Park** ≤ 🚗 🏠 📶 🛗 rm, 📶 📶 **P** 💳 🌐

*Clunie Bridge Rd ⊠ PH16 5JY – 𝒞 (01796) 473 248 – www.thegreenpark.co.uk*
*– Closed 25 December* Aa
**51 rm** (dinner included) � – ♦£ 73/103 ♦♦£ 146/206
**Rest** – (light lunch residents only) (booking essential at dinner for non-residents)
Menu £ 16/21 – Carte £ 21/29
• Family run 1860s summer retreat on Loch Faskally. Rooms in the old house are
decorated in floral patterns; impressive up-to-date wing has good, contemporary
facilities. Unhurried dinners at lochside setting.

**East Haugh House** 🚗 🍴 📶 📶 📶 💳 🌐

*Southeast : 1.75 mi off A 924 (Perth Rd) ⊠ PH16 5TE – 𝒞 (01796) 473 121*
*– www.easthaugh.co.uk – Closed 1 week Christmas*
**14 rm** ⊵ – ♦£ 118/178 ♦♦£ 118/258 – 1 suite
**Rest** *Two Sisters* – see restaurant listing
• 17C turreted stone house in 2 acres of gardens; originally part of the Atholl Estate. Traditionally appointed bedrooms, named after fishing flies, are split between
the house and two lodges. They also own fishing rights to Dalmarnock Beat.

**Craigatin House and Courtyard** without rest 🚗 🛗 📶 📶 **P**

*165 Atholl Rd ⊠ PH16 5QL – 𝒞 (01796) 472 478* 💳 🌐 🌐
*– www.craigatinhouse.co.uk – Closed Christmas* Ae
**12 rm** ⊵ – ♦£ 65/75 ♦♦£ 75/95 – 1 suite
• Built in 1822 as a doctor's house, now a stylish boutique hotel. Stunning modern open-plan lounge and breakfast room centred around a wood burning stove
and overlooking the garden. Contemporary, minimalist bedrooms; some in the
old stables.

**Beinn Bhracaigh** without rest ≤ 🚗 📶 **P** 💳 🌐 🌐

*Higher Oakfield ⊠ PH16 5HT – 𝒞 (01796) 470 355 – www.beinnbhracaigh.com*
*– Closed 22-28 December* Bn
**11 rm** ⊵ – ♦£ 50/90 ♦♦£ 77/100
• Spacious stone house built in 1880 and run by passionate owners. Immaculately kept interior with good comforts; most rooms boast lovely views of the
Tummel Valley. Breakfast includes French toast and pancakes with maple syrup
and bacon.

**Dunmurray Lodge** without rest 🚗 📶 **P**

*72 Bonnethill Rd ⊠ PH16 5ED – 𝒞 (01796) 473 624 – www.dunmurray.co.uk*
*– Mid-March to mid-November* Bc
**4 rm** ⊵ – ♦£ 55/70 ♦♦£ 65/80
• Imposing 19C former doctors surgery, close to town, boasting views across to
the mountains. Smart lounge and neat bedrooms with co-ordinated décor; the
best outlooks are from the front. Bright, neatly laid breakfast room features very
locally sourced produce.

**Two Sisters** – at East Haugh House Hotel 🚗 **P** 💳 🌐

*Southeast : 1.75 mi off A 924 (Perth Rd) ⊠ PH16 5TE – 𝒞 (01796) 473 121*
*– www.easthaugh.co.uk – Closed 1 week Christmas*
**Rest** – (restricted opening lunch in winter) Carte £ 22/31
• Charming fishermen's bar and bright, laid-back restaurant, located in a lovely
17C turreted house. Seasonal Scottish menu is served in both areas; cooking is
clean and exact, with fish and game to the fore and fresh, home-baked breads.

**at Killiecrankie** Northwest : 4 mi by A 924 - A - and B 8019 on B 8079
– ⊠ Pitlochry

**Killiecrankie House** 🌿 ≤ 🚗 📶 **P** 💳 🌐 📶

*⊠ PH16 5LG – 𝒞 (01796) 473 220 – www.killiecrankiehotel.co.uk*
*– Closed 3 January-15 March*
**9 rm** (dinner included) ⊵ – ♦£ 115/195 ♦♦£ 250/290 – 1 suite
**Rest** – (bar lunch) Menu £ 38
• Quiet and privately run, a converted 1840 vicarage with a distinct rural feel.
The sizeable bedrooms come in co-ordinated patterns and overlook pleasant
countryside. Warm, red dining room; garden produce prominent on menus.

SCOTLAND

## PLOCKTON – Highland – **501** D11 📖 Scotland — 29 B2

▶ Edinburgh 210 mi – Inverness 88 mi
◉ Village★
◉ Wester Ross★★★

---

🍺 **Plockton Hotel** with rm  ⪡ 🖥 🏠 ⅏ 🐾 ℃ 🌐 𝖵𝖨𝖲𝖠 ⓪ 𝖠𝖤
*41 Harbour St ⊠ IV52 8TN –* 𝒞 *(01599) 544 274 – www.plocktonhotel.co.uk*
**15 rm** 🖵 – †£ 40/90 ††£ 100/130  **Rest** – Carte £ 16/38
♦ Formerly two cottages on the lochside, now a family-run pub with small terrace and restaurant. Cooking uses local Highland or Scottish produce, with fresh seafood dishes a speciality. Bedrooms, in the pub and annexe, boast bay views to the front.

---

## PORT APPIN – Argyll and Bute – **501** D14 – ⊠ Appin — 27 B2

▶ Edinburgh 136 mi – Ballachulish 20 mi – Oban 24 mi

---

🏨 **Airds** ⏃  ⪡ 🖥 🔄 🕪 𝖯 𝖵𝖨𝖲𝖠 ⓪ 𝖠𝖤
⊠ *PA38 4DF –* 𝒞 *(01631) 730 236 – www.airds-hotel.com – Closed
Monday-Tuesday November, December and January*
**11 rm** (dinner included) 🖵 – †£ 194/235 ††£ 317/460
**Rest** – *(booking essential for non-residents)* Menu £ 53 (dinner) – Carte £ 27/33
♦ Former ferry inn boasting loch/mountain views and warm, welcoming interior. Two sumptuously furnished, open-fired sitting rooms display antiques. Intimate, floral-themed bedrooms provide good comforts. Excellent views from well-laid dining room. Classical cooking with a modern edge; 7 course tasting menu available.

---

## PORT CHARLOTTE – Argyll and Bute – **501** A16 – see Islay (Isle of)

---

## PORT ELLEN – Argyll and Bute – **501** B17 – see Islay (Isle of)

---

## PORTMAHOMACK – Highland – **501** I10 — 30 D2

▶ Edinburgh 194 mi – Dornoch 21 mi – Tain 12 mi

---

🍴 **Oystercatcher** with rm  🏠 𝖯 𝖵𝖨𝖲𝖠 ⓪ 𝖠𝖤
*Main St ⊠ IV20 1YB –* 𝒞 *(01862) 871 560 – www.the-oystercatcher.co.uk
– restricted opening in winter*
**3 rm** 🖵 – †£ 45/78 ††£ 108
**Rest** – Seafood – *(closed Sunday dinner, Wednesday lunch, Monday and Tuesday) (booking essential)* Menu £ 33 (dinner) **s** – Carte £ 37/79 **s**
♦ Personally run bistro and piscatorially themed main dining room in a lovely setting. Numerous seafood menus, offering a vast choice and some unusual combinations. Simple bedrooms.

---

## PORTPATRICK – Dumfries and Galloway – **501** E19 – pop. 585 — 25 A3
– ⊠ Stranraer

▶ Edinburgh 141 mi – Ayr 60 mi – Dumfries 80 mi – Stranraer 9 mi
🏌 Golf Course Rd, 𝒞 (01776) 81 02 73

---

🏨 **Knockinaam Lodge** ⏃  ⪡ 🖥 🕭 ⅏ rm, 𝖯 𝖵𝖨𝖲𝖠 ⓪ 𝖠𝖤
✿ *Southeast : 5 mi by A 77 off B 7042 ⊠ DG9 9AD –* 𝒞 *(01776) 810 471
– www.knockinaamlodge.com*
**10 rm** (dinner included) 🖵 – †£ 165/215 ††£ 340/440
**Rest** – *(booking essential for non-residents) (set menu only)* Menu £ 40/58 ⅋
**Spec.** Steamed fillet of sea bass with gazpacho emulsion. Fillet of beef with truffle pomme purée, trio of shallots and a tarragon reduction. Raspberry panna cotta with a strawberry doughnut.
♦ Charming country house in a private cove. Classical guest areas include openfired sitting rooms and a wood-panelled bar; a relaxed atmosphere pervades. Traditionally furnished bedrooms boast antiques. Gold-hued dining room offers sea views and a carefully judged, 5 course daily menu of top quality, seasonal produce.

## RANNOCH STATION – Perth and Kinross – **501** G13     **27** B2
▶ Edinburgh 108 mi – Kinloch Rannoch 17 mi – Pitlochry 36 mi

⌂ **Moor of Rannoch** 🍂     ⬚ 🚗 **P** *VISA* 🌐
✉ *PH17 2QA* – ✆ *(01882) 633 238* – *www.moorofrannoch.co.uk* – *23 March-October*
**5 rm** ☕ – ♦£ 62/92 ♦♦£ 92
**Rest** – *(dinner only)* Carte £ 21/32 **s**
♦ Immaculately whitewashed 19C property "in the middle of nowhere", next to railway station with link to London! Comfy, sofa-strewn lounges. Rustic rooms with antiques. Home-cooked menus in characterful dining room with conservatory.

## RATAGAN – Highland     **29** B2
▶ London 572 mi – Edinburgh 187 mi – Inverness 65 mi

⌂ **Grants at Craigellachie**     ⬚ 🚗 **P** *VISA* 🌐
✉ *IV40 8HP* – ✆ *(01599) 511 331* – *www.housebytheloch.co.uk* – *restricted opening November-Easter*
**4 rm** (dinner included) ☕ – ♦£ 95/103 ♦♦£ 160/175
**Rest** – *(closed Sunday) (dinner only) (booking essential for non residents)* Carte £ 31/39
♦ Set in an idyllic spot beside Loch Duich; compact modern bedrooms are divided between the main house and a building in the rear garden. Local produce and Mediterranean influences inform the menu. Interesting wine list and a good selection of malt whiskies.

## ST ANDREWS – Fife – **501** L14 – pop. 14 209 ▮ Scotland    **28** D2
▶ Edinburgh 51 mi – Dundee 14 mi – Stirling 51 mi
🛈 70 Market St ✆ (01334) 47 20 21, www.standrews.co.uk
⛳ Duke's Craigtoun Park, ✆ (01334) 47 43 71
◉ City★★ • Cathedral★ (⁂★★) AC**B**• British Golf Museum AC**A**M1• St Andrews Preservation Trust B**M**2 • St Andrews Aquarium AC**A**M3 • MUSA University of St Andrews Museum B**M**4 • West Port★**A**
🎫 Leuchars (parish church★), NW : 6 mi by A 91 and A 919. The East Neuk★★, SE : 9 mi by A 917 and B 9131 B – Crail★★ (Old Centre★★, Upper Crail★) SE : 9 mi by A 917 B – Kellie Castle★ **AC**, S : 9 mi by B 9131 and B 9171 B – Ceres★, SW : 9 mi by B 939 - E : Inland Fife★ A

🏨🏨🏨 **Old Course H. Golf Resort and Spa**   ⬚ 🌐 🍸 🛗 ⬚ 🎬 🖥 ⬚ 🍴 ⬚
*Old Station Rd* ✉ *KY16 9SP* – ✆ *(01334)*     ⬚ 🍸 🎿 **P** *VISA* 🌐 AE ①
*474 371* – *www.oldcoursehotel.co.uk*        **Ab**
**123 rm** ☕ – ♦£ 220/390 ♦♦£ 250/420 – 21 suites
**Rest** *Road Hole* **Rest** *Sands Grill* – see restaurant listing
♦ Vast resort hotel on a world-famous championship golf course, overlooking the bay. Spacious guest areas with stylish Scottish theme; superb spa, leisure and meeting facilities. Chic, comfortable bedrooms: some sumptuous, some contemporary.

🏨🏨🏨 **Fairmont St Andrews**   ⬚ 🚗 🌀 🌐 🍸 🛗 🎬 🖥 ⬚ 🍴 rm, 🅰🅲 🍸 🎿 **P**
*Southeast : 3 mi on A 917* ✉ *KY16 8PN*       *VISA* 🌐 AE ①
– ✆ *(01334) 837 000* – *www.fairmont.com/standrews*
**203 rm** ☕ – ♦♦£ 90/150 – 6 suites
**Rest** *Squire* – ✆ *(01334) 837 441 (dinner only)* Menu £ 25 – Carte £ 24/37
**Rest** *Esperante* – ✆ *(01334) 837 271 (closed Monday-Tuesday) (dinner only)* Menu £ 50
♦ Modern, purpose-built property set in 520 acres. Spacious guest areas display a subtle Scottish theme. Extensive conference and leisure facilities; two golf courses; superb spa and wellness centre. Well-appointed bedrooms with smart bathrooms. Informal Squires in vast atrium. Mediterranean menu in Esperante.

## ST ANDREWS

**Botanic Garden** [A 915] *KIRKCALDY* **A**       **B** [A 917] *CRAIL, ANSTRUTHER*

SCOTLAND

---

🏨🏨 **Rufflets Country House** ⚜    ⬅ 🚗 🔊 🕭 rm, 🍽 🛜 🖐 🄿
*Strathkinness Low Rd, West : 1.5 mi on B 939* ⊠ *KY16 9TX*     VISA ⓿⓿ AE ⓪
*– 𝒞 (01334) 472 594 – www.rufflets.co.uk*
**22 rm** 🖃 – †£ 125/225 ††£ 200/260 – 2 suites
**Rest** *Terrace* – Menu £ 13/35 – Carte £ 27/53
♦ Handsome 1920s house set in ornamental gardens. Traditional drawing room
with cosy fireside sofas. Thoughtfully appointed bedrooms that mix classic and
contemporary styles. Terrace restaurant offers fine vantage point to view the lawns.

⛫ **Fairways** without rest                                              🍽
*8a Golf Pl.* ⊠ *KY16 9JA – 𝒞 (01334) 473 319 – www.fairwaysofstandrews.co.uk*
**3 rm** 🖃 – †£ 60/80 ††£ 80/95                                           **A**z
♦ Run by the same friendly owners as older sister 6 Murray Park and the closest
guesthouse in town to the famous 'Old Course'. Bedrooms are contemporary
and offer good modern facilities; the suite boasts a balcony and overlooks the
18th hole.

⛫ **Six Murray Park** without rest                          🍽 🛜 VISA ⓿⓿ ⓪
*6 Murray Pk.* ⊠ *KY16 9AW – 𝒞 (01334) 473 319 – www.sixmurraypark.co.uk*
**8 rm** 🖃 – †£ 40/80 ††£ 80/95                                           **A**n
♦ Victorian terraced property with smart window boxes. Modern bedrooms boast
bold feature walls and good facilities, including flat screen TVs and iPod docks.
Hot daily specials are taken in the linen-laid, leather-furnished breakfast room.

⛫ **Five Pilmour Place** without rest                        🚗 🛜 VISA ⓿⓿ AE
*5 Pilmour Pl.* ⊠ *KY16 9HZ – 𝒞 (01334) 478 665 – www.5pilmourplace.com*
*– February-November*                                                       **A**x
**6 rm** 🖃 – †£ 58/75 ††£ 105/160
♦ Terraced Victorian house with neatly lawned rear garden. Flag-floored hall
leads to clubby lounge and communal breakfast room. Bedrooms range in size
and come with boldly coloured feature walls and good facilities; one has a claw-
foot bath.

**↑ Aslar House** without rest  🖨 📶 📡 📶 _VISA_ ⊕
_120 North St ⊠ KY16 9AF – 𝒞 (01334) 473 460 – www.aslar.com – Closed 2-20_
_January and 20-28 December_ A
**6 rm** 🖵 – †£ 47/90 ††£ 94/100
• Victorian terraced house in the town centre, run by a friendly, enthusiastic couple. Open-plan lounge and breakfast room. Neat, tidy bedrooms offer good modern facilities. Largest rooms are at the top; one has a lounge inside the turret.

**XXX Seafood**  ⇐ 🏠 AC _VISA_ ⊕ AE
_The Scores ⊠ KY16 9AB – 𝒞 (01334) 479 475 – www.theseafoodrestaurant.com_
**Rest** – Seafood – _(booking essential)_ Carte £ 22/45 Ac
• Overhanging the town's beach, with super views, as all four sides are made
of glass. A very pleasant attitude and attention to detail accompanies agreeable,
top quality, regularly changing seafood menus.

**XXX Road Hole** – at Old Course Hotel Golf Resort and Spa  ⇐ AC 🅿
_Old Station Rd ⊠ KY16 9SP – 𝒞 (01334) 474 371_  _VISA_ ⊕ AE ⓘ
_– www.oldcoursehotel.co.uk_ Ab
**Rest** – _(Closed January, February, Sunday and Monday)_ _(dinner only)_ Carte approx. £ 42
• Fine dining restaurant within a smart golf resort and spa, boasting views out
across St Andrews golf course and the bay. Menus are largely classically based
but display some modern touches.

**XX Sands Grill** – at Old Course Hotel Golf Resort and Spa  ⇐ AC 🅿
_Old Station Rd ⊠ KY16 9SP – 𝒞 (01334) 474 371_  _VISA_ ⊕ AE ⓘ
_– www.oldcoursehotel.co.uk_ Ab
**Rest** – _(dinner only)_ Carte approx. £ 27
• Informal grill restaurant located in a stylish golf resort and spa next to St Andrews golf course. Menus comprise mainly of seafood and steak dishes, with all
meats cooked in the Josper oven.

---

**ST BOSWELLS** – The Scottish Borders – **501** L17 – pop. 1 199  **26 D2**
– ⊠ Melrose 🛈 Scotland

▶ Edinburgh 39 mi – Glasgow 79 mi – Hawick 17 mi – Newcastle upon Tyne 66 mi
📷 St Boswells, 𝒞 (01835) 82 35 27
🔲 Dryburgh Abbey★★ AC (setting★★★), NW : 4 mi by B 6404 and B 6356 – Tweed
Valley★★. Bowhill★★ AC, SW : 11.5 mi by A 699 and A 708

**↑ Whitehouse** 🌢  ⇐ 🖨 📶 📡 🅿 _VISA_ ⊕
_Northeast : 3 mi on B 6404 ⊠ TD6 0ED – 𝒞 (01573) 460 343_
_– www.whitehousecountryhouse.com_
**3 rm** 🖵 – †£ 60/75 ††£ 90/110
**Rest** – Menu £ 29
• Former dower house built in 1872 by the Duke of Sutherland, boasting excellent views across the estate. Traditionally furnished bedrooms; cosy, country
house feel. Many people come for the on-site shooting/fishing. Local game and
wild salmon feature at dinner.

**↑ Clint Lodge**  ⇐ 🖨 📡 🅿 _VISA_ ⊕ AE
_North : 2.25 mi by B 6404 on B 6356 ⊠ TD6 0DZ – 𝒞 (01835) 822 027_
_– www.clintlodge.co.uk – Closed 1 week Christmas_
**5 rm** 🖵 – †£ 50 ††£ 75/110
**Rest** – Menu £ 33
• Former shooting lodge with superb river and hill views. Characterful interior
boasts antiques and fishing memorabilia. Traditionally decorated bedrooms; luxurious No. 4 and south facing rooms are the best. Daily changing 5 course dinner
served at beautiful table.

**ST FILLANS** – Perth and Kinross – **501** H14      **28** C2

Edinburgh 65 mi – Lochearnhead 8 mi – Perth 29 mi

🏠   **Achray House**     ⬅ 🍴 📶 **P** VISA ⓪⓪
PH6 2NF – ☏ (01764) 685 231 – www.achrayhouse.com – Closed January and first 2 weeks December
**8 rm** 🍽 – ♦£ 89/109 ♦♦£ 176/200
**Rest** – (closed Monday-Tuesday November-March) Menu £ 9/27
♦ Superbly located Edwardian villa affording stunning views over Loch Earn. Bright breakfast room and inviting lounge with open fires and Douglas Fir polished wood floor. Modern bedrooms have bespoke pine furniture and contemporary bathrooms. Simple restaurant offers classical dishes crafted from local produce.

**ST MARGARET'S HOPE** – **501** L7 – see Orkney Islands (Mainland)

**ST MONANS** – Fife – **501** L15 – pop. 3 965      **28** D2

Edinburgh 47 mi – Dundee 26 mi – Perth 40 mi – Stirling 56 mi

XX   **Craig Millar @ 16 West End**     ⬅ 🍴 VISA ⓪⓪ 🆎
16 West End ⌂ KY10 2BX – ☏ (01333) 730 327 – www.16westend.com – Closed Monday-Tuesday March-September and restricted opening October-March
**Rest** – Seafood – (booking essential) Menu £ 26/40
♦ Unassuming former pub with attractive interior and charming team. Characterful lounge and smart, linen-laid restaurant with small terrace and great views over the harbour and sea. Experienced chef offers clean, refined, flavoursome dishes.

**SANQUHAR** – Dumfries and Galloway – **501** I17 – pop. 2 028      **25** B2

London 368 mi – Edinburgh 58 mi – East Kilbride 51 mi – Hamilton 43 mi

XX   **Blackaddie House** with rm     🍴 **P** VISA ⓪⓪ 🆎
Blackaddie Rd ⌂ DG4 6JJ – ☏ (01659) 50 270 – www.blackaddiehotel.co.uk
**9 rm** 🍽 – ♦£ 65/80 ♦♦£ 120
**Rest** – Menu £ 27 (lunch) – Carte £ 35/51
♦ 16C stone house by the river. Lunch offers good value classics. Dinner is more elaborate and features complex, original cooking. Ingredients are luxurious and dishes, well presented. Simpler bar menu also available. Bedrooms are named after whisky distilleries.

**SCALASAIG** – Argyll and Bute – **501** B15 – see Colonsay (Isle of)

**SCALPAY** – Western Isles – **501** A10 – see Lewis and Harris (Isle of)

**SCARISTA** – Western Isles – **501** Y10 – see Lewis and Harris (Isle of)

**SCOURIE** – Highland – **501** E8 – ⌂ **Lairg** ▌ Scotland      **30** C1

Edinburgh 263 mi – Inverness 107 mi

Cape Wrath★★★ (⬅★★) **AC**, N : 31 mi (including ferry crossing) by A 894 and A 838 – Loch Assynt★★, S : 17 mi by A 894

🏠   **Eddrachilles** ⌂     ⬅ 🍴 ⓪ ⚡ **P** VISA ⓪⓪ 🆎
Badcall Bay, South : 2.5 mi on A 894 ⌂ IV27 4TH – ☏ (01971) 502 080 – www.eddrachilles.com – April-September
**11 rm** 🍽 – ♦£ 77/80 ♦♦£ 104/110
**Rest** – (bar lunch) Menu £ 30
♦ Remotely set, converted 18C manse with views of the countryside, Badcall Bay and its islands. Cosy, well-kept bedrooms. Snug bar and flag-floored dining room; delightful outlook from conservatory lounge. Daily menu with strong French slant. Meats cured on-site.

**SCRABSTER** – Highland – **501** J8 – see Thurso

# SHETLAND ISLANDS – 501 P/Q3 – pop. 21 988 🏴 Scotland

✈ Sumburgh Airport : ☎ (01950) 460905, S : 25 mi of Lerwick by A 97 - Tingwall Airport: 01595) 840246, NW: 6m. of Lerwick by A971

⛴ from Foula to Walls (Shetland Islands Council) 1-2 weekly (2 h 30 mn) – from Fair Isle to Sumburgh (Shetland Islands Council) 1-2 weekly (2 h 40 mn)

⛴ from Lerwick (Mainland) to Aberdeen and via Orkney Islands (Stromness) (P and O Scottish Ferries) – from Vidlin to Skerries (Shetland Islands Council booking essential 3-4 weekly (1 h 30 mn) – from Lerwick (Mainland) to Skerries (Shetland Islands Council) 2 weekly (booking essential) (2 h 30 mn – from Lerwick (Mainland) to Bressay (Shetland Islands Council) frequent services daily (7 mn) – from Laxo (Mainland) to Isle of Whalsay (Symbister) (Shetland Islands Council) frequent services daily (30 mn) – from Toft (Mainland) to Isle of Yell (Ulsta) (Shetland Islands Council) frequent service daily (20 mn) – from Isle of Yell (Gutcher) to Isle of Fetlar (Oddsta) and via Isle of Unst (Belmont) (Shetland Islands Council) – from Fair Isle to Sumburgh (Mainland) (Shetland Islands Council) 3 weekly (2 h 40 mn)

👁 Islands★ - Up Helly Aa (last Tuesday in January) – Mousa Broch★★★ AC (Mousa Island) – Jarlshof★★ - Lerwick to Jarlshof (≤★) – Shetland Croft House Museum★ AC

---

**SCOTLAND**

## MAINLAND – Shetland Islands                                          31 B2

▶ London 559 mi – Edinburgh 148 mi

## LERWICK – Shetland Islands – pop. 6 830 🏴 Scotland                   31 B2

ℹ Lerwick ☎ (08452) 255 1 21, www.visitscotland.com

⛳ Shetland Gott Dale, ☎ (01595) 84 03 69

👁 Clickhimin Broch★

📷 Gulber Wick (≤★), S : 2 mi by A 970

### Kveldsro House                                          ✗ ⁽¹⁾ P VISA AE ⓪
*Greenfield Pl ⊠ ZE1 0AQ – ☎ (01595) 692 195 – www.shetlandhotels.com
– Closed 1-2 January and 25-26 December*
**17 rm** ⊡ – ♦£ 105 ♦♦£ 130
**Rest** – *(bar lunch Monday-Saturday, carvery lunch Sunday)* Carte £ 21/34 s
♦ Spacious Georgian house hidden in the town centre; its name means 'evening peace'. Cosy sitting room with original ceiling mouldings, comfy bar with views of the islands and traditionally styled bedrooms. Menus offer mainly island produce; portions are hearty.

### Glen Orchy House                                        & rm, ⁽¹⁾ P VISA
*20 Knab Rd ⊠ ZE1 0AX – ☎ (01595) 692 031 – www.guesthouselerwick.com*
**24 rm** ⊡ – ♦£ 65/90 ♦♦£ 90
**Rest** – Thai – *(booking essential) (residents only)* Carte £ 18/23
♦ Family-run hotel set in a 1904 former convent. Neat, well-kept guest areas include an honesty bar and spacious, comfortable lounge. Simple, cosy bedrooms – those in the wing boast underfloor heating. Homely dining room; unusually, cooking is totally Thai-based.

## VEENSGARTH – Shetland Islands                                         31 B2

### Herrislea House                                         ✎ ⁽¹⁾ P VISA
*⊠ ZE2 9SB – ☎ (01595) 840 208 – www.herrisleahouse.co.uk
– Closed 12 December-8 January*
**9 rm** ⊡ – ♦£ 85/110 ♦♦£ 120/130
**Rest** – *(dinner only) (booking essential for non-residents)* Carte £ 19/32
♦ Large, family-run hotel set just out of town. Unusual African hunting theme with mounted antlers, animal heads and skins on display. Cosy, individually designed bedrooms; some with valley views. Fresh cooking uses local produce and meats from the family crofts.

776

**SHIELDAIG** – Highland – **501** D11 – ✉ **Strathcarron** ▐ Scotland          **29** B2

▶ Edinburgh 226 mi – Inverness 70 mi – Kyle of Lochalsh 36 mi

ⓖ Wester Ross ★★★

⌂ **Tigh An Eilean**          ⟨ ⁽ᵗ⁾ VISA ◐◑ AE
  ✉ IV54 8XN – 𝒞 (01520) 755 251 – www.tighaneilean.co.uk – *Restricted opening in winter*
  **11 rm** � – ♦£ 70/110 ♦♦£ 140
  **Rest** – *(booking essential for non-residents) (bar lunch)* Menu £ 45 (dinner) – Carte £ 15/25
  ♦ In a sleepy lochside village, an attractive, personally run 19C inn with fine views of the Shieldaig Islands. Cosy, well-kept bedrooms and a comfy lounge with a homely feel. Linen-clad dining room showing eclectic variety of art; Scottish produce to the fore.

---

**SKIRLING** – The Scottish Borders – **501** J17 – ✉ **Biggar** ▐ Scotland          **26** C2

▶ Edinburgh 29 mi – Glasgow 45 mi – Peebles 16 mi

ⓖ Biggar★ - Gladstone Court Museum★, Greenhill Covenanting Museum★,
  S : 3 mi by A 72 and A 702. New Lanark★★, NW : 16 mi by A 72 and A 73

⋔ **Skirling House**          ⟨⟩ ⟨⟩ ⁂ ⁽ᵗ⁾ P VISA ◐◑
  ✉ ML12 6HD – 𝒞 (01899) 860 274 – www.skirlinghouse.com – *Closed January, February and 1 week November-December*
  **5 rm** ⊒yy – ♦£ 60/85 ♦♦£ 140   **Rest** – Menu £ 32
  ♦ On the green in an attractive hamlet; a personally run, Scots Pine, Arts and Crafts house. Beautiful Florentine carved ceiling and eclectic range of memorabilia in drawing room. Simple, characterful bedrooms with extras. Accomplished cooking uses home-grown produce; daily 4 course menu can be taken in the conservatory.

---

**SKYE (Isle of)** – Highland – **501** B11 – pop. 9 232 ▐ Scotland          **29** B2

⇔ from Mallaig to Isles of Eigg, Muck, Rhum and Canna (Caledonian MacBrayne Ltd) (summer only) – from Mallaig to Armadale (Caledonian MacBrayne Ltd) (summer only) 1-2 weekly (30 mn)

⇔ from Mallaig to Armadale (Caledonian MacBrayne Ltd) 1-5 daily (30 mn) – from Uig to North Uist (Lochmaddy) or Isle of Harris (Tarbert) (Caledonian MacBrayne Ltd) 1-3 daily (1 h 50 mn) – from Sconser to Isle of Raasay (Caledonian MacBrayne Ltd) 9-10 daily (except Sunday) (15 mn)

ⓞ Island★★ - The Cuillins★★★ – Skye Museum of Island Life★ **AC**

ⓖ N : Trotternish Peninsula★★ – W : Duirinish Peninsula★ – Portree★

**BERNISDALE** – Highland

⋔ **Spoons** without rest ⟿          ⟨ ⟨⟩ ⁂ ⁽ᵗ⁾ P VISA ◐◑ AE
  75 Aird Bernisdale ✉ IV51 9NU – 𝒞 (01470) 532 217
  – www.thespoonsonskye.com – *Closed 1 week February, 1 week October and 20-27 December*
  **3 rm** ⊒yy – ♦£ 105/125 ♦♦£ 135/155
  ♦ Luxurious, purpose-built guest house in unspoilt hamlet, with airy, wood-floored lounge and breakfast room overlooking the loch. Bedrooms are individually decorated in a crisp, modern style and provide every conceivable extra. Superb 3 course breakfasts, with eggs from the charming owners' chickens.

**BROADFORD** – Highland          **29** B2

⋔ **Tigh an Dochais**          ⟨ ⟨⟩ ⁂ ⁽ᵗ⁾ P VISA ◐◑ AE
  13 Harrapool, on A 87 ✉ IV49 9AQ – 𝒞 (01471) 820 022
  – www.skyebedbreakfast.co.uk – *April-November*
  **3 rm** ⊒yy – ♦£ 80 ♦♦£ 90   **Rest** – Menu £ 25
  ♦ Striking house with award-winning architecture, overlooking Broadford Bay and the Applecross Peninsula. Comfortable lounge has well-stocked bookshelves. Modern, minimalist bedrooms boast superb views and good facilities, including underfloor heating and plenty of extras. Communal, home-cooked meals by arrangement.

**DUISDALEMORE** – Highland                                                 **29** B2

🏨 ▮ **Duisdale House** ॐ                          ⇦ 🖫 ⓓ ℀ rm, ☂ 🅿 𝗩𝗜𝗦𝗔 ⬤⬤
*Sleat, on A 851.* ✉ *IV43 8QW* – ☏ *(01471) 833 202* – *www.duisdale.com*
**18 rm** ☟ – ♦£ 85/190 ♦♦£ 160/280 – 1 suite
**Rest** – Menu £ 22/42 – Carte £ 13/45
♦ Stylish, up-to-date hotel with lawned gardens, hot tub and coastal views. Comfortable bedrooms boast bold décor, excellent bathrooms and a pleasing blend of contemporary and antique furniture. Modern cooking makes good use of local produce. Smart uniformed staff.

**DUNVEGAN** – Highland                                                    **29** B2

⌂ ▮ **Roskhill House** without rest                        🖫 ℀ ☂ 🅿 𝗩𝗜𝗦𝗔 ⬤⬤
 *Roskhill, Southeast : 2.5 mi by A 863* ✉ *IV55 8ZD* – ☏ *(01470) 521 317*
– *www.roskhillhouse.co.uk* – *Closed 15 December-16 February*
**5 rm** ☟ – ♦£ 52/60 ♦♦£ 76/86
♦ Welcoming 19C croft house with small garden, set in peaceful location close to the water. Formerly the old post office, the lounge boasts exposed stone, wooden beams and an open fire. Fresh, bright bedrooms have a contemporary edge and smart, modern bathrooms.

%% ▮ **Three Chimneys & The House Over-By** with rm ॐ          ⇦ 🖫 ⅙
*Colbost* ✉ *IV55 8ZT* – ☏ *(01470) 511 258*                       🅿 𝗩𝗜𝗦𝗔 ⬤⬤ 𝗔𝗘
– *www.threechimneys.co.uk* – *Closed 6-21 January*
**6 rm** ☟ – ♦£ 196/295 ♦♦£ 196/295
**Rest** – Seafood – *(closed Sunday lunch November-March) (booking essential)*
Menu £ 37/60
♦ Immaculately kept crofter's cottage in stunning lochside setting. Three characterful low-beamed dining rooms display modern artwork. Choose from accomplished, classical seafood-orientated dishes or 7 course tasting menu. Split-level bedrooms are spacious and stylishly understated; great outlook from residents' lounge.

**EDINBANE** – Highland                                                    **29** B2

🏨 ▮ **Greshornish House** ॐ                         ⇦ 🖫 ⓓ ℀ 🅿 𝗩𝗜𝗦𝗔 ⬤⬤
*North : 3.75 mi by A 850 in direction of Dunvegan* ✉ *IV51 9PN*
– ☏ *(01470) 582 266* – *www.greshornishhouse.com* – *Restricted opening in winter*
**6 rm** ☟ – ♦£ 125/155 ♦♦♦£ 150/185
**Rest** – *(Closed Monday, and Tuesday in winter) (booking essential)*
Menu £ 23/40 – Carte £ 25/48
♦ Early 18C lochside house in 10 acres. Comfy panelled drawing room; old billiard room with snooker table, piano, books and games. Country house style bedrooms; some four-posters/loch views. Breakfast in conservatory; seasonal, island dinners in candlelit dining room.

**FLODIGARRY** – Highland – ✉ Staffin                                      **29** B2

🏨 ▮ **Flodigarry Country House** ॐ                    ⇦ 🖫 ↘ 🅿 𝗩𝗜𝗦𝗔 ⬤⬤
 ✉ *IV51 9HZ* – ☏ *(01470) 552 203* – *www.flodigarry.co.uk* – *Closed 3 January-8 February and 5 November-21 December*
**18 rm** ☟ – ♦£ 105/135 ♦♦£ 150/210
**Rest** – *(dinner only and Sunday lunch)* Carte £ 40/60 **s**
♦ Victorian house and cottage annexe which was once Flora MacDonald's home. Comfy, antique-filled interior with excellent island views over gardens that run down to the coast. Cosy, homely bedrooms. Characterful bar and part-panelled dining room; classical menu.

**SCOTLAND**

**PORTREE** – Highland – pop. 1 917

🚹 Bayfield Rd ✆ (08452) 25 51 21, www.visitscotland.com

### Cuillin Hills ⌖ ≼ 🚃 🕪 & 👖 🕸 **P** 🚇 **VISA** **◉◉** **AE**
Northeast : 0.75 mi by A 855 ⊠ IV51 9QU – ✆ (01478) 612 003
– www.cuillinhills-hotel-skye.co.uk
**26 rm** ⚏ – †£ 210 ††£ 310
**Rest** – (bar lunch Monday-Saturday, buffet lunch Sunday) Menu £ 35
– Carte £ 18/34 **s**
◆ Yellow-washed 19C hunting lodge in 15 acres of gardens and grounds; overlooking the bay and hills. Comfy lounge and stylish open-plan bar. Bedrooms offer good facilities; the best are to the front. Bright dining room offers good outlook and traditional menus.

### Bosville ≼ 🕪 **VISA** **◉◉** **AE**
Bosville Ter ⊠ IV51 9DG – ✆ (01478) 612 846
– www.macleodhotels.co.uk/bosville
**19 rm** ⚏ – †£ 69/120 ††£ 88/260
**Rest** *Chandlery* – see restaurant listing
**Rest** *Bistro* – Carte £ 17/33
◆ Boldly painted, purpose-built hotel in town centre. Wood-furnished bar – formerly the village bank – and small, traditionally decorated, first floor lounge. Modern bedrooms with co-ordinating fabrics and good facilities. Accessible menu served in popular bistro.

### Almondbank without rest ≼ 🚃 🕪 **P** **VISA** **◉◉**
Viewfield Rd, Southwest : 0.75 mi on A 87 ⊠ IV51 9EU – ✆ (01478) 612 696
**4 rm** ⚏ – †£ 60 ††£ 76
◆ Friendly guesthouse with large lawned gardens, set on a sloping bank and boasting lovely views across the bay. Spacious lounge and linen-laid breakfast room. Immaculately kept bedrooms.

### XX Chandlery – at Bosville Hotel **VISA** **◉◉** **AE**
Bosville Ter ⊠ IV51 9DG – ✆ (01478) 612 846 – www.macleodhotels.co.uk
**Rest** – (dinner only) Menu £ 44
◆ Hotel restaurant displaying deep red walls, linen-laid tables and high-backed chairs. Concise 3 course set menu offers classically based meat and seafood dishes. Friendly service.

**SLEAT** – Highland

**30** C1

### Kinloch Lodge ⌖ ≼ 🚃 🕪 ⊙ 🕪 **P** **VISA** **◉◉**
⊠ IV43 8QY – ✆ (01471) 833 214 – www.kinloch-lodge.co.uk
**14 rm** (dinner included) ⚏ – †£ 149/199 ††£ 280/440 – 1 suite
**Rest** – (booking essential for non-residents) Menu £ 35/60 **s** 🕸
**Spec.** Home-cured and steamed organic salmon with beetroot, crème fraîche and dill dressing. Rabbit stuffed with venison and prunes, Kinloch croquette and brandy sauce. Orange crème, warm dark chocolate sauce and apricot fudge.
◆ 17C lochside hunting lodge surrounded by heather-strewn moorland. Antique-filled country house interior with comfy lounges. Individually styled bedrooms boast good facilities/extras. Menus offer 2 choices per course and showcase local island produce. Classical cooking displays some clever modern touches. Good service.

**STRUAN** – Highland

**29** B2

### Ullinish Country Lodge ⌖ ≼ 🚃 🕾 **P** **VISA** **◉◉**
West : 1.5 mi by A 863 ⊠ IV56 8FD – ✆ (01470) 572 214
– www.theisleofskye.co.uk – Closed January and 1 week November
**6 rm** ⚏ – †£ 120 ††£ 170 **Rest** – (dinner only) Menu £ 49
◆ Personally run, 17C whitewashed house in windswept location, affording lovely loch/hill views. Comfy lounge filled with ornaments and books about the area. Warmly decorated bedrooms boast good facilities and extras. Formal dining room offers complex 5 course menu.

## TEAGUE – Highland                                              29 A2

⌂ **Toravaig House**                    ⟨ 🚗 ⚡ 📶 **P** 🆅🆂🅰 ⊗⊗
*Knock Bay, on A 851* ✉ *IV44 8RE –* 𝒞 *(01471) 820 200 – www.skyehotel.co.uk*
**9 rm** 🍽 – ♦£ 80/150 ♦♦£ 130/230
**Rest** – *(booking essential for non-residents)* Menu £ 28/49
♦ Stylish whitewashed house with neat gardens, set on the road to the Mallaig ferry. Cosy, open-fired lounge with baby grand piano and heavy fabrics. Individually designed bedrooms boast quality materials and furnishings. Good service with extras. Two-roomed restaurant offers concise, classical menu of island produce.

## WATERNISH – Highland                                           29 A2

✗ **Loch Bay Seafood**                              **P** 🆅🆂🅰 ⊗⊗ ⊕
*1 MacLeod Terr, Stein* ✉ *IV55 8GA –* 𝒞 *(01470) 592 235*
*– www.lochbay-seafood-restaurant.co.uk – Easter-October*
**Rest** – Seafood – *(closed Sunday and Monday) (booking essential)*
Carte £ 23/32
♦ Whitewashed cottage in a tiny hamlet overlooking the loch. Small room with low-backed chairs and benches. Concise menu of simply prepared seafood and blackboard specials. Friendly service.

🍴 **Stein Inn** with rm ⌘                    ⟨ 🛋 📶 **P** 🆅🆂🅰 ⊗⊗
*MacLeod Ter, Stein* ✉ *IV55 8GA –* 𝒞 *(01470) 592 362 – www.stein-inn.co.uk*
*– Closed 1 January and 25 December*
**5 rm** 🍽 – ♦£ 46/58 ♦♦£ 110
**Rest** – Seafood – *(residents only Monday dinner except Bank Holidays)*
Carte £ 15/22
♦ Set in a tiny fishing village, this characterful inn is the oldest on Skye. Menus are formed around the latest local produce available, with lighter toasties and salads on offer at lunchtime. Bedrooms are simple, well-kept and boast lovely bay outlooks.

## SLEAT – Highland – see Skye (Isle of)

## SORN – East Ayrshire – 501 H17                                 25 B2
▶ Edinburgh 67 mi – Ayr 15 mi – Glasgow 35 mi

🍴 **Sorn Inn** with rm                          📶 **P** 🆅🆂🅰 ⊗⊗
*35 Main St* ✉ *KA5 6HU –* 𝒞 *(01290) 551 305 – www.sorninn.com – Closed 10 days January and Monday*
**4 rm** 🍽 – ♦£ 40/50 ♦♦£ 50/70   **Rest** – Menu £ 14 (lunch) – Carte £ 19/27
♦ Unassuming whitewashed inn set in a small backwater village. Very much a family affair – the father checks you in and the son cooks. Choose either the smart bar or larger dining room. Extensive menu includes a variety of British dishes plus a choice of more elaborate international offerings. Neat, simple bedrooms represent good value.

## SPEAN BRIDGE – Highland – 501 F13                              30 C3
▶ Edinburgh 143 mi – Fort William 10 mi – Glasgow 94 mi – Inverness 58 mi
ℹ The Kingdom of Scotland, by Fort William, Inverness-shirev 𝒞 (0845) 2 25 51 21, www.visitscotland.com
⛳ Spean Bridge GC Station Rd, 𝒞 077 471 4 70 90

⌂ **Corriegour Lodge**              ⟨ 🚗 ⚡ 📶 **P** 🆅🆂🅰 ⊗⊗ 🅰🅴 ⊕
*Loch Lochy, North : 8.75 mi on A 82* ✉ *PH34 4EA –* 𝒞 *(01397) 712 685*
*– www.corriegour-lodge-hotel.com – Easter-November*
**12 rm** 🍽 – ♦£ 90 ♦♦£ 90   **Rest** – *(dinner only)* Menu £ 50
♦ 19C hunting lodge with pretty gardens, in great lochside location; owner's father is the local gamekeeper. Homely, curio-filled sitting room; high quality beds, linens and fabrics. Every dining table has a loch view; classical 4 course menu features local meats.

⌂ **Distant Hills** without rest     🚗 ⁇ ⁇ 🅿 VISA ⬤
*Roy Bridge Rd, East : 0.5 mi on A86* ✉ *PH34 4EU* – ℰ *(01397) 712 452*
*– www.distanthills.com – March-October*
**7 rm** ⌷ – †£ 43/73 ††£ 72/85
♦ Welcoming guesthouse with friendly owners, who suggest walks and provide packed lunches. French windows in large lounge lead to stream-side seating. Modern bedrooms. Wide-ranging breakfasts.

⌂ **Corriechoille Lodge** ⌂     ⬅ 🚗 ᵹ rm, ⁇ ⁇ 🅿 VISA ⬤
*East : 2.75 mi on Corriechoille rd* ✉ *PH34 4EY* – ℰ *(01397) 712 002*
*– www.corriechoille.com – Closed November-March, Sunday and Monday*
**4 rm** ⌷ – †£ 48 ††£ 76    **Rest** – Menu £ 27
♦ Charming, part-18C house in remote location, boasting large gardens and views over the Grey Corries and Aonach Mor. Comfy lounge and spacious, pine-furnished bedrooms; two wooden bothy lodges provide more intimacy. Homely cooking; the fish is smoked on site.

XX **Russell's at Smiddy House** with rm     ⁇ 🅿 VISA ⬤
*Roybridge Rd* ✉ *PH34 4EU* – ℰ *(01397) 712 335* – *www.smiddyhouse.co.uk*
*– Restricted opening in winter*
**4 rm** ⌷ – †£ 70/95 ††£ 90/115
**Rest** – *(dinner only) (booking essential)* Menu £ 35
♦ Passionately run restaurant in an appealing Highland village. Snug lounge and two intimate, candlelit dining rooms. Classical menus of tried-and-tested combinations which rely on natural flavours. Cosy, well-equipped bedrooms boast comfy beds and fine linens.

X **Old Pines** with rm ⌂     ⬅ 🕭 ᵹ rm, ⁇ 🅿 VISA ⬤ AE ⓘ
*Northwest : 1.5 mi by A 82 on B 8004* ✉ *PH34 4EG* – ℰ *(01397) 712 324*
*– www.oldpines.co.uk – February-October*
**7 rm** ⌷ – †£ 70/80 ††£ 90/120
**Rest** – *(booking essential for non-residents)* Carte £ 21/35
♦ Log cabin style building that blends well with the Highland scenery. Comfy lounge; simple dining room with tables arranged around the windows. Classical menus offer lots of local seafood and beef. Up-to-date, pine-furnished bedrooms feature traditional quilts.

---

**SPITTAL OF GLENSHEE** – Perth and Kinross – **501** J13     28 C2
– ✉ **Blairgowrie** ▌ Scotland
▶ Edinburgh 69 mi – Aberdeen 74 mi – Dundee 35 mi
⛷ Glenshee (❄ ★★) (chairlift **AC**)

🏛 **Dalmunzie Castle** ⌂     ⬅ 🚗 🕭 ⥿ ✕ 🎦 ⬆ 🅿 VISA ⬤
✉ *PH10 7QG* – ℰ *(01250) 885 224* – *www.dalmunzie.com*
*– Closed 1 week Christmas*
**17 rm** (dinner included) ⌷ – †£ 105/180 ††£ 170/295
**Rest** – *(bar lunch)* Menu £ 16/45
♦ Edwardian hunting lodge in a magnificent spot, encircled by mountains. Traditional rooms mix antique and pine furniture. Bar with cosy panelled alcove and leather chairs. Modern dining room with views down the valley.

---

**STANLEY** – Perth and Kinross – **501** J14 – see PERTH

---

**STEVENSTON** – North Ayrshire – **501** F17 – pop. 9 129     25 A2
▶ Edinburgh 82 mi – Ayr 19 mi – Glasgow 36 mi

⌂ **Ardeer Farm Steading** without rest     ⁇ ⁇ 🅿 VISA ⬤ ⓘ
*Ardeer Mains Farm, East : 0.75 mi by A 738 and B 752, on no through rd*
✉ *KA20 3DD* – ℰ *(01294) 465 438* – *www.ardeersteading.co.uk*
**8 rm** ⌷ – †£ 35 ††£ 48/52
♦ Smart, family-owned farmhouse on the edge of a 100 acre working farm. Large, cream leather furnished lounge and breakfast room boast pleasant country views. Immaculately kept contemporary bedrooms display sleek, modern lines. Complimentary pick-up from station.

SCOTLAND

▶ Edinburgh 37 mi – Dunfermline 23 mi – Falkirk 14 mi – Glasgow 28 mi

🛈 41 Dumbarton Rd ✆ (08707) 20 06 20, www.visitstirling.org

◎ Town★★ – Castle★★ **AC** (Site★★★, external elevations ★★★, Stirling Heads★★, Argyll and Sutherland Highlanders Regimental Museum★) B – Argyll's Lodging★ (Renaissance decoration★) B **A** – Church of the Holy Rude★ B **B**

◐ Wallace Monument (✳★★) NE : 2.5 mi by A 9 - A - and B 998. Dunblane★ (Cathedral★★, West Front★★), N : 6.5 mi by A 9 A

**Park Lodge**      🍴 🛁 P VISA ©® AE

*32 Park Ter* ⌧ *FK8 2JS* – ✆ *(01786) 474 862* – *www.parklodge.net*
*– Closed Christmas and New Year*      Ba

**9 rm** ⌂ – ♦£ 60/75 ♦♦£ 75/85

**Rest** – Menu £ 17/26 **s** – Carte £ 18/26

♦ Lovely part-Georgian, part-Victorian, creeper-clad house, with mature garden and fruit trees to the rear. Warm, intimate bar and sitting room. Traditional, individually designed bedrooms; the four-poster room being particularly popular. Formal dining room has a beautiful ornate ceiling and traditional menu.

**SCOTLAND**

## STIRLING

⚐ **Number 10** without rest                                    🔲 🕸 ⸮

*Gladstone Pl* ⊠ *FK8 2NN –* ℰ *(01786) 472 681 – www.cameron-10.co.uk*
**3 rm** ⌸ – ♦£ 40/50 ♦♦£ 60/65                              B**v**

♦ Light-stone Victorian townhouse with attractive rear garden and surprisingly spacious interior; set in a quiet street. Linen-laid breakfast room displays ornate coving. Individually furnished bedrooms have good facilities and tartan themes.

⚐ **West Plean House** without rest 🖇             🔲 🔾 🕸 ⸮ **P** **VISA** ⸜⸝

*South : 3.5 mi on A 872 (Denny rd)* ⊠ *FK7 8HA –* ℰ *(01786) 812 208*
*– www.westpleanhouse.com – Closed 15 December-15 January*
**3 rm** ⌸ – ♦£ 48/80 ♦♦£ 78/80

♦ Attractive house with long history – its latest extensions added in 1803 – on a working farm in a peaceful, rural location. Beautiful tiled hall, classic country house lounge and communal breakfast room. Warm, traditionally styled bedrooms.

---

**STONEHAVEN** – Aberdeenshire – **501** N13 – **pop. 9 577** ▯ Scotland      **28** D2

▶ Edinburgh 109 mi – Aberdeen 16 mi – Montrose 22 mi

◉ Dunnottar Castle ★★, S : 1.5 mi by A 92

⚐ **Beachgate House** without rest             ⸝ 🕸 ⸮ **P**

▨ *Beachgate Ln* ⊠ *AB39 2BD –* ℰ *(01569) 763 155 – www.beachgate.co.uk*
**3 rm** ⌸ – ♦£ 60/80 ♦♦£ 85

♦ Well-run guesthouse located on the seashore and looking out over Stonehaven Bay. Super views from well-appointed, first floor lounge. Comfortable bedrooms are furnished in a luxurious, modern style. Breakfast, taken at linen-laid tables, includes fresh poached fish or a full Scottish with hen or duck eggs.

🍴🍴 **Tolbooth**                                             **VISA** ⸜⸝

*Old Pier, Harbour* ⊠ *AB39 2JU –* ℰ *(01569) 762 287*
*– www.tolbooth-restaurant.co.uk – Closed first 3 weeks January, 25 December, Sunday October-April and Monday*
**Rest** – Seafood – Menu £ 15 (lunch) – Carte £ 33/44

♦ Stonehaven's oldest building, delightfully located by the harbour. Rustic interior with lovely picture window table. Various menus available, with the emphasis on local seafood.

---

**STORNOWAY** – Western Isles – **501** A9 – see Lewis and Harris (Isle of)

---

**STRACHUR** – Argyll and Bute – **501** E15 – **pop. 628**          **27** B2

▶ Edinburgh 112 mi – Glasgow 66 mi – Inverness 162 mi – Perth 101 mi

🏨 **Creggans Inn**                                   ⸝ 🔲 ⸮ **P** **VISA** ⸜⸝

⊠ *PA27 8BX –* ℰ *(01369) 860 279 – www.creggans-inn.co.uk*
**13 rm** ⌸ – ♦£ 75/85 ♦♦£ 120/140 – 1 suite
**Rest** *Loch Fyne Dining Room* – see restaurant listing
**Rest** *Mac Phunn's Bar* – Carte £ 22/37

♦ Well-established inn located on the shores of Lock Fyne and boasting enviable views. Spacious, well-kept bedrooms; traditional décor is in keeping with the building's age. Conservatory popular for afternoon teas while taking in the view. Pubby bar with pool tables and accessible menu of local ingredients.

🍴🍴 **Loch Fyne Dining Room** – at Creggans Inn Hotel      ⸝ 🔲 **P** **VISA** ⸜⸝

⊠ *PA27 8BX –* ℰ *(01369) 860 279 – www.creggans-inn.co.uk*
**Rest** – (dinner only) Menu £ 37

♦ Vast restaurant in a long-standing inn on the shore of Loch Fyne. Warm décor, linen-clad tables and great watery views. Formal 4 course menu changes daily and offers traditionally based dishes.

### ✗ Inver Cottage  ⟨ icons ⟩ 🅿 VISA ⓒⓓ

*Strathlaclan, Southwest : 6.5 mi by A 886 on B 8000 ✉ PA27 8BU – ℰ (01369) 860 537 – www.invercottage.com – Closed late December-March, Monday and Tuesday except July-August*

**Rest** – Carte £ 19/33

◆ Lochside former crofter's cottage boasting water/mountain views. Small bar and casual tables for drinks/afternoon tea; simple, airy restaurant. Constantly evolving menu uses only local produce.

---

## STRATHPEFFER – Highland – 501 G11 – pop. 918          30 C2

▶ Edinburgh 174 mi – Inverness 18 mi

ℹ Pump Room Museum ℰ (01997) 42 14 15, www.visitscotland.com

🔟 Strathpeffer Spa Golf Course Rd, ℰ (01997) 42 12 19

### ↑ Craigvar *without rest*  ⟨ icons ⟩ 🅿 VISA ⓒⓓ

*The Square ✉ IV14 9DL – ℰ (01997) 421 622 – www.craigvar.com – Closed 8-21 October and 23 December-12 January*

**3 rm** ⌂ – †£ 45/70 ††£ 80/84

◆ Attractive Georgian house overlooking the main square of a delightful spa village. Traditional guest areas include a comfy lounge and linen-laid breakfast room. Spacious bedrooms have a modern edge and plenty of personal touches. Proudly run by a charming owner.

---

## STRATHYRE – Stirling – 501 H15 – ✉ Callander ▌ Scotland          27 B2

▶ Edinburgh 62 mi – Glasgow 53 mi – Perth 42 mi

◉ The Trossachs★★★ (Loch Katrine★★) SW : 14 mi by A 84 and A 821 – Hilltop viewpoint★★★ (❄★★★) SW : 16.5 mi by A 84 and A 821

### ✗✗ Creagan House *with rm*  ⟨ icons ⟩ 🅿 VISA ⓒⓓ AE

*on A 84 ✉ FK18 8ND – ℰ (01877) 384 638 – www.creaganhouse.co.uk – Closed 18 January-8 March, 7-22 November and 24-26 December*

**5 rm** ⌂ – †£ 75 ††£ 130

**Rest** – *(Closed Wednesday and Thursday) (dinner only)* Menu £ 32

◆ Personally run baronial dining room in 17C former farmhouse. Concise fixed price menu of fine seasonal Scottish produce; classical dishes prepared with care. 'Smokie in a Pokie,' a speciality. Watch red squirrels in the garden from the cosy bedrooms.

---

## STROMNESS – 501 K7 – see Orkney Islands (Mainland)

---

## STRONTIAN – Highland – 501 D13          29 B3

▶ Edinburgh 139 mi – Fort William 23 mi – Oban 66 mi

ℹ Acharacle ℰ (08452) 25 51 21, www.visitscotland.com

### 🛏 Kilcamb Lodge ⟨ leaf ⟩  ⟨ icons ⟩ 🅿 VISA ⓒⓓ

*✉ PH36 4HY – ℰ (01967) 402 257 – www.kilcamblodge.co.uk – Closed January*

**10 rm** *(dinner included)* ⌂ – †£ 145/208 ††£ 229/309

**Rest** – Menu £ 18/50

◆ Charming lochside hunting lodge, with 19 acres of gardens and woodland running down to a private shore. Traditional interior boasts rich fabrics, log fires and up-to-date bedrooms. Formal restaurant offers a traditional menu; seafood and game feature highly.

---

## STRUAN – Highland – see Skye (Isle of)

---

## SWINTON – The Scottish Borders – 501 N16 – pop. 472 – ✉ Duns          26 D2

▶ Edinburgh 49 mi – Berwick-upon-Tweed 13 mi – Glasgow 93 mi
– Newcastle upon Tyne 66 mi

SCOTLAND

🏠 **Wheatsheaf** with rm     🚗 ⅄ ⚒ **P** *VISA* ⚈
*Main St* ✉ *TD11 3JJ – 𝒞 (01890) 860 257 – www.wheatsheaf-swinton.co.uk*
*– Closed 24-26 December*
**10 rm** ⌂ **– †**£ 75 **††**£ 112
**Rest** *– (closed lunch Monday-Thursday)* Carte £ 22/40
♦ Substantial stone inn overlooking the village green. Lunch menu offers pub classics; concise evening à la carte is more adventurous. Both feature local produce, including meat from nearby farms and fish from Eyemouth. Bedrooms are spacious, cosy and well-equipped.

---

**TAIN** – Highland – **501** H10 – **pop. 4 540**     **30** D2
▶ Edinburgh 191 mi – Inverness 35 mi – Wick 91 mi
🔟 Tain Chapel Rd, 𝒞 (01862) 89 23 14
◐ Tarbat Portmahomack, 𝒞 (01862) 87 12 78

🏠 **Golf View House** without rest     ≤ 🚗 ⚒ ⟨ᵖ⟩ **P** *VISA* ⚈
*13 Knockbreck Rd* ✉ *IV19 1BN – 𝒞 (01862) 892 856*
*– www.tainbedandbreakfast.co.uk – mid-March to October*
**5 rm** ⌂ **– †**£ 45/55 **††**£ 65/75
♦ 19C former manse near the golf course. Neat lawned garden with comfy seating in wooden bothy hut. Leather-furnished lounge and bright, modern bedrooms; front rooms have water/mountain views.

**at Nigg** Southeast : 7 mi by A 9, B 9175 and Pitcalnie Rd.

🏠 **Wemyss House** ॐ     🚗 ⚒ ⟨ᵖ⟩ **P** *VISA* ⚈ 𝔸𝔼 ①
*Bayfield, South : 1 mi past church* ✉ *IV19 1QW – 𝒞 (01862) 851 212*
*– www.wemysshouse.com*
**3 rm** ⌂ **– †**£ 90/95 **††**£ 90/95
**Rest** – Menu £ 35
♦ Remote, rurally set guesthouse with charming owners, well-maintained gardens and pleasant views. Cosy sitting room with grand piano. Spacious, immaculately kept bedrooms. Freshly prepared dishes use local ingredients. Excellent quality breakfasts.

**at Cadboll** Southeast : 8.5 mi by A 9 and B 9165 (Portmahomack rd) off Hilton rd
– ✉ Tain

🏠 **Glenmorangie House** ॐ     ≤ 🚗 ⚑ ⤳ ⚒ ⟨ᵖ⟩ **P** *VISA* ⚈ 𝔸𝔼
*Fearn* ✉ *IV20 1XP – 𝒞 (01862) 871 671 – www.theglenmorangiehouse.com*
**9 rm** (dinner included) ⌂ **– †**£ 220 **††**£ 400 – 3 suites
**Rest** *– (dinner only)* Menu £ 55
♦ Charming 17C house owned by the famous distillery. Antiques, hand-crafted local furnishings and open peat fires feature; there's even a small whisky tasting room. Luxuriously appointed bedrooms show good attention to detail; those in the courtyard cottages are suites. Communal dining from classical Scottish-based menu.

---

**TALMINE** – Highland – **501** G8 – ✉ Lairg     **30** C1
▶ Edinburgh 245 mi – Inverness 86 mi – Thurso 48 mi

🏠 **Cloisters** without rest ॐ     ≤ 🚗 ⅄ **P**
*Church Holme* ✉ *IV27 4YP – 𝒞 (01847) 601 286 – www.cloistertal.demon.co.uk*
*– Closed 25 December and 1 January*
**3 rm** ⌂ **– †**£ 35 **††**£ 60
♦ Converted church boasting great views over Tongue Bay and the Rabbit Islands. Homely interior packed with memorabilia. Leather-furnished lounge, snug breakfast area and simple, well-kept bedrooms.

---

**TARBERT** – Western Isles – **501** Z10 – see Lewis and Harris (Isle of)

**SCOTLAND**

**TARBET** – Argyll and Bute – **501** F15 – ⊠ Arrochar          **27** B2

▶ Edinburgh 88 mi – Glasgow 42 mi – Inverness 138 mi – Perth 78 mi

⊼    **Lomond View Country House** without rest    ≤ 🚗 🍴 📶 **P**
      on A 82 ⊠ G83 7DG – 𝒸 (01301) 702 477      **VISA** ⓒⓞ ⓘ
      – www.lomondview.co.uk
      **3 rm** ⊑ – †£ 65/75 ††£ 80/90
      ♦ Purpose-built guesthouse which lives up to its name: there are stunning loch
views. Spacious sitting room. Light and airy breakfast room. Sizeable, modern
bedrooms.

---

**TAYVALLICH** – Argyll and Bute – **501** D15 – ⊠ Lochgilphead          **27** B2

▶ Edinburgh 148 mi – Glasgow 103 mi – Inverness 157 mi

🍴    **Tayvallich Inn**      ≤ 🍴 **P** **VISA** ⓒⓞ
      ⊠ PA31 8PL – 𝒸 (01546) 870 282 – www.tayvallichinn.co.uk – Closed Monday
November-March
      **Rest** – Carte £ 19/32
      ♦ Dine in bar, more formal dining room or on decked terrace, with views over
the bay. Menu focuses on locally caught fish and shellfish, but also lists classic
pub dishes like steak and chips.

---

**TEANGUE** – Highland – see Skye (Isle of)

---

**THORNHILL** – Dumfries and Galloway – **501** I18 – pop. 1 633          **25** B2

▮ Scotland

▶ Edinburgh 64 mi – Ayr 44 mi – Dumfries 15 mi – Glasgow 63 mi

◩ Drumlanrig Castle ★★ (cabinets ★) **AC**, NW : 4 mi by A 76

⊼    **Gillbank House** without rest    🚗 ⅄ 📶 **P** **VISA** ⓒⓞ
      8 East Morton St ⊠ DG3 5LZ – 𝒸 (01848) 330 597 – www.gillbank.co.uk
      **6 rm** ⊑ – †£ 50 ††£ 75
      ♦ Red stone house built in 1895; originally the Jenner family home.
Lovely stained glass front door, spacious, light-filled interior and airy breakfast
room with distant hill views. Large, simply furnished bedrooms: two with feature
beds; all with wet rooms.

---

**THURSO** – Highland – **501** J8 – pop. 7 737 ▮ Scotland          **30** D1

▶ Edinburgh 289 mi – Inverness 133 mi – Wick 21 mi

🚢 from Scrabster to Stromness (Orkney Islands) (P and O Scottish Ferries) (2 h)

🛈 Riverside 𝒸 (0845) 2 25 51 21, www.visitscotland.com

🏴 Newlands of Geise, 𝒸 (01847) 89 38 07

◩ Strathy Point ★ ( ≤ ★★★) W : 22 mi by A 836

🏨    **Forss House** ♨      🚗 ⅄ 🎣 **P** **VISA** ⓒⓞ **AE** ⓘ
      Forss, West : 5.5 mi on A 836 ⊠ KW14 7XY – 𝒸 (01847) 861 201
      – www.forsshousehotel.co.uk – Closed 24 December-2 January
      **14 rm** ⊑ – †£ 115 ††£ 165    **Rest** – (dinner only) Carte £ 32/39 **s**
      ♦ Traditional Scottish hotel centred around fishing and offering timeshares on
the river. Rods and mounted fish sit beside deer heads and open fires. Good-sized
bedrooms – annexe rooms are most modern. Elegant dining room serves classic
menu; seafood a speciality.

⊼    **Murray House**      🍴 📶 **P**
      1 Campbell St ⊠ KW14 7HD – 𝒸 (01847) 895 759 – www.murrayhousebb.com
      – Closed Christmas-New Year
      **5 rm** ⊑ – †£ 30/60 ††£ 60/70    **Rest** – (by arrangement) Menu £ 15
      ♦ A centrally located and family owned Victorian town house. Pine furnished
bedrooms are colourfully decorated and carefully maintained. Modern dining
room with home-cooked evening meals.

**at Scrabster** Northwest : 2.25 mi on A 9

X **Captain's Galley** *VISA* ◉◉
*The Harbour* ⊠ *KW14 7UJ* – *ℰ (01847) 894 999* – *www.captainsgalley.co.uk*
*– Closed 1-2 January, 25-26 December, Sunday and Monday*
**Rest** – Seafood – *(dinner only) (booking essential)* Carte £ 47/57
♦ Rustic seafood restaurant on the pier, with vaulted stone dining room, cosy lounge and old chimney from its former smokery days. Owner was once a fisherman, so has excellent local contacts; he keeps some produce in creels in the harbour. Classical daily menu.

---

**TIGHNABRUAICH** – Argyll and Bute – **501** E16                                            **27** B3
▶ Edinburgh 113 mi – Glasgow 63 mi – Oban 66 mi

🏠 **Royal An Lochan** ⇐ **P** *VISA* ◉◉
⊠ *PA21 2BE* – *ℰ (01700) 811 239* – *www.theroyalanlochan.co.uk*
**11 rm** ⚏ – †£ 75/125 ††£ 125/150
**Rest** – Carte £ 15/30 **s**
♦ Spacious 19C hotel located in a peaceful village, overlooking the Kyles of Bute. Comfortable bedrooms; some with excellent outlooks. Charming bar with nautical theme serves snack menu. Formal conservatory restaurant offers water views and mainly seafood dishes.

---

**TIRORAN** – Argyll and Bute – **501** B14 – see Mull (Isle of)

---

**TOBERMORY** – Argyll and Bute – **501** B14 – see Mull (Isle of)

---

**TONGUE** – Highland – **501** G8 – pop. 552 – ⊠ Lairg 🚩 Scotland          **30** C1
▶ Edinburgh 257 mi – Inverness 101 mi – Thurso 43 mi
◉ Cape Wrath★★★ (⇐ ★★) W : 44 mi (including ferry crossing) by A 838 – Ben Loyal★★, S : 8 mi by A 836 – Ben Hope★ (⇐ ★★★) SW : 15 mi by A 838 – Strathy Point★ (⇐ ★★★) E : 22 mi by A 836 – Torrisdale Bay★ (⇐ ★★) NE : 8 mi by A 836

🏠 **Tongue** ⇐ 🚗 ⌘ **P** *VISA* ◉◉ *AE*
*Main St* ⊠ *IV27 4XD* – *ℰ (01847) 611 206* – *www.tonguehotel.co.uk* – *Closed 1 December-28 February*
**18 rm** ⚏ – †£ 45/75 ††£ 90/110
**Rest** – *(bar lunch)* Menu £ 28 – Carte £ 18/34
♦ Fiercely Scottish former hunting lodge overlooking the Kyle of Tongue; Highland shooting and fishing memorabilia abounds. Snug, open-fired lounge and contemporary bedrooms. Snacks served in linen-laid bars; classical menus of local ingredients in dining room.

---

**TORRIDON** – Highland – **501** D11 – ⊠ Achnasheen 🚩 Scotland          **29** B2
▶ Edinburgh 234 mi – Inverness 62 mi – Kyle of Lochalsh 44 mi
◉ Wester Ross★★★

🏠 **Torridon** 🐾 ⇐ 🚗 ⌘ 🐕 🎣 👤 ⅙ 🍴 **P** *VISA* ◉◉ *AE*
*South : 1.5 mi on A 896* ⊠ *IV22 2EY* – *ℰ (01445) 791 242*
*– www.thetorridon.com – Closed January and Monday-Tuesday November-March*
**18 rm** ⚏ – †£ 130/225 ††£ 195/430 – 1 suite
**Rest** – *(bar lunch) (booking essential)* Menu £ 50 **s**
♦ Family-owned and run former hunting lodge; remotely set, with wonderful views of Loch Torridon and mountains. Ornate ceilings, peat fires and Highland curios. Some very contemporary bedrooms; others more classic in style. Traditional wood-panelled restaurant uses fine local produce, some from the grounds.

**Torridon Inn** ⌂ 🚲 🐕 🍴 ♿ 🅿 VISA ⦿ AE
*South : 1.5 mi on A 896* ✉ *IV22 2EY* – ✆ *(01445) 791 242*
*– www.thetorridon.com – Closed mid-December-February and Monday-Thursday November-March*
**12 rm** – ♦£ 99 ♦♦£ 99, ☕ £ 6.50 **Rest** – Carte £ 16/32 **s**
♦ Peaceful, rural location in grounds of Torridon House. Spacious, functional bedrooms in annexe; the larger ones ideal for families. Characterful, rustic restaurant serving classic pub dishes.

---

# TROON – South Ayrshire – **501** G17 – pop. 14 766      25 A2

▶ Edinburgh 77 mi – Ayr 7 mi – Glasgow 31 mi
🚢 to Northern Ireland (Larne) (P and O Irish Sea) 2 daily
⛳ Troon Municipal Harling Drive, ✆ (01292) 31 24 64

 **Lochgreen House** ⌂ 🚲 📶 ♿ 🕴 🍴 🧖 🅿 VISA ⦿ AE
*Monktonhill Rd, Southwood, Southeast : 2 mi on B 749* ✉ *KA10 7EN* – ✆ *(01292) 313 343 – www.costley-hotels.co.uk*
**37 rm** ☕ – ♦£ 113/154 ♦♦£ 215/241 – 1 suite
**Rest** *Tapestry* – see restaurant listing
♦ Attractive, coastal Edwardian house in mature grounds. Lounges exude luxurious country house feel. Large rooms, modern or traditional, have a good eye for welcoming detail.

XXX **Tapestry** – at Lochgreen House Hotel 🚲 AK 🅿 VISA ⦿ AE
*Monktonhill Rd, Southwood, Southeast : 2 mi on B 749* ✉ *KA10 7EN* – ✆ *(01292) 313 343 – www.costley-hotels.co.uk*
**Rest** – Menu £ 18/30 – Carte £ 35/55
♦ Spacious dining room with baronial feel. Elegant chandeliers; large pottery cockerels. Classical, modern cooking, with a strong Scottish base.

**at Loans** East : 2 mi on A 759 – ✉ Troon

**Highgrove House** 🏠 ≤ 🚲 🍴 🕴 🍴 🅿 VISA ⦿ AE
*Old Loans Rd, East : 0.25 mi on Dundonald rd* ✉ *KA10 7HL* – ✆ *(01292) 312 511 – www.costleyhotels.co.uk*
**9 rm** ☕ – ♦£ 69/85 ♦♦£ 85/110
**Rest** – Menu £ 12 – Carte £ 18/38
♦ Immaculate whitewashed hotel in elevated position, offering superb coastal panorama. Comfy floral bedrooms; 1 and 2 have the best views. Tartan carpets remind you where you are. Large restaurant with floor to ceiling windows and granite columns.

---

# TURNBERRY – South Ayrshire – **501** F18 – ✉ **Girvan** ▌Scotland    25 A2

▶ Edinburgh 97 mi – Ayr 15 mi – Glasgow 51 mi – Stranraer 36 mi
🏰 Culzean Castle★ **AC** (setting★★★, Oval Staircase★★) NE : 5 mi by A 719

**Turnberry** ⌂ ≤ 🚲 🍴 🍴 ⦿ 🔆 ♨ £₆ 📶 🕴 ♿ rm, AK rest, 🕴 🧖 🅿
*on A 719* ✉ *KA26 9LT* – ✆ *(01655) 331 000*     VISA ⦿ AE ⦿
*– www.luxurycollection.com/turnberry – Closed 4-12 January*
**194 rm** ☕ – ♦£ 160/300 ♦♦£ 180/400 – 4 suites
**Rest** *1906* – see restaurant listing
**Rest** *Tappie Toorie* – (lunch only) Menu £ 15 (Sunday) – Carte £ 24/35
**Rest** *James Miller* – (booking essential) Menu £ 65 – Carte £ 27/58
♦ Resort-style, Edwardian railway hotel boasting a smart spa and 3 championship golf courses. Spacious inner with some areas in a light, contemporary style. Luxurious bedrooms; suites have stunning coast and course views. Cocktails and snacks in Ailsa; French classics in 1906; pub favourites in simpler Tappie Toorie; ambitious, modern offerings in intimate James Miller.

XXX **1906** – at Turnberry Hotel ◁ 🚗 Ⓐ Ⓟ 💳 ⓒⓓ Ⓐⓔ Ⓞ
*on A 719* ⌗ *KA26 9LT* – ℰ *(01655) 331 000*
*– www.luxurycollection.com/turnberry – Closed 4-12 January*
**Rest** – *(dinner only)* Carte £ 34/49

◆ Named after the year that the Turnberry opened, this smart hotel restaurant boasts lovely views across the sea. Classical French menus feature dishes true to the spirit of Auguste Escoffier.

---

**UDNY GREEN** – Aberdeenshire                                      28 D1
▶ London - 554 mi – Edinburgh 143 mi – Aberdeen 15 mi – Arbroath 67 mi

XX   **Eat on the Green** 🚗 Ⓐ Ⓟ 💳 ⓒⓓ
⌗ *AB41 7RS* – ℰ *(01651) 842 337 – www.eatonthegreen.co.uk – Closed Monday, Tuesday and Saturday lunch*
**Rest** – Menu £ 25 (lunch) – Carte dinner £ 32/44

◆ Converted pub by the village green, with snug seating area and two smart dining rooms. Accomplished, flavourful dishes make good use of seasonal, local produce. Polished service.

---

# UIST (Isles of) – 501 X/Y11 – pop. 3 510

🚢 from Lochmaddy to Isle of Skye (Uig) (Caledonian MacBrayne Ltd) 1-3 daily (1 h 50 mn) – from Otternish to Isle of Harris (Leverburgh) (Caledonian MacBrayne Ltd) (1 h 10 mn)

SCOTLAND

**NORTH UIST** – Western Isles                                      29 A2
▶ London 639 mi – Edinburgh 254 mi

**CARINISH** – Western Isles                                       29 A2

🏠   **Temple View** ◁ 🚗 📶 Ⓟ 💳 ⓒⓓ
⌗ *HS6 5EJ* – ℰ *(01876) 580 676 – www.templeviewhotel.co.uk*
**10 rm** ⌷ – †£ 55/75 ††£ 95/105
**Rest** – *(bar lunch)* Menu £ 24 **s** – Carte £ 18/24 **s**

◆ Victorian house with uncluttered interior and modern yet homely style. Small bar, sitting room and sun lounge. Simple, comfortable bedrooms with moor views to rear and sea/13C ruins of Trinity Temple to front. Cosy dining room offers popular seafood specials.

**LANGASS** – Western Isles

🏠🏠   **Langass Lodge** 🍽 ◁ 🚗 📶 🐟 ₺ rm, 📶 Ⓟ 💳 ⓒⓓ
⌗ *HS6 5HA* – ℰ *(01876) 580 285 – www.langasslodge.co.uk – Closed 1 January, 24-25 and 31 December*
**12 rm** ⌷ – †£ 60/90 ††£ 95/140
**Rest** – *(dinner only)* Menu £ 48

◆ Former Victorian shooting lodge nestled in heather-strewn hills and boasting distant loch views. Characterful bedrooms in main house; more modern, spacious rooms with good views in wing. Eat in comfy bar or linen-clad dining room from simple, seafood based menu.

**LOCHMADDY** – Western Isles                                      29 A2

🏠🏠   **Tigh Dearg** 🚗 🏠 ₺ ₺ rm, 📶 Ⓟ 💳 ⓒⓓ
⌗ *HS6 5AE* – ℰ *(01876) 500 700 – www.tighdearghotel.co.uk*
**9 rm** ⌷ – †£ 79/129 ††£ 80/169
**Rest** – *(October-March closed Sunday and dinner only)* Carte £ 19/34

◆ Stylish hotel with sleek, boutique style. Well-equipped gym, sauna and steam room. Chic, modern bedrooms offer good facilities. Forward-thinking owner continually reinvests. Smart bar and dining room; menus display plenty of seafood. Bikes available for hire.

## ULLAPOOL – Highland – 501 E10 – pop. 1 308 📱 Scotland    30 C2

▶ Edinburgh 215 mi – Inverness 59 mi

🛳 to Isle of Lewis (Stornoway) (Caledonian MacBrayne Ltd) (2 h 40 mn)

🛈 20 Argyle St 𝒞 (0845) 2 25 51 21, www.ullapool.com

◉ Town ★

◉ Wester Ross ★★★ - Loch Broom ★★. Falls of Measach ★★, S : 11 mi by A 835 and A 832 - Corrieshalloch Gorge ★, SE : 10 mi by A 835 – Northwards to Lochinver ★★, Morefield (≤ ★★ of Ullapool), ≤ ★ Loch Broom

⌂    **Point Cottage** without rest    ≤ 🚗 ℀ 🛝 🅿

🍽  22 West Shore St ✉ IV26 2UR – 𝒞 (01854) 613 702
– www.ullapoolbedandbreakfast.co.uk – closed Christmas-New Year
**3 rm** 🖵 – ♦£ 50/60 ♦♦£ 60/70
♦ 18C converted fisherman's cottage on the shores on Loch Broom, not far from the ferry terminal. Simple, homely interior; cosy, floral bedrooms boast lovely views. Snug sitting room is filled with oil paintings, locals maps and guides. Friendly, chatty owner.

⌂    **Ardvreck** without rest 🌭    ≤ 🚗 ℀ 🛝 🅿 VISA ⓒⓑ ⓞ

Morefield Brae, Northwest : 2 mi by A 835 ✉ IV26 2TH – 𝒞 (01854) 612 028
– www.smoothhound.co.uk/hotels/ardvreck – March-November
**10 rm** 🖵 – ♦£ 37/70 ♦♦£ 75/80
♦ Modern house set away from the town centre, affording amazing views over the loch and mountains. Bedrooms are fresh and up-to-date; local watercolours feature. Friendly, accommodating owner.

## VEENSGARTH – see Shetland Islands (Mainland)

## WALKERBURN – The Scottish Borders – pop. 647    26 C2

▶ Edinburgh 30 mi – Galashiels 23 mi – Peebles 8 mi

🏠    **Windlestraw Lodge** 🌭    ≤ 🚗 ⌇ 🛝 🅿 VISA ⓒⓑ

on A 72 ✉ EH43 6AA – 𝒞 (01896) 870 636 – www.windlestraw.co.uk
– Closed 1 week February, 25 December and 1 January
**6 rm** (dinner included) 🖵 – ♦£ 140 ♦♦£ 300    **Rest** – (dinner only) Menu £ 46
♦ Attractive Arts and Crafts property built in 1906, boasting original fireplaces, old plaster ceilings and great valley views. Stylish, tastefully modernised bedrooms. Comfy bar, plush lounge and attractive, wood-panelled dining room offering daily changing menu.

## WATERNISH – Highland – 501 A11 – see Skye (Isle of)

## WESTRAY (Isle of) – 501 K/L6 – see Orkney Islands

## WICK – Highland – 501 K8 – pop. 9 713 📱 Scotland    30 D1

▶ Edinburgh 282 mi – Inverness 126 mi

✈ Wick Airport : 𝒞 (01955) 602215, N : 1 m

🛈 Whitechapel Rd 𝒞 (0845) 2 25 51 21, www.visitscotland.com

🔞 Reiss, 𝒞 (01955) 60 27 26

◉ Duncansby Head ★ (Stacks of Duncansby ★★) N : 14 mi by A 9 – Grey Cairns of Camster ★ (Long Cairn ★★) S : 17 mi by A 9 – The Hill O'Many Stanes ★, S : 10 mi by A 9

⌂    **Clachan** without rest    🚗 ℀ 🛝

🍽  13 Randolph Pl, South Rd, South : 0.75 mi on A 99 ✉ KW1 5NJ – 𝒞 (01955)
605 384 – www.theclachan.co.uk – Closed 2 weeks Christmas-New Year
**3 rm** 🖵 – ♦£ 55 ♦♦£ 70
♦ Detached house on edge of town, in an area formerly housing herring workers during the 1930s. Rebuilt and having undergone a contemporary makeover, it now boasts stylish, modern bedrooms and a smart breakfast room hung with period photos. Accommodating owner.

X **Bord De L'Eau**
*2 Market St (Riverside) ⊠ KW1 4AR – ℰ (01955) 604 400 – Closed first 2 weeks
January, 25-26 December, Sunday lunch and Monday*
**Rest** – French – Carte £ 22/35
♦ Long-standing riverside bistro with simple dining room and conservatory.
Framed Eiffel Tower prints and French posters on the walls. Authentic, classic Gallic dishes; plenty of local seafood.

---

**WORMIT** – Fife – **501** L14 – ⊠ Fife                                    **28** C2
▶ Edinburgh 53 mi – Dundee 6 mi – St Andrews 12 mi
🏌 Scotscraig Tayport Golf Rd, ℰ (01382) 55 25 15

X **View** ≤ 🍴 **P** *VISA* ⊚⊙
*Naughton Rd ⊠ DD6 8NE – ℰ (01382) 542 287 – www.view-restaurant.co.uk
– Closed 2 weeks November, 25-26 December, 1-2 January, Sunday dinner,
Monday and lunch Tuesday*
**Rest** – Carte £ 29/45
♦ Unassuming former pub in a small village, boasting superb views over the
Tay railway bridge to Dundee. Extensive menu and daily specials board offer
homemade small plates that can be served in succession or all at once; quality
ingredients.

SCOTLAND

**ABERAERON** (Aber Aeron ) – **Ceredigion** – **503** H27 – **pop. 1 520**          33 B3
▶ Cardiff 90 mi – Aberystwyth 16 mi – Fishguard 41 mi

🏠🏠 **Ty Mawr Mansion Country House** 🦢          🍴 🐕 🍸 rest, 📞 🅿️
Cilcennin, East : 4.5 mi by A 482 ⊠ SA48 8DB – ℰ (01570)          📶 💳 ⊙⊙ ⊙⊙
470 033 – www.tymawrmansion.co.uk – Closed 27 December-16 January
**8 rm** 🛏 – ♦£ 130/240 ♦♦£ 240/320 – 1 suite
**Rest** – (closed Sunday dinner) (dinner only and Sunday lunch) Menu £ 27
– Carte £ 34/48
◆ Grade II listed Georgian stone mansion in 12 acres of delightful grounds. Several well-appointed lounges with high ceilings. Spacious bedrooms boast marble bathrooms and a good level of facilities. Small basement cinema offers dining packages. Smart restaurant has a concise menu of bold, wide-ranging dishes.

🏠 **3 Pen Cei** without rest          ⇐ 🍸 📶 💳 ⊙⊙
3 Quay Par ⊠ SA46 OBT – ℰ (01545) 571 147 – www.pencei.co.uk – Closed
25-26 December
**5 rm** 🛏 – ♦£ 90 ♦♦£ 140
◆ Brightly painted, modern-style guest house on the harbourfront, formerly the headquarters of the Packet Steam Company. Spacious bedrooms are named after nearby rivers; Aeron has a bathroom with a free-standing bath and large walk-in shower.

🏠 **Llys Aeron** without rest          🍴 🍸 🎵 🅿️ 💳 ⊙⊙ 🅰️🅴
🍽 Lampeter Rd, on A 482 ⊠ SA46 OED – ℰ (01545) 570 276 – www.llysaeron.co.uk
– Closed 25-26 December
**3 rm** 🛏 – ♦£ 50/70 ♦♦£ 75/105
◆ Charmingly run Georgian guesthouse with conservatory lounge. Modern bedrooms come in warm pastel shades and boast large bathrooms. Breakfast room overlooks the walled garden; choose from extensive Aga-cooked options, alongside local honey and homemade preserves.

🍴 **Harbourmaster** with rm          ⇐ & rm, 🍸 🎵 💳 ⊙⊙
Quay Par ⊠ SA46 OBA – ℰ (01545) 570 755 – www.harbour-master.com
– Closed 25 December
**13 rm** 🛏 – ♦£ 65/185 ♦♦£ 170/195     **Rest** – Carte £ 32/41
◆ Vibrant blue pub with modern bar-lounge, traditional dining room and lovely harbour views. Choice of bar menu or more substantial evening à la carte, supplemented by daily specials. Comfortable, brightly decorated bedrooms; some boast huge windows or terraces.

---

**ABERDOVEY** (Aberdyfi) – **Gwynedd** – **503** H26 – **pop. 869**          32 B2
▶ London 230 mi – Dolgellau 25 mi – Shrewsbury 66 mi
🟢 Snowdonia National Park★★★

🏠 **Llety Bodfor** without rest          ⇐ 🎵 🅿️ 💳 ⊙⊙ ⊙⊙
Bodfor Terr ⊠ LL35 OEA – ℰ (01654) 767 475 – www.lletybodfor.co.uk – Closed
1-29 December
**8 rm** – ♦£ 40/110 ♦♦£ 100/120, 🛏 £ 10
◆ Two 19C seafront houses, now a guest house with a difference: a relaxed atmosphere prevails but the design is stylish and contemporary. Spacious New England themed bedrooms boast bay views. Breakfast is served three doors down.

---

**ABERGAVENNY** (Y-Fenni) – **Monmouthshire** – **503** L28          33 C4
– **pop. 14 055**
▶ London 163 mi – Cardiff 31 mi – Gloucester 43 mi – Newport 19 mi
ℹ️ Monmouth Rd ℰ (01873) 85 32 54, www.abergavenny.org.uk
🔟 Monmouthshire Llanfoist, ℰ (01873) 85 26 06
👁 Town★ - St Mary's Church★ (Monuments★★)
🟢 Brecon Beacons National Park★★ – Blaenavon Ironworks★, SW : 5 mi by A 465
and B 4246. Raglan Castle★ **AC**, SE : 9 mi by A 40

**Llansantffraed Court**

*Llanvihangel Gobion, Southeast : 6.5 mi by A 40 and B 4598 off old Raglan rd*
✉ *NP7 9BA* – ℰ *(01873) 840 678 – www.llch.co.uk*
**21 rm** ⌂ – ♦£ 85/115 ♦♦£ 125/145    **Rest** – Menu £ 20/33 – Carte £ 31/38
♦ Historic country house beside ornamental pond and fountain, in 19 acres of grounds. Large lounges and bar. Dark-hued bedrooms with smart bathrooms: room 19 has double aspect mountain/valley views. Classical menus showcase local ingredients.

**Angel**

*15 Cross St* ✉ *NP7 5EN* – ℰ *(01873) 857 121 – www.angelabergavenny.com – Closed 25 December*
**33 rm** – ♦£ 74/80 ♦♦£ 96, ⌂ £ 5 – 2 suites
**Rest** – *(closed dinner 24-31 December)* Carte £ 22/36
♦ Georgian former coaching inn run by friendly, attentive team. Smart exterior and very modern guest areas: traditionally styled bedrooms undergoing refurbishment. Contemporary bar and restaurant with courtyard offer extensive bistro menu and popular afternoon teas.

**Hardwick** with rm

*Old Raglan Rd, Southeast : 2 mi by A 40 on B 4598* ✉ *NP7 9AA* – ℰ *(01873) 854 220 – www.thehardwick.co.uk – Closed 1 week January and 25 December*
**8 rm** ⌂ – ♦£ 100 ♦♦£ 170
**Rest** – *(booking essential)* Menu £ 27 (lunch) – Carte £ 31/50
♦ Whitewashed former pub overlooking the mountains. Rustic bar and three dining rooms – one cosy and open-fired with wood beams, another with a glass-fronted wine cellar and the third, with large windows and an airy feel. Extensive menus of robust, flavoursome dishes with Italian influences. Spacious, modern bedrooms boast light oak furnishings and excellent bathrooms.

**Charthouse**

*Llanvihangel Gobion, Southeast : 5 mi by A 40 on B 4598* ✉ *NP7 9BA* – ℰ *(01873) 840 414 – www.thecharthouse-abergavenny.co.uk – Closed 25-26 December, 1 January, Sunday dinner and Monday*
**Rest** – Carte £ 30/37
♦ Former pub with beamed ceilings, wood burning stove, stylish tongue and groove panelling and pleasant terrace. Daily à la carte offers refreshingly unfussy, modern dishes that let ingredients speak for themselves. Relaxed, friendly service.

## at Llanddewi Skirrid Northeast : 3.25 mi on B 4521

**Walnut Tree** (Shaun Hill)

✉ *NP7 8AW* – ℰ *(01873) 852 797 – www.thewalnuttreeinn.com – Closed 1 week Christmas, Sunday and Monday*
**Rest** – *(booking essential)* Menu £ 24 (lunch) – Carte £ 37/42
**Spec.** Chicken consommé with scallops and herb pasta. Turbot in spiced mussel and clam broth. Orange and almond cake.
♦ A reinvigorated, long-standing Welsh institution set in a valley. Welcoming staff and always bustling with regulars. It takes skill to make cooking look this simple; it's seasonal and each dish bursts with flavour.

## at Cross Ash Northeast : 8.25 mi on B 4521

**1861**

✉ *NP7 8PB* – ℰ *(01873) 821 297 – www.18-61.co.uk – Closed first 2 weeks January, Sunday dinner and Monday*
**Rest** – Menu £ 24/32 – Carte £ 32/43
♦ Victorian former pub; now a cosy restaurant, with contemporary furnishings and exposed brick fireplace. Classically based menus make use of good quality local produce. Personable service.

WALES

**at Nant-Y-Derry** Southeast : 6.5 mi by A 40 off A 4042 – ⊠ Abergavenny

✗ **Foxhunter**  P VISA ◉◉
⊠ NP7 9DD – ℰ (01873) 881 101 – www.thefoxhunter.com – *Closed 25-26 December, 1 January, Sunday dinner and Monday*
**Rest** – Menu £ 24 (lunch) – Carte £ 31/37
♦ Former station master's house with fresh, bright feel, flagstone floors and wood burning stoves. Dishes range in style from classic British to fusion and come in large, hearty portions.

**at Llanover** South : 5.5 mi by A 40 off A 4042

⌂ **Llansabbath Country House** without rest ⬙  ⟵⟶ ⅌ ᛃ P VISA ◉◉
⊠ NP7 9BY – ℰ (01873) 840 068 – www.llansabbathcountryhouse.co.uk
– *Closed Christmas and New Year*
**5 rm** ⬚ – †£ 70 ††£ 90/105
♦ Former farmhouse renovated in a modern style. Large lounge with wood burning stove; conservatory breakfast with eggs from hens who roam the garden. Comfortable bedrooms have all mod cons.

---

**ABERGELE** – Conwy – **503** J24 – pop. 17 574  **32** C1
▶ London 229 mi – Cardiff 182 mi – Liverpool 51 mi – Manchester 75 mi

**at Betws-yn-Rhos** Southwest : 4.25 mi by A 548 on B 5381

⌂ **Ffarm Country House** without rest  ⟵⟶ ⅋ ⅌ ᛃ⟆ P VISA ◉◉
⊠ LL22 8AR – ℰ (01492) 680 448 – www.ffarmcountryhouse.co.uk – *Closed 1 week Christmas*
**8 rm** ⬚ – †£ 79/90 ††£ 98/188
♦ Gothic-style country house; stylish, comfortable and personally run. Beautiful tiled hall with vaulted wood ceiling. Tastefully furnished bedrooms are named after wine regions.

---

**ABERSOCH** – Gwynedd – **502** G25 – pop. 805 – ⊠ Pwllheli  **32** B2
▶ London 265 mi – Caernarfon 28 mi – Shrewsbury 101 mi
⛳ Golf Rd, ℰ (01758) 71 26 36
◉ Lleyn Peninsula★★ – Plas-yn-Rhiw★ **AC**, W : 6 mi by minor roads. Bardsey Island★, SW : 15 mi by A 499 and B 4413 – Mynydd Mawr★, SW : 17 mi by A 499, B 4413 and minor roads

✗✗ **Venetia** with rm  P VISA ◉◉ ◉
Lon Sarn Bach ⊠ LL53 7EB – ℰ (01758) 713 354 – www.venetiawales.com
– *Closed 1 January-10 February and 25-26 December*
**5 rm** ⬚ – †£ 103/133 ††£ 118/148
**Rest** – Italian – *(dinner only)* Carte £ 25/33
♦ Smart, modernised detached house boasts minimalist bar/lounge and stark white dining room. Classic Italian dishes, well presented in a distinctly modern style, with fish a speciality. Friendly, efficient service. Comfortable, well-equipped bedrooms.

**at Bwlchtocyn** South : 2 mi – ⊠ Pwllheli

⌂⌂ **Porth Tocyn** ⬙  ⟵ ⟵⟶ ⬙ ⅋ ᛃ P VISA ◉◉
⊠ LL53 7BU – ℰ (01758) 713 303 – www.porthtocyn-hotel.co.uk – *April-October*
**17 rm** – †£ 72/176 ††£ 99/176, ⬚ £ 6.75
**Rest** – *(bar lunch Monday-Saturday, buffet lunch Sunday)* Menu £ 42
♦ Set high on the headland overlooking Cardigan Bay, a traditional hotel that's been in the family for 3 generations. Comfy lounges. Mix of classical and more modern bedrooms; some with balconies or sea views. Great leisure and children's facilities. Modern menus display interesting, soundly executed dishes.

WALES

## ABERYSTWYTH (Aberestuuth) – Ceredigion – 503 H26    32 B2
– pop. 21 877

▶ London 238 mi – Chester 98 mi – Fishguard 58 mi – Shrewsbury 74 mi

ℹ Terrace Rd ℰ (01970) 61 21 25, www.aberystwyth-online.co.uk

🏌 Bryn-y-Mor, ℰ (01970) 61 51 04

👁 Town★★ - The Seafront★ – National Library of Wales (Permanent Exhibition★)

◄ Vale of Rheidol★★ (Railway★★ AC) - St Padarn's Church★, SE : 1 mi by A 44.
Devil's Bridge (Pontarfynach)★, E : 12 mi by A 4120 – Strata Florida Abbey★ AC
(West Door★), SE : 15 mi by B 4340 and minor rd

🏠  **Gwesty Cymru**    ≼ 🏠 ॐ ⁿ VISA ⊕⊕
*19 Marine Terr ⊠ SY23 2AZ – ℰ (01970) 612 252 – www.gwestycymru.com*
*– Closed 23 December-5 January*
**8 rm** ⊑ – ♦£ 65/133 ♦♦£ 87/183
**Rest** – *(closed Tuesday lunch) (booking essential)* Carte £ 28/33
♦ Georgian Grade II listed building on the promenade, with a nice front terrace
and sea views. Thoughtfully designed, contemporary bedrooms are colour-
themed in décor and furnishings; impressive bathrooms. Small basement dining
room serves dishes using Welsh produce, with some international influences.

## ANGLESEY (Isle of) (Sîr Ynys Môn) – Isle of Anglesey – 503 G/H24    32 B1
– pop. 68 900

▶ London 270 mi – Cardiff 205 mi – Liverpool 92 mi – Birkenhead 86 mi

## BEAUMARIS – Isle of Anglesey – ⊠ Isle Of Anglesey    32 B1

▶ London 253 mi – Birkenhead 74 mi – Holyhead 25 mi

🏌 Baron Hill, ℰ (01248) 81 02 31

👁 Town★★ - Castle★ AC

◄ Anglesey★★ – Penmon Priory★, NE : 4 mi by B 5109 and minor roads. Plas
Newydd★ AC, SW : 7 mi by A 545 and A 4080

🏠🏠  **Ye Olde Bull's Head Inn**    ॐ ⁿ VISA ⊕⊕ ᴀᴇ
*Castle St ⊠ LL58 8AP – ℰ (01248) 810 329 – www.bullsheadinn.co.uk*
*– Closed 24-25 December*
**13 rm** ⊑ – ♦£ 85/110 ♦♦£ 100/120
**Rest** *Brasserie* **Rest** *Loft* – see restaurant listing
♦ Characterful 1670s coaching inn. Bedrooms are split between the main house
and adjacent block; the former, traditional and named after Dickens' characters;
the latter, more colourful and contemporary. Vast inglenook fireplace in the
lounge.

🏠  **Cleifiog** without rest    ≼ 🚗 ॐ VISA ⊕⊕
*Townsend ⊠ LL58 8BH – ℰ (01248) 811 507 – www.cleifiogbandb.co.uk*
*– Closed Christmas-New Year*
**3 rm** ⊑ – ♦£ 65 ♦♦£ 95
♦ Delightful seafront guesthouse overlooking the mountains and Menai Strait.
Cosy, antique-furnished lounge with watercolours hung on wood-panelled walls.
Comfy bedrooms with fine linens, large bathrooms and local toiletries. Excellent
breakfasts. Welcoming owner.

🍴🍴  **Loft** – at Ye Olde Bull's Head Inn    VISA ⊕⊕ ᴀᴇ
*Castle St ⊠ LL58 8AP – ℰ (01248) 810 329 – www.bullsheadinn.co.uk*
*– Closed 25-26 December, 1 January, Sunday and Monday*
**Rest** – *(dinner only)* Menu £ 41
♦ Formal restaurant set in an old coaching inn, with plush, open-fired lounge and
dining room in the old loft above. Elegant décor, exposed beams and immacu-
lately laid, candlelit tables. Ambitious dishes feature lots of different ingredients.

WALES

797

✕ **Brasserie** – at Ye Olde Bull's Head Inn                    *VISA* **⚫⚫** **AE**
*Castle St ⊠ LL58 8AP – 𝒞 (01248) 810 329 – www.bullsheadinn.co.uk*
*– Closed 24-25 December*
**Rest** – *(bookings not accepted)* Carte £ 20/31
♦ Large brasserie set in the rear of a charming 17C coaching inn. Relaxed, contemporary feel with a Welsh slate floor, local stone fireplace and light wood tables. Extensive international menu.

**BENLLECH** – Isle of Anglesey – ⊠ Isle Of Anglesey                    **32** B1

⌂ **Hafod** without rest                                   🚗 ⚄ **P**
*Amlwch Rd ⊠ LL74 8SR – 𝒞 (01248) 853 092 – Closed 24-26 December*
**4 rm** ⊊ – ♦£ 50/55 ♦♦£ 70/72
♦ 19C house with large lawned garden and view out over the bays. Cosy lounge and traditional breakfast room; fantastic parquet floor and original staircase. Good-sized bedrooms have open fires.

**CEMAES (Cemais)** – Isle of Anglesey – ⊠ Isle Of Anglesey                    **32** B1

⌂ **Hafod Country House** without rest             ⪕ 🚗 ⚄ **P** *VISA* **⚫⚫**
*South : 0.5 mi on Llanfechell rd ⊠ LL67 0DS – 𝒞 (01407) 711 645*
*– www.anglesey-countryhouse.co.uk – April-September*
**3 rm** ⊊ – ♦£ 40/50 ♦♦£ 65/75
♦ Charming Edwardian house on outskirts of a fishing village, on far side of the island. Lovely garden with pair of majestic oaks. Spacious interior with original tiled floors, delightful staircase, antique-filled lounge and homely bedrooms.

**LLANERCHYMEDD** – Isle of Anglesey – ⊠ Isle Of Anglesey                    **32** B1

⌂ **Llwydiarth Fawr** without rest ⅏         ⪕ 🚗 🐎 🎣 🍸 📞 **P** *VISA* **⚫⚫**
*North : 1 mi on B 5111 ⊠ LL71 8DF – 𝒞 (01248) 470 321*
*– www.llwydiarthfawr.com*
**4 rm** ⊊ – ♦£ 60 ♦♦£ 85/100
♦ Sizeable Georgian house in 1,000 acres of farmland. Country house feel with impressive hallway/landing, plush drawing room and fine views. Individually decorated bedrooms boast extras.

**MENAI BRIDGE** – Isle of Anglesey – ⊠ Isle Of Anglesey                    **32** B1

⌂ **Neuadd Lwyd** ⅏                        ⪕ 🚗 ⚄ **P** *VISA* **⚫⚫**
*Penmynydd, Northwest : 4.75 mi by B 5420 on Eglwys St Gredifael Church rd*
⊠ *LL61 5BX – 𝒞 (01248) 715 005 – www.neuaddlwyd.co.uk – Closed 28*
*November-20 January*
**4 rm** (dinner included) ⊊ – ♦£ 155/215 ♦♦£ 205/265    **Rest** – Menu £ 45
♦ This fine 19C rectory, set in a beautiful rural location, has had a sleek and stylish refit, lending it a luxurious air. Elegant interiors are matched by stunning bedrooms. Freshest Welsh ingredients incorporated into tasty evening meals.

**RHOSCOLYN** – Isle of Anglesey – ⊠ Isle Of Anglesey

🍴 **White Eagle**                              ⪕ 🚗 🍴 **P** *VISA* **⚫⚫**
⊠ *LL65 2NJ – 𝒞 (01407) 860 267 – www.white-eagle.co.uk*
**Rest** – Carte £ 22/33
♦ Spacious pub with cosy bar, modern dining room, decked terrace and stunning sea views. Monthly menu offers everything from sandwiches and salads to pub classics and more sophisticated fare.

**VALLEY** – Isle of Anglesey – ⊠ Isle Of Anglesey

🏠 **Cleifiog Uchaf**                        🚗 🐎 🎣 🍸 📞 **P** *VISA* **⚫⚫** **AE**
*off Spencer Rd ⊠ LL65 3AB – 𝒞 (01407) 741 888 – www.cleifioguchaf.co.uk*
**6 rm** ⊊ – ♦£ 69/79 ♦♦£ 95/145 – 2 suites
**Rest** – *(closed Sunday and Monday) (dinner only)* Carte £ 23/45
♦ Restored 16C longhouse, simply and stylishly furnished. Bedrooms boast character beds and every mod con including flat screens, DVDs and Roberts radios. Slate-floored, bistro-style dining room for classical combinations of locally sourced, seasonal ingredients.

WALES

## BALA – Gwynedd – 503 J25 – pop. 1 980 – ✉ Gwynedd
▶ London - 213 mi – Cardiff 160 mi – Liverpool 75 mi – Stoke-on-Trent 84 mi

⌂ **Abercelyn Country House** without rest 　🚗 ⅌ **P** VISA ⓒⓓ
*Llanycil, Southwest : 1 mi on A 494* ✉ *LL23 7YF –* ℰ *(01678) 521 109*
*– www.abercelyn.co.uk – February-October*
**3 rm** ⚏ – ♦£ 53/60 ♦♦£ 72/90
◆ Attractive former rectory, with pleasant garden and brook. Warmly decorated bedrooms, named after surrounding mountains. Eggs from owners' hens, plus homemade jams and breads.

## BEAUMARIS – 504 H24 – see Anglesey (Isle of)

## BEDDGELERT (Bedkelerd) – Gwynedd – 502 H24 – pop. 535　　32 B1
▶ London 249 mi – Caernarfon 13 mi – Chester 73 mi
◨ Snowdonia National Park★★★ - Aberglaslyn Pass★, S : 1.5 mi on A 498

⌂ **Sygun Fawr Country House** ⁇　　≤ 🚗 ⅃ ⅌ **P** VISA ⓒⓓ
*Northeast : 0.75 mi by A 498* ✉ *LL55 4NE –* ℰ *(01766) 890 258*
*– www.sygunfawr.co.uk – Closed 3 January-10 February and 16-27 December*
**12 rm** ⚏ – ♦£ 41 ♦♦£ 107
**Rest** – *(closed Monday-Tuesday to non-residents) (dinner only) (booking essential)* Carte £ 18/26
◆ Part-16C stone-built house, located halfway up a mountain and boasting views over the Gwynant Valley towards Snowdon. Charming open-fired interior with snug sitting room and spacious conservatory. Good-sized bedrooms with a cosy, homely feel. Traditional dining room offers a range of hearty, regional dishes.

## BENLLECH – 502 H24 – see Anglesey (Isle of)

## BETWS GARMON – Gwynedd　　32 B1
▶ Cardiff 194 mi – Betws-y-Coed 25 mi – Caernarfon 5 mi

⌂ **Betws Inn**　　≤ 🚗 ⅌ ⅋ **P** VISA ⓒⓓ
◨◀ *Northwest : 1 mi on A 4085* ✉ *LL54 7YY –* ℰ *(01286) 650 324*
*– www.betws-inn.co.uk*
**3 rm** ⚏ – ♦£ 60/80 ♦♦£ 70/90　**Rest** – Menu £ 25 **s**
◆ Rustic former coaching inn surrounded by the towering mountains of Snowdonia. Superb inglenook fireplace on display in the cosy lounge; exposed stone walls and pine dresser in the breakfast room. Warm, beamed bedrooms boast half-tester or four-poster beds and modern bathrooms. Home-cooked meals feature local produce.

## BETWS-Y-COED – Conwy – 502 I24 – pop. 848　　32 B1
▶ London 226 mi – Holyhead 44 mi – Shrewsbury 62 mi
🛈 Royal Oak Stables ℰ(01690) 71 04 26, www.betws-y-coed.co.uk
◨ Clubhouse, ℰ(01690) 71 05 56
◉ Town★
◨ Snowdonia National Park★★★. Blaenau Ffestiniog★ (Llechwedd Slate Caverns★ **AC**), SW : 10.5 mi by A 470 – The Glyders and Nant Ffrancon (Cwm Idwal★), W : 14 mi by A 5

⌂ **Tan-y-Foel Country House** ⁇　　≤ 🚗 ⅌ ⅋ **P** VISA ⓒⓓ
*East : 2.5 mi by A 5, A 470 and Capel Garmon rd on Llanwrst rd* ✉ *LL26 ORE*
*–* ℰ *(01690) 710 507 – www.tyfhotel.co.uk – Closed December and restricted opening January*
**6 rm** ⚏ – ♦£ 90/145 ♦♦£ 125/245
**Rest** – *(closed Monday) (dinner only)* Menu £ 49 ❀❀
◆ Personally run, part-16C country house in 4 acres of grounds, affording stunning views over the Vale of Conwy and Snowdonia. Individually designed modern bedrooms with smart bathrooms. Snug lounge and contemporary breakfast room. Much of the produce used at dinner is grown in the owners' greenhouse.

WALES

↑ **Bryn** without rest  ⇐ 🏃 ⚡ (¹) **P** VISA ⊕
*Lôn Muriau, Llanrwst Rd, Northeast : 1 mi by A 5 on A 470* ✉ *LL24 0HD*
*–* ℰ *(01690) 710 627 – www.bryn-bella.co.uk*
**5 rm** ⚏ – ♦£ 80/85 ♦♦£ 80/85
◆ Comfy, well-kept guesthouse with pleasant garden, valley views and every conceivable extra in the bedrooms. Keen owners provide reliable local info. Fresh, tasty eggs from their rescued hens.

↑ **Pengwern** without rest  ⇐ 🏃 ⚡ (¹) **P** VISA ⊕
*Allt Dinas, Southeast : 1.5 mi on A 5* ✉ *LL24 0HF –* ℰ *(01690) 710 480*
*– www.snowdoniaaccommodation.co.uk – Closed 24 December-2 January*
**3 rm** ⚏ – ♦£ 62/68 ♦♦£ 77/83
◆ Former Victorian artist 'colony' with a comfy, homely and stylish lounge, warmly decorated breakfast room and individually appointed bedrooms, two with superb valley vistas.

**at Penmachno** Southwest : 4.75 mi by A 5 on B 4406 – ✉ Betws-Y-Coed

↑ **Penmachno Hall** ⑤  ⇐ 🏃 ⚡ (¹) **P** VISA ⊕
*on Ty Mawr rd* ✉ *LL24 0PU –* ℰ *(01690) 760 410 – www.penmachnohall.co.uk*
*– Closed Christmas-New Year*
**3 rm** ⚏ – ♦£ 100 ♦♦£ 100  **Rest** – Carte £ 18/38
◆ Former rectory built in 1862, set in a pleasant rural location and boasting delightful views. Breakfast-cum-sitting room is filled with books and portraits; boldly coloured bedrooms are personally decorated by the friendly owners. Lovely mature gardens. Snug dining room offers traditional menus, serving 2 courses on weekdays and 5 on Saturdays.

**BETWS-YN-RHOS** – Conwy – **502** J24 – **see Abergele**

**BODUAN** – Gwynedd – **see Pwllheli**

**BRECHFA** – Carmarthenshire – **503** H28  **33** B3
▶ London 216 mi – Cardiff 71 mi – Birmingham 183 mi – Liverpool 164 mi

🏠 **Ty Mawr**  🏃 (¹) **P** VISA ⊕ AE
✉ *SA32 7RA –* ℰ *(01267) 202 332 – www.wales-country-hotel.co.uk*
**6 rm** ⚏ – ♦£ 70 ♦♦£ 128
**Rest** – *(dinner only) (booking essential)* Menu £ 29
◆ 16C stone-built farmhouse set in the centre of the village, next to the river. Personally run, it boasts charm and character aplenty, with exposed brick, wooden beams, open fires, a comfortable lounge and spacious, pine-furnished bedrooms. Modern menu has a Welsh twist; produce is homemade or from the valley.

**BRECON** – Powys – **503** J28 – **pop. 7 901**  **33** C3
▶ London 171 mi – Cardiff 40 mi – Carmarthen 31 mi – Gloucester 65 mi
🎫 Cattle Market Car Park ℰ (01874) 62 24 85, www.breconbeacons.org
⛳ Cradoc, Penoyre Park, ℰ (01874) 62 36 58
⛳ Newton Park Llanfaes, ℰ (01874) 62 20 04
◎ Town★ - Cathedral★ **AC** – Penyclawdd Court★
◎ Brecon Beacons National Park★★. Llanthony Priory★★, S : 8 mi of Hay-on-Wye by B 4423 - Dan-yr-Ogof Showcaves★ **AC**, SW : 20 mi by A 40 and A 4067 – Pen-y-Fan★★, SW : by A 470

↑ **Canal Bank** without rest  🏃 (¹) **P**
*Southeast : 0.5 mi by B 4601 turning right over bridge onto unmarked road after petrol station* ✉ *LD3 7HG –* ℰ *(01874) 623 464*
*– www.accommodation-breconbeacons.co.uk*
**3 rm** ⚏ – ♦£ 60/90 ♦♦£ 98
◆ Delightfully stylish and peaceful 18C canalside cottage. Charming garden with pergola and access to River Usk. Organic breakfasts. Immaculate rooms with extra attention to detail.

WALES

⌂ **Cantre Selyf** without rest   ◻ ✗ ⓣ P̲ VISA ⚊
*5 Lion St ⊠ LD3 7AU – ℰ (01874) 622 904 – www.cantreselyf.co.uk – Closed Christmas and New Year*
**3 rm** ⌱ – †£ 60 ††£ 90
♦ Charming, centrally located 17C townhouse with peaceful garden, period bedrooms and modern shower rooms. Contemporary colours blend with original Georgian features and antiques throughout.

⌂ **Felin Glais** ⌁   ◻ ⓣ P̲ VISA ⚊ AE ⓞ
*Aberyscir, West : 4 mi by Upper Chapel rd off Cradoc Golf Course rd turning right immediately after bridge ⊠ LD3 9NP – ℰ (01874) 623 107 – www.felinglais.co.uk – Closed 25 December*
**4 rm** ⌱ – †£ 85 ††£ 95   **Rest** – Menu £ 40 s
♦ 17C house and barn in tranquil hamlet. Spacious interior with pleasant 'lived in' feel; rooms filled with books and knick-knacks. Homely bedrooms; good toiletries; towels and bedding from Harrods. Owners interest in cooking is evident in the lengthy menu: order dinner two days ahead.

**at Pwllgloyw** Northwest : 4 mi on B 4520 (Upper Chapel rd) – ⊠ Powys

🍴 **Felin Fach Griffin** with rm   ◻ ⌂ P̲ VISA ⚊
⊛ *Felin Fach, Northeast : 4.75 mi by B 4602 off A 470 ⊠ LD3 0UB – ℰ (01874) 620 111 – www.felinfachgriffin.co.uk – Closed 25 December*
**7 rm** ⌱ – †£ 75/85 ††£ 115   **Rest** – Menu £ 19/27 – Carte £ 25/33 ⚬
♦ Rather unique pub with extremely laid back atmosphere. Following the motto "simple things, done well", dishes are straightforward, tasty and arrive in refined, well presented portions. Bedrooms boast super-comfy beds and excellent bedding.

**WALES**

**BRIDGEND** (Pen-y-Bont) – Bridgend – **503** J29 – pop. 39 429   **33** B4
▶ London 177 mi – Cardiff 20 mi – Swansea 23 mi
🖈 Bridgend Designer Outlet Village ℰ (01656) 65 49 06, www.bridgend.gov.uk

**at Laleston** West : 2 mi on A 473 – ⊠ Bridgend

🏨 **Great House**   ◻ ⌂ ʖⓢ ⓣ ♨ P̲ ⚊ AE ⓞ
*High St ⊠ CF32 0HP – ℰ (01656) 657 644 – www.great-house-laleston.co.uk*
**12 rm** ⌱ – †£ 85 ††£ 140
**Rest** *Leicester's* – (closed Sunday dinner and bank holidays) Menu £ 15/22 – Carte £ 22/50
♦ Welcoming 15C, Grade II listed property; the home of the Lordship of Laleston and reputedly a gift from Elizabeth I to the Earl of Leicester. Characterful bar and lounge. Individually styled bedrooms with extras; those in the coach house are most modern. Restaurant offers a seasonal menu of regional produce.

**BWLCHTOCYN** – Gwynedd – **502** G25 – see Abersoch

**CAERNARFON** – Gwynedd – **502** H24 – pop. 10 066   **32** B1
▶ London 249 mi – Birkenhead 76 mi – Chester 68 mi – Holyhead 30 mi
🖈 Castle St. ℰ (01286) 67 22 32, www.caernarfononline.co.uk
🖈 Aberforeshore Llanfaglan, ℰ (01286) 67 37 83
◉ Town★★ - Castle★★★ AC
🄶 Snowdonia National Park★★★

🏠 **Plas Dinas** ⌁   ◻ ⌂ ⓣ P̲ VISA ⚊ AE
*South : 2 mi on A 487 ⊠ LL54 7YF – ℰ (01286) 830 214 – www.plasdinas.co.uk – Closed Christmas and New Year*
**10 rm** ⌱ – †£ 79/199 ††£ 89/250
**Rest** – (closed Sunday and Monday) (dinner only) (residents only) Menu £ 30
♦ Former family home of Lord Snowdon, set in large gardens and full of antiques, oils and family portraits. Spacious lounge with piano. Smart bedrooms boast designer touches and immaculate bathrooms. Café-style dining from concise menu of unfussy, hearty dishes.

**at Seion** Northeast : 5.5 mi by A 4086 and B 4366 on Seion rd – ⊠ Gwynedd

XX **Ty'n Rhos Country House** with rm  ⫷ 🖅 🕪 🄰 🅿 VISA ⓬ AE ⓞ
*Southwest : 0.25 mi ⊠ LL55 3AE – 𝒞 (01248) 670 489 – www.tynrhos.co.uk*
**14 rm** ⌷ – ♦£ 65/120 ♦♦£ 90/150
**Rest** – *(booking essential at lunch)* Menu £ 23/38 – Carte £ 25/38
♦ Formal restaurant with contemporary furnishings, French windows and views over Anglesey. Classic country house cooking uses local, seasonal produce to create hearty old favourites. Modern bedrooms, some with views/terraces.

**at Groeslon** South : 3 mi by A 487

⌂ **Y Goeden Eirin** ⤫  ⫷ 🖅 🕪 🕅 🅿
*Dolydd, North : 0.5 mi ⊠ LL54 7EF – 𝒞 (01286) 830 942*
*– www.ygoedeneirin.co.uk – Closed Christmas-New Year*
**3 rm** ⌷ – ♦£ 70 ♦♦£ 90
**Rest** – Menu £ 28
♦ Attractive stone house between mountains and sea. Picture windows in lounge; interesting artwork and furniture. Charming bedrooms – those in annexe have stable doors and slate-floored bathrooms. Dining room boasts original oils, grand piano and fresh, seasonal dishes.

**at Llandwrog** South : 4.25 mi by A 487 on A 499

XX **Rhiwafallen** with rm  🖅 🄰🄲 rest, 🅿 VISA ⓬ AE
*North : 1 mi on A 499 ⊠ LL54 5SW – 𝒞 (01286) 830 172*
*– www.rhiwafallen.co.uk – Closed 25-26 December, 1 January, Sunday dinner and Monday*
**5 rm** – ♦£ 80 ♦♦£ 150
**Rest** – *(dinner only and Sunday lunch)* Menu £ 35
♦ 19C farmhouse run by enthusiastic young couple; dine in slate-floored conservatory with pleasant view. Seasonal, monthly changing menu; well presented, modern-style dishes based on classic combinations. Stylish, contemporary bedrooms, with bathrooms to match.

---

**CAERSWS** – Powys – **502** J26  **32** C2
▣ London 194 mi – Aberystwyth 39 mi – Chester 63 mi – Shrewsbury 42 mi

**at Pontdolgoch** Northwest : 1.5 mi on A 470 – ⊠ Newtown

⌂ **Talkhouse** with rm  🖅 🍴 🕅 🅿 VISA ⓬ ⓞ
*Newtown ⊠ SY17 5JE – 𝒞 (01686) 688 919 – www.talkhouse.co.uk – Closed 2 weeks January, Monday and Tuesday*
**3 rm** ⌷ – ♦£ 70 ♦♦£ 125
**Rest** – *(booking essential)* Carte £ 25/35
♦ 17C coaching inn with comfy lounge and cosy bar; dining room overlooks garden. Daily changing menu offers hearty portions and bold flavours. Cottage-style bedrooms with antique furniture; Myfanwy is the best.

WALES

# CARDIFF

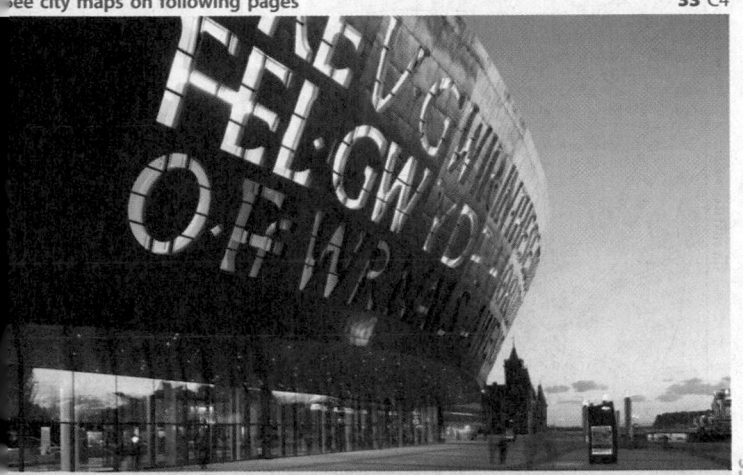

WALES

**Cardiff** – pop. 316 793 – **503** K29 – ⬛ Wales

▶ London 155 – Birmingham 110 – Bristol 46 – Coventry 124

## 🛈 Tourist Information

The Old Library, The Hayes, Working St ✆(0870) 1 21 12 58, www.visitcardiff.com

## Airport

✈ Cardiff (Wales) Airport : ✆ (01446) 711111, SW : 8 m. by A 48 AX

## Golf Courses

⛳ Dinas Powis Old Highwalls, ✆(029) 2051 27 27

## ◎ SIGHTS

**In the town :** City★★★ • National Museum and Gallery★★★ **AC** BY • Castle★ **AC** BZ • Llandaff Cathedral★ AV**B** • Cardiff Bay★ (Techniquest★ **AC**) AX

**On the outskirts :** Museum of Welsh Life★★ **AC**, St Fagan's, W : 5 mi by A 4161 AV • Castell Coch★★ **AC**, NW : 5 mi by A 470 AV

**In the surrounding area :** Caerphilly Castle★★ **AC**, N : 7 mi by A 469 AV • Dyffryn Gardens★ **AC**, W : 8 mi by A 48 AX

---

🏨🏨 **St David's H. & Spa** ⟨≤ 🖼 🌐 ⅏ 𝄞 🛗 & 🕪 ❤ 🏊 🅿
*Havannah St, Cardiff Bay* ⊠ *CF10 5SD* – ✆ *(029)* 🆅🆂🅰 ⓒⓓ 🅰🅴 ⓞ
*2045 4045* – *www.principal-hayley.com/thestdavids* CUa
**120 rm** – 🛏£ 85/325 🛏🛏£ 114/600, � £ 18.50 – 12 suites
**Rest** *Tempus at Tides* – see restaurant listing
♦ Modern, purpose-built hotel set on the waterfront, affording lovely 360° views. Good-sized, minimalist bedrooms have a slightly funky feel; all boast balconies and bay outlooks. Smart spa features seawater pools and a dry floatation tank.

🏨🏨 **Hilton Cardiff** 🖼 ⅏ 🛗 & rm, 🕪 ❤ 🏊 🅿 🆅🆂🅰 ⓒⓓ 🅰🅴 ⓞ
*Kingsway* ⊠ *CF10 3HH* – ✆ *(029) 2064 6300* – *www.hilton.co.uk/cardiff*
**193 rm** – 🛏£ 99/170 🛏🛏£ 120/170, ⊐ £ 18 – 4 suites BZx
**Rest** *Razzi* – Menu £ 19/28
♦ Imposing former tax office in the city centre, with excellent views of the castle, law courts and city hall. Large atrium; well-equipped function rooms and leisure club. Spacious bedrooms offer good comforts – some have fabulous outlooks. Choice of bars. Conservatory style restaurant with international menu.

# CARDIFF

## Park Plaza

🖥 📶 ℹ️ 🔗 & rm, 🏧 ※ rm, 🛜 🔋 *VISA* 🅭 🆎

*Greyfriars Rd* ⌧ *CF10 3AL* – ℰ *(029) 2011 1111*
– *www.parkplazacardiff.com*

BY**s**

**129 rm** – �$£ 89/280 �$�$£ 99/290,
☕ £ 12.95

**Rest** *Laguna Kitchen and Bar* – ℰ (029) 2011 1103 – Menu £ 19 (lunch)
– Carte £ 17/36

♦ Formerly municipal offices, now a light, airy hotel with stylish lounge, extensive conference facilities and vast leisure centre boasting 8 treatment rooms. Modern bedrooms have international power sockets, laptop safes and slate bathrooms.

## CARDIFF

0 — 200 m
0 — 200 yards

WALES

### Radisson Blu Cardiff ≤ ᴸᵃ 🎴 ㄍ rm, AC 🛎 "📶" ṠÁ 🚗 VISA ⊚⊚ AE ①

*Meridian Gate, Bute Terr.* ⊠ *CF10 2FL*
– ℰ *(029) 2045 4777*
– *www. radissonblu.co.uk/hotel-cardiff*                              BZ**a**
**215 rm** ⬙ – †£ 99/150 ††£ 120/240
**Rest** *Filini* – Italian – *(closed Sunday) (dinner only)*
Carte £ 19/46
♦ Large glass building in great central location. Spacious, modern guest areas, excellent meeting facilities and smart bar. Modern, slightly minimalist bedrooms in three styles – Fresh, Fashion and Chic – all boast slate-tiled bathrooms and city views. Simply furnished restaurant offers accessible Italian menu.

805

# CARDIFF BAY

🏨 **Parc**　　　　　　🖼️ 🛗 AK (¹) 🧖 VISA ⓪ AE ⓪

*Park Pl* ⊠ *CF10 3UD* – 🕾 *(0871) 376 9011* – *www.thistle.com/theparchotel*
**139 rm** – †£ 250/340 ††£ 350, ☑ £ 15.95 – 1 suite　　　　　BZr
**Rest** *Crown Social* – see restaurant listing
♦ Centrally located, commercial hotel hidden behind a Victorian façade. Marble tiled lobby, fashionable bar and contemporary bedrooms with dark wood fur nishings – modern art hangs on the walls. 3 large functions rooms; each has its own bar.

🏠 **Lincoln House** *without rest*　　　　🈂️ (¹) P VISA ⓪ AE ⓪

*118-120 Cathedral Rd* ⊠ *CF11 9LQ* – 🕾 *(029) 2039 5558*
– *www.lincolnhotel.co.uk*　　　　　　　　　AV e
**23 rm** ☑ – †£ 70/85 ††£ 90/110 – 1 suite
♦ Two lovingly restored houses with original features still in situ. Comfy bed rooms boast contemporary fabrics and wallpapers; some have period furniture/ four-posters. Ultra-modern attic penthouse.

✕✕ **Tempus at Tides** – *at St David's Hotel & Spa*　　⇐ AK 🐕 P VISA ⓪ AE ⓪

*Havannah St, Cardiff Bay* ⊠ *CF10 5SD* – 🕾 *(029) 2045 4045*
– *www.principal-hayley.com/thestdavids*　　　　　　CUa
**Rest** – Menu £ 26 – Carte £ 34/59
♦ Stylish hotel restaurant whose dining terrace affords stunning views out over the bay. Contemporary cooking displays international influences. Live entertain ment towards the end of the week.

XX **Crown Social** – at Parc Hotel     AK ⇄ VISA ⦿ AE ⓪
*Park Pl* ⊠ *CF10 3UD* – ✆ *(029) 2078 5593* – *www.crownsocial.co.uk*
**Rest** – Carte £ 20/34     BZ**n**
♦ Smart hotel restaurant with two dark-wood furnished dining areas and small private room showing live kitchen footage. Precise, well-presented and flavoursome dishes range from nibbles and sharing plates to 6 or 8 course on the tasting menu.

X **Woods Brasserie**     ⛲ AK 🖥 VISA ⦿ AE
*The Pilotage Building, Stuart St, Cardiff Bay* ⊠ *CF10 5BW* – ✆ *(029) 2049 2400*
*– www.woods-brasserie.com – Closed 25-26 December, dinner*
*Sunday October-June and bank holidays*     CU**b**
**Rest** – *(booking essential at dinner)* Menu £ 18 (lunch) – Carte £ 29/38
♦ Modern brasserie dishes and European influences from an open kitchen. Bay view from the first floor terrace. Popular for business lunches and bay visitors in the evening.

X **Mint & Mustard**     AK VISA ⦿ AE
☻ *134 Whitchurch Rd* ⊠ *CF14 3LZ* – ✆ *(029) 2062 0333*
*– www.mintandmustard.com – Closed 25-26 December and Sunday*
**Rest** – Indian – *(dinner only)* Carte £ 24/30     AV**n**
♦ Warm, welcoming Indian restaurant with modern, laid-back feel; a real hit with the locals. The keen chef-owner's training in Kerala is reflected in the extensive menu of original, authentic dishes. Spicing is subtle yet effective and combinations work well. Desserts are tasty and attractively presented.

X **Garçon**     ⛲ AK 🖥 ⇄ VISA ⦿ AE
*9 Upper Mermaid Quay* ⊠ *CF10 5BZ* – ✆ *(029) 2049 0990*
*– www.garcon-resto.co.uk – Closed first week January, 24-26 December, dinner*
*Sunday and bank holiday Mondays*     CU**s**
**Rest** – French – Menu £ 16 (lunch) – Carte £ 27/48
♦ Traditional French brasserie with a large marble-topped bar, mirrored panelling, powder blue banquettes and a pleasant terrace – set on the top floor of a quayside complex. Classical Gallic dishes with gutsy flavours; good value set menu.

X **Patagonia**     VISA ⦿ ⓪
*11 Kings Rd* ⊠ *CF11 9BZ* – ✆ *(029) 2019 0265*
*– www.patagonia-restaurant.co.uk – Closed 24 December-18 January, Sunday*
*and Monday*     AX**v**
**Rest** – *(dinner only)* Menu £ 31
♦ Friendly neighbourhood restaurant set over two floors, with brightly coloured walls and eclectic artwork. Short menu offers wholesome and tasty modern European cooking.

X **'Bully's**     AK VISA ⦿
*5 Romilly Cres.* ⊠ *CF11 9NP* – ✆ *(029) 2022 1905* – *www.bullysrestaurant.co.uk*
*– Closed 1-10 January, 1-10 April, 27 August-4 September, 24-26 December,*
*Sunday dinner, Monday and Tuesday*     AX**x**
**Rest** – French – Menu £ 18 (weekday lunch) – Carte £ 24/51
♦ Welcoming neighbourhood bistro run by a passionate, hands-on owner. Simply furnished interior boasts a fascinating array of memorabilia. Classical cooking displays a strong Gallic edge; carefully prepared dishes feature quality ingredients.

X **chai st**     AK VISA ⦿ ⓪
☻ *132 Whitchurch Rd* ⊠ *CF14 3LZ* – ✆ *(029) 2062 0333* – *www.chaistreet.com*
*– Closed 25-26 December and Monday*     AV**c**
**Rest** – Indian – *(lunch only)* Carte £ 13/16
♦ Trendy, vibrant sister to Mint & Mustard, with modern Bollywood pop art and bold printed canvases on the walls. Keen, helpful team serve excellent value Indian street food. Highlights are the large, daily changing 'Thali' platters: tapas-style portions served in small stainless steel dishes on a large tray.

WALES

### New Conway
🛏 AC VISA ⦿

*53 Conway Rd* ✉ *CF11 9NW* – ☎ *(029) 2022 4373* – *www.theconway.co.uk*
**Rest** – Carte £ 25/34
AVa
◆ Neighbourhood pub with pleasingly simple approach to food which sees fresh
seasonal, local produce used to create tasty pub classics like toad in the hole or
apple and raisin crumble.

**at Penarth** South : 3 mi by A 4160 - AX – ✉ Cardiff

### Holm House
🛋 ❄ ⚛ P VISA ⦿

*Marine Par* ✉ *CF64 3BG* – ☎ *(029) 2070 1572* – *www.holmhouse.com*
**12 rm** 🛏 – ♦£ 120 ♦♦£ 425
**Rest** *Neale's* – *(dinner only and lunch Friday-Sunday)* Menu £ 20 (lunch)
– Carte £ 35/44
◆ Built in 1920s for son of local shipbuilder. Part art deco, part modern styling
displaying flock wallpapers and bold colours; some bedrooms boast feature baths
and oversized windows. Restaurant with views to distant Holm Islands; weekly
menus of simple, wholesome combinations.

### Olive Tree
AC ❄ VISA ⦿ AE

*21 Glebe St* ✉ *CF64 1EE* – ☎ *(029) 2070 7077* – *www.the-olive-tree.net*
– *Closed 25-27 December, Sunday dinner and Monday*
**Rest** – *(dinner only and Sunday lunch)* Menu £ 23 (weekday dinner)
– Carte £ 27/38
◆ Rewarding discovery tucked away in the centre of town. Relaxing feel aug-
mented by vivid artwork. Warm, friendly service of good value, seasonal, fre-
quently changing dishes.

---

## CARMARTHEN – Carmarthenshire – 503 H28 – pop. 14 648 33 B3

▶ London 219 mi – Fishguard 47 mi – Haverfordwest 32 mi – Swansea 27 mi
🈯 113 Lammas St ☎ (01267) 23 15 57, www.visitcarmarthenshire.co.uk
◉ Kidwelly Castle★ – National Botanic Garden★

**at Felingwm Uchaf** Northeast : 8 mi by A 40 on B 4310 – ✉ Carmarthen

### Allt y Golau Uchaf without rest
🛋 ❄ ⚛ P

*North : 0.5 mi on B 4310* ✉ *SA32 7BB* – ☎ *(01267) 290 455*
– *www.alltygolau.com* – *Closed 20 December-2 January*
**3 rm** 🛏 – ♦£ 45 ♦♦£ 68
◆ Georgian farmhouse rebuilt in Victorian times, up a steep slope on a 2 acre
smallholding. Well-kept, rustic interior. Neat, pine-furnished bedrooms with homely
feel. Extensive breakfast features local meats and eggs from the hens out back.

**at Llanllawddog** Northeast : 8 mi by A485

### Glangwili Mansion without rest ⌖
🛋 ❄ ⚛ P VISA ⦿

✉ *SA32 7JE* – ☎ *(01267) 253 735* – *www.glangwilimansion.co.uk* – *Closed 24-25,
31 December and 1 January*
**3 rm** – ♦£ 90/100 ♦♦£ 125/135
◆ Part-16C mansion rebuilt in Georgian style, in a great location on the edge of
the forest. Spacious, modern interior with sleek tiled floors and modern art. Airy
lounge and breakfast room; bright, bold bedrooms with modern oak furnishings.

**at Nantgaredig** East : 5 mi on A 40 – ✉ Carmarthen

### Y Polyn
🛋 🏡 ❄ P VISA ⦿ AE

*South : 1 mi on B 4310* ✉ *SA32 7LH* – ☎ *(01267) 290 000*
– *www.ypolynrestaurant.co.uk* – *Closed Sunday dinner and Monday*
**Rest** – Menu £ 15/30 – Carte £ 21/30
◆ Welcoming dining pub in a great rural location by a stream. Hearty, wholesome dishes are classically based with modern touches. À la carte or 'express'
lunch and fixed price dinners.

---

**CLYNNOG-FAWR** – Gwynedd – pop. 100                                      **32** B1

▶ London 273 mi – Cardiff 179 mi – Dublin 47 mi – Birmingham 148 mi

🏠 **Y Beuno** with rm                                      ॐ rest, 🅿 VISA ⚫ ◑
⊠ LL54 5PB – ℰ (01286) 660 785 – www.ybeuno.com – *Restricted opening in winter*
**7 rm** ☐ – †£ 75/85 ††£ 105/135
**Rest** – *(closed lunch Monday-Thursday in low season)* Carte £ 23/34
♦ Sizeable pub set close to the coast, with delightfully rustic bar and series of snug, homely rooms. Experienced French chef – choose a classic Gallic daily special or in summer, a fresh, unfussy seafood dish. Bedrooms are comfy and modern; some boast bay views.

---

**COLWYN BAY** (Bae Colwyn) – Conwy – **502** I24 – pop. 30 269          **32** B1

▶ London 237 mi – Birkenhead 50 mi – Chester 42 mi – Holyhead 41 mi
🛈 Information Point, Cayley Promenade, Rhos-on-Sea ℰ (01492) 54 87 78, www.ukinformationcentre.com/north-wales
🏌 Abergele Tan-y-Goppa Rd, ℰ (01745) 82 40 34
🏌 Old Colwyn Woodland Ave, ℰ (01492) 51 55 81
◉ Welsh Mountain Zoo★ AC (≤★)
◎ Bodnant Garden★★ AC, SW : 6 mi by A 55 and A 470

🏠 **Rathlin Country House** without rest              🚗 ⚓ ॐ ᵚ 🐾 🅿 VISA ⚫
48 Kings Rd, Southwest : 0.25 mi on B 5113 ⊠ LL29 7YH – ℰ (01492) 532 173 – www.rathlincountryhouse.co.uk – Closed 24-25 December
**3 rm** ☐ – †£ 69/75 ††£ 85/95
♦ Large Arts and Crafts house set in mature gardens, boasting ornate ceilings, leaded windows, oak panelling and parquet floors. Outdoor pool and sauna. Individually furnished bedrooms display modern touches; one even has a steam shower. Extensive breakfast menu.

🏠 **Pen-y-Bryn**                                      🚗 ⚓ 🅿 VISA ⚫ AE
Pen-y-Bryn Rd, Upper Colwyn Bay., Southwest : 1 mi by B 5113 ⊠ LL29 6DD – ℰ (01492) 533 360 – www.penybryn-colwynbay.co.uk – Closed 25 December
**Rest** – Carte £ 17/24
♦ Modern, laid-back pub set on a residential street; its unassuming façade concealing impressive bay views. Extensive all-day menu ranges from pub classics to more adventurous fare.

**at Rhos-on-Sea** Northwest : 1 mi – ⊠ Colwyn Bay

🏠 **Plas Rhos** without rest                          ≤ ॐ 🐾 🅿 VISA ⚫ AE
Cayley Promenade ⊠ LL28 4EP – ℰ (01492) 543 698 – www.plasrhos.co.uk – February-mid-December
**7 rm** ☐ – †£ 50/75 ††£ 90/100
♦ 19C house on first promenade from Colwyn Bay. Homely front lounge with bay view. Breakfasts feature local butcher's produce. Immaculately kept rooms: superior ones to front.

---

**CONWY** – Conwy – **502** I24 – pop. 3 847                               **32** B1

▶ London 241 mi – Caernarfon 22 mi – Chester 46 mi – Holyhead 37 mi
🛈 Conwy Castle Visitor Centre ℰ (01492) 59 22 48, www.touristnetuk.com/wa/northwales
🏌 Penmaenmawr Conway Old Rd, ℰ (01492) 62 33 30
◉ Town★★ - Castle★★ AC – Town Walls★★ - Plas Mawr★★
◎ Snowdonia National Park★★★ – Bodnant Garden★★ AC, S : 8 mi by A 55 and A 470 – Conwy Crossing (suspension bridge★)

WALES

🏨 **Castle**                    ⁛ 🛗 🅿️ 𝗩𝗜𝗦𝗔 ⊙⊙ 🅰🅴

High St ⊠ LL32 8DB – 𝒞 (01492) 582 800 – www.castlewales.co.uk
– Closed 2-10 January
**27 rm** ⊑ – ♦£ 89/166 ♦♦£ 160/166 – 1 suite
**Rest Dawson's** – (closed to non-residents dinner 25 December) Carte £ 27/41
♦ Adjoining brick and flint coaching inns within walled town, on site of forme
Cistercian abbey. Comfy firelit country house sitting room; mix of classic/moder
bedrooms. Some castle views. Contemporary dining room offers extensive men
of brasserie classics.

✗✗ **Signatures**                              🅿️ 𝗩𝗜𝗦𝗔 ⊙⊙

Northwest 1 mi by A 55 ⊠ LL32 8GA – 𝒞 (01492) 583 513
– www.signaturesrestaurant.co.uk – Closed Monday and Tuesday
**Rest** – (dinner only) (booking advisable) Menu £ 24 (weekdays) – Carte £ 30/4
♦ Unusually set on an upmarket static caravan site. Smart dining room boast
flocked wallpapers and elegantly laid, polished tables. All-encompassing menu o
fers a daily set selection and signature dishes are marked out. Well-versed team.

🍴 **Groes Inn** with rm          ≤ 🚗 🛋 ⁛ 🅿️ 𝗩𝗜𝗦𝗔 ⊙⊙ 🅰🅴 ⓪

South : 3 mi on B 5106 ⊠ LL32 8TN – 𝒞 (01492) 650 545 – www.groesinn.com
– Closed 25 December
**14 rm** ⊑ – ♦£ 95/105 ♦♦£ 160/190   **Rest** – Carte £ 18/42
♦ Characterful inn, beautifully set overlooking the estuary, in the foothills o
Snowdonia. Local Welsh and British dishes arrive in neat, generous portions
more adventurous restaurant menu. Tastefully styled bedrooms boasts views
some have terraces and balconies.

**at Llansanffraid Glan Conwy** Southeast : 2.5 mi by A 547 on A 470
– ⊠ Conwy

🏠 **Old Rectory Country House** without rest ⦾    ≤ 🚗 ⁛ 🅿️ 𝗩𝗜𝗦𝗔 ⊙⊙

Llanrwst Rd ⊠ LL28 5LF – 𝒞 (01492) 580 611
– www.oldrectorycountryhouse.co.uk – Closed 24-25 and 31 December
**5 rm** ⊑ – ♦£ 99/119 ♦♦£ 99/159
♦ Personally run country house with attractive gardens and estuary views. Beautifully furnished Georgian-style sitting room displays china and antiques. Bedrooms, split between the house and annexe, boast comfy feature beds and luxury
bathrooms. Good breakfasts.

**at Rowen** South : 3.5 mi by B 5106

🏠 **Tir Y Coed** ⦾                   🚗 🛋 ⁛ 🅿️ 𝗩𝗜𝗦𝗔 ⊙⊙ 🅰🅴 ⓪

⊠ LL32 8TP – 𝒞 (01492) 650 219 – www.tirycoed.com
**7 rm** ⊑ – ♦£ 110 ♦♦£ 125/175   **Rest** – (dinner only) Menu £ 37
♦ In secluded valley at foothills of Snowdonia, with balcony terrace overlooking
mature garden. Tastefully furnished bedrooms. Intimate, candlelit dining room
features fine collection of Victorian lithographs. Daily changing menu reflects the
best of local produce.

---

**COWBRIDGE** (Y Bont Faen) – The Vale of Glamorgan – **503** J29      **33** B4
– pop. 3 616
▶ London 170 mi – Cardiff 15 mi – Swansea 30 mi

✗✗ **Huddarts**                                    𝗩𝗜𝗦𝗔 ⊙⊙

69 High St ⊠ CF71 7AF – 𝒞 (01446) 774 645 – www.huddartsrestaurant.co.uk
– Closed 26 December-9 January, 1 week spring, 1 week autumn, Sunday dinner
and Monday
**Rest** – Menu £ 26 (lunch) – Carte dinner £ 28/32
♦ Honest restaurant on high street of an ancient market town; husband cooks
and wife looks after the friendly service. Traditional décor with a stone fireplace
and Welsh tapestries. Carefully executed, classical dishes and good presentation.

WALES

## CRICCIETH – Gwynedd – 502 H25 – pop. 1 826

▶ London 249 mi – Caernarfon 17 mi – Shrewsbury 85 mi
🖼 Ednyfed Hill, *ℰ* (01766) 52 21 54
🇬 Lleyn Peninsula★★ – Ffestiniog Railway★★

🏠 **Mynydd Ednyfed Country House** ⤫ ⫸ ⟐ ☆ ⫿⫿ **P** 𝚅𝙸𝚂𝙰 ⊚⊚
*Caernarfon Rd, Northwest : 0.75 mi on B 4411* ⊠ *LL52 0PH –* *ℰ* *(01766) 523 269*
*– www.criccieth.net – Closed 22 December-5 January*
**8 rm** ⯒ – †£ 70/75 ††£ 98/120   **Rest** *– (dinner only)* Carte £ 20/29
♦ Cosy, personally run 17C country house in eight acres of gardens and woodland. Traditional bedrooms - some with four-posters and fine bay views; all with
stylish modern bathrooms. Dinner served in conservatory, which also boasts
great outlook.

## CRICKHOWELL (Crucywel) – Powys – 503 K28 – pop. 2 166

▶ London 169 mi – Abergavenny 6 mi – Brecon 14 mi – Cardiff 40 mi
🇮 Beaufort St *ℰ* (01873) 81 19 70, www.crickhowellinfo.org.uk
🇬 Brecon Beacons National Park★★. Llanthony Priory★★, NE : 10 mi by minor roads

🏘 **Gliffaes Country House** ⤫ ⫸ 🕮 ☜ ☆ ☆ ⫿⫿ ☆ **P** 𝚅𝙸𝚂𝙰 ⊚⊚ 𝙰𝙴 ⓞ
*West : 3.75 mi by A 40* ⊠ *NP8 1RH –* *ℰ* *(01874) 730 371*
*– www.gliffaeshotel.com – Closed 2 January-1 February*
**23 rm** ⯒ – †£ 93/115 ††£ 248
**Rest** *– (light lunch Monday-Saturday)* Menu £ 39 **s**
♦ Impressive country house built in 1886 in semi-Italianate style, set in 32 acres
of delightful grounds that lead down to the river. Spacious, well-appointed
lounges and great views from terrace. Smart, individually styled bedrooms; some
with balconies. Victorian-style restaurant; menus showcase Welsh produce.

🏨 **Bear** ⫸ ⫿⫿ ☆ **P** 𝚅𝙸𝚂𝙰 ⊚⊚ 𝙰𝙴
*High St* ⊠ *NP8 1BW –* *ℰ* *(01873) 810 408 – www.bearhotel.co.uk – Closed 25*
*December*
**34 rm** (dinner included) ⯒ – †£ 75/126 ††£ 92/163 – 1 suite
**Rest** *Bear* – see restaurant listing
♦ Well-maintained 15C coaching inn full of nooks and crannies. Comfortable
bedrooms, some with jacuzzis; most characterful are in main house and feature
beams, four-posters and fireplaces.

🏡 **Glangrwyney Court** ⫸ 🕮 ☆ ☆ ⫿⫿ **P** 𝚅𝙸𝚂𝙰 ⊚⊚
*Southeast : 2 mi on A 40* ⊠ *NP8 1ES –* *ℰ* *(01873) 811 288*
*– www.glancourt.co.uk*
**5 rm** ⯒ – †£ 65/95 ††£ 130/145   **Rest** *–* Carte £ 31/35
♦ Passionately run guesthouse with large lounge and high-ceilinged breakfast
room. Fresh flowers and objets d'art cover every surface. Bedrooms boasts rich
fabrics, good facilities and country views. Dinner by arrangement or transport to
the local pub arranged.

🏡 **Ty Gwyn** without rest ⫸ ☆ **P**
*Brecon Rd* ⊠ *NP8 1DG –* *ℰ* *(01873) 811 625 – www.tygwyn.com*
*– February-November*
**3 rm** ⯒ – †£ 45/50 ††£ 75
♦ A homely place boasting spotlessly kept, simply furnished bedrooms, with
comfort and character. Well-tended garden with stream. Enthusiastic owner has
vast local knowledge.

🍴 **Bear** ⫸ **P** 𝚅𝙸𝚂𝙰 ⊚⊚ 𝙰𝙴
*High St* ⊠ *NP8 1BW –* *ℰ* *(01873) 810 408 – www.bearhotel.co.uk – Closed 25*
*December*
**Rest** – Carte £ 22/35
♦ Keenly run coaching inn serving classical, tried-and-tested menu available both
in characterful bar and more formal restaurant. Swift, assured service from young,
cheery team.

## CROSS ASH – Monmouthshire – see Abergavenny

**CROSSGATES** – Powys – **503** J27 – see Llandrindod Wells

**DEGANWY** – Conwy – **502** I24 – see Llandudno

**DOLFOR** – Powys – **503** K26                                        **32** C2

▶ London 199 – Cardiff 93 – Oswestry 34 – Ludlow 39

⚐ **Old Vicarage**                    ⟨€ ⌂ ⁒ ⁗ ℙ 𝖵𝖨𝖲𝖠 ⓒⓞ Æ⟩
North : 1.5 mi by A 483 ⊠ SY16 4BN – ℰ (01686) 629 051
– www.theoldvicaragedolfor.co.uk
**4 rm** ⌨ – †£ 65/75 ††£ 95/110   **Rest** – Menu £ 25/30
♦ Characterful 19C detached house with large gardens; formerly a vicarage. Cosy bedrooms, named after nearby rivers, mix period furniture with modern colours. Concise menu of home-cooked dishes features local produce and veg from garden. Preserves/chutneys for sale.

**DOLGELLAU** – Gwynedd – **502** I25 – pop. 2 407              **32** B2

▶ London 221 mi – Birkenhead 72 mi – Chester 64 mi – Shrewsbury 57 mi

🛈 Eldon Sq ℰ (01341) 42 28 88, www.dolgellau-snowdonia.co.uk

🏌 Hengwrt Estate Pencefn Rd, ℰ (01341) 42 26 03

◉ Town ★

🖼 Snowdonia National Park ★★★ - Cadair Idris ★★★ - Precipice Walk ★,
NE : 3 mi on minor roads

🏨 **Penmaenuchaf Hall** ॐ           ⟨€ ⌂ 𝄢 🤿 ⌂ ⁗ ℙ 𝖵𝖨𝖲𝖠 ⓒⓞ ①⟩
*Penmaenpool, West : 1.75 mi on A 493 (Tywyn Rd) ⊠ LL40 1YB – ℰ (01341) 422 129 – www.penhall.co.uk – Closed 12-22 December and 4-19 January*
**14 rm** ⌨ – †£ 100/150 ††£ 250   **Rest** – Menu £ 19/43 – Carte £ 43/49
♦ Personally run Victorian house with wood panelling, ornate ceilings and original stained glass. Country house style bedrooms; some with balconies. Beautiful grounds and superb mountain and estuary views. Friendly staff and family feel. Formal conservatory dining room with garden outlook.

⌂ **Ffynnon** without rest            ⟨⌂ ⁒ ⁗ ℙ 𝖵𝖨𝖲𝖠 ⓒⓞ Æ⟩
*Love Ln, (off Cader Rd) ⊠ LL40 1RR – ℰ (01341) 421 774
– www.ffynnontownhouse.com*
**6 rm** ⌨ – †£ 130 ††£ 175
♦ A haven of luxury; lovingly restored and modernised, yet retaining many original features. Stylish sitting room and spacious, tastefully decorated suites, boasting every mod con.

⚐ **Tyddyn Mawr** without rest ॐ        ⟨€ ⌂ 𝄢 🤿 ⁒ ⁗ ℙ⟩
🏛 *Islawdref, Cader Rd, Southwest : 2.5 mi by Tywyn rd on Cader Idris rd
⊠ LL40 1TL – ℰ (01341) 422 331 – www.wales-guesthouse.co.uk
– February-November*
**3 rm** ⌨ – †£ 55 ††£ 78
♦ Set on secluded working sheep farm, stunningly situated beneath Cader Idris mountain. Immaculate bedrooms boast superb views and plenty of extras; one has a balcony, another, a terrace. Five course breakfast taken beside impressive inglenook. Great hospitality.

**at Llanelltyd** Northwest : 2.25 mi by A 470 on A 496

🍽🍽 **Mawddach**                    ⟨€ 🤿 ℙ 𝖵𝖨𝖲𝖠 ⓒⓞ⟩
⊠ LL40 2TA – ℰ (01341) 424 020 – www.mawddach.com – Closed 2 weeks November, 1 week January, 1 week spring, Sunday dinner, Monday and Tuesday
**Rest** – Carte £ 26/32
♦ Stylish barn conversion on family farm. First floor dining room with huge glass wall and superb view. Straightforward cooking uses beef and lamb from the farm; more adventurous dinner menu.

## EAST ABERTHAW (Aberddawan) – The Vale of Glamorgan       33 B-C4
– **503** J29 – ✉ Barry

▶ London 180 mi – Cardiff 20 mi – Swansea 33 mi

🍺 **Blue Anchor Inn**                                       **P** 💳 ⓪⓪
✉ CF62 3DD – ℰ (01446) 750 329 – www.blueanchoraberthaw.com
– *Closed Sunday dinner*
**Rest** – Carte £ 17/28
♦ Thatched stone-built pub dating back to 1380, with characterful bar and vast
upstairs restaurant. Traditional, wholesome dishes boast straightforward presenta-
tion and plenty of flavour.

---

## FELINGWM UCHAF – Carmarthenshire – see Carmarthen

---

## FISHGUARD – Pembrokeshire – **503** F28 – pop. 3 193       33 A3

▶ London 265 mi – Cardiff 114 mi – Gloucester 176 mi – Holyhead 169 mi
🚢 to Republic of Ireland (Rosslare) (Stena Line) 2-4 daily (1 h 50 mn/3 h 30 mn)
🛈 The Square ℰ (01437) 77 66 36, www.visitpembrokeshire.com
🌄 Pembrokeshire Coast National Park★★

🏠 **Manor Town House** without rest       ← 🚗 ⚡ ⑨ 💳 ⓪⓪
11 Main St ✉ SA65 9HG – ℰ (01348) 873 260 – www.manortownhouse.com
– *Closed 24-26 December*
**6 rm** ⌂ – ♦£ 60/75 ♦♦£ 105/165
♦ Well-run, listed Georgian townhouse, boasting fabulous harbour views from
its garden. Cosy lounges and personally styled, antique-furnished bedrooms;
some art deco, some Victorian. Tasty breakfast includes a waffle menu.
Charming owners.

---

## GRESFORD = Groes-ffordd – Wrexham – **502** L24 – see Wrexham

---

## GROESLON – Gwynedd – see Caernarfon

---

## HARLECH – Gwynedd – **502** H25 – pop. 1 233       32 B2

▶ London 241 mi – Chester 72 mi – Dolgellau 21 mi
🛈 High St ℰ (01766) 78 06 58, www.harlech-snowdonia.co.uk
⛳ Royal St David's, ℰ (01766) 78 02 03
◉ Castle★★ **AC**
🌄 Snowdonia National Park★★★

✕✕ **Castle Cottage** with rm       💳 ⓪⓪
Pen Llech, by B 4573 ✉ LL46 2YL – ℰ (01766) 780 479
– www.castlecottageharlech.co.uk – *Closed 2 weeks November*
**7 rm** ⌂ – ♦£ 85 ♦♦£ 170
**Rest** – *(dinner only) (booking essential)* Menu £ 39
♦ Attractive cottage behind Harlech Castle, with cosy yet surprisingly contemporary interior. Classical, daily changing menus display passionately sourced local
produce and modern touches. Bedrooms are spacious and comfy; some boast
stunning castle/mountain views.

---

## HAVERFORDWEST (Hwlffordd) – Pembrokeshire – **503** F28       33 A3
– pop. 13 367

▶ London 250 mi – Fishguard 15 mi – Swansea 57 mi
🛈 Old Bridge ℰ (01437) 76 31 10, www.visitpembrokeshire.com
⛳ Arnolds Down, ℰ (01437) 76 35 65
◉ Scolton Museum and Country Park★
🌄 Pembrokeshire Coast National Park★★. Skomer Island and Skokholm Island★,
SW : 14 mi by B 4327 and minor roads

WALES

### Lower Haythog Farm ॐ      🚗 🕭 💥 🟊 ℗

*Spittal, Northeast : 5 mi on B 4329* ⊠ *SA62 5QL –* ℰ *(01437) 731 279*
*– www.lowerhaythogfarm.co.uk*
**5 rm** ☕ – ✦£ 45/65 ✦✦£ 75/85    **Rest** – Menu £ 25
♦ Friendly atmosphere, traditional comforts and a warm welcome at this 250 acre working dairy farm with accessible woodland walks. Well-kept and comfortable throughout. Dining room in homely, country style reflected in hearty, home-cooked food.

### Paddock ॐ      🚗 🟊 ℗

*Northeast : 5 mi on B 4329* ⊠ *SA62 5QL –* ℰ *(01437) 731 531*
*– www.thepaddockwales.co.uk*
**3 rm** ☕ – ✦£ 55/70 ✦✦£ 75/90    **Rest** – Menu £ 28
♦ Very modern new build guesthouse set on working farm; minimalist ground floor bedrooms feature chunky furniture and Egyptian cotton bedding. Comfy lounge with books, magazines and board games. Set 2 or 3 course dinner makes good use of local produce.

---

## HAY-ON-WYE (Y Gelli) – Powys – **503** K27 – pop. 1 846    **33** C3
▶ London 154 mi – Brecon 16 mi – Cardiff 59 mi – Hereford 21 mi
🇮 Oxford Rd ℰ (01497) 82 01 44, www.hay-on-wye.co.uk
🖼 Rhosgoch Builth Wells, ℰ (01497) 85 12 51
◎ Town ★
🖼 Brecon Beacons National Park★★. Llanthony Priory★★, SE : 12 mi by minor roads

### Old Black Lion with rm      🍴 💥 🟊 ℗ 𝗩𝗜𝗦𝗔 ⓒⓞ 𝖠𝖤

*26 Lion St* ⊠ *HR3 5AD –* ℰ *(01497) 820 841 – www.oldblacklion.co.uk – Closed 24-26 December*
**10 rm** ☕ – ✦£ 53/70 ✦✦£ 90    **Rest** – Carte £ 23/34
♦ Characterful part-13C inn with lots of old world charm. Traditional menu offers tasty, honest dishes, hearty portions and plenty of choice, with more favourites on the board. Bedrooms boast either antique furnishings or rich colours and modern bathrooms.

### Three Tuns      🍴 𝗩𝗜𝗦𝗔 ⓒⓞ 𝖠𝖤

*4 Broad St* ⊠ *HR3 5DB –* ℰ *(01497) 821 855 – www.three-tuns.com*
**Rest** – *(closed 25 December)* Carte £ 22/32
♦ Grade II listed 16C pub, reputedly the oldest building in town. Wide-ranging menus: bar and terrace offer blackboard classics; formal upstairs dining room comes into its own in the evening.

---

## HOWEY – Powys – see Llandrindod Wells

---

## KNIGHTON (Trefyclawdd) – Powys – **503** K26 – pop. 2 851    **33** C3
▶ London 162 mi – Birmingham 59 mi – Hereford 31 mi – Shrewsbury 35 mi
🇮 West St ℰ (01547) 52 87 53, www.visitknighton.co.uk
🖼 Ffrydd Wood, ℰ (01547) 52 86 46
◎ Town ★
🖼 Offa's Dyke ★, NW : 9.5 m

 ### Milebrook House      🚗 💥 🟊 ℗ 𝗩𝗜𝗦𝗔 ⓒⓞ

*Ludlow Rd, Milebrook, East : 2 mi on A 4113* ⊠ *LD7 1LT –* ℰ *(01547) 528 632*
*– www.milebrookhouse.co.uk – Closed December-February*
**10 rm** (dinner included) ☕ – ✦£ 114 ✦✦£ 194
**Rest** – *(closed Sunday dinner and Monday lunch)* Menu £ 19/34 – Carte £ 31/35
♦ Part-Georgian dower house located in the Teme Valley; once home to explorer Wilfred Thesiger. Several well-appointed lounges; spacious, comfortable bedrooms furnished in country house style. Superb formal gardens boast lovely exotic plants. Traditional restaurant with menu showcasing kitchen garden produce.

WALES

**LAKE VYRNWY** – Powys – **502** J25 – ⊠ **Llanwddyn**　　　　**32** C2

⊒ London 204 mi – Chester 52 mi – Llanfyllin 10 mi – Shrewsbury 40 mi

⊒ The Shop in the Corner, Vyrnwy Craft Workshops  ℰ (01691) 87 03 46,
www.lake-vyrnwy.com

⊒ Lake ★

🏠　**Lake Vyrnwy** ⌚　　⪤ 🖨 🕭 🎝 ☎ 🐾 ಓ ⅏ ╳ 🖫 🌡 rm, 🛁 **P** **VISA** ⫴ **AE**
⊠ SY10 0LY – ℰ (01691) 870 692 – www.lakevyrnwyhotel.com
**51 rm** � ⊒ – ♔£ 116/126 ♔♔£ 213/225 – 1 suite
**Rest** – Menu £ 40 (dinner) **s** – Carte lunch £ 19/26 **s**
**Rest Tavern** – Carte £ 19/26 **s**
  ◆ Victorian country house, stunningly located overlooking Lake Vyrnwy and a
sporting estate. Bedrooms range in style – most are traditionally furnished and
some have balconies; one even has a roll-top bath looking down the lake. Restaurant opens out onto a terrace and offers classical menus, while the Tavern
serves informal pub favourites.

**LALESTON** – Bridgend – **503** J29 – see Bridgend

**LAMPHEY** = Llandyfai – Pembrokeshire – **503** F28 – see Pembroke

**LLANARMON DYFFRYN CEIRIOG** – Wrexham – **502** K25　　**32** C2
- ⊠ Llangollen (denbighshire)

⊒ London 196 mi – Chester 33 mi – Shrewsbury 32 mi

🏡　**Hand at Llanarmon** with rm　　🖨 🗟 🕭 rm, **P** **VISA** ⫴
⊠ LL20 7LD – ℰ (01691) 600 666 – www.thehandhotel.co.uk
**13 rm** ⊒ – ♔£ 50/70 ♔♔£ 108/128   **Rest** – Menu £ 20 – Carte £ 21/33
  ◆ Rustic, personally run inn providing a warm welcome and wholesome meals to
travellers through the lush Ceiriog Valley. Generous portions of fresh, flavoursome
cooking. Cosy bedrooms with hill views and modernised bathrooms.

**LLANDDERFEL** – Gwynedd – pop. 4 500　　　　**32** C2

⊒ London 210 mi – Cardiff 157 mi – Birmingham 97 mi – Liverpool 72 mi

🏠　**Palé Hall** ⌚　　🖨 🕭 🎝 🖫 🗟 rm, ╳ **P** **VISA** ⫴
Palé Estate – ℰ (01678) 530 285 – www.palehall.co.uk – Closed January
**15 rm** ⊒ – ♔£ 90/155 ♔♔£ 125/210 – 2 suites   **Rest** – Menu £ 25/38
  ◆ Mid-Victorian house boasting fine oil paintings and Scottish hunting lodge feel,
set in 17 acres of parkland. Beautiful wood-panelled hall and traditional lounges.
Bedrooms boast period fireplaces and antique furniture. Elegant dining room offers classical menu.

**LLANDDEWI SKIRRID** – Monmouthshire – see Abergavenny

**LLANDEILO** – Carmarthenshire – **503** I28 – pop. 1 731　　**33** B3

⊒ London 218 mi – Brecon 34 mi – Carmarthen 15 mi – Swansea 25 mi

◎ Town ★ – Dinefwr Park ★ **AC**

Ⓖ Brecon Beacons National Park ★★ – Black Mountain ★, SE : by minor roads – Carreg
Cennen Castle ★ **AC**, SE : 4 mi by A 483 and minor roads

🏠　**Plough Inn**　　⪤ 🖨 🕭 🗟 🐾 ಓ 🖫 🗟 rm, 🔟 ๙ 🛁 **P** **VISA** ⫴ **AE**
Rhosmaen, Northeast : 1 mi on A 40 ⊠ SA19 6NP – ℰ (01558) 823 431
– www.ploughrhosmaen.com – Closed 26 December
**14 rm** ⊒ – ♔£ 70 ♔♔£ 90   **Rest** – Menu £ 16/19 – Carte £ 17/25
  ◆ Powder blue building boasting contemporary interior and pleasant country
views to the rear. Modern bedrooms are spacious, comfy and well-equipped: deluxe rooms have whirlpool baths. Snacks and light lunches in the conservatory; more substantial dinners served in the vaulted restaurant.

WALES

↑ **Fronlas** without rest      🛇 📶 VISA 👁
*7 Thomas St.* ✉ *SA19 6LB –* 𝒞 *(01558) 824 733 – www.fronlas.com*
**4 rm** ⬓ – **†**£ 80/100 **††**£ 100/120
• Old Edwardian house furnished in a very contemporary, minimalist style. Smar bedrooms display funky wallpapers, bold fabrics and stylish bathrooms. They op erates a sustainable ethos with solar panels, recycling bins and organic breakfasts

---

**LLANDENNY** – Monmouthshire – **503** L28 – see Usk

---

**LLANDOVERY** – Carmarthenshire – **503** I28 – **pop. 2 235**    33 B.
▶ London 207 mi – Cardiff 61 mi – Swansea 37 mi – Merthyr Tydfil 34 mi

🏠 **New White Lion**      ⅙ rm, 🛇 📶 P VISA 👁
*43 Stone St* ✉ *SA20 0BZ –* 𝒞 *(01550) 720 685 – www.newwhitelion.co.uk*
*– Closed 25-27 December*
**6 rm** ⬓ – **†**£ 80 **††**£ 120
**Rest** – *(dinner only) (booking essential residents only)* Menu £ 28
• Laid-back, Grade II listed former pub set in a small town; now a stylish hotel Comfortable lounge with honesty bar. Smart, individually designed bedroom are named after folklore characters and boast contemporary fabrics and furnish ings. Cosy, designer dining room where menus feature local, seasonal produce.

---

**LLANDRILLO** – Denbighshire – **502** J25 – **pop. 1 048** – ✉ Corwen   32 C2
▶ London 210 mi – Chester 40 mi – Dolgellau 26 mi – Shrewsbury 46 mi

XXX **Tyddyn Llan** (Bryan Webb) with rm 🍃      🛏 ⅙ rm, 📶 P VISA 👁
✉ *LL21 0ST –* 𝒞 *(01490) 440 264 – www.tyddynllan.co.uk – Closed last 2 weeks*
🕸 *January*
**13 rm** (dinner included) ⬓ – **†**£ 150 **††**£ 300
**Rest** – *(dinner only and lunch Friday-Sunday) (booking essential)*
Menu £ 35/50 🕮
**Spec.** Dressed crab with fennel and pea shoot salad. Local pork 4 ways with shal-lot and thyme purée. Panna cotta with blood orange and Grappa.
• Personally run country house with pretty gardens. Dine in one of two spacious rooms. Menu offers considerable choice; cooking is classical in style and dishes are expertly balanced, using sensible combinations. Tidy, well-equipped bedrooms.

---

**LLANDRINDOD WELLS** – Powys – **503** J27 – **pop. 5 024**    33 C3
▶ London 204 mi – Brecon 29 mi – Carmarthen 60 mi – Shrewsbury 58 mi
🛈 Memorial Gardens 𝒞 (01597) 82 26 00, www.llandrindod.co.uk
🔢 Llandrindod Wells The Clubhouse, 𝒞 (01597) 82 38 73
🄶 Elan Valley★★ (Dol-y-Mynach and Claerwen Dam and Reservoir★★, Caban Coch Dam and Reservoir★, Garreg-ddu Viaduct★, Pen-y-Garreg Reservoir and Dam★, Craig Goch Dam and Reservoir★), NW : 12 mi by A 4081, A 470 and B 4518

🏨 **Metropole**      🛏 🖥 🀫 📶 ⅙ rm, 🄺 rest, 📶 🛀 P VISA 👁 AE
*Temple St* ✉ *LD1 5DY –* 𝒞 *(01597) 823 700 – www.metropole.co.uk*
**112 rm** ⬓ – **†**£ 82/111 **††**£ 105/125 – 2 suites
**Rest** *Radnor* – *(dinner only)* Menu £ 24 **s** – Carte £ 25/32 **s**
**Rest** *Spencer's* – Carte £ 23/28 **s**
• Brightly painted hotel run for many years by the Baird-Murray family. Some modern bedrooms, others more traditional; the tower rooms are particularly pop-ular. Swimming pool is in the Victorian-style conservatory. Dishes in formal Radnor showcase local produce. Contemporary bar and brasserie offers an all-day menu.

**at Crossgates** Northeast : 3.5 mi on A 483 – ✉ Llandrindod Wells

↑ **Guidfa House** without rest      🛏 🛇 📶 P VISA 👁
✉ *LD1 6RF –* 𝒞 *(01597) 851 241 – www.guidfahouse.co.uk*
**6 rm** ⬓ – **†**£ 65/90 **††**£ 85/95
• Georgian gentleman's residence with pleasant garden, smart breakfast room and period lounge displaying an original cast iron rose on the ceiling. Bright, airy bedrooms; the best is in the coach house. Friendly owners serve tea on arrival.

WALES

**at Howey** South : 1.5 mi by A 483 – ⊠ Llandrindod Wells

⚐ **Acorn Court Country House** without rest ⌂
*Chapel Rd, Northeast : 0.5 mi* ⊠ *LD1 5PB* – ℰ *(01597) 823 543*
*– www.acorncourt.co.uk – Closed 25-26 December*
**3 rm** ☲ – ♦£ 38/60 ♦♦£ 70/78
• Chalet-style house in 35 acres, with views over rolling countryside towards the river and lake. Welcoming owner and real family feel. Simple lounge and breakfast room; spacious, well-kept bedrooms with extras. Try the Welsh whisky porridge.

---

**LLANDUDNO** – Conwy – 502 I24 – pop. 15 250                **32 B1**

▶ London 243 mi – Birkenhead 55 mi – Chester 47 mi – Holyhead 43 mi
ℹ Mostyn St ℰ (01492) 57 75 77, www.visitllandudno.org.uk
⛳ Rhos-on-Sea Penrhyn Bay, ℰ (01492) 54 96 41
⛳ 72 Bryniau Rd West Shore, ℰ (01492) 87 53 25
⛳ Hospital Rd, ℰ (01492) 87 64 50
◉ Town★ - Pier★ B – The Great Orme★ (panorama★★, Tramway★, Ancient Copper Mines★ AC) AB
◎ Bodnant Garden★★ AC, S : 7 mi by A 470 B

Plan on next page

**WALES**

🏨 **Bodysgallen Hall** ⌂
*Southeast : 2 mi on A 470* ⊠ *LL30 1RS* – ℰ *(01492) 584 466*          VISA ⓒ AE
*– www.bodysgallen.com*
**13 rm** – ♦£ 149/349 ♦♦£ 169/425, ☲ £ 7.50 – 18 suites – ♦♦£ 220/425
**Rest *Dining Room*** – see restaurant listing
**Rest *1620*** – *(closed Sunday lunch)* Carte £ 26/32 **s**
• Stunning country house with 13C tower, surrounded by 200 acres of delightful gardens and parkland, and boasting a superb outlook to the mountains beyond. Welcoming, open-fired hall and characterful wood-panelled lounge. Antique-furnished bedrooms: some set in cottages; some affording splendid Snowdon views.

🏨 **Empire**
*73 Church Walks* ⊠ *LL30 2HE* – ℰ *(01492) 860 555* – *www.empirehotel.co.uk*
*– Closed 16-30 December*                                                Ae
**50 rm** ☲ – ♦£ 70/95 ♦♦£ 130 – 1 suite
**Rest *Watkins and Co.*** – see restaurant listing
• Family-run, Victorian hotel with grand columned façade, its interior hung with chandeliers and Russell Flint prints. Well-equipped gym and good-sized pool. Antique-furnished bedrooms feature brass or cast iron beds and have good facilities.

🏨 **Osborne House**
*17 North Par* ⊠ *LL30 2LP* – ℰ *(01492) 860 330* – *www.osbornehouse.co.uk*
*– Closed 16-30 December*                                                Ac
**8 rm** – ♦£ 150/210 ♦♦£ 150/210
**Rest *Osborne's Cafe Grill*** – see restaurant listing
• Smart townhouse overlooking the bay. All of the bedrooms are large, luxurious suites and have stunning, almost whimsical styles; they boast canopied beds, spacious sitting rooms with Victorian fireplaces and marble bathrooms with double-ended, roll-top baths.

🏨 **St Tudno**
*North Par* ⊠ *LL30 2LP* – ℰ *(01492) 874 411* – *www.st-tudno.co.uk*          Ac
**17 rm** ☲ – ♦£ 75/95 ♦♦£ 98/104 – 1 suite
**Rest *Terrace*** – see restaurant listing
• Long-standing, personally run seaside hotel, set opposite the old Victorian pier. Classical sitting room and warm bar-lounge afford bay views. Simply furnished bedrooms with mini-bars and Molton Brown toiletries; some have whirlpool baths.

## LLANDUDNO

GREAT ORME'S HEAD

HAPPY VALLEY

Toll road

GREAT ORME CABIN LIFT

GREAT ORME TRAMWAY

0 ——— 400 m
0 ——— 400 yards

VENUE CYMRU

CONWY **A 546**  **A 546** CONWY **A 470**

### Escape Boutique B&B without rest
⟨ 🛋 🍴 📶 **P** 𝗩𝗜𝗦𝗔 ⓪ 𝗔𝗘

*48 Church Walks ⊠ LL30 2HL – 𝒞 (01492) 877 776 – www.escapebandb.co.uk*
*– Closed 1 week Christmas*                                          **An**
**9 rm** 🖵 – ♟£ 73/123 ♟♟£ 88/136

♦ Attractive Arts and Crafts house with stained glass windows, parquet floors and a chic, modern interior that sets it apart. Spacious, contemporary bedrooms; the lounge is suitably stylish.

### Bryn Derwen without rest
🍴 📶 **P** 𝗩𝗜𝗦𝗔 ⓪

*34 Abbey Rd ⊠ LL30 2EE – 𝒞 (01492) 876 804 – www.bryn-derwen.co.uk*
*– February-October*                                                **Av**
**9 rm** 🖵 – ♟£ 55 ♟♟£ 92

♦ Well-run, welcoming house built in 1878 for a wealthy family. Original features remain, including an ornate pitch pine staircase. Well-appointed lounge and spacious, individually designed bedrooms. Beauty salon offers a range of treatments.

Take note of the classification: you should not expect the same level of service in a �X or 🏠 as in a XXXXX or 🏨🏨🏨.

⌂ **Lympley Lodge** without rest   &#x2709; ⚘ ⓦ **P**
*Colwyn Rd, East : 2.5 mi on B 5115* ⊠ *LL30 3AL*
*– ℰ (01492) 549 304 – www.lympleylodge.co.uk*
*– Closed mid-December-February*
**3 rm** ☲ *–* 🛏£ 55 🛏🛏£ 85
♦ Detached Victorian house close to the Little Orme headland; built in 1870 as a summer residence for a local family. Antique-filled lounge with promenade views. Individually themed bedrooms come with good extras and sea outlooks. Hearty breakfasts of local produce taken at antique tables.

⌂ **Abbey Lodge** without rest   &#x2709; ⚘ ⓦ **P**
*14 Abbey Rd* ⊠ *LL30 2EA – ℰ (01492) 878 042*
*– www.abbeylodgeuk.com – March-October*   A**x**
**4 rm** ☲ *–* 🛏£ 40 🛏🛏£ 70/75
♦ Welcoming terraced property – built in the early 1850s as a gentleman's residence. Individually decorated, pine-furnished bedrooms; all with baths. Cosy lounge and communal breakfasts from extensive menu. Pleasant rear garden boasts views up to the Great Orme.

⌂ **Sefton Court** without rest   &#x2709; ⚘ ⓦ **P** ⓥⓘⓢⓐ ⓒⓞ ⓞ
*49 Church Walks* ⊠ *LL30 2HL – ℰ (01492) 875 235*
*– www.seftoncourt-hotel.co.uk – Closed December-January*   A**n**
**10 rm** ☲ *–* 🛏£ 50/55 🛏🛏£ 72/80
♦ Substantial Victorian house in an elevated position, affording good town views. Original features include pretty stained glass windows and interesting friezes. Contemporary bedrooms provide a pleasant contrast with their stylish wallpapers.

XXX **Dining Room** – at Bodysgallen Hall Hotel   ← &#x2709; ⓚ **P** ⓥⓘⓢⓐ ⓒⓞ ⒶⒺ
*Southeast : 2 mi on A 470* ⊠ *LL30 1RS – ℰ (01492) 584 466*
*– www.bodysgallen.com – Closed Sunday dinner and Monday*
**Rest** *– (booking essential)* Menu £ 23/44
♦ Delightful, two-roomed dining room overlooking stunning gardens, located within a beautiful country house which part-dates from the 13C. Formal, classically based dishes. Smart dress required.

XX **Watkins and Co.** – at Empire Hotel   ⒶⒸ **P** ⓥⓘⓢⓐ ⓒⓞ ⒶⒺ ⓞ
*73 Church Walks* ⊠ *LL30 2HE – ℰ (01492) 860 555*
*– www.empirehotel.co.uk – Closed 16-30 December*   A**e**
**Rest** *– (dinner only and Sunday lunch)* Menu £ 22
♦ Smart dining room with wooden floor and linen-covered chairs, set on the site of a former wine merchants, in a grand, column-fronted hotel. Appealing set menu supplemented by daily specials.

XX **Terrace** – at St Tudno Hotel   ⓥⓘⓢⓐ ⓒⓞ ⒶⒺ ⓞ
*North Par* ⊠ *LL30 2LP – ℰ (01492) 874 411*
*– www.st-tudno.co.uk*   A**c**
**Rest** *–* Carte £ 27/38 **s**※
♦ Unique restaurant with murals of Lake Como running the length of the wall and chandeliers adorned with flowers. Set within a personally run seaside hotel and offering a modern, seasonal menu.

XX **Osborne's Cafe Grill** – at Osborne House Hotel   ⒶⒸ ⓔⓖ **P**
*17 North Par* ⊠ *LL30 2LP – ℰ (01492) 860 330*   ⓥⓘⓢⓐ ⓒⓞ ⒶⒺ ⓞ
*– www.osbornehouse.co.uk – Closed 16-30 December*   A**c**
**Rest** *–* Menu £ 19 *–* Carte £ 20/45
♦ All-day hotel restaurant with opulent lounge and ornate dining room boasting Corinthian columns and gilded mirrors. All-encompassing menu ranges from tasty afternoon tea to British classics.

WALES

**at Deganwy** South : 2.75 mi on A 546 - A - ✉ Llandudno

🏨 **Quay H. & Spa**    ≤ 🔲 ⓦ 🏊 Ló ▯ & ☆ ¶¶ 🍴 **P** 𝘝𝘐𝘚𝘈 ⓒⓞ 𝖠𝖤
*Deganwy Quay* ✉ *LL31 9DJ* – 𝒞 *(01492) 564 100* – *www.quayhotel.com*
**55 rm** ⌂ – ▮£ 95/145 ▮▮£ 115/215 – 19 suites
**Rest** *Grill Room* – see restaurant listing
◆ Smart hotel by the Conwy Estuary, in a modern marina development. Large guest areas have superb outlook over the harbour and castle. Extensive meeting facilities, great pool and well-run spa. Contemporary bedrooms include 3 private towers.

🍴🍴 **Grill Room** – at Quay Hotel & Spa    ≤ **P** 𝘝𝘐𝘚𝘈 ⓒⓞ 𝖠𝖤
*Deganwy Quay* ✉ *LL31 9DJ* – 𝒞 *(01492) 564 100* – *www.quayhotel.com*
**Rest** – Carte £ 11/30
◆ Stylish, nautically-themed, first-floor hotel restaurant, boasting stunning views over the harbour, castle and mountains. Extensive menu offers locally sourced meat, fish and grill dishes.

🍴 **Nikki Ip's**    𝖠𝖢 𝘝𝘐𝘚𝘈 ⓒⓞ
*57 Station Rd* ✉ *LL31 9DF* – 𝒞 *(01492) 596 611* – *www.nikkiips.com* – *Closed 25 December and 1 January*
**Rest** – Chinese – *(booking essential)* Menu £ 12/29 – Carte £ 21/35
◆ Choice of casual eatery/bar or friendly restaurant with estuary views. Dim sum and concise set menu at lunch; extensive à la carte and specials at dinner. Fresh, tasty ingredients; good flavours.

---

**LLANDWROG** – Gwynedd – **503** H24 – **see Caernarfon**

---

**LLANDYRNOG** – Denbighshire – **503** J/K24    **32** C1
▶ Cardiff 158 mi – Denbigh 7 mi – Ruthin 6 mi

🏠 **Pentre Mawr** ॐ    ≤ 🚗 🐎 ⤖ ℑ ☆ **P** 𝘝𝘐𝘚𝘈 ⓒⓞ
*North : 1.25 mi by B 5429 taking left hand fork after 0.75 mi* ✉ *LL16 4LA* – 𝒞 *(01824) 790 732* – *www.pentremawrcountryhouse.co.uk* – *Closed Christmas*
**7 rm** ⌂ – ▮£ 100/110 ▮▮£ 130/190
**Rest** – Menu £ 35
◆ Set in 200 acres. Choice of 17C farmhouse with cosy open-fired lounges, country house atmosphere and antique-furnished bedrooms; or luxury African-themed canvas lodges with private terraces and hot tubs. Dinner served in wood-floored conservatory; local ingredients a feature.

---

**LLANELLTYD** – Gwynedd – **503** I25 – **see Dolgellau**

---

**LLANERCHYMEDD** – **502** G24 – **see Anglesey (Isle of)**

---

**LLAN FFESTINIOG** – Gwynedd    **32** B2
▶ London 234 mi – Bangor 35 mi – Wrexham 52 mi
◉ Llechwedd Slate Caverns ★ **AC** N : 4 mi by A 470

🏠 **Cae'r Blaidd Country House** ॐ    ≤ 🚗 ☆ ¶¶ **P** 𝘝𝘐𝘚𝘈 ⓒⓞ
*North : 0.75 mi by A 470 on Blaenau Rd* ✉ *LL41 4PH* – 𝒞 *(01766) 762 765* – *www.caerblaidd.fsnet.co.uk* – *Closed January*
**3 rm** ⌂ – ▮£ 49 ▮▮£ 79    **Rest** – *(dinner only)* Menu £ 20 **s**
◆ Sizeable Victorian house in remote setting, boasting panoramic mountain views. Spacious guest areas; light, airy bedrooms – two with superb outlooks. Welcoming owners are mountain guides. Daily changing dishes of local produce served at large communal table.

---

**LLANFIHANGEL** – Powys – **see Llanfyllin**

WALES

## LLANFIHANGEL-Y-CREUDDYN – Ceredigion – 503 I26      33 B3

▶ London 235 mi – Cardiff 109 mi – Birmingham 121 mi – Liverpool 123 mi

### 🏠 Y Ffarmers      �cc VISA ⬤⬤
✉ SY23 4LA – ☎ (01974) 261 275 – www.yffarmers.co.uk – Closed first week
January, Monday except bank holidays and Sunday dinner
**Rest** – *(dinner only and lunch Thursday-Sunday)* Carte £ 17/29
• Life in the remote, picturesque valley revolves around this passionately run village pub, with its locals bar and homely restaurant opening onto the garden. Concise, monthly menu of satisfying, original dishes; regional and valley produce.

---

## LLANFYLLIN – Powys – 502 K25 – pop. 1 267      32 C2

▶ London 188 mi – Chester 42 mi – Shrewsbury 24 mi – Welshpool 11 mi
🄶 Pistyll Rhaeadr★, NW : 8 mi by A 490, B 4391, B 4580 and minor roads

### 🍴 Seeds      VISA ⬤⬤
5 Penybryn Cottages, High St ✉ SY22 5AP – ☎ (01691) 648 604 – Closed
Monday
**Rest** – *(restricted opening in winter)* Menu £ 28 (dinner) – Carte lunch £ 20/33
• Converted 16C red-brick cottages in sleepy town, run by hands-on husband and wife team. Simple, rustic interior featuring old kitchen range; matched by unfussy, flavoursome, classical dishes.

**at Llanfihangel** Southwest : 5 mi by A 490 and B 4393 on B 4382 – ✉ Llanfyllin

### 🏠 Cyfie Farm ⚜      ⬅ �cc 🕭 🕅 🕱 🕮 P VISA ⬤⬤ AE ⓞ
South : 1.5 mi by B 4382 ✉ SY22 5JE – ☎ (01691) 648 451
– www.cyfiefarm.co.uk – March-October
**4 rm** ⬚ – ♦£ 90 ♦♦£ 130    **Rest** – Menu £ 28
• 17C longhouse and barn conversions, set in a great spot and boasting far-reaching views across the Meifod Valley. Mix of bedrooms and self-catering cottages; some with beams and wood-burning stoves. Spacious lounges and communal dining room, with porridge cooked overnight on the Aga and cordon bleu dinners.

---

## LLANGAMMARCH WELLS – Powys – 503 J27      33 B3

▶ London 200 mi – Brecon 17 mi – Builth Wells 8 mi – Cardiff 58 mi

### 🏨 Lake Country House and Spa ⚜      ⬅ 🚗 🕭 🕲 🖼 📺 🕱 ✄ 🍴
East : 0.75 mi ✉ LD4 4BS – ☎ (01591)    🖼 ♿ rm, 🍴 🛁 P VISA ⬤⬤ AE ⓞ
620 202 – www.lakecountryhouse.co.uk
**22 rm** ⬚ – ♦£ 220 ♦♦£ 270 – 8 suites
**Rest** – *(booking essential)* Menu £ 24/39⚛
• Extended, part-timbered 19C country house, in 50 acres of mature gardens and parkland, with a pond, lake and river. Comfy lounges and well-appointed bedrooms with antiques and extras; some set in the lodge. Impressive spa overlooks the river. Personally run, with excellent service. Breakfasts in the orangery; elegant restaurant for classical, candlelit dinners.

---

## LLANGOLLEN – Denbighshire – 502 K25 – pop. 3 093      32 C2

▶ London 194 mi – Chester 23 mi – Holyhead 76 mi – Shrewsbury 30 mi
🄸 Castle St ☎ (01978) 86 08 28, www.llangollen.org
🄵 Vale of Llangollen Holyhead Rd, ☎ (01978) 86 09 06
◎ Town★ - Railway★ **AC** - Plas Newydd★ **AC**
🄶 Pontcysyllte Aqueduct★★, E : 4 mi by A 539 - Castell Dinas Bran★, N : by footpath
– Valle Crucis Abbey★ **AC**, N : 2 mi by A 542. Chirk Castle★★ **AC** (wrought iron
gates★), SE : 7.5 mi by A 5 – Rug Chapel★ **AC**, W : 11 mi by A 5 and A 494

WALES

**Gales**  🛋 ⌖ ⛲ 🖺 **P** VISA ◎ AE ①

*18 Bridge St ✉ LL20 8PF – ℰ (01978) 860 089 – www.galesofllangollen.co.uk*
*– Closed 24 December-2 January*
**15 rm** – 🛏£ 60 🛏🛏£ 80, ⌷ £ 5
**Rest** – *(closed Sunday dinner)* Carte £ 17/29
• Pair of family-run, brick-built townhouses with characterful wine theme throughout. Spacious beamed bedrooms boast modern bathrooms and complimentary port. Below are a wine/kitchenware shop and atmospheric wood-panelled wine bar with wide-ranging blackboard menu.

---

## LLANGRANNOG – Ceredigion – 503 G27          33 B3

▶ London 241 mi – Caerdydd / Cardiff 96 mi – Aberystwyth / Aberyswyth 30 mi – Caerfyrddin / Carmarthen 28 mi

**Grange** without rest 🍃  🚗 **P**

*Pentregat, Southeast : 3 mi by B 4321 on A 487 ✉ SA44 6HW – ℰ (01239) 654 121 – www.grangecountryhouse.co.uk*
**4 rm** ⌷ – 🛏£ 45/55 🛏🛏£ 75/85
• Originally the manor house of the adjacent estate. Traditionally furnished guest areas; afternoon tea from real silver teapot on arrival. Well-maintained bedrooms boast roll-top baths.

---

## LLANGYBI – Monmouthshire – 503 L29 – see Usk

---

## LLANLLAWDDOG – Carmarthenshire – see Carmarthen

---

## LLANOVER – Monmouthshire – see Abergavenny

---

## LLANRHIDIAN – Swansea – 503 H29 – see Swansea

---

## LLANSANFFRAID GLAN CONWY – Conwy – 502 I24 – see Conwy

---

## LLANUWCHLLYN – Gwynedd – 503 I/J25          32 B2

▶ Cardiff 147 mi – Dolgellau 13 mi – Llangollen 27 mi

**Eifionydd** without rest  ≤ 🚗 ⌖ 🏠 **P** VISA ◎

*✉ LL23 7UB – ℰ (01678) 540 622 – www.visitbala.com – March-October*
**4 rm** ⌷ – 🛏£ 40/70 🛏🛏£ 70/100
• Comfortable guesthouse located in a small hamlet and boasting beautiful rear views across a stream to the mountains beyond. Pleasant sun lounge, conservatory and breakfast room. Immaculately kept, individually decorated bedrooms with compact, modern bathrooms.

---

## LLANWRTYD WELLS – Powys – 503 J27 – pop. 649          33 B3

▶ London 214 mi – Brecon 32 mi – Cardiff 68 mi – Carmarthen 39 mi
ℹ The Square ℰ (01591) 61 06 66, www.llanwrtyd.com
◉ Abergwesyn-Tregaron Mountain Road★, NW : 19 mi on minor roads

**Lasswade Country House**  ≤ 🚗 🔧 ⌖ 🏠 **P** VISA ◎ AE

*Station Rd ✉ LD5 4RW – ℰ (01591) 610 515 – www.lasswadehotel.co.uk*
**8 rm** ⌷ – 🛏£ 65/80 🛏🛏£ 80/120
**Rest** – *(dinner only)* Menu £ 35
• Keenly run, detached Edwardian house, close to town, with book-filled lounge and conservatory breakfast room. Comfortable, uncluttered bedrooms come in light hues and boast pleasant countryside views. Concise menu features their own hot-smoked salmon, Elan Valley mutton and sustainable local produce.

XX  **Carlton Riverside** with rm                                    ¶⁰ _VISA_ ◯◯
*Irfon Cres* ⊠ *LD5 4SP –* ℰ *(01591) 610 248 – www.carltonriverside.com*
*– Closed 22-30 December and Sunday*
**5 rm** ⊒ – ♦£ 50/75 ♦♦£ 100
**Rest** – *(dinner only)* Menu £ 25 – Carte approx. £ 40
♦ Traditional stone building in the centre of the village, overlooking the River Irfon. Two comfy lounges and small bar filled with books and modern art; well-
spaced tables in the dining room. Two set menus and elaborate à la carte utilise
local produce. Courteous service. Simple, well-priced bedrooms.

---

**LLYSWEN** – Powys – 503 K27 – ⊠ Brecon                              33 C3
▶ London 188 mi – Brecon 8 mi – Cardiff 48 mi – Worcester 53 mi
◻ Brecon Beacons National Park★★

🏛🏛🏛  **Llangoed Hall** ⧈              ⇐ ⊜ 🕭 ⟍ ⅌ ¶⁰ ⅍ P _VISA_ ◯◯ AE
*Northwest : 1.25 mi on A 470* ⊠ *LD3 0YP –* ℰ *(01874) 754 525*
*– www.llangoedhall.com*
**23 rm** ⊒ – ♦£ 175/205 ♦♦£ 195/225
**Rest** – *(booking essential for non-residents)* Menu £ 25/45 **s**
♦ Homely country house by the River Wye, built by Sir Clough Williams-Ellis
and restored by the late Sir Bernard and Laura Ashley. Spacious rooms mix period
and modern furnishings. Impressive art collection includes Whistler. Restaurant
serves classical dishes with a modern edge.

---

**MACHYNLLETH** – Powys – 503 I26 – pop. 2 147                        32 B2
▶ London 220 mi – Shrewsbury 56 mi – Welshpool 37 mi
🛈 Penrallt St ℰ (01654) 70 24 01, www.ukinformationcentre.com/central-wales
◻ Felingerrig, ℰ (01654) 70 20 00
◉ Town★ - Celtica★ **AC**
◻ Snowdonia National Park★★★ - Centre for Alternative Technology★★ **AC**,
  N : 3 mi by A 487

🏛  **Ynyshir Hall** ⧈                         ⇐ ⊜ 🕭 P _VISA_ ◯◯ AE
*Eglwysfach, Southwest : 6 mi on A 487* ⊠ *SY20 8TA –* ℰ *(01654) 781 209*
*– www.ynyshir-hall.co.uk*
**6 rm** ⊒ – ♦£ 205/335 ♦♦£ 295/345 – 3 suites
**Rest** – *(closed lunch Monday and Tuesday) (booking essential)* Menu £ 25/73
♦ Part-Georgian house set within 1,000 acre RSPB reserve. Bright, individually ap-
pointed bedrooms, cosy drawing room with art, antiques and Welsh pottery.
Charming and very attentive service. Intimate and comfortable dining room.

---

**MENAI BRIDGE** – 502 H24 – see Anglesey (Isle of)

---

**MOLD (Yr Wyddgrug)** – Flintshire – 502 K24 – pop. 9 568           32 C1
▶ London 211 mi – Chester 12 mi – Liverpool 22 mi – Shrewsbury 45 mi
🛈 Earl Rd ℰ (01352) 75 93 31, www.visitmold.com
◻ Pantmwyn Clicain Rd, ℰ (01352) 74 03 18
◻ Old Padeswood Station Rd, Old Padeswood, ℰ (01244) 54 77 01
◻ Padeswood & Buckley Station Lane, The Caia, ℰ (01244) 55 05 37
◻ Caerwys, ℰ (01352) 72 12 22
◉ St Mary's Church★

🏠  **Tower** without rest ⧈               ⇐ ⊜ 🕭 ⟍ P _VISA_ ◯◯ AE
*Nercwys, South : 1 mi by B 5444, Nercwys rd on Treuddyn rd* ⊠ *CH7 4EW*
*–* ℰ *(01352) 700 220 – www.towerwales.co.uk – March-November*
**3 rm** ⊒ – ♦£ 90 ♦♦£ 120
♦ Impressive fortified house with pond and extensive grounds, dating from 1465
and in family almost as long. Huge high-ceilinged bedrooms boast character
beds, antiques and vast modern showers.

WALES

WALES

✗ **56 High Street**                                      VISA ⦿

*56 High St. ⊠ CH7 1BD – 𝒞 (01352) 759 225 – www.56highst.co.uk – Closed 1 January, Sunday and Monday*
**Rest** – Menu £ 15/18 – Carte £ 28/40
• Intimate neighbourhood restaurant in busy market town, run by brother and sister. Extensive menus evolve over time. Dishes range from classical to modern, with a focus on sustainable seafood.

🍺 **Glasfryn**                              🚗 🌳 **P** VISA ⦿ AE

*Raikes Ln, Sychdyn, North : 1 mi by A 5119 on Civic Centre rd (Theatr Clwyd) ⊠ CH7 6LR – 𝒞 (01352) 750 500 – www.glasfryn-mold.co.uk – Closed 25 December*
**Rest** – Carte £ 22/33
• Sizeable red-brick pub with Arts and Crafts styling and pleasant town outlook. Menu offers plenty of choice from pub to culinary classics. Portions are generous and service is swift.

---

**MONMOUTH** (Trefynwy) – Monmouthshire – **503** L28 – pop. 8 547        **33** C4
🚩 London 135 mi – Abergavenny 19 mi – Cardiff 40 mi
◉ Town ★

**at Whitebrook** South : 8.25 mi by A 466 – ⊠ Monmouth

✗✗✗ **Crown at Whitebrook** with rm ⤾         🚗 AC rm, ⁽ᵗ⁾ **P** VISA ⦿ AE
£3      ⊠ NP25 4TX – 𝒞 (01600) 860 254 – www.crownatwhitebrook.co.uk – Closed 2 weeks Christmas
**8 rm** ⌂ – †£ 90/120 ††£ 135/170    **Rest** – (booking essential) Menu £ 30/50
**Spec.** Grey mullet, smoked eel, avocado and shiso. Loin of wild rabbit, almond, gingerbread and pear. Banana bread with walnuts and condensed milk.
• Attentively run by smart, personable staff. Lounge bar with deep leather sofas and immaculately laid dining room. The kitchen effectively employs modern techniques to produce original, flavoursome dishes. Smart bedrooms in contemporary colours.

**at Rockfield** Northwest : 2.5 mi on B 4233 – ⊠ Monmouth

✗ **Stonemill**                                   🚗 🌳 **P** VISA ⦿

*West : 1 mi on B 4233 ⊠ NP25 5SW – 𝒞 (01600) 716 273 – www.thestonemill.co.uk – Closed 2 weeks January, 25-26 December, Sunday dinner and Monday*
**Rest** – Menu £ 16/20 – Carte £ 21/33
• Converted 16C stone cider mill with exposed timbers, and leather sofa in sitting area/bar. Attentive service. Well-sourced modern seasonal dishes feature produce from small local suppliers.

---

**MONTGOMERY** (Trefaldwyn) – Powys – **503** K26 – pop. 1 059        **32** C2
🚩 London 194 mi – Birmingham 71 mi – Chester 53 mi – Shrewsbury 30 mi
◉ Town ★

✗✗ **The Checkers** (Stéphane Borie) with rm           🌳 ⁽ᵗ⁾ VISA ⦿
£3      *Broad St ⊠ SY15 6PN – 𝒞 (01686) 669 822 – www.thecheckersmontgomery.co.uk – Closed 2 weeks January, 1 week autumn, 25 December, Sunday and Monday*
**3 rm** – †£ 85/110 ††£ 95/150    **Rest** – Carte £ 28/40 **s**
**Spec.** Cheddar cheese soufflé with roasted red peppers. Pork belly with roasted pear, creamed potato and braising jus. Lemon crème brûlée with candied ginger ice cream.
• Charming 18C former coaching inn, set in the main square of a hilltop town. Spacious panelled bar and lounge; stylish restaurant opens onto a terrace. Monthly changing menus of classical dishes that are executed with a deft touch; flavours are sharply defined. Elegant, antique-furnished bedrooms.

**NANTGAREDIG** – Carmarthenshire – **503** H28 – see Carmarthen

**NANT-Y-DERRY** – Monmouthshire – see Abergavenny

Guesthouses ⋔ don't provide the same level of service as hotels. They are often characterised by a warm welcome and a décor which reflects the owner's personality. Those shown in red ⋔ are particularly pleasant.

**NARBERTH** – Pembrokeshire – **503** F28 – pop. 1 869                    **33** A4

▶ London 234 mi – Cardiff 88 mi – Swansea 51 mi – Rhondda 79 mi

**Grove** ⧸        ≤ ⇌ ⏃ ⏾ ⚙ ᵗᵖ **P** 𝒱𝒾𝒮𝒜 ⓪ 𝔸𝔼
*Molleston, South : 2 mi by A 478 on Herons Brook rd* ⊠ *SA67 8BX –* ℰ *(01834) 860 915 – www.thegrove-narberth.co.uk*
**9 rm** ⧖ – †£ 200/260 ††£ 210/270 – 3 suites
**Rest** – *(booking essential at lunch)* Menu £ 23/40 **s**
♦ Part-Stuart, part-Victorian house and adjacent 15C longhouse, set in a charming rural location. Bedrooms blend boldly coloured walls and fabrics with traditional furnishings; spacious bathrooms boast every modern amenity. Seasonal menus offer creative, modern dishes with a classical base.

⋔  **Canaston Oaks** without rest        ⇌ ⏃ ⅋ ⚙ ᵗᵖ **P** 𝒱𝒾𝒮𝒜 ⓪
*Canaston Bridge, West : 3 mi by B 4314 and A 40 on A 4075* ⊠ *SA67 8DE* – ℰ *(01437) 541 254 – www.canastonoaks.co.uk*
**7 rm** ⧖ – †£ 90 ††£ 125
♦ Converted longhouse and outbuildings set in 35 acres of gardens and grasslands leading down to the river. Set around a courtyard water feature, wood-furnished bedrooms boast fridges and DVD players; some have jacuzzis, others, patio areas.

**NEWPORT** – Newport – **503** L29 – pop. 116 143                    **33** C4

▶ London 145 mi – Bristol 31 mi – Cardiff 12 mi – Gloucester 48 mi

🛈 John Frost Sq ℰ (01633) 84 29 62, www.newport.gov.uk

🛈 Caerleon Broadway, ℰ (01633) 42 03 42

🛈 Parc Coedkernew Church Lane, ℰ (01633) 68 09 33

👁 Museum and Art Gallery★ AX **M** - Transporter Bridge★ **AC** AY - Civic Centre (murals★) AX

🕌 Caerleon Roman Fortress★★ **AC** (Fortress Baths★ - Legionary Museum★ - Amphitheatre★), NE : 2.5 mi by B 4596 AX – Tredegar House★★ (Grounds★ - Stables★), SW : 2.5 mi by A 48 AY. Penhow Castle★, E : 8 mi by A 48 AX

🏨🏨🏨 **Celtic Manor Resort**        ≤ ⏃ 🖥 ⊕ ⏃ ᵗᵖ ♨ ᐟ 🎾 🖼 ▯ ⅋ 🛗 rm, 🏊 𝔸𝒞 ⚙ ᵗᵖ
*Coldra Woods, East : 3 mi on A 48* ⊠ *NP18 1HQ*        🄰 **P** 𝒱𝒾𝒮𝒜 ⓪ 𝔸𝔼 ⓪
– ℰ *(01633) 413 000 – www.celtic-manor.com*
**315 rm** – †£ 268/1500 ††£ 268/1500, ⧖ £ 17.95 – 19 suites
**Rest** *Crown at Celtic Manor*
**Rest** *Rafters* – see restaurant listing
**Rest** *Olive Tree* – Buffet – *(dinner only and Sunday lunch)* Menu £ 33 **s**
**Rest** *Patio* – French – *(dinner only)* Carte £ 24/56 **s**
♦ Vast resort hotel in 1,400 acres, boasting 3 golf courses, an impressive pool and spa, two floors of function rooms and even a shopping arcade. Classical bedrooms range from standard to presidential suites and boast smart marble bathrooms. Modern fine dining in The Crown, grills in Rafters, buffet and carvery in main restaurant Olive Tree, French bistro menu in Patio.

WALES

XXX **Crown at Celtic Manor** – at Celtic Manor Resort Hotel    🔊 🏧 **P**

*Coldra Woods, East : 3 mi on A 48* ✉ *NP18 1HQ*    VISA ⦿ AE ①
– 𝒞 *(01633) 413 000 – www.celtic-manor.com*
– *Closed Sunday and Monday*
**Rest** – Menu £ 50 **s**

♦ Set within a huge resort hotel, a contemporary fine dining restaurant with dedicated bar. Modern cooking; express lunch contrasts with more elaborate and pricier tasting and à la carte menus.

X **Chandlery**    VISA ⦿ AE ①

*77-78 Lower Dock St* ✉ *NP20 1EH*
– 𝒞 *(01633) 256 622 – www.thechandleryrestaurant.com*
– *Closed Sunday dinner and Monday*    AY**a**
**Rest** – Menu £ 18 (lunch)
– Carte £ 28/41

♦ 18C former chandlery near the river, with cosy bar, lounge and dining room downstairs, and airy, antique-furnished restaurant above. Good value set lunch and daily offers; adventurous à la carte and 6 course tasting menu. Regular events.

X **Rafters** – at Celtic Manor Resort Hotel    🔊 🏧 **P** VISA ⦿ AE

*Coldra Woods, East : 3 mi on A 48* ✉ *NP18 1HQ*
– 𝒞 *(01633) 413 000 – www.celtic-manor.com*
**Rest** – Carte £ 27/51 **s**

♦ Modern restaurant with solid cedar wood beams, set in the clubhouse of a sizeable resort hotel. Serves breakfast, lunch, snacks and wide selection of steaks at dinner. Smart-casual dress code.

---

**NEWPORT** (Trefdraeth) – **Pembrokeshire** – **503** F27 – **pop. 1 162**    **33** A3

▶ London 258 mi – Fishguard 7 mi
🅸 Long St 𝒞 (01239) 82 09 12, www.newport-pembs.co.uk
🅶 Newport Links, 𝒞 (01239) 82 02 44
🅶 Pembrokeshire Coast National Park★★

🏠 **Cnapan**    🚗 🖓 🛰 **P** VISA ⦿

*East St, on A 487* ✉ *SA42 0SY*
– 𝒞 *(01239) 820 575 – www.cnapan.co.uk*
– *Closed 25-26 December and January-mid-March*
**5 rm** ☐ – ♥£ 54 ♥♥£ 88
**Rest** – *(closed Tuesday) (dinner only) (booking essential)* Menu £ 34

♦ Keenly run, well-maintained, part-Georgian house with traditionally furnished lounge and bar. Fresh, compact bedrooms with white walls, coloured throws and slightly old-fashioned feel. Candlelit restaurant opens onto spacious garden and offers extensive home-cooked menu.

XX **Llys Meddyg** with rm    🚗 🛰 **P** VISA ⦿ ①

*East St* ✉ *SA42 0SY* – 𝒞 *(01239) 820 008 – www.llysmeddyg.com*
– *Closed 1 week January, 1 week November, Sunday except bank holiday weekends and Monday*
**8 rm** ☐ – ♥£ 70/85 ♥♥£ 100/180
**Rest** – *(booking essential at lunch)* Menu £ 33

♦ Centrally located restaurant with kitchen garden behind. Eat in the formal dining room or characterful, laid-back cellar bar; the owner's father's art is displayed throughout. Simple, classical lunches and more innovative, modern dinners. Contemporary, Scandinavian-style bedrooms are located in the annexe.

## NEWTOWN – Powys – **503** K26 – pop. 10 358 – ⊠ Blaenau Gwent    **32** C2

▶ London 194 mi – Cardiff 98 mi – Birmingham 81 mi – Wolverhampton 69 mi

↑ **Highgate** without rest 🌲    ≤ 🚗 ⟡ 🌸 ⁋ **P.** **VISA** **CO** **AE** **①**
*Bettws Cedewain, Northeast : 2.5 mi by B 4568 off B 4389* ⊠ *SY16 3LF*
*– 𝒞 (01686) 623 763 – www.highgatebandb.co.uk. – Closed Christmas-New Year*
**4 rm** 🖵 – ♦£ 45/55 ♦♦£ 90
• Timbered farmhouse built in 1631, with colourful gardens, stables for your
horse and superb views across rolling fields. Tastefully furnished, it boasts good-
sized bedrooms and a warm, welcoming feel. Homemade breads and preserves
feature at breakfast.

## OLD RADNOR (Pencraig) – Powys – **503** J27 – pop. 400    **33** C3

▶ London 180 mi – Cardiff 81 mi – Birmingham 86 mi – Liverpool 121 mi

🍴 **Harp Inn** with rm    ≤ 🍴 **P.** **VISA** **CO**
⊠ *LD8 2RH – 𝒞 (01544) 350 655 – www.harpinnradnor.co.uk – Closed Monday*
*except bank holidays and restricted opening in winter*
**5 rm** 🖵 – ♦£ 50/55 ♦♦£ 80/85
**Rest** – *(dinner only and lunch Saturday-Sunday)* Carte £ 22/28
• 15C stone inn that welcomes its drinkers and diners alike. Charming, flag-
floored, open-fired inner, its beams hung with hop bines; glorious views from the
terrace. 'Seasonality' and 'sustainability' are key; menus are concise but original.

## PARKMILL – Swansea – **503** H29 – see Swansea

## PEMBROKE (Penfro) – Pembrokeshire – **503** F28 – pop. 7 214    **33** A4

▶ London 252 mi – Carmarthen 32 mi – Fishguard 26 mi
**Access** Cleddau Bridge (toll)
🛳 to Republic of Ireland (Rosslare) (Irish Ferries) 2 daily (4 h) – to Republic of Ireland
(Cork) (Swansea Cork Ferries) daily (8 h 30 mn)
🇮 Commons Rd 𝒞 (01646) 62 23 88, www.pembrokeshire.gov.uk
🏌 Pembroke Dock Military Rd, 𝒞 (01646) 62 14 53
◉ Town ★★ - Castle ★★ **AC**
🖲 Pembrokeshire Coast National Park ★★ - Carew Castle ★ **AC**, NE : 4 mi by A 4075.
Bosherston (St Govan's Chapel ★), S : 7 mi by B 4319 and minor roads – Stack
Rocks ★, SW : 9 mi by B 4319 and minor roads

↑ **Poyerston Farm** without rest    🚗 ⁋ **P.**
*Cosheston, Northeast : 2.75 mi by A 4075 on A 477* ⊠ *SA72 4SJ*
*– 𝒞 (01646) 651 347 – www.poyerstonfarm.co.uk – February-October*
**3 rm** 🖵 – ♦£ 45/55 ♦♦£ 70/80
• Victorian farmhouse with well-tended gardens, on a working dairy farm in 220
acres. Intimate breakfast room, airy conservatory and cosy lounge. Immaculate
bedrooms with light oak furnishings and extras. Warm welcome from experienced owner.

**at Lamphey** East : 1.75 mi on A 4139 – ⊠ Pembroke

🏠 **Lamphey Court** 🌲    🚗 ⟡ 🖵 🌐 🌀 ⅃𝈓 ✗ ⟡ ⁋ 🖧 **P.** **VISA** **CO** **AE** **①**
⊠ *SA71 5NT – 𝒞 (01646) 672 273 – www.lampheycourt.co.uk*
**39 rm** 🖵 – ♦£ 88/100 ♦♦£ 110/160
**Rest** – Menu £ 28
• Large Georgian mansion surrounded by parkland, built by Charles Mathias in
an idyllic location. Well-furnished throughout with fine mahogany in the coordi-
nated bedrooms. Formal restaurant with a good country house style menu.

WALES

**PENARTH** – The Vale of Glamorgan – **503** K29 – see Cardiff

---

**PENMACHNO** – Conwy – **502** I24 – see Betws-y-Coed

---

**PONTDOLGOCH** – Powys – see Caersws

---

**PORTHCAWL** – Bridgend – **503** I29 – pop. 15 640      **33** B4
- London 183 mi – Cardiff 28 mi – Swansea 18 mi
- John St ℰ (01656) 78 66 39, www.bridgend.gov.uk
- Glamorgan Heritage Coast★

⌂    **Foam Edge** without rest        ⪕ ⁒ ⁒ **P**
     9 West Dr ⊠ CF36 3LS – ℰ (01656) 782 866 – www.foam-edge.co.uk
     – Closed 25 December
     **3 rm** � – †£ 40/70 ††£ 90
     ♦ Unassuming house by the promenade masks stylish, modern interior with superb Bristol Channel views. A family home in essence, with comfy lounge and communal breakfast. Bedrooms in pastel hues.

---

**PORTMEIRION** – Gwynedd – **502** H25      **32** B2
- London 245 mi – Caernarfon 23 mi – Colwyn Bay 40 mi – Dolgellau 24 mi
- Village★★★ **AC**
- Snowdonia National Park★★★ - Lleyn Peninsula★★ – Ffestiniog Railway★★ **AC**

🏨    **Portmeirion**        ⪕ ⌂ ⌂ ⌂ ⁒ ⁒ ⌂ **P** 𝗩𝗜𝗦𝗔 ⚬⚬ 𝖠𝖤 ⓪
     ⊠ LL48 6ET – ℰ (01766) 770 000 – www.portmerion-village.com
     **28 rm** (dinner included) ⊠ – †£ 100/216 ††£ 145/279 – 14 suites
     **Rest** – (booking essential for non-residents) Menu £ 40
     – Carte £ 24/38
     ♦ Unique Italianate village built on a private peninsula and boasting wonderful estuary views: the life work of Sir Clough Williams-Ellis. Appealing 1930s hotel and snug, well-appointed bedrooms spread about the village. Dining room features lovely parquet floor.

🏨    **Castell Deudraeth**        ⪕ ⌂ ⌂ 🛏 𝖠𝖢 rest, ⁒ ⌂ ⌂ **P** 𝗩𝗜𝗦𝗔 ⚬⚬ 𝖠𝖤
     ⊠ LL48 6EN – ℰ (01766) 772 400 – www.portmeirion-village.com
     **9 rm** ⊠ – †£ 180/250 ††£ 215/285 – 2 suites
     **Rest** Grill – Carte £ 27/58
     ♦ Impressive crenellated manor house displaying original stone fireplace. Relaxed, informal atmosphere; fine Snowdonia views. Huge bedrooms boast chic, contemporary décor and kitchen areas. Choose from brasserie classics in conservatory or pleasant walled garden.

> Large towns and cities include detailed plans locating hotels and restaurants.
> Use the given coordinates (ex.: **12**BMe) to find them easily.

---

**PWLLGLOYW** – Powys – see Brecon

---

**PWLLHELI** – Gwynedd – **502** G25 – pop. 3 861      **32** B2
- London 261 mi – Aberystwyth 73 mi – Caernarfon 21 mi
- Station Sq ℰ (01758) 61 30 00, www.ukinformationcentre.com/north-wales
- Golf Rd, ℰ (01758) 70 16 44
- Lleyn Peninsula★★

828

XX **Plas Bodegroes** with rm ☜  ☐ **P** VISA ⚫
*Northwest : 1.75 mi on A 497* ✉ *LL53 5TH* – ℰ *(01758) 612 363*
– *www.bodegroes.co.uk* – *March-November*
**10 rm** ☐ – ♦♦£ 110 ♦♦♦£ 180
**Rest** – *(closed Monday except bank holidays) (dinner only and Sunday lunch)*
*(booking essential)* Menu £ 20/45☷
• Delightful Grade II listed Georgian house in secluded gardens. Local art dec-
orates the pale green dining room. Classically based cooking, using good quality
local ingredients. Contemporary, Scandinavian-style bedrooms.

**at Boduan** Northwest : 3.75 mi on A 497 – ✉ Pwllheli

↑ **Old Rectory** without rest ☜  ☐ ❄ 📶 **P** VISA ⚫
✉ *LL53 6DT* – ℰ *(01758) 721 519* – *www.theoldrectory.net* – *Closed Christmas*
**3 rm** ☐ – ♦£ 75/95 ♦♦£ 85/110
• Lovely part-Georgian family home with paddock, run by charming owner.
Comfy lounge with carved wooden fireplace; cakes on arrival. Tasteful bedrooms
boast period furnishings and garden views.

**RHOSCOLYN** – **503** G24 – see Anglesey (Isle of)

**RHOS-ON-SEA** = Llandrillo-yn-Rhos – Conwy – **502** I24 – see Colwyn Bay

**RHYL** – Denbighshire – **502** J24 – pop. 24 889                                    **32** C1
▶ Cardiff 182 mi – Chester 34 mi – Llandudno 18 mi
ⓒ Rhuddlan Castle★★, S : 3 mi by A 525 – Bodelwyddan★★, S : 5 mi by A 525 and
minor rd – St Asaph Cathedral★, S : 5 mi by A 525. Llandudno★, W : 16 mi by A
548, A 55 and B 5115

XX **Barratt's at Ty'n Rhyl** with rm  ☐ 📶 **P** VISA ⚫
*167 Vale Rd., South : 0.5 mi on A 525* ✉ *LL18 2PH* – ℰ *(01745) 344 138*
– *www.barrattsoftynrhyl.co.uk*
**3 rm** ☐ – ♦£ 70 ♦♦£ 95
**Rest** – *(dinner only and Sunday lunch) (booking essential)* Carte approx. £ 39
• Rhyl's oldest house boasts comfortable lounges with rich oak panelling. Dine in
either the conservatory or original house. Ambitious cooking displays a classic
base. Bedrooms are individually designed.

**ROCKFIELD** – Monmouthshire – **503** L28 – see Monmouth

**ROWEN** – Conwy – see Conwy

**RUTHIN** (Rhuthun) – Denbighshire – **502** K24 – pop. 5 218                      **32** C1
▶ London 210 mi – Birkenhead 31 mi – Chester 23 mi – Liverpool 34 mi
◨ Ruthin-Pwllglas, ℰ (01824) 70 22 96
ⓒ Llandyrnog (St Dyfnog's Church★), Llanrhaeder-yng-Nghinmeirch (Jesse
Window★★), N : 5.5 mi by A 494 and B 5429. Denbigh★, NW : 7 mi on A 525

↑ **Firgrove**  ❄ 📶 **P** VISA ⚫
⌂ *Llanfwrog, West : 1.25 mi by A 494 on B 5105* ✉ *LL15 2LL* – ℰ *(01824) 702 677*
– *www.firgrovecountryhouse.co.uk* – *February-November*
**3 rm** ☐ – ♦£ 60 ♦♦£ 90    **Rest** – Menu £ 35
• Attractive stone-built house set in stunning gardens. Sit in the snug by the cosy
inglenook fireplace in winter or in the delightful glasshouse in summer. Two comfortable four-poster bedrooms and a self-contained cottage offer valley pleasant
views. Communal, home-cooked dinners showcase locally sourced farm produce.

WALES

↑↑ **Eyarth Station** without rest ♨  ← 🚗 ⌛ ⁇ 🅿 VISA ⓸
*Llanfair Dyffryn Clwyd, South : 1.75 mi by A 525* ✉ *LL15 2EE*
– ℰ *(01824) 703 643 – www.eyarthstation.co.uk – February-December*
**6 rm** ⌛ – †£ 50/80 ††£ 75/80
♦ Former railway station: platform at heart of house, tracks under conservatory.
Simple pine-furnished bedrooms feature railway memorabilia. Panoramic windows in lounge afford great rural views.

XX **Manorhaus** with rm  🏠 ⁇ 🛁 ⁇ VISA ⓸ AE
*Well St* ✉ *LL15 1AH –* ℰ *(01824) 704 830 – www.manorhaus.com*
**8 rm** ⌛ – †£ 68/98 ††£ 90/145
**Rest** – *(dinner only and lunch Saturday-Sunday)* Menu £ 35
♦ Boutique restaurant and gallery in 17C townhouse, displaying frequently
changing Bauhaus art. Chic lounge and modern conservatory dining room laid
with designer tableware. Seasonal, country-style menu and modern presentation.
Snug bedrooms boast good facilities.

X **On the Hill**  VISA ⓸ AE
*1 Upper Clwyd St* ✉ *LL15 1HY –* ℰ *(01824) 707 736*
– *www.onthehillrestaurant.co.uk – Closed last 2 weeks January, last 2 weeks
September, 1 week May, Sunday, Monday and lunch Tuesday*
**Rest** – *(booking essential)* Menu £ 15 *(lunch)* – Carte dinner £ 21/31
♦ Immensely charming 16C house located in a busy market town, and boasting
characterful sloping floors, exposed beams and buzzy, bistro atmosphere. Accessible menu of keenly priced, internationally influenced classics. A real family
business.

**ST ASAPH** – Denbighshire – **503** J24 – pop. 3 491  **32 C1**
▶ London 223 mi – Cardiff 176 mi – Liverpool 46 mi – Manchester 69 mi

↑↑ **Tan-yr-Onnen**  🚗 ⅙ rm, ⁇ 🅿 VISA ⓸
*Waen, East : 1.5 mi by A 55 and B 5429 on Tremeirchion rd* ✉ *LL17 0DU*
– ℰ *(01745) 583 821 – www.northwalesbreaks.co.uk – Closed 25-26 December*
**6 rm** ⌛ – †£ 69 ††£ 125  **Rest** – Menu £ 29
♦ Spacious house with large rear garden filled with trees and shrubs. Immaculately kept bedrooms are of a good size and well-equipped; three of them have
their own sitting rooms. Large conservatory and lounge also offer plenty of seating. Full Welsh breakfasts and homely dinners served in pleasant dining room.

**ST CLEARS** – Carmarthenshire – **503** G28 – pop. 1 587  **33 B3**
▶ London 221 mi – Cardiff 76 mi – Swansea 37 mi – Llanelli 33 mi

↑↑ **Coedllys Country House** without rest ♨  ← 🚗 ⅛ ⁇ ⁇ 🅿 VISA ⓸
*Llangynin, Northwest : 3.5 mi by A 40 turning first left after 30 mph sign on
entering village.* ✉ *SA33 4JY –* ℰ *(01994) 231 455*
– *www.coedllyscountryhouse.co.uk – Closed 23-27 December*
**4 rm** ⌛ – †£ 50/65 ††£ 90/100
♦ Idyllic country house and animal sanctuary with picture perfect façade. Delightful owner keeps everything immaculate. Superb breakfasts. Bedrooms with an unerring eye for detail.

**ST DAVIDS** (Tyddewi) – Pembrokeshire – **503** E28 – pop. 1 959  **33 A3**
– ✉ **Haverfordwest**
▶ London 266 mi – Carmarthen 46 mi – Fishguard 16 mi
🅸 Oriel Y Parc ℰ (01437) 72 03 92, www.stdavids.co.uk
🅵 St Davids City Whitesands Bay, ℰ (01437) 72 17 51
⊙ Town ★ – Cathedral ★★ - Bishop's Palace ★ **AC**
🅶 Pembrokeshire Coast National Park ★★

## 🏨 **Warpool Court** 🦢 ⟨ 🚆 🕭 🖵 🗞 🍴 🌡 **P** VISA ⬤ AE

*Southwest : 0.5 mi by Porth Clais rd* ✉ *SA62 6BN –* ☏ *(01437) 720 300*
*– www.warpoolcourthotel.com – Closed November and first 2 weeks December*
**22 rm** ☕ – 🛏£ 110 🛏🛏£ 330
**Rest** *Warpool Court* – see restaurant listing
♦ Characterful clifftop property built in 1860 to house the cathedral choir. Traditional bar and light, airy lounges. Over 3,000 hand-painted Celtic and heraldic tiles feature. Bedrooms range in style; one boasts nice sea views from its bath.

## 🏠 **Ramsey House** ⟨ 🚆 🍴 🌡 **P** VISA ⬤ ①

*Lower Moor, Southwest : 0.5 mi on Porth Clais rd* ✉ *SA62 6RP –* ☏ *(01437)*
*720 321 – www.ramseyhouse.co.uk – Closed January, December and restricted*
*opening November and February*
**6 rm** ☕ – 🛏£ 60/110 🛏🛏£ 100/110
**Rest** – Menu £ 35
♦ Unassuming bungalow hiding stylish, contemporary interior with superb comforts, small lounge and bar. Bedrooms display modern colour schemes and state-of-the-art shower rooms. Traditional menus offer tasty three course dinners.

## ✖✖ **Warpool Court** – at Warpool Court Hotel 🚆 🕭 **P** VISA ⬤ AE

*Southwest : 0.5 mi by Porth Clais rd* ✉ *SA62 6BN –* ☏ *(01437) 720 300*
*– www.warpoolcourthotel.com – Closed November and first 2 weeks December*
**Rest** – *(light lunch/dinner)* Menu £ 40
♦ Smart restaurant boasting sea views, set in a 19C house originally built to accommodate the cathedral choir. Daily changing menus are classically based and feature plenty of local produce.

## ✖ **Cwtch** VISA ⬤ AE

*22 High St* ✉ *SA62 6SD –* ☏ *(01437) 720 491 – www.cwtchrestaurant.co.uk*
*– Closed 25 December and Sunday-Monday November-March*
**Rest** – *(dinner only) (booking advisable)* Menu £ 30
♦ Popular, friendly restaurant; its name meaning 'hug' in Welsh. Rustic dining room boasts stone walls, crammed bookshelves and log-filled alcoves. Classical British dishes arrive in generous portions; each comes with a wine recommendation.

WALES

## **ST GEORGE** (Llan Sain Siôr) – Conwy 32 C1

▶ London 227 mi – Cardiff 180 mi – Dublin 62 mi – Birmingham 113 mi

## 🏠 **Kinmel Arms** with rm 🍴 **P** VISA ⬤

*The Village* ✉ *LL22 9BP –* ☏ *(01745) 832 207 – www.thekinmelarms.co.uk*
*– Closed 1 January, 25 December, Sunday, Monday and bank holidays*
**4 rm** – 🛏£ 115 🛏🛏£ 115/175
**Rest** – Carte £ 23/41
♦ Early 17C stone inn hidden away in a hamlet by the entrance to Kinmel Hall. Delightful open-fired bar and two spacious dining areas; the latter offering much more formal service and food.

## **SAUNDERSFOOT** – Pembrokeshire – **503** F28 – pop. 2 946 33 A4

▶ London 241 mi – Cardiff 90 mi – Pembroke 12 mi

## 🏨 **St Brides Spa** ⟨ 🕭 🐟 ♨ 🖦 ⧉ 🌡 🛠 **P** VISA ⬤ AE

*St Brides Hill* ✉ *SA69 9NH –* ☏ *(01834) 812 304 – www.stbridessspahotel.com*
**40 rm** ☕ – 🛏£ 110/125 🛏🛏£ 230/280 – 6 suites
**Rest** *Cliff* – see restaurant listing
♦ Nautically styled hotel overlooking the harbour and bay, displaying wood panelling and pastel shades. Impressive spa boasts marine and outdoor infinity pools. Well-appointed bedrooms and apartments feature mosaic and limestone bathrooms.

**Cliff** – at St Brides Spa Hotel  ≤ 😒 **P** _VISA_ ∞ **AE**
_St Brides Hill_ ⊠ _SA69 9NH_ – 𝒞 _(01834) 812 304_ – _www.stbridesspahotel.com_
**Rest** – _Carte £ 23/38_
• Smart yet casual fine dining restaurant within a New England style hotel boasting a beautiful terrace and stunning views over Carmarthen Bay. Good range of appealing modern European dishes.

---

**SEION** – Gwynedd – see Caernarfon

---

**SENNYBRIDGE (Pontsenni)** – Powys                    33 B3
▪ London 189 mi – Cardiff 43 mi – Birmingham 127 mi – Liverpool 147 mi

**Blaencar Farm** without rest 🕭        🕭 🍸 **P**
_South : 1 mi off A 4067_ ⊠ _LD3 8HA_ – 𝒞 _(01874) 636 610_ – _www.blaencar.co.uk_
– _Closed 25 December_
**3 rm** ⊡ – ✝£ 45 ✝✝£ 70
• Set on a 450 acre working farm; its name meaning 'Mouth of the Brook'. Superb welcome from hands-on owner, who is a fountain of local knowledge. Dark-wood furnished breakfast room, lounge with log burner and simple, comfortable bedrooms.

---

**SKENFRITH** – Monmouthshire – **503** L28                    33 C4
▪ London 135 mi – Hereford 16 mi – Ross-on-Wye 11 mi

**Bell at Skenfrith** with rm        🚗 🤽 😒 🎇 **P** _VISA_ ∞
⊠ _NP7 8UH_ – 𝒞 _(01600) 750 235_ – _www.skenfrith.co.uk_
– _Closed last week January and first week February_
**11 rm** ⊡ – ✝£ 120 ✝✝£ 220
**Rest** – _(closed Tuesday November-Easter) (booking essential)_ Menu £ 20 (lunch) – Carte £ 26/36🕭
• Well-run pub in verdant valley offering clean, fresh cooking with an innovative, modern twist and using ingredients from the organic kitchen garden. Excellent choice of champagnes and cognacs; warm and unobtrusive service. Understated elegance in super-comfy bedrooms.

---

**SWANSEA** – Swansea – **503** I29 – pop. 173 868                    33 B4
▪ London 191 mi – Birmingham 136 mi – Bristol 82 mi – Cardiff 40 mi
🖪 Plymouth St 𝒞 (01792) 46 83 21, www.swansea.info
🔞 Morriston 160 Clasemont Rd, 𝒞 (01792) 79 65 28
🔞 Clyne Mayals 120 Owls Lodge Lane, 𝒞 (01792) 40 19 89
🔞 Langland Bay, 𝒞 (01792) 36 17 21
◉ Town★ - Maritime Quarter★ B – Maritime and Industrial Museum★ B
– Glynn Vivian Art Gallery★ B – Guildhall (British Empire Panels★ A **H**)
🖸 Gower Peninsula★★ (Rhossili★★), W : by A 4067 A. The Wildfowl and Wetlands Trust★, Llanelli, NW : 6.5 mi by A 483 and A 484 A

Plans pages 833, 834

**Morgans**        🛎 ⅙ rm, ⴉ 🍸 🤳 🖇 **P** _VISA_ ∞ **AE**
_Somerset Pl_ ⊠ _SA1 1RR_ – 𝒞 _(01792) 484 848_ – _www.morganshotel.co.uk_
**42 rm** ⊡ – ✝£ 250 ✝✝£ 250                    B**b**
**Rest** – _(closed Monday-Wednesday)_ Menu £ 14/22
• Impressive Edwardian building by the docks; once the harbour offices. Beautiful façade and charming interior with original plasterwork, stained glass and soaring cupola. Sizeable modern bedrooms in main house; Town House rooms more compact. Restaurant boasts original hand-painted mural and a modern menu.

WALES

# SWANSEA

WALES

## XX   Didier & Stephanie's                    AC VISA ⊚⊚
56 St Helens Rd ⊠ SA1 4BE – 𝒞 (01792) 655 603 – Closed Sunday and Monday
**Rest** – French – (booking essential) Menu £ 18 (lunch) – Carte £ 29/32        **A a**
♦ Well-run neighbourhood restaurant in a pleasant Victorian building, with light,
airy interior, smart wood panelling, original plaster ceiling and small bar to the
rear. French owners offer interesting menus of flavoursome Gallic classics.

## X    Slice                                    VISA ⊚⊚
73-75 Eversley Rd, Sketty, West : 2 mi by A 4118 ⊠ SA2 9DE
– 𝒞 (01792) 290 929 – www.sliceswansea.co.uk
– Closed 3 weeks January, 2 weeks summer, 2 weeks autumn, 1 week spring,
Christmas-New Year and Monday-Wednesday                                **A x**
**Rest** – (booking essential) Menu £ 22/34
♦ Former haberdashery in a residential suburb; the name reflecting its tapered
shape. Simple polished tables and unfussy, honest cooking. Concise set menus
feature homemade bread and ice cream, home-grown veg and home-smoked
fish and meat.

## at Parkmill West : 8.5 mi on A 4118

## XX   Maes-Yr-Haf with rm                    ⁽ᵗⁱ⁾ P VISA ⊚⊚ AE
⊠ SA3 2EH – 𝒞 (01792) 371 000 – www.maes-yr-haf.com
– Closed Monday in low season
**5 rm** � – ♥£ 80/100 ♥♥£ 130/140   **Rest** – Menu £ 20 (lunch) – Carte £ 27/36
♦ Minimalist restaurant within an old farmhouse in a wooded valley, set by a
small stream leading down to the sea. Contemporary interior is matched by ad-
venturous modern cooking that showcases seasonal produce from the Gower
Peninsular. Well-kept bedrooms boast stylish furnishings and smart bathrooms.

SWANSEA

A 483 | B | A 4067 | A 48 | A 4217 | (A 48) | C

WALES

## at Llanrhidian West : 10.5 mi by A 4118 - A - on B 4271 – ⌧ Reynoldston

### Fairyhill ⌂

Reynoldston, West : 2.5 mi by Llangennith Rd ⌧ SA3 1BS
– ℰ (01792) 390 139 – www.fairyhill.net
– Closed 2-27 January and 25-26 December

**8 rm** ☞ – †£ 160 ††£ 280

**Rest** – Menu £ 25/45 ⊞

♦ Georgian country house in 24 acres of grounds, with a lake and well-man-icured gardens. Charming guest areas include a cosy bar and contemporary lounge complete with piano. Eclectic, individually styled bedrooms offer good extras and holistic treatments are popular. Dining room and terrace serve a modern, seasonal menu of Gower produce. Friendly, accommodating service.

XX **Welcome To Town**  $P$ $VISA$ $\infty$
✉ SA3 1EH – ✆ (01792) 390 015 – www.thewelcometotown.co.uk
– *Closed last week October, Christmas-New Year, Tuesday November-April,*
*Sunday dinner and Monday*
**Rest** – *(booking essential)* Carte £ 34/48
♦ 17C whitewashed building – formerly a pub, gaol and courthouse – located
on a picturesque peninsula. Traditional interior with well-spaced tables. Ap-
pealing, classically based dishes display modern touches and champion local
Gower produce.

---

**TALSARNAU** – Gwynedd – **502** H25 – pop. 647 – ✉ **Harlech**   **32** B2
▶ London 236 mi – Caernafon 33 mi – Chester 67 mi – Dolgellau 25 mi
⬡ Snowdonia National Park★★★

🏠 **Maes-y-Neuadd** ⬧   $\Leftarrow$ $\not\equiv$ $P$ $VISA$ $\infty$
*South : 1.5 mi by A 496 off B 4573* ✉ LL47 6YA – ✆ (01766) 780 200
*– www.neuadd.com*
**14 rm** � – ♦£ 133/145 ♦♦£ 276/296 – 1 suite
**Rest** – Menu £ 18/40 – Carte lunch £ 19/32
♦ Part-14C country house with pleasant gardens in delightful rural seclusion.
Furnished throughout with antiques and curios. Charming service. Individually
styled bedrooms. Traditional dining room with linen-clad tables.

---

**TREMEIRCHION** – Denbighshire – **502** J24 – ✉ **St Asaph**   **32** C1
▶ London 225 mi – Chester 29 mi – Shrewsbury 59 mi

🏠 **Bach-Y-Graig** without rest ⬧   $\not\equiv$ $\mathcal{I}$ $\mathcal{D}$ $\mathcal{P}$ $VISA$ $\infty$
*Southwest : 2 mi by B 5429 off Denbigh rd* ✉ LL17 0UH – ✆ (01745) 730 627
*– www.bachygraig.co.uk*
**3 rm** � – ♦£ 50/55 ♦♦£ 75/84
♦ Attractive brick-built farmhouse dating from the 16C, set on a working farm, in
a quiet spot, with woodland trails nearby. Large open fires and wood-furnished
bedrooms with cast iron beds.

---

**USK** – Monmouthshire – **503** L28 – pop. 2 318   **33** C4
▶ London 144 mi – Bristol 30 mi – Cardiff 26 mi – Gloucester 39 mi
⬡ Alice Springs Usk Kemeys Commander, ✆ (01873) 88 07 08
⬡ Raglan Castle★ **AC**, NE : 7 mi by A 472, A 449 and A 40

🏠 **Glen-Yr-Afon House**   $\not\equiv$ $\mid\Xi\mid$ $\xi$ $\P$ $\xi\mathbb{A}$ $P$ $VISA$ $\infty$ $AE$
*Pontypool Rd* ✉ NP15 1SY – ✆ (01291) 672 302 – www.glen-yr-afon.co.uk
**27 rm** � – ♦£ 99 ♦♦£ 159
**Rest** *Clarkes* – see restaurant listing
♦ Extended Victorian villa with well-tended gardens, set just across the bridge
from town. Comfortable, traditionally styled guest areas and well-booked function rooms. Mix of country house and more contemporary bedrooms; one is
four-poster.

XX **Clarkes** – at Glen-Yr-Afon House Hotel   $\not\equiv$ $AC$ $P$ $VISA$ $\infty$ $AE$ $①$
*Pontypool Rd* ✉ NP15 1SY – ✆ (01291) 672 302 – www.glen-yr-afon.co.uk
**Rest** – Carte £ 22/36
♦ Stylish, formal dining room in an extended Victorian villa. Monthly changing à
la carte has a distinct Welsh edge, and offers a few modern dishes alongside a
largely traditional selection.

**at Llandenny** Northeast : 4.25 mi by A 472 off B 4235 – ✉ Usk

🍴 **Raglan Arms**   $\widehat{\mathcal{M}}$ $\mathcal{K}$ $P$ $VISA$ $\infty$ $AE$
✉ NP15 1DL – ✆ (01291) 690 800 – www.raglanarms.com – *Closed 25-26*
*December*
**Rest** – *(closed Sunday dinner and Monday)* Carte £ 29/36
♦ Cosy village pub with fireside sofas and simply laid tables. Local produce em-
ployed in a range of cooking styles; lunchtime main courses offer particularly
good value.

WALES

**at Llangybi** South : 2.5 mi on Llangybi rd – ✉ Ceredigion

🏠 **White Hart**  ⬆ 🅿 VISA ⊙⊙
✉ NP15 1NP – ℰ (01633) 450 258 – www.thewhitehartvillageinn.com
– *Closed Monday except bank holidays*
**Rest** – *(closed Sunday dinner)* Carte £ 29/38
♦ Characterful 16C pub with interesting history, 11 fireplaces and priest's hole. Blackboard lunch and more ambitious evening à la carte offer well-prepared, precisely presented, restaurant-style dishes; most produce is from within 10 miles.

---

**VALLEY** – **503** G24 – see Anglesey (Isle of)

---

**WHITEBROOK** – Monmouthshire – see Monmouth

---

**WHITTON** – Powys – **503** J27 – pop. 300  33 C3

▶ London 185 mi – Cardiff 84 mi – Birmingham 84 mi – Liverpool 108 mi

🏠 **Pilleth Oaks** ◈  ⬅ 🚐 ⬆ ⬇ ⬇ ℛ 🅿
*Northwest : 1.25 mi on B 4356* ✉ LD7 1NP – ℰ (01457) 560 272
– *www.pillethoaks.co.uk*
**3 rm** ⬜ – ♦£ 40 ♦♦£ 70  **Rest** – Carte £ 15/22
♦ Smart, double-gabled country house in 100 acres, overlooking two lakes and the surrounding hills. Traditional, antique-filled interior with elegant lounge; comfortable bedrooms – one with a balcony. Welcoming owner offers tea on arrival. Communal dining at a smart oak table; desserts are worth investigating.

---

**WOLF'S CASTLE** (Cas-Blaidd) – Pembrokeshire – **503** F28 – pop. 616  33 A3
– ✉ Haverfordwest

▶ London 258 mi – Fishguard 7 mi – Haverfordwest 8 mi
◷ Pembrokeshire Coast National Park★★

🏠 **Wolfscastle Country H.**  🚐 ⅩⅩ rest, ⑪ 🛁 🅿 VISA ⊙⊙ AE
✉ SA62 5LZ – ℰ (01437) 741 225 – www.wolfscastle.com
– *Closed 24-26 December*
**20 rm** ⬜ – ♦£ 82 ♦♦£ 150  **Rest** – Menu £ 17/18 – Carte £ 21/34
♦ Former manor house that's been greatly expanded over the years and is popular for weddings and conferences. Tidy, well-equipped bedrooms – some with four-posters; some recenlty refurbished. Traditional bar. Contemporary restaurant offers everything from snacks to the full 3 courses.

---

**WREXHAM** (Wrecsam) – Wrexham – **502** L24 – pop. 42 576  32 C1

▶ London 192 mi – Chester 12 mi – Liverpool 35 mi – Shrewsbury 28 mi
🔢 Lambpit St ℰ (01978) 29 20 15, www.wrexham.gov.uk
🔟 Chirk, ℰ (01691) 77 44 07
🔟 Clays Golf Centre Bryn Estyn Rd, ℰ (01978) 66 14 06
🔟 Moss Valley Moss Rd, ℰ (01978) 72 05 18
🔟 Pen-y-Cae Ruabon Rd, ℰ (01978) 81 01 08
🔟 Plassey Oaks Golf Complex Eyton, ℰ (01978) 78 00 20
◉ St Giles Church★
◷ Erddig★★ **AC** (Gardens★★), SW : 2 m – Gresford (All Saints Church★), N : 4 mi by A 5152 and B 5445

**t Gresford** Northeast : 3 mi by A 483 on B 5445

**Pant-yr-Ochain**      🍺 🏠 **P** *VISA* **◎** **AE**

*Old Wrexham Rd, South : 1 mi* ✉ *LL12 8TY –* ✆ *(01978) 853 525*
*– www.pantyrochain-gresford.co.uk – Closed 25 December*

**Rest** – Carte £ 20/31

♦ Classic country manor house with mature, manicured gardens leading down to a lake. Daily changing menu offers hearty, wholesome, all-day dishes, ranging from pub classics to more modern fare.

WALES

# Ireland

# Northern Ireland

**ANNAHILT** = Eanach Eilte – **Lisburn** – **712** N/O4 – **see Hillsborough**

---

**BALLINTOY** – Moyle – **712** M2                                    35 C

▶ Belfast 59 mi – Ballycastle 8 mi – Londonderry 48 mi – Lisburn 67 mi

↑  **Whitepark House** without rest                 ⌨ ⚒ 📶 **P** *VISA* **⦵**
   *150 Whitepark Rd, West : 1.5 mi on A 2 ⊠ BT54 6NH – ℰ (028) 2073 1482*
   *– www.whiteparkhouse.com*
   **3 rm** ⌣ – ♛£ 75  ♛♛£ 100
   ♦ Charming 18C house with lovely wall hangings, framed silks and other Asian a
   tefacts from the personable owner's travels. Comfy, open-fired lounge and indivi
   ually decorated, antique-furnished bedrooms. Breakfast around communal table.

---

**BALLYCLARE** (Bealach Cláir) – Newtownabbey – **712** N/O3           35 D
– pop. 8 770

▶ Belfast 14 mi – Newtownabbey 6 mi – Lisburn 23 mi

XX  **Oregano**                                          ⌨ **AC** ⇔ **P** *VISA* **⦵**
🅛  *29 Ballyrobert Rd, South : 3.25 mi by A 57 on B 56 ⊠ BT39 9RY – ℰ (028)*
    *9084 0099 – www.oreganorestaurant.co.uk – Closed 11-13 July, 24-27*
    *December, Saturday lunch and Monday*
    **Rest** – Menu £ 15/18 – Carte £ 24/34
    ♦ Very remotely set, unassuming Victorian house concealing a spacious, mod
    ern bar and lounge, and a stylish restaurant hung with contemporary art. Goc
    value modern British cooking uses local produce and displays some European i
    fluences. Flavours are honest, clean and clear.

---

**BALLYMENA** (An Baile Meánach) – Ballymena – **712** N3              35 C
– pop. 28 717 🔖 Ireland

▶ Belfast 27 mi – Dundalk 78 mi – Larne 21 mi – Londonderry 51 mi

🛈 1-29 Bridge St ℰ (028) 2563 59 00, www.ballymena.gov.uk

🔟 128 Raceview Rd, ℰ (028) 2586 12 07

🖸 Antrim Glens★★★ - Murlough Bay★★★ (Fair Head ⩽★★★), NE : 32 mi by A 26,
   44, A 2 and minor road - Glengariff Forest Park★★ **AC** (Waterfall★★), NW : 13 m
   by A 43 – Glengariff★, NE : 18 mi by A 43 - Glendun★, NE : 19 mi by A 43, B 14
   and A2 – Antrim (Round Tower★) S : 9.5 mi by A 26

**at Galgorm** West : 3 mi on A 42

🏨  **Galgorm Resort and Spa** ⌖          ⌨ ⥁ ⤳ 📺 ⊕ 🛁 🎱 ⚒ 🛎 P
    *136 Fenaghy Rd, West : 1.5 mi on Cullybacky rd ⊠ BT42 1EA*  *VISA* **⦵** **AE**
    *– ℰ (028) 2588 1001 – www.galgorm.com*
    **75 rm** ⌣ – ♛£ 105/155  ♛♛£ 105/245
    **Rest** *River Room* **Rest** *Gillies* – see restaurant listing
    ♦ Victorian manor house with newer extensions, set in large grounds. Stylish in
    terior with plenty of lounge space, huge function capacity and excellent spa/lei
    sure club. Modern bedrooms boast state-of-the-art facilities; some have balconie

XXX  **River Room** – at Galgorm Resort and Spa    ⌨ ⥁ & **AC** **P** *VISA* **⦵** **AE**
     *136 Fenaghy Rd, West : 1.5 mi on Cullybacky rd ⊠ BT42 1EA – ℰ (028)*
     *2588 1001 – www.galgorm.com*
     **Rest** – *(closed Monday-Tuesday) (dinner only and Sunday lunch)* Menu £ 25
     (lunch) – Carte £ 33/40
     ♦ Formal fine dining room set in a stylishly furnished, whitewashed Victoria
     manor house. Floor to ceiling windows provide panoramic views across the Rive
     Mein. Menus are classically based.

X  **Gillies** – at Galgorm Resort and Spa        ⌨ ⥁ ⤳ & **AC** **P** *VISA* **⦵** **AE**
   *136 Fenaghy Rd, West : 1.5 mi on Cullybacky rd ⊠ BT42 1EA – ℰ (028)*
   *2588 1001 – www.galgorm.com*
   **Rest** – Carte £ 19/36
   ♦ Laid-back, split-level steakhouse with large outside dining area; set within
   smartly appointed, whitewashed Victorian manor house. Extensive all-day menu
   Live music in the bar at weekends.

▶ Belfast 15 mi – Newtownards 5 mi

🛈 34 Quay St 𝒞 (028) 9127 00 69, www.bangor-local.com

◉ North Down Heritage Centre★

◉ Ulster Folk and Transport Museum★★ **AC**, W : 8 mi by A 2. Newtownards : Movilla Priory (Cross Slabs★) S : 4 mi by A 21 - Mount Stewart★★★ **AC**, SE : 90 mi by A 21 and A 20 – Scrabo Tower ('≤★★) S : 6.5 mi by A 21 – Ballycopeland Windmill★, SE : 10 mi by B 21 and A 2, turning right at Millisle – Strangford Lough★ (Castle Espie Centre★ **AC** - Nendrum Monastery★) - Grey Abbey★ **AC**, SE : 20 mi by A 2, A 21 and A 20

---

🏨 **Clandeboye Lodge**     🚗 🖼🔞 🛗 & ⚲ ⟨⟨⟩⟩ 🏊 **P** 🌊 ⓜ ⒶⒺ ①
10 Estate Rd, Clandeboye, Southwest : 3 mi by A 2 and Dundonald rd following signs for Blackwood Golf Centre ⊠ BT19 1UR
– 𝒞 (028) 9185 2500 – www.clandeboyelodge.com
– Closed 24-26 December
**43 rm** ⌕ – ♥£ 70/85 ♥♥£ 85/130
**Rest** *Clanbrasserie* – see restaurant listing
♦ Well-run property on the site of a former estate school house, surrounded by 4 acres of woodland and well-placed for country and coast. Airy, open-plan guest areas and contemporary bedrooms. Huge array of function rooms in separate block.

⌂ **Cairn Bay Lodge** without rest     ≤ 🚗 ⚲ ⟨⟨⟩⟩ **P** 🌊 ⓜ
278 Seacliffe Rd, East : 1.25 mi by Quay St ⊠ BT20 5HS
– 𝒞 (028) 9146 7636 – www.cairnbaylodge.com
– Closed 6-27 February
**5 rm** ⌕ – ♥£ 45/70 ♥♥£ 70/90
♦ Large, whitewashed Edwardian house overlooking the bay. Comfy guest areas feature unusual objets d'art and ornaments; spacious, individually styled bedrooms boast plenty of extras. Friendly owners leave homemade cake on the landing. Small beauty/therapy facility.

⌂ **Shelleven House** without rest     ⚲ ⟨⟨⟩⟩ **P** 🌊 ⓜ
59-61 Princetown Rd ⊠ BT20 3TA – 𝒞 (028) 9127 1777
– www.shellevenhouse.com
**11 rm** ⌕ – ♥£ 37/60 ♥♥£ 70/80
♦ Double-fronted, three-storey, Victorian end terrace, in a smart residential area close to the marina. Open-plan lounge and breakfast room; excellent breakfasts. Well-kept bedrooms vary in shape and size; front rooms boast great coast views.

✗✗ **Boat House**     🈂 🄰🄲 🌊 ⓜ ⒶⒺ ①
Seacliff Rd ⊠ BT20 5HA – 𝒞 (028) 9146 9253 – www.theboathouseni.co.uk
– Closed 1 week October, 1 January, Monday and Tuesday
**Rest** – Menu £ 22 (lunch and early dinner)/25 – Carte £ 28/40
♦ Delightful former lifeboat station with harbourside terrace. Experienced brothers source quality local produce. Inventive tasting menu and classical, seasonal à la carte with Dutch twists.

✗✗ **Jeffers at Blackwood**     🄰🄲 **P** 🌊 ⓜ ⒶⒺ
Blackwood Golf Centre, Southwest: 3 mi by A 2 and Dundonald Rd ⊠ BT19 1GB
– 𝒞 (028) 9185 3818 – www.jeffersbythemarina.com
– Closed 25-26 December, 1 January, 12 July, Sunday and Monday
**Rest** – (booking advisable) Menu £ 25 – Carte £ 20/37
♦ Set within Blackwood Golf Centre, this is a restaurant of two halves: upstairs is an all-day affair serving breakfast and light snacks; downstairs is a formal dining room with red banquettes, a semi-open kitchen and traditional grill menu.

NORTHERN IRELAND

843

XX **Clanbrasserie** – at Clandeboye Lodge Hotel    🖼 & P VISA ⊙ AE ⊙
*10 Estate Rd, Clandeboye, Southwest : 3 mi by A 2 and Dundonald rd following*
*signs for Blackwood Golf Centre* ✉ *BT19 1UR* – ✆ *(028) 9185 2500*
*– www.clandeboyelodge.com – Closed 24-26 December*
**Rest** – *(bar lunch Monday-Saturday)* Menu £ 20 – Carte £ 20/30
♦ Airy, high-ceilinged dining room in a well-run hotel that's surrounded by
acres of woodland. Stylish, minimalist décor: dine beside the fire in winter or al
fresco in summer. Modish menus.

X **Jeffers by the Marina**    AC VISA ⊙
*7 Grays Hill* ✉ *BT20 3BB* – ✆ *(028) 9185 9555* – *www.jeffersbythemarina.com*
*– Closed second week July, 25-26 December and Monday except bank holidays*
**Rest** – Menu £ 23 – Carte £ 22/33
♦ Smart restaurant with granite-topped tables and white tiles and newspape
clippings on the walls. Extensive menu has a strong seafood base and good value
specials evolve throughout the day.

🛏 **Coyle's**    VISA ⊙ ⊙
*44 High St* ✉ *BT20 5AZ* – ✆ *(028) 9127 0362* – *www.coylesbistro.co.uk* – *Closed*
*25 December*
**Rest** – *(closed Monday)* Carte £ 19/30
♦ Friendly, laid-back, typically Irish pub; a great place for a quiet drink and a
good meal. Bar menu offers classics and some international influences; bistro
menu steps things up a gear.

🛏 **Salty Dog** with rm    🖼 ℅ ⊛ VISA ⊙
✉ *BT20 5EY* – ✆ *(028) 9127 0696* – *www.thesaltydogbistro.com* – *Closed 25-26*
*December*
**15 rm** ⬜ – †£ 50/70 ††£ 80/95
**Rest** – *(booking advisable)* Menu £ 19 (lunch) – Carte £ 19/28
♦ Large Victorian pub at the head of the harbour, affording pleasant sea views
Smart, modern interior, polished tables and glass-fronted terrace. Unfussy cooking
of local produce – set menu evolves throughout the day. Good-sized bedrooms
come with period charm.

# BELFAST

Belfast – pop. 276 459 – **712** O4 – Ireland

Dublin 103 – Londonderry 70

## Tourist Information

Donegal Pl ℰ (028) 9024 66 09, www.gotobelfast.com

## Airports

Belfast International Airport, Aldergrove : ℰ (028) 9448 4848, W : 15 ½ m. by A 52 AY

George Best Belfast City Airport : ℰ (028) 9093 9093

## Ferries and Shipping Lines

to Isle of Man (Douglas) (Isle of Man Steam Packet Co. Ltd) (summer only) (2 h 45 mn) – to Stranraer (Stena Line) 4-5 daily (1 h 30 mn/3 h 15 mn), (Seacat Scotland) March-January (90 mn) – to Liverpool (Norfolkline Irish Sea) daily (8 h 30 mn)

## Golf Courses

Balmoral 518 Lisburn Rd, ℰ (028) 9038 15 14

Belvoir Park Newtonbreda 73 Church Rd, ℰ (028) 90 49 16 93

Fortwilliam Downview Ave, ℰ (028) 9037 07 70

## SIGHTS

**In the town :** City★ • Ulster Museum★ AZ**M1** • City Hall★ BY • Donegall Square★ BY**20** • Botanic Gardens★AZ • St Anne's Cathedral★ BX • Crown Liquor Saloon★ BY • Sinclair Seamen's Church★ BX • St Malachy's Church★ BY

**In the surrounding area :** Carrickfergus Castle★★ **AC** NE : 9.5 mi by A 2

**On the outskirts :** Belfast Zoological Gardens★★ AC, N : 5 mi by A 6 AY

**BELFAST**

NORTHERN IRELAND

847

# INDEX OF STREET NAMES IN BELFAST

NORTHERN IRELAND

## Merchant                 🍴 🛎 🍸 🛗 👤 ⚿ rm, 🅰🅲 ⚓ 📶 🐾 🚭 VISA 🅼🅾 AE

*16 Skipper St* ✉ *BT1 2DZ* – ℰ *(028) 9023 4888*
*– www.themerchanthotel.com*                                          **BX**×

**60 rm** ⌁ – †£ 150/240 ††£ 150/350 – 2 suites
**Rest** *Great Room* – see restaurant listing
**Rest** *Berts* – (dinner only and lunch Saturday and Sunday) Menu £ 20
– Carte £ 25/35

♦ Former Ulster Bank HQ with an impressive Victorian façade. Plush, inti-
mately styled bedrooms; those in the annexe are more contemporary. Rooftop gym comes with an outdoor hot tub and skyline view; afterwards relax
in the swish cocktail bar. Choice of fine dining or brasserie classics accompanied by live jazz.

## Fitzwilliam                          ⚓ 👤 🍸 🛗 👤 🅰🅲 ⚿ 📶 🐾 VISA 🅼🅾 AE

*Great Victoria St* ✉ *BT2 7BQ* – ℰ *(028) 9044 2080*
*– www.fitzwilliamhotelbelfast.com*                                     **BY**e

**129 rm** – †£ 190 ††£ 200, ⌁ £ 19 – 1 suite
**Rest** *Menu by Kevin Thornton* – see restaurant listing

♦ Stylish, contemporary hotel next to Grand Opera House, boasting striking
bold colours and comfy bedrooms with good facilities; the higher you go,
the better the view. Afternoon teas in snug lobby and comfort food in brightly
coloured bar.

## Malmaison                                    👤 👤 👤 📶 🐾 VISA 🅼🅾 🅞

*34-38 Victoria St* ✉ *BT1 3GH* – ℰ *(028) 9022 0200* – *www.malmaison.com*
**62 rm** – †£ 160 ††£ 160, ⌁ £ 14.50 – 2 suites                        **BY**v
**Rest** *Brasserie* – see restaurant listing

♦ Converted Victorian seed warehouse with ornate exterior. Original features
blends with modern furnishings throughout. Dark-hued reception leads to a
snug bar; stylish bedrooms offer good facilities – one boasts a 9' bed and
snooker table.

**Radisson Blu**  ≤ ᴵ⛫ & AC ⵚ ⟨⟨⟩⟩ ⵚ P VISA ⓒⓞ AE ⓘ
*3 Cromac Pl, Cromac Wood* ⌧ *BT7 2JB* – ⌀ *(028) 9043 4065*
*– www.radissonblu.co.uk/hotelbelfast* BY**z**
**119 rm** – ♦£ 95/184 ♦♦£ 170/196 – 1 suite
**Rest Filini** – Italian influences – *(closed Sunday)* Menu £ 20 (lunch)
– Carte £ 25/40
♦ Stylish, modern hotel on the site of former gasworks. Smart, up-to-date facilities. Two room styles – Urban or Nordic; both boast fine views over city and waterfront. Restaurant/bar with floor-to-ceiling windows and part-open kitchen.

 **Ten Square**  ᴵ⛫ & AC ⵚ ⟨⟨⟩⟩ ⵚ VISA ⓒⓞ AE
*10 Donegall Sq South* ⌧ *BT1 5JD* – ⌀ *(028) 9024 1001* – *www.tensquare.co.uk*
*– Closed 25 December* BY**x**
**22 rm** – ♦£ 155 ♦♦£ 175, ⌧ £ 12
**Rest Grill Room** – see restaurant listing
♦ Sizeable Victorian property in the town centre, hidden behind city hall. Stylish, modern bedrooms display bold feature walls and offer a good level of facilities. Large first floor function room is popular for both meetings and weddings.

 **Malone Lodge**  ⌂ ᴸ⌂ ᴵ⛫ & AC rest, ⵚ ⟨⟨⟩⟩ ⵚ P VISA ⓒⓞ AE ⓘ
*60 Eglantine Ave* ⌧ *BT9 6DY* – ⌀ *(028) 9038 8000*
*– www.malonelodgehotelbelfast.com* AZ**n**
**90 rm** ⌧ – ♦£ 70/140 ♦♦£ 70/140 – 3 suites
**Rest The Green Door** – *(closed Sunday dinner)* Carte £ 20/25
♦ Well-run, privately owned hotel in peaceful 19C terrace. Bedrooms display good facilities, with smart corporate bedrooms in main house and executive rooms/apartments in various annexes. Wood-furnished bar; simple restaurant offering classical menus.

 **Crescent Townhouse**  & ⵚ ⟨⟨⟩⟩ ⵚ VISA ⓒⓞ AE
*13 Lower Cres* ⌧ *BT7 1NR* – ⌀ *(028) 9032 3349* – *www.crescenttownhouse.com*
*– Closed 24-26 December, 1 January and 11-12 July* BZ**x**
**17 rm** ⌧ – ♦£ 75 ♦♦£ 85/100
**Rest Metro Brasserie** – see restaurant listing
♦ Centrally located Regency-style townhouse run by a welcoming team. Snug first floor lounge hung with oils. Well-equipped, spacious bedrooms are split between the old house and newer extension; some boast four-poster beds and huge bathrooms.

 **Ravenhill House** without rest  ⵚ ⟨⟨⟩⟩ P VISA ⓒⓞ
*690 Ravenhill Rd* ⌧ *BT6 0BZ* – ⌀ *(028) 9020 7444* – *www.ravenhillhouse.com*
*– Closed 20-31 December, 1-7 January, 1-15 July and 27 August-2 September*
**5 rm** ⌧ – ♦£ 50/55 ♦♦£ 75 AZ**s**
♦ Friendly, red-brick Victorian house with bay windows, set in the city suburbs. Bright, homely lounge and wood-furnished breakfast room. Colourful bedrooms boast good facilities. Organic breakfasts feature homemade muesli and wheat for the bread is home-milled.

 **Roseleigh House** without rest  ⵚ ⟨⟨⟩⟩ P VISA ⓒⓞ ⓘ
*19 Rosetta Park, South : 1.5 mi by A 24 (Ormeau Rd)* ⌧ *BT6 0DL* – ⌀ *(028)*
*9064 4414* – *www.roseleighhouse.co.uk* – *Closed Christmas-New Year*
**6 rm** ⌧ – ♦£ 45 ♦♦£ 65 AZ**r**
♦ Imposing Victorian house close to the Belvoir Park golf course and in a fairly quiet residential suburb. Brightly decorated and well-kept bedrooms with modern amenities.

XXX **Great Room** – at Merchant Hotel  & AC VISA ⓒⓞ AE
*16 Skipper St* ⌧ *BT1 2DZ* – ⌀ *(028) 9023 4888* – *www.themerchanthotel.com*
*– Closed Saturday lunch* BX**x**
**Rest** – Menu £ 23/27 – Carte dinner £ 30/50
♦ Grand old banking hall, set behind the impressive Victorian façade of the former Ulster Bank HQ. Impressive ornate plasterwork and original stained glass windows. Ambitious French-based menu.

NORTHERN IRELAND

XX **Menu by Kevin Thornton** – at Fitzwilliam Hotel   `VISA` `CO` `AE` `①`
*Great Victoria St* ⊠ *BT2 7BQ* – ℰ *(028) 9044 2080*
*– www.fitzwilliamhotelbelfast.com*   BY
**Rest** – *(dinner only) (booking essential)* Carte £ 30/42
♦ Three-roomed restaurant on 1st floor of stylish hotel; large centre table seat
one large party or several smaller; if you're a couple, choose a booth. Classi
dishes cooked in modern Irish style.

XX **James Street South**   `AE` `CO` `VISA` `CO` `AE`
*21 James St South* ⊠ *BT2 7GA* – ℰ *(028) 9043 4310*
*– www.jamesstreetsouth.co.uk – Closed 25-26 December, 1 and 12 January,*
*Easter Sunday and Monday, 12 July and Sunday lunch*   BY
**Rest** – Menu £ 17 (lunch) – Carte £ 28/42
♦ Smart backstreet restaurant with Victorian façade, slate-floored bar and bright
modern dining room. Good-sized menus offer tasty dishes of simply cooked loca
produce. Efficient service.

XX **Cayenne**   `AE` `CO` `⇔` `VISA` `CO` `AE` `①`
🈯 *7 Ascot House, Shaftesbury Sq* ⊠ *BT2 7DB* – ℰ *(028) 9033 1532*
*– www.cayenne-restaurant.co.uk – Closed 25-26 December, 1 January, 12-13 July*
*and Tuesday*   BZ
**Rest** – Asian influences – *(dinner only and lunch Thursday, Friday and Sunday*
*(booking essential)* Menu £ 16/28 – Carte £ 28/44
♦ Stylish restaurant with leather-furnished lounge and large dining room displaying Asian/Oriental touches. Choice of good value set or more adventurous à la
carte menus, offering unfussy, flavoursome cooking with an Asian base. Service
is friendly and efficient.

XX **Shu**   `AE` `⇔` `VISA` `CO` `AE`
*253 Lisburn Rd* ⊠ *BT9 7EN* – ℰ *(028) 9038 1655* – *www.shu-restaurant.com*
*– Closed 24-26 December, 1 January, 11-13 July and Sunday*   AZz
**Rest** – Menu £ 28 – Carte £ 26/35
♦ Modern L-shaped restaurant in affluent residential district, with cream/dark
wood décor and lively, vibrant atmosphere. Modern British cooking is guided by
seasonality and availability of local produce.

XX **Deanes**   `AE` `CO` `VISA` `CO` `AE`
*36 Howard St* ⊠ *BT1 6PF* – ℰ *(028) 9033 1134* – *www.michaeldeane.co.uk*
*– Closed Sunday and bank holidays*   BYn
**Rest** – Menu £ 18 (lunch and early dinner) – Carte £ 31/43
♦ Three places in one. Stylish brasserie serves interesting, classically based dishes
with original modern style. Smaller eatery offers more casual seafood dining. Limited opening in upstairs restaurant, which has elaborate, inventive, 5 or 7 course
tasting menus.

XX **Grill Room** – at Ten Square Hotel   `&` `AE` `VISA` `CO` `AE`
*10 Donegall Sq South* ⊠ *BT1 5JD* – ℰ *(028) 9024 1001* – *www.tensquare.co.uk*
*– Closed 25 December*   BYx
**Rest** – Carte £ 18/35
♦ Set within an attractive building, in a great central location. Menus feature
fresh fish, seafood and locally reared, prime-aged, grain-fed beef. Entertainment
in the vibrant bar at weekends.

XX **Brasserie** – at Malmaison Hotel   `&` `AE` `VISA` `CO` `AE` `①`
*34-38 Victoria St* ⊠ *BT1 3GH* – ℰ *(028) 9022 0200* – *www.malmaison.com*
**Rest** – Menu £ 18 – Carte £ 27/30   BYv
♦ Located within a fine old warehouse, with high beamed ceilings, richly coloured décor and intimate booths. Choice of à la carte or daily changing set
menu; ingredients are strictly regional.

NORTHERN IRELAND

## ✗ **No 27** — AK VISA ⬤ AE

*27 Talbot St ⌂ BT1 2LD – ℰ (028) 9031 2884 – www.no27.co.uk – Closed 24-26 December, 1 January, 12-13 July, Sunday and Monday* BX**a**

**Rest** – Carte £ 27/41

♦ Bustling restaurant opposite the cathedral; sleekly styled with wooden floor, modern lighting and open kitchen. Simple lunch choices; daily changing dinner menu of modern, globally influenced dishes. Fresh market produce.

## ✗ **Deanes Deli** — AK VISA ⬤ AE

*42-44 Bedford St ⌂ BT2 7FF – ℰ (028) 9024 8800 – www.michaeldeane.co.uk – Closed 25-26 December, 1 January, Easter, 1 week July and Sunday*

**Rest** – Menu £ 28 – Carte £ 25/33 BY**a**

♦ Spacious, glass-fronted city centre restaurant serving a mix of comfort food and globally influenced dishes, with a good choice of daily specials. Bustling, chatty atmosphere. Small coffee shop serves homemade cakes.

## ✗ **Ginger Bistro** — ⬤ᴥ VISA ⬤

*7-8 Hope St ⌂ BT2 5EE – ℰ (028) 9024 4421 – www.gingerbistro.com – Closed Christmas, New Year, Easter, 3 days mid-July, lunch Monday, Sunday and bank holidays* BYZ**i**

**Rest** – Carte £ 26/32

♦ Keenly run neighbourhood eatery with modern artwork for sale and bespoke fish-themed paintings. Eclectic menus display worldwide influences; good value lunch/pre-theatre. Owner is passionate about using only Irish ingredients.

## ✗ **Molly's Yard** — ⬡ ⬤ᴥ VISA ⬤

*1 College Green Mews, Botanic Ave ⌂ BT7 1LW – ℰ (028) 9032 2600 – www.mollysyard.co.uk – Closed 24-26 December, 1 January and Sunday*

**Rest** – *(booking essential)* Carte £ 19/31 BZ**s**

♦ Friendly split-level bistro in former coach house and stables, with exposed brickwork and pleasant courtyard. Menus display fresh, unfussy, modern bistro fare; simpler dishes at lunch. Fine locally brewed ales and stouts.

## ✗ **Mourne Seafood Bar** — AK VISA ⬤ AE

*34-36 Bank St ⌂ BT1 1HL – ℰ (028) 9024 8544 – www.mourneseafood.com – Closed 24-26 December, 1 January, 17 March, Easter Sunday and Monday, and dinner Sunday-Monday* BY**c**

**Rest** – Seafood – *(booking essential at dinner) (lunch bookings not accepted)* Carte £ 17/26

♦ Popular, split-level seafood restaurant with small shop and cookery school. Blackboard menus offer a huge array of fresh dishes; go for the specials or the Carlingford oysters and a pint of stout. Large rear bar serves tapas-style dishes.

## ✗ **Metro Brasserie** – at Crescent Townhouse Hotel — & AK VISA ⬤ AE

*13 Lower Cres ⌂ BT7 1NR – ℰ (028) 9032 3349 – www.crescenttownhouse.com – Closed 24-26 December, 1 January and 12-13 July* BZ**x**

**Rest** – *(dinner only)* Carte £ 18/28

♦ Large, modern brasserie on the ground floor of a Regency-style townhouse hotel. Accessible modern dishes and dedicated vegetarian menu. Pub quiz on Thursdays and DJ on Saturdays in the bar.

Each starred restaurant lists three specialities that are typical of its style of cuisine. These may not always be on the menu but in their place expect delicious seasonal dishes. Be sure to try them.

**BENBURB** – Dungannon – **712** L4 – see Dungannon

## BUSHMILLS (Muileann na Buaise) – Moyle – **712** M2 – pop. 1 319    35 C
– ✉ **Bushmills** 🏴 Ireland

▶ Belfast 57 mi – Ballycastle 12 mi – Coleraine 10 mi

🏌 Bushfoot Portballintrae 50 Bushfoot Rd, ℰ (028) 2073 13 17

🎯 Giant's Causeway★★★ (Hamilton's Seat ⬍★★) N : 2 mi by A 2 and minor road
- Dunluce Castle★★ **AC** W : 3 mi by A 2 – Carrick-a-rede Rope Bridge★★★ **AC**, E
8 mi by A 2 – Magilligan Strand★★, W : 18 mi by A 2, A 29 and A 2 – Gortmore
Viewpoint★★, SW : 23 mi by A 2, A 29, A 23 and minor road from Downhill
– Downhill★ (Mussenden Temple★), W : 15 mi by A 2, A 29 and A 2

### 🏠 Bushmills Inn                  �⭘ ⚙ ⁑ 📶 **P** 𝗩𝗜𝗦𝗔 ⓸ 𝗔𝗘
9 Dunluce Rd ✉ BT57 8QG – ℰ (028) 2073 3000 – www.bushmillsinn.com
– Closed 25 December
**41 rm** ⌗ – ♦£ 98/158 ♦♦£ 138/298
**Rest** *Restaurant* – see restaurant listing
• Proudly run, part-17C whitewashed inn that successfully blends the old with the
new. Lovely cinema, state-of-the-art function rooms and spacious, modern bed
rooms boasting up-to-date facilities. Old whiskey bar features an open peat fire.

### ✗✗ Restaurant – at Bushmills Inn              **P** 𝗩𝗜𝗦𝗔 ⓸ 𝗔𝗘
9 Dunluce Rd ✉ BT57 8QG – ℰ (028) 2073 3000 – www.bushmillsinn.com
– Closed 25 December
**Rest** – *(carvery lunch Sunday)* Carte £ 22/38
• Three-roomed restaurant and old whiskey bar complete with peat fire, set in
proudly run, smartly refurbished 17C inn. Choose from main room, garden room
or charming booths. Traditional menu.

## COLERAINE (Cúil Raithin) – Coleraine – **712** L2 – pop. 24 089    35 C
🏴 Ireland

▶ Belfast 53 mi – Ballymena 25 mi – Londonderry 31 mi – Omagh 65 mi

ℹ Railway Rd ℰ (028) 7034 47 23, www.causewaycoastandglens.com

🏌 Castlerock 65 Circular Rd, ℰ (028) 7084 83 14

🏌 Brown Trout 209 Agivey Rd, Aghadowey, ℰ (028) 7086 82 09

🎯 Giant's Causeway★★★ (Hamilton's Seat ⬍★★), NE : 14 mi by A 29 and A2
- Dunluce Castle★★ **AC**, NE : 8 mi by A 29 and A 2 – Carrick-a-rede-Rope
Bridge★★★ **AC**, NE : 18 mi by A 29 and A2 – Benvarden★ **AC** E : 5 mi by B 67
– Magilligan Strand★★, NW : 8 mi by A 2 - Gortmore Viewpoint★★, NW : 12 mi by
A 2 and minor road from Downhill - Downhill★**AC** (Mussenden Temple★), NE :
7 mi by A 2

### ⌂ Greenhill House without rest 🌿          🚗 ⤿ ⚙ ⁑ 📶 **P** 𝗩𝗜𝗦𝗔 ⓸ 𝗔𝗘
24 Greenhill Rd, Aghadowey, South : 9 mi by A 29 on B 66 ✉ BT51 4EU
– ℰ (028) 7086 8241 – www.greenhill-house.co.uk – Closed 1 November-31
December
**6 rm** ⌗ – ♦£ 45 ♦♦£ 70
• An agreeably clean-lined Georgian house with large windows overlooking
fields. Game and course fishing available locally. Neat bedrooms replete with extra touches.

## COMBER (An Comar) – Ards – **712** O4 – pop. 8 933    35 D2
▶ Belfast 10 mi – Newtownards 5 mi – Lisburn 17 mi

### ⌂ Anna's House without rest 🌿          ⬍ 🚗 ⤿ �ይ ⚙ ⁑ 📶 **P** 𝗩𝗜𝗦𝗔 ⓸
Tullynagee, 35 Lisbarnett Rd., Southeast : 3.5 mi by A 22 ✉ BT23 6AW – ℰ (028)
9754 1566 – www.annashouse.com – Closed Christmas-New Year
**4 rm** ⌗ – ♦£ 60/65 ♦♦£ 110
• Farmhouse with cosy lounge and comfy bedrooms with lovely vistas. Glass-
walled extension has geo-thermal heating and lake views. Organic breakfasts utilise produce from garden.

▶ Belfast 14 mi – Ballymena 20 mi

**Ballyrobin**                    📶 ⅙ rm, 🛜 🎖️ 📶 P VISA ⓒⓞ AE
144-146 Ballyrobin Rd, North : 7 mi by A 26 ⊠ BT29 4EG – 𝒞 (028) 9422 2211
– www.ballyrobincountrylodge.com – Closed 25 December
**21 rm** – ♦£ 45/83 ♦♦£ 72/86, ⌷ £ 8.95    **Rest** – Carte £ 17/29
♦ Smart, country style lodge, just a stone's throw from the airport and offering a
week's free parking. Stylish, modern bedrooms are luxuriously appointed. Eat in
one of the cosy rooms in the original pub building or the conservatory-style extension. Menus offer hearty portions of good old Irish dishes.

**Caldhame Lodge** without rest          🚗 ⅙ 🎖️ 📶 P VISA ⓒⓞ
102 Moira Rd, Nutts Corner, Southeast : 1.25 mi on A 26 ⊠ BT29 4HG – 𝒞 (028)
9442 3099 – www.caldhamelodge.co.uk
**8 rm** ⌷ – ♦£ 40/45 ♦♦£ 60/70
♦ Purpose-built guesthouse near the airport, with pleasant mix of lawns and
paved terracing. Comfy, slightly kitsch guest areas include a leather-furnished
lounge filled with family photos and a conservatory breakfast room. Good-sized
bedrooms boast warm fabrics.

---

**DERRY/LONDONDERRY** = Doire – Sligo – **712** K2/3 – see Londonderry

---

▯ Ireland

▶ Belfast 18 mi – Ballymena 44 mi

🖼 Warren Rd, 𝒞 (028) 9188 36 24

◉ Ballycopeland Windmill★ **AC** S : 4 mi by A 2 and B 172. Mount Stewart★★★ **AC**,
SW : 10 mi by A 2 and minor road SW – Movilla (cross slabs★), Newtownards, SW :
7 mi by B 172

**Grace Neill's**                         🛋 P VISA ⓒⓞ
33 High St ⊠ BT21 0AH – 𝒞 (02891) 884 595 – www.graceneills.com
**Rest** – Menu £ 18 (lunch) – Carte £ 18/38
♦ Characterful beamed pub – the oldest in Ireland – decorated with antiques and
old pictures. Extensive, largely classical menu, with express lunches and daily fish
and seafood specials.

**Pier 36** with rm                    🛋 🎖️ P VISA ⓒⓞ AE
36 The Parade ⊠ BT21 0HE – 𝒞 (028) 9188 4466 – www.pier36.co.uk – Closed
25 December
**7 rm** ⌷ – ♦£ 50 ♦♦£ 99    **Rest** – Carte £ 18/38
♦ Spacious harbourside pub, set opposite a lighthouse. Extensive menus feature
a mix of classic, modern and international influences, and plenty of fresh, local
seafood. Good weekday deals. Simple, comfy bedrooms boast sea views.

---

▯ Ireland

▶ Belfast 23 mi – Newry 31 mi – Newtownards 22 mi

◉ Cathedral★ **AC** - Down County Museum★ **AC**

◉ Struell Wells★ **AC**, SE : 2 mi by B 1 - Ardglass★ (Jordan's Castle**AC**), SE : 7 mi by B
1 – Inch Abbey★ **AC**, NW : 2 mi by A 7 – Quoile Countryside Centre★ **AC**, E : 2 mi
by A 25 – Castle Ward★★ **AC** (Audley's Castle★), E : 8 mi by A 25

NORTHERN IRELAND

⌂ **Pheasants' Hill Farm** without rest  🗜 🕭 ⟨⟨ᵠ⟩⟩ 🅿 VISA ⓒⓞ
*37 Killyleagh Rd, North : 3 mi on A 22 ⊠ BT30 9BL – 𝒞 (028) 4461 7246*
*– www.pheasantshill.com – Closed 10 December-3 January*
**3 rm** ⌣ – ♦£ 75 ♦♦£ 85
◆ Simple guesthouse surrounded by a 20 acre organic smallholding, complete with rare breeds livestock and a small shop selling their meats. Cosy, homely bedrooms come with pine furnishings and compact shower rooms. Hearty breakfasts.

# DUNDRUM (Dún Droma) – Down – **712** O5 – pop. 1 065 ▮ Ireland     35 D3

▶ Belfast 29 mi – Downpatrick 9 mi – Newcastle 4 mi
◎ Castle★ **AC**
⚙ Castlewellan Forest Park★★ **AC**, W : 4 mi by B 180 and A 50 - Tollymore Forest Park★ **AC**, W : 3 mi by B 180 - Drumena Cashel and Souterrain★, W : 4 mi by B 180

⌂ **Carriage House** without rest  🗜 ⟨⟨ᵠ⟩⟩ 🅿
*71 Main St ⊠ BT33 0LU – 𝒞 (028) 4375 1635*
*– www.carriagehousedundrum.com*
**3 rm** ⌣ – ♦£ 45/50 ♦♦£ 75/80
◆ Welcoming, lilac-washed terraced house with colourful window boxes and attractive rear garden. Comfy, traditionally styled guest areas. Simple bedrooms with plain décor and antique furniture.

✗ **Buck's Head Inn**  🗜 🏠 VISA ⓒⓞ AE
*77-79 Main St ⊠ BT33 0LU – 𝒞 (028) 4375 1868*
*– www.bucksheadrestaurant.com*
**Rest** – Seafood – Menu £ 30 (dinner) – Carte £ 20/29
◆ Informal restaurant with attractive terrace and garden. Have drinks in the lounge then choose a dining room; the front bar is a good spot to dine. Good-sized menus of unfussy, traditional cooking with a local seafood base.

✗ **Mourne Seafood Bar**  🏠 VISA ⓒⓞ AE
*10 Main St ⊠ BT33 0LU – 𝒞 (028) 4375 1377 – www.mourneseafood.com*
*– Closed dinner 24 December, 25 December and Monday-Tuesday in winter*
**Rest** – Seafood – (booking essential in summer) Carte £ 25/29
◆ Informal, rustic restaurant, set on main street; wood-furnished interior with coastal oil paintings. Classical seafood cooking, with oysters and mussels from owners' beds a speciality.

# DUNGANNON (Dún Geanainn) – Dungannon – **712** L4     35 C2
– pop. 11 139 ▮ Ireland

▶ Belfast 42 mi – Ballymena 37 mi – Dundalk 47 mi – Londonderry 60 mi
⚙ The Argory★, S : 5 mi by A 29 and east by minor rd. Ardboe Cross★, NW : 17 mi by A 45, B 161 and B 73 – Springhill★ **AC**, NE : 24 mi by A 29 – Sperrin Mountains★ : Wellbrook Beetling Mill★ **AC**, NW : 22 mi by A 29 and A 505 - Beaghmore Stone Circles★, NW : 24 mi by A 29 and A 505

⌂ **Grange Lodge** ⌾  🗜 ⟨⟨ᵠ⟩⟩ 🅿 VISA ⓒⓞ
*7 Grange Rd, Moy, Southeast : 3.5 mi by A 29 ⊠ BT71 7EJ – 𝒞 (028) 8778 4212*
*– www.grangelodgecountryhouse.com – Closed 20 December-1 February*
**5 rm** ⌣ – ♦£ 60/69 ♦♦£ 85/89     **Rest** – (closed Sunday) Menu £ 36
◆ Attractive Georgian country house set in a peaceful area and surrounded by mature, well-kept gardens, where guests can have afternoon tea. Antique-furnished guest areas display fine sketches and lithographs. Snug, well-appointed bedrooms are immaculately kept and come with good extras. Flower-filled dining room serves traditional menu of unfussy Irish dishes.

: **Benburb** South : 8 mi by B 45 and B 130

✗ **Priory House**                    *VISA* **◎◎** **AE**
*14 Main Street – ℰ (028) 3754 7767 – www.prioryhouserestaurant.com
– Closed 1 January, Good Friday, 2 weeks spring, 25-26 December, Monday and
Tuesday*
**Rest** – Menu £ 25 – Carte £ 22/32
♦ Laid-back, almost bohemian-style bistro and restaurant set within a 200
year old priory that's attached to an art school. Interesting antiques, clocks
and pottery abound. Simple, rustic Irish cooking; dinner is of a more ambitious
nature.

**NNISKILLEN (Inis Ceithleann)** – Fermanagh – 712 J4 – pop. 13 599    34 A2
Ireland

◨ Belfast 87 mi – Londonderry 59 mi
◨ Wellington Rd ℰ (028) 6632 31 10, www.enniskillen.com
◧ Castlecoole, ℰ (028) 6632 52 50
◨ Castle Coole★★★ **AC**, SE : 1 m – Florence Court★★ **AC**, SW : 8 mi by A 4 and A 32
– Marble Arch Caves and Forest Nature Reserve★ **AC**, SW : 10 mi by A 4 and A 32.
NW by A 26 : Lough Erne★★ : Cliffs of Magho Viewpoint★★★ **AC**- Tully Castle★
**AC** – N by A 32, B 72, A 35 and A 47 : Devenish Island★ **AC** - Castle Archdale
Forest Park★ **AC** - White Island★ - Janus Figure★

*(NORTHERN IRELAND — printed vertically in right margin)*

🏨🏨🏨 **Lough Erne Resort**    ≤ 🚗 🐕 🏊 🔌 ⑨ 𝔰 🕰 🏨 🛗 🖖 ✿ 𝄢 📶 🛄 🅿
*Belleek Rd, Northwest : 4 mi on A 46 ⊠ BT93 7ED*    *VISA* **◎◎** **AE** ①
*– ℰ (028) 6632 3230 – www.lochernegolfresort.com*
**89 rm** ⌂ – ✝£ 130/202 ✝✝£ 150/402 – 31 suites – ✝✝£ 280/340
**Rest** *Catalina* – see restaurant listing
**Rest** *Lochside* – (dinner only) Carte £ 19/45
♦ Vast, luxurious golf and leisure resort, set between two loughs. Bedrooms
have a glitzy feel and are extremely well-appointed; suites and lodges are
dotted about the place. Beautiful Thai spa and huge pool boasting a stunning
mosaic wall. Fine dining or steaks and tapas-style small plates in the clubhouse.

🏨🏨🏨 **Manor House** ☙    ≤ 🚗 🔌 𝔰 🕰 🖖 🛗 🖖 ✿ 📶 🅿 *VISA* **◎◎** **AE**
*Killadeas, North : 7.5 mi by A 32 on B 82 ⊠ BT94 1NY – ℰ (028) 6862 2200
– www.manorhouseresorthotel.com*
**79 rm** ⌂ – ✝£ 73/125 ✝✝£ 81/140 – 2 suites
**Rest** *Belleek* – Menu £ 18/28
**Rest** *Cellar Door* – Carte approx. £ 28
♦ Impressive manor house overlooking Lough Erne. Characterful guest areas
and well-equipped leisure and meeting facilities. Traditional bedrooms in main
house, more modern rooms in extensions. Formal dining room boasts ornate
plasterwork and offers classical menus; more casual all-day dining in the old
vaults.

🏠 **Cedars**                    🚗 ✿ 📶 🅿 *VISA* **◎◎**
*301 Killadeas Rd., Irvinestown, North : 10 mi by A 32 on B 82 ⊠ BT94 1PG
– ℰ (028) 6862 1493 – www.cedarsguesthouse.com
– Closed 1 week Christmas*
**10 rm** ⌂ – ✝£ 45/55 ✝✝£ 100/110
**Rest** *Rectory Bistro* – (closed Monday-Tuesday) (dinner only and Sunday lunch)
Carte £ 23/31
♦ Good value, converted 19C former rectory with pleasant gardens. Exudes im-
pression of spaciousness; country-style décor. Individually designed bedrooms:
ask for numbers 2 or 5. Rustic bistro serves hearty cuisine.

XXXX **Catalina** – at Lough Erne Resort  🚗 🍴 ⚓ P VISA ☮
*Belleek Rd, Northwest : 4 mi on A 46* ✉ *BT93 7ED –* 𝒞 *(028) 6632 3230*
*– www.lochernegolfresort.com*
**Rest** – *(dinner only and Sunday lunch)* Menu £ 40 – Carte £ 45/55
♦ Fine dining restaurant boasting great views over Lough Erne, set within a larg
luxurious, resort hotel. Contemporary menu showcases top quality ingredien
from local and artisan producers.

---

**GALGORM** Antrim – Ballymena – **712** N3 – see Ballymena

---

**HILLSBOROUGH** (Cromghlinn) – Lisburn – **712** N4 – pop. 3 400          35
▌ Ireland
▶ Belfast 12 mi
ℹ The Square 𝒞 (028) 9268 97 17, www.discovernorthernireland.com
◉ Town ★ – Fort ★
◙ Rowallane Gardens ★ **AC**, Saintfield, E : 10 mi by B 178 and B 6. The Argory ★, W
25 mi by A 1 and M 1

🏠 **Plough Inn**                                                    P VISA ☮ AE ①
*3 The Square* ✉ *BT26 6AG –* 𝒞 *(028) 9268 2985 – www.bar-retro.com – Closed
25 December*
**Rest** – Menu £ 12/20 – Carte £ 15/25
♦ Family-run 18C coaching inn that's three establishments in one: a bar with a
joining dining room, café and bistro. Dishes range from light snacks and pub cla
sics to modern, international fare.

🏠 **Parson's Nose**                                                    🍴 VISA ☮
*48 Lisburn St.* ✉ *BT26 6AB –* 𝒞 *(028) 9268 3009 – www.theparsonsnose.co.uk*
*– Closed 25 December*
**Rest** – *(booking advisable)* Menu £ 17/22 – Carte £ 21/34
♦ Characterful Georgian property built by the first Marquis of Downshire. Rusti
open-fired bar; restaurant above overlooks a lake in the castle grounds. Unashan
edly traditional menus and generous portions; the daily fish specials are a hit.

**at Annahilt** Southeast : 4 mi on B 177 – ✉ Hillsborough

🏠 **Fortwilliam** without rest                                    🚗 🍴 📶 P VISA ☮
*210 Ballynahinch Rd, Northwest : 0.25 mi on B 177* ✉ *BT26 6BH –* 𝒞 *(028)*
*9268 2255 – www.fortwilliamcountryhouse.com*
**4 rm** ⌂ – ✝£ 45 ✝✝£ 70
♦ Attractive bay-windowed farmhouse with neat gardens, set in 80 acres
land. Keenly run and comfortable throughout. Individually designed bedroom
boast pleasant outlooks and extras; two have private bathrooms.

🏠 **Pheasant**                                                    🍴 P VISA ☮ AE ①
*410 Upper Ballynahinch Rd, North : 1 mi on Lisburn rd* ✉ *BT26 6NR –* 𝒞 *(028)*
*9263 8056 – www.thepheasantrestaurant.co.uk – Closed 12 July and 25-26*
*December*
**Rest** – Menu £ 10/12 – Carte £ 15/30
♦ Sizeable yellow-washed pub with gothic styling and typical Irish feel. Menu
offer local, seasonal produce, with seafood a speciality in summer and game fea
turing highly in the winter.

---

**HOLYWOOD** (Ard Mhic Nasca) – North Down – **712** O4          35 D.
– pop. 12 037 ▌ Ireland
▶ Belfast 7 mi – Bangor 6 mi
⛳ Holywood Demesne Rd, Nuns Walk, 𝒞 (028) 9042 21 38
◙ Cultra : Ulster Folk and Transport Museum ★★ **AC**, NE : 1 mi by A 2

**Culloden** ← �̅ ⬙ 🖪 ⓦ 🖫 🛏 ⬙ 🅰 rest. ⬙ ⬙ 🅿 ⱽⁱˢᵃ ⬀ 🅰🅴 ⓘ
*142 Bangor Rd, East : 1.5 mi on A 2* ⬙ *BT18 0EX* – ℰ *(028) 9042 1066*
*– www.hastingshotels.com*
**102 rm** ⬙ – †£ 190  ††£ 240 – 3 suites
**Rest** *Cultra Inn* – see restaurant listing
**Rest** *Mitre* – *(dinner only and Sunday lunch)* Menu £ 30/45 – Carte Monday-
Friday £ 31/38
♦ Gothic mansion with well-maintained, sculpture-filled gardens and lough
views. Charming, antique-filled interior boasts open fires and fine frescoes. Mix
of characterful bedrooms with pleasant views or more contemporary rooms.
Smart spa. Classical menus and good views in Mitre; informal dining in Cultra Inn.

**Rayanne House** ← 🚗 ⬙ ⬙ 🚛 🅿 ⱽⁱˢᵃ ⬀ ⓘ
*60 Demesne Rd, by My Lady's Mile Rd* ⬙ *BT18 9EX* – ℰ *(028) 9042 5859*
*– www.rayannehouse.com* – *Closed 24 December-15 January and August*
**11 rm** ⬙ – †£ 70/95  ††£ 110/130
**Rest** – *(dinner only) (residents only)* Menu £ 35/48 – Carte £ 25/45
♦ Victorian red-brick house in peaceful residential area. Homely, antique-filled
guest areas. Stylish, contemporary bedrooms with country house feel, good facilities, smart bathrooms and extras. Formal dining room with seasonal menu; interesting breakfasts.

**Beech Hill** without rest ⬙ ← 🚗 ⬙ 🅿 ⱽⁱˢᵃ ⬀ 🅰🅴
*23 Ballymoney Rd, Craigantlet, Southeast : 4.5 mi by A 2 on Craigantlet rd*
⬙ *BT23 4TG* – ℰ *(028) 9042 5892* – *www.beech-hill.net*
**3 rm** ⬙ – †£ 55/60  ††£ 90/100
♦ Country house in rural location. Pleasant clutter of trinkets and antiques in
guest areas which include a conservatory. Neat, traditionally styled bedrooms: a
very fine home.

**Fontana** ⱽⁱˢᵃ ⬀
*61A High St* ⬙ *BT18 9AE* – ℰ *(028) 9080 9908* – *Closed 25-26 December, 1-2
January, Saturday lunch, Sunday dinner and Monday*
**Rest** – Menu £ 18 (lunch) – Carte £ 17/32
♦ Smart, first floor restaurant, accessed via a narrow, town centre passageway.
Modern British cooking displays Mediterranean influences; specials include local
fish, in unfussy, flavoursome combinations. Good value set lunch and midweek
dinner.

**Cultra Inn** – at Culloden Hotel 🚗 ⬙ ⬙ 🅰 🅿 ⱽⁱˢᵃ ⬀ 🅰🅴 ⓘ
*142 Bangor Rd, East : 1.5 mi on A 2* ⬙ *BT18 0EX* – ℰ *(028) 9042 5840*
*– www.hastingshotels.com*
**Rest** – Carte approx. £ 25
♦ Informal restaurant located within the grounds of a famous, antique-filled
Gothic mansion overlooking Belfast Loch. Picnic benches for alfresco dining.
Choose between light bites and grills.

**KILLINCHY** – Ards – 712 O4                                        35 D2
▶ Belfast 16 mi – Newtownards 11 mi – Lisburn 17 mi – Bangor 16 mi

**Balloo House - Restaurant** 🅿 ⱽⁱˢᵃ ⬀
*1 Comber Rd, (1st floor), West : 0.75 mi on A 22* ⬙ *BT23 6PA* – ℰ *(028)
9754 1210* – *www.balloohouse.com* – *Closed 25 December*
**Rest** – *(closed Sunday and Monday) (dinner only) (booking essential)* Menu £ 27
– Carte £ 29/38
♦ Intimate, first floor restaurant with high beamed ceilings and linen-laid tables.
Flavourful classic cooking has modern touches; hearty yet refined dishes feature
local produce.

NORTHERN IRELAND

**LARNE** (Latharna) – Larne – **712** O3 – pop. 18 228 📱 Ireland    **35** D2

▶ Belfast 23 mi – Ballymena 20 mi

🛳 to Fleetwood (Stena Line) daily (8 h) – to Cairnryan (P & O Irish Sea) 3-5 daily (1 h/2 h 15 mn)

🛈 Narrow Gauge Rd ℰ (028) 2826 00 88, www.larne.gov.uk

🅱 Cairndhu Ballygally 192 Coast Rd, ℰ (028) 2858 39 54

◉ SE : Island Magee (Ballylumford Dolmen★), by ferry and 2 mi by B 90 or 18 mi by A 2 and B 90. NW : Antrim Glens★★★ - Murlough Bay★★★ (Fair Head ⩽★★★), N : 46 m by A 2 and minor road – Glenariff Forest Park★★ **AC** (Waterfall★★), N : 30 mi by A 2 and A 43 - Glenariff★, N : 25 mi by A 2 - Glendun★, N : 30 mi by A 2 – Carrickfergus (Castle★★ - St Nicholas' Church★), SW : 15 mi by A 2

⌂    **Manor House** without rest    ⍣ 🄿 VISA ⊚⊚
    *23 Olderfleet Rd, Harbour Highway* ✉ *BT40 1AS*
    *– ℰ (028) 2827 3305 – www.themanorguesthouse.com*
    *– Closed 25-26 December*
    **8 rm** ⌷ – ♦£ 30/35 – ♦♦£ 55/60
    ♦ Large Victorian house filled with antiques; the owner has been here nearly 50 years. Lounge boasts immense Chinese vase and gilded art; snug dining room has flocked walls. Cosy, immaculate bedrooms reached via original carved staircase.

---

**LIMAVADY** (Léim an Mhadaidh) – Limavady – **712** L2 – pop. 12 135    **34** B1
📱 Ireland

▶ Belfast 62 mi – Ballymena 39 mi – Coleraine 13 mi – Londonderry 17 mi

🛈 7 Connell St ℰ (028) 7776 03 07, www.limavady.gov.uk

🅱 Benone Par Three Benone 53 Benone Ave, ℰ (028) 7775 05 55

◉ Sperrin Mountains★ : Roe Valley Country Park★ **AC**, S : 2 mi by B 68 - Glenshane Pass★, S : 15 mi by B 68 and A 6

✗    **Lime Tree**    VISA ⊚⊚ AE
    *60 Catherine St* ✉ *BT49 9DB – ℰ (028) 7776 4300*
    *– www.limetreerest.com – Closed Sunday and Monday*
    **Rest** – *(dinner only)* Menu £ 18 (early dinner weekdays)/26 – Carte £ 28/38
    ♦ Keenly run neighbourhood restaurant, where a traditional exterior hides smart modern hues. Good-sized menus of unfussy classical dishes, with seafood a speciality. Meats and veg are from the village. Friendly, detailed service.

---

**LISNASKEA** – Fermanagh – **712** J5 – pop. 2 739    **34** B3

▶ London 388 mi – Belfast 83 mi – Enniskillen 17 mi – Dublin 91 mi

✗✗✗    **Watermill** with rm    ☰ 🄺 AC rest, ☏ 🄿 VISA ⊚⊚
    *Kilmore Quay, Southwest: 3 mi by B 127* ✉ *BT92 ODT*
    *– ℰ (028) 6772 4369 – www.watermillrestaurant.org*
    *– Closed 2-17 January*
    **7 rm** ⌷ – ♦£ 59/79 – ♦♦£ 79
    **Rest** – French – *(closed Monday and Tuesday) (dinner only) (booking advisable)*
    Menu £ 20 (early dinner) – Carte £ 28/43
    ♦ Charming brick new-build with thatched roof, delightful terrace and superb water gardens flowing down to Lough Erne. Rustic inner boasts immaculately laid tables and a 25,000 litre aquarium. Classical Gallic menu is served by white-gloved waiters. Comfortable, airy bedrooms; some look out across the water.

▶ Belfast 70 mi – Dublin 146 mi

✈ City of Derry Airport : ℰ (028) 7181 0784, E : 6 mi by A 2

🖹 44 Foyle St ℰ (028) 7126 72 84, www.derryvisitor.com

🚉 City of Derry 49 Victoria Rd, ℰ (028) 7134 63 69

◉ Town★ - City Walls and Gates★★ – Guildhall★ **AC** – Long Tower Church★ – St Columb's Cathedral★ **AC** – Tower Museum★ **AC**

◖ Grianan of Aileach★★ (≼★★) (Republic of Ireland) NW : 5 mi by A 2 and N 13. Ulster-American Folk Park★★, S : 33 mi by A 5 - Ulster History Park★ **AC**, S : 32 mi by A 5 and minor road – Sperrin Mountains★ : Glenshane Pass★ (≼★★), SE : 24 mi by A 6 - Sawel Mountain Drive★ (≼★★), S : 22 mi by A 5 and minor roads via Park – Roe Valley Country Park★ **AC**, E : 15 mi by A 2 and B 68 – Beaghmore Stone Circles★, S : 52 mi by A 5, A 505 and minor road

---

 **City**    ≼ 🖾 🐾 ⅃ᴃ 🖪 ⅆ 🕸 rest, 🎇 ⅋ ⅍ 🅿 𝗩𝗜𝗦𝗔 ⓒⓞ 𝐀𝐄

*Queens Quay* ⊠ *BT48 7AS –* ℰ *(028) 7136 5800 – www.cityhotelderry.com*
*– Closed 24-26 December*
**145 rm** ⳨ *–* †£ 79/109 ††£ 86/129 – 1 suite
**Rest** *Thompson's on the River – (bar lunch Monday-Saturday)* Menu £ 21 **s**
*– Carte dinner £ 24/30* **s**
♦ Large, centrally located hotel with underground car park, next to the river and looking towards the bridge. Modern interior with vast lobby, plenty of seating areas and well-equipped leisure centre. Smart bedrooms; those on the upper floors have great outlooks. Formal dining room affords pleasant water views.

---

**Beech Hill Country House** ✎    ⚗ ⅄ ⟋ 🎇 🖪 ⅆ ⅋ ⅍ 🅿
*32 Ardmore Rd, Southeast : 3.5 mi by A 6* ⊠ *BT47 3QP*    𝗩𝗜𝗦𝗔 ⓒⓞ 𝐀𝐄
*–* ℰ *(028) 7134 9279 – www.beech-hill.com*
*– Closed 24-25 December*
**25 rm** ⳨ *–* †£ 105 ††£ 140 – 2 suites
**Rest** *Ardmore –* Menu £ 20/30 **s** *–* Carte £ 32/43 **s**
♦ 18C country house, now personally run but once a US marine camp; one lounge is filled with memorabilia. Accommodation varies from vast rooms to more traditional, rural ones. Restaurant housed within conservatory and old billiard room. Fine garden.

---

 **Ramada H. Da Vinci's**    🖪 ⅆ 🕸 rest, 🎇 ⅋ ⅍ 🅿 𝗩𝗜𝗦𝗔 ⓒⓞ 𝐀𝐄 ⓞ

*15 Culmore Rd, North : 1 mi following signs for Foyle Bridge* ⊠ *BT48 8JB*
*–* ℰ *(028) 7127 9111 – www.davincishotel.com*
*– Closed 24-25 December*
**70 rm** *–* †£ 50/90 ††£ 50/90, ⳨ £ 8.95
**Rest** *Grill Room – (dinner only and Sunday lunch)* Carte £ 17/25
♦ Set beside a characterful Irish pub – now the trendy hotel bar – at the northern edge of the city. Photos of stars who've stayed here fill one wall. Well-equipped, uniform bedrooms improve with grade. Charming brasserie displays rustic beams and exposed brickwork.

---

🍴🍴 **Browns**    🕸 𝗩𝗜𝗦𝗔 ⓒⓞ

*1 Bonds Hill* ⊠ *BT47 6DW –* ℰ *(028) 7134 5180*
*– www.brownsrestaurant.com – Closed Monday, Saturday lunch and Sunday dinner*
**Rest** *– (booking advisable)* Menu £ 18 – Carte £ 25/35
♦ Long-standing neighbourhood restaurant. Plush lounge and intimate dining room with black and white photos and some banquette seating. Cooking is surprisingly modern and technical, and relies on local produce, home-baking and home-smoking.

## MAGHERA (Machaire Rátha) – Magherafelt – 712 L3 – pop. 3 711    35 C2

▶ Belfast 40 mi – Ballymena 19 mi – Coleraine 21 mi – Londonderry 32 mi

### 🏠 Ardtara Country House 🍃    🚗 & 💇 ⁿⁱ P VISA ⓒ AE
*8 Gorteade Rd, Upperlands, North : 3.25 mi by A 29 off B 75 ⊠ BT46 5SA*
*– 𝒞 (028) 7964 4490 – www.ardtara.com*
*– Closed 25-26 December*
**9 rm** 🛏 – ♦£ 60/65 ♦♦£ 100/130
**Rest** – *(closed Sunday lunch) (booking essential for non-residents)* Menu £ 20/32
♦ 19C house with a charming atmosphere. The interior features 'objets trouvés'
collected from owner's travels; original fireplaces set off the individually styled
bedrooms. Restaurant set in former billiard room with hunting mural and panelled walls.

---

## NEWCASTLE (An Caisleán Nua) – Down – 712 O5 – pop. 7 444    35 D3
🟦 Ireland

▶ Belfast 32 mi – Londonderry 101 mi
ℹ 10-14 Central Promenade 𝒞 (028) 4372 22 22, www.newcastle.gov.uk
◉ Castlewellan Forest Park★★ AC, NW : 4 mi by A 50 – Tolymore Forest Park★ AC,
W : 3 mi by B 180 – Dundrum Castle★ AC, NE : 4 mi by A 2. Silent Valley
Reservoir★ (◁★ - ) - Spelga Pass and Dam★ - Kilbroney ForestPark (viewpoint★)
– Annalong Marine Park and Cornmill★ AC, S : 8 mi by A 2 – Downpatrick :
Cathedral★ AC, Down Country Museum★ AC, NE : 20 mi by A 2 and A 25

### 🏨 Slieve Donard    ◁ 🚗 🔳 🌐 🏦 ℔ 💇 🍴 🛏 & 💇 ⁿⁱ 🛁 P VISA ⓒ AE
*Downs Rd ⊠ BT33 0AH – 𝒞 (028) 4372 1066 – www.hastingshotels.com*
**172 rm** 🛏 – ♦£ 130/190 ♦♦£ 170/200 – 6 suites
**Rest Oak** – *(dinner only and lunch July-August)* Carte £ 30/40
**Rest Percy French** – Carte £ 20/27
♦ Grand railway hotel right beside the beach, boasting marble-floored lobby,
interesting museum, superb leisure facilities and excellent sea and mountain
views. Spacious bedrooms in classic or contemporary styles; good mod cons.
Formal Oak offers classical menu. More accessible fare in casual bar-restaurant Percy French.

### 🏨 Burrendale H. & Country Club    🚗 🔳 🌐 🏦 ℔ 🍴 🛏 & 🗚 rest,
*51 Castlewellan Rd, North : 1 mi on A 50*    💇 ⁿⁱ 🛁 P VISA ⓒ AE ⓪
*⊠ BT33 0JY – 𝒞 (028) 4372 2599 – www.burrendale.com*
**67 rm** 🛏 – ♦£ 80 ♦♦£ 140 – 1 suite
**Rest Vine** – *(dinner only and Sunday lunch)* Carte £ 24/27 **s**
**Rest Cottage Kitchen** – Carte £ 18/32 **s**
♦ Privately owned hotel between the Mourne Mountains and Irish Sea, close to
the Royal County Down Golf Course. Well-equipped, contemporary bedrooms. Excellent leisure facilities and vast spa offering a comprehensive range of treatments. Large, open-plan bar and lounge, traditional linen-laid restaurant or all-
day dining in Cottage Kitchen.

---

## NEWTOWNARDS (Baile Nua na hArda) – Ards – 712 O4    35 D2
– pop. 27 821

▶ Belfast 10 mi – Bangor 144 mi – Downpatrick 22 mi

### 🏠 Edenvale House without rest 🍃    ◁ 🚗 💇 ⁿⁱ P VISA ⓒ
*130 Portaferry Rd, Southeast : 2.75 mi on A 20 ⊠ BT22 2AH*
*– 𝒞 (028) 9181 4881 – www.edenvalehouse.com*
*– Closed Christmas and New Year*
**3 rm** 🛏 – ♦£ 50 ♦♦£ 90
♦ Attractive Georgian farmhouse with pleasant mountain views. Traditionally
decorated, with comfy drawing room and wicker-furnished sun room. Spacious,
homely bedrooms boast good facilities.

**PORTRUSH** (Port Rois) – Coleraine – **712** L2 – **pop. 6 372** ▮ Ireland    **35** C1

▶ Belfast 58 mi – Coleraine 4 mi – Londonderry 35 mi

🛈 Sandhill Drive 𝒞 (028) 7082 33 33, www.portrush.org.uk

🏌 Royal Portrush Dunluce Rd, 𝒞 (028) 7082 23 11

◨ Giant's Causeway★★★ (Hamilton's Seat ≤★★, E: 9 m by A 2) - Carrick-a-rede Rope Bridge★★★, E: 14 mi by A 2 and B 15 - Dunluce Castle★★ **AC**, E: 3 mi by A 2 – Gortmore Viewpoint★★, E: 14 mi by A 29, A 2 and minor road - Magilligan Strand★★, E: 13 mi by A 29 and A 2 – Downhill★ (Mussenden Temple★), E: 12 mi by A 29 and A 2

⛩    **Beulah** without rest                                  ⌖ ⌖ **P** 𝗩𝗜𝗦𝗔 ⓒⓒ ⓞ
     16 Causeway St ✉ BT56 8AB – 𝒞 (028) 7082 2413
     – www.beulahguesthouse.com
     **9 rm** ⌂ – ♦£ 40/50 ♦♦£ 60/70
     ♦ Terraced Victorian house in perfect central location. Sound Irish breakfasts. Homely guest lounge. Colourful, co-ordinated and immaculately kept modern bedrooms.

**PORTSTEWART** (Port Stióbhaird) – Coleraine – **712** L2                       **35** C1

▶ Belfast 60 mi – Ballymena 32 mi – Coleraine 6 mi

⛩    **York**                                        ⌖ ⌖ ⌖ ⌖ **P** 𝗩𝗜𝗦𝗔 ⓒⓒ
     2 Station Rd, on A2 ✉ BT55 7DA – 𝒞 (028) 7083 3594
     – www.theyorkportstewart.co.uk
     **8 rm** ⌂ – ♦£ 59/79 ♦♦£ 99/115    **Rest** – Menu £ 9 (lunch) – Carte £ 19/30
     ♦ Smart, contemporary hotel overlooking the North Coast. Stylish bedrooms offer good mod cons; the two front rooms are the largest, with terraces and excellent views. Trendy, marble-floored bar with vivid red stools. Ground floor restaurant offers extensive menus and has a large terrace.

**WARRENPOINT** (An Pointe ) – Newry and Mourne – **712** N5                     **35** C3
– **pop. 7 000**

▶ Belfast 44 mi – Newry 7 mi – Lisburn 37 mi

✗✗    **Restaurant 23**                                    ≤ 𝗔𝗖 𝗩𝗜𝗦𝗔 ⓒⓒ
 ☺    Balmoral Hotel (1st floor), 13 Seaview ✉ BT34 3NJ – 𝒞 (028) 4175 3222
     – www.restaurant23.com – Closed 25 December
     **Rest** – Menu £ 15 (weekday dinner) **s** – Carte £ 29/31 **s**
     ♦ Long-standing restaurant that moved from the high street to the first floor of a seafront hotel. Trendy bar and lounge; dining room with boldly patterned wallpapers, red banquettes and fantastic lough views. Neatly presented, unfussy classics at lunchtime; carefully executed, enticing modern dishes at dinner.

Republic of Ireland

## ACHILL ISLAND (Acaill) – Mayo – 712 B5/6 ▮ Ireland

▶ Dublin 288 km – Castlebar 54 km – Galway 144 km
🛈 Achill Sound ✆ (098) 4 53 84, www.achilltourism.com
🏌 Achill Island Keel, ✆ (098) 4 34 56
◉ Island ★

**DOOGORT (Dumha Goirt) – Mayo – ⊠ Achill Island**

⌂   **Gray's**   🚗 **P** 𝚟𝚒𝚜𝚊 ◉◉ **AE**
– ✆ (098) 43 244 – www.grays-guesthouse.ie – April-September
**14 rm** ⌷ – ✝ € 40/56 ✝✝ € 80/100   **Rest** – (dinner only) Menu € 26/32
♦ A row of tranquil whitewashed cottages with a homely atmosphere; popular with artists. Cosy sitting rooms with fireplaces and simple but spotless bedrooms. Local scene paintings adorn dining room walls.

**KEEL – Mayo – ⊠ Achill Island**

🏠   **Achill Cliff House**   ≼ 🕅 🕅 ⸱⸱⸱ **P** 𝚟𝚒𝚜𝚊 ◉◉ **AE**
– ✆ (098) 43 400 – www.achillcliff.com – Closed 10 January-12 February and 23-26 December
**10 rm** ⌷ – ✝ € 60/90 ✝✝ € 80/100
**Rest** – (dinner only and Sunday lunch) Menu € 27 – Carte € 36/47
♦ Whitewashed modern building against a backdrop of countryside and ocean. Within walking distance of Keel beach. Well-kept, spacious bedrooms with modern furnishings. Spacious restaurant with sea views.

---

## ADARE (Áth Dara) – Limerick – 712 F10 – pop. 982 ▮ Ireland

**38 B2**

▶ Dublin 210 km – Killarney 95 km – Limerick 16 km
🛈 Mains St ✆ (061) 39 62 55, www.ireland-travel-guide.com
◉ Town ★ – Adare Friary ★ - Adare Parish Church ★
◎ Rathkeale (Castle Matrix ★ **AC** - Irish Palatine Heritage Centre ★) W : 12 km by N 21 – Newcastle West ★, W : 26 km by N 21 – Glin Castle ★ **AC**, W : 46.5 km by N 21, R 518 and N 69

🏨🏨   **Adare Manor H. and Golf Resort** ⤸   ≼ 🚗 🐾 🍴 🛏 **18** 🛗
– ✆ (061) 396 566 – www.adaremanor.com   🕅 ⸱⸱⸱ 🛁 **P** 𝚟𝚒𝚜𝚊 ◉◉ **AE** ◉
– closed 24-26 December
**60 rm** ⌷ – ✝ € 290/493 ✝✝ € 290/493
**Rest Oakroom** – see restaurant listing
**Rest The Carriagehouse** – Carte € 30/46 s
♦ Part-19C Gothic mansion in 750 acres of riverside parkland; home to the Irish Open. Spacious, elaborately decorated guest areas. Most characterful bedrooms are in the main house and boast fireplaces, wood-panelling and ornate plasterwork. Choose between formal Oakroom or more casual Carriagehouse for dinner.

🏨🏨   **Dunraven Arms**   🚗 🔲 🏋 🛗 ⸱⸱⸱ 🛁 **P** 𝚟𝚒𝚜𝚊 ◉◉ **AE** ◉
Main St – ✆ (061) 605 900 – www.dunravenhotel.com
**86 rm** ⌷ – ✝ € 100/155 ✝✝ € 195
**Rest Maigue Restaurant** – see restaurant listing
♦ Greatly extended Irish coaching inn dating back to 1792. Various small lounges and good-sized, classical bedrooms – some with four-posters and colourful garden outlooks – are dotted about the place. Busy bar and annexed conference suite.

🍴🍴🍴   **Oakroom** – at Adare Manor Hotel and Golf Resort   🚗 🔾 **P** 𝚟𝚒𝚜𝚊 ◉◉ **AE** ◉
– ✆ (061) 396 566 – www.adaremanor.com – closed 24-26 December
**Rest** – (dinner only) Carte € 51/70 s
♦ Formal dining room and intimate conservatory boasting pleasant water views, located in a part-19C Gothic mansion on the banks of the River Maigue. Classically based menus follow the seasons.

XX **Wild Geese**                                                    VISA ◐◉ AE ◍

*Rose Cottage – 𝒞 (061) 396 451 – www.thewild-geese.com – Closed 24-26*
*December, 2 weeks January, Sunday dinner and Monday*
**Rest** *– (dinner only and Sunday lunch) (booking essential)* Menu € 25/35 (early
dinner) – Carte € 35/48
 ◆ Traditional 18C cottage on main street. Friendly service and cosy welcoming
atmosphere. Varied menu with classic and international influences uses much
fresh local produce.

XX **Maigue Restaurant** – at Dunraven Arms Hotel            ⬚ P VISA ◐◉ AE ◍

*Main St – 𝒞 (061) 396 633 – www.dunravenhotel.com*
**Rest** *– (dinner only and Sunday lunch)* Menu € 30 – Carte € 31/44
 ◆ Linen-clad restaurant with crystal chandeliers, set in a greatly extended 18C Irish coaching inn. Menus are firmly rooted in tradition and a beef trolley is
wheeled around at every service.

X **White Sage**                                               ⬚ VISA ◐◉ AE ◍
☺
*Main St – 𝒞 (061) 396 004 – www.whitesagerestaurant.com – Closed last 2*
*weeks January, 24-26 December, Good Friday, Sunday and Monday (except bank*
*holidays)*
**Rest** *– (dinner only) (booking advisable)* Menu € 32 (weekday dinner)
– Carte € 35/45
 ◆ Set in a row of 300 year old thatched cottages, with a spacious, candlelit inner,
a small rear terrace and a pleasant alfresco seating area in front. The experienced
chef creates tasty European-based dishes using regionally sourced produce. Service is charming.

---

**ARAN ISLANDS** (Oileáin Árann) – Galway – **712** C/D8 – pop. 1 280          **38** B1
▮ Ireland

▶ Dublin 260 km – Galway 43 km – Limerick 145 km – Ennis 111 km

**Access** Access by boat or aeroplane from Galway city or by boat from Kilkieran,
Rossaveel or Fisherstreet (Clare) and by aeroplane from Inverin

🇮 Inis Mor 𝒞 (099) 6 12 63, www.aranislands.ie

⬚ Islands★ – Inishmore (Dún Aonghasa★★★)

**INISHMORE** – Galway

🏨 **Óstán Árann**                           ≤ ⬚ ⬚ 🍴 & rm, ⤴ P VISA ◐◉

*Kilronan – 𝒞 (099) 61 104 – www.aranislandshotel.com – mid-February to*
*October*
**22 rm** ⬚ – ✝ € 59/79 ✝✝ € 78/118
**Rest** *– (bar lunch)* Menu € 20 **s** – Carte € 26/40 **s**
 ◆ Comfortable, family-owned hotel with great view of harbour. Bustling bar with
live music most nights in high season. Spacious, up-to-date bedrooms are decorated in bright colours. Traditional dishes served in wood-floored restaurant.

🏠 **Pier House**                                  ≤ ⬚ ⤴ P VISA ◐◉

*Kilronan – 𝒞 (099) 61 417 – www.pierhousearan.com – March-October*
**12 rm** ⬚ – ✝ € 50/80 ✝✝ € 80/100
**Rest** *The Restaurant* – see restaurant listing
 ◆ Smart hotel in a great location overlooking Kilronan pier, not far from the
ferry point and village centre; take advantage of the wonderful outlook from
the comfortable lounge. Cosy bedrooms come with good mod cons and some
share the view.

🏡 **Ard Einne Guesthouse** ⬚                    ≤ ⬚ ⤴ rm, P VISA ◐◉

*Killeany – 𝒞 (099) 61 126 – www.ardeinne.com – Closed December-January*
**8 rm** ⬚ – ✝ € 55/90 ✝✝ € 80/120   **Rest** – Menu € 27
 ◆ Close to the airport, an attractive chalet-style guesthouse set back on a hill and
boasting superb views of Killeany Bay; relax in the comfy lounge while taking it
all in. Uniformly decorated bedrooms have pine furnishings and afford great outlooks. Homely cooking with a menu featuring lots of island fish.

X  **The Restaurant** – at Pier House Hotel  ← 🚗 🛋 **P** VISA ⦿
*Kilronan* – ℰ *(099) 61 417* – *www.pierhouserestaurant.com* – *March-October*
**Rest** – *(light lunch)* Menu € 25 – Carte € 30/44
♦ Well-regarded hotel restaurant with cosy, intimate interior; popular for celebrating occasions. Light lunches and more substantial dinners where they offer homely country cooking with a modern edge. Try the blackboard seafood specials.

---

**INISHMAAN** – Galway                                          **38** B1

XX  **Inis Meáin Restaurant & Suites** with rm 🌿  ← 🚗 🌊 🍴 📶 **P**
– ℰ *(086) 826 60 26* – *www.inismeain.com* – *March-September, 2*  VISA ⦿
*night minimum stay*
**4 rm** 🛏 – 👫 € 250/400 – 1 suite
**Rest** – *(closed Sunday-Tuesday) (dinner only) (booking essential)* Carte € 30/60
♦ Striking stone building in futuristic design, owned and run by charming native of this unspoilt island and his wife. Unpretentious modern cooking exploits finest local ingredients, including seafood caught in currachs and delicious home-grown potatoes. Minimalist bedrooms feature natural furnishings. Breakfast is delivered to your room.

---

**ARDMORE** (Aird Mhór) – Waterford – **712** I12 – pop. 412          **39** C3
▶ Dublin 240 km – Waterford 71 km – Cork 60 km – Kilkenny 123 km

🏨  **Cliff House**  ← 🛋 🔳 ⦿ 🌿 🧖 🍴 🏊 🤿 📶 🚴 **P** VISA ⦿ AE ①
– ℰ *(024) 87 800* – *www.thecliffhousehotel.com* – *Closed 24-26 December*
**36 rm** 🛏 – 🚹 € 175/200 👫 € 200/225 – 3 suites
**Rest** *House* 🥢 – see restaurant listing
**Rest** *Bar* – Menu € 32/40 – Carte € 33/49
♦ Stylish hotel on the cliffside, overlooking the bay. Slate walls, Irish fabrics and bold colours feature throughout; lower floor houses a relaxing spa. Modern bedrooms boast backlit glass artwork: some have balconies; all have smart bathrooms and a view. Comfy bar and slate-floored terrace offer an extensive menu.

XXX  **House** – at Cliff House Hotel  ← 🛋 **P** VISA ⦿ AE ①
🥢  – ℰ *(024) 87 800* – *www.thecliffhousehotel.com* – *Closed 24-26 December*
**Rest** – *(Restricted opening in low season) (dinner only)* Menu € 65
**Spec.** Organic Bantry Bay salmon with beetroot textures. Skeaghanore duck with Earl Grey raisins. Dark chocolate mousse with olive oil crumbs.
♦ Smart hotel restaurant, where full length windows provide every table with an impressive coastal view. Irish/garden produce features in concise menus; cooking is technically strong and complex. Creative, original dishes combine good flavours and textures.

---

**ARTHURSTOWN** (Colmán) – Wexford – **712** L11 – pop. 159          **39** D2
▶ Dublin 166 km – Cork 159 km – Limerick 162 km – Waterford 42 km

🏨  **Dunbrody Country House** 🌿  ← 🚗 🐾 🛋 🚹 rm, 🍴 📶 **P**
– ℰ *(051) 389 600* – *www.dunbrodyhouse.com*  VISA ⦿ AE ①
– *Closed 19-27 December and Monday-Tuesday except July-August*
**16 rm** 🛏 – 🚹 € 145/165 👫 € 245/325 – 6 suites
**Rest** – *(closed Sunday and Monday ) (dinner only and Sunday lunch) (booking essential for non-residents)* Menu € 35/65 – Carte € 40/65
♦ Part-Georgian former hunting lodge that once belonged to the Marquis of Donegal. Comfortable lounge and large bar with marble-topped counter. Spacious bedrooms are furnished in a period style. Classical restaurant offers modern menu with some Mediterranean influences; dishes feature top quality Irish produce.

## ASHFORD (Áth na Fuinseog) – Wicklow – 712 N8 – pop. 1 349    39 D2

▶ Dublin 43 km – Rathdrum 17 km – Wicklow 6 km

⌂ **Ballyknocken House** 🌾    🍴 🕭 🍽 ⅌ 𝐏 𝗩𝗜𝗦𝗔 ⓒⓞ
*Glenealy, South : 4.75 km on L 1096 – ℰ (0404) 44 627 – www.ballyknocken.com
– February-November*
**7 rm** ⌨ – ♦ € 90/94 ♦♦ € 110/118
**Rest** – *(dinner only Friday-Saturday)* Menu € 45
♦ Part-Victorian house with neat gardens and adjoining cookery school, located next to the family farm. Traditional lounge and good-sized bedrooms
with antique furnishings, modern feature walls and bright fabrics; some have
claw-foot baths. Traditional dishes of local produce taken at gingham-clothed
tables.

## ATHLONE (Baile Átha Luain) – Westmeath – 712 I7 – pop. 17 544    37 C3

▌ Ireland

▶ Dublin 120 km – Galway 92 km – Limerick 120 km – Roscommon 32 km

🛈 St Peter's Sq ℰ (090) 647 21 07, www.athlonechamber.ie

🖼 Hodson Bay, ℰ (090) 6 49 20 73

🅲 Clonmacnois★★★ (Grave Slabs★, Cross of the Scriptures★) S : 21 km by N 6 and N
62 – N : Lough Ree (Ballykeeran Viewpoint★)

🏛 **Sheraton Athlone**    🔲 📶 📶 🕭 🗐 ♿ 🅰🅲 🍽 📡 🏋 🛆 𝗩𝗜𝗦𝗔 ⓒⓞ 🅰🅴
*Gleeson St – ℰ (090) 645 1000 – www.sheratonathlone.com – Closed 25
December*
**166 rm** ⌨ – ♦ € 155 ♦♦ € 230 – 1 suite
**Rest** – Menu € 25/40 – Carte € 36/43
♦ 12 storey glass tower beside the shopping centre. Bedroom grades increase
with floor number: all have excellent mod cons; some boast super lough and river
views. Very smart leisure, spa and aquatics area. Eat in laid-back café, chic bar or
elegant restaurant.

⌂ **Shelmalier House** without rest    🛆 📶 🍽 📡 𝐏 𝗩𝗜𝗦𝗔 ⓒⓞ
*Retreat Rd., Cartrontroy, East : 2.5 km by Dublin rd (N 6) – ℰ (090) 647 22 45
– www.shelmalierhouse.com – March-November*
**7 rm** ⌨ – ♦ € 40 ♦♦ € 70
♦ Well-run guesthouse with homely décor, sauna and hot tub. Clean, comfortable
bedrooms, most with polished wood floors – Room 3 is best. Extensive breakfast
menu includes a daily special.

✗ **Left Bank Bistro**    🅰🅲 𝗩𝗜𝗦𝗔 ⓒⓞ 🅰🅴
*Fry Pl – ℰ (090) 649 44 46 – www.leftbankbistro.com – Closed 1 week Christmas,
Sunday and Monday*
**Rest** – Menu € 25 (early dinner) – Carte € 24/40
♦ Keenly run bistro with airy interior, rough floorboards, brick walls and open-
plan kitchen. Extensive menus offer an eclectic mix, from Irish beef and local fish
specials through to Asian fare.

✗ **Kin Khao**    🅰🅲 𝗩𝗜𝗦𝗔 ⓒⓞ
*Abbey Lane – ℰ (090) 649 88 05 – www.kinkhaothai.ie – Closed 24-26 December*
**Rest** – Thai – *(dinner only and lunch Wednesday-Friday and Sunday)*
Menu € 10/20 – Carte € 22/36
♦ Vivid yellow building with red window frames, hidden down a side street,
close to the castle. Small downstairs bar; tapestries hang in main room. Good
choice of authentic Thai dishes and daily specials – try the owner's recom-
mendations.

**at Glasson** Northeast : 8 km on N 55 – ⊠ Athlone

**Glasson Golf H. & Country Club** ⌖
West : 2.75 km – ℰ (090) 648 51 20
– www.glassongolfhotel.ie
**65 rm** – † € 100/160 †† € 190/240
**Rest** – (bar lunch) Menu € 38 **s** – Carte € 21/43 **s**
♦ Greatly extended period house with views over the golf course and Lough Ree.
The owner was born here and several family generations are now involved. Many
visitors are golfers and golfing memorabilia fills the walls. Spacious, modern bedrooms; some with huge balconies. Classical menu served in dining room.

**Wineport Lodge** ⌖
Southwest : 1.5 km – ℰ (090) 643 90 10 – www.wineport.ie – Closed 24-26
December
**28 rm** – † € 125/155 †† € 210/240 – 1 suite
**Rest** – (dinner only and Sunday lunch) Carte € 30/59
♦ Superbly set, with the bedroom wing following the line of the lough shore and
each room boasting a waterside terrace or balcony. Luxurious bedrooms range in
size; it's worth paying the extra for the Captain's Suite. 2 treatment rooms and a
rooftop hot tub for relaxation. Extensive menus of seasonal produce.

**Glasson Stone Lodge** without rest
– ℰ (090) 648 50 04 – www.glassonstonelodge.com – May-October
**6 rm** – † € 50 †† € 70
♦ Smart guesthouse built from Irish limestone. Pine features strongly; bedrooms
boast thoughtful extras and locally made furniture. Breakfast includes homemade
bread and fruit from the garden.

**Fatted Calf**
– ℰ (09064) 85 208 – www.thefattedcalf.ie – Closed 25 December, Good Friday
and Monday except bank holidays
**Rest** – Carte € 22/44
♦ Well-run pub with attractive wood-panelled bar hung original Guinness and Gil-
beys signs and a locals snug complete with pool table. Dishes range from hand-
made sausages to local rabbit terrine; tasty specials are a feature in the evening.

---

**AUGHRIM** (Eachroim) – Wicklow – **712** N9 – pop. 1 145                    **39** D2
▶ Dublin 74 km – Waterford 124 km – Wexford 96 km
🛈 Ballinasloe ℰ (090) 9 76 39 39, www.wicklowtourism.ie

**Brooklodge H & Wells Spa** ⌖
Macreddin Village, North : 3.25 km – ℰ (0402) 36 444
– www.brooklodge.com
**89 rm** – † € 140/160 †† € 200/240 – 1 suite
**Rest Strawberry Tree Rest Armento** – see restaurant listing
♦ Sprawling hotel in 180 peaceful acres in the Wicklow Valley. Flag-floored reception, comfy lounge, informal café and bar. Smart, modern bedrooms with
large bathrooms; some in an annexe, along with the conference rooms. State-of-
the-art spa.

**Strawberry Tree** – at Brooklodge Hotel & Wells Spa
Macreddin Village, North : 3.25 km – ℰ (0402) 36 444
– www.brooklodge.com
**Rest** – (dinner only) Menu € 65
♦ Formal restaurant with intimate, atmospheric feel, set on a village-style estate.
Menus feature wild and organic ingredients sourced form local artisan suppliers.
Communal 'Feasts' available.

REPUBLIC OF IRELAND

AUGHRIM

## Armento – at Brooklodge Hotel & Wells Spa
*Macreddin Village, North : 3.25 km –* ℰ *(0402) 36 444 – www.brooklodge.com – closed Monday except March-August, Tuesday October-February and Wednesday November-March)*
**Rest** – Italian – *(dinner only)* Menu € 30
♦ Informal Italian restaurant set in a smart hotel on a secluded 180 acre estate. Southern Italian menus feature artisan produce imported from Armento and pizzas cooked in the wood-fired oven.

## AVOCA (Abhóca) – Wicklow – 712 N9 – pop. 734 ▌ Ireland    39 D2
▶ Dublin 75 km – Waterford 116 km – Wexford 88 km
◐ Avondale★, N : by R 752 – Meeting of the Waters★, N : by R 752

### Keppel's Farmhouse without rest
*Ballanagh, South : 3.25 km by unmarked rd –* ℰ *(0402) 35 168 – www.keppelsfarmhouse.ie – mid-May to mid-October*
**5 rm** � – ♦ € 45/50 ♦♦ € 70/80
♦ Small farmhouse with colourful garden and friendly owners. Neat, brightly decorated bedrooms with compact shower rooms and lovely views over the vale. Large home-cooked and buffet breakfasts feature duck and hen eggs from their own flock.

## BAGENALSTOWN (Muine Bheag) – Carlow – 712 L9 – pop. 2 532    39 D2
▶ Dublin 101 km – Carlow 16 km – Kilkenny 21 km – Wexford 59 km

### Kilgraney Country House
*South : 6.5 km by R 705 (Borris Rd) –* ℰ *(059) 977 52 83 – www.kilgraneyhouse.com – March-October*
**7 rm** ⊆ – ♦ € 135 ♦♦ € 240 – 2 suites
**Rest** – *(closed Monday-Wednesday March-June and September-October, and Tuesday-Wednesday July and August) (dinner only) (booking essential)* Menu € 52
♦ Georgian country house adopting a truly holistic approach. Period features blend with modern, minimalist furnishings; the mood is calm and peaceful. Small tea room, craft gallery and spa with relaxation room; pleasant herb, veg, zodiac and monastic gardens. Modern menus of clean, fresh cooking with European influences.

## BALLINA (Béal an Átha) – Mayo – 712 E5 – pop. 10 490 ▌ Ireland    36 B2
▶ Dublin 241 km – Galway 117 km – Roscommon 103 km – Sligo 59 km
ℹ Cathedral Rd ℰ (096) 7 08 48, www.towns.mayo-ireland.ie
🏌 Mossgrove Shanaghy, ℰ (096) 2 10 50
◐ Rosserk Abbey★, N : 6.5 km by R 314. Moyne Abbey★, N : 11.25 km by R 314 - Pontoon Bridge View (≤★), S : 19.25 km by N 26 and R 310 – Downpatrick Head★, N : 32 km by R 314

### Ice House
*The Quay Village, Northeast : 2.5 km by N 59 –* ℰ *(096) 23 500 – www.theicehouse.ie – closed 24-26 December*
**32 rm** ⊆ – ♦ € 110/220 ♦♦ € 150/250 – 6 suites
**Rest** – *(dinner only and Sunday lunch)* Menu € 29/39 – Carte € 34/49
♦ A former ice vault for local fishermen with two modern extensions. Terrific river views. The bedrooms a quirky mix of the old and the new; some with full-length windows. Modern menus in restaurant.

### Crockets on the Quay with rm
*The Quay, Northeast : 2.5 km by N 59 –* ℰ *(096) 75 930 – www.crocketsonthequay.ie – Closed 25 December and Good Friday*
**8 rm** – ♦ € 30 ♦♦ € 50, ⊆ €10
**Rest** – *(dinner only and lunch Saturday and Sunday)* Carte € 26/36
♦ Vibrant orange pub with a lively atmosphere, which hosts regular poker, quiz and music nights. Tasty, generously proportioned dishes include local Irish steaks. Serves dinner only. Modest, well-kept bedrooms; those over the restaurant are the quietest.

REPUBLIC OF IRELAND

## BALLINADEE (Baile na Daidhche) – **Cork** – **712** G12 – pop. 425      **38** B3

▶ Dublin 185 km – Cork 25 km – Limerick 86 km – Galway 148 km

⌂ **Glebe Country House** ⌖      🚗 🛜 **P** **VISA** 🄫 ⓓ
– ℰ *(021) 477 82 94 – www.glebecountryhouse.com – Closed Christmas*
**4 rm** ⌷ – **†** € 45/50 **††** € 90/100    **Rest** – Menu € 35 **s**
♦ Creeper-clad rectory dating back to 1854. Handsomely furnished drawing room; well-chosen fabrics and fine wooden beds in pretty bedrooms, one with French windows opening into the garden. Classical county house cooking with veg from the garden and fish from the local boats.

## BALLINASLOE (Béal Átha na Sluaighe) – **Galway** – **712** H8      **36** B3
– pop. 6 303  📕 Ireland

▶ Dublin 146 km – Galway 66 km – Limerick 106 km – Roscommon 58 km

ℹ Bridge St ℰ (0909) 64 26 04, www.ballinasloe.com

🔟₈ Rossgloss, ℰ (0905) 4 21 26

🔟₉ Mountbellew, ℰ (090) 9 67 92 59

🄶 Clonfert Cathedral★ (west doorway★★), SW : by R 355 and minor roads. Turoe Stone, Bullaun★, SW : 29 km by R 348 and R 350 – Loughrea (St Brendan's Cathedral★), SW : 29 km by N 6 – Clonmacnoise★★★ (grave slabs★, Cross of the Scriptures★) E : 21 km by R 357 and R 444

🏠 **Melodys at Moycarn**      🚗 🛜 🛏 �④ rm, ⚿ ᴚ **P** **VISA** 🄫
*Shannonbridge Rd, Southeast : 2.5 km by N 6 off R 357 – ℰ (090) 964 50 50
– www.moycarnlodge.ie – Closed 25-26 December*
**15 rm** ⌷ – **†** € 39/49 **††** € 78/99    **Rest** – Carte € 19/32
♦ Purpose-built hotel run by friendly, experienced owners, with pleasant gardens and terrace overlooking the river – where there's free berthing for guests. Light, airy bedrooms; five open onto a large shared balcony boasting river views. Rustic bar and restaurant offer accessible menu of traditional dishes.

## BALLINGARRY (Baile an Gharraí) – **Limerick** – **712** F10 – pop. 348      **38** B2
📕 Ireland

▶ Dublin 227 km – Killarney 90 km – Limerick 29 km

🄶 Kilmallock★ (Kilmallock Abbey★, Collegiate Church★), SE : 24 km by R 518 – Lough Gur Interpretive Centre★ **AC**, NE : 29 km by R 519, minor road to Croom, R 516 and R 512 – Monasteranenagh Abbey★, NE : 24 km by R 519 and minor road to Croom

🏠 **Mustard Seed at Echo Lodge** ⌖      🚗 🛜 ⚿ ᴚ **P** **VISA** 🄫 🄰🄴
– ℰ *(069) 68 508 – www.mustardseed.ie – Closed late January-mid February and 24-26 December*
**14 rm** ⌷ – **†** € 130 **††** € 240 – 2 suites    **Rest** – *(dinner only)* Menu € 63
♦ Converted convent with very neat gardens and peaceful appeal. Cosy lounge with fireplace and beautiful fresh flowers. Individually furnished rooms with mix of antiques. Meals enlivened by home-grown herbs and organic farm produce.

## BALLINROBE (Baile an Róba) – **Mayo** – **712** E7 – pop. 2 098      **36** B3

▶ Dublin 163 km – Castlebar 18 km – Galway 31 km – Westport 20 km

🏠 **JJ Gannons** with rm      🛜 ᴚ rm, 🄰🄲 ⚿ ᴚ **P** **VISA** 🄫
*Main St – ℰ (094) 954 10 08 – www.jjgannons.com – Closed 25 December*
**10 rm** ⌷ – **†** € 65/70 **††** € 135/150
**Rest** – Menu € 25 (dinner) – Carte € 21/40
♦ Run by the third generation of the Gannon family, with an atmospheric front bar and a smart, spacious restaurant. Satisfyingly traditional dishes, fish specials and eager service. Spacious, comfortable bedrooms have a bright, minimalist style.

**BALLSBRIDGE** = Droichead na Dothra – Dublin – **712** N8 – see Dublin

---

**BALLYBOFEY** (Bealach Féich) – **Donegal** – **712** I3 – pop. 4 176     37 C1

▶ Dublin 238 km – Londonderry 48 km – Sligo 93 km

🏌 Ballybofey & Stranorlar The Glebe, 𝒞 (074) 3 10 93

  🏨  **Kee's**     🔲 🕸 ♨ 🛗 ⅙ 🍴 🖫 ℗ 𝗩𝗜𝗦𝗔 ⅏ 𝗔𝗘 ①
      *Main St, Stranorlar, Northeast : 0.75 km on N 15 –* 𝒞 *(074) 913 10 18*
      *– www.keeshotel.ie*
      **53 rm** 🖵 – 🛉 € 96/106 🛉🛉 € 158/178    **Rest** – Carte € 25/50 **s**
      ♦ Long-standing, family-run hotel in town centre. Bedrooms in newer building
      are more spacious and modern. Atmospheric bar and raised lounge area. Popular
      favourites served in informal, wood-furnished restaurant.

---

**BALLYBUNION** (Baile an Bhuinneánaigh) – **Kerry** – **712** D10     38 A2
– **pop. 1 365** 📗 Ireland

▶ Dublin 283 km – Limerick 90 km – Tralee 42 km

🏌 Ballybunnion Sandhill Rd, 𝒞 (068) 2 71 46

◉ Rattoo Round Tower★, S : 10 km by R 551. Ardfert★, S : 29 km by R 551, R 556
and minor road W – Banna Strand★, S : 28 km by R 551 – Carrigafoyle Castle★,
NE : 21 km by R 551 – Glin Castle★ **AC**, E : 30.5 km by R 551 and N 69

  🏠  **Teach de Broc Country House**     🛗 ⅙ ⌀ 🍴 ℗ 𝗩𝗜𝗦𝗔 ⅏ ①
      *Link Rd, South : 2.5 km on Golf Club Rd –* 𝒞 *(068) 27 581*
      *– www.ballybuniongolf.com – March-October*
      **14 rm** 🖵 – 🛉 € 80/100 🛉🛉 € 120/150
      **Rest *Strollers*** – *(light lunch)* Menu € 25 (Sunday lunch) – Carte € 24/40
      ♦ Stylish house by the Ballybunion golf course. Spacious, modern interior boasts
      a nicely furnished bar-lounge with outdoor seating. Bedrooms are extremely com-
      fortable and have smart bathrooms. Elegant dining room with smartly laid tables
      offers wide-ranging menu.

  🏠  **19th Lodge** without rest     🚗 ⅙ 🆔 ⌀ 🍴 ℗ 𝗩𝗜𝗦𝗔 ⅏
      *–* 𝒞 *(068) 27 592 – www.ballybuniongolflodge.com – Closed Christmas, restricted*
      *opening in winter*
      **14 rm** 🖵 – 🛉 € 70/130 🛉🛉 € 100/180
      ♦ Comfortable house overlooking the fairways of the famed course and filled
      with golfing memorabilia. Comfy first floor lounge; pleasant, classical décor
      throughout. Executive bedrooms boast both showers and spa baths. Substantial
      breakfasts.

---

**BALLYCASTLE** (Baile an Chaisil) – **Mayo** – **712** D5 – pop. 215     36 B2
📗 Ireland

▶ Dublin 267 km – Galway 140 km – Sligo 88 km

◉ Cáide Fields★, **AC**, NE : 8 km by R 314

  🏨  **Stella Maris** ⌀     ≼ 🚗 ⅙ rm, ⌀ 🍴 ℗ 𝗩𝗜𝗦𝗔 ⅏ ①
      *Northwest : 3 km by R 314 –* 𝒞 *(096) 43 322 – www.stellamarisireland.com – 24*
      *April-September*
      **12 rm** 🖵 – 🛉 € 170 🛉🛉 € 250
      **Rest** – *(dinner only) (booking essential)* Carte € 35/55
      ♦ Former coastguard station and fort in a great spot overlooking the bay. Public
      areas include a long conservatory. Attractive rooms with antique and contempo-
      rary furnishings. Modern menus in stylish dining room.

---

**BALLYCONNELL** (Báal Atha Conaill) – **Cavan** – **712** J5 – pop. 747     37 C2

▶ Dublin 143 km – Drogheda 122 km – Enniskillen 37 km

🏌 Slieve Russell, 𝒞 (049) 952 64 58

**Slieve Russell**

*Southeast : 2.75 km on N 87* – ℰ *(049) 952 64 44*
– *www.slieverussell.ie*     VISA ◑◑ AE ⓪

**220 rm** ⌷ – ♦ € 109 ♦♦ € 158 – 2 suites

**Rest Conall Cearnach** – *(Sunday lunch and open dinner Friday-Saturday during off-peak season)* Menu € 27/50 **s** – Carte € 34/56 **s**

**Rest Setanta** – ℰ *(049) 952 50 14 (closed Sunday lunch) (dinner only and lunch Saturday and Monday)* Menu € 19 (lunch) **s** – Carte € 29/53 **s**

♦ Impressive façade in mock-Georgian style, with neo-classical lobby. Bedrooms overlooking grounds are large and luxurious with every modern convenience. Restaurants named after Irish folk heroes. Classical dishes in formal Conall Cearnach. Relaxed, stylish Setanta offers eclectic Mediterranean menu.

---

**BALLYCOTTON (Baile Choitín)** – **Cork** – **712** H12 – **pop. 412**     **39** C3

Ireland

▶ Dublin 265 km – Cork 43 km – Waterford 106 km

Cloyne Cathedral★, NW : by R 629

**Bayview**     ← ◻ ◐ ▤ ◈ **P** VISA ◑◑ AE ⓪

– ℰ *(021) 464 67 46* – *www.thebayviewhotel.com* – *May-October*

**33 rm** – ♦ € 70/149 ♦♦ € 70/149, ⌷ € 15 – 2 suites

**Rest** – *(bar lunch Monday-Saturday)* Carte € 41/57

♦ A series of cottages in an elevated position with fine views of bay, harbour and island. Bar and lounge in library style with sofas. Spacious, comfy rooms with ocean views. Warm, inviting dining room.

---

**BALLYFARNAN (Béal Átha Fearnáin)** – **Roscommon** – **712** H5     **37** C2
– **pop. 182**

▶ Dublin 111 km – Roscommon 42 km – Sligo 21 km – Longford 38 km

**Kilronan Castle** 🐾     ← ◻ ◐ ▤ ◈ ▥ ◈ 🎧 ◻ ◐ ▤ ◈ 🎧 **P**

*South East : 3.5 km on Keadew rd* – ℰ *(071) 961 80 00*
– *www.kilronancastle.ie*     VISA ◑◑ AE ⓪

**84 rm** – ♦ € 145/165 ♦♦ € 165/185

**Rest Douglas Hyde** – *(dinner only and Sunday lunch)* Menu € 45
– Carte € 40/50

♦ Imposing restored castle, with wood panelling, antiques, portraits and a suit of armour. Opulent red and gold bedrooms offer a high level of comfort. Impressive hydrotherapy centre. Grand dining room; traditional menu uses local produce.

---

**BALLYFIN** – **Laois** – **712** J8     **39** C1

▶ Dublin 69 km – Portlaoise 11 km – Cork 114 km – Limerick 67 km

**Ballyfin** 🐾     ← ◻ ◐ ▤ ◈ ▥ 🎧 ◻ ◐ rm, 🎧 ◈ **P** VISA ◑◑ AE ⓪

– ℰ *(057) 875 58 66* – *www.ballyfin.com* – *March-December*

**13 rm** *(dinner included)* ⌷ – ♦ € 600/950 ♦♦ € 1150/1400 – 2 suites

**Rest** – *(residents only)*

♦ Immaculate Regency mansion built in 1820 and set in 600 acres. Stunning interior with gold leaf decorated drawing room and library featuring 7,000 antique books. Elegant, antique-furnished bedrooms boast marble bathrooms. Excellent service. 5 course tasting menu of classical dishes with contemporary touches.

Ireland

▶ Dublin 347 km – Cork 88 km – Killarney 72 km

🔟 Bantry Bay Donemark, ℰ (027) 5 05 79

◉ Bantry Bay★ - Bantry House★ **AC**, S : 5 km by R 584. Glengarriff★ (Ilnacullin★★, access by boat) NW : 13 km by N 71 - Healy Pass★★ (≤★★) W : 37 km by N 71, R 572 and R 574 – Slieve Miskish Mountains (≤★★) W : 46.75 km by N 71 and R 572 – Lauragh (Derreen Gardens★ **AC**) NW : 44 km by N 71, R 572 and R 574 – Allihies (copper mines★) W : 66.75 km by N 71, R 572 and R 575 – Garnish Island (≤★) W : 70.75 km by N 71 and R 572

### 🛏 Seaview House                    ⊞ & rm, ¶¶ **P** 𝘝𝘐𝘚𝘈 ⓪ 𝖠𝖤
– ℰ (027) 50 462 – www.seaviewhousehotel.com – Mid March-mid November
**25 rm** ⊇ – ♦ € 75/95 ♦♦ € 140/200
**Rest** – (dinner only and Sunday lunch) Menu € 35/45
♦ Well-run, whitewashed Victorian house that upholds tradition in both its décor and service. Pleasant drawing room and cosy bar. Bedrooms feature antique furnishings; some boast sea views. Attractive gardens lead down to the bay shore. Classical menu served at elegant polished tables laid with silver tableware.

### ⌂ Ballylickey House without rest         ≤ ⊞ 🐾 ⤴ ¶¶ **P** 𝘝𝘐𝘚𝘈 ⓪
– ℰ (027) 50 071 – www.ballylickeymanorhouse.com – May-September
**6 rm** ⊇ – ♦ € 90/100 ♦♦ € 110/180
♦ Attractive country house with beautiful gardens reaching down to the sea. Spacious, individually furnished bedrooms are split between the house and 'chalets'. Smart, period-style breakfast room displays pleasant art. Heated outdoor pool.

▶ Dublin 174 km – Lifford 46 km – Letterkenny 39 km

### 🛏 Ballyliffin Lodge           ≤ ⊞ 🔲 ⓪ ⋒ 🛗 🛗 & 𝖠𝖢 rest, 🍴 ℭ ♨ **P**
Shore Rd – ℰ (074) 937 82 00 – www.ballyliffinlodge.com         𝘝𝘐𝘚𝘈 ⓪ 𝖠𝖤
– Restricted opening in winter
**40 rm** ⊇ – ♦ € 105/124 ♦♦ € 160/198
**Rest** – Menu € 25 – Carte approx. € 32
♦ Remote hotel with well-kept gardens, affording superb outlook over the countryside to the beach. Cosy bedrooms – ask for one facing the front – and great spa with lovely pool. Relax in the snug bar or have afternoon tea and take in the view from the lounge. Large dining room offers an all-encompassing menu.

▶ Dublin 190 km – Cork 79 km – Waterford 63 km

◉ Clonmel★ (St Mary's Church★, County Museum★ **AC**), N : 16 km by R 671 – Lismore★ (Castle Gardens★ **AC**, St Carthage's Cathedral★), SW : 26 km by R 671and N 72 – W : Nier Valley Scenic Route★★

### 🏠 Hanora's Cottage 🌿              ≤ ⊞ 🐾 **P** 𝘝𝘐𝘚𝘈 ⓪
Nire Valley, East : 6.5 km by Nire Drive rd on Nire Valley Lakes rd – ℰ (052) 613 61 34 – www.hanorascottage.com – Closed 1 week Christmas
**10 rm** ⊇ – ♦ € 80 ♦♦ € 160
**Rest** – (closed Sunday and bank holiday Mondays) (dinner only and Sunday lunch) (booking essential for non-residents) Menu € 40
♦ Dating back to 1891 and named after the owner's grandmother, who it once belonged to; a great base for exploring the Comeragh Mountains. Spacious, brightly painted bedrooms with characterful furnishings and spa baths, No.11 overlooks the river. Comfy dining room offers a menu of classically inspired dishes.

REPUBLIC OF IRELAND

⌂  **Glasha Farmhouse** ⚲   ⟨ 🚗 🍴 📺 **P** **VISA** 💳

*Northwest : 4 km by R 671 – ℰ (052) 613 61 08 – www.glashafarmhouse.com*
*– January-November*
**6 rm** 🍽 – ♦ € 50/60 ♦♦ € 90/100   **Rest** – Menu € 40
♦ Large farmhouse set between the Knockmealdown and Comeragh Mountains. Guest areas include a spacious lounge, airy conservatory and patio. Comfy bedrooms; some with jacuzzis. Welcoming owners have good local knowledge. Home-cooked meals; picnic lunches available.

# BALLYMORE EUSTACE (An Baile Mór ) – **Kildare** – **712** J2     **39** D1
– pop. 725

▶ Dublin 48 km – Naas 12 km – Drogheda 99 km

🏩 **Ballymore Inn**                                  **P** **VISA** 💳 **AE**

*– ℰ (045) 864 585 – www.ballymoreinn.com*
**Rest** – Menu € 22/35 – Carte € 28/39
♦ Remote village pub with spacious bar and Parisian brasserie style dining area. Generous portions include tasty homemade bread, pizzas, tarts and pastries. Small artisan producers favoured.

# BALLYNAHINCH (Baile na hInse) – **Galway** – **712** C7 – ✉ **Recess**     **36** A3
🟩 Ireland

▶ Dublin 225 km – Galway 66 km – Westport 79 km
🟩 Connemara★★★ – Roundstone★, S : by R 341 – Cashel★, SE : by R 341 and R 340

🏰  **Ballynahinch Castle** ⚲   ⟨ 🚗 🍴 🦆 ♨ ※ 🍴 ☏ **P** **VISA** 💳 **AE** ⓪

*– ℰ (095) 31 006 – www.ballynahinch-castle.com – Closed February and 1 week*
*at Christmas*
**37 rm** 🍽 – ♦ € 240/300 ♦♦ € 300/420 – 3 suites
**Rest** – *(dinner only) (booking essential for non-residents)* Menu € 48 **s**
♦ Part-17C, grey-stone castle within extensive grounds, set in an unrivalled location by the river. Log-fired entrance and well-appointed sitting rooms. Modern country house style bedrooms with up-to-date facilities. Pub attracts the locals. Restaurant offers classical 4 course dinners overlooking the river.

# BALLYVAUGHAN (Baile Uí Bheacháin) – **Clare** – **712** E8 – pop. 224     **38** B1
🟩 Ireland

▶ Dublin 240 km – Ennis 55 km – Galway 46 km
🟩 The Burren★★ (Scenic Route★★, Aillwee Cave★ **AC** (Waterfall★★), Corcomroe Abbey★, Poulnabrone Portal Tomb★) – Kilfenora (Crosses★, Burren Centre★ **AC**), S : 25 km N 67 and R 476. Cliffs of Moher★★★, S : 32 km by N 67 and R 478

🏰 **Gregans Castle** ⚲   ⟨ 🚗 🍴 ☏ 📺 **P** **VISA** 💳 **AE**

*Southwest : 6 km on N 67 – ℰ (065) 707 70 05 – www.gregans.ie – 11*
*February-27 November*
**16 rm** 🍽 – ♦ € 152/195 ♦♦ € 195/245 – 4 suites
**Rest** – *(bar lunch) (booking advisable)* Menu € 60/90 **s**
♦ Part-18C country house with superb views of The Burren and Galway Bay. Open-fired hall, rustic bar-lounge and elegant sitting room. Antique-furnished bedrooms: one in the old kitchen with panelled ceiling and four-poster; two opening onto the garden. Good service, with tea on arrival. Conservatory dining room offers elaborate modern menu with a Scandinavian edge.

🏠 **Drumcreehy House** without rest          ⟨ 🚗 🍴 **P** **VISA** 💳

*Northeast : 2 km on N 67 – ℰ (065) 707 73 77 – www.drumcreehyhouse.com*
*– Closed 25-26 December, restricted opening in winter*
**10 rm** 🍽 – ♦ € 58/100 ♦♦ € 84/100
♦ Well-run, pristine house overlooking Galway Bay. Stylish lounge with honesty bar. Named and colour themed after flowers, bedrooms are excellent value: spacious, comfortable and furnished in German stripped oak. Pleasant terrace. Excellent choice at breakfast.

REPUBLIC OF IRELAND

↑↑ **Ballyvaughan Lodge** without rest                     ⚙ ⽳ **P** **VISA** **⦿**
– 𝒞 (065) 707 72 92 – www.ballyvaughanlodge.com – Closed 25-26 December
**11 rm** – ♦ € 35/45 ♦♦ € 75/85
   • Welcoming guesthouse with colourful flower display and decking. Comfy, light-filled lounge. Bedrooms boast co-ordinating fabrics and furnishings. Quality farmers' market produce at breakfast.

↑↑ **Cappabhaile House** without rest          ≤ ⌿ ⚙ ⽳ **P** **VISA** **⦿** **AE**
Southwest : 1.5 km on N 67 – 𝒞 (065) 707 72 60 – www.cappabhaile.com
– April-September
**10 rm** ⌑ – ♦ € 55/75 ♦♦ € 84/90
   • Proudly run, grey-stone house with nice gardens, offering great views over The Burren. Spacious lounge-cum-breakfast room; comfy, good-sized bedrooms. Pool table and regular live music sessions.

---

**BALTIMORE** (Dún na Séad) – **Cork** – **712** D13 – **pop. 377** ▯ Ireland    **38** A3
▶ Dublin 344 km – Cork 95 km – Killarney 124 km
◫ Sherkin Island★ (by ferry) – Castletownshend★, E : 20 km by R 595 and R 596
   – Glandore★, E : 26 km by R 595, N 71 and R 597

REPUBLIC OF IRELAND

⌂ **Casey's of Baltimore**          ≤ ◍ rest, ⚙ ⽳ **P** **VISA** **⦿** **AE** **◍**
East : 0.75 km on R 595 – 𝒞 (028) 20 197 – www.caseysofbaltimore.com – Closed 20-27 December
**14 rm** ⌑ – ♦ € 70/120 ♦♦ € 120/180    **Rest** – Menu € 24 – Carte € 25/49 **s**
   • Popular hotel near seashore. Cosy bar with open fires and traditional music at weekends, with beer garden overlooking bay. Large, well-decorated rooms with pine furniture. Great sea views from dining room.

↑↑ **Baltimore Townhouse** without rest          ⚙ ⽳ **P** **VISA** **⦿** **AE** **◍**
– 𝒞 (028) 20 197 – www.baltimoretownhouse.com – Closed 20-27 December
**6 rm** ⌑ – ♦ € 100/160 ♦♦ € 100/160
   • Six open plan suites comprising of a bedroom, living area, small kitchen and bathroom. Check in at Casey's on your way into the village; where your breakfast is also served.

↑↑ **Slipway** without rest                     ≤ ⌿ ⚙ **P**
The Cove, East : 0.75 km – 𝒞 (028) 20 134 – www.theslipway.com
– May-September
**4 rm** ⌑ – ♦ € 60/72 ♦♦ € 72/80
   • Relaxed, informal guesthouse with yellow façade and lovely views of local harbour, particularly from veranda outside breakfast room. Simple, individualistic, well-kept rooms.

---

**BANDON** (Droichead na Bandan) – **Cork** – **712** F12 – **pop. 5 822**          **38** B3
▶ Dublin 181 km – Cork 20 km – Carrigaline 28 km – Cobh 33 km

↑↑ **Kilbrogan House** without rest          ⌿ ⚙ ⽳ **P** **VISA** **⦿**
Kilbrogan Hill, North : 1 km on Macroom rd (R 589) – 𝒞 (023) 884 49 35
– www.kilbrogan.com – March-October
**4 rm** ⌑ – ♦ € 50 ♦♦ € 80
   • Georgian townhouse set above the town and boasting a stunning original staircase, fine cornicing in the lounge and a turn-of-the-century conservatory overlooking pleasant gardens. Simple, antique-furnished bedrooms. Breakfast from the Aga.

⌂ **Poacher's Inn**                                        **P** **VISA** **⦿**
Clonakilty Rd, Southwest : 1.5 km on N 71 – 𝒞 (023) 884 1159
– www.poachersinnbandon.com
**Rest** – Menu € 25 – Carte € 25/40
   • Cosy neighbourhood pub that's popular with the locals. Light snack menu in the bar and snug; hearty, classical seafood dishes in the upstairs restaurant, which opens later in the week.

**BANSHA** – South Tipperary – **712** H10 – pop. 288        **39** C2

▶ Dublin 121 km – Clonmel 21 km – Cork 59 km – Limerick 31 km

🏠   **Rathellen House** 🌿      ⪕ 🚗 🕸 📶 **P** **VISA** ⚫

*Southeast : 3.5 km. by N 24 on Coopers Cottage rd –* ✆ *(062) 54 376*
*– www.rathellenhouse.com*
**6 rm** 🛏 – 🛉 € 60/65 🛉🛉 € 90/110
**Rest** *– (dinner only) (residents only set menu)* Menu € 40
♦ Very comfortable, Georgian-style house with classic country house feel, set in
peaceful location. Variously-sized bedrooms feature antique furniture and pleasant
countryside/mountain outlooks; bathrooms boast heated flooring. Formal dining
room with antique tables; home-cooked meals utilise local, often organic produce.

---

**BARNA** (Bearna) – Galway – **712** E8 – pop. 12 795        **36** B3

▶ Dublin 227 km – Galway 9 km

🏨   **Twelve**      🍴 ⪕ 🆎 📶 🛁 **P** **VISA** ⚫ **AE** ①

*Barna Crossroads –* ✆ *(091) 597 000 – www.thetwelvehotel.ie*
**38 rm** 🛏 – 🛉 € 100/145 🛉🛉 € 110/155 – 10 suites
**Rest** *West* – see restaurant listing
**Rest** *The Pins* – Menu € 25 – Carte € 25/35 **s**
♦ Unassuming exterior hides a keenly run boutique hotel. On-site bakery in the
pubby bar. Stylish, modern bedrooms with large gilt mirrors, mood lighting and
designer 'seaweed' toiletries in the bathrooms; some boast bars or giant spa
baths. Ambitious fusion menu in West; modern European dishes in The Pins.

XX   **West** – at Twelve Hotel      ⪕ 🆎 **P** **VISA** ⚫ **AE** ①

*Barna Crossroads –* ✆ *(091) 597 000 – www.thetwelvehotel.ie*
**Rest** *– (closed Monday and Tuesday) (dinner only)* Menu € 25 **s**
– Carte € 35/45 **s**
♦ Stylish restaurant with booth seating, set in a smart boutique hotel. Fusion
menu offers ambitious, innovative dishes and features plenty of locally landed
seafood. Chef's table in the kitchen.

X   **O'Grady's on the Pier**      ⪕ 🆎 **VISA** ⚫ **AE**

*–* ✆ *(091) 592 223 – www.ogradysonthepier.com – Closed 24-26 December*
**Rest** *– Seafood – (booking essential)* Carte € 31/47
♦ Converted quayside pub on two floors with great views of Galway Bay. Cheerful, attentive staff and daily menus of simple, flavourful seafood have earned
good local reputation.

---

**BARRELLS CROSS** – Cork – **712** G12 – **see Kinsale**

---

**BEAUFORT** = Lios an Phúca – Kerry – **712** D11 – **see Killarney**

---

**BIRR** (Biorra) – Offaly – **712** I8 – pop. 5 081 📗 Ireland        **39** C1

▶ Dublin 140 km – Athlone 45 km – Kilkenny 79 km – Limerick 79 km
🛈 Wilmer Rd ✆ (057) 912 09 23, www.heritagetowns.com
📍 The Glenns, ✆ (057) 9 12 00 82
◉ Town★ – Birr Castle Demesne★★ **AC** (Telescope★★)
◉ Clonfert Cathedral★ (West doorway★★), NW : 24 km by R 439, R 356 and minor
roads – Portumna★ (Castle★ **AC**), W : 24 km by R 489 – Roscrea★ (Damer House★
**AC**) S : 19.25 km by N 62 – Slieve Bloom Mountinas★, E : 21 km by R 440

🏠   **Maltings** without rest      🕸 📶 **P** **VISA** ⚫

*Castle St –* ✆ *(057) 912 13 45*
**10 rm** 🛏 – 🛉 € 40/80 🛉🛉 € 70/80
♦ Characterful stone-built house once used to store malt in the production of
Guinness. Set on the riverside, its breakfast-room-cum-lounge overlooks the castle grounds. Simple, pine furnished bedrooms. Homemade soda bread, scones
and jams.

**BLACKLION** (An Blaic) – Cavan – **712** I5 – pop. 174

▣ Dublin 194 km – Drogheda 170 km – Enniskillen 19 km

▣ Blacklion Toam, ℰ (071) 9 85 30 24

XXX **MacNean House** with rm      🏧 rest, *VISA* ◉◉
Main St – ℰ (071) 985 30 22 – www.macneanrestaurant.com – Closed January
**19 rm** ⬓ – ✝ € 80/100 ✝✝ € 85/100
**Rest** – (closed Monday-Tuesday and Sunday dinner) (dinner only and Sunday
lunch) (booking essential) Carte approx. € 70
♦ Stylish, modern restaurant in a smart townhouse, with plush seating, linen-clad
tables and subtle cream décor. Choice of three menus; refined, complex dishes
use good quality ingredients and skilled techniques. Keenly run, with friendly local team. Comfortable, contemporary bedrooms.

---

**BLARNEY** (An Bhlarna) – Cork – **712** G12 – pop. 2 400 – ⊠ Cork     **38** B3
▮ Ireland

▣ Dublin 268 km – Cork 9 km

◉ Blarney Castle★★ **AC** – Blarney Castle House★ **AC**

⌂ **Killarney House** without rest      🚗 ⚡ 🛜 **P** *VISA* ◉◉
Station Rd, Northeast : 1.5 km on Carrignavar rd. – ℰ (021) 438 18 41
– www.killarneyhouseblarney.com
**6 rm** ⬓ – ✝ € 38/50 ✝✝ € 60/68
♦ Spacious, modern guesthouse set above attractive village. Very comfortable
lounge. Breakfast room equipped to high standard. Sizeable, immaculately kept
rooms.

**at Tower** West : 3.25 km on R 617 – ⊠ Cork

🏠 **Ashlee Lodge**      🏦 🕭 🏧 🛜 **P** *VISA* ◉◉ 🝙 ◑
– ℰ (021) 438 53 46 – www.ashleelodge.com – closed 20 December-20 January
**10 rm** ⬓ – ✝ € 65/95 ✝✝ € 70/240
**Rest** – (closed Sunday and Monday) (dinner only) Carte approx. € 39 **s**
♦ Smart hotel with open-fired lounge complete with board games and honesty
bar. Comfy bedrooms offer all you could want; some have whirlpool baths. Outdoor Canadian hot tub, sauna and in-room treatments. Dining room offers freshly
prepared, home-cooked dishes.

---

**BORRIS** – Carlow – **712** L10 – pop. 582     **39** D2
▣ Dublin 121 km – Carlow 36 km – Waterford 66 km

🏨 **Step House**      ≤ 🚗 ⤢ 🛌 🕭 ⚡ 🛜 🍴 **P** *VISA* ◉◉
– ℰ (059) 977 32 09 – www.stephousehotel.ie – Closed 9-26 January and 25
December
**19 rm** ⬓ – ✝ € 90/110 ✝✝ € 190/220 – 1 suite
**Rest Reubens** – see restaurant listing
♦ Welcoming, family-run, Georgian townhouse, located in a small heritage village.
Spacious, modern bedrooms with gilt furniture and a slightly kitsch feel; the pent-
house boasts a terrace and lovely mountain views. Red leather furnished bar.

XX **Reubens** – at Step House Hotel      🚗 🕭 **P** *VISA* ◉◉ ◑
– ℰ (059) 977 32 09 – www.stephousehotel.ie – Closed 9-26 January and 25
December
**Rest** – (dinner only Friday-Saturday and Sunday lunch) Carte € 33/49
♦ Atmospheric hotel restaurant with vaulted ceilings and archways; set in the
kitchens of the old McMurrough Kavanagh Estate dower house. Interesting mod-
ern menu of local and artisan ingredients.

*(sidebar, vertical)* REPUBLIC OF IRELAND

## BOYLE (Mainistir na Búille) – Roscommon – 712 H6 – pop. 2 522

▮ Ireland

▶ Dublin 175 km – Longford 53 km – Sligo 45 km

ℹ King House 𝒞 (071) 966 21 45, www.visitboyle.net

◉ King House★ **AC**

◉ Boyle Abbey★ **AC**, E : 2 km by N 4 – Lough Key Forest Park★ **AC**, E : 3.25 km by N 4. Arigna Scenic Drive★ (⩻★), NE : 20 km by N 4, R 280 and R 207 – Curlew Mountains (⩻★), NW : 3.5 km by N 4

---

⌂ **Rosdarrig House** without rest      ☷ ⁽ⁱⁱ⁾ **P** **VISA** ◎◎
*Carrick Rd, (East : 1.5 km) – 𝒞 (071) 966 20 40 – www.rosdarrig.com*
*– April-October*
**5 rm** ⌷ – ♦ € 40/45 ♦♦ € 70
◆ Neat house on the edge of town, close to the abbey, where friendly owners offer genuine Irish hospitality. Comfy lounge and linen-laid breakfast room. Pleasant bedrooms overlook the garden.

---

## BRIDGE END – Donegal – 712 J2 – pop. 298

▶ Dublin 158 km – Lifford 25 km – Belfast 78 km – Londonderry 5 km

ⅩⅩ **Harrys**      **AC** **P** **VISA** ◎◎
*– 𝒞 (074) 936 85 44 – www.harrys.ie*
**Rest** – Menu € 20 (dinner) – Carte € 30/38
◆ Long-standing, passionately run restaurant with large, open-plan interior and modern bistro feel. Menus evolve with the seasons, offering flavoursome, classically prepared dishes. Traceability is key: they hang and mature their own steaks.

---

## BUNDORAN (Bun Dobhráin) – Donegal – 712 H4 – pop. 1 964

▮ Ireland

▶ Dublin 259 km – Donegal 27 km – Sligo 37 km

ℹ Main St 𝒞 (071) 9 84 25 39, www.discoverbundoran.com

◉ Creevykeel Court Cairn★, S : 5 km by N 15 – Rossnowlagh Strand★★, N : 8.5 km by N 15 and R 231

---

🏨 **Fitzgerald's**      ⩻ ▤ ⅍ ⁽ⁱⁱ⁾ **P** **VISA** ◎◎
*– 𝒞 (071) 984 13 36 – www.fitzgeraldshotel.com – Restricted opening in winter*
**16 rm** ⌷ – ♦ € 55/80 ♦♦ € 80/120
**Rest** *The Bistro* – *(closed Monday-Tuesday) (dinner only)* Carte € 25/38 **s**
◆ Family owned hotel in centre of popular seaside town overlooking Donegal Bay. Reception rooms warmed by wood-burning stove. Sumptuous sofas abound. Sea-facing front bedrooms. Linen-clad, informal Bistro with carefully compiled menu.

---

## BUNRATTY (Bun Raite) – Clare – 712 F9 ▮ Ireland

▶ Dublin 207 km – Ennis 24 km – Limerick 13 km

◉ Town★★ – Bunratty Castle★★

---

🏠 **Bunratty Manor**      ☲ ⌂ ⅊ rm, ⅍ ⁽ⁱⁱ⁾ **P** **VISA** ◎◎ **AE**
*– 𝒞 (061) 707 984 – www.bunrattymanor.net – Closed 1 week Christmas*
**20 rm** ⌷ – ♦ € 79/99 ♦♦ € 99/120
**Rest** – *(closed Monday) (dinner only and Sunday lunch)* Carte € 30/45
◆ Smart hotel not far from the castle and folk park, in a busy tourist town. Good-sized, brightly decorated bedrooms display colourful fabrics; most bathrooms have showers only. Comfy lounge. Traditional bar with courtyard offers both pub and restaurant-style menus.

---

⌂ **Bunratty Grove** without rest      ☲ ⅍ ⁽ⁱⁱ⁾ **P** **VISA** ◎◎
*Castle Rd., North : 3 km on Buratty Castle rd – 𝒞 (061) 369 579*
*– www.bunrattygrove.com*
**6 rm** ⌷ – ♦ € 35/50 ♦♦ € 50/65
◆ Purpose-built guesthouse with mature gardens, set in a peaceful area out of town. Tidy, well-kept lounge and pine-furnished breakfast room. Good-sized bedrooms with polished wood floors.

REPUBLIC OF IRELAND

## CAHERLISTRANE (Cathair Loistreáin) – Galway – **712** E7

▶ Dublin 256 km – Ballina 74 km – Galway 42 km

🏠 **Lisdonagh House** 🌿     ← 🛋 🔌 🎣 ⁽ᵖ⁾ **P** **VISA** **co** **AE**
*Northwest : 4 km by R 333 off Shrule rd –* ℰ *(093) 31 163 – www.lisdonagh.com*
*– May-October*
**9 rm** ⌑ – ♦ € 80/98 ♦♦ € 140/180     **Rest** – *(dinner only)* Menu € 45
♦ Ivy-clad Georgian house with lough views. Traditional country house interior boasts eye-catching mural and open-fired lounges. Antique-furnished bedrooms have marble bathrooms; first floor rooms are larger and brighter. Formal dining room offers home-cooked meals.

---

## CAHERSIVEEN (Cathair Saidhbhín) – Kerry – **712** B12 – pop. 1 294

📗 Ireland

▶ Dublin 355 km – Killarney 64 km

🟢 Ring of Kerry★★

🏨 **QC's** with rm     🛋 **P** **VISA** **co** **①**
*3 Main St –* ℰ *(066) 947 22 44 – www.qcbar.com – Closed*
*Monday-Wednesday in winter and Sunday lunch*
**5 rm** – ♦ € 60/70 ♦♦ € 90/110
**Rest** – Seafood – *(dinner only and lunch in summer)* Menu € 20 (dinner)
– Carte € 31/46
♦ Cosy little pub with characterful flagged floors, exposed stone walls and a strong nautical theme. Seafood-orientated menus offer fresh, unfussy classics and some more unusual daily specials; the family also own a local fish wholesalers. Spacious, well-equipped bedrooms are located just around the corner.

🍺 **O'Neill's (The Point) Seafood Bar**     ← 🛋 **AC** **P**
*Renard Point, Southwest : 2.75 km by N 70 –* ℰ *(066) 947 21 65 – Closed*
*November-February*
**Rest** – *(bookings not accepted)* Carte € 28/38
♦ Striking blue pub beside the Valentia Island ferry terminal; run by the O'Neill family for over 150 years. Traditional Irish cooking; generous dishes with a strong seafood base. Unusually, no chips or desserts and no credit card payments.

---

## CAMPILE (Ceann Poill) – Wexford – **712** L11 – pop. 347 📗 Ireland

▶ Dublin 154 km – Waterford 35 km – Wexford 37 km

🟢 Dunbrody Abbey★, S : 3.25 km by R 733 – J F Kennedy Arboretum★, N : 3.25 km by R 733. Tintern Abbey★, SE : 12.75 km by R 733 – Duncannon Fort★, S : 12.75 km by R 733

🏠 **Kilmokea Country Manor** 🌿     ← 🛋 🔌 🎣 🖥 🎬 ⅃₄ 🍽 & rm, **P**
*West : 8 km by R 733 and Great Island rd –* ℰ *(051) 388 109*     **VISA** **co**
*– www.kilmokea.com – February-4 November*
**6 rm** ⌑ – ♦ € 75/150 ♦♦ € 180/300
**Rest** – *(booking essential for non-residents)* Menu € 50 (dinner) – Carte lunch approx. € 28
♦ Georgian rectory set in 20 acres, 7 of which are formal gardens open to the public. Small antique-furnished drawing room with oils and piano. Bedrooms, some in the old coach house, are more contemporary. Conservatory tea rooms and smart restaurant with daily changing classical menu of organic garden produce.

---

## CAPPOQUIN (Ceapach Choinn) – Waterford – **712** I11 – pop. 740

📗 Ireland

▶ Dublin 219 km – Cork 56 km – Waterford 64 km

🟢 Lismore★ (Lismore Castle Gardens★ **AC**, St Carthage's Cathedral★), W : 6.5 km by N 72. The Gap★ (← ★) NW : 14.5 km by R 669

## Richmond House with rm

*Southeast : 0.75 km on N 72 – &#x1F4DE; (058) 54 278 – www.richmondhouse.net – Closed 2 weeks Christmas-New Year, Sunday and Monday*

**9 rm** &#x2615; – &#x1F6B9; € 70/100 &#x1F6B9;&#x1F6B9; € 130/190
**Rest** – *(dinner only)* Menu € 33/55 – Carte approx. € 33 **s**

♦ Built for Earl of Cork and Burlington in 1704; retains Georgian style with stately, cove-ceilinged dining room: local produce to the fore. Individually decorated period rooms.

**at Millstreet** East : 11.25 km by N 72 on R 671 – &#x2709; Cappoquin

## Castle Country House without rest &#x2615;

*– &#x1F4DE; (058) 68 049 – www.castlecountryhouse.com – mid-March-October*
**5 rm** &#x2615; – &#x1F6B9; € 50/65 &#x1F6B9;&#x1F6B9; € 90/100

♦ Extended farmhouse on working dairy and beef farm with 15C origins. Rural location and lovely gardens. Individual bedrooms with cottage style decor.

---

# CARAGH LAKE (Loch Cárthaí) – Kerry – 712 C11 &#x1F4D8; Ireland    38 A2

&#x25B6; Dublin 341 km – Killarney 35 km – Tralee 40 km

&#x1F18; Dooks Glenbeigh, &#x1F4DE; (066) 9 76 82 05

&#x1F4F7; Lough Caragh ★

&#x1F532; Iveragh Peninsula ★★ (Ring of Kerry ★★)

## Ard-Na-Sidhe &#x2615;

*– &#x1F4DE; (066) 976 91 05 – www.ardnasidhe.com – May-October*
**18 rm** &#x2615; – &#x1F6B9; € 144/211 &#x1F6B9;&#x1F6B9; € 168/288
**Rest** – *(dinner only) (booking essential for non-residents)* Carte € 40/59

♦ 1913 Arts and Crafts house, set on the shores of Lough Caragh and surrounded by mountains. Subtle yet stylish modernisation has retained much of its original character. Smart, antique-furnished bedrooms; Garden Rooms are more traditional. Dining room offers classically based dishes with subtle modern twists.

## Carrig Country House &#x2615;

*– &#x1F4DE; (066) 976 91 00 – www.carrighouse.com – March-November*
**16 rm** &#x2615; – &#x1F6B9; € 125/140 &#x1F6B9;&#x1F6B9; € 150/250 – 1 suite
**Rest** – *(dinner only) (booking essential for non-residents)* Menu € 45

♦ Victorian former hunting lodge set down a wooded drive, located on the lough shore and surrounded by mountains. Cosy country house interior with traditionally furnished guest areas. Individually decorated bedrooms boast antique furnishings. Beautiful views from the dining room; fresh, country house cooking.

---

# CARLINGFORD (Cairlinn) – Louth – 712 N5 – pop. 623 &#x1F4D8; Ireland    37 D2

&#x25B6; Dublin 106 km – Dundalk 21 km

&#x1F4F7; Town ★

&#x1F532; Windy Gap ★, NW : 12.75 km by R 173 – Proleek Dolmen ★, SW : 14.5 km by R 173

## Four Seasons

*– &#x1F4DE; (042) 937 35 30 – www.4seasonshotelcarlingford.ie*
**59 rm** &#x2615; – &#x1F6B9; € 69/115 &#x1F6B9;&#x1F6B9; € 69/180
**Rest** – *(bar lunch Monday-Thursday)* Menu € 25 (dinner) – Carte € 31/38

♦ Purpose-built, town centre hotel, with large leisure centre and spa. Smartly maintained gardens boast a wrought iron pergola and lovely mountain backdrop. Well-equipped bedrooms; 'Executives' are of a good size, with separate bath and shower. Large bar leads into intimate, formal dining room with Irish menu.

## Beaufort House without rest &#x2615;

*– &#x1F4DE; (042) 937 38 79 – www.beauforthouse.net – Closed 25 December*
**5 rm** &#x2615; – &#x1F6B9; € 65/100 &#x1F6B9;&#x1F6B9; € 100/120

♦ Modern house on the shores of the lough. Spacious lounge displays local art and old maritime charts; large, comfortable bedrooms boast water or mountain views. Welcoming owners also run a sailing school.

↑ **Carlingford House** without rest   ⌿ 🛇 ⟨⟨ᵗ⟩⟩ 🅿 𝘃𝘪𝘴𝘢 ⦿
– ℰ (042) 937 31 18 – www.carlingfordhouse.com – Closed Christmas
**5 rm** ⌸ – † € 65 †† € 90/140
• Early Victorian house close to the old ruined abbey; the owner was born, and has always lived, here. Smart, understated bedrooms are immaculately kept. Snug lounge and pleasant breakfast room; tasty locally smoked salmon and bacon.

**CARLOW** (Ceatharlach) – Carlow – **712** L9 – pop. 20 724   **39** D2
▶ Dublin 80 km – Kilkenny 37 km – Wexford 75 km
🛈 College St ℰ (059) 9 13 15 54, www.carlowtourism.com
🔞 Carlow Dublin Rd, Deer Park, ℰ (059) 9 13 16 95

↑ **Barrowville Town House** without rest   ⌿ 🛇 ⟨⟨ᵗ⟩⟩ 🅿 𝘃𝘪𝘴𝘢 ⦿ 𝘈𝘌
⟨⟩ Kilkenny Rd, South : 0.75 km on N 9 – ℰ (059) 914 33 24 – www.barrowville.com
– Closed 24-26 December
**7 rm** ⌸ – † € 50/80 †† € 90/120
• Attractive Georgian house located on the main road into town. Comfy, characterful drawing room with heavy fabrics, period ornaments and grand piano. Breakfast in the conservatory, overlooking the pretty rear garden. Spacious, brightly decorated bedrooms offer a good level of comfort and modern facilities.

**CARNAROSS** (Carn na Ros) – Meath – **712** L6 – ⌧ Kells   **37** D3
▶ Dublin 69 km – Cavan 43 km – Drogheda 48 km

XX **Forge**   ⌿ 🅿 𝘃𝘪𝘴𝘢 ⦿ 𝘈𝘌
Pottlereagh, Northwest : 5.5 km by N 3 on Oldcastle rd – ℰ (046) 924 50 03
– www.theforgerestaurant.ie – Closed 24-26 and 31 December, 1 January, last week July, first week August, Sunday dinner, Monday and Tuesday
**Rest** – (dinner only and Sunday lunch) Menu € 30 – Carte € 39/46
• Former forge tucked away in rural isolation. Family run, traditionally styled restaurant serving tried-and-tested dishes with modern twist: ample, good value choice.

**CARNE** – Wexford – **712** M11   **39** D3
▶ Dublin 169 km – Waterford 82 km – Wexford 21 km

⟨⟩ **Lobster Pot**   ⟨⟨ᵗ⟩⟩ 🅐🅒 🅿 𝘃𝘪𝘴𝘢 ⦿ 𝘈𝘌
Ballyfane – ℰ (053) 913 11 10 – Closed 25-26 December, January, Good Friday and Monday except bank holidays
**Rest** – Seafood – (dinner only and Sunday lunch) Carte € 25/45
• Popular pub filled with a characterful array of memorabilia. Large menus feature tasty, home-style cooking. Fresh seafood dishes are a must try, with oysters and lobster cooked to order the specialities. No children after 5pm.

**CARRICKMACROSS** (Carraig Mhachaire Rois ) – Monaghan   **37** D2
– **712** L6 – pop. 4 387 ▯ Ireland
▶ Dublin 92 km – Dundalk 22 km
🔞 Nuremore Hotel & CC, ℰ (042) 9 66 14 38
◉ Dún a' Rí Forest Park★, SW : 8 km by R 179 – St Mochta's House★, E : 7 km by R 178 and minor road S

🏠🏠🏠 **Nuremore** ⟨⟩   ← ⌿ ⟨⟩ ⟨⟩ 🔲 ⊕ ⟨⟩ 🛗 ✕ 🔞 ⟨⟩ ⓖ 🛇 ⟨⟨ᵗ⟩⟩ ⟨⟩ 🅿
South : 1.5 km on N 2 – ℰ (042) 966 14 38   𝘃𝘪𝘴𝘢 ⦿ 𝘈𝘌 ⓪
– www.nuremore.com
**72 rm** ⌸ – † € 105/125 †† € 140/180
**Rest Restaurant** – see restaurant listing
• Long-standing Victorian house with extensive gardens and golf course. Classical interior with formal bar and comfy lounge serving three-tiered afternoon tea. Good leisure facilities and smart pool. Peaceful bedrooms, many have rural views.

REPUBLIC OF IRELAND

XXX **Restaurant** – at Nuremore Hotel    AC P VISA OO AE ①
*South : 1.5 km on N 2 – &* (042) 966 14 38 – www.nuremore.com
**Rest** – *(dinner only and lunch Saturday-Sunday)* Menu € 30/40
• Traditional split-level dining room within a well-established Victorian hotel. For mally set, linen-laid tables are well-spaced and service is attentive. Menus show case luxurious seasonal ingredients and dishes are stylishly presented.

X **Courthouse**    AC VISA OO
*1 Monaghan St – &* (042) 969 28 48 – www.courthouserestaurant.ie – *Closed one week January, 25-26 December, Easter Friday, Monday (except bank holidays) and Tuesday*
**Rest** – Carte € 26/39 **s**
• Relaxed, rustic restaurant featuring wooden floors, exposed ceiling rafters and bare brick. Carefully prepared, flavourful dishes; good value midweek menu. Friendly efficient service.

REPUBLIC OF IRELAND

**CARRICK-ON-SHANNON** (Cora Droma Rúisc) – Leitrim – **712** H6    **37** C.
– pop. 3 163 ▌ Ireland
▶ Dublin 156 km – Ballina 80 km – Galway 119 km – Roscommon 42 km
ℹ Visitor Information Centre The Marina &*(0719) 62 01 70, www.carrickonshannon.ie
▣ Carrick-on-Shannon Woodbrook, &*(071) 966 70 15
◉ Town★
◗ Lough Rynn Demesne★

命命 **Landmark**    ⏢ ᬅ rm, AC rest, ⌘ ℡ ♨ P VISA OO AE
*on N 4 – &* (071) 962 22 22 – www.thelandmarkhotel.com – *Closed 25 December*
**60 rm** ⬜ – ♦ € 90/125 ♦♦ € 130/198
**Rest** *Boardwalk* – Carte € 23/37
• Next to the Shannon, with a water feature in reception and water-themed pictures throughout. Traditional style bedrooms; some overlooking the river. Styl ish cocktail lounges with stunning modern design. Boardwalk boasts pleasant river views.

▐◻ **Oarsman**    ᬅ VISA OO
*Bridge St – &* (071) 962 1733 – www.theoarsman.com – *Closed 25-26 December, Easter Friday, Sunday and Monday*
**Rest** – Menu € 20/35 – Carte € 21/43
• Traditional, family-run pub filled with pottery, bygone artefacts and fishing tackle. Cooking is simple and produce, locally sourced. Comfortable restaurant area opens later in the week.

**CARRIGALINE** (Carraig Uí Leighin) – Cork – **712** G12 – pop. 12 835    **38** B3
▶ Dublin 262 km – Cork 14 km
▣ Fernhill, &*(021) 437 22 26

命命 **Carrigaline Court**    ⏢ ▨ ᬅ ♨ ⏢ ᬅ rm, AC rest, ⌘ ℡ ♨ P
*Cork Rd – &* (021) 485 21 00 – www.carrigcourt.com    VISA OO AE ①
– *Closed 23-27 December*
**89 rm** ⬜ – ♦ € 80/140 ♦♦ € 140/220 – 2 suites
**Rest** *The Bistro* – *(dinner only) (meals served in bar Sunday-Thursday)*
Carte € 30/50 **s**
• Purpose-built hotel in the heart of town. Excellent leisure centre boasting a 20m pool and well-equipped events facilities. Luxurious suites and spacious, modern bedrooms with queen-sized beds. Atmospheric bar for snacks and light meals; formal restaurant has eclectic décor and offers an international menu.

**CARRIGANS** (An Carraigain) – Donegal – **712** J3 – pop. 191     **37** C1

▶ Dublin 225 km – Donegal 66 km – Letterkenny 230 km – Sligo 124 km

⌂    **Mount Royd** without rest     🚗 ⅍ 🕪 **P** 𝘝𝘐𝘚𝘈 ⓒⓞ
– ℰ (074) 914 01 63 – www.mountroyd.com – Closed 1 week Christmas, restricted opening in winter
**4 rm** 🍽 – 🛉 € 40 🛉🛉 € 70
♦ Remotely set, creeper-clad house with well-tended gardens, lovely rear terrace and fountain. Immaculately kept throughout with snug lounge and pleasant break-fast room. Cosy bedrooms; one leading to a terrace. Tasty locally smoked salmon.

---

**CASHEL** (An Caiseal) – Galway – **712** C7 🔖 Ireland     **36** A3

▶ Dublin 278 km – Galway 66 km

◉ Town ★

ⓒ Connemara ★★★

🏠🏠🏠    **Cashel House** 🌿     🚗 🕭 🗮 ✕ **P** 𝘝𝘐𝘚𝘈 ⓒⓞ 𝔸𝔼
– ℰ (095) 31 001 – www.cashel-house-hotel.com – Closed 2 January-6 February
**30 rm** 🍽 – 🛉 € 75/295 🛉🛉 € 150/250
**Rest** – (bar lunch Monday-Saturday) (booking essential for non-residents)
Menu € 30/32 – Carte € 35/49
♦ Built 1840; a very comfortable and restful country house, warmly decorated with delightful gardens. General de Gaulle stayed in one of the luxurious country house rooms. Dining room, with Queen Anne style chairs, opens into elegant con-servatory.

---

**CASHEL** (Caiseal) – South Tipperary – **712** I10 – pop. 2 936 🔖 Ireland     **39** C2

▶ Dublin 162 km – Cork 96 km – Kilkenny 55 km – Limerick 58 km

🛈 Heritage Centre, Town Hall, Main St ℰ (062) 6 25 11, www.cashel.ie

◉ Town ★★★ – Rock of Cashel ★★★ **AC** – Cormac's Chapel ★★ – Round Tower ★
– Museum ★ – Cashel Palace Gardens ★ – GPA Bolton Library ★ **AC**

ⓒ Holy Cross Abbey ★★, N : 14.5 km by R 660 – Athassel Priory ★, W : 8 km by N 74.
Caher (Castle ★★, Swiss Cottage ★), S : 18 km by N 8 – Glen of Aherlow ★, W :
21 km by N 74 and R 664

🏠🏠🏠    **Cashel Palace**     🚗 🕭 🛏 ⅍ 🛁 **P** 𝘝𝘐𝘚𝘈 ⓒⓞ 𝔸𝔼 ⓞ
Main St – ℰ (062) 62 707 – www.cashel-palace.ie – Closed 23-26 December
**19 rm** 🍽 – 🛉 € 95/130 🛉🛉 € 130/234
**Rest** – (carvery lunch Monday-Saturday) Carte € 41/54
♦ Queen Anne house, once home to an archbishop, with pleasant gardens and path leading to the famous rock. Pillared entrance hall and high-ceilinged guest areas with ornate plasterwork and open fires. Traditional bedrooms; some in the old coach house. Characterful vaulted bar, buttery and elegant restaurant.

🏠🏠    **Baileys of Cashel**     🛗 ⅊ rm, 𝔸𝔺 ⅍ 🕪 **P** 𝘝𝘐𝘚𝘈 ⓒⓞ 𝔸𝔼
42 Main St – ℰ (062) 61 937 – www.baileyshotelcashel.com – Closed
23-28 December
**20 rm** 🍽 – 🛉 € 70/80 🛉🛉 € 110/120    **Rest** – Carte € 25/40
♦ Extended Georgian townhouse, used as grain store during Irish famine. Con-temporary bedrooms are furnished to a high standard. Small lounge with library; bar area in basement. Restaurant with open plan kitchen serves modern Euro-pean cooking.

⌂    **Aulber House** without rest     🚗 ⅊ ⅍ 🕪 **P** 𝘝𝘐𝘚𝘈 ⓒⓞ
Deerpark, Golden Rd, West : 0.75 km on N 74 – ℰ (062) 63 713
– www.aulberhouse.com – March-October
**12 rm** 🍽 – 🛉 € 50 🛉🛉 € 80/100
♦ Modern house in Georgian style, within walking distance of Rock of Cashel and 13C Cistercian abbey ruins. Well-maintained gardens with wooden gazebo. Open-fired lounge, bespoke mahogany staircase and open-plan landing. Comfy bed-rooms; many with king-sized beds.

### Chez Hans 🅿 VISA ⓶ ⓪

*Rockside, Moor Ln. – ℰ (062) 61 177 – www.chezhans.net – Closed 2 weeks January, 25 December, Sunday and Monday*
**Rest** – *(dinner only) (booking essential)* Menu € 35 (early weekday dinner)
– Carte € 45/57
• Imposing former Synod Hall built in 1861, with stained glass lancet windows and vast, high-ceilinged inner. Carefully prepared and creatively presented dishes rely on local produce.

### Cafe Hans 🅰🅲 🅿

*Rockside, Moore Lane St – ℰ (062) 63 660 – Closed 2 weeks late January, 25 December, 1 week October, Sunday and Monday*
**Rest** – *(lunch only) (bookings not accepted)* Carte approx. € 25
• Just down the road from The Rock of Cashel, a vibrant, popular eatery set next to big sister 'Chez Hans' and run by the same family. Closely set tables and art covered walls. Tasty, unfussy dishes crafted from local ingredients. Arrive early as you can't book.

## CASTLEBALDWIN (Béal Átha na gCarraigíní) – Sligo – 712 G5   36 B2
– ✉ Boyle (roscommon) 📙 Ireland

▶ Dublin 190 km – Longford 67 km – Sligo 24 km

Ⓒ Carrowkeel Megalithic Cemetery (≼★★), S : 4.75 km. Arigna Scenic Drive★, N : 3.25 km by N 4 - Lough Key Forest Park★ **AC**, SE : 16 km by N 4 – View of Lough Allen★, N : 14.5 km by N 4 on R 280 – Mountain Drive★, N : 9.5 km on N 4 – Boyle Abbey★ **AC**, SE : 12.75 km by N 4 - King House★, SE : 12.75 km by N 4

### Cromleach Lodge ⌂ ≼ 🚗 🔌 🍷 🌐 🏊 🛗 ♨ 🅿 VISA ⓶ ⓪

*Ballindoon, Southeast : 5.5 km – ℰ (071) 916 51 55 – www.cromleach.com – Closed November and Monday-Thursday December to March*
**57 rm** ⌁ – † € 75 †† € 90/170
**Rest Moira's** – see restaurant listing
• Remotely located hotel in great position, affording superb views over Lough Arrow. Large, luxurious bedrooms – some modern, some classic – deluxe rooms have views and either a balcony or terrace, and are well worth the extra.

### Moira's – at Cromleach Lodge Hotel ≼ 🚗 🔌 🍷 🅿 VISA ⓶ ⓪

*Ballindoon, Southeast : 5.5 km – ℰ (071) 916 51 55 – www.cromleach.com – Closed November and Monday-Thursday December to March*
**Rest** – *(closed Monday-Tuesday)* Menu € 55 (dinner) – Carte € 50/54
• Spacious, contemporary restaurant with views to Lough Arrow. Rear booths ideal for large groups. Fixed price menu of modern Irish cooking, with local produce to the fore.

## CASTLEGREGORY (Caisleán Ghriaire) – Kerry – 712 B11 – pop. 205   38 A2
▶ Dublin 330 km – Dingle 24 km – Killarney 54 km

### Shores Country House without rest ≼ 🚗 🛁 🕊 🅿 VISA ⓶ 🅰🅴

*Conor Pass Rd, Cappateige, Southwest : 6 km on A 560 – ℰ (066) 713 91 95 – www.shorescountryhouse.com – Closed 2 December-10 January*
**6 rm** ⌁ – † € 45/90 †† € 60/90
• Modern guesthouse, beautifully set between Stradbally Mountain and a spectacular beach. Friendly owner has added a touch of fun to the place. Stylish bedrooms, some with antique beds; all with good attention to detail. Plush breakfast room. Quality furnishings.

## CASTLELYONS (Caisleán Ó Liatháin) – Cork – 712 H11 – pop. 203    38 B2

▶ Dublin 219 km – Cork 30 km – Killarney 104 km – Limerick 64 km

### 🏠 Ballyvolane House ঙ    ⟨ 🚗 🔄 🔌 ⟩ ¶ P̄ VISA ⓸⃝ AE
*Southeast : 5.5 km by Midleton rd on Britway rd – ℰ (025) 36 349*
*– www.ballyvolanehouse.ie – Closed 24 December-4 January*
**6 rm** ⌇ – ♦ € 120/125 ♦♦ € 170/210    **Rest** – *(dinner only)* Menu € 35/55
♦ Stately 18C Italianate mansion mentioned in local legend, with lakes in parkland. Name means "place of springing heifers". Antique-filled rooms, some with Victorian baths. Dining room with silver candlesticks and balanced dishes.

## CASTLEMARTYR (Baile na Martra) Cork – Cork – 712 H12    39 C3
– pop. 978

▶ Dublin 174 km – Cork 20 km – Ballincollig 25 km – Carrigaline 24 km

### 🏨 Castlemartyr ঙ    ⟨ 🚗 🔄 🔌 🔲 ⦿ 🐟 ✦ 📺 🌀 👥 🔌 AC ¶ 🚿 P̄
*– ℰ (021) 464 40 50 – www.castlemartyrresort.ie – Closed*    VISA ⓸⃝ AE
*Monday-Thursday November to March*
**77 rm** – ♦ € 195/230 ♦♦ € 210/260 – 26 suites
**Rest** *Bell Tower* – see restaurant listing
♦ Impressive 17C Georgian manor house in 220 acres, complete with lakes, castle ruins and golf course. Columned, parquet-floored hall; superb original ceiling in bar. Luxurious bedrooms boast marble bathrooms and every mod con. Stunning spa.

### 🍴🍴🍴 Bell Tower – at Castlemartyr Hotel    🚗 🔄 🔌 AC P̄ VISA ⓸⃝ AE
*– ℰ (021) 464 40 50 – www.castlemartyrresort.ie – Closed Monday-Thursday*
*November to March*
**Rest** – *(dinner only)* Menu 65 **s** – Carte € 33/60 **s**
♦ Formal hotel dining room in a grand 17C manor house that's set in 220 acres. Cooking is modern and sophisticated but with a strong classical base. Affords pleasant views out across the garden.

## CASTLEPOLLARD (Baile na gCros ) – Westmeath – 712 K6    37 C3
– pop. 1 004

▶ Dublin 63 km – Mullingar 13 km – Tullamore 37 km – Édenderry 36 km

### ⛰ Lough Bishop House ঙ    🚗 🔄 🚿 ¶ P̄
*Derrynagarra, Collinstown, South : 6 km by R 394 taking L 5738 opposite church*
*and school after 4 km – ℰ (044) 966 13 13 – www.loughbishophouse.com*
*– Closed Christmas-New Year*
**3 rm** ⌇ – ♦ € 55/75 ♦♦ € 110    **Rest** – Menu € 30
♦ Charming 18C farmhouse on tranquil, south-facing hillside. Hospitable owners and their dogs greet you; tea and cake are served on arrival. Simple bedrooms with neat shower rooms; no TVs. Communal dining: home-cooked dishes include meats and eggs from their farm.

## CASTLETOWNSHEND (Baile an Chaisleáin) – Cork – 712 E13    38 B3
– pop. 188 📗 Ireland

▶ Dublin 346 km – Cork 95 km – Killarney 116 km

◎ Glandore★, NE : 10 km R 596 – Sherkin Island★ **AC**, W : 15 km by R 596 and R 595 and ferry

### 🍺 Mary Ann's    🔄 VISA ⓸⃝
*Main St – ℰ (028) 36 146 – www.westcorkweek.com/maryanns/ – Closed 9*
*January-1 February, Monday-Tuesday October-March and 24-26 December*
**Rest** – *(bookings not accepted)* Carte € 20/42
♦ Bold red pub set up a steep street in a sleepy village. Simple rustic interior and a lovely garden with enclosed dining area. All-encompassing menus display a seafood base and Asian influences.

▶ Dublin 114 km – Drogheda 93 km – Enniskillen 64 km
ℹ Central Library, 1st Floor, Farnham St ☏ (049) 4 33 19 42, www.cavantourism.com
ⓖ Killykeen Forest Park★, W : 9.5 km by R 198

**Radisson Blu Farnham Estate**  ⟨ icons ⟩
*Farnham Estate, Northwest : 3.75 km*
*on R 198* – ☏ (049) 437 77 00 – www.farnhamestatecom
**154 rm** ☐ – ♦ € 105/195 ♦♦ € 130/220 – 4 suites
**Rest** *Botanica* – *(dinner only and Sunday lunch)* Menu € 40 – Carte € 32/50
◆ Set in extensive parkland, boasting every impressive outdoor activity and an impressive spa. Original Georgian features are combined with contemporary furnishings. Luxury bedrooms offer superb views. Traditional menus feature local seasonal ingredients.

**Cavan Crystal**  ⟨ icons ⟩
*Dublin Rd, East : 1.5 km on N 3* – ☏ (049) 436 0600
– www.cavancrystalhotel.com – Closed 24-26 December
**85 rm** ☐ – ♦ € 75/120 ♦♦ € 100/200
**Rest** *Opus One* – see restaurant listing
◆ Modern hotel next to – and owned by – the Cavan Crystal factory. Impressive atrium and spacious, stylish lounge-bar. Good meeting and leisure facilities. Up-to-date bedrooms in uniform designs.

**Opus One** – at Cavan Crystal Hotel  ⟨ icons ⟩
*Dublin Rd, East : 1.5 km on N 3* – ☏ (049) 436 0600
– www.cavancrystalhotel.com – Closed 24-26 December
**Rest** – *(light lunch)* Carte € 28/41
◆ Contemporary first floor restaurant in a smart hotel. Fresh, unfussy dishes at lunch; more ambitious dishes with unusual combinations and textures in the evening. Quality ingredients used in modern techniques.

**at Cloverhill** North : 12 km by N 3 on N 54 – ⊠ Belturbet

**Olde Post Inn** with rm  ⟨ icons ⟩
– ☏ (047) 55 555 – www.theoldepostinn.com – Closed 24-28 December
and Monday including bank holidays
**6 rm** ☐ – ♦ € 55/65 ♦♦ € 100/120
**Rest** – *(dinner only and Sunday lunch)* Menu € 35/56 – Carte € 41/55
◆ Keenly run former village post office; now a characterful restaurant with large rafters and exposed stone and brick. Attractive wooden conservatory. Seasonally changing menu of well presented, contemporary Irish cooking. Stylish, modern bedrooms.

**CELBRIDGE** – Kildare – **712** M7 – pop. 17 262  **39** D1
▶ Dublin 13 km – Naas 16 km – City Centre 14 km – Rathmines 17 km

**La Serre** with rm  ⟨ icons ⟩
*The Village at Lyons, South : 4.5 km. by Ardclough rd on Newcastle rd.* – ☏ (01)
630 35 00 – www.villageatlyons.com – Closed 25-30 December, Monday, Tuesday
and bank holidays
**14 rm** ☐ – ♦ € 180/310 ♦♦ € 180/310 – 3 suites
**Rest** – Menu € 30 – Carte € 55/65
◆ Charming restaurant within The Village at Lyons. Dine in the ornate 17C conservatory or rustic courtyard. Constantly evolving modern menus let quality ingredients speak for themselves. Contemporary bedrooms are set around a small lake; some have four-posters.

**CLAREMORRIS** (Clár Chlainne Mhuiris) – Mayo – **712** E/F6  **36** B2
– pop. 2 595
▶ Dublin 149 km – Castlebar 18 km – Galway 39 km – Newbridge 41 km

🏨 **McWilliam Park**  🖹 🛖 ₤₆ 🖹 ₺ rm, 🅰 rest, 🕉 🕪 �R 🅿 💳 ⓒⓔ AE ⓞ
*Knock Rd, East : 2 km on N 60 – ℰ (094) 937 80 00 – www.mcwilliampark.ie*
**101 rm** ⬜ – ♦ € 110/130 ♦♦ € 130/170 – 2 suites
**Rest** – *(carvery lunch Monday-Saturday)* Menu € 21/35 **s** – Carte € 28/41 **s**
♦ Named after a local 18C landowner, this busy, purpose built hotel is located on the outskirts of town, convenient for the N17, Knock and the airport. Modern bedrooms. Stylish restaurant offers dishes made using local produce.

---

**CLIFDEN** (An Clochán) – Galway – 712 B7 – pop. 1 497 ▌ Ireland        36 A3
▶ Dublin 291 km – Ballina 124 km – Galway 79 km
🛈 Galway Rd ℰ (095) 2 11 63, www.clifden.galway-ireland.ie
◉ Connemara★★★, NE : by N 59 – Sky Road★★ (≤ ★★), NE : by N 59 – Connemara National Park★, NE : 1.5 km by N 59 – Killary Harbour★, NE : 35 km by N 59 – Kylemore Abbey★ **AC**, N : 18 km by N 59

🏨 **Clifden Station House**  🖹 🕫 🛖 ₤₆ 🖹 ₺ rm, ✈ 🕉 🕪 🚫 🅿
*– ℰ (095) 21 699 – www.clifdenstationhouse.com*  💳 ⓒⓔ AE ⓞ
**78 rm** ⬜ – ♦ € 88/140 ♦♦ € 100/240
**Rest** – *(closed weekdays November-February) (bar lunch)* Menu € 30
– Carte € 30/45
♦ Purpose-built hotel on site of the old Galway-Clifden railway line, in a modern complex. Residents only kids club, leisure and wellness centre. Uniform bedrooms with good facilities. Local seafood orientated menus in restaurant. BBQs on the platform in summer.

🏨 **Ardagh** ⌂                    ≤ 🚿 🅿 💳 ⓒⓔ
*Ballyconneely Rd, South : 3 km. on R 341 – ℰ (095) 21 384*
*– www.ardaghhotel.com – Easter-October*
**21 rm** ⬜ – ♦ € 40/120 ♦♦ € 90/150
**Rest** – *(dinner only)* Menu € 35 – Carte € 40/65
♦ Neat hotel with modern interior, overlooking a small bay. Three lounges. Pleasant bedrooms – many with bold fabrics and colourful headboards designed by the owner; some with window seats and views. Bright restaurant affords excellent outlook; seafood a speciality.

🏠 **Dolphin Beach Country House** ⌂      ≤ 🚿 🕭 🛖 🕉 🅿 💳 ⓒⓔ
*Lower Sky Rd, West : 5.5 km. by Sky Rd – ℰ (095) 21 204*
*– www.dolphinbeachhouse.com – March-October*
**9 rm** ⬜ – ♦ € 60/100 ♦♦ € 130/160
**Rest** – *(dinner only) (residents only)* Menu € 37 **s**
♦ Terracotta-coloured former farmhouse in peaceful hillside location. Mediterranean villa style interior with bright décor and red stone tiles. Good-sized bedrooms with artwork by friendly owner. Traditional home-cooked meals; wonderful bay views from dining room.

🏠 **Quay House** without rest                ≤ 🕉 💳 ⓒⓔ
*Beach Rd – ℰ (095) 21 369 – www.thequayhouse.com – mid-March-October*
**14 rm** ⬜ – ♦ € 70/110 ♦♦ € 130/150
♦ Cream-washed former harbourmaster's house and monastery, overlooking the bay. Relaxed, bohemian interior with antiques and wild animal memorabilia. Comfy, spacious bedrooms; those in the wing have kitchenettes. Homemade bread and local cheese feature at breakfast.

🏠 **Sea Mist House** without rest          🚿 🕉 🕪 🅿 💳 ⓒⓔ AE
*– ℰ (095) 21 441 – www.seamisthouse.com – March-December, restricted opening in winter*
**4 rm** ⬜ – ♦ € 50/80 ♦♦ € 75/100
♦ Centrally located stone-built house with traditional lounge and pleasant gardens. Simple, modern bedrooms boast colourful fabrics and co-ordinating drapes; no TVs. Conservatory breakfast area.

⌂ **Buttermilk Lodge** without rest     ⪦ ⌗ ⁗ 🛜 **P** **VISA** ◉ **AE**
*Westport Rd – ℰ (095) 21 951 – www.buttermilklodge.com – Closed 25*
*December and January*
**11 rm** ⌷ – † € 50/75 †† € 80/100
♦ Immaculately kept guesthouse. Lounge has games, hot drinks and a real turf
fire; a cow theme predominates. Homely, colour co-ordinated bedrooms. Friendly
owners offer local info/packed lunches.

⌂ **Tower View** without rest ⌚     ⪦ ⌗ ⁗ 🛜 **P**
*Lower Sky Rd, West : 4 km by Sky Rd – ℰ (095) 21 965*
*– www.towerview.clifden.com – May-September*
**3 rm** ⌷ – † € 35/45 †† € 65/70
♦ Yellow-painted house overlooking Clifden Bay. Well-priced, cosy bedrooms are
spotlessly kept, with plain décor, bright fabrics and fully tiled bathrooms. All have
views but no TVs.

---

**CLOGHEEN** (An Chloichín) – **South Tipperary** – **712** I11 – **pop. 509**     **39** C2
▶ Dublin 122 km – Tipperary 23 km – Clonmel 21 km – Dungarvan 28 km

✕✕ **Old Convent** with rm     ⪦ ⌗ **P** **VISA** ◉
*Mount Anglesby, Southeast : 0.5 km on R 668 (Lismore rd) – ℰ (052) 746 55 65*
*– www.theoldconvent.ie – Closed 24 December-31 January and*
*Sunday-Wednesday except bank holidays*
**7 rm** ⌷ – † € 125/150 †† € 170/200
**Rest** – (dinner only) (booking essential) (set menu only) Menu € 65
♦ Home to the Sisters of Mercy for over 100 years, this converted convent retains
a serene feel. Dine in the candlelit former chapel on seasonal 8 course tasting
menu. Comfortable bedrooms, decorated in calming colours.

---

**CLONAKILTY** (Cloich na Coillte) – **Cork** – **712** F13 – **pop. 4 154**     **38** B3
▯ Ireland
▶ Dublin 310 km – Cork 51 km
🛈 25 Ashe St ℰ (023) 8 83 32 26, www.clonakilty.ie
▣ Dunmore Muckross, ℰ (023) 3 46 44
◉ West Cork Regional Museum★ **AC**
◉ Courtmacsherry★, E : 12 km by R 600 and R 601 – Timoleague Friary★, E : 8 km by
R 600. Carbery Coast★ (Dromberg Stone Circle★, Glandore★, Castletownshend★)
by N 71 and R 597

🏚 **Inchydoney Island Lodge and Spa**     ⪦ ⌂ ▤ ◉ ⁘ ⑃ ▤ ⌧
*South : 5.25 km by N 71 following signs*     **AC** rest, ⁗ 🛜 ⑃ **P** **VISA** ◉ **AE**
*for Inchydoney Beach – ℰ (023) 883 31 43 – www.inchydoneyisland.com*
*– Closed 23-26 December*
**63 rm** ⌷ – † € 145/170 †† € 190/250 – 4 suites
**Rest** *Gulfstream* – see restaurant listing
**Rest** *Dunes Bistro* – Carte € 23/47 **s**
♦ Superbly located on a remote headland and boasting stunning views over the
beach and out to sea. Contemporary bedrooms come with balconies or terraces
and all you could ask for. Smart spa boasts a seawater pool. Dine in the formal
restaurant or from a more accessible menu in the nautically styled bistro-bar.

✕✕ **Gulfstream** – at Inchydoney Island Lodge and Spa     ⪦ ⌖ **AC** **P** **VISA** ◉ **AE**
*South : 5.25 km by N 71 following signs for Inchydoney Beach – ℰ (023)*
*883 31 43 – www.inchydoneyisland.com – Closed 24-26 December*
**Rest** – (dinner only) Menu € 59
♦ Formal hotel dining room located on the first floor of a vast hotel on the headland. Modern menus feature plenty of fresh local seafood. Affords superb views
over the beach and out to sea.

📷 **An Súgan** with rm   &. rm, ⚭ 🏧 🆑
*41 Wolfe Tone St – ℰ (023) 883 3719 – www.ansugan.com*
**7 rm** ☐ – 🛉 € 30/60 🛉🛉 € 70/100
**Rest** – Menu € 25 (dinner) – Carte € 22/43
♦ Charming, personally run, salmon-pink pub with characterful dining rooms. Menus are based around daily arrivals of fresh local fish/seafood; some meat dishes also feature. Bedrooms, in the old harbourmaster's house, boast bold feature walls and flat screen TVs.

**CLONEGALL (Cluain na nGall)** – Carlow – **712** M9 – pop. 231     **39** D2
🚇 Dublin 73 km – Carlow 20 km – Kilkenny 39 km – Wexford 30 km

✗ **Sha Roe Bistro**   🏧 🆑
☺ *Main St – ℰ (053) 937 56 36 – Closed January, 1 week April, 1 week October, Sunday dinner, Monday and Tuesday*
**Rest** – *(dinner only and Sunday lunch) (booking essential)* Menu € 34 (lunch) – Carte € 32/43
♦ Rurally set restaurant with good reputation, run by an enthusiastic couple. Rustic lounge; small dining room with enormous inglenook and chef's table. Classically based menus display modern touches. Produce is local – cheese comes from the weekly farmers' market.

**CLONTARF** = Cluain Tarbh – Dublin – **712** N7 – see Dublin

**CLOVERHILL** = Droim Caiside – Cavan – **712** J5 – see Cavan

**COBH (An Cóbh)** – Cork – **712** H12 – pop. 11 303 📖 Ireland     **38** B3
🚇 Dublin 264 km – Cork 24 km – Waterford 104 km
📷 Ballywilliam, ℰ (021) 81 23 99
👁 Town★ – St Colman's Cathedral★ – Lusitania Memorial★
📷 Fota Island★ (Fota House★★ **AC**, Fota Wildlife Park★ **AC**), N : 6.5 km by R 624 – Cloyne Cathedral★, SE : 24 km by R 624/5, N 25, R 630 and R 629

🏠 **Knockeven House** without rest   🖼 ⚭ 📶 **P** 🏧 🆑
*Rushbrooke, West : 2 km by R 624 – ℰ (021) 481 17 78 – www.knockevenhouse.com – Closed 15-26 December*
**4 rm** ☐ – 🛉 € 65/85 🛉🛉 € 90/100
♦ Spacious, yellow-painted Victorian house with comfortable lounge and communal breakfast room. Traditional bedrooms feature antique furniture; flat screen TVs provide a modern touch.

**CONG (Conga)** – Mayo – **712** E7 – pop. 150 📖 Ireland     **36** A3
🚇 Dublin 257 km – Ballina 79 km – Galway 45 km
ℹ Old Courthouse ℰ (094) 9 54 65 42, www.congtourism.com
👁 Town★
📷 Lough Corrib★★. Ross Errilly Abbey★ (Tower ≤★) – Joyce Country★★ (Lough Nafooey★) W : by R 345

🏰 **Ashford Castle** ॐ   ≤ 🖼 🐎 🏊 ♨ 🚴 ✗ 🖼 🛗 ⚭ 🔧 **P** 🏧 🆑 🅰🅴 ①
*– ℰ (094) 954 60 03 – www.ashford.ie*
**78 rm** ☐ – 🛉 € 175/950 🛉🛉 € 175/950 – 5 suites
**Rest Cullen's at the Cottage** – see restaurant listing
**Rest George V Room** – *(dinner only) (residents only)* Menu € 67 – Carte € 49/76
♦ Hugely impressive lochside castle in formal gardens, dating from 1228. Handsome, antique-furnished guest areas. Well-appointed bedrooms display warm fabrics; some four-posters. Activities include archery, falconry and clay pigeon shooting. Elegant George V requires a jacket and tie; casual meals in Cullen's.

🏠 **Lisloughrey Lodge** ◌ ☜ ☞ ☓ ⎙ 🛌 🎇 💺 🕸 🥂 ⛵ 🛥 🅿
*The Quay, Southeast : 2.25 km by R 345 off R 346 – ☎ (094)* VISA ⓒⓞ AE
*954 54 00 – www.lisloughrey.ie – Closed January, Christmas, Monday and
Tuesday*
**41 rm** ⌁ – ♦ € 85/185 ♦♦ € 135/225 – 9 suites
**Rest** *Salt* – Carte € 44/51
• Georgian house in 10 acres of gardens. Guest areas boast contemporary feature walls and brushed velvet sofas. Bright, modern bedrooms have smart bathrooms and bold colour schemes; most are located in the courtyard. Three-roomed
restaurant serves a modern menu.

🏠 **Michaeleen's Manor** without rest ⎙ 🎇 ☓ 💺 🅿 VISA ⓒⓞ
*Quay Rd, Southeast : 1.5 km by R 346 – ☎ (094) 954 60 89
– www.quietman-cong.com*
**6 rm** ⌁ – ♦ € 50 ♦♦ € 75
• Named after the lead character in the film 'The Quiet Man', filmed in the village; comfortable, brightly decorated bedrooms follow suit. Homely lounges
airy breakfast room.

🏠 **Ballywarren House** ☜ ⎙ ⛵ 🅿 VISA ⓒⓞ AE
*East : 3.5 km on R 346 – ☎ (094) 954 69 89 – www.ballywarrenhouse.com
– Closed 1 week spring and 1 week autumn*
**3 rm** ⌁ – ♦ € 98/124 ♦♦ € 136/148 **Rest** – Menu € 45 **s**
• Passionately run by a charming couple who ensure each guest's stay is special.
Open fires, galleried landing and oak staircase. Bedrooms boast luxurious linen
and lovely views. Aga-cooked breakfast and tasty homemade dinners.

🍴🍴 **Cullen's at the Cottage** – at Ashford Castle Hotel ⎙ 🔥 🅿
*– ☎ (094) 954 60 03 – www.ashford.ie* VISA ⓒⓞ AE ⓞ
**Rest** – (May-September) Carte € 23/51
• All-day restaurant set in a whitewashed, thatched cottage, in the grounds of an
imposing restored castle. Homely inner; enjoy castle views from the outside tables. Modern, bistro-style menu.

---

**CORK (Corcaigh)** – Cork – **712** G12 – pop. 119 418 ▯ Ireland **38** B3
▶ Dublin 248 km
✈ Cork Airport : ☎ (021) 4313131, S : 6.5 km by L 42 X
🚢 to France (Roscoff) (Brittany Ferries) weekly (14 h/16 h) – to Pembroke (Swansea
Cork Ferries) 2-6 weekly (8 h 30 mn)
🛈 Grand Parade ☎ (021) 4 25 51 00, www.cork-guide.ie
🏁 Douglas, ☎ (021) 4 89 10 86
🏁 Mahon Blackrock Cloverhill, ☎ (021) 4 29 25 43
🏁 Monkstown Parkgarriffe, ☎ (021) 4 84 13 76
🏁 Little Island, ☎ (021) 4 35 34 51
◎ City★★ – Shandon Bells★★ Y, St Fin Barre's Cathedral★★ **AC** Z, Cork Public
Museum★ X **M** – Grand Parade★ Z , South Mall★ Z , St Patrick Street★ Z ,
Crawford Art Gallery★ Y – Elizabethan Fort★ Z
◎ Dunkathel House★ **AC**, E : 9.25 km by N 8 and N 25 X. Fota Island★ (Fota
House★★ **AC**, Fota Wildlife Park★ **AC**), E : 13 km by N 8 and N 25 X – Cobh★ (St
Colman's Cathedral★, Lusitania Memorial★) SE : 24 km by N 8, N 25 and R 624 X

Plans pages 891, 892

🏠 **Hayfield Manor** ⎙ 🖥 🌀 🛌 💺 💺 🅰🅲 ⛵ 🛥 🅿 VISA ⓒⓞ AE ⓞ
*Perrott Ave, College Rd – ☎ (021) 484 59 00 – www.hayfieldmanor.ie*
**84 rm** ⌁ – ♦ € 380 ♦♦ € 380 – 4 suites X♠
**Rest** *Orchids* **Rest** *Perrotts* – see restaurant listing
• Luxurious country house with wood-panelled hall, impressive staircase and antique-furnished drawing rooms – the perfect spot for afternoon tea. Plush bedrooms have plenty of extras, including putting machines. Well-equipped residents spa.

### 🏠 **Lancaster Lodge** without rest
*Lancaster Quay, Western Rd – ℰ (021) 425 11 25 – www.lancasterlodge.com*
*– Closed 23-28 December*                                                      **Zi**
**48 rm** ☕ – † € 79/119  †† € 79/138
♦ Purpose-built hotel with crisp, modern interior. Bedrooms are chintz-free, pleasingly and sparingly decorated. Largest rooms on the fourth floor; rear rooms are quieter.

### ⌂ **Garnish House** without rest
*Western Rd – ℰ (021) 427 51 11 – www.garnish.ie*                               **Xr**
**21 rm** ☕ – † € 50/80  †† € 75/120
♦ Justifiably proud of gourmet breakfast: 30 options include pancakes and porridge. Guests are welcomed with home-made scones in cosy rooms; those at the rear have quiet aspect.

### XXX **Augustine's**
*Clarion Hotel, Lapps Quay – ℰ (021) 427 93 75 – www.augustines.ie*
*– Closed Good Friday, 25 December, Sunday and Monday*                          **Zu**
**Rest** – *(dinner only)* Carte € 36/52
♦ Smart, spacious ground floor restaurant set in corporate hotel. Modern, carefully crafted dishes made with quality seasonal produce. Formal but friendly service from uniformed staff.

### XXX **Flemings** with rm
*Silver Grange House, Tivoli, East : 4.5 km on N 8 – ℰ (021) 482 16 21*
*– www.flemingsrestaurant.ie – Closed 23-26 December*                           **Xu**
**3 rm** ☕ – † € 75/80  †† € 110
**Rest** – *(closed Monday lunch) (booking essential)* Menu € 34/36
*– Carte € 42/57*
♦ Classical cuisine, French bias; uses local produce, organically home-grown vegetables, herbs. Two dining rooms in keeping with Georgian character of house. Period furnished bedrooms.

REPUBLIC OF IRELAND

CORK

### ☆☆☆ Orchids – at Hayfield Manor Hotel

🚗 ⚫ AC P VISA ⦾ AE ⦿

*Perrott Ave, College Rd – ℰ (021) 484 59 00 – www.hayfieldmanor.ie*
**Rest** – *(closed Monday-Wednesday and Sunday dinner) (dinner
only and Sunday lunch) (booking essential)* Menu € 65
– Carte € 44/62

X**z**

• Sophisticated formal dining room in a well-appointed country house. Pillars
dominate the room, which is laid with crisp white tablecloths. Menus offer refined
dishes with some modern twists.

### ☆☆ Jacques

AC VISA ⦾ AE

*Phoenix St – ℰ (021) 427 73 87 – www.jacquesrestaurant.ie – Closed 25
December-3 January, Sunday and bank holidays*
**Rest** – *(dinner only)* Menu € 25 *(early dinner)*
– Carte € 33/49

Z**c**

• A long, warmly decorated room with modern tables on which old Irish classics
are delivered. Farm ducks, wild game, fresh fish and organic vegetables are used
in the cooking.

XX **Gourmandises**  *VISA* ⓒⓑ AE ⓪
*17 Cook St – ℰ (021) 425 19 59 – www.lesgourmandises.ie – Closed 1 week March, 1 week August, Sunday dinner (except bank holiday weekend) and Monday* Z**v**
**Rest** – French – *(dinner only and Sunday lunch) (booking essential)*
Menu € 30/45
♦ Well-run restaurant with spacious, high-ceilinged interior; formerly a Turkish bath. Experienced chef produces accomplished, detailed dishes with a classical French base and original touches.

XX **Perrotts** – at Hayfield Manor Hotel  ⇛ & AC P VISA ⓒⓑ AE ⓪
*Perrott Ave, College Rd – ℰ (021) 484 59 00 – www.hayfieldmanor.ie*
**Rest** – Menu € 32 (lunch) – Carte € 40/56 X**z**
♦ Conservatory restaurant overlooking the gardens of a luxurious country house. Smart but comfortably furnished, with adjoining wood-panelled bar. Menu offers a modern take on brasserie classics.

X **Cafe Paradiso** with rm  (ⁱ) VISA ⓒⓑ
*16 Lancaster Quay, Western Rd – ℰ (021) 427 79 39 – www.cafeparadiso.ie – Closed 25-28 December* Z**o**
**2 rm** ⊒ – ♦ € 100 ♦♦ € 120
**Rest** – Vegetarian – *(dinner only and lunch Friday and Saturday) (booking essential)* Menu € 35 (dinner) – Carte € 29/47
♦ Stylish little restaurant with grey/green colour scheme, friendly service and intimate atmosphere. Extensive choice of interesting, original, vegetarian dishes which feature plenty of flavours and textures. Spacious, modern bedrooms come in bright, bold colours.

X **Fenn's Quay**  AC VISA ⓒⓑ AE
*5 Sheares St – ℰ (021) 427 95 27 – www.fennsquay.ie – Closed 24-27 December, 1 January, Sunday and bank holidays* Z**n**
**Rest** – Menu € 28 (dinner) – Carte € 31/40
♦ Modest little bistro with whitewashed brick walls, closely set tables and loyal following. Simple, flavoursome cooking offers 'tart of the day', as well as more substantial dishes at dinner.

X **Farmgate Cafe**  VISA ⓒⓑ ⓪
*English Market (1st floor), Princes St – ℰ (021) 427 81 34 – www.farmgate.ie – Closed Sunday and bank holidays* Z**s**
**Rest** – *(lunch only)* Menu € 22 – Carte € 24/29
♦ Long-standing café on 1st floor of the English Market. Small daily changing menu of food from the stalls below or from the counties of Munster; all simple, homemade and fresh.

**at Cork Airport** South : 6.5 km by N 27 - X – ✉ Cork

⌂⌂⌂ **International Airport**  ⧮ & rm, AC ⅏ (ⁱ) ⅍ P VISA ⓒⓑ AE
*Gate 2 – ℰ (021) 454 98 00 – www.corkinternationalairporthotel.com – Closed 23-27 December*
**141 rm** ⊒ – ♦ € 180 ♦♦ € 180 – 4 suites
**Rest** *Strata* – *(closed Friday-Saturday) (carvery lunch)* Carte € 21/37 **s**
♦ Quirky hotel with aviation theme and various eateries. Decent-sized bedrooms come in Deluxe and Executive versions. The superb Pullman lounge resembles the cabin of a plane. Modern restaurant has interesting smoking terrace.

**CORK AIRPORT** = Aerfort Chorcai Cork – Cork – **712** G12 – see Cork

REPUBLIC OF IRELAND

## CORROFIN (Cora Finne ) – Clare – **712** E9 – pop. 485     **38** B1

▶ Dublin 228 km – Gort 24 km – Limerick 51 km

↑   **Fergus View** without rest     ⩾ 🚗 🍽 🅿
*Kilnaboy, North : 3.25 km on R 476 – ℰ (065) 683 76 06 – www.fergusview.com*
*– March-October*
**6 rm** � – ♦ € 50/53 ♦♦ € 78
♦ Charming bay-windowed house with open-fired lounge, cosy breakfast room
and country views. Bright, immaculately kept bedrooms: tiny bathrooms; no TVs.
Delightful owners offer superb hospitality.

---

## CROMANE – Kerry – **712** C11 – pop. 125     **38** A2

▶ Dublin 201 km – Tralee 23 km – Cork 73 km – Limerick 78 km

✗✗   **Jacks Coastguard**     ⩾ 🚗 🆎 🅿 💳 ⦿
*– ℰ (066) 976 91 02 – www.jackscromane.com – Closed 7 January-9 February,*
*Monday-Wednesday except June-October and Tuesday*
**Rest** – Seafood – Carte € 32/48
♦ Remotely set former coastguard station, now a bright, glitzy, split-level restau-
rant with panoramic windows and lovely bay views. Seafood-orientated menu
offers well-presented, classic combinations. Smart bar-lounge; live piano at
weekends.

---

## CROOKHAVEN (An Cruachán) – Cork – **712** C13 – pop. 1 669     **38** A3

▶ Dublin 373 km – Bantry 40 km – Cork 120 km

↑   **Galley Cove House** without rest ⌗     ⩾ 🚗 🍽 🍸 🅿
*West : 0.75 km on R 591 – ℰ (028) 35 137 – www.galleycovehouse.com – Closed*
*March 16 to October 31*
**4 rm** ⊔ – ♦ € 45/55 ♦♦ € 75/90
♦ Detached house just outside the town, affording superb southerly views over
the sea towards Fastnet Rock. Conservatory breakfast room and simple, pine-
furnished bedrooms with bright colour schemes; all have a sea outlook. Hospitable owners.

---

## CROSSHAVEN – Cork – **712** H12 – pop. 1 373     **38** B3

▶ Dublin 170 km – Cork 15 km – Limerick 78 km – Galway 140 km

🛏   **Cronin's**     🏠 💳 ⦿ 🆎 ⓪
*– ℰ (021) 483 18 29 – www.croninspub.com – Closed 25 December and Good*
*Friday*
**Rest** – Seafood – *(lunch only and dinner Friday-Saturday)* Carte € 15/35
♦ Classic Irish pub in the same family since 1970 and now run by the 3rd genera-
tion. Interesting artefacts and boxing memorabilia. Unfussy seafood dishes feature
local produce. Limited opening in restaurant, which offers more ambitious fare.

---

## CROSSMOLINA (Crois Mhaoilíona) – Mayo – **712** E5 – pop. 930     **36** B2
▌ Ireland

▶ Dublin 252 km – Ballina 10 km

◎ Errew Abbey★, SE : 9.5 km by R 315. Cáide Fields★ **AC**, N : 24 km by R 315 and R
314 W – Killala★, NE : 16 km by R 315 and minor road – Moyne Abbey★, NE :
18 km by R 115, minor road to Killala, R 314 and minor road – Rosserk Abbey★,
NE : 18 km by R 115, minor road to Killala, R 314 and minor road

🏠   **Enniscoe House** ⌗     ⩾ 🚗 🕭 🍽 🅿 💳 ⦿
*Castlehill, South : 3.25 km on R 315 – ℰ (096) 31 112 – www.enniscoe.com*
*– Closed 7 January-31 March and 1 November-27 December*
**6 rm** ⊔ – ♦ € 130/150 ♦♦ € 220/260
**Rest** – *(dinner only) (booking essential for non-residents)* Menu € 50/56 **s**
♦ Georgian manor, overlooking Lough Conn, on Enniscoe Estate with walled gar-
den and heritage centre. Hallway boasts original family tree; antique beds in
flower-filled rooms. Home cooked country dishes served in the dining room.

**DALKEY** (Deilginis) – Dún Laoghaire-Rathdown – **712** N8 – pop. 8 076    **39** D1

Ireland

▶ Dublin 13 km – Bray 9 km

◉ Killiney Bay (≤ ★★), S : by coast road

XX   **Jaipur**      AK VISA ◎◎ AE
    21 Castle St – ℰ (01) 285 0552 – www.jaipur.ie – closed 25 December
    **Rest** – Indian – *(dinner only and Sunday lunch)* Menu € 16 (lunch)
    – Carte € 27/42
    ♦ Central location and smart, lively, brightly coloured, modern décor. Well-
    spaced, linen-clad tables. Warm, friendly ambience. Contemporary Indian dishes.

---

**DINGLE** (An Daingean) – Kerry – **712** B11 – pop. 1 772   Ireland    **38** A2

▶ Dublin 347 km – Killarney 82 km – Limerick 153 km

◉ Town ★ – St Mary's Church ★ – Diseart (stained glass ★ **AC**)

◉ Gallarus Oratory ★★, NW : 8 km by R 559 – NE : Connor Pass ★★ – Kilmalkedar ★,
NW : 9 km by R 559. Dingle Peninsula ★★ – Connor Pass ★★, NE : 8 km by minor
road – Stradbally Strand ★★, NE : 17 km via Connor Pass – Corca Dhuibhne
Regional Museum ★ **AC**, NW : 13 km by R 559 – Blasket Islands ★, W : 21 km by R
559 and ferry from Dunquin

Plan on next page

🏠   **Emlagh Country House** without rest     ≤ 🚗 🛗 ᴋ AK ℅ 📶 P
    – ℰ (066) 915 23 45 – www.emlaghhouse.com – 18     VISA ◎◎ AE
    March-October     **Yd**
    **10 rm** ⊆ – † € 90/130 †† € 180/220
    ♦ Built to resemble a Georgian country house, with mock period features. Per-
    sonally run, it has a comfortable, relaxing feel. Large, luxurious bedrooms are col-
    our themed around local plants and boast antique furnishings and feature beds;
    choose from a sea view or terrace. Homemade breads and jams at breakfast.

🏠   **Castlewood House** without rest     ≤ 🚗 🛗 ᴋ ℅ 📶 P VISA ◎◎
    The Wood – ℰ (066) 915 27 88 – www.castlewooddingle.com – Closed 6-20
    January and 6-27 December     **Yw**
    **12 rm** ⊆ – † € 55/99 †† € 99/160
    ♦ Well run, spacious and comfortable house. Individually decorated bedrooms;
    some with antique brass beds, others more contemporary. All have jacuzzi bath;
    most have view.

🏠   **Greenmount House** without rest     ≤ 🚗 ℅ 📶 P VISA ◎◎
    Gortonora – ℰ (066) 915 14 14 – www.greenmounthouse.ie – Closed 20-27
    December     **Zc**
    **15 rm** ⊆ – † € 50/120 †† € 80/160
    ♦ Large, yellow painted, extended house located above the town. Two comfort-
    able lounges and a conservatory-style breakfast room. Newest bedrooms most
    comfortably appointed.

🏠   **Heatons**     ≤ 🚗 ᴋ rm, ℅ 📶 P VISA ◎◎
    The Wood – ℰ (066) 915 22 88 – www.heatonsdingle.com – Closed 4 January-1
    February     **Yc**
    **16 rm** ⊆ – † € 49/95 †† € 70/130
    **Rest *Shore View*** – Carte approx. € 35
    ♦ Large, family run house, a short walk from town and overlooking the harbour.
    Well-appointed lounge and conservatory breakfast room. Modern bedrooms; one
    with a small balcony and good views. Comprehensive breakfasts include home-
    made scones. Linen-laid restaurant offers concise modern menu of local ingredi-
    ents.

**REPUBLIC OF IRELAND**

⌂ **Coastline** without rest    ⇐ 🚗 ⚔ 🛜 **P** 𝘝𝘐𝘚𝘈 ⊕ ➊

*The Wood* – ℰ (066) 915 24 94 – www.coastlinedingle.com – February-November
**8 rm** ⌂ – ♦ € 45/55  ♦♦ € 74/94                                        **Y**x

♦ Hard to miss modern guesthouse with bright pink façade. Comfy, homely interior with lots of local info. All rooms have pleasant view; those at the front face
Dingle harbour.

XX **Global Village**  ⓐⓀ VISA ⓞⓞ ⒶⒺ
*Upper Main St – ℰ (066) 915 23 25 – www.globalvillagedingle.com – mid-March to mid-November*  **Za**
**Rest** – Seafood – *(dinner only) (booking essential)* Menu € 28 (early dinner) **s** – Carte € 33/52 **s**
♦ Homely restaurant with local artwork and relaxed vibe. Wide-ranging menu makes good use of seasonal, organic and home-grown produce; fantastic fresh fish dishes feature. The well-travelled owner has visited 42 different countries!

X **Chart House**  ⓐⓀ VISA ⓞⓞ
☺ *The Mall – ℰ (066) 915 22 55 – www.thecharthousedingle.com – Closed 2 January-12 February, 22-27 December, and Monday in low season*  **Zf**
**Rest** – *(dinner only) (booking essential)* Menu € 25/33 – Carte € 25/43
♦ Attractive stone cottage at the entrance to the town. Charming, open-plan inner with rustic flint walls, wood floors and large bar boasting stained glass dividers. Chunky wood tables and friendly, effective service. Local ingredients; meat dishes are particularly good.

X **Out of the Blue**  ⌂ ⓐⓀ VISA ⓞⓞ
*Waterside – ℰ (066) 915 08 11 – www.outoftheblue.ie – mid-March to October*  **Zn**
**Rest** – Seafood – *(dinner only and Sunday lunch) (booking essential)* Carte € 38/48
♦ Simple, brightly painted building, with a relaxing, rustic charm, located 50yds from harbour. Daily changing menu of classic fish dishes. Jolly service from a well-versed local team.

**REPUBLIC OF IRELAND**

---

**DONEGAL** (Dún na nGall) – **Donegal** – **712** H4 – **pop. 2 339** 📗 Ireland  **37** C1

▶ Dublin 264 km – Londonderry 77 km – Sligo 64 km

🛬 Donegal Airport ℰ (074) 9548284

ℹ Quay St ℰ (074) 9 72 11 48, www.donegaldirect.ie

◎ Donegal Castle★ **AC**

⬡ Donegal Coast★★ - Cliffs of Bunglass★★, W : 48.25 km by N 56 and R 263 – Glencolmcille Folk Village★★ **AC**, W : 53 km by N 56 and R 263 - Rossnowlagh Strand★★, S : 35.5 km by N 15 and R 231 – Trabane Strand★, W : 58 km by N 56 and R 263

🏨 **Solis Lough Eske Castle** ॐ  🖼 🔊 🖽 ⓦ ⑩ 🏋 🛌 🖥 ♿ ⓦ 🔌 🅿
*Northeast : 6.5 km by N15 (Killybegs rd) – ℰ (074)*  VISA ⓞⓞ ⒶⒺ ⓞ
*972 51 00 – www.solisloughheskecastle.com*
**95 rm** 🍽 – †€ 185/235 ††€ 185/235 – 1 suite
**Rest** *Cedars* – see restaurant listing
♦ Beautifully restored 17C castle with many extensions, surrounded by 43 sculpture-filled acres. Fantastic spa; swimming pool overlooks an enclosed garden. Mix of contemporary and antique-furnished bedrooms, superior are worth the extra cost.

🏨 **Harvey's Point** ॐ  ≤ 🖼 🔊 ⚲ 🖥 ♿ 🗊 🔌 🅿 VISA ⓞⓞ
*Lough Eske, Northeast : 7.25 km. by T 27 (Killybegs rd) – ℰ (074) 972 22 08 – www.harveyspoint.com – Restricted opening in winter*
**66 rm** 🍽 – †€ 198/250 ††€ 198/250 – 4 suites
**Rest** *Restaurant* – see restaurant listing
♦ Sprawling, classical hotel in restful loughside setting, with wood-panelled rooms and leather-furnished lounge. Bedrooms in wing have high level of facilities; more traditional courtyard rooms.

REPUBLIC OF IRELAND

**Ardeevin** without rest ⚐　　　　　　　≼ 🍴 🕸 🎙️ **P** VISA

*Lough Eske, Barnesmore, Northeast : 9 km by N 15 following signs for Lough Eske Drive – ℰ (074) 972 17 90 – www.members.tripod.com/ardeevin – 18 March-November*
**6 rm** ⌷ – 🛏 € 45/50 🛏🛏 € 65/70

◆ Friendly, brightly painted house set in peaceful gardens and boasting beautiful views over Lough Eske; personally run by the friendly owner. Warm, pleasantly cluttered guest areas are filled with ornaments and curios. Individually designed bedrooms display quality furnishings and thoughtful extras.

XXX　**Restaurant** – at Harvey's Point Hotel　　≼ 🍴 🕭 AC **P** VISA ⊚

*Lough Eske, Northeast : 7.25 km. by T 27 (Killybegs rd) – ℰ (074) 972 22 08 – www.harveyspoint.com – Closed Wednesday dinner and restricted opening November-March*
**Rest** – Menu € 59 (dinner) – Carte lunch  € 27/39

◆ Large, formal restaurant with semicircular glass side providing lovely lough views; try for a window table. Traditional cooking, local ingredients and a few international touches. Attentive, structured service.

XX　**Cedars** – at Solis Lough Eske Castle Hotel　　🍴 🕭 ⅃ AC ⇨ **P** VISA ⊚ AE ①

*Northeast : 6.5 km by N15 (Killybegs rd) – ℰ (074) 972 51 00 – www.solislougheskecastle.com*
**Rest** – (dinner only and Sunday lunch) Menu € 55 – Carte € 37/70

◆ Stylish, modern grill restaurant located in a 17C castle close to the loch. Slate terrace boasts views over the lawns and woodland. Extensive grill menu features locally sourced meats and fish.

 On a tight budget? Take advantage of special prices at lunch.

---

**DOOGORT** = Dumha Goirt – Mayo – **712** B5/6 – **see Achill Island**

---

**DOOLIN** (Dúlainm) – Clare – **712** D8 ▯ Ireland　　　　　**38** B1

▶ Dublin 275 km – Galway 69 km – Limerick 80 km

◪ The Burren★★ (Cliffs of Moher★★★, Scenic Route★★, Aillwee Cave★ **AC** (Waterfall★★), Poulnabrone Portal Tomb★, Corcomroe Abbey★, Kilfenora Crosses★, Burren Centre★ **AC**)

　**Tír Gan Éan House** without rest　　　🗐 ⅃ AC 🕸 **P** VISA ⊚

*– ℰ (065) 707 57 26 – www.tirganean.ie – Easter to October*
**11 rm** ⌷ – 🛏 € 50/100 🛏🛏 € 90/140

◆ Stylish hotel on main road into the village; part of a small holiday cottage complex. Open-plan guest areas include a comfy lounge and bar. Modern bedrooms are decorated in browns/creams and have a high level of facilities.

XX　**Cullinan's** with rm　　　　　　　🍴 🎙️ **P** VISA ⊚

*– ℰ (065) 707 41 83 – www.cullinansdoolin.com – Closed mid-December to mid-February, Sunday dinner and Wednesday*
**8 rm** ⌷ – 🛏 € 40/70 🛏🛏 € 70/100
**Rest** – (dinner only) (booking essential) Menu € 30 (early dinner) – Carte € 35/45

◆ Orange building in the middle of the Burren; run by a keen husband and wife team. Two walls of full length windows offer excellent views. Classical cooking uses Irish produce and portions are generous. Comfy, pine-furnished bedrooms; some overlook a small river.

**DROGHEDA** (Droichead Átha) – **Louth** – **712** M6 – **pop. 35 090**

Ireland

▶ Dublin 46 km – Dundalk 35 km

*i* Mayoralty St *𝒞* (041) 9 83 70 70, www.drogheda.ie

 Seapoint Termonfeckin, *𝒞* (041) 9 82 23 33

Towneley Hall Tullyallen, *𝒞* (041) 984 22 29

◉ Town★ – Drogheda Museum★ – St Laurence Gate★

◷ Monasterboice★★, N : 10.5 km by N 1 – Boyne Valley★★, on N 51
– Termonfeckin★, NE : 8 km by R 166. Newgrange★★★, W : 5 km by N 51 on N 2
– Mellifont Old Abbey★ **AC** - Knowth★

---

### The D

             *ℱ⑥* 🖭 & 🆔 rest, ⅀ ℅ ⅍ **P** *VISA* ⓒⓞ **ᴁ**

*Scotch Hall, Marsh Rd. – 𝒞 (041) 987 77 00 – www.thed.com – Closed 23-30 December*

**104 rm** ⬚ – 🕇 € 69/130 🕇🕇 € 69/130

**Rest** – Menu € 27 (lunch) – Carte € 26/50

◆ Stylish hotel adjacent to shopping centre on banks of the Boyne. Modish, minimalistic interiors include two comfy bars and spacious bedrooms with a cool, clinical appeal. Popular menus in the airy dining room.

---

### Scholars Townhouse

               🚗 🖭 & ⅀ ℅ **P** *VISA* ⓒⓞ **ᴁ**

*King St, by West St and Lawrence St turning left at Lawrence's Gate – 𝒞 (041) 983 54 10 – www.scholarshotel.com – Closed 25-26 December*

**16 rm** ⬚ – 🕇 € 59/69 🕇🕇 € 79/89    **Rest** – Menu € 30 – Carte € 32/62

◆ Well-run, privately owned hotel; formerly a 19C priest's house. Appealing bar and cosy lounge; smart wood panelling and ornate coving feature throughout. Comfy, well-kept bedrooms. Dine on classically based dishes under impressive mural of the Battle of Boyne.

# DUBLIN

See city maps on following pages

**Dublin – pop. 2 400 437 – 712** N7 – ▮ Ireland

▶ Belfast 166 – Cork 248 – Londonderry 235

## 🛈 Tourist Information

Suffolk St ☏ (01) 605 77 00, www.visitdublin.com

## Airport

✈ Dublin Airport : ☏ (01) 814 1111, N : 9 km by N 1 BS

## Ferries

▬ to Holyhead (Irish Ferries) 4 daily (3 h 15 mn) – to Holyhead (Stena Line) 1-2 daily (3 h 45 mn) – to the Isle of Man (Douglas) (Isle of Man Steam Packet Co. Ltd) (2 h 45 mn/4 h 45 mn) – to Liverpool (P & O Irish Sea) (8 h)

## Golf Courses

🏌 Elm Park Donnybrook, Nutley House, ☏ (01) 269 34 38

🏌 Milltown Lower Churchtown Rd, ☏ (01) 497 60 90

🏌 Royal Dublin Dollymount North Bull Island, ☏ (01) 833 63 46

## ◎ SIGHTS

**In the town :** City★★★ • Trinity College★★ JY • Old Library★★★ • Christ Church Cathedral★★ HY • St Patrick's Cathedral★★ HZ• National Museum★★ KZ • National Gallery★★ KZ • Newman House★★ JZ• Custom House★★ KX • Kilmainham Gaol Museum★★ AT**M6**• Phoenix Park★★ AS • National Botanic Gardens★★ BS • Tailors' Hall★ HY • City Hall★ HY • Temple Bar★ HJY • Liffey Bridge★ JY • Merrion Square★ KZ • Number Twenty-Nine★ KZ**D** • Grafton Street★ JYZ • Powerscourt Centre★ JY • O'Connell Street★ JX • Hugh Lane Municipal Gallery of Modern Art★ JX**M4**• Bluecoat School★ BS**F** • Guinness Museum★ BT**M7**

**On the outskirts :** The Ben of Howth⋘★, NE : 9.5 km by R 105 CS

**In the surrounding area :** Powerscourt★★ **AC**, S : 22.5 km by N 11 and R 117 EV • Russborough House★★★, SW : 35.5 km by N 81 BT

### ᐱᐱᐱ Shelbourne     𝟙𝓈 📶 ♿ 🄰🄲 ☏ 🈶 🚗 𝓥𝓘𝓢𝓐 ⑳ 🄰🄴 ⓪

*27 St Stephen's Grn.* ⊠ *D2* – ℰ *(01) 663 45 00*
– *www.theshelbourne.ie*       **JZc**
**250 rm** – ♦ € 192/244 ♦♦ € 192/260, � €29 – 12 suites
**Rest** *Saddle Room* – see restaurant listing
• Landmark Georgian hotel with elegant guest areas, contemporary furnishings and state-of-the-art facilities. Bedrooms in original house are most characterful. High level of services and extras.

### ᐱᐱᐱ Merrion     🚗 📺 𝟙𝓈 📶 🄰🄲 ⚄ 🈶 𝕾🄰 𝓥𝓘𝓢𝓐 ⑳ 🄰🄴 ⓪

*Upper Merrion St* ⊠ *D2* – ℰ *(01) 603 06 00*
– *www.merrionhotel.com*       **KZe**
**133 rm** – ♦ € 460 ♦♦ € 480, ⊇ €29 – 10 suites
**Rest** *Cellar* – Modern – ℰ *(01) 603 06 30 (closed Saturday lunch)* Menu € 20 **s**
– Carte € 35/49 **s**
**Rest** *Cellar Bar* – *(closed Sunday)* Carte approx. € 34 **s**
• Elegant hotel boasting opulent lounges and stylish cocktail bar. Spacious bedrooms – some with original features, some more corporate in style – boast smart marble bathrooms and good facilities. Characterful barrel-ceilinged bar offers accessible menu.

### ᐱᐱᐱ Westin     𝟙𝓈 📶 ♿ 🄰🄲 ⚄ 🈶 𝕾🄰 𝓥𝓘𝓢𝓐 ⑳ 🄰🄴 ⓪

*Westmoreland St* ⊠ *D2* – ℰ *(01) 645 10 00*
– *www.thewestindublin.com*       **JYn**
**153 rm** – ♦ € 399 ♦♦ € 399, ⊇ €19.95 – 10 suites
**Rest** *Exchange* – *(closed Sunday dinner and Monday) (dinner only and lunch Saturday-Sunday)* Carte € 25/45
**Rest** *Mint* – Carte € 25/50
• Built in 1860 as a bank; now a smart hotel set over 6 period buildings, with comfy lounges, impressive conference rooms and good facilities. Classical bedrooms boast heavy fabrics and marble bathrooms. Modern European cooking in semi-formal Exchange. Accessible menu in The Mint, a characterful room which was once the bank's vaults.

### ᐱᐱ  Dylan     🚲 📶 ♿ 🄰🄲 ⚄ 🈶 🄿 𝓥𝓘𝓢𝓐 ⑳ 🄰🄴 ⓪

*Eastmoreland Pl* ⊠ *D4* – ℰ *(01) 660 30 00*
– *www.dylan.ie* – *Closed 24-26 December*       **EUa**
**44 rm** – ♦ € 175/395 ♦♦ € 175/395, ⊇ €27
**Rest** – Menu € 20/40 – Carte € 40/60
• Modern boutique hotel with vibrant use of colour. Supremely comfortable, individually decorated bedrooms boast an opulent feel and a host of unexpected extras. French-influenced menus served in warm, stylish dining room.

### ᐱᐱ Brooks     🈵 𝟙𝓈 📶 ♿ 🄰🄲 ⚄ 🈶 𝕾🄰 𝓥𝓘𝓢𝓐 ⑳ 🄰🄴

*Drury St* ⊠ *D2* – ℰ *(01) 670 40 00* – *www.brookshotel.ie*       **JYr**
**97 rm** ⊇ – ♦ € 385 ♦♦ € 385 – 1 suite
**Rest** *Francesca's* – see restaurant listing
• Smart, boutique-style townhouse hidden down a backstreet. Traditional basement lounge and stylish bedrooms with modern artwork; executives boast fresh flowers and other homely touches. Experienced owner keeps a keen eye over proceedings.

### ᐱᐱ  Clarence     ⬅ 𝟙𝓈 📶 ♿ ⚄ 🈶 𝕾🄰 🚗 𝓥𝓘𝓢𝓐 ⑳ 🄰🄴 ⓪

*6-8 Wellington Quay* ⊠ *D2* – ℰ *(01) 407 08 00*
– *www.theclarence.ie* – *Closed 25-26 December*       **HYa**
**44 rm** – ♦ € 109/199 ♦♦ € 159/219, ⊇ €9.50 – 5 suites
**Rest** *Tea Room* – see restaurant listing
• Attractive riverside hotel, formerly a warehouse. Stylish and well-run, with art deco reception, comfy lounge and famous domed bar. Plainly decorated, understated bedrooms; good facilities.

# DUBLIN

 **Fitzwilliam** ← ⅃ᴬ 🕭 🅐🅒 🕯 🐾 🔋 🌀 _VISA_ 🆎 🅐🅔 🅞

St Stephen's Grn. ⊠ D2 – ℰ (01) 478 70 00 – www.fitzwilliamhoteldublin.com
**136 rm** – ♦ € 380 ♦♦ € 380, � €22 – 3 suites                                JZ**d**
**Rest** _Thornton's_ ✽ – see restaurant listing
**Rest** _Citron_ – (closed Sunday lunch) Menu € 19/24 – Carte dinner € 32/49
◆ Stylish U-shaped hotel set around huge roof garden – the largest in Europe.
Contemporary bedrooms display striking bold colours and good facilities; half
overlook garden; half, the green. Modern first floor brasserie with international
menu.

 **Ashling** 🕭 & rm, 🕯 🔋 🅿 _VISA_ 🆎 🅐🅔

Parkgate St. ⊠ D8 – ℰ (01) 677 2324 – www.ashlinghotel.ie – Closed 24-26
December                                                                          BS**a**
**225 rm** – ♦ € 79/199 ♦♦ € 89/340, ⊻ €14
**Rest** – Menu € 30 – Carte € 27/35
◆ Smartly refurbished hotel with sleek, modern frontage and cheery team;
set close to the tram and rail links. Mix of classic and contemporary bedrooms; front rooms boast river and Guinness Brewery views. Large bar-lounge
serves all-day menu. Restaurant offers carvery lunches and accessible evening
à la carte.

*(map of Dublin with areas including GLASNEVIN, NATIONAL BOTANIC GARDENS, GLASNEVIN CEMETERY, DRUMCONDRA, MARINO, MARINO CASINO, KILLESTER, ST ANNE'S PARK, HOWTH, CLONTARF, North Bull Island, TRINITY COLLEGE, CASTLE, RINGSEND, SANDYMOUNT, HAROLD'S CROSS, RATHMINES, DONNYBROOK, HERBERT PARK, UNIVERSITY COLLEGE, BOOTERSTOWN, DUBLIN BAY, etc.)*

REPUBLIC OF IRELAND

HOWTH · DOUGLAS, HOLYHEAD · LIVERPOOL, MOSTYN

N 81 R 114 BLESSINGTON B R 117 ENNISKERRY C BRAY N 11 DUN LAOGHAIRE R 118

---

## La Stampa
🕙 🛗 AC rm, ⚄ rm, (((•))) VISA ⚈ AE

*35-36 Dawson St ⊠ D2 – 𝒞 (01) 677 44 44 – www.lastampa.ie – Closed 25-26 December* JZ**a**

**36 rm** – 🛏 € 110/150 🛏🛏 € 110/150, � € 14.95 – 1 suite

**Rest The Dining Room by Conrad Gallagher** – French – Menu € 19
– Carte € 22/76

• Georgian townhouse with Art Nouveau exterior and quirky, eclectic décor. Stylish guest areas and characterful spa with Far Eastern feel. Spacious bedrooms feature bespoke Asian or opulent French furnishings; the suite has a Moroccan theme. Grand dining room with interesting menu of original modern cooking.

---

## Number 31 without rest
🚗 ⚄ (((•))) VISA ⚈ AE

*31 Leeson Cl. ⊠ D2 – 𝒞 (01) 676 50 11 – www.number31.ie* EU**c**

**21 rm** ⊒ – 🛏 € 90/150 🛏🛏 € 175/190

• Unique house with retro styling, personally run by hospitable couple. Sunken lounge with open fire; quirky, comfortable bedrooms. Communal breakfast includes The Full Irish.

REPUBLIC OF IRELAND

**DUBLIN**

IRISHTOWN

SEAN
MOORE
PARK

DUBLIN
BAY

SANDYMOUNT

BALLSBRIDGE

MARTELLO
TOWER

MERRION

LONSKEAGH

REPUBLIC OF IRELAND

# DUBLIN

REPUBLIC OF IRELAND

REPUBLIC OF IRELAND

N 1 (N 2)

Garden of Remembrance

119

126

Parnell Square

ROTUNDA HOSPITAL CHAPEL

Garden of Remembrance

Gardiner

Sean

Mac

Dermott

St

North

St

25

CONNOLLY

Sheriff St

PRO-CATHEDRAL

100

Talbot

Street

IRISH LIFE MALL CENTRE

Amiens

Anna Livia Fountain

DUBLIN SPIRE

O'CONNELL ST

Street

Henry

Street

Liffey

Street

Abbey

T

T

Street

P

P

Street

P

CUSTOM HOUSE

157

Custom

House

Quay

LIFFEY

Quay

Eden

O'Connell Bridge

HA'PENNY BRIDGE

Millennium Bridge

TEMPLE BAR

181

68

BANK OF IRELAND

Walk

Aston Quay

Burgh

187

51

68

n 46

45

Quay

City

Quay

69

TARA

171

Moss

St

Townsend

St

Pearse

TRINITY COLLEGE

College

Park

Street

186

PEARSE

f

m

d

b

P

r

M

k

POWERSCOURT CENTRE

e

c

GRAFTON

STREET

Dawson

St

58

x

a

M

Clare St

Fenian

St

65

88

6

k

a

r

Mansion House

e

s

n

c

87

NATIONAL MUSEUM

k

NATIONAL GALLERY

M

North

West

MERRION SQUARE

East

South

Z

STEPHENS GREEN CENTRE

d

Fusiliers' Arch

North

Lord Ardilaun

William Butler Yeats

p

St Stephens's Green

German Monument

e

104

x

a

n

Baggot

D

112

b

University Church

NEWMAN HOUSE

South

Harcourt

Leeson St Lower

Pembroke

St

Fitzwilliam

Street

Lower

06

60

U

W

c

J

N 11

K

T 44

CAR FERRY TERMINAL

REPUBLIC OF IRELAND

### Kellys *without rest*

*First Floor, 35 South Great Georges St* ⊠ *D2* – ℰ *(01) 648 0010*
*– www.kellysdublin.com*                                                          JY**b**
**16 rm** 🖵 – 🛉 € 79/110 🛉🛉 € 120/175

• Shabby-chic hotel set among trendy boutiques and bars, in a bustling area. Stripped paint and white emulsioned walls hung with funky artwork; airy, open-plan lounge and bar; spacious, minimalist bedrooms. Breakfast in the restaurant below.

### Trinity Lodge

*12 South Frederick St* ⊠ *D2* – ℰ *(01) 617 09 00* – *www.trinitylodge.com*
**23 rm** – 🛉 € 59/150 🛉🛉 € 89/195, 🖵 €7.50                        JY**x**
**Rest *Georges*** – ℰ *(01) 679 70 00 (closed dinner Monday-Tuesday and Sunday)*
Carte € 20/27 **s**

• Elegant, centrally located Georgian townhouses near local landmarks. Airy, well-furnished bedrooms with good level of comfort: the larger deluxe rooms are worth asking for. Modern restaurant and popular wine bar.

### Eliza Lodge

*23-24 Wellington Quay* ⊠ *D2* – ℰ *(01) 671 80 44* – *www.elizalodge.com*
**18 rm** – 🛉 € 49/89 🛉🛉 € 59/199, 🖵 €9                              JY**u**
**Rest *Italian Corner*** – Italian – ℰ *(01) 671 91 14* – Carte € 24/41

• Friendly, family-owned hotel ideally situated for lively Temple Bar area. Uniform bedrooms; those at the top have the best outlook over the city and river; two have balconies. Bright restaurant serves popular Italian menus overlooking the Liffey.

### XXXX  Patrick Guilbaud (Guillaume Lebrun)

ε3 ε3  *21 Upper Merrion St* ⊠ *D2* – ℰ *(01) 676 41 92*
*– www.restaurantpatrickguilbaud.ie – Closed 25-26 December, 17 March, Sunday*
*and Monday*                                                                      KZ**e**
**Rest** – French – Menu € 50 (lunch) – Carte € 93/149 🕮
**Spec.** Red king crab cannelloni, wasabi crème fraîche. Squab pigeon, sauce soubise. Granny Smith vacherin, pistachio ice cream.

• Smart, stylish and personally run restaurant within a restored and sympathetically extended Georgian house; decorated with contemporary Irish art. Accomplished and harmonious cooking, with cleverly complementing flavours and textures.

### XXXX  Shanahan's on the Green

*119 St Stephen's Grn* ⊠ *D2* – ℰ *(01) 407 09 39* – *www.shanahans.ie*
*– Closed Good Friday, 25-26 December and Sunday*                    JZ**p**
**Rest** – Beef specialities – *(dinner only and lunch Friday-Saturday) (booking essential)* Menu € 45 – Carte € 45/100

• Sumptuous Georgian townhouse; upper floor window tables survey the Green. Supreme comfort enhances your enjoyment of strong seafood dishes and choice cuts of Irish beef.

### XXXX  Thornton's – *at The Fitzwilliam Hotel*

ε3  *128 St Stephen's Grn.* ⊠ *D2* – ℰ *(01) 478 70 08* – *www.thorntonsrestaurant.com*
*– Closed 24 December dinner-5 January, Sunday, Monday except December,*
*lunch Tuesday and Wednesday*                                          JZ**d**
**Rest** – Modern – Menu € 25/79 **s** 🕮
**Spec.** Bere Island king scallop with truffle mousse. Noisette of Sika deer, potato gnocchi and Valrhona sauce. Apple tarte Tatin, pressed apple terrine and cider granité.

• Elegant hotel restaurant where smart glass panels divide the room; eye-catching food photos adorn the walls. Choice of classical à la carte, or modern tasting menu displaying innovative texture and flavour combinations. Knowledgeable service.

XXX **L'Ecrivain** (Derry Clarke)                    🏫 AC ⇔ VISA ⓒ AE
☺ *109A Lower Baggot St* ⊠ *D2* – ℰ *(01) 661 19 19*
*– www.lecrivain.com – Closed Sunday and bank holidays*                KZ**b**
**Rest** – Contemporary – *(dinner only and lunch Thursday and Friday) (booking essential)* Menu € 25/65 – Carte approx. € 86
**Spec.** Scallops with pork cheek and Jerusalem artichoke. Loin of veal, pumpkin and portobello mushroom. Opéra chocolate tasting plate.
• Three-floored, former warehouse with piano bar, whiskey-themed private dining room, mezzanine and attractive terrace. Refined cooking arrives with modern touches and contemporary presentation. Service is formal but comes with personality.

XXX **Chapter One** (Ross Lewis)                      AC 🏩 ⇔ VISA ⓒ
☺ *The Dublin Writers Museum, 18-19 Parnell Sq* ⊠ *D1* – ℰ *(01) 873 22 66*
*– www.chapteronerestaurant.com – Closed 2 weeks August, 2 weeks Christmas, Sunday, Monday and bank holidays*                JX**r**
**Rest** – Modern – *(booking essential)* Menu € 38/65 **s**
**Spec.** Scallops with smoked bacon and spring onion, vermouth and potato mousseline. Angus rib of beef bordelaise with watercress purée, bone marrow and baby gem lettuce. Warm chocolate mousse, caramel jelly and lime ice cream.
• Long-established, popular restaurant in basement of historic building; contemporary lounge/bar and two smart dining rooms. Seasonal, classically-based cooking demonstrates skill and understanding. Attentive, formal service.

XXX **Forty One**                                     🏫 🏩 ⇔ VISA ⓒ AE
*41 St. Stephen's Grn.* ⊠ *D2* – ℰ *(01) 662 00 00*
*– www.fortyone.ie – Closed Good Friday, 25-30 December, Sunday and Monday*
**Rest** – Modern European – *(booking advisable)* Menu € 28/68        KZ**x**
– Carte € 53/83
• Richly furnished, intimate restaurant set in an attractive, creeper-clad 18C townhouse, tucked away in a corner of St Stephen's Green. Accomplished, classical cooking uses luxurious ingredients.

XXX **Cliff Townhouse** with rm                       AC rest, ℅ 🎵 VISA ⓒ AE
*22 St. Stephen's Grn.* ⊠ *D2* – ℰ *(01) 638 39 39*
*– www.theclifftownhouse.com – Closed 25-27 December and 1 January*
**9 rm** ⊑ – 🛉 € 135/155 🛉🛉 € 155/175                            JZ**s**
**Rest** – Modern European – *(booking advisable)* Menu € 25/40 – Carte € 37/60
• Impressive Georgian townhouse overlooking the green. Large dining room with marble-topped bar and blue leather seating. Good value fixed price menus offer straightforward, classical combinations. Bedrooms display contemporary colour schemes and good comforts.

XXX **Saddle Room** – at Shelbourne Hotel             AC ⇔ VISA ⓒ AE ⓞ
*27 St Stephen's Grn.* ⊠ *D2* – ℰ *(01) 663 45 00*
*– www.theshelbourne.ie*                                          JZ**c**
**Rest** – Grills – Menu € 26/40 – Carte € 49/63
• Smart restaurant with well-spaced, linen-laid tables: some are set by the window; some are in booths; and some, in glass-walled private rooms. Open kitchen specialises in seafood and steaks.

XXX **One Pico**                                      AC ⇔ VISA ⓒ AE
*5-6 Molesworth Pl* ⊠ *D2* – ℰ *(01) 676 03 00*
*– www.onepico.com – Closed bank holidays*                        JZ**k**
**Rest** – Modern – Menu € 25 – Carte € 51/66
• Wide-ranging cuisine, classic and traditional by turns, always with an original, eclectic edge. Décor and service share a pleasant formality, crisp, modern and stylish.

REPUBLIC OF IRELAND

⇔ VISA ◉◉ AE

*1 Windsor Terr. ✉ D8 – ✆ (01) 420 05 55 – www.locksbrasserie.com – Closed 25 December-7 January and bank holidays* DU**a**
**Rest** – Modern European – *(dinner only and lunch Thursday-Sunday)* Carte € 30/53

♦ Attractive, well-lit restaurant with a relaxed atmosphere and professional, engaging staff. Dining is split over two floors, with comfy banquette seating and a cocktail bar. Menu of modern European classics; well-presented dishes make use of fine ingredients.

XX **Pearl Brasserie**

AC VISA ◉◉ AE

*20 Merrion St Upper ✉ D2 – ✆ (01) 661 35 72 – www.pearl-brasserie.com – Closed 25 December and Sunday* KZ**n**
**Rest** – French – Carte € 32/58

♦ Basement restaurant with small bar-lounge and two surprisingly airy dining rooms; choose one of the stylish booths set in the old coal bunkers. Modern menus of elaborate, stylishly presented dishes and a simpler market menu. Formal service.

XX **Pichet**

AC VISA ◉◉ AE

*14-15 Trinity St ✉ D2 – ✆ (01) 677 10 60 – www.pichetrestaurant.com – Closed 1-10 January* JY**g**
**Rest** – Modern European – *(booking advisable)* Menu € 25 – Carte € 30/50

♦ Popular brasserie with buzzy atmosphere; its long, narrow room dominated by an open-plan kitchen. Front café-cum-bar – complete with cake and pastry counter – for light snacks. Neat, flavoursome modern European cooking from good value, daily changing menus. Wines available by the glass or in a 500ml 'pichet'.

XX **Dax**

VISA ◉◉ AE

*23 Pembroke St. Upper ✉ D2 – ✆ (01) 676 14 94 – www.dax.ie – Closed 1 week Easter, 2 weeks August, 10 days Christmas, Saturday lunch, Sunday, Monday*
**Rest** – *(booking essential)* Menu € 29/35 – Carte approx. € 79 KZ**c**

♦ Simply furnished restaurant hidden in the basement of a Georgian terraced house not far from Fiztwilliam Square. Rustic inner with smart linen-laid tables and wine cellar. French-inspired menus include a six course 'surprise' selection.

XX **Dobbin's**

AC ⇔ VISA ◉◉ AE ◯

*15 Stephen's Lane, (off Stephen's Place) off Lower Mount St ✉ D2 – ✆ (01) 661 95 36 – www.dobbins.ie – Closed 24 December-2 January, Saturday lunch, Sunday dinner, Mondays (except December) and bank holidays* EU**s**
**Rest** – Traditional – *(booking essential)* Menu € 23 (lunch)/25 – Carte € 38/53

♦ Smart, well-established restaurant in residential area. Small bar with booths leads to spacious, neatly laid dining room with warm, modern décor. Large menu displays international influences.

XX **Tea Room** – at The Clarence Hotel

VISA ◉◉ AE ◯

*6-8 Wellington Quay ✉ D2 – ✆ (01) 407 08 13 – Closed 25-26 December*
**Rest** – Modern – *(booking essential)* Menu € 15/25 HY**a**
– Carte € 23/42

♦ Spacious hotel restaurant, where small mezzanine level overlooks larger main room with central banquette island. Ambitious cooking displays Gallic influences. Polite, formal service.

XX **Les Frères Jacques**

AC VISA ◉◉ AE

*74 Dame St ✉ D2 – ✆ (01) 679 4555 – www.lesfreresjacques.com – Closed 24-30 December, Saturday lunch, Sunday and bank holidays* HY**x**
**Rest** – French – Menu € 18/38 – Carte € 51/69

♦ Long-standing restaurant on narrow cobbled alley, with typical French styling and team. Classical Gallic cooking with seafood a speciality: daily fresh fish and lobster tank on display.

## Peploe's
XX                  AC VISA ⚫⚪ AE

*16 St Stephen's Grn.* ⊠ *D2 – ℰ (01) 676 31 44 – www.peploes.com – Closed Good Friday and 25-29 December*    **JZe**

**Rest** – Mediterranean – *(booking essential)* Menu € 25 – Carte € 36/53

♦ Well-run, atmospheric brasserie named after Scottish artist and set in former bank vault. Small bar; main room with smart mural and linen-laid tables. Extensive menu with influences from the Med.

## Bleu
XX                  AC VISA ⚫⚪ AE

*Joshua House, Dawson St* ⊠ *D2 – ℰ (01) 676 70 15 – www.onepico.com – Closed 25-26 December*    **JZr**

**Rest** – Modern European – Menu € 21/25 – Carte € 32/43

♦ Stylish, modern eatery on a bustling street. Smart and contemporary interior, with framed mirrors a feature. The appealing, varied menu keeps its influences within Europe.

## Town Bar and Grill
XX              AC 🍴 VISA ⚫⚪ AE

*21 Kildare St* ⊠ *D2 – ℰ (01) 662 4800 – www.townbarandgrill.com – Closed Good Friday, 25-27 December and bank holidays*    **JZn**

**Rest** – Italian influences – *(booking advisable)* Menu € 25 (lunch) – Carte € 35/58

♦ Located in the old cellar's of a famous city wine merchant. Small bar and high stools at entrance, more intimate tables to the rear. Eclectic menu of grills and bold Italian dishes, with the occasional Asian influence. Pianist at weekends.

## Fallon & Byrne
XX               VISA ⚫⚪ AE

*First Floor, 11-17 Exchequer St* ⊠ *D2 – ℰ (01) 472 10 00 – www.fallonandbyrne.com – Closed Good Friday, 25-26 December and Sunday dinner*    **JYf**

**Rest** – Bistro – Menu € 25/30 – Carte € 20/44

♦ Food emporium boasting vast basement wine cellar, ground floor full of fresh quality produce, and first floor French style bistro with banquettes, mirrors and tasty bistro food.

## Bang
XX           🌂 AC ⇕ VISA ⚫⚪ AE

*11 Merrion Row* ⊠ *D2 – ℰ (01) 400 42 29 – www.bangrestaurant.com – Closed first week January, Easter, Monday lunch and Sunday*    **KZa**

**Rest** – Modern – *(booking essential)* Menu € 25/37 – Carte € 35/45

♦ Stylish three floor restaurant displaying impressive modern art by leading Irish/international artists. Good value lunch/early evening menus; more luxurious, modern dishes on the à la carte.

## Francesca's – at Brooks Hotel
XX          ₺ AC 🍴 VISA ⚫⚪ AE

*Drury St* ⊠ *D2 – ℰ (01) 670 40 00 – www.brookshotel.ie*    **JYr**

**Rest** – Modern – *(closed to non-residents 25 December) (dinner only)* Menu € 28 – Carte € 31/51

♦ Fine dining room with an open-plan kitchen, set in a smart, boutique-style townhouse. Interesting menu offers plenty of choice and relies on local produce; good value pre-theatre selection.

## Pig's Ear
X   ⊛            VISA ⚫⚪ AE

*4 Nassau St* ⊠ *D2 – ℰ (01) 670 38 65 – www.thepigsear.ie – Closed first week January, Sunday and bank holidays*    **KYa**

**Rest** – Modern European – Menu € 20/25 – Carte € 33/49

♦ Split-level, bistro-style restaurant, in a Georgian city centre house with a striking pink door. Porcine-themed memorabilia features throughout. Well-priced, refined bistro cooking has French influences and relies on Irish produce. Attentive, personable service.

REPUBLIC OF IRELAND

## X  La Maison 🛜 AC VISA 💿
*15 Castlemarket ⊠ D2 – ℰ (01) 672 7258 – www.lamaisonrestaurant.ie – Closed 25 December to 1 January* JY**c**
**Rest** – French – *(bookings not accepted)* Menu € 26 – Carte € 25/42
• Appealing French bistro with light blue façade, tables on the pavement and original posters decorating the walls inside. Breton-born chef offers carefully prepared, seasonal Gallic classics at a good price, which are brought to the table by a personable team.

## X  Rustic Stone 🛜 AC VISA 💿
*17 Great George's St ⊠ D2 – ℰ (01) 707 9596 – www.rusticstone.ie*
**Rest** – Modern – Menu € 30/50 (dinner) – Carte € 22/62 JY**m**
• Split-level restaurant offering something a little bit different. Good quality ingredients are cooked simply to retain their natural flavours and menus point out the healthier options; some meats and fish arrive on a sizzling hot stone.

## X  L'Gueuleton 🛜 VISA 💿
*1 Fade St ⊠ D2 – ℰ (01) 675 37 08 – www.lgueuleton.com – Closed 25-27 December, 1 January and Easter Friday* JY**d**
**Rest** – French – *(bookings not accepted)* Carte € 32/47
• Rustic restaurant with beamed ceilings, Gallic furnishings and rear terrace. Interesting French menus use local, seasonal produce. Flavoursome country cooking; friendly, efficient service.

## X  Camden Kitchen ♻ 💿 ①
*3a Camden Mkt, Grantham St ⊠ D8 – ℰ (01) 476 01 25*
*– www.camdenkitchen.ie – Closed 25-26 December, Sunday dinner and Monday*
**Rest** – Modern – Menu € 18 (early dinner) – Carte € 31/39 JZ**x**
• Appealing bistro with canopied façade and rustic inner, set over two floors. Open kitchen serving gutsy menu of robust, modern dishes. Relaxed, friendly service from a young team.

## X  Saba AC VISA 💿 AE
*26-28 Clarendon St ⊠ D2 – ℰ (01) 679 2000 – www.sabadublin.com – Closed Good Friday and 25-26 December* JY**k**
**Rest** – Thai – Menu € 20/30 – Carte € 25/36
• Very trendy, buzzy Thai restaurant and cocktail bar. Simple yet stylish rooms with refectory tables in the centre and banquette seating around the walls. Fresh, clean, visual cooking from all all-Thai team who like to keep things authentic.

## X  Port House VISA 💿 ①
*64a South William St ⊠ D2 – ℰ (01) 677 0298 – www.porthouse.ie – Closed 25 December* JY**e**
**Rest** – Spanish – Carte € 16/43
• Characterful Spanish tapas bar serving a vast array of authentic, flavoursome dishes. Rustic, candlelit interior with exposed brick, semi-vaulted ceiling and tightly packed tables; small bar upstairs. Imported meats, cheeses and olives.

## at Ballsbridge

## 🏠🏠🏠  Four Seasons ⧉ 🖥 💿 🛜 🏋 🖢 ♿ AC ⛾ 🔬 🅿 🚗 VISA 💿 AE
*Simmonscourt Rd. ⊠ D4 – ℰ (01) 665 4000 – www.fourseasons.com/dublin*
**156 rm** – ♦ € 185/289 ♦♦ € 255/329, ⊇ €29 – 40 suites FU**e**
**Rest** *Seasons* – Menu € 35 **s** – Carte € 46/65 **s**
• Set in grounds of the RDS arena. Elegant guest areas, state-of-the-art meeting rooms and impressive ballrooms boast ornate décor, antiques and Irish art. Spacious bedrooms; plenty of extras. Fine dining with fountain/garden views in Seasons.

**Herbert Park** 　　　　　　　　　🏊 📶 ⚕ AC ☎ 📞 ♨ P VISA ⬟ AE
☒ D4 – ☏ (01) 667 2200 – www.herbertparkhotel.ie 　　　　　　FU**m**
**151 rm** – 🛏 € 119/250 🛏🛏 € 119/385, ☕ €19.50 – 2 suites
**Rest** *The Pavilion* – Menu € 35
♦ Contemporary hotel overlooking suburban park, with smart marble-floored reception, stylish seating areas and chic bar. Modern bedrooms display quality furnishings and marble bathrooms. Sizeable, formal restaurant offers interesting menu.

**Schoolhouse** 　　　　　　　　　🚗 🍴 📶 AC ☎ 📞 P VISA ⬟ AE ⬤
2-8 Northumberland Rd ☒ D4 – ☏ (01) 667 5014
– www.schoolhousehotel.com – Closed 24-27 December 　　　　FU**k**
**31 rm** – 🛏 € 109/129 🛏🛏 € 109/159, ☕ €15
**Rest** *Olivier's at The Schoolhouse* – see restaurant listing
**Rest** *Schoolhouse Bar* – Carte € 25/50
♦ Dating back to 1861 and formerly the St Stephens Parochial School. Spacious, well-kept bedrooms – most in the extension – boast William Morris designed fabrics and locally built Macintosh-style furniture; some have half-tester beds. Busy bar with vaulted ceiling and stone fireplaces offers pub-style menus.

**Merrion Hall** without rest 　　　　　　🚗 📶 AC ☎ 📞 P VISA ⬟ AE ⬤
54-56 Merrion Rd. ☒ D4 – ☏ (01) 668 1426
– www.merrionhall.com 　　　　　　　　　　　　　　　　FU**b**
**30 rm** ☕ – 🛏 €90/159 🛏🛏 € 129/399
♦ Red-brick Victorian house boasting spacious, antique-furnished guest areas with a Georgian feel. Comfortable bedrooms have a traditional edge; those to the rear are quieter.

**Ariel House** without rest 　　　　　　　　　☎ 📞 P VISA ⬟ AE
50-54 Lansdowne Rd ☒ D4 – ☏ (01) 668 5512
– www.ariel-house.net – Closed 22 December-3 January 　　　FU**n**
**37 rm** ☕ – 🛏 € 69/130 🛏🛏 € 79/300
♦ Personally run Victorian townhouse with comfy, traditionally styled guest areas and antique furnishings. Warmly decorated bedrooms have modern facilities and smart bathrooms; some four-posters.

**Aberdeen Lodge** without rest 　　　　🚗 ☎ 📞 P VISA ⬟ AE ⬤
53-55 Park Ave. ☒ D4 – ☏ (01) 283 8155
– www.halpinsprivatehotels.com 　　　　　　　　　　　GV**e**
**16 rm** ☕ – 🛏 € 90/169 🛏🛏 € 139/359
♦ Two Victorian townhouses in smart suburban setting, knocked through into one impressive hotel. Comfy lounge, warm homely atmosphere and well-equipped bedrooms – some with garden views.

**Pembroke Townhouse** without rest 　　📶 ☎ 📞 P VISA ⬟ AE ⬤
90 Pembroke Rd ☒ D4 – ☏ (01) 660 0277
– www.pembroketownhouse.ie – Closed 2 weeks Christmas-New Year
**48 rm** – 🛏 € 199 🛏🛏 € 310, ☕ €15 　　　　　　　　FU**d**
♦ Formerly three Georgian houses, now a friendly hotel with traditional styling, comfy lounge and sunny breakfast room. Bedrooms vary in shape and size: duplex rooms are the cosiest.

**Glenogra House** without rest 　　　　　☎ 📞 P VISA ⬟ AE ⬤
64 Merrion Rd ☒ D4 – ☏ (01) 668 3661
– www.glenogra.com – Closed 24-27 December 　　　　　FU**w**
**13 rm** ☕ – 🛏 € 69/199 🛏🛏 € 89/199
♦ Personally run red-brick Victorian house with informal reception, comfy lounge and homely furnishings. Simply decorated bedrooms vary in shape and size; all boast modern facilities.

REPUBLIC OF IRELAND

913

XX **Olivier's at The Schoolhouse** – at Schoolhouse Hotel

2-8 Northumberland Rd ⊠ D4 – ✆ (01) 667 5014

– www.oliviers.ie – Closed 24-27 December                                    FU

**Rest** – (closed Saturday lunch, Monday dinner and Sunday) (brunch Saturday and Sunday) (booking essential at dinner) Menu € 28/40 **s**

– Carte € 39/60 **s**

♦ Formal restaurant taking pride of place in the old classroom of a former school. Original vaulted ceiling and stone fireplaces. Classical menu, written in French and English, has strong Gallic influences and showcases luxurious ingredients.

XX **Bloom Brasserie**

11 Upper Baggot St ⊠ D4 – ✆ (01) 668 7170

– www.bloombrasserie.ie – Closed 25 December, Sunday and bank holidays                                                                       EU»

**Rest** – Modern European – Menu € 25 – Carte € 25/48

♦ Sizeable basement brasserie with cool, contemporary styling, vibrant art and garden terrace. Menus offer a mix of traditional and more modern dishes; with an additional small plate selection in the evening.

🍴 **Chop House**

2 Shelbourne Rd ⊠ D4 – ✆ (1) 660 23 90

– www.thechophouse.ie                                                            FU»

**Rest** – Modern European – Carte € 26/49

♦ Imposing square pub with small side terrace, dark bar and bright, airy conservatory. Relaxed lunchtime menu; more ambitious dishes in the evening, when the kitchen really comes into its own.

## at Rathmines

XX **Zen**

89 Upper Rathmines Rd ⊠ D6 – ✆ (01) 497 94 28

– www.zenrestaurant.ie – Closed 25-27 December                          DVt

**Rest** – Chinese – (dinner only and Friday lunch) Carte € 18/31

♦ Renowned family run Chinese restaurant in the unusual setting of an old church hall. Imaginative, authentic oriental cuisine with particular emphasis on spicy Sichuan dishes.

## at Dublin Airport North : 10.5 km by N 1 - BS - and M 1 – ⊠ Dublin

🏨 **Carlton H. Dublin Airport**

Old Airport Rd., Cloughran, on R 132 Santry rd – ✆ (01) 866 7500

– www.carlton.ie/dublinairport – Closed 24-26 December

**117 rm** – ♦ € 89/129 ♦♦ € 89/129, � €13.50 – 1 suite

**Rest** *Kittyhawks* – Menu € 18/20 **s** – Carte € 25/40 **s**

♦ Modern commercial hotel with spacious marbled reception and comfy guest areas. Uniform bedrooms display good facilities and smart bathrooms. Some rooms overlook airfield; some have balconies. Informal all-day brasserie offers popular menu.

🏨 **Bewleys**

Baskin Ln. , East : 1.5 km on N 32 – ✆ (01) 871 1000

– www.bewleyshotels.com – Closed 25 December

**466 rm** – ♦ € 89/199 ♦♦ € 89/199, � €12

**Rest** *The Brasserie* – Menu € 20/25 – Carte dinner € 25/60

♦ Immense eight floor hotel, ten minutes from the airport, with selection of small meeting rooms. Immaculately kept bedrooms; good value for money. Wide-ranging menu served in The Brasserie.

**at Clontarf** Northeast : 5.5 km by R 105 – ⊠ Dublin

 **Clontarf Castle**    ⛵ 🛉 ᴛ AC 🖧 ⁿ° ᴚ P VISA ⬤ AE
Castle Ave. ⊠ D3 – ℰ (01) 833 2321 – www.clontarfcastle.ie    CSa
**111 rm** – 🛉 € 79/299, 🛉🛉 € 99/299, ⬚ €10
**Rest Fahrenheit Grill** – (dinner only) Menu € 25 – Carte € 35/51
♦ Set in an historic castle, partly dating back to 1172. Striking medieval style entrance lobby. Modern rooms and characterful luxury suites with cutting edge facilities. Grand restaurant reminiscent of a knights' banqueting hall; local meats and seafood feature.

**at Dundrum** Southeast : 8 km by N 11 - CT – ⊠ Dublin

XXX **Harvey Nichols First Floor Restaurant**    AC ⇆ VISA ⬤ AE
Harvey Nichols, Town Sq., Sandyford Rd ⊠ D16 – ℰ (01) 291 0488
– www.harveynichols.com – Closed 25 December, Sunday dinner and Monday
**Rest** – Menu € 25/30 – Carte € 29/39
♦ Up the lift to ultra-stylish bar and plush, designer-led restaurant. Attentive, professional service. Dishes are modern, seasonal and confident with a fine dining feel.

XX **Ananda**    AC VISA ⬤ AE
Town Sq. ⊠ D14 – ℰ (01) 296 00 99 – www.anandarestarant.ie – Closed 25 December and lunch Monday-Wednesday
**Rest** – Indian – Menu € 16 (lunch) – Carte € 31/49
♦ Meaning 'bliss' in ancient Sanskrit. Stylish restaurant located in city centre arcade. Beautiful décor, attractive fretwork and gorgeous lighting. Flavourful modern Indian cuisine.

**at Sandyford** Southeast : 12 km by N 11 and R 112 off R 133 - CT – ⊠ Dublin

 **Beacon**    🛏 🛐 ᴛ AC rest, 🖧 ⁿ° ᴚ 🕿 VISA ⬤ AE
Beacon Court, Sandyford Business Region ⊠ D18 – ℰ (01) 291 5000
– www.thebeacon.com – Closed 24-25 December
**87 rm** – 🛉 € 80/300, 🛉🛉 € 99/300, ⬚ €15 – 1 suite
**Rest My Thai** – Thai – Carte € 25/33 s
♦ Ultra-stylish hotel with uniquely quirky entrance lobby featuring a chandelier on the floor and bed with central seating! Modish bar, low-key meeting rooms, sleek bedrooms. Funky, relaxed restaurant serving authentic Asian dishes.

XX **China Sichuan**    🛏 AC VISA ⬤
The Forum, Ballymoss Rd. ⊠ D18 – ℰ (01) 293 5100 – www.china-sichuan.ie – Closed 25-31 December, Good Friday, lunch Saturday and bank holidays
**Rest** – Chinese – Menu € 25 – Carte € 25/50
♦ Established in 1979 and now run by the third generation of the family. Smart, modern interior matched by creative menus, where Irish produce is used in tasty Chinese-influenced dishes. Sichuan specialities pay homage to their heritage.

**at Foxrock** Southeast : 13 km by N 11 - CT – ⊠ Dublin

XX **Bistro One**    VISA ⬤
3 Brighton Rd ⊠ D18 – ℰ (01) 289 7711 – www.bistro-one.ie – Closed 25 December-3 January, Sunday and Monday
**Rest** – (booking essential) Menu € 25 – Carte € 27/35
♦ Long-standing neighbourhood restaurant; popular with the locals. Daily changing lunch and dinner menus display a mix of Irish and Mediterranean influences. Good use of local produce.

REPUBLIC OF IRELAND

---

**DUNBOYNE** (Dún Búinne) – Meath – **712** M7 – pop. 5 713                    37 D

▶ Dublin 17 km – Drogheda 45 km – Newbridge 54 km

**Dunboyne Castle**    🚗 🏖 🏠 🛁 🖥 ⚕ 🛗 🛝 📶 ⛳ 📶 **P** **VISA** **OO** **AE** **①**
– 𝒞 (01) 801 35 00 – www.dunboynecastlehotel.com
**141 rm** ⌂ – ♦ € 270 ♦♦ € 340 – 4 suites
**Rest** – (dinner only and Sunday lunch) Menu € 25 – Carte € 35/47
♦ Georgian house with vast, modern extensions and formal gardens, set in 26 acres. State-of-the-art meeting rooms with the latest conference equipment. Stylish spa and plunge pool. Spacious bedrooms boast good mod cons; some have balconies. Sizeable formal dining room offers classically based Irish dishes.

---

**DUNCANNON** (Dún Canann) – Wexford – **712** L11 – pop. 291                    39 D2
▌Ireland

▶ Dublin 167 km – New Ross 26 km – Waterford 48 km

◎ Fort★ **AC**

⊙ Dunbrody Abbey★ **AC**, N : 9 km by R 733 – Kilmokea Gardens★ **AC**, N : 11 km by R 733 – Tintern Abbey★ **AC**, E : 8 km by R 737 and R 733. Kennedy Arboretum★ **AC**, N : 21 km by R 733

XX    **Aldridge Lodge** with rm    🚗 ⚘ **P** **VISA** **OO**
😊    South : 1 km by Hook Head Rd – 𝒞 (051) 389 116 – www.aldridgelodge.com
– Closed 3 weeks January and 24-25 December
**3 rm** ⌂ – ♦ € 55 ♦♦ € 90
**Rest** – (closed Monday and Tuesday) (dinner only) (booking essential)
Menu € 39 s
♦ New-build house run by cheery owner. Constantly evolving menu offers tasty homemade bread and veg from the kitchen garden. Focus on good value fish and shellfish – the owner's father is a local fisherman – with some Asian and fusion influences. Simply furnished bedrooms with hot water bottles and home-baked cookies.

X    **Sqigl**    🍴 **VISA** **OO**
Quay Rd. – 𝒞 (051) 389 700 – www.sqiglrestaurant.com – Closed
November-Easter and Sunday-Wednesday
**Rest** – (dinner only) (booking essential) Menu € 38 – Carte € 28/41
♦ Stone-built restaurant; a converted barn standing adjacent to a popular bar in this coastal village. Faux leopard skin banquettes. Modern European cuisine with amiable service.

---

**DUNDALK** (Dún Dealgan) – Louth – **712** M5/6 – pop. 35 085                    37 D2
▌Ireland

▶ Dublin 82 km – Drogheda 35 km

🏖 Killinbeg Killin Park, 𝒞 (042) 9 33 93 03

⊙ Dún a' Rí Forest Park★, W : 34 km by R 178 and R 179 – Proleek Dolmen★, N : 8 km by N 1 R 173

X    **Left Bank**    📶 **VISA** **OO**
43-44 Park St – 𝒞 (042) 933 8851 – www.leftbankdundalk.com
– Closed 25-26 December, Monday dinner and bank holidays
**Rest** – (closed Monday dinner) Menu € 14/22 – Carte € 20/36
♦ Well-run bistro in a busy market town. Large bar and raised dining room with tightly packed tables and booth seating; chiller cabinet offers home-made pastries and cakes to take home. All-purpose menu offer carefully prepared, hearty dishes.

REPUBLIC OF IRELAND

### ☖ Crowne Plaza   ← 🚗 🛏 L♨ 🖼 ♿ 🔲 ✄ 🗼 👧 🅿 🆚 ⑤ 🅰🅴 ⓘ

*Green Park, South : 2.5 km on N 52 – ℰ (042) 939 49 00 – www.cpdundalk.ie*
*– Closed 25 December*
**128 rm** – ♦ €55/99 ♦♦ €69/109, 🍽 €15 – 1 suite
**Rest** – *(bar lunch Monday-Saturday)* Menu €35 **s** – Carte €30/45 **s**
♦ Modern 14-storey hotel tower block, close to the main shopping centre, with stylish ground floor bar/lounge and good conference facilities. Uniform bedrooms boast views of surrounding countryside; ask for one higher up. Top floor restaurant offers seasonal menu of classic dishes and has superb 360° vista.

### ⌂ Rosemount without rest   🚗 🗼 🅿

*Dublin Rd, South : 2.5 km on R 132 – ℰ (042) 933 58 78*
*– www.rosemountireland.com – Closed 25 December*
**6 rm** 🍽 – ♦ €40 ♦♦ €65
♦ Attractive guesthouse with flower-filled gardens; run by welcoming couple. Laura Ashley and Brown Thomas fabrics/furnishings feature throughout. Individually styled bedrooms; some with sofas and flat screen TVs. Freshly cooked breakfasts; tea and cake on arrival.

**at Jenkinstown** Northeast : 9 km by N 52 on R 173

### 🍺 Fitzpatricks   🚗 🗼 🅿 🆚 ⑤

*Rockmarshall, Southeast : 1 km – ℰ (042) 937 61 93*
*– www.fitzpatricks-restaurant.com – Closed Good Friday, Monday*
*September-May (except bank holidays) and 25 December*
**Rest** – Menu €28 – Carte approx. €33
♦ Hugely characterful pub with beautiful flower displays and intriguing memorabilia. Extensive menu of hearty, flavoursome dishes and plenty of classics; local seafood and steaks a speciality.

---

**DUNDRUM** = Dún Droma – Dún Laoghaire-Rathdown – **712** N8 – see Dublin

---

**DUNFANAGHY** (Dún Fionnachaidh) – Donegal – **712** I2 – pop. 316   **37** C1
– ✉ Letterkenny ▌ Ireland

▶ Dublin 277 km – Donegal 87 km – Londonderry 69 km

🏁 Dunfanaghy Letterkenny, ℰ (074) 913 63 35

◉ Horn Head Scenic Route★, N : 4 km. Doe Castle★, SE : 11.25 km by N 56 – The Rosses★, SW : 40.25 km by N 56 and R 259

### ☖ Arnolds   ← 🚗 🔲 rest, ✄ 👧 🅿 🆚 ⑤ 🅰🅴 ⓘ

*Main St – ℰ (074) 913 62 08 – www.arnoldshotel.com – Easter-October*
**30 rm** 🍽 – ♦♦ €130/150
**Rest** *Sea Scapes* – *(bar lunch)* Menu €40 – Carte €24/41
♦ Pleasant traditional coaching inn with a variety of extensions. Spacious lounge area and a charming bar with open fires. Family run with traditional bedrooms. Informal Sea Scapes serves wide-ranging menus.

### ✕✕ Mill with rm   ← 🚗 🔲 rest, 🅿 🆚 ⑤ 🅰🅴

*Southwest : 0.75 km on N 56 – ℰ (074) 913 69 85 – www.themillrestaurant.com*
*– Closed mid-December to mid-March, mid-week March, April and November*
*and part December*
**6 rm** 🍽 – ♦ €70 ♦♦ €130   **Rest** – *(Closed Monday) (dinner only)* Menu €45
♦ Converted flax mill on the waterside, with lovely garden edged by reeds and great view of Mount Muckish. Homely inner with conservatory lounge and knick-knacks on display throughout. Antique-furnished dining room has a classical Georgian feel. Traditional menus showcase seasonal ingredients and fish features highly. Cosy, welcoming bedrooms come in individual designs.

**DUNGARVAN** (Dún Garbhán) – Waterford – **712** J11 – pop. 8 362    **39** C:
🔲 Ireland

▶ Dublin 190 km – Cork 71 km – Waterford 48 km

🏠 Knocknagrannagh, ℰ (058) 4 16 05

🏠 Gold Coast Ballinacourty, ℰ (058) 4 22 49

👁 East Bank (Augustinian priory, ≤ ★)

🅖 Ringville (≤ ★), S : 13 km by N 25 and R 674 – Helvick Head★ (≤ ★), SE : 13 km by N 25 and R 674

XX    **Tannery** with rm                        🅰🅺 rest, ⁰🎷 𝘝𝘐𝘚𝘈 ⊙⊙ 🅰🅴
*10 Quay St, via Parnell St – ℰ (058) 45 420 – www.tannery.ie – Closed 2 weeks January, 25-26 December and Good Friday*
**14 rm** – 🛉 € 60/70 🛉🛉 € 100/110
**Rest** – *(dinner only and lunch Friday and Sunday)* Menu € 30 – Carte € 37/53
♦ Long-standing restaurant in delightful coastal location, affording grea views of the castle, sea and sunsets. Large conservatory, vast decked terrace and snug bar with seafaring memorabilia. Spacious dining room has dark linen cloths; classical menu features mussels and oysters from the bay. Contemporary bedrooms have gilt mirrors, plush fabrics and very comfy beds.

**DUNKINEELY** (Dún Cionnaola) – Donegal – **712** G4 – pop. 363    **37** C1
▶ Dublin 156 km – Lifford 42 km – Sligo 53 km – Ballybofey 28 km

XX    **Castle Murray House** with rm ⌂      ≤ 🚗 🕭 ⁰🎷 🅿 𝘝𝘐𝘚𝘈 ⊙⊙
*St John's Point, Southwest : 1.5 km by N 56 on St John's Point rd – ℰ (074) 973 70 22 – www.castlemurray.com – Closed 24-25 December, restricted opening in winter*
**10 rm** ⌂ – 🛉 € 60/70 🛉🛉 € 120/130
**Rest** – *(closed dinner Monday-Thursday in winter) (dinner only and Sunday lunch, light lunch in summer)* Carte € 45/55
♦ In delightful, picturesque position with view of sea and sunsets from the lounges and the pleasant dining room. Good local seafood. Comfortable and contemporary styled bedrooms.

**DUN LAOGHAIRE** (Dún Laoghaire) – Dún Laoghaire-Rathdown    **39** D1
– **712** N8 – pop. 23 857 🔲 Ireland
▶ Dublin 14 km
🚢 to Holyhead (Stena Line) 4-5 daily (1 h 40 mn)
🏠 Dun Laoghaire Eglinton Park, ℰ (01) 280 39 16
🅖 ≤ ★★ of Killiney Bay from coast road south of Sorrento Point

XX    **Rasam**                                      𝘝𝘐𝘚𝘈 ⊙⊙
*1st Floor (above Eagle House pub), 18-19 Glasthule Rd – ℰ (01) 230 0600 – www.rasam.ie – Closed 25-26 December and Good Friday*    e
**Rest** – Indian – *(dinner only)* Menu € 25 (dinner) – Carte € 40/50
♦ Located above Eagle House pub, this airy, modern, stylish restaurant shimmers with silky green wallpaper. Interesting, authentic dishes covering all regions of India.

X    **Alexis Bar and Grill**                      🕭 🅰🅺 𝘝𝘐𝘚𝘈 ⊙⊙
*17-18 Patricks St. – ℰ (01) 280 8872 – www.alexis.ie – Closed 25 December, Good Friday, Saturday lunch and Monday*    b
**Rest** – Menu € 16/25 – Carte € 29/44
♦ Modern bistro towards the back of town, run by an experienced owner. Simply furnished interior with tightly packed tables and buzzy vibe; sunny courtyard to the rear. Unfussy, value for money menus change daily and reflect the seasons.

REPUBLIC OF IRELAND

### ✗ Cavistons
AC VISA ⊕⊙ AE

58-59 Glasthule Rd – ✆ (01) 280 9245 – www.cavistons.com – Closed 1 week
Christmas, Sunday and Monday **a**
**Rest** – Seafood – (lunch only and dinner Friday and Saturday) (booking essential) Menu € 16 (early lunch) – Carte € 26/45
• Simple, informal restaurant attached to the well-established seafood shop which specialises in finest piscine produce. Mermaid friezes and quality crustacean cuisine.

### ✗ Tribes
AC VISA ⊕⊙ AE Ⓞ

57a Glasthule Rd – ✆ (01) 236 5971 – www.tribes.ie – Closed Good Friday
and 24-26 December **x**
**Rest** – (dinner only and Sunday lunch) (booking advisable) Menu € 24/27
• Personally run neighbourhood restaurant next to Cavistons. Smart, original interior harmonises seamlessly with creative modern European menus that evolve slowly over time.

---

**DUNLAVIN** (Dún Luáin) – Wicklow – **712** L8 – pop. 849 **39** D2
▶ Dublin 50 km – Kilkenny 71 km – Wexford 98 km
🏨 Rathsallagh, ✆ (045) 40 33 16

REPUBLIC OF IRELAND

 **Rathsallagh House** ⟨⟩ ← 🚗 🐕 ⚡ ✂ 📺 & 🟡 ⚓ 🅿 VISA ⓪ AE ①
*Southwest : 3.25 km on Grangecon rd –* 𝒞 *(045) 403 112 – www.rathsallagh.com*
**28 rm** 🛏 – 🛏 € 110/300 🛏🛏 € 200/350 – 1 suite
**Rest** – *(dinner only and Sunday lunch , bar lunch Monday-Saturday)*
Carte € 34/50
♦ Collection of converted 18C stables and farm buildings in peaceful, rural location. Extensive grounds include a golf course; working farm to the rear. Characterful, open-fired lounges and cottagey bar. Spacious country house bedrooms with
good facilities. Large formal restaurant serves classically based menu.

---

**DUNMORE EAST** (Dún Mór) – **Waterford** – **712** L11 – **pop. 1 547**     **39** C2
– ✉ **Waterford** 📗 Ireland
▶ Dublin 174 km – Waterford 19 km
📷 Dunmore East, 𝒞 (051) 38 31 51
👁 Village★

🏠 **Beach** without rest                         ← & ✂ 🟡 🅿 VISA ⓪ AE ①
*1 Lower Village –* 𝒞 *(051) 383 316 – www.dunmorebeachguesthouse.com*
*– March-December*
**7 rm** 🛏 – 🛏 € 45/60 🛏🛏 € 80/90
♦ Modern house overlooking a large cove, with the beach just metres away. Inside,
it has an almost Mediterranean feel, with bedrooms displaying whitewashed walls
and ash furniture. Superb views from conservatory lounge-cum-breakfast room.

---

**DURRUS** (Dúras) – **Cork** – **712** D13 – **pop. 313**              **38** A3
▶ Dublin 338 km – Cork 90 km – Killarney 85 km

✕✕ **Blairscove House** with rm ⟨⟩          ← 🚗 🅿 VISA ⓪ AE ①
*Southwest : 1.5 km on R 591 –* 𝒞 *(027) 62 913 – www.blairscove.ie – 18
March-October*
**4 rm** 🛏 – 🛏🛏 € 160/260
**Rest** – *(closed Sunday and Monday) (dinner only) (booking essential)*
Menu € 58 **s**
♦ Charming 18C house just a stone's throw from the sea, boasting fantastic panoramic views, pretty gardens, a courtyard and lily pond. Stylish bar and large candlelit dining room with stone walls. Starters and desserts are in buffet format,
while the seasonal main courses are cooked on a wood-fired char-grill. Luxurious,
modern bedrooms are dotted about the place.

✕ **Good Things Café**                         🚗 🏠 🅿 VISA ⓪
☺ *Ahakista Rd, West : 0.75 km on Ahakista rd –* 𝒞 *(027) 61 426
– www.thegoodthingscafe.com – Closed August - late September*
**Rest** – *(booking essential)* Carte € 22/48
♦ Cookery school with simple, unpretentious restaurant open for weekends in
July and most Friday nights March to early December. Sit among shelves of cook-
ery books overlooking an open kitchen. Unfussy menu offers seasonal classics
with Mediterranean and Moroccan influences.

---

**ENNISCORTHY** (Inis Córthaidh) – **Wexford** – **712** M10 – **pop. 9 538**   **39** D2
📗 Ireland
▶ Dublin 122 km – Kilkenny 74 km – Waterford 54 km – Wexford 24 km
🛈 Millpark Rd 𝒞 (0539) 23 46 99, www.enniscorthytourism.com
📷 Knockmarshal, 𝒞 (053) 9 23 31 91
👁 Enniscorthy Castle★ (County Museum★)
📷 Ferns★, NE : 13 km by N 11 – Mount Leinster★, N : 27.25 km by N 11

**Monart**  🕭 🏵 🚗 🖥 🌐 🐾 ⚡ ⛉ 🖳 rest, ⚘ 🕻 P 🖭 💳 ⓐ🅔
*The Still, Northwest : 3 km by N 11 (Dublin rd) – 𝒞 (053) 923 8999*
*– www.monart.ie – Closed 19-27 December*
**68 rm** ⬜ – ♦ € 112/255 ♦♦ € 184/430 – 2 suites
**Rest** *Garden Lounge* – Carte € 25/43
**Rest** *The Restaurant* – *(dinner only and Sunday lunch)* Menu € 30/38
– Carte € 39/59
♦ Spa resort in 100 acres; enter via the elegant Georgian house and experience various therapies in state-of-the-art treatment rooms. Bedrooms all have views; many have balconies. Enjoy lighter dishes in the Garden Lounge or out on the terrace. Formal dining in The Restaurant.

**Ballinkeele House** 🦢 ⬅ 🕭 🕩 ⚘ P 🖭 💳
*Ballymurn, Southeast : 10 km by R 744 and Vinegar Hill rd on Curracloe rd*
*– 𝒞 (053) 913 81 05 – www.ballinkeele.ie – Closed December-January*
**5 rm** ⬜ – ♦ € 95/105 ♦♦ € 85/90 **Rest** – Menu € 45 **s**
♦ High ceilinged, firelit lounge plus sizeable rooms with period-style furniture and countryside views add to the charm of a quiet 1840 manor, well run by experienced owners. Dining room enriched by candlelight and period oils.

Your discoveries and comments help us to improve the guide.
Please write and let us know about your experiences -
good or bad!

**ENNISKERRY (Áth an Sceire)** – Wicklow – **712** N8 – pop. 1 881      **39** D1
🔲 Ireland

▶ Dublin 25 km – Wicklow 32 km
🔟 Powerscourt Powerscourt Estate, 𝒞 (01) 204 60 33
👁 Powerscourt★★ **AC** (Waterfall★★, **AC**)

**Ritz Carlton** 🦢 ⬅ 🕭 🕩 🐾 🖥 🌐 🐾 🖳 🖫 ⚡ ⛉ ✈ 🖭 🕻 🚿 P
*West : 1.5 km by Powerscourt rd – 𝒞 (01) 274 88 88* 💳 ⓐ🅔
*– www.ritzcarlton.com*
**106 rm** – ♦ € 255 ♦♦ € 315, ⬜ € 29 – 94 suites – ♦♦ € 305/365
**Rest** *Gordon Ramsay at Powerscourt* **Rest** *Sugar Loaf* – see restaurant listing
♦ Impressive curved building overlooking Sugar Loaf Mountain. Stylish guest areas, state-of-the-art conference facilities and superb spa. Luxurious bedrooms with marble bathrooms; some have balconies. Activities include archery and falconry.

XXX **Gordon Ramsay at Powerscourt** – at Ritz Carlton Hotel      🕭 🕩
*West : 1.5 km by Powerscourt rd – 𝒞 (01)* 🏵 ⛉ 🖭 P 🖭 💳 ⓐ🅔 ⓞ
*274 93 77 – www.ritzcarlton.com*
**Rest** – *(dinner only and lunch Saturday-Sunday)* Carte € 55/69
♦ Smart restaurant boasting superb mountain views and a chef's table, set in an impressive estate hotel. Classic Ramsay dishes in the main room and on the terrace; sharing boards in the wine bar.

XX **Sugar Loaf** – at Ritz Carlton Hotel      ⬅ 🕭 🕩 ⛉ 🖭 P 🖭 💳 ⓐ🅔 ⓞ
*West : 1.5 km by Powerscourt rd – 𝒞 (01) 274 88 88 – www.ritzcarlton.com*
**Rest** – Carte € 49/58
♦ Spacious Georgian-style lounge set in a smart hotel on the Powerscourt Estate. Light, airy room affords pleasant views out over Wicklow. All-day menu offers light choices and afternoon tea.

**FENNOR** – Waterford – **712** K11    **39** C2

▶ Dublin 115 km – Waterford 12 km – Cork 75 km – Limerick 89 km

✕ **Copper Hen**    **P** **VISA** **◎◎** **AE**
*Mother McHugh's Pub – ℰ (051) 330 300 – www.thecopperhen.ie – Closed 1 week January, 1 week autumn, 25-26 December, Monday-Wednesday, Sunday dinner and bank holidays*
**Rest** – *(dinner only and Sunday lunch) (booking advisable)* Menu € 25 – Carte € 25/34
◆ Simple, likeable little restaurant above a pub, with rustic décor and a brightly coloured fireplace; set on the coast road from Tramore to Dungarven. Keenly priced menus offer hearty, unfussy classics. Owners raise their own pigs.

---

**FETHARD** (Fiodh Ard) – South Tipperary – **712** I10 – pop. 1 374    **39** C2
▌ Ireland

▶ Dublin 161 km – Cashel 16 km – Clonmel 13 km

◙ Cashel★★★ : Rock of Cashel★★★ **AC** (Cormac's Chapel★★, Round Tower★), Museum★ **AC**, Cashel Palace Gardens★, GPA Bolton Library★ **AC**, NW : 15 km by R 692 – Clonmel★ : County Museum★ **AC**, St Mary's Church★, S : 13 km by R 689

⌂ **Mobarnane House** ⌘    ⪕ ⪜ ⟁ ※ ⅌ **P** **VISA** **◎◎**
*North : 8 km. by Cashel rd on Ballinure rd – ℰ (052) 613 19 62 – www.mobarnanehouse.com – March-October*
**3 rm** ⌕ – ♦ € 125 ♦♦ € 150/190
**Rest** – *(dinner only) (residents only)* Menu € 48 **s**
◆ Very personally run classic Georgian house with mature gardens in quiet rural setting, tastefully restored to reflect its age. Ask for a bedroom with its own sitting room. Beautiful dining room for menus agreed in advance.

---

**FOTA ISLAND** (Oileán Fhóta) – Cork – **712** H12    **38** B3
▶ Dublin 263 km – Cork 17 km – Limerick 118 km – Waterford 110 km

🏨 **Fota Island**    ⪕ ⪜ ⟁ ⊛ ⬚ ⬚ ⬚ ⬚ & rm, ⱪ ⅌ ⚓ **P** **VISA** **◎◎** **AE** **①**
*– ℰ (021) 488 37 00 – www.fotaisland.ie – Closed 25-26 December*
**127 rm** ⌕ – ♦ € 129/149 ♦♦ € 145/165 – 4 suites
**Rest** *Fota* – *(dinner only)* Carte € 25/41
◆ Resort hotel set within Ireland's only wildlife park. Extensive business and leisure facilities include a golf course and state-of-the-art spa. Spacious, well-appointed bedrooms; most with island views. Stylish restaurant offers modern takes on classical dishes.

---

**FOXROCK** = Carraig an tSionnaigh – Dún Laoghaire-Rathdown – **712** N7 – see Dublin

---

**FURBOGH/FURBO** (Na Forbacha) – Galway – **712** E8 – pop. 1 236    **36** A3
▶ Dublin 228 km – Galway 11 km

🏨 **Connemara Coast**    ⪕ ⪜ ⟁ ⅏ ⬚ ※ & ⚶ ⅌ ⚓ **P** **VISA** **◎◎** **AE**
*– ℰ (091) 592 108 – www.sinnotthotels.com – Closed 23-27 December*
**141 rm** ⌕ – ♦ € 130/200 ♦♦ € 178/350 – 1 suite
**Rest** *The Gallery* – *(bar lunch)* Menu € 40 **s** – Carte € 40/50 **s**
◆ Sprawling hotel geared to families, with super views of Galway Bay, The Burren and Aran from the spacious bedrooms. Comprehensive leisure facilities. Club for kids. Two dining options; The Gallery for adults only.

REPUBLIC OF IRELAND

REPUBLIC OF IRELAND (side tab)

▶ Dublin 217 km – Limerick 103 km – Sligo 145 km

✈ Carnmore Airport : 𝒞 (091) 755569, NE : 6.5 km

🛈 Discover Ireland Centre, Aras Failte, Forster St 𝒞 (091) 53 77 00,
www.galwaytourism.ie

⛳ Galway Salthill Blackrock, 𝒞 (091) 52 20 33

◎ City★★ – St Nicholas' Church★ BY - Roman Catholic Cathedral★ AY – Eyre
Square : Bank of Ireland Building (sword and mace★) BY

◎ NW : Lough Corrib★★. W : by boat, Aran Islands (Inishmore - Dun Aenghus★★★)
BZ - Thoor Ballylee★, SE : 33.75 km by N 6 and N 18 D – Dunguaire Castle,
Kinvarra★ **AC**, S : 25.75 km by N 6, N 18 and N 67 D – Aughnanure Castle★, NW :
25.75 km by N 59 - Oughterard★ (⩽★★), NW : 29 km by N 59 - Knockmoy
Abbey★, NE : 30.5 km by N 17 and N 63 D – Coole Park (Autograph Tree★), SE :
33.75 km by N 6 and N 18 D - St Mary's Cathedral, Tuam★, NE : 33.75 km by N 17
D – Loughrea (St Brendan's Cathedral★), SE : 35.5 km by N 6 D - Turoe Stone★,
SE : 35.5 km by N 6 and north by R 350

Plans on following pages

REPUBLIC OF IRELAND

---

**🏨 Glenlo Abbey** 🦢    ⩽ ⇌ 🐾 🐕 📷 🏊 & ℅ rm, ⸙ ⛷ **P** 🆚 ⊙ 🅰 ⓪
*Bushypark, Northwest : 5.25 km on N 59 – 𝒞 (091) 526 666*
*– www.glenlo.com – March to December*
**42 rm** ⯑ – ♦ € 130/200 ♦♦ € 170/400 – 4 suites
**Rest *River Room*** – Menu € 35 – Carte € 28/54
**Rest *Pullman*** – (dinner only Thursday-Sunday) Menu € 28/35 – Carte € 28/54
♦ Imposing 18C grey-stone country house with impressive grounds and church-/
bay views. Very comfortable lounge, leading into chapel. Spacious, traditional
bedrooms. Formal restaurant boasts golf course views. Pullman, a converted railway carriage, offers modern dishes with an Asian base.

---

**🏨 Radisson Blu**    ⩽ 🏕 🖻 🌐 🍴 ♨ Ⓕ♨ 🏊 & 🔟 ℅ ⸙ ⛷ 🚗 🆚 ⊙ 🅰
*Lough Atalia Rd – 𝒞 (091) 538 300*
*– www.radissonhotelgalway.com*                                              **D**a
**259 rm** ⯑ – ♦ € 175/195 ♦♦ € 550/600 – 2 suites
**Rest *Marinas*** – Menu € 22/40 – Carte € 36/49
♦ Striking atrium leads to ultra-modern meeting facilities and very comfortable
and refurbished accommodation. Higher spec rooms on the 5th floor have glass
balconies. International dining; accessible, rapid lunch menu.

---

**🏨 G**    🌐 🍴 🏊 & rm, 🔟 ℅ ⸙ 🔉 🚗 🆚 ⊙ 🅰
*Wellpark, Dublin Rd – 𝒞 (091) 865 200*
*– www.theghotel.ie – Closed 24-27 December*                                  **D**g
**100 rm** ⯑ – ♦ € 130/320 ♦♦ € 150/320 – 1 suite
**Rest *Matz at the G*** – (dinner only and Sunday lunch) Menu € 35/55
– Carte € 39/56
♦ Uber-hip boutique hotel with cutting edge design from renowned milliner Philip Treacy. Vividly assured sitting room styles; décor imbued with fashion shoot
portraits. Cool, slinky bedrooms. Stunning spa. Modern Irish cooking in colourful
restaurant.

---

**🏨 Clayton**    🖻 🍴 🏊 ♨ & rm, 🔟 ℅ 🔉 🏊 **P** 🆚 ⊙ 🅰
*Ballybrit, East : 4 km on N 6 – 𝒞 (091) 721 900*
*– www.clayton.ie – Closed 24-27 December*
**196 rm** ⯑ – ♦ € 99/350 ♦♦ € 120/350
**Rest** – (dinner only) Menu € 35 – Carte € 20/38
♦ Striking angular building on edge of city, with stylish, modern interior and bar
with buffet carvery. Smart white bedrooms have a minimalistic feel, with dark
wood furniture. Large first floor restaurant offers traditional menu.

# GALWAY

Scale: 0 — 200 m / 200 yards

## Ardilaun

🛏 🍽 📺 🅿️ 🧖 ♨ 🛗 ♿ 🅰️🅲 rest, 📞 ᴙ 🅿️ 𝚅𝙸𝚂𝙰 ⓒⓞ 🅰🅴 ①

Taylor's Hill – ℘ *(091) 521 433 – www.theardilaunhotel.ie – Closed 22-26 December*

Ca

**120 rm** ⬚ – 🛉 € 79/150 🛉🛉 € 99/290 – 5 suites

**Rest *Camilaun*** – *(dinner only and Sunday lunch)* Menu € 20/32 – Carte € 32/112

**Rest *Blazer's Bar and Bistro*** – Menu € 29 (dinner) – Carte € 20/33

• Georgian style country house hotel in five acres of gardens and ancient trees. Informal bar. Extensive leisure facilities. Spacious rooms; ask for one of the newer ones. Stylish, formal Camilaun. Seafood, including oysters, feature strongly in the bar-bistro.

GALWAY

### Park House

Forster St, Eyre Sq – ℰ (091) 564 924 – www.parkhousehotel.ie – Closed 24-26 December

BY**c**

**84 rm** ⌷ – † € 109/350 †† € 109/350

**Rest** – Menu € 42 (dinner) – Carte € 30/56

♦ Popular grey-stone hotel in city centre. Marble reception and comfy seating areas. Boss Doyle's Bar is busy and spacious. Dark wood bedrooms with rich, soft fabrics. Strong international flavours define restaurant menus.

### House

Spanish Par – ℰ (091) 538 900 – www.thehousehotel.ie – Closed 24-26 December

**39 rm** ⌷ – † € 169/199 †† € 169/199 – 1 suite

BZ**e**

**Rest** – (bar lunch) Carte € 17/26 s

♦ Luxury boutique hotel, blending contemporary design with a cosy, relaxed style. Bedrooms are divided between cosy, classy and swanky. Modern menus take on a global reach; try to get a seat on the outdoor deck.

### Ardawn House without rest

College Rd. – ℰ (091) 568 833 – www.ardawnhouse.com – Closed 20-27 December

D**b**

**9 rm** ⌷ – † € 45/90 †† € 80/160

♦ Sample Irish hospitality at this family-run guest house. Individually decorated bedrooms and comfy lounge. Extensive breakfast menu served at linen-clad tables.

XX **Kirwan's Lane**        ⟨⟩ AK VISA ⊙⊙ AE

*Kirwan's Lane – ℰ (091) 568 266 – Closed 25-28 December, Sunday dinner in winter and Sunday lunch*        BZs

**Rest** – Carte € 20/40

♦ Well-regarded, long-standing restaurant with pleasant terrace, in an old medieval lane. Modern menus have a classical base, with simpler offerings at lunch downstairs seafood bar offers an extensive selection of dishes. Formal service.

XX **Vina Mara**        AK VISA ⊙⊙ AE

*19 Middle St – ℰ (091) 561 610 – www.vinamara.com – Closed 24-27 December*

**Rest** – Menu € 20/28 – Carte € 29/42        BYn

♦ Spacious restaurant in warm welcoming colours – smart yet informal; attentive service. Mediterranean style dishes with Irish and other touches. Affordable but limited lunch choice.

X **Ard Bia at Nimmos**        VISA ⊙⊙ AE

*Spanish Arch – ℰ (091) 561 114 – www.ardbia.com – Closed 25-26 December*

**Rest** – *(light lunch) (booking essential at dinner)* Carte € 29/45    BZu

♦ Simple restaurant in two-storey building with buzzy, bohemain feel. Generous full-flavoured dishes have Mediterranean and Irish influences. Lighter lunches; upstairs used at weekends.

---

## GARRYKENNEDY – North Tipperary – **712** G9      **39** C2

▶ Dublin 176 km – Killaloe 14 km – Youghal 2 km

🏠 **Larkins**        ⟨⟩ ⟨⟩ **P** VISA ⊙⊙

*– ℰ (067) 23 232 – www.larkinspub.com – Closed 25 December, Good Friday and Monday-Tuesday November-April*

**Rest** – Carte € 20/37

♦ Thatched, whitewashed pub in a charming loughside location. Traditional interior plays host to folk music sessions and Irish dancers. Simple, unfussy bar menu; more ambitious à la carte.

---

## GARRYVOE (Garraí Uí Bhuaigh) – Cork – **712** H12 – pop. 560    **39** C3

– ✉ Castlemartyr

▶ Dublin 259 km – Cork 37 km – Waterford 100 km

🏨 **Garryvoe**       ⟨⟩ ⟨⟩ ⟨⟩ ⟨⟩ ⟨⟩ ⟨⟩ ⟨⟩ ⟨⟩ **P** VISA ⊙⊙ AE ①

*– ℰ (021) 464 67 18 – www.garryvoehotel.com – Closed 25 December*

**81 rm** ⊑ – †€ 74/149 ††€ 74/149 – 1 suite

**Rest** *Samphire* **Rest** *Lighthouse Bistro* – see restaurant listing

♦ Modernised hotel overlooking Ballycotton Bay. Contemporary interior features plenty of natural wood and slate. Bedrooms are spacious and comfortable – most boast balconies and sea views. A well-equipped fitness centre completes the picture.

XX **Samphire** – at Garryvoe Hotel       ⟨⟩ ⟨⟩ **P** VISA ⊙⊙ AE ①

*– ℰ (021) 464 67 18 – www.garryvoehotel.com – Closed 25 December*

**Rest** – *(dinner only and Sunday lunch)* Carte € 38/50

♦ Formal restaurant in a modern hotel overlooking Ballycotton Bay. Menus feature meats from nearby farms and plenty of the famed local seafood that is landed on the village pier every morning.

X **Lighthouse Bistro** – at Garryvoe Hotel     ⟨⟩ **P** VISA ⊙⊙ AE ①

*– ℰ 464 67 18 – www.garryvoehotel.com – Closed 25 December*

**Rest** – Carte € 29/43

♦ Relaxed restaurant set within an up-to-date hotel and affording views out across the sea towards the Ballycotton lighthouse. Accessible menus consist largely of simply prepared pub classics.

**GLASLOUGH** = Glasloch – Monaghan – **712** L5 – see Monaghan

**GLASSON** = Glasán – Westmeath – **712** I7 – see Athlone

**GLOUNTHAUNE** – Cork – **712** G12 – pop. 900          **38 B3**

▶ Dublin 160 km – Cork 7 km – Limerick 68 km – Galway 130 km

🍴 **Rising Tide**          🚗 🏠 **P** VISA 🌐
– ℰ *(021) 435 32 33 – www.therisingtide.ie – Closed Good Friday and 25 December*
**Rest** – Seafood – Carte € 34/48
♦ Friendly little pub in pleasant waterside village. Bright, modern interior with nautical knick-knacks and village memorabilia. Fresh, unfussy cooking; seafood plays a prominent role at dinner.

**GOLEEN** (An Góilín) – Cork – **712** C13          **38 A3**

▶ Dublin 230 km – Cork 74 km – Killarney 67 km

🏠 **Heron's Cove**          ≤ 🦢 📶 **P** VISA 🌐 AE ①
*The Harbour* – ℰ *(028) 35 225 – www.heronscove.com – Closed Christmas*
**5 rm** 🍽 – ♦ € 60/70 ♦♦ € 70/80
**Rest** – *(dinner only)* Menu € 30 – Carte € 32/49
♦ Long-standing guesthouse hidden away in a pretty location and overlooking a tiny harbour. Bedrooms are tidy and pleasantly furnished: all overlook the waterfront and most have a balcony. If you're lucky you might see herons at the water's edge.

**GOREY** (Guaire) – Wexford – **712** N9 – pop. 7 193 📗 Ireland          **39 D2**

▶ Dublin 93 km – Waterford 88 km – Wexford 61 km

🛈 Main St ℰ (055) 942 12 48, www.discoverireland.ie

🏌 Courtown Kiltennel, ℰ (055) 2 51 66

🔵 Ferns★, SW : 17.75 km by N 11

🏨 **Marlfield House** ॐ          ≤ 🚗 🐾 🏠 🎿 ✂ 🍽 rest, 📶 **P** VISA 🌐 AE ①
*Courtown Rd, Southeast : 1.5 km on R 742* – ℰ *(053) 942 11 24*
*– www.marlfieldhouse.com – Closed 3 January -February*
**19 rm** 🍽 – ♦ € 80/190 ♦♦ € 210/250
**Rest** – *(dinner only and Sunday lunch)* Menu € 25/64
♦ Attractive Regency house surrounded by large informal gardens and woodland. Various stylish, classical lounges and drawing rooms with warm décor, heavy fabrics and antiques. Well-appointed bedrooms in period styles, with a good level of facilities and pleasant views over the grounds. Smart dining room and orangery offer refined, traditional dishes with modern touches.

**GRAIGUENAMANAGH** (Gráig na Manach) – Kilkenny – **712** L10          **39 D2**
– pop. 1 376 📗 Ireland

▶ Dublin 125 km – Kilkenny 34 km – Waterford 42 km – Wexford 26 km

🔵 Duiske Abbey★★ **AC**

🔵 Jerpoint Abbey★★ **AC**, W : 15 km by R 703 and N 9 – Inistioge★, SW : 8 km by minor road – Kilfane Glen and Waterfall★ **AC**, SW : 17 km by R 703 and N 9

🍴 **Waterside** with rm          ≤ 📶 VISA 🌐 AE
*The Quay* – ℰ *(059) 972 42 46 – www.watersideguesthouse.com – Closed January and 25 December*
**10 rm** 🍽 – ♦ € 55/69 ♦♦ € 90/98
**Rest** – *(closed Monday-Thursday) (dinner only and Sunday lunch)* Carte € 25/40
♦ 1871 stone-built corn store at the foot of Brandon Hill and the Blackstairs Mountains, overlooking the River Barrow. Bright, modern bar and restaurant. Concise à la carte offers modern Irish-influenced dishes with Mediterranean touches. Simply furnished bedrooms have exposed beams and pleasant river views.

**GREYSTONES** (Na Clocha Liatha) – **Wicklow** – **712** N8 – **pop. 14 569**    **39** D

🏛 Ireland

▶ Dublin 35 km

🏘 Greystones, 𝒞 (01) 287 41 36

◪ Killruddery House and Gardens★ **AC**, N : 5 km by R 761
– Powerscourt★★ (Waterfall★★) **AC**, NW : 10 km by R 761, minor road, M 11 and minor road via Enniskerry. Wicklow Mountains★★

XX **Chakra by Jaipur**    ᴀᴄ 𝘝𝘐𝘚𝘈 ⓒⓞ ᴀᴇ
*Meridan Point Centre (1st floor), Church Rd – 𝒞 (01) 201 72 22 – Closed 25 December*
**Rest** – Indian – *(dinner only and Sunday lunch)* Menu € 22 (early dinner) – Carte € 27/47
♦ Red and ochre restaurant overlooked by elephant god, Ganesh, on 1st floor of modern shopping centre. Vibrant Indian cooking represents all regions; a blend of old and new.

---

**GWEEDORE** (Gaoth Dobhair) – **Donegal** – **712** H2    **37** C

▶ Dublin 278 km – Donegal 72 km – Letterkenny 43 km – Sligo 135 km

🏨 **Gweedore Court**    ≤ ⤳ 🔲 ⊕ 🏤 ♨ 💄 ⴹ 💺 ♀ ⬙ 🐾 🛁 𝙿 𝘝𝘐𝘚𝘈 ⓒⓞ
*on N 56 – 𝒞 (074) 953 29 00 – www.gweedorecourthotel.ie – Closed January and 20-27 December*
**66 rm** ⬚ – ♦ € 69/89 ♦♦ € 69/89
**Rest** – *(dinner only and Sunday lunch) (bar lunch Monday-Saturday)* Menu € 35 – Carte € 19/38
♦ Rebuilt 19C house sharing grounds with a Gaelic craft centre. Spacious accommodation in classic patterns; east-facing rooms enjoy superb views of Glenreagh National Park. Classic menu matched by traditional surroundings and period-inspired décor.

---

**HORSE AND JOCKEY** (An Marcach) – **North Tipperary** – **712** I10    **39** C2

▶ Dublin 146 km – Cashel 14 km – Thurles 9 km

🏨 **Horse and Jockey**    🔲 ⊕ 🏤 💄 💺 ⬙ rm, ✴✴ ♀ ⬙ 🛁 𝙿 𝘝𝘐𝘚𝘈 ⓒⓞ ᴀᴇ ①
*– 𝒞 (0504) 44 192 – www.horseandjockeyhotel.com – Closed 25 December*
**67 rm** ⬚ – ♦ € 80/100 ♦♦ € 100/150 – 1 suite
**Rest** *Silks* – Carte € 28/42 **s**
♦ Much extended hotel with stylish, state-of-the-art meeting rooms, superb spa and great gift shop. Bar full of horse racing pictures on walls. Spacious, contemporary bedrooms. Easy going dining room with traditional menus.

---

**HOWTH** (Binn Éadair) – **Fingal** – **712** N7 – **pop. 8 186** – ✉ **Dublin**    **39** D1

🏛 Ireland

▶ Dublin 22 km – Swords 17 km – Belfast 172 km – Cork 276 km

🏘 Deer Park Hotel Howth Castle, 𝒞 (01) 832 60 39

◉ The Cliffs★ (≤★)

XX **Aqua**    ≤ ᴀᴄ 𝘝𝘐𝘚𝘈 ⓒⓞ ᴀᴇ
*1 West Pier – 𝒞 (01) 832 0690 – www.aqua.ie – Closed Good Friday, 25-26 December, and Monday-Tuesday in winter*
**Rest** – Seafood – Menu € 25/30 – Carte € 36/45
♦ Glass sided, first floor restaurant in former yacht club, with super bay views. Intimate bar filled with local photos, whetting the appetite for accomplished dishes of fresh seafood. Chefs on view.

XX **King Sitric** with rm  ≤ AK rest, ¶¹ VISA ©©
*East Pier – 𝒞 (01) 832 5235 – www.kingsitric.ie – Closed 25-26 December*
**8 rm** ⬚ – **†** € 145 **††** € 205
**Rest** – Seafood – *(closed dinner Sunday, Tuesday and bank holidays) (dinner only and Sunday lunch)* Menu € 35 – Carte € 43/64
♦ Established in 1971 and one of Ireland's original seafood restaurants. Enjoy locally caught produce in first floor dining room with bay views. Modern, comfy bedrooms.

---

**NISHMAAN** = Inis Meáin – Galway – **712** D8 – see Aran Islands

**NISHMORE** = Árainn – Galway – **712** C/D8 – see Aran Islands

**ENKINSTOWN** = Baile Sheinicín – Louth – see Dundalk

---

**KANTURK** (Ceann Toirc) – Cork – **712** F11 – pop. 1 915 ▌ Ireland  **38** B2
▶ Dublin 259 km – Cork 53 km – Killarney 50 km – Limerick 71 km
▣ Fairy Hill, 𝒞 (029) 5 05 34
◉ Town★ - Castle★

⌂ **Glenlohane** without rest ⬚  ≤ ⬚ ⬚ ⬚ ⬚ P VISA ©© AE
*Southeast : 4 km. by R 580 on Cecilstown rd – 𝒞 (029) 50 014
– www.glenlohane.com*
**3 rm** ⬚ – **†** € 75 **††** € 150
♦ In the family for over 250 years, a Georgian country house at the centre of wooded parkland and a working farm. Library and cosy, en suite rooms overlooking the fields.

---

**KEEL** = An Caol – Mayo – **712** B5/6 – see Achill Island

---

**KENMARE** (Neidín) – Kerry – **712** D12 – pop. 1 701 ▌ Ireland  **38** A3
▶ Dublin 338 km – Cork 93 km – Killarney 32 km
ℹ Heritage Centre 𝒞 (064) 664 12 33, www.kenmare.com
▣ Kenmare, 𝒞 (064) 4 12 91
◉ Town★
◎ Ring of Kerry★★ - Healy Pass★★ (≤★★), SW : 30.5 km by R 571 and R 574 AY – Mountain Road to Glengarriff (≤★★) S : by N 71 AY - Slieve Miskish Mountains (≤★★), SW : 48.25 km by R 571 AY – Gougane Barra Forest Park★★, SE : 16 km AY - Lauragh (Derreen Gardens★ **AC**), SW : 23.5 km by R 571 AY – Allihies (Copper Mines★), SW : 57 km by R 571 and R 575 AY – Garnish Island (≤★), SW : 68.5 km by R 571, R 575 and R 572 AY

Plan on next page

▲▲▲ **Park** ⬚  ≤ ⬚ ⬚ ⬚ ⬚ ⬚ ⬚ ⬚ ⬚ ⬚ ⬚ ⬚ ⬚ rm, ¶¹ P VISA ©© AE ①
– 𝒞 (064) 664 12 00 – www.parkkenmare.com – *Easter-October and 23 December-3 January*  BY**k**
**46 rm** ⬚ – **†** € 225/275 **††** € 440/846
**Rest** *Park* – *(dinner only)* Menu € 68
♦ Substantial country house dating from 1897 and offering superb views over the bay and hills. Cosy cocktail lounge and charming drawing room filled with portraits and antiques. Tastefully furnished bedrooms boast smart marble bathrooms. Stylish, intimate spa. Linen-laid dining room; classically based dishes with a modern touch and local ingredients to the fore.

## KENMARE

 **Sheen Falls Lodge** ⟨⟩  ≤ 🚗 🐕 🐟 📺 🛋 💆 ✕ 🍴 ᕼ ✕ 🎿 🏋 ⽛ P
*Southeast : 2 km. by N 71 –* ℰ *(064) 664 16 00*      𝚅𝙸𝚂𝙰 ⓪⓪ 𝙰𝙴 ①
*– www.sheenfallslodge.ie – Closed January*
**57 rm** ⌁ – 🛉 € 310/455 🛉🛉 € 310/455 – **9 suites**
**Rest *La Cascade*** *– (dinner only)* Carte € 60/77
• Luxurious hotel in an idyllic spot, where the falls drop away into the bay.
Welcoming, wood-fired lobby, book-filled library and lovely airy indoor pool.
Well-appointed bedrooms overlook the falls. Comprehensive service. Light
lunches in cocktail bar; classical menu with a modern touch in formal restaurant.

 **Brook Lane**                          ᕼ & rm, ✕ ⟪⟫ 🎿 P 𝚅𝙸𝚂𝙰 ⓪⓪
*Northwest : 1.5 km. by N 71 on N 70 –* ℰ *(064) 664 20 77*
*– www.brooklanehotel.com*
**22 rm** ⌁ – 🛉 € 75/90 🛉🛉 € 100/239
**Rest *Casey's*** *–* Menu € 26 (dinner) *–* Carte € 25/45
• Stylish, personally – run hotel close to the town centre. Contemporary bedrooms
offer a good level of comfort and range from 'Standard' to 'Luxury', the latter
boasting impressive fabric headboards and designer touches. Informal bar and
restaurant offer classic Irish and seafood dishes; regular live music.

**Shelburne Lodge** *without rest*                    🚗 ✕ ✕ ⟪⟫ P 𝚅𝙸𝚂𝙰 ⓪⓪
*East : 0.75 km. on R 569 (Cork Rd) –* ℰ *(064) 664 10 13*
*– www.shelburnelodge.com – 10 March to mid-November*
**9 rm** ⌁ – 🛉 € 75/110 🛉🛉 € 130/160
• Georgian farmhouse with pleasant lawns and herb garden. Antiques stylishly
combined with contemporary colours and modern art. Firelit lounge and cosy
rooms. Affable hosts.

⇧ **Sallyport House** without rest  ⇦ 🚗 🏷 🛜 **P**
*South : 0.5 km. on N 71 – 𝒞 (064) 664 20 66 – www.sallyporthouse.com*
*– April-October*
**5 rm** ⏟ – 🛏 € 75/85 🛏🛏 € 100/140
• Unassuming 1930s house hiding a charming interior packed with antiques and Irish art. Pleasant lounge with local information; breakfast, served from the characterful sideboard, features pancakes, stewed fruits and smoked salmon. Traditionally furnished bedrooms are immaculately kept and boast water views.

XX **Mulcahys**  🅰🅲 **VISA** ◷◷ **AE** ◑
*36 Henry St – 𝒞 (064) 664 23 83 – Closed 25 December, Tuesday, and Monday and Wednesday October-April*  AYc
**Rest** – *(dinner only)* Carte € 34/49
• Contemporary restaurant named after its passionate, hands-on owners. Vibrant modern art, exposed stone walls and intimate candlelight. Seasonal ingredients prepared with care and a modern touch; well-judged flavours and good presentation.

XX **Lime Tree**  🅰🅲 **P** **VISA** ◷◷
*Shelbourne St. – 𝒞 (064) 664 12 25 – www.limetreerestaurant.com*
*– Easter-October and weekends only in winter*  BYh
**Rest** – *(dinner only)* Menu € 30 – Carte € 31/47
• Bright restaurant with exposed stone walls, open fire and country-style décor, set in a 19C former schoolhouse; modern art on display both here and in the first floor gallery. Simply laid tables with unfussy modern Irish dishes to match.

X **Packies**  **VISA** ◷◷ **AE**
*Henry St – 𝒞 (064) 664 15 08 – Closed mid-January to mid-March and Monday*
**Rest** – Seafood – *(dinner only) (booking essential)* Carte € 31/53  AYb
• Locally popular, personally run little place with understated rustic feel. Handwritten menu of fresh, modern Irish dishes prepared with care and super local seafood. Friendly staff.

---

**KILBRITTAIN** (Cill Briotáin) – **Cork** – **712** F12 – pop. 185  **38** B3
▶ Dublin 289 km – Cork 38 km – Killarney 96 km

⇧ **Glen Country House** without rest ⌂  ⇦ 🚗 🐾 🏷 🛜 **P** **VISA** ◷◷
*Southwest : 6.5 km. by R 600 – 𝒞 (023) 884 98 62 – www.glencountryhouse.com*
*– April-October*
**5 rm** ⏟ – 🛏 € 65/75 🛏🛏 € 100/130
• Early Georgian house in 300 acres of mature parkland; the family have farmed the land for over 350 years. Comfy lounge and antique-filled breakfast room. Smart bedrooms with distant sea views.

---

**KILCOLGAN** (Cill Cholgáin) – **Galway** – **712** F8 – ✉ Oranmore  **36** B3
▶ Dublin 220 km – Galway 17 km

🍴 **Moran's Oyster Cottage**  🏷 **VISA** ◷◷ **AE**
*The Weir, Northwest : 2 km. by N 18 – 𝒞 (091) 796 113*
*– www.moransoystercottage.com – Closed Good Friday and 24-26 December*
**Rest** – Seafood – Carte € 30/60
• Attractive whitewashed pub with golden thatch, hidden away in a tiny hamlet – a very popular place in summer. Largely cold seafood dishes, with oysters a speciality and tasty homemade bread.

REPUBLIC OF IRELAND

🔲 Ireland

▶ Dublin 114 km – Cork 138 km – Killarney 185 km – Limerick 111 km

🔒 Shee Alms House 𝒞 (056) 7 75 15 00, www.kilkennytourism.ie

🏘 Glendine, 𝒞 (056) 776 54 00

🏘 Callan Geraldine, 𝒞 (056) 772 51 36

🏞 Castlecomer Drumgoole, 𝒞 (056) 444 11 39

◉ Town★★ – St Canice's Cathedral★★ – Kilkenny Castle and Park★★ **AC** – Black Abbey★ – Rothe House★

◎ Jerpoint Abbey★★ **AC**, S : 19.25 km by R 700 and N 9 – Kilfane Glen and Waterfall★ **AC**, S : 21 km by R 700 and N 9 – Kells Priory★, S : 12.5 km by R 697 – Dunmore Cave★ **AC**, N: 11.25 km by N 77 and N 78

---

🏨 **Kilkenny**   🚗 🔲 🕍 🛁 🛏 ⛄ rm, 🌿 🔟 rest, 🍽 rm, 🎵 🔐 🅿 🚗 ☎ 🅰🅴 ⓘ
*College Rd, Southwest : 1.25 km by Patrick St on Ormonde Rd (N76) – 𝒞 (056) 776 20 00 – www.hotelkilkenny.ie*
**138 rm** 🍽 – 🛏 € 170/190 🛏🛏 € 190
**Rest** *Taste* – Menu € 30 **s**
♦ Unassuming modern property just outside the city centre, with contrastingly stylish, contemporary interior. Well-equipped leisure centre and smart function rooms. Funky colour schemes feature throughout. Bright bedrooms have a slightly kitsch style. Mediterranean-influenced menus in pink-hued restaurant.

🏠 **Butler House** without rest   🚗 🌿 🎵 🔐 🅿 🆅🆂🅰 ☎ 🅰🅴 ⓘ
*15-16 Patrick St. – 𝒞 (056) 776 57 07 – www.butler.ie – Closed 23-29 December*
**12 rm** 🍽 – 🛏 € 60/120 🛏🛏 € 99/180 – 1 suite
♦ Substantial, part-Georgian house. Spacious accommodation with 1970s style furnishings – superior bow-fronted bedrooms located to the rear, overlooking neat, geometric lawned gardens.

🏠 **Rosquil House** without rest   🛁 🌿 🎵 🅿 🆅🆂🅰 ☎
*Castlecomer Rd., Northwest : 1 km. – 𝒞 (056) 772 14 19 – www.rosquilhouse.com*
**7 rm** 🍽 – 🛏 € 36/50 🛏🛏 € 75/95
♦ Purpose-built guesthouse on the main road out of the city. Comfy, leather-furnished lounge filled with books and local information; linen-laid breakfast room to the rear. Simply furnished bedrooms boast flat screen TVs. Welcoming owners.

🏠 **Blanchville House** without rest 🦢   ≤ 🚗 🦆 🌿 🌿 🎵 🅿 🆅🆂🅰 ☎ 🅰🅴
*Dunbell, Maddoxtown, Southeast : 10 km by R 712 – 𝒞 (056) 772 71 97 – www.blanchville.ie – March-October*
**5 rm** 🍽 – 🛏 € 65 🛏🛏 € 120
♦ Large, rurally set Georgian manor house with a Peel Tower in the garden. Classical, fire-lit drawing room with heavy fabrics; traditionally styled, antique-furnished bedrooms. Tea and homemade cakes on arrival.

🏠 **Fanad House** without rest   🚗 🛁 🎵 🅿 🆅🆂🅰 ☎
*Castle Rd., South : 0.75 km. on R 700 – 𝒞 (056) 776 41 26 – www.fanadhouse.com*
**12 rm** 🍽 – 🛏 € 50/65 🛏🛏 € 70/120
♦ Striking green house close to the town centre, run by a friendly owner and looking out towards the castle. Formal reception area and bright, wood-floored breakfast room. Simple, wood-furnished bedrooms come in neutral colours.

🍴🍴🍴 **Campagne**   🍽 🔟 🆅🆂🅰 ☎ 🅰🅴
*5 The Arches, Gashouse Ln. – 𝒞 (056) 777 28 58 – www.campagne.ie – Closed 2 weeks January, Sunday dinner and Monday*
**Rest** – *(dinner only and lunch Friday-Sunday) (booking advisable)* Menu € 29 (lunch and early dinner) **s** – Carte € 42/49 **s**
♦ Hidden close to the railway arches, away from the city centre. Crescent shaped dining room with bright contemporary art. Modern French and Irish cooking; tasty, unfussy dishes.

XXX **Ristorante Rinuccini** 　　AC VISA ⊕ AE ①
*1 The Parade – ℰ (056) 776 15 75 – www.rinuccini.com – Closed 26-27 December*
**Rest** – Italian – Carte € 30/51
• Named after the 17C papal nunci, this family-owned restaurant is bigger than it looks, and has long been a local favourite. Cooking is classical Italian and service is thoughtful.

XX **Zuni** with rm 　　🛋 📶 & AC 📶 P VISA ⊕ AE
*26 Patrick St – ℰ (056) 772 39 99 – www.zuni.ie – Closed 25 December*
**13 rm** ⌷ – ♦ € 60/90 ♦♦ € 85/150 　**Rest** – Carte € 29/44
• Chic modern restaurant in a great city centre location. Small wood-furnished café-bar opens out into bright room with mirrored walls, leather panels and a terrace to once side. Eclectic modern menus of Irish produce and with a Mediterranean or Asian twist. Bedrooms continue the smart, contemporary theme.

---

**KILLALOE (Cill Dalua)** – Clare – **712** G9 – pop. 1 035 ▌ Ireland　　**38** B2

▶ Dublin 175 km – Ennis 51 km – Limerick 21 km – Tullamore 93 km

👁 Town★ – St Flannan's Cathedral★

🅖 Graves of the Leinstermen (≤★), N : 7.25 km by R 494 – Castleconnell★, S : 16 km by R 494 and R 466 – Clare Glens★, S : 24 km by R 494, R 504 and R 503. Nenagh (Castle★), NE : 19.25 km by R 496 and N 7 – Holy Island★ **AC**, N : 25.75 km by R 463 and boat from Tuamgraney

XX **Cherry Tree** 　　≤ ⟨⟩ P VISA ⊕ AE
*Lakeside, Ballina, follow signs for Lakeside Hotel – ℰ (061) 375 688*
*– www.cherrytreerestaurant.ie – Closed first week January, Good Friday, 25-26 December, Sunday dinner, Sunday lunch November-April and Monday*
**Rest** – *(dinner only and Sunday lunch)* Menu € 26 – Carte € 38/45
• Contemporary, relaxing interior, polite staff and a wide range of original, well-sourced modern Irish dishes on offer from an open kitchen. Seasonal produce of the essence.

---

**KILLARNEY (Cill Airne)** – Kerry – **712** D11 – pop. 14 603 ▌ Ireland　　**38** A2

▶ Dublin 304 km – Cork 87 km – Limerick 111 km – Waterford 180 km

✈ Kerry (Farranfore) Airport : ℰ (066) 976 4644, N : 15.25 km by N 22

ℹ Beech Rd ℰ (064) 663 16 33, www.killarney.ie

Mahoney's Point, ℰ (064) 3 10 34

👁 Town★★ – St Mary's Cathedral★ CX

🅖 Killarney National Park★★★ (Muckross Friary★, Muckross House and Farms★) AZ - Gap of Dunloe★★, SW : 9.5 km by R 562 AZ – Ross Castle★ **AC**, S : 1.5 km by N 71 and minor rd – Torc Waterfall★, S : 8 km by N 71 BZ. Ring of Kerry★★ – Ladies View★★, SW : 19.25 km by N 71 BZ – Moll's Gap★, SW : 25 km by N 71 BZ

Plans pages 934, 935

🏨 **Europe** ⌁ 　　≤ 🚣 ⟨⟩ 🛥 ⅀ 🗔 ⊕ 🎾 ⅃♭ 🛋 & ⚒ 🏊 😊 P VISA ⊕ AE
*Fossa, West : 4.75 km. by R 562 on N 72 – ℰ (064) 667 13 00*
*– www.theeurope.com – 10 May-8 October*
**181 rm** ⌷ – ♦ € 182/264 ♦♦ € 230/278 – 6 suites
**Rest** *Panorama* **Rest** *Brasserie* – see restaurant listing
• Vast hotel in a superb lakeside location, boasting views over Lough Leane and Macgillycuddy's Reeks. Opulent guest areas, impressive events facilities and sublime 3-level spa. Lavishly appointed bedrooms; Lake Rooms afford the best outlook.

## 🏨 Killarney Park

🚗 🖥 🏖 🏊 ⅃♨ ✕ 🍴 ⌖ ➔ 🅰 ᵈ ᵉ 🔌 🅿 VISA ⓿ 🅰🅴

– 𝒞 (064) 663 55 55 – www.killarneyparkhotel.ie
– Closed 24-26 December                                    DX**k**
**65 rm** 🍽 – ♦ € 250/350 ♦♦ € 250/350 – 3 suites
**Rest Park** – see restaurant listing

♦ Large, luxurious hotel run by a keen, well-versed team. Plush library and lavish drawing room; clubby wood-panelled bar for linen-laid lunches. Bedrooms range in style, mixing modern furnishings with original features and offering everything you could want. Smart spa and leisure facilities add to the appeal.

## 🏨 Aghadoe Heights H. and Spa 🐾

≤ 🚗 🖥 🏖 🏊 ⅃♨ ✕ 🍴 🅰 ᵈ

Northwest : 4.5 km. by N 22 – 𝒞 (064) 663 17 66            🔌 🛏 🅿 VISA ⓿ 🅰🅴 ⓪
– www.aghadoeheights.com – Weekends only January-April
**72 rm** 🍽 – ♦ € 105/160 ♦♦ € 160/220 – 2 suites
**Rest Lake Room** – see restaurant listing

♦ Striking glass-fronted hotel in an enviable position, looking out over lakes, mountains and countryside. Luxurious interior with stylish cocktail bar, evening pianist and impressive spa. Spacious bedrooms; most have balconies or terraces.

## 🏨 Ross

🍴 ⌖ 🅰 ᵈ ᵉ 🔌 🅿 VISA ⓿ 🅰🅴

– 𝒞 (064) 663 18 55 – www.theross.ie – Closed 24-26 December            DX**b**
**29 rm** 🍽 – ♦ € 160/220 ♦♦ € 160/275
**Rest Cellar One** – (closed weekdays in winter) (bar lunch) Menu € 36
– Carte € 27/50

♦ Striking modern hotel in the centre of town, overlooking the famous Killarney 'Horse and Carriages'. Contemporary bar and lounge with multi-level design. Stylish, boldly coloured bedrooms are comfortable and well-equipped. Vibrant basement restaurant with curved timbers, intimate lighting and global menu.

REPUBLIC OF IRELAND

The map shows Killarney with streets and points of interest including St Mary's Cathedral, St Mary's Church, Franciscan Friary, Methodist Church, Killarney National Park.

## Cahernane House 🏡

⬅ 🚗 🔧 ✗ 🛏 📶 ♨ 🅿 VISA ⑩ AE ①

*Muckross Rd – ☏ (064) 663 18 95 – www.cahernane.com – Closed December-16 March*                                                                                      AZ**d**

**37 rm** 🍽 – 🛏 € 95/145  🛏🛏 € 140/190 – 1 suite

**Rest** *Herbert Room* – see restaurant listing

◆ Fine Victorian house built in 1877, set in a peaceful location and affording westerly mountain views. Characterful open-fired library and drawing room with stags' heads, portraits and antiques. Bedrooms range from classical to contemporary.

Fancy a last minute break?
Check hotel websites to take advantage of price promotions.

935

### Randles Court ▢ ☆ ▤ ⅢⅢ rest, ᵀⁱ ⅏ 🅿 🆅🅸🆂🅰 ⓪ 🅰🅴 ⓪

*Muckross Rd – ℰ (064) 663 53 33 – www.randlescourt.com – Closed 18-27
December and 2 January-10 February*                                        DY**p**
**75 rm** ⌂ – ♦ € 75/150 ♦♦ € 120/350
**Rest** *Checkers* – *(dinner only and lunch Saturday-Sunday)* Menu € 45 (dinner)
– Carte € 38/51
♦ Family run hotel, centred on a rectory built in 1906. Good leisure facilities.
Rooms, at their best in the modern extension, and comfy lounge subtly reflect
the period style. Good choice of local produce in chequerboard floored restaurant.

### Killarney Royal ▤ ⅢⅢ ᵀⁱ 🆅🅸🆂🅰 ⓪ 🅰🅴 ⓪

*College St – ℰ (064) 663 18 53 – www.killarneyroyal.ie – Closed 25-26 December*
**29 rm** ⌂ – ♦ € 75/169 ♦♦ € 89/225                                      DX**g**
**Rest** – *(bar lunch)* Menu € 21/30 – Carte approx. € 35
♦ Classically styled, centrally located hotel; in the family for four generations.
Large, luxurious bedrooms boast air conditioning and putting machines. Take afternoon tea in the comfy, well-appointed lounge. Bistro-bar displays pleasing Parisian brasserie styling. Formal restaurant offers traditional menu.

### Fairview without rest ▤ ♿ ℂ ᵀⁱ 🆅🅸🆂🅰 ⓪ 🅰🅴

*College St. – ℰ (064) 663 41 64 – www.fairviewkillarney.com – Closed 24-25
December*                                                                 DX**a**
**29 rm** ⌂ – ♦ € 60/110 ♦♦ € 90/250
♦ Stylish townhouse with smart, leather furnished lounge. Bright, up-to-date bedrooms exude distinctively individualistic flourishes; penthouse has whirlpool bath
and roof terrace.

### Earls Court House without rest ◺ ▤ ♿ ℂ 🅿 🆅🅸🆂🅰 ⓪ 🅰🅴

*Woodlawn Rd. – ℰ (064) 663 40 09 – www.killarney-earlscourt.ie – 15
February-15 November*                                                     DY**t**
**30 rm** ⌂ – ♦ € 100/120 ♦♦ € 120/180
♦ Large, well-run hotel behind an unassuming façade. Afternoon tea served on
arrival, in one of two comfortable, antique-furnished lounges. Spacious bedrooms feature half-tester or four-poster beds and some have balconies and
mountain views.

### Kathleens Country House without rest ◺ ⅏ ᵀⁱ 🅿 🆅🅸🆂🅰 ⓪ 🅰🅴

*Madams Height, Tralee Rd., North : 3.75 km. on N 22 – ℰ (064) 663 28 10
– www.kathleens.net – May-September*
**17 rm** ⌂ – ♦ € 55/90 ♦♦ € 105/140
♦ Cosy lounge with broad, pine-backed armchairs facing an open fire and neat
bedrooms in traditional patterns – an extended house run by the eponymous
owner for over 20 years.

### Killarney Lodge without rest ◺ ⅢⅢ ⅏ ᵀⁱ 🅿 🆅🅸🆂🅰 ⓪ 🅰🅴

*Countess Rd. – ℰ (064) 663 64 99 – www.killarneylodge.net – 10 March-October*
**16 rm** ⌂ – ♦ € 85/95 ♦♦ € 100/130                                      DX**u**
♦ Modern house close to the town centre, run by a welcoming couple. Immaculately kept, well-furnished bedrooms; No.6 boasts lovely mountain views. Bright
little breakfast room where homemade bread and scones feature. Afternoon tea
on arrival.

### XXXX Panorama – at Europe Hotel ≤ ◺ 🕭 ♿ 🅿 🆅🅸🆂🅰 ⓪ 🅰🅴

*Fossa, West : 4.75 km. by R 562 on N 72 – ℰ (064) 667 13 00
– www.theeurope.com – 10 May-8 October*
**Rest** – *(closed Sunday dinner)* Carte € 42/59
♦ Large, formal restaurant in a luxuriously appointed hotel. Panoramic windows
afford superb views across the lough towards the mountains. Classical, international menu offers plenty of choice.

XXXX **Park** – at Killarney Park Hotel    ⟨icons⟩
   – 𝒞 (064) 663 55 55 – www.killarneyparkhotel.ie
   – Closed 24-26 December     DX**k**
   **Rest** – (dinner only) Menu € 55 – Carte € 32/58
   ♦ Elegant fine dining restaurant boasting chandeliers, ornate cornicing and linen-laid tables, set in a luxurious hotel. Menus are distinctly classical in style. A pianist completes the picture.

XXX **Lake Room** – at Aghadoe Heights Hotel and Spa    ⟨icons⟩
   Northwest : 4.5 km. by N 22 – 𝒞 (064) 663 17 66
   – www.aghadoeheights.com – Weekends only January-April
   **Rest** – Menu € 55 (dinner) – Carte € 45/55
   ♦ Set in a luxury hotel and boasting a stylish cocktail bar and lounge with evening pianist. Stunning panoramic views over the lakes and mountains. Classical dishes executed with a modern touch.

XX **Cucina Italiana**    ⟨icons⟩
   17 St Anthonys Pl – 𝒞 (064) 662 65 75
   – Closed January-February     DX**c**
   **Rest** – Italian – (dinner only) Menu € 28 (early dinner) – Carte € 33/54
   ♦ Stylish, modern restaurant set over two floors, in the centre of town. Hearty, authentic Italian cooking has a strong Neapolitan feel and features plenty of daily specials. Effective service from smart Italian staff.

XX **Chapter Forty**    ⟨icons⟩
   40 New St. – 𝒞 (064) 66 71 833 – www.chapter40.ie – Closed 24-26
   December, Sunday and Monday     CX**a**
   **Rest** – (dinner only) Menu € 25/35 – Carte € 31/48
   ♦ Contemporary, split-level restaurant with rich burgundy walls, polished wood floors and smart high-backed cream chairs. Visually appealing, classically based dishes are prepared with a lightness of touch; try the 'tasting plate' starter.

XX **Brasserie** – at Europe Hotel    ⟨icons⟩
   Fossa, West : 4.75 km. by R 562 on N 72 – 𝒞 (064) 667 13 00
   – www.theeurope.com – 10 May-8 October
   **Rest** – Carte € 32/64 **s**
   ♦ Set within a luxurious, lakeside hotel, a modern take on a classical brasserie. Accessible all-day menu ranges from light snacks to steaks cooked on an open grill. Terrace for alfresco dining.

XX **Herbert Room** – at Cahernane House Hotel    ⟨icons⟩
   Muckross Rd – 𝒞 (064) 663 18 95 – www.cahernane.com – 17 March-November
   **Rest** – (closed Sunday-Monday except in summer) Menu € 35/48    AZ**d**
   – Carte approx. € 30
   ♦ Formal hotel restaurant and atmospheric bar, set within a fine Victorian house in a pleasant rural location. Classically based dishes display some modern influences. Excellent mountain views.

**at Beaufort** West : 9.75 km by N 72 off Glencar rd – ✉ Killarney

🏠 **Dunloe Castle** ॐ    ⟨icons⟩
   – 𝒞 (064) 664 41 11 – www.thedunloe.com – April-October
   **100 rm** 🖵 – ♦ € 160/210 ♦♦ € 180/230 – 2 suites
   **Rest** – (light lunch) Carte € 26/63 **s**
   ♦ Creeper-clad modern hotel offers sizeable, well-equipped rooms and smart conference suites, not forgetting an impressive view of the Gap of Dunloe and Macgilllicuddy's Reeks. Restaurant serves Irish classic dishes.

## KILLENARD – Laois – 712 D11

▶ Dublin 48 km – Portlaoise 19 km – Naas 25 km – Carlow 36 km

**Heritage**     🚗 🐾 ⚓ 🖼 🍷 🏠 🎣 ✖ 🎦 🔌 🛗 rm, 🚹 🄰🄲 🕴 ☎ 🧖 **P**
– ℰ *(057) 864 55 00* – *www.theheritage.com* – *Closed 20-26*    **VISA** **⑩** **AE**
*December*
**95 rm** ⏢ – 🛉 € 325 🛉🛉 € 325/550 – 3 suites
**Rest** *Sol Oriens* – see restaurant listing
**Rest** *Arlington* – *(dinner only and Sunday lunch)* Menu € 45 **s**
◆ Vast resort hotel with plush, spacious interior. Impressive range of facilities, from huge conference centre, superb leisure club and spa to outdoor pursuits and Ballesteros-designed golf course. Beautifully furnished, sumptuous bedrooms. Traditional fine dining in Arlington and family friendly atmosphere in Italian Sol Oriens.

✖ **Sol Oriens** – at Heritage Hotel     🚗 🐾 🄰🄲 **P** **VISA** **⑩** **AE**
– ℰ *(057) 864 55 00* – *www.theheritage.com* – *Closed 20-26 December, Monday and Tuesday*
**Rest** – Italian – *(dinner only)* Carte € 23/42
◆ Purpose-built Italian restaurant located in the grounds of a vast resort hotel. Informal, family friendly room with open-plan kitchen. Menu offers a range of pizzas, pastas and Irish steaks.

## KILMALLOCK (Cill Mocheallóg) – Limerick – 712 G10 – pop. 1 443

🛡 Ireland

▶ Dublin 212 km – Limerick 34 km – Tipperary 32 km

◎ Abbey★ - Collegiate Church★

◉ Lough Gur Interpretive Centre★ **AC**, N : 16 km by R 512 and minor road
– Monasteranenagh Abbey★, N : 24 km by R 512 to Holycross and minor road W

⌂ **Flemingstown House** ⌖     ⩽ 🚗 🖼 **P** **VISA** **⑩**
*Southeast : 4 km on R 512* – ℰ *(063) 98 093* – *www.flemingstown.com*
– *February-October*
**5 rm** ⏢ – 🛉 € 70 🛉🛉 € 120   **Rest** – *(residents only)* Carte € 40/45
◆ Creeper clad, extended 19C house in centre of 200 acre working farm. The attractively decorated bedrooms boast countryside vistas and pieces of antique furniture. Satisfying homemade fare served in comfy dining room.

## KINLOUGH (Cionn Locha) – Leitrim – 712 H4 – pop. 690

▶ Dublin 220 km – Ballyshannon 11 km – Sligo 34 km

✖ **Courthouse** with rm     📶 **VISA** **⑩**
*Main St.* – ℰ *(071) 984 23 91* – *www.thecourthouserest.com* – *Closed 1 week spring and 24-26 December*
**4 rm** ⏢ – 🛉 € 35/45 🛉🛉 € 70/80
**Rest** – Italian – *(dinner only and Sunday lunch)* Menu € 25 – Carte € 35/45
◆ Former courthouse with stained glass entrance. Sardinian chef-owner creates extensive, seasonally changing classical menu of honest, authentic Italian dishes – including local fish/shellfish. Informal atmosphere; friendly service. Simple, good value bedrooms.

## KINSALE (Cionne tSáile) – Cork – 712 G12 – pop. 4 099 🛡 Ireland

▶ Dublin 286 km – Cork 27 km

🛈 Pier Rd ℰ *(021) 4 77 22 34, www.kinsale.ie*

◎ Town★★ – St Multose Church★ Y – Kinsale Regional Museum★ **AC** Y **M1**

◉ Kinsale Harbour★ ( ⩽★ from St Catherine's Anglican Church, Charles Fort★).
Carbery Coast★, W : 61 km by R 600

REPUBLIC OF IRELAND

```
R 600 (N 27) CORK
R 600
```

CARMELITE

Lower Catholic Way

Cork

ST JOHN'S

Friars St.

The New Rd

The Glen

Hill

Barrack

Featherbed

Lane

Road

Eastern Quay

Long Quay

River Rd

High Rd

Pearse St.

ST-MULTOSE

The

The Ramparts

Blind

Winter's Hill

Gate

The Mall

O'Connell St.

Compass Hill

Lower Road

**KINSALE**

TOWN PARK

Pier

KINSALE

HARBOUR

Pier Head

CASTLE PARK

**REPUBLIC OF IRELAND**

0        200 m
0        200 yards

**Perryville House** without rest

Long Quay – ℰ (021) 477 27 31 – www.perryvillehouse.com – 15 April-October
**22 rm** ⊇ – ♦ € 120/150 ♦♦ € 200/300                              **Yf**
• Luxuriously appointed house in the heart of town, overlooking the harbour; named after the family that built it in 1820. Two antique-furnished drawing rooms, smart boutique and coffee shop. Tastefully styled bedrooms; 'Luxury' boast feature beds, chic bathrooms and harbour views. Comprehensive breakfasts.

**Blue Haven**

3-4 Pearse St – ℰ (021) 477 22 09 – www.bluehavenkinsale.com – Closed 25 December                                                              **Yc**
**17 rm** ⊇ – ♦ € 65/140 ♦♦ € 110/190
**Rest** *Fish market* – see restaurant listing
**Rest** *Bistro* – Menu € 40 – Carte € 26/47
• Small but well-established hotel right in the heart of town. Cosy, vibrant interior features interesting artwork. Comfortable bedrooms are named after vineyards and have a subtle contemporary edge. Chic, clubby lounge with art deco styling; adjoining all-day bistro resembles the hull of an upturned boat.

## Old Bank Townhouse without rest

10-11 Pearse St. – *(021) 477 40 75 – www.oldbankhousekinsale.com – Closed 24-25 December*  Yd

**16 rm** – ✦ € 65/140 ✦✦ € 110/190 – 1 suite

• Substantial Georgian townhouse in the heart of town. The local post office and a café (where breakfast is served) occupy the ground floor; above is cosy, classically furnished lounge. Traditional bedrooms; No.17 boasts great harbour views.

## Old Presbytery without rest

43 Cork St. – *(021) 477 20 27 – www.oldpres.com – mid-February to mid-November*  Ya

**9 rm** – ✦ € 70/120 ✦✦ € 90/180

• 18C building once housing priests from the nearby church; a few ecclesiastical pieces remain. Cosy lounge with piano and gramophone; upstairs breakfast room boasts unusual chairs. Bedrooms feature brass or cast iron beds and Irish pine.

## Desmond House without rest

42 Cork St. – *(021) 477 35 35 – www.desmondhousekinsale.com – 10 March-October*  Yx

**4 rm** – ✦ € 70/100 ✦✦ € 100/140

• Built by a Spanish merchant in 1780 and once belonging to the church – it still displays a tiny alter on the landing. Attractive, parquet-floored breakfast room, where homemade bread and scones feature. Comfortable bedrooms boast jacuzzis.

## Max's

48 Main St. – *(021) 477 24 43 – www.maxs.ie – Closed mid-December-March, Sunday except June-September and Tuesday*  Zm

**Rest** – Seafood – *(dinner only)* Carte € 35/49

• Intimate restaurant on quaint main street; well-known by locals. Simple yet smart interior with polished floor and part-panelled walls. Unfussy, classical seafood menu offers good choice, try the 'Fresh Catches'. Efficient, engaging team.

## Fish market – at Blue Haven Hotel

3-4 Pearse St – *(021) 477 22 09 – www.bluehavenkinsale.com – Closed 25 December*  Yc

**Rest** – Menu € 25/35 – Carte € 29/50

• Informal restaurant located in small, well-run hotel in the town centre. Original artwork hangs on the walls. Seafood-orientated menu specialises in fresh fish and shellfish from local waters.

## Fishy Fishy Cafe

Pier Rd – *(021) 470 04 15 – www.fishyfishy.ie*  Zx

**Rest** – Seafood – *(bookings not accepted at lunch)* Carte € 33/39 s

• Friendly informal restaurant that's a local institution. Dine at the bar and watch the kitchen shuck oysters, in the main room amongst 'fishy' memorabilia or alfresco on the lovely terrace. Concise, all-day menus offer well-prepared, good value seafood dishes and tasty specials; owner collects the fish daily.

## Toddies at The Bulman

Summercove, East : 2 km. by R 600 – *(021) 477 21 31 – www.thebulman.ie – Closed 25 December, Good Friday and Sunday dinner*

**Rest** – Carte € 25/45

• Rustic pub with nautical theme and views over Kinsale and the bay. Lunch, served in the bar, offers simple pub classics; dinner, in the more formal restaurant, presents carefully prepared, globally influenced dishes.

**at Barrells Cross** Southwest : 5.75 km on R 600 - Z – ✉ Kinsale

🏠 **Rivermount House** without rest 🌿     ⟨ 🛏 🐾 ⚙ 📶 **P**
Northeast : 0.75 km. – ℘ (021) 477 80 33 – www.rivermount.com – 16 March-October
**6 rm** – † € 50/90 †† € 80/90
♦ Spacious, purpose-built house overlooking the River Bandon, not far from the town. Distinctive modern style throughout, with attractive embossed wallpapers, quality furnishings and designer touches. Bedrooms display high attention to detail and boast immaculate bathrooms.

---

**KNOCK (An Cnoc)** – Mayo – **712** F6 – pop. 745 📘 Ireland     **36** B2
▶ Dublin 212 – Galway 74 – Westport 51
🛫 Ireland West Airport, Knock : ℘ (094) 9368100, NE : 14.5 km by N 17
ℹ Town Centre ℘ (094) 9 38 81 93, www.discoverireland.ie
👁 Basilica of our Lady, Queen of Ireland ★
🅖 Museum of Country Life ★★ **AC**, NW : 26 km by R 323, R 321 and N 5

Hotels see : **Cong** SW : 58 km by N 17, R 331 R 334 and R 345

---

**LAHINCH (An Leacht)** – Clare – **712** D9 – pop. 607 📘 Ireland     **38** B1
▶ Dublin 260 km – Galway 79 km – Limerick 66 km
⛳ Lahinch, ℘ (065) 7 08 10 03
🅖 Spanish Point Miltown Malbay, ℘ (065) 7 08 42 19
🅖 Cliffs of Moher ★★★ – Kilfenora (Burren Centre ★ **AC**, High Crosses ★), NE : 11 km by N 85 and R 481

🏨 **Vaughan Lodge**     🛏 📶 ⚙ ⚙ 📶 **P** 𝖵𝖨𝖲𝖠 ⦿ 𝖠𝖤 ⓪
Ennistymon Rd – ℘ (065) 708 11 11 – www.vaughanlodge.ie – April-October
**20 rm** ⌷ – † € 95/155 †† € 130/260
**Rest** – (closed Sunday and Monday) (dinner only) Carte € 34/62
♦ Stylish roadside hotel. Bright, modern interior boasts a leather-furnished lounge with flat screen TV and plenty of malts behind the bar. Smart, spacious bedrooms – in browns and creams – offer good facilities. Linen-laid dining room serves seafood-based menus.

🏠 **Moy House** 🌿     ⟨ 🛏 🐾 ⚙ **P** 𝖵𝖨𝖲𝖠 ⦿ 𝖠𝖤 ⓪
Southwest : 3 km on N 67 (Milltown Malbay rd) – ℘ (065) 708 28 00
– www.moyhouse.com – March-October
**8 rm** ⌷ – † € 145/250 †† € 225/280 – 1 suite
**Rest** – (dinner only) Menu € 55
♦ Italian-style clifftop villa, overlooking the bay. Traditional interior with a comfy drawing room, honesty bar and small library; antiques, oil paintings and heavy fabrics/drapes feature. Individually designed, classically styled bedrooms boast good extras; most have views. Friendly, attentive service. Formal dining.

---

**LEENANE (An Líonán)** – Galway – **712** C7 – ✉ Clifden 📘 Ireland     **36** A3
▶ Dublin 278 km – Ballina 90 km – Galway 66 km
👁 Killary Harbour ★
🅖 Joyce Country ★★ – Lough Nafooey ★, SE : 10.5 km by R 336 – Aasleagh Falls ★, NE : 4 km. Connemara ★★★ – Lough Corrib ★★, SE : 16 km by R 336 and R 345 – Doo Lough Pass ★, NW : 14.5 km by N 59 and R 335

🏠 **Delphi Lodge** 🌿     ⟨ 🛏 🐾 ⚙ 📶 🛏 **P** 𝖵𝖨𝖲𝖠 ⦿
Northwest : 13.25 km by N 59 on Louisburgh rd – ℘ (095) 42 222
– www.delphilodge.ie
**12 rm** ⌷ – † € 132 †† € 198/264   **Rest** – Menu € 49
♦ Georgian sporting lodge in a stunning loughside setting with extensive gardens and grounds. Haven for fishermen. Country house feel and simple bedrooms. Communal dining table: fisherman with the day's best catch sits at its head.

REPUBLIC OF IRELAND

## LEIGHLINBRIDGE (Leithghlinn an Droichid) Carlow – Carlow — 39 D2
– 712 L9 – pop. 674

▶ Dublin 63 km – Carlow 8 km – Kilkenny 16 km – Athy 22 km

### 🏠 Lord Bagenal     🛉 ♿ 🆑 ⚓ ⓦ 🛁 P VISA ⚫ AE ⓘ
*Main St – ℰ (059) 977 40 00 – www.lordbagenal.com – Closed 25-26 December*
**39 rm** ⚏ – 🛉 € 65/85 🛉🛉 € 110/190   **Rest** – *(carving lunch)* Menu € 35
♦ Eye-catching hotel on the banks of the River Barrow; originally a coaching inn, now with vast modern extensions. Characterful bar and excellent collection of Irish art on display throughout. Up-to-date bedrooms. Traditional menus in Lord Bagenal bar and restaurant.

## LETTERFRACK (Leitir Fraic) – Galway – 712 C7 ▓ Ireland — 36 A3

▶ Dublin 304 km – Ballina 111 km – Galway 91 km

◉ Connemara★★★ - Sky Road★★ (≤★★) – Connemara National Park★ – Kylemore Abbey★, E : 4.75 km by N 59

### 🏠 Rosleague Manor ⚜     ≤ 🐎 ⚓ ⓦ 🛁 P VISA ⚫
*West : 2.5 km. on N 59 – ℰ (095) 41 101 – www.rosleague.com*
*– mid-March-mid-November*
**20 rm** ⚏ – 🛉 € 80/155 🛉🛉 € 130/250   **Rest** – *(dinner only)* Carte € 34/44
♦ Foliage-clad country house in mature grounds, boasting excellent bay and mountain views. Spacious, antique-filled drawing rooms and wicker-furnished conservatory. Large, classically styled bedrooms with flat screen TVs. Formal dining room overlooks the gardens.

## LETTERKENNY (Leitir Ceanainn) – Donegal – 712 I3 – pop. 17 586 — 37 C1
▓ Ireland

▶ Dublin 241 km – Londonderry 34 km – Sligo 116 km

🛈 Neil T Blaney Rd ℰ (074) 9 12 11 60, www.letterkennyguide.com

🏌 Dunfanaghy, ℰ (074) 913 63 35

◉ Glenveagh National Park★★ (Gardens★★), NW : 19.25 km by R 250, R 251 and R 254 – Grianan of Aileach★★ (≤★★) NE : 28 km by N 13 – Church Hill (Glebe House and Gallery★ **AC**) NW : 16 km by R 250

### 🏠 Radisson Blu     🖼 ⚘ 🆚 🛉 ♿ 🆑 rest, ⚓ ⓦ 🛁 P VISA ⚫ AE ⓘ
*Paddy Harte Rd – ℰ (074) 919 44 44 – www.radissonblu.ie/hotel-letterkenny*
**114 rm** ⚏ – 🛉 € 55/155 🛉🛉 € 89/220
**Rest** – *(early dinner and Sunday lunch)* Menu € 28 **s** – Carte € 25/38 **s**
♦ Corporate accommodation on the edge of town. Bedrooms are identically appointed, all are clean, modern and spacious, and 'Business Class' come with extras. Bar serves all-purpose, daily changing menu. Brasserie-style dining room offers dishes to match.

## LIMERICK (Luimneach) – Limerick – 712 G9 – pop. 90 757 ▓ Ireland — 38 B2

▶ Dublin 193 km – Cork 93 km

✈ Shannon Airport : ℰ (061) 712000, W : 25.75 km by N 18 Z

🛈 Arthur's Quay ℰ (061) 3 17 52 2Y, www.limericktourist.com

◎ City★★ - St Mary's Cathedral★ Y – Hunt Museum★★ **AC** Y - Georgian House★ **AC** Z – King John's Castle★ **AC** Y - Limerick Museum★ Z **M2** – John Square★ Z **20** – St John's Cathedral★ Z

◉ Bunratty Castle★★ **AC**, W : 12 km by N 18 – Cratloe Wood (≤★) NW : 8 km by N 18 Z. Castleconnell★, E : 11.25 km by N 7 - Lough Gur Interpretive Centre★ **AC**, S : 17.75 km by R 512 and R 514 Z – Clare Glens★, E : 21 km by N 7 and R 503 Y – Monasteranenagh Abbey★, S : 21 km by N 20 Z

KILLALOE R 463

REPUBLIC OF IRELAND

DUBLIN R 445 NENAGH

WATERFORD Z TIPPERARY (N 24) R 512 FERMOY

LIMERICK

300 m
300 yards

CORK N 20 (N 21) TRALEE

## Savoy

🖥 🛏 ⅃⚹ 🍴 ⚹ AC 📶 🏊 P VISA ⚫⚫ AE

Zc

*Henry St.* – 𝒞 *(061) 448 700* – *www.savoylimerick.com*

**94 rm** – 🛏 € 99/155 🛏🛏 € 155/250, ⚏ €14

**Rest** *Market Square Brasserie* – see restaurant listing

• Corporate hotel named after the theatre that previously stood on the site. Spacious guest areas and bar; good-sized, uniform bedrooms with smart, modern bathrooms. Hands-on owner and his charming team provide good old-fashioned hospitality.

943

### Limerick Strand    ⫷ 🖼 🏛 🛏 🖼 🚲 Ⓐ🅒 🍸 📶 🦽 🚗 𝗩𝗜𝗦𝗔 ⓒⓞ 🅰🅔 ⓞ

Ennis Rd. – 𝒞 (061) 421 800 – www.strandlimerick.ie – Closed 25 December
**184 rm** – 🛏 € 89/179 🛏🛏 € 89/179, 🖵 €12
**Rest** *River Restaurant* – (bar lunch) Menu € 25/27 – Carte € 26/43    Y2

♦ Extensive function and leisure facilities. Modern bedrooms come in dark wood and autumnal browns and oranges; Junior suites have balconies. Terrace bar overlooks River Shannon. River Restaurant serves mix of traditional and more modern dishes.

### Absolute H. & Spa    🏠 🖼 🏛 🛏 🚲 rm, Ⓐ🅒 🍸 ☏ 🦽 🚗 𝗩𝗜𝗦𝗔 ⓒⓞ 🅰🅔 ⓞ

Sir Harry's Mall – 𝒞 (061) 463 600 – www.absolutehotel.com    Ya
**99 rm** – 🛏 € 199 🛏🛏 € 199, 🖵 €12.50   **Rest** – Menu € 17/25 – Carte € 22/39

♦ Stylish, modern hotel and spa on outskirts of city centre; designed like an old mill to reflect the area's industrial heritage. Clever use of space in light-coloured bedrooms. Restaurant serves traditional menu and overlooks river.

### Radisson Blu H. & Spa    🖼 🖼 🏛 🛏 🍴 🖼 🚲 Ⓐ🅒 rest, 🍸 📶 🦽 🅿

Ennis Rd, Northwest : 6.5 km by N 18 – 𝒞 (061) 456 200    𝗩𝗜𝗦𝗔 ⓒⓞ 🅰🅔 ⓞ
– www.radissonblu.ie/hotel-limerick
**152 rm** – 🛏 € 79/159 🛏🛏 € 89/169, 🖵 €10 – 2 suites
**Rest** *Porters* – (buffet lunch) Carte € 28/45

♦ Modern hotel with tastefully used chrome and wood interiors. Well-equipped conference rooms and a leisure centre which includes tennis court. Smart, state-of-the-art bedrooms. Informal Porters restaurant with traditional menus.

### No 1 Pery Square    🖼 🖼 🍸 📶 𝗩𝗜𝗦𝗔 ⓒⓞ 🅰🅔

Pery Sq – 𝒞 (061) 402 402 – www.oneperysquare.com    Za
**19 rm** 🖵 – 🛏 € 89/195 🛏🛏 € 89/195 – 1 suite
**Rest** *Brasserie One* – see restaurant listing

♦ Charming, personally run house in the historic Georgian quarter of the city. Beautiful spa facility and wine shop in cellar. Well-proportioned, luxuriously appointed bedrooms.

### ✕✕ Brasserie One – at No 1 Pery Square Hotel    𝗩𝗜𝗦𝗔 ⓒⓞ 🅰🅔

Pery Sq – 𝒞 (061) 402 402 – www.oneperysquare.com – Closed dinner Sunday and Monday    Za
**Rest** – Menu € 25/29 – Carte € 25/48

♦ Set on first floor of hotel, with well-spaced tables, Georgian-style furniture and semi-open kitchen. Tasty bistro dishes with a modern slant. Good service from a well-versed team.

### ✕✕ Market Square Brasserie – at Savoy Hotel    Ⓐ🅒 𝗩𝗜𝗦𝗔 ⓒⓞ 🅰🅔

Henry St. – 𝒞 (061) 316 311 – www.savoylimerick.com – Closed 25 December, Sunday, Monday and bank holidays    Ze
**Rest** – (dinner only) (booking essential) Menu € 49 – Carte € 50/60

♦ Richly decorated restaurant that's relocated to the Savoy Hotel. Intimate atmosphere created by fabric-covered walls and low lighting. Modern menus offer good quality produce and a variety of textures in hearty, boldly flavoured dishes.

---

## LISCANNOR (Lios Ceannúir) – Clare – **712** D9 – pop. 71 ▌ Ireland    **38** B1

▶ Dublin 272 km – Ennistimmon 9 km – Limerick 72 km

◉ Cliffs of Moher★★★, NW : 8 km by R 478 – Kilfenora (Burren Centre★ **AC**, High Crosses★), NE : 18 km by R 478, N 67 and R 481

### Vaughan's Anchor Inn with rm    🏠 🍸 🅿 𝗩𝗜𝗦𝗔 ⓒⓞ

Main St – 𝒞 (065) 708 15 48 – www.vaughans.ie – Closed 25 December
**7 rm** 🖵 – 🛏 € 50 🛏🛏 € 70   **Rest** – Seafood – Carte € 28/48

♦ Lively, family-run pub in a picturesque fishing village near the Cliffs of Moher. Old favourites at lunch and more elaborate meals in the evening, with the emphasis firmly on seafood. Bedrooms boast bright local artwork, colourful throws and modern bathrooms.

**LISDOONVARNA** (Lios Dúin Bhearna) – Clare – **712** E8 – pop. 767    **38** B1

▌ Ireland

▶ Dublin 268 km – Galway 63 km – Limerick 75 km

◉ The Burren★★ (Cliffs of Moher★★★, Scenic Route★★, Aillwee Cave★ **AC** (Waterfall★★), Corcomroe Abbey★, Kilfenora Crosses★)

---

🏠 | **Sheedy's Country House**     🚐 ⚹ rm, 🎏 📶 **P** 🚾 ⓪ ⒶⒺ
– *𝒞 (065) 707 40 26 – www.sheedys.com – Easter-September*
**11 rm** ⌷ – ♦ € 100/200 ♦♦ € 119/200
**Rest** – *(dinner only) (booking essential for non-residents)* Carte € 35/50
♦ Mustard-yellow house in village centre, with kitchen garden in front. Comfy library, wicker-furnished sun lounge and traditional bar. Bedrooms display plain décor with flowery fabrics and good facilities. Classical menu offered in dining room; exacting service.

---

🏠 | **Wild Honey Inn** with rm     🚐 ⚹ rm, 🚾 ⓪
③ | *South : 0.5 km on Ennistimon rd – 𝒞 (065) 707 43 00 – www.wildhoneyinn.com*
*– Closed January-12 February, 24-26 December, and restricted opening November-December and February-April*
**14 rm** ⌷ – ♦ € 55/60 ♦♦ € 80/90
**Rest** – *(closed lunch Monday and Tuesday) (bookings not accepted)*
Carte € 24/40
♦ Roadside inn close to the limestone landscape of The Burren and the Cliffs of Moher. Short, simple lunch menu; wider selection of classics at dinner. Specials best display the chef's talent and are truly satisfying. Neatly kept, simply furnished bedrooms and comfortable residents' lounge; ground floor rooms have patios.

---

**LISMORE** (Lios Mór) – Waterford – **712** I11 – pop. 1 240    **39** C2

▶ Dublin 227 km – Cork 56 km – Fermoy 26 km

---

✕ | **O'Brien Chop House**     🏠 🚾 ⓪
③ | *Main St – 𝒞 (058) 53 810 – www.obrienchophouse.ie – Closed Monday-Tuesday except July-August, Wednesday-Thursday in low season and Sunday dinner except before bank holidays*
**Rest** – *(booking advisable)* Menu € 25 (weekdays) – Carte € 28/45
♦ Timeless Victorian bar leading through to a rustic restaurant with bare wooden floorboards and whitewashed walls. Very appealing, value-for-money menu offers wholesome Irish dishes, which make excellent use of locally sourced produce. Polite, friendly service.

---

**LISTOWEL** (Lios Tuathail) – Kerry – **712** D10 – pop. 4 338 ▌ Ireland    **38** B2

▶ Dublin 270 km – Killarney 54 km – Limerick 75 km – Tralee 27 km

ℹ St John's Church 𝒞 (068) 2 25 90, www.listowel.ie

◉ Ardfert★ **AC**, SW : 32 km by N 69 and minor roads via Abbeydorney – Banna Strand★, SW : 35 km by N 69 and minor roads via Abbeydorney – Carrigafoyle Castle★, N : 17 km by R 552 and minor road – Glin Castle★ **AC**, N : 24 km by N 69 – Rattoo Round Tower★, W : 19 km by R 553, R 554 and R 551

---

✕ | **Allo's Bistro** with rm     🏠 🚾 ⓪
*41 Church St – 𝒞 (068) 22 880 – Closed Good Friday, 25-26 December, Sunday and Monday*
**3 rm** – ♦ € 50/60 ♦♦ € 70/90    **Rest** – *(booking essential)* Carte € 28/40
♦ Former pub, now a simple, well-run restaurant with characterful feel. Series of homely rooms and friendly, efficient service. Wide-ranging menus rely on regional produce, with theme nights Thursdays and adventurous gourmet menu at weekends. Individually designed, antique-furnished bedrooms boast feature beds.

▶ Dublin 124 km – Drogheda 120 km – Galway 112 km – Limerick 175 km
**i** Market Square  𝒞 (043) 4 25 77, www.longfordtourism.ie

🏠 **Viewmount House** ⚓     🚗 ᴧ ⚒ ⚑ **P** **VISA** **🅾🅾** **AE**
*Dublin Rd, Southeast : 1.5 km by R 393 – 𝒞 (043) 334 19 19*
*– www.viewmounthouse.com*
**14 rm** 🛏 – **†** € 50/70 **††** € 100/140 – 5 suites
**Rest VM** – *(closed Good Friday, 25 December, Sunday dinner, Monday and Tuesday) (dinner only and Sunday lunch)* Menu € 35 *(early dinner Wednesday-Thursday)*/53
♦ Fine Georgian house in 4 acres, with charming period style and many original features still on display. Ornate vaulted ceiling in breakfast room; impressive staircase leads to the lounge. Bedrooms boast antique beds – opt for a duplex room. Rustic formal dining room set in the old stables; traditional menu.

---

▶ Dublin 14 km – Drogheda 38 km
**27** Beechwood The Grange,  𝒞 (01) 846 16 11
◎ Castle★★
◎ Newbridge House★ **AC**, N : 8 km by R 106, M1 and minor road

XXX **Bon Appétit** (Oliver Dunne)     **AC** **VISA** **🅾🅾** **AE**
🟢 *9 St James Ter, (1st floor) – 𝒞 (01) 845 0314 – www.bonappetit.ie – Closed first 2 weeks January, first 2 weeks August, and Sunday-Tuesday*
**Rest** – Modern – *(dinner only) (booking essential)* Menu € 60
**Spec.** Oxtail and apricot croquette, black truffle mayonnaise and celeriac purée. Roast halibut with creamed broccoli and Morteau sausage. Raspberry tartlet with lemon curd and ginger ice cream.
♦ Set in a delightful converted Georgian terrace. Sumptuous, subtly lit bar and elegant, formal dining room with fine china and linen-laid tables. Cooking uses classic combinations and has a French accent. Efficient service, with good attention to detail.

XX **Jaipur**     **AC** **VISA** **🅾🅾** **AE** **①**
*5 St James Terr – 𝒞 (01) 845 5455 – www.jaipur.ie – Closed 25 December*
**Rest** – Indian – *(dinner only)* Carte € 27/43
♦ Basement restaurant in terraced Georgian parade. Tasty, contemporary Indian cooking with Tandoori Jhinga (large prawns marinated in Indian spices) a speciality. Friendly, efficient service.

XX **Brasserie at Bon Appétit**     **AC** **VISA** **🅾🅾** **AE**
*9 St James Terr., (basement) – 𝒞 (01) 845 0314 – www.bonappetit.ie – Closed Sunday dinner and Monday*
**Rest** – *(dinner only and Sunday lunch) (booking essential)* Menu € 24/30 – Carte € 31/40
♦ Stylish modern restaurant in the basement of a terraced Georgian house, below the more formal 'Bon Appétit'. Largely modern dishes on the menu with a few French classics; selection of small plates in trendy bar. Pleasant, efficient service.

---

▶ Dublin 240 km – Cork 34 km – Killarney 64 km – Limerick 66 km
**18** Ballyellis,  𝒞 (022) 2 11 45
◎ Town★ – St James' Church★
◎ Annes Grove Gardens★, E : 17.75 km by N 72 and minor rd – Buttevant Friary★, N : 11.25 km by N 20 – Doneraile Wildlife Park★ **AC**, NE : 9.5 km by N 20 and R 581 – Kanturk★ (Castle★), W : 16 km by N 72 and R 576

**Longueville House** ✍
*West : 5.5 km by N 72 – ☎ (022) 47 156 – www.longuevillehouse.ie – Closed 25-27 December*
**20 rm** 🖃 – ♦ € 85/150 ♦♦ € 180/190
**Rest** *Presidents* – *(closed Monday and Tuesday) (dinner only and Sunday lunch) (booking essential)* Menu € 50 (weekdays)/65
◆ Part-Georgian manor house built in William and Mary style, set in mature grounds and affording pleasant views over Dromineen Castle. Lovely oak-floored hall, superb flying staircase and stunning drawing room hung with chandeliers. Well-appointed bedrooms boast antique furniture and a high level of facilities. Grand restaurant; accomplished, elaborate French cooking.

---

# MIDLETON (Mainistir na Corann) – Cork – 712 H12 – pop. 10 048       39 C3
▶ Dublin 259 km – Cork 19 km – Waterford 98 km
🔢 Jameson Heritage Centre ☎ (021) 4 61 37 02, www.midletononline.com
🔢 East Cork Gortacrue, ☎ (021) 4 63 16 87
🔢 Cloyne Cathedral ★ **AC**, S : 8 km by R 630 and R 629

✗ **Farmgate Restaurant & Country Store**       VISA ⓒⓞ ⓞ
*Coolbawn – ☎ (021) 463 27 71 – www.farmgate.ie – Closed 24 December-3 January, Sunday and Monday*
**Rest** – Carte € 21/48
◆ Busy and appealingly rustic, with entrance through shop and local art on display. Market-bought produce, simply cooked; perhaps an Irish stew, some tasty squid or a freshly baked tart.

---

# MILLSTREET = Sráid an Mhuilinn – Waterford – 712 I11 – see Cappoquin

---

# MOHILL (Maothail) – Leitrim – 712 I6 – pop. 931       37 C2
▶ Dublin 98 km – Carrick-on-Shannon 11 km – Cavan 41 km – Castlerea 44 km

 **Lough Rynn Castle** ✍
*East : 4 km by R 201 off Drumlish rd – ☎ (071) 963 27 00 – www.loughrynn.ie*
**43 rm** 🖃 – ♦ € 89/195 ♦♦ € 109/195
**Rest** *Sandstone* – Menu € 28/42
◆ 18C country house in 60 acres. Impressive interior with numerous lounges. Original features include a grand fireplace and parquet floor in the Baronial Hall. Large, well-appointed bedrooms in the house/stables. Formal dining room offers ambitious French cuisine.

---

# MONAGHAN (Muineachán) – Monaghan – 712 L5 – pop. 6 710       37 D2
▶ Dublin 133 km – Belfast 69 km – Drogheda 87 km – Dundalk 35 km
🔢 Clones Rd ☎ (047) 8 11 22, www.monaghantown.ie

**at Glaslough** Northeast : 9.5 km by N 12 on R 185 – ✉ **Monaghan**

 **Castle Leslie** ✍
*Castle Leslie Estate – ☎ (047) 88 100 – www.castleleslie.com – Closed 24-26 December*
**20 rm** 🖃 – ♦ € 203 ♦♦ € 270/320       **Rest** – *(dinner only)* Menu € 65
◆ Impressive castle set in 1,000 acres of parkland: home to 4th generation of the Leslie family. Ornate, comfortable, antique-furnished guest areas and individually styled bedrooms. Intimate, linen-laid dining room overlooks the lough and offers classically based menus.

947

REPUBLIC OF IRELAND

**Lodge at Castle Leslie Estate** 🐾    🏇 🐕 🐎 🏞 ⑩ 🖥 ⅃ 🏊 🏋 **P**
– *𝒞 (047) 88 100 – www.castleleslie.com – Restricted opening*    VISA ⓩ AE
*in winter*
**28 rm** 🛏 – ♦ € 128/143 ♦♦ € 170/190 – 1 suite
**Rest** *Snaffles* – *(dinner only)* Menu € 48 – Carte € 36/49
♦ Victorian former hunting lodge in 1,000 acres with equestrian centre. Plenty of antiques and equine-themed pictures; relaxed and informal atmosphere. Stylish and contemporary bedrooms, some with balconies. Snaffles mezzanine brasserie has open kitchen and serves Mediterranean-meets-Irish cooking.

---

# MULLINGAR (An Muileann gCearr) – Westmeath – 712 J/K7    37 C3
– pop. 18 416 ▮ Ireland

▶ Dublin 79 km – Drogheda 58 km
🇮 Market Sq. 𝒞 (0449) 34 86 50, www.midirelandtourism.ie
◎ Belvedere House and Gardens★ **AC**, S : 5.5 km by N 52. Fore Abbey★, NE : 27.25 km by R 394 – Multyfarnhan Franciscan Friary★, N : 12.75 km by N 4 – Tullynally★ **AC**, N : 21 km by N 4 and R 394

🏨 **Mullingar Park**    🖥 ⑩ ⋔ ⅃ 🖥 ⅃ rm, Ⓐ rest, 🏊 🖤 🏋 **P** VISA ⓩ AE
*Dublin Rd, East : 2.5 km on Dublin Rd (N 4) – 𝒞 (044) 933 7500*
*– www.mullingarparkhotel.com – Closed 25-26 December*
**94 rm** 🛏 – ♦ € 85/160 ♦♦ € 130/250 – 1 suite
**Rest** – Menu € 24/30 **s** – Carte dinner € 31/47 **s**
♦ Large, contemporary hotel close to a business park and the main road to Dublin. Well-equipped, modern bedrooms in uniform style. Comprehensive leisure and spa facilities. Horseshoe bar-lounge and spacious formal dining room offering classical Irish cooking.

🏠 **Marlinstown Court** without rest    🖥 🏊 🖤 **P** VISA ⓩ
*Dublin Rd, East : 2.5 km on Dublin Rd (N 4) – 𝒞 (044) 934 00 53*
*– www.marlinstowncourt.com – Closed 23-27 December*
**5 rm** 🛏 – ♦ € 40/50 ♦♦ € 70/75
♦ Clean, tidy guesthouse close to junction with N4. Modern rear extension. Light and airy pine-floored lounge and breakfast room overlooking garden. Brightly furnished bedrooms.

---

# MULRANNY (An Mhala Raithní) – Mayo – 712 C6    36 A2
▶ Dublin 270 km – Castlebar 35 km – Westport 29 km

🏨 **Mulranny Park**    ≤ 🖥 🐕 🖥 ⋔ ⅃ 🖥 ⅃ rm, ⚹⚹ Ⓐ rest, 🏊 🏋 **P**
*on N 59 – 𝒞 (098) 36 000 – www.mulrannyparkhotel.ie – Closed*    VISA ⓩ
*7-21 January and 25-26 December*
**40 rm** 🛏 – ♦ € 65/105 ♦♦ € 130/160 – 21 suites
**Rest** *Nephin* – see restaurant listing
**Rest** *Waterfront Bistro* – Carte € 22/35 **s**
♦ Purpose-built business oriented hotel behind 19C façade: lovely Clew Bay views. Impressive leisure and conference facilities. Airy rooms with slightly minimalist interiors. Waterfront Bistro has informal, relaxing ambience.

🍴🍴🍴 **Nephin** – at Mulranny Park Hotel    ≤ 🖥 🐕 Ⓐ **P** VISA ⓩ
*on N 59 – 𝒞 (098) 36 000 – www.mulrannyparkhotel.ie – Closed 7-21 January*
*and 25-26 December*
**Rest** – *(dinner only and Sunday lunch)* Menu € 39 **s** – Carte € 49/56 **s**
♦ Large, lively restaurant with fine southerly views. Modern, intricately presented cooking offers interesting combinations based around well sourced, quality ingredients.

**NAAS (An Nás)** – Kildare – **712** L/M8 – **pop. 20 044** ▯ Ireland                    **39** D1

▮ Dublin 30 km – Kilkenny 83 km – Tullamore 85 km

▮ Kerdiffstown Naas, ℰ (045) 87 46 44

▮ Russborough ★★★ **AC**, S : 16 km by R 410 and minor road – Castletown House ★★
**AC**, NE : 24 km by R 407 and R 403

ᐧᐧᐧᐧ **Killashee House H. & Villa Spa** ⌖          ⟀ ⥀ ⬚ ⬡ ⬢ ᴸᵇ ▯ & rm,
*Kilcullen Rd, South : 3 km on R 448*          ⒶⒸ rest, ⌘ ⥁ ⥈ ▣ ⍘ ⍘ ⍘
– ℰ (045) 879 277 – www.killasheehouse.com – Closed 25-26 December
**129 rm** ⌑ – ⴲ € 110/150 ⴲⴲ € 160/250 – 12 suites
**Rest** *Jack's* – see restaurant listing
**Rest** *Turners* – *(dinner only Friday-Saturday)* Carte € 21/44
♦ Impressive, part-1860s hunting lodge surrounded by vast grounds. Spacious,
traditionally styled guest areas; good event facilities; superb leisure club and spa.
Country house style bedrooms – those in the main house are most characterful.
Elegant fine dining overlooking the garden or brasserie menu in Jack's.

Ⅹ  **Vie de Châteaux**                         ⌂ ⒶⒸ ⤬ ⍘ ⍘ ⍘
*The Harbour* – ℰ (045) 888 478 – www.viedechateaux.ie – Closed 24 December-5
January, lunch Saturday-Sunday and bank holidays
**Rest** – French – *(booking essential)* Menu € 25/29 – Carte € 32/44
♦ Stylish, popular restaurant with open-plan kitchen and a brasserie feel. Concise,
keenly priced menu moves with the seasons; mainly French dishes but with some
Mediterranean influences.

Ⅹ  **Jack's** – at Killashee House Hotel & Villa Spa      ⟀ ⥀ ⒶⒸ ▣ ⍘ ⍘ ⍘
*Kilcullen Rd, South : 3 km on R 448* – ℰ (045) 879 277 – www.killasheehouse.com
– Closed 24-25 December
**Rest** – Menu € 19/28 – Carte € 26/38
♦ Informal brasserie located within an impressive Victorian hunting lodge. Con-
temporary, open-plan interior with white leather chairs and dark wood bar. Fam-
ily friendly menu of familiar classics.

**at Two Mile House** Southwest : 6.5 km by R 448 – ✉

ⅩⅩ **Brown Bear**                              ⌂ ⒶⒸ ▣ ⍘ ⍘ ⍘
– ℰ (045) 883 561 – www.thebrownbear.ie – Closed 25-30 December and 19
February-4 March
**Rest** – *(dinner only and lunch Saturday and Sunday)* Menu € 28
– Carte € 43/48
♦ Smart restaurant set in a small village and boasting a pubby locals bar and
split-level dining room with leather furnishings and a subtle brasserie feel. Two-
choice set menu or an à la carte of complex, ambitious dishes with a Gallic twist.

---

**NAVAN (An Uaimh)** – Meath – **712** L7 – **pop. 24 851** ▯ Ireland          **37** D3

▮ Dublin 48 km – Drogheda 26 km – Dundalk 51 km

▮ Moor Park Mooretown, ℰ (046) 2 76 61

▮ Royal Tara Bellinter, ℰ (046) 902 52 44

▮ Brú na Bóinne : Newgrange ★★★ **AC**, Knowth ★, E : 16 km by minor road to
Donore – Bective Abbey ★, S : 6.5 km by R 161 – Tara ★ **AC**, S : 8 km by N 3.
Kells ★ (Round Tower and High Crosses ★★, St Columba's House ★), NW : by N 3
– Trim ★ (castle ★★), SW : 12.75 km by R 161

▯ **Ma Dwyers** without rest                   ⌘ ▣ ⍘ ⍘ ⍘ ⍘
*Dublin Rd, South : 1.25 km on N 3* – ℰ (046) 907 79 92
**26 rm** ⌑ – ⴲ € 40/50 ⴲⴲ € 75
♦ Surprisingly spacious detached house on the main road into town. Comfortable lounge and large breakfast room. Bright, up-to-date bedrooms, in uniform
style, provide good value. Showers only.

## NEWMARKET-ON-FERGUS (Cora Chaitlín) – Clare – **712** F7     **38** B
– pop. 1 542 ▮ Ireland

▶ Dublin 219 km – Ennis 13 km – Limerick 24 km

🛅 Dromoland Castle, ℰ (061) 36 84 44

🅖 Bunratty Castle★★ **AC**, S : 10 km by N 18 – Craggaunowen Centre★ **AC**, NE : 15 km by minor road towards Moymore – Knappogue Castle★ **AC**, NE : 12 km N 18 and minor roads via Quin – Quin Friary★ **AC**, N : 10 km by N 18 and minor road to Quin

🛏🛏🛏 **Dromoland Castle** �’     ≤ 🚗 🕭 🐟 🔍 ⊗ 🐎 ⅃♨ ℅ 🖼 📶 👌 rm,
*Northwest : 2.5 km on R 458 – ℰ (061)*     🕳 📶 🛢 **P** **VISA** **⊙** **AE** **①**
*368 144 – www.dromoland.ie*
**94 rm** – 🛏 € 449/878 🛏🛏 € 449/878, ⬲ €24 – 5 suites
**Rest** *Earl of Thomond* – (dinner only) Menu € 68
**Rest** *Fig Tree* – Carte € 25/44
• Impressive 16C castle in 375 acres. Various antique-filled, country house lounges; comfy, classical bedrooms with heavy fabrics, iPod docks and flat screen TVs. Popular golf/leisure/wellness facilities. Formal fine dining in the restaurant. More casual meals in Fig Tree.

## NEWPORT (Baile Uí Fhiacháin) – Mayo – **712** D6 – pop. 590     **36** A2
▮ Ireland

▶ Dublin 264 km – Ballina 59 km – Galway 96 km

🛈 Westport ℰ (098) 2 57 11, www.mayo-ireland.ie

🅖 Burrishoole Abbey★, NW : 3.25 km by N 59 – Furnace Lough★, NW : 4.75 km by N 59. Achill Island★, W : 35 km by N 59 and R 319

🛏🛏 **Newport House** �’     🚗 🕭 🐟 🕊⁾ **P** **VISA** **⊙** **AE**
*– ℰ (098) 41 222 – www.newporthouse.ie – 19 March-October*
**16 rm** ⬲ – 🛏 € 115/140 🛏🛏 € 190/240
**Rest** – (dinner only) Carte € 42/62 **s** ⅋
• Mellow ivy-clad Georgian mansion; grand staircase up to gallery and drawing room. Bedrooms in main house or courtyard; some in self-contained units ideal for families and those with dogs. Enjoy the fresh Newport estate produce used in the dishes served in the elegant dining room.

## OUGHTERARD (Uachtar Ard) – Galway – **712** E7 – pop. 1 305     **36** A3
▮ Ireland

▶ Dublin 240 km – Galway 27 km

🛈 Main Street ℰ (091) 55 28 08, www.oughterardtourism.com

🛅 Gortreevagh, ℰ (091) 55 21 31

◎ Town★

🅖 Lough Corrib★★ (Shore road - NW - ≤★★) – Aughnanure Castle★ **AC**, SE : 3.25 km by N 59

🛏🛏 **Currarevagh House** �’     ≤ 🚗 🕭 ℅ **P** **VISA** **⊙** **AE**
*Northwest : 6.5 km on Glann rd – ℰ (091) 552 312 – www.currarevagh.com*
*– April to mid-October*
**12 rm** ⬲ – 🛏 € 80/135 🛏🛏 € 150/160
**Rest** – (dinner only) (set menu only) Menu € 45
• Victorian manor on Lough Corrib, set in 180 acres. Period décor throughout plus much fishing memorabilia. Two lovely sitting rooms. Comfortable, well-kept bedrooms. Four course dinner menu makes good use of garden produce.

### Ross Lake House 🕭 🛋 ✗ ℅ P VISA ⦾ AE

*Rosscahill, Southeast : 7.25 km by N 59 – ℘ (091) 550 109
– www.rosslakehotel.com – 17 March-October*
**12 rm** ⬜ – † € 105/125 †† € 150/170 – 1 suite
**Rest** – *(dinner only)* Menu € 45

◆ Personally run Georgian country house with attractive gardens, set in a
wooded estate. Traditionally styled bedrooms; Strefens suite and Killaguile are
the best. Begin the evening in the cocktail bar before dining by candlelight at
smartly set, cloth-clad tables.

### Railway Lodge without rest 🕭 ≼ 🛋 ⸜⸜ P VISA ⦾

*West : 0.75 km by Costello rd taking first right onto unmarked road – ℘ (091)
552 945 – www.railwaylodge.net*
**4 rm** ⬜ – † € 60/70 †† € 100/110

◆ Stylish house in remote farm setting, with beautifully kept, elegantly furnished
interior. Themed bedrooms boast books, stripped wood furniture and an eye for
detail. Helpful owner provides good local knowledge. Homemade bread and
scones; tea served on arrival.

### Waterfall Lodge without rest 🛋 ⸜ ✗ ⸜⸜ P

*West : 0.75 km on N 59 – ℘ (091) 552 168 – www.waterfalllodge.net*
**6 rm** ⬜ – † € 50 †† € 80

◆ Heavily restored Victorian house with fishing river running through the garden.
Infectiously enthusiastic owner. Sympathetically styled bedrooms with rug-cov-
ered floors and modern bathrooms; some four-posters. Pancakes, French toast
and smoked salmon at breakfast.

REPUBLIC OF IRELAND

---

## PARKNASILLA (Páirc na Saileach) – Kerry – 712 C12 📗 Ireland     38 A3

▶ Dublin 360 km – Cork 116 km – Killarney 55 km

◉ Sneem★, NW : 4 km by N 70. Ring of Kerry★★ : Derrynane National Historic
Park★★, W : 25.75 km by N 70 – Staigue Fort★, W : 21 km by N 70

### Parknasilla     ≼ 🛋 ⸜ 🖼 ⊕ ⌂ ⸝ ✗ 🖼 🅰 rest, ✗ P VISA ⦾ AE ⓪

*– ℘ (064) 667 56 00 – www.parknasillahotel.ie – April-early January*
**79 rm** ⬜ – † € 149/199 †† € 198/240 – 4 suites
**Rest** *Pygmalion* – ℘ (064) 45 122 *(dinner only) (booking essential for non
residents)* Carte € 42/48

◆ Grand hotel built in 1896 by The Railways, superbly set in 500 acres and
overlooking Kenmare Bay. Traditional styled lounges and cocktail bar; impressive grounds and range of leisure activates. Bedrooms vary from classical to
stylish and modern. Formal restaurant with portraits; menus display modern
touches.

---

## PORTLAOISE (Port Laoise) – Laois – 712 K8 – pop. 14 613     39 C2

▶ Dublin 88 km – Carlow 40 km – Waterford 101 km

### Ivyleigh House without rest     🛋 ✗ ⸜⸜ P VISA ⦾

*Bank Pl, Church St – ℘ (057) 862 20 81 – www.ivyleigh.com – Closed 25
December*
**6 rm** ⬜ – † € 50/70 †† € 80/115

◆ Traditional listed Georgian property set in the city centre, run by a welcoming owner. Comfortable lounge and communal dining area, with antique furniture and ornaments on display throughout. Good-sized bedrooms decorated in a period style. Homemade breads, preserves, granola and muesli at
breakfast.

## PORTMAGEE (An Caladh) – Kerry – **712** A12 – pop. 375 ▯ Ireland    38 A2

▶ Dublin 365 km – Killarney 72 km – Tralee 82 km
⬤ Ring of Kerry★★

⌂ **Moorings**    ← AK rest, ⚒ ⓧ P VISA ⚫ AE
– ℰ *(066) 947 71 08* – www.moorings.ie – Closed 24-25 December
**16 rm** ⬚ – ♦ € 60/100 ♦♦ € 90/140
**Rest** – *(closed Monday except bank holidays) (bar lunch)* Carte € 31/60
♦ Cosy, personally run hotel overlooking the harbour and bridge, and made up a series of little cottages. First floor lounge offers great views, as do some of the pleasant bedrooms; 4 and 6 boast jacuzzis. Characterful bar with music nights. Nautically themed restaurant with seafood straight from local boats.

---

## PORTMARNOCK (Port Mearnóg) – Fingal – **712** N7 – pop. 8 979    39 D1
▯ Ireland

▶ Dublin 8 km – Drogheda 45 km
⬤ Malahide Castle★★ **AC**, N : 4 km by R 124 – Ben of Howth★, S : 8 km by R 124 – Newbridge House★ **AC**, N : 16 km by R 124, M 1 and minor road east

🏢 **Portmarnock H. and Golf Links**    ← ⬛ ⚒ ℉♯ ⬛ ▯ & AK rest,
Strand Rd – ℰ *(01) 846 0611*    ⚒ rm, 📞 ⚒ P VISA ⚫ AE ①
– www.portmarnock.com – Closed 24-28 December, Sunday and Monday
**138 rm** – ♦ € 89/129 ♦♦ € 89/129, ⬚ € 16.95 – 3 suites
**Rest** *Osborne Brasserie* – *(closed Sunday and Monday) (dinner only)*
Menu € 25 – Carte € 38/45 **s**
♦ Large golf-oriented hotel with challenging 18-hole course. Original fittings embellish characterful, semi-panelled Jamesons Bar. Very comfortable, individually styled rooms. Smart brasserie with traditional menus.

---

## RATHDRUM – Wicklow – **712** N9 – pop. 2 235    39 D2
▶ Dublin 60 km – Wicklow 17 km – Drogheda 127 km

✗✗ **Bates**    ⬛ VISA ⚫
3 Market St – ℰ *(0404) 29 988* – www.batesrestaurant.ie – *(dinner only and Sunday lunch) Closed lunch September- May,25 December, 1 January and Monday*
**Rest** – Menu € 24 (Sunday lunch)/27 – Carte € 29/51
♦ Champions local produce, with counter selling local cheese, home-cured meats and Italian staples. Various menus offer boldly flavoured dishes with Italian influences, which arrive in hearty portions.

---

## RATHMELTON (Ráth Mealtain) – Donegal – **712** J2 – pop. 1 051    37 C1
▯ Ireland

▶ Dublin 248 km – Donegal 59 km – Londonerry 43 km – Sligo 122 km
◉ Town★

⌂ **Ardeen** without rest ⬚    ⬛ ⚒ ⚒ ℉♯ P VISA ⚫
turning by the Village Hall – ℰ *(074) 915 12 43* – www.ardeenhouse.com
– Easter-September
**5 rm** ⬚ – ♦ € 45/55 ♦♦ € 90
♦ Victorian house on edge of the village, with peaceful gardens and river nearby. Welcoming owner and homely, personally styled interior. Open-fired lounge with local info; polished communal breakfast table. Cosy, immaculately kept bedrooms.

---

## RATHMINES = Ráth Maonais – Dublin – **712** N8 – see Dublin

**RATHMULLAN** (Ráth Maoláin) – Donegal – **712** J2 – pop. 469       **37** C1
- ✉ **Letterkenny** ▯ Ireland

▶ Dublin 265 km – Londonderry 58 km – Sligo 140 km

◉ Otway Saltpans, ℰ (074) 915 16 65

◉ Knockalla Viewpoint★, N : 12.75 km by R 247 – Rathmelton★, SW : 11.25 km by R 247

🏠🏠🏠 **Rathmullan House** ⌘       ≤ ⌂ 🕭 ↘ 🔲 ⅍ ⚒ **P** ꭦꭥꓮ ⚌ ꭓꭓ
*North : 0.5 mi on R 247* – ℰ *(074) 915 81 88* – *www.rathmullanhouse.com*
*– Closed 6 January-10 February, restricted opening in winter*
**34 rm** ☕ – ♦ € 80/175 ♦♦ € 160/250
**Rest** *Weeping Elm* – *(bar lunch)* Menu € 45 – Carte € 45/55
 ♦ Part-19C, family run country house with fine gardens, set in a secluded site on Lough Swilly. Various lounges provide pleasant spots for lunch. Stylish, individually styled bedrooms. Restaurant offers serious dinner menus taken at linen-clad tables; kitchen garden produce features.

---

**RATHNEW** = Ráth Naoi – Wicklow – **712** N8 – **see Wicklow**

---

**RIVERSTOWN** (Baile idir Dhá Abhainn) – Sligo – **712** G5 – pop. 310       **36** B2

▶ Dublin 198 km – Sligo 21 km

🏠 **Coopershill** ⌘       ≤ ⌂ 🕭 ↘ ⅍ ⚒ rm, **P** ꭦꭥꓮ ⚌ ⓪
*– ℰ (071) 916 51 08 – www.coopershill.com – April-October*
**8 rm** ☕ – ♦ € 144/157 ♦♦ € 218/244
**Rest** – *(dinner only) (booking essential for non-residents)* Menu € 45
 ♦ Magnificent Georgian country house set within a 500 acre estate; home to six generations of one family. Antique-furnished communal areas and bedrooms exude charm and character. Family portraits and antique silver adorn the dining room, with much of the produce featured on the menus coming from the estate.

---

**ROSCOMMON** (Ros Comáin) – Roscommon – **712** H7 – pop. 5 017       **36** B3
▯ Ireland

▶ Dublin 151 km – Galway 92 km – Limerick 151 km

🛈 Harrison Hall ℰ (090) 6 62 63 42, www.visitroscommon.com

🏠 Moate Park, ℰ (09066) 2 63 82

◉ Castle★

◉ Castlestrange Stone★, SW : 11.25 km by N 63 and R 362 – Strokestown★ (Famine Museum★ **AC**, Strokestown Park House★ **AC**), N : 19.25 km by N 61 and R 368 – Castlerea : Clonalis House★ **AC**, NW : 30.5 km by N 60

🏠🏠🏠 **Abbey**       ⌂ 🔲 ♨ ♨ ⚒ ⅍ **P** ꭦꭥꓮ ⚌ ꭓꭓ ⓪
*on N 63 (Galway rd)* – ℰ *(090) 662 62 40* – *www.abbeyhotel.ie* – *Closed 24-26 December*
**50 rm** ☕ – ♦ € 160/180 ♦♦ € 280/300
**Rest** – Menu € 35 (dinner) – Carte € 29/41
 ♦ Part-18C, family-run manor house with impressive castellated façade; overlooking ruins of 13C Abbey. Most characterful bedrooms in original house; some boast feature beds and roll-top baths. Good function and leisure facilities. Large bar and formal restaurant.

---

**ROSSLARE** (Ros Láir) – Wexford – **712** M11 – pop. 1 359 ▯ Ireland       **39** D2

▶ Dublin 167 km – Waterford 80 km – Wexford 19 km

🛈 Kilrane ℰ (053) 3 32 32, www.rosslare.ebookireland.com

🚢 Rosslare Strand, ℰ (053) 913 22 03

◉ Irish Agricultural Museum, Johnstown Castle★★ **AC**, NW : 12 km by R 740, N 25 and minor road. Kilmore Quay★, SW : 24 km by R 736 and R 739 – Saltee Islands★, SW : 24 km by R 736, R 739 and ferry

**Kelly's Resort** ≤ 🚗 🖥 📶 🏠 ♨ ✕ 🍷 🔒 👤 📶 🄰🄲 rest, 🍽 **P** 🆅🅸🆂🅰 ⓒⓞ 🄰🄴
– 𝒞 (053) 913 21 14 – www.kellys.ie – Closed 7th December to 1st February
**118 rm** 🛏 – 🛉 € 77/198 🛉🛉 € 154/198
**Rest** *La Marine* – see restaurant listing
**Rest** *Beaches* – Menu € 25/45 ❀
♦ Started life in 1895 as a beachfront 'refreshment house', now a sprawling lei
sure-orientated hotel run by the 4th family generation. Various lounges, large
bar and sizeable spa. Well-appointed bedrooms; the newer rooms being the larg
est. Formal Beaches offers exceptional wine list; Gallic-influenced bistro.

✕ **La Marine** – at Kelly's Resort Hotel 🚗 🔒 🄰🄲 **P** 🆅🅸🆂🅰 ⓒⓞ 🄰🄴
– 𝒞 (053) 913 21 14 – www.kellys.ie – Closed 5 December - 19 February
**Rest** – Carte € 24/36
♦ Bistro-style restaurant located within a large beachfront hotel, boasting an
open-kitchen and glass-fronted wine cellar. A large zinc-topped bar from France
takes centre stage, while the menu offers a selection of tasty brasserie classics.

**ROSSLARE HARBOUR** (Calafort Ros Láir) – **Wexford** – **712** N11 **39** D2
– pop. 1 041
▶ Dublin 169 km – Waterford 82 km – Wexford 21 km
to France (Cherbourg and Roscoff) (Irish Ferries) (17 h/15 h) – to Fishguard (Stena
Line) 1-4 daily (1 h 40 mn/3 h 30 mn) – to Pembroke (Irish Ferries) 2 daily (3 h
45 mn)
ℹ Kilrane 𝒞 (053) 3 32 32, www.rosslareharbour.ie

**Churchtown House** without rest 🌿 🚗 🍷 📶 **P** 🆅🅸🆂🅰 ⓒⓞ 🄰🄴
Tagoat, West : 4.75 km by N 25 on R 736 (Rosslare rd) – 𝒞 (053) 913 25 55
– www.churchtownhouse.com – April-October
**6 rm** 🛏 – 🛉 € 85/110 🛉🛉 € 120/140
♦ Part-18C house with extension, set in a spacious, well-kept garden. Traditional
country house style lounge and wood furnished breakfast room. Individually dec
orated bedrooms.

**ROUNDSTONE** (Cloch na Rón) – **Galway** – **712** C7 – pop. 207 **36** A3
Ireland
▶ Dublin 293 km – Galway 76 km – Ennis 144 km
◉ Town ★
Connemara ★★★: Sky Road, Clifden ★★, W : 24 km by R 341 and minor road
– Cashel ★, E : 15 km by R 341 – Connemara National Park ★ **AC**, N : 40 km by R
341 and N 59 – Kylemore Abbey ★ **AC**, N : 44 km by R 341 and N 59

**O'Dowds** ≤ 🆅🅸🆂🅰 ⓒⓞ
– 𝒞 (095) 35 809 – www.odowdsbar.com – Closed 25 December
**Rest** – Seafood – (booking advisable) Carte € 22/31
♦ Busy pub in pretty harbourside town; popular with tourists and locals alike.
Owned by the O'Dowd family for over 100 years, it specialises in fresh, simply
cooked fish and shellfish; try the local crab. Sit in the cosy, fire-lit bar or wood-pa
nelled restaurant.

**ROUNDWOOD** – **Wicklow** – **712** N9 – pop. 518 **39** D2
▶ Dublin 25 km – Wicklow 12 km – Belfast 137 km – Limerick 144 km

✕✕ **Woods** **P** 🆅🅸🆂🅰 ⓒⓞ
Main St – 𝒞 (01) 281 70 78 – www.woodsbistro.ie – Closed 25 December and
Monday
**Rest** – (dinner only and Sunday lunch) Menu € 24/27 – Carte € 29/51
♦ Stone-built property high in the Wicklow Mountains. One half is a bar, the other,
a pleasant restaurant with wooden, hunting lodge style furnishings. Simple, un
fussy menus provide plenty of choice; excellent homemade breads and desserts.

**SANDYFORD** = Áth an Ghainimh – Dún Laoghaire-Rathdown – **712** N8 – see Dublin

---

**SHANAGARRY** (An Seangharraí) – Cork – **712** H12 – **pop. 297**          **39** C3
– ⊠ Midleton ▌ Ireland

▶ Dublin 262 km – Cork 40 km – Waterford 103 km
◉ Cloyne Cathedral★, NW : 6.5 km by R 629

**Ballymaloe House** ⤵          ≤ ⚘ ◊ ⊼ ✻ ⅋ 🔥 rm, ✻ rest, 🎿 **P**
*Northwest : 2.5 km on R 629 – ℰ (021) 465 25 31*          *VISA* ⊗ AE ①
*– www.ballymaloe.ie – Closed 2 weeks January and 24-26 December*
**30 rm** ⊑ – ♦ € 110/130 ♦♦ € 170/250
**Rest** – *(booking essential)* Menu € 37/75
♦ With pre-18C origins, this is the very essence of a country manor house. Family-run for 3 generations, it boasts numerous traditionally styled guest areas, comfy, classical bedrooms and a famed cookery school. 5 course daily menu offers local, seasonal produce.

---

**SKERRIES** (Na Sceirí) – Fingal – **712** N7 – **pop. 9 535** ▌ Ireland          **39** D1

▶ Dublin 30 km – Drogheda 24 km
🛈 Skerries Mills ℰ (01) 849 52 08, www.tasteofskerries.com
🏌 Skerries Hacketstown, ℰ (01) 849 15 67
◉ Malahide Castle★★ **AC**, S : 23 km by R 127, M 1 and R 106 – Ben of Howth (≤★), S : 23 km by R 127, M 1 and R 106 – Newbridge House★ **AC**, S : 16 km by R 217 and minor road

**Redbank House**          🔥 ⅋ *VISA* ⊗ AE ①
*5-7 Church St – ℰ (01) 849 1005 – www.redbank.ie – Closed 24-27 December*
**18 rm** ⊑ – ♦ € 45/75 ♦♦ € 60/120     **Rest** – Menu € 25 – Carte € 47/55
♦ Long-standing hotel and restaurant comprising of an old bank, a butcher's and a cottage, not far from the lively harbour. Original bedrooms have a classical style; newer rooms overlook a small courtyard and are more up-to-date. Extensive, traditional menus of local seafood; wine cellar in the old bank vault.

---

**SLANE** – Meath – **712** M6 – **pop. 823**          **37** B3

▶ Dublin 34 km – Navan 8 km – City Centre 35 km – Craigavon 69 km

**Tankardstown** ⤵          ⚘ ◊ 🔥 ✻ ⅋ **P** *VISA* ⊗ AE
*Northwest : 6 km by N 51off R 163 – ℰ (041) 982 46 21 – www.tankardstown.ie*
*– Closed January and 25-26 December*
**6 rm** ⊑ – ♦ € 150 ♦♦ € 315 – 7 suites
**Rest Brabazon** – see restaurant listing
**Rest Bistro** – *(closed Monday-Tuesday) (lunch only and Saturday dinner)*
Carte € 25/50
♦ Fine Georgian manor house on mature country estate; extensively restored to a luxurious level. Large, antique-furnished bedrooms in the house; some with silk-lined walls. Rooms in courtyard boast kitchens. Vaulted ceilings and relaxed all-day dining in Bistro.

**Brabazon** – at Tankardstown Hotel          🔥 **P** *VISA* ⊗ AE
*Northwest : 6 km by N 51 off R 163 – ℰ (041) 982 46 21 – www.tankardstown.ie*
*– Closed January and 25-26 December*
**Rest** – *(closed Monday-Tuesday) (dinner only and Sunday lunch)* Carte € 29/40
♦ Relaxed, rustic restaurant set in former piggery of the manor house, with modern interior, painted wooden tables and pleasant terrace overlooking the landscaped courtyard. Contemporary cooking makes use of good quality ingredients.

▶ Dublin 214 km – Belfast 203 km – Dundalk 170 km – Londonderry 138 km

🛫 Sligo Airport, Strandhill : 𝒞 (071) 9168280

🛈 Temple St 𝒞 (071) 9 16 12 01, www.sligotourism.ie

🏌 Rosses Point, 𝒞 (071) 917 71 34

◉ Town★★ – Abbey★ **AC** – Model Arts and the Niland Gallery★ **AC**

◉ SE : Lough Gill★★ – Carrowmore Megalithic Cemetery★ **AC**, SW : 4.75 km
– Knocknarea★ (⩽★★) SW : 9.5 km by R 292. Drumcliff★, N : by N 15 - Parke's
Castle★ **AC**, E : 14.5 km by R 286 – Glencar Waterfall★, NE : 14.5 km by N 16
– Creevykeel Court Cairn★, N : 25.75 km by N 15

---

🏨🏨🏨　**Clarion**　　🚗 🖃 ⊛ 🏛 ℔ 🖢 🖢 rm, 👬 𝔸ℂ rest, 🍽 ⁽ᵗᵖ⁾ 🏊 🅿 🚾 ⓞⓞ 𝔸𝔼

*Clarion Rd, Northeast : 3 km by N 16 – 𝒞 (071) 911 90 00*
*– www.clarionhotelssligo.com – Closed 24-28 December*
**95 rm** 🖃 – ♦ € 65/99 ♦♦ € 110/129 – 67 suites
**Rest** *Kudos* – Carte € 25/45
**Rest** *Sinergie* – Carte (Friday-Saturday) € 25/45
◆ Extensive Victorian building with granite façade: now the height of modernity
with excellent leisure club, impressive spacious bedrooms and a large choice of
smart suites. Two former churches – now function rooms – in the grounds. Informal Asian inspired Kudos. Modern European menus at Sinergie.

---

⌂　**Tree Tops** without rest　　🚗 🍽 ⁽ᵗᵖ⁾ 🅿 🚾 ⓞⓞ 𝔸𝔼

*Cleveragh Rd, South : 1.25 km by Dublin rd – 𝒞 (071) 916 01 60*
*– www.sligobandb.com – Closed 25 December and 1 January*
**5 rm** 🖃 – ♦ € 40/52 ♦♦ € 70/76
◆ Pleasant guesthouse in residential area. Stunning collection of Irish art. Cosy
public areas include small lounge and simple breakfast room. Neat, comfortable
rooms.

---

✗✗　**Montmartre**　　𝔸ℂ 🚾 ⓞⓞ 𝔸𝔼 ⓞ

*Market Yard – 𝒞 (071) 916 99 01 – www.montmartrerestaurant.ie – Closed 9-30*
*January, 24-26 December, Sunday and Monday*
**Rest** – *(dinner only)* Menu € 27 (early dinner)/37 – Carte € 30/48
◆ Smart, modern restaurant near cathedral with small bar at entrance and plenty
of light from windows. Efficient, formal staff serve broadly influenced classic
French food.

---

🍴　**Hargadons**　　🕁 𝔸ℂ 🚾 ⓞⓞ 𝔸𝔼

*4/5 O'Connell St – 𝒞 (071) 915 3709 – www.hargadons.com*
**Rest** – *(closed Sunday)* Menu € 11 (lunch) – Carte € 21/28
◆ Hugely characterful pub with sloping floors, narrow passageways, dimly lit ante-
rooms and a lovely "Ladies' Room" complete with its own serving hatch. Cooking
is warming and satisfying, offering the likes of Irish stew or bacon and cabbage.

---

**SPANISH POINT** (Rinn na Spáinneach) – Clare – **712** D9　　**38** B2
– ✉ Milltown Malbay

▶ Dublin 275 km – Galway 104 km – Limerick 83 km

---

🏠　**Red Cliff Lodge**　　🚗 🍽 rm, ⁽ᵗᵖ⁾ 🅿 🚾 ⓞⓞ ⓞ

*– 𝒞 (065) 708 57 56 – www.redclifflodge.ie – February-December*
**6 rm** 🖃 – ♦ € 100/120 ♦♦ € 120/170　　**Rest** – Carte € 33/44
◆ Thatched cottage with spacious courtyard bedrooms. Comfortable, modern
lounges boast bold feature walls and antique furniture. Breakfast comes in a
wicker basket delivered to your room. Informal menu of Irish produce; dine on
the terrace in the warmer months.

## STEPASIDE – Dún Laoghaire-Rathdown

▶ Dublin 10 km – Dún Laoghaire 7 km – Belfast 121 km – Cork 164 km

※※ **Box Tree** 　　　　　　　　　　　　　　　AC VISA ◎◎ AE
Enniskerry Rd ⊠ D18 – ℰ (01) 205 20 25 – www.theboxtree.ie – Closed Good
Friday and 25-26 December
**Rest** – Menu € 24/26 – Carte € 29/46
♦ Smart bistro in a small village. Daily menus offer unfussy, classically based dishes
with modern presentation. Staff are eager to please and the good value wine list is
well thought out. Home-grown ingredients can be exchanged for dinner.

⏸ **Wild Boar** 　　　　　　　　　　　　　　AC VISA ◎◎ AE
Enniskerry Rd ⊠ D18 – ℰ (01) 205 2025 – www.thewildboar.ie – Closed Good
Friday and 25 December
**Rest** – Carte € 21/34
♦ Modern pub, unusually set beneath a small, new-build apartment block. Dining
takes place in a former wine merchants shop, and ranges from breakfast and after-
noon tea to filling dinners. Quality ingredients are cooked with care and passion.

## STRAFFAN (Teach Srafáin) – Kildare – 712 M8 – pop. 439 ▮ Ireland

▶ Dublin 24 km – Mullingar 75 km

🛈 Naas Kerdiffstown, ℰ (045) 87 46 44

🅖 Castletown House, Celbridge★ **AC, NW** : 7 km by R 406 and R 403

🏨🏨🏨 **K Club** ⑤ 　　🚗 🕦 🤝 ⛺ 🔲 🏖 ⑩ 🏊 ♫₈ 🎣 🎒 & rm, 🛠 🍴 ⚽ 🅿
– ℰ (01) 601 72 00 – www.kclub.ie – Closed 8 January-8 　　VISA ◎◎ AE ①
February
**60 rm** ⎚ – ♥ € 295/395 ♥♥ € 345/445 – 9 suites
**Rest** *Byerley Turk* – ℰ (01) 601 72 21 (restricted opening in winter) (dinner
only and Sunday lunch) (booking essential for non-residents) Menu € 79
**Rest** *Legends* – ℰ (01) 601 73 10 (closed Sunday-Tuesday) Carte € 38/58
**Rest** *River Room* – ℰ (01) 601 72 21 (dinner only and Sunday lunch)
Carte € 49/76
♦ Part early 19C country house overlooking River Liffey, with gardens, arboretum
and championship golf course. Huge leisure centre. Exquisitely sumptuous rooms.
Opulent food in the formal Byerley Turk. Informal Legends has views of the golf
course. Accessible menu offered in the River Room.

🏨🏨 **Barberstown Castle** 　　🍴 🕦 ⎚ & rm, 🛠 🍴 ⚽ 🅿 VISA ◎◎ AE
North : 0.75 km – ℰ (01) 628 81 57 – www.barberstowncastle.ie – Closed January
and 24-26 December
**57 rm** ⎚ – ♥ € 150 ♥♥ € 230
**Rest** – (dinner only) (booking essential) (residents only Friday-Saturday)
Menu € 45/55 – Carte € 24/35
♦ Whitewashed Elizabethan and Victorian house with 13C castle keep and gardens. Country house style lounges exude style. Individually decorated, very comfortable bedrooms. Dine in characterful, stone-clad keep.

## TAHILLA (Tathuile) – Kerry – 712 C12 – pop. 193 ▮ Ireland

▶ Dublin 357 km – Cork 112 km – Killarney 51 km

🅖 Ring of Kerry★★ – Sneem★, **NW** : 6.5 km by N 70

🏠 **Tahilla Cove** without rest ⑤ 　　🍴 🕦 🅿 VISA ◎◎
– ℰ (064) 664 52 04 – www.tahillacove.com – Easter to mid-October
**9 rm** ⎚ – ♥ € 100 ♥♥ € 150
♦ Family home where the owner was brought up; great setting in a calm private
cove with views over the harbour and mountains. Cosy bar and lounge with eclectic knick-knacks. Traditionally furnished bedrooms; most have patios and views.

## TERMONBARRY – Roscommon – 712 I6 – pop. 518 ▮ Ireland

▶ Dublin 130 km – Galway 137 km – Roscommon 35 km – Sligo 100 km

🅖 Strokestown★ (Famine Museum★ **AC**, Strokestown Park House★ **AC**), **NW** : by N 5

REPUBLIC OF IRELAND

TERMONBARRY

### Keenan's
– *℘ (043) 332 60 52 – www.keenans.ie – Closed 25-26 December and bank holidays*
**12 rm** ⌑ – ♦ € 65/75 ♦♦ € 89/110
**Rest** – *(closed Sunday dinner)* Menu € 25/35 – Carte € 26/41
♦ Modern hotel on the banks of the Shannon, with cosy residents lounge. Stylish bedrooms have flat screens and showers; some have river views; some also have balconies. Large contemporary restaurant offers à la carte menu; characterful bar serves pub classics.

---

## THOMASTOWN (Baile Mhic Andáin) – Kilkenny – 712 K10      39 C2
– pop. 1 837 – ⊠ Kilkenny  Ireland
▶ Dublin 124 km – Kilkenny 17 km – Waterford 48 km – Wexford 61 km
◉ Jerpoint Abbey★★, SW : 3 km by N9 – Graiguenamanagh★ (Duiske Abbey★★ **AC**) E : 16 km by R 703 – Inistioge★, SE : 8 km by R 700 – Kilfane Glen and Waterfall★ **AC**, SE : 5 km by N 9

### Abbey House *without rest*
*Jerpoint Abbey, Southwest : 2 km on N 9 – ℘ (056) 772 41 66*
*– www.abbeyhousejerpoint.com – Closed 20-30 December*
**6 rm** ⌑ – ♦ € 50/75 ♦♦ € 75/85
♦ Neat inside and out, this whitewashed house in well-kept gardens offers simple but spacious rooms and pretty wood furnished breakfast room. Read up on area in lounge.

---

## TIMOLEAGUE – Cork – 712 F13 – pop. 323      38 B3
▶ Dublin 189 – Cork 28 – Limerick 90 – Galway 151

### Dillon's
*Mill St. – ℘ (023) 884 63 90 – www.dillons.ie – Closed 9 January-10 February, Monday, Tuesday and dinner Wednesday October-April*
**Rest** – Carte £ 35/45
♦ Sweet little restaurant in a small coastal village, with quarry tiled floor and pleasant courtyard. Fresh, seasonal cooking offers unfussy, traditionally based dishes. Menus evolve as new ingredients arrive; fish is from the local boats.

---

## TOORMORE (An Tuar Mór) – Cork – 712 D13 – pop. 207 – ⊠ Goleen    38 A3
▶ Dublin 355 km – Cork 109 km – Killarney 104 km

### Fortview House *without rest*
*Gurtyowen, Northeast : 2.5 km on Durrus rd (R 591) – ℘ (028) 35 324*
*– www.fortviewhousegoleen.com – May-September*
**3 rm** ⌑ – ♦ € 50 ♦♦ € 100
♦ Well-kept guesthouse just outside the village, run by bubbly owner. Built to look older than it really is, with stone walls, coir carpets and aged pine furniture providing a real country feel. Homemade breakfasts taken in the rear room overlooking the garden.

---

## TOWER – Cork – 712 G12 – see Blarney

---

## TRALEE (Trá Lí) – Kerry – 712 C11 – pop. 22 744  Ireland    38 A2
▶ Dublin 297 km – Killarney 32 km – Limerick 103 km
🖥 Denny St ℘ (066) 7 12 12 88, www.tralee.ie
◉ Kerry - The Kingdom★ **AC**
◉ Blennerville Windmill★ **AC**, SW : 3.25 km by N 86 – Ardfert★, NW : 8 km by R 551. Banna Strand★, NW : 12.75 km by R 551 - Crag Cave★ **AC**, W : 21 km by N 21 – Rattoo Round Tower★, N : 19.25 km by R 556

*REPUBLIC OF IRELAND*

🏠 **Grand**  ⬛ rest, 🍴 ⁽ᵗ⁾ 💆 VISA ⓒⓞ AE ⓞ
*Denny St – ℰ (066) 712 14 99 – www.grandhoteltralee.com – Closed 25 December*
**44 rm** ☑ – 🛆 € 75/95 🛆🛆 € 130/170
**Rest** – Menu € 25 (dinner) – Carte € 27/41
♦ Opened in 1928 and located right in the heart of this bustling town. Small first floor lounge and comfy, contemporary bedrooms; those to the rear are quietest. Traditional bar, once the post office, is a popular spot, offering hearty all-day dishes. Global menu and Irish specialities in classical dining room.

🏠 **Brook Manor Lodge** without rest  🚗 🍴 ⁽ᵗ⁾ P VISA ⓒⓞ
*Fenit Rd, Spa, Northwest : 3.5 km by R 551 on R 558 – ℰ (066) 712 04 06 – www.brookmanorlodge.com – March-November*
**8 rm** ☑ – 🛆 € 55/85 🛆🛆 € 85/110
♦ Modern purpose-built manor in meadowland looking across to the Slieve Mish mountains: good for walks and angling. Breakfast in conservatory. Immaculate bedrooms.

**RAMORE** (Trá Mhór) – **Waterford** – **712** K11 – **pop. 9 634** ▯ Ireland    **39** C2
▰ Dublin 170 km – Waterford 9 km
◳ Dunmore East★, E : 18 km by R 675, R 685 and R 684

🏠 **Glenorney** without rest  ≤ 🚗 🍴 ⁽ᵗ⁾ P VISA ⓒⓞ
*Newtown, Southwest : 1.5 km by R 675 – ℰ (051) 381 056 – www.glenorney.com – March-November*
**6 rm** ☑ – 🛆 € 50/80 🛆🛆 € 80/90
♦ Smart yellow house in pretty gardens, set on the hillside, overlooking the bay. Homely lounge leads to dark wood breakfast room; book-filled sun lounge is a pleasant spot. Simply furnished bedrooms. Breakfast includes pancakes, French toast and homemade preserves.

**TRIM** (Baile Átha Troim) – **Meath** – **712** L7 – **pop. 6 870** ▯ Ireland    **37** D3
▰ Dublin 43 km – Drogheda 42 km – Tullamore 69 km
🅳 Castle St ℰ (046) 9 43 72 27, www.meathtourism.ie
🆁 County Meath Newtownmoynagh, ℰ (046) 943 14 63
◉ Trim Castle★★ – Town★
◳ Bective Abbey★, NE : 6.5 km by R 161

🏠 **Trim Castle**  🛗 ⅙ 🍴 ⁽ᵗ⁾ 💆 P VISA ⓒⓞ AE
*Castle St – ℰ (046) 948 30 00 – www.trimcastlehotel.com – Closed 25 December*
**68 rm** ☑ – 🛆 € 135/165 🛆🛆 € 150/180
**Rest** *Jules* – see restaurant listing
♦ Modern family hotel opposite the castle. Homeware shop, café, bar and restaurant. Good-sized bedrooms in contemporary hues – front rooms have the view. Discounted use of local leisure facilities; great outlook from delightful roof garden.

🏠 **Highfield House** without rest  🚗 ⁽ᵗ⁾ P VISA ⓒⓞ
*Maudlins Rd. – ℰ (046) 943 63 86 – www.highfieldguesthouse.com – Closed 22 December-1 February*
**10 rm** ☑ – 🛆 € 55 🛆🛆 € 75/80
♦ Substantial 18C stone house close to the river and castle. Well-appointed lounge and breakfast room, delightful terraced courtyard and boldly coloured bedrooms. Breakfast is comprehensive.

🍴🍴 **Jules** – at Trim Castle Hotel  ⬛ P VISA ⓒⓞ AE
*Castle St – ℰ (046) 948 30 00 – www.trimcastlehotel.com – Closed 25 December*
**Rest** – (closed Monday-Thursday) Menu € 20 (lunch)/25 – Carte € 25/47
♦ Set in the centre of a pleasant market town, a stylish dining room on the first floor of a modern family hotel. Open Friday and Saturday only. Good value menus of traditional European dishes.

**TWO MILE HOUSE** – see Naas

📖 Ireland

▶ Dublin 154 km – Cork 117 km – Limerick 124 km

🛫 Waterford Airport, Killowen : 𝒞 (051) 846600

🛈 The Granary, The Quay, Cork Rd 𝒞 (051) 87 58 23, www.waterfordtourism.com

🚇 Newrath, 𝒞 (051) 87 67 48

💿 Town★ - City Walls★ – Waterford Treasures★ **AC** Y

🎨 Waterford Crystal★, SW : 2.5 km by N 25 Y. Duncannon★, E : 19.25 km by R 683 ferry from Passage East and R 374 (south) Z – Dunmore East★, SE : 19.25 km by 684 Z – Tintern Abbey★, E : 21 km by R 683, ferry from Passage East, R 733 and 734 (south) Z

REPUBLIC OF IRELAND

LIMERICK, KILKENNY, DUBLIN N 9

WEXFORD, NEW ROSS R 6

WATERFORD

Waterford Crystal · R680 CORK, R 675 : TRAMORE    DUNMORE EAST R 683

**Waterford Castle H. and Golf Resort** 🦢  ＜ 🚗 ⑩ 💥 🎧 🎵
*The Island, Ballinakill, East : 4 km by R 683,*  💥 🏊 🅿 𝚅𝙸𝚂𝙰 ⓪ 🅰🅴 ⓪
*Ballinakill Rd and private ferry – 𝒞 (051) 878 203*
*– www.waterfordcastle.com – Closed 24-26 December and restricted opening in January*
**14 rm** ☕ – 🛉 € 110/180 🛉🛉 € 260/415 – 5 suites
**Rest** *Munster Dining Room* – see restaurant listing
♦ Attractive part-15C castle and smart lodges, set on a charming 320 acre private island in the river. Carved stone and wood-panelled hall displays antiques and old tapestries. Elegant, classical bedrooms boast characterful period bathrooms.

 **Athenaeum House**  🚗 🎍 🎧 🆎 rest, 💥 ⓒ🕯 💥 🅿 𝚅𝙸𝚂𝙰 ⓪ 🅰🅴
*Christendom, Ferrybank, Northeast : 1.5 km by R 771 – 𝒞 (051) 833 999*
*– www.athenaeumhousehotel.com – Closed 25-26 December and January*
**29 rm** – 🛉 € 120/140 🛉🛉 € 150/170, ☕ €15  **Zn**
**Rest** *Athenaeum House* – Menu € 25 (dinner) – Carte € 26/42
♦ In a quiet residential area, this extended Georgian house has retained some original features; elsewhere distinctly modern and stylish. Well equipped rooms exude modish charm. Eclectic mix of dishes in restaurant overlooking garden.

 **Fitzwilton**  🎧 占 rm, 💥 🕯 𝚅𝙸𝚂𝙰 ⓪ 🅰🅴 ⓪
*Bridge St – 𝒞 (051) 846 900 – www.fitzwiltonhotel.ie*
*– Closed 23-28 December*  **Yb**
**89 rm** ☕ – 🛉 € 79/109 🛉🛉 € 125/159
**Rest** *Chez K's* – Menu € 19/25 – Carte € 22/45
♦ Central hotel featuring glass façade and trendy bar. Bedrooms are modern, with a good finish: some are more spacious than others; those at the back are much quieter. Contemporary restaurant offers international dishes made with Irish ingredients.

 **Foxmount Country House** without rest 🦢  🚗 ⑩ 💥 💥 🅿 𝚅𝙸𝚂𝙰 ⓪
*Passage East Rd, Southeast : 7.25 km by R 683, off Cheekpoint rd*
*– 𝒞 (051) 874 308 – www.foxmountcountryhouse.com*
*– mid March-mid November*
**4 rm** ☕ – 🛉 € 65 🛉🛉 € 120
♦ Ivy-clad house, dating from the 17C, on a working farm. Wonderfully secluded and quiet yet within striking distance of Waterford. Neat, cottage-style bedrooms.

💥💥💥 **Munster Dining Room** – Waterford Castle Hotel and Golf Resort  🚗
*The Island, Ballinakill, East : 4 km by R 683,*  ⑩ 🅿 𝚅𝙸𝚂𝙰 ⓪ 🅰🅴 ⓪
*Ballinakill Rd and private ferry – 𝒞 (051) 878 203*
*– www.waterfordcastle.com – Closed 24-26 December and restricted opening in January*
**Rest** – *(bar lunch Monday-Saturday)* Menu € 65 – Carte lunch € 30/48
♦ Oak wood panelled hotel dining room boasting an ornate ceiling and evening pianist, set in a part-15C castle on an island in the river. Classically based menus fully support local producers.

💥💥 **La Bohème**  🎧 🔄 𝚅𝙸𝚂𝙰 ⓪ 🅰🅴
*2 George's St – 𝒞 (051) 875 645 – www.labohemerestaurant.ie*
*– Closed 25-27 December, Sunday, Monday and bank holidays*  **Yc**
**Rest** – French – *(dinner only) (booking essential)* Menu € 29 (early weekday dinner)/35 – Carte € 40/56
♦ Careful restoration of this historic building has created an atmospheric, candlelit dining room. Classic French cooking, traditionally prepared, includes daily market specials.

REPUBLIC OF IRELAND

▶ Dublin 262 km – Galway 80 km – Sligo 104 km

ℹ James St 𝒞 (098) 2 57 11, www.westporttourism.com

◉ Town★★ (Centre★) – Westport House★★ **AC**

ⓖ Ballintubber Abbey★, SE : 21 km by R 330. SW : Murrisk Peninsula★★ – Croagh Patrick★, W : 9.5 km by R 335 – Bunlahinch Clapper Bridge★, W : 25.75 km by R 335 - Doo Lough Pass★, W : 38.5 km by R 335 – Aasleagh Falls★, S : 35.5 km by 59

🏨🏨🏨 **Knockranny House H. & Spa**       ⟨ 🚲 🔲 ☺ 🐾 ⅃₆ 🛗 ᵴ rm, 🅰 rest

*Castlebar Rd., Knockranny, East :1.25 km on N 5*       ⚐ 🕯 🏖 **P** 🚗 🚗 🚗 🚗
*– 𝒞 (098) 28 600 – www.khh.ie – Closed 24-27 December*
**87 rm** ☕ – 🛉 € 110/150 🛉🛉 € 150/230 – 10 suites
**Rest** – *(Bar lunch Monday-Saturday)* Menu € 54 – Carte € 63/65 ⯐
• Purpose-built hotel in elevated position, overlooking the town, mountain and bay. Furnished in contemporary yet classic style and offering excellen comforts. Large, smart bedrooms; some with marble bathrooms or four-pos ters. Superb spa. Formal restaurant; experienced chef and original, modern Ir ish dishes.

🏨🏨 **Ardmore Country House**       ⟨ 🚲 ⚐ 🕯 **P** 🚗 🚗 🚗

*The Quay, West : 2.5 km on R 335 – 𝒞 (098) 25 994*
*– www.ardmorecountryhouse.com – April-October*
**13 rm** ☕ – 🛉 € 100/130 🛉🛉 € 100/150
**Rest** – *(dinner only) (booking essential residents only on Sunday)* Menu € 35 – Carte € 35/40
• Attractive, personally run hotel in commanding setting with views across gardens and Clew Bay. Neat, comfortable bedrooms have a sumptuous yet homely feel. Passionate chef-owner produces traditional dishes using local in gredients.

🏨🏨 **Westport Country Lodge** ⯐       🚲 🕭 🛗 ᵴ rm, 🅰 ⚐ 🕯 **P** 🚗 🚗

*Aghagower, Southeast : 4 km by R 330 – 𝒞 (098) 56 030*
*– www.westportlodge.com*
**21 rm** ☕ – 🛉 € 45/90 🛉🛉 € 70/140       **Rest** – Carte € 21/29
• Hotel set in 36 acres, with 9 hole pitch and putt. Rooms have big beds, flat screens and mod cons; many also have countryside views out towards Croagh Pa trick. Contemporary bar and dining room. Unpretentious homemade food, with classics given a modern touch.

🏠 **Augusta Lodge** without rest       🚲 ⚐ 🕯 **P** 🚗 🚗 🅾

*Golf Links Rd, North : 0.75 km by N 59 – 𝒞 (098) 28 900*
*– www.augustalodge.ie – closed 23-27 December*
**10 rm** ☕ – 🛉 € 35/70 🛉🛉 € 60/90
• Family run, purpose-built guesthouse, convenient for Westport Golf Club; play the piano in the lounge while admiring the golfing memorabilia. Homely, simple bedrooms.

✗ **An Port Mór**       ⟺ 🚗 🚗

*Brewery Pl, Bridge St – 𝒞 (098) 26 730*
*– www.anportmor.com – Closed 24-26 December, Monday except July-August and bank holidays*
**Rest** – *(dinner only)* Carte € 30/44
• Tucked away down a small alleyway and named after the chef's home village. Compact interior with shabby-chic, Mediterranean-style décor. Classically based menu showcases local produce in elaborate dishes; seafood specials on the blackboard.

## ⌂▯ Sheebeen 🛉 **P** VISA ⓄⓄ

*Rosbeg, West : 3 km on R 335 – ☎ (098) 26 528 – www.croninssheebeen.com – Closed Good Friday, 25 December and lunch weekdays November-mid March*
**Rest** – Carte € 23/42

♦ Thatched roadside pub to west of town. Cosy front bar has some tables but main dining is upstairs. Fresh, accurate cooking; go for the fresh local fish and seafood specials.

---

## WEXFORD (Loch Garman ) – Wexford – **712** M10 – pop. 18 163  **39** D2
Ireland

◪ Dublin 141 km – Kilkenny 79 km – Waterford 61 km

◪ Crescent Quay ☎ (053) 2 31 11, www.wexfordweb.com

◪ Mulgannon, ☎ (053) 4 22 38

◪ Town★ - Main Street★ YZ - Franciscan Friary★ Z – St Iberius' Church★ Y **D** - Twin Churches★ Z

◪ Irish Agricultural Museum, Johnstown Castle★★ **AC**, SW : 7.25 km X – Irish National Heritage Park, Ferrycarrig★ **AC**, NW : 4 km by N 11 V – Curracloe★, NE : 8 km by R 741 and R 743 V. Kilmore Quay★, SW : 24 km by N 25 and R 739 (Saltee Islands★ - access by boat) X – Enniscorthy Castle★ (County Museum★ **AC**) N : 24 km by N 11 V

Plans pages 963, 964

REPUBLIC OF IRELAND

### Whites

Abbey St – ℰ (053) 912 23 11 – www.whitesofwexford.ie
– *Closed 24-27 December*
**157 rm** ⌷ – ♦ € 150 ♦♦ € 250/310
**Rest** *Whites* – *(dinner only and carvery lunch in bar)* Menu 25
– Carte € 28/41 **s**

♦ Modern hotel built around a paved central courtyard. Spacious public area
with popular meeting rooms, superb leisure facilities and very comfortable bed
rooms. Internationally influenced menu served in contemporary dining room
carvery lunches in the busy bar.

**WEXFORD**

**Ferrycarrig**   ⟨ 🚗 🖼 🏠 🛴 🎒 ⅏ rm, AC rest, ⅏ 🛈 🛄 P VISA ⚌ AE ①

*Ferrycarrig, Northwest : 4.5 km on N 11 – 𝒞 (053) 912 09 99*
*– www.ferrycarrighotel.ie*                                                    V**a**
**98 rm** ⌑ – 🛏 € 90/135  🛏🛏 € 170/250 – 4 suites
**Rest** *Reeds* – *(booking essential at lunch)* Menu € 30 (dinner) – Carte € 30/43
♦ Imposing hotel idyllically set on River Slaney and estuary. Public areas on enchanting waterfront curve. Good leisure facilities. Modern rooms with super views and balconies. Lively, informal Reeds.

⩙ **Rathaspeck Manor** without rest ⬎        🚗 🖼 ⅏ P VISA ⚌
*Rathaspeck, Southwest : 6.5 km by R 730 off Murntown rd – 𝒞 (053) 914 16 72*
*– www.rathaspeckmanor.com – March-October*                                    X**k**
**4 rm** ⌑ – 🛏 € 55/75  🛏🛏 € 100/130
♦ Georgian country house with 18-hole golf course half a mile from Johnstone Castle. Period furnishings adorn the public rooms. Comfortable, spacious bedrooms.

⩙ **McMenamin's Townhouse** without rest        ⅏ 🛈 P VISA ⚌ ①
*6 Glena Ter. – 𝒞 (053) 914 64 42 – www.wexford-bedandbreakfast.com*
*– January-November*                                                          X**n**
**4 rm** ⌑ – 🛏 € 55/65  🛏🛏 € 90/120
♦ Homely Victorian townhouse retaining many original features. Friendly, hands-on owners. Legendary breakfasts include homemade breads, preserves, omelettes and drop scones.

✗ **Jacques Bistro**        🏠 AC ⇔ VISA ⚌ AE
*Selskar – 𝒞 (053) 91 23 004 – www.greenacres.ie – Closed 25-26 December, 1*
*January, Easter, restricted opening on Saturday and Sunday*                    Y**x**
**Rest** – French – Menu € 25 (weekdays) – Carte € 27/46 🍷
♦ Modern, split-level bistro with a deli and patisserie selling cheese, charcuterie, homemade pastries and breads. Well-priced French wines fill the shelves. Simple lunch menu offers salads and platters; flavoursome Gallic dishes at dinner.

---

**WICKLOW (Cill Mhantáin)** – Wicklow – **712** N9 – pop. 10 071        **39** D2
🇮 Ireland
▶ Dublin 53 km – Waterford 135 km – Wexford 108 km
🛈 Fitzwilliam Sq 𝒞 (0404) 6 91 17, www.visitwicklow.ie
🅖 Mount Usher Gardens, Ashford★ **AC**, NW : 6.5 km by R 750 and N 11 – Devil's Glen★, NW : 12.75 km by R 750 and N 11. Glendalough★★★ (Lower Lake★★★, Upper Lake★★, Cathedral★★, Round Tower★★, St Kevin's Church★★, St Saviour's Priory★) – W : 22.5 km by R 750, N 11, R 763, R 755 and R 756 – Wicklow Mountains★★ (Wicklow Gap★★, Sally Gap★★, Avondale★, Meeting of the Waters★, Glenmacnass Waterfall★, Glenmalur★, – Loughs Tay and Dan★)

✗✗ **Black 'N' Blue Grill**        VISA ⚌
*Church St – 𝒞 (0404) 66 800 – www.blacknbluegrill.ie – Closed Monday*
**Rest** – *(dinner only and Sunday lunch)* Menu € 27 **s** – Carte € 36/52 **s**
♦ Well-run, split-level, former bakery. Characterful restaurant with exposed stone, beams and an old cast iron oven; open-fired lounge in the basement. Menus fuse Mediterranean, Californian and Asian influences in tasty, well-presented dishes.

**at Rathnew** Northwest : 3.25 km on R 750 – ⊠ Wicklow

 **Tinakilly House** ⬎        ⟨ 🚗 🎒 🎒 ⅏ rm, AC rest, ⅏ 🛄 P VISA ⚌ AE
*on R 750 – 𝒞 (0404) 69 274 – www.tinakilly.ie*
**50 rm** ⌑ – 🛏 € 141/164  🛏🛏 € 191/237 – 1 suite
**Rest** *Brunel* – *(dinner only and Sunday lunch)* Carte € 37/50
♦ Part Victorian country house with views of sea and mountains. Grand entrance hall hung with paintings. Mix of comfortable room styles, those in main house most characterful. Large dining room with rich drapes, formal service.

🏠 **Hunter's**      🛋 ⚜ ⁽ᵖ⁾ ᴬ P VISA ⚙

*Newrath Bridge, North : 1.25 km by Dublin rd on R 761 – 𝒞 (0404) 40 106*
*– www.hunters.ie – Closed 24-26 and 31 December*
**16 rm** ⬜ – 🛏 € 65/110 🛏🛏 € 130/190    **Rest** – Menu € 25/45
♦ 18C former coaching inn run by the 5th generation of the same family. Traditionally styled throughout with homely lounges displaying flowery fabrics and
drapes. Neat, country house style bedrooms boast sleigh beds and antique furnishings. Formal dining room offers menu of traditionally based dishes.

---

**YOUGHAL** (Eochaill) – **Cork** – **712** I12 – **pop. 6 785** 🎋 Ireland     **39 C**

▶ Dublin 235 km – Cork 48 km – Waterford 75 km
🅳 Market Sq 𝒞 (024) 2 01 70, www.youghal.ie
🔟8 Knockaverry, 𝒞 (024) 9 27 87
👁 Town ★ – St Mary's Collegiate Church ★★ – Town Walls ★ - Clock Gate ★
🅖 Helvick Head ★ ( ≤ ★ ), NE : 35.5 km by N 25 and R 674 – Ringville ( ≤ ★ ), NE :
32.25 km by N 25 and R 674 – Ardmore ★ - Round Tower ★
- Cathedral ★ (arcade ★ ), N : 16 km by N 25 and R 674 – Whiting Bay ★, SE :
19.25 km by N 25, R 673 and the coast road

XX    **Aherne's** with rm     ⁽ᵖ⁾ P VISA ⚙ AE ①

*163 North Main St – 𝒞 (024) 92 424 – www.ahernes.com – Closed 23-27*
*December*
**12 rm** ⬜ – 🛏 € 110/130 🛏🛏 € 130/210
**Rest** – Seafood – *(bar lunch)* Menu € 25/40 – Carte € 27/51
♦ In the third generation of the family and dating back to 1910. Traditional bar,
smart cocktail bar and contemporary dining room. Freshly prepared local seafood
appears in tasty, unfussy dishes. Large, antique-furnished bedrooms and welcoming open-fired lounge.

# The MICHELIN Guide
*A collection to savor!*

Belgique & Luxembourg
Deutschland
España & Portugal
France
Great Britain & Ireland
Italia
Nederland
Portugal
Suisse-Schweiz-Svizzera
Main Cities of Europe

*Also:*

Chicago
Hokkaido
Hong Kong Macau
Kyoto Osaka Kobe
London
New York City
Paris
San Francisco
Tokyo

# International Dialling Codes

Note: When making an international call, do not dial the first (0) of the city cod (except for calls to Italy).

| from \ to | Ⓐ | Ⓑ | ⒸⒽ | ⒸⓏ | Ⓓ | ⒹⓀ | Ⓔ | ⒻⒾⓃ | Ⓕ | ⒼⒷ | ( |
|---|---|---|---|---|---|---|---|---|---|---|---|
| **A Austria** | | 0032 | 0041 | 00420 | 0049 | 0045 | 0034 | 00358 | 0033 | 0044 | 0 |
| **B Belgium** | 0043 | | 0041 | 00420 | 0049 | 0045 | 0034 | 00358 | 0033 | 0044 | 0 |
| **CH Switzerland** | 0043 | 0032 | | 00420 | 0049 | 0045 | 0034 | 00358 | 0033 | 0044 | 0 |
| **CZ Czech Republic** | 0043 | 0032 | 0041 | | 0049 | 0045 | 0034 | 00358 | 0033 | 0044 | 0 |
| **D Germany** | 0043 | 0032 | 0041 | 00420 | | 0045 | 0034 | 00358 | 0033 | 0044 | 0 |
| **DK Denmark** | 0043 | 0032 | 0041 | 00420 | 0049 | | 0034 | 00358 | 0033 | 0044 | 0C |
| **E Spain** | 0043 | 0032 | 0041 | 00420 | 0049 | 0045 | | 00358 | 0033 | 0044 | 0 |
| **FIN Finland** | 0043 | 0032 | 0041 | 00420 | 0049 | 0045 | 0034 | | 0033 | 0044 | 0C |
| **F France** | 0043 | 0032 | 0041 | 00420 | 0049 | 0045 | 0034 | 00358 | | 0044 | 0C |
| **GB United Kingdom** | 0043 | 0032 | 0041 | 00420 | 0049 | 0045 | 0034 | 00358 | 0033 | | 0C |
| **GR Greece** | 0043 | 0032 | 0041 | 00420 | 0049 | 0045 | 0034 | 00358 | 0033 | 0044 | |
| **H Hungary** | 0043 | 0032 | 0041 | 00420 | 0049 | 0045 | 0034 | 00358 | 0033 | 0044 | 0C |
| **I Italy** | 0043 | 0032 | 0041 | 00420 | 0049 | 0045 | 0034 | 00358 | 0033 | 0044 | 00 |
| **IRL Ireland** | 0043 | 0032 | 0041 | 00420 | 0049 | 0045 | 0034 | 00358 | 0033 | 0044 | 0C |
| **J Japan** | 00143 | 00132 | 00141 | 001420 | 00149 | 00145 | 00134 | 001358 | 00133 | 00144 | 00 |
| **L Luxembourg** | 0043 | 0032 | 0041 | 00420 | 0049 | 0045 | 0034 | 00358 | 0033 | 0044 | 0C |
| **N Norway** | 0043 | 0032 | 0041 | 00420 | 0049 | 0045 | 0034 | 00358 | 0033 | 0044 | 00 |
| **NL Netherlands** | 0043 | 0032 | 0041 | 00420 | 0049 | 0045 | 0034 | 00358 | 0033 | 0044 | 0C |
| **PL Poland** | 0043 | 0032 | 0041 | 00420 | 0049 | 0045 | 0034 | 00358 | 0033 | 0044 | 00 |
| **P Portugal** | 0043 | 0032 | 0041 | 00420 | 0049 | 0045 | 0034 | 00358 | 0033 | 0044 | 00 |
| **RUS Russia** | 81043 | 81032 | 81041 | 810420 | 81049 | 81045 | 81034 | 810358 | 81033 | 81044 | 81C |
| **S Sweden** | 0043 | 0032 | 0041 | 00420 | 0049 | 0045 | 0034 | 00358 | 0033 | 0044 | 00 |
| **USA** | 01143 | 01132 | 01141 | 001420 | 01149 | 01145 | 01134 | 01358 | 01133 | 01144 | 01 |

*Direct dialling not possible*

| (?) | (I) | (IRL) | (J) | (L) | (N) | (NL) | (PL) | (P) | (RUS) | (S) | (USA) | |
|---|---|---|---|---|---|---|---|---|---|---|---|---|
| 36 | 0039 | 00353 | 0081 | 00352 | 0047 | 0031 | 0048 | 00351 | 007 | 0046 | 001 | **A Austria** |
| 36 | 0039 | 00353 | 0081 | 00352 | 0047 | 0031 | 0048 | 00351 | 007 | 0046 | 001 | **B Belgium** |
| 36 | 0039 | 00353 | 0081 | 00352 | 0047 | 0031 | 0048 | 00351 | 007 | 0046 | 001 | **CH Switzerland** |
| 36 | 0039 | 00353 | 0081 | 00352 | 0047 | 0031 | 0048 | 00351 | 007 | 0046 | 001 | **CZ Czech Republic** |
| 36 | 0039 | 00353 | 0081 | 00352 | 0047 | 0031 | 0048 | 00351 | 007 | 0046 | 001 | **D Germany** |
| 36 | 0039 | 00353 | 0081 | 00352 | 0047 | 0031 | 0048 | 00351 | 007 | 0046 | 001 | **DK Denmark** |
| 36 | 0039 | 00353 | 0081 | 00352 | 0047 | 0031 | 0048 | 00351 | 007 | 0046 | 001 | **E Spain** |
| 36 | 0039 | 00353 | 0081 | 00352 | 0047 | 0031 | 0048 | 00351 | 007 | 0046 | 001 | **FIN Finland** |
| 36 | 0039 | 00353 | 0081 | 00352 | 0047 | 0031 | 0048 | 00351 | 007 | 0046 | 001 | **F France** |
| 36 | 0039 | 00353 | 0081 | 00352 | 0047 | 0031 | 0048 | 00351 | 007 | 0046 | 001 | **GB United Kingdom** |
| 36 | 0039 | 00353 | 0081 | 00352 | 0047 | 0031 | 0048 | 00351 | 007 | 0046 | 001 | **GR Greece** |
|  | 0039 | 00353 | 0081 | 00352 | 0047 | 0031 | 0048 | 00351 | 007 | 0046 | 001 | **H Hungary** |
| 036 |  | 00353 | 0081 | 00352 | 0047 | 0031 | 0048 | 00351 | 007 | 0046 | 001 | **I Italy** |
| 036 | 0039 |  | 0081 | 00352 | 0047 | 0031 | 0048 | 00351 | 007 | 0046 | 001 | **IRL Ireland** |
| 136 | 00139 | 001353 |  | 001352 | 00147 | 00131 | 00148 | 001351 | 007 | 001146 | 0011 | **J Japan** |
| 036 | 0039 | 00353 | 0081 |  | 0047 | 0031 | 0048 | 00351 | 007 | 0046 | 001 | **L Luxembourg** |
| 036 | 0039 | 00353 | 0081 | 00352 |  | 0031 | 0048 | 00351 | 007 | 0046 | 001 | **N Norway** |
| 036 | 0039 | 00353 | 0081 | 00352 | 0047 |  | 0048 | 00351 | 007 | 0046 | 001 | **NL Netherlands** |
| 036 | 0039 | 00353 | 0081 | 00352 | 0047 | 0031 |  | 00351 | 007 | 0046 | 001 | **PL Poland** |
| 036 | 0039 | 00353 | 0081 | 00352 | 0047 | 0031 | 048 |  | 007 | 0046 | 001 | **P Portugal** |
| 036 | 81039 | 810353 | 81081 | 810352 | * | 81031 | 81048 | 810351 |  | 81046 | 8101 | **RUS Russia** |
| 036 | 0039 | 00353 | 0081 | 00352 | 0047 | 0031 | 0048 | 00351 | 007 |  | 001 | **S Sweden** |
| 136 | 01139 | 011353 | 01181 | 011352 | 01147 | 01131 | 01148 | 011351 | 0117 | 011146 |  | **USA** |

# Index of towns

975

# Major hotel groups

Central reservation telephone numbers

| | |
|---|---|
| ACCOR HOTELS (NOVOTEL) | 0871 6630624 |
| DE VERE HOTELS PLC | 0845 3752808 |
| DOYLE COLLECTION | 0870 9072222 |
| HILTON HOTELS | 08705 515151 |
| HOLIDAY INN & CROWNE PLAZA WORLDWIDE | 0800 40 50 60 *(Freephone)* |
| HYATT HOTELS WORLDWIDE | 0845 8881234 |
| INTERCONTINENTAL HOTELS | 0800 0289387 *(Freephone)* |
| MACDONALD HOTELS PLC | 08457 585593 |
| MARRIOTT HOTELS | 00800 1927 1927 *(Freephone)* |
| MILLENNIUM & COPTHORNE HOTELS PLC | 0845 3020001 |
| RADISSON HOTELS WORLDWIDE | 0800 374411 *(Freephone)* |
| SHERATON HOTELS & RESORTS WORLDWIDE | 0800 353535 *(Freephone)* |

# Maps
## Regional maps of listed towns

## Map Key
### Places with at least one

| | |
|---|---|
| ● | hotel or restaurant |
| ✿ | starred establishment |
| ◉ | « Bib Gourmand » restaurant |
| ◯⌂ | « Bib Hotel » |
| ✗ | particularly pleasant restaurant |
| ▯ | particularly pleasant pub |
| ▤ | particularly pleasant hotel |
| ⌂ | particularly pleasant guesthouse |
| ✍ | particularly quiet hotel |

# Distances in miles

(except for the Republic of Ireland: km). The distance is given from each town to other nearby towns and to the capital of each region as grouped in the guide. To avoid excessive repetition some distances have only been quoted once – you may therefore have to look under both town headings.
The distances quoted are not necessarily the shortest but have been based on the roads which afford the best driving conditions and are therefore the most practical.

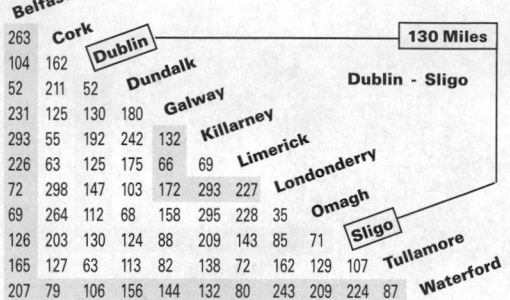

| Belfast | Cork | Dublin | Dundalk | Galway | Killarney | Limerick | Londonderry | Omagh | Sligo | Tullamore | Waterford |
|---|---|---|---|---|---|---|---|---|---|---|---|
| 263 | | | | | | | | | | | |
| 104 | 162 | | | | | | | | | | |
| 52 | 211 | 52 | | | | | | | | | |
| 231 | 125 | 130 | 180 | | | | | | | | |
| 293 | 55 | 192 | 242 | 132 | | | | | | | |
| 226 | 63 | 125 | 175 | 66 | 69 | | | | | | |
| 72 | 298 | 147 | 103 | 172 | 293 | 227 | | | | | |
| 69 | 264 | 112 | 68 | 158 | 295 | 228 | 35 | | | | |
| 126 | 203 | 130 | 124 | 88 | 209 | 143 | 85 | 71 | | | |
| 165 | 127 | 63 | 113 | 82 | 138 | 72 | 162 | 129 | 107 | | |
| 207 | 79 | 106 | 156 | 144 | 132 | 80 | 243 | 209 | 224 | 87 | |

130 Miles

Dublin - Sligo

# Distances between major towns/cities

Box note:

> **433 Miles**
> Edinburgh – Southampton

Diagonal city labels (in order): **Aber**, **Ayr**, **Birmingham**, **Blackpool**, **Brighton**, **Bristol**, **Cambridge**, **Cardiff**, **Carlisle**, **Coventry**, **Dover**, **Dumfries**, **Dundee**, **Edinburgh**, **Glasgow**, **Inverness**, **Ipswich**, **Kingston-upon-Hull**, **Leeds**, **Leicester**, **Liverpool**, **London**, **Manchester**, **Middlesbrough**, **Newcastle**, **Norwich**, **Nottingham**, **Oban**, **Oxford**, **Plymouth**, **Portsmouth**, **Sheffield**, **Southampton**, **Stoke-on-Trent**, **Swansea**, **Wick**

Mileage chart (each row lists the distances from that town to the towns named above it, read left-to-right):

| From | distances to preceding towns (in the order listed above) |
|---|---|
| Ayr | 182 |
| Birmingham | 424 328 |
| Blackpool | 329 233 127 |
| Brighton | 597 501 178 300 |
| Bristol | 505 409 98 208 175 |
| Cambridge | 488 392 100 222 178 158 |
| Cardiff | 528 430 118 229 98 122 206 |
| Carlisle | 230 134 196 101 369 277 192 261 |
| Coventry | 442 346 23 145 159 94 87 124 214 |
| Dover | 605 509 202 324 105 203 45 123 298 181 |
| Dumfries | 210 59 229 134 402 311 243 311 55 208 410 |
| Dundee | 66 125 359 265 532 441 277 359 132 264 530 146 |
| Edinburgh | 127 87 292 198 467 374 227 311 82 253 472 78 56 |
| Glasgow | 147 38 291 197 464 373 225 310 53 291 470 79 88 47 |
| Inverness | 105 208 449 354 622 531 385 469 273 449 630 235 157 171 171 |
| Ipswich | 537 441 151 243 132 179 60 208 317 95 127 401 281 219 252 195 |
| Kingston-upon-Hull | 416 320 93 191 188 161 90 188 141 52 208 141 92 110 134 158 128 |
| Leeds | 182 86 119 72 194 200 128 216 117 55 211 55 73 99 141 92 73 61 |
| Leicester | 498 402 53 126 152 133 44 181 207 24 140 152 124 190 171 139 66 79 99 |
| Liverpool | 619 524 86 66 270 162 236 167 102 84 319 119 232 295 291 342 255 84 79 170 |
| London | 580 484 107 119 54 116 65 159 250 90 82 236 190 171 291 45 50 181 187 79 210 |
| Manchester | 390 294 79 53 236 152 135 203 102 41 255 72 135 161 161 66 102 44 41 71 35 210 |
| Middlesbrough | 565 469 151 141 366 263 207 333 126 145 384 128 207 193 203 184 135 54 63 145 159 251 146 |
| Newcastle | 382 286 141 147 366 263 203 333 65 156 384 156 128 92 193 203 161 54 57 90 187 284 113 44 |
| Norwich | 561 465 218 227 154 210 42 236 242 147 126 242 283 264 277 283 283 54 159 160 233 113 219 253 259 |
| Nottingham | 561 465 49 80 241 162 66 227 181 45 233 128 283 186 192 141 92 187 233 50 54 128 82 193 186 303 |
| Oban | 205 104 454 355 651 570 525 614 433 569 730 336 258 104 105 341 665 479 480 436 663 541 586 384 421 662 384 |
| Oxford | 382 286 69 154 84 69 93 142 208 24 121 214 293 237 240 341 84 161 160 45 159 59 102 236 203 197 92 525 |
| Plymouth | 565 469 201 240 146 119 210 119 346 153 156 317 430 240 237 346 197 303 187 138 236 213 193 352 303 307 250 525 119 |
| Portsmouth | 382 286 119 190 54 69 237 154 201 81 73 186 237 187 192 525 54 203 184 69 159 73 145 320 203 197 128 525 81 154 |
| Sheffield | 561 465 81 154 210 175 175 190 154 119 336 156 277 233 277 283 233 54 63 81 175 54 41 193 190 156 54 525 153 240 238 |
| Southampton | 433 (Edinburgh – Southampton) 190 201 54 69 210 119 187 119 233 250 250 247 277 525 161 203 187 54 236 79 167 236 236 197 161 525 69 119 20 233 |
| Stoke-on-Trent | 186 81 48 75 218 134 150 167 126 57 293 117 238 233 258 283 252 101 102 63 57 184 41 161 203 253 54 525 128 263 250 57 210 |
| Swansea | 183 175 142 187 190 81 237 69 240 154 187 277 283 264 303 525 197 264 264 187 190 233 238 352 303 383 187 525 154 187 187 233 187 233 |
| Wick | 687 507 690 705 744 730 662 744 569 730 730 541 271 258 308 104 665 570 570 476 663 570 623 421 384 662 541 384 623 744 476 570 476 623 651 |

993

● FOLKESTONE
(CHANNEL TUNNE
● SOUTHAMPTON
● TYNEMOUTH

**Glasgow - Barcelona** | 1287 Miles |

GLASGOW

DUBLIN

BIRMINGHAM

CARDIFF

LONDON

København

Hamburg

Amsterdam

Berlin

Warsza

Düsseldorf

Praha

Lille

Bruxelles
Brussel

Frankfurt

Cherbourg-Octeville

Luxembourg

Strasbourg

Bratislava

Paris

München

Wien

Nantes

Basel

Bern

Genève

Zagreb

Clermont-Ferrand

Lyon

Milano

Bordeaux

San Sebastián

Toulouse

Marseille

Roma

Porto

Madrid

Barcelona

E

Lisboa

Valencia

Palermo

Málaga

| Birmingham | Cardiff | Dublin | Glasgow | London | |
|---|---|---|---|---|---|
| 231 | 455 | 399 | 336 | 304 | **Amsterdam** |
| 1017 | 1043 | 1184 | 1287 | 891 | **Barcelona** |
| 665 | 690 | 832 | 935 | 539 | **Basel** |
| 773 | 799 | 941 | 724 | 648 | **Berlin** |
| 725 | 750 | 892 | 995 | 599 | **Bern** |
| 735 | 760 | 902 | 1005 | 609 | **Bordeaux** |
| 1059 | 1085 | 1227 | 1330 | 934 | **Bratislava** |
| 1492 | 1518 | 1660 | 1763 | 1367 | **Brindisi** |
| 319 | 345 | 486 | 590 | 194 | **Bruxelles-Brussel** |
| 161 | 156 | 329 | 448 | 86 | **Cherbourg** |
| 637 | 663 | 804 | 907 | 511 | **Clermont-Ferrand** |
| 440 | 466 | 608 | 711 | 315 | **Düsseldorf** |
| 566 | 591 | 733 | 836 | 440 | **Frankfurt am Main** |
| 703 | 729 | 870 | 974 | 578 | **Genève** |
| 509 | 691 | 677 | 605 | 540 | **Hamburg** |
| 701 | 883 | 868 | 796 | 731 | **København** |
| 264 | 290 | 431 | 535 | 139 | **Lille** |
| 1455 | 1481 | 1623 | 1726 | 1330 | **Lisboa** |
| 452 | 478 | 619 | 722 | 326 | **Luxembourg** |
| 667 | 693 | 834 | 937 | 541 | **Lyon** |
| 1165 | 1191 | 1333 | 1436 | 1040 | **Madrid** |
| 1495 | 1521 | 1663 | 1766 | 1370 | **Málaga** |
| 861 | 887 | 1028 | 1132 | 736 | **Marseille** |
| 874 | 900 | 1042 | 1145 | 749 | **Milano** |
| 798 | 824 | 965 | 1069 | 673 | **München** |
| 563 | 589 | 731 | 834 | 274 | **Nantes** |
| 1787 | 1813 | 1955 | 2058 | 1662 | **Palermo** |
| 369 | 395 | 536 | 640 | 244 | **Paris** |
| 1360 | 1386 | 1527 | 1631 | 1234 | **Porto** |
| 879 | 905 | 1047 | 1150 | 754 | **Praha** |
| 1240 | 1266 | 1407 | 1510 | 1114 | **Roma** |
| 879 | 905 | 1046 | 1149 | 753 | **San Sebastián** |
| 580 | 605 | 747 | 850 | 454 | **Strasbourg** |
| 794 | 820 | 962 | 1065 | 669 | **Toulouse** |
| 1229 | 1255 | 1397 | 1500 | 1104 | **Valencia** |
| 1119 | 1144 | 1286 | 1070 | 993 | **Warszawa** |
| 1006 | 1032 | 1174 | 1277 | 881 | **Wien** |
| 1117 | 1143 | 1285 | 1388 | 992 | **Zagreb** |

# Great Britain & Ireland in 39 maps

**31** SHETLAND & ORKNEY

Shetland Islands

Orkney Islands

NORTH SEA

**29 30** HIGHLAND & THE ISLANDS

Aberdeen

**27 28** CENTRAL SCOTLAND

Dundee

Edinburgh

Glasgow

**25 26** BORDERS, EDINBURGH & GLASGOW

**24** NORTHUMBERLAND, DURHAM

Newcastle upon Tyne

Sunderland

**21**

**34 35** NORTHERN IRELAND

Belfast

ATLANTIC OCEAN

# Cornwall, Devon, Isles of Scilly

**A**

**B**

BR

**1**

Bryher

Tresco

St. Martin's

St. Mary's

**Isles of Scilly**

Clo

Hartland

Bude

Crackington Haven

Boscastle

**2**

Rock

C O R N W A L

Padstow

St. Issey

Wadebridge

A 30

Mawgan Porth

Watergate Bay

A 30

Bodmin

Newquay

Summercourt

Liskea

St Blazey

Tregrehan

Golant

Looe

St. Austell

Fowey

Polperro

Truro

Mevagissey

St. Ives

Zennor

Veryan

Gorran Haven

Marazion

Portscatho

Penzance

St. Hilary

St. Mawes

Perranuthnoe

Falmouth

Mousehole

Porthleven

Helston

Cury

St. Keverne

Coverack

**3**

Lizard

**A**

**B**

# 3 Somerset, Dorset, Gloucestershire, Wiltshire

**A**

**B**

**1**

WALES
(plans 32 33)

Merthyr
Tydfil

Swansea

Newport

NEL

Cardiff

Severn Estuary

Backwell

**2**

Weston-super-Mare

Minehead

Porlock

Dunster

Holford

East

Exford

Winsford

Luxborough

Tarr Steps

S O M E R S E

Dulverton

Somerton

CORNWALL, DEVON,
ISLES OF SCILLY
(plans 1 2)

Taunton

Langport

Long Sutton

Tintinhull

Ye

Bar

**3**

Hinton
St. George

Beaminster

Powerstock

Charmouth

Bridpo

Lyme Regis

Burton Bradstock

Abbotsl

Lyme Bay

Place with at least:

- • a hotel or a restaurant
- 🏵 a starred establishment
- 😊 a "Bib Gourmand" restaurant
- 🏠 a "Bib Hotel"
- ✕ a particularly pleasant restaurant
- ᐱ a particularly pleasant guesthouse
- 🏠 a particularly pleasant hotel
- 🌙 a particularly quiet hotel
- 🍺 a particularly pleasant pub

**A**

**B**

# The MICHELIN Guide
*A collection to savor!*

# Channel Islands

1

*ENGLISH CHANNEL*

*LA MANCHE*

**Alderney**
Braye

Cherbourg-
Octeville

**Guernsey**    Catel

Kings Mills

St. Saviour

St. Martin
Fermain Bay
St. Peter Port

Herm
**Herm**

Sark
**Sark**

**FRANCE**

2

Rozel Bay
St. Saviour
Gorey
La Pulente
St. Brelade's Bay
St. Aubin
La Haule
Grouville
Green Island
**Jersey**
St. Helier

3

A    B

# 6 Hampshire, Isle of Wight, Surrey, West Sussex

OXFORDSHIRE, BUCKINGHAMSHIRE
(plans 10 11)

**A**    **B**

**1**

SOMERSET, DORSET, GLOUCESTERSHIRE, WILTSHIRE
(plans 3 4 )

Avon

Newbury

Highclere

Old Burghclere

Baughurst

A 339

Hurstbourne Tarrant

A 34

A 303

Preston Candov

Longstock

Totford

Stockbridge

Sparsholt

Winchester

H A M P S H I

Salisbury

West Meon

**2**

Romsey

Droxford

Fordingbridge

A 27

Shedfield

Netley Marsh

Southampton

Wickham

A 31

Lyndhurst

Ringwood

Beaulieu

Ems

Brockenhurst

New Milton

Lymington

Portsmouth

Barton-on-Sea

Milford-on-Sea

Hay
Isla

Bournemouth

Yarmouth

Wootton Bridge

Seaview

Godshill

Shanklin

**3**

Isle of Wight

Bonchurch

Niton

Ventnor

**A**    **B**

**A** **B**

LONDON

**1**

BEDFORDSHIRE
HERTFORDSHIRE, ESSEX
(plans **12** **13**)

Farningham

R. TH

A 19

A 2

M 26    M 20    West Malling

Aylesfor

Maidstone

Boughton Monchelsea

**K E N T**

HAMPSHIRE,
ISLE OF WIGHT,
SURREY, WEST SUSSEX
(plans **6** **7**)

Crawley

Royal
Tunbridge Wells

**2**

Forest Row

Cranbrook

Bener

Iden Gre

**E A S T   S U S S E X**

Fletching

Newick

Uckfield

Bodiar

Rushlake Green

Broad

East Hoathly

Battle

Westfi

Lewes

Herstmonceux

A 27    A 259    Hastings
St. Leona

Hove

Brighton

Alfriston

Eastbourne

**3**

**A** **B**

# 10 Oxfordshire, Buckinghamshire

HEREFORDSHIRE,
WORCESTERSHIRE,
SHROPSHIRE,
STAFFORDSHIRE,
WARWICKSHIRE
(plans 18 19)

SOMERSET, DORSET,
GLOUCESTERSHIRE,
WILTSHIRE
(plans 3 4)

Banbury

Deddington

Chipping Norton

Church Enstone

Kingham

Kirtlington

Woodstock

Hampton Poyle

Murcott

Burford

Minster Lovell

OXFORDSHIRE

Oxford

Clanfield

Thames

Toot Bald

Buckland Marsh

Abingdon

Stadhar

Sutton Courtenay

Wantage

Harwell

Wallingford

Swindon

Aston Tirro

Moulsford

Lambourn Woodlands

East Garston

Chieveley

Yattendon

Newbury

**Place with at least:**

- • a hotel or a restaurant
- ❀ a starred establishment
- ☺ a "Bib Gourmand" restaurant
- ⌂ a "Bib Hotel"
- ✗ a particularly pleasant restaurant
- ↑ a particularly pleasant guesthouse
- ⌂ a particularly pleasant hotel
- ⌂ a particularly quiet hotel
- ⌂ a particularly pleasant pub

HAMPSHIRE,
ISLE OF WIGHT,
SURREY, WEST SUSSEX
(plans 6 7)

# Bedfordshire, Hertfordshire, Essex

**13**

C · D

Bury St Edmunds

**NORFOLK, SUFFOLK, CAMBRIDGESHIRE**
(plans **14** **15**)

Ipswich

🍴🏠 Dedham

Mistley 🍺 Harwich

Great Dunmow

Coggeshall

Fuller Street

Kelvedon 😊

**E S S E X**

Great Totham

St Osyth

Hatfield Peverel

Chelmsford

Hullbridge

Burnham-on-Crouch

Brentwood

Rayleigh

Leigh-on-Sea

Southend-on-Sea 📷

rndon the Hill

R. THAMES

Rochester

**EAST SUSSEX, KENT**
(plans **8** **9**)

Maidstone

C · D

1

2

3

Place with at least:
- • a hotel or a restaurant
- 🌸 a starred establishment
- 😊 a "Bib Gourmand" restaurant
- 📷 a "Bib Hotel"
- 🍴 a particularly pleasant restaurant
- 🏠 a particularly pleasant guesthouse
- 🏠 a particularly pleasant hotel
- ⌂ a particularly quiet hotel
- 🍺 a particularly pleasant pub

# 14 Norfolk, Suffolk, Cambridgeshire

**A**      **B**

*The Wash*

✿ Hunstanton

Snettisham •

**1**   DERBYSHIRE, LEICESTERSHIRE, NORTHAMPTONSHIRE, RUTLAND, LINCOLNSHIRE, NOTTINGHAMSHIRE

(plans **16 17**)

Spalding ○

King's Lynn ●

A 47

🦐 Grim

A 10

• Stamford

Ufford •

*Welland*

*Nene*

A 47

*Great Ouse*

Peterborough •

Elton •

A 1(M)

Stilton •

**C A M B R I D G E S H I R E**

**2**

Ely ●

Keyston 🏚

*Gt. Ouse*

• Huntingdon

A 10

Buckden •

A 14

Tudder •

A 14

A 428

Eltisley •

Bourn •

**Cambridge**
✿ ✿

• Little Wilbraham 😊

*Cam*

---SHIRE

Place with at least:

| | |
|---|---|
| • | a hotel or a restaurant |
| ✿ | a starred establishment |
| 😊 | a "Bib Gourmand" restaurant |
| 🏨 | a "Bib Hotel" |
| 🍽 | a particularly pleasant restaurant |
| 🏠 | a particularly pleasant guesthouse |
| 🏡 | a particularly pleasant hotel |
| 🐤 | a particularly quiet hotel |
| 🍺 | a particularly pleasant pub |

**3**

BEDFORDSHIRE, HERTFORDSHIRE, ESSEX
(plans **12 13**)

Bishop's Stortford ○

A 120

**A**      **B**

C
D
1

Scunthorpe

Ludford • • Louth

• Belchford

Lincoln
Horncastle
A 158

L I N C O L N S H I R E

rk-on-Trent
A 17
Hough-
on-the-Hill
• South Rauceby

The Wash

• Great Gonerby

tham •

A 16

mondham

Clipsham

Holbeach

A 17

King's Lynn

smore
TLAND
akham

Hambleton
Stamford

Easton on The Hill

Peterborough

ingham
A 43

NORFOLK, SUFFOLK,
CAMBRIDGESHIRE
(plans 14 15)

Oundle
A 605

2

3

Derbyshire,
Leicestershire,
Northamptonshire,
Rutland, Lincolnshire,
Nottinghamshire

Bedford

BEDFORDSHIRE,
HERTFORDSHIRE,
ESSEX
(plans 12 13)

C
D

C

D

Chesterfield

**19**

Mansfield

**DERBYSHIRE, LEICESTERSHIRE,
NORTHAMPTONSHIRE, RUTLAND,
LINCOLNSHIRE, NOTTINGHAMSHIRE**
(plans **16 17**)

Alstonefield

• Cheddleton 🍴

Stoke-on-Trent

Place with at least:
- • a hotel or a restaurant
- ❀ a starred establishment
- 😊 a "Bib Gourmand" restaurant
- 🍴 a "Bib Hotel"
- ✕ a particularly pleasant restaurant
- ⋔ a particularly pleasant guesthouse
- 🏨 a particularly pleasant hotel
- ⤴ a particularly quiet hotel
- 🏚 a particularly pleasant pub

Uttoxeter •

**TAFFORDSHIRE**

1

• Stafford

Burton-upon-Trent •

Lichfield •

erhampton

A 5

Leicester

2

• Sutton Coldfield

Clent •

Birmingham
❀ ✕

Solihull •

• Hampton
in Arden

Nuneaton

Coventry

Hockley •Dorridge
Heath

Redditch

Lapworth

Chadwick
End

Kenilworth
🍴

oitwich Spa

Callow Hill

Henley-
in-Arden

• Hunningham

• Royal Leamington Spa ❀ 🏨

Warwick 🍴

RCESTERSHIRE

Aston Cantlow

**WARWICKSHIRE**

Northampton

Pershore •

🏨⋔
Stratford-
upon-Avon

Ettington •

Halford •

Pillerton Priors

⋔

Oxhill 🍴

3

Ilmington •

Armscote •

⤴🏨 Broadway

• Great Wolford

• Long Compton

Gt. Ouse

**SOMERSET,
DORSET,
GLOUCESTERSHIRE,
WILTSHIRE**
(plans **3 4**)

C

D

## 20 Cheshire, Lancashire, Isle of Man

**CUMBRIA**
(plans 21)

**ISLE OF MAN**

Ramsey

Port Erin

Douglas

Port St Mary

Barrow-in-Furness

**YORKSHIRE**
(plans 22 23)

Nether Burrow

Arkholme

Morecambe

Lancaster

**LANCASHIRE**

Forton

Skipt

Bolton-by-Bowland

Whitewell

Thornton

Clitheroe

Blackpool

Little Eccleston

Longridge

Whalley · Wiswell

Lytham St Anne's

Preston

Langho

Blackburn

Southport

Eccleston

Chorley

Ramsbottom

Rochdale

Aughton

Standish

Bury

Oldham

Prestwich

Hali

Manchester

Liverpool

Urmston

Chorlton-cum-Hardy

West Didsbury

Birkenhead

Port Sunlight

Altrincham

Sale

Didsbury

Stockport

Marple

West Kirby

Irby

Lymm

Alderley Edge

Knutsford

Prestbury

Buxt

Chester

Sandiway

**CHESHIRE**

Swettenham

**WALES**
(plans 32 33)

Tarporley

Tattenhall

Bunbury

Congleton

Tilston

Wrexham

Nantwich

Malpas

Stoke-on-Trent

**HEREFORDSHIR
WORCESTERSHI
SHROPSHIRE,
STAFFORDSHIR
WARWICKSHIR**
(plans 18 19)

# Cumbria

**B**

**21**

**A**

**1**

BORDERS,
EDINBURGH & GLASGOW
(plans 25 26)

Dumfries

Longtown 🔲

Brampton 🏠

Carlisle

NORTHUMBERLAND,
DURHAM
(plan 24)

**2**

Cockermouth

Bassenthwaite �]

Braithwaite 🌙

Penrith 🔲

Lorton 🌙

Portinscale 🏠

*Derwent water*

Keswick

Pooley Bridge 🕸🏠🌙

Watermillock 🌙

Buttermere 🌙

itehaven

*Ullswater*

Ullswater

Appleby-
in-Westmorland

Grasmere

Ambleside 🏠🏠

Kirkby Stephen 🌙

Hawkshead

Far Sawrey 🏠

Windermere 🕸🏠

Bowness-on-Windermere 🏠🌙

Crosthwaite 🗎

Bowland Bridge

Newby Bridge

Witherslack

Kendal

YORKSHIRE
(plans 22 23)

Grange-over-Sands

Ulverston

Cartmel
🕸 🍴

Arnside

Kirkby
Lonsdale 🍴

Lancaster

**3**

CHESHIRE,
LANCASHIRE,
ISLE OF MAN
(plan 20)

Blackpool

Place with at least:
- a hotel or a restaurant
🕸 a starred establishment
😊 a "Bib Gourmand" restaurant
🔲 a "Bib Hotel"
🍴 a particularly pleasant restaurant
🏚 a particularly pleasant guesthouse
🏠 a particularly pleasant hotel
🌙 a particularly quiet hotel
🗎 a particularly pleasant pub

Preston

**A**

**B**

# Northumberland, Durham

**A**     **B**

of Forth

**1**

BORDERS,
EDINBURGH & GLASGOW
(plans 25 26)

Berwick-upon-Tweed

Cornhill-on-Tweed

Milfield

Belford

Bamburgh
Seahouses

Wooler

Chatton

Jedburgh

Teviot

Alnwick

Warkworth

Rothbury

Longhorsley

Kirkwhelpington

Morpeth

Kielder Resr.

North Tyne

**NORTHUMBERLAND**

Barrasford

Matfen

Ponteland

Tynemouth

Haltwhistle

Hexham

Heddon on
the Wall

Newcastle-upon-Tyne

Corbridge

Hedley on the Hill

Sunniside

Gateshead

Sunderland

Chester-
le-Street

Seaham

**DURHAM**

Cowshill

Eastgate

Wear

Durham

Castle Eden

Middleton-
in-Teesdale

Romaldkirk

Middlesbrough

CUMBRIA
(plan 21)

Barnard Castle

Tees

Winston

Yarm

Maltby

**2**

**3**

YORKSHIRE
(plans 22 23)

Swale

Thirsk

Ure

Ripon

**A**     **B**

CENTRAL SCOTLAND
(plans **27** **28**)

**1**

Loch Lomond

Forth

Dunl

Stir

Balloch

Dunoon

Cardross

WEST
DUNBARTONSHIRE

EAST
DUNBARTONSHIRE

FALK

Rothesay

Bishopton
INVERCLYDE

RENFREWSHIRE

NORTH
LANARKSHI

Glasgow

Lochranza

Fairlie

NORTH
AYRSHIRE

EAST
RENFREWSHIRE

Dalry

Kilbrannan Sound

Brodick

Stevenston

EAST
AYRSHIRE

Clyde

Lamlash

**Isle of Arran**

Firth of Clyde

Troon

Ayr

Annbank

Sorn

SOUT

LANAR

**2**

Turnberry

SOUTH
AYRSHIRE

Sanquhar

Thornhill

Ballantrae

DUMFRIES

Newton Stewart

Castle Douglas

Portpatrick

Luce Bay

Kirkcudbright

Auchencairn

**3**

Wigtown Bay

So

A

B

St. Andrews

C

D

Kirkcaldy

Firth of Forth

Dunfermline

1

thgow

Leith

Gullane

North Berwick

Ingliston

Dunbar

Edinburgh

EAST LOTHIAN

Kirknewton

A 1

Currie

Dalkeith

WEST
LOTHIAN

MIDLOTHIAN

Chirnside

S C O T T I S H

Swinton

R. Tweed

B O R D E R S

Skirling

Peebles

Walkerburn

Ednam

Innerleithen

Tweed

Melrose

Kelso

St. Boswells

Teviot

Kirk Yetholm

Wooler

Jedburgh

2

Moffat

NORTHUMBERLAND,
DURHAM
(plan 24)

Annan

Esk

Kielder Resr.

N D

G A L L O W A Y

North Tyne

mfries

A 75

rkbean

Firth

Carlisle

3

CUMBRIA
(plan 21)

Eden

Penrith

Derwent water

Keswick

Ullswater

C

D

Place with at least:

● a hotel or a restaurant

✿ a starred establishment

😊 a "Bib Gourmand" restaurant

🍽 a "Bib Hotel"

✗ a particularly pleasant restaurant

↟ a particularly pleasant guesthouse

🏠 a particularly pleasant hotel

🍃 a particularly quiet hotel

🍺 a particularly pleasant pub

A

B

**HIGHLAND & THE ISLANDS**
(plans 29 30)

1

*The Little Minch*

*Snizort*

*Sound of Raasay*

*Loch Torridon*

*Loch Maree*

*Loch Fannich*

*SEA OF*

*THE HEBRIDES*

Isle of Skye

*Cuillin Sound*

Kyle of
Lochalsh

*Loch Bracadale*

*Loch Quoich*

*Loch Morar*

*Loch Arkaig*

*Loch Lochy*

*Sound of Rhum*

*Sound of
Arisaig*

*Loch Shiel*

Fort William

*Caledonian Canal*

*Backwater Resr*

*Loch La_*

HEBRIDES

Tobermory

Isle of Mull

*Sound of Mull*

Gruline

Tiroran

Port Appin

Eriska

Barcaldine

Connel

*Loch Etive*

Rann
Stat

2

INNER HEBRIDES

Oban

Kilchrenan

**ARGYLL
AND
BUTE**

Balquhidd

Isle of Seil

Arduaine

*Loch Awe*

Strathy

**STIRLIN**

Isle of Colonsay

Scalasaig

Crinan

Strachur

Tarbet

*Loch Lom_*

Tayvallich

Isle of Jura

Tighnabruaich

Dunoon

Greenock

Ballygrant

Kilberry

Ascog

Port Charlotte

Bowmore

Isle
of Bute

Isle of Islay

Port Ellen

Isle
of Gigha

Carradale

Kilmarnock

**EA_**

3

Peninsula

of

Kintyre

Isle
of Arran

*Firth of Clyde*

Ayr

Coleraine

**NORTHERN
IRELAND**
(plans 34 35)

**BORDERS,
EDINBURGH
& GLASGOW**
(plans 25 26)

A

B

A    B

THE MINCH

Galson

Isle of Lewis and Harris

Breasclete

Stornoway

1

OUTER HEBRIDES

West Loch Tarbert

WESTERN ISLES

Ardhasaig

Tarbert

Scarista

Scalpay

Sound of Harris

Gruin Bay

North Uist

Langass

Lochmaddy

Carinish

Sound of Monach

The Little Minch

Loch Snizort

Flodigarry

Waternish

Loch Torridon

Torridon

Edinbane

Bernisdale

Shieldaig

2

Isles of Uist

Dunvegan

Struan

Portree

Sound of Raasay

Applecross

Inner Sound

A 87

SEA OF

THE HEBRIDES

Loch Bracadale

Plockton

Balmacara

Broadford

Isle of Skye

Cuillin Sound

Sleat

Ratagan

South Uist

Sound of Barra

Duisdalemore

Teangue

Sound of Sleat

North Bay

Castlebay

Isle of Barra

Sound of Rhum

Loch Morar

A 830

INNER

Sound of Arisaig

Loch Shiel

3

HEBRIDES

Strontian

Or

Duror

Kingairloch

Sound of Mull

Lochaline

Loch Linnhe

Isle of Mull

Firth of Lorn

Oban

A    B

**A**     **B**

**1**

Unst

Yell

*St. Magnus Bay*

Muckle Roe     Whalsay
Papa Stour

Mainland

Veensgarth   Bressay
     Lerwick

Foula

SHETLAND
ISLANDS

**2**

Westray    *The North*    North Ronaldsay
Pierowall    *Sound*
    Cleat

         Sanday
*Westray Firth*    Eday
Mainland       Stronsay
   Dounby
  Harray   *Stronsay Firth*

Stromness    Shapinsay
    Kirkwall
      *Scapa Flow*    ORKNEY
          ISLANDS
Hoy      Burray
St Margaret's Hope
       South Ronaldsay
  *Pentland Firth*    Cleat

Thurso

    Wick

HIGHLAND
& THE ISLANDS
(plans 29 30)

**3**

Place with at least:

- • a hotel or a restaurant
- ❀ a starred establishment
- 😊 a "Bib Gourmand" restaurant
- 🏠 a "Bib Hotel"
- ✗ a particularly pleasant restaurant
- ⌂ a particularly pleasant guesthouse
- 🏠 a particularly pleasant hotel
- ॐ a particularly quiet hotel
- 🍸 a particularly pleasant pub

**A**     **B**

# Wales

**32**

Place with at least:

- • a hotel or a restaurant
- ✿ a starred establishment
- ⊞ a "Bib Gourmand" restaurant
- ⊡ a "Bib Hotel"
- ✕ a particularly pleasant restaurant
- ⬈ a particularly pleasant guesthouse
- ▥ a particularly pleasant hotel
- ⬉ a particularly quiet hotel
- ⊡ a particularly pleasant pub

CHESHIRE, LANCASHIRE, ISLE OF MAN (plan 20)

HEREFORDSHIRE, WORCESTERSHIRE, SHROPSHIRE, STAFFORDSHIRE, WARWICKSHIRE

Liverpool

Birkenhead

Liverpool Bay

Chester

Shrewsbury

Wrexham

Rhyl
Abergele
Colwyn Bay

St George
St Asaph
Tremeirchion
Mold

Llandyrnog

Ruthin

FLINTSHIRE

DENBIGHSHIRE

Llangollen

Llandderfel
Llandrillo

Llanarmon Dyffryn Ceiriog

Llanfihangel

Lake Vyrnwy

Llanfyllin

P O W Y S

Montgomery

Newtown

Caersws

Pontdolgoch

Severn

Llandudno

Conwy

CONWY

Betws-y-Coed

Penmachno

Bala

GWYNEDD

Llan Ffestiniog

Llanuwchllyn

Machynlleth

Cemaes

Llanerchymedd
Benllech

Beaumaris

ISLE OF ANGLESEY

Valley

Menai Bridge

Caernarfon

Betws Garmon

Beddgelert

Talsarnau

Dolgellau

Harlech

Aberdovey

Rhoscolyn

Caernarfon Bay

Llandwrog

Clynnog-Fawr

Boduan

Pwllheli

Criccieth

Portmeirion

Abersoch

Bwlchtocyn

CHANNEL

NORTH CHA...

1

Ballintoy ⌂

Portstewart
Portrush
Bushmills

Coleraine
37

**MOYLE**

**BALLYMONEY**

*Bann*

Maghera

Ballymena

**MAGHERAFELT**

A 26

Larne

A 8

M 22

☺ Ballyclare

**NEWTOWNABBEY**

M 2

**OOKSTOWN**

**ANTRIM**

*Lough Neagh*

Crumlin ●

*Belfast Lough*

☺ Hollywood

A 2

Bangor ☺

**NORTH DOWN**

Donaghadee

2

⌂ Dungannon

M 1

● Belfast
☺ ☺ ☺

Newtownards

**CASTLEREAGH**

Comber

M 1

**CRAIGAVON**

Hillsborough ●

A 1

*Bann*

Killinchy ●

*Strangford Lough*

**BANBRIDGE**

A 24

**DOWN**

A 3

Downpatrick ●

Dundrum ●

Newcastle ●

**NEWRY AND MOURNE**

*Dundrum Bay*

3

Warrenpoint ☺

*Carlingford Lough*

○ Dundalk

A 1

*Dundalk bay*

C

D

A     B

1

*Gwee*

*Donegal*

*Broad Haven*

Ballycastle

*Killala Bay*

*Sligo Bay*

Sligo

**SLIGO**

*Blacksod Bay*

Keel   Doogort

Crossmolina   Ballina

Rivers

Castlebaldwin

**Achill Island**

*L. Conn*

*Moy*

Boyle

Mulrany

Newport

**ROSCOMMO**

*Clew Bay*

Westport

N 5

**MAYO**

Knock

Claremorris

*Killary Harbour*

Leenane

*Lough Mask*

Ballinrobe

Clifden

Letterfrack

Ballynahinch

Recess

Cong

Roscommon

Cashel

*Lough Corrib*

Caherlistrane

*Clare*

Roundstone

Oughterard

**GALWAY**

Furbogh

Barna

Galway

Ballinasloe

M 6

**Aran Islands**

*Galway Bay*

Kilcolgan

N 6

**REPUBLIC OF IRELAND**
(plans **38 39**)

A     B

# Republic of Ireland

REPUBLIC
OF IRELAND
(plans 36 37)

Killa...
Lough
Mask
Lough
Corrib
Clare
Clifden

Galway

**1**

Galway Bay

Inishmore
**Aran Islands**
Inishmaan
Ballyvaughan
Doolin
Lisdoonvarna
Liscannor
Corrofin
Lahinch

Spanish Point

**C L A R E**

Killalo

Newmarket on Fergus
Bunratty
Limeric...

River Shannon

*Mouth of
the Shannon*
Ballybunnion
Adare

**LIMERICK**

Listowel
Ballingarry

Maigue

*Tralee
Bay*
Castlegregory
Kilmallock

**2**

Tralee

Dingle
Cromane

*Dingle Bay*

Caragh
Lake
Killarney
Kanturk
Mallow
Castley...

**Valencia
Island**

Cahersiveen    **KERRY**

*Blackwater*

**C O R K**

Portmagee

Kenmare
Glounthaune
Blarney
Cork
Fo...
Isl...

Tahilla
Parknasilla

*Lee*

Carrigaline
C...
Crosshav...

Ballylickey

*Bandon*
Bandon
Ballinadee
Kilbrittain
Kinsale

*Bantry Bay*

Durrus
Clonakilty
Timoleague
Barrells Cross

*Dunmanus Bay*
Toormore
Goleen
Crookhaven
Castletownshend

Baltimore

**3**

*Roaringwater Bay*

C    E    L    T

Great Britain : Based on the Ordnance Survey of Great Britain with the permission of the Controller of Her Majesty's Stationery's Office © Crown Copyright 100000247

Northern Ireland : Reproduced from the OSNI map with the permission of the Controller of HMSO © Crown Copyright 2010 Permit Number 110050

Ireland : Based on Ordnance Survey Ireland Permit No. 8763 © Ordnance Survey Ireland / Government of Ireland

---

## Manufacture française des pneumatiques Michelin

Société en commandite par actions au capital de 504 000 004 EUR.
Place des Carmes-Déchaux – 63 Clermont-Ferrand (France)
R.C.S. Clermont-Fd B 855 200 507

**© Michelin, Propriétaires-Éditeurs**
Dépôt légal octobre 2011

Printed in Italy - septembre 2011

Printed on paper from sustainably managed forests

Compogravure : JOUVE, Saran (France)

Impression et Finition : La Tipografica (Varese)

Our editorial team has taken the greatest care in writing this guide and checking the information in it. However, practical information (prices, addresses, telephone numbers, internet addresses, etc) is subject to frequent change and such information should therefore be used for guidance only. It is possible that some of the information in this guide may not be accurate or exhaustive as at the date of publication. We therefore accept no liability in regard to such information.